To Alex & Emily, with [illegible] and appreciation. October, 1978.

HERITAGE OF BRITAIN

HERITAGE OF BRITAIN

Great Moments in the Story of an Island Race

Published by

THE READER'S DIGEST ASSOCIATION LIMITED

London   New York   Montreal   Sydney   Cape Town

Touch the cool stones of Britain's most mysterious cathedral, Stonehenge. You are touching the past.

No written records were left by the countless generations of men and women who lived on this island before the coming of the Romans.

But the face of the land is marked by what has endured of their works.

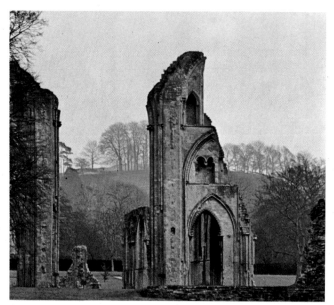

Gaze on ruins which speak of vanished greatness, places where centuries of human effort have ended in slow decay or sudden disaster.

Above, are the ruins of Glastonbury Abbey which flourished for 1000 years and became the wealthiest religious foundation in Britain. The riches of such abbeys led to their destruction.

In November 1539 the last abbot was hanged and his great church was plundered of all its treasures.

But enough remains. In this grass-grown sanctuary you can still visualise the splendours of the monastic age – and imagine the drama of that day when 1000 years of British history died with the Abbot of Glastonbury.

Wander round museums and galleries – and view relics which have witnessed our history.

Among the treasures of the Ashmolean Museum at Oxford, for instance, is this lantern – the lantern with which Guy Fawkes tried to change a nation's destiny.

Walk where history was made. Everywhere in Britain are places where the spirit of the past lingers.

This iron bridge at Coalbrookdale can carry you back through two tumultuous centuries. For here was born the Industrial Revolution, which was to transform the face of the world.

Look at jewellery, the yellowed paper and faded ink of old manuscripts, or even the household utensils familiar to our great-grandparents.

Such things are links binding us to the past, part of a chain which reaches back for **250,000** years.

This brooch was made to be worn at Queen Victoria's diamond jubilee. It has the power to recall that distant June day when the British people gave thanks for their worldwide empire.

Reminders of our national heritage lie all around us.

Castles and cathedrals, personal relics, souvenirs and stately homes – all have played a part in our island story.

Such relics provide the inspiration for this book, each one acting as a 'talisman' to form a living link with the past.

HERITAGE OF BRITAIN

was edited and designed by
The Reader's Digest Association Limited, London

First Edition Copyright © 1975
The Reader's Digest Association Limited
25 Berkeley Square, London W1X 6AB

Printed in Great Britain

CONSULTANT EDITORS

The Publishers wish to express their gratitude to the following
for their assistance in the preparation of HERITAGE OF BRITAIN:

PRE-HISTORY, ROMANS AND ANGLO-SAXONS
Barry Cunliffe MA, PhD, FSA
*Professor of European Archaeology,
Oxford University and Fellow of Keble
College, Oxford*

H. R. Loyn MA, DLitt
*Professor of Medieval History,
University College of South Wales and
Monmouthshire*

MEDIEVAL AND VICTORIAN
J. P. C. Sumption BA
*Fellow in Modern History at Magdalen
College, Oxford*

THE TUDORS
Penry Williams MA, DPhil
*Fellow and Tutor in Modern History,
New College, Oxford*

EARLY STUARTS
J. P. Kenyon BA, PhD
*Professor of Modern History,
University of Hull*

LAST STUARTS AND TWENTIETH CENTURY
Robert Lacey MA

EARLY GEORGIAN
Geoffrey Holmes MA, BLitt, FRHistS
*Professor of History,
Lancaster University*

GEORGE III AND THE REGENCY
J. C. Clarke MA, DPhil
Fellow, All Souls College, Oxford

BATTLES OF THE TWO WORLD WARS
Correlli Barnett MA, FRSL

HERITAGE OF ART
Richard Ormond MA
*Assistant Keeper,
The National Portrait Gallery*

Dr Roy Strong FSA
Director, Victoria and Albert Museum

HERITAGE OF ARCHITECTURE
John Julius Norwich FRSL
*Member of the Executive and the
Properties Committee of The National
Trust*

HERITAGE OF SCIENCE
Nigel Hawkes BA

Jonathan Miller MB, BCh
*Research Fellow in the History of
Medicine, University College, London*

HERITAGE OF MUSIC
Sir Neville Cardus CBE

HERITAGE OF LITERATURE
Lettice Cooper
Vice-President of the English P.E.N.

John Lehmann BA, CBE, FRSL
President, Royal Literary Fund

Peter Quennell CBE

LAND OF HISTORY
Neville Williams
MA, DPhil, FRHistS, FSA
Secretary of the British Academy

CONTENTS

PAGEANT
OF THE
CENTURIES

250,000 BC – AD 1975

The heritage of Britain has been shaped by a series of epic and colourful events. These historic episodes range from bloody battles at home and abroad to such peaceful and significant happenings as the arrival of the first Christian missionaries or the stirrings of the Industrial Revolution which was to transform the world. Britain's heritage is also made up of the achievements of men and women of genius in art and architecture, music, literature and science. *Pageant of the Centuries* records these great moments in our island's story, in the world of action and in the arts and sciences, from the earliest times to the present day.

UNCHANGING RITUAL *Century by century, Britons have marvelled at the splendour of royal occasions. Here 16th-century Londoners watch their boy king Edward VI ride by under a golden canopy on the eve of his coronation.*

Dawn of the island's story

For nearly a quarter of a million years nomad hunters struggle for survival in an untamed land before farmers from the Continent set Britain on the road to civilisation

The story of mankind in Britain goes back a quarter of a million years to a time when men's whole lives were a bitter struggle against gnawing hunger or unexpected death. Slowly, through the aeons of time, they learnt to master new skills, and began the long struggle to control their environment. It was the beginning of the epic journey to civilisation.

In the late Ice Age, when Britain was still joined by land to Europe, bands of hunter nomads roamed what is now southern England. At first they possessed only primitive flint axes like those found at Swanscombe in Kent. Slowly, they evolved finer and more effective hunting weapons. But still, during the worst times when ice, snow and blizzards swept the land, their shelters were caves like Kent's Cavern in Devon (pp. 14–15).

Between 4000 and 3000 BC, groups of primitive farmers arrived in Britain, this time by sea, for Britain had become an island. They began to sweep away the island's mantle of virgin forest, to grow grain and raise their cattle, sheep and pigs. At last man was not wholly dependent on nature. He was beginning to control his own food supply.

Now that some men could grow and store more than they needed to eat, others could set up specialist industries like the flint mines of Grime's Graves in Norfolk (pp. 16–17); and, as men settled and population grew, there was leisure to ponder the mysteries of life and build impressive, complex monuments, such as Stonehenge (pp. 18–19).

The Metal Age produced a race of wealthy chieftains in Britain. Adorned in their finery of gold and amber, they were buried in great mounds like the Bush Barrow near Stonehenge (pp. 20–21).

About 600 BC iron began to replace bronze as the metal for tools and weapons. An exuberant and beautiful art developed (pp. 22–23) under the patronage of chieftains. These were the fierce warriors who confronted Julius Caesar when he invaded England in 55 BC.

ACHIEVEMENT OF THE FIRST BRITONS

For more than 1000 years, the building and re-building of the awe-inspiring sanctuary at Stonehenge on Salisbury Plain reflected the development and progress of early man in Britain. Recent surveys and excavations have shown that the great monument was more than a religious meeting place. It may have been a gigantic observatory, the result of early man's strong determination to learn more about the mysterious forces which affected his everyday life. Mastery of the movements of the heavens would enable him to anticipate the seasons' changes – a tremendous break-through in a predominantly agricultural age. Stonehenge survives as a reminder of this brilliant ingenuity and determination to conquer the unknown.

Men battle for survival in an age of ice and snow

Forty thousand years ago, Britain was in the last stages of the Ice Age. A great ice-sheet covered the north. Small groups of hunters roamed the arctic wastes to the south. Sometimes the blizzards and bitter winds drove these people – and often their animal prey – into the shelter of caves. Kent's Cavern, near Torquay, is one such refuge.

To this complex of narrow passages and vast chambers of limestone came generations of highly skilled hunters for more than 20,000 years. They possessed a sophisticated arsenal. They had spears and spear-throwers, long shafts which effectively increased the length of a man's arm so that he could throw spears greater distances. They also used bone harpoons and weapons with fine flint cutting edges set in wooden handles.

Hunter and hunted

Often, after a kill, the hunters dragged their quarry back to the cave. The bones left on the cave floor over passing centuries provide evidence of the generations who had found a refuge in these caves.

Remains of mammoths, woolly rhinoceroses, cave bears, horses, hyenas, red deer and reindeer have been discovered. They date from the last spell of intense cold, which began about 17,000 years ago.

A fragment of human jaw with three teeth in place was also unearthed. The teeth differ from those of a man of today only in their degree of wear and freedom from disease. They were worn down by the tough food of the hunters.

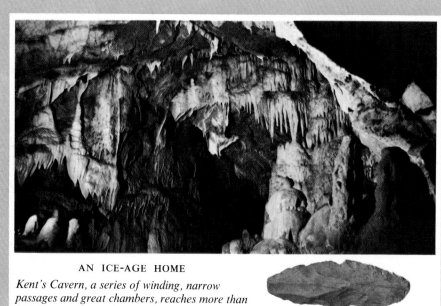

AN ICE-AGE HOME

Kent's Cavern, a series of winding, narrow passages and great chambers, reaches more than 300 ft into a limestone hill near Torquay in Devon. Festoons of stalactites hang from the roof. Here, 40,000 years ago, Old Stone Age people sheltered. They used tools of flint, antler and bone (right).

THE HUNTERS AND THEIR KILL *The hunters of the Old Stone Age were skilled at organising group expeditions to hunt the great beasts of the Ice Age. Their survival depended on their courage and skill. At Kent's Cavern, hunters prepare to skin and joint a dead cave bear, using flint tools. Animals' warm skins gave the hunters comfort in an inhospitable world.*

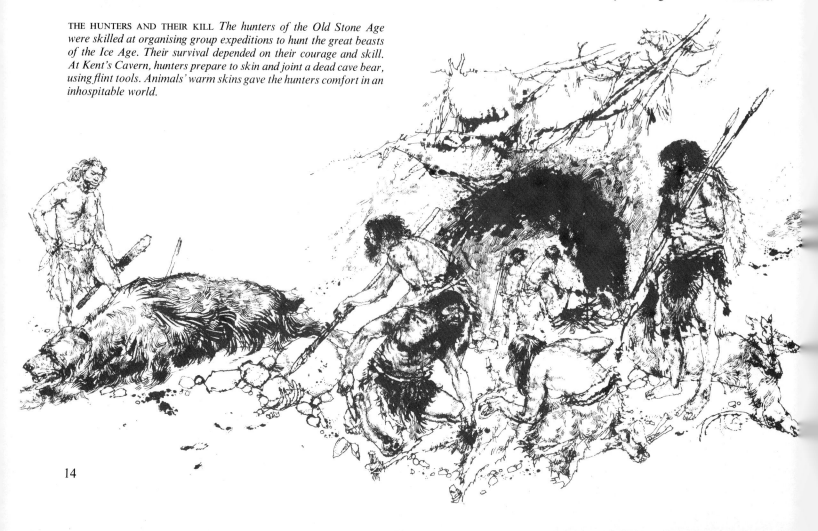

THE FIRST KNOWN BRITON

When Britain was still joined to the Continent 250,000 years ago, the first known inhabitant lived in the valley where the Kent town of Swanscombe now stands. He and his tribe shared the forests with the prehistoric animals that meant two things to them: meat and danger. There were straight-tusked elephants, gigantic cattle called aurochs, two species of fearsome rhinoceroses, horses and red deer.

The gravel pit where Swanscombe man's only remains – the skull bones (below) – were found.

Moving in for a kill, Swanscombe hunters trap a deer.

Armed only with wooden spears, the Swanscombe hunters tracked their prey in the forests of oak, elm and viburnum. After a kill, they skinned and butchered the animal on the spot using hand-held flint axes, skilfully chipped to give cutting edges. Flints were so plentiful and easily chipped that, once used, they were often simply thrown away.

Swanscombe man probably had beetling brows and a massive jaw. Only three of his skull bones have survived, but experts believe that he was not very different from men of today. His brain was much the same size.

His life was precarious. Disease and hunting accidents must have taken a heavy toll. The bones which have been found belong to someone who died young – probably aged only 20–25.

The most tantalising question about Swanscombe man is whether he understood the secret of fire. Pieces of charcoal and fire-shattered flints have been found with his bones and tools, but they may have been the result of forest fires.

These early Britons made clothes of fur and skin, sewn together with bone needles. They also knew how to use and control fire.

Their elaborate tools, their skill in tracking and killing their prey, and the speed with which they adapted to the changes of the Ice Age suggest a highly developed people. The inhabitants of Kent's Cavern were just that – the first Modern Men to live in Britain. They belonged to the *Homo sapiens sapiens* group, which includes all present-day people. Their sophisticated culture ushered in the final phase of the Old Stone Age.

During the Ice Age, the sea level constantly changed, and Britain was periodically joined to the Continent. The hunters spent much of their time on the move, following their prey as it migrated with the seasons. But arctic Britain was inhospitable, the edge of the habitable world. It attracted few hunters, and there were probably fewer than 2000 people in Britain south of the ice-sheet. Traces of them have been found in caves in the Mendips, in South Wales and Derbyshire.

BRITAIN'S FIRST ART *A Stone Age hunter scratched this horse on bone at Creswell Crags in Derbyshire, almost 40,000 years ago.*

The hunters had to devote most of their energy to survival. Yet they possessed a high degree of artistic skill. This can be seen in many of the articles they used. The carefully made barbed harpoons and spear-throwers reveal a people who took pleasure in functional design.

The so-called ceremonial staff from Gough's Cave at Cheddar in Somerset is a fine example of their craftsmanship. The patiently whittled antler rod, 6½ in. long with a hole at one end, was perhaps an arrow-straightener.

Life after death

The hunters adorned themselves with strings of animal teeth and mollusc shells. They had a reverence for the dead, and almost certainly believed in life after death.

This deep-rooted belief has been revealed by a discovery at Paviland Cave in the Gower peninsula of South Wales. There the early Britons buried one of their young men with great care. The corpse, that of a tall man aged about 25, with the head missing, was laid out and covered with powdered red ochre. Stones were set at each end, and around were placed an ivory bracelet, ivory rods, perforated shells and an elephant's skull, probably for his use in the afterlife. Was this burial a special case – honours afforded to a man of high status – or was it perhaps a sacrifice to the gods? Whatever the motives, these relics show that the creative powers of these Britons were directed beyond the needs of sheer subsistence.

Britain in the harsh grip of the Ice Age

About 1 million years ago, the climate of the Northern Hemisphere began to deteriorate. In Europe and Asia the Ice Age had begun.

But the Ice Age was not a continuous period of ice and snow. Four major phases of intense cold, the glaciations, were separated by three warmer periods. It was during the second of these that Swanscombe man lived.

At the height of a glaciation, Britain was uninhabitable, with an ice-sheet up to 1000 ft thick in the north. During the second glaciation it reached the Thames Valley.

South of the ice, glaciers gouged out the valleys. Biting winds swept the frozen ground where only dwarf pines and lichens could grow. This tundra was the home of reindeer, woolly rhinoceroses, cave bears and mammoths. It was during the last glaciation that Modern Men lived at Kent's Cavern.

As it became warmer, the ice retreated northwards. Grasses and sedges, and later pine and birch forest, replaced the tundra.

During the first and third of these warmer periods, the climate was hotter than today. Hippopotamuses and rhinoceroses roamed the forests of firethorn and oak.

EXTINCT BEASTS *The mammoth and woolly rhinoceroses of the tundra died out when the weather grew warmer and the forests took over.*

BRITAIN BECOMES AN ISLAND *About 8000 BC, as the ice retreated, water flooded from the North Sea across the land-bridge and into the Channel. The gateway from the Continent was closed.*

Skilled miners create Britain's first industry

A PREHISTORIC PITHEAD

Local superstition has named this site, near Thetford in Norfolk, Grime's Graves – the digging place of the devil ('Grim'). But in reality it was one of the first industrial sites in Britain. More than 4500 years ago, men of the New Stone Age mined for flint there. The chalk figure of a woman (right) was perhaps a fertility symbol worshipped by the miners.

UNDERGROUND
Men at work in the flint mines. Equipped with only simple tools – picks and axes – these prehistoric miners excavated 10,000 cu. ft of earth and stone from one of the mines' many shafts and galleries.

Perhaps the greatest break-through in the story of the British islands took place gradually over 1000 years of history. After more than 200,000 years, in which the inhabitants of Britain had lived by hunting and gathering wild plants and fruits, a new way of life slowly evolved.

The new age came about because of a great wave of migration from the Continent about 3500 BC. The migrants were Britain's first farmers. They forged primitive agricultural settlements out of the untamed wilderness of their new country.

Over centuries their knowledge and experience spread throughout the country as farming slowly supplanted hunting as the principal source of food. Agriculture, however, needed new and different implements with which to tend the fields. This need led to the creation of Britain's first industry – flint mining.

The flints which were dug out of the ground were chipped and polished into the tools of the new age – axes for felling trees, primitive farming implements and weapons for defence. They represent a significant step in the evolution of organised life, the beginning of the long process of turning England into pasture and arable land, and helping to create a society where trade flourished.

An underground maze

Of the 17 flint mines which have been found in southern England, the most remarkable is Grime's Graves, near Thetford in Norfolk, a 93 acre area of intensive mining which was being worked over 4500 years ago.

Since the best flint lay buried 40 ft below the surface under thick layers of sand, clay and chalk, the miners had to sink deep shafts to reach it. No fewer than 600 shafts were dug at Grime's Graves, varying in depth from shallow open-cast workings 10–15 ft deep to astonishing pits 40 ft deep and over 40 ft wide. The complex system of tunnels and galleries followed the thin flint seams and formed an elaborate underground maze.

These gigantic workings were all excavated with the most primitive of tools. All the miners had to dig with were picks made of deer antlers, or polished flint axe-heads fitted into wooden handles.

Wooden shovels were probably used to clear away surface sand and clay, and the flint was raised to the surface in wicker or skin baskets attached to ropes. These were brought up from deep, dark chambers lit by torches or chalk lamps fuelled by animal fat.

Now and then things went wrong. One shaft which failed to find a good vein of flint was turned into an underground shrine, possibly to placate the gods of fertility who were believed to watch over production.

Close to the entrance to one of the galleries, chalk blocks were piled to form a pedestal. On top of this was placed a chalk figure of a pregnant woman. Near by stood a chalk phallus and carved chalk spheres. Towards the centre of the shaft, another pedestal, this time of flint, bore seven of the antler picks and a small chalk cup, possibly for making offerings to the gods.

The miners were also traders whose wares were peddled over a wide distance along the upland ridgeways which connected the scattered farming communities. The rough stone was not cut to its final shape until it reached the customer, who would grind and polish his tool to a smooth surface.

The rough pieces of stone were exchanged for corn, skins, pottery or other necessities of life. Some flint travelled great distances. Tools of Welsh stone have been found as far east as Essex.

Considerable skill and ingenuity marked these early mining exploits. Grime's Graves is proof that, even at this early stage of history, full-time craftsmen-specialists already existed. The beginnings of industry and of trade had come to Britain.

TECHNOLOGY IN STONE

In the absence of detailed records, stone tools provide valuable clues to the development of technology in prehistoric Britain. Some 300,000 years separate the crude 'choppers' of the early hunters from the finely shaped arrow-heads which were fashioned by farmers modern enough to practise metal-casting.

Chipped core of flint, shaped c. 300,000 BC.

Swanscombe man's hand-axe, c. 250,000 BC.

A Wiltshire farmer's flint dagger, c. 2000 BC.

Polished stone battle-axe, c. 2000 BC.

Flint arrow-head, made c. 1800 BC.

A new society takes root on the fertile downs

No one will ever know why the first farmers embarked on the dangerous journey to Britain, but their arrival in the south of England brought about one of the greatest of all changes in the history of the island.

In 4000 BC, Britain was still populated by men who hunted their food and ate wild fruit and roots – just as their ancestors had done for at least 200,000 years. But by 3000 BC, self-sufficient farming communities had spread to most parts of the country.

The farmers brought with them in their small boats not only the seeds of barley and of wheat, but sheep and cattle. They brought new types of stone tools including sickles.

With their flint axes, they hacked out clearings in the thick woods, which covered most of the country. The logs and underbrush were burnt and the seeds sown into the ash-enriched earth. In southern Britain, the well-drained chalk and limestone hills proved to be exceptionally fertile.

But these first farmers were mainly dependent for their daily livelihood on their herds of sheep and cattle, whose need for grazing helped to replace forest with grassland. Because their animals needed a constant supply of fresh grazing-land, the first farmers were semi-nomadic, moving on when grazing was exhausted.

Life on the land

Life was scarcely easier for them than for the hunting people they were supplanting. Clearing the land, breaking the soil, sowing and reaping was in many ways a more arduous form of existence. Crops and animals were prey to natural disasters such as bad weather or outbreaks of disease. But, for the first time, the food supply was at least partially under human control.

In good years, enough grain could be grown to last through a lean winter. In the autumn, cattle could be butchered to provide meat for many weeks. Clothing made from their hides gave admirable protection against the winter cold. So the farmers persisted, and the hunter-gatherer bands gradually disappeared or were absorbed into their numbers.

The tools of the new farmers were extremely primitive. Digging sticks were used for planting and hoeing. Later, knowledge of the ard – a crude plough pulled by men or oxen – reached Britain from the Continent. Sickles and various other cutting tools and scrapers, made from fine flint blades and mounted in bone or wood handles, were also used. Axes served to help build timber and thatch huts.

To store grain, and perhaps milk, the farmers needed containers. The art of pottery making was thus brought to Britain. At first, the dishes that were made were plain and undecorated. But by about 3300 BC decorations had begun to be scratched on the clay.

As food supplies became more abundant, the farming societies grew rapidly. Across the inhabited world, herding and agriculture helped to increase the population to many times what it had been in the hunting and gathering era of about 8000 BC. The same area of land could support many more farmers than hunters. And, as farming techniques improved, a more settled life became possible.

An increasingly large and complex society soon began to construct its first full-scale monuments. On several hilltops in southern Britain, such as Windmill Hill in Wiltshire and Hembury in Devon, large earthwork enclosures were erected. Around them were dug a series of ditches, which in places were bridged by solid causeways.

An elaborate society

These causewayed camps were certainly not inhabited all the year round. They may have served as tribal gathering places for barter, feasting or worship. There, scattered communities could reaffirm their rules and relationships with each other.

During the same period, a definable social structure began to emerge in Britain. The top rung of the ladder was occupied by prominent men and their families, who received burials of marked splendour.

Whole communities might work together to build their tombs – long earthen mounds or barrows from 30 to 100 yds long. Beneath each, several people were buried and their high status was commemorated by the white chalk, which shone for years before grass grew again on these mounds. These honoured dead headed a now quite elaborate society. The basis had been laid for the dramatic cultural developments of the next 1000 years.

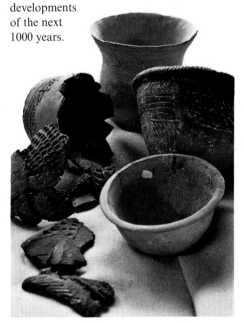

FARMERS' ART *Earthenware pots fashioned by the early farmers who settled in Wiltshire. The first pots were plain and dish-like.*

The mystery of Britain's Stone Age masterpiece

A STONE AGE CATHEDRAL
Dawn at Stonehenge, Britain's greatest prehistoric monument. The ruins of this unique sanctuary have aroused the awe of visitors for centuries. The Normans acclaimed it one of the wonders of Britain. Archaeologists now believe that the stone circle was built about 4–5000 years ago. But its precise purpose still remains a mystery.

High on the windswept downs of Wiltshire are the ruins of one of Britain's first and in some ways most impressive cathedrals. Over a span of nearly 1000 years, generations of prehistoric men toiled at the building of the great stone circles of Stonehenge.

But the reason for their long years of activity, the inspiration that drove them to build and rebuild this massive monument, has never been discovered. In all its stark grandeur, Stonehenge remains one of the greatest mysteries in the story of man.

The first steps

Work began at Stonehenge sometime after 3000 BC, when primitive farming communities living on the Wiltshire downs excavated a circular ditch with a 6 ft high wall of chalk inside, enclosing a circular area more than 280 ft across. Just inside, a circle of 65 pits was dug. They probably resulted from religious ceremonies, and were discovered in the 17th century. Some of the pits have since been found to contain cremated human bones.

Around 600 years passed before the next stage of building at Stonehenge began. About 2200 BC, at least 80 bluestones, each weighing up to 4 tons, were set up in a double circle.

These stones originated in the Prescelly Mountains in Dyfed, more than 150 miles away. Some experts believe that they were carried to southern England by ice and flood

SUMMIT OF ACHIEVEMENT *The climax in the centuries of building at Stonehenge came when the workmen added the 7 ton lintel stones which ran round the top of the circle of standing stones. Here the builders are shown raising one of the lintels, inch by inch, on a series of timber platforms. When the lintels were level with the tops of the standing stones, they were levered into their final position.*

waters during an Ice Age. Others consider that the builders themselves may have brought them on rafts by sea and river to the Avon Valley, and then dragged them overland to Stonehenge.

Even before this second version of Stonehenge was completed, it was replaced by a grand new design. The bluestones were apparently taken down and stockpiled near by. Great sarsen stones – blocks of sandstone found on the Marlborough Downs – were loaded on to sledges and dragged the 20 miles to the site over rollers of logs.

The task was enormous. Recent experiments have shown that 200 men would have been needed to move the largest stone even on level ground. When the stones finally reached the site, the work of erection began. The outer circle, about 100 ft in diameter, was composed of 30 upright stones, each weighing about 25 tons. Its 30 lintels weighed about 7 tons each.

For the uprights, foundation pits would have been dug with one side sloping. Then, each stone was probably dragged out on rollers until its base projected above the bottom of the pit. By levering the other end up, the stone could be slid into the hole.

The next stage was to raise it into a vertical position by levering from an adjacent timber stack and by hauling. When all the uprights were in position, work on the lintels could begin. It is probable that they were raised inch by inch on a stack of timber and finally slid sideways on to the top of the standing stones.

Culminating achievement

As the last lintel fell into place, the building of Stonehenge reached its climax, the highest achievement of prehistoric people in Europe. A few years later the bluestones were finally placed to form the 'inner sanctum' of the Stonehenge that stands today.

The monument was now complete, about 1000 years after the digging of the first ditch. Clearly it fulfilled a major role in the life of the inhabitants of the Salisbury Plain. But the nature of that role is shrouded in mystery.

The mathematical accuracy of the stones' positioning has led some experts to suggest that Stonehenge was designed as an elaborate observatory. Priests could have used its stones in relation to the rising and setting sun to measure time – and then to plot the times to sow crops, to slaughter cattle and to perform other necessary acts of the farming year. The observatory could also have helped them to predict eclipses of the sun and moon – events regarded with superstitious awe.

But the prime motive for these centuries of dedicated activity must have been religious. Even in the first years of its long life, Stonehenge was a place of mystery – a temple dedicated to the unknown power which governs the sun and moon, the wheeling galaxies of the night sky and all the miraculous workings of life on earth.

Lasting memorials to prehistoric genius

The new way of life brought to Britain by immigrant farmers had led to enormous social changes. Closely knit, settled communities had grown up, ruled by prominent families. These had led, about 3000–2500 BC, to the building of great hill-top camps as meeting places, and to the construction of collective tombs for men of wealth and power. The next 500 years saw the creation of Britain's first monumental architecture.

Men began building huge earthwork enclosures, or henges, at Avebury, Durrington Walls and Marden, all in Wiltshire. At Avebury, one of the largest henges in Britain, the outer bank has a diameter of 1400 ft. The henge at Durrington is 1600 ft across.

The henges acted as religious centres for large areas and they were used for over 500 years. They were rather like medieval cathedrals. Both resulted from enormous communal effort and centralised organisation motivated by religious aspirations.

The exuberance and vision of the same farming people also led to the building of Silbury Hill, in Wiltshire, the largest man-made structure in prehistoric Europe. Earth and layers of chalk blocks were piled up to a height of 130 ft. But excavations over many years have revealed no clue to its purpose.

By this time, society had become sufficiently organised to supply the immense labour force necessary for these great projects. Agriculture had reached a stage where men could be spared from the fields for long stretches. This had been achieved in a mere 1500 years – the time since the introduction of farming.

Britain's first scientists

Some experts believe that late in this period Britain produced its first scientists – men capable of undertaking extended periods of observation of the sun, the moon and the stars. They used their knowledge to construct stone circles in which the stones were meticulously placed, to form gigantic mathematical instruments. These arrangements may have been used for the measurement of time, and to predict phases of the moon and even eclipses.

Britain's first scientists belonged to farming communities, with a way of life determined by the seasons. In Britain, with its uncertain climate, their accurate methods of dating the seasons must have been particularly valuable. At Stonehenge their technical skill and deep religious instincts created a monument that remains one of the wonders of the world.

WORK OF GENERATIONS *Silbury Hill, in Wiltshire, was the largest man-made structure in prehistoric Europe. It covers 5½ acres.*

STONE AGE SANCTUARY *At Avebury, Wiltshire, Europe's largest stone circle lies within a henge, a circular ditch and bank enclosing 28 acres.*

BURIAL PLACE *This 'dolmen' or tomb of great stones at Llanglydwen in Dyfed was once covered by a great mound of earth.*

MOUNTAIN MONUMENT *Rimmed by mountains in the Lake District, Castlerigg stone circle, formed of 38 stones, is 100–110 ft across.*

A warrior chieftain takes his treasures to the grave

MONUMENT TO A BRONZE AGE CHIEF
On Normanton Down, near Stonehenge, Wessex tribesmen erected this round barrow over the remains of their leader about 3500 years ago. The rich ornaments and weapons buried with him, such as this gold belt hook (right), suggest that he was a man of great importance. But the outstanding symbol of the chieftain's power was his mace (below), headed with polished stone and decorated with carved bone.

The barrows that dot the downlands of southern Britain are an enduring legacy of an age when the first organised societies were formed in Britain. The rulers of these early societies were invested with a power and grandeur that their subjects believed would continue even after death itself. This was the motive that prompted the lavish burial ceremonies that produced the downland barrows.

One such ceremony took place about 1650 BC, when a group of tribesmen carried the body of their ruler across Salisbury Plain to a sacred burial ground within sight of Stonehenge. When they reached the appointed place, the mourners laid their dead chieftain – a tall, stout man – on his back, with his head towards the south. He was regally dressed, and splendidly armed as befitting a leader and a warrior. The care taken over this no doubt indicated the status his people believed he would hold in the next world.

The possessions buried with him in the Bush Barrow were products of a new form of society – one which created an aristocracy commanding technical skills never seen before in Britain. The chieftain's followers did not rely on brittle, blunt-edged stone tools, nor on the primitive metal implements of their predecessors. Their smiths worked the copper, tin and gold of Britain into ornaments of great beauty – fit for the use of a king.

Ornaments for a king

Two daggers were placed at the chief's right side. One was made of copper, with a blade nearly 10 in. long, and one of bronze, with a blade nearly 1 ft in length. Both had wooden handles, and both were sheathed. The pommel of the smaller one was decorated with thousands of tiny gold pins arranged in intricate patterns – a work of delicate and skilful craftsmanship.

A hook of gold adorned his belt. Just above the chief's left shoulder, in a position convenient for a right-handed grip, the tribesmen laid his bronze-headed axe. A knife, also of bronze, rested in his hand, and above his head lay an object made of wood, metal rivets and bronze – probably a shield.

Not far away, again on his right-hand side, was reverently placed what must have been the chieftain's symbol of office – a wooden staff, decorated with finely wrought ivory and topped with a large polished stone: his ceremonial mace. Only one other example has been found – a macehead made of stone, decorated with gold bosses, from a royal burial in Dorset.

When the funeral itself was over, the mourners turned their attention to the final

A ROYAL FUNERAL *On a sacred plain within sight of Stonehenge, a Wessex chieftain is buried in full regalia. His followers provided him with the finest luxuries of the Bronze Age. At his side they laid daggers of copper and bronze, and his ceremonial mace. A breastplate and belt hook, both of gold, adorned his body. With his bronze battle-axe at the ready and his shield above his head, the chief would be fully equipped for the afterlife.*

The age of metal transforms life in Britain

Two hundred years before the people of Wessex buried their chieftain in the Bush Barrow, the first metal-using races came to Britain. They brought with them knives and axeheads made of copper, and gold jewellery. More importantly, they brought the knowledge needed to extract these metals, to make useful alloys and to fashion them. The Metal Age had begun in Britain, and now the island's valuable tin, copper and gold ores could be worked into useful tools and beautiful ornaments.

Copper produced by smelting ore is soft enough to be hammered into shape, but hard enough to take a cutting edge. And so it was an obvious starting-point for the prehistoric smiths. They soon discovered that by adding a small amount of tin it was possible to make a much harder alloy – bronze.

Tools made of bronze would make a sharper point and cut much more cleanly than copper or flint. Unlike stone, bronze tools could be recast if they broke, re-straightened if they bent, and sharpened over and over again.

To begin with, copper and tin – and therefore bronze – must have been rare in Britain. But gradually the knowledge and use of the new material spread, as the copper ore supplies of Ireland, Wales and northern England were opened up, and tin from Cornwall became more accessible.

At first, bronze seems to have been used for luxury goods only. Bronze beads and even small knives, found in the early graves, were status symbols, rather than practical tools. Tools for everyday use were still made of flint.

A few centuries later, more effective daggers were made, together with flat bronze axes. These were the weapons buried with the Wessex chieftain in the Bush Barrow.

In the early stages, the objects were cast by pouring the molten metal into open moulds of stone or clay. Then they were hammered or trimmed into final shape. But as supplies of bronze increased, so did the range of products and the technical skill of the smiths.

Another new metal

Fostered by contacts with metal-working on the Continent, British trade and production in bronze reached its peak in the 8th century BC. But during the next two centuries, knowledge of an even better metal was beginning to spread to the island. It was iron – abundant, widespread and much more durable.

Producing iron tools involved an elaborate process of high-temperature smelting, reheating and forging – a process which remained unknown to generations of British bronzesmiths. The secrets of iron-making were gradually carried across Europe from the eastern Mediterranean.

From about 500 BC, British warriors, like their Continental neighbours, were equipped with iron stabbing swords and, occasionally, iron-fitted chariots. But these people knew more than fighting. They were Celts – as famous for their delight in decoration as they were notorious for their ferocity. They hammered their iron not only into weapons, but into the finest art of prehistoric Britain.

---

rites. Over the body they raised a 25 ft high bowl-shaped mound of earth and chalk, which served both to protect the corpse of their chief and to commemorate the position he had enjoyed during his lifetime.

The dead ruler was a member of the Wessex people, warrior aristocrats with contacts as far afield as Brittany, Ireland and Northern Europe. Their lands were inhabited by farmers and traders whose traditions and way of life dated back several centuries, and by more recent immigrants with a rudimentary knowledge of metal-working.

Wealth and power

The Wessex people brought the rich metal resources of Britain under their control, and founded a culture of exceptional wealth and power. Their prosperity was founded on a network of far-flung trading connections. Goods were exchanged with the inhabitants of Ireland, Scandinavia, Brittany and central Europe, and they perhaps even made trading agreements with the people of the eastern Mediterranean.

Their homeland on the Wiltshire Downs was ideally situated for trade. Northwards lay the shores of the Bristol Channel, from which boats crossed to Ireland. Southwards, they were within easy reach of the English Channel and Continental trade routes.

In this way the Wessex chieftains could exchange the grain, wool and hides produced by their peasant subjects for the precious metals of Ireland, Cornwall, Wales and northern England. And these goods, in turn, would be traded for the luxuries of all Europe. In addition to wealth, trade brought them increased knowledge and power.

Their brilliant organisational abilities, their exceptional technical skills and, above all, their mastery of metal, made the Wessex people the master craftsmen of their age.

THE METAL-SMITH'S ART

As supplies of bronze increased in prehistoric Britain, so did the technical abilities of the bronze-smiths. The *cire perdue*, or lost wax, method of casting was a sophisticated technique developed in the later Bronze Age. By 1000 BC, it was commonly used as an improvement on the old process of pouring molten metal into open moulds of stone or clay and then trimming the rough-cast object.

Cire perdue casting involved modelling the required object in beeswax. The model was encased in clay, and then the whole was gently heated to melt the wax and bake the clay hard. When the wax had been removed, the void was filled with molten bronze.

Using this technique, British craftsmen could produce a range of implements with more varied shapes than by simple mould-casting. Axeheads, daggers and, later, all manner of objects including sword-blades and shield-mounts, were made in this way. They provided lasting proof of the bronze-smith's art in Britain.

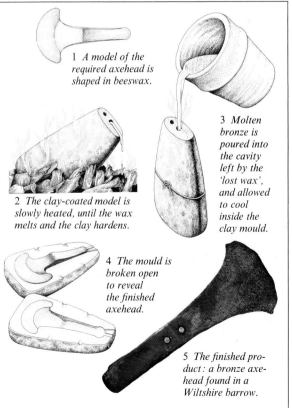

1 *A model of the required axehead is shaped in beeswax.*

2 *The clay-coated model is slowly heated, until the wax melts and the clay hardens.*

3 *Molten bronze is poured into the cavity left by the 'lost wax', and allowed to cool inside the clay mould.*

4 *The mould is broken open to reveal the finished axehead.*

5 *The finished product: a bronze axehead found in a Wiltshire barrow.*

THE EXUBERANT ARTS OF A WARRIOR PEOPLE

Like the Celtic character, Celtic art was energetic, exuberant and explosive, and yet at the same time full of humour.

The Celts, a warrior people, spread across much of Europe by the 5th and 4th centuries BC. Many established themselves in well-defended hill-forts in the south and west of England. Often highly complex constructions, the hill-forts were protected by a system of multiple ditches and ramparts. Within these virtually impregnable hill-top fortresses the members of a tribe and their animals lived.

By about 200 BC, an essentially British style of Celtic art began to appear under Continental influence. Individual 'schools' of artists, working under the patronage of wealthy chieftains, developed their own distinctive styles.

When Julius Caesar came to Britain in 55 BC, British craftsmen were lavishing their skills on objects used to display wealth and status – weapons, shields, helmets and horse trappings. Specialists worked full-time to pro-duce magnificent products for the wealthy and excelled in metalwork, particularly iron and bronze. Even articles for everyday use, such as pots, weaving-combs and spindlewhorls, were enlivened with simple elegant patterns.

The artists took their inspiration from nature, often repeating the gentle curves of the rolling hills in rounded, flowing patterns. A straight line or a sharp angle was almost unknown in the richly embossed and usually abstract designs.

Behind it all lay the suspicion of humour. sometimes called the 'Cheshire cat' style. After a short gaze almost any design will dissolve into the shape of a human face. Sometimes you see the whole, sometimes just the grin.

CHIEFTAIN'S HELMET *An exuberant pattern decorates this helmet. Made by a British bronze-smith about 50 BC, it was found in the Thames at Waterloo Bridge, London.*

MIRROR FOR A LADY *A riot of swirling patterns gives a typically Celtic design to the back of this bronze mirror. It was made just before the Roman invasion of AD 43, and was found near Desborough in Northamptonshire.*

ART AT ITS FINEST *At Battersea in London the River Thames yielded up this gleaming golden-bronze shield. Made in the 1st century AD, it is decorated with red glass studs and swirling patterns which the craftsman hammered into relief from the reverse side.*

MAGNIFICENT TRAPPINGS *This bronze mask, showing a brilliantly stylised horse, may have decorated a chariot. It came from the tribal centre of the Brigantes at Stanwick, Yorkshire.*

A CELTIC IMAGE *Excavations at Gloucester uncovered this superb head of a man, carved in limestone in the 1st century AD. The protruding eyes and nose and the heavy locks of hair suggest a Celtic god. The tapering shape of the face was much admired by the Celts.*

JEWELLER'S ARTISTRY *A Celtic craftsman made this gold torc, or collar, about 50 BC. He put a coin of the time inside one of the terminals. The torc, fashioned from eight strands of twisted wire, was found at Snettisham, Norfolk.*

CELTIC ARCHITECTS IN TIME OF WAR

About 2000 years ago, as the legions pushed the Roman Empire northwards, the whole of Celtic Europe was on the move in their path. A chieftain and his supporters, probably about 50 people in all, sailed to Shetland from the Orkneys in search of a safe place for a farmstead. They took over the Iron Age farming community which lived in round stone houses protected by a circular wall on the lake island of Clickhimin.

The newcomers then set about building a broch – a communal farmhouse within a massive stone tower. For, in that time when danger was always near, they found that the island site alone was not enough for their protection.

It was an enormous task. The outside of the broch was 65 ft in diameter and it stood 40–50 ft high. Large quantities of building stone, ferried from the mainland, were needed. It was stockpiled in the yard, the builders living in temporary huts near by.

The main entrance, at ground level, was a 17 ft long passage through the wall, opening into the central courtyard. A solid wooden door, with a guard-room just beyond it, made the entrance virtually impregnable.

The central courtyard, about 33 ft across, was surrounded by tiers of timber rooms. These were two or three storeys high, and they backed on to the inside of the tower wall.

A staircase, built into the thickness of the wall, led from the first floor to the top of the tower. Two small rooms inside the wall at ground level provided storage space, or perhaps additional living-rooms.

The work of the community was done on the ground floor. There was a central stone-lined hearth in the courtyard, and jobs such as smithing, corn-grinding and weaving were done in the rooms around it. These also housed the cattle in winter. The people themselves lived and slept in the upper storeys.

The Clickhimin community prospered. From the safety of their fortress home, the tribesmen traded skins, wool, hides, corn and slaves for iron and bronze weapons and goods from the south.

Over 500 brochs like that at Clickhimin are known in Scotland. The Celtic architects put all the emphasis on strength and security, and the brochs must have been among the strongest fortresses in all prehistoric Europe.

But, by about AD 150, the Romans had defeated the tribes of central Scotland, and the main threat to the broch people was over. The great defensive farmsteads were no longer needed.

The best preserved of all the brochs built by the Celts stands on a lonely headland on Mousa, one of the Shetland Islands. Its walls are 43 ft high.

Celtic tribesmen built Clickhimin broch in Shetland about 2000 years ago. Their ingenuity and skill combined to produce an elaborate, circular farmhouse within a massive, defensive wall. This was a safe, strong home in a time of constant warfare, and its inhabitants prospered in its shelter.

Britain prospers under Rome's rule

The Roman conquerors bring to Britain all the benefits of their civilisation – superb roads, well-planned cities, luxurious villas – and 300 years of peace

The march of civilisation from Rome made its first, hesitant steps in ancient Britain in 55 BC. The ambitious general Julius Caesar landed with an army and began to explore this uncharted isle of the north. Caesar found a misty, fertile land, partly cultivated and filled with warring tribes. His pen recorded for history his first glimpse of this strange country: 'The population is exceedingly large and the cattle very numerous. Tin is found inland and small quantities of iron near the coast. There is timber of every kind, except beech. Most of the tribes of the interior do not grow corn, but live on milk and meat and wear skins. All the Britons dye their bodies with woad, which makes them a blue colour, and this gives them a terrifying appearance in battle.'

Caesar's curiosity about this strange race was not satisfied by his first brief visit. He made a second expedition the following year. It was constantly harassed, but eventually the British submitted. Caesar gladly accepted tribute and sailed back to Roman Gaul (pp. 28–29).

But Caesar never reached the heart of the island, and it was not until AD 43 that the invasion of Britain began in earnest. Then the disciplined legions gathered the stubborn islanders into the Roman Empire. The invasion was planned as a triumph for the Emperor Claudius. From the south-east, the Roman army fanned out, conquering the British in fierce battles around their fortified hill towns such as Maiden Castle in Dorset (pp. 30–31).

Within four years a frontier had been established from Lincoln to Exeter. To the west, constant troubles with the British tribes lured the legions out on punitive expeditions. And there was a brutal lesson to be learnt before the virile people of the south-east were fully absorbed into the empire. In AD 60 a rebellion broke out, led by a widowed queen, Boudicca. Great areas of the new province were devastated (pp. 32–33).

But the rebellion was quickly smashed. The *pax romana* – the peace of

MEMORIAL TO THE POWER OF ROME

Hadrian's Wall, stretching relentlessly across the moors, valleys and crags of northern England, is the most impressive and lasting legacy of Rome in Britain. The Emperor Hadrian began the wall in AD 122, and its 73 mile length from the Tyne to the Solway was completed in eight years. This feat of military engineering kept the northern barbarians at bay.

The construction of the wall was a turning point in Rome's policy towards its empire. Hadrian decided that further expansion would serve no purpose. He was determined to create a world of stability and peace within the existing frontiers. In Britain he succeeded. Behind the protecting wall, Roman civilisation flourished for more than 250 years.

JULIUS CAESAR *In 55 BC, Julius Caesar, Rome's most famous military commander, led his army across the Channel to Britain. A year later he returned, but failed to make a lasting conquest.*

CLAUDIUS AND VESPASIAN *The unmilitary Claudius (left) ordered the conquest of Britain in AD 43. During the campaign he visited Britain for 16 days, but he left the fighting to able commanders such as the young Vespasian (right), who was also to become emperor.*

HADRIAN *This Roman coin was minted to commemorate Hadrian's visit to Britannia in AD 122. He ordered a great wall to be built to defend the northern frontier.*

SEVERUS AND CONSTANTINE *In AD 208 Septimius Severus and his son Caracalla (left) brought the Imperial court to York and drove the barbarians back across Hadrian's Wall. In York, nearly 100 years later, Constantine (right) was proclaimed emperor.*

Rome which reached across the world – had come to Britain. With peace came unity, law and order, majestic buildings, roads, trade and – for the fortunate few – a luxurious way of life that was not to be surpassed for 1900 years.

At Fishbourne, near Chichester, a huge palace was built about AD 75 and fitted out in sumptuous style, with baths, gardens and mosaic floors by a team of expert craftsmen who perhaps came from Rome itself (pp. 34–35).

The 2nd century was a time of unprecedented prosperity and expansion. Everywhere the villa owners were improving their estates and properties, many of them adding the comforts of central heating and simple mosaic floors. In the growing towns trade flourished. As British tastes became more Romanised, local artists and craftsmen augmented the flood of imported goods.

At York, the most northerly city of the empire grew up. It was really two cities: the fortress from which the army patrolled the northern frontier, and a bustling civilian centre. And in AD 208 the city played host to a great soldier and ruler. Emperor Septimius Severus brought his family and the Imperial court there. Severus was determined to subdue the savage tribesmen who were harrying the northern frontier. For more than two years he led his vast empire from York, and died there in AD 211 (pp. 36–37).

Severus was not the only emperor to visit York. More than 80 years earlier, in AD 122, Hadrian came there during his tour of the empire's borders. He began Hadrian's Wall – a defensive frontier which stretches from sea to sea across the 'neck' of Britain. For more than 250 years it marked the boundary with the tribal lands to the north (pp. 38–39).

But Hadrian's Wall was also the frontier of the empire. There the advance of Rome stopped. Beyond it lay primitive peoples waiting and watching for their moment to seize upon the treasures of Roman civilisation.

Enemies from all sides

The great wall and the courageous campaigns of Severus did much to stabilise the northern frontier. But late in the 3rd century the coasts of the island were ravaged by Saxon pirates. To meet this danger, a system of forts was built along the east coast – the Saxon Shore. To the first forts at Brancaster and Reculver, eight more were added to extend the system.

But as the power of Rome ebbed, generals fought each other for the emperor's throne. They drained the army in Britain of men desperately needed for defence against the increasing boldness of the barbarians – the Picts, Scots, Franks and Saxons. By 410 the army had virtually withdrawn from the island, and the Emperor Honorius wrote to the towns of Britain telling them to look after their own defence. The promising land which had tempted Caesar more than 450 years earlier was now left to the barbarian hordes.

During the next decades the cities which had brought the ease and order of Rome to the remote northern island withered away. Many were totally abandoned for centuries. In Britain it was soon as if the splendour of Roman civilisation had never been.

But something remained. Lost beneath a protective layer of earth and vegetation, superb mosaic floors and busts of emperors, gods and goddesses lay undamaged for centuries. Fifteen hundred years later archaeologists were to uncover these riches of Roman civilisation – a reminder of the achievements of Britain's era as a province in the great empire (pp. 40–41).

There was another still more potent legacy. Among the many religions brought to Britain by the Romans, one faith took so firm a hold on the hearts of the inhabitants that it survived the deluge. Retreating before the pagan invaders, Britain's first Christians withdrew into the mountains and remote valleys of the west. There they clung to the faith which was to unite the kingdoms of Anglo-Saxon Britain 250 years later.

Coloniae: towns for soldiers who had completed their service

Cantonal capital: centre of regional administration

Lesser walled town

Spa

Other major settlement

Legionary fortress

Fort

Fortlet

Roman Fort of the Saxon Shore

Marching camp in Scotland

Villa

Other sites

Roman wall

ICENI   Native tribe

Roads: Course certain

Roads: Course uncertain

ROMAN FORTS ON AND NEAR HADRIAN'S WALL

1 CASTRA EXPLORATORUM Netherby

2 BLATOBULGIUM Birrens

3 MAIA Bowness

4 Broomholm

5 CAMBOGLANNA Birdoswald

6 BANNA Bewcastle

7 VERCOVICIUM Housesteads

8 CILURNUM Chesters

9 PONS AELIUS Newcastle

Westernisles

Moray Firth

Auchinhove

CARNONACAE

CREONES DECANTAE

CALEDONII

EPIDII

VACOMAGI

TAEZALI

PINNATA CASTRA
Inchtuthil

HORREA CLASSIS
Carpow

VENICONES

Firth of Forth

ANTONINE WALL   Cramond

DAMNONII

Firth of Clyde

SELGOVAE

VOTADINI

NOVANTAE

Tyne
Irthing
HADRIAN'S WALL
Stanegate

LUGUVALIUM
Carlisle

CORSTOPITUM
Corbridge

Tees

MONAVIA INS
Isle of Man

Scarborough

OCELLI PROM
Flamborough Head

ISURIUM BRIGANTUM
Aldborough

Langton

Ouse

EBURACUM
York

PETUARIA
Brough

PARISI

B R I G A N T E S

PENNINES

THE WOLDS

Humber

Caer Gybi

MONA INS
Anglesey

DECEANGLI

DEVA
Chester

SEGONTIUM
Chernarvon

ORDOVICES

CORNOVII

LINDUM
Lincoln

CORITANI

BRANODUNUM
Brancaster

VIROCONIUM
CORNOVIORUM
Wroxeter

RATAE CORITANORUM
Leicester

Ermine Street

VENTA ICENORUM
Caistor St Edmund

ICENI

GARIANNONUM
Burgh Castle

LAVOBRINTA
Forden Gaer

DEMETAE

DOBUNNI

Watling Street

CATUVELLAUNI

CAMULODUNUM
Colchester

Walton
Castle

SILURES

GLEVUM
Gloucester

Lydney

Rykneld Street

CORINIUM DOBUNNORUM
Cirencester

Wheathampstead

Park Street

VERULAMIUM
St Albans

LONDINIUM
London

OTHONA
Bradwell-on-Sea

ISCA
Caerleon

VENTA SILURUM
Caerwent

Brislington

AQUAE SULIS
Bath

Salisbury
Plain

ATREBATES

CALLEVA ATREBATUM
Silchester

Cullompstone

REGULBIUM
Reculver

RUTUPIAE
Richborough

DUROVERNUM
CANTIACORUM
Canterbury

DUBRIS
Dover

LEMANIS
Lympne

Strait of Dover

DUROTRIGES

Hinton
St Mary

Hod Hill
Frampton

CLAUSENTUM
Bitterne

VENTA BELGARUM
Winchester

Bignor

Medway

The Weald

CANTIACI

DUMNONII

ISCA
DUMNONIORUM
Exeter

Maiden
Castle

Spettisbury
Castle

DURNOVARIA
Dorchester

PORTUS ADURNI
Porchester

Fishbourne

Selsey
Bill

NOVIOMAGUS
REGNENSIUM
Chichester

Angmering

ANDERITA
Pevensey

Walmer

VECTIS INS
Isle of Wight

0   50   100
miles

ROMAN BRITAIN *The network of military roads built in their province by the Romans was not to be surpassed until the 19th century.*

Julius Caesar comes and sees - but fails to conquer

THE BEACH WHERE CAESAR LANDED

Caesar and his army struggled for a foothold near Walmer, in Kent, in 55 BC. The shelving shingle beach was their first obstacle. The legionaries, each staggering under 88 lb. of equipment, waded through deep water in the face of British resistance.

About 9 a.m. on August 26, 55 BC, a fleet of warships appeared off the Kent coast. On the clifftops thousands of British charioteers, stone-slingers and spearmen watched grimly as the Roman fleet pitched and rolled in the Channel swell.

A force of 10,000 Romans was approaching the island's shore, under the command of Julius Caesar. At 46, he was already in control of the newly won territory of Gaul – and ambitious for even higher office.

He needed an audacious gesture to further his popularity with the Roman Senate and people. And he knew that the idea of Roman legions landing in the remote and fabulous island would win him fame in Rome.

Mysterious island

The Romans knew little of Britain. It was reported to be rich. There was talk of gold and pearl fishing. Its slaves were highly valued, and it exported tin and copper.

Apart from that it was a place of mystery, the centre of the Druidic religion which the Romans had met in Gaul. But, more practically, it provided a refuge for Caesar's enemies.

The invasion force set sail from Gessoriacum (Boulogne) in Gaul at midnight. But confronted by the cliffs bristling with British warriors, Caesar chose to bide his time. Eventually, he chose his spot, a shelving beach probably near what is now Walmer.

The Britons had followed the Roman fleet along the shore and were waiting on the beach – footsoldiers armed with swords, spears and slings, and charioteers. The Britons watched as the first Roman soldiers, weighed down by their armour, began to wade ashore.

The clamouring defenders dashed into the sea to hurl themselves on the advancing soldiers, or to throw volleys of spears at the struggling enemy. Roman morale wavered. As Caesar himself wrote, his men were totally unused to this kind of warfare – 'with the result that they did not show the same alacrity and enthusiasm as they did on dry land'.

The situation was now critical, but suddenly the standard-bearer of the Tenth Legion jumped overboard bearing the Roman eagle aloft. No legionary would let his standard fall into the hands of an enemy. The troops lost their hesitation and rushed after him.

The brilliant commander

For the Romans, the main problem was lack of mobility in the face of an enemy which commanded the beach and could easily regroup. Caesar ordered his scout ships to rush with reinforcements to any point where help was needed. Gradually and painfully the Romans gained a foothold on dry land. Finally, they charged, totally shattering British resistance. But they were robbed of final success, for the cavalry, so essential for the rout of a broken enemy, had been delayed in the crossing. The long day ended in uncertainty.

Nightfall brought near disaster. A sudden gale combined with unusually high tides wrecked many of Caesar's transport ships anchored offshore, and damaged his warships which were beached on the shingle.

Caesar had taken a calculated risk when he had set out for Britain. It was dangerously late for campaigning in the wet northern climate. He had brought no winter supplies, so the loss of his ships made his plight desperate.

Next morning Caesar set about the task of

ROMAN BEACH-HEAD *Fierce British resistance dismayed the invaders, but they were rallied by the standard-bearer of the Tenth Legion.*

saving his expedition. Craftsmen began salvaging what ships they could, while forage parties were sent out in search of corn.

The British responded with attacks on the forage parties, and on Caesar's camp. But they were no match for disciplined legionaries.

One night in mid-September, Caesar and his men slipped away to Gaul. He had come, and seen – but not conquered.

Caesar did not like to leave a job unfinished. He spent the winter months planning. He now knew that the British were capable of combining in the face of an invader. He had also learnt what kind of resistance he could expect.

By July of the following year, 54 BC, he was ready with a massive force – about 800 vessels laden with men, horses and equipment.

Caesar's triumph

But this time the Roman landing was unopposed. After establishing a base camp, Caesar's army broke out of Kent, taking the battle north of the Thames into Hertfordshire, the territory of the Catuvellauni. Eventually, Caesar succeeded in capturing the principal Catuvellauni stronghold (possibly the earthwork still surviving at Wheathampstead). The war-lord Cassivelaunus, who had temporarily united the British, was forced to come to terms, and agreed to pay tribute.

Caesar now felt that he had achieved enough. His own ambitions lay closer to Rome. Once again he withdrew his forces in September – and this time he did not return.

It was the last Britain was to see of the Roman legions for nearly a century. Caesar, his honour and curiosity satisfied, won his 'Triumph' – public recognition in Rome of a major victory. For him, at least, Britain had served its purpose.

THE GENIUS OF CAESAR

When Julius Caesar invaded Britain in 55 BC, he was 46 years old and a highly successful politician and general. But his ambition was boundless, and he saw an invasion of Britain as a chance to enhance his reputation.

In Rome, he had fought his way up the political ladder to the highest rank he could attain – that of Consul. In 58 BC, aged 43, he was appointed Governor of Gaul.

In the three and a half years before he invaded Britain, he subjugated France, Belgium and the Rhinelands in a series of brilliant victories. His two British expeditions added to his fame. But Rome had another great man in Caesar's son-in-law, Pompey. The rivalry between the two led to civil war. Five years after his second visit to Britain, Caesar, now aged 52, crossed the Rubicon into Italy to begin a titanic struggle for mastery of Rome.

He won decisive victories in Spain, Greece, Africa and Egypt, where the entrancing Queen Cleopatra became his mistress. By 45 BC, Pompey and his supporters were defeated. But Caesar himself was soon to fall. Only a year later, at the age of 57, he was assassinated by a group of jealous senators.

Caesar's murder on the Ides (15th) of March, 44 BC, was commemorated on a coin (above) showing the conspirators' knives. A statue (right) depicts him as a Consul.

The lure of the misty off-shore isle

The fierce tribesmen who had made Caesar's two visits to Britain so precarious were to enjoy almost a century of independence. The Catuvellauni stopped paying tribute to Rome. But peaceful trade between Britain and the Continent flourished, and the Romans saw no need of a permanent conquest.

Yet the lure of the unconquered islands beyond the frontiers of civilisation remained. The poet Horace called Britons 'the remotest inhabitants in the world'.

The more prosperous Britons were not so keen on being remote. They developed a taste for Roman luxuries such as wine, oil and delicacies like *garum*, a kind of fish-paste, as well as glass and pottery.

Relations with Rome varied from tribe to tribe. But, on the whole, peaceful relations were maintained. In AD 16, when some Roman soldiers were shipwrecked in eastern England, they were immediately returned to the Continent in safety.

Troublesome island

Emperor Augustus thought of conquering Britain, encouraged by the pleas of rival British tribal leaders who were threatened by the rising power of the Catuvellauni under their king, Cunobelinus – Shakespeare's 'Cymbeline'. But pressures elsewhere in the empire prevented any positive action.

The mad Emperor Caligula, in AD 41, actually assembled an invasion force at Boulogne in Gaul, but changed his mind.

That same year, Caligula was assassinated and Cunobelinus died. While the old king had lived, Rome had been happy with the growing trade links and friendly relations he had established. But now the Catuvellauni had once again, as in Julius Caesar's day, become a menace to Rome's northern frontier, Gaul.

Gallic trouble-makers fled to their fellow tribesmen across the Channel and used Britain as a base. In addition, Britain was the training centre for the fanatically anti-Roman Druid priests. The island had become a menace to the peace of the Roman Empire. The new emperor, Claudius, decided to bring the troublesome island under his imperial sway.

VICTIM OF WAR *Caesar's campaigns of conquest were paid for in human suffering. This Roman statue shows the death of a hostile tribesman.*

Heroism in defeat as Britons make their last stand

SIEGE COMMANDER *The conqueror of Maiden Castle was Vespasian, a soldier, who in AD 69 became Roman Emperor. He made his military reputation in the conquest of Britain.*

DEFENDERS' STRONGHOLD

Defending their island against the Roman conquest, the British made a fierce stand at Maiden Castle, near Dorchester. Archaeologists have uncovered grim evidence of the skeletons of horribly mutilated bodies buried in shallow graves after the battle.

Rising from the green Dorset hills 2 miles from Dorchester stands the ancient fortress of Maiden Castle, the scene of one of the fiercest battles of the Roman conquest of Britain. The fall of this massive bastion in AD 44 was the death-blow to British resistance in south-west Britain.

The task of subjugating the south-western tribes had been given to Vespasian, a brilliant and vigorous general who, 25 years later, was to become Emperor of Rome. Vespasian was only 33 when the invasion of Britain began. He came from a humble family – his father had been a tax collector in Asia. But he was already making a name for himself as a soldier, and he had recently distinguished himself in a decisive battle on the River Medway in Kent by outflanking the British.

His task was formidable. The British tribesmen wisely chose to avoid set battles, confining themselves to skirmishes against parties foraging for corn, or ambushes on small patrols. The tribesmen preferred to dig in on the hill-forts, many of which had been tribal centres for over 500 years. These forts were surrounded by lines of deep ditches, the earth

THE FINAL RESISTANCE *In a hail of spears and sling-shot, the Romans stormed the eastern gate of Maiden Castle. The gates were broken by a Roman 'tortoise', which advanced under cover of a barrage of* ballista *arrows.*

from which was built up into ramparts up to 45 ft high. Ramparts swept inwards towards gateways which, in turn, were protected in front by ramparts topped with fighting platforms. Maiden Castle had as many as seven lines of defence before its West Gate.

Vespasian and his Second Augustan Legion first established a supply base at the head of Chichester harbour, in the territory of the friendly local king, Tiberius Claudius Cogidubnus. From here he took the Isle of Wight, which offered little or no resistance. Then he began the systematic reduction of the tribes, moving relentlessly across the land, with a supply fleet in constant support.

One by one he mopped up pockets of resistance. The historian Suetonius says that he fought 30 battles, subdued two powerful tribes and captured 20 *oppida*, or fortified towns.

Slaughter by the sword

But the greatest trial of Roman strength came at Maiden Castle, a massive fortress half a mile long, with ramparts towering 125 ft above the surrounding fields, and topped with wooden stockades. The ramparts were manned by fierce Durotriges, a tribe adept at sling warfare, who left behind them after the battle an ammunition dump of 22,000 sling-stones.

The Roman answer to stones was *ballistae*, spring guns of wood, animal hair and gut that fired deadly metal arrows with a range three times that of a British sling-shot. Under a barrage, the defenders retreated until they were among their families and livestock in the inner defences. And the Romans advanced in *testudo*, the close 'tortoise' of legionaries sheltering under their interlocked shields, relentlessly cutting down anything that stood in their path. They reached some circular huts in the courtyard before the gates, which they set alight. Then, as the smoke billowed about, they stormed the gates.

The Romans must have been aroused to fury by the resistance of the British, for in a confusion of savagery, they hacked down the defending warriors, their womenfolk, their children and the old.

Archaeologists have uncovered the grim result of this battle, a series of hastily dug shallow graves near the scene of the fight – 23 men and 11 women buried amid the ashes of the burnt huts. The bodies had been bundled in carelessly, though the necessary food and drink for their journey into death were placed in most of the graves.

But the skeletons are a fearful testimony of the ferocity of the battle – mutilated limbs, and skulls with gaping sword slashes. One skull had no fewer than nine savage wounds, and one skeleton had the head of a *ballista* bolt still embedded in its backbone.

The conquerors built a town at Dorchester, and there the survivors of the massacre were re-settled. It was 300 years before anyone built again on the hill at Maiden Castle.

The Romans return to conquer Britain

When Claudius replaced his mad nephew Caligula as ruler of the Roman Empire in AD 41, he inherited a shambles. He had to restore public confidence and, above all, he had to show the legions that had made him emperor that he could act decisively.

The conquest of Britain served all his political aims. By enlarging the empire, rather than restoring order in an existing part of it, he would be entitled to a triumph – a sure way to please the Roman citizenry. Also, the death of Cunobelinus, king of the Catuvellauni tribe, had created unrest which threatened Gaul.

Claudius, aged over 50, was anxious for military honour. In August AD 43, an invasion force, four legions and auxiliaries numbering over 40,000 men, landed unopposed on the Kent coast – possibly at Richborough. In command was Aulus Plautius, who was to be Britain's first military governor.

His objective was Camulodunum, modern Colchester, now the Catuvellaunian capital. By arrangement, Claudius remained in Rome waiting for the message which would bring him to Britain to complete the campaign.

Plautius advanced through Kent to the Medway, where the British first opposed him. He then had to fight his way to the Thames, where he halted and sent the arranged message to Claudius.

Claudius left the luxury of his palace in Rome immediately and set sail for Marseilles. The contemporary historian Suetonius says that he was nearly wrecked on the way. From Marseilles he travelled for 13 days by carriage and litter through France to Boulogne.

He brought with him two warlike novelties for the British – an elephant corps, and 12 camels.

Claudius joined his army on September 5.

VICTORS' ARROGANCE *Roman stone-carvers often chose to depict scenes showing the victory of their legionaries over British tribesmen.*

Two days later he led the attack on the British. The battle may have been fought on Brentwood Hill, between London and Colchester, with a marsh on one flank and a dense thicket of hawthorn on the other.

Now Claudius's military menagerie came into its own. The elephants easily penetrated the hawthorn bushes. The smell of the alien camels maddened the native horses and threw the British charioteers into confusion.

In the ensuing rout 4700 Britons were killed and 8000 were taken prisoner. The Romans lost only 380 dead with 600 wounded. Colchester fell, and Caractacus – the outstanding British warrior – had to flee for his life.

Claudius triumphant

Claudius spent only 16 days in Britain. He received the submission of the conquered tribes and hurried back to Rome to claim his triumph. The Senate awarded him the title of Britannicus because, in the words of an inscription still in Rome, 'without any mishap, he received in unconditional surrender, eleven conquered British kings'.

Plautius now completed his task unhindered by the imperial court. With the Twentieth Legion in reserve at Colchester, the remaining three fanned out and occupied the land behind the frontier Claudius had laid down – a line from Lincoln to the south Devon coast. The new defences were served by the 190 mile Fosse Way, Britain's first military frontier road. Along it were forts manned by detachments of troops.

Beyond this line were the wild unconquered tribesmen. But within the new frontiers the process of ruling – and civilising – the islanders could now begin.

THE STUTTERING CONQUEROR

When Claudius became emperor in AD 41, he was over 50 and already the object of unkind fun. He was ridiculed because of his stutter. He limped, and drooled when he spoke. He was laughed at for his bookish interests. His illustrious family despised him. Claudius had managed to survive the purges, cruelty and intrigue of the reigns of Augustus, Tiberius and Caligula because nobody took him seriously. Yet he was to reign as emperor for 13 years, covering the first crucial decade of Roman occupation of Britain. And he accomplished liberal reforms throughout the empire from which the conquered island benefited.

The bronze head of Claudius (left), found in a Suffolk river in 1902, could have been torn from a statue in Boudicca's revolt.

A woman inspires the British to revolt against Roman might

RELIC OF REBELLION

The carving on this tombstone of a Roman officer, Longinus, shows him trampling a defeated Briton with his horse – an expression of the arrogance which was a cause of Boudicca's uprising. When Boudicca's furious mob sacked Colchester 11 years after Longinus's burial, they defaced his tomb and threw down its headstone.

Rome nearly lost Britain, its new imperial possession, in AD 60. Only 17 years after the invasion, in one of the bloodiest episodes in the island's history, the subject Britons rose against their new masters.

The revolt was against Roman injustice and corruption. Its tragic heroine, Boudicca, was a formidable woman, according to the Roman historian Dio Cassius: 'In appearance terrifying, in the glance of her eye most fierce, and her voice was harsh; a great mass of the tawniest hair fell to her hips.'

Unfair extortion of tax money and massive redistribution of land to Roman veterans had already angered the British. But the revolt finally centred around Boudicca herself.

Her husband, the Roman vassal-king Prasutagus of the Iceni, a tribe living in East Anglia, had willed his estates jointly to Boudicca and Emperor Nero. In this way he hoped to circumvent the law by which the lands of vassal kings without sons passed directly to Rome. But when he died, Roman officials not only seized his domains, but took the lands of Icenian nobles as well. Roman legionaries then sacked the royal palace, flogged Boudicca and raped her two daughters.

The Iceni exploded in rebellion at the outrage, and the uprising quickly spread to other tribes in south-east England. The rebels' timing was perfect. A large part of the occupying army under the command of the province's governor, Suetonius Paulinus, was occupied in massacring the Druids in North Wales, two weeks' march away from East Anglia.

Tacitus, the historian, noted in surprise that the British did not object to a woman as a leader. Her streaming hair acted as a banner to the horde following her war chariot.

Their first target was Colchester (Camulodunum), a city settled by Roman veterans, who were hated for their arrogance. The unwalled town was overwhelmed in two days, and Boudicca began to exact a terrible revenge.

Blood and fire

The last defenders took refuge in a temple built in honour of the Roman Emperor Claudius. There they were slaughtered to a man and the temple was burnt down.

Paulinus, who by now was marching his legions back from North Wales, rode ahead with a detachment of cavalry, and found London in a state of panic.

The governor made the agonising decision to abandon London to its fate. The evidence of Boudicca's wrath on the undefended town is a thick layer of ashes which lies under the soil of much of the present-day City of London.

The same fate awaited Verulamium (St Albans) – the next centre to fall. Modern excavations have revealed the burnt-out remains of a row of timber-built shops. The flames must have engulfed the entire block in a matter of minutes.

Tacitus estimated that 70,000 people died in

ANTI-ROMAN FURY *Enraged by insults to their queen, Boudicca, the Icenian tribe rose against Roman rule in AD 60. They sacked London and Colchester, and burnt St Albans (below).*

these bloody episodes. He records: 'The barbarians would have no capturing, no selling, nor any kind of traffic usual in war. They would have nothing but killing, by sword, cross, gibbet or fire.'

But Boudicca had over-extended her resources. Food supplies had been neglected, and her undisciplined followers were beginning to break up into plundering bands. The Roman Legions from Wales were now within striking distance of the British.

The two forces met in the south Midlands. Paulinus drew up his force of about 17,000 men in a defile with his flanks protected on three sides by woods, and an incline in front up which the British would have to charge. The British warriors outnumbered the Romans three to one. But they were hampered by their families whom they had brought with them – an undisciplined horde of over 100,000 people.

The final defeat

It was Roman discipline that won the day. The British were annihilated; 80,000 were slain. Boudicca escaped to the woods, where it is believed she poisoned herself.

There was a short period of vengeance on the Iceni, but in Rome Emperor Nero supported a policy of conciliation towards the vanquished tribesmen. Instead of continued reprisals there was pardon and reform.

Boudicca had won a posthumous victory. In the aftermath of her moment of triumph, a system of justice and order was established which was to last for over three centuries.

Bringing the 'Pax Romana' to Britain

Before Britain became a province of the Roman Empire, it was split into warring tribes. But the Romans established a system of law and order which gave the island its first taste of national unity, and opened up communications so that trade could flourish. Under Rome, Britain was to enjoy three centuries of unprecedented peace and prosperity.

Romans encouraged their subject nations to adopt their ways. The historian Tacitus records how the conquerors tamed the wild Britons. He reported: 'In place of distaste for the Latin language came a passion to command it. In the same way, our national dress came into favour, and the toga was everywhere to be seen. And so the Britons were gradually led on to the amenities that make vice agreeable – arcades, baths and sumptuous banquets. They spoke of such novelties as "civilisation", when they were only a feature of enslavement.'

Rome comes to Britain

Though the essence of Roman civilisation was racial toleration, it was also firmly based on a class society. There were Roman citizens and there were slaves. But it was always possible for non-Italians to gain the privilege of Roman citizenship by merit, influence or service to Rome.

It was in the towns, the centres of Roman influence and administration, their civilisation had its main impact. Ordered streets, with shops and temples and a central forum, sprang up with amazing speed. The estimate of 70,000 dead in London, St Albans and Colchester during Boudicca's rising, only 17 years after the invasion of Claudius, gives some idea of how quickly these new towns had grown.

With equal speed and efficiency, the Romans constructed their network of over 6000 miles of roads. Not until the turnpike roads of the late 18th century was a comparable attempt made at road-building. By the end of the first century, a traveller could journey from Colchester to Constantinople as fast as at any time before the reign of Queen Victoria.

Trade flourished under the protection of the Roman legions, not only within the island, but between Britain and the rest of Europe. Amphorae (large jars) of wine and oil were shipped from the Mediterranean in bulk, ceramics and glass from Germany, France and even Egypt. Local enterprises flourished. Potteries sprang up everywhere. Their products were on sale in the market towns, together with the work of other native craftsmen working in metal, wood and leather.

If Tacitus was right in regarding this civilisation as 'enslavement', it was a form of slavery which provided a good life for many Britons.

ROMAN LUXURY *Pottery figures from a child's grave at Colchester show diners reclining in the Roman manner. The standing man is reading to the diners from a scroll.*

A palace proclaims the power and luxury of Rome

The building of a Roman palace at Fishbourne in Sussex must have amazed the British. Only 30 years before, when Claudius established Roman rule in the island, they had witnessed the brute strength of their conquerors. Now the British were to see another side of their rulers – elegance and luxury on a scale far beyond their imaginations.

Nothing like the new palace had been seen before in Britain. There had been a stone-built country house on the site during the reign of the Emperor Nero (AD 54–68). But the builders and craftsmen who were called in about AD 75 had orders to construct a palace fit for a king.

'King and Legate'

Nobody can be certain who was the owner of the Fishbourne Palace, but the most likely answer is Tiberius Claudius Cogidubnus, a powerful ally of Rome. He was a king of the Regni, a tribe which occupied present-day Hampshire and Sussex. The Regni had allowed their territory to be used as a base for Vespasian's advance into western England.

The contemporary Roman historian Tacitus wrote that Cogidubnus 'maintained his unswerving loyalty (to Rome) down to our own time', and that his loyalty had been rewarded by the gift of estates. An inscription found in 1723 in Chichester, a mile from Fishbourne, describes him as 'King and Legate to the Emperor'. These titles would have made him eligible for a seat in the Roman Senate.

The palace was built to impress – but by its luxury and ostentation not by its military strength. A visitor approached it from the east along the Chichester road, which led directly to the columned front of a monumental entrance hall 80 ft wide and over 110 ft long. At the far end of the hall there was a pool with a fountain. Beyond this again was a large formal garden 270 ft across, enclosed by the four wings of the palace.

The entrance hall was well lit by windows and the walls were painted in bright, simple

THE BOY ON A DOLPHIN

The finest of the many superb mosaic floors found at Fishbourne Palace shows a winged boy playfully riding on a dolphin (above). The marble head of a boy (right), possibly represents the son of the palace's owner. The statue is of continental workmanship and dates from the 1st century AD.

ROMAN MAGNIFICENCE *The huge Roman palace at Fishbourne near Chichester was built c. AD 75, probably to house a native king protected by Rome. The columned entrance (centre), ornate courtyard and the audience chamber and offices (back wing) were intended to overawe and impress British subjects.*

LASTING MEMORIAL TO THE ROMANS

The Romans brought with them to Britain one form of art which they had made very much their own – the mosaic. Mosaic floors, made of fragments of hard stone, were designed to last – and they have proved the most enduring of all the works of Roman Britain. Many beautiful floors have survived almost intact, while buildings of brick and stone which surrounded them have crumbled away leaving little trace.

Mosaic floors were used to decorate town houses, country villas and to pave bath-houses. In Britain the wide range of local stones contributed to the fine colour and rich variety of the mosaics.

The construction of a fine mosaic, using thousands of small fragments of carefully selected material, was a long and complicated work. Only the richest people could afford this elegant luxury, and the presence of fine mosaic floors is a sure

The spirit of autumn, from a floor mosaic in the city of Corinium, now Cirencester. This fine mosaic was made in the 2nd century.

sign that a town house or villa was owned by a man of high status. Mosaics in towns became common from AD 150–200 onwards. Most of the mosaics in towns and villas date from the 4th century, when town life flourished and villa life was at its most luxurious.

Gradually, British craftsmen learnt the art from their Roman masters. Some of their mosaics portray animals and flowers, as well as a host of the gods and goddesses which the Romans introduced to Britain. They provide a fascinating glimpse of life in Roman Britain.

This elaborate scallop-shell design comes from a 2nd-century floor mosaic in a Roman house at Verulamium, now St Albans, Hertfordshire.

The leisurely life of a prosperous ruling class

The luxurious way of life which was introduced to Britain at Fishbourne spread to other splendid villas in many parts of Britain. It was a way of life far removed from the customs of the native tribesmen-peasants – an expression of the supreme power of the Romanised ruling classes.

Most of the great villas reached their peak of comfort and artistic elegance during the first half of the 4th century. About 700 villas have been discovered in Britain. Although most of these were relatively modest farm houses, a minority were clearly the luxurious mansions of successful and wealthy people.

They incorporated such comforts as very large warm baths, and reception rooms with under-floor central heating. One villa, at Bignor in Sussex, had a summer drawing-room, facing south with a fountain playing in its centre, and another equally splendid living-room with central heating for the winter. Both chambers had mosaic floors depicting scenes from Roman mythology and walls painted with imitation marble.

All the larger villas were self-sufficient, with adjoining buildings for slaves and ranges of barns for the animals. They were surrounded by great estates of well-cultivated fields, and these lands were the source of most of the corn, fruit and vegetables which were offered for sale in the market towns.

Inside, the villas were furnished with statues, armchairs of wood or wicker-work, bronze chests, ornamental tables and comfortable couches with cushions covered with bright woven cloth. These were the hallmarks of the luxurious life Rome imported to Britain.

A BRITON AT WORK *This bronze statuette of a Romano-British ploughman and his oxen was discovered at Piercebridge, County Durham.*

FARM TOOLS *Farmers had iron implements such as this ploughshare (left) and a two-pronged hoe (right), which were used in cultivation.*

---

colours. The overwhelming effect of grandeur was given by the sheer scale of the interior.

Directly opposite the entrance hall, and at a slightly higher level, stood the vaulted audience chamber reached from the garden by a flight of steps leading to a columned porch.

This west wing seems to have been the official part of the building, and the two large rooms on either side of the audience chamber may have been dining-rooms.

The north wing lay largely hidden behind a colonnade. It was a series of suites of rooms looking inwards on to two separate private courtyards. Its luxury suggests it was intended for honoured guests. Less spacious suites in the east wing may have been for minor officials.

The south wing of the house was probably the private living quarters of the owner and his family. It had two colonnades, one looking over the main garden, the other south over a garden which sloped down to the sea.

Evidently, the owner valued scenery and solitude; but equally he liked luxury, for his wing was convenient to the bath suite with its hot, tepid and cold baths and plunges. Strangely enough, the palace was not centrally heated. Perhaps the architect who designed it was not used to building for an English climate.

The palace covered over 230,000 sq. ft, an area roughly five times that of Canterbury Cathedral. Glass was brought from Egypt, pottery from Germany and France, marble from Turkey, Greece, Italy and Spain. Stone

came from the Weald of Kent, Selsey Bill, the Isle of Wight and Gloucestershire. Much of the building material passed through the busy harbour at Fishbourne.

Gardens of splendour

Tons of locally produced iron nails, roof tiles and vast quantities of oak were used. But perhaps the most staggering aspect of the palace was not so much the grandeur of its plan, but the immense trouble taken over its interior.

Almost all of its 80 or so rooms were floored with mosaics – the earliest found in Britain. Most of them were in traditional Roman patterns, occasionally featuring sea creatures. Many were of exceptional quality – as fine as any of the elaborate floors to be seen in the houses of Imperial Rome.

The gardens were no less magnificent. With their bubbling fountains fed from a header tank through underground ceramic pipes, their statues and their formal hedge-lined paths, they rivalled those in Rome itself.

Some time towards the end of the first century, the owner of Fishbourne Palace died and the house was divided into smaller units. Nearly 200 years later, when further alterations were in progress, the palace was destroyed by fire. Careless workmen may have started the blaze; or perhaps the palace was one of the first victims of Saxon pirate-marauders. But enough has survived to give a picture of the palace which symbolised the luxury of Rome.

A northern city becomes the heart of the Roman Empire

From the northern regions of Britain in the second century of Roman rule came a desperate threat to the African-born emperor, Septimius Severus. In AD 208 Severus marched with his army and his court to York. For two years this garrison town became the heart of his sprawling empire, while Severus subdued the rebellious tribes.

Fight for survival

Severus was a usurper. He seized the throne in AD 193 by a daring, forced march on Rome from his African province after the murder of Emperor Pertinax. But only three years later he was challenged by a new contender – Clodius Albinus, governor of Britain. Albinus sailed to Gaul to press his claims, draining the island of its defensive troops. The two claimants clashed at Lyons in France. Severus won the day. Albinus committed suicide and left his rival undisputed emperor.

But the price was heavy. Northern Britain had been left to the mercy of the Brigantes, a plundering tribe from the Pennines. Other tribes had poured over Hadrian's Wall. Anarchy spread. The task of ending the chaos and saving Britain for the Roman Empire was to occupy much of the rest of Severus's life.

At first, while he returned to Rome to ensure his power, Severus sent generals to pacify the restless province. But after ten years it was still not under control. By AD 208 Severus was 50 years old, and in failing health. But he was a keen soldier and could not resist the lure of the empire's most testing battlefield – the hills of North Britain. He descended on York with his wife and two sons, Caracalla and Geta.

York was a major frontier city of the empire. It was in two parts. North of the Ouse lay the fortress; to the south a cosmopolitan town with shops, law courts and forum.

A splendid palace was built for Severus. From there, in two summers, Severus marched to subdue the defiant tribes north of Hadrian's

LEGACY OF EMPIRE
The Multangular Tower at York is one of the most imposing Roman buildings still standing in Britain. Constantine the Great probably raised his standard in its shadows, for it was built about the time of his father. York was an important provincial city. Across the Ouse from the garrison, trade flourished in the business sector. Among the local crafts, even before the reign of Severus, was the making of fine jewellery from jet (left) – a hard stone found at Whitby. Jet was favoured by fashion-conscious Romans.

THE EMPEROR'S LAST JOURNEY *The body of Septimius Severus is borne in state to his grave outside the walls of York. Hard campaigning against northern tribes had hastened his death.*

Generations of Roman emperors believed that the best way to preserve the loyalty of their far-flung subjects was to provide them with 'panem et circenses' – bread and circuses. Even in Britain, one of the most remote provinces of the empire, there was a constant succession of popular entertainments.

A stage mask found at Caerleon, Gwent.

Most Roman cities had amphitheatres outside the walls. They were used for plays and pantomimes. In the arenas inside the cities, sporting events and real tragedies were played out. Men and animals were torn or hacked to death in gladiatorial clashes which drew cheering, bloodthirsty crowds. Many pots made in Roman Britain show gladiators fighting, and depict tales of their feats.

Gladiators locked in combat, on a vase c. AD 200.

Rome's civilisation takes root in British soil

Where the legions came and conquered, the Romans built towns. They were to stamp the order of Rome on barbarian Britain.

To the towns came lawyers and tax collectors. They bound the people of the empire into the legal and fiscal network of Rome.

Roman towns were built to a chessboard pattern. They often began as collections of soldiers' families and traders beside fortresses. Streets carved the towns into blocks, and at the centre was the forum – the town square. Along one side of the forum stood the basilica, or town hall, and the other sides were lined with shops and colonnades.

Benefits of Roman life

In the basilica the taxmen, administrators and the local council met, and legal disputes were settled by Roman justice. The language of the law was Latin.

In the streets behind the forum the industrial market was established where potters, blacksmiths, tile-makers, carpenters and weavers all worked. There were also bakeries and laundries, and in the bigger towns and cities slaves were used to deliver goods.

To the forum, farmers from the villas and estates outside the towns brought grain, meat, butter, cheese, milk and eggs to sell. Their cries mingled with those of traders selling wines, textiles from northern Italy, red Samian pottery from Gaul, glass-ware, leather boots and medicines of the East. The loose exchange of corn and crops for fish and skins had been replaced by Europe's first common market.

The main public buildings of the Roman towns were built of stone and a form of mortar resembling concrete. The bigger ones had their own courtyards and baths. On social occasions local dignitaries met to dine on oysters, salmon, poultry, game and fruit.

Most houses had access to running water, piped from wells through the town by skilled plumbers. All were served by main drains. More prosperous citizens were able to afford their own central heating, supplied by a hot-air hypocaust.

Fashion played an important part in the lives of women in Roman Britain. While men conducted business in the forum, their wives frequently met at the hairdressers' salons.

Chalk was used to whiten the face and arms, red ochre to colour lips and cheeks, and powdered ash for eyebrows. In Rome the writer Martial knew of one woman who had false teeth, a wig and false eyebrows. No doubt such fashions also reached Britain.

But the Romans also brought a deeper culture to Britain. The first schools opened in British cities soon after the invasion. By AD 300 there were probably schools flourishing in the major towns.

Tutors gave lessons in elegant salons. Here, the descendants of the old tribal chiefs studied Latin, literature and art. Tacitus noted that young Britons showed 'an enthusiastic desire' for learning. In the space of a few generations the island and its people had been transformed.

Wall. In two ruthless campaigns he drove the Caledonians as far as the Moray Firth. Though he failed to conquer them completely, his action gave time for the legions to restore the Wall. His fighting spirit contributed to the peace of Britain for the next 200 years.

It also hastened the end of his life. The ailing emperor's return to York was marked by an omen of doom. The contemporary Roman writer Spartianus recalls that as Severus was borne by litter to the town, black sacrificial animals escaped from the Temple of Bellona – Goddess of War – and followed him to the gates of his palace. It was Severus's last journey. He died that winter at York, and was buried outside the city wall.

It had been the old emperor's wish that his two sons, Caracalla and Geta, should rule jointly after his death. They hastened back to Rome. Within a few months Caracalla had murdered Geta, and had slain thousands of his supporters. But his bloody reign was ended in its turn by an assassin in AD 217.

The Imperial spotlight fell once again on York nearly 100 years later. In AD 306 another emperor, Constantius, died in York and was succeeded by his son – Constantine the Great. Constantine took two decisions which assured him of a lasting place in history. Firstly, he made his capital in the eastern city which took his name – Constantinople.

His other decision was even more momentous. In AD 313 he became the first emperor to permit Christianity – a turning-point for the civilised world.

The splendid Roman bath at Aquae Sulis – modern-day Bath – was rediscovered in the 19th century.

Every town of any substance in Britain had its public baths – the clubs and community centres of Roman civilisation.

Some baths, like the famous ones at Bath, were built over warm, natural springs, containing many valuable salts. The Romans recognised their health-giving properties and established the first resort town there – Aquae Sulis.

In other towns the waters and steam rooms were heated by the hypocaust, which carried hot air through ducts from a central furnace.

Roman Britons went to their baths in the afternoons. They could play games or sports in the courtyards, gossip in the steam rooms, or tone up with a cold plunge and massage.

Flasks of body oil and strigils – back-scrapers – were provided for their use. Separate sessions were held for men and women. There was a small admission charge, but soldiers and children were often allowed in free.

This iron strigil, a body-scraper used by bathers to remove oil, was found at Walbrook in London.

A glass flask which held oil for anointing the body. Also found at Walbrook in London.

A great wall marks the limits of Rome's Empire

WORLD RULER *This 2nd-century bronze head of Hadrian was found in the Thames at London Bridge, probably hurled there by Saxon raiders.*

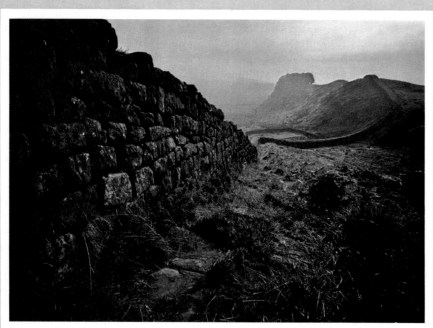

ORDERED BY AN EMPEROR

The great wall which Emperor Hadrian ordered to be built across northern Britain more than 18 centuries ago. This section at Housesteads shows how the engineers designed it to take advantage of hills and slopes which would be difficult for an enemy to storm.

FRONTIER DUTY *The legionary fort at Housesteads as it probably looked when still under construction. The soldiers are living in leather tents until their barrack blocks are built. Beyond the west gate a squad of troops marches along the military road that linked forts and milecastles spaced along the wall. An ox cart ambles through the gate with supplies, while sentries on the ramparts keep watch for attackers.*

One of the most impressive monuments of the might of Rome is Hadrian's Wall, stretching across the neck of northern England. It is also one of the world's most effective fortifications – for it played a vital role in providing Britain with nearly 300 years of peace.

During the first 70 years of the Roman occupation of Britain, this, the wildest frontier of the empire, was ravaged by tribesmen from the north and threatened from the south by the restless Brigantes of Yorkshire.

The master builder

Into this turmoil in the year AD 122 stepped Emperor Hadrian. He was a man of new ideas. And the greatest of these was to see that the mighty empire could expand no further.

Until Hadrian, the driving force of Rome had carried its civilisation ever further forward into the untamed areas of the world. With Hadrian came an age of containment. He turned the legionaries into defenders – and it was in Britain that he met the greatest test of his policy which changed the history of the Roman Empire.

He decided to build a wall to 'separate the barbarians from the Romans'. It was a mammoth task, one of the greatest ever undertaken by Roman power. But it took only seven years.

Altogether, at least 8500 men were employed to build the wall. They worked in 'centuries', groups of 80 men, piling the stones 15 ft high. Every Roman mile (1620 yds) they built a milecastle, and in between two watch towers. And 16 large forts, about 5 miles apart, were built to house the garrison.

Each group worked on a 40 yd section, then moved on. The great barrier crept across the hills, taking advantage of every major slope and craggy outcrop of rock.

This was a dangerous and lonely posting for the legions. The climate was cold. The work was hard. It is probable that the soldier builders had to down tools to fight off the wild raiders, who must have resented this un-natural barrier across land they held to be their own. Possibly it was this opposition that forced the Romans to cut the thickness of the wall from 10 ft to 8 ft to speed the work.

The men quarried more than 27 million cu. ft of stone, and dug a ditch 9 ft deep and 27 ft wide along the north side of the wall. But at its western end, nearly half its 80 Roman miles, the wall was built of turves because there was no suitable stone available. When the wall was finished, a great ditch known as the *vallum* was dug on the south side, perhaps because the Romans could not even be sure of the loyalty of the tribes in their rear, such as the Brigantes.

Abandoned to the wind

For 250 years Hadrian's sturdy fortification served its purpose well. But its success depended on the constant manning of garrisons with loyal and well-disciplined men. But in the 4th century the forces were no longer available.

Generals feuding for the Imperial throne drained away troops. Others were ordered away to fight Goths, Vandals and Huns battering on borders much nearer to Rome. In AD 407, the last effective Roman forces left Britain for the Continent.

No final, glorious battle decided the fate of the wall. It was simply abandoned to the wind, rain, wild flowers and the barbarian. After nearly 350 years of peace and civilisation, Roman Britain had finally come to an end.

Fight for survival as Roman power crumbles

The Roman way of life in Britain did not end overnight. It withered away gradually under the pitiless onslaught of invaders and the draining of resources as the legions were withdrawn for Continental campaigns.

But the barbarian invasion of 367 marked a turning point. From then on life in the province sank towards the chaos of the Dark Ages. Forty years later Britain ceased to be part of the Roman world.

During 300 years of Roman rule, the Britons had become accustomed, at least in the south-east, to prosperity and peace. Great villas, or farming estates, worked by an ample supply of peasants and slaves, produced food for the flourishing cities.

But things were changing. The central government in Rome was now weak. Barbarian attacks were increasingly strong and more frequent. And above all, the powerful army had aspirations of its own. The men not involved in frontier duties were free to indulge in the activities of victorious troops in conquered lands, the most attractive being the acquisition of booty. In 383 and again in 406, British commanders took their troops to the Continent, to pillage and to bid for the Imperial throne. Each episode ended in disaster.

A brief respite came in 396–8 when Stilicho, a Vandal-born general of brilliance, re-organised British defences. But in 401, Stilicho and his army left Britain to defend Italy, the heart of the empire itself.

By 407 matters had reached crisis point. Three times in 25 years Britain had been depleted of its army. Confidence had never fully returned after 367. Now the morale of the country was in tatters. Villas were abandoned; their fields reverted to scrub. The country-dwellers fled to the safety of the walled cities. But trade on which city life depended rapidly declined with the slump in agriculture and growing hazards of travel.

In 410 the Saxons raided the coasts once more. The Britons seized the opportunity to break away from Rome, establishing their own administration as best they could. Centralised government had evidently broken down completely. In the death agony of Roman Britain, the towns wrote to Emperor Honorius asking for help, only to be told that from now on they must look after their own defences. Britain was on its own.

BARBARIANS *A carved Pictish stone slab found at Aberlemno in Angus, shows Pict fighting men on foot and horseback.*

ROME'S RULE ENDS – BUT A RICH LEGACY SURVIVES

As Roman civilisation collapsed under the successive blows of barbarian hordes, its splendid buildings were devastated and all their riches laid waste.

In the towns, abandoned by fleeing citizens, trees and bushes pushed their way through the pavements and dislodged the columns and pediments of forums and temples. In many of the villas which had carried luxurious Roman living to the remotest corner of the empire, cattle were stabled in the magnificent tiled bathrooms and formal chambers. Within a few generations the civilisation which had brought Britain one of the longest and most settled periods in its history was buried beneath rubble and scrub.

But many of its finest creations proved miraculously immune to the ravages of time. Hundreds of years later, marvellous works of art and architecture were unearthed from the layers of earth and undergrowth. Intricately patterned mosaics, fresco paintings, relief sculptures and busts to unknown gods in magnificent temples had been preserved.

Some of the great wealth of Roman art came to light by patient archaeological research, others by pure chance. It was workmen digging a drain who discovered Fishbourne Palace, near Chichester, with its rich mosaic floors; and in Suffolk a ploughman turned up the Mildenhall Treasure, one of the finest hoards of Roman silver ever found. It was apparently buried by a rich family before they took flight from the barbarian invaders.

Much of the decorative work of the early period of Roman occupation was done by foreign craftsmen and artists. They were brought in to embellish the villas which sprung up in south-east Britain after the Claudian invasion. Soon, British craftsmen learnt the newly imported skills and established flourishing schools of mosaic work, glass and pottery manufacture, sculpture, painting and metal work.

Nothing inspired the Roman artists and sculptors as much as the many gods and goddesses they brought with them from Imperial Rome, and these figures and busts are among the most fascinating and beautiful pieces of Roman art in Britain.

Gods of the empire

The Romans also adopted many of the Celtic gods, some interchangeable with their own. Mars, the Roman God of war, corresponded closely with the Celtic deities Belatucadrus and Calumus. Throughout the north of England Roman soldiers built shrines to Celtic gods, no doubt seeking the protection of these powerful local deities in their campaigns against the fierce neighbouring tribesmen.

Some of these shrines were complex buildings filled with treasures such as the splendid

MASTERPIECES IN GLASS

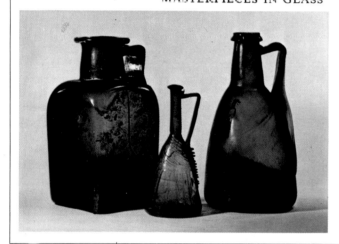

Glass-blowing, which was invented about the 1st century, transformed the use of glass from a luxury only the rich could afford into a thriving industry, which supplied glass vessels and medallions for practical and decorative use. Much of the early glass came from the Rhineland; other objects from as far away as Egypt. Many pieces, some of them with fragile handles or intricate designs, survived in the ruins of Roman Britain.

CHRISTIAN HOUSEHOLD *The Romans introduced Christianity to Britain during the 3rd century, and it spread quickly. These paintings, found in* *Lullingstone Villa, are of the sacred monogram, made from the first two Greek letters of Christ's name, and of a man praying.*

temple, built on a hilltop above Lydney, to Nodens, a hunter-god of the Forest of Dean. Nodens's temple, decorated with mosaic panels and filled with religious ornaments and sculpture, was made up of a nave and a series of chapels and aisles. The outbuildings included public baths, shops and a hostelry for pilgrims to the shrine.

The Romans also imported gods which they had adopted from other parts of their empire. A Persian god, Mithras, became the object of a thriving cult in Britain and temples to him were built throughout the island. A sculpture unearthed in London shows the god as a handsome youth with long curly hair, and other portrayals depict him slaying a bull, symbolising the conquest of nature. His followers too, many of them rich merchants, were expected to show their willingness to conquer the wild elements in human nature. The cult involved severe physical and mental tests.

The most lasting legacy

Among the strange cults the Romans brought to Britain was the primitive faith which was eventually to triumph and lead to a new civilisation. Introduced to Britain in the 3rd century, Christianity flourished under the Romans and inspired its own art, the finest examples of which were found in the Roman villa at Lullingstone in Kent.

As the barbarians advanced on their trail of pillage and destruction the Christians fled to the hills, where they fostered and kept alive their faith. And there, in the remoter reaches of the country, Christianity grew, to become the greatest legacy of Roman civilisation.

THE MILDENHALL TREASURE

During the last troubled years of Roman rule in Britain, in the late 4th and early 5th centuries, Saxon raids from the Continent became ever more menacing. A wealthy family living at Mildenhall in Suffolk panicked – and buried their hoard of silver treasure for safety. They were never to recover it.

Nearly 16 centuries later, during the Second World War, a ploughman working at Mildenhall set his plough 4 in. deeper than was usual. He struck an object – and found a hoard of encrusted objects which he gave to his employer. Believing them to be made of lead or pewter, the farmer left them, neglected, in his home. But in 1946 an inquest declared the find to be treasure trove and their true value came to light.

The Mildenhall Treasure is probably the most important collection of Roman works of art ever to be found in Britain. It consists of 34 pieces of highly ornamented silverware, priceless in value. When cleaned, the pieces were found to be in an almost perfect state of preservation, made of the finest-quality silver. The bulk of the collection dates from the 4th century, but some could be as early as the 2nd, indicating that the family heirlooms were collected over several generations.

The centrepiece of the hoard, which was found 30 yds from the remains of a 4th-century Roman building, is a magnificent dish, nearly 2 ft in diameter and weighing 18¼ lb. A relief shows the head of Oceanus, god of the sea, in the centre, with other gods and sea monsters surrounding him. Other pieces of the treasure include dishes, goblets, a fine bowl with a lid and eight spoons, five of which are of the kind that may have been used as christening gifts.

Most of the treasures were either made in Rome or in Gaul; but some items, like a fluted bowl, were probably worked in Britain.

The Mildenhall Treasure is a magnificent reminder of the high state of Roman culture in Britain, and an intriguing sidelight on the history of the troubled times when it was so hurriedly buried by its wealthy Romano-British owners.

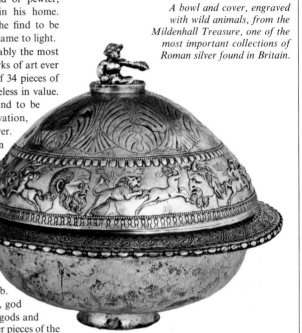

A bowl and cover, engraved with wild animals, from the Mildenhall Treasure, one of the most important collections of Roman silver found in Britain.

A FAMILY OF GODS *Throughout much of Roman history, Roman religion allowed considerable freedom of worship, and the Romans imported to Britain many different gods from all over their empire. The many statues they left behind show their variety – a Jupiter (left), a Sphinx and a Lar, or simple household god. A head of Mithras (right) was found at the Walbrook Temple to Mithras in London. It had been made in Italy of marble and was buried in London by the god's followers, with other cult objects, during a period of persecution by Christians.*

Invaders forge a united nation

Waves of land-hungry warriors come to Britain, first as raiders, then as settlers who build the villages of England and slowly create a realm united by the Christian faith

With the Anglo-Saxon invasions of the 5th century, a new era opened in British history. It lasted for six centuries and ended in apparent disaster at the Battle of Hastings in 1066. Yet during this time, these newcomers of West Germanic stock – Angles, Saxons, Jutes and Frisians – created the pattern of villages that was to endure to modern times.

The Anglo-Saxons came from areas outside the Roman Empire, from the coastline which stretches from Jutland to the mouth of the Rhine. They brought an alien way of life with them, and their settlement was not unopposed or easy. The native British, now more Celtic than Roman, were still capable of putting up stout resistance.

Various ancient hill-forts became the bases of British war leaders for their campaigns against the invaders. One of these, Cadbury Castle in Somerset (pp. 46–47), holds a mystery that remains unsolved. According to legend, it was the home of Arthur, the heroic leader of the Britons in their struggle.

For a time the British managed to halt the tide of settlement and conquest. But, by the late 6th century, the Anglo-Saxons had resumed the offensive. After victory at the Battle of Dyrham in 577, they were well poised to overrun all of Britain to the borders of Wales, Devon and Cornwall. They also advanced into the lowlands of the north-west, and as far as the Firth of Forth and modern Edinburgh in the north-east.

After about 600, the Saxons in Britain were organised into several small kingdoms. In the early days Northumbria, formed by the merging of two

A SYMBOL OF SAXON FAITH

The Anglo-Saxons first came to Britain as pagan raiders about AD 400. Three centuries later they had peopled and tamed much of England. It was they who began the clearing of Britain's ancient forests in earnest. They cleared far more than the Romano-Britons before them.

During these centuries, the Saxons embraced Christianity. And, although still divided into many kingdoms, they established a united Church. It was to be the inspiration of their finest works of art, such as this 10th-century ivory depicting the Crucifixion (inset). Their faith also inspired works of architecture. The tower of Sompting church in West Sussex has survived for 1000 years as evidence of their skill. It is similar to towers built in the Rhinelands in the same period. The use of Roman bricks at Sompting shows how Saxon England grew out of the ruins of Roman Britain. The village of Sompting, with its church, was among hundreds of settlements founded by the Saxons. These communities, and the well-tended fields which surrounded them, were the lasting legacy of the Anglo-Saxons.

PLOUGHING AND SOWING *The Anglo-Saxons were, above all things, a farming people. These pictures, from a Saxon calendar made in the 11th century, are a rare contemporary record of Saxon life. A man ploughs in the month of January. His plough, drawn by four oxen, has a blade to cut the sod in front of the share, and a wheel for control. The Saxons brought this type of heavy plough from the Continent. It was a boon in the lowlands of the English Midlands, where the Saxons prospered.*

CUTTING WOOD *The Saxons relied on wood. It was their only fuel and their main building material. Carts and wagons, and all manner of tools and utensils were made of wood. The Romans, and the Celts before them, had made little inroad into the forests of Britain. It was the Saxons who began the long process of turning woods and marshes into fields, making slow but lasting changes in the landscape. The Saxon artist showed men cutting wood in February.*

RAKING, DIGGING AND SOWING *March was one of the busiest months of the Saxon year. After winter frosts, the soil was ready for final digging and sowing. The peasant was required to work up to three days a week in unpaid service to his lord at this time of year. He was expected to 'lie at his lord's fold as often as it falls his lot', and to plough and plant 5 acres a week at his own expense. The rest of the time he could look to his own livelihood.*

SHEEP TENDING *Every Saxon farmer – lord and peasant alike – owned sheep. And Saxon wool gained a high reputation for its quality. This rich heritage was to become the foundation of English wealth in the Middle Ages. In May, the lambing season nearly over, shepherds and their seasonal helpers had to be constantly on the lookout for the wild beasts – wolves and foxes – which preyed on their flocks.*

kingdoms in the north – Deira and Bernicia – was the most powerful. The East Angles of Norfolk and Suffolk formed a somewhat isolated kingdom. In the south-east, Kent, Sussex and Essex were among the earliest kingdoms.

The formation of the two most important of these early kingdoms, Mercia and Wessex, was slower and more complicated. It was not until the second quarter of the 7th century that the Mercians, led by their pagan and war-loving ruler, Penda, built up a powerful military confederation over the Midlands. Wessex was an earlier creation. But, like Mercia, it was not until late in the 7th century that it achieved the power its founders sought.

All these kingdoms were converted to Christianity in the course of the 7th century. The missionary zeal of St Augustine (pp. 48–49), who was sent by Pope Gregory the Great, brought the people of the south-east into the Church, in direct contact with Rome. Meanwhile, St Aidan, from St Columba's island monastery of Iona in Scotland, helped St Oswald of Northumbria to convert his people, following Celtic practices. Representatives of those favouring Roman and Celtic customs met to resolve their differences at Whitby in 663–4, at the great synod called by King Oswy of Northumbria. After that, all the kingdoms turned to Rome for inspiration and guidance. In this way, unification of the kingdoms through Christianity was achieved about 300 years before political unity.

For the Anglo-Saxons, the rich lands of England had been worth fighting for. Their careful agriculture brought wealth. The treasures found at Sutton Hoo in East Anglia (pp. 50–51) show the wealth attained by a Saxon king.

The threat from across the North Sea

Generation by generation over the succeeding centuries, the divided kingdoms of Saxon England moved towards unity. Mercia came close to achieving it under King Offa.

But national unity was not to be won by English effort alone. It took a new, external threat to force unity upon England. After 800, the heathen Vikings – notably the Danes – were an ever-increasing menace.

Northumbria, the Christian stronghold of the north, suffered severely. After the sacking of the monastery of Lindisfarne (pp. 52–53) the Christian torch, lit by St Oswald, came close to being extinguished.

It fell to another kingdom to take up the struggle against the menace. The hour produced the man – Alfred, ruler of Wessex (pp. 54–55). By an all-out military effort, he and his successors were able first to contain and finally to reconquer the lands that had fallen under Scandinavian control.

The Anglo-Saxons were not totally concerned with war. They were primarily a farming people. But during the 8th century, their vigour and vitality began to manifest itself in town life. London flourished.

The Church was powerful under both Celtic and Roman churchmen. St Dunstan of Canterbury inspired the foundation of many monasteries in the 10th century, which were to have a lasting effect on religious and social life.

Scholarship also flourished. Monks such as Bede produced works in Latin. But authors also wrote in Anglo-Saxon – the beginnings of the English language. The epic poem 'Beowulf', telling a great warrior's story and more than 3000 lines in length, was composed in the 8th century.

Learning was encouraged by kings such as Alfred, who assembled a notable group of scholars. They translated many works from Latin, and books 'most needful for men to know' were made accessible to the English in their own language. The *Anglo-Saxon Chronicle* also took shape at this time.

But, despite Alfred's victories, Scandinavian influence was long-lasting, and in the late 10th and early 11th centuries a fresh move brought the Danes success. From 1016 to 1042 a Christian Danish dynasty ruled England.

The Anglo-Saxons now produced their last king of the direct Saxon line – Edward the Confessor. Under his rule art flourished, carrying on a long tradition of Anglo-Saxon craftsmanship (pp. 58–59). And his own contribution was the creation of Westminster Abbey (pp. 56–57), a towering monument to the Christianity the Anglo-Saxons had come to treasure.

On Edward's death in early 1066, the throne passed to his brother-in-law, Harold, Earl of Wessex, the strongest man in the kingdom. But, as the *Anglo-Saxon Chronicle* recorded, he 'met little quiet in it as long as he ruled the realm'. In 1066 England was wealthy and potentially powerful. Its throne was a rich temptation to any warrior. William of Normandy played for high stakes when he landed on the Sussex shore that autumn.

ANGLO-SAXON BRITAIN *Saxon settlement in Britain began in the 5th century. It was another 500 years before the Saxon kingdoms were welded into the united kingdom of England.*

SYMBOLS

· Saxon settlement (pre-AD 500)

• Other Saxon settlement (with current name)

Area conquered by AD 600

Danelaw boundary established by Alfred and Guthrum the Dane in 886

KENT Kingdom

Line of Offa's Dyke

REAPING *Everyone in Saxon England knew the importance of a good harvest. Here, three peasants cut corn with sickles; a fourth binds it into sheaves. Three more harvesters load sheaves on to a cart. The great Saxon estates, the vills, were arranged so that they included woods, meadows, arable land and common-land grazing. The strips of cultivated field were allotted to the lord, peasants and tenants, so that every man had some good land and some less fertile.*

HUNTING WITH THE FALCON *Young birds and animals were hunted at their fattest and most succulent in October. Hunting with falcons and hawks reached England from the Continent in the mid-9th century. The sport soon became popular with the nobility, and laws governing it were strictly enforced. Pheasants, partridges, quails, ducks, teals, woodcocks, hares and rabbits abounded in the countryside.*

THE WARM FIRE OF WINTER *In November, the harvest gathered in and the farm animals safely in the byre, the Saxon peasant could relax. Some animals would be killed and their meat salted to preserve it. But after the twelve days of Christmas festivities, Anglo-Saxon peasant's fare was monotonous – bread and porridge, with occasional milk, fish and cheese and, rarely, salt meat and dried fruit.*

THRESHING AND WINNOWING *Work out of doors was shunned in December. In the barn, the peasants would carefully beat out the corn to separate the grains from the ears. Then came the job of sifting the corn to get rid of the chaff. After that, the precious corn was bagged for storage, ready to be taken to the mill.*

45

A hilltop fortress keeps its age-old secret

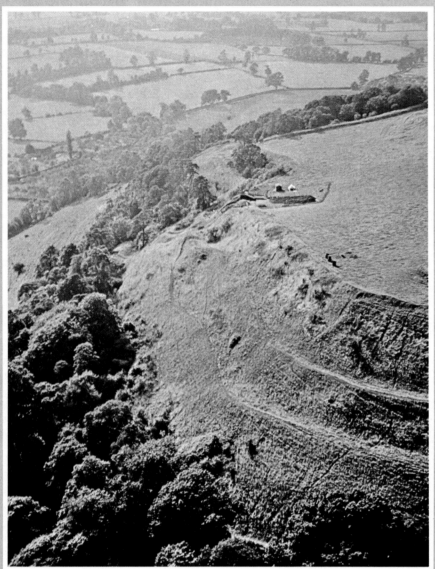

WAS THIS CAMELOT?

Cadbury Castle, Somerset, viewed from the air. In recent years, archaeologists have been at work on the site, trying to discover whether this pre-Roman hill-fort was the head-quarters of Arthur, the legendary hero of British resistance to the Saxons.

Above the Somerset village of South Cadbury, close to the Dorset border, stands an ancient hill-fort which has become the subject of the most romantic mystery in British history. For a tradition which reaches back for at least 500 years links this quiet spot with the legendary castle of Camelot and its ruler, King Arthur.

Cadbury Castle, as the fort is named, was originally built by the Iron Age inhabitants of the area. It is constructed to a pattern found in many places in southern Britain, crowning a 500 ft hill whose sides are covered with massive banks and ditches, designed to discourage an enemy from storming the 18-acre enclosure at the summit.

But it was not strong enough to defy the Romans. When Vespasian led his legions in the conquest of south-western Britain, he took the fortress by storm. During the four centuries of Roman rule it fell into decay but, as the Romans withdrew, Cadbury was re-occupied by the Britons of the area for defence against both the pagan Anglo-Saxon invaders and the many rival British kingdoms.

From this era of bloody war and sudden death dates a mystery which has never been solved. According to the Tudor historian and chronicler John Leland: 'At . . . South Cadbury standeth Camelot, sometime a famous town or castle . . . The people can tell nothing there but that they have heard say that Arthur much resorted to Camelot.'

Was Cadbury the home of Arthur? Did this great British war-leader in fact exist? A medieval story-teller, Geoffrey of Monmouth, wrote of Arthur, his battles and of his magic sword. Other writers added the romance of the Round Table, the ill-starred love of Lancelot and Guinevere, and the magician Merlin.

But these legends were not of their own creation. They drew upon older sources – the ancient memories of the Celtic peoples of Wales, Cornwall and Brittany – which originated in the Dark Ages of the 5th to 9th centuries. Then, the British ancestors of these Celts were engaged in a long and bitter struggle to preserve their homeland from the Anglo-Saxon invaders.

Arthur the war lord

Most historians today agree that Arthur existed, though he was probably not a king. He may have been leader of a band of highly mobile men. This would account for his ability to move swiftly through Britain to win the dozen victories associated with his name.

The monk Nennius, writing in the 9th century to extol the Welsh, described Arthur as *dux bellorum* (battle chief) in his *History of the Britons*. At Mount Badon, probably near Swindon, he won his greatest victory over the Saxons. In that battle, Nennius recorded, 960 men fell 'in one onslaught of Arthur's'. The triumph was so overwhelming that the Saxons made no further encroachments on

AS IT WAS *The British chief who reoccupied Cadbury in the 5th century rebuilt much of its defences. The most striking features of his improvements were a timber gate-tower, built about 470, and a great hall.*

the scene of major rebuilding operations at exactly the period when Arthur must have lived.

The man who ordered the rebuilding of Cadbury was clearly an exceptionally powerful British chief. He was strong enough to raid far-off Saxon settlements in search of slaves and booty, for early Saxon ornaments have been found at Cadbury.

The castle also fits the Arthurian legend because of its geographical location and the size and scale of its defences. On the present archaeological evidence, Cadbury gives the best idea of what Arthur's base must have been like, with its great feasting hall.

Modern legend

Despite all the accumulated evidence of modern archaeology, the mystery of South Cadbury may never be solved. Even at Cadbury today, archaeological fact merges into legend. A local tradition claims that Arthur sleeps beneath the hill, and will rise again when his country calls.

Arthur's reputation was not confined to Britain. Writing about 1170, the chronicler Alanus de Insulis recorded: 'What place is there within the bounds of the empire of Christendom to which the winged praise of Arthur the Briton has not extended? The peoples of the east speak of him as do those of the west, though separated by the breadth of the whole earth.'

British territory for the next 50 years. But it was at this point Arthur passed into legend. According to the Celts, he never died but was merely sleeping. One day he would wake again to drive the Saxons into the sea. As late as 1113, when a group of French monks laughed at this story in Cornwall, the local people were so angered that they attacked them.

Arthur's fortress

Other legends told of Arthur's lavish court at Camelot. Many sites have been suggested for this fabulous palace. Cadbury is perhaps the most probable. It was never the spectacular building chronicled by the medieval romancers, but there is no doubt that it was

A land threatened by invaders from all sides

After the Romans withdrew from Britain in the 5th century AD, the Britons faced many enemies. Although Germanic pirates had been raiding the east coast for some generations, it seemed to the British that their island was chiefly threatened by Picts from the north and by Scots from Ireland. So their rulers followed the example the Romans had set and hired German princes and their warbands to fight off the Picts.

Unwittingly the British themselves had taken the first step that was to lead to their doom. German warriors were established from the Vale of York to Southampton Water.

These tribesmen brought their families with them and were given land to till in return for military defence. But only 50 years after they arrived, the policy began to break down. The newcomers had come to realise the weakness of their employers. No doubt there was pressure from land-hungry fellow-tribesmen on the Continent as well. A series of revolts began.

Saxon triumph

The British kingdoms did their best to hold out against this pressure – especially in the west. But their alliance was broken by defeats at Dyrham in Gloucestershire in AD 577 and at Chester in 616. By the late 7th century, most of England was under the rule of Angle or Saxon kings.

The native British, however, were not expelled or exterminated. Though some fled to the far marches of Wales, the west and the north, historians now believe that much of the English settlement was peaceful – a slow take-over of the decaying Romano-British villages and estates. Both Celtic Briton and Germanic Saxon had a part in the making of England.

ARTIST'S RECORD *In this 11th-century illustration of Noah's ark, a monk based his work on the longboats used by the Saxon invaders.*

'THE ONCE AND FUTURE KING'

One of the first authors to collect many of the myths and legends surrounding the heroic figure of Arthur, King of the Britons (left), was Geoffrey of Monmouth. In his *History of the Kings of Britain*, written in the 1130's, the reign of Arthur was the highlight. According to Geoffrey, Arthur was crowned as King of the Britons at the age of 15 and led his people to triumphs over both the Saxons and the Picts. These were won with the aid of the king's magic sword, which Geoffrey called Caliburn but later writers renamed Excalibur.

Arthur went on to conquer Ireland, Iceland, the Orkneys, Norway and Gaul. But his treacherous nephew Mordred allied himself with the Saxons against his uncle. Arthur and Mordred eventually met in battle. Though Mordred was slain, Arthur himself received a deadly wound and was carried away to the Isle of Avalon in the far west and rested there until it healed.

Many other writers added more stories to the legend. These included the tragic love of Lancelot and Guinevere, the quest for the Holy Grail, and the legend of the Round Table. But on one fable they all agreed: Arthur would return in a time of trouble when his people called upon him. He was, in truth, 'the once and future king'.

A medieval illustration shows Arthur's Round Table in all its glory as Galahad, the purest knight of all, is introduced to membership.

St Augustine rekindles the flame of Christianity

CRADLE OF CHRISTIANITY
The first church of St Martin at Canterbury was built during the Roman occupation. Two centuries later, St Augustine used it on his mission to convert the pagan Saxons. The church was rebuilt in succeeding centuries, but parts of the Roman walls survive.

Early in 597, a ship dropped anchor off the Isle of Thanet in north-east Kent. From it there landed a band of 40 men. They were Christian monks and they had been led on their long journey to Britain by the Prior of St Andrews in Rome. His name was Augustine, and his mission was to convert the heathen peoples of Britain to Christianity.

Augustine's mission had been long in preparation. About 20 years before he and his companions set out, Gregory, who was then the pope's representative at Constantinople, had noticed some fair-haired boys being offered for sale in the slave-market. He asked the name of their race.

'They are called Angles,' the slave-dealer replied. 'That is appropriate,' Gregory said, 'for they have angelic faces, and so it is right that they should become fellow-heirs with the angels in Heaven.'

The chosen leader

From that time onwards, Gregory was determined to bring Christianity to the Angles. In 590 he was elected pope. At last he had the power to authorise the mission he had so long desired. And to lead this hazardous venture, he chose Augustine.

In many ways the choice was surprising, for Augustine seems to have been a cautious man, with more than a touch of arrogance. Gregory, however, knew and trusted him.

Such was the man who set foot on the Kent shore early in 597. One of the first to hear of his arrival was Ethelbert, King of Kent and overlord of all the English south of the Humber. Augustine and his companions were swiftly summoned to his presence. This was the crucial moment. If Augustine could

CONVERSION OF A KING *Augustine (left, with cross) was made welcome by King Ethelbert of Kent (seated, centre), whose wife Bertha (left of king) was already a Christian. Augustine's words bore fruit. He later baptised Ethelbert.*

persuade the king to listen, his mission stood a fair chance of success.

He had one great advantage on his side – apart from his gifts as a preacher. Ethelbert was married to Bertha, a Christian princess from France, who had come to Kent some years before, accompanied by her bishop, Liudhard.

Augustine and his companions marched boldly up to the king, carrying a silver cross and chanting prayers. The king greeted them politely, but he had taken care to meet them in the open in case these mysterious strangers cast spells on him.

Augustine then explained the purpose of his mission, and preached to the assembled court. Finally, Ethelbert rose. According to the Venerable Bede, he replied: 'Your words and promises are fair indeed. But they are new and strange to us and I cannot accept them and abandon the age-old beliefs of the whole English nation. But since you have travelled far . . . we shall not harm you. We will receive you hospitably . . . Nor do we forbid you to preach and to convert.'

The king then gave Augustine a house in the old Roman town of Canterbury. There, he used the church of St Martin, built by Christians during the Roman occupation 200 years earlier. Ethelbert became so impressed by the faith and teaching of the missionaries that he himself was baptised.

Foundations of the Church
This was the turning-point of Augustine's mission. Ethelbert's example encouraged many of his subjects to take the same step. On Christmas Day 597, more than 10,000 men and women were baptised by Augustine.

From Canterbury, Augustine sent out men to establish new bishoprics. One of them, Justus, became the first Bishop of Rochester and another, Mellitus, founded the see of London. Ethelbert's nephew, Saebert, King of Essex, followed his uncle's example and became a Christian. All over south-east England the idols fell and the cross was set up in their place.

But the fires of paganism still burnt strongly in Saxon hearts. Saebert died, and his pagan sons forced Mellitus to flee to Gaul. Even in Kent, Ethelbert's successor reverted to the old beliefs for a short while.

For their part, the Christians were learning the wisdom of building on pagan foundations. Pope Gregory advised Augustine not to 'pull down the heathen temples . . . Let them become temples of the true God, so the people will have no need to change their place of concourse'.

In spite of everything, the Church survived. Within a few generations, Anglo-Saxon missionaries were themselves setting out to convert the heathen Saxons of Germany. English missionaries were to become the bearers of the faith to countless pagans. Christian England had been born.

Britain's Christians return to the Roman fold

Augustine, his monks and his converts were not the only Christians in Britain. In the far west, in the north and in Wales survived the Celts – the Britons whom the Angles and Saxons had driven out. The Anglo-Saxons called them 'Welsh' or foreigners.

Though they had been cut off from Rome, the British had remained loyal to the Christian faith they had adopted when their land was part of the Roman Empire.

With the arrival of Augustine, there were now two Christian Churches in Britain. But he was not the man to reconcile any differences between them. Newly arrived from Rome, he was suspicious of the customs that had grown up in the Celtic Church.

Differences resolved
The Celts calculated the date of Easter in a different way. Their monks shaved their heads in a different pattern. Their approach to baptism differed, and abbots were more important than bishops in their church organisation.

All this worried Augustine. He saw differences and may have suspected heresy. When he eventually conferred with the leaders of the Celtic Church at Aust on the River Severn, he offended them by his arrogance.

The British agreed to another meeting, but made up their minds to test his good faith. They decided to let Augustine enter the conference chamber first. If he then rose to greet them, it would show that he respected their rank and they would continue to negotiate. If he failed to do so, they would refuse to agree to his demands. Augustine remained seated,

and the Celtic churchmen continued angrily to defend their customs.

By the 650's, however, Celtic Christians had come to play a major part in the task of conversion, especially in Northumbria. In 663 King Oswy of Northumbria summoned the leaders of both Churches to meet at Streoneshealh (Whitby). There, the two sides calmly debated the great issue.

The Celtic case was put by Colman. He argued that the Church should observe the customs hallowed by tradition. The Roman case was put forward by the forceful Bishop Wilfrid. The Celtic fathers were holy men, but should they – a few men on a corner of a remote island – be preferred before the universal Church of Christ? King Oswy supported Wilfrid: 'If Peter indeed held the keys of the kingdom of Heaven, King Oswy had no wish to offend him.'

The verdict was in favour of Rome, and one account says that Oswy was smiling as he gave it. Agreement had at last been achieved. And more important still, a strong link with Europe had been re-established.

BURIED TREASURE *Found in a grave at Stanton, near Ixworth, in Suffolk, this gold cross is inset with thick pieces of garnet.*

GREAT HISTORIAN *The Venerable Bede, a monk of Jarrow, completed the masterpiece of the age, his* Ecclesiastical History, *in 731.*

PAGAN SURVIVALS *The Franks Casket, carved in whalebone in the early 8th century, shows the smith of pagan legend, Wayland, at his forge.*

Riddle of a royal treasure buried in the Suffolk sands

In about AD 625, the people of the small Saxon kingdom of East Anglia prepared a sumptuous burial in their royal cemetery at Sutton Hoo in Suffolk. It was one of the most magnificent royal burials in Western Europe, for the treasure they buried was fit for a king.

Into a pit on a sandy heath above the Deben estuary, the Saxons lowered a ship. It was old and already repaired, a great open rowing boat with places for 40 oarsmen and a steersman. In a wooden cabin amidships the mourners placed a king's treasure. Lastly, the sand from the pit was put back over the ship, and a mound of turf and sand was piled over it.

The site held its secret until 20th-century archaeologists discovered the burial. They found remains of the weapons of a warrior, including his axe, his jewelled sword, his magnificent ornamental helmet, his shield and a great stone sceptre tipped with a bronze stag.

All these clues pointed to a king. But archaeologists have found no definite trace of a body among the precious cargo of the burial ship. Some experts believe that the ship with all its treasures was placed here without its royal master – perhaps as a cenotaph to a king.

Some of the king's garments were certainly included among the weapons. A parade dress of linen and leather had perished, but jewelled

A ROYAL RESTING PLACE

A sandy heath at Sutton Hoo in east Suffolk concealed the priceless treasures of a 7th-century Saxon king. All the things he would need as warrior and king were buried with the great sea-going ship which may have carried him to war.

BURIAL OF A KING'S SHIP *The loyal subjects of a 7th-century Saxon king of East Anglia dug a great oval pit in their royal cemetery. It lay about 100 ft above the Deben estuary and one-third of a mile from the water. Then they dragged up from the river a ship, 89 ft long and 14 ft in beam. It was run out over the pit on rollers, and then carefully lowered into the ground. After placing the dead king's treasure in the ship, they covered it with a great mound.*

A KING'S HELMET *Helmets, like this one of decorated bronze and iron, unearthed at Sutton Hoo, were the prerogative of Anglo-Saxon kings.*

ROYAL GOLD *This great buckle was part of a king's parade dress which was buried at Sutton Hoo. It is of solid gold and weighs nearly 15 oz.*

clasps and the mounts of a purse or sporran, all locally made of gold and garnet, survived.

The ship also held vessels the king would need to extend royal hospitality beyond the grave. There were cauldrons and the richest collection of hanging bowls ever found.

The silverware, including a great dish with a set of ten bowls and two christening spoons, had all been made in the Mediterranean area.

Who was the warrior king? Gold coins from mints in many parts of the Continent suggest that the mound was made in about AD 625. So the owner of the hoard may have been Raedwald, king of East Anglia (c. 610–c. 625). It is known that the kingdom experienced a brief period of importance during his reign.

A changing world

Another tantalising question is whether the burial was pagan or Christian. It was not customary to bury objects in the grave of a Christian; worldly goods were not needed in the Christian life after death. The rich military gear reflects the pagan spirit of the burial. But the christening spoons were there too.

It is known that Raedwald himself maintained both pagan and Christian altars. During his reign Christianity was spreading with faltering steps among the pagan English. The burial at Sutton Hoo came at the transition point in the island's history, as the worship of old gods gave way to the new faith. Buried in the sands of Suffolk was the pagan age itself, with all its barbaric splendour.

A society in which each man knew his place

Across the face of Britain, the Anglo-Saxons stamped a new system of village life with its own social pyramid. At the top were rich kings and nobles who, in pagan times, were buried with their treasure. The Sutton Hoo burial was a monument to such a king.

The Saxons made their settlements in the fertile river valleys. They were ruled by warrior kings or local war lords. These great men lived in halls, some up to 80 ft long by 40 ft wide, where feasts and meetings were held. Here, wandering minstrels sang and recited news and gossip, and tales of heroic deeds.

Beneath these lords and their families was the solid middle class of churls. Today this word has a derogatory meaning, but in Saxon times, churls were freemen, living in well-built wooden houses. They held plots of land, and in return they were expected to fight for their lord and to provide him with a share of their crops. They were buried with a spear, a knife and perhaps a shield. Their wives' graves contained a number of bronze brooches.

These solid yeomen citizens were skilled farmers. They cleared more of England's forest than the Romano-British before them. And their intensive farming gave a sound economic basis to early England.

At the bottom of the social pyramid were the serfs, who spent their whole lives in servitude. They possessed little and went to their graves with nothing but a simple iron knife. They lived in rude huts with sunken floors.

A man's worth

This highly stratified society was reflected in Anglo-Saxon writings. Poems such as 'Beowulf' tell of the rich and splendid lives of kings and warrior heroes. Legal documents reveal the scale of values placed on human life.

Every man had his price or *wergild* – the sum of money to be paid to his kinsfolk if he was slain. The *wergild* of a nobleman would be at least three times that of a churl, and a humble serf would be worth only a quarter that of a churl. This social system became more complicated as time went on, but it was to be the basis of English life for more than 600 years.

A KING'S LASTING MEMORIAL

Of all the kings who ruled in Anglo-Saxon England, the one who left the most lasting memorial on the face of the land was Offa, king of the kingdom of Mercia from 757–796.

Offa described himself as Rex Anglorum – 'King of the English' – because he was overlord of all the Anglo-Saxon kingdoms south of the Humber. He ruled Wessex by marriage alliances, and Kent and Essex by force of arms.

London, already a great Mercian trading city, grew steadily under his rule because he fostered trade relations with the Continent, including the Holy Roman Empire of Charlemagne.

Mercia's supremacy vanished under Offa's successors, but two things lived on. One was Offa's great dyke, built from sea to sea between the Dee and Severn estuaries. It marked the boun-

dary he had carved at sword point between English Mercia and British Wales. The other was his coinage. Offa's silver penny was so good in weight, size and artistry that it set the pattern for the standard English coin for 600 years.

Mercians, 'the boundary people', built Offa's Dyke, the great earthen bank which can still be seen cutting through the Welsh border country. The bank, 10 ft high and 30 ft wide, reaches 120 miles from Dee to Severn, with few gaps. Offa's feat of engineering is shown (above right) at Spoad Hill.

Heathen Vikings desecrate the shrine of St Cuthbert

WHERE THE VIKINGS LANDED
In the summer of AD 793, Viking raiders streamed across this beach on Holy Island from their longships. Near by stood an unprotected treasure-house – the monastery of Lindisfarne, founded by St Aidan, with the rich shrine of St Cuthbert, a 7th-century bishop.

Strange and terrifying omens were reported in the sky over Northumbria in AD 793. According to the *Anglo-Saxon Chronicle*, compiled about a century later, frightened people saw 'immense whirlwinds and flashes of lightening, and fiery dragons . . . flying in the air'. Soon after the omens they suffered a terrible famine. But this was nothing to the horror that was coming through the mists of the North Sea.

On June 8, 793, a band of Norwegian Vikings beached their longships on the North Shore at Holy Island and sacked the wealthy monastery of Lindisfarne, which had flourished on the island for over 150 years. They slaughtered cattle to restock their ships, murdered many of the monks, stripped the monastery of most of its treasures and sailed away with their loot and all the monks worth taking as slaves.

Terror from the sea

This was the first great Viking raid on England, and horror at the wanton savagery of it swept across the Christian world. Alcuin, a Northumbrian scholar working on the Continent at the court of Charlemagne, thought that God was punishing loose living in high places. He wrote in protest to Ethelred, King of Northumbria: 'Lo, it is nearly 350 years that we and our fathers have inhabited this most lovely land, and never before has such terror appeared in Britain as we have now suffered from a pagan race, nor was it thought that such an inroad from the sea could be made. Behold, the church of St Cuthbert spattered with the blood of the priests of

God, despoiled of all its ornaments; a place more venerable than all in Britain is given as prey to pagan peoples . . . Foxes pillage the chosen vine, the heritage of the Lord has been given to a people not his own; and where there was praise of God, are now the games of the Gentiles; the holy festivity has been turned to mourning . . .

'Behold, judgment has begun, with great terror, at the house of God, in which rests such lights of the whole of Britain. What should be expected for other places . . . I do not think this sin is theirs alone who dwell in that place.'

A 12th-century historian wrote of the attack with horror: 'The pagans from the northern regions came . . . like stinging hornets and spread on all sides like fearful wolves, robbed, tore and slaughtered not only beasts of burden, sheep and oxen, but even priests and deacons, and companies of monks and nuns. And they came to the church of Lindisfarne, laid everything waste with grievous plundering, trampled the holy places with polluted steps.'

The pagans gained a rich prize. For the monastery founded in 635 by St Aidan, a Celtic monk from Iona, had become a brilliant centre of art and learning. Inspired bishops like the saintly Cuthbert led the community. Cuthbert had come from his hermitage on Farne Island to be bishop in 685–7, and was buried at Lindisfarne.

To glorify God, the monks adorned their chapel with rich ornaments, collected fine vestments and holy relics and jewelled caskets. They built a library by copying books. The beautifully illuminated Lindisfarne Gospel-

Book was written when Eadfrith was bishop (698–721). His successor saw that the book was bound in finely tooled leather. Later the covers were adorned with gold, silver and gems.

The sacking of Lindisfarne came without any real warning, for until then the monks had hardly heard of Vikings. But the following year, when the raiders returned to plunder the monastery at Jarrow, 50 miles further south, the monks were ready for them. Many Vikings were killed and their leader was captured and put to death. In addition, a storm in the North Sea wrecked several of the Viking ships. Some 40 years passed before they struck the English coast again.

Settling on English soil

But when they did return, they came in strength and they came to stay. In 835 heathen men, as the *Chronicle* calls the Danes, ravaged Sheppey. And after that, hardly a year passed without a new attack, sometimes by Vikings already settled in Ireland and the Scottish isles. Both Rochester and London were attacked with great savagery in 842. And the raiders plundered the south coast as far as Cornwall.

These raids were carried out from temporary bases established along the coast. From these the Vikings ravaged the surrounding countryside, leaving English shores when they had gathered enough booty. They seldom penetrated more than 15 miles inland.

But things were to change. In 851 the Danes stayed during winter on English soil for the first time, on the Isle of Thanet. Fourteen years later, they began campaigns that brought them within an ace of conquering all England.

THE RAVAGES OF HEATHEN MEN *The* Anglo-Saxon Chronicle *says of the Viking raid on Lindisfarne: '. . . the ravages of heathen men miserably destroyed God's church on Lindisfarne, with plunder and slaughter.' A 12th-century writer said: '. . . the pagans . . . came like stinging hornets and . . . like fearful wolves.'*

SAINT OF THE NORTH

Cuthbert, 'the man of the Lord', as the Venerable Bede called him, was born about 635. He died on March 28, 687. His coffin was beautifully carved with pictures of the Apostles (left).

The 'youth beloved of God' spent his early years as a shepherd in the Lammermuir Hills of Scotland. One night, in 651, he saw a vision of a holy man carried to heaven by angels. The next morning, when the devoted Cuthbert heard that St Aidan of Lindisfarne had died that night, he resolved to dedicate his life to the service of God.

He journeyed to Melrose and was received into the monastery there, where he served under Eata, one of Aidan's disciples. When Eata went to Ripon as bishop, Cuthbert went with him.

Eventually the two came to Lindisfarne. But in 679, Cuthbert retired to a stone cell on Farne Island. There he lived a frugal life of prayer.

Six years later, King Ecgfrith of Northumbria visited the hermit and asked him to become bishop of Lindisfarne as successor to Eata. Cuthbert reluctantly agreed, but in less than two years he returned to his island retreat, where he died.

The monks of Lindisfarne brought Cuthbert's body to their monastery, and laid it in a stone coffin on the south side of the altar. The shrine soon became a rich place of pilgrimage.

The silver fragment (above) once decorated a portable altar. It was found in St Cuthbert's coffin with his cross of gold (left).

After ravaging East Anglia and all of eastern England, the 'Great Danish Army' invaded Northumbria in 867. Three years later, King Edmund of East Anglia was martyred when the Danes took his kingdom. Mercia too was overrun, and the three kingdoms were forced to make peace on Danish terms.

Understandably, the monks of Lindisfarne were afraid. Though they had recovered from the sacking of 793, by 875 their fear of Vikings was so great that they fled from the monastery never to return. They took with them their most sacred treasures – the gospel-book and the bones of St Cuthbert. They carried his relics from refuge to refuge until they eventually settled and built a new church at Chester-le-Street near Durham.

Northern invaders settle in Britain

The Viking invasions of Britain reached their peak in 870-1. Then a great trial of strength took place – the 'year of battles', as the *Anglo-Saxon Chronicle* called it. In the thick of the fighting, Ethelred of Wessex died, and was succeeded by Alfred. But it was not until 878 that Alfred could confine the Danes to eastern England – the Danelaw.

As elsewhere in Europe, the Scandinavians in Britain, though initially ravagers and destroyers, contributed much of their own gifts. And, above all, they inspired their enemies to unite against them.

In Scotland their attacks led the Picts of eastern Scotland and the Scots of Dalriada (Argyll) to unite under Kenneth MacAlpin (843–58). This union marked the birth of the kingdom of Scotland.

But the Vikings' impact was most direct of all on England. The Danelaw, where they settled and imposed their legal customs, survived even after the Norman Conquest. And today, place-names ending in -by (a village) and -thorpe (a hamlet) are a legacy of the Danish settlers.

Union of two peoples

The Vikings forced the Saxons to unite. Eventually, the kingdom of Alfred's great-grandson Edgar (959–75) came to include also the Danes themselves.

Political success was accompanied by legislative and administrative success. Recognition was given to the special laws and customs of the Danes, but the monarchy, supported by the Church, emerged as a unifying force.

The country was divided into shires on the Wessex pattern. Great officers, ealdormen, were appointed to look after royal rights in every part of the kingdom. By the end of Edgar's reign, Hundred Courts (or courts of sub-divisions of shires, known as wapentakes in Danish areas) met every four weeks. They had become vital in keeping the peace.

And though local differences and distinctions remained important, the idea of a united kingdom of England was fast achieving reality.

VIKING WARRIORS *A procession of Viking warriors, armed with swords and axes, is seen on this 9th-century stone slab from Lindisfarne.*

A warrior king saves England for Christianity

JEWEL FOR A KING

The Alfred Jewel (right) is now in the Ashmolean Museum, Oxford. It bears the inscription: 'Alfred had me made.' The king is shown on the coin (left).

On a May morning in 878, two armies met at Edington, near Westbury in Wiltshire. And the outcome was a decisive victory for Alfred, King of Wessex, and his West Saxons, over the heathen Danes led by their king, Guthrum. The last great threat that the whole of England would pass under heathen control was averted. And Guthrum himself accepted the Christian faith.

By the middle 870's, the Danes, with ten years' hard campaigning behind them, had shown signs of settling permanently in the ravaged lands of England. The victorious heathens shared out land in the Saxon kingdoms of East Anglia, Northumbria and Mercia. According to the *Anglo-Saxon Chronicle*, they now 'proceeded to plough and support themselves'.

Alfred stands alone

The days when the Danes were just raiders by sea and marauders on land were over. And now they looked enviously towards the fruitful lands of Wessex.

At the beginning of 878, things could not have looked blacker for the 29-year-old Alfred. For in the early days of January, soon after twelfth night, the Danes made one last effort in a surprise attack against Wessex.

They captured Alfred's royal encampment at Chippenham and overran the greater part of the kingdom, virtually all east of Selwood, on the borders of Wiltshire and Somerset. They 'settled there, and drove a great part of the people across the sea'.

The rest submitted – all except Alfred. The *Chronicle* records that he 'journeyed in difficulties through the woods and fen-fastnesses with a small force' to Athelney, an island in the Somerset marshes.

The plight of Alfred and his men was wretched. Bishop Asser, in his *Life of King Alfred* written about 893, tells how Alfred 'had nothing to live on except what he could seize by frequent raids, either secretly or openly, from the pagans and even from the Christians who had surrendered to the rule of the pagans'. At the time of writing, Asser was a member of Alfred's household and must have gained much of his information from the king himself.

At Athelney, Alfred and his faithful men gained a precious breathing space. A giant raid by the Vikings from Pembrokeshire was defeated at the Battle of Countisbury Hill, near Lynmouth, beaten off by the men of Devon commanded by the ealdorman Odda.

Even so, the young king must have been near despair. His people probably believed he had deserted them. The situation called for all the forbearance and staying power that he could muster. And in the crisis Alfred showed these qualities to the full.

It was while he was at Athelney that Alfred is said to have sheltered one day with a peasant woman. He was in disguise and she left him to look after the cakes which she was baking.

DECISIVE VICTORY *The Danes falter before a wedge-shaped formation of Saxons led by Alfred. Standing shield to shield the Saxons win victory at the Battle of Edington in 878.*

According to legend, she returned to find Alfred deep in thought and the cakes burnt to a cinder. Not unnaturally, she scolded her careless watchman. Perhaps the king had been thinking of the campaign he was about to launch, or perhaps he had been engrossed in the book of psalms and prayers from which, Asser says, he was never parted.

Alfred was never physically strong. Asser says that 'he was harassed, nay, rather disturbed, day and night with illnesses unknown to all the physicians in the island'. Later, Asser speaks of 'his daily infirmities of the body'.

Alfred made Athelney a stronghold. Then, seven weeks after Easter, the king and his warriors rode out to battle. Somewhere east of Selwood, all the people of Somerset, Wiltshire and much of Hampshire gave him a tumultuous welcome. The *Chronicle* says 'they rejoiced to see him'. According to Asser, they welcomed him like a man who had come back from the dead.

The army went on to challenge the Danish host at Edington, 15 miles south of the Danes' encampment at Chippenham – once Alfred's fortress. The battle was long and hard-fought.

Saviour of England

Asser wrote that Alfred 'closed his ranks, shield locked with shield, and fought fiercely against the entire heathen host in long and stubborn stand. At last by God's will he won his victory, slew very many and pursued the rest to their place of refuge, striking as he went . . . Then pitched camp boldly with all his army before the gates of the fortress held by the heathen'.

Guthrum and his Danes held out a fortnight. At the end of the siege, according to Asser: 'They sought peace on these terms, that the king should receive from them distinguished hostages, as many as he wished, and should not give one to them. Never before, indeed, had they made peace with anyone on such terms.'

The Danes also swore that they would leave Alfred's kingdom and that their king would be baptised. The *Chronicle* says that they kept their promise. Three weeks later King Guthrum with 30 of his most important warriors came to Alfred at Aller, near Athelney, where the king stood sponsor to him at his baptism. The *Chronicle* adds that Guthrum 'was 12 days with the king, and he honoured him and his companions greatly with gifts'.

Finally, in 880, the Danes moved to East Anglia, where they settled down and shared out the land in peace.

Between 892 and 896, England suffered a fresh set of savage attacks, but Alfred rallied resistance, and maintained his hold over Wessex, West Mercia and London which he had occupied since 886. On October 26, 899, he died in the faith that he had done so much to serve. He had saved England, not only for the English but for Christianity.

Alfred's realm passes to a Danish dynasty

Alfred, the victor at Edington, was a great reformer. He reorganised the army efficiently and set up a whole complex of fortified towns – the burhs. For his navy, Alfred had built a new type of longship, twice as long as existing Saxon ships and much swifter. Alfred also drew up a great code of laws for all his kingdom.

Alfred's son, Edward the Elder, and his daughter, Aethelflaed of Mercia, brought the Danish lands under their control. His grandson, Athelstan, crushed the last resistance at Brunanburh in 937. Edgar, Alfred's great grandson, was the first ruler to be crowned king of all England – Danes included.

A Danish dynasty was to succeed to his crown. Edgar's son Ethelred 'the Unready' was completely defeated by the Danes under Sweyn Forkbeard and his son Canute. When Ethelred's son Edmund Ironside died in November 1016, Canute was left as sole king.

Although a heathen, Canute was quickly converted to Christianity and, in 1027, made a pilgrimage to Rome. And he proved a worthy successor to the best Saxon rulers.

Wulfstan, Archbishop of York, helped draft the laws of Canute. This collection of laws became the basis of English legal procedure well into Norman times.

Although England was now part of a great Scandinavian empire, its interests were not neglected. Administration, encouragement of monasteries, and the coinage continued along Saxon lines. For a quarter of a century, under its Danish kings, the country was given peace.

DANISH KING *Canute and his queen present a cross to a church at Winchester. He ruled England from 1016 to 1035.*

The saintly king's legacy-
a shrine for the nation

Edward the Confessor, King of England (1042–66), ordered the building of a great abbey church at Westminster. Over many years, craftsmen and labourers toiled at the construction of a building that would match the king's dream. It was not only to be a lasting memorial to Edward's faith in God, but also an abiding legacy to the country over which he ruled.

Edward's plans for his church were grand and far reaching. Above all, he wanted it to be spectacular. It was to be completely different from any other church in the kingdom – and infinitely more magnificent.

In this aim, Edward succeeded. Though the abbey he so lovingly planned has now almost completely vanished in subsequent centuries of

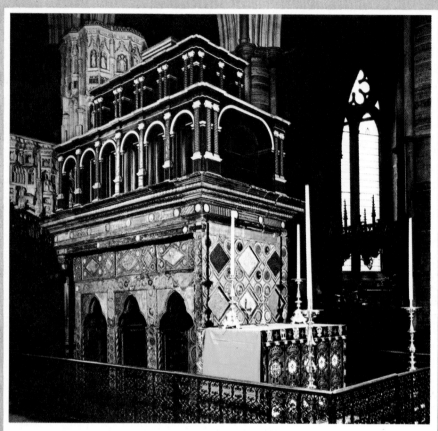

LEGACY OF THE CONFESSOR

Edward the Confessor lies beneath this magnificent tomb in Westminster Abbey, the church which he built. He was buried there on January 6, 1066, only a few days after the abbey was consecrated. The new church, described by a contemporary as 'a princely house, lofty and noble', was the last and greatest achievement of the Anglo-Saxons.

ROYAL SAINT *Edward the Confessor, ruler of England from 1042 to 1066, was canonised as St Edward in 1161 because of his piety.*

BUILDING THE ABBEY *Edward confers with a mason during the great work at Westminster. Edward himself took a personal interest in every detail of the construction and spent much of his royal revenues on the work. But he did not see the consecration of the abbey on December 28, 1065 – he was too ill to be there. He died eight days later.*

reconstruction, the spirit of the saintly ruler who founded Westminster continues to hover over this national and Christian shrine.

Edward the Confessor was the son of Ethelred II, in whose reign England was again deeply ravaged by the Scandinavians. Edward was only 11 or 12 years old when his half-brother, Edmund Ironside, died in November 1016, and during the years when Canute of Denmark and his successors ruled England (1016–41) he and his brother, Alfred, lived in exile in Normandy.

It was there that Edward first saw the architecture that was to inspire him to create a great abbey in his homeland. The dukes of Normandy, kinsmen of his mother, were great builders, and he resolved to create a work that would match their magnificence. But he was unable to fulfil his ambitions until he returned to England in 1041 and was recognised by Harthacnut, Canute's son, as heir to the throne. The following year, Harthacnut died during the marriage feast of his standard bearer, Tofig the Proud, at Lambeth. Edward was immediately chosen king in London by 'all the people'. He was consecrated at Winchester on Easter Day the next year.

But it is probable that a decade went by before Edward was able to start his great work at Westminster.

A king's legacy

The first task was to rebuild the monastery there, a short distance upstream from the thriving town of London. Then work commenced on the abbey itself. From all accounts, Edward's church was a fine building in the Romanesque style he had come to admire in Normandy. It was vast – over 320 ft long, about the length of the present church – and the largest church in the realm.

Finally, in 1065, the great abbey, although incomplete, was consecrated. But Edward was too ill to be present. The *Anglo-Saxon Chronicle* tells how 'King Edward came to Westminster at Christmas and had dedicated the minster which he had himself built to the glory of God and St Peter and all of God's saints. The consecration of the church was on Holy Innocents' Day (December 28). And he died on the eve of Epiphany (January 5, 1066) and was buried on the Feast of Epiphany in the same minster'.

Almost a year after Edward was laid to rest in his own great church, it was the scene of another royal occasion – perhaps the most significant in the abbey's incomparable history. After overthrowing Harold, William, Duke of Normandy, and Conqueror of England, had himself consecrated king there on Christmas Day 1066.

The church, which had been the last and greatest achievement of Anglo-Saxon England, provided a link between the old dynasty and the new. It has remained the rightful place for the coronation of England's monarchs ever since.

England on the eve of the Norman Conquest

Edward the Confessor left behind him a prosperous and flourishing kingdom – one that William, Duke of Normandy was anxious to rule.

Much of England's wealth came from her rich farmlands. Great manors, or estates, existed. Living on these were important thegns (nobles), whose duties were mostly of a military character, peasants, and 'unfree' labourers who were not allowed to bear arms and had limited legal rights.

The bulk of the peasantry were not 'unfree'. But a man owed much to his lord: unpaid labour and rent in money and kind. And he paid his hearth-penny, a tax on every dwelling, to the Church, like any freeman.

Town life also flourished. London, the largest city of the kingdom, had over 15,000 inhabitants. And within the bustling towns, both great and small, men were organised into trading guilds. Craftsmen and merchants were as common as smallholders and peasants.

For its day and age, England was a well-run country. The king was responsible for government, and he could consult powerful churchmen and laymen in his council – the witenagemot or witan. The king was wealthy, owning much land and profitable rights. He imposed gelds, or land taxes, on his people.

The coinage was the most stable in Western Europe. Savage penalties against fake coining or the issue of inferior coins were enforced.

By 1066 the machinery of local government was complete. The king's reeve, the shire-reeve or sheriff, looked after royal rights in each shire. The king's will was made known to the ealdormen and thegns at the shire court through solemn writs.

Order and prosperity

Shires were divided into hundreds, and much of the routine legal work was transacted in the Hundred Courts. Freemen within the hundreds were arranged in tithings, groups of ten men who took corporate responsibility for the good behaviour of the men in their group.

The *Anglo-Saxon Chronicle* tells how, after Edward the Confessor's death in January 1066, 'Earl Harold was now consecrated king and he met little quiet in it as long as he ruled the realm'. His prosperous, well-ordered kingdom was a rich prize for any conqueror.

THE RITUAL OF CORONATION

Since the crowning of William the Conqueror in 1066, Westminster Abbey has been the setting for the coronation of every English king and queen – with the exceptions of Edward V, one of the princes in the Tower, and Edward VIII, who abdicated before his coronation in 1936.

But the mystic ritual which plays such a vital part in the Coronation Service was already long-established when Edward the Confessor ordered the building of the national shrine at Westminster. A service had already been devised by AD 973 for the first ruler to be crowned king of all England. On Whit Sunday of that year, Edgar was consecrated king at Bath by Archbishop Dunstan of Canterbury.

An early account gives the details of the service: 'Two bishops led him (Edgar) to the church walking one on either hand and chanting . . . He wore his crown, but laid it aside before the high altar. As he did so, Archbishop Dunstan began the 'Te Deum', which was sung, by the multitude of monks and clergy.

When the hymn was ended two bishops raised the king from the ground and, at the dictation of Dunstan, he took a threefold oath;

To guard the church of God
To forbid Violence and Wrong
And to keep Justice, Judgment and Mercy . . .

After this, the king was anointed . . . Then Dunstan placed a ring on the king's hand . . . put the crown upon his head and gave him his blessing . . . lastly the mass was sung.'

The act of anointing the king with holy oil was considered even more important than the act of coronation. It set Edgar apart from other men and gave him a direct relationship with God. This ritual persists in the Coronation Service today.

Archbishop Dunstan of Canterbury crowns Edgar as ruler of all England at Bath in 973.

THE ARTISTS WHOSE WORKS WERE DEDICATED TO GOD

Inspired by Christianity, the Anglo-Saxons produced outstanding and beautiful works of all kinds. But both in pagan and Christian days, the art of the jeweller in gold, silver, garnet and enamel reigned supreme. Exquisite brooches, decoration for sword handles and harnesses and, later, pendant crosses, shone out in a period sometimes called the 'Dark Ages' – the time of confusion that followed the break-up of the Roman Empire.

With the coming of Christianity, the vigorous artistic impulses of the Saxons were channelled into the production of great stone crosses and, above all, into the making of books. Three works made in Northumbria around AD 700 rank among the greatest European manuscripts of all times. They are the *Book of Durrow*, the *Lindisfarne Gospels* and the *Book of Kells*.

Beauty in church and home

The Saxon artists of Northumbria were inspired by traditions from both the Mediterranean lands and Celtic Ireland. Their great tradition of art and learning was finally destroyed by the onslaught of the Viking raiders.

But in the south of England another school of superlative Christian art was flourishing. The founding of Benedictine monasteries, fostered by the great kings and churchmen of Wessex in the 10th century, inspired a new age of book-making there. Groups of scribes, who produced fine manuscripts in both Latin and Anglo-Saxon, assembled at monasteries in Winchester, Canterbury and Worcester. Their work survived the upheavals of the Norman conquest and continued into the 12th century. Their manuscripts were graced by delicately coloured pictures and vigorous line-drawings.

England also had a high reputation for its skill in metal work, ivory carving and textiles. Elaborately embroidered hangings adorned the walls of churches and the great halls of kings and nobles.

Most Saxon building was in wood. But the log nave of the Church of St Andrew at Greensted-juxta-Ongar in Essex is all that has weathered the succeeding centuries. However, several fine stone churches have survived as evidence that the Saxons were the masters of a graceful and simple style of building, which expressed their own profound faith in God.

FORGOTTEN CHURCH *The Church of St Laurence at Bradford-on-Avon, Wiltshire, was rediscovered in the 19th century after 700 years of secular use. It is a near-perfect survival from Saxon times, much of it from the 8th century. The arcading, carved 200 years later, was inspired by the churches of Charlemagne's great empire.*

MANUSCRIPT FROM NORTHUMBRIA *This 'carpet page' comes from the gospel book which was made at the island monastery of Lindisfarne about 700. This was during Northumbria's golden age of learning, literature and art, when missionaries from the kingdom took the fame of its scribes to the Continent. In 875, the Lindisfarne monks fled from savage Viking raiders to Durham, taking their priceless book with them.*

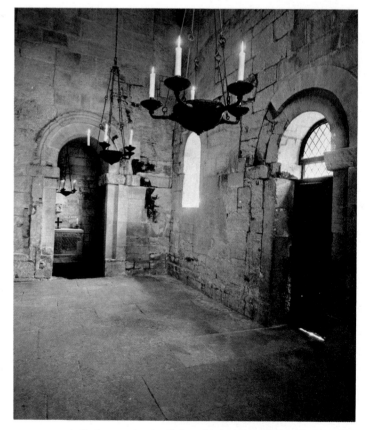

SAXON PIETY *In its sturdy simplicity, the interior of the Church of St Laurence is a perfect expression of Saxon religion. Only 25 ft long and completed about 703, the church is all that survives of the monastery of St Laurence, founded by St Aldhelm, Abbot of Malmesbury, in 676–706. Its windows are splayed inside so that the minimum of glass lets in the maximum amount of light.*

FATE OF THE DAMNED *This frightening view (left) of an angel locking up the jaws of death upon the tortured souls of the damned, represents the dark side of Anglo-Saxon religion. It also shows the rich detail and vivid imagination of an artistic tradition established in the kingdom of Wessex in the 10th century. It is the last of nine miniatures depicting the Last Judgment, described in Chapter 20 of the Book of Revelation.*

EXQUISITE IVORY *Anglo-Saxon artists produced superb ivory carvings. This figure of Christ was made from walrus ivory in the late 10th century. It is mounted on a cedarwood cross covered with gold filigree and enamels depicting the symbols of the four Evangelists. The whole is a reliquary. Beneath the figure is a cavity which, according to the inscription above it, must once have held a relic of the True Cross.*

THE CRAFTSMAN'S ART

The boisterous Saxons delighted in jewellery and all manner of personal adornment. They were fascinated by the bright colours so popular with the British people, and copied them.

Saxon nobles wore exquisite ornaments – brooches, pins and bracelets – and fine garments of silk, linen and wool. Alcuin, a Northumbrian monk at the court of Charlemagne, was horrified by the gaudiness of court dress and the tendency of priests and monks to copy it. Writing to Aethelheard, Archbishop of Canterbury in 797,

he urged: 'May you be zealous to do away with the most vain style of dress and the immoderate habit of feasting, as much as you can, from . . . all the clergy and all grades of ecclesiastical orders.'

But people of all classes enjoyed jewellery, particularly the brooches which they used to fasten their mantles and robes. And Saxon jewellers excelled in producing them.

Thousands of brooches worn by Anglo-Saxon peasants have been found in their pagan graves of the 5th and 6th centuries. They are made of

bronze, iron and occasionally of silver, in simple saucer, cruciform or disc shapes.

The more affluent Saxons owned finer brooches of gold and silver, often decorated with enamels of many colours, deep red garnets and bright blue lapis lazuli. In the 7th century, brooches made in the kingdom of Kent were highly prized. They have been found throughout England and even on the Continent. The techniques perfected by the Kentish jewellers set the pattern for British craftsmen right into the Middle Ages.

The Kingston brooch, with garnet and lapis lazuli pieces set in gold 'cloisons' or cells, is 3·3 in. across. It was made in Kent in the 7th century.

Saxon goldsmiths perfected the cloisonné technique in which enamels and jewels are set in cells made of metal. The Winster Moor brooch shows their skill.

The 9th-century Fuller brooch is of silver decorated with engraved lines filled with black resin (niello). The five senses are shown in the centre.

Faith and war in an age of kings

Inspired by William the Conqueror, a line of strong-willed monarchs, ruling by the sword, slowly forge a nation from the disunited peoples of England

On a cold October morning in 1066, England was dragged into a new world. As a result of the Norman victory at Hastings (pp. 64–65), a small and isolated island became part of the European continent. The British gained from Europe new ideas in war, government, religion and art. They were to contribute ideas of their own. But first the island was to be subjected to an alien military rule. It was just under 300 years before Normans and Anglo-Saxons began thinking of themselves as Englishmen.

In his 21 year reign, William the Conqueror demonstrated all the contrasts of medieval England. Though he was extremely religious, William nevertheless subjected England to a baptism of fire. It was he who taught the English that peace rested on violence – on revenge ruthlessly visited on all who dared to defy the will of the king.

Vast stone castles such as the Tower of London (pp. 66–67) helped to consolidate William's might. Great cathedrals and abbeys, such as Ely, Peterborough and Durham (pp. 70–71), stood out as citadels of Norman Christianity, commanded by harsh, uncompromising prelates, in the heart of a hostile land.

But William's abilities were not inherited by his heir, William Rufus. For 13 years this monarch presided over a nation torn by aristocratic quarrels and trampled down by foreign mercenaries. Many of his subjects must have heard with unconcealed relief of the death of Rufus in the New Forest in August 1100 (pp. 68–69), and of the accession of Henry I to the throne.

THE KING IS CROWNED

The line of kings planted on the English throne by William, Duke of Normandy, ruled by the sword. And they had another power at their command – the teaching of the Church that a king's authority came directly from God. The mystic ritual of the coronation service played a vital part in establishing this belief. This illustration of an English coronation, dating from the turn of the 13th century, shows the king seated, surrounded by his archbishops and bishops, while nobles and courtiers look on. The same ritual has continued to the present day. The coronation chair (inset) was first used by Edward II in 1308. Since then, every ruler of England – with the exceptions of Edward V and Edward VIII – has been crowned on it.

61

STRUGGLE *In the Middle Ages nobles constantly struggled with their royal overlords. Only a strong king could keep such men in their place. Here, John of Gaunt, the mightiest baron of his day, feasts with his retainers.*

CHIVALRY *A clash at a tournament. The code of chivalry dominated court life in medieval England. Edward III even re-founded King Arthur's legendary Round Table for his nobles.*

GUILDS *A master oversees a mason (right) and a carpenter (left). An apprenticeship could last as long as ten years.*

Henry's dour and stern manner won him few friends in his day. But his dictatorial rule, though hated by his barons, brought peace to English homes. His one failure had nothing to do with politics. His inability to sire more than one legitimate son brought danger. For stability depended on a peaceful succession, and in the Middle Ages even healthy men were likely to be struck down in the prime of their lives. Just such a fate intervened on November 25, 1120, when Henry's heir, the 17-year-old Prince William, was drowned crossing the Channel in the *White Ship* (pp. 72–73).

This calamity brought upon England nearly two decades of anarchy. For the succession was disputed by Stephen, Henry I's nephew, and Matilda, Henry's daughter. Their struggle lasted for 19 years – the 'dark winter', in which it was said that 'God and his saints slept'.

Kings, nobles and Church struggle for power

But Henry II, who succeeded Stephen in 1153, was a remarkable king. He gave his country an administrative system which was the envy of Europe. Henry's quick mind and tireless energy enabled him to rule an empire which covered two-thirds of France, as well as England and Ireland.

Henry usually acted on instinct, dealing rapidly with problems as they arose, outwitting his enemies by speed of action. But occasionally his instinct betrayed him. A few hasty words spoken to a group of knights at Christmas 1170 involved him in a crisis which was sensational even in a violent age – the murder of Archbishop Becket in Canterbury Cathedral (pp. 74–75).

England's next king, Richard I (the Lionheart), had little in common with his father. He took after his mother, the glamorous and passionate Eleanor of Aquitaine. Richard's triumphs on the Third Crusade (pp. 76–77) brought fame and renown to English arms. But his country paid a heavy price for this pursuit of chivalry. And Richard's brother, John, though reviled by posterity, was far more effective a king than his brother. He built on the work of his father to give England the firm government it needed. But like his father, John, too, had to face the bitter and lasting opposition of the Church. This, combined with the hostility of his barons, brought him down. In June 1215, John was forced to put his seal to Magna Carta at Runnymede (pp. 80–81). There, he signed away many of the powers so painfully won and maintained by his ancestors.

The downfall of John was above all the work of the Church, which was now equal to the strongest of kings. Its dominance was expressed in the first great Gothic cathedrals of England. Canterbury was rebuilt in pure French style from the money given by pilgrims to the shrine of Thomas Becket. Wells Cathedral (pp. 82–83) illustrated that English architects could adapt the new style to their own English tastes. And another significant event in this enlightened age was the foundation and slow development of England's first university at Oxford (pp. 78–79).

John's dark reign gave way in 1216 to the long and gloomy rule of his young son, Henry III. Though Henry's intentions were good, his unworldliness and incompetence exasperated his subjects. The expense and shame of a succession of calamitous foreign wars brought the king to his knees in 1258.

In that year, the barons embarked on a bold experiment in constitutional government. Summoned by a brilliant adventurer, Simon de Montfort, England's first Parliament (pp. 84–85) assembled in 1265. But this experiment was short-lived, for Henry's son, the able Edward I, soon restored royal power. Edward's ambition was to fulfil the dream of his ancestors by uniting the whole of the British Isles under his rule. Wales was conquered and English power there buttressed by a line of castles – buildings which rank with Hadrian's Wall among the most effective fortifications ever built in these islands (pp. 86–87). But even the mighty Edward met his match in Robert Bruce and his hosts of patriotic Scots.

Where Edward I had failed, his wretched son, Edward II, could scarcely be expected to succeed. At the Battle of Bannockburn in 1314 (pp. 88–89), Edward led his troops to England's most humiliating defeat since the Battle of Hastings. Hounded from his throne by his rebellious subjects and his estranged wife, he met a miserable death in Berkeley Castle in 1327.

Edward III was only 15 when he was called upon to rule over the ruins of his father's kingdom. But it was he who bound the nation together and led it in an enterprise which his successors carried on for more than a century – the struggle for their rights in the fields of France.

In June 1340 a great naval victory at Sluys laid the foundations of English sea power. At Crécy in 1346 (pp. 90–91) and Poitiers, ten years later, the proud armies of France were humbled by a handful of English longbowmen.

Even as Edward's armies were winning glory in France, his country was being devastated by the monstrous ravages of plague. In 1348–9 rats brought the Black Death to English shores (pp. 92–93). More than one-third of the population died in torment. The resulting unrest came to a head under the boy-king Richard II. In the Peasants' Revolt of 1381 (pp. 94–95), the serfs of Kent rose in rebellion, marched on London and confronted the king at Smithfield. Only Richard's presence of mind saved his throne. But in 1399 he lost his throne and a year later his life, when he was secretly put to death at Pontefract Castle. Despite the troubles of Richard's reign, English culture rose to new heights in the work of a new generation of English poets. Chief among them was Geoffrey Chaucer (pp. 96–97).

The reign of Henry IV was a period of reconstruction after the unity of England had been shattered by Richard II and his enemies. The great barons of the north, led by the Percy family, were crushed at Shrewsbury (pp. 98–99), and the foundations laid for England's campaigns of conquest under Henry's son. At Agincourt in 1415 (pp. 100–1), Henry V repeated the achievements of his great-grandfather, Edward III, by destroying a French army vastly superior to his own. The crown of France itself was soon within Henry's grasp. But he died prematurely in 1422 and his son, Henry VI, was not the man to fulfil his father's dreams. His inability to govern lost the English their empire in France and unleashed upon them the horrors of civil war. The Wars of the Roses (pp. 104–5), a struggle between the rival houses of Lancaster and York, were to convulse the realm for 30 years.

The need for a strong king

Henry redeemed himself, in the eyes of posterity at least, by his generous patronage of the arts. Two great educational foundations – Eton and King's College, Cambridge (pp. 102–3) – owe their existence to him. But these achievements mattered little to his people, who rejoiced when he was finally overthrown by Edward IV, the Yorkist claimant to the throne.

Edward tried to bring back strong rule to England. He encouraged the arts as well. In the houses of prosperous merchants and educated noblemen could be found the first books printed by William Caxton (pp. 106–7). But in a land torn by civil war, it would take more than the financial genius of Edward IV to restore the peace. His able but ruthless brother, Richard III, reopened old wounds when he seized the throne. Only after his death at Bosworth in 1485 (pp. 108–9) could the crown be restored to its former lustre, under a new dynasty.

In the Middle Ages, Englishmen came to believe that only the rule of strong kings could save them from anarchy. They were to have a full measure of such rule under the Tudors.

RELIGION *Monks worked on menial tasks, but the orders they belonged to controlled vast riches. The Cistercians were so wealthy that in 1198 they raised one-third of the ransom of 150,000 silver marks that Leopold of Austria demanded for the release of Richard I.*

TRADE *The cloth industry was medieval England's most important trade. In this miniature, painted in 1482, dyers dip cloth into heated cauldrons of red dye. Women, too, were employed in the textile trade – a 'spinster' was originally a single woman who earned her living by spinning yarn.*

SERFS *Peasants till the fields supervised by an overseer. Those working on the land were often bound to it for life. But in England the Black Death of the 1340's helped to end the system.*

Saxon and Norman meet to decide England's fate

BATTLEFIELD FOR A NATION
Nine centuries ago on this peaceful field at Telham Hill, East Sussex, the sound of clashing arms rang out as Norman and English soldiers met in battle to decide the fate of England. At the end of the battle, King Harold was dead and the English army routed.

As dawn broke on October 14, 1066, a thin column of men wound their way out of Hastings towards nearby Telham Hill. They were the soldiers of the last conquering army ever to set foot in England. Their commander, William, Duke of Normandy, had for years cast covetous eyes across the English Channel and awaited patiently the moment to strike at his island neighbour. Now, his moment had come.

On the summit of a neighbouring hill lay the camp of the defending English army, led by King Harold. At any other time these strong-limbed Saxon warriors would have been formidable enemies, but on that morning they were exhausted and disorganised. Three weeks earlier they had defeated Harold Hardrada, the King of Norway, in a pitched battle at Stamford Bridge in north Yorkshire. Then on the news of the Norman invasion they had marched 250 miles south. Such was the speed of their march that many of Harold's archers and infantrymen had fallen behind through sheer exhaustion.

A moment's cool calculation would have persuaded Harold that it was a mistake to rush headlong into battle. He could have held off, fortified London and left Duke William to fritter away his supplies and his energy in laying waste southern England. But no English leader of those days could risk the dishonour of appearing to stand by while English villages were ravaged. The invader had to be hurled back, not starved into retreat.

Preparing for battle
While the English recovered from the march, the Normans listened to their duke. 'Now is the time for you to show your strength,' he told them. 'You are fighting not only for victory but for survival.'

King Harold had hoped to take the Normans by surprise. But the English were slow to prepare for action, and by 9.00 a.m. they had still not lined up ready for battle. It was William who had the advantage of surprise.

First, the Norman archers advanced to within bow-shot and opened fire. Then, placing a bag of holy relics round his neck, the Norman commander led his army of horsemen and infantry in three groups down Telham Hill and up the slope towards the English position. The English foot soldiers hurriedly assembled and formed a wall of shields to resist the enemy advance. As the Norman light infantry came within 70 ft of the English ranks they let loose a hail of javelins.

Then the two armies clashed, and the English battle-axes sang through the air, biting deep into Norman bone. In the fierce hand-to-hand struggle, two of Harold's brothers were among the first to fall. But the English shield-wall held firm and the Norman attack wavered. The Breton troops on the left of the Norman line turned and fled. Then, a rumour flew through the Norman ranks that William himself had been killed, and his half-brother, Odo, Bishop of Bayeux, desperately tried to halt the flight of the invaders. Harold was on the point of gaining a spectacular victory.

'I shall yet be victorious'
Instead of making a disciplined advance, however, the English allowed their enthusiasm to get the better of them. They swarmed down the hill on foot in full pursuit of the Norman horsemen. It was a fatal mistake. Drawn up in ordered ranks, the English infantry were more than a match for William's cavalry. But once they broke ranks, the Norman knights had only to turn and cut their assailants to pieces.

Seizing his opportunity, William raised his helmet in the air. 'Look at me! I am still alive, and by the grace of God I shall yet be victorious.' His followers took heart and charged the English once again. This time their attack was irresistible. Alarming gaps were carved in the English ranks, and no reinforcements could be found to fill them.

Finally, four Norman knights broke through to where Harold and the élite corps of his army were gathered. The king desperately tried to fight them off, but he could not parry four thrusts simultaneously. One knight struck Harold to the ground with his lance. Two others hewed at his prostrate body, and the fourth cut off the king's head.

As the news of Harold's death spread through their ranks, the already demoralised English gave up the fight. Thousands fled from the field in disarray to take refuge in the surrounding woods. Many more were butchered where they stood. A small band rallied near where Harold had fallen and fought a hopeless rearguard action against their pursuers.

Hastings need not have been the end for Saxon England, but the Saxon nobles could

COMETS AND CATASTROPHES

During the Middle Ages, man's faith in the Christian religion was unshakeable. Therefore, natural phenomena in the skies such as comets and eclipses were often looked upon as divine intervention and greeted with awe and terror. The appearance in 1066 of Halley's Comet, named after the 17th-century astronomer who charted its orbit, had exactly that effect. It was regarded as a sign that God was about to punish King Harold for breaking an oath which he had sworn to William of Normandy some years before, when he was shipwrecked in France, promising to support the duke's claim to the English throne. By accepting the throne himself in January 1066, Harold had broken his word and thus, it was believed, faced divine vengeance. And to many, the outcome of the Battle of Hastings, in which Harold was killed and Saxon England fell to William and his Norman invaders, seemed to justify their forebodings of disaster.

A photograph of Halley's Comet, during its most recent appearance in 1910. This was the sight that so frightened the English in 1066.

In this detail from the Bayeux Tapestry, a court astrologer warns King Harold that the comet will bring disaster in its wake.

not agree who was to be king. Edgar, the next in line to the throne, was only nine years old. While the Saxons disputed, William advanced cautiously, capturing Dover and Canterbury. Then the Saxon forces at Winchester – the stronghold where the royal treasure was kept – surrendered. With the whole of south-east England in his hands, William conferred with the Saxon leaders at Berkhampstead. There, according to an 11th-century edition of the Anglo-Saxon Chronicle, 'he was met by Bishop Aldred (the Archbishop of York), Prince Edgar, Earl Edwin, Earl Morcar and all the best men from London... they gave him hostages and swore oaths of fealty and he promised to be a gracious lord to them'. England's fate was decided – the Normans had come to stay.

A KING FALLS *A new interpretation of the Bayeux Tapestry has shattered the myth of Harold's death. It is now known that Harold is to the right of the Norman horseman (centre) falling beneath the hooves as he defends himself with an axe. Above him is the inscription* Harold Rex Interfectus Est *('King Harold is killed'). Previously it was thought that the man with an arrow in his eye, to the horseman's left, was the king. The myth was originated by the Norman Abbot of Bourgeil, who mistook the figures while writing on the battle 30 years later. But it is now known that medieval artists always showed death by a falling or prostrate figure.*

William I: Rule by fear, fire and the sword

William the Conqueror won his throne by force and he defended it by force. Any opposition to his rule was brutally crushed. Not only the English suffered, for the king also dealt harshly with Normans who showed too much ambition or independence of mind.

William was justly proud of having conquered England. He lost no opportunity of displaying his power, especially when he wanted to impress foreign ambassadors with his importance. During his reign he made a point of solemnly wearing his crown in public to receive the veneration of his subjects.

Instant obedience to the Norman king

William's appearance suited his personality. He was tall, broad and thick-set, and was noted for his moroseness. His voice was harsh, and his manner of speaking clipped and concise. He spoke as if he expected – and required – instant obedience.

He practised a strict piety and was an enthusiastic founder of churches and monasteries. Indeed, at the end of his life he feared that the brutality he had displayed during his career, would deprive him of salvation. On his death-bed he confessed that he had 'subjugated England by slaughter and by persecuting it beyond endurance'.

Almost with his last breath, he added: 'I have cruelly oppressed my subjects, unjustly disinherited them, and killed large numbers of them by famine and violence. May God forgive me for my sins.'

In spiritual and humane terms they were sins indeed, but as conqueror and king they had been the basis of his success in establishing his rule over England.

FACE OF THE CONQUEROR *A stone sculpture of William I, England's first Norman king. He treated the English harshly and only repented of his deeds on his death-bed.*

The Tower–a fortress to subdue capital and kingdom

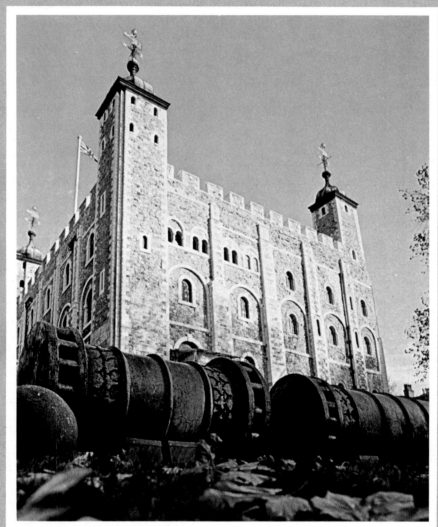

BUILT BY THE CONQUEROR
For nearly 1000 years, the Tower has played a key role in Britain's history. Built by William I to overawe London, it has been fortress, royal residence, prison, place of execution, armoury and a home for the crown jewels. The White Tower (above) is its oldest part.

The Tower of London is the enduring symbol of the Norman Conquest. Its sturdy grey mass of stone stands out across the River Thames as a monument to the last successful invasion in Britain's history.

When William, Duke of Normandy, embarked on his conquest of England in 1066, he already had vast experience of warfare. For generations his ancestors had fought to retain their hold on the duchy of Normandy, and to expand into the neighbouring provinces.

They had learnt that a district could be conquered by force, but then lost as soon as an army withdrew. William knew that a few carefully placed castles, designed to be manned

by small garrisons, could hold a nation in thrall. His first action on landing in England was to build a wooden castle – the parts for which he had brought across the Channel – at his landing place.

A network of castles to crush resistance

In the years following the Conquest, Norman castles sprang up in every place where William feared the slightest opposition from his new subjects. As he moved northwards in 1068, William built castles at Warwick and Nottingham. On his return march to London he ordered castles to be constructed at Lincoln, Cambridge and Huntingdon. Most of these

castles were not built of stone, however. They consisted of a ditch and an earthwork rampart (the 'bailey') topped by a wooden palisade. In the centre was a tall mound (the 'motte') with a wooden keep – the last refuge of the garrison. They were cheap and quick to build, and easy to repair.

But in places of special importance, William built stone keeps. The first of these was begun at Exeter in 1068, after the town's citizens had twice rebelled. William paced out the site himself. Another was built at Colchester.

Building the White Tower

But the most impressive stone keep of all was the White Tower of the Tower of London, so-called because its walls were originally whitewashed. London was the largest and wealthiest city in the land. Its citizens – numbering some 30,000 – had resisted the Normans for some weeks after Hastings, and William needed more than a primitive wooden castle to overawe them. Within the city walls, he built Baynard's castle (on the Embankment). Then, to the east of the city, just outside the walls, arose the White Tower.

It was typical of an age of warlike bishops that the architect William chose to build the White Tower was a churchman. Gandulf, Bishop of Rochester, had won a reputation as a military architect by building a fortress-like tower beside his cathedral.

Apart from its windows, the White Tower looks much the same today as it did when it was built to Gandulf's design. It was extremely large by the standards of the day, for it had to house not only a strong Norman garrison, but occasionally the king and his bustling court with its crowds of clerks and servants.

The Tower was four storeys high. The ground floor was given over entirely to store-

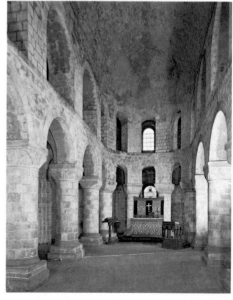

PLACE OF WORSHIP *The stern severity of the Chapel of St John in the Tower was a fitting place of worship for the Norman garrison.*

A ROYAL STRONGHOLD *The Tower of London is seen in all its late medieval glory in this 15th-century manuscript. Many kings – including William Rufus, Henry I, Henry III and Edward I – improved on the Conqueror's work, to make the Tower the most powerful fortress in Europe.*

rooms, enabling the garrison to withstand a long siege. The entrance was on the first floor and was approached across a broad moat. On the upper floors the king and his officials lived when they stayed in London.

The first stage of the building was finished in 1078. But in 1091, when the Tower was 'by tempest and wind sore shaken', William Rufus, the Conqueror's son, had it strengthened. Henry I, Henry III and Edward I added further improvements. By 1307 there had been built around the Norman fortress a series of gateways, ramparts and towers that made the Tower of London one of the largest and most invulnerable strongholds in Europe.

Long after the Norman conquerors had won acceptance, the shadow of the Tower still loomed over England's history. It became the destination of the ruler's enemies – and the site of many executions. To most Englishmen the Tower was a place of misery and dread.

'In truth there is no sadder spot on the earth,' wrote the 19th-century historian, Thomas Babington Macaulay. 'Thither have been carried, through successive ages, by the rude hands of gaolers, without one mourner following, the bleeding relics of men who had been the captains of armies, the leaders of parties, the oracles of senates, and the ornaments of courts.'

A RECORD OF WEALTH

Domesday Book is the record of the great national survey ordered by William I in 1085, to discover the true wealth and probable future wealth of England. Royal officials journeyed throughout the land, detailing the property owned by everyone from the king downwards.

The survey was carried out quickly but with such thoroughness that, according to a chronicler, 'not even one ox, or one cow or pig escaped notice'. When the information had been gathered, returns were submitted for individual 'hundreds' – subdivisions of counties.

The two volumes of Domesday Book cover most of England. London, however, was omitted, together with the far north, which had not been conquered when the survey was made. The original volumes were first of all kept at Winchester, and later brought to Westminster.

A copy of Domesday Book. It was written by French clerks who were accurate and speedy.

The mailed fist of the Normans rules England

Even after William the Conqueror's decisive victory at Hastings, it seemed that final triumph was a long way off. London still held out. William must have known that if resistance continued, his communications with Normandy were vulnerable and his sources of supply uncertain.

But at this crucial moment Saxon England's leaders surrendered to William. On Christmas Day 1066 he was crowned King of England.

It was not until 1068 that the Conqueror faced his first real challenge. It came from the north. In January, a Norman army was massacred in Durham. A few weeks later, the Normans fled from York, leaving it to be occupied by the rebels. This was the most serious defeat suffered by the Normans in England. Yet such was the English leaders' indecision that at the news of the Conqueror's approach the rebellion collapsed.

In the heart of the Fens

The last men to resist the Norman oppressors held out in the fens of East Anglia. There, a Lincolnshire thegn (lord), Hereward the Wake, brought together refugees from every part of England, and at the end of 1070 launched a campaign against the Normans.

The Isle of Ely, Hereward's chief refuge, was protected on all sides by treacherous and uncharted marshes. But from the early summer of 1071 the isle was continuously besieged by William's army. Faced with starvation, the defenders' morale crumbled, and within a few weeks the king was master of Ely. Only Hereward himself escaped.

William's suppression of English resistance was brutal. The north was punished for rebellion by being laid waste with fire and sword. But the Conqueror achieved his object. Norman rule was to be permanent.

SAXON HERO *A 19th-century illustration of Hereward the Wake, who led Saxon resistance to the Norman conquerors. He held out in the fens of Lincolnshire for a year.*

The huntsman king meets a mysterious death

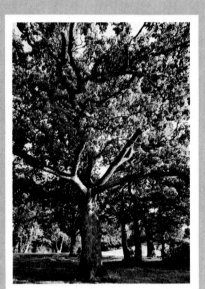

DEATH IN THE NEW FOREST
William Rufus met his death in 1100 where this tree now stands, near Minstead. He was killed by an arrow while hunting – but whether it was fired deliberately remains a mystery.

The last year of William Rufus's reign was a time of strange portents, omens of murder and whispers of treason. Tortured minds imagined they had seen devils in the New Forest and wells flowing with blood on the Berkshire Downs.

But William Rufus was not a superstitious man. He laughed aloud when such omens were reported to him. Even when a monk arrived at his court and predicted that the king was about to die, William did no more than giggle to his courtiers: 'He is a monk and dreams for money. Give him 100 shillings.' It was August 1, 1100, and William's last night on earth.

Omens of disaster

That night at Brockenhurst, where William was staying in preparation for hunting in the New Forest, the king had a nightmare. He dreamt that he was being bled by his private surgeon, and that the blood gushed up to the ceiling and shut out the light of the sun. Waking in terror, he called his chamberlains and ordered them to stand guard over his bed while he slept, and to keep a candle burning in his chamber. But, despite these precautions, William was unable to sleep. He rose at dawn, dressed and announced his intention of going hunting. His attendants protested. They regarded dreams and omens as serious matters,

and urged the king to devote the morning to business. William grudgingly postponed the hunt until the afternoon.

That afternoon, William Rufus rode out of Brockenhurst into the New Forest. With him were his usual host of flatterers and sycophants, chief among them a French noble, called Walter Tirel. Tirel was a soldier of fortune, drawn to England by tales of Rufus's extravagant court, who had swiftly won the king's favour.

William liked to hunt with the crossbow. It was less accurate than the traditional English longbow, but easier to shoot from the saddle. On that afternoon he had six bolts, newly forged by a local smith. Two of these he gave to Tirel. 'Here, have these,' he said, 'it is only right that the sharpest bolts should go to the sharpest shot among us.'

As the laughing party of courtiers rode out of Brockenhurst, a monk stood in their path. He carried a message from the Abbot of Gloucester, warning the king of a dream in which one of his monks had been told that England was shortly to have a new king. William guffawed and rode on. 'Is it not strange that such a wise old abbot should write me such trifles when I have so many other things to attend to?' he asked Tirel. 'Does he think that I am like the English, who abandon all their plans whenever they hear of the snoring dreams of some old hag?'

The fatal moment

The party now divided, but William and Tirel stayed together and rode westwards through the forest. At the far end of a clearing, a stag moved in front of a clump of bushes. The king took aim and shot his bolt. The beast was hit but only wounded. As it fled, William turned his horse after it and Tirel followed him. The stag ran directly into the setting sun and William could scarcely see to aim a second shot. He shielded his eyes with his hands and spurred on his horse. Then came a high-pitched twang and a bolt struck the king in his side, just below the heart. He slumped in the saddle and groped at his side in a vain attempt to break off the shaft. Then he fell to the ground. Tirel rode up and dismounted. The king was unable to speak and was plainly

MURDER OR ACCIDENT? *William Rufus falls in this Victorian illustration. The fatal arrow was believed to have been shot by Walter Tirel, a courtier, who fled to France. Some said Tirel had quarrelled with William, others that he was part of a plot; but Tirel claimed his innocence.*

dying. Tirel remounted his horse and galloped away from the scene.

Did Walter Tirel, who had never sworn allegiance to the king, kill him in the New Forest on August 2, 1100? Tirel was the only man known to have been in the vicinity when the king died. With one accord his contemporaries accused him of the deed.

Some men thought that it was an accident. Perhaps Tirel had himself been aiming at the stag and struck the king in error. But others hinted darkly of a plot. Walter Tirel was a fine shot, and it seemed unlikely that his bolt would have gone so far astray. He had quarrelled with the king the previous night. William had boasted that he would invade France and celebrate Christmas at Poitiers. Tirel's patriotic pride had been offended and he had poured scorn on the idea. It seemed that the quarrel had been made up. But did Tirel's temper fail him? Or were there other conspirators waiting for the king in the forest that fading August evening – perhaps in the employ of William's ambitious young brother, Henry? Henry was certainly quick to take advantage of his brother's death. Instead of pursuing Tirel, he hastened to Winchester and seized the treasury. It is one of the deepest mysteries that English history holds.

SPORT OF KINGS

A peasant hunts with the poor man's longbow.

Hunting was the favourite pastime of the Norman kings of England, and they went to great lengths to indulge their pleasure. By the end of the 12th century, one-third of England had been set aside as royal forest – a term which at that time meant simply an area devoted to hunting. The New Forest, created by William the Conqueror, was one of the earliest. Deer and wild boar were preserved for the king's sport alone, but his barons and abbots were allowed to hunt lesser game, such as hare and fox.

Penalties for poaching in Norman times were savage. The man killing this deer risked execution if his crime were ever to be discovered.

William II: 'Wanton, lascivious and corrupt'

UNLOVED IN LIFE *This early 14th-century illumination – the first-known portrait of William Rufus – depicts the king's violent end. But William's death was never avenged, for his corrupt, aggressive and blasphemous life had won him the hatred and enmity of his people.*

The King of England for 13 years after the death of the Conqueror, William Rufus – so-called because of his flame-red hair – was unfortunate in his choice of enemies. In addition to the traditional enemies of the Norman kings – their over-mighty barons – he also took on the Church. And though William had the upper hand in this quarrel, it was the Church who had the last word, for it was by churchmen that the chronicles of medieval England were written. 'A wicked, avaricious, evil-living man,' wrote one. 'Wanton, lascivious and corrupt,' agreed another. And the Church had much to complain about in William's reign. Anselm, Archbishop of Canterbury, was forced to spend most of the reign in exile, while the king plundered churches and stole their lands.

From love to hatred

William's worst mistake was that he recklessly threw away the popularity he had enjoyed when he first became king. In 1087, one of William's barons, Odo of Bayeux, rebelled against his accession, but the people of England flocked to support their new king. In return, William made sweeping promises of reform and good government – but, as soon as the danger had passed, he conveniently forgot all his handsome words. And when Archbishop Lanfranc, Anselm's predecessor, rebuked him, William responded angrily: 'Who can be expected to keep all his promises?' In 1093, William fell ill. At death's door, he accepted Anselm as archbishop and again promised to reform. But on his recovery he once more broke his word.

The stern unbending moralists of the day were disgusted by the frivolity of William's court. His generosity to his favourites drew a great number of ambitious, self-seeking young men, many of them foreigners, whose behaviour the English considered offensive and unmanly. But a graver charge levelled against the king was that the sycophants who came to his court were allowed to ride roughshod over all others. Although he held several Church offices, William's chief minister, the notorious Rannulf Flambard, mercilessly extorted money from the Church. But the most unpopular men at William's court were his mercenary soldiers. When the news of the king's approach reached any English village, the populace would leave their homes and take to the forests rather than submit to their brutality.

A man of contrasts

The Norman kings were men of striking contrasts, and none more so than William Rufus. For however much his contemporaries blackened his reputation, they could not deny that he had some redeeming features. Even as he confiscated the wealth of the Church with one hand, he returned it with the other in the form of lavish religious foundations. Despite his faults, Rannulf Flambard was an efficient administrator – and he paid for the building of the choir of Durham Cathedral. William placed his mercenaries and courtiers above the law, but where others were concerned he enforced justice. In his day, the law was obeyed by every man in England – except for the king and his immediate followers.

Above all, William Rufus regarded his father, the great Conqueror, with an almost superstitious reverence and constantly emulated him. He was perhaps the cleverest of the Norman kings, yet his character remained elusive, a tissue of paradoxes. He had only himself to blame if few men mourned him.

A FORTRESS CHURCH STANDS GUARD ON THE BORDER

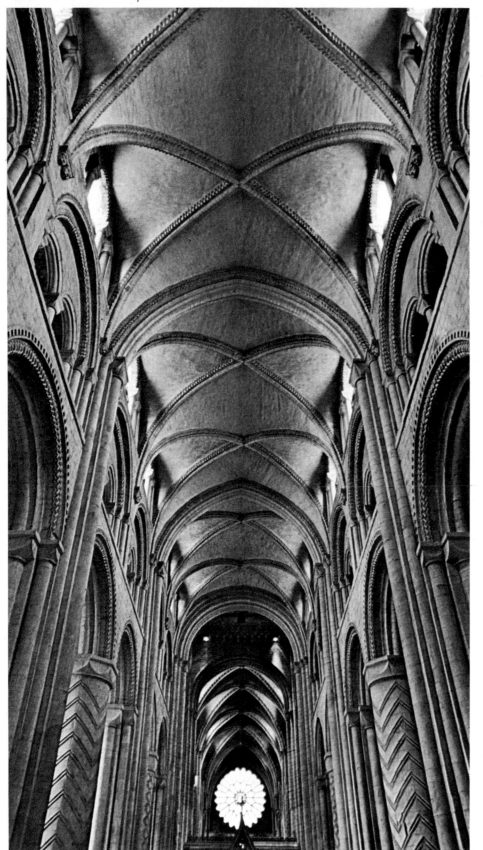

MASSIVE GRANDEUR *Durham Cathedral is England's greatest masterpiece of early-Norman architecture. It was begun in 1093 as a shrine for St Cuthbert, the most famous saint of the north. This view of the aisle shows the ribbed vaulting of the massive roof. The earliest of its kind in Europe and the only one in England, the roof was considered a construction miracle in its day.*

WRITER'S TRIBUTE *Situated on a hill above the River Wear, few cathedrals have a more impressive setting than Durham. Sir Walter Scott paid it tribute on a bridge-stone (above).*

Sir Walter Scott's description of Durham Cathedral was 'half church of God, half castle 'gainst the Scot'. The words of the 19th-century novelist aptly describe the magnificent building that soars above the River Wear and dwarfs even the castle beside it.

Durham Cathedral was built in an age when both the faith and the mortal bodies of Christians were in constant danger from the ravages of the heathen. In 875 the monks of Lindisfarne, off the Northumbrian coast, were driven by the Danes from their island sanctuary. They took with them their most precious relic, the body of their 7th-century bishop, St Cuthbert. In 999, a year of grim foreboding when many men awaited the end of the world, they settled at Durham – and found prosperity and peace.

Built around a shrine

A century later, in 1093, the first Norman bishop, William of St Carileph, began to build a cathedral around the shrine of the saint. By 1133, enough of the construction work was finished to give St Cuthbert's body a resting place in safety at the heart of one of the strongest citadels of the Church. It still retains the air of a fortress. In medieval times, lit only by flickering candles, it must have had the appearance of a gloomy cave.

Strength and simplicity are the keynotes of

Durham's style. The massive pillars, for all their ornate carved decoration, are emphatically structural. They look as though they could support the world itself.

These pillars and the round arches between them are solidly Norman. But above, the arches forming the vaulted roof of the nave are pointed, a device developed by the 12th-century masons of Durham to bring greater height and light to the upper parts of the structure. This is the first appearance in Europe of the pointed arch – the feature that was to be the secret of the world's greatest works of architecture during the next four centuries. Durham is not only the triumphant climax of the Norman style, but also the first hint of the Gothic.

Influences from the East

Soon, St Cuthbert's shrine became the most popular in the north of England. Though only men were admitted to the tomb itself (women being forbidden to cross the strip of black marble in front of the font), pilgrims of both sexes flocked to Durham – and pilgrims meant profit for the Church.

As the money flowed in, so the cathedral grew – notably to the west, where the lovely Galilee Chapel was built in 1175. At that time it was lovelier still, its 12 broad arches supported only on marble columns. The stone shafts are 15th-century reinforcements.

There is something curiously Islamic about those arches. Their zigzag ornamentation, always described as typically Norman, is really Moorish in origin, brought back to England by early Crusaders. This exquisite chapel was chosen as the final resting place of the Venerable Bede, the 7th-century scholar who became the father of English history. The fame of Bede's *Ecclesiastical History of the English*

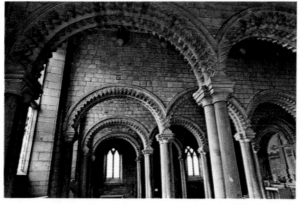

ISLAMIC ARCHES *The Galilee Chapel, built in 1175, shows the Moorish influence brought back by early Crusaders. It houses the tomb of the Venerable Bede.*

SAINT'S BLESSING *A 12th-century portrait of St Cuthbert painted on the Galilee Chapel's wall.*

People had won worldwide renown for the northern church. In displaying his sacred tomb, Durham reinforced its claim as the citadel of the Holy Church in the north.

The work of enhancing Durham's stern grandeur continued in the following centuries, even though its bishops were busy with other concerns. They had authority over the Palatinate of Durham, which extended from the Tees to the Tyne and also included other lands far to the north on the Scottish border. Within these boundaries the bishop was responsible for administration, justice, coinage, supervision of markets and levying troops. Soldier-bishops, such as Anthony Bek and Thomas of Hatfield, who both led armies against the Scots, were more common than architect-bishops.

Nevertheless, Durham Cathedral did grow and did change. In the 1230's, Bishop Richard le Poore, who had already built one cathedral at Salisbury, enlarged the East End, adding the Chapel of the Nine Altars, where the more

ornate Gothic style contrasts strikingly with the simplicity of the original Norman building.

The 14th century brought new riches, with the gift of the great screen behind the High Altar which is encrusted with more than 100 gilded and painted alabaster figures. In this last great age of Durham's building, twin towers were set up at the West End and a central spire was raised to dominate the city.

But in 1429 the spire was struck by lightning, charring the wooden belfry and irreparably damaging the stonework. The monks of Durham were apparently too poor to pay for the necessary rebuilding and resorted to sending one of their number out into the world to beg for money, armed with a silver-gilt crucifix and a piece of cloth in which the body of St Cuthbert had been wrapped.

Presumably these relics failed to stir the people of the palatinate to pious generosity, for nothing was done until 1455, by which time the whole structure was in danger of collapse. Even then work proceeded slowly; and it was 1499 before the great tower was finished. After four centuries of building, Durham was complete.

Survival through the ages

With this achievement, the era of medieval building closed. A less constructive age was dawning. On December 31, 1540, the monastery was dissolved and its treasures were confiscated – a catastrophe for which even the opening of St Cuthbert's tomb and the discovery of his body 'incorrupt, with his face bare and his beard as it had been a fortnight's growth', must have been poor compensation. Four hundred years of tradition were destroyed. More disasters were to follow. In 1650, 4000 Scottish soldiers, captured by Oliver Cromwell after the Battle of Dunbar and imprisoned in the cathedral, burnt the choir stalls for fuel.

And yet, miraculously, Durham has survived. Firm on its river-girt rock, it seems to breathe indestructibility and confidence, honouring its God, sheltering its saints – and keeping the Scots in their place.

SYMBOL OF SANCTUARY

A bronze knocker in the form of a frightening mask leers from the north door of Durham Cathedral. To a fugitive, this curious example of 12th-century metalwork once meant safety. By clinging to it he could claim sanctuary – safety from the civil law.

Medieval law gave right of sanctuary to a fugitive once he reached the church – provided that he observed rules which were set out in minutest detail. He had to confess to the priests and also had to surrender his arms and pay an admission fee.

At Durham the fugitive had to toll a special bell as a formal signal that he claimed sanctuary. The civil law then allowed the fugitive to take an oath of 'abjuration of the realm', whereby he undertook to quit the kingdom. In a long white robe, armed only with a cross, he was then allowed only nine days in which to leave the shores of England. In other churches, a stone seat was placed near the altar for fugitives; examples of these 'frith-stools' (peace stools) are at Beverley and Hexham.

Few examples of Norman metalworkers' art have survived which can compare with this 12th-century sanctuary knocker. The grotesque and frightening face once had coloured enamel eyes.

Shipwreck sets England on the road to civil war

But for the pride of a 17-year-old prince, England might have been spared 19 years of bloody civil war – years during which, as the chroniclers said, 'God and his saints slept'. A Norman prince had to grow to manhood quickly, and William of England, grandson of the mighty Conqueror, was no exception. Although just turned 17, he had won his spurs at the side of his father, Henry I, during bitter fighting and tortuous diplomacy in Normandy. He had faced death in battle, though his chin was not yet darkened by a beard. Broad shouldered and quick with a jest, he was as great a favourite with the ladies as he was popular with the soldiers. As heir to the crown, he was courted by the young nobility of the nation and by any man with a name or fortune to make.

Such was the prince who, on November 25,

1120, refused to share a ship with his father for the voyage back to England from Barfleur in Normandy. England's name was feared and respected throughout Europe, and the young prince had played his part in making it so. It was beneath his dignity to have to take only the second place on a voyage. So he bade his father farewell and ordered the *White Ship* to be prepared ready for sea.

A voyage doomed to disaster

The *White Ship* was the finest vessel in England of its time – large, stoutly built and recently re-equipped. But the ships of those days were still perilously small and flimsy. Each week brought new tidings of ships lost in the Channel, dashed against submerged rocks or carried away by strong currents. Men avoided the sea whenever possible. Very few of them could swim for more than a few yards, and a disaster at sea meant certain death for most of

THE LINE OF DISASTER

A contemporary illuminated 'family tree' shows how the sinking of the White Ship *off the Normandy coast in November 1120 changed history. The manuscript, at the British Museum, includes Henry I (top) and the line to his son William, who drowned in the disaster. After that, the tree shows Matilda, Stephen and Henry II.*

DISASTER IN THE CHANNEL *As the* White Ship *struck a hidden rock, panic broke out on board. Prince William and a handful of companions managed to escape in a small boat. But the prince ordered it to return to rescue his sister and it was swamped by other passengers trying to clamber on board.*

the passengers. Men confessed their sins and prepared for death before even the shortest of sea voyages.

The crew of the *White Ship* – who had spent the evening in drunken revelry – promised the young prince that they would quickly overtake the king's party and arrive first in Southampton. It was already dark before they ran down the beach, singing and laughing, and launched the ship from the shore. With the prince, embarked all those who paid court to him as a rising star. There were several of Henry's illegitimate children, a nephew of the German emperor, earls and barons, important churchmen and civil servants on board.

Aground on the rocks

The *White Ship* sped out into the Channel, its drunken crew steering an erratic course towards England. But the night concealed the hazards of the Normandy coast. As the passengers retired to their beds, the ship struck a submerged rock. It shuddered violently. The timbers of the side broke, and the vessel began to list heavily. With cries of panic the passengers rushed on deck and tried to help the sailors to free the ship with boat-hooks. Others seized oars, in a desperate attempt to row the ship off the rocks before its hull was crushed by the pounding sea.

The first thought of William's attendants was for the prince's safety. A small boat was quickly launched and William, with a few companions, boarded it. The shore was only a few hundred yards away, and the royal party might have escaped safely. But at that moment an illegitimate sister of the prince cried out to him not to leave her to her death. Prince William took pity on her, and ordered the

sailors to row back. The *White Ship* was now sinking rapidly, its timbers breaking up under the pounding waves. Many people were clinging to pieces of wood in the bitterly cold water and, as the prince's boat came into view, the panic grew. They all struggled to climb on board or hold on to the sides. The boat swayed from side to side and finally capsized.

For days afterwards, richly dressed bodies were washed up on the Normandy coast. Few of the victims were ever identified; most were never found. A butcher from Rouen, the humblest of the ship's passengers, was the only one who survived.

'No ship ever brought such misery to England,' proclaimed a chronicler, 'none was ever so notorious in the history of the world.' The absence of an heir threatened to destroy the whole fabric of Norman monarchy. For with the death of Henry's only legitimate son, no man could be sure that the law of the realm would not die with him.

An oath to secure the succession

Henry I had 22 children, 20 of whom were bastards. William's death left only Henry's daughter, Matilda, to represent the direct line of the Norman kings. Anxious to secure her succession, Henry made his barons swear an oath in 1121 that they would support her.

But they did so reluctantly, since they were unwilling to accept the prospect of a woman on the throne. And when Henry died in December 1135, they rallied to the support of the first claimant to arrive in England from Normandy – Stephen, Henry's nephew. The citizens of London declared him their king. And in January, his election as king was confirmed by Pope Innocent III.

NINETEEN LONG WINTERS

Quick action by Stephen (left) in seizing the throne saved England from the haughty, tactless and grasping Matilda. It did not ensure that the rule of law which his uncle, Henry I, had upheld would be maintained. Though Stephen was kind and generous, he lacked the ruthlessness necessary in a medieval ruler. There was, as the *Peterborough Chronicle* recorded, 'treason soon in the land, for every man that could forthwith robbed another'. Stephen's uncertain rule lasted from 1135 to 1154. It went down in history as the 'nineteen long winters when God and his saints slept'. The rule of law that Henry I had striven so hard to establish seemed doomed to perish in these years of anarchy, pillage and destruction.

Stephen was not entirely to blame. Matilda landed in England determined to take the crown. To gain support, he gave away royal

lands and relaxed his uncle's tight rein. But such weakness lost him the respect of his feudal lords and inspired a series of civil wars. It was a price that a stronger man might not have been forced to pay. But it secured Stephen the throne and, by a treaty of settlement, the succession passed peacefully to the greatest of medieval English monarchs, Matilda's son, Henry II.

A scene from the 12th-century illuminated Bury Bible depicts the siege of a walled town during the breakdown of law and order in the unsettled 19-year reign of King Stephen.

Henry I: A king sees his hopes shatter

Henry I, the youngest son of William the Conqueror, shared his father's practical, down-to-earth attitudes; he had all the qualities of greed and ruthlessness that characterised the Norman kings of England. He was brusque and plain-speaking. He ate and drank in plenty. He slept heavily and snored loudly. In addition to his two legitimate children, he had 20 illegitimate ones.

Despite his gross manners, in politics Henry was the subtlest of his family. He preferred to gain his ends by negotiation, persuasion and diplomacy, rather than by brute force. By such methods he won Normandy from his brother, Robert, at the beginning of his reign in 1086, and made England a power to be reckoned with on the European continent.

Keeping the peace

Like his father, Henry spent much of his time dealing with rebellions by his barons. He preferred diplomacy, but this had often to be discarded for suppression. Henry was at all times intensely suspicious, constantly in fear of plots and treason. He suspected his closest servants of planning his death. He regularly changed the position of his bed, and armed guards stood at every door of his chamber. His sword always hung beside his bed.

Not all Henry's enemies were rebellious barons. The longest and most bitter struggle of his reign was with Anselm, the saintly Archbishop of Canterbury. Henry insisted on controlling the Church himself, for bishops at that time were powerful and wealthy men, and he demanded the right to appoint his friends to important Church posts. But it was not until 1107, after seven years of intrigue and diplomacy, that he got his way.

Search for an heir

But Henry's most serious problem remained unsolved. Although his mistresses bore him innumerable sons, his wife bore him only one before her death in 1120. When that son was drowned in the *White Ship* in the same year, Henry was left without a male heir. Legend has it that after the disaster he never smiled again; he may well have realised that the hopes of his dynasty had foundered with the ship. He married again within eight weeks of the disaster, but his second wife, Adelaide, daughter of Godfrey VII, Count of Lorraine, failed to produce a male heir.

This lack of a son was the direct cause of the civil wars that were to follow Henry's death. No one, in the Middle Ages, could feel secure until a new king had come to the throne and renewed all the old laws. On December 1, 1135, Henry died after a meal of lampreys, his favourite sea-food. The anarchy that followed lasted for 19 bitter years.

The clash that led to murder in the cathedral

WHERE BECKET FELL

Today, a plaque marks the spot in Canterbury Cathedral where, on December 29, 1170, Archbishop Thomas Becket paid with his life for his opposition to Henry II. He was put to death by four of Henry's impetuous courtiers, who had taken at face value their king's angry demands to be rid of 'this miserable priest' who 'insults me to my face'.

As the year 1170 closed, a conflict which had been dividing England for six years reached its climax. The Archbishop of Canterbury, Henry II's erstwhile friend Thomas Becket, had defied the king's demands to control the power of the Church.

These demands were far-reaching. Henry had forbidden the clergy to exercise their time-honoured right of appeal to Rome as the final authority in matters concerning the Church; he had diverted the papal tax known as 'Peter's Pence' – it was used for the building of St Peter's in Rome – to his own purposes. Finally, he had gone as far as ordering the priests of England to take an oath against the pope.

Becket had held out against this pressure. He went into exile and took refuge in the abbey of Pontigny in France. At the beginning of December, however, he had met the king in Normandy and agreed to be reconciled. But on his return to Canterbury, Becket publicly excommunicated his enemies from the pulpit of the cathedral on Christmas Day 1170.

Henry's patience was exhausted. The Archbishop of York and the Bishops of London and Salisbury hastened to him, to report that Becket was determined to discipline those churchmen who had supported the crown. In a moment of exasperation, Henry railed at the 'idle cowards of my court who stand by while this miserable priest insults me to my face'. These hasty words were to inspire a deed which shocked the whole of Christendom.

Four knights, Reginald FitzUrse, William de Tracy, Hugh Mauclerk, and Richard le Breton – took the king at his word. To rid him of this troublemaker would surely be a great service to the realm. They hastily left the royal court, which at that time was in Normandy, and set sail for England. There, they planned to arrest the archbishop and imprison him to await the king's pleasure. Or, if this was impossible, they would kill him.

The final quarrel

At 4 p.m. on December 29, 1170, the knights reached Canterbury. A bustling crowd of on-lookers had gathered outside the cathedral, drawn by news of Becket's latest defiance of the king, and by sinister rumours of violence and murder. FitzUrse ordered his retainers to guard the gates of the cathedral precinct. He and his three companions then entered the great courtyard and demanded that the monks take them to the archbishop.

Thomas Becket was in his study next to the great hall. Reginald FitzUrse was the first to speak: 'We have a message for you from the king. He commands that you and your followers shall leave his realm. After your insolence there can be no peace between you.' The knights menacingly approached the archbishop. Voices were raised and finally they strode out, shouting 'To arms! To arms!' On this signal, their followers outside the gates swarmed into the courtyard, replying with the cry 'King's men!'

From his study, Becket heard the sound of splintering wood and the muffled shouts of the king's soldiers. His clerks pleaded with him to take refuge in the cathedral, and almost dragged him out through the cloisters and into the north-west transept.

But Becket refused to be hurried. He was proud of his dignity as primate of England, and would not save himself by flight. As the monks tried to bolt the cathedral door he stopped them, crying: 'The Church of God is not a fortress. Open it!'

'I am no traitor'

Seconds later, the knights burst through the doors. 'Where is Thomas Becket, traitor to his king and kingdom?' demanded FitzUrse. From the steps leading to the High Altar Becket replied: 'I am here, no traitor but a priest of God and an archbishop.'

A sword glinted in the candlelight, and the archbishop reeled as a blow struck him in the shoulder. FitzUrse raised his axe and struck at his head. Another of the knights, William de Tracy, stepped forward and dealt Becket such a blow that his sword broke in two with its force. As soldiers ran jubilantly out into the cloister, Hugh Mauclerk placed his foot on the dead man's neck and scattered his brains on the floor with the point of his sword. 'Here,' he cried, 'is one traitor who will not rise again.'

But Becket had the final word. An eye-witness to the tragedy, William fitzStephen, wrote that 'the sun's gaze was averted, its rays hidden from the earth and the day veiled in darkness...a terrible storm cloud overhung the firmament, the rain fell suddenly and swiftly and the thunder rolled round the Heavens. After this, the sky turned a deep red in token of the blood which had been shed and in horror at the outrage.'

This was the stuff of legend. Within three years Becket had been canonised by Pope Alexander III, and his tomb had become a shrine for pilgrims from all over Europe. Henry himself was forced to do public penance – being whipped in Canterbury Cathedral on the site of Becket's murder. But this did not stop him in his purpose. He succeeded in bringing the English Church under royal control – a position which his successors never lost.

Becket had failed in his great struggle. His martyrdom had been in vain. But for 360 years his memory lived on. Then Henry VIII had the shrine destroyed. But even this action could not destroy the legend of a man of God who perished for his beliefs.

RECORD IN PICTURES *A medieval illumination tells the story of the events leading up to and following Becket's death. At the top, the knights overhear the king and plot to kill the archbishop. Below, Becket is murdered and pilgrims are seen praying at his tomb.*

Henry II: Rebuilding after the anarchy

Henry II, the man whose hasty words led to the death of Thomas Becket, had inherited a kingdom shattered by two decades of civil war, and a discredited and despised crown. His consuming aim was to re-establish royal power and prestige, and his achievements made him one of the most successful rulers of medieval England.

Henry recognised that he had to ensure that his subjects lived in peace and security if he was to keep their loyalty. To do this, he introduced trial by jury, a turning point in English history. For the first time, the king's justice was made available to all – high or low-born. A brilliant administrator, Henry also built up a large professional civil service to make sure that his policies were effectively carried out.

Might of the crown

Henry was determined to make his crown the one power in the land. The over-mighty barons, who had terrorised England under the weak Stephen, were soon brought to heel. Only the Church, under the obstinate leadership of Thomas Becket, held out in refusing to meet Henry's demands. In particular, the king was determined to take some of the powers that the Church courts possessed. All men, he argued, should be equal before the law – the king's law. This was what Becket refused to yield him – and the subsequent quarrel was to lead to the archbishop's martyrdom.

Henry's other failure was within his own family. He married Eleanor of Aquitaine for her wealth; but then he unceremoniously deserted her for the charms of a beautiful mistress, Rosamund Clifford. Eleanor never forgave him, and she passed her hatred on to their four sons – Richard, Henry, Geoffrey and John. And the king's last years were tormented by the rebellions that his children fostered against him. In 1183, Henry and Geoffrey joined the nobles of Aquitaine in a rising against their father and their brother, Richard. No sooner had Henry II dealt with this than Richard himself turned against him and eventually joined with the French king to wage war against his father.

Alone and friendless, the ageing Henry was forced to beg for peace. Stricken with fever, he met Richard and Philip of France and agreed to all their terms. But it was not Richard's treachery that broke his father's heart. For he learnt from Philip that his favourite son, John, had also conspired against him. 'Enough,' he cried, 'now let things go as they may. I care no more for myself or for the world!' Two days later he died on July 6, 1189.

Henry's proud spirit had been broken and many of his achievements shattered. But his greatest work survived – the rule of law – as his gift to future generations.

CULT OF A MARTYRED SAINT

No single deed shocked medieval Christendom more than the murder of the saintly Archbishop Thomas Becket in his cathedral at Canterbury, in December 1170. Immediately, Becket was acclaimed as a martyr, and within three years Pope Alexander III had canonised him. In 1174, Henry II himself visited the tomb to do penance

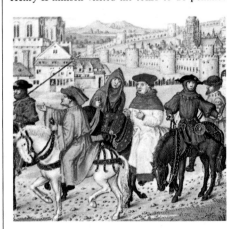

Pilgrims confer outside the walls of Canterbury in this 15th-century illustration. St Thomas's tomb attracted thousands from all over Europe.

for the deed his hasty words had inspired. From then on, the shrine of St Thomas was one of the greatest centres of pilgrimage in the Christian world. Kings, princes, nobles, merchants, priests and peasants journeyed there, all anxious to see one of the miracles said to occur at the shrine. Such a journey was immortalised 300 years later by England's greatest medieval poet, Geoffrey Chaucer, in his *Canterbury Tales.*

Becket's fame spread still further. In the Holy Land, an order of Christian knights was founded in his memory. Even in the remoteness of Iceland a long poem, 'Thomas Saga Erkibyskups' (The Saga of Archbishop Thomas), was written telling the story of his life. Relics, too, were in great demand. Among the chief 'miracle-workers' on sale were phials supposed to contain drops of the martyred Becket's blood, collected by his faithful monks from beneath the High Altar immediately after his death.

But in the 1530's, when England broke with the Roman Catholic Church, Henry VIII ordered the shrine to be destroyed, and confiscated all the rich gifts which had been lavished on it over the centuries. The memory of St Thomas, however, he could not destroy. It still lives on in the Canterbury of today.

England's king leads an army to the Holy Land

THE 'LIONHEART'S' MEMORIAL

Within weeks of Richard I's coronation as king, he planned his first Crusade to the Holy Land. For Richard, war was to become a way of life. It is as a warrior that he is remembered, as this contemporary tile from Chertsey Abbey shows. But Richard's campaigns were an expensive burden for his people, and a source of growing discontent. He once remarked that he would sell London if he could find a buyer.

NO QUARTER *Richard imposed harsh surrender terms after the fall of Acre. The king gave the infidel Muslims no quarter; he regarded their lives as forfeit, and on August 20, 1191, watched (on the balcony, left) as 2700 of them were being put to the sword.*

For 200 years, the fervent Christianity that dominated medieval Europe inspired a great military movement – the Crusades to the Holy Land. Under the red cross of the Crusaders, monarchs and nobles – and, on occasion, peasants and children – marched to rescue the 'Holy Places' of Christendom from the hands of the infidel Muslims.

The Crusades started in 1095, when knights from Europe first set sail for Palestine. They captured Jerusalem and set up four Crusader kingdoms, building vast fortresses, such as Krak des Chevaliers in Syria, to secure their hold on their new possessions.

But Crusader rule was not to last. The Muslims rallied and, by 1189, the Crusaders were close to being driven out of the sacred land they had given so much to conquer. Jerusalem had fallen to the armies of the Muslim leader, Saladin, and only two cities in the whole of Palestine remained in Christian hands.

It was at this decisive moment, within weeks of his coronation as King of England, that Richard I drew up his plans to intervene. Nowhere in Europe did the romantic fascination of men with the Holy Land have a stronger pull than in England. Now Richard launched an expedition to Palestine. He left England in December 1189 and on June 6, 1191, he landed in Palestine.

The first task was to recapture the great fortified port of Acre, an essential base for the Crusaders if they were to avoid being driven into the sea. When Richard arrived, their siege had been going on for two years. But a man who had won the reputation of 'the first soldier of Europe' and boasted the proud nickname of 'Lionheart', was not willing to brook delay. He immediately took command and, by the first week of July, it was clear that the city could hold out no longer. On July 12, Acre surrendered to the triumphant Crusaders.

But the fall of Acre was only the first stage in the battle for the Holy Land. Both sides – Christian and Muslim – realised that the decisive conflict was still to come.

Leaving garrison in Acre, Richard marched the Crusader army south along the coast, hoping to be able to turn inland towards Jerusalem. But Saladin barred the Crusaders' path, and the Christians' high hopes soon gave way to despair. The desert sun beat down pitilessly on the heavily armoured knights; many of the recent arrivals perished from sunstroke or malaria. Stragglers were swept up by squads of Muslim horsemen.

Battle on the plain

By early September, it was clear that the Muslims intended to force a battle. This took place on a narrow plain north of the town of Arsuf, some 2 miles from the sea and bounded on both sides by forest.

Richard drew up his army with bowmen in the front and the cavalry behind them. The Knights Templar, so dreaded by the Muslims that prisoners were never ransomed, but always beheaded, were on the right flank. Now Richard and his troops waited for the Muslim assault. When it came, the Crusaders held their ground, and eventually their adversaries began to tire. But Richard refused to order a counterattack. The Christian army was to wait until the full force of the Muslim attack had been spent. The Knights Templar, however, lacked the

Richard I: Champion of Christendom's cause

Richard I, the Crusader king, was the least English of all England's monarchs. He spent no more than six months in his native country during his ten-year reign. These were unhappy years for England – years of destructive conflict between those who governed in Richard's absence; years of crushing taxation as the absent king drew on English wealth to finance his ambitious enterprises abroad.

Richard's brilliant victories in Palestine did something to compensate England for the unrest that followed his departure. But he had all the hot-tempered and impetuous characteristics of his family. During his Crusade, he quarrelled with Duke Leopold of Austria, who never forgave him for throwing the Hapsburg standard into the moat at Acre.

This last dispute had far-reaching consequences. On his return to Europe in 1192, Richard was shipwrecked on the Adriatic coast and forced to travel disguised as a common soldier through Leopold's territories. But he was recognised and arrested at an inn near Vienna. Leopold cast him into prison and demanded a ransom of 150,000 silver marks.

The king's brother, John, took advantage of his capture to raise rebellion. And Richard's loyal subjects faced the bill for his ransom. The money was raised in a few months, but Richard stayed no more than two months in the land that had bought his freedom. The rest of his reign was spent campaigning to defend his lands in France, until he was killed by an arrow fired from the castle of Chalus on April 6, 1199.

CHRISTIANITY'S CHAMPIONS

The example set by Richard I in 'taking the Cross' was soon followed by many of his nobles. Enthusiasm for the Crusade was whipped up by preachers and minstrels and many volunteers came forward; those men who refused to follow their king were often presented with a distaff and some wool, implying that they were no better than women. The pope, for his part, offered the Crusaders indulgences, absolving them from their sins.

Though the Crusaders failed to liberate the Holy Land, their expeditions produced a lasting legacy. For they gained from the Arabs some of the secrets in science and mathematics that the West had lost during the Dark Ages, after the fall of the Roman Empire.

The Crusader John de Holcombe's tomb, in Dorchester Abbey, Oxfordshire, is a fine example of medieval craftsmanship.

king's patience and decided to force his hand. Two of them charged towards the enemy, to be followed by others. Then suddenly the whole body of the Christian cavalry spurred their horses forward.

Suppressing his anger at this disobedience, Richard took personal command of the assault. The Muslims wavered, then broke ranks and fled. Saladin's reputation for invincibility was shattered.

This was the high point of Richard's Crusade. The road to Jerusalem was open, and the Crusaders jubilantly advanced towards their goal. But 12 miles from the city the army was halted – not by their foes but by quarrels between its commanders. Philip Augustus, who had already returned from Palestine to France after quarrelling with the imperious Richard, had attacked Normandy. In England, Richard's brother, John, ambitious for supreme power, was plotting against him.

On receiving this news, Richard had no choice but to order a retreat back to the coast. Realising that the disunity of his forces made military victory impossible, he began negotiations with the Muslim leaders, Saladin and Safadin. These came to nothing and once more Richard advanced on Jerusalem. This time, he led an advance party to within sight of the city walls. But again quarrels forced the Crusaders to retreat. Finally, a treaty was agreed between the Christian and Muslim leaders, which gave the Crusaders a strip of land along the coast of Palestine. They were also ceded the ports of Acre and Jaffa, and pilgrims were to be allowed to visit Jerusalem. The peace was to last three years.

Richard had failed to fulfil his dream. No English king would liberate Jerusalem – nor would one again go on Crusade. The city was to remain in Muslim hands until the First World War, more than seven centuries later.

ABSENTEE KING *Richard spent only six months of his reign in England. After his return from the Crusades he fought in France, where he met his death in action.*

A king's anger creates Britain's first university

A SEAT OF LEARNING
The Mob Quad at Merton College is Oxford's oldest quadrangle, completed between 1304 and 1311. Founded by the statesman William de Merton in 1274, Merton was the first Oxford college to be endowed on a large scale. William, however, made conditions as to the use of his funds; the first eight fellows of Merton were his nephews.

RECEIVING INSTRUCTION *A master and pupils at New College, from a 14th-century manuscript. The college's founder, William of Wykeham, aimed to educate leaders for Church and state.*

Most of the great beginnings of the Middle Ages were attended by bloodshed and violence. The story of Oxford University, the first capital of English learning, was no exception. But out of the strife that accompanied the university's early history were to come ideas that would transform the Western world.

Britain's oldest university owes its origin to the quarrel between Henry II and his Archbishop of Canterbury, Thomas Becket. In 1167, enraged that the exiled archbishop had found safe refuge in France, Henry decreed that all English scholars studying on the Continent were to return home.

Many of them, students and teachers alike, gathered at Oxford. There they tried to re-create the scholarly atmosphere they had known at Paris and the other universities of France. But it was not until 1209 that a sudden flash of violence prompted them to take the first steps to found a university.

Uncertain beginnings
The town's citizens had never much liked the students who gathered there in such numbers. They were noisy and boisterous, and they drank too much. Besides, they were mostly in holy orders and so aroused the townspeople's longstanding dislike of the clergy.

When a woman was killed by a scholar the town rose in uproar. Led by the mayor, the townsmen arrested several students. Two of them were speedily hanged, and in protest the university closed. Some students went to Reading, some went back to Paris – and some went to the small fenland town of Cambridge, to found a new university there in 1231.

The scholars were less disturbed by their migration than the Oxford merchants, who found they missed the students' custom. In 1214 the townsmen apologised for their action, and invited the scholars back. For the rest of the century, the university flourished.

According to the contemporary historian Matthew Paris there were 3000 scholars at the university in this period, though today it is thought that the true figure was 1500. They ranged in age from 14 to 40.

The organisation of the university was still rudimentary. There was no formal entrance examination for students, who merely enrolled to study with a Master of Arts. Nor did the university at that time possess buildings or

SOURCE OF KNOWLEDGE
From the earliest years of the new universities, books were regarded as the most precious of treasures. In medieval Oxford, manuscripts were so valuable that the volumes containing them were chained up. Printing made books cheaper in the 15th century. In 1610, Sir Thomas Bodley, a diplomat, arranged with the Stationer's Company that the university should receive a copy of every book printed. His library – the Bodleian – is today the greatest in the world.

Henry V's brother, Duke Humphrey, founded this library to house his manuscripts.

Some of the rare books in Merton library are still chained to prevent their removal.

colleges of its own. Its students lived either in individual lodgings or groups of them banded together to rent houses. Each of them had, however, to be supervised by a graduate.

The course of study consisted of grammar, rhetoric and logic, together with geometry, arithmetic, astronomy and music. And, because books were scarce and expensive, students were taught in lectures, where they took dictation, and by disputation – a process of formal argument in which students had to refute their teachers' propositions.

After three years the students became 'questionists', winning the right to 'dispute' with Bachelors of Arts. A year later, after a verbal examination by the Masters of Arts, they became Bachelors themselves. After passing this test they were licensed to give lectures.

Three more years passed before the Bachelors could take their Masterships, and two more years of study known as 'Necessary Regency' followed. The few who survived went on to study for a Doctorate – a course which lasted at least seven years. Doctors were in great demand as officials and diplomats.

Founding great colleges

This course of study was very expensive. And rich men soon realised that the best way they could help Oxford's students was to found colleges in which they could live and work. In 1260, a wealthy baron, John de Balliol, founded Balliol College as a penance for raiding Durham Cathedral. Twenty years later, the Great University Hall (now University College) opened its doors to students.

But the grandest of all was New College, founded by William of Wykeham. From the time he became Bishop of Winchester in 1367, William planned two foundations to commemorate his fame – Winchester School and a college in Oxford. Work began in Oxford in 1379; it was largely completed by 1386.

William gave Oxford one of its leading landmarks – the college quadrangle. As a former Surveyor of the King's Works, he was keenly interested in building. He was the first to insist that a college's buildings should all be arranged round a courtyard. This feature has dominated Oxford's colleges ever since.

Town versus gown

The first Oxford students were clerics, but they were not men of peace. The bitter struggle between 'town and gown' was regularly fought out in battles in the High Street. In February 1298 the students armed themselves and assembled in the High Street. After attacking every citizen they could see, they rampaged through the town, breaking into houses and stealing from the occupants. Far from punishing the students for their crimes, the university court appointed to settle this dispute ordered the townspeople to pay £200 damages.

But in spite of such troubles, the 13th century was one of the most distinguished periods

in Oxford's history. Philosophers such as Duns Scotus, and scientists such as Roger Bacon made Oxford the greatest university in Europe. Duns Scotus was the most famous British theologian of the Middle Ages. Through his contributions to medieval philosophy, he won the nickname 'the subtle doctor'.

Bacon was a Franciscan friar. He set up a laboratory known as The Folly, where he conducted many scientific experiments. His work covered the fields of optics, mathematics, astronomy and chemistry. Despite the opposition of his religious superiors, Bacon refused to let his quest for truth be suppressed. At first he had the secret support of Pope Clement IV, who was interested in Bacon's *Opus Majus* – an encyclopedia of all the known sciences.

But when Clement died in 1268, Bacon lost his protector. His enemies intensified their attacks, and in 1277 the Franciscans threw him into prison. But until his death, 17 years later, Bacon continued to write as defiantly as ever, putting forward his revolutionary ideas.

These, and other men, inaugurated a tradition of thought and scholarship which, protected by kings and ministers, has endured to the present day. When the riches of Oxford were threatened at the time of the Reformation, Henry VIII said. 'I tell you, Sirs, that I judge no land in England better bestowed than that which is given to our universities. For by their maintenance our realm shall be well governed when we be dead and rotten.'

Ordeal by combat gives way to trial by jury

Violence in the Middle Ages was part of daily life. 'Every day,' a royal proclamation complained in the 12th century, 'our subjects commit murder, robbery and arson across the length and breadth of our land and escape with impunity.'

The records of the courts show that this was no exaggeration. One of Henry I's judges once had 44 thieves hanged in the space of a morning. Another, in the reign of John, tried 114 murderers in a single session.

Such crime figures would tax the resources of a modern police force. But in the Middle Ages there were no police at all. And to the crimes of the people had to be added the endless quarrels of their masters – the great landowners. To meet this problem the foundations of a great legal system were laid.

It had long been the custom to settle legal issues by ordeal or combat. But nobody cared for these ancient methods. Litigants disliked them because they were uncertain. Kings opposed them because they were violent and disorderly. The Church condemned them because they were barbarous.

Trial by jury

In 1166, Henry II issued a decree known as the assize of Clarendon, announcing that he would send his judges round England to settle disputes by hearing the verdict of 'twelve free and law-abiding men'. He introduced other legal reforms in the assize of Northampton in 1176 and the assize of arms in 1181.

Henry II's juries were, however, very different from those of today. Their members were not only expected to come before the judge free of all prejudices and preconceptions. They were also supposed to know at first hand who was guilty, or, if they did not know, they were expected to find out. Their role was to be detectives, prosecutors, witnesses and jurors.

The earliest juries had many faults. Those called to serve on them found it time-consuming and expensive. Often, they refused to come to court at all and had to be fined and bullied into doing so. A more serious fact was that, since they were local men, jurors were liable to be friends or enemies of the accused.

But gradually the defects were eliminated, and men came to see how much more reliable this was. In 1215, the Church dealt a final blow to trial by ordeal by forbidding the priests to have anything to do with it. In time, trial by combat, too, lapsed into oblivion, though it was not formally abolished until 1819.

It was only by slow and hesitant steps that the medieval courts and juries came to resemble those of our own day. But the seed sown by medieval lawyers took firm root in English soil. The jury was to become the keystone of the English legal system.

On a Thames-side meadow England's freedom is born

BIRTHPLACE OF LIBERTY
No name is more closely linked to the tradition of English freedom than Runnymede in Berkshire. There, in 1215, the barons and churchmen of England forced their reluctant king, John, to seal the first charter promising liberty to his subjects.

A ROMANTIC VIEW *John, his barons, and Archbishop Langton confer in this Victorian illustration of their meeting at Runnymede, while an official prepares to seal the charter. It had taken civil war to force John to agree to its demands.*

Step by step in the spring and summer of 1215, an all-powerful feudal monarch was driven to grant his subjects rights and liberties which set his country on the path to constitutional government. John, ruler of all England, had, by the severity of his rule, driven the barons of feudal England to forget their long-standing quarrels and unite in the struggle against him. Such men had their own particular grudges against John, and their motives were suspect in the eyes of the people. But it was John's misfortune that their cause was joined by a man of outstanding reputation, Stephen Langton, Archbishop of Canterbury. In the great events that were to follow, his voice was to prove decisive.

Revolt was a part of life in medieval England. There were always nobles who felt aggrieved at their exclusion from royal favours, which were too few to go round. But John's rule was more bitterly resented than most of his predecessors, for reasons for which the king was not entirely to blame.

An enormous debt and expensive wars in an age of inflation compelled him to exact from the barons far heavier payments than his predecessors had demanded. And his sense of royal duty induced him to temper justice in favour of women, children and the poor – often at the expense of the rich.

Nor had the Church reason to love John. For six years, from 1207–13, Langton had been forced to live abroad in exile until, at last, the king recognised him as Archbishop of Canterbury. During that time John attacked the Church without mercy, confiscated part of its wealth and forced seven English bishops to flee to the Continent.

There was thus a powerful and widespread opposition in the making when, in 1213, the king left England to campaign in France. His absence gave the barons time to plan their moves carefully, and the disastrous outcome of his wars against Philip Augustus, King of France, provided them with their opportunity.

But the Great Charter – Magna Carta – which the reluctant John was forced to seal on the banks of the Thames at Runnymede in June 1215, was nearly never presented to the king at all. At first, John had been prepared to listen and compromise, but soon his ungovernable temper got the better of him. In May 1215, he hysterically rejected the rebellious demands of the barons, shouting at their messenger: 'Take away your absurd, impertinent piece of paper and trouble me no longer.' Civil war was the result.

This war began disastrously for John's opponents. They laid siege to Northampton, but were forced to abandon it after 15 days. Meanwhile, the king had not been idle. He sent fast riders to the barons who had not yet joined the revolt, offering them favours and promising to mend his ways if they would join him. At this moment, the rebels seemed to be facing total defeat.

London – the key to success

Then they made a decision that was to change the fate of their campaign – and the course of English history. They marched on London. The king's French mercenaries, commanded by the Earl of Salisbury, hurried to reach the capital first, but they arrived too late. Early on the morning of May 17, the rebel barons stood before the walls of the city. The majority of Londoners were loyal to the king, for he had recently granted them a charter of liberty. But while they were at Mass, a small body of wealthy citizens, who sympathised with the rebels, opened the gates. By the time Mass was over, the city had fallen.

Overnight, John's cause was lost. Once London had fallen, the uncommitted nobles flocked to join the rebellion. Unrest spread over the entire country. The men of Devon rose; in Northampton, mobs looted the homes of suspected royalists. By the beginning of June an invincible force had gathered in London to confront the king. Moreover, Philip Augustus, King of France, had promised to send the rebels aid.

John realised that he had to yield if he was to keep his throne. Even the most loyal of his nobles, chief among them the wise William Marshal and the able administrator Hubert de Burgh, urged him to make concessions. He moved his headquarters to Windsor Castle, where he could feel secure behind the stout walls of the keep. The barons set up their camp at Staines, their forces controlling the London

road and protected from attack by the marshes of the Thames.

Between Windsor and Staines, in the water meadows of Runnymede, the two sides met. John's fate had already been resolved before the walls of London, so there was little room for argument. Each baron received the royal kiss of peace, and took food and drink with the king to cement their new-found friendship. John then solemnly set his seal upon the great charter – Magna Carta.

Foundation stone of English liberty

Later generations of Englishmen came to regard Magna Carta as the foundation stone of English liberty. But, alone among the great documents of human freedom, it has no sweeping statement of principle, no general declaration of the rights of all men. The barons who drew up much of the document were hard, practical men, with no time for theories. Most of its clauses – 'headings which the barons seek and the lord king grants' – recited their specific complaints against the lawless behaviour of King John, and ended with a promise that it would not be repeated.

But indiscriminately mixed with these detailed and specific complaints were principles of law, which in future ages were to be regarded as the backbone of English liberties. John was not to levy unauthorised taxes or fine men excessive amounts for trivial offences. His officers could no longer seize crops without paying for them. Knights were not to be forced to serve the king overseas. The Church could not be oppressed, nor its wealth confiscated. And, most important of all, 'to no one will we sell, deny or delay right or justice'.

These clauses were largely the work of Stephen Langton. It was his great achievement, in persuading the barons to insert clauses benefiting others, to expand a purely baronial agreement into a great national charter touching all classes of the realm.

Throughout its length, Magna Carta insisted that the king could not be above the law. In the future, he must govern his subjects according to its terms and not according to his own whim. If a monarch were to break the terms of the charter, his subjects would be released from their obligations to obey him and could legally bring about his overthrow.

But the most important thing about Magna Carta was not what it said, but the fact that it was granted at all. Wrested from the hands of an unwilling monarch, it marked the point at which the feudal monarchy of England was forced for the first time to recognise the limits of royal power. Every medieval king of England up to the time of Edward IV confirmed the charter. And long after its detailed provisions were forgotten, the spirit of Magna Carta was to guide the development of the English constitution. As a 13th-century chronicler wrote: 'The barons stood against the king for the liberty of the Church and realm.'

John: A king trapped by his ambition

Until John (right) succeeded to the throne of England in 1199, few, if any, took him seriously. Even when he tried to overthrow his brother Richard I while he was on Crusade in Palestine, the latter did not punish him. 'Think no more of it, John,' he said. 'You are only a child who has been led astray.'

In May 1199, John finally came to the throne. He immediately indulged his taste for luxury and display. He feasted regularly and dressed magnificently. He took frequent baths – a most unusual practice in those days – and even possessed a dressing gown. But the long years of waiting had soured his mind, and he came to the throne with a powerful inferiority complex. No English king ever had so strong a desire to assert his authority. Nor was there one who was so untrusting.

A royal failure

If John had managed to win success, no doubt opposition to him would never have materialised. But he discovered that his power was weaker than that of his great father, Henry II. Philip Augustus, King of France, was the ablest monarch in Europe; he won Normandy from John in a few months. Pope Innocent III held half of Europe in his power; John was no match for him. Stephen Langton, Archbishop of Canterbury and chief architect of Magna Carta, was the most formidable bishop ever to challenge an English king.

The king's mailed fist

Thwarted by these powerful enemies, John's response was to turn on his barons, who felt the full weight of his rule. He constantly bullied and threatened them, menacing their lands and taking their eldest sons hostage for good behaviour.

Even the remotest of John's subjects could not feel safe. The king was perpetually on the move – appearing without warning to punish or browbeat some unsuspecting victim. His secretive ways and his suspicious nature finally drove many of his nobles to join together in rebellion. Men who had fought against each other for decades were now united by hatred of John. All the grievances of England against John and his predecessors were visited on him in a few short months. Out of this hatred Magna Carta was born.

John survived the granting of the charter by only a year. In October 1216, while campaigning against rebels in the Midlands, he died of fever at Newark. He was buried in Worcester Cathedral, where his body still lies.

TWO CENTURIES OF GENIUS DEVOTED TO GOD'S GLORY

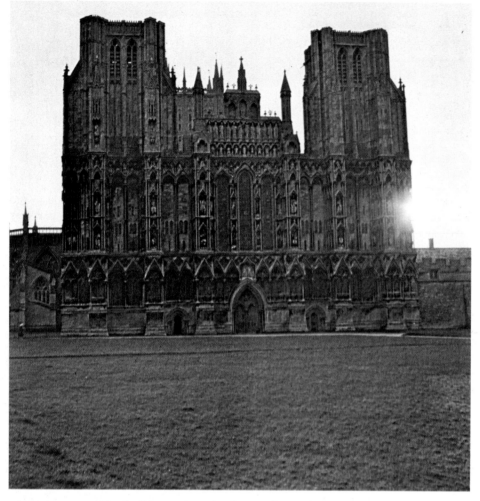

PAGEANT IN STONE *Nearly 400 statues are fitted into niches on the West Front of Wells Cathedral. The original concept of this cavalcade of angels, bishops and kings was that of Bishop Jocelin Trotman, who died in 1242; his grand plan was completed 40 years later.*

UNCHANGING VIEW *Many of the buildings shown in this picture of Wells, drawn in 1464, have changed little in the last five centuries.*

There is something comfortable about Wells; no greater contrast could be imagined than that between the citadel church of Durham on its crag above the dark River Wear and this graceful West Country cathedral, breathing harmony and composure. Wells gives the impression of a place which avoided the violent episodes of our history.

Built to honour God
There was a Norman cathedral at Wells but, about 1180, Bishop Reginald de Bohun, who conceived the grand design of the present building, decided to start on a new site. 'The honour due to God should not be tarnished by the squalor of His house,' he said.

The result was a building full of space, air and light, with the typical ribbed vaults and pointed arches of the new Gothic style of building, vastly different from the dark, fortress-like Norman churches with their round arches and massive pillars.

Building began about 1185, and was largely completed by Bishop Jocelin Trotman after Reginald became Archbishop of Canterbury. Jocelin's work was hindered by a quarrel with King John which forced him to spend five years in exile, but the accession of Henry III brought an upward turn to the fortunes of the bishop and his cathedral. Henry gave 60 oaks 'from our woods at Cheddar for the work of the church at Wells', and also made an annual donation to the building fund.

Bishop Jocelin's greatest project was a West Front designed to display nearly 400 statues – the richest sculpture gallery in England. Conceived by Jocelin as a magnificent array of religious and lay figures united into one vast panorama, it was not completed until 1282 – 40 years after the bishop's death.

His successors were faithful to his great inspiration, and every niche of the vast design was eventually filled with a statue. Most of them were more than life size, depicting angels, apostles, prophets, saints, bishops, kings, noblemen and ladies. They were laboriously carved and hoisted into the seven tiers of niches carefully prepared for them.

Above the central doorway is a representation of the coronation of the Virgin Mary. Soaring above that again is Christ in glory. The holy figures are flanked by a cavalcade of statues paying their devotions. Although this wonderful façade has not escaped the ravages of time and the Reformation, it remains a unique survival of medieval piety.

A style dominated by simplicity
The central tower was built in the 1300's, and the western towers were added in the late 14th and early 15th centuries; but they were intended from the start, and their architects plainly conceived them as developments in the mood of the original building. The result is a single harmonious unity, the most perfect example of the simplicity that characterises early-English cathedral architecture.

From the outside, the great church possesses infinite tranquillity; but within there is unexpected drama. The moment the visitor passes through the west door he is struck by the effect of the great arch of the crossing which stands immediately ahead. Here the two sides of the cathedral converge halfway to the roof, intersect, and then – magically – continue, snaking upward to form another, inverted, arch above. On each side of the intersection are two huge eye-like roundels. The motif is repeated at the entry to each transept.

These marvellous arches were not a part of the original plan. The buttresses were improvised to solve a crisis in about 1340, when the walls began to crack under the weight of the new central tower.

The nave itself has its splendours – the piers at once massive and delicate, each consisting of 24 clustered shafts. The details are of incom-

DESIGN REVOLUTION *The inverted arches of the nave were a brilliant innovation, designed when the church began to collapse in 1340.*

TIME-WORN STEPS *The Prior's Staircase, worn down by the tread of generations of the faithful, was built in the early 14th century.*

GLORY OF WELLS *The vaulted roof of the 14th-century Chapter House is one of the greatest architectural triumphs of the cathedral.*

parable craftsmanship and originality. The capitals of the columns were each individually carved by craftsmen who possessed a ready sense of humour as well as skill. Some are even devoted to the theme of toothache.

Beyond the crossing, the contrast is complete. Comparative simplicity gives way to flamboyance, with stone tracery climbing over every available inch of wall to tangle its tendrils in a fantasy of net-vaulting in the roof. This eastern end was subjected to a major rebuilding in the mid-14th century and it is late-Gothic architecture at its best. Most of the craftsmen who built our cathedrals are anonymous, but it is known that the man responsible for all this brilliance in carved stone was the local master-mason, William Joye. He also designed the serenely beautiful central tower and the airy Lady Chapel.

This octagonal chapel was originally conceived as a separate building. Its tall, five-light windows are fine examples of late-Gothic tracery, and all but one of them are filled with fragments of early-14th-century glass.

Unspoilt by time

The pictures in these windows have disappeared, but the rich kaleidoscope of colours – ruby, ultramarine, golden-brown, olive green and white – is immensely satisfying. When it was decided to join the Lady Chapel to the cathedral, Joye created a linking building of great beauty, using slender shafts of marble to enhance the sense of spaciousness.

Yet still the best is to come. The Chapter House is approached by a breathtaking flight of broad stone steps which curve up to a double-arched doorway of miraculous delicacy. Within is one of the most beautiful rooms to be found anywhere. Each wall of the octagonal chamber is pierced by an enormous

and intricate window. From the central pier of Purbeck marble spring the 32 ribs of the vault. A stone bench running right round the wall could seat the 50 canons who, generation after generation, have met here to discuss the affairs of the cathedral. Here, perhaps more than anywhere else, one feels the spirit of Wells – the quiet serenity that soothes and refreshes all who visit this lovely place.

This feeling of serenity spreads outwards from the great cathedral. For Wells inhabits

its own little island of peace. All the neighbouring buildings are of the same mellow, golden stone – the Chain Bridge and the gate houses, the gigantic cloister, the moated Bishop's Palace, and the fascinating Vicars' Close, the only complete medieval street left in Britain. All are charming in themselves, and together, in the shadow of the cathedral itself, they form a single unspoilt unity – a little enclosed world of lawns and water and mellowed stone in which the Middle Ages last for ever.

SCENES FROM COUNTRY LIFE

In the 13th century, England had a native school of sculptors whose skill and ingenuity has never been surpassed. These medieval stone-carvers were working for the glory of God, not for their own fame, and it was rare for them to leave behind even a record of their names. But their carvings in such cathedrals as Wells form an enduring memorial.

Two styles of sculpture are superbly represented at Wells: the spiritual figures in their niches on the West Front, and the equally effective but far more worldly carvings which decorate the capitals and columns inside the cathedral. These interior sculptures are not only marvels of skill; they also capture for eternity the vigorous life of England in the Middle Ages, when the vast majority of the population lived in villages, and even the largest city, London, had only 60,000 inhabitants.

Some of the carvings seem to echo the ancient theme of fertility and harvest; rich foliage entwines round bunches of grapes and other fruits. Other sculptures depict scenes from daily life in Somerset. A farmer wakes up to discover a fox making off with his goose. Four carvings tell the story of two men being caught stealing fruit. A cobbler eternally mends shoes while, near by, a poor woman who cannot afford shoes pulls a thorn from her foot.

FIRST AID *A carved capital in the nave shows a barefooted peasant woman pausing to pull out a thorn which has got stuck in her foot.*

STOP THIEF! *An angry farmer belabours a bearded robber caught stealing fruit from his orchard.*

People and peers meet in Britain's first Parliament

THE BIRTHPLACE OF PARLIAMENT

Westminster Hall, near the House of Commons, is the oldest-surviving part of the great royal palace of Westminster. It was the scene of the historic assembly of Henry III's barons and bishops in 1265 when England's first Parliament was called.

PARLIAMENTARY PIONEER *Simon de Montfort, pictured here on his seal, was the leading opponent of Henry III. He forced the king to summon the first Parliament.*

Englishmen have long been sustained by a belief in the sturdy independence of the English character. This belief has been demonstrated time and again throughout their history in demands for the protection of their liberties. But it was in the creation of Parliament – one of the greatest gifts that Britain has given to the world – that a new force was given to England's own struggle for freedom and liberty.

It was under Henry III that, for the first time, this force made itself felt in English history. On a March morning in 1265, a historic assembly gathered together in the dim light of Westminster Hall. The bishops, abbots and barons of England had met to draw up terms of peace between Henry III and his subjects, who had rebelled at his incompetence and extravagance.

There was nothing new in such a meeting.

A similar assembly had forced Henry's father, King John, to agree to Magna Carta 50 years before. But on this day in 1265, a new force shared the stage with these hereditary rulers. Seated in the hall were two knights from each shire, and two leading citizens from each of the most important towns of the realm. In the presence of this imposing body – England's first Parliament – Henry swore to mend his ways and reform his government.

This astounding achievement – the single-handed creation of Parliament – was the work of one man, Simon de Montfort. Simon was a French adventurer who, 30 years before, had arrived penniless at Henry III's court. He soon won the king's friendship, married Henry's sister, and became one of the most powerful nobles in the kingdom. But with success, Simon became arrogant. He tried to impose his will on the king, and finally the two men

quarrelled. Simon then turned to his fellow barons who, under his leadership, drew up the Provisions of Oxford and forced a council upon Henry to control the affairs of the kingdom he had failed to rule.

But the upstart Simon was almost equally distrusted by his new allies. To bolster his power, he determined to bring into the government men of the rising middle classes – the 'Commons' of England. Knights from the shires and prosperous merchants from the towns were in any case becoming a force which no king or baron could afford to ignore. Their support had become indispensable.

A power to rival the throne

Now, as the Parliament deliberated in the king's own palace, Simon had reached the summit of success. A subject had challenged the might of his monarch and won. But the victory was to be short-lived. His main ally, Gilbert de Clare, Earl of Gloucester, now regarded Simon's use of power with increasing distaste. Joining the royal cause, Clare freed the king's son, Edward, from Simon's captivity at Hereford. Edward cut off Simon's force behind the Severn, and at the Battle of Evesham in August 1265 killed Simon and most of his followers.

But the Parliament that Simon had created lived on. From the small beginnings that he had witnessed in Westminster Hall was to grow a mighty power, which would help to depose a king within the course of the following century.

Paradoxically, Parliament owed its survival to the statesmanlike qualities of Simon's most bitter enemy, Henry's son and successor, Edward I. In 1275, Edward called his first Parliament, and others followed at regular intervals throughout his reign.

Edward realised that in his efforts to bring peace to England after bitter years of civil war, he could use Parliament as a symbol of national unity. King, Lords and Commons collaborated to reform the outdated laws of England, and Edward consulted his Parliaments on all the great issues of state. Moreover, to fulfil his dream of uniting Britain under one rule, Edward needed money – and Parliament was the quickest and most efficient body through which to raise the taxes he needed to wage war in Wales and Scotland.

Parliament, however, had yet to assert its independence. This great stride forward started in the 14th century – a century of war in which the rulers of England needed vast taxes to support their ambitious attempts to conquer France. The never-ending demands for grants and subsidies put a powerful weapon into Parliament's hands, and it was not slow to use it. Taxes were voted only after the king had promised to remedy grievances. And by the 1350's, the Commons were pressing Edward III to agree to their demands to control the principal source of royal revenue – the *maletot*, a tax on wool.

This tax was of vital importance. By this time the wealth of England was largely vested in the curly fleeces of the sheep that grazed on vast acres of land throughout the kingdom. In 1360, Edward finally gave way; he agreed that the *maletot* should not be levied without the consent of Parliament. The Commons had won the first battle to control taxation.

With this advance, the Commons soon grew bolder. In 1376, they even tried to put Edward's corrupt ministers on trial. And 24 years later, they played a leading part in forcing his grandson, Richard II, to abdicate.

The Parliaments of Henry IV proved to be even more aggressive than their predecessors. The king was forced to alter his policies and cut down his extravagance. Only the renewed onset of the popular war with France saved the Lancastrian monarchy from a major conflict.

But when the war with France ended in defeat in the 1440's, the old bitterness returned. Parliament's position was strengthened further by the Wars of the Roses, when its members were wooed by the rival contenders for the throne – the Houses of York and Lancaster.

Power of Parliament

By the time the Tudors mounted the English throne, Parliament had developed into a body that was willing and able to challenge royal authority. In 1523, even Henry VIII's close friend, Thomas More, could deliver to Henry's chief minister, Wolsey, a stinging rebuff, when the cardinal tried to order him to use his powers as Speaker of the House of Commons to silence its complaining members. More proclaimed that he had 'neither eyes to see nor ears to hear but as this house shall direct me whose servant I am'. Parliament was now an integral part of English life – and, as the Stuarts were to discover when they tried to do without it – it was indispensable.

Henry III: His rule led to civil war

Henry III was a man of mediocre abilities. The tragedy of his reign was that he possessed a burning ambition and an exalted idea of his own grandeur.

Henry longed to be the dominant figure on the European stage. His eyes turned particularly towards France, where he dreamt of reviving the French empire his father, John, had lost. He married a French wife, Eleanor of Provence, in 1236 and filled his court full of her friends and relations. But his barons were uninterested in Henry's ambitions, and resented the taxes they paid to finance his wars.

In 1254, Henry embarked on the crowning folly of his reign – the attempted conquest of Sicily, the crown of which had been offered to his son, Edmund, by the pope. In four years his kingdom was bankrupt, and his power had been wrested from his hands by his nobles.

In 1258, led by the idealistic Simon de Montfort, Earl of Leicester, the nobles set up a committee of 24 barons, which governed the country for almost two years. Others toured England unearthing evidence of corruption and misgovernment.

Henry's attempt at a counter-stroke failed miserably, when his army was routed at Lewes in 1264. Yet slowly the barons' enthusiasm waned. They turned against de Montfort – especially after his creation of Parliament – and gradually deserted him.

Finally, Henry gathered enough support to strike back at the hated earl who had once been his closest friend. On August 4, 1265, Simon was slain at the Battle of Evesham. England had learnt that it could not do without a king, even though that king was deluded and incompetent.

A KING AND HIS PARLIAMENT *This 16th-century illustration is the earliest-known portrayal of Parliament in its medieval infancy. Edward I presides, flanked by the kings of Scotland (left) and Wales (right). Edward made great use of Parliament to reform English law.*

UNWISE KING *Henry III's effigy from his tomb in Westminster Abbey. He ruled England for 54 turbulent years. Though a sincere man, his political folly turned his subjects against him.*

Eight mighty fortresses to hold a turbulent kingdom

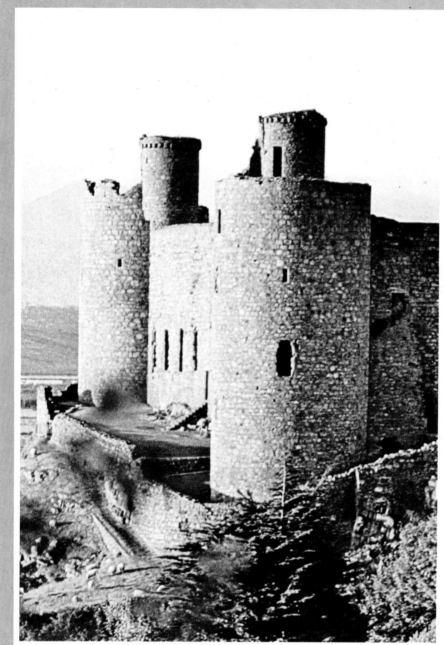

PROUD HARLECH – A MASTERPIECE IN STONE

Edward I ordered Harlech Castle to be built in 1283 as part of his plans to subdue the fiery Welsh. The defences of this clifftop fortress were designed to withstand any weapon that the ingenuity of medieval man could bring to bear.

CHAIN OF COMMAND *The chain of eight massive stone strongholds constructed in the 25 years after 1277 were Edward I's ultimate weapons against the threat of a Welsh uprising. They were also his ultimate memorial, for they still stand. Most of the castles were carefully sited so that they could be provisioned from the sea by the English.*

An anonymous chronicler wrote 'the kingdom of Wales has been overthrown', after one of his country's greatest princes, Rhys ap Tewdr, had been killed in a Norman ambush in 1093. The Normans had crushed England almost overnight; now the end for Wales seemed near. Yet this turbulent principality managed to preserve its independence until Edward I's invasion of 1282.

Many factors combined to delay the progress of subjugation. Chief among them were the terrain and the weather. The Berwyn Mountains stood in the path of Henry II's determined invasion in 1165, and the incessant rain of the principality soon doused the ardour of Norman chivalry. The Welsh princes, too, soon became adept at using English quarrels to their own advantage. Under a strong king, they would make vague promises of obedience, but under a weak one they intrigued with rebel barons to win concessions.

This form of diplomacy the Welsh understood well, for their own land was divided into many kingdoms. And, paradoxically, it was the achievement of unity under the proud and ambitious Llywelyn ap Gruffydd, ruler of Gwynedd, that brought upon them an invasion they could not resist.

The last leader

In 1277, after Llywelyn had refused to pay him homage, Edward I launched his armies into Wales. The traditional Welsh tactics of guerrilla warfare availed them little when confronted by a leader of Edward's genius. The proud Llywelyn was humbled and forced to

Workers from all over England were recruited to help build Edward I's castles in Wales.

THE IMPREGNABLE CASTLE

The building of invincible castles was an art that the English learnt on their Crusades to the Holy Land. The principle they brought back was the concentric idea – that, within the main enclosure of a castle, second and third lines of defence should be provided. If the enemy captured the outer wall, the rest of the fortress could still hold out.

It was this form of castle that Edward I built in Wales. His castles combined an outer curtain of massive walls and towers with a complex barbican protecting the gatehouse of the inner ring of defence. The old square towers were replaced by round ones, which had few blind spots and which deflected boulders more easily.

The main weapon these castles had to face before the invention of cannon was the siege engine – the siege catapult, a form of giant crossbow on wheels, and the trebuchet, a lever device operated by men pulling on ropes, which could launch stones of a quarter of a ton.

make peace. But he could not face the loss of the power he had laboured so long to build up and, urged on by his brother, David, he rose in revolt in March 1282. Eight months later, Llywelyn was killed in a skirmish near Builth. He became known to the Welsh as *ein elyw olaf* (our last leader), for Wales was then annexed to England.

Edward was determined to hold what he had so painstakingly won. He made his young son Prince of Wales to please his Welsh subjects in 1301. But his main task was to build impregnable fortresses so that never again would Norman rule be threatened.

A chain of castles

In the space of 25 years Edward I built a vast chain of castles in Wales – the greatest feat of royal building in British history. The strongholds of Harlech, Caernarvon, Conway, Beaumaris, Flint, Rhuddlan, Builth and Aberystwyth embodied all the lessons that military architects had learnt over the centuries. They were erected in fulfilment of Edward's vow to enforce law and order upon the Welsh. And in their massive strength they were a tribute to the people he had just conquered; only the finest castles in the world

could withstand the courage and cunning of this wild warrior race.

The master of the king's works in Wales came from Savoy, Master James of St George d'Esperance, Europe's most renowned military architect. James had been with Edward in Gascony and Scotland, and he was paid the exceptionally high salary of three shillings a day. Under him worked an army of officials, clerks, masons and labourers. The scale of the enterprise – the total cost was estimated at £80,000 – brought one of Europe's wealthiest kings to the verge of bankruptcy.

A report sent to London in 1296 gives a glimpse of the operations at Caernarvon. Some 400 skilled masons were continuously at work, and 1000 unskilled labourers assisted them in making the mortar and lime. There were also 200 carters, 30 smiths and carpenters and a guard of 30 men. Great stone blocks were brought to Caernarvon by sea; 30 boats and 160 wagons were needed to keep the builders supplied. Only a few miles away, the same feverish activity could be seen at Beaumaris.

Such was the rivalry between the castle-builders, that they even diverted royal money in the effort to complete their work first. At the beginning of 1296, a royal ship carrying the wages for the masons at Caernarvon was intercepted by the men working at Beaumaris. The workers at Caernarvon complained to the king of the sharp practices of their rivals. The moat had been begun, the walls were 24 ft high and 15 ft thick, but the work was behind schedule. Would not Edward help them by sending more money and materials? But the calls on the royal purse were many and pressing; in the event, Beaumaris was ready for a garrison in the summer of 1298, more than a year before Caernarvon.

Maintaining the conquest

The medieval art of castle-building reached its highest point in these lonely outposts of English power on the northern coast of Wales. Edward's castles were built to withstand any siege weapon that medieval man could bring to bear – the ram, the bore, the catapult and the mine. But, more important, the whole structure was designed to make any attack both difficult and dangerous. Each wall, each tower, each gateway was built with this in view. And later they were further refined.

Vast as they were, Edward's castles were designed so that they could be defended by a small force. The great fortresses of Harlech, Conway and Caernarvon were each normally manned by only 30 to 60 men. They served their purpose well. Edward had fought a bitter war to bring the Welsh under his rule, but never again would that rule be seriously threatened. No longer would a sudden rising like that of 1294–5 take the English off their guard. For, as James of St George wrote to his master: 'You know well that Welshmen will be Welshmen even if they appear to be pacified.'

Edward I: He fought to rule a united Britain

CROWNING A KING *The coronation of Edward I. His dream was to unite the three countries of the British Isles under his rule.*

Edward I was the most formidable king to rule medieval England. In his long reign he achieved more than any king since the Conqueror. He transformed the law of England, and made his crown the richest and most powerful in Europe.

Edward's success was chiefly due to his ability to pick his subordinates. In Robert Burnell, his Chancellor, he had an assistant of conspicuous ability and undoubted loyalty. Under Burnell there worked a talented corps of royal civil servants. Edward knew the value of such men, and rewarded them with high salaries in their lifetimes and Masses in the royal chapel after their deaths.

Other kings before him had shown Edward's energy; others had displayed his political skill. But Edward also had extraordinary good luck. Nicholas Trevet, a close friend of the king, believed that Edward's life was charmed and his enterprises favoured by God. This luck stood by him on the battlefield, and in his complex dealings with Wales and Scotland.

Edward's over-riding ambition was to unite Britain under one rule, concluding the conquest that William I had begun more than two centuries before. His great-grandfather, Henry II, had invaded Ireland and won the region around Dublin known as 'the Pale'; and his father, Henry III, had made a tenuous claim to the overlordship of Scotland.

Edward first turned his attention to Wales. His success there was given permanence by the enduring strength of the castles he built. Next he marched into Scotland, taking advantage of the internal disputes among the Scots in the 1290's. But the Scots found a war leader of equal genius in Robert Bruce, and the ageing Edward was repeatedly frustrated in his attempts to hold the lands he had won in battle. In July 1307, he was leading his army in a last great campaign when he died just south of the border – leaving his mission to a son who was ill-equipped for the task.

Robert Bruce triumphs in Scotland's day of victory

CAUSE OF THE BATTLE

In 1314 the hard-pressed English garrison at Stirling Castle anxiously waited for their king to drive off the Scots under Robert Bruce. Edward II's determination to relieve Stirling led to his complete defeat at Bannockburn, within sight of the castle walls.

The great stone castle of Stirling stands on a rock overlooking the marshy plain of Bannockburn, guarding the principal crossing of the River Forth. On Midsummer's Day, 1314, English eyes looked anxiously across the plain from the castle walls, hoping to see the approaching banners of the English army. For its commander, Sir Philip Mowbray, had agreed to surrender it to the Scots under Robert Bruce unless an English army appeared before sunset on that day.

Seven years had passed since the death of Edward I, who had brought most of Scotland under his rule. Edward's last wish had been that his bones be carried at the head of the army that was to make the conquest secure. But Edward II had ignored the request and allowed the Scots, under Robert Bruce, to win back almost all they had lost. Now Stirling was the last strongpoint in English hands.

Only hours before the castle was due to surrender, Edward arrived on the banks of the Bannock, 3 miles south of the castle. With him was an enormous army of some 15,000 to 20,000 men. North of the Bannock, across the old Roman road leading to the Highlands, stood the Scottish army. Early in the evening, Mowbray rode into Edward's camp and urged him not to attack. The agreement had already

DISASTER AT BANNOCKBURN *A 15th-century illustration of the Battle of Bannockburn (right). Beneath the walls of Stirling Castle the grim struggle for the mastery of Scotland was brought to its conclusion. The rashness of Edward II was the crucial factor in his army's crushing defeat at the hands of Robert Bruce (above). For Bruce, his victory meant complete independence for Scotland, and also established him firmly as king. The pope recognised him as King of Scots in 1323 and five years later the English made formal peace. Bruce died in 1329 at the age of 53; his dying wish was that his heart be taken for burial in the Holy Land.*

been honoured and the castle relieved. To advance was to risk defeat, and honour would then compel Mowbray to give up the castle to the Scots in accordance with his bargain.

The impetuous Edward resolved to fight. He had little choice. For he had much cavalry, and it was composed of noblemen eager to display their valour and their skill. Many of them were from northern counties and were only partially under the control of a king for whom they had little respect. A cavalry unit led by Sir Humphrey Bohun was despatched to reconnoitre the Scottish position. At the summit of a hill, Bohun encountered Robert Bruce and charged him with a lance. Bruce felled Bohun with a battle-axe and the rest of the English party retreated. Demoralised by this unfortunate incident, the English army made camp for the night.

Disaster on the banks of the Bannock
The next morning the fateful encounter took place. The same incautious enthusiasm that had made Edward reject Mowbray's advice the day before now led him into a fatal blunder. The Scots held the higher ground and the English were exhausted by their march. But when the 24-year-old Earl of Gloucester implored him to wait, Edward taunted him with treachery. 'I shall show you,' replied Gloucester, 'that I am neither a traitor nor a liar.' He mounted his horse and flung his cavalry on the tight phalanx of Scottish pikemen. The horses were impaled by the pikes, and the English charge disintegrated into a fierce hand-to-hand battle. Gloucester's rash advance blocked the English archers' line of fire, and they found themselves shooting into their own men's backs. The English infantry was thrown into hopeless confusion.

Victory for the Scots
Then, suddenly, a host of Scottish irregulars swarmed down a hill behind the Scots, and the English, mistaking them for reinforcements, fell back in retreat. 'On them, on them,' cried the Scots, 'they fail!' The English fled in disorder towards the marshes and the Bannock, where many hundreds were killed.

Edward himself rode hard for Stirling Castle. But Mowbray refused to admit him to safety and prepared to hand over the castle to the Scots. Pursued by the vengeful Scots cavalry, Edward then turned east and reached Dunbar to board a ship and sail for England. Other fugitives were not so lucky. The Earl of Hereford and 1600 men were captured at Bothwell Castle. Robert Baston, a monk whom Edward had brought with him to record his victory in verse, was also taken prisoner and forced by his Scottish captors to rhyme the story of their triumph. And the Privy Seal of England, which was with Hereford's party, fell into Scottish hands – a symbol of the completeness of the Scots' victory. One day had secured the independence of Scotland.

Edward II: Fated to lose both throne and life

Edward II came to the throne of England in 1307. He was 23 years old, 'fair of body and of great strength', witty in conversation, and engaged to a beautiful French princess. Yet his life as king was devoid of noble purpose or ambition and, in the end, his stubborn folly delivered him into the murderous hands of his enemies.

In the whole span of the Middle Ages, only three English kings were deposed by violence – Edward II, Richard II and Henry VI. All three had in common a failing which largely contributed to their fate. They all had a taste for incompetent favourites who were loathed and despised by the nobles and people alike. But Edward's choice of favourite was the worst of all. His infatuation with a young French knight, the grasping and effeminate Piers Gaveston, brought him both unpopularity and rebellion.

In the last years of his reign, Edward I had banished Gaveston from his court. But after the old king's death, Edward II's first action was to recall Gaveston from exile and make him Earl of Cornwall. The French upstart was the most favoured and powerful subject in the kingdom. His pride, said a contemporary chronicler, 'would have been unforgivable in a king's son'. Sure of Edward's favour, he deliberately insulted the barons and gave them nicknames to amuse his royal friend and master. The Earl of Warwick became the 'Black Hound of Arden', the Earl of Lancaster, 'Churl', the Earl of Lincoln, 'Burstbelly' and the Earl of Gloucester 'Horeson'.

Edward II had too little sense to realise that the great landowners, traditionally the king's closest advisers, would deeply resent the intrusion of a foreign upstart. So outraged did the barons – and the queen he scorned – become with Edward's infatuation, that in 1308 they forced the king to banish Gaveston. But the unrepentant king recalled him to court a year later. The result was immediate civil war.

The barons now forced Edward to agree to the appointment of Lords Ordainers – a council of nobles led by the king's cousin, Thomas, Earl of Lancaster, to oversee the government of the kingdom. Their first

action was to demand that Gaveston be sentenced to perpetual banishment. But he defied the Ordainers and returned from exile again in 1311.

This time, Gaveston was not to escape. The Ordainers promised him safe conduct to France if he surrendered and, trusting in their word, he did so. But, as he was being taken south from Scarborough Castle, he fell into the hands of his bitterest enemy, the Earl of Warwick. After being led through the streets of Warwick, he was taken to Blacklow Hill, outside the town, and executed.

Edward's reputation did not recover after Gaveston's death. His rustic tastes – singing and dancing, swimming and rowing – were too unbecoming in a monarch. And the shattering defeat at Bannockburn discredited him in the most important task of his reign, the protection of the north and the subjection of Scotland.

The king's chief hope was that the barons would fall out amongst themselves. In 1322 this hope was realised, when a moderate party among the Ordainers, led by the Earl of Pembroke, became so disgusted with Lancaster's incompetence that they joined the king. Lancaster launched a rebellion to regain his lost power, but this ended in his defeat and execution at Pontefract. But Edward lacked the personality to command loyalty. He immediately showered on Hugh le Despenser the favours he had given Gaveston.

A gruesome death
That was the prelude to disaster. Edward's queen, Isabella, now turned finally against him. She sailed home to France on the pretext of negotiating with her brother, Charles IV. There, she became the mistress of the exiled Roger Mortimer and in the autumn an army led by the queen and her lover overran the kingdom. Edward was captured and imprisoned in Berkeley Castle in the custody of Lord Berkeley and Sir John Maltravers. There he was murdered by means which have never been discovered. Rumours spoke of an agonising death accompanied by tortures – intricate enough not to leave a mark on his body.

Such a dreadful death of the Lord's anointed king led to pious calls for Edward's canonisation. They went unheeded. 'Keeping in prison, villainous and opprobrious death cause not a martyr,' wrote a monk, 'but if the holiness of life before be correspondent.'

But the queen and Mortimer were not long to survive their triumph. For Edward's son, the young Edward III, was resolved to revenge himself on his father's murderers. In October 1333, he struck. Mortimer was arrested at Nottingham Castle and, three weeks later, executed. Queen Isabella, whose pleas to 'have pity on gentle Mortimer', were rejected by her son, was sent to a nunnery. Edward II had enjoyed a posthumous revenge.

A handful of longbowmen crush the flower of France

VICTORY FOR THE INVADERS *The Battle of Crécy in 1346 was a triumph for the invading armies of Edward III. But shortage of food and supplies forced Edward to retreat to the coast and so he could not follow up his great victory.*

HERO OF AN AGE OF CHIVALRY

Edward III's eldest son, Edward, the Black Prince, characterised the age of chivalry in the 14th century. He won his spurs on the battlefield of Crécy when he was only 16 years old. And 10 years later he scored another victory against the French at Poitiers. A magnificent effigy of the prince (above) and his battle-scarred shield (right) can be seen at Canterbury Cathedral, where he was buried in 1376. Edward won the name Black Prince because of the black armour he wore at Crécy in 1346. His courage and dash made him a popular hero, but he did not live to inherit the throne. The long years of war took their toll on his health. He died aged 46 – a year before his father followed him to the grave.

The Hundred Years' War between England and France was a war against odds for the English, who were always outnumbered by their enemy. But this fact did not stop them winning victory after victory in the field. The first of these came on the afternoon of August 26, 1346, when the vast unwieldy mass of the French army marched towards Crécy, 32 miles south of Boulogne.

Although it had been hastily recruited, this 40,000-strong host was one of the largest armies ever raised in France. The enemy force, the invading troops of Edward III, was scarcely one-third the size. Shortly after 4 p.m. the French army arrived at the rising ground east of Crécy, and stared in disbelief at the well-drawn lines of the English gathered on the hillside opposite them.

For the French this was a rude shock. They had believed the English to be several miles away, and King Philip had not intended to fight that day. He decided not to attack until the light of morning, when the famished and

exhausted English soldiers would be hard put to resist the shock of his cavalry.

But the proud nobility of France were not accustomed to disciplined waiting. They had already divided amongst themselves the prisoners they would take. One would have the King of England, another the Earl of Northampton. As Philip's staff officers rode along the marching columns ordering the army to halt, they found confusion everywhere. Units had been parted from their commanders. Foreign mercenaries could not understand what was being shouted at them. Worse still, a number of French knights disobeyed the order to halt and pressed forward, propelling their reluctant crossbowmen – Genoese mercenaries from Italy – before them.

A rain of arrows

This spectacle of disorder was watched in silence by the waiting English ranks. In front stood the longbowmen, drawn up in wedge-like formations, their arrows implanted in the

ground before them. They held their fire. By 6 p.m. the French had reached a point 150 yds away – within range of the deadly English longbow. Edward watched from his command post in a windmill. Then a sharp command rang out. The longbowmen fired, and for a few moments the sky was darkened by a rain of arrows speeding into the French line. The Genoese crossbowmen fell in vast numbers beneath the deadly rain. As the chronicler Froissart recounted, the longbowmen 'shot their arrows with such force and quickness that it seemed as if it snowed'.

Then, from the middle of the English line, three cannons spat fire, and hurled enormous stone balls at the oncoming French. Never before had cannon been used on a battlefield. The Genoese crossbowmen had never seen, never expected, such a thing. They turned to flee, but found their path blocked by the French cavalry.

A battle now raged within the French army itself. King Philip shouted in fury 'kill me these scoundrels, for they stop up our road without reason'. His brother, the Duc d'Alençon, ordered his horsemen to cut down the panic-stricken Genoese, but, as they moved to do so, the heavily armoured French infantry, in a desperate lunge to reach the front, trampled the Genoese underfoot. Chaos rapidly spread in the French ranks as all remaining order was lost.

All the while there was no relief from the shower of English arrows. As each bowman used his last arrow, he rushed forward to remove another from the body of a fallen enemy. At length, the French men-at-arms waded forward through the carnage to engage the English in hand-to-hand battle.

The brunt of the French troops' charge was borne by the young Prince of Wales, known as the Black Prince. His guardian, Godfrey Harcourt, pleaded with the king to commit his reserves and protect his heir. But Edward needed to keep his reserves intact while he waited for the outcome of a powerful counter-attack, which the Earl of Arundel had just launched on the other flank. 'Is the prince dead or injured?' he asked. The answer was no. 'Then let the lad win his spurs alone, for if God wills it, this day shall be his.' And so it was. The Black Prince held off assault after assault, and at the end of the day the slaughter in front of his division was greater than any-where else. This feat was not accomplished without some danger. At the height of the battle the prince was thrown to the ground by his foes. But he was rescued by an officer who covered him with the banner of Wales.

By nightfall, over 10,000 Frenchmen had perished. Among the dead were many of the greatest knights and nobles of feudal France. Edward was less than pleased at the slaughter of the French barons and knights, as he would have preferred to capture them alive and receive a ransom for their release. But in an age in which courage was deeply revered, no death was more widely mourned and admired than that of Philip's ally, the blind King of Bohemia. At the climax of the battle he ordered his knights to lead his horse forward in a fatal charge so that he might strike a blow with his own hands.

When night came, Philip found that he was left with fewer than 60 knights. He had been slightly wounded and his horse had been shot from under him. One of the knights put Philip on another horse and forced him to leave the battlefield, explaining to the king that there would be another day for revenge against the English foe. But for the crown of France, Crécy was 'a mournful day indeed'.

A triumph for English arms

Crécy made a hero of Edward III; his judg-ment and control had been faultless. It established his son, the Black Prince, as the ideal knight of Europe's age of chivalry. But above all it proved the superiority of English tactics – the combination of longbowmen and dismounted men-at-arms over the outdated crossbow and the cavalry charge. Ten years later, this superiority was re-emphasised when the French were again overwhelmingly de-feated at Poitiers. Amongst those captured on this proud day for English arms was John II, King of France, who was carried captive to England. He was eventually ransomed for 3 million gold crowns.

But Edward III could not translate military triumph into territorial empire. Like the Romans when confronted with the might of Hannibal, the French adopted guerrilla tactics to wear their enemy down. In this they suc-ceeded, for in 1360 Edward III agreed to the Treaty of Brétigny, which forced him to abandon his ambitions to the crown of France.

However, the dream of complete conquest was not dead in English hearts. It was left to Edward's great-grandson, Henry V, to try to bring the dream to fulfilment.

Edward III: A warrior king's Age of Chivalry

In a century of deep discord between king and subject – Edward's predecessor and suc-cessor were both deposed – Edward III was loved and respected by his people. He gave to a knightly society the opportunity to prove itself at arms. Under Edward II the barons had expended their energies in rebellion against the crown; under Edward III they used them in its service.

The pomp and pageantry of chivalry flourished under Edward as never before. The new chivalry reached its peak in 1348 when the king, flushed with his victories in France, proclaimed the new Order of the Garter, which took its name from the occasion when Edward stooped to pick up the garter of the Countess of Salisbury, and rebuked his laughing courtiers with the words, 'Honi soit qui mal y pense' – 'Evil to him who evil thinks'.

Edward pursued his ambition to be King of France for three decades. Lords and squires delighted in the chance to prove their courage and to make a fortune from prisoners' ran-soms. Financiers grew rich from contracts for loans and supplies. Nor was war simply the sport of kings. The skill and endurance of the common men who wielded the long-bows and manned the ships were plain to see. Edward was vain, ostentatious and extrava-gant – but these were the very qualities which his people admired.

WAR KING *Edward III at prayer. He is seen in armour with the arms of England and France quartered on his surcoat.*

REVOLUTION IN WAR

By 1357 – after two great victories at Crécy and Poitiers – Englishmen were confident of their military superiority over their French adver-saries. Nothing contributed more to that confidence than the development of the long-bow. Its range was accurate up to 250 yds, and its rate of fire was much quicker than that of the conventional crossbow. The lumbering cavalry which had previously dominated the battlefield was helpless against it.

The longbow also brought about the decline of the feudal chivalry which placed a premium on exploits of personal bravery. The chain mail worn by noblemen afforded little protection against its arrows. As the nobles of France found, to take the offensive against skilled archers was to court disaster.

Longbowmen at target practice. Their weapons were to be the mainstay of English armies for the following 200 years, and won the famous victories of Crécy, Poitiers and Agincourt.

England's agony – the Black Death claims one in three

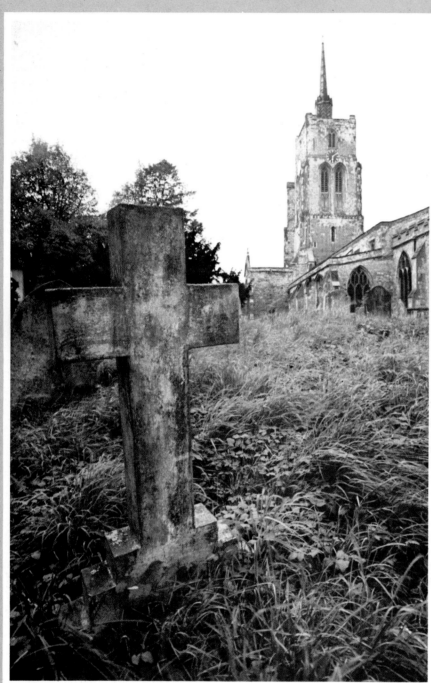

BURIAL-PLACE FOR THE VICTIMS
St Mary's Church, Ashwell, Hertfordshire, where victims of the Black Death lie buried. An inscription carved on the church tower reads: 'Miserable, wild, distracted, the dregs of the people alone survive.' A legend says that if the burial site – a grassed-over pit in the background – is disturbed, the plague will re-emerge.

THE TOLL MOUNTS *Grave-diggers work feverishly as the ravages of the Black Death increase. The plague started in China in 1333 and it slowly spread along the trade routes to Europe. In 1348 it reached England; by the time it died down a year later, one-third of the population had perished.*

Life in the Middle Ages was a battle for survival for the majority of Englishmen. Sickness, disease and death were a constant threat. In the mid-14th century, the average Englishman could expect to live only to the age of 38 years. Nor was medical science advanced enough to offer much hope of improving this situation. Such doctors as there were based their knowledge on ancient Greek textbooks, chief among them those written by Aristotle, Hippocrates and Galen. But these concentrated on theory rather than practice, and the only treatment for disease was a variety of herbal remedies. Surgery was primitive and hygiene almost unknown.

Thus, in times of trial and peril, men looked to God and the Church rather than to science for aid and assistance. But, as the terrible plague of the Black Death swept through England in 1348, God seemed to have deserted the English. The poet William Langland wrote that priests 'had no power these pestilences to lette, for God is def now a days'.

Cargoes of germs

Towards the end of June in that fateful year, two merchant ships arrived in the small Dorset harbour of Melcombe (present-day Weymouth), carrying the seeds of disaster in their cargo. For they brought from the Continent the germs of bubonic plague – the Black Death – which had ravaged the population of Europe.

The English knew the plague was spreading towards them, but their primitive medical science was no barrier to the advance of the most virulent epidemic in Western history. The disease, carried by flea-infested black rats, thrived and spread rapidly in every direction, striking Southampton, Exeter, the Midlands and London within weeks.

Everywhere its symptoms inspired terror in men's hearts. Horrible swellings of the glands, the size of grapefruits, appeared without warning and, as the whole body slowly turned black, the swellings festered for four or five

A doctor tends a patient in this medieval manuscript (left), while some of the instruments used by surgeons – scalpels, probes, splints and saws – are shown above. But primitive medieval medicine could do little against the ravages of the plague.

London – the breeding ground for pestilence

On the eve of the Black Death, 60,000 people were crammed into medieval London. Filth accumulated in the streets and armies of rats bred in dark alleys. Sewage was flung into streets designed with a central channel to carry it to the nearest stream. Householders were required by law to clean the patches in front of their houses, and 'scavengers' were appointed to rake up the rubbish. At times the stream which flowed past the Fleet prison was so choked with garbage and human excrement, that no water could penetrate to the prison moat. And seven years after the plague, Edward III was still complaining that rubbish on the waters of the Thames obstructed the passage of the royal barge.

The squalor of the city did much to explain the rapid strides made by the plague in London. Not only did Londoners live among disease-carrying rats; but they also suffered from malnutrition, which weakened their resistance to disease. Rich citizens had orchards and vegetable gardens; the rest depended on food brought from the countryside, which placed a heavy strain on the primitive agricultural system and road network. In times of nation-wide famine, it was always the poor of London who suffered the first pangs of hunger. The city's three slaughterhouses – St Nicholas Shambles, Walbrooke and East Cheap – prepared cattle for the butchers in indescribably filthy conditions. During the plague they were thought to be so great a source of infection that they were moved out to Knightsbridge.

days before death released the victim from his sufferings. Ignorant and frightened men asserted that the disease was carried in a great black cloud, or that it was spread by travelling Jews who poisoned the wells.

Violence and crime increased in the towns; resentment against the clergy and the rich erupted into ugly riots. Men grew sceptical of the Christian argument that all things were just in God's mysterious creation, and the frail fabric of medieval society began to break down.

By January 1349 the epidemic had London in its grip. Edward III dissolved Parliament and the court left London in haste for the countryside, where there was less risk of infection. The rich fled to their country houses, the bishops to their summer palaces.

The Abbot of Westminster was among the first to flee, but his flight failed to save him; he was one of the first to die, and 27 of his monks followed him to the grave. Three successive Archbishops of Canterbury died in the space of 12 months. London's cemeteries were too small to take the hundreds of dead who

arrived every day. For many years after the plague an inscription could be seen on the site of the Spittle Croft cemetery: 'This churchyard was consecrated in the year of Our Lord 1349 when the Great Plague was raging; wherein were buried more than fifty thousand of the dead whose souls God have mercy upon.'

The plague created social problems. Men were afraid to travel and consequently little food reached the towns, adding starvation to the sufferings of those whose poverty made escape impossible. Many Englishmen, in any case, had their resistance to the disease lowered by previous years of famine.

Consequences of the plague

The burial of the dead aroused bitter ill-feeling. The Church insisted that only consecrated churchyards could be used, while the people were convinced that even beneath the ground bodies were a source of infection. At Winchester, a burial service was disturbed by a mob who demanded that the victims be buried outside the town walls.

In the countryside, too, the population was halved in some places. Landowners' profits fell sharply as labourers who knew that they were in short supply demanded two or three times their usual wages. In vain, the government tried to intervene, issuing the Statute of Labourers, a measure which laid down that wages should be fixed at pre-plague rates. It also tried to control prices. But the policy failed in both these aims, and during the next 30 years peasant unrest built up, eventually to explode in the Peasants' Revolt of 1381. Recruitment to the armies of Edward III suffered grievously. Priests could not be found to say Mass in poor parishes.

The destruction of one-third of England's population of 3 million, and the laying waste of over 1000 villages, was a disaster unparalleled in modern times. 'Truly,' remarked one chronicler, 'no sin of man could be so awful as to deserve such a punishment of God.'

Punishing the profiteers

Meat was often putrid by the time it reached the family table. Milk, produced in cramped dairies on the south bank of the Thames, was a luxury. Numerous officials, armed with sheets of regulations, fought a constant war against dishonest food sellers. Sellers of putrid ale were put in the stocks. In 1319, a butcher from West Ham was caught in the act of selling meat from diseased cattle. He was put in a pillory and the carcasses burnt under him – but history does not record whether he survived this treatment. Fraudulent bakers appeared before the courts at each session.

It was small wonder that the wealthy merchants, nobility and clergy preferred to live outside the city walls, building their houses by the Thames and enjoying the luxury of private latrines jutting over the river. The first fashionable suburb of London was Fleet Street, where Edward III's brother, John of Gaunt, built his Savoy Palace. The Archbishop of Canterbury had his country estate at Lambeth, and the Abbot of Westminster had his in Hampstead. But the city of London itself, a contemporary chronicler remarked, was 'no place for the decent sort of men'.

The peasants of England rise to demand new rights

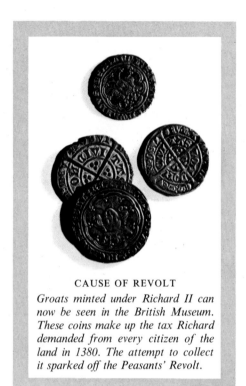

CAUSE OF REVOLT
Groats minted under Richard II can now be seen in the British Museum. These coins make up the tax Richard demanded from every citizen of the land in 1380. The attempt to collect it sparked off the Peasants' Revolt.

On Friday June 15, 1381, a cavalcade of some 200 courtiers and soldiers escorted Richard II out of the north gate of Westminster Abbey, riding towards Smithfield. For three days Richard's capital had been sacked and looted by several thousand enraged peasants from Essex and Kent. These peasants had risen spontaneously in rebellion, and now demanded that the king listen to their grievances. They would no longer submit to the yoke of serfdom. They demanded the repeal of the unjust laws which held down their wages. Most of all, they would not pay the grinding taxes needed for the king's futile wars in France.

The revolt begins

Trouble had started a year before, when Richard's government had imposed a new poll (head) tax on his subjects. Its burden fell heaviest on the poor, and the first attempt to collect it was a disaster. In the spring of 1381, a force of commissioners was sent out to collect the balance of the tax, and this was the spark that fired the Peasants' Revolt.

The first rising took place in Essex. When the tax-collectors arrived at Brentwood the villagers declared that 'they would have no dealings with them nor pay them a penny'. Violence soon broke out and swiftly spread to Kent. Gangs of peasants waylaid the commissioners, burnt down manor houses and destroyed the charters which bound them to their masters. Soon, towns were falling to the rebels and on June 10 they sacked the Archbishop's palace at Canterbury.

Little resistance could be offered. Most of the army was in France, Wales and Scotland. John of Gaunt, the king's all-powerful uncle, was himself in Edinburgh negotiating with the Scottish king.

Many of the citizens of London itself sympathised with the rebels and they easily won entrance. Within hours of their arrival, the Savoy Palace in the Strand, residence of the hated John of Gaunt, lay in ashes. The equally unpopular Archbishop of Canterbury, Simon of Sudbury, together with Robert Hales, the royal treasurer, had been dragged from sanctuary in the Tower chapel. Sudbury pleaded in vain with the rebels, and the unmoved peasants killed him on Tower Hill.

The peasants, however, claimed that they had not risen against their monarch. Their rallying cry was 'King Richard and his true commons'. It was his corrupt ministers, not the king, who had to be hunted down and killed. But even so, the 14-year-old king was taking his life in his hands in riding to meet the rebels at Smithfield.

From the Tower battlements, Richard had watched, impotent, as the flames of the Savoy reddened the sky. For the first time this frail boy had asserted himself against his tutors and advisers, and had agreed to discuss his subjects' grievances.

Smithfield lay outside the walls of London – a large open space, which, even then, served as London's cattle market. There, Richard found the insurgents drawn up in ranks. He took up his station opposite them and called on their leader to come forward. A discharged soldier from Maidstone, Wat Tyler, whose ready tongue had earned him the revolt's leadership, rode forward with a single companion.

Flushed with the success of the revolt, Tyler was in no mood to compromise with his king. He demanded the abolition of serfdom, the hunting laws and bishoprics, and the confiscation of Church property. 'Let no man be the lord of another,' Tyler shouted, 'but all should be equal under the king.' But Richard stalled before these extreme demands and Tyler began to grow abusive.

Then, one of the king's attendants cried out that he recognised Tyler as 'the greatest thief and robber in all Kent'. The rebel leader turned to his companion and ordered him to strike down the heckler. The companion hesitated, however, and Tyler himself rode in among the royal retinue, sword in hand. But

CLASH AT SMITHFIELD *In a medieval illustration, Richard II watches as William Walworth, Lord Mayor of London, stabs Wat Tyler in the shoulder. Tyler's quick wits had won him the leadership of the Peasants' Revolt. Without him, it swiftly collapsed.*

his way was barred by the Lord Mayor of London, William Walworth.

A scuffle followed. Tyler stabbed at the mayor, but in vain, for Walworth was wearing mail beneath his cloak. Drawing his own sword, the mayor stabbed the rebel leader in the shoulder while a royal squire rode forward and ran him through. Mortally wounded, Tyler turned his horse towards the ranks of the peasants, crying out, 'Treachery!' Then he fell to the ground in full view of the assembled crowd.

'Sirs, will you shoot your king?'

For a few moments it seemed as if none of the royal party would escape alive. Then, just as the peasants were drawing their bows to avenge their dead leader, Richard suddenly rode out towards them, his hand raised, and cried: 'Sirs, will you shoot your king? I will be your chief and captain and you shall have from me all that you ask for.' Followed by the insurgents, Richard then rode off towards Clerkenwell fields, while the mayor galloped back into the city to raise a rescue force.

For nearly an hour, Richard talked against time with the roughest of his subjects. Chief among them was John Ball, a half-mad excommunicated priest from Kent, whom the rebels had released from the archbishop's prison at Canterbury. At Blackheath he had preached to them of social equality and political revolution, taking as his text:

> *Whan Adam delved, and Eve span,*
> *Who was thanne a gentilman?*

But at last the king saw the mayor's forces advancing towards the rebels and slowly encircling them. Richard called a halt to the debate and declared the meeting dissolved.

Gradually, the peasants dispersed – but this was by no means the end of the revolt. Many villages around London were plundered and destroyed. In Cambridge, Corpus Christi College was gutted. Parchments, charters and priceless documents were burnt by the mob in Market Square, as an old woman, Margery Starre, cried: 'Away with the learning of the clerks, away with it !' But with the crushing of the revolt in London, the government could move to quell the rebels in the rest of the kingdom. By the end of the year, Richard's proud boast on the morrow of Smithfield had come true: 'Let us rejoice and praise God, for I have this day recovered my lost heritage.'

POWER BEHIND THE THRONE

During Richard II's boyhood, England was virtually ruled by the king's uncle, John of Gaunt, Duke of Lancaster (below). Gaunt was a brilliant administrator, but Richard himself resented such domination. Gaunt's power, however, made him indispensable. His death in 1399 brought about the king's fall. For Richard had exiled Gaunt's son, Henry Bolingbroke, who now claimed his father's lands which Richard had confiscated. Refused this, he deposed the king and seized the throne.

Richard II: The tragic reign of a boy king

Richard II was a child for the first eight years of his reign, and by temperament he remained a child all his life. Richard's coronation was a magnificent spectacle of pomp and ceremony, but behind the pageantry England was ruled by a parliamentary council, dominated by the king's uncle, the powerful John of Gaunt. He had seized control during Edward III's illness and continued to dominate the land during Richard's minority.

Richard, in theory Lord of all England, chafed at the restrictions imposed upon him. A physical weakling, he found it impossible to live up to the standards that his father, the Black Prince, had set. Yet he was taught that he must do so to fulfil the divinity which 'doth hedge in a king'. The conflict in Richard's character was resolved only during the Peasants' Revolt, the supreme moment of Richard's life.

It was not until he reached the age of 18 in 1385 that Richard freed himself from his tutors. But the effect of this long period of frustration on his character was disastrous. For the rest of his life he reacted with hysterical passion when anyone tried to argue with him, or control his policies.

A royal misfit

Richard liked to move in a small circle of friends. To outsiders he was moody and suspicious, especially after the death of his first wife, Anne of Bohemia, in 1394, which removed the last restraint on his self-control. When the Earl of Arundel arrived late for the funeral at Westminster Abbey, Richard assaulted him. The king's arrogant bearing grew ever stronger throughout the rest of his life.

These failings of character brought Richard into conflict with the nobility and with Parliament. In 1386, Parliament deprived Richard of much of his power by appointing a commission to control the government. But Richard refused to accept defeat and mustered a small army, which was routed at Radcot Bridge in December 1387. A new Parliament, called the 'Merciless Parliament', met in 1389 and convicted several of Richard's friends of 'treason'; two of them were hanged, drawn and quartered, and others of them were beheaded.

Richard recovered control by promising to be more conciliatory in the future. But he never forgot how he had been treated, and nine years later he began to take his revenge. His enemies were exiled, executed or imprisoned, and their estates confiscated. Among them was the Earl of Arundel, the man Richard had attacked four years before.

Rebellion and overthrow

So confident was Richard that in 1399, when John of Gaunt died, he seized his lands and then left the kingdom to lead his armies in a campaign in Ireland. This was the moment for which the king's many enemies had been waiting. In June, Henry Bolingbroke, John of Gaunt's son, returned from exile in France. He landed on the Humber and rapidly collected an army to march against the king. Among his chief supporters were the Earl of Northumberland, head of the powerful Percy family, and Ralph Neville, Earl of Westmorland. With frightening suddenness, Richard's power disintegrated in his hands. His few friends betrayed him, and he took refuge in Conway Castle with a force of only 100 men.

Even the walls of Conway could not protect him, and within a few weeks Richard surrendered himself into the hands of his rival. In September a deed of abdication was extracted from the once-proud king, and Henry placed the crown on his own head. The rest of Richard's life was spent in a solitary dungeon deep in Pontefract Castle. There, in 1400, he was either starved or smothered to death by his gaoler – an obscure end to England's most eccentric monarch. The absolute monarchy he had tried to create perished with him.

FORCED ABDICATION *Richard II hands his crown and sceptre to his cousin, Henry Bolingbroke, in this 15th-century illustration. Richard overcame one threat to his throne in the Peasants' Revolt. But he could not resist his rebellious nobles when they rose against him in 1399.*

A POET'S ACHIEVEMENT – TO CATCH THE SPIRIT OF HIS AGE

The title 'Father of English Poetry' belongs by tradition to a 14th-century Londoner who wrote poetry in the intervals of a busy public career. For over 500 years, Geoffrey Chaucer – courtier, diplomat, civil servant and poet – has held a unique place in the minds of his countrymen. It was he who first gave literary expression to the English sense of humour in his masterpiece *The Canterbury Tales*. This work, written in the late 1380's, is a timeless comedy of medieval life and manners and mixes bawdy farce, gentle satire and shrewd observation of human beings. In its rich profusion of characters drawn from life, this poem gives a unique insight into the medieval world.

First poet of English

Chaucer's poetic genius, flowering in the springtime of English culture, raised the native tongue to a dignity and importance that hitherto only such languages as French and Latin had enjoyed. He established through his art the distinctive strengths and beauties of English – its music, economy, its flexible ease and its blend of vigour and delicacy. These qualities appear in such lines as the opening of the Prologue to *The Canterbury Tales*:

> *Whanne that Aprille with his shoures sote*
> *The droghte of Marche hath perced to*
> *the rote . . .*
> *And smale fowles maken melodye,*
> *That slepen al the night with open ye . . .*
> *Than longen folk to goon on pilgrimages.*

In modern translation:

> *When April with its sweet showers*
> *has pierced the drought of March to*
> *the root . . .*
> *and small birds make melody,*
> *that sleep all night with open eye . . .*
> *then folk long to go on pilgrimages.*

Chaucer's presence fills the pages of *The Canterbury Tales*, giving the reader an intimate sense of a kindly, shrewd and penetrating mind. Yet little is known of Chaucer's private life. He was born about 1340, the son of a London wine merchant. Before he was 20 he accompanied Edward III to the French wars, where he was captured and ransomed.

On his return to England, Chaucer became a valet in the royal household, and was the

PLUMP POET *A portrait of Chaucer from an early edition of* The Canterbury Tales. *In it the Host of the inn describes Chaucer as being 'elvish' in appearance, absent-minded and tending to middle-aged stoutness – 'he in the waist is shaped as well as I'.*

particular favourite of Edward's second and third sons, Lionel, Duke of Clarence, and John of Gaunt, Duke of Lancaster. Soon, Chaucer was sent on diplomatic missions to Italy, Flanders and France. At home, he served, apparently with distinction, under both Richard II and his supplanter, Henry IV. He held such mundane but lucrative and necessary offices as Clerk of the Works and Comptroller of the Customs and Subsidy of Wools, Skins and Tanned Hides in the Port of London. He died in 1400 and was the first of England's poets to be buried in Westminster Abbey.

A lover of life

Chaucer married Philippa Roet, a lady of the court, but passages in some of his works suggest that he discovered little happiness in marriage. When he was about 40 he was threatened with a law suit concerning his alleged abduction of a woman called Cecilia Champaigne. He had a son, 'Little Lewis', possibly an illegitimate child, for whose benefit he prepared a treatise on the astrolabe, an instrument used in medieval astronomy.

The few personal glimpses we have of Chaucer are supplied by the poet himself in his own works. It is clear that he loved flowers, particularly the common daisy, and was deeply attracted to women. The jolly Host in *The Canterbury Tales* describes the poet as 'elvish' in appearance and tending to corpulence – 'he in the waist is shaped as well as I'.

What matters most for posterity is that Chaucer was a great lover of life, and that he could describe the world he knew and enjoyed so well in language unsurpassed for richness and rhythm. A worldly man himself, Chaucer's poetic vision of life was worldly· too. The people he writes about are real people, economically described in telling detail. That is why the characters of *The Canterbury Tales* – like

---

PIONEERS OF A NEW LANGUAGE

The language which was to express some of the world's greatest literature was born in England in the 14th century. While Chaucer was turning the everyday speech of London into the language of poetry, two other writers were using the common tongue for a more uplifting purpose. John Wyclif and William Langland forged the language into a weapon in their struggle against the Roman Catholic Church and its popes.

In medieval England, Latin was the language of the Church and the Bible. It was spoken and written exclusively by scholars and churchmen. But when John Wyclif inspired a group of fellow-scholars to make the first complete translation of the Bible into English in 1382, he was not merely championing his native tongue.

To Wyclif, Latin was the symbol of Church authority, as distinct from the authority of God. By replacing Latin with the English language, he sought to create a national Church which could speak directly to the common people. Although a scholar and a priest, Wyclif attacked enforced confessions, penances and indulgences – the system by which priests took money for pardoning sins. He even proposed that the Church should do without popes and bishops.

Another reformer who chose the English language for his attack on the princely rulers of Church and state was William Langland, a clerk and poet, who wrote 'Vision of Piers Plowman'. He tried to show simple souls the way to salvation.

VISIONARY *A page from a manuscript of William Langland's 'Vision of Piers Plowman', written about 1362. This manuscript dates from 1427 and is kept in the Bodleian Library, Oxford.*

REBEL PRIEST *Wyclif was called a heretic because he wanted all men to read the Bible. But he was protected by powerful nobles.*

TOUGH SEADOG *The ship's captain who made the pilgrimage had much to repent of. Chaucer tells how he stole wine from foreign traders and was merciless with prisoners. 'If, when he fought, the enemy vessel sank, he sent his prisoners home; they walked the plank.'*

GENTLE LADY *According to Chaucer, the well-bred prioress showed every sign of enjoying her pleasant life. She was remote from the troubles and bustle of the world with her lapdogs and her cultivated manners. But she was very likeable – 'all sentiment and tender heart'.*

PILGRIM'S WARNING *The canon's yeoman had grown thin and shabby in the service of a cleric who practised witchcraft and alchemy. The yeoman warned his fellow-travellers against trying to turn base metal into gold: it led to 'empty moneybags and addled brains'.*

Whatever the flavour of the tales – ribald or tragic, heroic or ironic – the men and women who tell them spring from the printed page. These portraits are as true to life as the poet can make them: the Nun who had such a zest for courtliness that she would 'her upper lip wipe so clean, that not a trace of grease was to be seen'; or the Pardoner, with his false relics – pigs' bones and the like – with which he imposes on the poor and makes 'monkeys of the priest and congregation'.

Imagination and realism

Such merry realism contrasts with the moving lyricism of others of *The Canterbury Tales*. Not until Shakespeare reached maturity does any other English writer display so rare a blend of imaginative and realistic gifts. Chaucer's eye was almost as keen as Shakespeare's. It had the same dispassionate clarity, the same wonderfully unfailing sharpness for observation of detail.

Only two of the stories told on the road to Canterbury appear to have been drawn entirely from Chaucer's imagination. The rest were traditional tales or free adaptations from the works of other writers. But the credit for the realistic characterisation in the tales and the depth of philosophical thought that underpins the poem, belongs to Chaucer alone.

He did not live to complete *The Canterbury Tales*. His pilgrims arrive at their destination, but do not make the return journey to London. We never learn which of them wins the free meal at the Tabard Inn in Southwark, which the Host promised would be the reward for the teller of the best tale with the 'fullest measure of good morality and general pleasure'.

The Host's decision, in any case, would not have been easy. With such rich profusion, every tale adds munificently to our own heritage of pleasure.

JOLLY HYPOCRITE *The friar was a pleasant, easy-going fellow. He never imposed harsh penances on sinners who came for confession. He was no stranger to innkeepers and was good company to all – except those who could not contribute to his needs.*

MONEY-GRABBER *The steward or reeve of the poem was a successful guardian of his lord's lands and wealth. He was even more successful in lining his own pocket. But a lifetime of terrorising tenants and peasants had left him 'old and choleric and thin'.*

the Miller with a wart at the tip of his nose, on which 'stood a tuft of hairs red as the bristles of a sow's ears' – and other poems are instantly recognisable, even today. Their outlook may be moulded by the Middle Ages, but in their greed, lust, cynicism, generosity and goodness they are timeless.

Chaucer's genius as the first English poet with the power to create a vivid world of fiction emerged in his poem *Troilus and Criseyde*, a moving study of young love blighted by infidelity, set against the background of the Trojan Wars. In its narrative, drive and the directness of its dialogue it resembles a novel, written long before that literary form was even thought of.

But the work for which Chaucer is most famous – and justly so – is his account of that magnificent cavalcade of medieval personali-

ties, *The Canterbury Tales*. The story tells how some 30 pilgrims make the journey from London to the shrine of Archbishop Thomas Becket at Canterbury. As they go, each of them tells a tale. The travellers include the Merchant, the Knight, the Miller, the Nun, the Pardoner, the Franklin, the Squire, and the Wife of Bath.

Chaucer's characters provide an engaging cross-section of contemporary life. Although the poet moved in court circles, he chose his personages from the middle and poorer classes. The coarse, the proud, the sanctimonious and the over-hearty – they are all there, and their creator pokes good-humoured fun at almost all of them, gently exposing their weaknesses and idiosyncrasies but never stripping them of their dignity as human beings. The procession that moves across Chaucer's pages is as bright as the figures on a medieval manuscript.

Proud lords of the north fight to overthrow their king

![STRONGHOLD OF THE MASTERS OF THE NORTH]

STRONGHOLD OF THE MASTERS OF THE NORTH

Alnwick Castle, Northumberland, was the principal stronghold of the Percies. From its grim fortifications this proud family built up an almost-independent empire through war and diplomacy. At its height, their rule covered much of northern England.

In the Middle Ages, a man's place in life was largely determined by his birth. Moving between their enormous castles, leading private armies and administering the affairs of vast provinces, the nobles of northern England were often little less than kings; and sometimes even more so.

Of these families, destined by birth to play their part in the bloodstained politics of medieval power, none was stronger or more ambitious than the Percy family of Northumberland – described by Shakespeare as the 'proud Percies'. In their great pride, they overthrew one monarch and placed another on the throne, though they paid for this with the life of their greatest son, the brilliant Henry Percy, nicknamed Hotspur, on the bloody field of Shrewsbury.

Many things helped the Percies in their rise to wealth and fame. Among them were the threat the Scots constantly posed on the northern border, and the distance separating their domains from London. But most important was the native shrewdness of their race. High office brought the Percies the opportunity to enrich themselves, and they grasped it greedily. Such was the family that fought a private war with the crown of Scotland at its own expense, and once had the crown of England £52,000 in its debt.

The ablest and most arrogant members of the family were Hotspur and his uncle, Thomas Percy, Earl of Worcester. Both took a leading part in the rebellion that deposed Richard II, and placed Henry IV on the throne in 1399. With his courtly manners and explosive temper, Hotspur was idolised by his contemporaries. His reputation reached a peak in September 1402, when he crushed the Scots at Homildon Hill in Northumberland, capturing 80 noblemen. But, after his victory over the Scots, Hotspur complained that Henry IV had failed to repay the money the

INTRIGUE FOR POWER *Richard II (mounted, centre) surrenders to Bolingbroke in 1399. In front of him stands Henry Percy, Earl of Northumberland, whose decision to join the rebels ensured the success of their cause. But three years later, he and his family turned against the king.*

THE NORTH'S MASTERS *The Percies dominated the north in medieval times. Their castles and the major battles they fought are shown (left).*

Percies had spent fighting the campaign. So he refused to hand over the Earl of Douglas, most powerful of the nobles captured at Homildon, arguing that if Henry could not settle his debts, then Hotspur was entitled to receive the earl's ransom.

The two men quarrelled and Hotspur, with his father, the Earl of Northumberland, and his uncle, rose in rebellion. The Percies denounced as a usurper the king whom they had helped to the throne and announced that Richard II had not died at Pontefract, but was still alive. Negotiations were swiftly opened with the rebellious Welsh forces of Owen Glendower.

Hotspur's plan was to recruit fighting men from Cheshire and North Wales – regions where loyalty to Richard II's memory remained strong – and then march on Shrewsbury, where Henry IV's son, Prince Hal, was camped. Having seized the prince, Hotspur would wait for the forces his father was mustering in the north and for his Welsh allies under Glendower. The united armies would then advance to confront the king. But the king and his able Scottish lieutenant, George Dunbar, led his forces in a rapid march north, and managed to reach Shrewsbury a few hours ahead of the Percies. The fate of Henry's crown, the dynasty he was trying to establish, and the fortunes of the mightiest of his subjects were now to be decided in a single day's violent conflict.

A fight to the finish

Even though Henry had thwarted his original plan, Hotspur resolved to give immediate battle. On Saturday July 21, 1403, the king received the Percies' last defiant challenge. 'We do intend to prove with our own hands personally against thee, Henry, Duke of Lancaster, unjustly presuming and named King of England, without right of title, but only of thy guile.'

The two armies now prepared for action. Hotspur had stationed his troops on high ground, and the king's forces had to charge up a hill to get to grips with them. As the 16-year-old Prince of Wales charged up the slope, he and his men faced a hail of arrows from the Percy archers. For the first time, English troops had to face the weapon with which they had wrought such havoc on the battlefields of France. But Henry's men were undeterred and soon came to close quarters with their enemy.

The fighting lasted until nightfall. The armies were evenly matched, but at the end of the day Hotspur's cause was lost and he himself lay dead upon the field.

Nor did the other members of Hotspur's family escape. His uncle was beheaded two days later, and the old earl, Hotspur's father, had no choice but to throw himself on the king's mercy. It was to be many years before the north would see a Percy ruling again in the proud manner of his ancestors.

Henry IV: The usurper king's uneasy reign

KING BY THE GRACE OF GOD *Henry IV's seizure of the throne from his cousin receives the blessing of the Church in this contemporary illustration of his coronation in 1399. Henry looked forward to a long and successful reign, but it was short and constantly troubled by revolt.*

When Henry IV forced his cousin, the 32-year-old Richard II, to abdicate in 1399 and took his place on the English throne, the wealth of the Duchy of Lancaster and the power of the Plantagenets were united in a single pair of highly capable hands. The events of 1399 ought to have made the English monarchy unchallengeable. Instead they ushered in a period of turbulence and rebellion, of royal bankruptcy and constant crisis.

Henry should have found it easy to win recognition for his new authority. According to the chronicler Adam of Usk, he had rescued England from a ruler whose crimes included 'perjuries, sacrileges . . . exactions from his subjects and cowardice'. But within a few months of his accession, Henry faced threats on every side. In Wales, he had to deal with a formidable national rebellion under the leadership of Owen Glendower. In the north, the mighty Percies turned against him. Despite the fact that the two nations were supposedly at peace, the French launched murderous raids on the south coast and landed troops in Wales. Henry's success in parrying each of these threats to his crown was striking evidence of his force of character and political skill.

Worn down by the cares of office

But the king was not to enjoy his victory for long. Although only 32 when he came to the throne, Henry's constant cares made him prematurely old. Once handsome and active, he became ill-tempered and lost much of his intellectual drive.

In 1405, Henry was further weakened by a mild stroke, which his contemporaries thought to be leprosy, God's punishment for ordering the execution of Archbishop Scrope

for treason. For much of the rest of his reign, he was forced to look on as a bitter struggle for power raged about him. One faction, led by the king's younger son, Thomas, and by Thomas Arundel, the aristocratic Archbishop of Canterbury, dominated the government for almost five years. In 1410, however, they were edged out of power by Prince Hal, the young Prince of Wales, and his friends. Only when Henry's half-brother, Henry Beaufort, Bishop of Winchester, tactlessly suggested he should abdicate did the king emerge from his retirement to take personal command of affairs and dismiss the prince from the council.

Henry's energy was entirely taken up by threats to his crown. But although violence was the dominant theme of Henry's reign, the king had a degree of sensibility and refinement which was wholly absent in those around him. He was fond of music in an age when English music was pre-eminent in Europe. He patronised the poets Chaucer and Gower, doubling the former's pension, and invited Christine de Pisan, the first professional authoress in the world, to visit England after reading her poetry. Before his accession, he had been to Danzig, Venice and the Holy Land.

Pained by constant illness, Henry finally collapsed in the early spring of 1413, after an exhausting session of Parliament. His last words were a curious epitaph for such a harsh realist. He begged forgiveness for his usurption of the crown, and told his assembled household that, had he lived, he would have led a Crusade. According to Shakespeare, it had been prophesied that Henry would die in Jerusalem – but in fact he died at the early age of 46 in the Jerusalem Chamber at Westminster Abbey, in March 1413.

'Cry God for Harry, England and St George'

ENGLAND'S IMMORTAL HERO

Henry V's overwhelming victory over the might of France at Agincourt made him the hero of his people – and his reputation as a leader increased after his early death, at the age of 35. This stone relief of the king in full armour is in Westminster Abbey.

E ngland's long struggle for the mastery of France lasted for more than a century, but only once did the English come close to complete success. In 1415 Henry V, who, as legend had it, had been a wastrel as Prince of Wales, launched his country once again into a gigantic gamble – with the final conquest of its rich and powerful neighbour as the prize. Henry had a united island behind him in this cause. Parliament and the Church agreed willingly to extra taxation. Volunteers flocked to the colours, for war meant a chance of adventure, ransom and plunder.

Clash to decide the fate of France
The struggle came to a head on October 25, 1415, when the English and French armies clashed on the field of Agincourt. The night before the battle was stormy, as the two opposing forces camped on the open ground by the forest of Agincourt, 20 miles inland from Boulogne. The French army, numbering according to some accounts as many as 50,000 men under the Constable d'Albret, lay between the English and the coast, blocking their line of march towards Calais and their winter quarters. The French were in high spirits. Their laughing and shouting disturbed the quiet of the night, and drink flowed in abun-

dance. The French commanders were playing dice – the stakes being the English prisoners they confidently expected to capture on the field the next day.

But a grim silence hung over the English tents. Henry's negotiations with the French had failed, and the king knew that he had to defeat them or face captivity and perhaps even death. The weakness of the English army – it was barely 4000 strong – gave little cause for hope. Its men were hungry, and many were suffering from dysentery contracted at the siege of Harfleur. One of its leaders, Sir Walter Hungerford, gloomily confided that he wished he could have 10,000 of the best archers in England with him. A contemporary chronicle reported that Henry angrily replied: 'You are wrong. I do not need a single extra man, for my hope is in God, and if my cause is just I shall prevail whatever the size of my following.' This was the origin of Shakespeare's 'a little touch of Harry in the night'.

Agincourt had been chosen with care by the French. Their army included large contingents of cavalry, and the flat, narrow plain, bounded on either side by thick woodland, was ideal cavalry country. But the French had forgotten the rain. By the morning, the ploughed fields that separated the two armies had become a

HENRY V *Only premature death deprived the cleverest and most ambitious of the Lancastrian kings from winning the throne of France.*

muddy marsh. Rising at dawn, Henry heard Mass and then made his final plans for the battle. Knowing how heavily he was outnumbered, he and his subordinate commanders, the Duke of York and Lord Canoys, decided to concentrate almost all their men to hold the open ground between the woodlands, and so prevent the French from outflanking the English line. Only a tiny reserve was left to secure the camp in the rear. Henry also took great care over the placing of the archers. They were ordered to provide themselves with 6 ft wooden stakes, which they could dig into the ground as a defence against the French cavalry. Now all the English could do was wait.

CLASH ON THE BATTLEFIELD *English cavalry, pikemen and archers throw the French into confusion in this 15th-century miniature of Agincourt. The French chose the battlefield because it seemed to be ideal cavalry country. But mud and England's bowmen upset their calculations.*

Henry V: A captain of genius wins France

Few kings of England have been as idolised both in their lifetimes and by posterity as Henry V. In England's long struggle to win France, Henry came within an ace of achieving the ambitions of his ancestors. Only his death at the age of 35 cheated him of triumph.

Henry's path was eased by the disordered state of France after 40 years of corrupt government and civil war. His ambitions began modestly, but they became ever greater as each attack he made met with less and less resistance. When he first struck at Normandy in 1415, Henry had only a speedy raid in mind. But, for the second time in a century, a vastly superior French army was shattered by a small force of English longbowmen.

After his victory at Agincourt, Henry went on in 1417 to attack Normandy. Then, in 1419, the powerful Duke of Burgundy recognised Henry as King of France. Within a few months, the whole country was under English control. Fine generalship and shrewd diplomacy had brought Henry to unequalled heights of power. But dysentery struck Henry down on August 31, 1422, leaving a baby son – Henry VI – to succeed him. Two months later the French king followed Henry to the grave. If Henry V had lived a few weeks longer, he might have been King of France. But his son was to lose all he had gained.

Meanwhile, the French had arranged themselves in three lines. After a long pause, in which each side waited for the other to attack, the first French line of heavily armoured infantry advanced. But the impetus of their charge was broken by the mud before they had even crossed half the distance to the English line. Henry ordered his archers to shoot. The devastating flights of arrows that had slaughtered French men-at-arms at Crécy and Poitiers again caused appalling casualties. By the time the surviving French finally reached the English position, they were exhausted.

A desperate hand-to-hand struggle followed. The French attacked fiercely with swords, while the English archers dropped their bows and resisted with axes. Soon, confusion was spreading among the French, who slowly fell back. But this retreat embroiled them with their second line which had by then been ordered forward. A wall of bodies built up, from the top of which the English slaughtered their foes in hundreds.

The carnage lasted for two hours before the third and final French line – the cavalry – hurled itself on the English. This attack caught Henry's forces unawares. For a moment, there seemed the danger of a breakthrough, and behind the English lines were several hundred French prisoners, many of high rank, not yet disarmed. Henry was forced to make a rapid and ruthless decision. While he faced the final French assault, 200 archers were ordered to kill the prisoners. But as the hapless captives were butchered, the fate of the battle was decided. Almost as soon as it reached the English archers the cavalry attack collapsed, and the French horsemen turned and fled.

Towards the French throne

The rain, the longbow and their own heavy equipment had broken France's feudal chivalry. The French had lost 7000 men, among them the finest of their nobility. Their country was left defenceless and leaderless in the face of England's ambitious 28-year-old king. In contrast, the English had lost under 100, and the only lord to fall was the Duke of York.

A one-sided struggle continued for the next four years. The French now had not only to contend with an invader. Their old insane king, Charles VI, had to watch helplessly as the two great families of Armagnac and Burgundy added civil war to his country's other miseries. Finally, in 1420, it was agreed that Henry should marry Katherine de Valois and be formally recognised as heir and regent of France. On May 21, the treaty confirming this was ceremoniously signed in the cathedral at Troyes. Henry used the seal of his great-grandfather, Edward III, for the ceremony. But he had far outshone Edward's achievements, for he had brought England to one of the highest points of success in its long history.

AGE OF ARMOUR

By the beginning of the 15th century, old-fashioned chain mail had been replaced by plate armour (above). This armour was complex and difficult to forge; its great centres were Milan in Italy and Augsburg and Nuremberg in Germany. But at Agincourt, even the new armour was found to be vulnerable to the deadly power and accuracy of the longbow. Armour, however, continued to be worn in battle until guns and gunpowder finally put an end to its usefulness in the 16th century.

A SOARING MONUMENT TO ENGLAND'S AGE OF FAITH

TOWERING PINNACLES *Henry VI expressed his piety and love of learning by building King's College Chapel, seen here from the River Cam.*

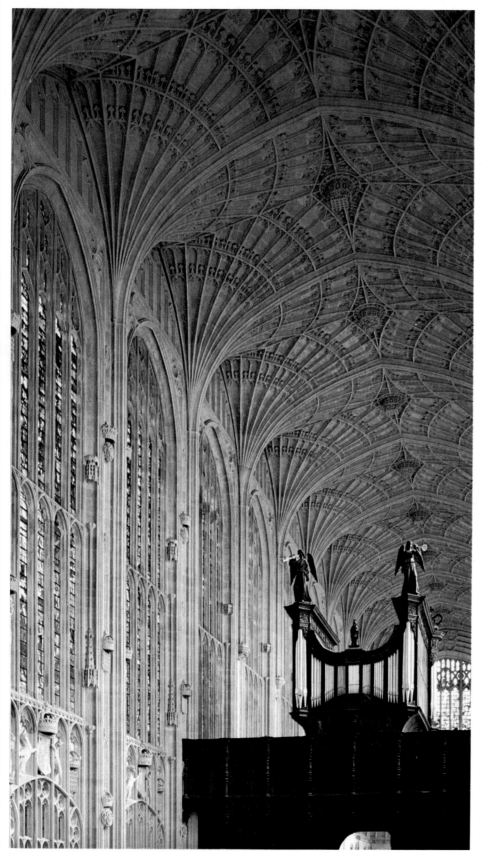

A KING'S LEGACY *Henry VI is remembered best for two glorious buildings which he created at Cambridge and Eton. In this view towards the east window of King's College Chapel his ideas are carried out to perfection. The fan-vaulting is à masterpiece of the late-Gothic style.*

In his 50 years of disastrous rule, Henry VI left only one tangible legacy – the buildings which expressed his own qualities of Christian faith and devotion to learning. The chapels he called into being at King's College, Cambridge, and at Eton College embody the highest ideals of medieval Christendom. In them the Gothic style, which had dominated Europe for four centuries, had its last flowering.

Only the east end of Eton College Chapel was completed, and plans for an enormous nave were eventually abandoned. But the work at King's College was carried through by Henry and two of his Tudor successors to perfection. The chapel is almost 100 yds long. Its great length and astonishing height serve to emphasise the soaring aspirations of Gothic architecture. The eye is led upward to the exuberant fan-vaulting, and then towards the great east window and the high altar. The effect is undeniably beautiful, and deeply impressive.

The work of two dynasties

Henry was only 19 when he gave orders for the beginning of the work at King's College in 1440. He paid frequent visits to the site and supervised the progress of the building. The provision of adequate labour and materials for his great works at Eton and King's was probably the only matter over which he exercised royal authority. While Yorkists and Lancastrians vied for the crown, Henry was issuing letters patent for the conscription of labourers to work on these two projects.

King's College Chapel was too enormous to be finished in Henry's lifetime, but he left in his will meticulous instructions for its completion, even including methods to be used to discipline 'any mason or other labourer who shall be found unprofitable or of any such ill demeanour whereby the works shall be hindered'. Hindered they unfortunately were, owing to the disturbed times. The chapel was not completed until 90 years later, during the reign of Henry VIII. Yet, throughout these nine decades, the original inspiration was zealously preserved. King's is all of a piece, an ordered whole in a sense that is unique among medieval buildings; and it has survived the centuries unmarred – even in such details as its brilliantly coloured windows and carved ornaments.

A building of inspiring beauty

Seen from the river, the twin west towers soar heavenwards, the great west window scarcely contained between them. This is perhaps one of the best known and best loved of English views.

The inside of the vast building is even more breathtaking than its exterior. It is a marvel of spaciousness and light. The long, narrow nave and choir are incredibly high and crowned by superb fan-vaulting.

This incomparable roof is the work of two masons, John Wastell and Henry Semerk. In 1513 they were commissioned to create 'a good, sure and sufficient vault for the great church . . . after the best handling and form of good workmanship according to a plan'. They did their work well. The vault is an artistic and technical masterpiece.

The great roof runs the full length of the building, for the nave is separated from the choir by a carved wooden screen. This screen is a perfect match for the stonework. Its richly detailed carvings, by an unknown French or Italian craftsman, are among the finest woodwork in Europe. The repeated cyphers of AB and HR show that they were made between 1533 and 1536, when Henry VIII was married to Anne Boleyn. Apart from this woodwork and the brilliance of the glowing windows, the decoration of the church is simple. A few boldly carved designs are repeated again and again, providing an impression of confidence and cohesion.

By a startling irony the chapel, which was to express the piety of its founder, is stamped in all its details with the insignia of the more worldly Henry VIII. These dramatic carvings express the aspirations of the Royal House of Tudor – the rose and crown of their dynasty, the portcullis, the strange royal beasts and the fleur-de-lis, signifying the Tudors' claim to the throne of France.

King's College Chapel is quite as big as many Gothic cathedrals. In a sense, it is as impressively beautiful as any of them. Yet its mood is different. The clue lies in these secular carvings and the tell-tale initials of Henry VIII and the queen he married in violation of the old laws of Christendom. King's College Chapel fulfils its founder's aims as an intensely religious building; but it also evokes a later mood in which piety was allied with a new spirit of patriotism.

A VANISHED ART

The soaring windows of King's College Chapel mark the swan song of an ancient craft.

Depicting biblical stories in coloured glass was a medieval way of teaching Christian stories to the illiterate. To the minds of simple people they seemed to have a magic power – for the passing clouds and the movement of the sun across the sky made the stiff figures of saints pulse with apparent life and movement.

All over England, religious buildings, from great abbeys and cathedrals to remote parish churches, were enriched with these testimonies of faith. But stained-glass windows were to prove the most vulnerable of all the creations of the Middle Ages. When England became Protestant, mobs stormed the churches smashing 'graven images', which they believed had no place there. Within a few years much of the work of five centuries of glass-making was destroyed.

By good fortune, King's College Chapel escaped unscathed. The multi-coloured windows have survived unharmed to this day, the most impressive survival of stained glass in Britain, and a brilliant testimony to a vanished art.

TELLING A STORY *Unlettered peasants learnt their Bible from the pictures in stained-glass windows.*

A KING'S AMBITION

Henry VI's idea when he founded Eton College in 1440 and King's College, Cambridge, the same year was that the scholars of Eton should be transferred to King's 'when sufficiently imbued with the rudiments of grammar'.

Seen from the Thames or across the playing fields, Eton College Chapel soars as imposingly as King's. If Henry had had his way it would have been only the choir of an immense church. But his ambitious plans languished after he was deposed and eventually murdered.

The wall-paintings in the chapel were the work of two English artists, William Baker and a man called Gilbert, and were finished by 1488. They were whitewashed over by the college barber in 1560, rediscovered in 1847 and covered again by Victorian Gothic stalls. Workmen destroyed the upper row in the process. Only in 1923 were the paintings finally revealed and, after expert restoration, they can be seen for what they are – the finest 15th-century murals in Britain.

HIDDEN ART *The Eton murals are visible in all their splendour after being lost for centuries.*

ETON THROUGH THE EYES OF AN ARTIST *The 18th-century Italian artist Canaletto found inspiration in the English scene. He painted this view of Eton College Chapel from across the River Thames.*

Two families fight for the throne in 30 years of war

SYMBOL OF CIVIL WAR

This helmet, now to be seen in the Victoria and Albert Museum, once protected the head of an English infantryman on the bloody battlefields of the Wars of the Roses. In that turbulent age, thousands of common soldiers perished as kings and mighty barons fought for power in a struggle that was to last for 30 years.

THE FATEFUL CHOICE *In a 19th-century illustration from Shakespeare's* Henry VI, *English nobles choose sides by plucking white and red roses – the badges of York and Lancaster.*

For 30 years, from the middle of the 15th century, England was torn by a vicious and violent struggle between rival claimants to the throne. The source of this conflict lay in the deep bitterness of dynastic rivalry. From the sons of Edward III had sprung two great families, the houses of York and Lancaster. Each family believed that it had a legitimate claim to the throne. Each found support among the barons and nobles of the nation, who were greedy for wealth and power.

But open conflict did not break out until the 1450's. By that time, the once profitable Hundred Years' War with France had ended in defeat and disaster and the English economy lay stagnant. The incomes of the barons fell, while their appetite for extravagant display never ceased to increase. And, where once strong kings had dominated their subjects, the weak and feeble-minded Henry VI was a figure no man could fear. This pathetic member of the House of Lancaster seemed an easy prey to greedy Yorkist eyes. His crown and his royal gold glinted in invitation to his enemies. But there were few battles in these years of civil

GREAT PEER, GREAT QUEEN *Two of the chief figures of the wars – the Earl of Warwick (left) and Henry's queen, Margaret of Anjou.*

strife – scarcely half a dozen in three decades. The clash came far above the heads of ordinary people, in the palaces of southern England and the grim castles of the north and west.

There, dominating men and women pitted themselves against their rivals in contests of willpower and ingenuity. There was the Earl of Suffolk, Henry VI's grasping and corrupt minister, and the most influential man in the court. His impeachment and murder in 1450

removed a strong minister, and thus was a decisive step on the road to open conflict. There was Margaret of Anjou, Henry's hated French queen, who led her troops into battle herself, and whose resourcefulness and determination almost saved her husband's throne. Above them all towered the figure of Richard Neville, Earl of Warwick, known as 'the Kingmaker'. Warwick was the subtlest as well as the most unscrupulous politician of 15th-century England. For 20 years the mightiest supporter of the Yorkist cause, he was to change sides dramatically in a desperate bid to preserve his personal power.

York and Lancaster

Until the 1450's, the energies of England's great families had been spent in the French wars. But when the Hundred Years' War ended in final defeat, the nobles transferred their ambitions, passions and quarrels from the soil of France to that of England itself. The seeds of the conflict that was to set father against son for 30 years were sown in Parliament. There, in 1450, was voiced the demand that Richard, Duke of York, wealthiest man in England after his cousin the king, and a champion of reform, should be recognised as heir to the throne. When three years later Henry VI suffered his first attack of insanity, his subjects rejoiced as Richard succeeded in making himself regent. But he did so in the face of relentless opposition from the queen, and her friends among the corrupt ministers of the court. As soon as the king recovered his sanity, she released her supporters from prison and banished York from the court.

Richard turned to force. But the first Battle of St Albans in May 1455 was inconclusive. It was not until the war of 1459–61 that intrigue gave way to open conflict. In two decisive battles, at Wakefield and St Albans, the Yorkists were defeated and Richard of York was himself numbered among the dead. Margaret of Anjou had his head crowned with a paper crown, and then had it placed above the gates of York to mark her triumph.

This was the queen's victory, and it was the queen who threw it away. Her own arrogance lost her whatever support she had once enjoyed. Moreover, Richard's son, Edward,

BLOODY DEFEAT *At Tewkesbury in 1471, the Yorkists (left) crush their Lancastrian enemies. A scene from a contemporary manuscript.*

BATTLE *During the years of civil war, battles were few in number.*

SCOTLAND

⊛ Lancastrian victory
⊛ Yorkist victory

⊛ Hexham 1464

E N G L A N D

⊛ Towton 1461

Wakefield ⊛ 1460

⊛ Blore Heath 1459

⊛ Bosworth 1485

Mortimers Cross ⊛ 1461

⊛ Ludford 1459

Edgcote ⊛ 1469

⊛ Northampton 1460

Tewkesbury ⊛ 1471

⊛ St. Albans 1455 ⊛ 1461

⊛ Barnet 1471

W A L E S

0   50   100
miles

took up his father's cause. The Lancastrians met defeat in their turn, and when Edward seated himself upon the throne in Westminster Hall on March 4, 1461, there were few who regretted the passing of the red rose of Lancaster. The old king, Henry VI, remained at large, a wandering fugitive with a small band of attendants, for a few years longer. But his cause was irrevocably lost. Even the mighty Earl of Warwick could not remake a king whom he had once unmade, and his attempt at Barnet (1471) to do so led to his own death. But the campaign was not over.

The final reckoning

Lancastrian hopes now rested not on Henry, but on his redoubtable queen and her young son, the 17-year-old Prince Edward, who both landed at Weymouth from France on the day of Warwick's defeat.

Undeterred by the news of Barnet, the queen at once started recruiting a new army, and soon was on the march towards Gloucester, where she planned to cross the River Severn to join forces with the Welsh levies of Jasper Tudor, Earl of Pembroke. But Gloucester held out for the Yorkist cause, and Edward IV hurried to its relief. Margaret now decided to cross the river to meet her allies at Tewkesbury, where Edward's pursuing army caught up and attacked her.

The clash between the two armies was for a time indecisive, but in the end the Lancastrians suffered a crushing defeat, largely through the inactivity of one of their leaders, Lord Wenlock. He failed to order his troops forward to support the forces of the Duke of Somerset. Wenlock had already changed sides twice in the course of the wars, and might well have been planning to do so again. But he did not live to receive the rewards of his treachery, for Somerset himself beat out Lord Wenlock's brains with a battle-axe. All was now lost, and the panic-stricken Lancastrian soldiers began to throw down their arms. Many were slaughtered trying to cross the river.

The Yorkists offered no quarter – not even to the highest. For Prince Edward, too, met his end at Tewkesbury. According to some accounts, he perished on the battlefield, crying in vain for mercy to his treacherous brother-in-law, Clarence. But more probably, he was betrayed to the Yorkists by his hosts in a house where he had taken refuge. His death, and the murder of his father in the Tower of London three weeks later, seemed to end Lancastrian hopes of ruling England.

But this was not to be the end of the story. In 1485, the seemingly triumphant Yorkists were challenged by the last of the Lancastrian line, the young Prince Henry Tudor. And with the death of Richard III, the last of the Plantagenets, on Bosworth Field, there came to the throne a new dynasty which was to reunite a divided land and lead it back to greatness – the House of Tudor.

Henry VI: His kingdom was 'not of this world'

'The king is but a natural fool, and no man to be ruling this land.' From the lips of a farm labourer, John Merfield, in the market-place of Brightling in Sussex one summer afternoon in 1450, came this condemnation of his royal master, Henry VI. Merfield paid a heavy price for his indiscretion, for he was found guilty of high treason and put to death. But future events were to show how much truth there was in his words. Early in the autumn of 1453, the 32-year-old Henry suffered the first attack of the insanity which was to dog the rest of his life. The first fit lasted only 16 months. But it dramatically confirmed a fact which had been long suspected by the king's councillors – that he was incapable of controlling the government of his kingdom.

A man set apart from his age

The truth was that Henry had never behaved as a king was expected to do. 'His sole delight was to immerse himself day and night in the law of God,' recorded his chaplain. Henry's councillors constantly complained of the long hours he passed in prayer, when pressing matters of state required his attention.

Henry's childlike simplicity had its attractive side. But his reign was disastrous. He wanted his nobles to live in peace with one another, but he did not command them to do so on his authority as their king. He preached feebly at them, and then resigned himself to events.

Even his Tudor descendants never suggested that Henry was an impressive monarch. But they claimed that miracles had occurred at his tomb, and tried to have him canonised as a saint. Certainly his kingdom was 'not of this world'.

SAINTLY KING *Henry VI was no man to control England's turbulent nobility. He helplessly watched his country slide into the civil war that was to cost him his throne.*

Caxton's vision brings Britain into a new age

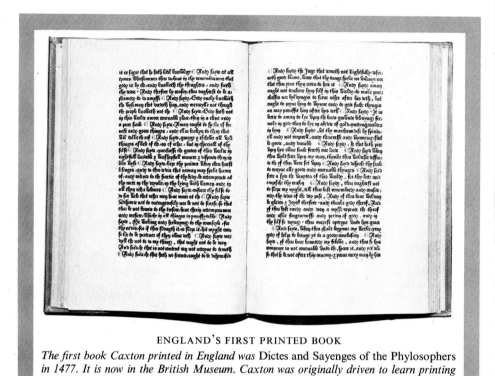

ENGLAND'S FIRST PRINTED BOOK

The first book Caxton printed in England was Dictes and Sayenges of the Phylosophers *in 1477. It is now in the British Museum. Caxton was originally driven to learn printing by the time-consuming tedium of copying out translations in longhand.*

PRESENTED AT COURT *A contemporary manuscript shows Edward IV receiving* Dictes and Sayenges of the Phylosophers *from his brother-in-law, Earl Rivers, who translated it into English from the French. Caxton printed the book on his press at Westminster.*

The book which Edward IV accepted from a kneeling courtier, in a simple ceremony in November 1477, was a milestone in British history. The king's brother-in-law, Anthony Woodville, Earl Rivers, presented him with a copy of *Dictes and Sayenges of the Phylosophers*, which the earl had himself translated from the original French. What made the occasion so special was not the book's contents, but that it was the first book to be printed in England.

A man of vision
The man who brought this revolutionary invention to England was William Caxton, a rich wool merchant. Caxton had become a printer almost by accident. In 1469 he started to translate a French history of Troy, but found copying in longhand so tedious that his 'pen became worn, his hand weary, his eye dimmed'. With typical energy and determination, he decided, at the age of 48, to learn the newly developed craft of printing.

Before this time, books had been produced by hand. Specially trained scribes laboured for months and sometimes years to make beautiful illuminated manuscripts. Most of these dedicated men worked in monasteries, so the works they produced were largely concerned with religion – lives of the saints and works of devotion. Almost all such books were written in Latin.

But this process was not only long and arduous – it was also extremely expensive. Only the fortunate few could afford the luxury of a library. Books were so valuable, and so few in number, that even in the universities they were kept chained to the shelves.

A German, Johann Gutenberg, had set up the first printing press in Europe in the city of Mainz in about 1440, and by the time Caxton decided to learn printing most of the larger German cities had their own presses. It was to Cologne that Caxton went to learn his craft between 1470 and 1472.

Being a rich man, Caxton could afford to establish his own press at Bruges in 1474. A year later, he published his first book, *The Recuyell of the Historyes of Troye* – the one which he had found so difficult to copy a few years before. This was followed by another translation, *The Game and Playe of the Chesse*, which appeared in 1476.

Caxton now resolved to give up the wool trade and devote himself to full-time printing, writing and publishing. Towards the end of 1476, he returned to England and set up his press in a building near Westminster Abbey. Since he was both a shrewd businessman and a conscientious scholar, Caxton had a double reason for going into business – to make money and to spread knowledge.

The book presented to the king was only the first of nearly 100 titles he printed at Westminster between 1476 and his death in 1491. Caxton catered for all tastes. His customers were aristocrats, clergymen, students, middle-class landowners and merchants. Books on chivalry and romance, manners and morality, history, philosophy and religion, were all available for a few pence. Among them was an encyclopedia, *The Myrrour of the World*, the first illustrated book to be printed in England. Maintaining a high standard of accuracy and clarity, Caxton also printed nearly all existing English literature, including the first great English poem, Chaucer's *Canterbury Tales*, and Sir Thomas Malory's *Morte d'Arthur*, the story of Arthur and the legendary quest for the Holy Grail. He also published many more translations from abroad. These included great works from the past, such as those of the Roman author Cicero, and Aesop's fables.

One language for the nation
One of Caxton's main problems was to decide how to establish a standard form of English which he could use in his books. He had no dictionaries to guide him. Latin was still the language of the educated. There were as many dialects spoken as there were regions of England. Caxton wrote of the difficulties he faced in his preface to a translation of Virgil's *Aeneid*: 'Certayn marchauntes were in a shippe in Tamyse and for lacke of wynde thei taryed

POWER OF PRINT

The first hand-presses were modelled on the wine presses used in the Rhine Valley, where printing in Europe began. With only minor modifications, the hand-press was to be used for 350 years after Caxton brought it to England. On his press, he printed a total of over 18,000 pages.

Until the coming of the printing press, only the wealthy could afford to buy books. Manuscripts were copied out laboriously by hand, and at 14th-century prices cost about £35 each to produce – several hundred pounds today.

The greatest power of the printing press was to bring knowledge within the grasp of an ever-widening and ever more eager public. But at first many people regarded the new technique with distaste, and would employ scribes to copy a printed book back into manuscript. Nor did rulers and governments view the rapid growth of printing with favour, for it meant that books and pamphlets could be produced cheaply and in quantity. Thus the way was opened for the spread of new ideas which would revolutionise society.

This model of Caxton's first hand-press was made in 1812. It is now in the Science Museum. From Caxton's press grew the printing industry of today.

atte Forlond (the North Foreland in Kent) and wente to lande for to refreshe them; And one of theym . . . cam in-to an hows and axed for mete; and specyally he axyed after eggys; and the goode wyf answerde that she coude speke no Frenshe . . . And theene at laste another sayd that he wolde haue "eyren" then the goode wyf sayd that she vnderstod hym wel. Loo, what sholde a man in thyse dayes now wryte, "egges" or "eyren"?'

Caxton chose to use the English of the court and capital. And in a century, largely due to his efforts, this became the accepted written word of England.

Caxton established a long-standing link with the Church because ecclesiastics were the most literate section of the community, and therefore potential buyers of books. One of Caxton's earliest pieces of work was a poster advertising the *Sarum Ordinale*, a church service handbook.

Not merely a printer, Caxton continued to pursue his own scholarly work with great vigour. In 1481 he began the massive task of translating and modernising an earlier Latin version of a work called *The Polychronicon*, completing it in the astonishing time of 18 months with 800 pages of about 400 words each, with a final supplementary section. In all, it consisted of 340,000 words.

Like so many inventions, printing came into being because it was needed. By the mid-15th century, books were in such demand that their production could no longer be left to monks and scholars laboriously copying manuscripts in longhand. And the invention spread with surprising speed – from the Rhine Valley to every European country, including Russia, by the end of the century. By 1500, more than 1700 presses had produced more than 40,000 editions.

When Caxton died towards the end of 1491, his printing business was continued by Wynkyn

de Worde, his manager and foreman. De Worde remained at Westminster for a few years. Then, he moved to St Bride's, Fleet Street, where there were good business prospects among the many ecclesiastics who had settled between St Paul's and Temple Bar.

If Caxton's emphasis was on quality, de Worde's was on quantity: not without good reason is he known as 'the father of Fleet Street'. Unlike Caxton, de Worde was solely dependent on printing for his livelihood, and books came thick and fast from his press.

By the time he died in 1535, de Worde had printed 800 items, almost half of them for use in grammar schools.

Power of the press

Some of the printing practices of the day were irresponsible. Inaccuracy was common, and often deliberate. One picture block might be made to serve several purposes, appearing over several captions and illustrating different subjects, even being printed several times in one book.

In the Middle Ages the printed word made possible the religious pamphlets of the Reformation, and provided the materials for the wide-ranging scholarship of the Renaissance. The medieval court which witnessed the presentation of Caxton's book could not know of the occasion's far-reaching consequences for Britain. The invention of printing was as shattering in its impact on the medieval world as the invention of gunpowder. Printing brought new ideas flooding into the long-isolated kingdom in an explosion of knowledge seldom paralleled in human history. It was to remove scholarship from the restraining hands of the monks, and assist in the liberation of mankind. In that process of liberation, Caxton's successors in London, Oxford and Cambridge played a significant part.

Edward IV: A youth wins the throne for York

In a snowstorm on Easter Sunday 1461, Edward, Duke of York, defeated Henry VI at Towton. Three months later he was crowned king. He was just 19 years old.

Edward was well equipped to meet the challenge of bringing order to a country which for six years had been torn by civil war. He was nearly 6 ft tall, and his striking good looks gave him the physical presence of a king. And he also possessed administrative skill. From the start, Edward declared his intention of reforming the royal finances so that he could avoid raising unpopular taxes. He reorganised the government, repressed disorder and supported English merchants overseas.

Yet within eight years of his coronation, Edward was a fugitive. Supremely confident in his own ability, he had tried to manage without the support of his most powerful subject, his uncle, the Earl of Warwick, known as 'the Kingmaker'. In 1469, Warwick allied himself with the exiled Henry VI, and forced his nephew to flee the kingdom.

But a year later Edward returned. Two brilliant victories at Barnet and Tewkesbury in 1471 shattered the Lancastrian armies. Warwick himself was killed and the luckless Henry put to death in the Tower. Edward was now free to complete his reforms.

In his later years, Edward's nature was coarsened by the wars and the betrayals he had experienced. Nevertheless, when he died of a fever in 1483, he had earned a place among England's notable statesmen and soldier kings. His great misfortune was that he died before his sons were old enough to rule the country in his place.

ROYAL REFORMER *Edward IV established the House of York on the throne by deposing his Lancastrian rival, Henry VI. His aim was to end the disorder brought by civil war.*

'Treason! Treason!'–Richard falls fighting at Bosworth

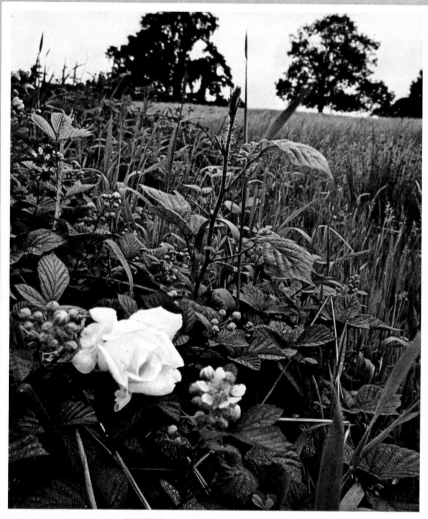

WHERE A ROYAL DYNASTY FELL
Nearly five centuries ago, Bosworth Field, outside Market Bosworth in Leicestershire, rang with the clash of steel as two English armies battled for the throne. Fighting bravely after being betrayed by his allies, the last Plantagenet, Richard III, perished. By the end of the day a new dynasty, the House of Tudor, had won the throne. Its monarchs were to unite their divided realm and lead it to greatness over the next century.

On the green fields outside the village of Market Bosworth, some 10 miles from Leicester, two armies clashed on an August day in 1485. The battle was to close an epoch in English history and bring to power the brilliant Tudor dynasty.

The dawn of August 22, 1485, found the 10,000-strong army of Richard III camped in a strong position on the summit of Ambien Hill. The bulk of Richard's forces occupied the centre and took their commands from the king himself. In front of them stood a large body of archers under the Duke of Norfolk, and behind them the private army of Henry Percy, Earl of Northumberland.

Plotting by the leaders

This imposing array, it seemed, could scarcely fail to vanquish Henry Tudor's army, gathered on the plain below. Was not Henry's hurriedly collected force only half the size of Richard's? Was not the king one of the boldest and most skilled commanders of the day?

But treason was in the air. Invasion had been threatening ever since Richard had ascended his brother's throne. When Henry Tudor landed at Milford Haven on August 7, the army at his back was scarcely 2000 strong, and the majority of his troops were convicted French felons, persuaded to enlist by the bribe of a free pardon. Only two English noblemen – Henry's uncle, Jasper Tudor, and the Earl of Oxford – rallied to the rebel cause.

For months, however, Henry's agents had been sounding out possible sympathisers and re-awakening the ashes of Lancastrian loyalty. Rhys ap Thomas, the Welsh leader who had sworn to Richard that the usurper would only reach England over his dead body, had already gone over to Henry, taking with him the recruits he had raised for the Yorkist cause. Richard was now tormented by one question: how far could his nobles be trusted?

This especially applied to the third army on the field that August morning. It was the 3000-strong host of Lord Stanley and his brother, Sir William. Lord Stanley was the steward of Richard's household, and a great man in his native Lancashire.

When Henry Tudor landed in Wales to claim the throne, Stanley had been absent

MEN OF VALOUR *Yorkists and Lancastrians clash in the Wars of the Roses. These bloody years saw the emergence of men of determined courage and ruthless ability. Such a man was Richard III (right), who, through his loyalty and generalship, helped his brother, Edward, to the throne. But Richard's reputation was blasted by his seizure of the crown after Edward's death in 1483 and the death of the princes in the Tower. King for only two years, he perished as he had lived, in violence at Bosworth Field in 1485.*

THE MYSTERY OF THE PRINCES IN THE TOWER

Of all the black deeds that have stained the name of the Tower of London, none is more infamous than the murder of Edward IV's young children in 1483. The elder boy, the 12-year-old Edward, was brought to the Tower in May, while he was still king. In June his 10-year-old brother, Richard, was taken from sanctuary in Westminster Abbey and carried off to join him. Gradually, the princes' lives became shrouded in secrecy. For some weeks inquisitive visitors to the Tower caught glimpses of the brothers as they played together in the garden. But by the end of the summer they had been confined in an inner room. Only the occasional fleeting appearance of a boyish face at a barred window confirmed that they were still alive. A doctor who attended them reported that they lived in constant fear. Then silence fell.

By the autumn the news leaked out that the princes were dead. Contemporary chroniclers hinted that the boys may have been murdered, though without suggesting who was responsible. But in 1485, Henry VII formally accused Richard of 'shedding infants' blood', and Tudor historians tried to substantiate this charge, aiming to strengthen the new dynasty. Sir Thomas More claimed that Sir James Tyrell, an ambitious crony of Richard's, had later confessed to having arranged for the princes to be suffocated on Richard's orders, and this is the story that has passed into legend – and Shakespeare.

Henry VII had as good a reason as Richard to eliminate all rivals to the throne; but the princes died in the autumn of 1483, while Henry was in exile on the Continent and far from ready to make his bid for power. So suspicion points inexorably at Richard; yet decisive evidence of his guilt has never been found. The most perplexing mystery in the history of England remains unsolved to this day.

A Victorian picture of Edward IV's sons in the Tower. Richard III's reputation has never recovered from the charge that he murdered them.

Richard III: The reign of the last Plantagenet

No king in English history has been the source of more mystery and controversy than Richard III. For many, Richard will always be the hunchbacked 'wicked uncle' of legend, who had his two nephews murdered in his greedy quest for the throne.

But for others, Richard is the most defamed man in history – an energetic and inventive politician, whose evil reputation was foisted on him by his Tudor successor, Henry VII, to justify his own seizure of the throne.

Sir Thomas More, who wrote a hostile biography of Richard 30 years after the king's death, claimed that he was a sinister figure from the moment of his birth. He wrote that Richard had been born 'feet forward, also not untoothed'. And from More, too, stemmed the description of Richard that was later made famous by Shakespeare – 'little of stature, ill-featured of limbs, crookbacked, his left shoulder higher than his right, hard-favoured of visage'. But though Richard was sickly and undersized as a child, and a sad contrast to his tall and handsome brothers, there is no evidence that he was the misshapen figure depicted by More.

Survival in a turbulent age

As a boy, Richard was well schooled in the sudden shifts of fortune that his turbulent century heaped upon the noble and powerful. Before he was ten, he had been a Lancastrian prisoner, had lost his father in battle and been a fugitive in Flanders with his mother. Finally, in March 1461 he saw the triumph of his family, when his brother Edward became king.

While Edward IV was on the throne, Richard's future was assured. The king showered lands and titles on his young brother and, from the age of 17, Richard was at Edward's side in every crisis. He shared the Yorkist command at the victories of Barnet and Tewkesbury. Then, at the age of only 18, he was sent to subdue the northern borderlands, and brought them under firm control.

Richard's greatest concern was that England should have a strong and orderly government. And when Edward IV died in April 1483, leaving the crown to his 12-year-old son, Richard feared a new civil war, with powerful noblemen vying for control of the realm through the boy king. His response was to seize the throne himself, ruthlessly crushing all resistance, and imprisoning little Edward and his 10-year-old brother Richard in the Tower. There, before the end of the year, the boys perished.

But Richard's crown was not secure, and he survived his nephews by only two years. On Bosworth Field his reign ended, as it had begun, with violence. Two days later Richard's body was flung into an unmarked grave.

from court. Richard's first act was to summon him to help repel the invaders. But Stanley wavered, opening secret negotiations with both sides. Richard's reaction was to arrest Stanley's eldest son, Lord Strange, and hold him hostage. But as the king surveyed his troops on the eve of the battle, he could only gaze anxiously at Stanley's camp and wonder on which side those 3000 retainers would fight.

The trumpets of the Tudor army sounded while Richard was still making his final plans for the battle. A large body of rebels advanced rapidly on the royal archers under Norfolk. After several minutes of savage fighting, Norfolk's line showed signs of breaking and the king, who had watched the engagement from the top of Ambien Hill, sent in a small force of reserves. The rebels fell back, but in the confusion Norfolk was reported slain. Disorder spread through the royal ranks and the king's commanders looked anxiously to their master for further reinforcements.

Richard sent a messenger ordering Stanley to join him. Stanley refused; he had decided not to intervene until he could see which side was winning. The king angrily ordered the execution of Stanley's son, but then realised that this would resolve any doubts in Stanley's mind and instantly countermanded the order.

Richard then called on Northumberland, whose forces were massed immediately behind him. The true weakness of the king's position suddenly became clear as Northumberland's reply was read out by a messenger. The earl would stay where he was until he saw what Stanley had decided.

The last charge

In desperation, Richard gathered his own personal retainers and men-at-arms together and pointed out the lonely figure of Henry Tudor at the other side of the battlefield. They would charge across the field in front of the massed immobile forces of the Stanleys and snatch a spectacular victory from the very hands of the usurping prince.

The royal cavalcade galloped swiftly across Sir William Stanley's front. Now Sir William saw that his moment had come. He entered the battle on Henry Tudor's side, and as the royal force reached the Welsh prince's personal guard, it found itself trapped by a grim alliance of the king's rival and his treacherous friends. Defeat was inevitable.

Fighting with a savage bravery to which even his enemies paid tribute, Richard fell within a few yards of his adversary, his body scarred by wounds. His last shouts were: 'Treason! Treason! Treason!'

Sir William Stanley dismounted and plucked the crown from the dead king's head to place it on that of Henry Tudor. As for Richard, his naked body was thrown over a horse and carried from the field.

The dawn of an age of adventure

After long years of civil war, England unites as a new dynasty – the brilliant House of Tudor – leads the way to future glory

In 1485, when the Tudor dynasty came to power, England was divided and bankrupt after 30 years of civil war. The country counted for little on the Continent, whether in diplomacy, commerce or war. But the spirit which had once won the English an empire in France was not dead. In just over a century, the brilliant Tudors directed it into new fields to revitalise their kingdom and make it the envy of the world.

The transformation of medieval anarchy into efficient government was no easy task. It owed much to the fact that three of the five Tudor monarchs were rulers of extraordinary ability, and much also to their continuing good luck. Their abilities showed themselves in their astute choice of servants and policies; their luck in the fact that they lived to an advanced age and left obvious heirs to succeed them.

Yet, when the first Tudor, Henry VII, fought his way to the throne at Bosworth Field, few Englishmen realised that an age of civil war, royal incompetence and bankruptcy was over. They saw no reason why another powerful baron should not seize the throne by force, just as Henry and others before him had done. But Henry soon proved to be one of England's most astute rulers. He quickly made his position at home unchallengeable.

Propaganda was the key to Henry's success. In order to be strong, the Tudors had to appear strong. Magnificent displays of wealth and power (pp. 114–15) were more than a way of life. They were instruments of state. So long as Englishmen thought that their king could defeat any rebellion, they were unlikely to join one. Henry VII at once grasped this point. And he easily disposed of the last Yorkist claimants to the throne – two impostors called Lambert Simnel and Perkin Warbeck.

Henry was active in other fields as well. He made a profitable trade agreement with Spain and by such encouragement of trade, and his patronage of explorers such as Cabot (pp. 116–17), he opened up a new chapter in England's history. The new wealth and the new spirit of confidence and

THE TUDORS AND THE WORLD

Hans Holbein, court painter to Henry VIII, depicted two emissaries sent from France to his master's court in his painting 'The Ambassadors'. They are surrounded by objects symbolising the 'new learning' of the Renaissance – including an astrolabe, a hymn book by Martin Luther, and a globe marked with the latest voyages of discovery. Under the Tudors, England ended its *long isolation from the Continent. The inquiring spirit of the Renaissance, with its self-confident belief in the ability of man to achieve all his aims, soon established itself. The impact of such men as Holbein and his friend the Dutch scholar Erasmus, who also visited Britain, inspired a culture which became the envy of the world under Henry VIII and his daughter, Elizabeth.*

END OF AN ERA *By Tudor times, the monasteries, once the power-houses of the Christian faith, had fallen into decay. Members of religious orders were criticised for their corruption – as in this picture of a monk drinking.*

RELIGIOUS EXILES *The followers of the new Protestant religion found themselves persecuted when Henry VIII's daughter, the Catholic Mary, came to the throne. Many – like the Duchess of Suffolk and her family (above) – were forced to flee into exile.*

HARD TIMES *A woodcut from* The Sorrowful Lamentation of the Pedlars, *published in the mid-16th century, bemoans the harshness of the times and the decay of trade. When Elizabeth came to the throne, thousands of labourers had been forced off the land by enclosures which were turning cultivated fields into pastures for sheep. A new Poor Law brought help to the ill and aged, but poverty was seen as a vice. The thousands of 'sturdy beggars' roaming the land were harshly treated. A persistent beggar could be sentenced to be whipped 'until his or her body be bloody', and the law even laid down that such offenders could be put to death.*

peace produced a new style of architecture. The rich could build for comfort, instead of for protection. The domestic intimacy of the house built by the Comptons at Compton Wynyates (pp. 118–19) was a striking contrast to the grimly turreted castles of medieval England.

Henry VII's son and heir lacked only one of his father's qualities – the habit of careful economy. But he had no need of it, for his father's wisdom had provided him with an enormous personal fortune and a realm blessed by ever-increasing prosperity. Henry VIII believed in display as a mark of power, and this was amply shown at the Field of the Cloth of Gold in 1520 (pp. 120–1). There, Henry met Francis I of France and their meeting was formal recognition that England had won back her status as a great power.

A tyrant king and his ministers

But to begin with, Henry left the hard business of policy-making to his astutely chosen ministers. Cardinal Thomas Wolsey, the first of these, was a supremely skilled politician, who enjoyed almost absolute power. His vanity, however, was to bring about his fall (pp. 124–5). It showed itself in the building of Hampton Court (pp. 122–3), a residence which threatened to outshine even the king's own palace.

Wolsey's successor, Thomas Cromwell, was if anything even more efficient. And his tasks were even more complex and demanding. First, he had to free Henry from his first wife, Catharine of Aragon, to enable him to marry Anne Boleyn (pp. 126–7). To achieve his master's 'Great Matter', Cromwell let nothing stand in his path. When all else failed, he broke his country's links with the Roman Catholic Church, an enterprise which abruptly altered the whole course of English history. In men such as the saintly Sir Thomas More (pp. 128–9), the English Reformation claimed some of the nation's finest figures as its victims. It overturned institutions as long established as the monasteries (pp. 130–1), and it rode roughshod over the popular indignation expressed by the rebels of the Pilgrimage of Grace.

Even Cromwell was not immune from the revolutionary power he had unleashed. In 1540 he fell foul of Henry and perished on the block. For, in the dark years of Henry's last decade, no one was safe. The men and women who lived through these years of tyranny were painted for posterity by the first great artist to work in England, Hans Holbein (pp. 132–3).

Golden age for England

Henry's tyranny, his six marriages and the Reformation itself stemmed from one over-riding concern. He feared that the Tudor achievement would crumble without a male heir. During the short reign of his sickly son, Edward VI, these premonitions were to be fulfilled. The kingdom was dominated by nobles who attempted to exploit the tensions caused by religious upheaval. Edward encouraged extreme Protestantism, but his sister, Mary, the next in line to the throne, was a devout Catholic. So, when Edward died, the ambitious Duke of Northumberland tried to place Lady Jane Grey on the throne. Her tragic rule was to last only nine days (pp. 134–5).

Though Mary came to the throne with popular support, she soon lost the love of her people. Try as she might, Protestantism had put down roots too firm to be stamped out. Mary found that she could not restore the monasteries, as their lands were now divided among thousands of small landowners. Her persecutions and burnings, especially of the Oxford Martyrs – Latimer, Ridley and Cranmer – only added to the national mood of discontent (pp. 136–7). Latimer proved to be a better prophet of the future than the bigoted queen, when he shouted from amidst the flames: 'We shall this day light such a candle . . . in England as I trust shall never be put out.' When Mary died childless in November 1558, she left behind a nation united in hatred of her and her principles.

Had Mary produced an heir, popular revulsion against Tudor rule might have led to the downfall of the dynasty. But her sister, Elizabeth, was quick to establish her popularity. Her coronation in 1559 (pp. 138–9) was a magnificent curtain-raiser to the achievements that were to follow. Elizabeth had all the dictatorial instincts of her family, but she also had qualities which none of them had enjoyed. She was subtle when they were brutal. Above all, she understood her people as no other Tudor had done. She knew that they must be guided and cajoled, not bullied and coerced. For four decades, the magic of Elizabeth's personality stamped every feature of English life. The men and women who played their part in this dazzling period of English history were given immortality in the tiny jewel-like portraits of Nicholas Hilliard (pp. 140–1).

But Elizabeth, too, faced many grave problems. And none was more intractable than that posed by her Catholic cousin, Mary, Queen of Scots. Having lost her throne after the murder of her husband, Darnley (pp. 142–3), Mary fled as an unwelcome exile to England. There, she was the focus of every conspiracy against Elizabeth's rule. For 19 years, Mary was kept in prison. Finally, Elizabeth was forced to have her executed (pp. 144–5).

'The lords and masters of the sea'

Elizabethan England, however, had a self-confidence that could afford to ignore the stresses of politics. On the oceans, a hardy breed of sea-faring adventurers pushed the frontiers of exploration outwards. Their pioneering voyages were crowned by Drake's circumnavigation of the world (pp. 146–7). 'The sea is full of English ships,' a Spanish official complained, 'for the English have become the lords and masters of the sea and care for no man else.' At home, this spirit of confidence and wealth found expression in houses of unparalleled flamboyance, such as Longleat (pp. 148–9).

When the crisis of Elizabeth's reign came in the 1580's, this self-confidence stood England in good stead. The simmering rivalry with Spain broke into open war in 1585. Three years of preparation by the Spanish culminated in the launching of the mighty Armada in 1588 to invade Britain. But, in one of the most remarkable victories in English history, the Spanish fleet was scattered by the genius of Elizabeth's sea-dogs (pp. 150–3).

This was the glorious climax of the Elizabethan age. It was the achievement not only of England's famous captains but of the common soldiers and sailors who shouted their love for the Virgin Queen at her great review at Tilbury. 'God send me such a company again, if need is,' the commander of the fleet, Lord Howard of Effingham, remarked. In the world of poetry and drama this feeling of confidence was matched by William Shakespeare (pp. 154–5), who gave his country and the world plays without rival.

The last years of Elizabeth's reign were clouded by personal and political troubles. She had long outlived the friends and councillors of her youth, and now she became infatuated with a young favourite, the Earl of Essex. But in 1601 he raised a revolt against her and she had no choice but to order his execution (pp. 156–7). For two more years she lived on – a monument to an age that had passed beyond recall. In Parliament, new voices were being raised, making demands with which she had little sympathy. Yet she never lost her hold on the hearts of her people. 'This I count above all,' she told the House of Commons, 'that I have reigned with your loves.' And in her achievements she had amply fulfilled the hopes with which her illustrious grandfather, Henry VII, had come to the throne 118 years earlier.

HIGH LIFE *Hunting in the royal park at Nonesuch, Surrey. The rich suffered little from the economic depression of the time.*

A HOPELESS CAUSE *Such was the patriotism of Elizabeth's England that appeals by Jesuit priests such as Edmund Campion (left) to overthrow the heretic queen met with little success. Campion went to the stake at Tyburn in 1581.*

FROM AMERICA *The merchant-venturers of Elizabethan England brought many strange things back to their homeland. Among them was the potato plant, which, according to tradition, was discovered by Sir Walter Raleigh in Virginia in the 1580's.*

NEW LEARNING *Pupils under instruction, in a contemporary woodcut. Tudor England saw a vast expansion in education. Edward VI encouraged the foundation of grammar schools, and under Elizabeth, his sister, Rugby and Harrow were established. But teaching was still centred on the classics, and modern languages and history were not studied.*

THE PEACOCK AGE

Life in Tudor England was governed by a rigid social system, which was held to follow God's divine laws. As there was a hierarchy in Heaven, from the Almighty down through the Seraphim and Cherubim to the lesser angels, so there was an order of authority and status on earth, from kings and queens through the social scales of gentleman, merchant and burgess to yeoman and lastly 'artificer and labourer'. Sir Thomas Elyot, author of a book on etiquette, warned that 'where order lacketh, there all thing is odious and uncomely'.

At the nerve centre of the political and artistic life of the nation lay the magnificence of the court. Henry VIII and Elizabeth were at pains to establish an impression of God-like monarchy. The court, with its pomp, ceremony and ostentation, became the centre of power and prestige, the lode-star for every artist, musician or actor hungry for fame. The landed gentry sent their children to court to acquire finesse.

The degrees of society were mirrored by its clothes. 'As for their outward show,' said Sir Thomas Smith, a prominent politician, 'a gentleman...must go like a gentleman, a yeoman like a yeoman, and a rascal like a rascal.' Fashions in clothes changed rapidly and only the very wealthy could afford to follow them. A damask gown could cost £81, and brocade was 10s 8d a yard, while a clergyman's salary might be less than £10 a year.

More than any other individual, Elizabeth herself summed up in her person the spirit of the age. Moving in splendour from one royal residence to another, her extravagant white gowns attesting to the virginity that had become a symbol of her power, she was supremely aware of her position as head of Church and state – God's chosen deputy on earth.

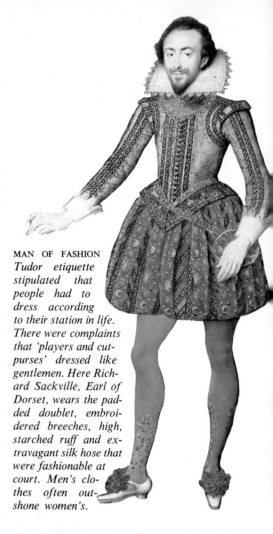

MAN OF FASHION *Tudor etiquette stipulated that people had to dress according to their station in life. There were complaints that 'players and cutpurses' dressed like gentlemen. Here Richard Sackville, Earl of Dorset, wears the padded doublet, embroidered breeches, high, starched ruff and extravagant silk hose that were fashionable at court. Men's clothes often outshone women's.*

FAMILY MEALS *Tudor children were dressed as miniature adults, in the elaborate brocades and starched ruffs of their parents. They were brought up with strict discipline to assume their destined place in society. In this painting, Lord Cobham's family sit at table, eating dessert, with the family pets, a parrot and a monkey. Elizabethan dessert generally consisted of fruit – here apples, pears and grapes – nuts and wine.*

TUDOR BEAUTY *Eliza-beth Vernon comb-ing her hair, in a sumptuously em-broidered court dress. Elizabe-than fashions became so ex-travagant and changed so rapidly that the writer Fynes Moryson accused his countrymen of 'becoming more sump-tuous than the proudest Persians'.*

COUNTRY SCENES *Elaborate tapes-tries and embroidery enhanced the ostentatious display of Tudor life. A bed belonging to the Earl of Dorset, in which Queen Elizabeth slept, had cloth-of-gold hangings said to have cost £8000. A detail from the Bradford table carpet (above) and an embroidered cush-ion from the late 16th century (left) depict country scenes. Em-broidered rugs and carpets were frequently used as table coverings.*

COURT MUSIC *At every level of society, people in Tudor England loved music, and under Henry VIII, a composer himself, the court came to be its leading patron. Here, in an illustration from Henry's own psalter, musicians are seen playing a pipe and tabor (drum), harp and virginal.*

A ROYAL MUSICIAN *Henry VIII created a fashion at court for composing musical tunes and setting verses to them. Although music was considered an essential part of an upper-class education, performances were only given in private. If a gentleman plays 'in a common audience', Sir Thomas Elyot wrote in his book on etiquette, 'it impairs his estimation, the people forgetting reverence when they behold him in the similitude of a common servant or minstrel'.*

115

A flag and a cross – and Britain's empire begins

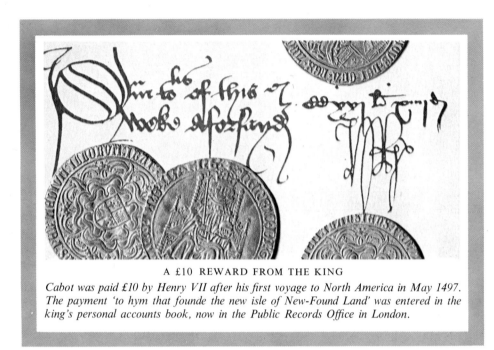

A £10 REWARD FROM THE KING

Cabot was paid £10 by Henry VII after his first voyage to North America in May 1497. The payment 'to hym that founde the new isle of New-Found Land' was entered in the king's personal accounts book, now in the Public Records Office in London.

In May 1497, five years after Christopher Columbus discovered the New World, a small ship, the *Mathew*, sailed west out of Bristol. Its captain, a Venetian named John Cabot, had arrived in England a few years before in search of support for voyages of exploration.

Cabot believed like Columbus that the route to the spice-rich islands of Asia lay westwards, and Columbus's discoveries seemed to confirm this theory. For when the Genoese explorer made his landfall, he was convinced that he had reached some barbaric islands off the coast of Asia. He did not realise that he had reached a new continent.

Across the Atlantic

Cabot promised his patron, Henry VII, that he would find new ocean routes to Cipangu (Japan) and Cathay (China). Henry, prepared to do anything that might further his nation's prosperity, had already considered enlisting Columbus himself in England's commercial interests. When Cabot appeared with his own promises, and with the resources of Bristol's experienced seamen behind him, Henry took up this offer. He granted Cabot and his sons a licence to travel north, east or west across the Atlantic Ocean.

Because of her shipping industry, Bristol had been one of England's richest towns for over 300 years. She exported leather and cloth to Europe. Fish, coal and iron were sent up the River Severn to the Midlands. Into Bristol came wine and silks from the Continent, tin

from Cornwall and fish from Iceland. Cabot had no difficulty in persuading Bristol's merchants to back his search for new riches.

So Cabot, with his one ship and 20 men, left Bristol in the early summer. He sailed to the south-western corner of Ireland, and then headed due west across the Atlantic. He made

land after 35 days – the first seafarer to cross the northern Atlantic since the Vikings in the early 11th century. But the details of his landing in the first English venture to North America are vague. No written account of the voyage survives. Cabot himself called the land that he sighted 'New-Found Land'; but it may have been Nova Scotia, somewhat to the south of Newfoundland.

Rewarded by the king

Having planted the royal standard and a crucifix, Cabot explored the coast for a month, noting the great forests of trees suitable for masts, and the 'infinite quantity of fish' in the sea. He then sailed for home and, having made a remarkably quick return passage in 15 days, he was back in Bristol by August 6, 1497.

Cabot believed that he had discovered the northern coasts of Asia, and promised that, by sailing further to the south-west, he would be able to reach China and the 'Spice Islands'. No one doubted him, and he received a hero's welcome. In London he was dubbed 'The Great Admiral', wore fine silk clothes and was followed everywhere by an admiring throng. Henry VII rewarded his daring in a more practical manner, giving him £10, a pension of £20 a year, and – most welcome of all – an assurance of a bigger fleet for a second voyage in the spring.

In May of the following year, Cabot sailed again, this time with five ships. He reached the east coast of Greenland in early June and named it Labrador's Land. As he sailed along the coast, looking for a passage, the cold grew intense and the icebergs bigger. On June 11 the crews refused to go on and Cabot had to put his ships about. He then explored Greenland's south coast and part of the west coast; but ice again blocked his path and he set a course to the west. He mistook Baffin Island for the Asiatic mainland and headed southwards, hoping to find Cipangu. In the end, he had to abandon the search because of shortage of stores. Cabot arrived back in England in the late autumn and died soon afterwards.

But Cabot had lit a slow-burning fuse. In 1502 a further expedition to his 'New-Found Land' brought back three men who were 'clothed in beasts' skins and ate raw flesh and spake such speech that no man could understand them'. These were the first Eskimoes to reach the civilised world. Then in 1509 John Cabot's son, Sebastian, set off to find a north-western passage to Asia, and reached what was later to be called Hudson Bay. Sebastian was a skilled navigator, confident both of his own abilities and the prospects for success. But the merchants who risked their money in financing these voyages wanted results. No man had yet sailed west and returned with the spices and riches of the Asian mainland.

A renewed challenge

When Sebastian returned, he found little enthusiasm and, worse, Henry VII had died. His son, Henry VIII, was more interested in war than discovery. Sebastian made for Spain, to seek new chances there.

For many years, English exploration lacked leadership and money. What ultimately returned England to the forefront of maritime enterprise was not that love of the unknown that meanwhile inspired her European neighbours: it was a simple desire for trade and

profit. From the middle of the century, when Europe's traditional economy began to fall apart, the old trades and markets collapsed. New ones had to be found in their place. The New World beckoned.

Sebastian Cabot returned to England in 1548. He himself had retired from active exploration, but was soon employed again by the Tudors to supervise the maritime affairs of their kingdom. He was the inspiration behind a new generation of explorers, working with a new breed of merchants. Together, they carried out the great feats of exploration that made the famous names of English discovery – such as Willoughby, Frobisher, Gilbert, Chancellor, all of whom searched for the fabled north-west passage from the Atlantic to the Pacific. To the merchant ready to take the risk, the lure of profits was potent: backed by a charter from the crown, he could invest a sum and hope for it to be returned a hundredfold. The sober merchant and the daring explorer together began the task of opening up the corners of the globe to English enterprise.

FAMILY AFFAIR *John Cabot and his three sons, Lewis, Sebastian and Santius, received royal authority in March 1496 'to seeke out, discover and finde isles, countries, regions or provinces of the heathens and infidels'. In return, Henry VII demanded one-fifth of the profits. A Victorian painting (left) shows John and Sebastian's departure from the quayside at Bristol. The contemporary map (above) shows the Cabots' transatlantic voyages to the New World.*

Henry VII: His thrift filled England's purse

Henry VII (left) was the first businessman to become King of England. For his virtues were not romantic or chivalrous; they were the lack-lustre ones of industry, patience and diplomacy. And they brought him success in bringing peace to the battle-scarred kingdom he now ruled.

Henry VII was too busy to be a dashing and romantic figure. He had determined to establish the Tudor dynasty and to lead the national recovery after the chaotic and depressed years of civil war. And for that great work Henry chose to wear a mask of inhumanity. He made himself remote and aloof in order to be more feared than loved; generosity might be taken for weakness.

Henry's early years hardened him to a life of struggle, and even after he gained the crown at Bosworth Field in 1485 his troubles were by no means over. He had to contend with Yorkist conspiracies such as the attempt to pass off Perkin Warbeck as Richard of York, the younger of the princes in the Tower. Only in 1506, when he arrested the Earl of Suffolk, the last surviving claimant to the throne, could he feel secure.

Henry's achievement in government was remarkable, if not spectacular. He rescued the crown from bankruptcy and avoided war. He raised the income from crown lands by 40 per cent. When he acquired the crown it was in debt; at his death in 1509 it showed a healthy credit balance.

Not that Henry was a miser. Behind the public mask was a king whose pleasures were varied and luxurious. He paid for a leopard for the Tower menagerie, and in a burst of extravagance 'to John van Delf, for garnishing of a salad £38 1s 4d'. Though he married Elizabeth of York for political reasons, he took pains to console her on the death of their eldest son, Prince Arthur, in 1502.

Under Henry, the country laid the foundations of future Tudor strength. Efficient and continuous government released the nation's energies to create wealth. Ocean-going ships and great houses were built. The wool and cloth industries prospered. Already, by 1497, the Venetian ambassador was impressed. 'In one single street, named the Strand, leading to St Paul's,' he reported, 'there are 52 goldsmiths' shops, so rich and full of silver vessels, great and small, that in all the shops of Milan, Rome, Venice and Florence together, I do not think there would be found so many of the magnificence that is to be seen in London.'

A HOUSE BUILT TO CELEBRATE THE JOYS OF A LAND AT PEACE

Waking from the long nightmare of the Wars of the Roses, England found prosperity and civil peace – and an enchanting style of architecture to match the mood of the age. During centuries of intense faith and constant threats of war, the genius of British architecture had been devoted to the building of invincible castles and soaring cathedrals. Now, in a more settled and secular age, the skill of the finest craftsmen was poured into a new art form: the making of beautiful houses.

Nowhere in England is more expressive of this new mood than Compton Wynyates, the romantic moated manor which took shape in a remote Warwickshire valley under the first two Tudor kings. It was the creation of two generations – the generations in which England moved into a new era.

Comptons had already lived at Compton Wynyates for 300 years, when Edmund Compton inherited the property in 1481. He married an heiress and soon started to rebuild his manor house, using brick rather than local stone – an expensive choice in the 15th century. It was he who gave the house its basic structure of the Big Hall and the four wings encircling a central courtyard. He retained the medieval moat around most of the house and built a second moat with drawbridge and portcullis at the western entrance.

The outside walls of Edmund's great house were 4 ft thick, built for strength in an age when most men had vivid memories of siege warfare. But the scores of wide windows, with their glittering diamond panes, expressed the builder's confidence in a more peaceful age.

Friendship with a king

Edmund died shortly after the building was completed. His son, William, was only 11 years old. But Henry VII took the boy under his protection, appointing him page to two-year-old Prince Henry, the charming and promising child who was to become Henry VIII.

In spite of the difference in their ages, the two boys became close friends. When Henry came to the throne in 1509 he made his friend the First Gentleman of the Bedchamber. During the first carefree years of Henry's reign, the two young men were constant companions. A courtier recorded that they would often challenge all comers 'with spear at the tilt one day, and at tourney with swords the other'.

They were comrades on the battlefield too. Their friendship was crowned in 1512 on the steps of the cathedral of Tournai in France, when the king knighted William for his gallantry at the Battle of Tournai. The young squire of Compton Wynyates was also granted the exceptional privilege of adding the Royal Lion of England to his coat of arms.

The king was a frequent visitor to his friend's home. The bedchamber which was made ready for Henry and Catharine of Aragon was simple and comfortable. Its diamond-paned windows overlooked the tranquil inner courtyard. Warm rugs and tapestries decorated the floors and walls.

On the ceiling, and set into a window, were the arms and insignia of Castile and Aragon. When Elizabeth I, James I and Charles I stayed at the house, their crests were added.

In the years that William Compton was making his house fit for a king, he added the richly decorated chapel, the entrance porch, the towers and the splendid roof of the Big Hall. He also embellished the house with beautiful bay windows and stained glass.

Like his father, William showed little interest in formal architecture. The house grew as convenience demanded, sprouting gables of

TUDOR LEGACY *Virtually unchanged since Tudor times, Compton Wynyates nestles among the hills of Warwickshire. It has belonged to the Compton family, in the direct male line, since the beginning of the 13th century. The present building is almost entirely the work of a father and son, Edmund and William Compton, who rebuilt the house during the reigns of two kings – Henry VII and Henry VIII.*

unequal height, turrets of differing shapes and more than 40 twisted chimneys. There was no hint of the Classic style which was soon to influence English building.

During these years of busy building at Compton Wynyates, honours and lucrative appointments were showered on Sir William Compton. In 1527 he was given the unusual privilege of wearing his hat in the king's presence. But the following year, at the age of 46, he died of fever.

Conflict of loyalties

Perhaps it was as well that William did not live into the years of his royal friend's tyranny and the breach with Rome. For by tradition the Comptons were as loyal to the Catholic Church as they were to the crown.

In the age of Elizabeth the family walked a tightrope of conflicting loyalties, but the queen made Henry Compton a baron. On August 26, 1572, Elizabeth arrived to stay at Compton Wynyates for a few days, and her chief minister, Lord Burghley, expressed satisfaction with all the arrangements. 'Surely, the entertainment is very great,' he wrote.

At the same time, the family remained faithful to Catholicism and sheltered many priests and Jesuits. The priest's room had three escape staircases, two leading to spacious hiding places, and the third to a council chamber with six exits.

Elizabeth showed her concern for the family towards the end of her long reign when she smoothed the troubled romance of William, the second Lord Compton. One of London's richest merchants, Sir John Spencer, objected to William as a husband for his daughter, Elizabeth. But the suitor smuggled the girl from her father's house in Canonbury, hidden in a baker's basket. The queen calmed Sir John's ruffled feelings. When the first child of the marriage was born, she even persuaded him to join her as a godparent.

A family at war

The many secret stairs, passages and small chambers of Compton Wynyates again proved of great importance in the Civil War, when it became a centre for wounded Royalist soldiers. Even when it was occupied by the Roundheads in 1644, Royalist troops remained securely hidden in secret corners, fed and cared for by the family.

After they were driven from their house by the Roundheads, the Comptons made an attempt to recapture it. If they failed to press home their attack, it was because they knew that even its thick walls could not withstand cannon balls and they were loath to bring down their treasured inheritance.

Instead they were forced into exile, returning to England only with the restoration of the monarchy. Compton Wynyates, now their home again, stood unchanged – a Tudor masterpiece preserved against the ravages of war.

SHELTERED SECLUSION *The courtyard at Compton Wynyates, mellow with old brick, has the atmosphere of a college quadrangle.*

TUDOR SPLENDOUR *Medieval in spirit, the Big Hall gains a feeling of Tudor ease and comfort from its windows and carved panelling.*

ROYAL BEDCHAMBER *Henry VIII and Queen Catharine of Aragon stayed in this bedroom when they visited William Compton. Their arms are displayed in the bedroom with those of Elizabeth I, James I and Charles I, who all slept here during visits to Compton Wynyates.*

FIT FOR A KING *The Compton family tradition was strictly royalist, and William Compton's friendship with Henry VIII lasted until William's death in 1528. Henry let him emblazon the royal arms over the house's entrance porch (above) with the loyal inscription 'The House of Henry VIII'.*

The young Henry's pomp and pageantry dazzle Europe

GIFT FOR A KING

This finely wrought combined clock and salt cellar, made of silver gilt, is believed to have been a gift from Francis I of France to Henry VIII. It formed part of the Tudor treasure, and can be seen in the Goldsmiths' Hall in London.

A French author glowingly described the Field of the Cloth of Gold, when the young kings of France and England met in the Val d'Orée at Ardres in the summer of 1520, in the following words: 'Banquets and feasts lavish enough for the celestial court itself. Pavilions, exceeding the miraculous pyramids of Egypt or the amphitheatres of Rome.' That meeting was certainly the most spectacular event in the reign of Henry VIII.

The 29-year-old Henry had been on the throne 11 years. Strong, virile, handsome and widely accomplished, he was in his prime and acclaimed by many as an Apollo among princes. He could sing and play on both the lute and the virginal; he was a brilliant horseman and a fine performer in tournaments with two-handed sword and battle-axe. He drew a good bow and excelled at tennis. During the early years of his reign, court entertainments were frequent and lavish.

The young king's claim that he could out-dance, out-drink and out-hunt any of his courtiers was no mere boast. Yet he also enjoyed the company of scholars, was interested in art, music (being himself something of a composer) and poetry, and had a high reputation in theological debate. The only attribute this paragon among Renaissance princes apparently lacked was an enthusiasm for the routine work of government.

Meeting of two kings

Fortunately he was relieved of this by the industry and enterprise of his Lord Chancellor, Thomas Wolsey. Allegedly the son of an Ipswich butcher, this shrewd, vain and worldly wise priest had risen rapidly in the royal service. He collected offices in Church and state until, by 1520, he was Lord Chancellor, Archbishop of York, papal legate, a cardinal of the Roman Church and the most powerful man in England after the king.

Wolsey shared his master's love of pomp and ceremony. He alone was responsible for the diplomatic extravaganza in the Val d'Orée.

GOLDEN KING *The young Henry VIII's flamboyance won him admiration. But he outlived his promise and sank into a tyrannical old age.*

FRENCH KING *Francis I met Henry VIII for the first time in 1520 at the Field of the Cloth of Gold. Both shared a love of hunting and tournaments, both were vain and extravagant and both of them died in 1547.*

He had two aims: to dazzle the French with a display of English magnificence and to draw the two kings into an alliance. One sour contemporary suggested that the cardinal had a third, overriding, motive: 'He longed like a peacock to display his many-coloured tail in the land of France.'

Wolsey threw himself into every detail of the preparations. Each of the 5800 people in the English royal entourage was selected with care. Elaborate arrangements were needed to carry them to France in comfort and to accommodate them there, together with their 3223 horses. A total of 340 beef cattle, 2200 sheep, 800 calves, 160,000 litres of beer and 125,000 litres of wine were requisitioned and transported to the site. Some 2000 craftsmen set to work constructing cunningly conceived palaces, banqueting chambers and chapels out of timber, glass and canvas. These buildings were decorated with hangings of tapestry and embroidered cloth, and gilded statues and fountains gushing wine made ostentatious display of English ingenuity and wealth.

The events of the festive fortnight began on June 7, when Henry VIII and Francis I of France met in the middle of the valley for the first time. The theme of the festivities that

MEMORABLE MEETING *Cardinal Wolsey organised the meeting of Henry VIII and Francis I at the Field of the Cloth of Gold to ally England and France. This 'narrative picture' shows Henry and Wolsey arriving (left) and the two kings meeting alone in Francis's tent (top).*

Henry VIII: Dominated by passion and power

Henry VIII was a man quick to become infatuated, and quick to become displeased. But the turmoil of his marital life owed more to dynastic needs than to passion.

His greatest concern was to produce a male heir to the throne. Catharine of Aragon, his righteous and patient first wife, only bore him a daughter, Mary. And, in 1527, Henry fell in love with the coy and flirtatious Anne Boleyn. For her he divorced Catharine and broke with the Roman Catholic Church. But this revolution was in vain. Anne Boleyn, too, failed to give him the son he craved. She lost the king's favour, was put on trial for adultery and witchcraft and was beheaded.

Her successor was a simple and shy Wiltshire girl, Jane Seymour. Hers was the greatest tragedy of all. Henry loved her deeply and she bore him the future Edward VI. But the ordeal of Edward's birth killed her, and the grieving king allowed his advisers to arrange a diplomatic marriage with Anne of Cleves. She was wed in haste and as quickly abandoned.

The fifth wife, Catharine Howard, was the most unjustly treated. She was beheaded in 1542 for adultery – a crime of which Henry was hardly innocent. But his sixth and last wife, Catharine Parr, survived when others more beautiful had fallen. She tended the ailing king until his death in 1547.

DIVORCED *Catharine of Aragon (1533).*

EXECUTED *Anne Boleyn (1536).*

DIED *Jane Seymour, after childbirth (1537).*

DIVORCED *Anne of Cleves (1540).*

EXECUTED *Catharine Howard (1542).*

SURVIVOR *Catharine Parr, died (1548).*

---

followed was the Feat of Arms, a series of almost daily engagements in which the two sovereigns and their nobles competed in tournaments and joustings before their ladies. No one participated more enthusiastically than Henry. The chronicler Edward Hall noted: 'The King of England this day ran so freshly and so many courses that one of his best coursers was dead that night.'

After dark there were feasts, followed by dancing and masques. The two kings often took part in the masques, which involved dressing in sumptuous gowns and masks, performing elaborate charades and, still disguised, dancing and flirting with lady guests before finally unmasking. At one such masque Henry appeared dressed in a cloth-of-gold gown lined with green taffeta, decorated with silver points. He had a false beard of fine gold wire.

On the final Saturday, Wolsey himself, assisted by other princes of the Church, said Mass in a chapel, 'richly behanged and garnished with divers saints and relics'. It is said that he was rather out of practice in his ecclesiastical duties, not having said a Mass for several years. But all passed off well and the holy occasion was enlivened by the appearance of a firework in the sky shaped like the dragon of Wales.

The monarchs said their farewells on June 24. The gorgeous palaces were dismantled. The 2800 richly draped tents that had housed the English nobility and gentry were struck. But the tangible results were not what Wolsey had hoped for. Francis's entourage had matched the splendour of the English contingent. The diplomatic achievement of the meeting was minimal: a treaty of friendship, with Henry's daughter, Mary, betrothed to the Dauphin as a seal of that treaty. Though the two kings swore eternal friendship, they parted in a mood of mutual suspicion.

Henry's irresistible will

Wolsey's elaborate and costly scheme to bring about a French alliance foundered on the rock of Henry's irresistible will. For the king's character was changing. Pressed by Wolsey to conclude a French alliance and by his wife, Catharine of Aragon, to make a treaty with her nephew, Charles V of Spain, Henry determined to make his own judgment.

What had previously passed for playful stubbornness was now revealing itself as indomitable wilfulness. The ruddy-cheeked boisterousness of youth was giving way to an early bloated, irascible middle age. The king was soon to show himself capable of ruthlessness and tyranny. Both Wolsey and Catharine would be broken by Henry's cruelty – and there would be many others.

The first signs of this profound change were seen immediately after Henry VIII left Guisnes. He rode straight to the Flemish town of Gravelines. There he met Charles V and, in surroundings far more modest than those of the Val d'Orée, he negotiated an Anglo-Spanish agreement which largely annulled the French treaty that Wolsey had striven to bring about at the Field of the Cloth of Gold.

THE 'PROUD PRELATE' BUILDS A PALACE FIT FOR A KING

The most sumptuous palace of Tudor England was built not for a monarch but for a subject – Cardinal Thomas Wolsey, the man who ruled both king and kingdom.

Rivalling his sovereign in wealth, and haughtier by far, Wolsey used the revenues from the appointments he amassed to satisfy his passion for building on an unprecedented scale. Hampton Court is the legacy of this Renaissance prince of the Church. Its creation and its later history illustrate the realities of power in the Tudor state, and the unhappy fate that awaited even the mightiest subject who forfeited the king's favour.

Thomas Wolsey, son of an Ipswich butcher, emerged from obscurity to become Lord Chancellor and, at the age of 41, cardinal. By then he controlled the reins of government of both Church and state.

A man totally devoted to power, he knew that success, in his age, depended on display. Appearances were everything; the man who seemed most powerful would command the most obedience. Wolsey rode on a mule to emphasise his humility, but the saddle was of crimson velvet and the stirrups of pure gold. When, in 1514, he wanted to build a country house, it had to be a palace on a scale never attempted in England.

Wolsey took great pains with the design. His master mason, Henry Redman, received detailed instructions which he passed on to the 2500 workmen. Every wall, every ceiling and every archway was embellished.

Hampton Court was a unique advertisement for Wolsey's wealth and power. It had 1000 rooms, and the cardinal was reputed to have given particular orders for the decoration of each one of them.

The great work was completed in the astonishingly short period of five years. By 1520 the 2500 workmen had been replaced by an army of servants who wore Wolsey's crimson velvet livery. The 280 silken beds were prepared. The cardinal was ready to receive his guests.

Naturally they were overawed. The French ambassador, who was entertained at Hampton with his retinue of 400 attendants, reported that 'the very bed-chambers had hangings of wonderful value and every place did glitter with innumerable vessels of gold and silver'.

Wolsey's supreme sacrifice

But in winning the admiration of the world the cardinal alienated the one man he could not afford to offend. Henry VIII was a frequent guest at the new palace, and Wolsey's compulsive displays of vanity filled him with resentment and jealousy.

Although Wolsey gloried in his achievement at Hampton, power was still his first love. When he understood Henry's feelings, he made the supreme sacrifice. To retain Henry's favour, he presented him in 1525 with Hampton Court, with all its furnishings and plate. It was the most magnificent gift ever made by a subject, and it broke Wolsey's heart.

The gesture, as it turned out, postponed Wolsey's fall, but could not save him. In November 1530, already mortally ill, he was arrested for treason at his palace near York. He died at Leicester Abbey on his way back to London for trial at Westminster.

PROUD PRELATE *The arms of Cardinal Wolsey are surmounted by his cardinal's hat. Wolsey built Hampton Court to rival the splendour of the palaces of his master, Henry VIII.*

Henry, meanwhile, was making the palace even more sumptuous than Wolsey had envisaged. He added new wings and courtyards together with tennis courts, bowling alleys and a tiltyard for jousting. But his most ostentatious creation was the Great Hall, with its elaborately carved roof and musicians' gallery.

Hampton Court was now to provide a stage for the tragic drama of Henry's long quest for a male heir. Craftsmen were once again busy at work, carving badges and coats of arms on towers, arches and ceilings. Some of Wolsey's carved cardinal's hats were replaced by the intertwined initials H and A, for Henry and Anne Boleyn. But within a few years Anne had gone to the Tower and the block.

It was at Hampton Court on October 12, 1537, that Jane Seymour, the third and best-loved of Henry's queens, gave birth to the long-awaited son, later Edward VI. But a fortnight later his mother died.

Hampton Court also witnessed the tragedy of Catharine Howard, Henry's fifth wife. Before she left for imprisonment in Syon House to await a state trial for adultery, she

TUDOR LUXURY *It took 2500 men five years to complete the original Hampton Court, at a cost of 200,000 gold crowns. It had 1000 rooms, with 280 silken beds kept always ready for visitors. Even the tapestries were changed once a week. Wolsey, who had a passion for hygiene,* incorporated 3 miles of lead pipes into the design to bring pure spring water from beyond the Thames. This 17th-century drawing shows some of the Tudor buildings which were demolished by Christopher Wren when he built the new state apartments for William III and Mary.

made a last desperate attempt to plead with her husband, who was at Mass. But the guards caught her at the chapel doors, and dragged her away, screaming. The king piously continued his devotions.

A Tudor survival

In later centuries people said they had seen a ghostly figure running towards the chapel and heard a woman's blood-chilling screams echoing down the empty corridors. Such unhappy hauntings and the pokey unfashionable Tudor rooms made the old palace unpopular.

Under William and Mary, Sir Christopher Wren was called in to build a new palace. He planned to demolish the whole of the Tudor palace to make way for 'improvements'. But William's death after a fall from his horse in the park put an end to Wren's hopes.

The threat passed, Hampton Court survived, and the centuries that followed have left no mark. Its flamboyant carvings and imposing gateways still bear witness to the rivalry of two of the proudest men in English history: the king and the Ipswich butcher's son.

Fall of the man who ruled king and kingdom

PROUD CARDINAL *For 17 years Thomas Wolsey dominated England's history as the principal minister to Henry VIII. He ruled 'both king and kingdom', wrote an ambassador.*

IN THE COLLEGE HE FOUNDED

Thomas Wolsey's personal missal, carefully illuminated and showing his coat of arms, can be seen at Christ Church College Library, Oxford. Wolsey's power and wealth made him 'the proudest prelate that ever breathed', according to one diplomat. He loved power and made bishops tie his shoelaces and dukes attend him when he washed his hands.

In November 1530 the magnificent Cardinal Thomas Wolsey lay dying. But his massive frame lay not in a great bed of state, surrounded by attendants, physicians and all the luxury to which he had long been accustomed. He had been banished from the court, stripped of his offices, his wealth and his estates, and now he lay in a simple chamber at Leicester Abbey. Had he lived a few weeks longer, he would have faced certain imprisonment and possible execution. The last words of this worldly priest revealed political as well as spiritual wisdom: 'If I had served God as diligently as I have done the king, He would not have given me over in my grey hairs.'

For 17 years Wolsey, a butcher's son, had stood at the centre of affairs in Church and state. After a long and faithful service, his king confiscated the greater part of his wealth, allowed his enemies to persecute him and permitted him to die disgraced.

Hatred at court

The hatreds and jealousies that inhabited the Tudor court brought down many great men, for all officials held power only as long as they held the king's favour. Wolsey not only enjoyed power and favour; he revelled in them. He amassed an enormous fortune, surrounded himself with luxury, lorded it over nobles, bishops and courtiers. And his magnificence made him widely unpopular. His enemies ranged from the Duke of Suffolk, who

remarked that 'the old saw is true that never a cardinal or legate did good in England', to the ballad-makers who composed popular songs against him. Wolsey's enemies on the Privy Council watched carefully for any breach between the king and the cardinal that they could turn to their advantage, but Henry realised Wolsey's value. He dismissed him only when the cardinal failed to secure an annulment by the pope of the king's marriage to Catharine of Aragon.

In the summer of 1527 Henry, desperately wanting to marry his mistress, Anne Boleyn, to have a male heir, decided to break with his wife. Wolsey as papal legate was called upon to arrange the necessary dispensation from Rome. But the king's divorce was not so easily arranged. The pope was in the power of the Holy Roman Emperor, Charles V, Catharine's nephew, and Church leaders at home and abroad opposed Henry's plan.

The negotiations meant that Wolsey was away from court for long periods, and this absence contributed to his ruin. He had underestimated Anne's power. She was at the centre of the plot to destroy him, seizing every opportunity to influence the king against the proud cardinal. After two years of negotiations had failed, Wolsey approached Henry at his hunting lodge of Grafton in Northamptonshire, and was received with 'amiable good cheer'. The cardinal's reception infuriated Anne. She told Henry over dinner: 'There is

never a nobleman within this realm, that if he had done but half as much as he had done, but he were well worthy to lose his head.'

At last the frustrated and angry king listened to the complaints brought against Wolsey by his eager enemies. In October 1529 the cardinal was accused in the Court of King's Bench of abusing his power as papal legate. Wolsey was found guilty and condemned to the loss of offices, lands and goods. Although these penalties were not enforced in full – he was allowed his liberty and restored to the Archbishopric of York – Wolsey was no longer papal legate nor Lord Chancellor.

The journey north

However, he still hoped to recover the favour of the king. 'I doubt not,' he told his servants, 'that the king ... will shortly restore me again to my livings.' But his opponents, who feared that his return to power would be followed by revenge upon themselves, demanded that Wolsey should be dispatched at once to his diocese of York, where he would be isolated from the court. 'Show him,' said the Duke of Norfolk, 'that if he go not away shortly, I will, rather than he should tarry still, tear him with my teeth.' In April, Wolsey left for his northern see.

As the cardinal made his uncomfortable journey northwards the king vacillated, sending tokens and messages of good will while at the same time seizing eagerly upon Wolsey's sumptuous gold plate and Flemish tapestries. When the Archbishop of York reached the diocese he had never seen – though he had been appointed to it 15 years before – he settled at Southwell Palace where, in spite of his loudly proclaimed poverty, 'he kept a noble house and plenty both of meat and drink for all comers'. In this, his vigilant

WEALTH, POWER AND GLORY *Wolsey revelled in power and lavish ostentation. His example greatly influenced the king, who grew to maturity under his guidance. In this contemporary illustration, the cardinal is seen riding in procession with his entourage.*

HUMILIATION AND SURRENDER *Stripped of his power Wolsey (seated) surrenders the Great Seal of England – the emblem of the Lord Chancellorship – to his enemies, the dukes of Norfolk and Suffolk. Wolsey broke down and cried when they produced the king's written order of dismissal. Only his death a year later saved him from the final disgrace of a public trial.*

enemies saw signs of renewed ambition. 'Some allege you keep too great a house,' warned Thomas Cromwell, his principal assistant who was later to become Henry's chief minister.

The warning was apt. As Wolsey moved towards York for his enthronement in November 1530, orders for his arrest and return to London were given. His grandiose progress, combined with the continued obstinacy of the pope, had enabled his enemies to stir the king to further action. Although Sir William Kingston, Constable of the Tower, who was sent to fetch Wolsey, insisted that the king bore him as much favour as ever, Wolsey was not deceived. 'All these comfortable words which ye have spoken be but for a purpose to bring me in a fool's paradise,' he observed.

The old man turned south, sick in his body and despairing in his soul. On reaching Leicester Abbey he had to be carried to his bed. He knew the end was near. 'By eight of the clock ye shall lose your master,' he told his attendant, George Cavendish. Just before 8 a.m. on the following morning he died. It was discovered that he had worn a hair shirt next to his skin under another of fine linen.

It was the end of an age. Wolsey was the last of the great princes of the Church who could manipulate the affairs of England. Henry VIII was creating a new order of society in which there would be no room for such a figure as Cardinal Wolsey. In the future, statesmen would only have loyalty – to the monarch they served.

Thomas Cromwell: The king's 'best servant'

The man who filled the vacuum left by Wolsey was not another churchman but a lawyer – Thomas Cromwell, son of a Putney blacksmith. After a wild youth, and a series of military adventures abroad, Cromwell became a solicitor and financial agent in London. By 1514 he had attracted Wolsey's notice and became his principal assistant.

Cromwell remained loyal to his master when he fell from power. But his abilities had won him Henry VIII's favour and he did not share in Wolsey's disgrace. After Wolsey fell, he was soon admitted to the Privy Council. There, he urged on the king a radical policy which would solve Henry's matrimonial problems.

All-powerful minister

Cromwell was the architect of the English Reformation. He drafted the statutes that brought about the breach with Rome, the annulment of Henry's marriage to Catharine of Aragon, the dissolution of the English monasteries and the transference of their wealth into the royal coffers. He steered the people towards Protestantism by sponsoring the translation and printing of the Bible.

As king's secretary and Lord Privy Seal, Cromwell was responsible for all government business. He was a tireless administrator. From his many agents at home and abroad a constant flow of reports poured in. Thanks to them, and to his favour with the king, he was able to direct every aspect of national affairs.

Yet, like Wolsey before him, Cromwell fell. In his years of power, Cromwell made many enemies. Some, like the Duke of Norfolk, hated him as an upstart. Others disliked his religious radicalism. Their chance to strike came in 1540 after he engineered the king's marriage with Anne of Cleves. When Henry met his bride he was repulsed by her plainness, and Cromwell knew he had blundered.

Fall from favour

In 1540 Cromwell was made Earl of Essex, but his days were numbered. His fate was sealed by the Duke of Norfolk, who arranged that his beautiful niece, Catharine Howard, should be Henry's fifth wife. On June 10, 1540, Cromwell was arrested.

From his room in the Tower he appealed to the king: 'What labours, pains and travails I have taken according to my most bounden duty God knoweth . . . As to your commonwealth, I have ever after my wit, power and knowledge travailed therein, having no respect to persons (your Majesty only excepted).' It availed him nothing. Thomas Cromwell was beheaded on the day that Henry VIII married Catharine Howard. But the king was soon to realise his mistake. Too late he lamented the loss of 'the best servant I ever had'.

The castle where a king was 'struck by the dart of love'

CASTLE OF COURTSHIP
Hever Castle in Kent satisfied two great loves of Henry's life. Not only could he woo Anne Boleyn in the secluded bay window of the long gallery, but he could also indulge his favourite sporting pastime of hunting and hawking with her. Henry demanded absolute security when on his countrywide travels, and a lock (right) – now at Hever – was carried by his entourage to be put on the door of the various royal bed-chambers.

TUDOR BEAUTY *Anne Boleyn's beauty was considered to be unconventional. It stemmed from her vitality, her huge black eyes and her hair which reached below her waist.*

ROYAL LOVERS *A 19th-century impression of the king courting Anne at Hever. Henry was often perplexed by her teasing replies to his love letters, which he often wrote in stilted French. Their courtship lasted six years.*

In the spring of 1527 extraordinary rumours were sweeping through Europe. Henry VIII of England, who six years before had been named Defender of the Faith by the pope for his attacks on Protestant heresy, was whispered to be on the point of defying the authority of Rome by divorcing his wife, Catharine of Aragon, for a new mistress, Anne Boleyn.

The rumours were well founded. Henry had ascended the throne 18 years earlier, a glorious youth heralding in a golden age. He had then taken Catharine, the widow of his elder brother, Arthur, as his wife. At first, the marriage had been blissfully happy, but, despite frequent pregnancies, the queen had failed to produce a male heir. Her only surviving child was a daughter, Mary.

As the queen grew plain, Henry began to look elsewhere for his pleasure. In 1519 one of Catharine's ladies-in-waiting, Elizabeth Blount, bore him a son. Two years later, Mary Boleyn, daughter of Thomas Boleyn, the lord of Hever Castle in Kent, became Henry's mistress. Rumour had it that this liaison also

resulted in the birth of a child. It was through Mary that Anne, too, came to court in 1522, and it was there that she first caught the eye of the king. But, on that occasion, her stay was to be short lived. She fell foul of the all-powerful Cardinal Wolsey, who had her banished. On hearing that he had described her as 'a foolish girl', Anne left for Hever vowing revenge on Wolsey for this insult.

Anne was soon in a position to make good her threats. For by 1526 Henry VIII was desperate to secure the succession. He had decided that his marriage to Catharine was a moral outrage. God was punishing him by withholding a son because Henry had married his brother's wife in defiance of the Bible.

A six-year courtship
It was at this moment that Anne returned to court. There, according to the contemporary historian George Cavendish, she soon 'flourished in great estimation and favour with the king'.

But, unlike her predecessors, Anne did not

quickly succumb to the royal charms and become Henry's mistress in her turn. Instead, her resistance brought about one of the most remarkable courtships in English history between monarch and subject.

Who was this girl who could so captivate England's king? Anne was no beauty in the conventional sense. But, with a dark charm that came from her Irish ancestry, she was a woman capable of arousing intense passion. Before the king, she had won other admirers – among whom were Henry Percy, heir to the Duke of Northumberland, and her cousin Thomas Wyatt, the best-known poet of the day. But once she had cast her spell on the king, other rivals had to withdraw – or risk death. The disappointed Wyatt wrote:

> There is written her fair neck round about
> Noli me tangere, *for Caesar's I am,*
> *And wild to hold, though I seem tame.*

The 18-year-old Anne was indeed 'wild to hold'. She confessed to her maid: 'I am resolved to have him – whatever may become of me.' Thus she rejected the advances of other suitors, an act which gave rise to Wyatt's *noli me tangere* (do not touch). But she was not prepared to give herself to Henry unless the king would give himself to her. And her deliberate aloofness made Henry insecure. In one of his love letters he wrote: 'I have been more than one year now struck by the dart of love, and being uncertain either of failure or of finding a place in your heart.'

For six long years, Henry was to court Anne in such terms. But Anne's unyielding determination to have all or nothing stood in the way of the king's passion. And his wife was equally determined to hold on to marriage and position.

Marriage – and the throne

Eventually, the king decided to act. Catharine was sent away from court and in May 1527 a commission was appointed to investigate the validity of her marriage. The next step was to apply to the pope for an annulment, leaving Henry free to marry Anne.

But the politics of Europe in the 1520's meant that the pope could not yield to Henry's wishes. For two years Wolsey negotiated, knowing that his fate depended on satisfactorily settling his master's 'great matter'. But for all his political agility, the wily cardinal could not find a way through the thickets of European diplomacy. In 1529 he was disgraced – and Anne had her long-awaited revenge.

Henry now embarked alone on the struggle to free himself from the pope's rule. This was to do more than bring him a new wife – it was to bring his country a new religion.

The king's desires were now common knowledge. The people murmured that their master was ruled by 'a common stewed whore'. But it made no difference. Catharine was ordered to give the royal jewels to Anne. At first the queen protested, telling Henry that she would not give them up 'to a person who is the scandal of Christendom and a disgrace to you'. Henry forced her to give way. Anne was made Marchioness of Pembroke, and given money, jewels and lands. Finally, towards the end of 1532, she yielded at last. Within weeks, she had conceived a child.

Pregnancy broke the deadlock, for Henry was determined that this heir should be legitimate. On January 25, 1533, he and Anne were secretly married by the Bishop of Lichfield – even though Henry was not to be formally freed from his first wife until May. But for Anne her royal courtship was over. And in her womb lay England's heir.

The 'wanton queen' meets a grim fate

Eight months after her marriage to Henry, Anne Boleyn went into labour at Greenwich on September 7, 1533. Despite astrologers' predictions that the child would be a boy, she gave birth to a healthy girl. The baby – destined to become England's greatest queen – was named Elizabeth after her grandmother.

The mishap did not at first weaken Anne's hold on Henry's affections. The next time, she would surely produce the male heir that he so ardently desired. But two years passed and, as Henry's impatience grew, Anne's many enemies began to plot her downfall. But their hopes were dashed when, in the autumn of 1535, she became pregnant again.

Doomed by her loss of favour

But in the New Year, two disasters took place that were to doom Henry's young wife. In January 1536, Catharine of Aragon died. Henry callously celebrated this by a round of festivities but, in a moment of insight, Anne realised how vulnerable she now was: 'I am her death, she is mine.' In the eyes of Catholic Europe, Henry was now a widower and free to marry again. Anne could not afford to disappoint him a second time.

On the day of Catharine's funeral, Henry was injured while jousting and was unconscious for two hours. When the news was broken to Anne she miscarried a three-and-a-half month old foetus 'which had the appearance of a male'.

Henry did not mince his words: he had 'been seduced by witchcraft and for this reason considered it (his marriage) void'. But the king's attentions had begun to wander even while Anne was carrying Elizabeth. And

during her second pregnancy, Henry left her in London, while he visited Sir John Seymour at Wolf Hall, Wiltshire. There the king fell in love with Seymour's daughter, the quiet, modest Jane. Tired of Anne's tempestuous jealousies and passions, the king decided to rid himself of her and marry Jane.

Once Henry had decided on this, Anne's downfall was swift and merciless. On April 24, 1536, her uncle, the Duke of Norfolk, was appointed to head a commission to find evidence against her. Most of this was manufactured by Thomas Cromwell, who had succeeded Wolsey as Henry's chief adviser. The most damning testimony was that of Mark Smeaton, a court musician. Under torture, he confessed to adultery with the queen and was sent to the Tower. He was followed by four leading courtiers – Henry Norris, Francis Weston, William Brereton and Anne's own brother, George. All of them protested their innocence. The next step was to arrest Anne herself. Henry was now adamant in his belief that Anne was a nymphomaniac, with more than 1000 lovers. And he also accused her of witchcraft. Despite their protestations, Anne and her five alleged lovers were condemned to death. At her trial in Westminster Hall, Anne defended herself bravely. Henry himself commented: 'She has a stout heart, but she shall pay for it.'

On May 19, Anne went to the scaffold on Tower Green with calmness and dignity. To the end, she protested her innocence. In her last letter to Henry, written just before her execution, she declared: 'To speak a truth, never a prince had a wife more loyal in all duty and in all affection than you have ever found in Anne Boleyn.'

BEHIND THE QUEEN *Anne Boleyn's family were quick to abandon her at her fall. Her father, Sir Thomas Boleyn (above), used her to gain power and wealth. Her uncle, the Duke of Norfolk (right), helped to try her.*

The king's truest friend meets a martyr's death

RELIC OF A MARTYR

The 'George', a gold pendant depicting St George slaying the dragon, is reputed to have been a gift to Sir Thomas More from his friend and fellow-scholar, Erasmus. Erasmus often visited More's house in Chelsea, which he called a 'Plato's Academy'. The reverse side of the pendant has a picture of Christ seated on a tomb. The pendant can be seen, with other More relics, at Stonyhurst College in Blackburn, Lancashire.

Illness made the prisoner look older than his 57 years. Slumped in a large chair, his shabby cloak drawn around him against the draughts that raced through the lofty hall, he listened as the sentence was read out:

'Our sentence is that Thomas More shall
be taken from this place by William
Kingston, the Constable, to the Tower
and thence shall be hanged, cut down
while yet alive, ripped up, his bowels
burned in his sight, his head cut off,
his body quartered and the parts set
up in such places as the King shall
designate.'

Thus the sharpest wit and the liveliest mind that graced the court of Henry VIII was condemned to a barbarous death. His humiliation was still not over. For some minutes he had to endure the taunts and reproaches of his judges – men who had once been his colleagues on the king's Privy Council. More's final words to his accusers were restrained and well considered:

'In this world there will ever be discord,
and variety of opinion. But I trust
that as Paul persecuted Stephen even to
death and yet both are now united in
heaven, so we too who are now at
variance in this world and differ in our
opinions, may be one in heart and mind
for ever in the world to come. In
this hope I pray to God to preserve you

all, and especially my lord the King,
and to deign always to send him faithful
counsellors.'

Thomas More, the leading scholar of his day, was educated at Oxford and the Inns of Court. He became a Member of Parliament and then a member of the Privy Council. He soon became a close companion of the king. Henry, like most of his contemporaries,

COURAGE AND WIT *Jestingly, More told the headsman that he would never 'get any credit' for beheading him for his neck was 'so short'.*

VTOPIAE INSVLAE FIGVRA

A map of Utopia, drawn for the 1516 first edition.

UTOPIA – AN IDEAL WORLD

Thomas More believed that an ideal world would have no wars, poverty, crime, injustice or any other ills. He created such a place in his political romance, *Utopia*, which, after its publication in 1516, soon became a best-seller of its day and won its author a European reputation. The book was praised by the Dutch philosopher Erasmus, the leading scholar of the day and a personal friend of More.

Tudor England served as the model for many of More's strictures. He criticised the greed of the rich, the poverty of the lower classes, the readiness of kings to make war and the harshness of laws under which petty theft was punished by death. In More's imaginary island of Utopia, everyone had an equal stake in wealth, food and property. The working day was limited to six hours and leisure time devoted to the study of the arts, literature and science. Every child was entitled to a comprehensive education; fighting was permitted only in self-defence; law-breakers were condemned to slavery until they promised to reform. The king was elected for life and could be removed if guilty of tyranny.

THE FAMILY MAN *More with his eldest daughter, Margaret, when she visited him shortly before his death. During his long months of imprisonment More's family pleaded with him to give in to the king's demands. When he refused they petitioned Henry for his pardon and release. But the king refused their pleas.*

found More's wit and honesty refreshing.

But More's most outstanding characteristic – and the one that eventually brought him to his death – was his complete intellectual independence. He followed his conscience. Once, he ran foul of Wolsey in the council chamber because he eloquently swayed the council away from the cardinal's policy. The enraged Wolsey dismissed the young lawyer as 'a stupid and foolish councillor'. 'Thanks be to God,' rejoined More instantly, 'that the King's Majesty has but one fool in his council.' More saw in Wolsey all that was decadent in the Church and he worked as hard as any for the cardinal's overthrow.

Torn by his conscience

On Wolsey's downfall in 1529, More was awarded the office of Lord Chancellor, and a brilliant political career lay before him. But already there were clouds on the horizon. More could not reconcile himself to the annulment of Henry's marriage to his first wife, Catharine. While he welcomed ecclesiastical reform, he was firm in his loyalty to the pope.

By 1532 More had come to realise that the king was unshakably set on a course that he could not follow. Henry's determination to gain supreme power over Church as well as state filled him with foreboding: 'If a lion knew his own strength,' he warned Cromwell, 'hard were it for any man to rule him.'

Shortly after this, More resigned his office of Chancellor and retired into private life so that he 'might continually remember the immortality of the life to come'. He was no crusader and he hoped to be freed from any

further political involvement. Now he was able to enjoy the company of his own family more than he had done during his years in office. At his house in Chelsea there was a large household – his wife, his four daughters and their husbands, his 11 grandchildren and sundry pets, for More was fond of animals. Erasmus, the great Dutch scholar and a close friend of More's, wrote of the household:

'In it is none, man or woman, but readeth or studieth the liberal arts. Yet is their chief care of piety. There is never any seen idle. The head of the house governs it, not by lofty carriage and frequent rebukes, but by gentleness and amiable manners.'

A battle of wills

But More was not to be left in peace. Henry wanted his active support and refused to tolerate such detachment. In April 1534 More was ordered to swear the Oath of Succession, declaring that Elizabeth (the king's daughter by Anne Boleyn) was heir to the throne. He refused to do so and was sent to the Tower.

The tide of the Reformation rolled on. Henry was proclaimed Supreme Head of the Church in England and, the following spring, More was required to take the Oath of Supremacy. The king had resolved on a trial of wills. When More remained adamant, Henry determined that he should die. On July 1, 1535, More was brought to Westminster Hall to face his trial for high treason.

He knew what to expect. Perjured testimony, exaggerated evidence, groundless accusations – all the stock-in trade of Tudor state trials was brought against him. Though much weakened by his long spell in the Tower, he answered carefully, clearly and unemotionally every point argued against him. His accusers pointed out that only More refused to agree to a policy accepted by all the bishops and nobles of the realm. More's reply was unequivocal: 'For one bishop whom you may produce for your side, I will bring forth a hundred saintly and orthodox prelates who subscribe to my opinion: for your one Parliament, and God knows of what sort it is, I have on my side all the councils that have been held in the whole Christian world for more than a thousand years: and for your one kingdom of England I have with me all the kingdoms of Christianity.'

More's eloquence could not save him from his fate, but the king was 'pleased of his clemency' to change the sentence to one of simple beheading.

On July 6, 1535, Thomas More was taken out for his execution on Tower Hill. Few men have faced death with greater composure. He even jested as he approached the scaffold steps: 'I pray thee see me safely up,' he said to the Constable of the Tower, 'and for my coming down let me shift for myself.' After praying aloud that God would send the king good council, he laid his head on the block and signalled the headsman to strike.

Henry's pride gives England a new Church

The English Reformation was in part a popular religious movement and in part a political manoeuvre. Throughout the country there was widespread dissatisfaction with the leaders of the Church – their wealth, their greed, their immorality, their abuses of power and privilege. This discontent was fanned by reformers such as William Tyndale, who wrote pamphlets supporting the supremacy of king and Bible over pope and church.

England's breach with Rome was brought to a head by the king's 'great matter' – his wish for a divorce and a male heir. When Henry failed to obtain an annulment of his marriage to Catharine of Aragon from the pope he determined to have the case decided by an English court. The rejection of this claim by the pope and by many English churchmen served only to make Henry more determined to have his way.

Henry's first move was to take his case to the House of Commons. The MPs drew up a list of complaints against ecclesiastical courts and clerical abuses, and Henry promised a parliamentary deputation that action would be taken. 'We thought,' he said, 'that the clergy of our realm had been our subjects wholly, but now we have well perceived that they be but half our subjects, yea, and scarce our subjects.' The bishops were forced to give up their opposition to his plans. Having cowed the clergy, Henry had opened the path to complete independence from Rome.

The breach with Rome

In 1533 Parliament passed the central statute of Henry's Reformation – the Act of Appeals. Beginning with the resounding claim that 'this realm of England is an empire', the Act asserted the total independence of England from the pope's jurisdiction. The following year, Parliament proceeded to strip the papacy of its other rights: papal taxes were allocated to the crown; the appointment of bishops was taken over by the king. By the Act of Supremacy the king was made 'Supreme Head' of the Church of England.

By this time Henry had divorced his first wife and married Anne Boleyn. In 1533 she presented him with a daughter, who was named Elizabeth. An Act of Succession was now passed declaring the child to be the legal heir to the throne, thus bastardising Henry's elder daughter, Mary. All prominent men in Church and state were required to swear on oath to support the succession and to reject the authority of the 'Bishop of Rome' to interfere in such matters. A few men, like Thomas More, were unable to take the oath and suffered accordingly. They died as martyrs – but nothing could stand in the way of Henry's ambition to be sole master in his own kingdom.

Glastonbury plundered as a 1000-year tradition ends

LANDMARK OF THE REFORMATION

The ruins of the chapel at Glastonbury Abbey dominate the Somerset countryside today as a lasting memorial to England's monastic past. Founded in the 6th century, Glastonbury was the greatest of the monasteries Henry VIII dissolved 1000 years later.

On a November day in 1539, Richard Whiting, the last Abbot of Glastonbury, was dragged up Tor Hill, above the town, and hanged. He died asking pardon of God and the king for his offences. His crime was that he was one of the handful of Church leaders who chose to resist the forcible Dissolution of the Monasteries by Henry VIII's commissioners.

Whiting was no fanatical conservative in religious affairs and – like many of his colleagues – he had accepted Henry's divorce and the Reformation. But, as a respectable and conscientious abbot, he was unbending in his refusal to give up his office and the spiritual duties it imposed.

Penalty for resistance

Glastonbury Abbey was the richest and most beautiful in the land. It was said by the royal commissioners to be 'the goodliest house of any sort that we have seen, a house fit for the king's Majesty and no man else'. So, when Whiting refused to obey the royal command to dissolve his monastery voluntarily, the king's servants sought evidence to convict him of treason. His monks were interrogated, and Whiting himself carried off to the Tower of London. But attempts to persuade him to

admit his guilt failed and he was sent back to Glastonbury. There he faced trial on a charge of 'robbing Glastonbury Church' – a bitterly ironic accusation, for Henry himself was about to commit just this offence on a huge scale. Whiting was found guilty of the trumped-up charge, and met a felon's death.

The abbot's execution was among the final acts in a revolution which was to change the face of England. It began in May 1535, when six royal officials toured the 850 monasteries of England and Wales, acting on a commission from the king. Within months reports on each house had been submitted to the minister responsible, Thomas Cromwell. Though the reports were not total fabrications, their function was predetermined. They were intended to discredit the monks by accusations of superstition and wickedness.

End of a tradition

Faced with these catalogues of corruption, Parliament was persuaded to adopt a Bill to suppress the smaller foundations: 'Forasmuch,' ran the statute, 'as manifest sin, vicious, carnal and abominable living is daily used and committed among the little and small abbeys,' all those with an income below £200 a year were to be dissolved. Their lands and goods were forfeit to the king, their inhabitants told to return to secular life or else transfer to the larger houses. This task was completed by the busy and highly efficient royal commissioners in the early months of 1537.

Soon afterwards, Cromwell's officials turned their attention to the larger houses – the rich

DISSOLUTION *This 19th-century oil-painting (above) shows the dissolution of a nunnery. Like all monasteries, it was valued in the* Valor Ecclesiasticus *(right), a survey organised by Thomas Cromwell (far right).*

and noble foundations such as Glastonbury. These were not dissolved by a single Act of Parliament, but by applying pressure to each house in turn. Most monasteries succumbed to the royal will, dissolving themselves voluntarily in 1538 and 1539.

For the monks and nuns themselves, the most obvious effect of the dissolution was the abrupt end to their way of life. At the time of the dissolution there were about 9000 monks and nuns, all of whom were suddenly uprooted from their life of prayer and contemplation and thrown out into the world. And for the nation, too, this abrupt end to a long-established and deeply cherished religious tradition was a sudden shock. Yet the break was less disturbing than might have been expected, for the truth was that the spiritual vitality of monasticism had already declined to a shadow of what it once had been.

There had been only eight new monasteries founded since 1400, and many of the older ones could no longer attract members. Traditional duties were being neglected. Charity and hospitality, once vital monastic functions, were no longer offered to those most in need, but to the undeserving friends and relatives of the monks themselves.

Other monastic tasks had been superseded. The writing of manuscripts and chronicles had, for instance, given way to the commercial production of printed books. And a few monasteries had forgotten their spiritual purpose altogether. Some great abbots were more active as businessmen and estate managers than as religious leaders.

A peaceful revolution

Only on a handful of occasions was there any popular resistance to the royal officials as they went about their work. At Exeter, when a man was sent to dismantle the priory church of St Nicholas, some citizens reacted with unusual indignation. John Hooker, a city official, later recorded the events: 'Certain women and wives in the city, minding to stop the suppressing of that house, came in all haste to the said church, some with spikes, some with shovels, some with pikes, and, the door being shut, they broke it open. And finding there the man pulling down the rood loft, they hurled stones unto him, in so much that he was driven to take to the tower for his refuge. And yet they pursued him so eagerly that he was enforced to leap out of a window, and very hardly he escaped the breaking of his neck, but yet he brake one of his ribs.'

But such anger was rare. The monastic way of life passed away with little disruption. Far more significant in the long run was the economic effect of loosening the Church's iron grip on the nation's wealth and land. The Church had owned something between one-fifth and one-third of all the land in England, and it was in order to wrest a share of this from the monasteries that Henry had decided on his policy of dissolution. It was not the first time that a financially weak monarchy had turned to the wealth of the Church to furnish royal revenue, but Henry's solution to the problem was far more radical than the methods of his predecessors.

New wealth for the nobles

Financial necessity had driven him to embark on this bold course, and he knew that his people's dislike of the extravagance and worldliness of the Church would make it much easier for him to attack the monasteries. But more was to come of it than he had intended. At first, the king had thought to retain the forfeited lands for the crown. But no sooner had the dissolutions begun than Cromwell and his agents were besieged by requests from noblemen and gentry anxious to purchase a share in this new wealth. One of them wrote unashamedly: 'As God knows I was and am as glad as any man of this realm of the suppression of these devourers of God's word and takers away of the glory of Christ, and I will gladly, if it might stand with the king's majesty's pleasure, buy certain parcels of this suppressed land in these parts, and I will sell part of my inheritance to pay.'

This eagerness to profit from the dissolution was the vital factor in the whole episode. Through the grant or sale of land, Henry VIII was able to buy loyalty to the new order that he was creating in England. This process could never be reversed. Even under the Catholic Mary Tudor, the Church could never win back the land it had lost.

AFTER THE DISSOLUTION

Both monastic buildings and lands were sold off after the dissolution. Many of the greatest monasteries fell into ruin, and their stonework was plundered by local people in search of building materials. Others were converted into magnificent houses by their new owners. But the most sought-after buildings were the outlying farms – ready-made manor houses for a new generation of landowners.

Mells Manor was once a farm owned by Glastonbury Abbey. It was bought by the abbey's steward, John Horner, after the dissolution.

The North rises to defend the 'old religion'

VICTIM OF CONSCIENCE *A judge presides over the execution of Abbot Thomas Beche – one of 216 men condemned after the Pilgrimage of Grace.*

The rapid changes in Church and state that followed Henry VIII's divorce from Catharine of Aragon created resentment and alarm among his subjects. And trouble soon broke out. Early in October 1536, at Louth in Lincolnshire, rumours that the king intended to seize Church jewels roused the fears of the parishioners. Support soon came from neighbouring villages, and in a few days a mob was on its way to Lincoln, under a banner displaying the five wounds of Christ.

The Lincolnshire rebels were ill-organised and were easily dispersed. But north of the Humber, their cause was taken up by Yorkshiremen under a persuasive and determined leader, the lawyer Robert Aske. With the support of prominent nobles, Aske· was able to rally 30,000 men at Pontefract to take part in his Pilgrimage of Grace.

Faced with this threat, Henry VIII played for time. His representative, the Duke of Norfolk, met the rebel leaders at Doncaster. Norfolk assured them that the monasteries would be restored and he also promised them a full pardon for their rebellion.

Content with this, Aske and the other leading rebels ordered their followers to disperse. This was a fatal mistake. Henry now sought revenge on those who had been so bold as to challenge Tudor might. He was given the chance when a further rising broke out in January 1537. Falling outside the period covered by the pardon, it allowed Henry to arrest Aske and his fellows, even though they had helped to suppress this second rising.

The helpless rebel leaders went meekly to their deaths on the scaffold, betrayed by Henry's duplicity. They had made two fatal mistakes: threatening a Tudor king and then trusting his word.

THE ARTIST WHO WITNESSED ENGLAND'S RULE OF TERROR

The years of terror at Henry VIII's court were witnessed by the first painter of genius to work in Britain. Hans Holbein knew all the chief actors in the drama of intrigue and tyranny, and he was able to record them for all time in works of art.

He was a man of cool candour and deep perception who dared to look long and hard into the flawed personality of the English king. As court painter, he also recorded some of the unfortunate women whose lives became enmeshed in the intrigue of the Tudor age. He portrayed both the ministers who perjured themselves to please their sovereign and the men of conscience who reckoned their souls more highly than their lives. Finally, he looked with compassion on Henry's son, Edward, the innocent prince to whom all eyes turned as the terrible reign drew to its close.

Holbein's art was new to Britain. It was born of the new philosophy of humanism which was sweeping through Europe. When he arrived in England at the age of 30, he carried a letter of introduction from Erasmus, the great Dutch philosopher, to Sir Thomas More, who was then the king's closest friend.

More and Erasmus shared a new belief in the dignity of man. They saw him as a being of God's special creation who had the ability to rise upward to the stars or sink to the level of brute beasts. This faith in the destiny of man found expression in the new art form which Holbein introduced into England – the portrait.

Holbein believed that the true soul of man could be mirrored in a portrait. The artist's mission was to look deeply into the faces of his sitters, and observe every clue to the personality within.

A new art for England

Holbein was already an established artist when he came to England. Born in South Germany, he had made a name for himself in Italy and Switzerland. He first came to England in 1527, with the introduction to Sir Thomas More, whose household might be said to epitomise the 'New Learning'. It was in this circle of humanists that the Renaissance portrait was introduced, first in the great portrait of More himself and secondly in a huge painting of Sir Thomas More and his family at their home in Chelsea. The picture contained ten faces, each a careful character study. This epic work of art has been lost, and only a preliminary sketch for it survives.

In the same period, Holbein drew Bishop Fisher, who, like Thomas More, was to suffer for his Catholic faith and his integrity. In this delicate study of keen intelligence and bewildered virtue, Holbein seems to capture a quality that was not of this world – just as he seems to have perceived brutality in the cold gaze of Henry Tudor.

For the next four years, Holbein was away

THE EYEWITNESS *A self-portrait reveals the cool, steady gaze of Hans Holbein, the artist who, as King's Painter, witnessed the years of terror at the court of Henry VIII. He introduced the art of portrait painting to Britain.*

from England in Basle, Switzerland, where his wife and family still lived. During his absence, Thomas More fell from favour, but when Holbein returned to London in 1532 he found an even more powerful patron in the king himself. He was appointed King's Painter in 1536.

Holbein's honesty was such that his picture of his royal patron is not a particularly favourable one. There is no flattery in the way Holbein depicts the small mouth, cold eyes and heavy jowls. There is simply an overwhelming impression of power.

Besides portraying the king, Holbein was also of use to him in the search for a bride,

HAPPY FAMILY *Sir Thomas More welcomed Holbein into his large, busy household in Chelsea, and in return, the artist painted his family. The finished painting was lost, but the original sketch shows an affectionate and frugal household which the philosopher Erasmus called 'a veritable school of Christian religion'. More is in the centre of the sketch with his wife on the right.*

FUTURE MARTYR *During his first London visit Holbein painted Bishop Fisher. The artist captured the qualities of unworldliness and integrity which were to cost Fisher his life.*

following the death of Jane Seymour in 1537. Nine continental candidates were seriously considered, and five of them agreed to sit for Holbein. In 1538 he travelled to Brussels to paint Princess Christina of Denmark, Duchess of Milan, a 16-year-old widow with a 'singular good countenance'. But Thomas Cromwell urged the claims of a German princess, Anne of Cleves. Cromwell assured the king that her beauty exceeded that of Princess Christina 'as the golden sun excelleth the silvery moon'.

Painting the 'Flanders mare'

Both Anne and her sister Amelia were available, and Holbein painted them both. Henry chose Anne, but when he saw her in the flesh he was disappointed. He exclaimed: 'I am ashamed that men have so praised her as they have done – and I like her not.'

Luckily, Holbein suffered no disgrace from this episode. Possibly the king recognised, in fairness to the artist, that no portrait could convey some of the more annoying qualities of the 'Flanders mare' – her inability to speak English, her dowdy taste in clothes, and her lack of interest in music and the other arts.

During the next four years Holbein was kept busy painting the king, his successive queens and the anxious courtiers. He also turned his hand to the painting of miniatures, which were to inspire Tudor England's second great court artist, Nicholas Hilliard.

Holbein was only 46 when he died of the plague in London. But in 12 eventful years he had given Britain an art form which was to become one of its greatest assets – the tradition of beautiful and profound portraits.

KING'S PAINTER *Holbein's superb mastery of the portrait reached its peak with his studies of Henry VIII. This portrait was painted in 1536, the year Holbein was made King's Painter. The cool glance, raised eyebrows and tight mouth reveal a man in love with power.*

ENGLAND'S HOPE *As Henry Tudor's reign drew to a close, the people of England looked to the sole male heir, young Prince Edward. In this touching portrait Holbein captured the pathos of an innocent child fated to inherit problems far beyond his understanding.*

THE 'FLANDERS MARE' *In the search for a new bride for the king, Holbein was sent to Germany to paint Anne of Cleves. His picture decided the king in her favour. But, on seeing his bride, Henry disgustedly called her a 'Flanders mare'. He divorced her within months of marriage.*

The tragic reign of England's nine-day queen

AN INTRIGUER'S EPITAPH
England's nine-day queen, Lady Jane Grey, went to the block because of the passion for power of her scheming father-in-law, John Dudley, Duke of Northumberland. He made this elaborate carving in his cell in the Tower of London. Dudley sought but failed to secure a pardon by renouncing the Protestant faith. 'A living dog is better than a dead lion,' he said.

In January 1553, Edward VI entered the last stage of the disease that was to end his short reign six months later. As the young king lay dying of tuberculosis, the Duke of Northumberland, Lord President of the Council, was busy spinning the threads of a complex plot, designed to secure for the future the position he now held as England's regent and power behind the throne.

His intrigue centred on a 15-year-old girl, Lady Jane Grey. Northumberland planned to make her England's next sovereign, and to rule through her as he had ruled through Edward. Such was the background to the briefest and most pathetic reign in English history.

Puppet on the throne

Ambitious, hard and unloved, Northumberland calculated his procedure with meticulous care. He selected a candidate for the throne who was a devout Protestant – the granddaughter of Henry VIII's sister. She was admirably suited to appeal to all Englishmen who feared that the recognised heir, Mary Tudor, would overturn the Reformation and return England to Rome. The links between Jane's family and his own had been cemented through a series of carefully arranged weddings culminating in Jane's marriage to his own son, Lord Guildford Dudley.

Finally, in June 1553, he persuaded the dying Edward VI to sign a will bequeathing his crown to Jane. The stage was set; now the duke need only move the players.

From the moment that Northumberland's choice fell upon her, Lady Jane was no more than a puppet. Her private life and her own personality receded into the shadows.

Yet had her fortune been less harsh, Jane would have been a considerable figure in her own right. Her character was far from weak. She was highly educated and zealously religious; gentle, but with a touch of real authority; innocent in an unaffected way, but no fool. With her grace and delicate beauty, she might have been an ornament to her age. But, instead, she was made the martyr to the iron self-will of a burningly ambitious man.

Edward VI died at last on July 6. Northumberland and his colleagues in the Privy Council kept his death a secret for four days while final preparations were made. Then they proclaimed Lady Jane as queen. At first she insisted that Mary was the 'rightful heir' and, according to contemporary accounts, fainted when the council told her that she was Edward's chosen successor. But she later submitted to what she thought was God's will. For greater security she was taken to the royal residence in the Tower of London. She was rowed down the river from Syon House on July 10. It was to be her first and last state journey.

A nine-day reign

At first, Jane had behind her the whole power of the state, carefully gathered by Northumberland into his own grasping hands. Her rival, Mary, the elder daughter of Henry VIII and the legitimate heir to the throne, had only narrowly escaped capture and imprisonment by the duke's forces, and seemed to have no other weapon than her own resolution. But this was to carry her through to victory.

When Jane was proclaimed queen, Mary fled with a handful of supporters to East Anglia. There she issued a stern order to the Privy Council, reminding them that her succession had long ago been confirmed by Act of Parliament, and insisting on their loyalty.

Claiming that Mary's support was confined to 'a few lewd, base people', Northumberland and his fellow-plotters prepared to send an army against her. The duke took command himself, although he was filled with doubt at leaving the source of his power in the hands of men he barely trusted. His parting words to the council echoed his profound suspicion. 'If you mean deceit,' he thundered, 'God will revenge the same.'

The duke had much to trouble him. 'The

TRAGEDY IN THE TOWER *A pathetic incident in Lady Jane Grey's last seconds on the scaffold is shown in this Victorian painting (top). After tying a handkerchief over her eyes, Jane (portrait above) searched with her hands for the block.*

people press to see us,' he wrote as he marched northwards, 'but no one sayeth God speed us.'

Every day came news of growing support for Mary. Noblemen and gentry rushed to join her. Royal ships and soldiers deserted to her cause. One by one, towns all over the country declared their allegiance to her. And as soon as Northumberland marched away from London, his own colleagues on the Privy Council started to look to their own safety.

Within days of his departure, the plot had fallen apart. The council left the Tower and proclaimed Mary as queen. Even Jane's own father, the Duke of Suffolk, turned against his

QUEEN'S LETTER *Jane demands support from the Marquess of Northampton against the 'untrewe dayme of Lady Mary, bastard daughter to our great Uncle Henry the eight'. But few nobles rallied to her cause.*

daughter. On July 19, he recognised Mary and put Jane under arrest. Five days later, Northumberland, now in Cambridge, conceded defeat. His great gamble had failed and his spirit was broken. He gave himself up and was imprisoned in the Tower.

London greeted Mary's victory with wild joy. 'For my time,' wrote an eyewitness, 'I never saw the like. The bonfires were without number, and what with the shouting and crying of the people, and ringing of bells, there could no one man hear what another said.' It was a triumph for Mary – a triumph too for the principles of orderly succession which Northumberland had sought to overthrow.

Living on borrowed time

At first Mary proved merciful in her victory. True, she could not let Northumberland live: he and two of his closest followers were

executed in August. But Jane and her husband, though sentenced to death, were spared, until in January 1554 Mary was given cause to reverse her generous and compassionate decision.

In that month she found herself facing a popular rebellion, threatening not only her personal safety but that of her dynasty too.

The hot-headed Sir Thomas Wyatt raised the standard of revolt in Kent and marched on London at the head of 4000 men. His action showed his contempt for Mary's decision to marry a Catholic foreigner – Philip of Spain. In agreeing to this match she had thrown away the support of patriots, and she was obliged to take Wyatt's threat very seriously.

Innocent on the block

A succession of misfortunes and bad judgments eventually led to disaster for Wyatt. But those luckless innocents in the Tower, Jane and her husband, fell victim to his gamble.

Five days after Wyatt's rebellion had been crushed, the young couple were taken out on to Tower Hill and beheaded. The 16-year-old Jane met her death with astounding courage and composure. She rejected the offer of a reprieve if she denounced the Protestant faith. And, as she was taken to the block, she recited the 51st Psalm: 'Have mercy upon me, O God, after thy great goodness.' On the scaffold, she denied that she had ever desired the crown and said she perished 'a true Christian woman'.

Beautiful, learned, obedient – above all, firm in her devotion to the Protestant faith – Jane had been a pawn in other men's hands. Her life and her death were forfeits in a vicious power-game of dynasty and religion.

Edward VI: A boy-king governed by his elders

Henry VIII's only legitimate son was born to his third wife, Jane Seymour, on October 12, 1537. Within two weeks, the queen was dead. For the first six years of his life, the young Prince Edward (right) was brought up 'among the women'.

Then, in 1544, his education was entrusted to two of the leading scholars of the day, Richard Cox and John Cheke. Edward emerged from their hands, learned, precocious and devoutly Protestant.

The old king died in January 1547, and his 10-year-old son was crowned on February 20 in an atmosphere of rejoicing. But the child-king had no real authority, for his power was held by others. First it was grasped by Edward's maternal uncle, Edward Seymour, Duke of Somerset, who had himself declared Lord Protector. Somerset was charitable towards the poor, but arrogant and overbearing to the rich and powerful. The leading nobles conspired to dislodge him in 1549, and three years later he was beheaded. His place was taken by John Dudley, Duke of Northumberland, a man skilled at ingratiating himself with the king, but greedy and ambitious for himself and his kinsmen as well.

By now the young king was beginning to form a personality of his own. But he had always been a sickly child and in January 1553, at the age of 15, he developed tuberculosis. By May Edward was now beyond any treatment that his doctors could give. And when the end came in July, the Swiss Protestant theologian John Calvin lamented: 'By the death of one youth, the whole nation has been bereaved of the best of fathers.'

PRAYERS FOR THE PEOPLE

The English *Book of Common Prayer* (title page below) was published in 1549. The literary masterpiece of its day, the book was largely written by Thomas Cranmer, Archbishop of Canterbury. His main aims were to end the superstitions which he believed had crept into church services, to have one standardised form of prayer and to have the prayers in English, not Latin, 'to the end that the congregation may thereby be edified'. The book's prose was soon common reading for both rich and poor.

Three brave martyrs 'light a candle' for their religion

TRIAL OF THREE MARTYRS
St Mary's Church, Oxford, was the scene of one of the most dramatic trials in English history. In 1555, three of England's leading Protestants, Thomas Cranmer, Archbishop of Canterbury, Nicholas Ridley and Hugh Latimer, were put on trial there for their faith. All three were condemned to be burnt at the stake.

During the reign of Mary Tudor, three men died horribly outside the walls of Oxford. They were Thomas Cranmer, Archbishop of Canterbury, the spiritual leader of the English Reformation; Hugh Latimer, the greatest Protestant preacher in England; and Nicholas Ridley, Bishop of London, a brilliant Protestant theologian.

Within days of the Catholic queen's accession, Ridley had been imprisoned in the Tower for declaring her illegitimate. Cranmer and Latimer had followed him there in the autumn. For almost two years they had been held under close guard until the government felt strong enough to take more drastic action.

In September 1555 the three were taken to Oxford, where they were tried and condemned for heresy. On October 16, Ridley and Latimer were led out to die. They met at the stake, where Ridley embraced his fellow-martyr and urged him to 'be of good cheer, brother, for God will either assuage the fury of the flames or else strengthen us to abide it'.

'Be of good comfort'
When they had both been chained to the stake, Ridley's brother was allowed to tie bags of gunpowder around their necks to give them a quicker and more merciful end. As the faggots were kindled, Latimer spoke the words which were to echo in religious history. 'Be of good comfort, Master Ridley, and play the man: we shall this day light such a candle by God's

NICHOLAS RIDLEY *As Bishop of London, he was arrested in 1553 for claiming in a sermon that Mary was illegitimate.*

HUGH LATIMER *He had been imprisoned by Mary's father, Henry VIII, because of his ardent Protestantism.*

THOMAS CRANMER *He refused to accept the return to Catholicism and denounced the Mass as 'a device of Satan'.*

MEETING THEIR FATE *Latimer (left) and Ridley prepare to be burnt at the stake. Latimer's courage never flagged; he proclaimed that, through their sacrifice, he and Ridley would 'light such a candle by God's grace in England, as I trust shall never be put out'.*

FINAL MESSAGE *Cranmer, too, met his fate with dignity. On the day of his execution, he renounced the denial of his faith that he had previously made, saying that it was his hand that had signed it, not his heart. At the stake, he deliberately thrust the offending hand into the flames.*

grace in England, as I trust shall never be put out!' Strengthened, they faced death.

Latimer died easily. As the flames sprang up, he seemed to bathe his hands in them for a few moments and then was dead. But Ridley suffered the most terrible agonies. The wood had been so badly laid that the fire burnt his legs long before it reached the gunpowder, which finally put an end to his ordeal.

Cranmer had been brought from his prison to watch the final moments of his friends' sufferings in the hope that he would be terrified into admitting his heresy. But the courage displayed by Ridley and Latimer served at first only to strengthen his convictions. In the long months of imprisonment that followed, however, Cranmer began to weaken. He was removed from his pleasant lodgings in Christ Church to a dungeon. Isolated from his friends, subject to constant persuasion from Catholics, he became ever more harassed by spiritual doubt. Finally, he signed a recantation – even though this would not save him from his fate.

Triumphantly the government arranged for him to make a public confession before his death. On a rainy day in March he was brought to St Mary's Church in full state. But during the previous night, his old beliefs had reasserted themselves, and he refused to go as a penitent to the stake. He renounced the confession he had signed and condemned the hand that had written it. 'For as much as my hand offended, writing contrary to my heart, my hand shall first be punished,' he proclaimed.

Cranmer was hurried to the stake and as the flames rose he thrust his right hand into the fire. He remained motionless until his death, calling out 'Lord Jesus, receive my spirit'.

'An example for future generations'

Latimer, Ridley and Cranmer were not the only victims of Mary's fanatical devotion to her faith, nor even the first of those who died. But they were by far the most prominent figures to be executed, and their deaths inflamed the growing hatred of Mary's rule. One English politician, Sir John Cheke, wrote to John Calvin, the great Swiss Protestant theologian, in October 1555, that the condemned Protestants 'by their example and constancy not only give encouragement to those of the present age, but form an eminent example for future generations'.

This was to prove true. The merciless religious persecution Mary encouraged was the most fatal error of her rule. Not only did she execute almost 300 people, but she even exacted vengeance on the dead, by digging up and burning the bodies of long-dead Protestants. With every martyrdom, her people's outrage intensified, and their loyalty weakened. Mary made her enemies into popular heroes, and by doing so she made it impossible for the Roman Catholic Church to survive as the established church after her death.

Mary Tudor: The sorrows of an unloved queen

Mary Tudor, who was to become the most unpopular queen in British history, had lived for many years in the cold light of her father's disfavour before she came to the throne in 1553. At the age of 11 she saw her mother, Catharine of Aragon, divorced by Henry VIII and her own right to the throne set aside by Act of Parliament.

Despite this persecution, Mary clung obstinately to her rights. When the Duke of Norfolk told her that the king demanded that she pay her respects to Anne Boleyn's daughter, Princess Elizabeth, she replied that she knew 'no other princess in England but herself'. Henry was infuriated by such defiance. He refused to see Mary, and gave orders that whenever he visited the houses in which both the young girls lived, she was to be kept confined in her room. Once, at Hatfield, Mary disobeyed this command and climbed a tower in time to see her father mounting his horse. He turned to see his daughter and 'saluted her courteously' before riding away.

In the end, Mary was forced to conform. In 1536 she swore the Oath of the Succession, recognising that her mother had been justly divorced. But, like many other members of her family, Princess Mary was a wily politician. She wrote secretly to the pope, assuring him that she had been forced to take the oath and receiving in return a promise of absolution from it. Among her powerful protectors was Catharine's nephew, the Holy Roman Emperor Charles V. In the next reign, when the threat to the Catholic Mary grew even stronger, the emperor threatened Edward VI with war 'if I would not suffer his cousin the Princess to make her Mass'.

Mary survived her father's rage, her brother's ardent Protestantism and the Duke of Northumberland's attempt to place Lady Jane Grey on the throne in her stead. Her years of trial had left her determined to restore the Roman Catholic religion and destroy heresy in her kingdom. And she thought that the nation's welcome on her accession was a sign of support for such policies. In this she was to be mistaken.

The fires of Smithfield

At first, Mary was deceptively successful. The Church of England was quickly suppressed by Parliament, and the Mass was restored. But Protestantism persisted. Determined 'to demand of the law to strike terror into all those who ventured to do evil', the queen launched the persecution that was to win her the nickname of 'Bloody Mary'.

A married priest, John Rogers, was the first to pay with his life for his loyalty to the Protestant faith. He was burnt at Smithfield in London on February 4, 1555 – the forerunner of 283 martyrs. His end gave birth to one of the many myths that were to establish the Marian martyrs in history. When some pigeons, disturbed by the smoke, flew over the pyre, Protestants claimed that it marked the presence of the Holy Ghost. Most of these tales were collected by a Protestant author, John Foxe. His *Book of Martyrs*, first published in France, became a best-seller in Elizabethan England.

In so far as it was possible, Rogers met an easy death. It was the practice for friends to bribe the executioner to place a bag of gunpowder around the victim's neck, so that he would not suffer the full torment of the fire. But the next martyr, John Hooper, Bishop of Gloucester and Worcester, was not so fortunate. At his burning, outside Gloucester Cathedral, the gunpowder failed to explode.

In her private life, Mary was simple, kindly and fond of children. She lacked guile or sophistication. An ambassador said of her: 'I know the queen – so easy to get round, so simple, so little experienced in worldly matters, such a novice in all things.'

Marriage without love

But although Mary could be outmanoeuvred, she could never be bullied. Despite the pleas of her advisers, she set her heart on a Spanish marriage. Early in 1554 she married, by proxy, Philip of Castile, heir to the Spanish throne. As the envoys sent to arrange the marriage rode through the streets of London, they were pelted with snowballs by the mob. A short-lived rebellion broke out in Kent. But Mary was not to be deterred, and in July the groom arrived in England.

But the marriage that Mary (below) had sought so ardently turned out to be unsuccessful. Although the queen adored her husband, he gave her but a cold response and spent little time with her. His aims were to secure support in his war with France and an heir to the throne. In the first he succeeded, but in the second he failed. This was the deepest disappointment to Mary as well. She died with none of her aims accomplished.

England rejoices as 'Gloriana' is crowned

PRAYER BOOK FOR A QUEEN
The illuminated service book that Elizabeth used during her coronation in January 1559 is now at the Norman Undercroft Museum, Westminster Abbey. The queen ordered the astrologer John Dee to choose the most propitious day for the service.

seethed with support for her. There were rumours of a spirit in the city wall which when addressed with the cry 'God save Queen Mary!' answered nothing, but when challenged 'God save the Lady Elizabeth!' replied 'So be it!' Treasonous handbills were scattered in the street, pledging support to Elizabeth against Mary. A dead cat dressed in the vestments of a Catholic priest was hung on a gallows in Cheapside. All these were the open signs of a wave of revulsion against Mary, her Spanish husband and her religion. But to Elizabeth they were the first faint signs of a more hopeful future.

November 1558 was the glorious fulfilment of that promise, as Elizabeth's accession was greeted with whole-hearted enthusiasm. And in January 1559, as her coronation procession passed through the streets of London, her reception was very different from the one she had received five years before.

In procession through the city

There had been little time to prepare. Scaffolding had to be erected at various points in the city for the performance of pageants. Above all, robes and costumes had to be made. Customs officers were ordered to confiscate all crimson silk that entered the ports. For each of the 39 ladies who would attend the queen, 16 yds of velvet were needed. The queen's own mantle was made out of 23 yds of gold and silver tissue, with fur trimming. All was made ready in two months at the enormous cost of £16,000 – equivalent to 8 per cent of the annual royal budget.

On Saturday, January 14, Elizabeth left the Tower to journey in procession through the city on her way to Westminster. London had been transformed, said one observer, into 'a Stage wherein was shewed the wonderful spectacle of a noble-hearted princess towards her most loving people'. At Fenchurch Street, the queen's procession came to a scaffold where a child recited doggerel verse in her honour. Passing on, she came to five pageants designed to celebrate the accession of a worthy and Protestant ruler.

In all this ceremony, personal touches were not forgotten. The queen showed 'perpetual attentiveness in her face'. She smiled at the

Early in the winter of 1558, the ailing Mary Tudor finally despaired that she would ever bear a child and reluctantly recognised her sister, Elizabeth, as heir to the throne of England. Only a few days later, on November 17, Mary was dead and Elizabeth proclaimed queen. In traditional style, bonfires were lit and banquets were held in the streets of London.

On November 28 Elizabeth left Hatfield in Hertfordshire, where she had received the news of her accession, entered London and took possession of the Tower.

The Tower, now Elizabeth's palace, had once been her place of captivity, when, in 1554, she was imprisoned by Mary on suspicion of being involved in a Protestant rebellion. As she entered London on that earlier occasion she could see the evidence of the failed revolt – the heads of the executed traitors displayed in the streets. And when she was led through the Traitor's Gate, she had been heard to whisper: 'Oh Lord! I never thought to have come in here as a prisoner.'

Although her imprisonment had not lasted long, the episode in the Tower had proved how afraid Mary had become. She had feared that her sister would be a spear-head for popular rebellion – and her alarm was justified. Even while Elizabeth lay in the Tower, London

CORONATION PROCESSION *A contemporary sketch shows Elizabeth on her way to Westminster Abbey. A magnificent blue carpet covered the route, but it was ruined by souvenir hunters.*

A contemporary drawing of Sir Edward Dymoke, who acted as champion at Elizabeth's coronation. To fulfil this time-honoured duty, he rode into Westminster Hall at the start of the coronation banquet, threw down his gauntlet and challenged anyone to dispute the queen's title. The post of champion was in the Dymoke family from the coronation of Richard II in 1377 until that of George IV in 1821. The position was then abolished.

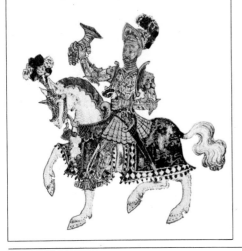

mention of her father's name, as the cry went up: 'Remember old Henry VIII!' Until she reached Westminster she kept with her a sprig of rosemary given to her by a poor woman.

Elizabeth spent the night at Westminster, and the next day, Sunday, the coronation ceremony took place. There was a more formal procession from Westminster Hall to the abbey. First came the ordinary gentlemen, then knights and aldermen, and up the ranks of English society to the bishops in their copes and mitres, the nobles with their coronets and the Duke of Norfolk bearing the crown in front of the queen.

A long and triumphant reign
Once inside the abbey, Elizabeth was acclaimed, preached to, anointed and at last crowned to the braying of trumpets. After this, the whole procession returned to Westminster Hall, where the queen was served with a banquet by the great officers of her household.

Elizabeth had begun her long and triumphant reign. Her country was now launched on one of the most glorious eras in its history. For more than a century afterwards, the date of Elizabeth's accession was celebrated as the great popular holiday of a Protestant nation.

VIRGIN QUEEN *The coronation portrait of Elizabeth from the Warwick Castle collection. Despite her many suitors, she remained unmarried, saying: 'It shall be sufficient for me that a marble stone shall declare that a queen, having reigned such a time, lived and died a virgin.'*

Elizabeth I: Mistress of her people's hearts

Elizabeth I possessed all the feminine qualities that are thought to be handicaps in a man's world. Yet this wilful, illogical and often infuriating woman achieved more in her reign of 45 years than any of her subjects could have dared to hope. For it was through her statesmanship and the magic of her personality that England was saved from political dismemberment and civil war.

Elizabeth was the child of a broken home. Her father, Henry VIII, had not only divorced her mother, Anne Boleyn; he had her executed and declared Elizabeth illegitimate. From then on, her fate varied with each change in her father's politics and with each of his marriages. Her childhood was dominated by tragedy and intrigue and she often lived in fear of death.

Her unhappiness continued into adolescence. Under her brother, Edward VI, the young Elizabeth came under suspicion for flirting with Thomas Seymour, who was executed for treason in 1549. With the accession of her Catholic sister, Mary, she was in grave danger as a Protestant and spent more than a year in prison in the Tower of London.

A queen and her people
But these tribulations were an invaluable lesson in political caution. By character and upbringing she was a complete ruler. Some of the finest scholars of the day had charge of her education. 'Her mind,' reported one of them, 'has no womanly weakness, her perseverance is equal to that of a man.' Once queen, she selected her ministers and servants with superb skill.

But Elizabeth was more than just a wise sovereign. Above all, she had the power to enchant and captivate her subjects – both the humble and the mighty. Year by year she made journeys round the country, and these tours became a meeting point for sovereign and people. At Norwich one year she heard a speech in appalling Latin given by a nervous schoolmaster. 'Be not afraid,' she called, as he began his ordeal, and then, when he came to the end: 'It is the best that ever I heard.' At Coventry the mayor presented her with a chalice filled with gold. Elizabeth was pleased: 'I have but few such gifts.' And the mayor dared to add: 'If it please your Grace there is a great deal more in it – the hearts of your loving subjects.' 'We thank you,' said the queen, 'It is a great deal more indeed.'

Early in her reign, Elizabeth admitted to a desire 'to do some act that would make my fame spread abroad in my lifetime'. This she did, and more. Not one act, but her entire reign and person were her undying memorial. Dubbed 'Gloriana' by the poet Edmund Spenser, she personified her country at the summit of its fame.

A JEWELLER ARTIST MIRRORS ELIZABETH'S GOLDEN COURT

All the romance of the Elizabethan age is captured in a miniature world in the work of Nicholas Hilliard, painter of some of the smallest and most exquisite works of art ever made by man. Hilliard was trained and practised as a jeweller and goldsmith. Many of his jewel-like masterpieces are little bigger than a postage stamp.

Hilliard was born at Exeter in 1547. His father, Richard, was a well-to-do goldsmith and a leader of the city's Protestant community. After the Catholic Mary came to the throne in 1553 he sent young Nicholas to Calvin's Geneva, citadel of the new faith. Such a strict upbringing seems to have left little trace on Hilliard's character. His prodigality later in life was to lead him into debt.

In 1564 he was apprenticed at the customary age of 14 to Robert Brandon, a prominent member of the London Goldsmiths' Company and goldsmith and jeweller to the new queen, Elizabeth I. Already young Nicholas was painting miniatures, and from the very start of his career he was primarily a painter.

A world captured in miniature

His earliest mature works bear the date 1572 and include one of Elizabeth herself, indicating that from the outset Hilliard's talent was cultivated by the court. From then on followed an uninterrupted flow of work until his death more than 40 years later, in 1619. In July 1576 he married his master's daughter, Alice Brandon. They were to have four sons and three daughters.

That autumn Hilliard's extravagance got him into financial difficulties, and he forsook the queen's service for that of one of her suitors, the French Duke of Alençon. Sir Amyas Paulet, English ambassador in Paris, set out Hilliard's motives. He wrote in a dispatch: 'He intends to increase his knowledge by this voyage, and upon hope to get a piece of money of the lords and ladies here for his better maintenance in England at his return.'

Wherever he went, Hilliard's astonishing art aroused envy and admiration. In France he met the poet Pierre Ronsard, who paid tribute to the English artist: 'The islands indeed seldom bring forth any cunning man, but when they do it is in high perfection.'

In February 1578 the queen asked Alençon for the return of her 'limner', or painter of miniatures. Later the same year Hilliard took over the lease of a house and shop in Gutter Lane, just off Cheapside, in the heart of the old City of London. The house was owned by the Goldsmiths' Company, and during the 35 years Hilliard lived there he fought a number of legal battles with them for the renewal of his lease. As late as 1600 even the Privy Council intervened on his behalf, pleading with the company to grant the queen's favourite artist a new lease at £3 a year.

Hilliard was often in financial difficulties. For an average miniature, showing the head and shoulders of the sitter, he would charge about £3. The cost would soar if he also provided a setting or background. Yet he frequently became involved in wild schemes to increase his fortune. Shortly after his return to England in 1578 he joined a speculator called Cornelius Devosse in a dubious enterprise to mine gold in Scotland.

A badly arranged contract to design and execute the second Great Seal of Elizabeth ended in a financial loss for Hilliard. He would cheerfully sign bonds for his friends'

SELF PORTRAIT *The style of Nicholas Hilliard greatly influenced the work of English painters.*

debts and was often near bankruptcy, but he never lacked supporters in high places. Elizabeth's principal ministers, Sir Francis Walsingham, Lord Burleigh and his son, Robert Cecil, were among those who bailed him out.

The Royal Limner left a remarkable account of his art in a work he wrote towards the end of his long life – *The Art of Limning*. It includes strict instructions on the best light in which to work, and urges the artist to wear only silk clothes so that no fluff falls on the wet paint – and, says Hilliard, 'take heed of the dandruff of the head shedding from the hair'.

He describes how he takes 'virgin parchment...as smooth as any satin' which he mounts on to card (often a playing card). After an initial underdrawing, painting begins with the laying-in of the flesh tints or 'carnations'. These were delicate washes of colour on to which the features were drawn.

There is a nervous sensitivity about the lines that twitch their way across the surface of the

ROYAL FAVOURITE *Hilliard painted Elizabeth's favourite, the Earl of Leicester, in 1576.*

MAN OF POWER *Sir Christopher Hatton, the Lord Chancellor, painted at the time of the Armada.*

DOOMED QUEEN *Mary, Queen of Scots. This miniature was painted after her execution.*

miniature. A single line can define an eyebrow, a complex of cross-hatching makes up the shadows in the flesh tints, or quivering, thickly massed lines duplicate the cascading curls of the elaborately crimped hair. Many times enlarged, the Elizabethan miniature is akin in the freedom of its technique to that used by the Impressionist painters of the late 19th century. The colours Hilliard used are, for the most part, blue and yellow, crimson and black, white and pink, orange and green. Jewels are often touches of real gold and silver which once sparkled in the light.

The mirror of the soul
Hilliard's tiny portraits of Elizabeth's courtiers are painted with the Renaissance conviction that the face is the mirror of the soul. The limner immortalised his subjects as they wished to see themselves, but the idealising approach of his art has none of the cynicism of the flatterer.

Hilliard was the first English-born artist to achieve international fame and he was inspired by a patriotic pride in English beauty, believing that in England 'even the hand and foot excelleth all pictures I ever saw'. His aim was to record 'these lovely graces, witty smilings and these stolen glances which suddenly like lightning pass, and another countenance taketh place'.

Three influences fashioned Hilliard's art.

The first was that of Hans Holbein, whose primary talent was in drawing. Hilliard wrote of Holbein: 'Holbein's manner of limning I have ever imitated, and hold it for the best.'

Holbein defined form through line alone, and this led to an abstract patterned style in which, for example, Queen Elizabeth was depicted less as a human being than as an arrangement of face, hair, hands, dress and jewellery.

From the contemporary French court portraitist and fellow miniaturist François Clouet, Hilliard learnt freshness of presentation. Finally he took a lesson in art from his royal mistress – Queen Elizabeth I.

At her first sitting Elizabeth observed that the Italian manner of painting was preferable because it avoided shadows, 'and therefore chose her place to sit in for that purpose in the open alley of a goodly garden, where no tree was near, nor any shadow at all'. The queen's opinion, Hilliard recorded, 'hath greatly bettered my judgment'.

The Elizabethan miniature belongs to a world of amorous dalliance between knights and ladies of the court. Hidden in boxes for secret contemplation, or encased in jewelled lockets and suspended over the heart, these precious ovals were designed as badges of loyalty or pledges of true love. They were frequently set in ivory, and the small closed cases look like ivory draughtsmen.

Tokens of love and loyalty
Sir James Melville, the Scottish soldier and diplomat whom Mary, Queen of Scots, sent as envoy to London, describes how Elizabeth kept a collection of miniatures in her bedroom, each one carefully wrapped and labelled with the name of the sitter.

'Upon the first that she took up was written *My Lord's Picture*,' he wrote in a dispatch. 'I held the candle, and pressed to see the picture so named. She seemed loath to let me see it; yet my importunity prevailed for a sight thereof, and found it to be the Earl of Leicester's picture.'

The queen was understandably reticent about the portrait of a man whom some believed to be her lover. But she was less secretive about her miniature of another of her ministers, Sir Robert Cecil. She wore it on her shoe.

Hilliard was the true founder of a style of miniature painting in which the English were to excel until the advent of photography in the Victorian age. Even at the age of 70 he was capable of producing work as fine as that he had produced as a young man.

Such extraordinary brilliance was not lost upon his contemporaries. They admired his patriotic vigour, bright palette and bold characterisation, and sonnets paid tribute to his power in evoking absent beauty.

But of all the eulogies, that which has most immortalised him is the passing salute by the poet John Donne in his poem 'The Storm':

> *a hand or eye*
> *By Hilliard drawn is worth a history*
> *By a worse painter made.*

CULT OF 'THE FAERIE QUEEN'
Nicholas Hilliard was said to have been able to depict Queen Elizabeth's face in four swift lines. This was because he had so much practice. The queen was inordinately vain, and accepted flattery with relish. Court painters were employed to promote the cult of the virgin queen-goddess, Gloriana. Their task was to depict her beauty and wealth so that all the world might marvel.

Poets, too, found a sure route to advancement through flattery. It was Edmund Spenser who first called the queen 'Gloriana', and who dedicated his poetic masterpiece 'The Faerie Queen' to her.

When her beauty faded, the queen seldom looked in a mirror. A courtier said that once, when she did so, she remarked bitterly 'how much she had been abused by flatterers whom she held in too great estimation'. Like the court poets, Hilliard's genius lay in his ability to transmute the everyday imperfect world, where even queens grow old, into a miniature 'faerie' realm where beauty never fades.

Elizabeth I was the centre of a galaxy of courtiers immortalised by Nicholas Hilliard.

MYSTERY PORTRAIT *This miniature is thought to be of the Earl of Essex, another royal favourite.*

PENSIVE MOOD *A flattering glimpse of Henry Percy, 9th Earl of Northumberland.*

Conspiracy and murder cost Mary the Scottish throne

EVIDENCE OF GUILT?
*Incriminating letters from Mary, Queen
of Scots, to Bothwell were found in a casket,
now in the Museum of Antiquities, Edinburgh.*

RICCIO DIES *David
Riccio (left) was pri-
vate secretary to Mary,
Queen of Scots, and
was suspected of being
her lover. In this paint-
ing (above), Mary's
husband, Darnley, con-
sumed by jealousy,
stabs Riccio to death
in front of the queen.*

Outside the city walls of 16th-century
Edinburgh stood a lonely house
known as Kirk o' Fields. Early in
February 1567 the despised and distrusted
husband of Mary, Queen of Scots, Lord
Darnley, settled in this lodging. And in the
early hours of February 10, the citizens of
Edinburgh were awoken by a thunderous
gunpowder blast. Kirk o' Fields had been
reduced to dust and rubble.

The next morning the body of Darnley was
discovered about 40 yds from the ruins. But
Darnley had been strangled, not blown up.
And his murder, shrouded in mystery, was the
centrepiece to a complex, tragic story that
eventually cost his wife her throne.

Exactly three years earlier, Henry Stuart,
Lord Darnley, had come to the Scottish court
at Holyrood. The ambition of this young
Catholic nobleman from England was to
marry his cousin, Mary, Queen of Scots.
Impressed by his tall and handsome appearance, his charm and his easy-going love of
pleasure, Mary failed to see that Darnley was
a feckless 19-year-old, who was spoilt, touchy
and vain. After nursing her suitor through an
attack of measles, Mary fell violently in love
with him. With astonishing recklessness, she
proposed to Darnley. On July 29, 1565, their
wedding was celebrated at Holyrood.

A short-lived honeymoon

The marriage enraged Elizabeth and her
Privy Councillors in England. Darnley had
English royal ancestry, and his marriage to
Mary strengthened the Scottish claim to
England's throne. In Scotland, too, there was
anger among the Protestant nobles, at the
upstart Catholic's sudden rise to power.
Thinking they could count on English assis-
tance, they mounted a rebellion against Mary.
But England refused to take this risk of a full-
scale war, and the rebels were easily crushed by
Mary with the aid of James Hepburn, the Earl
of Bothwell. Her marriage was safe.

Yet within a few months, Mary's affections
for her young husband cooled. Having
achieved his ambition, Darnley began to
reveal his true colours, displaying all the
worst vices of his Stuart ancestry. He was
proud, stupid, stubborn, unstable, given to
moodiness and fond of drink and women.
Mary's passion for him changed into deep
hatred. She excluded him from influence and
began to rely on two favourites: Bothwell,
and her Italian secretary, David Riccio.

Furious at his loss of authority, and even
more jealous of Mary's friendship with Riccio,
Darnley turned to conspiracy. He found allies
among the same noblemen who had resented
his elevation to the throne. Driven on by their
own ambitions, these nobles were now ready
to use Darnley to regain power for themselves.
They inflamed his jealousy against Riccio and,
in return for a pledge that the nobles would
not 'spare life nor limb' in avenging Darnley's

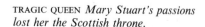

TRAGIC QUEEN *Mary Stuart's passions
lost her the Scottish throne.*

DARK DRAMA *A contemporary drawing (above) shows where Mary's husband, Darnley (left), was murdered in 1567. His house is a heap of rubble, and his body lies beneath a tree. Darnley's infant son, James, calls from his cradle for vengeance.*

honour, the slighted husband agreed to join their plot. On March 9, 1566, Darnley, heading a gang of the plotters, burst into the queen's apartments at Holyrood, where she was entertaining Riccio and other guests to supper. Under the eyes of the horrified queen, who was seven months pregnant, the conspirators seized the wretched Riccio and stabbed him to death.

Mary showed her anger in the one word she spat at her husband – 'Judas!' But her courage proved equal to the dangers of the situation. On the following day she calmly received the plotters, pardoned some of the rebels, and feigned a reconciliation with Darnley. That night, she slipped out of the palace with her husband and escaped to Dunbar Castle. Darnley denounced his fellow-plotters; the Earl of Bothwell hurriedly raised troops on Mary's behalf, and the outwitted conspirators fled to England.

Mary's strength of mind had saved the day. Only once again did she show her real feelings. As she fled from Holyrood, she passed a patch of waste ground where Riccio lay in his freshly dug grave. Lingering beside it in the moonlight, she poured forth her curses on her husband and his ancestors.

Relations between the two soon broke down again. In October Darnley refused to attend the baptism of their son, who was to become James I of England. Soon afterwards, he fell seriously ill, and went to stay in Glasgow.

For her part, Mary made it clear that she wished to end her marriage. A band of nobles, led by Bothwell, now conspired to rid the queen of her husband. But Mary's own part in the plot is uncertain. It was she who brought the ailing Darnley from Glasgow to Kirk o' Fields, possibly at Bothwell's request; but did she know that there were plans afoot to murder him there? Certainly her behaviour was not that of a woman plotting to murder her husband, for she came daily to his lodgings to care for him during his illness.

On the night of February 9, 1567, Mary visited Darnley before returning to Holyrood for a dance in celebration of her favourite valet, Bastian Pages. It was a Sunday and the last day of Darnley's life. On the following day, he was due to rejoin his wife at Holyrood.

Bothwell and his fellow-plotters had already mined Darnley's house with gunpowder. Now, shortly after midnight, they made their way silently to Kirk o' Fields to carry out the remainder of their conspiracy.

Murder at Kirk o' Fields

The house was quiet and Darnley lay asleep in bed. Abruptly, he was awakened by the sound of men moving about in the rooms below – the conspirators laying their fuse. Realising that his life was in danger, Darnley rushed to save himself, not even stopping to dress. He let himself down from the window by an improvised ladder and made off through the garden. But the conspirators caught up with him. Witnesses overheard his last desperate plea: 'Pity me, kinsmen, for the sake of Jesus Christ, who pitied all the world.'

But there was no compassion for Darnley. The murderers strangled him, then dropped the body beneath a tree. And as they carried out their deed, the house exploded.

The 20 year captivity of an exiled queen

The murder of Darnley was only the beginning of Mary Stuart's troubles. For it sparked off the events that were to lose her the Scottish throne and drive her into exile and captivity in England.

Whatever her part may have been in the death of her husband, Mary's subsequent behaviour convicted her of stupendous folly. And flight was soon Mary's only recourse.

On Sunday May 16, 1568, with nothing but the clothes she was wearing, Mary was rowed across the Solway Firth, fleeing from her kingdom to take refuge with her cousin, Elizabeth of England. Mary confidently expected to be back in Scotland at the head of an invading army by August. But she was never to return.

Mary's arrival was both an embarrassment and a threat to her Protestant cousin. She was a Catholic – and next in line to the throne. Nor could Elizabeth possibly send troops to crush the Protestant Scots. Gravely, her councillors debated what was to be done. Finally, the decision was made to keep Mary in captivity. For the next 20 years she was to be a prisoner.

For much of this time, Elizabeth was under constant pressure to put an end to her attractive but wayward cousin. Finally, Mary's fate was decided by the international politics of Europe. In 1580 the pope excommunicated Elizabeth and called on all Catholics to rally to overthrow her. Mary became the centre of every plot and every conspiracy. She was too dangerous to live.

Sir Francis Walsingham, the head of Elizabeth's secret service, slowly amassed evidence against the Queen of Scots. She was placed under stricter and stricter supervision. And finally, in 1587, Elizabeth was persuaded to place her on trial – for her life.

SCOURGE OF THE CATHOLICS

By his eloquence and force of character, John Knox (left) gave Scotland her stern Calvinist faith. A dour, dogmatic man, Knox worked tirelessly for Protestantism. In 1560 the Scots outlawed Catholicism, and Knox prepared a new Protestant liturgy. Even the reign of the Catholic Mary, Queen of Scots, could not weaken the new faith in its hold on the Scottish people. Among the most famous targets of Knox's blistering pen were Mary and her cousin, Elizabeth of England. He attacked them in his tract *The Monstrous Regiment of Women*. Knox died in 1572, with Protestantism triumphant in Scotland.

Scotland's tragic queen meets death on the scaffold

A QUEEN'S LEGACY

Mary, Queen of Scots, carried this golden rosary and Roman Catholic prayer book to her execution. Ignoring the Anglican priest, she said she would die defending her religion. Her possessions were handed to Anne Dacres, wife of the Earl of Arundel, at her death, and can be seen at Arundel Castle, the home of the Duke of Norfolk.

On October 25, 1586, a commission of 25 noblemen and Privy Councillors, sitting in the Star Chamber in London, found Mary Stuart, Queen of Scots, guilty of 'compassing and imagining matters tending to the destruction of the Queen of England'.

Mary might have suffered the same judgment at any time during the 20 years of her exile and imprisonment in England, for she had been the constant focus of Catholic bids to overthrow Queen Elizabeth. Though she had arrived in England as a fugitive seeking aid and mercy, Mary had enmeshed herself in an unceasing web of intrigue against the queen.

In these years Elizabeth had become Mary's staunchest protector. For although Elizabeth's closest advisers put increasing pressure on her to rid the land of 'the bosom serpent', as Sir Francis Walsingham described Mary, Elizabeth had refused to have her cousin and fellow-monarch put to death.

Now, in 1586, the men who guarded the security of the English queen finally forced the issue. Three months previously, Mary had been trapped into writing letters of encouragement to the latest group of Catholic plotters, led by Sir Antony Babington, who hoped to free Mary from her imprisonment and assassinate Elizabeth. The letters, smuggled out of Chartley House, Mary's place of captivity, in a beer-barrel, had been taken straight to Sir Francis Walsingham and decoded. Backed by the confession of her secretary – extorted by torture – they were enough to ensure Mary's condemnation.

But this was not the end of the matter. Though the commission appointed by the Privy Council might try Mary and sentence her to death, Elizabeth alone could sign her death warrant – and this the queen would not do. Both Houses of Parliament pressed for the execution of this 'daughter of sedition, the

A QUEEN DIES *A contemporary Dutch artist shows Queen Mary at her execution on February 8, 1587. As she knelt by the block in the Great Hall of Fotheringhay Castle, she cried three times: 'In manus tuas, Domine, confide spiritum meum' – 'Into thy hands, O Lord, I commend my spirit.'*

Mary Stuart: Doomed to lose throne and life

Great-granddaughter of Henry VII of England; daughter of James V of Scotland; wife of Francis II of France – Mary Stuart was the meeting point of three royal families. Yet the Queen Consort of France, the Queen of Scotland and heir to the throne of England ended her life on the block.

Mary inherited the Scottish throne just six days after her birth in 1542, when her father died following the Battle of Solway Moss against the English. At the age of five, she was sent by her French mother, Mary of Guise, to the royal court of France. There she was to receive the royal upbringing that the harsh, primitive society of Scotland could not provide.

At the age of 19, after the death of her first husband, Francis II, Mary returned to Scotland, a sophisticated, intelligent woman with an appetite for pleasure and a taste for reading. Though no great beauty, her impressive height of 6 ft and her golden hair made her a striking figure. Like most of the European nobility of the day Mary revelled in the pleasures of the chase, and was happy to find that in Scotland there were plenty of deer for sport. She played cards and indulged a mild fondness for gambling. She adored music and, most of all, loved to dance. For this she was pilloried by the Presbyterians. And when she fled to England she fared no better.

The queens who never met

In England, Mary was the prisoner of her cousin, Elizabeth, who had long been fascinated and somewhat jealous of the Scottish queen. Sir James Melville, Mary's ambassador to England, had told his mistress that Elizabeth's curiosity about her seemed unquenchable. She asked such questions as 'whether his queen's hair or hers was the best, and which of them two was fairest?'

Mary was confident of her ability to win Elizabeth's friendship when they met. But at first Mary was told that, until she had been cleared of complicity in Darnley's murder, it would be unwise for the two cousins to meet. And, as the long years of semi-captivity dragged on, Mary's assurance turned to doubt and finally to hatred.

As for Elizabeth herself, she saw Mary as the cause of many problems. From the moment she arrived in England she was a focus for plots and conspiracies. Finally, Elizabeth acted. In a letter appointing Mary's trial she wrote: 'You have in various ways and manners attempted to take my life and to bring my kingdom to destruction by bloodshed . . . These treasons will be proved to you and all made manifest.'

Mary's life was now forfeit. The tragedy of the two cousins who never met had come to its final conclusion.

---

mother of rebellion, the nurse of impiety, the handmaid of iniquity', as one member described the Scottish queen.

At the beginning of December, Elizabeth retreated a single step by issuing a public proclamation of the sentence against Mary. Yet later in the month when she received a long letter from Mary, which declared that she 'had a constant resolution to suffer death' as a martyr to her Catholic religion, Elizabeth wept.

A queen condemned by her cousin

But in January 1587 England was swept by rumours of yet another plot against the queen. Elizabeth could resist no longer. On February 1 she sent for William Davison, the Second Secretary of State, and signed the death warrant. Even at this last moment, Elizabeth shrank from sanctioning Mary's execution.

She was tempted to have Mary secretly murdered instead, so as to escape public blame for her death. But when this plan was suggested to Sir Amyas Paulet, Mary's gaoler, he refused indignantly: 'God forbid that I should make so foul a shipwreck of my conscience.'

Having waited so long, Elizabeth's councillors did not delay the execution any further. Without the queen's knowledge, the warrant was sent to Fotheringhay Castle in Northamptonshire, where Mary had been imprisoned since her trial.

On the evening of February 7, the messenger bearing the death warrant arrived at the castle. Mary had spent 20 of her 46 years as a prisoner, and had learnt to live with the expectation of sudden death. She received the news calmly. Turning to one of her ladies-in-waiting, she said: 'Well, Jane Kennedy, did I not tell you this would happen? I knew they would never allow me to live, I was too great an obstacle to their religion.'

The last evening of her life Mary spent putting her affairs in order and giving instructions for the disposal of her jewels and possessions. For a short time she lay down on her bed, closed her eyes, but did not sleep. In the Great Hall soldiers were building a wooden stage, which was draped in black. On it they placed the block itself, covered in black serge. Beside it was the axe.

At 8 a.m. on the sunny morning of February 8, Mary was brought into the Great Hall, where 300 spectators had gathered. There was a hush when she appeared. A tall, regal figure, the Scottish queen was dressed in black satin and wore a white headdress and veil.

Mary remained silent while the death warrant was read. When the Dean of Peterborough urged her to pray with him, she answered: 'I am settled in the ancient Catholic Roman religion, and mind to spend my blood defending it.' Ignoring his efforts, Mary then prayed aloud on her own. Her ladies-in-waiting helped her to undress down to her red satin petticoat. A white cloth, embroidered in gold, was placed over her eyes.

A few moments later the axe fell twice, severing her neck. When the executioner held up Mary's head, her auburn wig came away, revealing short grey hair.

Torn by pangs of conscience

When the news of Mary's death reached London, bells were rung and bonfires lit. But Elizabeth was enraged. She sent Davison to the Tower, and railed against her other councillors. It was convenient for her to blame others when the protests against the execution poured in from France and Spain. But she was also trying to appease the genuine guilt and shock she felt at the death of her cousin.

Elizabeth ordered that Mary should be buried at Peterborough Cathedral. But Mary's son, James I, moved his mother's body to Westminster Abbey. Her final resting place is not far from that of Queen Elizabeth.

The greatest sea-dog sails round the world

CAPTAIN COURAGEOUS *Sir Francis Drake, a yeoman's son who became an admiral, began as a humble apprentice in a coaster. At 18 he was a purser, and at 22 he had risen to captain. In 1577 he set off on the voyage which was to win him fame, fortune and a knighthood.*

One of the greatest adventures in England's maritime history began on December 13, 1577, when five ships, with a crew of 164 men and boys, sailed out of Plymouth harbour on the start of a voyage that was to take them around the world.

The expedition's commander was Francis Drake, a man of humble Devonshire birth who had already found fame and fortune as a pirate in the Caribbean. On his flagship, the *Pelican*, he lived like a nobleman, dining off silver dishes to the sound of trumpets. Armed with only 18 cannon and displacing only 120 tons, the *Pelican* was a small ship to venture

A STRANGE NEW FOOD *In the tropics, Drake and his men supplemented their rations with the fruits of the coconut palm. The natives, they discovered, used the contents as a major source of food, and they also made oil from the fleshy kernels. This drawing was made soon after Drake brought the fruit back to England.*

GIFT FROM A QUEEN

Sir Francis Drake gave Elizabeth I a coconut as a memento of his great voyage around the world. She was so fascinated by the fruit that she had a goblet made to hold it. The queen presented the goblet to Drake; it is now in Plymouth Art Gallery.

ENGLISH ACHIEVEMENT *A contemporary map shows the route Drake followed in his world voyage. He was the first Englishman to undertake such an arduous expedition, which lasted for two years and nine months. Drake started off with five ships, but only his flagship, the* Golden Hind, *completed the journey.*

on so arduous a voyage, but she still dwarfed the smallest ship – the 15 ton *Benedict*.

According to his instructions, Drake was to sail through the Straits of Magellan, at the southern tip of the South American continent, and head out into the Pacific in search of the mysterious *Terra Australis*. But, before the voyage began, Drake had a secret interview with Queen Elizabeth. She told him that she 'would be gladly avenged on the King of Spain for divers injuries'. Thus, the expedition was to be enlivened and enriched by raids on the Spanish Empire in South America.

Leadership quells a mutiny

The voyage out was slow and tedious. By June 1578, after more than six months at sea, trouble was brewing. The fleet had now reached Port Julien, near the southern tip of South America, and Drake's men had originally been told that they were bound for Alexandria. They now guessed the truth and many wanted to turn back. Moreover, they were angered by the idleness and arrogance of the merchant-gentlemen on the expedition.

This discontent was fomented by Drake's second-in-command, Thomas Doughty. He had been one of Drake's closest friends, but they had recently quarrelled. Now Doughty allegedly incited the crews to mutiny.

Drake's response was immediate. He arrested Doughty and put him on trial before a jury of 40 men. The verdict was inevitable; the sentence was death. Doughty was beheaded on the deck of the *Pelican*.

Drake now acted quickly to end the conflicts among his men. He ordered 'the gentlemen to haul and draw with the mariners' and continued: 'Let us show ourselves all to be of a company and let us not give occasion to the enemy to rejoice at our decay and overthrow.'

These brave words restored morale and the great decision was made. Abandoning two of his ships, Drake took the *Pelican*, the *Marigold* and the *Elizabeth* into the treacherous Straits of Magellan. They passed through the 300 mile passage in a record 16 days and entered the Pacific.

But there Drake and his ships ran into more trouble. In a prolonged north-easterly gale, the *Marigold* vanished. The *Pelican* – now renamed the *Golden Hind* – and the *Elizabeth* made for shelter on the coast. But no sooner had they dropped anchor than the *Golden Hind's* anchor-cable parted and she was forced to stand out to sea. The *Elizabeth* turned back for England.

Only the *Golden Hind* continued up the west coast of South America, where its appearance was to the Spanish 'like a visitation from Heaven'. They had come to regard the Pacific as their own private lake. But now Drake played havoc with Spanish ports and shipping on the Peruvian coast. His greatest moment was the capture of the treasure-ship, *Cacafuego*, on March 1, 1579. Its cargo – 80 lb. of gold, 26 tons of silver, 13 chests of pieces of eight, pearls, emeralds and rubies – was beyond price.

Rewarded by the queen

Drake now headed for home. First he sailed north in a vain search for the elusive north-west passage. Sailing south again, he stopped at the bay of what is now San Francisco to refit the *Golden Hind* before an audience of awe-struck Indians. They offered to make Drake their king. His response was to claim the land for England and name it New Albion.

Now the *Golden Hind* struck out across the Pacific. The crossing completed, Drake stopped at the Spice Islands where he loaded his ship with 6 tons of cloves, then fetching 5s a pound on the European market.

But on the last leg of the voyage, the *Golden Hind* ran aground on a reef near the Celebes. Drake had to throw half the precious cloves overboard, as well as eight guns, before the ship was refloated.

On September 26, 1580, after a voyage of 33 months, the *Golden Hind* put in at Plymouth. The voyage had been a resounding triumph. Its private backers received £47 for every £1 invested. The queen took £300,000. Drake himself, the first Briton to sail round the world, became a national hero. He was knighted by his sovereign aboard the *Golden Hind* in 1581. Seldom has a title carried more significance. In honouring Drake, Elizabeth flung down a challenge to the greatest power in Europe and invited her subjects to look to the sea for their future strength.

Intrepid explorers in search of fortune

'O brave new world!' Shakespeare called the Elizabethan age. And for the sea-dogs who searched for an empire it was. For the bold and adventurous there beckoned the riches of the east and the fabulous wealth of the Americas.

Among the great Elizabethan seamen were Sir Hugh Willoughby and Richard Chancellor. Both perished seeking a north-east passage to the east. But they established trade with Muscovy, and they were followed by Anthony Jenkinson, who journeyed to Persia. Soon, English merchants were exchanging woollens for rich Persian carpets.

The quest for the north-west passage inspired explorers too. In 1576 Martin Frobisher (above) reached the far north of Canada before being forced to turn back. He had found a back door to the lucrative fur trade of Canada.

But the lure of Spanish gold was the main driving force – and one of the men who fell victim to it was John Hawkins. His third voyage to the Caribbean in 1567 ended in disaster. Four ships were sunk by the Spanish.

Such disasters did not deter Elizabeth's bold captains. The example of her explorers and navigators showed future empire-builders the way to success.

PAINTING A NEW WORLD

Among the early English settlers in Virginia was the artist John White, who first landed at Roanoke Island in 1585. The following year, he and his companions were forced to return to England. In 1587, however, White was sent out again. But the privations that he and the colonists had to face were such that his fellow settlers sent him back to England to beg for aid. By the time he returned to Virginia all trace of the colony had vanished.

But the drawings White made of the American Indians survived. In this water-colour, two of them eat maize from a platter.

A MANSION BORN OF THE QUEST FOR PERFECTION

PARKLAND APPROACH *The impact of Longleat owes as much to its harmonious woodland setting as it does to the bold, grand exterior conceived by Sir John Thynne. The approach passes through parkland to the crest of a wooded hill which looks down on the house and the lakes beyond. Longleat is built around two inner courtyards, probably over the foundations of a monastery.*

DARING DESIGNER *Sir John Thynne, a compulsive builder and a perfectionist, spent 27 years building and rebuilding Longleat. His ideas broke many of the conventions of his time.*

For the first time since the days of the Romans, England under the Tudors was able to settle down to a long period of internal peace. From 1485 onwards, the upper classes began to spend the newly won wealth which came from the development of overseas trade by Britain's sea-going adventurers. And Englishmen were also expanding their cultural outlook beyond the English Channel. They were eager to learn from the glittering world of the Renaissance. From uncultivated warlords, the aristocrats changed to cultivated courtiers with clothes festooned with lace and rich embroidery. Velvet took the place of more serviceable broadcloth.

In their houses, as well as in their clothes, the change was astonishing. Here, if anywhere, was proof that the Middle Ages were over. No longer was the site of a major building chosen first and foremost for defence; its outlook became important, too. Instead of massive walls looking into a sheltered courtyard, there were thousands of panes of glittering glass looking outward to the world. Dark, small rooms were abandoned in favour of spacious-

ness and light, and the people of Tudor England put down carpets where their ancestors had been content to strew rushes. Windows were larger and had clear, rather than stained, glass. House fronts, once uncompromising, unscaleable stone, were now decorated with superimposed columns and the busts of Roman emperors in circular niches. Moats were filled in, to be replaced by lawns. The Englishman's home had ceased to be a castle.

A Renaissance palace in England

The great house which set the pattern of the new style of architecture was Longleat, the life work of a man who had reason to value light and air. Sir John Thynne built Longleat in the years that followed his release from the dark confines of the Tower of London, where he had been held prisoner for two years from 1551.

His house, with its enormous windows of clear glass commanding wide views in every direction, and its succession of lofty chambers forming long uncluttered vistas, symbolised his own sense of freedom – and also expressed the freedom of the Elizabethan age. Longleat

was the first great Renaissance palace to be built in England. And, though rivals soon sprang up to challenge it, it remained unquestionably the greatest.

Thynne began his career in the reign of Henry VIII, at a time when a young man could advance himself by gaining favour with one of the influential new men at court. Such undertakings were hazardous, for a rising star could also fall – and take all his followers into oblivion with him.

Thynne was introduced to the court by his uncle, William, a servant of Henry VIII, and he gained the favour of Edward Seymour, brother-in-law of the king, and became his steward. As his patron's fortunes improved, so did Thynne's. In 1547 Seymour, then Duke of Somerset, became Lord Protector, and in the same year Thynne was knighted on the battlefield of Pinkie where Seymour beat the Scots.

In 1549, during the reign of the boy king Edward VI, Seymour fell from power and a little over two years later was executed. Thynne followed his master to the Tower and almost to the block. He spent two years in prison but he was released in 1553 upon payment of a £6000 fine. He was ordered to retire to his country estate in Wiltshire where he devoted himself to building a new house, Longleat. The house was so named because of the watercourse, or *leat*, in the grounds.

Thynne, described by a contemporary as 'an ingenious man and a traveller', was an active builder for 30 years. Yet, apart from Longleat, little is known of his work. But as the Duke of Somerset's steward, he would probably have supervised the building of Somerset House, which began in 1547.

From the time of his release from prison until his death in 1580, Thynne never ceased in his attempts to make Longleat into the house of his dreams. One of his neighbours wrote a

WELCOMING THE GUESTS *Visitors are greeted at the main gate in this painting, dated 1676. The outward appearance of the house has hardly changed since it was built in the 16th century, although the walled forecourts and fountains disappeared during later 18th-century landscaping.*

HUNTING SCENES *The high walls of the Great Hall are decorated with a series of hunting scenes, painted in the 18th century by John Wootton. A gallery overlooks the hall with its sporting trophies and its strikingly carved mantelpiece, part of Thynne's house which still survives.*

satire in which the house itself complained of exhaustion: 'But now see him that by these thirtie yeares almost with such turmoyle of mynd byn thinking of me, framing and erecting me, musing many a tyme with great care and now and then pulling downe this or that parte of me to enlarge sometyme a foote, or some few inches, upon a conceyt, or this or that man's speech . . .'

Lifelong search for perfection
Thanks to the remarkably complete records and accounts which survive, it is known that Thynne rebuilt the house twice before it was destroyed by fire in 1567, and twice more afterwards. Its present façade, which dates from the end of his life, is a brilliantly confident display of the new Classicism. Its graceful bow windows feature three of the Classical orders, Corinthian, Doric and Ionic (described as 'Dorrick' and 'Yonk' in a note by one of the masons). Thynne was the first man to build in this style in England.

During this period he had as his master masons the Frenchmen Allen Maynard and Adrian Gaunt, and the Englishmen Robert Smythson and William Spicer, later to become Surveyor of the Queen's Works. Architects in the modern sense – designers rather than artificers – were still unknown in England, and if any one man can be said to be the true architect of Longleat, that man is Thynne himself.

Breaking with convention
From the start he showed extraordinary audacity. Longleat's main prospect faces south-south-east in defiance of the common rule of the time that houses should face the opposite way. The Elizabethans detested the south wind: Shakespeare made Caliban curse Prospero in *The Tempest* with the words 'a south-west blow on ye, and blister you all o'er'.

Thynne ignored this superstition, along with the tradition that the main rooms should face inwards towards a courtyard. The courts around which he built Longleat serve mainly as wells to gather light. The main rooms all face outwards to the park.

He also had the idea of putting little square pavilions on the roof to serve as 'banketting houses'. In the 16th century 'banquet' meant 'dessert'; Thynne and his guests would stroll up to the roof after dinner in the Great Hall for a final glass of wine and to watch the sun go down behind the Mendip Hills.

Sir John never saw the ultimate flowering of his noble house. He died before the final rebuilding was completed. Inside the house, only the Great Hall has remained fundamentally unchanged, with its hammerbeam roof and the great fireplace.

But from the outside, Longleat remains largely as Sir John envisaged it. It is also an example of the taste, wealth and vision of a nation in one of its proudest and most vigorous ages.

A band of heroes defeats the might of Spain

LEGENDS OF DRAKE'S DRUM
At the beating of this drum, Drake's sailors mustered for battle on the decks of his ship, the Revenge, *in 1588. After the defeat of the Spanish Armada, Drake's drum soon became the source of many popular legends. According to one, the drum will beat of its own accord if England ever faces a Spanish threat again. Another legend says that Drake, on his death-bed, vowed to return if the drum were beaten in warning of approaching danger. The drum is now in Buckland Abbey, near Plymouth.*

In the summer of 1588, all England awaited the long-prepared blow of the Spanish Armada. For three years, Philip II of Spain had been building a fleet which would bring his heretical enemies to their knees. And now word had reached the English that Philip was on the point of launching his 'enterprise of England' against them.

On May 20, 1588, the mightiest fleet the world had yet seen set sail from Lisbon. But then, as far as the English were concerned, it vanished into the unknown. It was not until July 19 that a pinnace sailed into Plymouth with the momentous news that the Armada had been sighted off the Isles of Scilly.

Beacons blazed along the Channel coast to warn of the approaching foe. The moment all Europe had been awaiting – the ultimate clash between Protestant England and Catholic Spain – was at hand. According to legend, Sir Francis Drake turned from a game of bowls on Plymouth Hoe and said: 'Let them wait their turn, there is time for that and to beat the Spaniards after.'

The Armada was a formidable fleet of 24 galleons, 40 merchantmen converted for war,

25 hulks to carry supplies and 36 smaller vessels. The Spanish plan was to win control of the Channel and then transport the Duke of Parma's waiting army across from Flanders to the English shore. Even under the most expert direction, this plan would have been difficult to carry out; and the Armada lacked such skill.

At its head was the Duke of Medina Sidonia, known as *el bueno* (the good). He was an honourable and courageous man, who had been forced a few months before, reluctantly and unhappily, into the command of Philip's great enterprise. 'I possess,' he said, 'neither aptitude, ability, health nor fortune.' Even before the Armada reached England, he was imploring his master to cancel the expedition. But Philip ordered him to proceed.

In the hope of a miracle

Opposed to Medina Sidonia was a fleet roughly equal to his own in power. The English had 21 first-line ships, 40 of the second line and a host of smaller vessels. They carried only 14,000 sailors – compared with the Armada's 30,000. But they had nearly 2000 cannon, compared with the Armada's 1000. And John Hawkins, the chief naval adviser to the government, had revolutionised the design of their ships. The towering castle-like ships of Henry VIII's day had been replaced by longer, narrower, faster galleons. Traditional

RIVAL MONARCHS *Personal as well as religious enmity divided the Catholic Philip of Spain (left) from the Protestant Elizabeth of England (below). The Armada was the climax of their hostility.*

naval strategy had been to board the enemy's ships and capture them. The new English method was to outmanoeuvre and sink them. The English ships had light guns that could hurl a 9 lb. shot half a mile.

Against England's navy, the Spanish relied on their faith. Philip had said to Medina Sidonia: 'If you fail, you fail; but the cause being the cause of God, you will not fail.' One Spanish captain, knowing the power of the English fleet, said: 'We are sailing against England in the confident expectation of a miracle.'

Such were the thoughts of the captains and crews of the Armada as it sailed up the Channel. But at first, God seemed to be on the Spaniards' side. For the English fleet was penned in Plymouth Harbour by tide and wind.

Now the skill of the English commanders played a decisive part. The fleet was led by Lord Howard of Effingham. Beneath him he had three subordinates of supreme ability – Francis Drake, John Hawkins and Martin Frobisher. By daring seamanship they got their ships out to sea.

But the English fleet was still at a disadvantage. For the moment, only 24 English ships of any size were in open waters. They faced a Spanish fleet of unexpected strength

THE BATTLE RAGES *A detail from a contemporary painting shows, in stylised form, the English and Spanish fleets in the thick of action in the Channel. This stage of the battle lasted a week. The English ships fly the red cross of St George at their mastheads. Lord Admiral Howard's flagship, the* Ark Royal, *is in the bottom left of the picture, raking a Spanish galley with its broadside. Its mainsail is emblazoned with the royal arms of England.*

and – even more sobering – awesome in its disciplined formation. Medina Sidonia had arranged his vessels in a crescent shape, with strong galleons at either tip. This formation demanded skilled seamanship on the part of the Spanish. It also meant that the vulnerable storeships and troop transports, clustered in the centre, were protected against an attack from the rear. If an English squadron tried to slip round, the Spanish galleons on either wing could drop back and quickly cut it off.

The battle begins

Although the English fleet lay between the Spanish and their destination, the Armada also had the benefit of the prevailing wind. It could maintain its formation with military precision, and it could sail into battle or break off the engagement at will.

The next step of the English commanders was to deprive their foes of this advantage. During the night of July 20, they performed another feat of outstanding naval skill, crossing the bows of the Spanish and sailing round to take the windward position. Meanwhile, the remaining English vessels were able to make their way out of Plymouth to join the main fleet sailing up the English Channel.

COURAGE OF A QUEEN
As the menace of the Spanish Armada drew close to England's shores, Elizabeth I addressed her army at Tilbury. In this contemporary picture, the queen rides among her troops, while the hoped-for destruction of the Armada is shown in the background. Elizabeth roused her men with the words: 'I know I have the body of a weak and feeble woman, but I have the heart and stomach of a king, and of a king of England too, and think foul scorn that Parma or Spain or any prince of Europe should dare to invade the borders of my realm; to which, rather than any dishonour shall grow by me, I will myself take up arms.'

The Spanish were dismayed by this achievement. Now Howard and his commanders had the initiative – and they never lost it. In accordance with the traditional rules of war, Howard sent forward his admiral's pinnace, the *Disdain*, to give the battle signal by firing her guns within sight of the enemy. Medina

Sidonia responded to this ceremonial challenge by hoisting aloft the standard of his expedition, consecrated to victory in Lisbon Cathedral three months before. It carried the arms of Spain between a picture of the Virgin Mary and the Crucifixion, with the motto 'Arise, O Lord and vindicate Thy cause'.

A week-long running battle followed, as the Armada moved in stately procession up the Channel. But Howard did not dare take his fleet into the heart of the Armada, which, despite the ferocity of the English attacks, stubbornly kept its formation. He reported: 'We durst not adventure to put in among them, their fleet being so strong.' Drake captured a flagship, and two other vessels were lost. But otherwise the Armada was intact when it anchored off Calais on July 27.

Driven by fire to disaster

Medina Sidonia had reached his first objective. He now awaited the arrival of the invasion force from Flanders. But the Duke of Parma, his invasion barges hemmed in by the ships of the Dutch rebels, was unable to join him. Medina Sidonia wrote in desperation, urging him to hurry: 'I am anchored here, two leagues from Calais, with the enemy's fleet on my flank. They can command me whenever they like and I shall be unable to do them much harm in return.' The appeal was in vain. Parma stayed where he was.

To the English, however, the situation still looked alarming. A powerful enemy fleet, which had survived all that they could bring against it, was still in the Channel. Some other weapon must be found.

The English commanders now met in council. Howard announced that he had sent a dispatch to Dover for hulks, which he would use as fireships. Crammed full of pitch, gunpowder, tar and anything else that would burn, such vessels were the terror of any fleet caught in harbour. But Drake was unwilling to wait. He offered one of his ships, the *Thomas*, for

COMMANDER OF THE FLEET *England's admiral, Lord Howard of Effingham (left), was a skilled but cautious commander, who knew how to make use of the talents of his brilliant subordinates, Francis Drake, John Hawkins and Martin Frobisher. In contrast, his adversary, the Duke of Medina Sidonia, was reluctant to command the Armada and pleaded with Philip II of Spain to be relieved from the post, stating that he had no experience of war on land or sea and that he suffered from sea-sickness. Surprisingly, Howard was also a Catholic. His loyalty to the throne proved the futility of Philip's cherished hopes that English Catholics would rise to back his invasion, for which Medina Sidonia's Armada was to have established a bridgehead in Kent.*

A CONTEMPORARY RECORD

In the first of a contemporary series of charts showing the Armada's progress, the Spanish fleet is seen off Cornwall. English and Spanish scout ships are also shown.

The English fleet sails out of Plymouth harbour in two squadrons. The plan was to menace the Armada from the rear. By this time, the Spanish had taken up their battle formation – a perfect crescent shape – which was designed to protect the weaker vessels in the fleet.

A skirmish off Portland Bill (left) was the first clash between the fleets. It temporarily breaks both their formations, then the Armada manages to reform and sets off up the Channel. The English, now in four squadrons, follow in close pursuit.

Driven from Calais by English fireships, the now disorganised Armada flees into the North Sea to start its disastrous voyage home. Spain lost 50 ships and 20,000 soldiers and sailors.

INVINCIBLE SAILOR *Francis Drake, Vice-Admiral of the English fleet, led the attack as the Armada sailed up the Channel.*

Drake, Hawkins and Frobisher – kept their heads and attacked the heart of the Armada. The Spanish were running out of ammunition and the English were able to batter away unmolested with their cannon at short range. The proud warships of the Armada, riddled with holes, began to sink lower into the water. Three galleons were put out of action, many more were crippled and hundreds of Spanish sailors killed or wounded.

On the following morning, the Armada stood on the verge of destruction. To the windward lay the English fleet, to leeward the treacherous shoals of the Dutch coast. 'It was,' wrote one Spaniard, 'the most fearful day in all the world, for the whole company lost all hope of success and looked only for death.' Even if the English did nothing, it seemed that the Armada must be driven to destruction on the shore.

Then, quite suddenly, the Armada was reprieved by the weather. The wind swung round to the south-west and the battered Spanish were able to sail unhindered into the North Sea. At a council-of-war on board their flagship, the Spanish admirals agreed that if the wind changed again they would return, but as long as it stayed in its present quarter they would sail north. For three days the English fleet followed the Armada northwards. Then on August 2, off the coast of Scotland, the wind changed again to north-west. The English lost contact and turned for home.

With the new wind the Armada might have renewed its threat. But it was a spent force, with no choice but to limp home. Driven headlong by the wind which had saved them

the purpose. Seven other ships were also prepared and, at midnight on July 28, were sent on the flood tide into the heart of the Spanish fleet.

The first two were intercepted, but the rest sailed on. The Spanish captains, terrified lest these blazing apparitions might explode, panicked. They cut their anchor cables and made for the open sea. The fireships drifted harmlessly to burn themselves out on the shore. But they had done their work; the close formation of the Armada had been broken.

The sun rose to reveal the Spanish ships scattered for miles along the coast. Howard at once brought the whole of his fleet into the attack. He and his squadron wasted time capturing a galleon which, in the night's panic, had run aground. But his subordinates –

FIRE IN THE NIGHT *The death-blow to the Armada came when the English sent fireships into the Spanish fleet as it lay anchored off Calais. Though Medina Sidonia did not lose a single ship, the effect of the attack was disastrous. His commanders panicked and fled in confusion.*

earlier, ship after ship foundered as the battered Armada sailed northwards.

Medina Sidonia issued sensible orders to his fleet, still more than 100 ships strong. They were to steer a course 30 miles north of Cape Wrath on the north-western tip of Scotland and keep well west of Ireland.

Those who followed his advice reached home. But others, desperately short of food and water, disobeyed and steered for Ireland in the hope of picking up supplies. Some 25 ships foundered on the rocky crags of western Ireland. Some Spaniards were drowned escaping from the wrecks while hundreds struggled ashore, only to be rounded up and slaughtered. The Lord Deputy of Ireland had sent out the order that all captives be put to death.

Doomed from the start

The great Armada had been humiliated. Spain had lost 50 ships and 20,000 men. On hearing the news, Philip II shut himself up in his magnificent palace, the Escorial, and gave himself up to prayer. Only his confessor dared to approach him. Medina Sidonia retired to his country estate.

Philip's navy was far from destroyed. Within a few years, it was stronger than ever. But the blow to Spanish prestige in Europe was irreparable. The invasion plan was misbegotten and doomed from the start. But what the world noted was that the mightiest empire on earth had been dealt a crushing blow by a small Protestant nation.

TREASURE FROM THE SEA

Pursued by the English and scattered by the winds, the defeated Armada sought a route home round Scotland and Ireland. The Spanish ships were carrying huge quantities of treasure: gold coin to pay the men, richly wrought religious objects, silver tableware, personal jewellery, charms and talismens. At least 25 of these floating treasure-ships were wrecked on the Irish coast, and for over three centuries their cargoes lay buried beneath the waves. But in June 1967 a carefully planned diving expedition off the coast of Ireland by a young Belgian diver, Robert Stenuit, began to bring to light the riches that had been lost to the sea.

Two finds from the wreck of the Girona, *a jewel in the shape of a salamander (above), carried as a charm against fire, and a relic box.*

Victors whose efforts were unrewarded

As the Spanish Armada vanished into the mists of the North Sea, the fleet that had defeated it put back into port. But the fate of the victors was almost as pitiable as that of the enemy they had vanquished.

As soon as the fleet got back to shore, disease swept through the ships. Lord Howard of Effingham implored the help of Lord Burghley, the queen's principal minister: 'Sickness (plague) and mortality begin wonderfully to grow amongst us,' he wrote.

Howard searched for lodgings for his men. But his search turned up nothing better than barns and outhouses. The Spanish had killed 100 men at the most; disease carried away thousands of Elizabeth's sailors.

Anxious to save money, the government ordered rapid demobilisation. Men who expected full pay were fobbed off with a small advance. Hawkins, the Treasurer of the Navy, bitterly accused Burghley of saving the pay of those who had died, though they left families behind them. Hawkins and Drake set up a fund, known as the 'Chatham Chest', to provide relief for the distressed sailors. This was an unprecedented act of private charity. But disentangling his official accounts, finding money from nowhere, and doing his best for the men proved too much for Hawkins. He asked to be relieved from his post: 'God, I trust, will deliver me of it ere it be long, for there is no other Hell.'

Elizabeth's broken promise

In the end, Howard paid off some of the men with treasure taken from a captured Spanish galleon, promising to repay the queen from his own purse if she objected. 'It were pitiful,' he explained, 'to have men starve after such a service.' And he appealed to Elizabeth's self-interest: 'If such men should not be cared for better than to let them starve and die miserably, we should very hardly get men to serve.'

Elizabeth had indeed previously pledged herself to pay for victory with hard cash. In her famous Tilbury speech, she had held out the promise of a rich reward to strengthen her people's fighting spirit: 'I know already for your towardness you deserve rewards and crowns, and we do assure you, in the word of a prince, they shall be duly paid you.'

But 'the word of a prince' proved fickle in this case. Elizabeth may well have regretted her apparent ingratitude. But she was the unwilling prisoner of her empty coffers. The cost of mobilising the entire English fleet to fight the Armada had almost bankrupted her treasury. Even during the battle, food and ammunition had run short. The real culprits were reluctant taxpayers and corrupt officials, who between them squeezed both the monarch and the forgotten heroes of 1588.

THE GENTLE POET WHO 'BESTRODE THE WORLD'

THE BARD *A portrait of Shakespeare on the title page of the First Folio edition of his works, with an introductory poem by Ben Jonson, published seven years after his death.*

The adventurous, freedom-loving Elizabethans were pioneers in almost every field – in seafaring and exploration, music, architecture, drama and poetry.

From this galaxy of talent, however, one man stands out supreme. William Shakespeare was not just a child of his own time, but a writer whose genius has won him an unparalleled position in English literature.

But while Shakespeare's plays are the best known in English literature, remarkably little is known of the writer himself. Certainly there was nothing in the early career of William Shakespeare to suggest his rise to greatness. He was 27 before he wrote anything of promise, and he seems to have gone through a difficult period in his youth.

Success in the capital

His father, a Warwickshire merchant, dealt in corn and malt, leather, hides and wool, and became so prominent in local affairs at Stratford-upon-Avon that he was made Bailiff (mayor). William, the third child of the family, was born at Stratford on April 22 or 23, 1564. Life must have been pleasant for him during the days of his father's prosperity.

In view of his father's position, William is almost certain to have attended Stratford Grammar School, where the boys were made to learn by heart great sections from classical Latin authors such as Cicero, Virgil and Ovid. The playwright Ben Jonson was later to sum up Shakespeare's school career as having left him with 'small Latin and less Greek'. But the plays that were to pour from his pen in later years leave no doubt that somewhere, probably at school, Shakespeare acquired a thorough grounding in Roman history.

When Shakespeare was 17, his father's fortune took a downward turn, and the family began to run into debt. A year later William was married – hurried into a wedding with Anne Hathaway, a woman eight years older than himself; their daughter Susanna was born within six months of the marriage.

About 1587 Shakespeare left Stratford. According to tradition he is said to have fled because he had been caught raiding the deer park of a neighbouring landlord, Sir Thomas Lucy. He had revenged himself for what he thought an over-severe punishment by writing

ALL THE WORLD'S A STAGE *The Globe theatre was built in Southwark in 1598 as a permanent home for the 'Lord Chamberlain's Men', the company of actors to which Shakespeare belonged.*

a lampoon on Lucy – and now feared the consequences. He took refuge in London where, for a time, he slipped into obscurity.

Given his dazzling gifts, it was an obscurity that could not last. He was attracted to the company of poets and actors, and by 1592 had made enough of an impact on the capital to attract enemies as well as friends. He was denounced by an envious rival, the ageing and embittered author Robert Greene, as a crafty imitator – 'an upstart crow, beautified with our feathers'.

A friend at court

But from this time Shakespeare's progress was smooth and rapid. He gained an influential patron at court, the brilliant young nobleman Lord Southampton; and he joined a company of players, the 'Lord Chamberlain's Men', in which he soon became a 'sharer', entitled to a proportion of their profits. By 1599 he was part-owner of a new playhouse called the Globe, at Southwark, and had already purchased New Place, one of Stratford's largest houses.

Shakespeare's friends concur in describing him as 'gentle', 'civil', 'friendly' and 'sweet'. He was 'honest, and of an open and free nature', wrote Ben Jonson. John Aubrey, the 17th-century gossip, wrote that besides being 'handsome' and 'well-shaped', he had shown 'a very ready and pleasant, smooth wit'.

Poems and plays

Many records remain of his public activities, but references to his private life are few. The Sonnets, however, published without his permission in 1609, give a wonderfully vivid, if puzzling, picture of his attachment to a young man (probably Lord Southampton) and of his sensual passion for a Dark Lady, who became his beloved friend's mistress.

Shakespeare spent the greater part of his life in London, though he paid regular visits to his Warwickshire home. Anne Shakespeare faded into the background after her hasty marriage. She bore him three children – first Susanna; and, in 1581, twins, a boy and girl named Hamnet and Judith. The poet was devoted to his son and Hamnet's death at the age of 11 left a permanent scar: a boy aged 10 or 11, pert, quick-witted and charming, is introduced into many of his plays. Hamnet's death aside, Shakespeare's adult career, as far as can be judged, was a happy one.

Shakespeare's writing career was to some extent conditioned by the need to satisfy the changing demands of the Elizabethan theatre; but it also followed its own line of development. He probed deeper and more daringly into experience as he grew older. And as his range of subject-matter widened, so his mastery of language and dramatic technique increased.

During 20 astonishingly creative years Shakespeare's output was enormous. His work can be divided into four main phases: his literary apprenticeship, closing in 1594, resulted in the two long narrative poems, 'Venus and Adonis' and 'The Rape of Lucrece', historical dramas such as *Henry VI* and *Richard III*, the tragedy of *Romeo and Juliet* and such comedies as *Comedy of Errors* and *The Taming of the Shrew*.

In the second phase, between 1594 and 1599, the mature Shakespeare wrote three of his greatest historical plays – *Henry V* and the two parts of *Henry IV* – and such masterly comedies as *Much Ado About Nothing* and *As You Like It*. The third period, ending about 1608, was the period of his great tragedies *Hamlet, Othello, Macbeth, King Lear* and *Antony and Cleopatra*. But if the playwright's thoughts took a pessimistic cast during early middle age, he threw off melancholy during his final phase. His last play, *The Tempest*, was also the finest of his romantic comedies.

About 1611, Shakespeare decided to retire to Stratford. He paid off the family debts, and on April 23, 1616, at the age of 52, he died of fever – said to have been the result of a 'merry meeting' with his fellow poets Michael Drayton and Ben Jonson, during which they drank too much. As his legacy to mankind he left the fruits of his creative years, 37 plays, two long narrative poems and his matchless sonnets.

THE MAGIC OF SHAKESPEARE

Shakespeare's work reveals an extraordinary insight into the workings of the heart. He probed the very recesses of human experience, and out of what he saw he created the most exquisite poetry, filled with compassion for every walk of life. His gift for capturing the essence of human character has never been equalled. The galaxy of men and women he created range from the heroic Othello, the subtle villain, Iago, the bewitching beauty, Cleopatra, and the ill-starred lovers Romeo and Juliet, to the rough-humoured Bottom and his fellow 'mechanicals' in *A Midsummer Night's Dream*.

On Mercy
> The Quality of mercy is not strain'd,
> It droppeth as the gentle rain from heaven
> Upon the place beneath: it is twice blest;
> It blesseth him that gives and him that takes.

(Portia in *The Merchant of Venice*)

On the finality of death
> Ay, but to die, and go we know not where;
> To lie in cold obstruction and to rot;
> This sensible warm motion to become
> A kneaded clod.

(Claudio in *Measure for Measure*)

On the beauties of the countryside
> I know a bank whereon the wild thyme blows,
> Where oxlips and the nodding violet grows
> Quite over-canopied with luscious woodbine,
> With sweet musk-roses, and with eglantine:
> There sleeps Titania some time of the night,
> Lull'd in these flowers with dances and delight;
> And there the snake throws her enamell'd skin,
> Weed wide enough to wrap a fairy in.

(Oberon in *A Midsummer Night's Dream*)

On the glory of England
> This royal throne of kings, this scepter'd isle,
> This earth of majesty, this seat of Mars,
> This other Eden, demi-paradise,
> This fortress built by Nature for herself
> Against infection and the hand of war,
> This happy breed of men, this little world,
> This precious stone set in the silver sea,
> Which serves it in the office of a wall,
> Or as a moat defensive to a house,
> Against the envy of less happier lands,
> This blessed plot, this earth, this realm, this
>   England,
> This nurse, this teeming womb of royal kings
> Fear'd by their breed and famous by their
>   birth,
> Renowned for their deeds as far from home,
> For Christian service and true chivalry,
> As is the sepulchre in stubborn Jewry,
> Of the world's ransom, blessed Mary's Son:
> This land of such dear souls, this dear, dear
>   land.

(John of Gaunt in *Richard II*)

Shakespeare's farewell
> Our revels now are ended. These our actors,
> As I foretold you, were all spirits and
> Are melted into air, into thin air:
> And, like the baseless fabric of this vision,
> The cloud-capp'd towers, the gorgeous palace
> The solemn temples, the great globe itself,
> Yea, all which it inherit, shall dissolve
> And, like this insubstantial pageant faded,
> Leave not a rack behind. We are such stuff
> As dreams are made on, and our little life
> Is rounded with a sleep.

(Prospero in *The Tempest*)

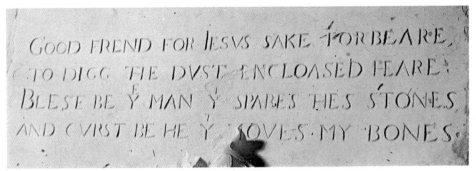

SHAKESPEARE'S TOMBSTONE *William Shakespeare was buried at Stratford in 1616. The inscription on his grave begins 'Good friend, for Jesus' sake forbear, To dig the dust enclosed here'.*

155

A weeping queen sends her favourite to the block

FROM FAVOUR TO FALL

Elizabeth's bold signature on Essex's death-warrant (above), now in the British Museum, contrasted with the queen's reluctance to send her favourite to his death. She recalled one warrant, and only the issue of a second sealed his fate. Essex's ring (right) is now in the Norman Undercroft Museum in Westminster Abbey. Legend has it that Elizabeth herself gave the ring to Essex, promising that she would pardon him of any offence if he sent it to her. But this did not save him from death for high treason.

At 10.30 a.m. on the morning of Sunday, February 8, 1601, Robert Devereux, the 2nd Earl of Essex, had all England at his mercy. He had several hundred swordsmen supporting him – romantic young knights who had fought beside him in his campaigns abroad, fiery Welsh squires from the Devereux estates on the Marches, disillusioned noblemen who felt that Queen Elizabeth had not rewarded them sufficiently. And the earl had only to turn left out of Essex House and lead his private army down the Strand towards the palace of Whitehall to menace the defenceless Queen Elizabeth and her loyal courtiers.

But Essex turned right – away from Whitehall and towards the city of London – and his chance was gone. He hoped to gather extra swordsmen there and to persuade the crowds who flocked to hear the Sunday sermon at St Paul's to respond to his appeal to purge the queen's government of its evil elements. He miscalculated. While he was trying to muster support in the city, Elizabeth's own forces had time to gather. By the time the earl finally turned to march on Whitehall it was clear that he would have to fight.

This miscalculation was typical of Robert Devereux's entire career. He was the supreme popular idol in the closing years of Elizabeth's reign. But he had no competition, for the heroic generation of Elizabethans had come to an end. And the loss of the queen's favour had forced him into revolt.

Romance with a queen

Much of Essex's appeal lay in the qualities that were to bring about his fall – his rashness and his impetuosity. Elizabeth herself was entranced by his dashing, madcap personality. His short temper, his flaring eyes, his unpredictable sulks, his inability to conceal his emotions – all this captivated her. She was 34 years older than Essex, and she felt able to forgive his boyish inconsistency.

For 12 years from 1587 a flirtatious romance between them pursued its explosive course. Elizabeth entrusted the young earl with a succession of responsible tasks – military commands in France and Ireland, naval commands against Cadiz and the Azores.

But Essex owed these favours to more than the power of a young man to entrance an ageing woman. His stepfather, the Earl of Leicester, used his influence at court to win Essex favour. There soon gathered round him a group of able and calculating men, chief among whom were the brothers Anthony and Francis Bacon. Both the Bacons were politicians of formidable talent and ambition.

'For the Queen! For the Queen!'

But Essex needed money as well as power. For the earl's extravagance far outran his income, and his only other sources of funds were the tax-farming offices given him by Elizabeth herself. And, given as a sign of favour, they could easily be withdrawn.

Essex, too, was unequal to the tasks Elizabeth gave him. Though he blustered and sulked his way out of many situations, in 1599 he went too far. He deserted the army he was leading in Ireland, returned secretly to court and broke into the queen's bedchamber. There, he accused his rivals, Walter Raleigh

DESTROYED BY FOLLY *Robert Devereux, Earl of Essex, painted in 1596 when he was 29 years old. Tall and handsome, Essex had an irresistible appeal for women. The ageing queen was so obsessed by him that, when they first met in 1587, she refused to let him out of her sight. Their romance lasted for 12 years.*

and Robert Cecil, of treason, claiming that they were being paid by Spain to ruin England. He was placed under house arrest.

Released at the end of 1600, Essex amplified his accusations. And they became his battle-cry on February 8, 1601, when in his impetuous revolt he tried to rally support in the city of London. 'For the Queen! For the Queen!' he shouted. 'A plot is laid against my life!'

Essex had no evidence for his cries. They sprang from jealousy, from his disappointed hopes – and from fear of bankruptcy, for the queen had at last cut off his income. London's Sunday church-goers ignored the earl's fevered shouts. His followers sheathed their swords and vanished. At the foot of Ludgate Hill his depleted and dispirited band was routed by a band of loyal militia.

A fortnight later Essex was executed. But whenever his name was mentioned in the remaining 25 months of her life, the queen was seen to weep.

SERVANTS OF THE QUEEN

No family in England gave more loyal service to Elizabeth I than the Cecils. William Cecil (above left), later Lord Burghley, was one of England's greatest statesmen. Elizabeth appointed him Secretary of State in 1558. 'This judgment I have of you,' she said, 'that you will not be corrupted by any manner of gifts.' Burghley lived up to this trust, and remained Elizabeth's faithful servant until his death in 1598. His son, Robert (above right), served the queen from 1591, but his quarrel with her favourite, Essex, kept him from high office until 1596. Robert continued his family's tradition of dedicated service under Elizabeth's successor, James I. He died in 1612.

Twilight years of the 'Virgin Queen'

Sir Walter Raleigh's graceful epitaph to Queen Elizabeth I was 'a lady whom time had surprised'. It seemed impossible to her contemporaries that 'Gloriana', the 'Virgin Queen', should age, let alone die. But after the defeat of the Armada in 1588 Elizabeth went into a sharper decline than her subjects realised or than she would admit.

In her sixties, the queen tried to hide her age with cosmetics, and one sharp-eyed courtier noted how she was 'continuously painted not only all over her face, but on her neck and breasts also, and that the same was in some places near half an inch thick'. The French ambassador described her face as 'very aged, long and thin. Her teeth are very yellow and unequal.... Many of them are missing so that one cannot understand her easily when she speaks quickly'. Her famous mane of red hair was a wig.

Elizabeth's infatuation with the Earl of Essex was similar to the deceit she tried to create with her beauty box. It was an attempt to escape backwards from reality to a world she had outlived. Hatton, Leicester, Burghley, her closest friends and advisers, had died, leaving her to cope with problems she could not solve. Inflation soared, so that by 1600 her royal income was worth half of what it had been when she came to the throne. The war against Spain and the campaign against the Irish rebels dragged on, draining her exchequer so that she died £400,000 in debt.

To rule 'with your loves'

And there was a new independent tone in the voice of the Parliament she approached for extra money. When, a frail old woman, she staggered under the weight of her ceremonial robes to open the Parliament of 1601, MPs ostentatiously stood back, and few saluted her with the customary 'God Save Your Majesty'. They were incensed by the financial privileges she had granted to favourites like Essex and Raleigh, and they made their anger felt.

But Elizabeth, unlike her successors James and Charles Stuart, knew when to give way graciously. Promising to reform the abuses the Commons had so bitterly attacked, she summoned them to Whitehall to make their peace with her. And on November 30, 1601, in the crowded Council Chamber, Elizabeth won back the hearts of her subjects.

'Though God hath raised me high,' she told them, 'yet this I count the glory of my crown, that I have reigned with your loves. It is not my desire to live or reign longer than my life and reign shall be for your good. And though you have had, and may have, many mightier and wiser princes sitting in this seat, yet you never have had, nor shall have, any that will love you better.'

Death in the chill morning

This 'Golden Speech' was a masterstroke. It was remembered through the next century of civil war and revolution as the model of a monarch's relationship with the nation – caring, considerate and involving obligations on both sides. It was Elizabeth's last address to her people, but the glory of her reign was not yet over. Within days came the news of the defeat of the Irish rebels. Six months later, an English squadron captured a Portuguese treasure-ship in an action that recalled the heroic days of Drake and his raids on the Spanish Main. Both in the character of the queen and the exploits of the nation, Elizabethan England remained brilliant to the very last.

Unwilling to acknowledge the imminence of her death, Elizabeth shunned any talk of her successor and delayed making her choice until the very last. But in the end a waiting messenger was sent galloping north by her last chief minister, Robert Cecil, to tell James Stuart that he would have the throne that his mother Mary, Queen of Scots, had died trying to ascend. Between the cold dark hours of 2 a.m. and 3 a.m. of March 24, 1603, Queen Elizabeth quietly turned her face to the wall and passed peacefully away, 'mildly like a lamb, easily like a ripe apple from the tree', in the words of her chaplain.

LAST JOURNEY *A contemporary painting of Elizabeth I's funeral procession, the coffin surmounted by an effigy of the queen dressed in full regalia, on its way to Westminster Abbey on April 28, 1603. Thousands of Londoners lined the streets in a moving demonstration of popular grief at the passing of their beloved sovereign.*

THE FIRST STUARTS: 1603–1660

Years of strife and bloodshed

*Too obstinate to accept the guidance of Parliament,
two Stuart kings divide the nation and set it on the road
to eight years of bitter and destructive civil war*

In 1603 a new dynasty, the House of Stuart, came to the throne at a fateful moment in England's history. It was the Stuarts' misfortune that they misunderstood the time itself and the character, beliefs and ambitions of the people they were called upon to rule.

The first Stuart, James I, boasted that he was 'an old, experienced king, needing no lessons'. But he and his son, Charles I, both found that their subjects meant to instruct them. Both of these kings obstinately believed in their 'Divine Right' to rule as they chose. Their subjects, however, had followed a different path, for previous monarchs had consulted their people in Parliament. The refusal of the Stuarts to understand this tradition of parliamentary liberty could have only one result – civil war.

In that war, the people emerged victorious. But, though they executed Charles I in 1649, they could find no satisfactory alternative to take the place of a monarch. And so, in 1660, the Stuarts returned.

As James I rode southwards from Scotland to claim his new throne in 1603, no such forebodings crossed his mind. He was supremely self-confident of his ability to rule England as he had ruled Scotland. The king was an intellectual in an age which had little time for subtlety. He also had little understanding of English history. His proposals for the toleration of Catholics were tactlessly presented to an unwilling Parliament, and swept away by the anti-Catholic hysteria which followed the discovery of the Gunpowder Plot to blow up the king in 1605 (pp. 162–3). What James lacked

CLIMAX OF REVOLUTION

On January 30, 1649, Charles I was executed outside Whitehall Palace. On his way to the scaffold, he passed through the Banqueting House, whose ceiling (inset) had been painted by Rubens 15 years before to glorify the Stuart monarchy. This detail shows Charles's father, James I, being received into Heaven.

Like his father, Charles believed that he could impose his will on his subjects. But, as an opponent said, 'No one was wise who permanently opposed himself to the people of England'. And when monarchy was restored in 1660 this vital lesson had been learnt. No English king could afford to be despotic. Subjects would always remember that, having overthrown one king, they could overthrow another.

159

TWO KINGDOMS *James I's seal shows the united arms of his two kingdoms, Scotland and England. But the English refused to pass a formal Act of Union, and it was to be another century before Parliament brought it about.*

KING AND CHURCH *James listens to a sermon in St Paul's churchyard. He was an ardent supporter of the Church of England, seeing it as a vital part of the system of government he was determined to defend. 'No bishop, no king,' he said. Opponents of the Church, such as the Puritans, were the first to feel his power.*

END OF AN ERA *By making friends with Spain, James ended a tradition which his people regarded as natural to Englishmen. Here, he welcomes back his son, Charles, from an abortive attempt to wed the King of Spain's daughter.*

was common sense, the supreme virtue of Elizabeth's wily counsellor, Robert Cecil, who also served James as chief minister. After Cecil's death in 1612, James abandoned all his policies. The one legacy Cecil left behind was Hatfield House (pp. 164–5), the incomparable work of wealth, taste and dynastic pride which he had built in Hertfordshire.

A king who divided the nation

One of James's first quarrels with his subjects concerned foreign policy. He had come to his inheritance penniless, and his extravagance soon brought the crown of England close to bankruptcy. His over-riding concern was to avoid the expense of foreign wars and so he made peace with Spain, reversing a policy which Englishmen had come to regard as a way of life.

There was, however, another reason for this clash of wills. The Puritans of England were prospering, and they wished to prosper further by destroying the Spanish monopoly of trade with the Americas. This, too, James resisted, and in 1618 the Puritans found their martyr in Sir Walter Raleigh (pp. 166–7), executed ostensibly for treason, but in fact at the behest of Spain.

Isolated from the real world by the flattery of his favourites, James was able to indulge his conceit. He was convinced that he could settle the bitter religious strife that was dividing his kingdom by imposing a compromise. But in 1617 James published a *Book of Sports*, which allowed certain games to be played on Sunday. For the Puritans, already harassed by zealous high-Church bishops, this was the final proof that James had turned his face against true religion. Three years later, the *Mayflower* set sail with its first cargo of Puritan exiles (pp. 168–9). The Pilgrim Fathers were bound for a new world, where they could worship freely.

At home, the question of government was setting king and people on a collision course. The first of the confrontations which were to lead England to civil war came when the House of Commons asserted its strength by impeaching the Lord Chancellor, Francis Bacon, in 1621.

Bacon was the most talented and original thinker who ever served a Stuart monarch. He combined a long and distinguished career in the government service with a leading place in the world of science and letters. His works, together with those of his contemporary, the biologist William Harvey, constitute the most enduring contribution of the age to the progress of scientific thought and discovery (pp. 170–1).

'So good a man, so bad a king'

When James finally died unlamented in 1625, it was thought that Charles would be a great improvement on his father. He was serious-minded and conscientious – a vast change from the ribald and drunken James. The new king, however, had inherited two characteristics from his father – an attachment to the same favourite, Buckingham, and an obstinate belief in his God-given right to rule unchallenged. These were to lead him to disaster.

In 1628 the House of Commons forced Charles to agree to the demands of the Petition of Right, which struck at the whole basis of Stuart monarchy. Its immediate effect was to arouse all Charles's inbred hatred of Parliament. The next year he set out on the ruinous course of 11 years of personal rule.

Charles began this experiment without Buckingham, who had met his death in 1628, assassinated by a deranged army officer. To replace him, Charles chose a group of serious-minded, efficient ministers – chief among them Thomas Wentworth, Earl of Strafford, and Archbishop Laud. The policy they were to follow they christened 'Thorough'. An enlightened king would rule, without fear or favour, for the benefit of all his subjects.

But finance was the king's undoing. Charles's legal advisers found ingenious methods of raising money without resort to Parliament, including an ancient levy called Ship Money. In one of the great constitutional cases in English history, a Buckinghamshire squire, John Hampden, challenged its legality in 1637 (pp. 172–3). The judges found for the king by a narrow margin – but nevertheless Charles's prestige suffered a terrible blow. Voices were now publicly raised against the court and, in an atmosphere of anger and distrust, England awaited the challenge that was to bring the king's rule down.

Ironically, this came not from England but from Scotland – the kingdom James I had left with such high hopes 36 years before. In May 1639, an army assembled to resist Laud's attempts to make the Church of England the official church of Scotland. Revolt broke out, and Charles realised that he had no choice but to recall Parliament.

Charles in private life was a different person from Charles the obstinate king. He had a real love of beauty. He aspired to create a Renaissance monarchy, adorned by noble buildings and fine paintings. From Italy and Holland, Charles brought a magnificent collection of paintings. And he persuaded Van Dyck, the greatest artist of the day, to settle in England, where he captured the grace and elegance of the Stuart court (pp. 178–9). He commissioned Rubens, who spent a year at his court, to paint the ceiling of the Banqueting House in Whitehall. This was Inigo Jones's first perfectly proportioned Classical building, but Jones's masterpiece was Wilton House in Wiltshire (pp. 176–7), built for the rich and powerful Herbert family.

'This is a time of shaking'

The Long Parliament, which was to outlive Charles, met in 1640. Instead of voting the king the taxes he needed, it began its work by putting Strafford, the pillar on which Charles's rule depended, on trial for his life (pp. 174–5). Charles had given his word that Strafford would 'in no wise suffer' for his loyal service to the crown. But the king's word was not equal to the pressure of a hostile Parliament, and he signed the death warrant. It was an action he regretted for the rest of his life. Laud was imprisoned in the Tower. Two extreme views had met head on; the result was civil war.

Charles had the advantage when the war began in 1642. But he failed to press this home, notably after the Battle of Edgehill (pp. 180–1). By 1645 Oliver Cromwell's New Model Army was in the field, and at the Battle of Naseby (pp. 182–3) the Royalist cause was shattered.

Parliament had won the war. What was it to do with the king it had defeated? Charles's stubborn refusal to accept peace terms, his treachery and duplicity, caused passions to flare still higher. In 1649 Cromwell and his followers were driven to try him and execute him (pp. 184–7).

To abolish monarchy was one thing; to find another form of government was a more difficult business. By 1653, when he dismissed the 'Rump Parliament' (pp. 188–9), Cromwell had become king in all but name. For the next five years, his army imposed a severe Puritan rule on the country.

But the rule of the army depended on Cromwell's strength and genius. When he died in 1658, it was clear that he had given England neither a permanent, stable form of government, nor the liberty for which the civil war had been fought. From that disillusionment, it was a short step to the restoration of the Stuarts in 1660.

The English Revolution was over. But it had left a legacy. The Puritan tradition had found its noblest voices in the writers John Bunyan and John Milton (pp. 190–1). And absolute monarchy had received a decisive check. Englishmen had made it plain that they would not be ruled by a despot.

UNPOPULAR MINISTER *The Duke of Buckingham on his death-bed after his assassination in 1628. First minister to both James and Charles I, he was arrogant and tactless.*

STUART DISPLAY *A float from the Lord Mayor's Show. Pomp, pageantry, display and splendour were actively encouraged by the Stuarts. But such ostentation was opposed by the Puritans, who saw it as offensive in the sight of God.*

FINAL CRISIS *Inspired by religious zeal, Scottish Calvinists sign the 'Solemn League and Covenant' in 1638. The Covenanters swore to resist Charles's attempts to impose Anglican ritual, and their success precipitated civil war.*

WORD WAR *King and Parliament found philosophers to support them. Thomas Hobbes (right) produced his defence of absolute monarchy in his* Leviathan *of 1651.*

A LESSON LEARNT *Charles II flees after defeat at Worcester in 1651. His exile taught him to abandon the Divine Right theory for which his father died.*

'Remember … remember the fifth of November'

FAWKES'S 'LANTHORN'

With this lantern, Guy Fawkes planned to kindle the gunpowder and wood the Gunpowder Plotters had stored under the Houses of Parliament in 1605. It was found in the cellar where Fawkes was arrested by the Earl of Suffolk and his men, and is now in the Ashmolean Museum, Oxford.

Seldom have a handful of men come so close to changing the course of history as did those who took part in the Gunpowder Plot of 1605. These young men, inspired by a fierce belief in the Roman Catholic faith, knew that their great plan would involve the deaths of over 300 Protestant leaders, including the king; and they had no compassion for these men. But they showed weakness over the inevitable killing of a handful of Roman Catholics – and it was this weakness which betrayed them in the last tense days before the plot reached its climax.

Deep in the cellars

At 11 p.m. on the dark night of November 4, 1605, a stately figure plodded through the maze of cellars and basements directly under the House of Lords, in the Palace of Westminster. It was the Earl of Suffolk, Lord Chamberlain of the King's Household, with two of his henchmen in close attendance.

Suffolk was there on the orders of the Privy Council, which had received an anonymous warning that violence was planned against James I when he came to open Parliament the next day. The chamberlain had been ordered to search one cellar in particular – one rented by a Catholic courtier, Thomas Percy.

Percy had a surprisingly large stock of coal and firewood there. And it was difficult for the council to see why he had ordered the skulking dark-haired manservant, who went by the name of John Johnson, to mount a 24 hour guard on his winter fuel supply.

As soon as Johnson opened the cellar door he was seized and overpowered. The coal and wood were thrown aside. Hidden beneath them were 36 barrels of gunpowder, connected to a slow fuse. In one corner was a dark lantern. Johnson was taken straight to the Tower, and on the rack confessed his real name – Guido (Guy) Fawkes.

Fawkes is the only Gunpowder Plotter whose name has passed into British folklore. But he was only a subordinate, brought over from Flanders where he had been serving with the Spanish army, because of his professional skill with explosives. He was called in by Thomas Winter, and behind Winter stood his cousin, Robert Catesby, the originator and leader of the plot.

Catesby and Winter were both well-born Catholics. By 1605 they were impoverished and desperate – a situation they blamed on the anti-Catholic laws. They had already tried to mend their fortunes by joining one madcap scheme – the Earl of Essex's rebellion against Queen Elizabeth in 1601 – only to suffer crush-

ENTER FAWKES *Guy Fawkes makes his way into the cellar rented by the plotters under the House of Lords. He stood guard over 'fuel' stocks for 24 hours under the false name of John Johnson.*

THE GUNPOWDER PLOTTERS *The Gunpowder Plotters confer in this contemporary illustration. Fawkes (third from right) was recruited in Flanders by another plotter, Thomas Winter. He had been serving there as an explosives expert with the Spanish army. He was hanged, drawn and quartered.*

ing fines. They had then approached James in Scotland with a proposal for religious toleration for their faith.

But James's half-promises meant little once he had achieved his ambition of succeeding to the English throne. In 1604 he reimposed the anti-Catholic laws. A desperate blow seemed the only answer.

The plotters thought that if they blew up the House of Lords when the king was opening the new session of Parliament, they would eliminate him, the Prince of Wales and all the leading ministers. They then hoped to seize the next heir, the five-year-old Prince Charles, and raise a general revolt. Governing in the young prince's name, they would reconvert England to Catholicism.

Betrayed by kindness

All was prepared by the end of 1604. Fawkes had arrived from Flanders, and Thomas Percy, who had been drawn into the plot at an early stage, had used his court connections to rent a cellar under the House of Lords.

But the meeting of Parliament that had been planned for February 1605 was postponed until the autumn, and discovery became an increasing risk. Catesby's persuasive tongue steadily won over more followers, until by November at least 13 men were in the secret.

It was in the last days of their long wait that the plotters made their fatal mistake, that of showing pity. They tried to save friends and relatives among the peerage, for Catholics could still sit in the House of Lords.

On October 26, one of these peers, Lord Mounteagle, received an anonymous letter of warning: 'Retire yourself into the country for ... they shall receive a terrible blow this Parliament and yet they shall not see who hurts them.' Mounteagle passed the letter to the Privy Council. Lord Suffolk was despatched to search the cellars.

A dismal fate

On the news that all was discovered, Catesby and Winter, with seven companions, took horse and rode hard for the Midlands. But a posse led by the Sheriff of Worcestershire tracked them down to Holbeach House in Staffordshire.

On the morning of November 8, the sheriff stormed the house, and four of the conspirators were killed. Among them was Robert Catesby, who crawled across the blood-stained floor to kiss a picture of the Virgin Mary before he died. Winter, his brother, Robert, and five others were brought back to London to stand trial with Fawkes. They were sentenced to be hanged, drawn and quartered.

To the last, they refused to repent. The tragedy was that, instead of helping the Catholics of England, the Gunpowder Plot nearly destroyed them. It was to be more than 200 years before Catholics would re-establish their good name and secure full legal toleration.

James I: Blinded by his own wisdom

On April 3, 1603, James VI of Scotland took leave of his subjects and started the long journey south to England. Scotland was a poor and barren land, and James had long envied his cousin, Queen Elizabeth, for the wealth and splendour of her court.

Now he would be able to indulge his passion for hunts, palaces and pageantry. His extravagant wife, Anne of Denmark, too, would have all she desired. The new king's first act on arriving at York was to write to the Privy Council demanding money.

As James drew nearer his new capital, the warmth of his reception went to his head like the rich wine of which he was so fond. 'The people of all sorts rode, ran, nay flew, to meet me,' he later wrote. But in truth, James's new subjects were expressing not so much joy at his arrival, as relief that the succession had been settled peacefully.

'The wisest fool'

Physically, James I, as he now styled himself, did not look the part of a king. His strong Scots accent was thickened by a deformity of the tongue, which was too large for his mouth, making him dribble and 'drink very uncomely'.

He was coarse and profane in his humour. When his bishops said that 'undoubtedly His Majesty spoke by the special assistance of God's spirit', a cynic added: 'the spirit was rather foul-mouthed.'

If James had been a more successful ruler, his lack of manners would not have mattered. But, though he announced that he was 'an experienced king, needing no lessons', his overweening self-confidence blinded him to some lessons that he did need.

James was an intelligent man who had read and thought deeply on questions of religion and government. His published works included a defence of absolute monarchy, a treatise on witchcraft, and even an attack on smoking tobacco. But in dealing with politicians, churchmen and Parliament, he combined pedantry with such ineptitude that the Spanish Ambassador, Count Gondomar, labelled him 'the wisest fool in Christendom'.

For the first seven years of his reign, James was saved from the consequences of his blunders by his principal minister, Robert Cecil, Earl of Salisbury, who tried to carry the Elizabethan ideal of good government into a new age. But James was not interested in government – least of all when it involved working with a critical Parliament. 'I am surprised,' he darkly muttered, 'that my ancestors should have allowed such an institution to come into existence.'

After Cecil's death in 1612, the men James preferred to trust were young courtiers whose sole claim to advancement was their physical beauty. The first of these was Robert Carr, Earl of Somerset. By 1616, however, Carr had

KING AND THINKER *James I was widely read and thoughtful. But, as ruler of England, he introduced policies that alienated his people.*

IN FAVOUR *Robert Carr, Earl of Somerset (left) and George Villiers, Duke of Buckingham were two of James's favourites, with nothing to commend them but good looks.*

been outshone by a new and brighter star, George Villiers, Duke of Buckingham.

James was now rapidly growing senile. He worshipped his 'sweet Steenie gossip' and lavished wealth upon him. Faced with mounting criticism of Buckingham, he wept, saying: 'Christ had his John and I have my George.' Buckingham, for his part, was James's 'most humble Slave and dogge'.

Buckingham, however, had enough wit not to rely on an obviously failing monarch. He cultivated the shy heir to the throne, the young Prince Charles, and the two men allied to force their views on the old king. With a last flash of intelligence, James told Charles, after he and Buckingham had pressed for the impeachment of Lionel Cranfield, Earl of Middlesex, the Lord Treasurer: 'You will live to have your bellyful of impeachments.' For the dying king realised that, by encouraging Parliament to attack royal ministers, his foolhardy son was opening the way for an attack on the crown itself.

MONUMENT TO AN AGE – BUILT BY A KING'S FIRST MINISTER

Hatfield is the Cecils; the Cecils are Hatfield. No great country house has seen more of our history in the making. The Cecil who built this magnificent palace was chief minister to James I. And Hatfield has served his family ever since – a house in which every room has been, at one time or another, a council chamber, and every passage a corridor of power.

In medieval times the manor of Hatfield belonged to the bishops of Ely, and in the 15th century an imposing palace was built there. One wing of this house, containing the banqueting hall, still stands 100 yds away from the later 17th-century building. It is perhaps the finest remaining example of English medieval brickwork.

But few bishops were to enjoy Hatfield. Henry VIII seized it and used it as a country home for his children. It was here that Edward VI and his sisters Mary and Elizabeth grew up, remote from the terrible events at their father's court. Here, too, under an oak tree, Elizabeth was told of her accession to the throne.

It was Elizabeth who made the Cecils, although it was not until after her death that they came to Hatfield as its owners. In a sense, though, the great dynasty began here. For the young queen's first official action, performed in the Great Hall at Hatfield, was to appoint William Cecil her chief Secretary of State.

'This judgement I have of you,' she said, 'that you will not be corrupted with any manner of gifts, and that you will be faithful to the state.' Her words were almost prophetic. For 40 years the devoted and wily courtier stood at the queen's right hand. And when he died, in 1598, he left a son, Robert, well able to take up the reins of government.

Robert Cecil, small and slightly deformed, was ridiculed by many about the court, but he was respected by both Elizabeth and her Stuart successor, James I, as a shrewd, calculating statesman. James heaped honours on him, made him Earl of Salisbury and left him in almost complete control of affairs of state.

Exchange with a monarch

In 1607 the king took a fancy to Cecil's fine house at Theobalds and offered to exchange it for Hatfield. As soon as Cecil took possession of his new domain, he determined to build a magnificent house which would suitably proclaim his power and wealth, and which would stand as a monument to all that was best in Jacobean taste and craftsmanship.

Cecil personally supervised the building of his masterpiece and used the vast power of his office to obtain the very best men and materials. Stone was brought from France and marble for statues from Italy. Timber was hewn on the vast estate, and millions of red bricks were made on the site by a master bricklayer named Jerome Taulcote.

The man charged with turning Cecil's ideas and designs into reality was Robert Lyminge, described as a 'surveyor' in surviving documents. Cecil, suffering frequent bouts of

JACOBEAN ELEGANCE *The South Front has changed little since its completion in 1611. Robert Cecil achieved its symmetry without using an architect. He himself worked on the plans with his clerk of works, Thomas Wilson, and his surveyor, Robert Lyminge. Cecil spent £40,000 on his magnificent house at Hatfield, but never lived to see it completed.*

illness, and perhaps fearing that he might not live to see the house completed, drove Lyminge on at breakneck pace. Notes and sketches were sent back and forth between master and servant by special messenger.

Lyminge had the best workmen money and influence could buy. There was Maximilian Colt, the Flemish sculptor who had created Queen Elizabeth's tomb in Westminster Abbey; a Frenchman, referred to by the English as 'Lewis Dolphin', made painted glass for the chapel; another Frenchman, Solomon de Caux, devised the complex system of waterworks and fountains; and a score of other master craftsmen came to Hatfield from Flanders, France and Italy.

Supreme achievement

Robert Cecil spent the colossal sum of £40,000 on his new house, which was completed in the incredibly brief period of five years. The date of completion, 1611, is triumphantly proclaimed in stone above the south porch.

In its essentials the house which was finished in that year has remained unchanged for three and a half centuries. It is the supreme achievement of Jacobean architecture and, in a deeper sense, it is also the final flowering of the Tudor style. The features which had been familiar parts of great English houses for the previous century are incorporated in this building with what now appears to be a kind of valedictory

---

ENGLAND'S FIRST BOTANIST

Among the craftsmen brought in by Robert Cecil to beautify Hatfield was John Tradescant. Described then as a gardener, he was really one of Britain's first great botanists.

Cecil set Tradescant on the course which was to enrich the gardens of England for succeeding ages. He sent him to hunt for rare plants and trees in distant countries. Tradescant's later employers, the Duke of Buckingham and James I, gave him the same encouragement. He brought back many rare flowers, a whole group of which were called 'Tradescantia', by the botanist Linnaeus. He toured Europe and America, and was the first to study Russian flora. In 1620 he was on a ship sent to harry Barbary pirates, but he forgot corsairs when he saw Morocco's flowers. A contemporary described him as 'a lover of all nature's varieties', and his collection of specimens included animals as well as flowers.

BOTANIST'S SKETCHBOOK *A detailed sketch (above) of a rare plum by Tradescant (left), the botanist who introduced many plants to Hatfield's gardens.*

workings of an old tradition; but the tradition is interpreted with an extravagance never before seen in England.

The Long Gallery more than fulfils its name – for it is 60 yds in length, although less than 7 yds wide. The great length is relieved by two magnificent fireplaces and, despite the extraordinary proportions, the room is very beautiful and even feels comfortable.

A lasting monument

The gardens were equally novel and extravagant. John Tradescant was commissioned to roam through half the countries of Europe in search of new flowers and shrubs. The Queen of France sent 500 fruit trees, and a vineyard was planted with 20,000 vines supplied by the wife of the French ambassador.

Visiting the mature gardens 50 years later, John Aubrey, the diarist, was deeply impressed. He wrote that the valley of Hatfield was now so beautiful that it must eclipse the Vale of Tempe, the mythological fields of perfection that were believed to be below Mount Olympus.

Sadly, it was not given to Robert Cecil to enjoy the splendour of his new creations. He slept for only eight nights in his house. The man whom Elizabeth had called her 'little elf' was stronger in wisdom and grasp of great affairs than in body. The burdens of serving an incompetent and ungrateful king were too much for his frail form, and he died at Marlborough in May 1612, aged 49.

Little of Robert Cecil's life work survived him; the men who managed the realm in his stead during the following 16 years were chosen for their charm and good looks rather than the Cecil qualities of dogged skill and high dedication. But the house he had built at Hatfield was a more lasting monument. If bricks and mortar can express an ideal, it has proved a powerful spokesman for the aspirations of his family. Its pervasive influence must surely have played a part in leading so many generations of Cecils to carry forward the family tradition – 'faithful to the state' – as the young Elizabeth had so wisely foretold.

MEDIEVAL MAGNIFICENCE *The lifetime of Robert Cecil straddled both the Tudor and Jacobean ages. But his nostalgia for the style of the Middle Ages is reflected in the Marble Hall, with its minstrels' gallery and carved screens. It takes its name from the chequered marble floor.*

GRAND STAIRCASE *The best available craftsmen were brought in by Cecil to beautify Hatfield House. There, they were given a free hand. The individualism of their work is reflected in the elaborate detail of this staircase with its richly carved pillars, lions and cherubs.*

ROYAL EXCHANGE *James I granted Hatfield to Robert Cecil in this Act of Parliament of 1607. He took Cecil's house at Theobalds in exchange.*

splendour; and there is little sign of the careful Classicism which was to dominate architecture during the next two centuries. Clearly, Robert Cecil had no wish to achieve the plain lines of perfect proportion; he was as little bound by the Classical forms as his contemporary William Shakespeare was in drama. He apparently relished intricate geometric patterns, rich materials and, above all, individual carvings made by craftsmen who felt free to express their own moods and fantasies, however grotesque or whimsical.

Hatfield's noblest rooms – the vast hall and the Long Gallery – seem almost self-consciously old-fashioned. Perhaps Cecil conceived them in a mood of nostalgia; for it was in such rooms that the affairs of England had been conducted during the long years of his father's greatness. In this mood of respect for the fruitful past, the builders of Hatfield created a fitting background for the incomparable collection of Tudor treasures, especially the portraits and personal relics of two queens – the Queen of England whom Robert Cecil's father had served so loyally, and the Queen of Scotland whose death he had felt obliged to encompass.

The Great Hall and Long Gallery are re-

The tragedy of the hero who outlived his age

FALLEN FAVOURITE *Writer, explorer and Elizabeth I's favourite, Raleigh fell from favour under James I. Many pleaded with the king to release him, but the king was deaf to such pleas.*

WRITTEN IN THE TOWER

While imprisoned in the Tower of London, Raleigh began writing his History of the World, *as well as studying chemistry and mathematics. But he only completed the first volume, covering the period from the Creation to 168 BC, and James I banned the book as an attack on royal authority. The book is now in the British Museum.*

FATAL DESTINY *Sir Walter Raleigh prepares to meet his fate in 1618 with the stoicism of the Romans he so admired. Ever since his condemnation for treason in 1603, he had lived on borrowed time, knowing that one false move would give James I the chance to send him to the scaffold.*

On the night of December 9, 1603, Sir Walter Raleigh sat writing in a cell in Winchester Castle:

Give me my scallop shell of quiet,
My staff of Faith to walk upon,
My scrip of joy, immortal diet . . .
And thus I'll take my pilgrimage.

The next morning Raleigh was to be executed on a trumped-up charge of treason. James I, new to the throne of England, had allowed himself to be panicked into condemning Elizabeth's former favourite to death.

Raleigh's arrogance had made him the most unpopular man in England before his trial. Mobs attacked his coach as it travelled to and from the prison. But the spirit with which he conducted his defence at his trial turned the people in his favour.

Reprieved but imprisoned

So, at the last minute, James had qualms. He was basically a merciful man, and he did not want to start off his reign by executing a popular hero. On the very morning of the execution, the sentence was suspended and Raleigh conveyed to the Tower instead.

But James's mercy was double-edged, for Raleigh was to live under the threat of execution for another 15 years. However, life in the Tower could have been worse. For he was allowed to live as unrestricted a life as was possible in such a prison.

Meanwhile, the outside world did not lose interest in this illustrious prisoner. Soon crowds were gathering daily on the riverside to watch him pace the battlements. James's wife, Anne, went to see Raleigh and was captivated by him. So was her brother, the King of Denmark, who pleaded in vain for his release. The young Henry, Prince of Wales, was another disciple. 'Who but my father would shut up such a bird?' he exclaimed.

But, as the years passed, the prospect of Raleigh's release faded. Perhaps the bitterest blow was the knowledge that the king's young favourite, Robert Carr, Earl of Somerset, now enjoyed the beauty of Raleigh's cherished home at Sherborne in Dorset, which the doting James I had given to him.

At last Raleigh found the key to his prison door in his dreams of *El Dorado*, a legendary gold mine which he insisted lay at the source of the Orinoco River in South America. By 1616, James was in desperate need of money, and in that year Raleigh was at last released on parole – to search for gold to save the crown from bankruptcy.

Release on parole

But the terms of release were hedged about with conditions. Raleigh had lived all his active life in a world in which England and Spain were bitter and bloody enemies. Now he came out into the daylight of a changed world. Spain was an ally which had to be placated – and the Orinoco lay in Spanish territory. He promised James that he could avoid conflict, and the king replied with a warning that any clash with the Spanish would cost Raleigh his head.

But at 66 Raleigh was an old man. He had already had two strokes, and the voice which had commanded instant obedience as captain of the old Queen's guard was now weak and faltering. When he reached the Orinoco in November 1617, he had to delegate command of the expedition inland to his eldest son, Wat, and his faithful lieutenant, Lawrence Keymis. They promptly sacked the town of San Thomé and Wat was killed. In grief and disappointment, Raleigh sailed home to his own death.

Once again James I faced the dilemma he had side-stepped 15 years before. He ordered a hearing before the Privy Council. No one wanted Raleigh to die; everyone knew he must. Even the Attorney-General, presenting the crown's case, said: 'Sir Walter Raleigh ... hath been as a star at which the world gazed; but stars may fall – nay, they must fall when they trouble the sphere wherein they abide.'

Raleigh had a week to prepare for execution, and he made the most of it. He was a classical figure and would make a classic death. He had studied the stoicism of the Romans, and had admired the easy, smiling wit with which the Tudors' victims had suffered.

James I had tried to divert public attention from the execution by fixing it for Lord Mayor's Day. But that morning a huge crowd greeted Raleigh as he left the Gatehouse. Dressed in sombre black, he mounted the scaffold and invited the onlookers to join him in prayer. As he knelt at the block he was asked if he would not prefer to face the east and the rising sun. He replied: 'The matter is not great which way we turn our faces, so our hearts be right.'

The executioner raised the severed head in silence, without shouting the usual formula: 'Behold the head of a traitor! God save the King!' Instead, a voice called out: 'We have not such another head in England.'

An adventurer grows old in the Tower

Dark, magnetically attractive to women and dramatically handsome, Walter Raleigh began his meteoric rise to fame in 1581, when, as a young gallant, he came to court at Greenwich, where he took the fancy of Elizabeth I. According to legend, he spread his cloak upon a muddy path for the queen to walk over on the occasion of their first meeting. His gallantry won him royal favour and soon appointments and lands were showered on him. The high point was reached in 1586, when he became Captain of the Guard. But Raleigh's self-centred arrogance left him without friends, and the queen's infatuation did the rest. In 1587 it was said that Raleigh was 'the best hated man of the world in court, city and country'.

Raleigh spent his new wealth like water. Over five years he spent £40,000 (£1 million today) in trying to establish a colony in his American possessions. Raleigh christened his settlements Virginia in honour of the queen, but his venture failed. All he had to show for it were potatoes and tobacco, both of which he helped popularise in England.

According to legend, once, in these years of favour, Raleigh had taken Queen Elizabeth's diamond ring and carved on the window pane: 'Fain would I climb, yet I fear to fall.' Taking back the ring, she had written: 'If thy heart fail thee, climb not at all.'

Raleigh had climbed high, but when the feared fall came in 1592, it was abrupt and painful. In that year, the queen discovered that he had been carrying on an intrigue with Bess Throckmorton, one of her Maids of Honour. She clapped him into prison, then banished him from court.

Raleigh kept busy enough in his enforced retirement. Much of the time he spent at his fine castle at Sherborne in Dorset, the estate which he saw as the basis of a great family dynasty. He wrote poetry, pursued his mathematical studies and discussed philosophy with the playwright Christopher Marlowe. But his main interest was still exploration. The Orinoco River, in what is today Venezuela, had come to dominate his thoughts. He sent an expedition there in 1594, and followed the next year. He sailed 400 miles up the river in an open boat, vainly seeking the fabulous gold mines of *El Dorado* (the golden land).

A tragic survival

The old glory was never to be fully recaptured. Though Raleigh and the ageing queen were reconciled in 1597, there was to be no place for him under a new king and a new dynasty. Robert Cecil, Elizabeth's Secretary of State, had persuaded James I that Raleigh was an atheist, a republican, a warmonger and a rake. From the moment of Elizabeth's death he was closely watched. In 1603, bewildered at his fall from power, Raleigh was trapped into talking treason against the new king. He was accused of plotting with Spain, tried and sentenced to death. His reprieve in 1603 gave him 15 more years of life. But the Elizabethan world in which he played so great a part had perished with the queen herself.

TOWARDS EL DORADO *On his way to seek the fabled riches of El Dorado in 1595, Raleigh captured the Spanish settlement of St Joseph, Trinidad. But he never found El Dorado; he ran out of supplies while sailing up the Orinoco River and was compelled to turn back to the coast.*

The Pilgrim Fathers sail in search of freedom

£60 worth of precious supplies. As a result, the founding fathers of the New World set out on their great adventure 'scarce having any butter, or oil, not a sole to mend a shoe, not every man a sword to his side'.

The two ships set sail on August 15, 1620, but they were forced to put back into port on two occasions, when the *Speedwell* sprang leaks. Finally, on September 16, the *Mayflower*, crammed with the *Speedwell's* passengers, set out from Plymouth alone. Her 101 passengers were divided into 35 Puritan 'Saints' and 66 'Strangers' – men driven, not by religious zeal, but by hardship, to leave a land which was then in the grip of poverty and famine.

The *Mayflower* was to be the pilgrims' home for more than two months. Only 90 ft long and 25 ft wide, she was a small vessel for so many passengers. Most of them had to sleep on the bare deck, without beds or hammocks, and protected by no more than a leaky canvas cover. Others had to content themselves with sleeping in the ship's longboat.

After a few days the *Mayflower* ran into stormy seas. One of the main beams amidships was bowed and cracked. Fortunately the passengers were able to mend it and the voyage continued. Despite sea-sickness, overcrowded cabins and violent winds, the pilgrims remained cheerful throughout the voyage, singing psalms and praying, confident that God would deliver them into safety.

Citizens of the New World

Only one sailor and one servant boy died on the voyage. One child was born in mid-Atlantic and appropriately christened Oceanus; and when the ship was in sight of land another

SHIP OF LIBERTY

This scale model of the Mayflower, *made early this century, can be seen in the Science Museum, London. The original* Mayflower, *which took the Pilgrim Fathers on their perilous voyage across the Atlantic, weighed only 180 tons, and was only 90 ft long.*

James I had been on the throne only a few months when he told the Puritans that, unless they conformed to the Church of England, he would 'harry them out of the land'. In 1608 a small group of pilgrims took refuge in Holland from threatened persecution, but even there they did not find the freedom they desired. And 12 years later, lured by the prospect of a free life in the new colony of Virginia, a few of them negotiated with a London merchant company, and prepared for a 3000 mile journey to the New World.

The 'Mayflower' sets sail

With their scanty resources they bought a small ship, the *Speedwell*, and crossed from Holland to Southampton. There the *Mayflower*, a square-rigged sailing ship chartered for the Atlantic crossing, awaited them. And there the pilgrims' troubles began.

The merchants insisted that for the first seven years in the New World the pilgrims should work for them; but the Puritans were determined to work their own farms and refused to sign the contract. No longer able to get advances from the merchants, they were forced to meet immediate expenses by selling boy was born – and given the name of Peregrine, which means Pilgrim. Oceanus was to die in infancy, but Peregrine lived to be 83, one of the first citizens of the New World.

Winter had already fallen when, on November 21, the *Mayflower* dropped anchor, not on Virginia's sunny, fertile shores as intended, but on the desolate northern wastes of Cape Cod. The crew spent half a day trying to turn south towards Virginia, but adverse winds and heavy breakers drove them back on Cape Cod. After a few days the pilgrims reluctantly decided to stay there. Attempts were made to venture inland, but finally they agreed to settle on the coast at a site they named Plymouth. On Christmas Day, 1620, they began building their new homes.

The weather had already played a decisive part in guiding the pilgrims to their new home. Now its menace was to drive them to an act of even greater significance in shaping the history of the New World. Without adequate provisions, and faced by months of winter in an unknown land, their chief need was to maintain unity and prevent demoralisation.

To silence the 'discontents and murmurings amongst some, and mutinous speeches in others', they improvised a system of government – and in their search for unanimity, they chose a method which allowed every man – whether master or servant, 'Saint' or 'Stranger' – an equal voice.

The result was the 'Mayflower Compact', the foundation stone of American government. This read: 'Having undertaken for the Glory of God, and the Advancement of the Christian Faith . . . a voyage to plant the first colony in the northern parts of Virginia,' 41 men, masters and servants agreed to 'covenant and combine ourselves together into a civil Body Politick . . . and by Virtue herof do enact, constitute, and frame such just and equal Laws, Ordinances, Acts, Constitutions, and Offices, from time to time, as shall be thought most meet and convenient for the general Good of the Colony.'

Struggle for survival

John Carver, a 'Saint', was chosen governor, the first popularly elected governor in English colonial history. The seed of American democracy had been sown by citizens, who had the audacity to believe that they could survive on their own.

But in the months to come the pilgrims' faith and resolution was to be sorely tested. As the severe winter set in, the settlers were overwhelmed by an illness which apparently combined scurvy, caused by their starvation diet, with pneumonia, caused by inadequate shelter – for they were living on meagre rations in dugouts, made of rough logs with turf roofs. Every few days throughout the long winter, the shivering survivors gathered around the shallow graves of their fellow adventurers. By spring their numbers had been reduced to a total of 51 men, women and children.

But still their troubles were not over. In April the *Mayflower* set sail for England, cutting off any prospect of escape, and in the same month their elected leader, John Carver, died. In his place, the colonists elected a remarkable Yorkshireman, William Bradford, whose leadership and practical gifts were ideally suited to a pioneer community. Bradford was re-elected 30 times before his death in 1657, and he found time in old age to write the classic *History of Plymouth Plantation*.

Under his guidance, the pilgrims won the friendship of the local Indians, and devoted every hour of the day to the task of reclaiming land and harvesting the fruits of their wild country. From the Indians they learnt how to plant corn, trap animals for their furs and tap maple trees for their sugary syrup.

In the summer, the first wedding in the colony took place between two Pilgrims who had lost husband and wife in the winter. By November the settlers were ready to celebrate the first anniversary of their landing. With 90 Indian braves as their guests, they sat down to what was to prove to be the first Thanksgiving Dinner – a feast of venison, wild goose, eel pie, lobster, corn bread and wild fruits, washed down by new-made wine.

These were the richly deserved fruits of their labours. In adjusting to the harvests of a new hemisphere, the pilgrims were already showing their will to become Americans.

THE PILGRIMS EMBARK *A Victorian painting shows a group of pilgrims leaving to join the* Mayflower, *under a banner reading 'Freedom of Worship'. Led by a minister, friends and well-wishers pray for the voyagers' safety.*

A new Bible to unite the nation

In commanding 54 scholars in 1604 to make a new translation of the Bible, James I launched a work which was to be both the inspiration and the bane of his kingdom.

The scholars worked in groups at Oxford, Cambridge and Westminster. By 1611 they were able to present the king with the fruits of their labours – describing the Holy Writ as 'that inestimable treasure which excelleth all the riches of the earth'.

The king knew well that such treasures are potent stuff. He hoped that his new translation, produced in fertile co-operation by Puritan ministers and Anglican bishops, would become a source of national unity.

But, ironically, the new Bible was not a source of peace. Its immediate impact was to encourage individual conscience and individual judgment. Charles I remarked that 'people are governed by the pulpit more than the Sword'. In their long Sabbath hours of compulsory church attendance, the subjects of James I and Charles I were inevitably influenced by the lesson that earthly powers and crowns cannot prevail against the armies of righteousness: 'How are the mighty fallen, and the weapons of war perished.'

Yet, despite its potent role in the drift to civil war, the success of the 'Good Book' was enduring. For at least four centuries it was to remain by far the most widely read and deeply loved work in the English language.

PEOPLE'S BIBLE *The frontispiece of the 1611 King James's Bible. Its translators tried to use popular language, employing only a vocabulary based on words in everyday use.*

THE GENIUS WHO DISCOVERED THE SECRETS OF THE HEART

MEDICAL GENIUS *William Harvey, a 17th-century physician, discovered the circulation of the blood.*

ROYAL DEMONSTRATION *As physician to Charles I, Harvey could have settled into the easy life of a courtier, but he continued with his experiments, carefully testing and then re-testing his theories. He is shown here demonstrating his theory of the circulation of the blood to the king.*

HARVEY REMEMBERED *After Cromwell became Lord Protector, Harvey concentrated on teaching at the Royal College of Physicians. Still treasured there are the pointer he used at lectures, his Padua University diploma, and the first edition of his book on the circulation of the blood.*

In the 17th century it was not only political ideas which were overthrown, but also the long-established concepts of philosophy and science. This second revolution was launched by Francis Bacon, but the man of science who turned theory into practice was another Englishman, William Harvey.

Harvey was one of those great men so totally immersed in their own work that they seem to stand apart from political and historical events. Yet he was the child of his time, born into the adventurous world of the Renaissance, when traditional knowledge and inherited beliefs were being challenged.

At the centre of this intellectual ferment was the University of Padua in Italy, where the Polish astronomer Copernicus had evolved his startling theory that the earth was not the centre of the universe, but revolved around the sun. It was there that Harvey received in 1602 his diploma as Doctor of Medicine and returned to England and the London College of Physicians.

Discovering nature's secrets

To the public, he appeared simply as a highly successful doctor, especially when, in 1626, he became personal physician to Charles I. But all the while in London and Oxford he was conducting a series of private experiments using modern scientific methods; and he had chosen as his subject the function of the key organ of the human anatomy, the heart.

Harvey was a reticent man who throughout his life shunned controversy. When less-enlightened critics attacked his theory, which he published in 1628, he showed great reluctance to defend himself. But slowly through the next decades his great discovery gained a hold wherever scientists were engaged in the study of human anatomy. He had opened a closed door in the understanding of the body and made possible the advances of modern medicine and surgery.

In Harvey's time the movement of blood was believed to be irregular in direction and speed. Some of it was believed to come from the liver. Also, it was thought to pass directly from the right to the left ventricle of the heart. Above all, there was no notion of the heart as a mechanical device, a muscular pump which controlled the flow of the blood.

Harvey hit upon this idea, and calculated that, at the normal pulse rate of 70 beats a minute, the heart pumped more than 50 gallons of blood an hour. Since that amount of blood weighs three times as much as a man, he reasoned that the blood must continually be re-circulated.

Earlier scientists had noticed little flaps on the veins. Harvey correctly identified them as one-way valves which prevent the blood from going backwards. By tying a tourniquet around a bare arm, and watching how the blood reacted, he proved that the blood passed from the heart along the arteries and returned through the veins.

As a result of such experiments, Harvey was able to overthrow most of the existing ideas about the circulation of the blood. He was never satisfied with his findings until he had checked his ideas by experiment.

A life of quiet dedication

Unlike his great contemporary, Bacon, who was for a period his patient, Harvey did not concern himself with the underlying philosophical problems of the scientific method. He was a practical man, but his lifework – a demonstration of deduction backed by experiment – was the first clear example of the scientific method which Bacon had foreshadowed.

Dr Harvey lived a life of quiet dedication, as a physician and as a scientist, and contemporary records provide few glimpses of his private life. Aubrey, the diarist, records that 'he did delight to be in the darke and told me he could then best contemplate'.

Another characteristic glimpse of him records his presence at the Battle of Edgehill in 1642, where he was supposed to be acting as tutor to Prince Charles, the 12-year-old heir to the throne, and his 9-year-old brother, Prince James. Undisturbed by gunfire and apparently unconcerned at the events which marked the beginning of the Civil War, Harvey spent the battle sitting under a hedge engrossed in a book – while his two young charges narrowly escaped capture or death.

But, despite appearances, Harvey's concentration was not limited to book-learning. His contribution to the heritage of science lay in his resolution to seek for truth by studying the wider 'book' of all created things. In doing so, he became the first of the long line of British experimental scientists who have contributed so much to world knowledge.

A PROPHET OF LEARNING AND THE SCIENTIFIC REVOLUTION

THEORIST OF SCIENCE *Detail of a portrait of Francis Bacon, whose theories laid the foundations of the modern scientific method.*

For hundreds of years, science and superstition went hand in hand. In medieval times, alchemists laboured in their laboratories, on tasks such as seeking an 'elixir' which would give its possessor eternal life, or the 'philosopher's stone', which would turn base metals into gold. In the course of their vain experiments they made many discoveries, but they were unable to realise the importance of what they had achieved. Firstly, they were bound by preconceived traditions, and secondly they lacked any sense of method. And without method, any systematic scientific advance was impossible.

So matters stood until an Englishman of genius, Francis Bacon, took things in hand. Bacon was not a practical scientist; he made no discoveries of his own. But his breadth of vision was such that his work illuminated the entire world of science and philosophy. Shrewd and sceptical, he overthrew the tyranny of ancient scholarship, smashed the intellectual idols of antiquity, and encouraged those interested in the secrets of nature to co-operate in establishing a new spirit of rational inquiry.

Born in 1561 in London, Bacon had a mind of extraordinary diversity. He was essayist, politician, legal authority, philosopher and, in the end, Lord Chancellor. It has even been said that he was the real author of Shakespeare's works. He thought of himself as a man who was over-awed neither by the old, nor by the new, and a hater of every kind of affectation: 'So I thought my nature had a kind of familiarity and relation with Truth,' he wrote on one famous occasion.

Bacon's dedication to this pursuit of truth, and his training as a lawyer, equipped him for his task as the prophet of the new age of science. He proceeded by applying the laws of evidence and burden of proof to scientific theory.

He isolated science from the muddled theories of medieval scholars and called for a truly scientific explanation of nature. And in doing so he pointed the way to the modern approach to scientific method – the process of experiment and observation leading to the laws of science.

Establishing 'scientific method'

Previously, what men regarded as knowledge was what had been handed down to them from ancient authorities such as Aristotle. Bacon's 'scientific method' was simple and revolutionary. First, the scientist, by observation, forms a hypothesis. Then he tests this hypothesis by repeated experiments. And if the experiments are successful he can claim that his hypothesis is a true fact. Knowledge thus becomes as Bacon wrote 'the fruit of experience. Man . . . is the servant and interpreter of nature'.

Unfortunately, Bacon's career failed to match his intellectual gifts. Though he eventually reached the highest office in the land as Lord Chancellor, this reward only came after years of humiliation and intrigue. To gain his ends he betrayed his friends, frequently dishonoured himself and, in the end, was indicted for taking bribes and removed from office.

Disgraced and disappointed, Bacon admitted that he would have done better to have remained faithful to his philosophical curiosity. He wrote that he knew that he was 'by inward calling to be fitter to hold a book than to play a part'. And so he retired to his lavish London house, with its 100 servants, and devoted his last years to the study of philosophy.

Bacon died at the age of 65, following his one recorded attempt to conduct a scientific experiment. It had occurred to him that meat might be preserved in ice instead of salt, and after stuffing a chicken carcass with snow, he caught a chill from which he died a few days later.

Bacon was disappointed with his own achievements. But he recognised that he had rung 'the bell which called the wits together'. And his dream of a meeting of great minds in the service of science and philosophy was fulfilled 34 years later, when the Royal Society was founded. He had laid the foundation for the great scientific revolution that was to change the face of the world.

In the name of 'justice' a commoner defies his king

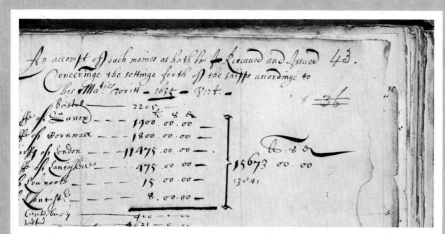

BALANCING THE BOOKS

A fragment of the royal accounts, now at the Public Records Office, London. It shows the large revenue that Charles I raised without the consent of Parliament by levying the tax of Ship Money in the 1630's. London was made to pay £11,475 and Bristol £2205.

TAX TO BUILD A NAVY *Ship Money provided the funds to equip the Royal Navy with magnificent ships such as the* Sovereign of the Seas *(above). Launched in 1637, it was England's first 100-gun battleship. John Hampden (left) refused to pay the tax in 1636. His trial in the next year attracted nationwide publicity, and proved to be the opening shot in the campaign which was to lead to civil war between king and Parliament. In this war Hampden was to die.*

Some of the greatest freedoms that Englishmen possess have been won as the direct result of one man's determination to stand up for his rights. Such a man was John Hampden, who in 1636 challenged the personal rule of Charles I by refusing to pay a tax known as Ship Money.

Hampden was a rich Buckinghamshire squire who had served in Parliament. He was a man of pleasant and cheerful disposition and had long been an opponent of unlimited royal power. In 1627 he spent a year in prison for refusing to contribute to a 'forced loan' for the king's war in France. Two years later, when the chief critic of Charles I, Sir John Eliot, was placed in the Tower, Hampden looked after his children. Eliot, a sick man, died in captivity, and Hampden never forgave the king. Ship Money was his opportunity for revenge.

The two flaws in the king's case

In the past this tax, which was for emergencies only, had been levied on coastal towns for the maintenance of the Royal Navy. In the 1630's the navy had been allowed to run down and there was no money to re-equip it. At this time piracy was a nagging threat to English merchant shipping.

In levying Ship Money to meet this situation, Charles appeared to have right and necessity on his side. But his case contained two weaknesses: he extended the tax to inland places and he acted in defiance of the recently accepted Petition of Right, which had declared non-Parliamentary taxation to be illegal. And Hampden was just the man to take up the

PETITION OF RIGHT

In February 1628, Parliament challenged Charles's bid to win supreme power with four demands. Taxation was not to be levied without Parliament's consent; no one was to be gaoled without trial; no troops to be billeted on private households; martial law to be abolished.

Together, these demands formed the Petition of Right. The king declared that the Petition of Right would 'dissolve the foundation of our monarchy'. But both Houses of Parliament voted in its favour and he was forced to give his assent. However, the agreement broke down within a year. It was finally wrecked by the Opposition leader, Sir John Eliot, who led a revolt against a royal command to adjourn the Commons for a week. Charles was outraged by this presumption. His response was to dissolve Parliament and rule without it for 11 years.

In this 19th-century painting, Members of Parliament prevent the Speaker from carrying out the king's demand to dissolve the 1629 Parliament. But Charles had his way, and ruled without it.

challenge. In 1637 he was summoned before the Court of Exchequer, charged with failure to pay Ship Money of 20 shillings on his lands at Stoke Mandeville, Bucks.

The sum was small, but the issues raised were of profound importance. The king's policies were on trial. As one of the judges said, this was 'one of the greatest cases that ever came in judgment'.

So an air of expectant uncertainty hung about the courtroom on November 6, 1637, as Oliver St John, a virtually unknown constitutional lawyer, rose to defend Hampden. With a brilliant display of learning and logic he rested his defence on two arguments.

First, if subjects were taxable at the royal pleasure, then all property was at the whim and mercy of the king. Secondly, although piracy had been vexatious, it was not an emergency. If the king needed money, the proper course was to call on Parliament.

A deadly blow to one-man rule

St John spoke for two days. The Solicitor General took four days to answer him. Then followed a battery of legal experts, each meticulously combing the past for precedents to support their pleas.

Hampden's refusal to pay his 20 shillings amounted to a challenge to the king to prove that he had the right to govern England without recourse to its long-established Parliament. In the end, the king's lawyers were unable to establish this right to the full satisfaction of the court, even though Hampden was ordered to pay his tax by a narrow majority of seven judges out of 12. And the five judges who gave their verdicts against the Crown dealt a blow to absolute monarchy from which it was never to recover.

As a result of the case, Hampden emerged as a public figure. Despite paying the fine the judges imposed, his struggle for principle had passed into history. When, three years later, Charles was finally forced to recall Parliament, its members made a hero of Hampden.

When war broke out, Hampden took up arms in defence of his principles. He was wounded in the shoulder during an insignificant skirmish in a cornfield at Chalgrove, near Oxford, in June 1643. Charles I offered to send a surgeon to help him, but it was too late. He died six days later, leaving moderate men on both sides with an acute sense of the wastefulness of war. A contemporary wrote: 'The loss of Colonel Hampden goeth near the heart of every man that loves the good of his king and country. The memory of him will more and more be had in honour and esteem.'

This last prophecy was fulfilled. Long after Hampden's death, the philosopher Edmund Burke put the question: 'Would twenty shillings have ruined Mr Hampden's fortune?' and gave a famous answer: 'No, but the payment of half twenty shillings on the principle it was demanded, would have made him a slave.'

Charles I: 'So good a man, so bad a king'

The young Charles I – unlike his father – was sober, dignified, handsome and courteous. It was said that he had never violated a woman, struck a man, or spoken an evil word. He lacked his father's intellectual grip and knowledge, but at first he appealed to a generation sickened by James I's vulgarity.

Charles was a small man – in some paintings he almost disappears into his riding boots; but he had a deeply rooted sense of his own dignity and importance. His delicate frame and feminine face were elongated by a pointed beard. His melancholy air almost seemed to mark him out for tragedy.

A sickly child, not in the direct line of succession, Charles was raised in seclusion until his brother Henry's death in 1612. He worshipped Henry and his sister Elizabeth who were both personally attractive.

When Henry died and Elizabeth married a German prince in 1613, Charles's transformation into heir apparent did not bolster his self-confidence, especially since James persisted in calling him 'baby Charles'. He over-compensated with pride and rigidity and he instinctively ignored unwelcome advice. His natural shyness and reserve were accentuated by a slight stammer.

Charles's awkwardness with people threw him heavily on those he could trust – men such

Archbishop Laud, one of Charles I's ministers, whose tactlessness helped to bring down his master.

as the Duke of Buckingham, whose disastrous influence led Charles to quarrel with Parliament. He came to rely on the duke even more when his marriage to the headstrong and homesick Henrietta Maria of France seemed to have failed.

James I had originally hoped to arrange a diplomatic marriage between Charles and the Spanish *Infanta* (Crown Princess). His plans had been frustrated, but the young Charles had not forgotten the languid, sensual beauty of the Hapsburg princess. She was very different from his bride, a gawky 16-year-old with buck teeth and enormous eyes, who burst into tears at the first sight of her husband.

Personal incompatibility was compounded by religious differences. Henrietta Maria was a devout Catholic. She refused even to attend her husband's Protestant coronation service, and insisted on having her own priests.

For two years Charles and Henrietta Maria lived virtually separate lives, while Charles continued to rely on Buckingham for affection and support. But this prop was removed when Buckingham was assassinated in 1628. His death left the king with no friends, only servants. In his despair, Charles turned to his young wife, but her advice was just as illfounded as the policies of the dead favourite. Coming from the autocratic court of France, she encouraged Charles's despotism.

Charles believed that Parliament's demands for reform would lead to revolution. In 1629 he abandoned parliamentary government. His belief in the 'Divine Right of Kings' was one of the few things he inherited from his father, coupled with a lofty view of the powers and the privileges of the Church.

From peace to civil war

Government without Parliament seemed to him not only natural but right. And by 1635 his attitude seemed to have been justified. England was at peace; the government's accounts had been balanced; one of his leading parliamentary opponents, Sir John Eliot, had died in the Tower, and another, Sir Thomas Wentworth, had been transformed under the new title of Earl of Strafford into his most loyal servant. Public prosperity was crowned by domestic happiness; he and his queen had achieved perfect harmony.

But this calm was not to last. In 1639 revolt in Scotland forced Charles to recall Parliament the next year. The king and his people were soon at loggerheads again. This time, however, the result was civil war.

Charles fought for seven years for his throne. But in 1649 he lost both the crown and his life. To the end, he was a man of principle. He refused to sacrifice his beliefs to keep his crown. And through his death, he paved the way for an eventual restoration of the Stuarts to the throne in 1660.

Supreme sacrifice – a minister dies to save his king

THE ULTIMATE SANCTION

The able and ruthless Earl of Strafford was executed in 1641, falling victim to a vengeful Parliament after seven years as Charles I's minister. He was the last holder of high office to fall victim to this axe and block, now to be seen in the Tower of London.

No event in the melancholy reign of Charles I so disturbed the king's conscience as the death of his most faithful servant, the Earl of Strafford, in 1641.

From 1633 to 1640 Strafford was the king's deputy in Ireland. There, riding rough-shod over the liberties of the people and the rights of property, he imposed the royal policy of 'Thorough' – royal rule without Parliament – with single-minded devotion and brutality.

In 1640, bankrupt and at war with his Scottish subjects, Charles was at last driven to recall Parliament after 11 years of absolute rule. To support him in his emergency he turned to Strafford, promising him that if he did his king this service he 'should not suffer in his person, honour or fortune'. It was a promise that Charles was forced to break. On November 10, Strafford arrived in London. Six months later he was dead, executed by an Act of Parliament.

The fall of Strafford is one of the most tragic stories in English history. An opponent of Charles's first minister, the Duke of Buckingham, in the 1620's, he had been imprisoned, like Hampden, in 1627. In the next year he was one of the most prominent voices in the parliamentary fight to force Charles to agree to the Petition of Right.

Lynchpin of the crown

But once Charles had accepted the Petition, Strafford decided that his duty was to support the crown. 'The authority of a king,' he said, 'is the keystone which closeth up the arch of order and government.'

Strafford thus brought upon himself all the odium of a turncoat. By 1640 his callous rule in Ireland had made him the most hated man in the kingdom. His very presence – his ravaged, parchment face suffused with the blood of rising anger, his body twisted by gout over his walking stick – inspired horror. Queen Henrietta Maria knew well of his loyalty to her husband, but she could not help recoiling from what she thought to be the smell of blood and mud about him.

When Parliament met in November 1640, after 11 years in which its pent-up anger had had no outlet, Strafford was the first object of attack. The members began proceedings to impeach him for 'high misdemeanours', for destroying the rule of law in Ireland. On the same day that the proceedings were started, Strafford went to the House of Lords to 'look my accusers in the face'. He was forbidden to speak, arrested and removed to the Tower.

'Thus he whose greatness in the morning owned a power over two kingdoms,' wrote a chronicler, 'in the evening straitened his person betwixt two walls.'

On his way to the Tower, the crowds cried out, 'What is the matter?' 'A small matter, I warrant you,' Strafford replied. What harm could come to him, he asked in a tender letter

END OF A DILEMMA *The Earl of Strafford (left) was Charles I's most devoted servant. 'The authority of a king,' he said, 'is the keystone which closeth up the arch of order and government.' But his devotion and efficiency aroused the anger of Parliament, and in 1641 it passed a Bill of Attainder which condemned him to death. Charles was in a dilemma. He had promised Strafford his protection, but to fulfil this promise would jeopardise his throne. Realising the king's difficulty, Strafford freed him from his promise and gave his life for the royal cause. He was executed (above) on Tower Hill on May 12, 1641.*

to his wife, when there was 'nothing capital' in the charge against him? Did he not have the confidence and the protection of his sovereign?

Strafford's trial opened in Westminster Hall on March 22, 1641. Not just Strafford, but the whole balance of power between the king and the Commons was at stake. The most damning accusation made against Strafford was Sir Henry Vane's unswerving testimony that he had advised the king to use the Irish army against his opponents in England, to 'reduce *this* kingdom'. But of that there was no proof and, by April 10, impeachment had failed.

Parliament was concerned, however, not with justice, but with political necessity. Strafford was the symbol of absolute monarchy, the enemy of the peace of the country. In Parliament's eyes his death was imperative. And so the House of Commons introduced a Bill of Attainder which, regardless of whether Strafford were guilty of a crime, simply declared it to be the will of Parliament that he should die.

On April 13, his head shrunk between his shoulders, his long grey beard making him look older than his years, Strafford made a last, two-hour speech in his defence. 'These gentlemen tell me they speak in defence of the Commonweal against my arbitrary laws; give me leave to say that I speak in the defence of the Commonweal against their arbitrary treason.' It was an heroic effort, but it failed. The Commons passed the Bill condemning him by a vote of 204 to 59.

King Charles now relied on the House of Lords not to condemn one of their own order for carrying out the orders of the king. But popular clamour raged against Strafford and, as mob violence grew, the Lords gave way.

A selfless sacrifice

Strafford's life now lay with the king. Without his assent the Bill of Attainder was not law. Charles had never taken to Strafford; like Queen Henrietta Maria he could not understand Strafford's rough manners. Yet, no man had rendered him such unstinting service.

In conscience, therefore, Charles could not break his word and give his assent to the Bill. Yet to refuse was to imperil the monarchy. To spare the king, Strafford, selfless to the end, wrote him a letter from the Tower, releasing the king from his promise: 'To set Your Majesty's conscience at liberty, I do most humbly beseech Your Majesty (for preventing of evils which may happen by Your refusal) to pass this bill.'

So, on May 12, 1641, before a crowd of 200,000 at Tower Hill, Strafford, in his last great service to the crown, surrendered his life. For the rest of his life the memory of that scene haunted Charles I. When, eight years later, he came to the same end on the scaffold, almost his last words were, 'An unjust sentence that I suffered for to take effect is punished now by an unjust sentence upon me'.

A nation prepares for bitter civil war

As he put his signature to the Bill which sent Strafford to his death, King Charles murmured tearfully, 'My Lord of Strafford's condition is happier than mine'. Yet the first signs were that Strafford's death was a blood sacrifice which might bring peace and happiness to the nation. Charles gave his assent to a number of reforming Bills, including one that abolished the Court of Star Chamber, and another that ended non-parliamentary taxation. At last, Parliament and the king seemed to have come to a settlement.

Moderate men, however, were alarmed when Parliament forced the king to agree that he would never dissolve it without its consent. Such an assault on the royal power rekindled Charles's hatred of Parliament. For the moment that hatred was impotent. Civil war was impossible because the king did not have command of an army.

Then, in November 1640, news reached London of an event which was to transform the situation. Ireland, released from Strafford's grip, had risen in rebellion. The king hoped that his quarrel with Parliament would be swallowed up in a loyalist reaction against the Irish rebels, that 'these ill news from Ireland may hinder some of these follies in England'.

But to put down the Irish uprising Charles needed to raise an army. And the Commons, who had long since learnt not to trust their king, insisted that unless he changed his councillors they would raise their own army to conquer Ireland. They also demanded a veto on army appointments.

Suddenly there was a spontaneous rally to the king. Throughout 1641 Charles cleverly exploited the new mood. He appealed as the anointed defender of the Established Church against those who wanted to do away with bishops and impose bleak Puritanism. There gathered around the king a party of 'constitutional Royalists', led in the Lords by Lord Digby and in the Commons by Edward Hyde, the future Earl of Clarendon. Hyde had voted for Strafford's death, but when the Church was attacked he turned to support the king. At the same time, Charles began to build up a small military force in London.

'The birds have flown'

Then, in January, Charles destroyed the goodwill which he was winning by one of the hasty acts which were so characteristic of him. With a small body of officers he marched into the Commons to arrest five Parliamentary leaders. But they had already fled. Declaring that 'the birds have flown', Charles retired in confusion. In fear for his safety, he now fled from London with the queen.

Charles's withdrawal to the north had the effect of dividing the nation into Royalists and Parliamentarians. By August, the king had secured enough supporters to strike. At Nottingham on August 22, 1642, he raised his standard. That was a symbolic and ancient summons to his subjects to come to his aid, but it was traditionally the symbol of a rebel proclaiming resistance to the government. Thus, it boded ill for Royalists that the anxious man who raised his standard behind a ruined castle, remote from the capital, was their king. But Englishmen had now to settle with their consciences on whose side they stood.

RAISING THE STANDARD *Having failed to arrest five of his leading enemies in Parliament, Charles fled from London with his queen and raised his standard at Nottingham. Here, he greets his followers. This was a crucial decision; from then on England was divided by civil war.*

AN ARCHITECT CAPTURES THE GLORY OF THE STUART SUNSET

Charles I's self-declared aim was to create the most civilised court in Europe, and during his 24 year reign he collected 1400 paintings and 400 pieces of sculpture. He patronised and encouraged the leading artists of his day, and in Inigo Jones the king had in his service the finest architect of the age.

It was Jones who transformed English architecture on Classical lines, creating a style whose influence was to last for nearly 300 years. Among his masterpieces are the Banqueting House at Whitehall, the Queen's House at Greenwich and St Paul's Church, Covent Garden.

Monument to an age

But the supreme monument to the Stuart age and to the vision of Inigo Jones is Wilton House, Salisbury. One of the king's chief nobles, Philip Herbert, Earl of Pembroke and Montgomery, turned Wilton into a house which rivalled the best the king could achieve. And Charles was not slow to show his admiration for the house. The diarist John Aubrey wrote that the king 'did love Wilton above all places; and came thither every Sommer'.

It is not surprising that Wilton House stood so high in the monarch's affections. The spirit of the carefree – and slightly unreal – 1630's is expressed in the graceful beauty of the principal rooms, which were created to the basic design of Inigo Jones.

The first Wilton House, on whose foundations Inigo Jones achieved his greatest triumph, was erected by William Herbert, grandfather of Philip, in the 1540's. It stood on the site of a great abbey which shared the fate of so many monastic buildings during Henry VIII's Reformation.

William Herbert was a soldier of fortune who had made his name in continental wars, and returned home to serve his king and to marry the sister of Henry VIII's sixth wife, Catharine Parr. The Tudor house of the powerful Herberts witnessed the first performance of Shakespeare's As You Like It, and it was there that the poet Sir Philip Sidney wrote his pastoral romance 'Arcadia'.

Only the tower in the centre of the East Front survives unchanged from William Herbert's great house. It was the fourth earl, Philip Herbert, who pulled down the south

block of the Tudor mansion, substituting for it a façade and a set of rooms that have no rival in the history of English architecture.

The king took an interest in the developments at Wilton, and Queen Henrietta Maria urged Inigo Jones, who was then Surveyor of the Royal Works, to submit designs. In the 1630's Jones was at the height of his fame, and most of the leading courtiers were competing for his services.

An artistic triumph

Jones was busy with the Queen's House at Greenwich, but found time to draw up a rough plan for Wilton and to instruct his French assistant, Isaac de Caux, to implement it. In 1635 the work was begun, the earl supervising every stage with frequent assistance from his royal visitors. Charles and his vivacious queen would stroll through the uncompleted state rooms, advising their host on points of detail.

According to a surviving drawing by de Caux of the South Front, the original idea was for a house twice the size of the present one. But the outbreak of the Civil War brought the building programme at Wilton to a halt.

The earl was uncertain which side to join. He was the king's friend and Lord Chamberlain, but all his sympathies lay with the Parliamentarians. Finally he threw in his lot with Parliament. The upheaval meant that

THE KING'S CHOICE *The South Front of Wilton House near Salisbury was rebuilt to the designs of Inigo Jones. The great beauty of the place and the hospitality of the Herbert family brought many famous people to Wilton. John Aubrey, the diarist, recorded: 'Wilton House was like a college, there were so many learned and ingeniose persons.' Charles I, whom Jones served as surveyor, loved the house 'above all places'.*

only the proposed east wing was built. But, strangely, this mutilation of the original plan produced an artistic triumph. De Caux's elevation of the east wing was brilliantly altered, probably by Inigo Jones himself. Towers at each end gave symmetry to the whole composition, and one of de Caux's great venetian windows became the central feature.

In 1647, like some divine retribution for his betrayal of the king, Philip saw his new house largely destroyed by fire. Undaunted, he immediately began the rebuilding. Inigo Jones, who was by now 75 years old, set to work on the magnificent state rooms which are still the chief of Wilton's glories. Neither he nor his patron lived to see them completed.

The work was continued by Jones's nephew and assistant, John Webb, who finished the task in 1653. The conception and designs are virtually all Jones's own, planned and executed with an exuberance belied by the house's restrained exterior. Jones once wrote that 'outwardly every wise man carries a gravity, yet inwardly has his imagination set on fire and sometimes licentiously flies out'.

Wilton embodies this philosophy to perfection. Outside all is harmony and restraint, but within the seven state rooms architects and decorators created an atmosphere of exuberant richness, largely in white and gold.

Most splendid of all is the Double Cube Room which is 60 ft long, 30 ft high and 30 ft wide. This glittering apartment is impressive without being intimidating; it has the feeling of a comfortable *salon* rather than a stately audience chamber. Carved and gilded fruit and flowers festoon the walls, and the lavish decoration is taken up into the moulded and painted ceiling. Equally ornate are the doors and the Italian marble fireplace.

Scarcely less impressive is the Single Cube Room, all the dimensions of which are 30 ft.

The smaller chambers – such as the Hunting Room and the Corner Room – are more intimate, though they, too, glow with sumptuous colours and rich fabrics.

In all the state rooms Jones's decorations have a weight and solidity, a feeling of essential Englishness about them. The English furniture makers, William Kent and Thomas Chippendale, working in the Double Cube Room, a century after it was built, brilliantly adapted their work to his style.

Two men of genius

Inigo Jones had another collaborator whose contribution to Wilton was far greater than that of Webb or de Caux. Sir Anthony van Dyck had painted his superb series of portraits of the Herberts between 1634 and 1636; and the Double Cube Room was specifically designed for these pictures, culminating in the family group that dominates the west wall. Nearly 20 ft wide, it is the largest family group painted by Van Dyck. There are few rooms anywhere in which paintings on canvas combine so effortlessly with gilding and plasterwork to form a single satisfying whole.

These two men of genius combined to make Wilton one of the most beautiful places in Britain; they also gave a lasting expression to the briefly sunlit episode when the ill-starred king and queen 'came thither every Sommer'.

STATELY COMFORT *For all its splendour, the Double Cube Room at Wilton House is still a room to be lived in. After a fire in 1647, it was redesigned to hold Van Dyck's portraits of the Herberts and the king's family. Its classical proportions were a triumph for the masterly Inigo Jones.*

BRITAIN'S FIRST ARCHITECT

Born in 1573, Inigo Jones spent most of his long life providing a graceful background for the Stuart court. He was kept busy designing court entertainments as well as the works of architecture which gave him lasting fame.

The ruinous extravagance of these entertainments made the architect deeply unpopular with the Puritans. At the end of the siege of Basing House in October 1645, he was stripped naked by Oliver Cromwell's troopers and carried away wrapped in a blanket.

When Jones died two years after the execution of Charles I, it was said that the cause of death was 'grief for the fatal calamity of his master'. But he had lived long enough to provide Britain with a body of buildings which satisfied his own high standards – 'solid, proportionable, masculine and unaffected'.

Inigo Jones (above) spent much time working on masques. He designed elaborate stage sets and costumes, such as this Fiery Spirit (right).

A MEMORIAL TO THE GRACE OF A DOOMED GENERATION

SORROWFUL KING *Van Dyck painted this triple portrait of Charles I for the sculptor Bernini, who used it as a guide when carving a bust of the king. Later writers fostered a legend that Bernini gazed at the painting and said: 'Something evil will befall this man; he carries misfortune in his face.' But Van Dyck himself would never have accepted this romantic interpretation of his work.*

CHILDREN APART *The confident royal manner is already apparent in five of Charles's children, painted in 1637. From the left, Mary, James, in girlish clothing, Charles, heir to the throne, stroking a pet almost as tall as himself, and Elizabeth playing with Anne, the baby of the family.*

The romantic image of Charles I and his court created by Anthony van Dyck is one of the most enduring in the history of art. In a series of breathtaking canvases, Van Dyck succeeded in immortalising and glamorising for ever the supporters of a lost cause, the valiant cavaliers and their ladies.

In the years he spent in Britain – 'the nine years of his mature genius – Van Dyck made a double contribution to the artistic heritage of his adopted land. He gave Britain the finest court portraits of any period and any country; and he introduced a new style of painting, a style which was to influence more than two centuries of English portraiture.

Chosen by the king

Van Dyck came from the Spanish Netherlands, that part of Europe now known as Belgium. He entered the studio of the great northern master, Peter Paul Rubens, and quickly became his most brilliant pupil. In 1621, at the age of 22, he was attracted to the service of the English crown and sent by James I to Italy to complete his training.

The English court then lost track of him until 1629, when Charles I bought one of his paintings. Three years later, Van Dyck was induced to settle in England and enter the royal service on unprecedented terms – a knighthood and an annual pension of £200. Apart from visits to his native Flanders in 1634 and 1640, Van Dyck lived in England until his death in 1641.

Almost overnight, the new artist at Whitehall revolutionised the style of portrait painting. Elizabethan paintings had enclosed the sitter in a tiny box, with little more than a carpet, chair and curtains as props. The effect was one of frozen immobility. Van Dyck's paintings opened up vistas into the beyond.

Models for the future

For the first time in English history, the picture frame became an open window through which the eye passed into a natural world governed by the rules of perspective.

Van Dyck's figures are always apparently in the act of moving or about to move. They stand elegantly in the midst of twilight landscapes, or walk through shadowy groves.

No painter was more successful in transforming his sitters into the heroes and heroines which they imagined themselves to be. By this imaginative sensitivity to his subject's secret aspirations, Van Dyck was a purveyor of ideals. In his lifetime, this rare skill naturally endeared him to his patrons. After his death they and their successors looked to other artists to give them something of the Van Dyck magic. His great works became the models which all aspiring portraitists knew they must emulate. He had established a tradition of fine portraiture which lasted for two centuries as one of the glories of British art. As a court artist, Van Dyck's first duty was

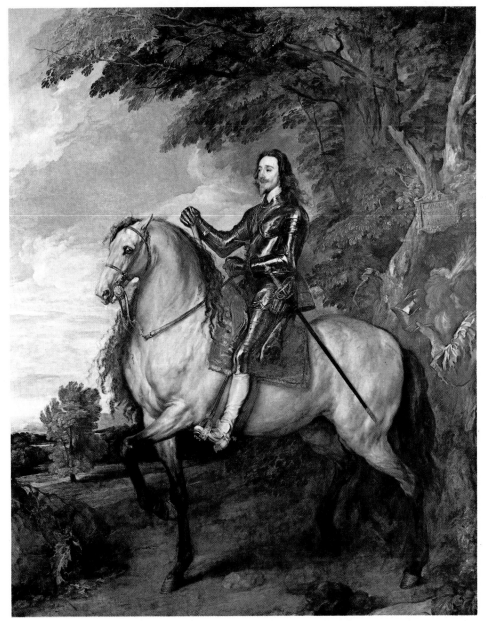

BORN TO RULE *There is a hint of melancholy in all Van Dyck's representations of the king. In this huge canvas, 12 ft high, he broke away from the older tradition of formal portraits and transformed his royal subject into a heroic knight of legend, the unchallenged master of all he surveyed.*

QUEEN OF LOVE *Henrietta Maria and her husband reigned over a world of masques, pageants and banquets which celebrated the ideals of courtly love and beauty. Their happy marriage provided a touching theme for Van Dyck.*

to present an acceptable view of his chief patron, the king. The image he created of Charles I was undoubtedly his master stroke, for it was not a work of mere flattery but rather an evocation of all that Charles wished to be. In reality, the limitations of Charles's own complex character – and the unhappy nature of the age itself – prevented him from realising his aspirations. Perhaps only in Van Dyck's canvases could he fulfil his ambitions as the ideal ruler of an ideal realm.

Later generations have seen in Van Dyck's renderings of Charles I's face the look of a man who foresaw his fate. At the time, however, the sad grandeur of the royal pose, with the heavy-lidded eyes and far-away look, were merely expressions of calm spiritual contemplation. Van Dyck presents a king who was dignified and solitary, with a touch of shadowed melancholy, then the most fashionable of

moods. But no suggestion of defeat or failure was intended – certainly no premonition of impending doom. Painted long before the civil war, the royal portraits were deliberate assertions of absolute power.

Van Dyck depicts him as the Lord's anointed in robes of state, as the ideal gentleman, elegantly leaning on his walking stick in a forest glade, as a Knight of the Garter, as the pious protector of the Church of England, and as a warrior on horseback.

Yet in all these aspects of the king, Van Dyck gave the royal face one consistent representation: elegant, refined and slightly disdainful. Above all, the expression conveyed an aura of intense spirituality, an appropriate mood for the divinely appointed ruler who was answerable to God alone.

The artist's genius touched Queen Henrietta Maria with the same divine radiance. Like her

husband, she was short; but you would not know it from Van Dyck's portraits. Sometimes she appears in the role of a love goddess, reforming a licentious court by the example of courtly love. Sometimes, in shimmering satin and pearls, she is the ideal lady of chivalry, a perfect spouse for Charles in his role as the gallant knight.

A world of make-believe
Henrietta Maria is also presented as the ideal mother, a fitting parent for the innocent royal children who grace Van Dyck's family portraits. These solemn infants are endowed with an artful artlessness and, like their parents, are set apart from ordinary mortals.

The world of Charles I and his queen was almost make-believe, a stage on which the principal actors played their parts behind masks. Van Dyck's genius conferred immortality on an exquisite and ideal world that never really existed. All too soon the masks were to be stripped away.

Even in matters of painting, Cromwell, the man of the future, was at odds with the court. He instructed the artist Peter Lely: 'I desire you would use your skill to paint my picture truly like me and not flatter me at all but remark all these roughnesses, pimples, warts and everything as you see me.'

Confident and invincible as Charles appears in his great horseback portrait, Cromwell – with his 'roughnesses, pimples, warts' – was fated to triumph. But nothing has been able to obliterate Van Dyck's dream world in which the melancholy king and his lovely queen reign for ever. The artist died in the year before the outbreak of war. It was fitting that he should not live to see his dreams shattered.

Edgehill—Cavaliers and Roundheads blunder into war

BATTLE HONOURS *Both sides claimed that they had won victory at the Battle of Edgehill. Charles himself had these medals of honour struck for the leaders of the Royalist army.*

WHERE THEY FIRST CLASHED
The peaceful setting of Edgehill in the Cotswolds was the scene of the first major battle of the Civil War in 1642. For the king, Edgehill was a lost opportunity. Thanks to the brilliance of his cavalry, commanded by his nephew, Prince Rupert, Charles had the better of the day. Had he pursued his advantage, he might have captured London. But instead he delayed and gave Parliament a chance to reorganise.

Edgehill, a sandstone ridge situated in the Cotswolds halfway between Birmingham and Oxford, commands one of the loveliest views in England. A rolling landscape of green fields and scattered copses unfolds to the Avon Valley. There, on a frosty October morning in 1642, the Royalist Cavaliers looked down upon the Parliamentary Roundheads in the valley, and prepared to fight the first pitched battle between Englishmen since the Battle of Bosworth Field more than a century and a half before.

The armies were about evenly matched: Parliament's 2000 cavalry and 11,000 foot against the king's 3000 cavalry and 9000 foot. For Charles I this first clash of the Civil War was critical: he needed to get his army past the Parliamentary forces, led by the inexperienced Earl of Essex, in order to advance on the Parliamentary stronghold of London.

The sunny morning dragged by. Neither side, it seemed, wanted to strike the first blow. Clothed in a black velvet coat with an ermine lining, Charles rode out among his troops and addressed them in characteristically stoical fashion: 'Come life or death, your King will bear you company, and ever keep this field, this place, and this day's service in his grateful remembrance.'

The battle begins
The signal for the fighting to begin came when Charles moved his cavalry halfway down the slope, and a nameless Roundhead gunner at last took it upon himself to fire the first shot – a shot that was to echo down English history. He sighted the king on Knowle Hill, took aim and fired. The cannon-ball fell short, but Charles reacted just as one of his forbears would have responded to a gauntlet thrown down at his feet. The Royalist army was given the signal to advance. In the centre, Sir Jacob Astley, the silver-haired veteran officer of the infantry, uttered a short prayer: 'O Lord, thou knowest how busy I must be this day. If I forget thee, do not thou forget me.'

At about 1 o'clock in the afternoon, a rumble of cannon signified that the Civil War had really begun. The cannonade lasted for about an hour, but did little damage. Then, on the right, Prince Rupert, the 23-year-old nephew of the king, and commander of the

NO TURNING BACK *King and Parliamentary leaders confront each other in this idealised engraving of the Battle of Edgehill. Seven bitter years of civil war were to follow this first action.*

Royalist cavalry, led the first of those brilliant charges which were, over the next three years, to establish him as the finest captain of horse in English history.

His troops trotted down the gentle descent for about a mile, jumped a narrow stream and then, breaking into a canter, headed straight for the Parliamentary cavalry. The sight of Rupert's force galloping towards them was too much for Essex's untrained horsemen. They turned and fled. And as Rupert's men gave chase down the road to Warwick, stragglers spread the news of Parliament's defeat.

'I fear them not!'

The reports were premature. The Cavaliers had made a fatal mistake, for their reserve cavalry, instead of staying to give cover to the infantry, had followed Rupert's charge and joined in the pursuit. No Royalist horsemen remained on the field to guard the infantry, guns and standard of the king.

Now Sir William Balfour, the commander of the Parliamentary reserves, and the most experienced soldier at Edgehill, seized his opportunity. Under cover of hedges, he led his reserve cavalry up the hill. Then, smashing through a brigade of the king's infantry, he reached the Royalist guns and tried to spike them with his own hands. The attempt failed, due to a shortage of nails, but he managed to kill the gunners and, by cutting the traces, to immobilise the guns.

When another brigade succumbed, the Royalist infantry was in danger of being swept away. Some of Balfour's troops came within yards of a spectacular prize: they stumbled across a party escorting the 12-year-old heir to the throne, Prince Charles, and his 9-year-old

brother James (later James II). Prince Charles drew a pistol and prepared to lead a charge. 'I fear them not!' he cried. But the boys were persuaded to ride off in haste.

At the centre of the king's own lifeguard, Sir Edward Verney, the Earl Marshal and bearer of the royal standard, fought hand to hand to save the sacred symbol of martial monarchy. But he was struck down, and the standard was snatched from his lifeless hand. Lord Lindsey, the Royalist infantry commander, whom Astley had replaced after a quarrel on the eve of the battle, was badly wounded and taken prisoner.

Balfour appeared to have won the day for the Roundheads. But once again the tide of battle turned. Prince Rupert, who had managed to arrest the impetuous chase of his men, arrived back on the battlefield just before dusk with half his cavalry. The Roundheads drew back, the royal standard was recovered and the shooting died away.

The action had been fierce. It had also been undisciplined. In the Parliamentary camp that night, the captured Lindsey, embittered towards the young royal favourite, Prince Rupert, vowed never to fight in the field with boys again. The next morning he died.

Missed opportunity

As night fell, and marauders moved in to strip the dead, men on both sides pondered the blunders that had been made in this first major engagement of the Civil War.

The man who learnt his lessons best was a Roundhead officer who had arrived late on the field of battle to find both sides in dispirited disorder. There, he discovered his destiny: to remodel the Parliamentary army and turn it into an invincible fighting force. His name was Oliver Cromwell. And the New Model Army he created was to bring him supreme power.

Each army lost about 2500 men, over half of them through desertion, and each side claimed the victory. The king had the better of the day; the road to London now lay open and undefended. Charles, however, shaken by the carnage he had seen – Verney dead, his young cousin, Prince d'Aubigny, mortally wounded, and 60 of his own footguard strewn in a heap around him – ignored Rupert's advice to press on to the capital. Instead, he fell back to Oxford. By the time he decided to advance on London, the Parliamentarians had found time to prepare. On November 4 Charles reached Reading, but it was another nine days before he reached the outskirts of London – Turnham Green. This was to be as close as he would get to recapturing his capital. There he was confronted by the 24,000-strong 'Trained Bands' of the City of London. A swift blow might have produced decisive results, but instead he decided to retreat. By a disastrous failure of nerve and foresight, Charles had squandered his best opportunity to win the war and save his crown.

Prince Rupert: Scourge of the king's enemies

'Clad in scarlet, very richly laid with silver lace, mounted upon a very gallant black barbary horse,' Prince Rupert of the Rhine, nephew of Charles I, was the most glamorous soldier of the English Civil War. A talented engraver and a competent scientist, he was above all an outstanding military commander, renowned for the lightning speed of his cavalry charges.

When the 23-year-old prince arrived in England from his Bohemian homeland in 1642, he was already a veteran of the Dutch and Swedish wars. He quickly established himself as the darling of the court. Charles appointed him General of the Horse. Rupert armed his men lightly and used them as shock troops, drilled to charge at a gallop rather than a trot, to keep their swords in their hands and to continue charging under heavy fire.

The Royalist cavalry remained undefeated until the Battle of Marston Moor in 1644. And Rupert's personal qualities – frankness and generosity, pride and spirit, speed of decision – won him the affection and loyalty of his troops. After the relief of Newark and York in 1644, the Duke of Newcastle hailed him as 'the Redeemer of the North and the Saviour of the Crown'.

But, in the end, the north was not to be redeemed or the crown saved. Against Cromwell's well-disciplined Ironsides, Rupert's tactics proved defective.

'Though the King's troops prevailed in the charge, and routed those they charged,' wrote the Earl of Clarendon, 'they seldom rallied themselves in order, nor could they be brought again to make a second charge.' It was the less romantic, but more methodical, Oliver Cromwell, who emerged as the greatest military leader of the age.

SOLDIER PRINCE *The impetuous and dashing Prince Rupert was a brilliant exponent of the cavalry charge at full gallop and under heavy fire.*

AMATEURS AT WAR

Edgehill was the first battle to be fought between Englishmen since the Wars of the Roses nearly 200 years before. At the beginning of the Civil War both sides were short of men and guns. More important, both lacked capable commanders. Most of the leaders at Edgehill were inexperienced soldiers who had won their positions by raising regiments of cavalry and infantry. As a mark of their independence, they took their own colours (below) into battle. It was not until Oliver Cromwell emerged as a leader of genius and cool common sense that an efficient army was organised.

Defeat at Naseby–and the king's cause is doomed

HALLMARK OF WAR

Oliver Cromwell's priming flask (above) is in the Cromwell Museum, Huntingdon. He used it in battle to charge his personal set of pistols. Cromwell shared all dangers with his men. It was said 'he loved his soldiers as his children, and his greatest care was to see them provided for with all the necessaries requisite'.

The spring of 1645 was a wet one. The broken land of small hills and valleys which lies between Naseby and Harborough was almost marshy when, on the night of June 13, 1645, the Royalist and Parliamentary commanders sought high ground on which to fight one another. Dawn found their ranks drawn up on opposing grassy ridges, separated by a small valley.

The king's forces looked resplendent in their polished breastplates and velvet livery, their bright banners fluttering in the wind. Against them were lined the untried, but disciplined and zealous, soldiers of Oliver Cromwell's New Model Army. The first great test of Cromwell's military skill was at hand. The 'poor handful of despised men', as a Puritan officer, Colonel Okey, called the New Model Army, was facing its baptism of fire. But Cromwell knew that they outnumbered the 7000-strong Royalists by two to one, and that victory could not be denied them.

The battle began when the Parliamentary army, not yet ready for battle, withdrew from the ridge of the hill, 'so that the enemy might not perceive in what form the battle was drawn, nor see any confusion therein'. Prince Rupert, mistaking this for retreat, charged.

His horsemen swept down the slope and up again, falling upon Colonel Ireton's front line. Musketry from the hedge merely dinted the

A description of His MAJESTIE'S ARMY of Horfe and Foot, and of his Excellencies Sr THOMAS FAIREFAX : as they were drawn into feveral Bodies at the
BATTAIL of NASBIE June the 14th 1645 .

TURNING POINT OF THE WAR *Cromwell's recently formed New Model Army was put to its first test at Naseby in June 1645. Charles's magnificently dressed troops put Cromwell's 'poor handful of despised men' to shame by comparison. But for the Royalists, the Battle of Naseby was* a total disaster. Charles himself left the field of battle while the fighting was still at its height. His army – and his future – was totally destroyed. Cromwell wrote to the Speaker of the House of Commons after the battle: 'Sir, this is none other than the hand of God.'

CHIEF OF THE ARMY *Sir Thomas Fairfax commanded the nationally organised New Model Army, which was to win the war for Parliament. Cromwell was its Lieutenant-General.*

advance, and Ireton was forced back upon Naseby. Two regiments broke completely and many of Ireton's men 'went clear away to Northampton and could never be stopped'. At the same time the king's infantry closed with the Parliamentary foot soldiers and forced them to give ground.

'Would you go upon your death?'

Cromwell now led his cavalry against Sir Marmaduke Langdale's 'Northern Horse'. Langdale's men did not scatter, but they were pushed back.

King Charles, with great courage, tried to hearten his infantry by going forward among them. A soldier, however, seized the king's bridle and, shouting 'Would you go upon your death?', turned the horse's head. Amid the dust of battle, the Royalist cavalry interpreted this as a sign to withdraw – and withdrawal turned into rout. Having kept the main body

of his cavalry intact after the first charge, Cromwell was now able to draw it together again for a second, decisive assault. Wave upon wave of Cromwell's horse pounded upon Langdale's forces, who buckled and galloped away for Leicester and Newark. The king's infantry was left unprotected and his Welsh levies, seeing no chance of victory, surrendered in whole companies.

Turning-point of the war

Officers saved themselves by flight, while Rupert's cavalry covered Charles's retreat from the field. By early afternoon, not a horse or man of the king's army, save those infantrymen taken prisoner, was to be seen.

In the royal coaches abandoned by the retreating cavalry, women were murdered and stripped of their belongings. The Parliamentary booty was reckoned at £100,000 in gold, silver and jewels. The saddest victims of the day were the massacred women, whom Cromwell's men called 'Irish women of cruel countenance' armed with knives. Probably they were Welsh soldiers' wives, appealing for mercy in a strange language, and defending themselves with the cutlery they had brought with them to cook for their menfolk.

Naseby saw the destruction of the king's army. He lost all his infantry, all his guns and most of his baggage train. In fact, though another year passed before he surrendered, he had lost his kingdom. The hand of God, so Cromwell believed, had at last revealed itself. 'When I saw the enemy draw up and march in gallant order towards us, and we a company of poor, ignorant men,' he afterwards confessed, 'I could not (riding alone about my business) but smile out to God in praises, in assurance of victory...O that men would therefore praise the Lord, and declare the wonders that He doth for the children of men.'

An army dedicated to the service of God

After the Battle of Edgehill, Cromwell told John Hampden what was wrong with Parliament's army. 'Your troopers are most of them old decayed serving-men, and tapsters, and such kind of fellows; do you think that the spirits of such base and mean fellows will ever be able to encounter gentlemen?'

In February 1645, Parliament created a new military system – the New Model Army – nationally organised and regularly paid. Its core was Cromwell's Eastern Association, a disciplined cavalry of East Anglian yeomen, unmatched by any other in the country.

'If you choose godly honest men to be captains of Horse,' Cromwell said, 'honest men will follow...I had rather have a plain russet-coated captain that knows what he fights for, and loves what he knows, than that which you call a gentleman, and is nothing else.' Cromwell's 'Ironsides' – they took their name from the epithet with which Rupert praised Cromwell after the Battle of Marston Moor – were inspired by the unshakeable Puritan conviction that God was on their side.

They were also well drilled and taught to charge without breaking their order in pursuit of the enemy. In May 1645, the New Model Army took the field, with Sir Thomas Fairfax as commander and Cromwell as his Lieutenant-General. At Naseby it won its spurs, and soon became the most powerful political force in the country, the instrument of Cromwell's rise to supreme power.

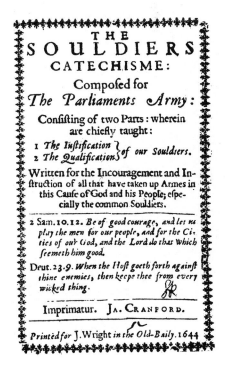

IN GOD WE TRUST *The Puritan Cromwell was convinced that God was on his side. The Almighty was invoked in the Soldiers' Catechism (above), specially produced for the troops.*

CAVALIER FLAMBOYANCE *Resplendent and often flamboyant dress was always a characteristic of the Cavaliers. Here it is worn to brilliant effect by three of Charles's supporters. From left to right they are Sir William Mainwaring, an unknown drummer and an officer, William Barnston. All of them feature in stained-glass windows in St Chad's Church, Farndon, Cheshire.*

Alone–the defeated king faces his accusers

SEAT OF JUDGMENT
In this chair, now in the Victoria and Albert Museum, Charles I heard himself accused by his opponents as 'a Tyrant, Traitor and Murderer...and public enemy'. He sat in it throughout his trial in Westminster Hall, presenting a figure of the utmost dignity.

CONTEMPORARY RECORD *Edward Bower painted this portrait of the king during the trial. Charles rose magnificently to the occasion and was always in perfect control of himself. If he had been unable to live like a king, he told a friend, he could at least die a gentleman.*

A KING ON TRIAL *In this contemporary engraving of the court-room scene, Charles (seated centre) is seen before the special commission chosen from 135 candidates. He refused to recognise the court.*

In 1649 the courts of Europe received shattering news from England. After six years of civil war, that country's Parliament had taken the momentous step of bringing the king, Charles I, to trial for treason – 'in the name of the people'.

English kings had been killed before, but only in battle or in obscure places. But in 1649 the passion which burnt in the hearts of the Roundhead army demanded the open trial of 'the chief author of our troubles'. Oliver Cromwell stated: 'We will cut off his head with the crown on it.'

The world was to witness the deed. The trial of Charles I was the first in history to receive full Press coverage. As the fanatical regicide, Colonel Harrison, said later: 'The

things that have been done have been done upon the stage, in the light of the Sun.'

Cromwell and his colleagues were driven to this last extremity by Charles's stubborn refusal to accept defeat. He would not surrender his principles either on the monarchy or on the Church, and negotiations were fruitless. Both Parliament and the army had learnt that Charles could not be trusted to keep his word.

On January 6, 1649, Parliament set up a special court to try the king. Its members were chosen from 135 candidates. Two weeks later, Charles was led into a packed Westminster Hall to hear the charge of treason read against him.

Dressed entirely in black and wearing the star and ribbon of the Garter, the king was

GUILTY MEN *Charles's death warrant was signed by 59 republicans. When the monarchy was restored in 1660, most of them escaped abroad. But ten of the leaders were tried as traitors and sentenced to be hanged, drawn and quartered. To the last, they refused to repent of their action.*

The men who sentenced their king to death

At the end of the first day of the king's trial, John Cook, the Solicitor-General, who was prosecuting the king, was hurrying through the dark streets of London, when he was stopped by a passer-by who said, 'I hear you are up to the ears in this business'. 'I am serving the people,' Cook answered. 'There's a thousand to one will not give you thanks,' muttered the stranger.

One at least of the Parliamentary leaders had recognised this popular mood. General Fairfax at the last shrank from killing a king. When his name was called on the roll of the court's commissioners, no answer came, save a cry from a heavily veiled woman in the gallery, who was later discovered to be Lady Fairfax: 'He has more wit than to be here.'

The day of reckoning

Fifty-nine republicans, whose convictions stifled doubts and fears, saw the matter through to its bloody end and signed the death warrant. Eleven years later, when Charles II was restored, 41 of them were still alive to answer for the deed.

Most of the regicides took refuge abroad or surrendered voluntarily and escaped execution. Colonel Tomlinson, who had marched the late king to the scaffold, produced a gold toothpick case which Charles I had given him as a keepsake and went free. Thomas Lister and Colonel Hutchinson purchased their freedom by kneeling at the bar of the House of Lords and pleading deep repentance.

But ten of the leading regicides refused to recant and were arraigned at the Old Bailey in the autumn of 1660. These men were still ready to die for their now unfashionable ideals.

Thomas Harrison, the first man to call Charles I 'that Man of Blood', died confident that he had followed 'the revealed will of God in his Holy Scriptures'. In a final gesture of defiance he struggled to his feet after being disembowelled to box his executioner on the ear. Colonel Axtell, asked on the scaffold if he had any regrets, replied, 'If I had a thousand lives I would lay them all down for the cause'. And John Cook, the man who had prosecuted Charles I, met the same end.

The execution of the regicides by the barbaric method of hanging, drawing and quartering bruised even the calloused sensibilities of the 17th century. On October 12, when four of them went to the scaffold in succession, the headsman broke down, leaving the fourth victim to his boy.

Charles II's mercy towards the contrite did not extend to the dead. The remains of Colonel Ireton, Cromwell's second-in-command, John Bradshaw and Cromwell himself, all of whom had died in the 1650's, were dug up and gibbeted outside Westminster Hall.

greyer than when Londoners had last seen him, seven years before. His cheeks had fallen in, and his expression was haggard.

Yet he was in perfect regal command of himself. It was this calm that his prosecutor, the Solicitor-General, John Cook, was determined to shatter. In his opening statement, Cook declared in ringing tones: 'I do accuse Charles Stuart, here present, of high treason and high misdemeanours, and I do, in the name of the Commons of England, desire the charge may be read to him.'

Charles tapped Cook on the shoulder with the silver head of his cane, as a sign that he wanted to speak. Cook took no notice. Then the head of the cane fell to the floor. There was a moment's pause as Charles waited for the customary attention due to a king. But no one came forward and he stooped to pick it up himself.

A battle of wits

The charge was then read. Charles was accused of having 'traitorously and maliciously levied war against the present Parliament and the people therein represented'. It denounced him as 'a Tyrant, Traitor and Murderer, and a public and implacable enemy to the Commonwealth of England'.

Charles rose magnificently to the occasion. If, as he said to a friend, he had been unable to live as a king, he might at least die a gentleman. He answered the charge with scorn and, in the intensity of the moment, his habitual stammer disappeared.

'I would know by what power I am called hither,' he asked with measured disdain. 'I would know by what authority, I mean lawful.' When the president of the court, John Bradshaw, blustered 'in the name of the people', Charles replied: 'I do stand more for the liberty of my people than any that come here to be my pretended judges.'

Charles refused to plead. He would not recognise a court which had no constitutional foundation. He believed that, as the fountainhead of justice, he stood for the true liberties of the people against an arbitrary and usurped authority. 'For if power without law may make laws ... I do not know what subject he is in England, that can be sure of his life or anything that he calls his own.'

By refusing to plead, Charles had cleverly disarmed the court of the opportunity to make anti-Royalist propaganda, for witnesses could not be brought in to support the case against him. Only their depositions could be read.

The judges were now engaged in anguished debate in their private meetings. Charles's pointed questions and stubborn refusal to plead were making a mockery of the trial – and his bearing and eloquence were winning him considerable sympathy. The ranks of the soldiers lining Westminster Hall might cry out 'Justice! Justice!' as the king was escorted away at the end of each public session. But a new and disturbing cry was also being raised – 'God save the king!'

Finally, on Sunday, January 21, the judges met in secret and came to a stern conclusion. Charles was to be given a last chance to plead. If he still refused, his silence would be taken as an admission of guilt and the court would proceed to pass sentence on the following Saturday. On that day, the king was brought to hear the inevitable sentence – that 'the said Charles Stuart, as a Tyrant, Traitor ... and public enemy, shall be put to death by the severing of his head from his body'.

The final exit

Charles made a last desperate attempt to speak. But Bradshaw cut him short: 'You have not owned us as a court.' Then he reminded the king that prisoners were never heard after the sentence had been passed. And as Charles once more began to speak, soldiers hustled him out of the courtroom. His last words were: 'I am not suffered for to speak: expect what justice other people will have.'

The axe falls ... and Charles gains a martyr's crown

DRESS FOR DEATH
For his execution, carried out on a cold January day, King Charles wore this extra shirt, so that he would not shiver and give the impression of fear on the scaffold. 'Death is not terrible to me,' he said. The shirt can now be seen in the London Museum.

On the morning of the day that he was to die, Charles I comforted his weeping gentleman-in-waiting, Thomas Herbert: 'This is my second marriage day; I would be as trim today as may be; for before night I hope to be espoused to my blessed Jesus.' Then he asked Herbert to put out an additional shirt. He would not have shivers from the cold attributed to fear. 'I fear not death. Death is not terrible to me. I bless my God I am prepared.'

Charles had been allowed three days, from the passing of the sentence on Saturday, January 27, to prepare himself for death on the following Tuesday. Much of that time he had spent in prayers with his chaplain, the gentle Bishop Juxon. He had also burnt his papers, and bequeathed the small remains of his personal property to members of his family.

On the Monday evening he was taken from the house next to Westminster Palace, where he had stayed during his trial, to St James's Palace. This was so that the hammering of the carpenters who were building the scaffold should not disturb his last night on earth. There he took leave of two of his children who were also prisoners of Parliament, the 10-year-old Henry, Duke of Gloucester, and the 13-year-old Princess Elizabeth.

Charles charged the boy not to be made king so long as his elder brothers, Charles and James, now safe in France, lived: 'Do not let them make thee king, for they will cut off your brothers' heads when they can catch them, and cut off thy head, too, at the last.'

He told Elizabeth that he had forgiven his enemies, and begged her not to grieve. He would die a glorious death, 'it being for the laws and liberties of this land, and for maintaining the true Protestant religion'.

He bade her tell her mother, Queen Henrietta Maria, that his thoughts had never strayed from her, and that his love would be the same to the last. Finally, he told her that he would die a martyr. The Lord would settle the throne upon his son.

A beating of drums

On the next morning Bishop Juxon arrived to celebrate Charles's last Holy Communion. The lessons appointed for the day – God's vengeance on the Egyptians for breaking faith with Moses, and Matthew's account of the Crucifixion – were texts so appropriate that Charles thought the bishop had deliberately inserted them into the service.

Then, at 10 a.m., the king, escorted by a company of infantry and accompanied by the mournful beating of drums, started out to walk across St James's Park, on the short journey to Whitehall, where the scaffold was

DEATH OF 'A MAN OF SORROWS' *A hushed crowd watches as Charles I is executed for high treason in Whitehall on January 30, 1649.*

erected. To reach the scaffold, Charles had to pass through the great Banqueting House, built for his father, James I, by Inigo Jones. In the seven years since it was last a royal palace, the building had fallen into sad decay. But the ceiling, which Charles himself had commissioned from Rubens, was undamaged. As the king walked through to his death he must have glimpsed its scenes depicting the glorification of his father as founder of the Stuart dynasty.

The last words

At 2 p.m. the king stepped out from a window on to the black-draped scaffold. At the block waited two masked men; around the scaffold's platform, soldiers stood guard against a rescue attempt or a riot.

Spectators filled the square and crowded the rooftops. Nothing disturbed Charles's heroic calm before his executioners. 'I go,' he said to Juxon, 'from a corruptible to an incorruptible crown.'

Reading from a slip of paper, he spoke to the few people within immediate earshot. He was about to die for his belief in divine monarchy, and he wanted the people not to forget the purpose of his sacrifice. His last words – taken down by shorthand writers on the scaffold – were a political testament.

'For the people . . . I must tell you, that their liberty and freedom consist in having of government those laws by which their life and their goods may be most their own. It is not for having a share in government, Sirs: that is nothing pertaining to them. A subject and a sovereign are clean different things.'

'Martyr of the people'

Then he spoke of the events which had brought him to his end: 'If I would have given way to have all changed according to the power of the sword, I needed not to have come here; and therefore I tell you (and I pray God it be not laid to your charge) that I am the martyr of the people.'

That said, the king folded his long hair under his cap, took off his cloak and doublet, handed the pendant of the Garter to Bishop Juxon, and bade the executioner to set the block fast. Lying down, he placed his head on the block and said to the headsman, 'Stay for the sign'. For weeks he had been called simply 'Sir', but the man answered, 'I will, an' it please your Majesty'.

They were the last words Charles heard. For a moment he knelt in prayer. Then, at his nod, the axe fell. His head was held up for all to see and a mighty groan was released from the crowd – 'such a groan', said one witness, 'as I never heard before, and desire I may never hear again'.

That night a visitor crept into the chamber in Whitehall where the king's coffin lay, lifted up the lid, stared a moment at the royal corpse, and muttered 'Cruel necessity'. It was Oliver Cromwell.

The legend created by 'A Man of Sorrows'

WINDSOR BURIAL *On February 9, 1649, the king's coffin was carried by four noblemen to its final resting place in the Garter Chapel in St George's, Windsor. Among the mourners was Bishop Juxon, a faithful friend, who had given Charles his last Holy Communion.*

As he prepared to meet his fate, Charles was still confident of the future. He hoped that his exiled heir, Prince Charles, might be home in time to take part in the burial ceremony. For the king believed that monarchy would survive despite his execution.

Charles's time-scale was to prove highly optimistic. The young Charles was to spend 11 long years 'on his travels' before the people of England were to welcome the restoration of the Stuart dynasty. His one attempt to regain the throne by military force was defeated at the Battle of Worcester in 1651. But, in the long run, the 'martyr king' showed a prophetic insight into the problems England would face in the bleak years that followed his death.

His enemies were less well prepared. On the first day of the trial, John Cook, the fervent prosecutor of the charges against the king, had boasted confidently: 'He must die, and monarchy must die with him.' But now, as Charles's coffin began its final journey through the falling snow to Windsor, it became all too clear that it was far easier to kill a king than to destroy monarchy itself.

Within a few days, Parliament tried to complete the work the executioner had begun. The institution of monarchy was formally abolished as being 'unnecessary, burdensome and dangerous to the liberty, safety and public interests of the people'. But no Act of Parliament could alter the fact that a society based on rank could not operate without a power at its apex. Nor could an Act of Parliament erase the deep instinct of the British people to show their reverence for the monarchy.

Within ten days of Charles I's execution, hawkers were peddling a book which was a classic of propaganda and the best-seller of the century. It was entitled *Eikon Basilike*, 'The Portraiture of His Sacred Majesty in His Solitudes and Sufferings'. It covered the events from the meeting of the Long Parliament to Charles's imprisonment. Edition after edition sold out. Royalists described it as an 'incomparable book', and its author as 'nearer the similitude of God than a man or king'.

Birth of a legend

Eikon Basilike was inspired by the thoughts and conversations of Charles and written by Francis Gauden, later Bishop of Ely. From its pages emerged the picture of a sublime human being, suffused with charity towards all, tragically misunderstood by a misguided nation. The book drew men to ponder the blood-guilt of the whole country, and helped to prepare men's minds for the Restoration. No matter who had done the deed, the work argued, every Englishman to some extent was guilty of the king's death and must work to avert the wrath of God.

The impact of *Eikon Basilike* continued after the Restoration. In 1660 a statute was passed making the day of execution, January 30, a day of fasting. And for the rest of the century, no Anglican parson forgot to rub home the lesson that the nation's guilt could be expiated only by unwavering obedience to the Lord's anointed servant.

'God's Englishman' seizes the reins of power

CROMWELL'S HAT

When Oliver Cromwell dissolved the Rump Parliament in April 1653, he was wearing this hat, now in the Cromwell Museum, Huntingdon. This was the decisive moment in Cromwell's rise to supreme power as Lord Protector. By abolishing Parliament, he either had to rule himself with the aid of the army he had created or face complete anarchy. But when Cromwell died, the system he had created perished with him.

'IN THE NAME OF GOD, GO !' *Disgusted by the failure of the self-seeking politicians of the Rump Parliament to carry out promised reforms, Oliver Cromwell (left) decided to dissolve it. On April 20, 1653, he called in his waiting soldiers and dismissed the members with the stinging words: 'You have sat too long here for any good you have been doing . . . In the name of God, go !' He later wrote: 'There was not so much as the barking of a dog.'*

Oliver Cromwell, 'clad in plain black clothes with grey worsted stockings', sat, as was his custom, on a back bench listening to the Long Parliament. The members were debating a new Bill which would continue the Parliament's existence indefinitely. For 15 minutes he sat, containing his indignation. Then, as the Speaker was about to put the question on whether the Bill should pass, he whispered to Major-General Harrison, 'This is the time I must do it', and rose to address the House.

Striding up and down the floor of the House, pointing now at one member, now at another, he harangued the assembly, chastising it for its corruption, its fraudulence, its injustice and its self-seeking.

'Perhaps you think,' he exclaimed, 'that this is not parliamentary language. I confess it is not; neither are you to expect any from me. You are no Parliament, I say you are no Parliament. I will put an end to your sitting.'

Time-servers in Parliament

The date was April 20, 1653. The Long Parliament, after 13 years a sorry remnant of what it once had been, was derisively called the 'Rump Parliament'.

Some of its members had been lost in the civil wars. The Presbyterians who had wished to come to an agreement with Charles I, rather than execute him, had been forcibly removed by Colonel Pride's 'purge' in December 1648. And more members had drifted away when the House of Lords and the monarchy were abolished in the spring of 1649.

The Rump Parliament, guardian of the rights of the people, contained only about 60 of its original 490 members.

Even this select group of men, who had compromised with each successive change of the revolutionary winds, failed to satisfy their real masters – Oliver Cromwell and the army. To these victorious 'soldiers of God', govern-

ENGLAND'S OVERLORD *Oliver Cromwell, painted by the contemporary miniaturist Samuel Cooper. Having destroyed monarchy, Cromwell was soon forced into taking supreme power.*

ment by Parliament was desirable, but not all-important.

Ever since the founding of the New Model Army in 1644, they had been inspired by a nobler vision, the prospect of an England blessed with civil liberty, and made glorious by religious toleration. In four years of lethargy the Rump did almost nothing.

'We cannot mention the Reformation of the Law,' Cromwell complained, 'but the lawyers cry out we mean to destroy property, whereas the law as it is now constituted serves only to maintain the lawyers, and to encourage the rich to oppress the poor.'

The last straw for the army, already impatient, was the Elections Bill, which would allow the existing members to retain their seats without being re-elected, and which would make them the sole judges of the fitness of those new members elected. Parliament rejected the proposal of Cromwell and the army that it dissolve itself and arrange for completely new elections. Cromwell knew well that it was the army and not the Parliament which had overthrown 'the bloody tyrant' Charles I on the fields of Marston Moor and Naseby. He knew now that the people were 'dissatisfied in every corner of the nation, and all men laying at our doors the non-performance of these things which had been promised and were of duty to be performed'. He felt that most people looked to the army to redress these wrongs, and once again he chose to lead the army in its mission.

Parliament dismissed

So, while on April 20, Cromwell upbraided the Commons, 30 of his musketeers waited outside the Chamber. 'Call them in,' ordered Cromwell, and Harrison went out and led them into the House. Cromwell now dismissed the assembled MPs: 'You have sat too long here for any good you have been doing. Depart, I say, and let us have done with you. In the name of God, go!'

Speaker Lenthall was taken from the Chair. With a scornful glance at the mace on the Speaker's table, Cromwell asked, 'What shall we do with this bauble?' Handing it to a soldier, he said, 'Here, take it away'.

Then, as the members of the Long Parliament filed out, he cried after them in a characteristic fit of self-justification: 'It is you that have forced me to this, for I have sought the Lord night and day, that he would rather slay me than put me upon doing this work.'

In the morning it was discovered that someone had written on the door of Westminster Palace: 'This house to let – unfurnished.'

Cromwell and the army had at long last emerged from the shadows to become the undisguised rulers of England. It was the beginning of England's only experiment with dictatorship – an experiment that was to last seven years. Cromwell was the only man with the wisdom, strength and will to make it work.

A country squire becomes England's dictator

MILITARY RULE *A Cavalier family faces interrogation by Cromwell's Major-Generals in the world-famous painting 'When did you last see your father?', by the 19th-century artist Yeams. Later ages saw Cromwell's military rule as harsh and tyrannical. But he only fell back on brute force because every other means he had used to try to establish peace, law and order had failed.*

The man who was Protector of the Realm of England, from 1651 until his death seven years later, was an unknown figure until fairly late in his life. A prosperous Huntingdonshire landowner, married to the daughter of a wealthy merchant, Oliver Cromwell made little impression on the turbulent times before the Civil War.

A courtier remembered him in the House of Commons in 1640 as 'a gentleman speaking whom I knew not, very ordinarily apparelled ... his linen was plain, and not very clean ... his countenance swollen and reddish; his voice sharp and untunable, and his eloquence full of fervour'.

Cromwell remained slovenly until the end and had no illusions or vanity, instructing the artist Peter Lely to paint him 'warts and all'. But the courtier's last observation was the key to Cromwell's character. For his fervour led him to throw himself into the holy cause against Charles I. And it led a self-taught soldier, whose only knowledge of war was his reading of the campaigns of the Swedish king, Gustavus Adolphus, to become the greatest general in Europe.

Like all great commanders, Cromwell had the ability to inspire his troops with his own zeal. When he raised his regiments, he looked for recruits who 'being well armed, within by satisfaction of their consciences and without by good iron arms, they would as one man stand firmly and charge desperately'.

Nor did he have any patience with the faint-hearts of his own side – men like the Earl of Manchester, who argued that 'if we beat the king 99 times, yet he is king still; but if the king beat us once, we shall all be hanged'. Cromwell replied: 'My lord, if this be so, why did we take up arms at first?'

Such determination won Cromwell rapid promotion. By 1644 he was Lieutenant-General of Horse for all the Parliamentary armies. But it was Marston Moor – where God delivered the Cavaliers 'as stubble to our swords' – that won him instant fame. He was the driving force in the creation of the New Model Army, the weapon forged by Parliament to win the war against the Royalists.

By 1649 Cromwell's prestige was unchallengeable. But ironically, in realising his aim to destroy the tyrant king, Cromwell confronted a problem which fervour and faith could not solve. Having destroyed the monarchy, he could find nothing to put in its place. The Parliament he had fought for failed, and he was forced back on to military rule.

Ruling a divided nation

His ambition was to unite the nation, but his reliance on armed force only divided it further. Desperately, his colleagues in the government tried to persuade him to take the crown. But even if Cromwell had been willing to accept this honour, the army would scarcely have approved it. Colonel Pride, the man who had purged Parliament in 1648, declared: 'He shall not ... and I will prevent it.'

By 1658 Cromwell's health was failing. The death of his favourite daughter, Elizabeth, on August 6 was the final blow. On Monday, August 30, his servants thought that the end had come. But England's Lord Protector lingered on until the Friday afternoon when he died of pneumonia.

Cromwell's dreams died with him. On his deathbed, his anxious colleagues pressed him to name his son, Richard, as his successor. But 'Tumbledown Dick', as he was derisively known, was no man to rule a kingdom. In May 1660, Charles II returned in triumph from his long exile, and the Cromwell family slipped back to the obscurity from which they had sprung.

A TINKER'S SON ON THE ROAD TO THE 'CELESTIAL CITY'

The political warfare and religious quarrels of the 17th century threw up a storm of violent literature. But out of the turmoil came one book – John Bunyan's *The Pilgrim's Progress* – which was to influence future generations. *The Pilgrim's Progress* is more than a tract; it is a record of Bunyan's journey through what he called 'the wilderness of this world' – of his own life-long pilgrimage in search of grace.

Bunyan was the son of a tinker and he wandered through his native Bedfordshire following his father's trade. Drafted into the Parliamentary army at the age of 16, he no doubt heard many impassioned sermons from the Ironside captains.

More important was the spiritual crisis which he underwent after leaving the army. It took the form of mysterious and threatening voices whispering to him prophecies that his soul was doomed to Hell. Bunyan came through that crisis of despair a transformed man, who saw his life's duty clearly before him: to preach the Word of God.

At the restoration of Charles II in 1660, preaching by anybody but the established clergy was strictly forbidden. Bunyan, however, would not submit to mere human laws.

'I was made to see,' he wrote, 'that if I would suffer rightly, I must pass sentence of death upon everything that can properly be called a thing of this life, even to reckon myself, my wife, my children, my health, my enjoyments all as dead to me, and myself as dead to them . . . I had this for consideration, that if I should now venture all for God, I engaged God to care for my concernments.'

A book based on life

So he chose to venture all for God, carried on preaching, and was sent to Bedford gaol where he remained for 12 years. With him in prison he had a copy of the Bible and of Foxe's *Book of Martyrs*, the Tudor account of earlier Protestants who suffered for their faith. In language inspired by these books, he now transformed his own life story into an

THE ROAD TO SALVATION *In this 18th-century illustration to* The Pilgrim's Progress, *Evangelist shows Christian the Way.*

FORBIDDEN PATHS *When Christian strays from the Straight and Narrow path, Evangelist redirects him on to the Path of Righteousness.*

TEST OF FAITH *The Pilgrim, with his shield of Faith, overcomes Appolyon, Satan's champion – a symbol of Bunyan's own spiritual struggle.*

FREEDOM *The Pilgrim and his friend, Hopeful, escape from Doubting Castle and the Giant Despair, by using the key of Promise.*

CHRISTIAN'S FAMILY *The Pilgrim's wife and children follow his path to salvation. Bunyan was himself a devoted husband and father.*

VICTORY OF RIGHTEOUSNESS *As Good triumphs over Evil, Doubting Castle is destroyed, the Giant Despair killed, and his head impaled.*

allegory, *The Pilgrim's Progress*. In this work of astonishingly effective story-telling, the good and evil influences which had affected Bunyan's life are given human personalities as the men and women met with by the hero Christian as he follows the narrow road which leads to the Celestial City.

Even the symbolic landscape of Christian's journey is based on the workaday world – the undramatic hills and valleys of Bedfordshire which Bunyan knew so well. A steep hill at Ampthill became Hill Difficult, up which Christian struggles to reach House Beautiful. A muddy part of Watling Street between Hockliffe and Dunstable was transformed into the Slough of Despond.

Though his progress is often illuminated by hope, Christian is driven forward by the same fear of ultimate damnation which had afflicted Bunyan in his youth. Like his author, he knows the anguish of doubt. But Bunyan's pilgrim surmounts all such obstacles and advances resolutely towards his just reward – the Kingdom of Heaven.

Bunyan's own life seems to have been crowned with similar blessings. His book brought him fame, though he was not so worldly as to be beguiled by success. During the next two centuries its popularity was enormous, and it probably ranked next to the Bible itself as the most widely read work in the English language.

'Death, where is thy sting?'
Bunyan spent his old age travelling the open roads once more – not as a tinker, but as a preacher. It was said that his fervour – and gift for telling stories – could attract an audience of a thousand people at 7 o'clock in the morning. It is pleasing to fancy that he may have faced death in 1688 as triumphantly as his own Mr Valiant-for-Truth:

'When the day that he must go hence was come, many accompanied him to the Riverside, into which as he went he said, Death, where is thy Sting? And as he went down deeper, he said, Grave, where is thy Victory? So he passed over, and all the Trumpets sounded for him on the other side.'

PURITAN GENIUS *John Bunyan, the tinker's son who wrote* The Pilgrim's Progress, *in a detail from a portrait made when he was 56.*

THE BLIND POET IN SEARCH OF HIS PURITAN PARADISE

The unfulfilled hopes of the English Revolution moulded the character of one of Britain's greatest poets. John Milton's active life spanned four decades of political turmoil, and ended in the collapse of all his hopes. This public failure was equalled by his many private sorrows. Out of this suffering he created some of the most resounding poetry in the English language.

From his earliest years, Milton was aware of his vocation. When he had graduated from Cambridge he spent six years at his father's house at Horton in Buckinghamshire, preparing himself by reading and study. In a poem of this period, 'Lycidas', he spoke of his ambition:

Fame is the spur the clear spirit doth raise
To scorn delight and live laborious days.

'Lycidas' and Milton's other early poems were superbly musical exercises, but the young poet still lacked a purpose.

Poet of Puritanism
In 1638 the 30-year-old poet returned from a cultural pilgrimage in Europe, and found England deeply divided by the great crisis of conscience soon to erupt in civil war. In this controversy he discovered the cause which was to give meaning to his life: the Puritan ideal. And in 1649 the poet was made the Commonwealth's semi-official spokesman. But at 44 Milton found himself totally blind.

Thus with the year
Seasons return; but not to me returns
Day, or the sweet approach of even or
* morn,*
Or sight of vernal bloom, or summer's
* rose,*
Or flocks, or herds, or human face divine.

With the help of secretaries, the blind poet fought on for his political beliefs right up to

ARTISTIC INSPIRATION *Like many works of art, the dramatic painting of 'Satan, Sin and Death', by the 18th-century Swiss artist Fuseli, was inspired by 'Paradise Lost'.*

the Restoration. But with the return of Charles II, everything he had championed was destroyed. Milton was imprisoned, but friends intervened to save him from execution; he escaped with a fine and the confiscation of most of his property.

Poor, blind, defeated and alone, Milton resolved to express in poetry the high ideals which had failed in politics. Contemplating a lifetime in which so much that was good had come to nothing, he chose to write on the theme of the Fall, and the loss of Paradise. He now compelled his daughters to learn all the languages he had once read, and he dictated to them the 10,566 lines of 'Paradise Lost', the work which was to assure him a place among the world's greatest poets.

The accomplishment of this vast task, with its successor 'Paradise Regained', apparently lightened Milton's private misery. The towering genius of these works was soon recognised. At home in his cottage at Chalfont St Giles, in Buckinghamshire, he found a measure of domestic peace with his third wife.

This unfamiliar note of 'peace of mind, all passion spent' was expressed in a last great poem, 'Samson Agonistes', based on the Old Testament story of the giant Samson. Like Samson, Milton was now blind. Like Samson, he had fallen into the hands of enemies and watched his life's great ideal brought into ridicule. But, at the last, it was given to Samson to triumph over his enemies, and the giant's flawed life was heroically vindicated. Milton, too, had now attained his goal, and it was his belief that in God's good time the cause for which he had fought so nobly and so long would surely triumph.

BLIND POET *John Milton, author of 'Paradise Lost', is shown in this detail from a portrait made after he went blind.*

191

King and people rule together

*'Good King Charles's golden days' open in a spirit
of toleration, but the issues which divide Britons are not
fully resolved until the Glorious Revolution of 1688*

In the latter half of the 17th century, the British made two decisions that have shaped their destiny ever since. In 1660 they resolved that they would be ruled by a king. And only three decades later, in 1688, they made their second momentous choice. They decided that their monarchy was to be a constitutional monarchy, limited by law and Parliament. At a time when many European countries were suffering under the lash of despotism, the British were establishing rights that were to make them the world's most free nation.

The British had also decided that they would have none of the dour Puritanism that Oliver Cromwell and his followers had imposed. Theatres were in business again. Maypoles were brought out once more. There was racing at Newmarket, yachting off the south coast, and skating on the pond in St James's Park – 'a very pretty art', as the diarist Samuel Pepys called it. The Puritan age gave way to a world in which men were not ashamed to enjoy themselves (pp. 196–7).

No one reflected this mood better than the new king, Charles II, who landed at Dover on May 25, 1660 (pp. 198–9). Even his friends were agreed that Charles was an idle pleasure-seeker. But he was also witty, intelligent, charming and a shrewd politician. His years of exile had made him determined 'never to go on my travels again'.

Having returned to England to the acclaim of his people, who recognised him, as one Cavalier wrote, as 'the truest lover of his subjects', he quickly set the pattern for life all over England. He had the magic touch of winning popularity, and in all his actions he practised an informality which delighted the nation. He even brought his dogs – the famous King Charles spaniels – into the council chamber. One of his courtiers who was bitten by them exclaimed: 'God bless your majesty but God damn your dogs!'

But life was not always easy for the king. Twice in his reign the citizens

THE MONARCHY TRANSFORMED

Sir James Thornhill painted this glorification of William III and Mary on the ceiling of the hall in the Royal Hospital at Greenwich. Enthroned above a sketch of the hospital they had endowed, the king and queen receive the crown and sceptre in triumph, while cherubs hold aloft a sun and wreaths of laurels.

But before Thornhill started his elaborate tribute to the power of the monarchy, the Glorious Revolution of 1688, which brought William and Mary to the throne in the place of James II, had revolutionised the role of the sovereign. Parliament had secured from them a guarantee that the crown would respect the rights of its subjects. In future, monarchs were to rule in partnership with Parliament.

193

WAR AT SEA *Commercial rivalry between Britain and Holland led to open war in 1665 for the second time in ten years. In the naval war that followed, both sides scored victories, but the ending was inconclusive. The Battle of Lowestoft (above) was Britain's most striking success.*

FRENCH ALLIANCE *Charles II's sister, Minette, Duchess of Orleans, negotiated the secret grants paid him by Louis XIV in the Treaty of Dover. Minette brought the treaty to England and Charles was so moved when she left that he followed her half way across the Channel.*

PHILOSOPHER OF REVOLUTION *The right of subjects to overthrow their rulers was defended by John Locke (above), who argued that government was a contract between ruler and ruled. These ideas were closely followed by the architects of the Glorious Revolution.*

of his capital faced disaster through two natural calamities. From the spring of 1665 to the autumn of 1666 England was gripped by an outbreak of plague more savage than any since the Black Death three centuries before. The primitive medicine of the day could offer little protection against the disease; at its height, the plague was killing more than 7000 Londoners a week (pp. 200–1), and it spread all over England.

Scarcely had the plague died down than a fresh disaster struck – the Great Fire of September 1666. By the time it had burnt itself out, the old city of London was in ruins. As he walked through the streets, Samuel Pepys could see 'nothing standing there, all the town burned and a miserable sight of St Paul's Church with all the roofs fallen'.

St Paul's was soon to rise again. Its rebuilding was the achievement of the greatest of all English architects, Sir Christopher Wren (pp. 204–5). And the city itself was rebuilt with remarkable speed. By 1670 most of the new buildings had been completed or were well under way. But shortage of money forced Charles II to abandon his support for Wren's plan to rebuild the whole of his capital.

From royal success to royal failure

This shortage of money was one of the chief problems of Charles's reign. Parliament could not be relied upon to vote him funds without making conditions. So, in 1670, Charles made a secret treaty with the French king, Louis XIV. Under it, he received subsidies from France in return for promising that he would publicly declare himself a Catholic at some future date. He would also aid Louis in his war against Holland.

Charles was not unwilling to oppose the Dutch, whose commercial rivalry had already led to war. But he knew full well that a suitable moment for his conversion to Catholicism would never arrive. Most of his subjects feared the Roman Catholic religion with a hatred that was fully revealed at the time of the Popish Plot (pp. 206–7).

Fired by the lying accusations of the infamous Titus Oates, the anti-Catholic hysteria brought on by the plot also led to Charles's greatest political crisis. Protestant politicians, led by the Earl of Shaftesbury, made a determined effort to exclude his Catholic brother, James, Duke of York, from the succession to the throne. In 1680 the House of Commons passed the Exclusion Bill, but it was thrown out by the House of Lords. A year later, another Parliament met at Oxford. It immediately introduced another Exclusion Bill and was promptly dissolved by the king. Charles had had enough of parliaments. He never summoned another.

Even at the height of the Exclusion crisis, Charles still found the time to be a patron of the arts and sciences. Music had become a national passion, and the king led the way with his patronage of Henry Purcell (p. 209), whose tuneful melodies enraptured his fellow citizens. And, as early as 1662, the king had become a patron of the newly founded Royal Society (p. 208), whose members included many of the best scientific minds in Europe. Among them was Isaac Newton, whose discoveries – especially in the field of gravitation – were to revolutionise mathematics and physics (pp. 212–13).

Charles's brother, James II, came to the throne in 1685. He was the first Catholic to rule Britain since the death of Mary Tudor in 1558. Despite his religion, he had everything in his favour at first. His subjects were loyal, and a subservient Parliament voted him a handsome subsidy. And when the Protestant Duke of Monmouth, Charles II's illegitimate son, raised a revolt in July 1685, it was easily crushed (pp. 210–11).

But James soon threw away these advantages. In 1687 he suspended the anti-Catholic laws and prepared to pack Parliament with his friends. And the following summer, he went too far. Six bishops were arrested and put on trial in London for petitioning the king against the concessions he had made to the Catholics. The London mob rallied to their support. On June 10 it was announced that James's wife had given birth to a son – a Catholic heir heralding a Catholic dynasty.

This – and the acquittal of the bishops – was the signal for revolt. Leading politicians turned to William of Orange and his wife, Mary, to save the country from James. In November William landed at Torbay in Devon. Deserted by his friends, James lost his nerve and fled to France and in February 1689 William and Mary were proclaimed king and queen of England (pp. 214–15). The Glorious Revolution had been accomplished.

Monarchs who worked with Parliament

Mary was James II's daughter by his first marriage. In English eyes, her great advantage was that she was a Protestant and that her husband was the most renowned Protestant ruler in Europe. There were other contrasts, too, between the new rulers and their predecessors. They were capable of working with Parliament. One of the first acts of the reign was a Bill of Rights, in which the arbitrary acts of Charles and James were declared illegal. The Bill is the nearest thing England has ever had to a written constitution.

But, though England welcomed the new rulers, loyalty to the exiled Stuarts remained strong in their homeland, Scotland. William's attempts to force the Scottish clans into submission only increased their bitterness. The massacre of Glencoe (pp. 216–17) left a bitter legacy.

William's real achievement was in foreign policy. His predecessors had been pensioners of Louis XIV, King of France. William, however, had spent most of his life fighting against Louis, and brought with him from Holland a bitter and passionate hatred of the French king. Immediately, William's war became England's war. And though William died before the climax of the struggle with France, it was his policies which laid the foundations of ultimate success.

End of a turbulent epoch

James II's younger daughter, Anne, who came to the throne on William's death in 1702, did not have William's sense of purpose or stern determination. But it was her reign which saw the mighty Louis humbled by England's greatest general, John Churchill, Duke of Marlborough. In a succession of victories – most notably Blenheim (pp. 218–19) – Marlborough achieved the most spectacular series of successes for British arms since the Hundred Years' War, 300 years before.

But Marlborough's success on the battlefield depended on support from home, particularly from his friends in the government and from his wife Sarah, who through her long-standing friendship with Anne was just as powerful as many a minister. Thus, Sarah's dramatic quarrel with the queen was more than a disagreement between two women. It brought the entire government down. The Tories came to power and made peace with France.

The death of Queen Anne in 1714 brought to an end in doubt and uncertainty one of the most eventful periods in British history. It was not a long period – scarcely more than half a century. There were men living in 1714 who could remember the restoration of Charles II. Such men had seen 54 years of dramatic change, including a revolution that had changed the concept of British monarchy. Henceforward, kings were to rule in partnership with Parliament. And these changes had established the liberties of Britons as never before.

END OF AN ERA *Although James II had been welcomed as monarch in 1685, his pro-Catholic policies rapidly destroyed his popularity. In 1688 leading politicians invited William of Orange to land in Britain. Here a spy listens as James decides to flee to France.*

SYMBOL OF PROSPERITY *The emblem used by the early Bank of England, which was founded in 1694 by a group of far-sighted financiers. The bank soon became popularly known as 'The Old Lady of Threadneedle Street'. Though it became increasingly linked with the government, it remained a private company until 1946.*

WAR LEADER *William III persuaded Britain and Holland to bury their old rivalry and join to resist France. Painted here as a mounted general, William led his troops in person. The wars, which ended in 1713 after his death, established Britain's supremacy in Europe.*

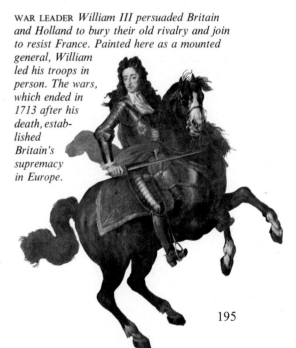

CHARLES'S GOLDEN DAYS

With the restoration of Charles II in 1660 came the return of the liberties and delights which had been denied to the British during the austere years of Puritan rule. The king himself, virile and with apparently inexhaustible energy, set the pace in the pursuit of pleasure. On the first night of his reign, he slipped away from the celebrations to spend the night in the arms of one of his mistresses. His palace of Whitehall was crowded 'like a fair all day'. He rode, hunted, danced and played tennis.

In the country, traditional pastimes such as hunting, wrestling, animal-baiting and primitive forms of football – all of which had been banned by the Puritans – reappeared. Horse racing drew large crowds, chiefly because of Charles's patronage of Newmarket, where he kept a string of Arab horses.

In London, a new game, pall mall, a form of croquet with the hoop hung 6 ft above the ground, gave its name to a London street. Tennis, ice-skating on the lake in St James's Park, cockfighting, gambling and the brothels provided other diversions. The London theatres, reopened by Charles, performed plays by such authors as John Dryden and William Congreve that were noted for their bawdy and unbridled themes. Fashionable women exposed their breasts and men's clothes were effeminate, foppish and exaggerated.

But not everyone was happy about the unchecked pursuit of pleasure. The diarist John Evelyn wrote 'with sorrow and pity' of 'the love of a voluptuous and sensual life, which a vicious court has brought into credit'. And, paradoxically, the greatest pursuer of pleasure after the king agreed with Evelyn. As early as August 1661 Samuel Pepys commented on 'the lewdness and beggary of the court which I am feared will bring all to ruin again'.

INDOOR GAMES *Gambling was a Restoration pastime. The Complete Gamster of 1709 shows contemporary versions of billiards, dice, backgammon, cockfighting and a game of cards.*

'BACCHANALIA' *The winter of 1683–4 was the coldest in living memory, and the people of London amused themselves by holding a 'Frost Fair' on the frozen Thames. One sunny afternoon, the diarist John Evelyn saw coaches plying across the ice, 'sleds, sliding with skates, a bull-baiting, horse and coach races, puppet plays and much tippling'. He concluded: 'It seems to be a Bacchanalian triumph.'*

THRILL OF THE CHASE *Fox hunting and hare coursing, traditional English sports, were frowned on under Cromwell, but sprang back into life under Charles II. Francis Barlow's engraving of 1671 from* Several Ways of Hawking, Hunting and Fishing *shows an unconventional approach.*

THE COMPLEAT ANGLER *Isaak Walton, an iron-monger by trade, was 60 when he published his classic book on the art of fishing in 1653.*

THEATRE OF LICENCE *Restoration drama was renowned for its bawdy and licentious plays. When Charles II reopened the London theatre, he granted a monopoly to two men, Sir Thomas Killigrew (above) and Sir William D'Avenant (below). Killigrew ran the 'King's Company of Players' at Drury Lane and D'Avenant, said to be an illegitimate son of William Shakespeare, the 'Duke of York's Company' at Lincoln's Inn Fields. Actresses were used in plays for the first time, replacing the boys who had previously played women's parts. One of the first was Nell Gwynne, who started her career by selling oranges at Drury Lane, and became the toast of the stage and Charles II's most famous mistress.*

LONDON'S PLAYWRIGHT *John Dryden (1631–1700), whose masterpiece,* All for Love, *was produced at the Drury Lane Theatre (left), designed by the architect Sir Christopher Wren in 1678.*

COFFEE-HOUSE CONSPIRACIES *A London coffee house in 1688. Charles II tried to suppress coffee houses in 1675 because he believed that they were a breeding ground for conspiracies. But he did not succeed and the coffee houses became the ancestors of the men's clubs of later times.*

After 12 years of exile Charles returns in triumph

A KING'S REFUGE
A former hunting lodge, Boscobel House in Salop, was the young Charles II's hiding place for six weeks after his defeat at Worcester in 1651. During the day, Charles hid in a hollow oak in the grounds – the oak (above) was grown from an acorn from the original tree. Nine years later, he regained the throne. The coat of arms (left) he chose in 1660 can be seen in the Victoria and Albert Museum.

As the ship that brought him from his exile bobbed at anchor beneath the white cliffs of Dover on the morning of May 25, 1660, Charles II was able for the first time to enjoy a real English breakfast as king in his own country. When the royal barge ground into the shingle of Dover beach and Charles stepped ashore, salutes rang out, echoed by artillery all round the coast. That evening the cannon in the Tower of London relayed the news of the landing to the capital, and Londoners danced in the streets for joy. Charles I's son had returned – and he had come without bloodshed.

The royal exile
Behind Charles's triumphant homecoming lay a dozen years of wandering as an exile in Europe. With the execution of his father in 1649, England had not only rejected the Stuart dynasty, but the institution of monarchy itself. Yet this bleak fact had in one sense at least worked to the young heir's advantage, for the monarchs of Europe, shocked at England's regicide, had been quick to recognise the new king's claim.

The first of Charles's attempts to regain the throne had been an abject failure. In alliance with the Scots, who had accepted him as their king, he had challenged Cromwell's army at Dunbar in September 1650 – but the Royalist forces had been brutally cut to pieces. A year to the day after this disaster, Charles's reconstituted army had been destroyed at Worcester, and the 21-year-old monarch had fled ignobly to France.

France, however, was not his home for long. For one thing, Charles and his ramshackle court were chronically short of money. Edward Hyde, who was Charles's chief minister, was so ashamed of his clothes that he would only venture out in the poorest quarters of Paris. Writing to a correspondent in 1653, Hyde lamented that: 'We are all here in the same beggarly condition you left us, which I think by long custom will grow second nature to us.'

But worse even than this was Charles's own behaviour, for the openness of his loose living and pursuit of pleasure scandalised the French. They sent him packing to Germany – where Charles still contrived to amuse himself: 'We pass our lives as well as people can do that have no more money, for we dance and play as if we had taken the Plate Fleet.'

So the exile's life continued, taking him in and out of the countries of north-west Europe. If Charles had no money, he had at least hope; and hope rose highest in him when, in September 1658, the news of Oliver Cromwell's death reached him in the Low Countries. But

the first plans for a speedy restoration of Charles collapsed in August 1659. Then, quite suddenly and unexpectedly, the English Republic began to fall apart.

Cromwell's son, Richard, soon proved unable to emulate the strength of the Republic's founder; another civil war seemed possible. In February 1660 General Monck, commander of the Republic's army in Scotland, brought his regiments down to London to help forestall the threatened collapse into anarchy.

A triumphant return
Some men feared that Monck was about to establish a new military dictatorship. But the general – 'old George' to his troopers – was not another Cromwell. He believed that the army should be the servant, not the master, of the people. He used his power not to impose his own will, but to hold the ring so that the will of the whole country could be realised.

On February 9, 1660, Monck called upon the unrepresentative clique who made up the 'Rump' Parliament to restore all the members they had excluded, and to make way for free elections and a new 'Free Parliament'. And,

---

A KING AND HIS MISTRESSES
The mistresses of Charles II enjoyed a high status on his list of daily priorities. On the day of his restoration, he slipped quietly away to spend the night in the arms of Barbara Villiers. She was rivalled by a Breton girl, Louise de Kéroualle, sent to London by Louis XIV to bring about an alliance between England and France. Both were made noblewomen, but both were eclipsed by the former orange seller, Nell Gwynne. The king met her in 1668, and the relationship lasted 17 years until his death. His last words to James, Duke of York, were reported to be 'Let not poor Nelly starve'.

Louise de Kéroualle, created Duchess of Portsmouth.

Barbara Villiers was made Countess of Castlemaine.

Nell Gwynne called the king 'Charles III' because she had two previous lovers called Charles. Samuel Pepys described her as 'pretty witty Nell'.

TRIUMPHANT RETURN *Charles II lands at Dover on the way to claim his crown after years of exile and poverty in Europe. He entered London on his 30th birthday. The diarist John Evelyn wrote that such joy had not been seen 'since the return of the Jews from Babylonian captivity'.*

Charles II: The rule of a 'merry monarch'

CAVALIER KING *Charles's mistresses were the talk of England. He also loved the arts, which flourished under his patronage.*

taking his cue from this, Charles – now at Breda in the Netherlands – wrote home that he too wished for and would be guided by a 'Free Parliament'.

Elections were held, and Parliament met. When Monck's cousin, William Morrice, moved that 'the constitution of England lay in King, Lords and Commons', his proposal was passed unanimously. Charles Stuart was invited to return forthwith to rule his country. His new subjects ran riot with their wild rejoicing, ringing the church bells and drinking the health of their monarch on bended knee – though the great diarist Samuel Pepys noted with some distaste that this last gesture seemed excessively slavish.

The king's mercy

Within a month Charles had arrived home. On May 29, his 30th birthday, he reached Blackheath on the outskirts of London, where the Lord Mayor and some 120,000 Londoners were waiting to lead him in procession through his capital. The diarist John Evelyn witnessed the king's entry into London – 'the ways strewed with flowers, the bells ringing, the streets hung with tapestry, fountains running with wine, trumpets, music and myriads of people. It was the Lord's doing.'

Though his Parliament was in the mood for revenge against the Republicans, Charles insisted that only the regicides – the men

actually instrumental in beheading his father 11 years previously – should pay for the hardships and injustices that the Royalists had suffered. The rotting corpse of Cromwell was dug up from its grave, to be hanged at Tyburn and then butchered and reinterred in the criminal pit. But apart from this the watchwords of the Stuart Restoration were to be mercy and reconciliation.

The great Parliamentary army was disbanded peacefully. The Church of England was re-established with little more acrimony than was inevitable in an age of deep religious faith. Men were allowed to keep property that they had purchased legitimately, no matter where their loyalties had lain in the past. And many other past actions and deeds were absolved by an Act of Indemnity and Oblivion. By the end of 1660, Englishmen could justly pride themselves on the accomplishment of a miracle – the bloodless restoration of a monarchy that had once been toppled with such violence and ferocity.

Charles continued to enjoy himself. 'He hates the very sight or thought of business,' wrote the diarist Samuel Pepys. But this was less than fair. The king proved himself capable of decisive and difficult action in his 25 years as ruler. He simply believed that pleasure was as important as work, and he distributed his time accordingly. It was a balance no other king of England has rivalled.

Few women could resist Charles II. 'His complexion is somewhat dark,' wrote a friend in 1660, 'but much enlightened by his eyes which are quick and sparkling . . . His hair, which he hath in great plenty, is of a shining black, not frizzled, but so naturally curling into great rings that it is a very comely ornament.' And Charles made no secret of his enslavement to what he described as 'a fantastical gentleman called Cupid'. He kept both court and country occupied with gossip about his latest love affairs.

Charles enjoyed being known as the 'merry monarch'; sculling alone down a river to clamber over a mistress's wall; dallying openly with the actress Nell Gwynne and bestowing a dukedom on the first of their two sons; gambling at the race course; sleighing, hunting, hawking and taking the helm to race his yachts up and down the Channel.

A plausible estimate of the number of mistresses Charles enjoyed even before he became king runs to 17, and Charles himself acknowledged 14 illegitimate children.

But he had no children by his wife, Catherine of Braganza, the sad and neglected victim of a diplomatic marriage of convenience, and this lack of a legitimate heir was to form the major constitutional issue of Charles's reign – the choice of his successor. For James, Duke of York, his brother and heir, was a Catholic, unacceptable to the Protestant majority of the nation, and the king risked everything to stand by him. In this he showed his great courage. For all his dallying, Charles had learnt the lesson of his father's reign: as he said, he was 'determined not to go on my travels again'.

199

'Lord have mercy upon us!' The plague sweeps England

On June 7, 1665, the famous diarist Samuel Pepys noticed with dismay that a number of houses in Drury Lane had been marked with red crosses on the doors, and the words 'Lord have mercy upon us'. These were the first signs of the plague Pepys had seen. 'It put me into an ill conception of myself,' he wrote, 'so that I was forced to buy some tobacco to smell and chew – which took away the apprehension.'

The crosses and inscriptions were the grim evidence that the plague had come to London, and the tobacco that Pepys hastened to buy – in the belief that it was an effective protection against infection – was no defence against the ravages of this dreaded disease. Before the Great Plague had run its course at the end of the year, at least 70,000 people had perished in London alone.

The first recorded case of this epidemic had occurred in November 1664, only yards from where Pepys saw the signs that the plague was gaining hold. Carried by rat fleas, the disease first showed itself as a small black blotch or lump on the victim's body. Fever and delirium followed, accompanied by agonising pain. Death or recovery took place within a few days. But in the squalid conditions of Restoration London, there were few who recovered.

The epidemic spread swiftly in the warm

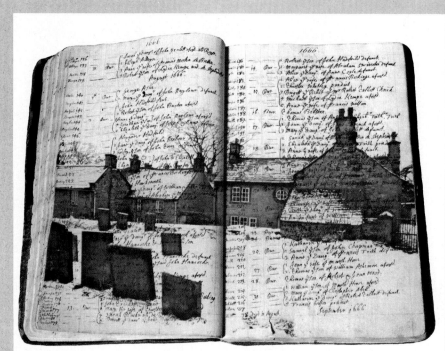

VILLAGE OF DEATH
The Derbyshire village of Eyam as it is today, with a page from the church's register listing the plague victims. The list includes Katherine Mompesson, the wife of the vicar who urged his people to stay in the village so as not to spread the disease. Only one woman tried to escape, but she was driven back by neighbouring villagers.

ANATOMISTS AT WORK *Two surgeons dissect the body of a plague victim, seeking in vain the cause of the disease which killed thousands of Londoners in 1665.*

weather. It was soon carried from London to other cities, including Norwich, Southampton, Portsmouth and, most dramatically, to the Derbyshire village of Eyam.

Eyam's ordeal by plague began just as London was emerging from the worst ravages. In September 1665 the local tailor, Edward Cooper, took delivery of a box of old clothes and patterns. Within two days the servant who unpacked the box was taken ill; four days later he was dead. Cooper himself died a fortnight later; before the end of the month there had been 26 more deaths in the village. By the time the ordeal ended, in October 1666, only 33 of Eyam's 350 inhabitants were alive. The rest had fallen victim to the plague.

MEDICINE AND DEATH *A doctor protects himself against the plague (right) by wearing a mask filled with spices which were believed to purify the air. But medicine could do little for the plague victims, who were hastily buried at night in mass graves (above). The labourers who carried out this gruesome task toured the streets, crying: 'Bring out your dead!'*

The reason for this appalling death-toll was an extraordinary but heroic decision by the village vicar, William Mompesson. Usually people would flee from the places where plague had struck, thus spreading it further. But Mompesson managed to persuade his fellow-villagers to deny themselves this path to safety. He knew that if the people of Eyam fled, they would carry the infection to others; and so he urged them to act as true Christians and remain.

A boundary line was marked out with stakes around the village. Within its limits the villagers settled in to meet their fate, living on food left at the boundary by men from neighbouring villages. For months, Eyam knew only pain, death and the grim struggle for survival. By mid-summer only one man, Marshall Howe, was strong enough to dig graves for the victims. And as his reward for this gruesome task, he claimed all the possessions of those he buried. Yet only one person tried to escape from the village.

Disease of the poor

The Great Plague had struck England after 30 years of relative immunity from the disease, and at the time men blamed the visitation on infected bales of merchandise shipped into London from the Middle East. But the truth was that the Black Death – the outbreak of plague which had decimated the subjects of Edward III just over three centuries earlier – had never entirely disappeared from England.

The disease was rooted in the squalid slums of the 'Liberties' – the shanty towns outside London's city wall – St Giles, Cripplegate, Whitechapel, Stepney, Westminster and Lambeth. It was likely to spread whenever large crowds gathered together. Thus the coronations of both James I and Charles I, and the accompanying festivities that drew tens of thousands into the capital, led to two terrible epidemics in 1603 and 1625.

Some 30,000 died after James's accession, and as many deaths provided a grisly memorial to Charles's first months as king. But the 1665 outbreak, bringing so many deaths after so long a period of immunity, came as a sudden and frightening shock. The pious were not slow to interpret it as God's judgment on the flagrant immorality of Charles II.

The plague was always the disease of the poor. Though it inconvenienced the upper classes, they were far less severely hit. Despite his fears, Samuel Pepys remained in London throughout the worst part of the epidemic – though he packed his wife off to the country and took advantage of her absence to pursue several love affairs. And even though scarcely a day passed without his noting some sign or sight of the plague's effects in London, Pepys's year was far from being ruined by the disaster. On December 31, 1665, he noted with satisfaction: 'I have never lived so merrily as I have done this plague time.'

A battle between superstition and science

The Manner of His Majesties Curing the Disease,
CALLED THE
KINGS-EVIL.

KING'S EVIL *A broadsheet shows Charles II laying his hands on a victim of scrofula – tuberculosis of the bones and lymphatic glands – which was thought at the time to be a skin disease. It was known as the 'King's Evil', because people believed that the king's touch could cure it.*

The Great Plague of 1665 laid bare the inadequacy of 17th-century medical science. The standard treatment for sufferers was an old herbal remedy – sage, rue, buttercup root, angelica root, snake root and saffron, infused in malaga. Not surprisingly, this had little effect in combating the disease and its cause remained unknown until the 19th century.

But some progress did come out of the tragedy. The physician Thomas Sydenham brought a new precision to the art of healing. The medieval practice of bleeding a patient was still the common remedy for any ailment, from a headache to a fever, and it was still administered by barbers – hence the red (blood) and white (bandage) of the traditional barber's pole. This ferocious treatment killed as often as it cured. But Sydenham argued that the symptoms of disease should be examined more carefully before this drastic treatment was indiscriminately applied. From his own studies he was able to show that measles and smallpox, for example, were different ailments and so required different treatments.

Surgeons and scientists

Sydenham's most important success came in the treatment of smallpox. He pioneered a method of cooling the patient's fever. Sydenham was the first surgeon to introduce opium into medical practice, and he also helped to popularise the use of quinine for malaria and iron for the treatment of anaemia. He also led the way in describing scarlet fever and in explaining the nature of hysteria and St Vitus's dance.

These were valuable and methodical advances, but the old superstitions and beliefs still lingered on. Sydenham's work won him more recognition abroad than in England. His arguments only antagonised his colleagues, and the College of Physicians would not elect him to membership. According to one of his friends, Andrew Browne, Sydenham 'died with accusation hanging over his head that he was an impostor and an assassin of humanity'. Richard Wiseman, Charles II's own surgeon, believed that his master's touch could cure the skin disease of scrofula – the 'King's Evil'. But Wiseman – himself a barber surgeon – was also reluctant to wield his scalpel, and examined factors such as the relative healthiness of the air in different localities. He discovered that patients thrived in Hampstead; but an invalid who improved in Knightsbridge was observed to relapse in Holborn.

Towards the truth

Religion and morality were hopelessly mixed up with true medicine. Rickets, the most prevalent disease of the age, was blamed on 'a soft and debauched way of living' – the very opposite of the truth, since it was caused by poor, not excessive, food. Human character and health were still explained in terms of the balance within the body of the four 'humours' – the sanguine, the phlegmatic, the choleric and the melancholic. Medical treatment was often varied according to the dominant 'humour' of each particular patient. Thus a short-tempered, choleric man who had constipation was prescribed rhubarb, while a melancholic patient was given sennapods for the same complaint.

But for all its essentially medieval beliefs, the reign of Charles II marked the era when medicine and surgery became established as serious sciences in their own right.

A spark from a baker's oven sets London ablaze

LONDON IN FLAMES *A contemporary painting by Jan Wyck shows Londoners taking to the Thames to save themselves and their possessions from the Great Fire. The Tower (right) stands unscathed, but old St Paul's (centre) blazes.*

WEAPONS AGAINST THE FIRE
London's only defence against the fire of 1666 was the simple equipment provided by private citizens. The hand-squirt (top) held no more than 2 pints of water; with the leather fire helmet (left) and bucket (right), it can be seen today in the London Museum.

An observer of the Great Fire of London in 1666 wrote that: 'You would have thought for five days that it had been Doomsday from the fire, the cries and howling of the people. My gardens were covered with ashes of paper, linens and plasterwork blown there by the tempest.' And he lived 6 miles from the city in what was then the country village of Kensington.

The fire started at about midnight on Saturday, September 1, in the oven of the king's baker, Thomas Farriner, in Pudding Lane. According to Farriner's own statement, he had checked the oven before retiring to bed that evening; but a few hours later he and his family were awoken by smoke and fumes, 'and, rising, did find the fire coming upstairs'. They escaped through a window to the next-door house. But the housemaid was too frightened of heights to use this route. She became the fire's first victim.

It was a dry autumn, and a strong east wind was blowing. Pudding Lane contained several warehouses packed with pitch, tar and cordage. The flames soon began to spread. At 3 a.m. on that fateful morning the Lord Mayor, Sir Thomas Bludworth, was called out to the blaze, but he dismissed it as insignificant and went back to bed. His folly caused a fatal delay

in the organisation of the fire-fighting force.

Four hours later some 300 houses had already been burnt down, according to the diarist Samuel Pepys. Pepys went out to take a look at the spectacle: 'Down to the waterside and there saw a lamentable fire. Everybody endeavouring to remove their goods, and flinging into the River or bringing them into lighters that lay off. Poor people staying in their houses as long as till the very fire touched them, and then running into boats or clambering from one pair of stair by the water-side to another. And the poor pigeons were loath to leave their houses, but hovered about the windows and balconies till they were burned and fell down.'

The city burns

Pepys noted that no one was making any effort to fight the fire: everyone was anxious only to save their possessions and run. The Lord Mayor, called out again at 10 a.m., was still unhelpful. He was asked to check the fire's raging progress by ordering the demolition of houses to create fire-breaks. But his response was merely: 'Who shall pay the charge of rebuilding the houses?'

So Pepys took matters into his own hands. As a government official, he went straight to

the king at Whitehall. Charles issued an instruction that the mayor should 'spare no houses but pull down before the fire every way'.

At last some strong action was to be taken. But by now the blaze was a mile long, consuming Fish Street Hill, Canning Street, Gracechurch Street, Lombard Street, Cornhill and Fenchurch Street. There was no stopping it. As darkness fell, Pepys watched from across the river: 'And saw the fire grow; and, as it grew darker, appeared more and more; and in corners and upon steeples, and between churches and houses, as far as we could see up the hill of the City, in a most horrid, malicious, bloody flame. We stayed till, it being darkish, we saw the fire as only one entire arch of fire from this side to the other side of the bridge, and in a bow up the hill for an arch of above a mile long: it made me weep to see it.'

On Tuesday the flames licked up into the tower of the old St Paul's Cathedral. The roof came cascading down into the aisles – a torrent of molten lead. The Tower of London was saved only because the houses round about it had by now been blown up.

Following Charles's orders, the same drastic measures were now being taken to stop the westward advance of the blaze at the Inner Temple. There the king himself and his brother James, Duke of York, were directly in charge of operations. The royal brothers organised bucket chains and worked fearlessly among the flames, commanding, reproving and, on occasions, rewarding their men's efforts from bags of guineas at their sides. 'All that is left of the city and suburbs,' wrote one

Charles's capital – A city devoted to pleasure

At the time of Charles II's Restoration in 1660, London was still very much a country town. On May Days, milkmaids danced in the Strand, and in July 1671 a mad cow ran amok in Whitehall. For, although the metropolis knew its traffic jams – Samuel Pepys was kept fuming for half an hour in his coach on successive days by hold-ups in Exchange Street – open green fields were always within walking distance. One favourite pastime of 17th-century Londoners was to saunter through the meadows to the surrounding villages – the cherry orchards of Rotherhithe, the cake-shops of Islington, and the woods of Vauxhall, loud with the song of nightingales in summer. With his wife out of London, the diarist Samuel Pepys drove out to the greenery of Highgate with Mary, the girl from The Harp and Ball – 'pretty and innocent and had what pleasure I would with her'.

observer, 'is acknowledged to be wholly due to the King and the Duke of York.' And the role played by Charles II in fighting the fire was celebrated by John Dryden, the leading poet and dramatist of the day:

> *Now day appears and with the day the King,*
> *Whose early care had robbed him of his rest;*
> *Far off the cracks of falling houses ring*
> *And shrieks of subjects pierce his tender*
> *breast.*

By the time the fire had burnt itself out on Thursday, September 6, it had consumed four-fifths of the area inside the City walls. Eighty-nine churches – including St Paul's – had been destroyed, and 13,200 houses. A north-countryman said that the capital reminded him of his native fells – a desolate expanse, marked only by odd heaps of blackened stone.

Rebuilding from the ruins

More than 100,000 Londoners had been made homeless: they were camping out on Moor-fields, where Charles rode among them to calm the rumours that England's enemies – the Dutch or the Jesuits – had deliberately started the fire.

But such rumours soon spread from London across England. The Oxford diarist Anthony Wood recorded: 'This fire did soe much affrighten the nation that all townes stood upon their owne defence day and night, and particularly Oxon... Three days after the fire began, a butcher driving certaine oxen over Carfax cried to his beasts when he was under the window "hiup! hiup!". Which, some taking for "fire!" run out of the church . . . with the semblance of death in their faces, some saying that they smelled smoke, others pitch etc... and could not be reconciled to their error a long while.'

Out of the destruction some good was to come. Charles II and his surveyor, Christopher Wren, saw the catastrophe as a chance to create a totally new, stone-built metropolis. But shortage of money, and obstruction from citizens intent on rebuilding on the sites of their old properties, meant that Wren did not have the free hand he wished for. Yet the architect did stamp his character on the capital in a fashion that endured until the Blitz of 1940: gracefully proportioned houses, memorably statuesque churches, and his crowning glory – the great dome-topped cathedral of St Paul's.

Taverns and lunatics

The River Thames was the dominant natural feature of Stuart London. It was the main highway of the capital, a bustling mass of barges and boats manned by watermen who made up a sturdy and independent fraternity some 2000 strong.

For fear of them, no second bridge could be built across the river to relieve the congested thoroughfare between the houses on London Bridge. And when hackney carriages became fashionable after the Restoration, the watermen successfully petitioned the king to limit this land-based method of plying for hire. Charles called the watermen his 'nursery of seamen', useful recruits for the navy – in contrast to the hackney coachmen, who simply blocked up the streets, transporting the fat and lazy.

Metropolitan tastes in entertainment were catered for by the naked lunatics on show at Bedlam, the moth-eaten lions kept in the Tower, and the countless taverns. The Trumpet, The Sugar Loaf and The Old Horse at Lambeth marsh, where Pepys made love to the wives of his subordinates at the Navy Board, were – along with hundreds more – the haunts of thousands of Londoners. For those who preferred to pay for their pleasures, there were flourishing brothels in such areas as Drury Lane and Moorfields.

But the old city was bursting at the seams. Noblemen became speculative builders, leasing off the simple yet elegant houses they erected on their London estates at profitable rents. The Earl of Southampton laid out Bloomsbury Square, while the Earl of St Albans accelerated the fashionable trend outside the city by developing St James's Square, the beginning of the West End. The London of today was slowly starting to take shape.

WREN'S MONUMENT RISES FROM THE ASHES OF LONDON

Britain's only Classical cathedral, St Paul's, is also the only one conceived and completed by one man within his own lifetime. Christopher Wren was 43 when he laid the foundation stone; he was 79 when the building was completed.

For those 36 years the cathedral was his whole life. Every detail was made to his specifications, every stone shaped and laid under his supervision.

In its grandeur and sheer architectural brilliance St Paul's is a towering monument to Wren's genius. But the continuation of the work from year to year, and its final triumphant vindication of his original vision, demonstrate Wren's other characteristic qualities – his subtlety as a diplomat, his skill as a politician and his fierce determination.

Destined for greatness

Wren was born in 1632, the son of the Dean of Windsor. Even from the start he seemed destined for greatness. At 21 he was described by the diarist John Evelyn as 'that miracle of youth'.

At 29 he became Professor of Astronomy at Oxford, and was a founder-member of the Royal Society, where Sir Isaac Newton claimed he was 'one of the greatest geometers of our time'. Casually, in his early thirties, he

turned his attention to architecture, when he was commissioned to design the Sheldonian Theatre at Oxford. There, he discovered the vocation which was to dominate his life.

Inspired by a visit to Paris, he returned to England in 1666 to submit a plan for a noble Classical dome to complete the restoration of old St Paul's Cathedral, ravaged by Cromwell's soldiers. But only ten days after Charles II approved Wren's plans, the Great Fire wrecked London, and the old cathedral. Wren's plans seemed to have been wrecked, too. But he soon realised he was being given the chance of a lifetime. He submitted a plan for a totally new city of piazzas and avenues to rival Paris, but he had a cool reception.

At last, in 1668, Wren received the message he had been waiting for – an invitation to give London an entirely new cathedral. The dean told him: 'You are so absolutely and indispensably necessary to us that we can do nothing, resolve on nothing without you.'

But one thing was still lacking – money. Wren knew that the great work he had in mind would cost hundreds of thousands of pounds, the equivalent of millions in modern money. In the meantime he was appointed Surveyor of the King's Works at £320 a year.

It was only in 1670 that Parliament gave Wren the means to start work – a tax on coal coming into London. At first it yielded only £5000 a year. But it was enough to make a start.

Rising from the ashes

Wren produced a design for a new St Paul's so much to Charles II's liking that a model was built, 18 ft long and at a cost of £600. Two days later Wren was knighted.

But the model appalled church officials. They were horrified at the huge dome and the Classical design for the building, with no recognisable choir or nave, and no spire. Wren, who was as a rule quite imperturbable, wept openly when they turned down his schemes. But he was too wily a diplomat to surrender. He drew a design with a puny dome and spindly steeple, calculated to satisfy the demands of his unimaginative clients.

On June 21, 1675, work began. Wren asked a man to fetch a flat stone to serve as reference point for all the cathedral measurements. The man returned with a broken slab from an old tomb. It was inscribed with the word 'RESURGAM' – 'I shall rise again'.

Wren subtly adapted the plans so that the building in process came to look more and more like the rejected grand model, and less like the absurd official design. When money ran out, he got himself elected an MP and persuaded Parliament to treble the coal tax.

AN ARCHITECT'S SKYLINE *London's skyline (below) painted by the Italian artist Canaletto was punctuated by Wren's spires, steeples and towers. Wren (right) designed 51 churches and many royal palaces and public buildings – including Chelsea Hospital. But his greatest ambition was to give London a dome to rival Michelangelo's dome of St Peter's, Rome. The dome of St Paul's fulfilled this dream.*

CITY'S CROWN *St Paul's dome still towers 365 ft above the skyline of the present-day city of London. The diameter of the dome is 112 ft, and it weighs 64,000 tons. Inside the outer dome is a brick cone which supports the lantern and cross – a landmark for Londoners.*

CLASSICAL MAGNIFICENCE *It was 20 years after the first stones were laid before Wren turned his attention to the interior of St Paul's. The picture shows the nave from the west, with the high altar in the background. Wren achieved a remarkable impression of radiant light.*

And other problems arose. The site had to be cleared. By January 1676, 753 cart-loads of rubbish had been carried away, and the carting went on for many more months. Work was painfully slow. Stone had to be brought by ship from the Portland quarries in Dorset. The enormous blocks were transferred into barges for the Thames journey, and finally dragged up to the cathedral.

The crowning glory

At last on December 5, 1697, the choir was opened for the first Sunday service held in the new cathedral. The dome, however, was still not begun. But all who saw Wren's drawings realised that London was to be crowned with a supreme work of architecture.

Eventually, tarred cloths were put up in April 1708 'to cover the workmen in hot and wet weather upon the Leading ye Roofe of the Dome'. For the next two years Londoners remained in ignorance of the work which was shrouded in the tangled jungle of scaffolding enclosing the whole cathedral. The first they saw of Wren's visionary building was the huge gold cross gleaming above the building works. When the scaffolding came down, the magnificent dome was at last revealed, crowning the

skyline of towers and spires and steeples which Wren had created.

The old architect was not strong enough to lay the last stone of the building in 1710. His son, Christopher, stood in for him. At the end of 1711 Parliament at last declared St Paul's to be complete. Wren's life work was done. He retired to his riverside house near the great palace he had been rebuilding for William of Orange at Hampton Court.

On February 25, 1723, few people noticed as a frail old man in a rich brown periwig and buff coat with gold frogging, was helped up the steps of St Paul's by his coachman. The 91-year-old architect was paying a visit to his supreme achievement.

For a long time he sat beneath the dome, watching the early spring sunlight play upon the stonework which had fulfilled his life's greatest ambition. Then he turned and hobbled slowly away.

It was his last visit. That afternoon he died peacefully and a few days later he was buried in the crypt of St Paul's. The Latin inscription carved on his black marble tomb expressed his own confidence: *Lector, monumentum requiris, circumspice* – 'Reader, you seek my memorial, look around you'.

MASTER CARVER

To add the final touches of magnificence to St Paul's, Wren assembled a team of master craftsmen – the Frenchman Jean Tijou, who made the cathedral's wrought-iron screens, the Danish sculptor Caius Gabriel Cibber, and Grinling Gibbons, the great woodcarver.

Born in Holland of British parents, Gibbons came to England when he was about 19, and worked first as a ship's carver in Deptford. There, in a 'poor solitary thatched cottage', he was 'discovered' by John Evelyn, the diarist. Evelyn introduced Gibbons to Charles II, who soon recognised his talents and appointed him his Master Carver and Sculptor.

Wren chose Gibbons to work on St Paul's, and the result was the beautiful, intricate carving of the choir stalls, an unparalleled example of the woodcarver's art. This detail (above) from one of the choir stalls shows Gibbon's mastery of his craft and his ability to capture the beauty of fruit and flowers in his carvings.

A trickster's witch-hunt plunges England into panic

NATION IN TERROR

A fictitious plot invented by Titus Oates reduced London to a state of hysteria in 1678. Houses were barricaded against an expected Catholic uprising. Even women carried pistols for protection. Catholic books and relics were publicly burnt. Priests were hunted down and the prisons were filled with suspects turned in by informers. And 30,000 innocent Catholics fled London to escape the mob. Oates's improbable tales gave licence to a host of rogues and adventurers, who took every opportunity to profit from the panic. The tiles (above), now in the Victoria and Albert Museum, London, show how completely an artist of the time had accepted the story that Oates had concocted.

For five years from 1678, the England of Charles II was whipped into a panic so intense that it almost provoked a revolution. The words of one man brought about the execution of some 35 victims, and the pitiless persecution of hundreds of others.

The man behind this panic was Dr Titus Oates, one of history's most successful confidence tricksters. And the field that he chose for his operations was that of religion – still the most volatile powder-keg of all.

The centrepiece to the whole story was Oates's allegation that the pope had commissioned the Jesuits to assassinate Charles II, massacre the English Protestants and overthrow the legitimate English government. After Charles had been killed – by shooting, stabbing or poisoning – his Catholic brother James, Duke of York, was to be set upon the throne. By this means the Church of Rome would again be supreme in England.

This so-called plot existed only in the mind of Oates. It was the scurrilous invention of a callous liar. Oates had been expelled from both school and university, though he had then gone on to take holy orders and practise as an Anglican vicar. In 1675 he had hastily signed up as chaplain aboard the frigate *Adventurer*, in order to escape a charge of perjury. But he soon lost his chaplaincy and, returning to London, mixed with notoriously low company.

Then suddenly, in 1677, he announced his conversion to Catholicism, and went off to Spain and France to study with the Jesuits.

His new course foundered within months. Expelled as an undesirable from the Jesuit school at St Omer in France, he returned to England again, burning with frustration and resentment. Here he took up with an old acquaintance, Israel Tonge – a fanatical, half-mad vicar, filled with hatred for the Jesuits, and the ideal partner for Oates. Between them, this disreputable pair of cranks concocted their wild story of a Popish Plot, and found the ear of the government.

Suiting the mood of the times

Oates hardly cut a trustworthy figure. According to a contemporary, the Jesuit historian John Warner, he had 'the speech of the gutter, and a strident and sing-song voice, so that he seemed to wail rather than to speak'. When he finally secured an audience with the king, Charles saw through him immediately, catching him out on two points of fact. Oates claimed to have met John of Austria, whom he described as tall and fair, but Charles knew that John was short and dark. Oates also claimed he had seen Père La Chaise, the French king's personal confessor, paying out £10,000 for Charles's assassination, in a particular house in Paris. Charles knew from

his own days of exile in Paris that the alleged house did not exist.

But though Oates was motivated only by his own malice and self-seeking ambition, he was assisted in his efforts by the political climate of the day. Ardent Protestant politicians took up the fears of a Popish Plot to advance their own party cause. And the plot was given credibility by two strange coincidences. Among the many people Oates had wildly accused of conspiracy was Edward Coleman, a secretary of James, Duke of York. And Coleman, an over-enthusiastic Catholic, had secretly written letters to Catholics on the Continent – including Père La Chaise. This action was imprudent, but not criminal, for

INNOCENT VICTIM *One of the victims of the Popish Plot was the Duke of York's secretary, Edward Coleman. A contemporary woodcut shows him being dragged to execution.*

JUST PENALTY *Oates was pilloried for the fraud which almost altered history.*

the letters said nothing about murder or rebellion. Yet the very fact of writing to such a man provided apparent corroboration for Oates's talk of a plot.

Under questioning, Coleman was urged to save his life by denouncing his fellow-conspirators. Pitifully, he cried that enough was known to condemn him, but he did not know enough to be saved. He was only too accurate.

Then, on October 17, 1678, Sir Edmund Berry Godfrey, the magistrate before whom Oates had first sworn the truth of his accusations, was discovered dead in a ditch at the foot of Primrose Hill, transfixed by his own sword. His murderers were never caught.

Godfrey's murder was the spark that ignited the powder-keg. Loyal Protestants had no doubt that the unlucky magistrate was the victim of Popish assassins. He became a martyr, and his corpse lay in state for two days while thousands filed past, swearing vengeance on his Jesuit murderers.

An enterprising cutler manufactured special 'Godfrey' daggers engraved 'remember the murder of Edmund Godfrey', to be used as protection. He sold 3000 of them in one day to his eager customers.

Hysteria now gripped London. A massacre was expected daily. The streets echoed to the tramp of militia patrolling by day and night. In such an atmosphere, ever wilder accusations were eagerly believed.

A pack of informers even more disreputable than Oates and Tonge sprang up to feed the national panic. Oates himself appeared before Parliament, where he shamelessly accused Charles's Catholic queen, Catherine of Braganza, of treason.

Revealed in his true colours

The panic persisted for months, and its rumbling aftermath was still being felt at the end of 1681. Before it subsided, many innocent Catholics had been packed off to prison to stand trial for their lives. Among those who were eventually executed were men as notable as Oliver Plunket, the Catholic Archbishop of Armagh and Primate of Ireland; and William Howard, Viscount Stafford. Twenty-one men were condemned by one judge alone, the infamous and brutal Chief Justice Scroggs.

Finally, England came to its senses and saw through Oates and his tissue of lies. In June 1684, James, Duke of York, secured a massive £100,000 damages for the libels that Titus Oates had circulated about him. Once he became king, James had further revenge, when his one-time accuser was whipped twice through the streets of London. Oates received over 3000 lashes on that bloody and painful journey in May 1685 – though Catholics thought it small compensation for the blood his perjury had shed. And Oates spent the last 20 years of his life in disreputable obscurity, hounded by poverty, debt and a dismal succession of petty scandals and intrigues.

Battle to 'exclude' the heir to the throne

The hysterical frenzy roused by the Popish Plot led to an event unprecedented in British history before or since. An attempt was made legally to exclude James, Duke of York, Charles II's brother and the heir to the throne, from the succession. For James was the country's leading Roman Catholic, accused by all those who joined in Titus Oates's murderous denunciations.

By the late 1670's, Charles II's over-enthusiastic friendship with Catholic France had produced a deep discontent in England. Another source of dissatisfaction was that a general election had not been held since 1660. The time was ripe for a challenge to the policies of Charles and his ministers.

An alliance of Protestant nonconformists, low churchmen and strict Parliamentary constitutionalists battled ever more fiercely to get a general election called. But when Titus Oates started whipping up Protestant emotions with his tales of popish conspiracy, their line of attack changed. Within weeks of James's secretary, Edward Coleman, being detected in correspondence with foreign Catholics, the Protestant party was proposing that Parliament should ban James from his brother's presence.

It was but a short step to seek the complete exclusion of James from the succession to the throne. This threat stirred Charles into action. He dissolved Parliament in January 1679, and in the next two years summoned and dissolved no fewer than four more Parliaments, in a vain attempt to secure an assembly that would support his brother. But with every fresh election, the Protestant opposition, led by the astute and unscrupulous Earl of Shaftesbury, made more progress.

Charles now found himself virtually deserted. Even two of his mistresses, Louise de Kéroualle and Nell Gwynne, took Shaftes-bury's side. But the desertion that pained Charles the most was that of his illegitimate son, the Duke of Monmouth, who hoped to be legitimised and become heir to the throne in James's place. In the end, however, the king triumphed. He refused to desert his brother, telling Shaftesbury 'I have the law and reason on my side'. The earl was now forced to choose between admitting his defeat or starting a rebellion on behalf of his own candidate for the succession, Monmouth.

The memories of the civil war were too fresh and too painful for such drastic action. Shaftesbury's plans were shattered and he was forced to flee the country. But the episode saw for the first time the emergence of definite political factions – the pro-Parliament, anti-Papist Whigs, and the monarchist, High Church Tories. Britain was launched on the road to her modern party system.

THE FIRST WHIG

One of Britain's first political parties, the Whig Party, was founded by Lord Shaftesbury (below), much of whose political life was devoted to challenging the power of the monarchy. But his career was a source of little pride to later Whigs. He began the Civil War as a Royalist, but finished as one of Cromwell's most trusted servants. After the Restoration he served Charles II. But his hatred of James, the king's brother and heir, and his anti-Catholic views, made him a natural ally for Titus Oates. When the plot collapsed, he was indicted for treason. He fled to take refuge in Protestant Holland, where he died at the age of 61 after only a year in exile.

PROTESTANT PROPAGANDA *A contemporary print shows the anti-Catholic demonstration organised by the Whig leader, the Earl of Shaftesbury, in the City of London on November 17, 1679. In the procession, demonstrators disguised as Jesuits, armed with knives, cardinals and the pope are shown pursuing the first 'victim' of the popish plotters, Sir Edmund Berry Godfrey.*

GREAT MINDS UNITE AND MODERN SCIENCE IS BORN

The restoration of the Stuart monarchy brought not only a deliverance from the moral restraints of the Puritan era, but also a new intellectual freedom. It was a golden age of philosophical and scientific study. Nor were learned pursuits restricted to scholars working in obscure corners at Oxford and Cambridge; patronage, encouragement and genuine interest came from the highest circles. The Royal Society, which symbolised the new spirit of inquiry, was formally constituted with the consent of Charles II only six months after he came to the throne in 1660.

The inspiration of the society came from Francis Bacon who had stressed the importance of experimental science, and the rejection of the ancient traditions which had bedevilled research and progress.

In the *New Atlantis*, he had put forward the idea of a Utopian College, consisting of men who were committed to 'the Knowledge of causes and the secret motion of things; and the enlarging of the bounds of Human Empire, to the effecting of all things possible'. Bacon's arguments were so persuasive that although he never succeeded in putting into practice what he preached, the next generation were infected by his enthusiasm.

In the 1640's a devoted band of Baconians met regularly at Oxford in the rooms of John Wilkins, Warden of Wadham College, for discussion and experimentation. Wilkins was determined to free science from the often ludicrous conventions of Classical philosophers. He wrote that it was 'a superstitious, a lazie opinion to think Aristotle's work the bounds and limits of human invention'. It was this

revolutionary attitude to the past which later prompted the Royal Society to choose as its motto *Nullius in verba*, which can be freely translated: 'We do not take anyone's word for it.'

Among the first members of the group were some of the men who were to transform the age: Christopher Wren, still in his twenties but already Oxford professor of astronomy, and Robert Boyle, who was beginning his experiments on the properties of air. On November 28, 1660, they moved to London to form themselves into a permanent society.

The king was deeply interested in the group from the start. He provided the members with objects for discussion: 'His Majestie has sent a small piece of glasse...which though strock with a hamer at the oval end would not breake, but breaking the taile or small part with your hand...the whole would crumble to dust.'

A unique meeting place

The diarist and a founder-member of the Royal Society, John Evelyn, recorded another meeting 'to whiche his Majestie has sente that wonderfull horn of the fish, which struck a dangerous hole in the keele of a ship, in the India sea, which being broake off with the violence of the fish, left in the timber, preserv'd it from foundring'.

In 1662 the king granted the society its first charter as the Royal Society of London for the Promotion of Natural Knowledge. He also presented it with a mace, and provided it with a permanent home at Chelsea and an annual supply of venison for its St Andrew's Day feast.

Where royalty led, others followed. The

OFFICIAL EXPERIMENTER *Robert Hooke, who was the Royal Society's first 'experimenter', used his own microscopes to discover vegetable cells.*

Royal Society became a unique meeting place of the worlds of fashion, politics and scholarship. There was scarcely a great Englishman of the age who was not a member – the dissolute Duke of Buckingham, the dashing general and cousin of the king, Prince Rupert, who himself used to conduct chemical experiments, Samuel Pepys, Christopher Wren, the Earl of Sandwich, the poet John Dryden and the

---

CREATED BY ROYAL PRIDE

The Royal Observatory owes its existence to a royal boast, and a royal fit of pique.

At a palace reception Charles II, stung by some remarks on maritime navigation made by a French visitor, publicly proclaimed that his astronomers could produce accurate tables describing the movements of the heavenly bodies.

But when he ordered the Royal Society to make good his boast, he was annoyed when it reported that it was impossible without a well-equipped observatory, of a kind that Britain did not possess. The king responded by ordering Christopher Wren to build an observatory close to the Palace of Greenwich, which was being rebuilt at the time. In 1675 a building, more beautiful than useful, was erected, and the first Astronomer Royal, John Flamsteed, was appointed at a salary of £100 a year.

The second Astronomer Royal was Edmond Halley, already famous for predicting the orbit of the comet which bears his name. He held the post from 1721 until his death in 1742.

The Octagon Room at the Royal Observatory, Greenwich, was designed by Christopher Wren. It was in this room, through painstaking study of the world's latitudes, that 'Greenwich Mean Time' was established.

towering genius of science, Isaac Newton. Nothing was barred from discussion; every aspect of pure and applied science, technical innovation and philosophical speculation might be explored. Samuel Pepys watched a hen stagger round the floor apparently inebriated with 'Florentine poison', and gazed upon a human foetus preserved in 'spirits of salt'. In March 1667 the transfusion of blood from a sheep to a dog was demonstrated.

Curiosities from Europe

In July 1668 the society considered various archaeological finds, discovered while foundations were being dug for a fort at Sheerness. A letter from Germany, read in April 1680, described a large quantity of hair 'an Inch in length, exceeding thick, and somewhat harsh and reddish', which had been observed growing on a corpse. The supply of interesting items presented to the members of the society was as endless as their curiosity was boundless.

The activities of the society were not confined to idle speculation. The government made frequent use of the services of this unique gathering of great minds. The Royal Society made recommendations on the sanitation system for the new city of London, and the implementation of these recommendations was in part responsible for the gradual stamping out of the plague.

Forum for great minds

But the Royal Society's greatest contribution to the world of science was in providing a forum for the sympathetic discussion of new theories, inventions and discoveries made by the great geniuses of the age. Robert Boyle set the world of chemistry on new lines by exploding the old theory of the four basic elements (earth, air, fire and water) and postulating that all matter is composed of indestructible atoms. Sir William Petty, one of the first practical economists, demonstrated the usefulness of statistics, and Edmond Halley was the first astronomer to make a serious study of the heavenly bodies visible from the Southern Hemisphere. In 1682 he observed the comet since named after him.

It was Halley who suggested to Newton that he should bring together his scientific findings in one book. The result, published with the sanction of the Royal Society, was Newton's *Principia*, probably the greatest step forward in the history of science.

By supporting scientific publications like the *Principia*, and by publishing its own discussions, the Royal Society became the living embodiment of Bacon's revolutionary vision – a community of men dedicated to extending human understanding. It succeeded brilliantly – unleashing a new spirit of inquiry which has lasted into modern days. For Englishmen in the last part of the 17th century, it seemed the world was full of secrets waiting to be unlocked, and that they held the key.

HENRY PURCELL'S TUNES CAPTIVATE STUART LONDON

Under the organ in Westminster Abbey lie the remains of one of the greatest and most original of English composers. For many years he had played there, and no more fitting burial place could be found. An inscription reads: 'Here lyes HENRY PURCELL Esqr. Who left this Life and is gone to the Blessed Place Where only his harmony can be exceeded.'

Purcell was a Londoner. He was born there in 1659 and he died there a short 36 years later. Much of his music was directly connected with the life of the capital. He was an honoured figure both at Westminster Abbey and at court, where the king kept his own choristers and musicians – the Chapel Royal. But his fame also reached out into the streets of London where thousands of people knew the songs and dance tunes he composed for the theatre.

Purcell's father was a Gentleman of the Chapel Royal and master of the choirboys at Westminster Abbey. Purcell became a Chapel Royal chorister at the age of six.

At the age of 15, he had become official music copier at Westminster Abbey under the famous organist and composer John Blow. When Purcell was 21, Blow resigned in his favour. Two years later Purcell was also appointed organist to the Chapel Royal.

Purcell's masterpiece, 'Dido and Aeneas', written about 1689, was the first true English opera. Composed for the pupils of a 'School for Young Gentlewomen' in Chelsea, it was deliberately simple, yet reached new heights of musical and dramatic expression.

Other stage works, like 'Dioclesian' and 'The Fairy Queen', were plays with incidental music which won him far greater success. In 'King Arthur' he collaborated with the poet John Dryden. The famous song 'Fairest Isle' is from this work.

Among Purcell's best-loved songs was 'Lillibulero', which inspired the soldiers who rallied to William III during his Glorious Revolution of 1688. In 20 years of composition he also wrote over 50 dramatic works, 80 religious works and a mass of incidental music and songs.

'Tears from all'

William III's wife, Queen Mary, was the monarch he liked best, and when she died, in February 1695, Purcell wrote a march and two anthems, including the famous 'Thou Knowest, Lord', for her funeral. 'I appeal to all that were present,' wrote one mourner, 'whether they ever heard anything so rapturously fine and Solemn! . . . which drew tears from all.'

Tears were shed again in the abbey nine months later when 'Thou Knowest, Lord' was played at Purcell's own funeral on November 26. His early death, probably from tuberculosis, robbed England of a supreme musical talent.

PUBLISHED PURCELL *The only stage work of Purcell's to be published during his lifetime was 'Dioclesian'. Despite the fact that the composer notated every copy sold by hand, the work made a loss. One of the few remaining portraits of the composer appears in the score.*

Rebellion, defeat and a king's bloody revenge

MASSACRE ON THE MOORS
The Duke of Monmouth's ambitions to the throne came to a bloody end at Sedgemoor, Somerset, in 1685. During a night attack on James II's army, his men became bogged down in a massive ditch and they were slaughtered where they stood by government troops.

In July 1685 vengeful government troopers were scouring the west of England. They sought remnants of those rebels who had risen against their lawful sovereign, James II, and had been cut to pieces at the Battle of Sedgemoor a few days before.

One such patrol found a man cringing miserably in a ditch. He did not resist, but trembled abjectly as his captors searched him. In his pockets they found all that he had to eat – a handful of peas snatched as he had fled from the battlefield. Suddenly they realised the importance of their capture. The man that pleaded for his life before them was none other than James, Duke of Monmouth, the leader of the revolt.

For Monmouth, Sedgemoor was the bitter culmination to a lifetime of thwarted ambition. A fortnight before the battle, Monmouth had proclaimed himself King of England, Wales, Scotland, France and Ireland. But now he stood revealed for something far less glorious – the inadequate victim of other men's ambitions and his own conceit.

Charles II, Monmouth's father, deserved much of the blame for his son's fate. Monmouth was the first and most favoured of his illegitimate sons, fathered when Charles was an 18-year-old exile in Holland. There was a rumour that a 'Black Box' contained proof of a marriage between Charles and Monmouth's mother, Lucy Walter, a prostitute. Charles denied any such marriage, but he did not deny his love for his handsome son, whom he brought proudly to England after the Restoration in 1660. He showered the boy with favours and titles, and married him to a wealthy heiress, Anne, Countess of Buccleuch.

Gamble for the throne

But Monmouth was scarcely worthy of these royal indulgences. He was headstrong, vain and ambitious. Pampered by the king, he began to attract interest as a possible heir to the throne. Politicians such as the Earl of Shaftesbury were working to exclude Charles's Catholic brother, James, from the succession. They encouraged the Protestant Monmouth to see himself as a future King of England. Monmouth lent himself willingly to such schemes, deceived by his own ambition and by his father's affection.

But Charles had no intention of altering the succession in Monmouth's favour. He sent his son into exile in Holland, and there he remained until his father died and James II came to the throne in February 1685.

Monmouth and his fellow exiles saw this as their opportunity. In the spring, they laid their plans for an invasion of England which, they hoped, would be met by a popular rising. On June 11, 1685, Monmouth and 82 followers

PROTESTANT HOPE *The Duke of Monmouth, illegitimate son of Charles II, was a Protestant and a good soldier, but little else.*

NIGHT RAID *The Battle of Sedgemoor was a short affair. Monmouth's men were hoping to surprise the royal troops by attacking at 1 a.m. But they were seen by a sentry, and in less than four hours the rebels had lost 1000 men and another 500 of them had been captured.*

TERROR OF THE 'BLOODY ASSIZE'

The notorious 'Bloody Assize' of Judge Jeffreys was seen at its worst during the trial of the ageing Dame Alice Lisle. She was accused of sheltering John Hickes, a minister who had fought for Monmouth at the Battle of Sedgemoor. Dame Alice, the widow of one of Cromwell's followers, did not deny that she had hidden Hickes at her home near Ringwood, Hampshire. But she claimed that she knew nothing of his support for Monmouth, and thought that Hickes, a well-known Dissenter, was a victim of government persecution. But at her trial at Winchester Assizes in 1685, Judge Jeffreys insisted she must have known that Hickes was a traitor. Despite his browbeating of witnesses, the judge could find no one who could prove that Dame Alice was lying. The jury were reluctant to convict her on the scant evidence, but Judge Jeffreys terrorised them into finding her guilty and ordered her to be burnt alive. She appealed to James II, who substituted beheading for burning. Dame Alice was executed on September 2.

Judge Jeffreys browbeats a witness during the trial of Dame Alice Lisle in 1685. At 40, he was the youngest-ever Lord Chancellor of England – and soon became known as the most brutal.

landed at Lyme Regis, a small port in Dorset. The gentry of Lyme – whose fears had been roused as, playing at bowls, they saw the rebels' three ships drop anchor in Lyme Bay – fled in horror from the town. But the humbler townsfolk, including many prisoners the rebels released from the town gaol, flocked to join the invader's banner. Within 12 hours, some 1500 men had rallied to Monmouth's call. Popular resentment against James II's Catholicism ran deep in this corner of England, and Monmouth's hopes of a spontaneous rebellion seemed about to be fulfilled.

But soon things started to go wrong. Not long after the landing, Monmouth's most trusted and experienced comrade, Heywood Dare, was shot in a brawl over a looted horse. The loss of such a leader was a poor start for the enterprise.

Nevertheless, for a fortnight the rebels' cause flourished. Their army marched triumphantly through the West Country, gathering strength at every step. When he set up camp outside Bristol at the end of June, Monmouth had about 7000 armed men.

But while Monmouth debated his next move, the government was not idle. Parliament voted James £400,000 to suppress the rebellion, and formally declared Monmouth a traitor. Royal forces, led by Lord Feversham and John Churchill, converged on the rebels.

Under this mounting pressure, Monmouth began to panic. His motley army of peasants was no match for the king's seasoned regiments. He withdrew from Bristol and his forces diminished in numbers as his frightened followers lost heart. Monmouth decided to risk all in a last desperate gamble.

On the night of July 5, the rebels launched an attack on the royalist encampment at Sedgemoor, near Bridgwater in Somerset. At first the royal army was caught by surprise – Feversham was in bed as the battle began. But luck was not on the rebels' side. A muddled order sent both their infantry and cavalry forces into a marshy ditch where, hopelessly entangled, they were massacred by the disciplined volleys of the royal regulars. By dawn the cause was lost, and Monmouth deserted his followers and fled from the battlefield.

A terrible retribution

Monmouth's foolhardy enterprise had a tragic sequel. Monmouth himself was executed on July 15, suffering terribly from the blunt axe wielded by his unskilful executioner. Those of his followers who survived the carnage of Sedgemoor were delivered up to the brutal Judge Jeffreys. In his notorious Bloody Assize Jeffreys ordered the execution of over 300 of the rebels. More than 1000 of them were transported to the colonies and countless others flogged or imprisoned.

But the appalling savagery of this retribution discredited James and his government. The self-seeking Monmouth was soon seen as a noble martyr for the Protestant cause. When, three years later, William of Orange made his own bid for the English throne, these were the memories that helped him to success.

James II: His obstinacy cost him his throne

The last of the Stuart kings, James II was short-sighted, arrogant and obstinate. 'This king,' wrote the French ambassador, 'is neither so self-controlled nor so great a man as has been supposed. He has all the faults of his father Charles I, but he has less sense, and he behaves more haughtily in public.'

James swiftly threw away his initial popularity. He made his subjects nervous. He increased the standing army from 6000 to 30,000 men, keeping 13,000 men at arms on Hounslow Heath to overawe the capital. When ministers – such as Lord Halifax – gave him advice he did not like, he sacked them as disloyal. Worst of all, his ardent Catholicism led him to embark on a campaign to make it the dominant religion in his kingdom. By his policies, he alienated the very men who had been his strongest supporters.

Piety was one explanation for his blundering. Mental degeneration caused by syphilis was more likely, for James – his religious fanaticism notwithstanding – was a greedy and indiscriminating womaniser.

England tolerated 'Squire James' and his clumsiness until his Italian wife, Mary of Modena, produced a son, who replaced the Protestant Mary as heir to the throne. Soon revolution broke out. But even when James was at the mercy of Mary's husband, William of Orange, in November 1688 he might have saved his throne, had he been prepared to agree to terms. Many Englishmen were unwilling to see an anointed king deposed. Compromise, however, had never been James's style, and he went into exile. If he could not have all, he preferred nothing.

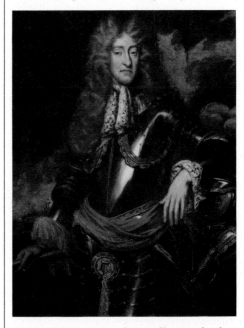

PROUD AND FOOLISH *James II was the last Stuart king to rule Britain. His obstinate refusal to compromise cost him his throne in 1688.*

A VISIONARY TRANSFORMS MAN'S VIEW OF THE UNIVERSE

When Isaac Newton was born prematurely on Christmas Day 1642 he was so small that his mother could have put him into a quart pot. For weeks after his birth he was not expected to live, and throughout infancy he had to wear a support around his neck to keep his head from lolling forward on to his shoulders.

A solitary child, endowed with a genius which only intensified his loneliness, he grew up believing that he was destined for future greatness. The date of his birth and the miracle of his survival seemed to him portentous. He came to feel that he had special access to the mind of the Almighty, and that in the mystical raptures of his private meditations the deepest secrets of the universe had been imparted to him alone.

Birth of science

Newton lived in an age in which 'science' can properly be said to have been born. The founding of the Royal Society, by Charles II in 1662, gave official support for the first time to scientific investigation in Britain. But while men of talent and enthusiasm abounded, it took Newton to make the crucial step from the vague theories of 'natural philosophy' to the hard mathematical laws and principles on which modern science is based.

While his contemporaries and the judgment of posterity have concurred in recognising Newton's genius, he himself said: 'If I have seen further, it is by standing on the shoulders of giants.' He considered the groundwork for his great discoveries had already been done by the great Italian, Galileo Galilei, who died the year he was born, and Johannes Kepler, who had died 12 years previously.

Both had made remarkable progress towards understanding the laws which govern the universe. But it was left to Newton, in his three fundamental Laws of Motion, to weld their discoveries together into a coherent whole.

At home in Woolsthorpe, a small village in Lincolnshire, Newton was expected to follow a farming career in the footsteps of his father, who had died before he was born. When his mother re-married, he was put into the care of his grandmother for the rest of his childhood. A delicate boy, he grew into a man to whom secrecy and solitude were second nature. He never married, had few intimate friendships and, though he remained a dutiful son, he formed few close emotional ties.

His academic record at King's School, Grantham, 7 miles away, was unspectacular. But he did show an aptitude for building models of all kinds. He made a water clock, a working model of a windmill and several sundials, displaying a skill at precision handiwork which later stood him in good stead.

In 1661, aged 19, he went to Trinity College, Cambridge, graduating without special distinction in 1665. But at Cambridge he met Isaac Burrow, Lucasian Professor of Mathematics, who took him on to help him prepare his book called *Optical Lectures*. Burrow recognised the first signs of Newton's outstanding talents, and wrote of him as 'a man of quite exceptional ability and skill'.

But it was when he was aged 23 and 24 that Newton's mind was to exert its exceptional power in a way never after repeated. The foundations for all his later thinking, all his major intuitions, were laid during these two extraordinarily fertile, creative years.

When the Great Plague of 1665 threatened Cambridge, Newton was forced to return to his parent's home in Woolsthorpe. Intellectually isolated, he embarked on an astonishing period of sustained mental activity. There is no doubt that Newton did possess superhuman powers of concentration. He was able to hold before his mind philosophical problems that would have exhausted a lesser intellect. 'I keep the subject constantly before me,' he wrote, 'and wait till the first dawnings open little by little into the full light.'

During 1665 and 1666 he calculated the basis for differential and integral calculus, the method which mathematicians have used ever since for solving complex problems. He deduced for the first time the nature and behaviour of light, and the law of gravitation. Legend has it that this discovery came to him as he sat watching an apple fall to the ground beside him in his mother's orchard.

The laws of the universe

Newton acknowledged himself the debt to those two years. 'In those days,' he wrote, 'I was in the prime of my age for invention, and minded mathematics and invention more than at any time since.' But although, by a brilliant combination of intellect and intuition, he had delved further than any scientist into the laws of the universe, he did not publish his findings, but kept them strictly to himself.

He returned to Cambridge in 1667 at the age of 25. His great creative burst was over, and the rest of his life was devoted to consolidating and expanding his ideas.

In 1669 Burrow resigned his post as Lucasian Professor in Newton's favour. Newton was feverishly engaged at the time on experiments into the nature of light. But his first major work came to the attention of the Royal Society only by hearsay. During his experiments, Newton had perfected the first reflecting telescope. The society heard about it, and begged to see it. Newton sent it to them in December 1671 and followed it in the February of 1672 with a paper outlining his optical theories.

Pondering the properties of light, Newton had deduced that all the colours of the spectrum combine to produce 'white' light. But if the blue light, for example, is separated out from the spectrum, it remains blue, even when refracted through a prism.

LAWS OF MOTION *Newton's masterpiece, the* Principia, *was widely acclaimed but little understood by his contemporaries. This diagram of a steam-driven engine illustrates simply his third law of motion – that for every action there is an equal and opposite reaction. It comes from a book published in 1747.*

GENIUS OF SCIENCE *Isaac Newton in his eighties.*

REFLECTING THE STARS
Newton's reflecting telescope, the prototype of all modern models, was made entirely by himself. It is preserved by the Royal Society.

SCHOLAR'S HAVEN *Newton's study in Woolsthorpe Manor, where he evolved most of his theories. He went there during the plague in 1665.*

EXPERIMENTS WITH LIGHT *Newton planned an experiment into the properties of light in this sketch from his notebook. He later published a book called* Opticks.

Newton's optical discoveries led him into a fierce controversy with Robert Hooke, the Secretary of the Royal Society. Thereafter he was reluctant to expose himself to criticism again. His theories on the idea of universal gravitation, in consequence, only came to the attention of the world by accident.

In the late summer of 1684 Edmond Halley, the astronomer who gave his name to Halley's comet, came to Cambridge to ask Newton a question which baffled Royal Society members. What, he asked, would be the orbit of a planet if it was attracted to the sun by a force obeying an inverse square law? Without hesitating, Newton replied 'An ellipse'.

A contemporary account continues the meeting: 'Struck with joy and amazement, Halley asked him how he knew it? "Why," saith he, "I have calculated it".'

Alchemy and the mint

But when Halley asked him to produce his calculation, Newton hunted vaguely around and said he could not find it. He did, however, promise Halley written proof. This promise bore fruit in the shape of perhaps the greatest scientific treatise the world had yet produced, *Philosophia Naturalis Principia Mathematica* – Mathematical Principles of Natural Philosophy, commonly known as the *Principia*.

Published in 1687 in Latin, the *Principia* was so dense and original that few of Newton's contemporaries were capable of grasping it. But for the next 250 years any other work done on the subject was only an enlargement of Newton's principles. Under his system, apples fell and planets rotated in accordance with unchanging laws. His three famous laws of motion formed the basis for all modern astronomy and physics.

The publication of the *Principia* left Newton, at 45, exhausted, once more deep in the public controversy he hated, and with his life's scientific work effectively over.

The remaining 40 years of his life was a slow emergence from the solitary struggle of discovery into the world of public affairs. But his nervous system was badly overstrained, and from 1693–4 he suffered a severe mental breakdown. He became convinced that all his friends had let him down and deceived him. One of his lifelong associations was with Charles Montagu, later Lord Halifax, whom he had first met at Cambridge. Montagu had become a very influential man, and was doing his utmost to find Newton a good position. Yet at the beginning of 1692 Newton was writing: 'Being convinced that Mr Montagu is false to me, I have done with him.' And another friend wrote: 'There is a man lost and so to speak dead for research, so I believe...'

Gradually he recovered. In 1697 Montagu obtained for him the position of Warden of the Mint, in London. The job could have been a mere sinecure, but Newton, with his usual enthusiasm, chose a complete overhaul of the British monetary system.

Public duties aside, he continued to scribble away at a study which had long fascinated him – on the occult.

It is hard to reconcile the worldly pompous official of these years with the rapt mystical hermit of earlier years. But Newton's life had always been a mass of contradictions. The man whose powers of logic had exposed the superstitious fantasies of generations had been secretly obsessed with the occult.

Ocean of truth

He wrote more than a million words on alchemy, and his library contained many books by the Rosicrucians, a secret brotherhood which believed in the magical side of alchemy, and mixed religion, disembodied spirits and chemistry.

In 1703, after the death of his old rival, Robert Hooke, Newton, to his delight, was finally made President of the Royal Society. He was knighted by Queen Anne in 1705, the first man of science to be so honoured. He ruled Britain's scientific world like a despot.

Long after his powers of sustained scientific thought had vanished, his interest in alchemy remained. It was as if the great man of science secretly rejoiced at the thought that beyond the world of science and scientific laws there existed an incalculable power, a mysterious force defying rational thought.

Before his death in 1727, at the age of 85, he told his nephew: 'I do not know what I may appear to the world, but to myself I seem to have been only like a boy, playing on the seashore... whilst the great ocean of truth lay all undiscovered before me.'

The 'Protestant wind' brings a glorious revolution

DOCUMENT OF REVOLUTION

One of the foundation stones of the British constitution is the Declaration of Rights, drawn up in 1689 after the last Stuart king, James II, had been deposed. The Declaration listed his misdeeds, including 'raising and keeping an Army within this Kingdom in time of peace and quartering soldiers contrary to the law'. William and Mary had to agree to the new curbs on their power contained in the Declaration – now in the Record Office of the House of Lords – before being given the throne. A Bill based on the Declaration was passed into law as the Bill of Rights in Parliament in 1689, although William made it clear that he resented the move as an undesirable limitation of his power. Lord Halifax, a leading Whig politician, said: 'The king had great jealousy at being governed.'

Early on the morning of November 5, 1688, Simon Jansen Hartevelt, captain of the Dutch ship *Den Briel*, cautiously edged his vessel into the harbour of Torbay in Devon. The navigation buoys round all Channel ports had been removed by order of James II, and Hartevelt's first attempt to gain the harbour had failed. But this time he was successful, and by noon 300 more Dutch ships had dropped anchor beside him.

On board the *Den Briel* was William of Orange, nephew and son-in-law of James. The other ships carried his army of more than 12,000 Dutch and British troops. High on a masthead flew a banner proclaiming 'The liberty of England and the Protestant religion'.

William was a Protestant prince who had married an English wife – Mary, the daughter of James II. He had come to England to restore liberty and to safeguard the Protestant succession. Privately, he hoped to win the throne.

His achievement became known as the Glorious Revolution – a bloodless revolution which established the foundations of England's constitutional monarchy.

Waiting in the wings

Unlike the Duke of Monmouth, whose invasion three years before had ended in ignominious failure, William had made careful preparations to ensure his success. Most important of these was the fact that he had waited for an invitation from powerful men before venturing to set foot in England.

William had refused to be drawn into overhasty action. So long as his wife remained heir to the throne, he could afford to wait for the Catholic James's death. For three years this hope sustained the English, too. James's policies were hated – but he was ageing. Then, in June 1688, came an event which shattered every Protestant's hopes. James's Italian wife, Mary of Modena, gave birth to a son. The boy

BLOODLESS COUP *A contemporary painting shows William of Orange landing from his fleet at Torbay on November 5, 1688. He then led his army to Exeter, where he waited for the political situation to become clearer and for leading politicians to join him. For William wanted his invasion to be bloodless and popular and had no intention of fighting a savage battle for the crown.*

was baptised into the Roman Catholic faith, and the pope was named godfather.

Appalled at the prospect of a continuing Catholic dynasty, seven of England's most notable Protestant politicians decided that the time had come for action. On June 30 they sent William a letter, reviewing the new situation, and ending: 'We, who subscribe this, will not fail to attend your Highness upon your landing.' It was an invitation to invasion. When at last William's powerful fleet set sail, the 'Protestant wind' – blowing from the east – sped it towards the Devon coast, while James's own navy was penned helplessly in the Thames estuary. Nor could James afford to disperse his army along the coasts. And so the landing on November 5 was accomplished without the slightest resistance.

William was no ordinary rebel. He had brought with him not just a band of personal followers, but a strong, disciplined, professional army. Five days after the landing, he marched his force in procession through the city of Exeter, in a manner calculated to encourage his supporters and overawe his opponents. First came 300 cavalry, then a squad of olive-skinned soldiers from the Dutch colony of Surinam, and then a unit of Lapland troops. Thousands more soldiers followed, and at the rear came 21 huge cannon, each one hauled by 16 horses.

The popular welcome expected by William was slow in coming. The people of the West Country had not forgotten the vengeance exacted by Judge Jeffreys the last time they supported a usurper. But as William moved nearer London, his numbers began to swell – and the importance of those who now flocked to his standard more than made up for their tardy conversion to the Protestant cause.

Among them, the most notable were Prince George of Denmark, husband of the king's younger daughter Anne, and – an even greater prize – John Churchill, James's most experienced general. As such desertions increased, James II's remaining supporters became confused and demoralised. James himself was shattered by the defection of two of his own children, Mary and Anne.

A peaceful revolution

Despairing of his cause, the king made arrangements to smuggle his infant son to France, and then decided that he too must flee to safety. As he fled by barge from London, James threw the Great Seal, the symbol of his sovereignty, into the Thames, so that no one could summon a Parliament in his name. And in the driving rain of a late December day, James slipped away unhindered to France.

Even in his last defiant gesture James had been unsuccessful. Five months later the seal was found by a fisherman.

James's flight was all that William needed. In February 1689, William's wife, Mary, returned to her English homeland. Parliament then formally offered the crown to both husband and wife as joint sovereigns. It was a solemn and momentous occasion, for Parliament did not make its offer as a humble suppliant, but as an equal partner in government.

In return for their crown, William and Mary subscribed to a Declaration of Rights drawn up by Parliament – a second Magna Carta, setting out the personal and political rights of all Englishmen. And, as William made his speech of acceptance, a new era in the history of the English constitution began.

William and Mary: A new role for monarchy

William of Orange and his attractive wife, Mary, accepted the English throne on terms which transformed the role of monarchy. Mary won the hearts of her people, but William's own part in the transformation won him little thanks. Only twice in the rest of his reign did he enjoy something like popularity with the English nation: after Mary's death in 1694; and in 1697, when he won peace with France. But, otherwise, this brave soldier and masterly statesman was unloved.

The English resented being dragged by William out of their isolation and into the struggle which dominated their foreign king's life – the need to save his beloved Holland from France. And William hardly went out of his way to coax and cultivate his subjects. He heaped wealth on his Dutch cronies and regarded the majority of British politicians as rogues or fools. Even in peacetime he left the country for months on end.

Had she lived, Mary might have taught her husband how to see his rule over the British as something more than a bleak necessity. For she had the charm, the friendliness, the natural touch, which he so painfully lacked.

After Mary's death from smallpox, William cared for little except his single-minded crusade against Louis XIV of France. Physically, he had never been robust. Now he degenerated alarmingly. At 45 he was already an old man, his lungs tortured by asthma and bronchitis. Little wonder that William began drinking heavily to make life bearable. And when he died in 1702, few Englishmen mourned him.

DUAL MONARCHY *William and Mary ruled together. He was reserved, with a chilling manner, while she was high spirited and romantic.*

Butchery in the glens leaves a legacy of hate

VALLEY OF DEATH

Glencoe, in the Highlands of Scotland, was described by the historian Thomas Babington Macaulay as a 'sad and awful place'. It was desolate, the land was infertile and the weather often rough. But for the rebellious MacDonalds, the towering hills made it a secure hide-out until 1692. Then they were tricked into billeting soldiers in their cottages – and were massacred by their hereditary enemies, the Campbells, just before dawn on a February morning as 'a proper vindication of public justice'.

In the spring and summer of 1691, the Highlands of Scotland were on the point of rebelling against English rule. The Scots still maintained a stubborn loyalty to the exiled Stuart king, James II, deposed in 1688 because of his pro-Catholic policies. To forestall open rebellion, the new king, William III, ordered that every clan must swear an oath of allegiance to him before New Year's Day, 1692. Failure would be punished by savage and brutal reprisals.

Faced with this threat, all the clan chiefs gave way – even such a wild, bloodthirsty tribe of cattle raiders as the MacDonalds of Glencoe.

The MacDonalds' tragedy was that they left their gesture of loyalty too late, even though this was not deliberate.

Their aged chief, MacIain MacDonald, had spared no effort to meet the deadline. On December 29, 1691, he rode through a snowstorm to take the oath at Fort William.

Built near the town of Inverlochy and named after the new king, Fort William was a forbidding strongpoint built to overawe the rebellious Scots. Its governor was a soldier, Colonel John Hill. But when MacIain presented himself before Hill to perform his distasteful duty, the governor announced that

he had no power to administer the oath. It must be sworn before a civil official, the Sheriff at Inveraray.

MacIain was appalled. Before him lay a journey of 60 miles to Inveraray – hard enough in good weather, impossible in the storm that was now raging as they talked. And time was running out.

MacIain did not reach Inveraray until January 2. There another disappointment met him: the Sheriff was away, staying with his family over Hogmanay. In mounting anxiety, MacIain awaited his return. Then, at last, on January 6, the Sheriff received him. He shook his head at the long delay, and only when he saw the chief break unashamedly into tears did he relent and allow the oath of loyalty to be taken.

Treachery in the glens

Those six days were to mean the death sentence for the MacDonalds of Glencoe. For, ever since July 1689, when clans loyal to James had wiped out government troops at Killiecrankie, in Perthshire, King William and his Scottish administrators had been anxious to teach the Highlanders a lesson. Old MacIain MacDonald led a clan that was small and unpopular. The king's callous and canny

advisers knew that brutal action against the clan would not lead to a general rising. So when the chief's belated oath was considered by the clerks to the Privy Council in Edinburgh, they refused to accept it.

'If MacIain of Glencoe and that tribe can be well separated from the rest,' William wrote, 'it will be a proper vindication of public justice to extirpate that sect of thieves.'

Late in the bitter month of January, 120 red-coated soldiers were dispatched to Glencoe. They were billeted in the tiny crofters' cottages of the valley on the pretext that Fort William had no room for them. The soldiers were mainly Campbells, under Captain Campbell of Glenlyon – bitter enemies of the MacDonalds. Yet they were accepted trustingly in Glencoe, for there was a hallowed Highland understanding that when hospitality has been offered and accepted, even the fiercest feud between guest and host must be laid aside.

After a fortnight of feasting and fraternisation came the execution order. The stark message was passed down from the regimental colonel to Captain Campbell of Glenlyon: 'You are hereby ordered to fall upon the rebels the MacDonalds of Glencoe and put all to the sword under 70. You are to have special care that the old fox (MacIain) and his sons do not escape your hands.'

After dark on February 12 the secret message was carried down the glen. Soldiers were called out into the snow from the cottage firesides to hear their instructions. They were to give no hint of their design until the appointed hour – 5 o'clock on the following morning.

At a few seconds after 5 a.m. the first cries rang out in the frosty air of the dark glen. The

TRAGEDY IN THE GLEN *A Victorian picture shows survivors of the massacre huddling in the snow as their homes blaze. The troops had been told to wipe out the MacDonalds, but many of them escaped. This was because the soldiers disobeyed orders and used muskets instead of swords on their victims. The gunfire awoke many clansmen who had time to run off to the hills.*

first man to die was Duncan Rankin, who lived near the chief's house. Fleeing from the soldiers, he was shot as he stumbled across the river. Soon came the turn of the 'old fox' himself. Ordering his men to MacIain's door, Lieutenant John Lindsay knocked and told a servant that the troops were leaving and wanted to thank the chief for his hospitality. MacIain awakened, climbed out of bed and told his wife to dress.

Soldiers immediately ran into the house, and shots rang out in the darkness. MacIain, hit in body and head, collapsed. He was still wearing his nightshirt, though he had pulled on his trousers. The Campbells stripped his wife naked and tore the rings from her fingers. Down the glen others were at work, bayoneting MacDonalds as they slept.

A child clung to the Campbell commander's knees and begged for mercy. The reply was a pistol shot at point-blank range. When the soldiers tired of using their weapons, they took to fire-raising. In one cottage alone, it was reported, 14 people burnt to death.

Even when facing their doom, the Mac-Donalds showed their courage. 'If I am to be killed by you,' said one villager, 'I would rather it were not beneath my own roof.' 'I've eaten your meat,' replied a soldier, 'I'll do you the favour and kill you without.' And this villager escaped his fate. As the soldiers closed in on him, he flung his plaid over their heads and fled into the snow.

The massacre was soon over. As the sacked cottages blazed, many MacDonalds heard the din, roused themselves and slipped away unseen. But for the weaker ones this freedom was short-lived. Naked in the snow, they died from exposure, as William III's Scottish Secretary of State, Lord Stair, had intended.

Legacy of hatred

Stair had callously set a midwinter deadline to the oath-swearing. He argued that this was 'the only season in which we are sure the Highlanders cannot escape and carry their wives, bairns and cattle to the hills . . . This is the proper time to maul them in the long winter nights'.

According to legend, not all the soldiers took eagerly to their task. One soldier, sickened by the order to kill a woman and her child hiding in the snow, slew an animal and showed his bloodstained sword to his officer as proof of his obedience.

As a systematic massacre, Glencoe was a failure. Both MacIain's sons escaped, and only 38 butchered bodies were found in the glen – less than one-tenth of MacIain's clan.

But as a symbol of William's cold-blooded and unscrupulous attitude towards his Scottish subjects, it had an enduring effect. No other single event did so much to strengthen Highland loyalty to the exiled James II and his descendants. It was this loyalty among the clans that was to lead to two later episodes in Scotland's tragic and heroic story, the Stuart rebellions of 1715 and 1745.

England and Scotland – from enmity to union

The Scottish Jacobites nursed a deep hatred for England, and the Dutch king, William III, in particular. They had accepted William and Mary as their king and queen in April 1689, more from disappointment at James's craven flight than out of any enthusiasm for the new joint monarchs. They responded warmly when James began fighting to win back his throne.

'Sold for English gold'

The Glencoe massacre and other examples of brutal government aroused undying bitterness in the Highland clans, and even led them to put aside their own differences to unite against their oppressors. But there was resentment, too, among the people of such cities as Edinburgh at England's economic power, and the harsh trading embargoes she imposed against the Scots. Two years after William's death, the Scottish Parliament passed an Act of Security, which prohibited an English monarch from ruling Scotland unless equal trading, political and religious rights were guaranteed. Ominously, it also provided for an independent Scottish army to be raised.

War between the two countries seemed a real possibility. But the English knew how to divide the Scots and rule them. The Lowlanders could be bought and the Highlanders starved into wretched compliance. An almost total union was agreed – on the basis of concessions to the Lowland townspeople. Sixteen Scottish peers and 45 MPs were to sit at Westminster. And although the Scots lost their own Parliament, they retained their own legal system.

The deal, ratified in the Act of Union of 1707, meant that Scotland had, in effect, traded her loyalty to the exiled King James for commercial equality.

The Highland clansmen, still unswervingly loyal to James, were disgusted. 'We are bought and sold for English gold,' they sang.

UNION ACCOMPLISHED *Queen Anne receives the Act of Union from the Duke of Queensberry. Its signing formally united England and Scotland.*

The first Churchill humbles the might of France

COMPLETE VICTORY *Marlborough's triumph at Blenheim established his reputation as the finest general in the world. The night before the battle, Marlborough (above) spent much of the time in prayer. At dawn he received Holy Communion. A Dutch tapestry (right) – now at Blenheim Palace – shows the duke on a white horse directing the battle from a hilltop. The battle lasted about eight hours and the French were routed. Their losses were enormous – 26,000 dead and 15,000 captured. The victory meant that the ambitious Louis XIV of France was forced to abandon his plans to dominate Europe, and the shadow that had hung over the Continent for three decades was lifted. But peace was not to be made until April 1713.*

By the beginning of the 18th century, England's lengthy quarrel with Louis XIV was reaching its climax. For 30 years the might of France had threatened the peace of Europe. But on August 13, 1704, English troops fighting at the south German village of Blenheim won their greatest victory since Agincourt, 300 years before. And their commander, John Churchill, Duke of Marlborough, shattered the legend of French military invincibility.

A new phase of war had started as soon as Queen Anne came to the throne in 1702. At first, England's ally the Netherlands had been the centre of the war, but by 1704 French interest had shifted to a greater prize – Vienna, capital of England's other ally, Austria.

Marching halfway across Europe

The Duke of Marlborough knew that the fall of Vienna would fatally weaken the alliance. Resisting Dutch demands that he stay and defend the Netherlands, he decided on a bold stroke that would take his army halfway across Europe to challenge the French on the Danube.

On this 600 mile, three-month-long march, Marlborough's main care was for the welfare of his 40,000 men – a motley collection of English, Dutch, German and Danish soldiers. He arranged a faultless supply system, even ensuring that every man was issued with new boots before the force entered hostile Bavaria. The Allied army thus reached the new theatre of war in peak fighting condition.

At Münster, on the Danube, Marlborough's troops were joined by a smaller Allied force under Prince Eugene of Savoy and prepared to block the path of the French and Bavarian army marching on Vienna. The Allies now had some 52,000 men – 9000 of them British. Their two commanders, the duke and the prince, were both skilled and experienced generals, confident of each other, and ideally suited to be partners in battle.

Marshal Tallard, the French commander, had no wish to join battle with Marlborough, and decided to take up a position so strong that it would deter an Allied attack. He drew up his 54,000 troops along the western bank of the River Nebel, about 6 miles from Münster. Protected by the Nebel and the Danube, and by the fortified village of Blenheim, he assumed that no enemy would be foolhardy enough to risk a battle.

But Tallard had reckoned without the cool daring of Marlborough and Eugene. Tallard's troops were not concentrated for the battle, and this left a fatal weakness in the French centre. Moreover, they were positioned too far back from the banks of the Nebel, giving room for the Allied army to regroup after crossing the river.

As the sun broke through the morning mist on August 13, the astonished French awoke to see the entire Allied army facing them, and preparing to cross the river.

Marlborough had to hold off his attack until Prince Eugene's force had reached its station on the wing. For five hours, 90 French guns poured a relentless fire on the waiting

Allied troops. Marlborough himself narrowly escaped being cut down by a cannon-ball as he rode on a tour of inspection. At last, all was ready, and at noon Marlborough gave the signal to advance.

The French commander in Blenheim, the Marquis de Clérambault, panicked immediately. He summoned up 18 battalions of reserves, thus trebling his original fighting strength. The result was that Blenheim became so overcrowded that his soldiers could hardly move. Rather than try to take the village, Marlborough simply left a contingent of his troops to encircle it, hemming in its 12,000 defenders and raining a damaging fire on them.

'A Glorious Victory'

The main fighting took place outside Blenheim. Here Marlborough showed his mastery of the combined cavalry and infantry action, drawing them up in alternate lines so that each supported the other.

Unable to match this, the French began to weaken and lose formation. Tallard failed to give either direction or inspiration to his men. At 5 p.m. the last triumphant scene of the battle was played out under Marlborough's unfailing direction. The Allied cavalry began to trot forward in close formation, their horses' strides lengthening into a gallop as they thundered towards the French cavalry lines.

The weight and impetus of the charge, and the bloody effect of the flashing Allied swords, was too much for the weary French. Soon they turned and galloped off in full flight.

The day was Marlborough's. Among the 15,000 prisoners taken by the Allies was Tallard himself, who was captured on his way to Blenheim village and brought to Marl-

THE QUEEN AND THE DUCHESS

The friendship of Queen Anne and Sarah Churchill, Duchess of Marlborough, was one of the most celebrated in British history. It started in childhood when the shy, poorly educated and plain Anne met the dominating, witty and beautiful Sarah.

When Sarah married John Churchill, Anne said that she would content herself with 'that little corner' of Sarah's heart which she hoped still remained unoccupied. But Sarah's great fault was her arrogance. Later, she was furious when she found Anne had a new favourite.

The two women quarrelled bitterly and Sarah even described Anne as a 'praying, godly idiot'. The friendship of Mrs Morley and Mrs Freeman – as the queen and duchess signed themselves in their intimate correspondence – came to an end in 1709. And with Sarah's fall from favour, her husband, too, lost his power.

Anne (left) and Sarah (right). Through their friendship the Whigs controlled the government.

borough. Still mounted on horseback, the duke took out an old tavern bill, and on the back scrawled a message to his wife Sarah: 'I have not time to say more, but to beg you will give my duty to the Queen, and let her know her Army has had a Glorious Victory.'

As Marlborough wrote, 12,000 panic-stricken men were still surrounded in the village of Blenheim. General Clérambault had not the courage to face the annihilation that confronted his troops – nor the disgrace that would greet any surrender. He mounted his horse, galloped through his infantry and plunged into the Danube and drowned.

The French losses at the Battle of Blenheim were catastrophic: four out of every five troops were killed or taken prisoner, compared with one in every five of the Allies.

When he heard the news of his army's defeat, the French king, Louis XIV, was so shocked that he issued an edict forbidding all mention of the battle.

It was eight days before the news of Blenheim reached England. One gallant officer, Colonel Parke, rode day and night until he reached London. Within a few minutes of his arrival, the cannon of the Tower boomed, the bells were set ringing and every citizen was on the streets. Englishmen had just cause for celebration. For, as the sun set on the field of Blenheim, it was said, the glory of their greatest enemy, Louis XIV, departed.

Anne: The sad story of the last ruling Stuart

It was sadly appropriate that Queen Anne – the last Stuart to rule Britain – was born in 1665, the year of the Great Plague. Her life was to be overshadowed by tragedy and constant ill-health.

Anne's great sorrow was her inability to bear living children, and 17 pregnancies in 16 years left her with no heir and a shattered constitution. By the time she succeeded her brother-in-law, William III, at the age of 37, she was a permanent invalid suffering frequent and agonising pain.

Although Anne's husband, Prince George of Denmark, was devoted to her, the person she felt closest to was Sarah Jennings, a former childhood playmate who had married John Churchill, the soldier who was to lead Anne's armies to great continental victories.

In many ways, the two women were opposites. Anne was quiet and withdrawn, with only average looks, while Sarah was a dominating woman of dazzling beauty. The friendship lasted for more than 30 years, although in later years Sarah found the queen a bore. She once said, after seeing Anne: 'It was extremely tedious to be so much where there could be no manner of conversation.' Eventually, the two women quarrelled and their relationship came to an end.

Anne was petty, argumentative, and had little education or intellect. Yet it was her very limitations that proved her strength and endeared her to her subjects. She echoed their dislike of France and their suspicion of Catholics. Even her personal characteristics – her greed, gout and fondness for hunting and gambling – were reassuringly commonplace after the dark foreign charm of the previous Stuart monarchs.

Establishing the succession

Anne's devotion to duty was formidable. For 14 years she dragged her sick body to endless council meetings, straining her afflicted eyes over state papers and striving to calm the bitter quarrels between Whig and Tory.

The last years of Anne's reign were preoccupied with the question of succession. Her Catholic half-brother, James, the 'Old Pretender', was a constant threat, although in 1701 Parliament had decreed that the throne should pass to the nearest Protestant heir – the House of Hanover.

Because she detested her Hanoverian cousins, Anne refused to let them set foot in England. But in the final days of her life she did ensure the peaceful Hanoverian succession, by sending an emissary to the future George I and assuring him of her friendship. She played a vital part in securing a peaceful change of dynasty – and so helped her country to avoid the agony of civil war.

A nation united under the Georges

A German dynasty, the House of Hanover, comes to the throne to preside over decades of growing prosperity crowned by triumph in war

In 1714 Queen Anne, the last Stuart monarch to rule Britain, died. A new dynasty came to the throne – an obscure family from the far-away Electorate of Hanover in Germany. The following year, George, Elector of Hanover, was crowned king, as George I. He could not even speak English, but he had been chosen by Parliament as the nearest Protestant heir to the childless Anne. His selection marked a turning point in British constitutional history. For the Hanoverians were strangers in a foreign land, and they had to rely on the guidance of their ministers and Parliaments more than any British monarch had ever done before.

The country the Hanoverians were called upon to rule was unrivalled in Europe in terms of power and prestige. The long years of war with Louis XIV of France had ended in triumph a year earlier. The Hanoverians were to bring to their new kingdom the blessing of a long-lasting peace. For a generation, under the leadership of Sir Robert Walpole, Britain deliberately set out to avoid conflict. His own clearly stated preference was for 'jaw, jaw, not war, war'. In 26 years of peace and prosperity Britain's economic strength reached new heights. And when the test of European war came again, this strength enabled Britain to triumph in the Seven Years' War.

During the entire period, however, the Stuarts and their supporters, the Jacobites, never gave up hope of winning back the throne. Prince James Edward Stuart, whose birth in 1688 had precipitated the Glorious Revolution, landed on December 22, 1715, at Peterhead in Scotland, from exile in

LONDON'S MEETING PLACE

The crowds who gathered on a summer evening in St James's Park (left) embodied the democratic spirit of early-18th-century London. In 1731 a Frenchman commented: 'St James's Park is the public walk of London and open to all. It is a strange sight to see the flower of the nobility and the first ladies of the court mingling in confusion with the vilest populace.'

In this painting, modestly dressed gentlefolk are seen drinking milk fresh from the grazing cows, while opulent aristocrats stroll beneath the trees of the Mall. Kilted Scots and lounging grenadiers supply a rougher note. In the distance rise the newly completed twin towers of Westminster Abbey. Even today St James's Park (inset) preserves much of this rural calm.

THE CUP THAT CHEERS *Tea first reached Britain in the 1650's, and tea-drinking had become a popular social habit by the early 18th century. Though all classes drank tea – it cost about a penny a cup in tea-houses – it was the aristocracy who brought its consumption in the home to a fine art. The taking of afternoon tea was soon to become a British ritual.*

CHURCHMEN *English bishops were reputed to be worldly and neglectful of their duties. Many preferred London life to their own dioceses. Bishop Hoadly (right) visited his diocese of Bangor three times in six years. Though a skilled theologian, most people knew him better as a famous glutton.*

CLERICAL CORRUPTION *Parish priests were more often hunting or drinking than preaching. In this satire by Hogarth, a short-sighted vicar reads to a slumbering congregation, while his clerk leers at a parishioner.*

France. His allies included high-placed Catholics and members of the Tory Party. But in February of the following year, after his generals had lost battles at Preston in England and Sheriffmuir in Scotland, James fled back to France. By April the rising had been completely suppressed (pp. 226–7).

The 1715 rebellion broke the Tory stranglehold on British politics which had dominated life during the last years of Anne's reign. The association of many high-ranking Tories with the Jacobites branded them as traitors and rebels in the eyes of George I and his successors. The Whigs took power and held it. For the following 50 years, they carved up all the offices of government, great and small, among themselves.

Prosperity in an era of peace

Political stability was reflected in the sophistication achieved in the arts. The city of Bath (pp. 228–9) was a temple to Georgian elegance. It had been visited by Queen Anne in 1702 and fashionable society soon followed her there. But the uncrowned king of Bath was Richard 'Beau' Nash, known as 'the Arbiter of Elegance'. Nash not only transformed the primitive amenities of this spa town, which had existed since Roman times, but laid down rules of etiquette which brooked no disobedience. Where Bath led, the rest of polite society followed (pp. 224–5). And Bath's architecture, too, was transformed by the work of a father and son of genius – the two Woods.

But this veneer of elegance did not conceal corruption and scandal in public life. Sir Robert Walpole (pp. 230–1), a country squire who rose to become Britain's first Prime Minister, came to prominence in the wake of a famous financial scandal, the South Sea Bubble crisis of 1720–1.

The South Sea Company had offered to take over the National Debt; its failure caused a catastrophic financial crisis. Walpole's bluff common sense – and his outstanding grasp of finance – extricated the country from threatening disaster. His twin aims of prosperity at home and peace abroad were to dominate British politics for the next 20 years. His dominance was such that his enemies gave him the title of Prime Minister. They meant it as a term of abuse, but the office was soon to pass into the British way of life.

The London over which Walpole presided was rapidly expanding, prosperous and uninhibited. The life of its citizens was captured in all its detail by William Hogarth (pp. 232–3), an engraver who soon became the most popular artist of the day. Satire was the language of the age, and Hogarth's most famous works revealed his biting wit. But they also showed compassion. He aimed, in his own words, 'both to entertain and to improve the mind', and portrayed harlots, rakes and the gin-drinking poor as unfortunate victims of their environment rather than as sinners. For, despite the prosperity fostered by Walpole during his period of power, Britain was still a nation of violent social contrasts.

A wealth of artistic talent and achievement

Hogarth was only one of the brilliant artistic talents of Georgian London. Writers such as Defoe and Fielding were producing their greatest works at this time. But the literary giant of the mid-18th century was Dr Samuel Johnson. His greatest work was his *Dictionary*, published in 1755. Even in this, Johnson's famous wit did not desert him; he described a lexicographer as: 'A writer of dictionaries, a harmless drudge.'

Johnson's friendship with James Boswell, a Scotsman 30 years younger than himself, was immortalised by the latter in one of the greatest biographies of English literature – *The Life of Samuel Johnson*. Boswell captured Johnson's dominance of London's literary life with such lively accuracy and wit that it is now impossible to think of one without the other (p. 236).

Music, too, flourished under the Hanoverians. The German-born composer George Frederick Handel made his home in London. His musical output was prodigious, including many operas for the London stage and a series of great biblical oratorios, culminating in the 'Messiah'. It was George II who brought the audience to its feet for the 'Hallelujah Chorus' at the first London performance in 1743. This tradition still survives today (p. 237).

While the arts flourished at home, the drive for empire went forward overseas. Walpole had to abandon his principle of peace in 1739 when London's merchants, avid for trade, forced him into a war against Spain, in order to open up the Spanish empire to their ships. He resigned three years later. But another politician, William Pitt, was to achieve as much success abroad as Walpole had done at home. The Spanish war was a prelude to almost a quarter of a century's struggle for worldwide dominance with Bourbon France.

In 1745, however, a sudden threat struck much nearer home. While most of the British army was engaged against France on the Continent, the Stuarts seized their last chance to win back the British throne. In July, Prince Charles Edward Stuart – 'Bonnie Prince Charlie' – landed in Scotland from France, in an attempt to win the throne for his father (pp. 234–5).

The handsome and courageous 25-year-old prince caught the imagination of the Highland clans, who were quick to rally to his standard. He found the British government completely unprepared. They were forced to recall their troops from the Continent to oppose him. By the end of October, however, Charles had captured Edinburgh and was ready to march into England.

Wars with France to win two empires

He got as far as Derby, only 130 miles from London. But he found no local support, the French failed him and his own troops were dwindling. Forced to withdraw to Scotland, the British army finally cornered his ill-fed and exhausted soldiers on the bleak moor of Culloden on April 16, 1746. The battle went against the prince, and after five months as a fugitive he escaped to France. The Jacobite threat had ended. And France made peace in 1748.

But this peace was to be short-lasting. In 1756 war with France broke out again. On this occasion, action was not confined to Europe but, more importantly, spread to the colonies. In India, Robert Clive made sure that the British would be masters of the sub-continent by winning the Battle of Plassey in 1757. And in Canada, where French and English had lived at dagger-point for 80 years, British dominance was assured by the capture of Quebec by the brilliant James Wolfe (pp. 238–9).

Britain's wealth and power was also expressed in stone. The landed aristocracy used their wealth to leave an indelible mark on the face of Britain with their magnificent houses, surrounded by landscape gardens which ensured perfect 'vistas' in every direction.

Stowe (pp. 240–1), in Buckinghamshire, was perfected by Lord Temple, his architect Robert Adam, and Capability Brown, the greatest landscape gardener of the day. It was the crowning glory of the age of the first two Georges, which came to an end in 1760. In that year, flushed with victory in war, enriched by trade and the wealth of empire, Britain stood on the brink of her greatest achievements yet as a world power. And the quiet confidence of the British people that their country would achieve still greater triumphs was best expressed in a letter by the contemporary diarist Horace Walpole. 'It really looks,' he wrote, 'as if we intended to finish the conquest of the world next campaign.'

ENGLAND'S PRIDE *The land was the source of wealth in the early 18th century. Though rich aristocrats were concentrating land and power within their own hands, the characteristic rural figure was still the squire, seen here in caricature. Disdaining fancy ways, the squire was a bluff farming man, rough-mannered and English to the core.*

AGRICULTURAL REVOLUTION *More than half England's inhabitants still lived off the land in the 1760's. Great strides in agriculture enabled farmers to feed the growing population. The first major innovator was Jethro Tull (top). He mechanised sowing with his seed-drill (above), which he built from parts of an organ soundboard.*

CHILDREN OF A NEW AGE *A free-ranging spirit of scientific inquiry laid the foundations for a revolution which was soon to change the face of Britain. Scientific inventions were now catching the popular imagination as never before. In this painting by Joseph Wright of Derby, a group of adults and children are examining an orrery, the intricate and often beautiful instrument which showed the movement of the planets.*

AGE OF VITALITY

The pleasures and pastimes of 18th-century life were as exuberant as the people themselves. At Bath, 'Beau' Nash was attempting to teach the fashionable to put aside their swords and riding boots.

The upper classes were eccentric, individual, sentimental, dramatic and tearful. They were emotional about their friends, cruel about their enemies – and above all they loved to gossip. And the age was rich in great eccentrics about whom gossip revolved.

Much time and trouble was spent on appearance, despite the difficulties of poor sanitation and the absence of baths. The British army in George II's reign used 65,000 tons of flour for powdering wigs every year. Etiquette was immensely important. Books like *The Dancing Master* gave instructions on 'How to take off your Hat and replace it'.

In town, public executions drew such excited crowds that they added a new phrase to the language – 'gala day', which is a corruption of 'gallows day'. The upper classes amused themselves with fighting duels, boxing, gaming, drinking and laying bets. When a passer-by fell down opposite Brook's Club in St James's, bets were laid as to whether he was alive or not – and those who said he was dead objected to the use of restoratives because it would interfere with the outcome of the bet. In the country they hunted and went shooting.

The poor in the country danced jigs and struggled to wrest a living from the land. In town they drank gin, as in Hogarth's famous cartoon 'Gin Alley', where the victims are shown 'drunk for a penny, dead drunk for 2d'.

Drink was one of the few pursuits that knew no class barriers. An astonished French visitor noted the British habit of solemnly sitting down to get drunk after dinner, and added that there was 'not an Englishman who is not supremely happy at this particular moment'.

POPULAR ENTERTAINMENT *The two loves of highwayman Macheath (centre)—Lucy Locket (left) and Polly Peachum (right)—plead for his life, in a scene from John Gay's famous work 'The Beggar's Opera'.*

ENGLISHMAN'S SPORT *The cartoonist Rowlandson drew this picture of a hunt meet. Fox-hunting, rather than older forms of the chase like stag-hunting, was now the popular pastime of country landowners.*

PLEASURE GARDENS *The upper classes, often in disguise, mingled with the common people at Vauxhall Gardens, strolling, drinking, gossiping and listening to the music. On the left side, in this aquatint by Rowlandson, Samuel Johnson and James Boswell sit drinking and chatting to* Johnson's friend and benefactor, Mrs Thrale, and the playwright Oliver Goldsmith. Dr Johnson so loved the life of the capital that he said: 'When a man is tired of London he is tired of life; for there is in London all that life can afford.'

SPECTACLE *Acrobats at open-air fairs were wildly popular.*

DANCING BEARS *The booths at Smithfield or Bartholomew Fair drew crowds with such attractions as puppet-shows, rope-dancers, tumblers, dancing bears, dogs and monkeys, or 'A little Farey Woman, from Italy, being Two Foot Two Inches high'.*

STREET HAWKERS *Many poor traders sold their wares on the street, from muffins to patent medicine, from 'scissors to grind' to live lobsters. Here a man and woman sell mops.*

'A HOT PUDDING, A PUDDING, A HOT PUDDING' *London streets were filled with the deafening noise of drums and flutes, penny-whistles and street-criers calling their wares. Foreigners were despised: they were abused, cheated and swindled, and even sometimes physically assaulted.*

VILLAGE DANCING *In the 18th century, the spread of land enclosure was gradually driving country folk, deprived of their livelihood, into the towns to find work. But village life still flourished. Here villagers, including a girl with a doll, watch a couple dancing outside an ale-house.*

TOWN DANCING *Under the rule of 'Beau' Nash, Bath became the hub of fashionable life. People went there to drink the waters for their health. They attended balls or drank tea in the Pump Room, carefully observing the unwritten code of conduct and dress. Here dancers try out the elegant steps of the minuet, a dance imported from the court of the French kings in Versailles.*

The Stuarts return–
in a revolt bound to fail

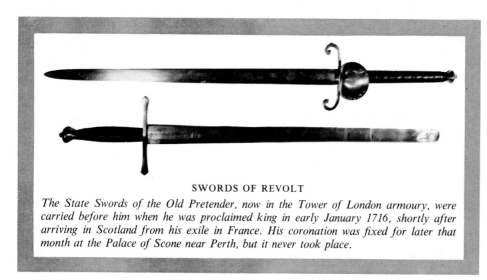

SWORDS OF REVOLT

The State Swords of the Old Pretender, now in the Tower of London armoury, were carried before him when he was proclaimed king in early January 1716, shortly after arriving in Scotland from his exile in France. His coronation was fixed for later that month at the Palace of Scone near Perth, but it never took place.

At Braemar on September 6, 1715, as the Stuart standard was being raised by the Earl of Mar to open his rebellion against the crown, the gilt knob which topped it was dislodged and fell to the ground. It was a disturbing omen for the rebels, hoping to topple Britain's new German king, and to restore Prince James Edward Stuart to the crown of his ancestors.

This Stuart prince – the son of England's last Catholic monarch, James II – was not the sort of man to inspire passionate devotion or win popular support. Like his opponent George I, James was more effective as a symbol than as a person. He had been brought up as an exile in France, and was now in his twenties. He was a colourless, cold character, pessimistic and subject to bouts of ill-health. His strongest personal trait was also his weakest political point, for he clung obstinately to his Catholic faith at a time when it was clear that no Catholic would ever rule England. Much of the blame for his attitude must go to his devout, almost bigoted Catholic mother, Mary of Modena. James was convinced that the justice of his claim was enough to guarantee his success.

The Jacobite dream

In this delusion James was encouraged by a bevy of ill-chosen courtiers, for their ambitions depended on his own. Inside this band of exiles, isolated at the court of the French king, Louis XIV, the hunger for future power spawned intrigue and back-biting. The Jacobites had dreams and ambitions, but no plans.

The death of England's Queen Anne in August 1714 seemed to change all this, and bring a sudden dawn of new possibilities, new personalities, and new initiatives. George I

was not loved in England. His succession was greeted with dismay. The election of January 1715 was marked by a wave of riots. Mobs ran wild in many towns, smashing windows and burning buildings, apparently in sympathy for the Stuarts. The Whig government was in disarray. Fearful of rebellion, it took a harsh repressive line which was more effective in aggravating hostility than in preventing it.

While the Whigs tried to grapple with the confusion, their opponents the Tories saw a chance to exploit it, for many of them believed that their own beliefs and political interests would be better served by a Stuart restoration. Their leader was Henry St John, Viscount Bolingbroke, a man of unrivalled talent among the Tories. His plan was to wait until discontent in England reached fever pitch, and

OLD PRETENDER *James Edward Stuart spent only six weeks on British soil before returning to his long life of exile in France.*

then execute a well-organised coup which would bring the Stuarts back to the throne.

But Bolingbroke was ill-served by his fellow Jacobites. Like James, they wanted action at all costs. Bolingbroke said of James: 'He was a man who expected every moment to set sail for England or Scotland, but who did not very well know for which.'

The Jacobites thought an immediate revolt in Scotland would be enough to spark off an English rising, and sweep James on to the throne in a wave of spontaneous enthusiasm. These muddlers like Ormonde, Middleton and Mar – 'those busy bees that buzz all day about me', as Bolingbroke later contemptuously described them – won the willing ear of James in France. Bolingbroke, alarmed for his own safety, fled to Paris in March 1715. Amid confusion, intrigue and indiscretion, the plans for action went ahead.

The exiles were utterly out of touch with reality in England. To rely on an automatic rising there was sheer folly, for the government was now recovering its sense of purpose and becoming daily more resolute. The English army was loyal and experienced, and the people themselves were calming down.

So blundering and unreliable were James's courtiers, that the English ambassador in France was able to discover the plot and warn his government. Finally, the keystone of the

ROYAL REVOLUTIONARY *A contemporary engraving shows the Old Pretender landing on Scottish soil at Peterhead three days before Christmas 1715. The Scots were not impressed by the sight of the young Stuart prince. One wrote: 'If he was disappointed with us, we were tenfold more so in him.'*

George I: A foreign king who spoke no English

'This is a very odd country' – such was the verdict of George I, Elector of Hanover, on the day after he arrived in England to take up his crown in August 1714.

England may well have seemed odd to a 55-year-old German prince, whose life had been a comfortable round of autocratic rule and keen soldiering in a small German state. But odder still was the way in which he came to be King of England. He was brought to the throne by an Act of Parliament, which had ignored the better claims of more than 50 other candidates to ensure a Protestant succession. A contemporary wrote: 'Fortune that made him king added nothing to his happiness, only prejudiced his honesty and shortened his days.'

And England's judgment on George was no less blunt than his on his new kingdom. The two mistresses he brought with him were nicknamed 'the Elephant' and 'the Maypole', in witness to their contrasting figures. His strange duo of Turkish servants became 'Mustafa and Mehemet'. His advisers, with their 'cacophonous, outlandish German names', were deeply resented.

Throughout his reign, George remained unmistakably a foreigner, happiest when visiting his Hanoverian home. He never mastered his new language, and had to talk to his ministers in French and Latin. Yet he took his royal duties seriously, especially where foreign policy was concerned. Unpopular as a man, he was an effective figurehead and a magnet for national loyalty against the troublesome background of Jacobite rebellion.

FIRST HANOVERIAN *George I suffered from chronic shyness. He hated all ceremony that made him the centre of attention.*

Jacobite scheme abruptly collapsed when Louis XIV died in August. With his death hope of French support for an invasion vanished.

Too little and too late

Such was the bleak background against which Mar left France to raise that ominous standard in Scotland on September 6. He had no difficulty in winning the Highlands to the Jacobite cause, for there loyalty to the exiled Stuarts had remained firm. But in every other respect the whole strategy of the rebellion went wildly astray.

Only in the north of England was there any popular response to the call for revolt; and even this was confined to a few half-hearted and badly led men who were easily dealt with by the government. As one rebel wrote: 'That party, who are never right hearty for the Cause till they are mellow over a bottle or two demonstrated that they did not care for venturing their carcases further than the tavern.'

On November 13 came the first real test for Mar's Scottish army – it was a test it did not surmount. At Sheriffmuir, near Perth, Mar's 10,000 men met a much smaller loyalist force commanded by the Duke of Argyll. Though the fighting itself was inconclusive, the result was a Jacobite defeat. For Mar was forced to retreat into the city of Perth, there to remain helpless and inactive while Argyll's army was swollen by reinforcements.

On December 22, James arrived in Scotland, landing at Peterhead in a fishing boat. He was ill with a fever, and cut a depressing figure for a leader. 'For me,' he said to his comrades, 'it is no new thing to be unfortunate, since my whole life from my cradle has been a constant series of misfortunes.'

James was both too late and too gloomy to revive his dispirited followers in Perth. In February 1716, the ruthless General Cadogan took over the command of the English army. The Jacobites lost their nerve and retreated into the Highlands, disfiguring their cause with pointless atrocities, and gradually disintegrating. Their enterprise was doomed. James, Mar and other leaders took ship for France and safety. But their followers were not so fortunate. By April the revolt had been crushed. Two rebel leaders were executed, others lost their estates and titles and some were exiled – all of them victims of the folly of the prince for whom they had risked so much.

GEORGIAN ELEGANCE CREATES A CITY MADE FOR PLEASURE

From 1702 onwards, the old Roman city of Bath underwent a meteoric rise to become the most fashionable and popular leisure resort in Georgian England. For over 50 years Bath reigned as the unchallenged summer capital of aristocratic society, dictating modes of dress, behaviour and good taste. Men and women of fashion and wit flocked to the town to take its famous waters, to gossip, to match-make, to see – and be seen.

The town, in its turn, put on a new face in keeping with its important new role. Almost completely rebuilt in the 18th century, it became famous for its early town planning, with its beautiful crescents and terraces and its superbly restrained and graceful public buildings. No other 18th-century city can equal its unity of architectural design.

Two factors combined to give Bath its special social appeal. The first was the hot mineral springs which gush out 250,000 gallons of water a day, heated to a constant 49°C. (120°F.). The second was the personality of one man – Richard 'Beau' Nash, a gambler who became Bath's uncrowned 'king'.

Ruled by one man

Born in Swansea of a poor middle-class family, Nash was a failed scholar, soldier and lawyer who excelled in only one area – the organisation of social ceremonies. He first became aide-de-camp to the then Master of Ceremonies, a Captain Webster, and when Webster was killed in a duel over a game of cards, Nash was his natural successor. He began a reign that transformed Bath from a provincial town into a fashionable centre unequalled in England.

Nash began by dressing the part, adopting an exaggerated elegance which soon earned him the nickname Beau. Instead of the popular white wigs of the times, he wore a black one topped with a jewelled cream beaver hat set at a rakish angle. His coat, decorated with braid and lace, was left open to show his embroidered waistcoat and ruffled shirt.

But those who dismissed Beau Nash as a mere fop were soon surprised. Nash showed his practical mind by supervising the paving, lighting and cleaning of the streets, punishing the insolence of sedan chair-carriers and driving beggars and thieves out of the city.

He also encouraged the wealthy men of Bath to put up new buildings, and himself initiated the building of the Pump Room, overlooking the King's Bath, where the company could assemble to gossip, and the Assembly Rooms, with a large, handsome ballroom and adjoining card room.

In both these buildings his word was law. He laid down a rigidly enforced code of be-haviour. He ridiculed the wearing of riding boots at fashionable gatherings, often asking the offender if he had 'forgot his horse'. Even royalty quailed before his frown – Princess Amelia, daughter of George II, was curtly refused one more dance after Nash had decreed the music should stop.

His twice-weekly balls in the Assembly Rooms were imitated throughout the country. The playwright Oliver Goldsmith wrote of them: 'The order, the decorum, the measured pomp, that distinguished the festivities of Bath were the pride and boast of the nation.'

Nash also forbade the wearing of swords. Bath became famous as the 'swordless city', prompting Richard Sheridan to write in *The Rivals*, a play set in the city: 'A sword seen in the streets of Bath would raise as great an alarm as a mad dog.'

The visitors' daily routine was a regimented one, beginning with bathing between 6 a.m. and 9 a.m. and followed by a general assembly in the Pump Room for gossip, three glasses of warm water and music. A public breakfast usually followed before the visitors returned in a sedan chair to their lodgings to change for a service in the abbey.

A late lunch, then another visit to the Pump Room and perhaps a walk filled in the afternoon, while evenings were spent at a ball, the theatre or the gambling table.

Two architects of genius

Under Nash's reign, Bath grew so prosperous that young men flocked there to seek their fortune. Some, like Ralph Allen, a Cornishman, and John Wood, a Yorkshireman, helped to change the face of Bath. Allen devised a way of exploiting the rich stone quarries outside Bath: Wood, and later his son, used the golden stone to cover Bath and its encircling hills in a succession of fine Palladian buildings.

Wood built for Allen his great mansion of Prior Park, a magnificent collonaded building set in terraces and landscaped gardens and made of Bath stone; built partly as an advertisement for the stone which was not then highly regarded.

In 1725 Wood devised a grand plan to develop the city in two parts, each with a central circus for sports, a royal forum for assemblies and an assortment of squares. The scheme was too ambitious for the corporation, and Wood set about building as much as he could privately. In 1727 he moved permanently to Bath, and lived there until his death 27 years later.

Queen Square, which took six years to build, was a perfect example of Wood's concept of a planned layout, with all the houses constructed of the same stone and built in the same proportions. He built a grand palace façade on the north side, with simpler houses on the south. On the slope at the east the houses followed a gently climbing pattern, and on the west were three large separate houses.

Wood then built a series of houses and buildings along what he termed 'parades', where the owners could walk and look out to views of the city or the countryside. He died, however, before he could finish his greatest project, the Circus, and it was left to his son, John Wood the Younger, to complete it. He faithfully followed his father's blue-print, right down to the exact number of magnificent coupled columns on the houses – 324 pairs in all. It was finally completed in 1765.

The young John Wood also contributed a pioneering architectural innovation to Bath – and to Britain. West of the Circus, he built an

CITY OF BEAUTY *An early-19th-century engraving shows Bath's spectacular beauty. The creation of this Georgian city was largely the work of two architects, John Wood the Elder and his son. They gave the city such masterpieces as the Circus, the Assembly Rooms and the Royal Crescent. Among other great 18th-century architects to work in the city was Robert Adam.*

incomparable ring of houses, facing on to a paved centre and overlooking the common. This was the Royal Crescent – the first to be built in the world.

So popular was the style of architecture created by the Woods that soon half a dozen other architects adopted the Palladian style and the use of golden Bath stone. Others such as the fashionable London architect Robert Adam, who designed the charming Pulteney Bridge inspired by Florence's Ponte Vecchio, brought new, complementary styles to the city.

Beau Nash, whose reign in Bath had inspired its new elegant look, died in 1761 at the age of 87 before many of its famous buildings were completed. The city whose life he had ruled for so long did not forget him. He was given a lavish funeral and a handsome memorial in the abbey. Goldsmith wrote: 'The whole kingdom became more refined by lessons originally derived from him.'

Bath continued as a popular resort throughout the rest of the century although its position of dominance was no longer unchallenged. Cheltenham and then Brighton rose to become rival centres. But although the world of fashion passed, it left behind in Bath an enduring monument to a unique age of elegance.

FOCAL POINT *The Pump Room, centre of life in Bath, was built immediately over the Roman reservoir into which gush the curing springs. Here people assembled to drink the waters.*

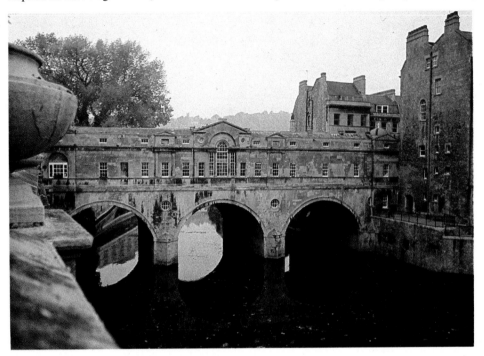

ITALIAN INFLUENCE *Pulteney Bridge was designed by Robert Adam in 1771, after the style of the Ponte Vecchio in Florence. It carries a broad carriageway with shops on either side, and was named after William Pulteney, an influential statesman, who became Earl of Bath.*

INSPIRED BY ROME *The superb Circus, planned by the elder Wood and completed by his son in 1765, has 30 houses built round a paved open space – inspired by the Colosseum in Rome.*

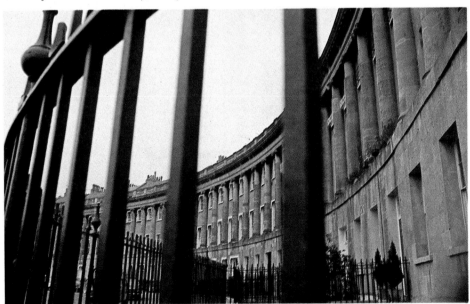

PALLADIAN MASTERPIECE *The Royal Crescent, often called the 'finest crescent in Europe', was built by John Wood the Younger between 1767 and 1775. The design was deeply influenced by the Classical style of imperial Rome and ancient Greece. It represented the summit of architectural achievement in Bath's hey-day as the fashionable haunt of the rich and powerful in the 18th century.*

MEETING PLACE *The Assembly Rooms, opened in 1771, were designed by John Wood the Younger. Here society met to breakfast, make new acquaintances and hear music or lectures. It was also the scene of magnificent balls.*

An English squire becomes the first Prime Minister

WALPOLE'S BIRTHPLACE
Sir Robert Walpole, a country squire and reckless spender, was born at Houghton Hall, Norfolk, which had been in his family for generations. At his death, he left debts of almost £40,000. But he saw little evidence of wealth during a childhood plagued by ill-health. His father only gave him 2s 6d pocket money a year.

Sir Robert Walpole, for 21 years the leader of England's government, was a politician of such overwhelming stature that he has become famous as 'the first Prime Minister'. The title itself was unknown in Walpole's lifetime, but this brilliant man forged the reality of the office from the turbulent stream of parliamentary politics. The title is a tribute to qualities of statesmanship and character that have rarely been equalled in England's history.

Throughout his life, Walpole was driven on by an inexhaustible personal dynamism, a thrusting urge for individual power. Yet for all his immense ambition and his exceptional talents and energy, he never lost touch with the feelings of the common people. Physically he was large and ungainly, given to enormous meals and long bouts of drinking. Many of his bills still survive and they show that in one year alone he spent at least £1500 on wines, equivalent to nearly £15,000 today. He also had a weakness for chocolates, which he bought by the hundredweight. He paid more for them than he did for his three footmen in a year. His other pleasures were equally gross: he was lecherous, coarse, fond of vulgar display, bewitched by money and extravagant possessions, inordinately proud of himself. In an age of fixed rank and hierarchy, he was a self-made man, and he basked in his success.

At his home, Houghton Hall in Norfolk, Walpole boasted that 'he always talked bawdy, because in that all men could join'. It was said

that throughout his life he looked first at his bailiff's reports on hunting and local news from his Norfolk estate, before turning to his official correspondence.

But mentally, Walpole was the reverse of crude. He had a powerful, incisive intellect, and an enormous capacity for hard work. An acute judge of character, he had a deep power of insight into other people's minds and emotions. This served him well – especially in his valuable friendship with George II's wife, Queen Caroline.

'All those men have their price'
In the 18th century, political conditions encouraged the lowest standards of behaviour: a man might make both career and fortune if he were only unprincipled enough. And Walpole knew precisely how to exploit this lust for easy power and money. He himself remarked of his followers, 'All those men have their price'. And, when his skill as a parliamentarian was not enough to win all the support he needed, he did not hesitate to bribe – though rarely with straight cash.

Walpole himself was not immune to the temptations of money. In 1720 he had succumbed, with thousands of others, to the speculative craze of the notorious South Sea Bubble. He made 1000 per cent profit on his investment. And because he was less compromised by the scandal than many in the government, Walpole managed to wriggle clear when the bubble burst, with his public

prestige intact. And this dubious episode proved the turning-point in his career. For Walpole was one of the few men free enough – or so the public believed – from the taint of corruption to take on, at the age of 45, the vacant government posts of Chancellor of the Exchequer and First Lord of the Treasury. From these two offices, Walpole was to create a Prime Minister's supremacy.

Until 1742, Walpole remained a giant on the political stage, effortlessly out-topping all rivals. His luck in 1721 was to find an England which had been raised, by his predecessors over the past two decades, to a new height of security and prestige in Europe. On this solid foundation, Walpole was able to construct his own policies of peace and prosperity. By upbringing a country squire, he treated England much like his own estate – fostering her wealth, avoiding the disruption and expense of war. His proud boast to Queen Caroline in 1734, a year of European turmoil, was, 'Madam, there are 50,000 men slain this year in Europe, and not one Englishman'.

'This dance it will no further go'
But so ruthless and arrogant was Walpole behind his bluff façade, and so shameless was his love of power and wealth that he soon became the most hated man in England. A mixed opposition of Tories and rebel Whigs had sought his scalp for years without success. Then, suddenly, in 1733, Walpole gave a hostage to fortune.

At this time, governments raised most of their revenue by taxing land. As a landowner himself, Walpole had long hoped to relieve his fellow squires of this burden. Instead he planned to rely on raising the taxes on the goods which everyone bought. And, because the existing customs duties at the ports yielded such a poor return – a third of them were evaded by massive smuggling – 'inland duties' seemed the answer.

Walpole's Excise Scheme of 1733 was designed to bring this strategy to fruition. By putting two major imports, tobacco and wine, straight into 'Bonded' warehouses, freeing them from customs, but subjecting them to a stiff excise if taken out for home consumption, Walpole could raise enough money to justify abolishing direct taxation outright.

On March 14, 1733, Walpole fired the first shot in what he was confident would be a triumphant battle. For years the government's majority had been cast-iron. The arguments for the Tobacco Bill seemed unanswerable.

But the Opposition was not interested in argument – only in emotion, prejudice and political advantage. For months, their pamphleteers and cartoonists, and their brilliant journal, *The Craftsman*, had carried on a publicity campaign of genius. The rumour had been fostered that Walpole was bent on taxing every necessity of life.

The Opposition's bogy-man was the excise

officer. To prevent evasion, local excise officers needed the power of search to ensure that no dutiable goods had slipped through the net. It proved easier than Walpole had imagined to convince his countrymen that this fore-shadowed a terrifying abuse of government authority. No man's house or goods would be safe. Trade would die. A vast bureaucracy would overturn the constitution.

Fired by this scurrilous but persuasive campaign, the people reacted with fear and fury. As Parliament debated the scheme, it was showered with petitions and protests – especially from London and other ports. Vicious cartoons were on display everywhere. The streets of London were decorated with posters, depicting such popular themes as the 'Vampire Excise' sucking greedily at the people's blood.

The mob ruled the streets, and even Walpole himself was manhandled. But though he was contemptuous of the clamour, his majorities gradually dwindled. At the end of four weeks,

he was left with the choice of abandoning the plan or losing power. Calling his supporters together, he told them, 'with a sort of un-pleased smile', that 'This dance it will no further go'. Walpole had acknowledged defeat.

Walpole's retreat, however, was planned and masterly. Though he had to shelve his cherished scheme and had the humiliation of seeing himself burnt in effigy, he recovered his majority and remained in office.

War – the final blow
But, in 1739, popular fervour forced Walpole to declare war on Spain. For Walpole, war spelt personal defeat: it was the collapse of all he had striven for. As he observed bitterly to the Duke of Newcastle, who led the anti-Spanish party in the cabinet, 'It is your war, and I wish you well of it'.

Walpole was no wartime leader, and in February 1742 he resigned. His era had passed; but it had been unmistakably his own.

George II: A king who knew his proper place

DOMINATED KING *When George II came to the throne he was expected to dismiss Walpole. His forceful wife, Queen Caroline, changed his mind.*

As far as most Englishmen were concerned, George II was not much of an improvement on his father. He, too, was born in Hanover, often absent there, and by no means fluent in English. Ribald placards posted on his palace of St James's testified to popular opinion: 'Lost or strayed out of this house, a man who left a wife and six children on the parish: whoever will give tidings of him shall receive four shillings and sixpence.'

A dapper little man, with a red face and bulging eyes, he had a Germanic passion for method. Business or pleasure – all had to conform to a strict routine, and he was often to be found outside his mistress's room, watch in hand, waiting for the hour of nine to strike.

Yet George did have some qualities which set him well above his father. George I had thought three hours a good day's work, but George II was a hard worker, with a pheno-menal memory, an eye for detail and an insight into European affairs. Most of all, he had in Queen Caroline a wife of lively intelli-gence and forceful character, who remained the power behind the throne until her death. According to Walpole, the king was 'for all his personal bravery as great a political coward as ever wore a crown and as much afraid to lose it'.

While Walpole and Caroline ruled, George himself took a back seat in government. Later, when forced to be more independent, George showed himself to be a man of quick temper and foul tongue. William Pitt the Elder in particular often aroused his anger. George never forgave him for his description of Hanover as 'that despicable Electorate'. The king hated to be ruled by the decisions of 'that d—d House of Commons'. But, quarrelsome and obstinate though he seemed, George played by the rules of the day. His saving virtue was that – as when he called the hated Pitt to high office – he knew 'when to sacrifice his private inclination to public interest'.

BRITAIN'S COLOSSUS *A satirical engraving of the time quoted from Shakespeare's* Julius Caesar *to describe Sir Robert Walpole: 'Why man, he doth bestride the narrow world like a Colossus; and we petty men walk under his huge legs and peep about to find ourselves dishonourable graves.'*

A COCKNEY REVEALS THE HEART OF GEORGIAN LONDON

In the mid-18th century London was a sprawling metropolis: crowded, disorderly, vigorous and often violent. Its vitality and wealth attracted talented men from all over the country. Its 600,000 people lived in extremes of sordid poverty and fabulous wealth.

This was the London in which William Hogarth was born and lived. Its glories and its miseries inspired him to paint – as no other artist had ever done before – a complete picture of his age. Sometimes satirical, sometimes tender, his incisive mind swept aside the polished veneer of Georgian life to express the full-bloodedness of the times and the passion and turbulence which lay underneath.

Born in Smithfield Market in 1697, Hogarth rarely left the city he so brilliantly portrayed. His training came not from study abroad but from his apprenticeship to a silver engraver

at the age of 15. By the time he was 20 he owned his own business. At 24 he had won full recognition. This success came from satirical engravings he made for sale at a shilling a copy.

Hogarth's wit was also appreciated by fashionable society, but it saw him more as a caricaturist than an artist. Hogarth, though, was determined to be taken seriously. He enrolled at an art school to learn oil painting. But this came to an abrupt end when he eloped with Jane, the beautiful 20-year-old daughter of his teacher, Sir James Thornhill.

With a wife to support, Hogarth turned to painting small 'conversation pieces' – informal family groups, which were then the vogue. He also found inspiration in the theatrical productions of his day. A scene from *The Beggar's Opera*, a lively work about pimps,

SELF PORTRAIT *Hogarth painted himself surrounded by cultural works by Shakespeare, Swift and Milton – and his pet dog, Pug.*

SOCIAL DRAMA *Hogarth won popularity and fame with his moral dramas – the series of paintings which exposed the follies of his time. In 'Marriage à la Mode', a dissolute noble and a rich girl contract a loveless marriage. It ends with her suicide (above) after the death of her husband and lover.*

prostitutes and thieves which had enraptured London, and his portrait of one of the great actors of the day – 'David Garrick as Richard III' – won him great success.

This interest in the theatre inspired him with an idea which was to give rise to some of his most brilliant works. He decided to present London life in dramatic terms, using his art to make 'scenes' and tell stories.

Hogarth had hit upon an art form which would take full advantage of his curiously varied qualities – his simple moral sense, his affectionate but deeply sceptical attitude to his fellow Londoners, and his ribald wit. In addition, his artistic skill was now at its peak and his four great 'morality plays', each in six or eight scenes, reveal his complete mastery of colour and form and his fantastic powers of invention. Each little detail of these crowded pictures contributes to the whole – and helps in the telling of their sad and sardonic stories.

The first, 'A Harlot's Progress', warned of the perils that could befall a young girl coming to London, her corruption by society and her eventual downfall. In 'A Rake's Progress' Hogarth turned to the themes of extravagance and dissipation. 'Marriage à la Mode,' probably his greatest achievement, attacked the evils of an arranged marriage, while 'Election', based on an actual election in Oxfordshire in 1754, vividly portrayed the debased state of English political life.

An artistic tradition

Pugnacious and combative by nature, Hogarth always felt that he had been denied his due honour as a serious artist. Ironically, this sense of injury probably helped to intensify his gifts as a satirist.

In 1754 he painted a self-portrait in which he included the works of Shakespeare, Swift and Milton – a demonstration of his literary tastes and his claim to rank with the great. But, characteristically, he showed he was not quite serious by including a handsome portrait of his dog, Pug.

Critical of London though he may have been, Hogarth was an intensely loyal man. His critical sense stemmed from a genuine desire to reform the city he loved, and he spent endless time and money managing various charities, particularly orphanages and hospitals.

His patriotism also expressed itself in his wish to establish English art and English artists in a world which assumed that only foreigners could paint. His own work, so firmly founded in the everyday reality of English life, proved once and for all that the English scene can be the stuff of artistic genius.

In this aggressive self-confidence, he laid the foundations for a national school of British art. In the next generation the great work was carried forward by Sir Joshua Reynolds, with the foundation of the Royal Academy, and by the triumphant and wholly English genius of George Stubbs and Thomas Gainsborough.

PAINTING FOR PLEASURE *The glowing oil painting 'The Shrimp Girl' was in Hogarth's studio when he died. Painted for his own pleasure, it reveals his humanity. After his death in 1764, his wife showed the picture to visitors with the comment: 'There's flesh and blood for you.'*

SATIRICAL ART *Hogarth's 'Chairing the Member' lampooned the election system. His fortune was based on the sale of the engravings he made of his pictures. An engraving cost a shilling a copy.*

233

So near but yet so far – the tragedy of the '45

GATHERING OF THE CLANS

Some 700 Cameron clansmen, the nucleus of an army which was to sweep to within 130 miles of London, rallied to Bonnie Prince Charlie's standard on August 19, 1745. A monument on the banks of Loch Shiel, in Glenfinnan, commemorates their gathering.

HIGHLANDERS' DEFEAT *Nine months after he landed in Scotland to claim the throne of Britain, Bonnie Prince Charlie, seen above in a detail from a contemporary portrait, was decisively defeated by a Hanoverian army on Culloden Moor on April 16, 1746. It was a one-sided battle. The Highlanders were outnumbered two to one, and an early artillery barrage decimated their ranks. Then the Highland charge, previously the terror of English troops, was broken by specially developed new tactics. A vivid impression (detail below) was painted shortly after the battle by David Morier.*

Charles Edward Louis Philip Casimir Stuart, 25-year-old son and heir of the Old Pretender, crossed the River Esk into England on November 8, 1745. Largely on his own eager initiative, he had embarked on a venture which was viewed with grave misgivings by some of his advisers, and with uneasiness by the army of 5000 Highlanders who were accompanying him so far from their native glens.

Yet the prince's confidence was understandable. The fiasco of his father's failure lay 30 years behind, and 'Bonnie Prince Charlie' was a figure of a quite different stamp from the moody and uninspiring James. He was a leader in reality as well as name, a brave fighter and a tireless soldier.

In the months that had already passed since his landing in the Hebrides on July 25, the prince had achieved wonders that augured well for the success of his expedition. He had arrived with only a handful of companions, with little money and few arms. But the clansmen flocked to Charles's standard, raised in Glenfinnan on August 19, 1745.

Marching south towards England
In this month, Charles's men marched southwards to Perth and Edinburgh, where Charles was proclaimed king. The English were not idle, however. Under General 'Johnny' Cope, a force of some 3000 men was massing east of Edinburgh to deal with Charles and his followers. But when the two armies clashed at Prestonpans on September 21, the Highlanders' charge was more than the English could face. 'The panic terror of the English surpassed all imagination,' wrote a participant. 'They threw down their arms that they might run with more speed.'

It was in this moment of national danger, that the actors at the Drury Lane Theatre, in London, added a new song to their programme on September 28. It was 'God Save the King'. For, when Charles crossed the border, only a hastily assembled force under General Wade obstructed his path south. Easily skirting round Wade and his men, Charles took the road to London.

At first all went well. There was surprisingly little panic as the Jacobites advanced. One observer described them as 'those shabby, scabby, scratchy, lowly, shitten rebels'. Many, however, of the well-to-do went to earth with their silver as news came in that Preston had been taken on November 27, Manchester on November 29, and Derby on December 4.

From Derby to London was a mere 130 miles, and the capital was briefly seized by intense terror on the 'black Friday' after Derby's fall. George II himself had the royal yacht made ready to take him to the Continent. But the prince's success was more apparent than real. Neither the expected French invasion, nor spontaneous Jacobite risings in England had taken place – no more than 300 Englishmen had enlisted with Charles. Wade's army was now a formidable force in Charles's rear; the ruthless Duke of Cumberland, recalled from Flanders, was in Staffordshire with 8000 men.

Retreat and disaster
Each step south now took the rebels further from their base, further from any reinforcements. To go beyond Derby was to invite destruction. Even as Londoners panicked, a Jacobite council of war recommended retreat, and Charles, in anguish, had to agree. On December 20 his army recrossed the border with Cumberland's troops in hot pursuit.

Back in the Highlands, the prince restored his numbers and his side's morale with local victories over government garrisons. But this was no permanent answer. The Jacobites were weary, demoralised, unpaid and facing an army almost twice their size.

On April 16, Charles decided to attack Cumberland's men on Culloden Moor. The plan was daring but ill-advised, for Cumberland had devised a new tactic to cope with the Highland charge. Instead of attacking the Scotsman in front of him, each Redcoat soldier bayoneted the exposed side of the Scotsman to the right. The English lost only 76 men to the 1200 of the Highlanders.

The clans never recovered from this bloody battle. Within 20 years the old clan system was dead, and Jacobitism had evaporated into a mere romantic dream.

Royal fugitive – with a price on his head

After the terrible day of slaughter at Culloden in April 1746, Prince Charles Edward fled westwards with a small band of followers. For the next five months he was to roam through the Highlands and islands. By horse, by boat, but chiefly on foot, he passed from one helping hand to another, with a price of £30,000 on his head.

First came ten dismal weeks in the Hebrides, flitting from island to island and back again, a naval patrol at his heels. There were nights spent at sea, others in the open fields. Exposure and privation made him 'ill-coloured, and overrun with the scab'.

By July, Charles was back on the mainland. In the next two months his desperate search for safety took him north as far as Glen Affrick, south to Ben Alder. His cheerless shelters – byres, caves, woods, mountaintops – pepper the Highlands. He must have walked hundreds of miles, but he bore his trials gallantly, whistling the Highland airs which, like his Gaelic phrases and his whisky bottle, endeared him to the clans.

These remained superlatively loyal, scorning the huge reward and risking life itself to preserve their beloved leader. At last, on September 19, Charles boarded a French ship to sail to safety. The 14 months of his great adventure were over. He lived for another 42 years, but slowly degenerated into a rambling drunkard. As he himself said: 'I should have died with my men at Culloden.'

ROMANTIC PRINCE

Bonnie Prince Charlie had the natural stamp of a romantic hero. He possessed not only good looks, but a personal charm and magnetism which his father had completely lacked. He was athletic, a golfer and an expert with the crossbow. He played the violin well and loved dancing. The Battle of Culloden Moor was a crushing military defeat, but it failed to destroy the legend of the dashing prince who had come so close to winning the throne for the Stuarts.

The romance was strengthened by the reign of terror conducted by the 'Butcher' Duke of Cumberland against the clans after the battle, and by the daring adventure of the prince's five months as a fugitive from the Hanoverian forces. This 'secret portrait' of him, a smudge which only takes shape when reflected on a curved cylinder, is an example of how his legend was kept alive through his years of exile from his 'lost kingdom'.

THE FRIENDSHIP WHICH GAVE DR JOHNSON IMMORTAL FAME

MAN OF LETTERS *Samuel Johnson, clumsy and uncouth, but one of the great minds of his age, was already a legend when he met Boswell.*

On Monday, May 16, 1763, one of the most momentous meetings in the history of English literature took place in a Covent Garden bookseller's back-parlour. James Boswell, an aspiring young author, was drinking tea with the bookseller, Tom Davies, and his wife, when Davies suddenly caught sight of Samuel Johnson through the glass door.

He 'announced his awful approach to me', wrote Boswell of the meeting, 'somewhat in the manner of an actor in the part of Horatio, when he addresses Hamlet on the appearance of the ghost'.

Johnson was 53, and already a legend. Author of the famous *Dictionary*, he was celebrated for his caustic wit and eccentric personal appearance. Boswell, a diminutive Scotsman, was only 22, brash and ambitious, and determined while in London to cultivate the English literary scene.

Boswell's opening gambit was inauspicious:

'Mr Davies mentioned my name...I was much agitated; and recollecting his prejudice against the Scotch...I said to Davies, "Don't tell him where I come from" – "From Scotland," cried Davies roguishly. "Mr Johnson," (said I) "I do indeed come from Scotland, but I cannot help it." I am willing to flatter myself that I meant this as a light pleasantry. But however that might be, this speech was somewhat unlucky; for with that quickness of wit for which he was so remarkable, he retorted, "That Sir, I find, is what a very great many of your countrymen cannot help." This stroke stunned me a good deal...'

When Johnson followed this snub with a second scathing remark, Boswell felt 'much mortified', but he 'remained upon the field . . . not wholly discomfited'.

It was difficult to deter Boswell and after this first meeting he soon summed up courage to call on Johnson in his 'uncouth' London rooms behind Fleet Street.

This time he was given an extremely amiable reception. 'Give me your hand,' Johnson requested as he bade the young man goodbye, 'I have a liking to you.'

No less likely friendship has existed in the history of English literature. Samuel Johnson came from the provincial middle-classes. His father, Michael, was a struggling bookseller in Lichfield, Staffordshire, who married late, and their first and only child, Samuel, at birth was a sickly, weak child. His wife was to describe him later as 'lean and lanky...with the scars of the scrofula deeply visible', and suffering from 'convulsive starts and gesticulations'.

Hampered by illness and lack of money, he was forced to leave Pembroke College, Oxford, after four terms to earn his living. In 1735 he married Elizabeth Porter, a widow 20 years older than himself, who brought him a small dowry, and he subsisted, until the publication of his great *Dictionary* in 1755, by teaching and journalism. He claimed that 'no man but a blockhead ever wrote, except for money'.

The *Dictionary* brought Johnson fame, and the final satisfaction of an honorary degree at Oxford. In 1762 he was awarded a royal pension of £300.

The Scot and the doctor

James Boswell, on the other hand, came from a long line of Lowland gentry. He was son and heir to Lord Auchinleck, a stern and unsympathetic Scottish law-lord, who thought his eldest son feckless, foolish and extravagant.

Boswell was indeed much given to dissipation and debauchery. He was a volatile character, whose moods quickly swung from riotous gaiety to black gloom.

In Johnson he found the second father, guide, protector and spiritual counsellor he had been seeking since childhood. He also found the subject which was to give purpose to his life. The book, the *Life of Samuel Johnson*, with which he crowned their friendship, has been acknowledged as one of the finest biographies in the English language.

Johnson was deeply affectionate and loyal to his friends. 'A man, Sir, should keep his friendship in constant repair,' he wrote, and he loved his fellow human beings, though he frequently derided and often abused them. He was an endless, indefatigable talker, often staying up until the small hours of the morning. 'There is in the world,' he declared, 'no

---

JOHNSON'S MEMORIAL

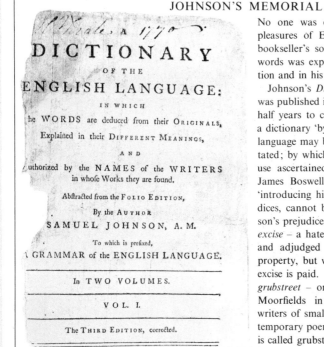

GREATEST ACHIEVEMENT *Title page of Johnson's* Dictionary. *The work took nearly nine years to compile. It revealed many of his prejudices, but brought him fame and a modest fortune.*

No one was ever more intoxicated with the pleasures of English than Samuel Johnson, a bookseller's son from Lichfield. His delight in words was expressed in a life-time of conversation and in his great *Dictionary*.

Johnson's *Dictionary of the English Language* was published in 1755, and took him eight and a half years to compile. His aim was to produce a dictionary 'by which the pronunciation of our language may be fixed, and its attainment facilitated; by which its purity may be preserved, its use ascertained, and its duration lengthened'. James Boswell wrote that Johnson's habit of 'introducing his own opinions, and even prejudices, cannot be fully defended'. Among Johnson's prejudices were:

excise – a hateful tax levied upon commodities, and adjudged not by the common judges of property, but wretches hired by those to whom excise is paid.

grubstreet – originally the name of a street in Moorfields in London; much inhabited by writers of small histories, dictionaries, and contemporary poems: whence any mean production is called grubstreet.

network – anything reticulated or decussated at equal distances, with interstices between the intersections.

oats – a grain, which in England is generally given to horses, but in Scotland supports the people.

pension – an allowance made to anyone without an equivalent – in England generally understood to mean pay given to a state hireling for treason to his country.

LONDON RISES TO HONOUR THE 'HALLELUJAH CHORUS'

BIOGRAPHER *James Boswell produced the great* Life of Samuel Johnson, *but died four years later, haunted by a sense of personal failure.*

real delight (excepting those of sensuality), but the exchange of ideas in conversation.'

During the 21 years of their friendship, these conversations were meticulously recorded by Boswell in the frank journals which he used later as the source books of his great biography.

In 1773 Boswell persuaded Johnson to accompany him on a walking tour of the Hebrides, despite the fact that Johnson loved London and detested Scotland, which he saw as '. . . a most dolorous country'.

His worst fears were realised: there was dried haddock for breakfast, the windows would not open, and the country 'grew more stoney, and continued naked of all vegetable decoration . . . an eye accustomed to flowery pastures and waving harvests is astonished and repelled by this wide extent of hopeless sterility'.

Through storm and discomfort Johnson was mainly philosophical, but he became moody when he lost his large oak walking-stick: 'It is not to be expected that any man in Mull, who has got it, will part with it. Consider, Sir, the value of such a *piece of timber* here!'

The victim of asthma and dropsy, Johnson's last illness was long and painful, but he refused to take opiates because he had prayed he might render his soul to God unclouded. He died in 1784 and was buried in Westminster Abbey.

Memorial of a friendship

Boswell never recovered from his friend's death. His drinking and debauchery became increasingly uncontrollable. However, by an extraordinary act of self-will, he forced himself to complete his *Life of Samuel Johnson*, which came out in 1791, and was immediately acclaimed a masterpiece.

Johnson had put the best part of his genius into his conversation. Boswell's great book rescued these brilliant conversations for posterity and provided the world with a record of a strange and fruitful friendship.

In the 18th century, London's artistic life achieved a sophistication it had not reached before. Painters like William Hogarth and writers such as Dr Samuel Johnson and the satirist Dean Swift were the leaders of a brilliant society. And to their number was added one of the greatest composers of the day – George Frederick Handel.

Handel was born in 1685 in the town of Halle in Saxony, where his father was the local barber and surgeon. Handel did not come from a musical family. His father intended him to become a lawyer, and the infant composer used to practise secretly on a clavichord in the attic while his parents slept. But he eventually won the right to follow a musical career.

From opera to oratorio

Handel settled in London in 1712, but two years after his arrival, the accession of George of Hanover to the English throne placed Handel in an awkward predicament. He had neglected his duties as court composer at Hanover, and the king was displeased. But he won his way back to favour by composing a suite of instrumental pieces, 'The Water Music', to accompany the royal family's progress by barge down the Thames from Whitehall to Limehouse. George was delighted; he welcomed Handel at the new court, and increased his royal pension by £200 a year. In England, Handel's early reputation was largely based on the Italian-style operas he wrote for the London stage. For a while this form of opera was all the rage, and the composer made a for-

tune. But even at the height of his operatic success, he was not without rivals – the chief of whom was the Italian Bononcini. The poet John Byrom wrote an epigram which was typical of the reaction of the time:

Some say, compared to Bononcini
That Mynheer Handel's but a ninny
Others aver, that he to Handel
Is scarcely fit to hold a candle.
Strange all this difference should be
'Twixt Tweedle-dum and Tweedle-dee!

In the end, it was a change in fashion rather than anything else which ended Handel's operatic enterprise. And though its collapse brought him ill-health and financial difficulties, it led him to devote his talents to a new field, the composing of the great religious works which were to win him immortality.

The series of biblical oratorios, from 'Esther' (1732) to 'Saul' (1739) and 'Israel in Egypt' (1739), culminated in his magnificent 'Messiah' which he composed in the amazingly short time of 23 days. At the first London performance in 1743, the king himself set the precedent of rising to his feet for the 'Hallelujah Chorus'.

On April 6, 1759, Handel attended a triumphal performance of 'Messiah' at Covent Garden. As the oratorio ended, he collapsed. Eight days later he died.

He had earned an honoured place in the nation he had made his own and had himself said, of the future George III, 'While that boy lives, my music will never want for a protector'. It has not wanted for a British protector since. And audiences listening to 'Messiah' today must often echo Handel's own feelings as he wrote it: 'I did think I did see all heaven before me, and the great God himself.'

HALLELUJAH! *Handel (above) directed performances of his most famous oratorio, 'Messiah', from this organ keyboard.*

Victory at Quebec wins Britain a new empire

A HERO'S RELIC

James Wolfe died from three bullet wounds as his men went on to capture Quebec. His body was brought home wrapped in his dressing-gown, now at Quebec House, Westerham, Kent.

In the middle of the 18th century, England and France were locked in a struggle that brought bloodshed and heroism to four continents. The prize at stake was not glory or prestige, nor even colonial conquest for its own sake: it was trade.

Scattered across the face of the globe were lands rich in the resources eagerly demanded by an economically expanding Europe – cotton and tea in India, slaves in Africa, sugar, tobacco and coffee in the Caribbean, fish and furs in North America. Few men were more aware of the value of trade than the British war minister, William Pitt. He was willing to subordinate all foreign policy to its demands. And few places were more crucial in Pitt's eyes than Canada – for Canada seemed the key to the commercial exploitation of the entire North American continent.

French and English interests had competed in Canada since the first settlers arrived in the 16th century. But England had carelessly thrown away her early military success there – much to the disgust of her American colonists. So, when in 1757 Pitt took over the conduct of the latest round of hostilities, the Seven Years'

War, he was determined not to let the prize slip from England's grasp again.

Whether Pitt could achieve his ambition hinged in the end on the fortunes of a remarkable expedition which crept, with infinite care, up the St Lawrence River in June 1759. Its target was the town of Quebec, 700 miles from the Atlantic Ocean, and the strategic gateway to a successful attack on Canada.

Quebec was a natural fortress which had defied a major English attack in Queen Anne's time. Many – including the French themselves – believed it to be impregnable.

The expedition's commanders were men of Pitt's own choice – young talents new to high command, and ready to rise to their leader's confidence. In charge of the 35 warships and 119 troop transports was Sir Charles Saunders, a brilliant sailor still in his mid-forties, who had once sailed round the world with the explorer Commodore Anson. The 8600 troops aboard Saunders' ships were the responsibility of an even younger leader, James Wolfe.

The great commander

Wolfe was a man born for a hero's life. In an age when advancement was so often won not by merit but by money, Wolfe had risen by his talents alone. He had been an officer at the age of 16, a captain at 17, lieutenant-colonel at 23, and now, at 32, he was a major-general. This dizzy climb to fame had brought him the enmity of less-favoured colleagues; but his own soldiers idolised him. Like many great commanders, Wolfe spared no pains to ensure the comfort of the ordinary fighting man, sharing his hardships and dangers. Although he was a man of frail constitution and gangling physique, he was full of reckless courage, tremendously energetic, agile and brimming with ideas. His temper was explosive, his aspirations boundless, his standards exacting. 'He looked upon danger,' said Horace Walpole, 'as the favourable moment that would call forth all his talents.'

Wolfe's whole attitude to soldiering was summed up in his memorable retort to a military engineer who boasted that he was 'slow and sure': 'Quick and sure, Sir – a much better maxim.' And yet this dashing soldier was also the man who admitted, on the eve of his last battle, that he would rather have penned Gray's famous *Elegy* than win a victor's crown in war.

Assisting the two leaders of the Quebec expedition was a notable array of other talents, including the young James Cook, soon to become England's most successful explorer. Cook had the task of reconnoitring the shoals

FALL OF QUEBEC *Under cover of darkness, Wolfe's troops sailed down the St Lawrence to storm the Heights of Abraham from a track up the hill-side. Within minutes the town (in the background) had fallen to Britain's Redcoats, and France's hold on Canada was broken.*

and shallows of the great river, right under the eyes of the French. The work took many months, but thanks to Cook's charts, the armada reached its destination unscathed – in itself an amazing feat of nerves and planning.

But this success was not matched elsewhere in Canada, where British armies were battling vainly against French forts and Indian warbands. Wolfe's expedition lacked the support it had relied on. The first assault on Quebec in July 1759 was a disastrous failure. Precious lives were lost; Wolfe himself fell sick with a fever; the great French general Montcalm was able to muster reinforcements and hasten to the defence of the city. On September 2, Wolfe, outnumbered and frustrated, wrote his despairing last dispatch to Pitt. He felt that his health was ruined, his expedition a failure, his career at a shameful end.

The crucial discovery

Suddenly the English had a stroke of luck which was to change their fortunes overnight. A scouting party, combing the riverbanks for a route into the citadel, made the crucial discovery: a small track led up to the Heights of Abraham overlooking the town. It was a track so sheer and narrow that the French had barely given its defence a thought. This was a vital weakness, and Wolfe used it brilliantly.

GENERAL'S DEATH *Mortally wounded as he led the attack on Quebec, James Wolfe learnt as he lay dying that victory was certain. On hearing the news he smiled and said: 'God be praised, now I can die in peace.' An eye-witness wrote: 'The smile never left his face until he died.'*

William Pitt: A genius plagued by ill-health

William Pitt, known to his contemporaries as 'the Great Commoner', was a man of deep and fertile contrasts. A grandson of a self-made magnate, 'Diamond Pitt', he was born outside the Whig aristocracy that ruled England in the 18th century. His personality was flamboyant, yet flawed by a manic instability which sometimes goes with genius.

Pitt was lonely and egotistical, and haunted by physical and mental ill-health, but he brought to politics an efficiency and honesty that set new standards in a lax and corrupt age. He was an inspired orator and England's first popular politician. He found firm support from the hard-headed businessmen whose pockets his fervent imperialism promised to line. Destructive in Opposition, he later led his country from crisis to victory.

Though Pitt entered the Commons in 1735, his rebel temperament deprived him of the highest office for 20 years. When at last he came to power, his recipe for national greatness was simple. Power came from wealth, and wealth from trade. France was England's great rival, to be driven from her trading posts abroad and swept from the seas.

In four years as war leader, Pitt smashed France's naval power and hit unerringly at her bases in India and the Americas. Horace Walpole said: 'We are forced to ask every morning what victory there has been for fear of missing one.' But in 1762 a new king, George III, decided to make peace. Pitt resigned in bitterness, his self-imposed task of saving the nation incomplete. And though he was later to recapture power, he was never again to achieve the greatness that had led his country to victory in the Seven Years' War.

ECCENTRIC GENIUS *William Pitt led Britain to victory in the Seven Years' War. But his later career was marred by outbreaks of physical ill-health, deep depression and insanity.*

Towards 2 a.m. on the morning of September 13, Wolfe's flagship, the *Sutherland*, raised the signal for the assault to begin. His 4000 troops had spent the night waiting in readiness on board the other ships; now the squadron floated noiselessly downstream with the tide, protected by a moonless sky. Challenged by a French sentry, the identity of the English force was disguised by a Highland officer who responded in fluent French.

The surprise was complete. The English swarmed up the path, and re-formed above in perfect order. When the French at last launched their counter-attack, they advanced carelessly, losing formation. Wolfe met them at the head of his men, reckless as ever.

Within minutes he had fallen, mortally wounded. An officer sought to encourage him, crying 'They run, see how they run!' 'Who runs?' demanded Wolfe, and was told: 'The enemy, Sir; Egad, they give way everywhere.' As he lay dying with victory assured, Wolfe issued a final order to cut off the French retreat. 'God be praised,' were his last words, 'now I can die in peace.'

It was a hero's death indeed, and a hero's burial at Greenwich followed. Wolfe had risen nobly to the challenge of leadership on the Heights of Abraham. His men went on to capture Quebec, and in 1760 all Canada fell to the English. Though Wolfe did not live to see it, his was the bravery that won an empire.

A NEW ART TRANSFORMS THE ENGLISH LANDSCAPE

The landed aristocracy of Georgian Britain regarded themselves as the most cultivated and educated class in the island's history. They were also perhaps the richest and most leisured. Many of them devoted their resources of time, money and educated taste to a single objective: the building of superb country houses which were to be the envy of their neighbours and the wonder of posterity.

They were not the first generation of British aristocrats to be preoccupied with the building of beautiful houses. But their aspirations went much further than even the most ambitious building schemes of their Stuart or Tudor ancestors. For the 18th-century landowner felt impelled to create not just another enormous mansion in the latest style, but a whole new landscape in which to enclose it. To fulfil the needs of these rich patrons a new kind of designer was born – the landscape gardener.

These gardeners and their patrons knew that they would seldom live to see the fulfilment of their dreams; their avenues of chestnuts and hilltop clumps of beeches took as much as a century to reach maturity. But the men of the 18th century were supremely confident that posterity would approve of all their works. Such confidence was justified; their mature gardens have won a place among Europe's supreme works of art – and no later generation has possessed the resources of patience or taste to rival their achievements.

Transforming the landscape
Of all the 18th century's many men of taste, few were more wealthy than Richard, the 1st Earl Temple, who inherited three fortunes, married into a fourth and made a fifth in politics. And of all the great estates created or improved in that century, none was more remarkable than the garden Temple brought to perfection at Stowe in Buckinghamshire. These gardens were the marvel of their age, and the men who helped in their design – William Kent, James Gibbs and Capability Brown – carried the inspiration of Stowe into countless estates in every part of England.

The work of transforming Stowe lasted for more than 50 years. It was begun by Temple's uncle, Lord Cobham, soon after he returned to England in 1715, enriched by his years as a general in Marlborough's wars and his marriage to an heiress. He employed, among others, the architect William Kent, and encouraged him to create an inspired succession of 'fantasy buildings'. To reach these carefully sited ornaments Kent laid out winding paths, and to show them to their best advantage he cleared informal vistas. In tune with the prevailing Classical mood he was trying to create,

Kent gave them such names as the Elysian Fields and the Grecian Valley.

By 1749, when Lord Temple inherited the property from his uncle, Stowe was already one of the finest country estates in the kingdom, due in the main to the labours of its head gardener, Lancelot 'Capability' Brown. Later one of the greatest landscape gardeners of his age, Brown left in 1751 to form his own business. Over the next 30 years Temple saw the fruits of Brown's years of planning and planting, the design which was to give Stowe its 'natural' grace.

Mountains of earth were moved, water courses were re-channelled, thousands of trees and shrubs were planted. An old watermill and other relics of an ancient village were demolished; the church was spared, but carefully screened from view by a dense grove of trees. Nothing was to clash with the ideal world which Temple determined to create.

An aristocrat's dream
By the time the work at Stowe had been completed, over 30 follies, temples, obelisks, ornaments and pavilions had been built and, perhaps most perfect of all, the Palladian bridge. Its proportions were designed to be seen mirrored among water-lilies, as an expression of perfect tranquillity.

But among all the attractions of Stowe, the most important was the great house itself. It had two roles to play in Temple's grand design: firstly, as the centre of the whole creation, the crowning glory of all the many views; secondly, as the main vantage point, from which the most breathtaking vistas opened out in each direction. Lord Temple was determined to give Stowe a house worthy of its surroundings. He asked Robert Adam, the greatest architect of the day, to design the South Front. The final building is an adaptation of Adam's plans.

It is this front that the visitor to Stowe sees first, framed in the Corinthian Arch, from a mile away across the lake. Its three linked pavilions in honey-coloured stone are simple enough, but the proportions are flawless. Dominating the wide landscape, they are the ultimate expression of the aristocratic ideal.

The view that unfolds from the South Front of the house, looking back towards the arch, is equally impressive. Stowe's dreaming world stretches out again, with all its individual works of art coming together as a perfectly balanced landscape. In it, even the movement of the wind in the trees, the shimmering light on the lake and the clouds in the sky seem to contribute to the ideal composition. Through this inspired union of art and nature, Stowe tells more about the tastes of the 18th century than any other house in England.

CROWNING GLORY *Determined to give Stowe a fitting house, Lord Temple himself adapted Robert Adam's designs for the South Front.*

CLASSICAL HEROES *Designed by William Kent in 1734, this temple honoured classical poets, philosophers, scholars and law-makers.*

TRIBUTE TO A QUEEN *This temple was named the Queen's Temple in gratitude to Queen Charlotte for her devoted nursing of George III in 1789.*

GARDEN ARCHITECTURE *John Vanbrugh's original Rotondo was adapted in 1721 to fit in with the fluid sweep of the newly landscaped gardens.*

THE PERFECTION OF STOWE *The superb 18th-century Palladian bridge dominates the lake in the grounds of Stowe. It is one of more than 30 works of architecture – temples, arches, follies, monuments and pavilions – all carefully positioned by the many designers who worked there.*

A SELF-MADE GENIUS

FAMOUS BRITONS *The Temple of British Worthies was built in 1735 to complement the Temple of Ancient Virtue across the river. Among the 16 busts of British celebrities are Bacon, Shakespeare and Milton.*

MEMORIAL *A monument in the grounds to the explorer Captain Cook.*

Of all the men who laboured to make Stowe the most perfect country house in England, Capability Brown (right) is the most renowned. He earned his nickname – 'Capability' – from the phrase he invariably used when looking at a garden: 'I see great capability of improvement here.'

Brown learnt his craft at Stowe, where he was made head gardener in March 1741 by Lord Cobham. He stayed on at Stowe for ten years before branching out into business on his own. He went on to transform more than 100 important gardens. Among his clients he numbered George III, for whom he worked at Kew.

Forsaking the old formal style of garden, Brown's two occupations were the provision of 'vistas' (views), and the creation of natural settings for his patrons' houses. William Cowper, the 18th-century poet, wrote of him:

The omnipotent Magician Brown appears.
He speaks; the lawn in front becomes a lake;
Woods vanish, hills subside and valleys rise
And streams – as if created for his use –
Pursue the track of his directing wand.

The concept of gardening he evolved at Stowe dominated much of the English countryside.

A SCULPTURED LANDSCAPE *Almost lost in mist, the Corinthian Arch, designed in 1765, crowns the horizon in this view looking from the house across the lake. The landscape gardeners of the time strove after a 'grand design' – a harmony between architecture and nature.*

THE AGE OF GEORGE III: 1760–1810

The 50 years of power and plenty

Victory in the Seven Years' War gives Britain mastery of the oceans and provides the impetus for Industrial Revolution

Stubborn, simple and well-meaning, the 22-year-old George III ascended the British throne in 1760, determined to follow his mother's advice to 'be a king'. He was the first British-born monarch to rule his country since 1714, and he believed that he possessed something that his two predecessors had lacked – the ability to understand the turbulent nation he had been called upon by God to lead.

In his own mind, George was convinced that his two Hanoverian predecessors, George II and George I, had been tricked by unscrupulous politicians into giving up many of the customary rights of a king. He, unlike them, had been born in England. He was determined to assert himself. And it was the Whig politicians, who had monopolised power since the Hanoverians had come to Britain in 1715, who were the targets of his hatred.

But great events far outside George's ken were now beginning to change the face of Britain. The Industrial Revolution was forcing millions into new occupations and new attitudes to their lives. Many Britons were beginning to question the established order of things and make demands for change. George, however, steadfastly set his face against reform – and in this much of the nobility followed him.

Nothing displayed the way the privileged lived more eloquently than Syon House (pp. 246–7). This was the home of the Duke of Northumberland, 'a person of extensive knowledge and correct taste', as his architect Robert Adam called him. But while Adam was creating the splendidly extravagant rooms of this mansion in Middlesex, the other England was revealing itself only a few miles away. A radical politician, John Wilkes (pp. 248–9), became the hero of the people when he defied king and court by standing up for the right of the Press to publish what it chose. Wilkes's long fight with George III and his ministers ended in an honourable draw, but not before a mob several thousand strong had rioted outside the prison where Wilkes was held

WEALTH FROM THE WORLD

East Indiamen, symbols of Britain's wealth under George III, lie at anchor at their dock in London. Their cargoes – sugar, cotton, rum, spices and tobacco – were all in great demand in mid-18th century Britain.

Britain's new wealth had largely been created by success in war. The nation's leader, Lord Chatham, taught his countrymen that trade

followed the flag. The genius of military commanders such as James Wolfe and Robert Clive had won Canada and India for the British.

Not only did these riches display themselves in houses and estates all over the country. They were also invested in the factories of the Industrial Revolution. The mastery of the seas helped make Britain the workshop of the world.

A NEW AGE *The new age of industry even utilised children in the mills and factories. But the miracles of the Industrial Revolution were enthusiastically welcomed by the British, who saw the development first of water-power and then of steam as the bringers of a new prosperity. The mill-owner Joseph Arkwright expressed this confidence when he boasted that the machine he had invented – the spinning-frame – would enable him to 'pay the National Debt'.*

TOWNS AND ROADS *The bustle of the Tottenham Court Road turnpike depicted by Rowlandson. Britain's primitive roads were ill-equipped to meet the demands of the industrial age. The late 18th century saw the beginnings of a great road-building programme to link the new cities of the Midlands and North with the capital.*

A WORLD OF ELEGANCE *For the rich, the late 18th century was an age of pleasure and elegance. The fashionable paid for their pleasures with the rents from vast acres of prosperous farmland and by shrewd investment in the new industries. However, this flamboyant display of wealth increasingly aroused the envy and the resentment of the poor, who were becoming attracted by radical ideas.*

captive. The outburst claimed 16 victims who were shot down by the government troops. This was the first stirring of discontent.

However, the real pressure for change was centred not in the capital but in the new towns springing up in the North and the Midlands. It was in George's reign that the foundations of Britain's industrial prosperity were laid. Roads that had been left unrepaired since the days of the Romans were now resurfaced. Canals, in which France had previously led the world, were built at an unprecedented speed. The first major canal (pp. 250–1) was commissioned by the Duke of Bridgewater, from the engineer James Brindley. The cost of transporting goods by canal was about one-third that of road transport. A network soon linked the new centres of industry.

With the coming of canals, new markets were open to enterprising businessmen who knew how to exploit their opportunities. Adam Smith, the first intellectual of capitalism, proclaimed the merits of the 'division of labour'. Shrewd merchants, such as Josiah Wedgwood, put Smith's theories into practice, establishing so-called 'manufactories' where primitive production lines were set up.

A slow progress towards democracy

Others found an outlet for their energies in the expanding British Empire. Victory in the Seven Years' War (1756–63) won Britain vast new territories in Canada and India. The empire now became a place where men wished to settle. Captain James Cook's great voyages of exploration in the Pacific (pp. 252–3) led the government to encourage settlement there.

Just as George III's government was starting to encourage these new settlements, it lost the oldest settlement of all. The North American colonies broke away to declare their independence in 1776. Bitter years of fighting followed. But these made little difference to the way of life in Britain itself. As the war reached its height, English painters were producing their finest work for their aristocratic patrons (pp. 254–5). In George Stubbs, Britain had a painter of horses of unequalled technical brilliance. Thomas Gainsborough applied the same acute powers of observation to his sensitive portraits of the rich and noble.

In 1781 the British surrendered at Yorktown (pp. 256–7). After this defeat, even George III recognised that victory was impossible. For George himself the blow was a bitter one. Not only was it an affront to his crown, but it was the direct result of the disastrous policies that he had obstinately pursued.

Defeat was to bring change to Britain itself. Discredited by its American policy, Lord North's government fell, and a year of crisis followed. In 1783 George resolved it by a bold stroke – he appointed Lord Chatham's 24-year-old son, William Pitt, as his Prime Minister. The appointment was ridiculed, but Pitt was to be no royal stooge. He embarked on a programme of financial reform and administrative reconstruction that was ultimately to spell the end of royal power as George III understood it.

Even Pitt found it difficult to carry his programme through when faced with determined royal obstruction. But George's patronage of the arts and sciences was more enlightened than his political policies. He commissioned the architect James Wyatt to remodel Windsor Castle in the Gothic style. He was an enthusiastic collector of books and paintings, and wrote articles about agriculture under a pseudonym. He followed his mother in encouraging the development of the botanical gardens at Kew (p. 258), where many significant advances in the scientific study of plants were made.

Such interest in scientific and technical problems was characteristic of educated Englishmen of the time. It was the common bond that united the members of the Lunar Society of Birmingham (p. 259), for example. James

Watt, a prominent member of the society, was typical of those who found a practical application for scientific knowledge. Developing and improving on the work of previous inventors, he built a revolutionary steam engine that was soon used to power the cotton-spinning factories springing up in Lancashire. The accelerating pace of industrial expansion required new fuels and new materials. Coal provided the power that turned Watt's engines. Cast iron to make the new machinery was produced in vast quantities at ironworks such as Coalbrookdale (pp. 260–1), where three generations of the Darby family were the most famous ironmasters in England.

The pace of change increases

Britain's aristocrats, however, still thought that agriculture was the only real source of wealth. Their education was based firmly on a study of Classical literature with a 'Grand Tour' of Europe as its traditional conclusion. The influence of the Classical tradition and of Italy – the centrepiece of any Grand Tour – can be seen in such great houses as Woburn Abbey in Bedfordshire (pp. 262–3), remodelled during the 1780's as a treasure house to display the magnificent collections of the wealthy dukes of Bedford.

The forces of change were given still more impetus when the French Revolution broke out in 1789. Many Britons welcomed it, and revolutionary clubs were founded in London and other cities. The ideas of the revolution struck an answering chord in the work of a new generation of poets (pp. 264–5) – Wordsworth and Coleridge, who deliberately set out to capture the authentic voice of ordinary people in their works, and Blake, whose vision made no concessions to the conventions of the day.

But the events in France – the execution of Louis XVI and his queen in the 'reign of terror', and the military menace posed by the revolutionary armies – made the rulers of Britain determined to stamp out the message of *Liberté, Egalité, Fraternité* (Liberty, Equality, Fraternity) both at home and abroad. In 1793 war broke out with France. The struggle which followed was to last – with one short break – for 23 years.

Fighting alone against revolution

As the French armies swept in their all-conquering path across Europe, Britain was left to fight alone. Invasion was the main danger, but it was overcome by the bravery and superiority of the Royal Navy. On October 21, 1805, a succession of victories was crowned by Nelson's triumph at the Battle of Trafalgar (pp. 266–9). Though Nelson himself was killed, he left his country a priceless legacy in his lasting improvements to the organisation and strategy of the Royal Navy. 'England has saved herself by her exertions,' Pitt declared after the victory, 'and will, as I trust, save Europe by her example.'

Pitt was not to see his prophecy fulfilled, for he died in the following year. Though Britain ruled the seas, France still dominated the entire continent of Europe. In 1808, however, British forces under Sir John Moore landed in Spain. Though Moore was defeated by Napoleon, his selfless bravery on the retreat to Corunna (pp. 270–1) saved his army. It was to return to drive the French from Spain and invade France itself.

The king in whose name victory was to be won was now incurably mad. For 50 years he had tried to dominate events. Though he had another ten years to live, he spent them in isolation at Windsor. Power passed to his hated eldest son who assumed the Regency. But even though George III had lost his battle to 'be a king', in his reign he had seen the foundations laid of the supremacy that was to take his country to world dominance.

THE VOICE OF THE MOB *Despite the spread of wealth, political power remained firmly in the hands of the aristocracy. The common man could only make his voice heard through violence, as in 1780 when the Gordon Riots (above) swept London. Led by Lord George Gordon, these started off as a peaceful protest against a plan to give Catholics some political rights, but they soon turned into an orgy of destruction which was only quelled by armed force.*

CONSTITUTION'S GUARDIAN *Edmund Burke, a prominent Whig, believed that the English constitution was incapable of improvement. He attacked George III for his attempts to increase royal power, and supported the American colonists.*

INTO BATTLE *The Prime Minister, William Pitt, rides George III into battle against revolution in this cartoon of 1793. In that year war broke out with revolutionary France, and a struggle began that was to last, with one short break, for 23 years. Pitt, too, had once been a reformer, but his fear of the revolutionary ideas which had overthrown the French monarchy led him to adopt a policy of repression. Measures such as the 'Gag Acts' restricted freedom of speech.*

A PALACE INSPIRED BY THE GLORY OF GREECE AND ROME

The aristocrats of George III's Britain spent fortunes on indulging their taste for flamboyant display. Riches from a newly won empire poured into their hands – together with the profits from their lands, and from the careful investments they made in the factories of the Industrial Revolution.

Inevitably, they compared themselves with the proud rulers of another empire, ancient Rome. The Romans, too, had thrived on the wealth of foreign territories, and prided themselves on the riches of their estates. The buildings which had provided a background to their lives had been made to last – and their ruined splendour provided the great inspiration of England's 18th-century aristocrats.

On their 'Grand Tours' of the Continent, young English nobles marvelled at the grave palaces and silent temples of Classical Rome. They returned with the resolution to provide their own lives with the grandeur and the beauty of a vanished imperial world.

A freshness of vision

In Britain in the 1760's an architect emerged who had the skill to exploit this demand for Classical palaces. He was Robert Adam, a man who had made his own Grand Tour, armed with a sketch book. But Adam was more than a correct follower of antique models. He was by far the most creative genius ever to work on the interiors of great houses in Britain – in such staggering displays of virtuosity and imagination as the five great reception rooms at Syon House, near London. There he evolved a style which was to revolutionise British architecture.

Robert Adam mastered the basic principles of his craft from his father, a prosperous Edinburgh architect. During his Grand Tour, which lasted for four years, Robert was greatly influenced by the ruins of Emperor Diocletian's palace at Spalato (now Split, in Yugoslavia). He returned home in 1758 bursting with ideas, self-confidence and a determination to make a name for himself.

Adam was now 30 years old. He went into partnership with his brothers, James and William, and together they took the fashionable world by storm. Robert's secret was his conviction that the whole effect of an interior could be marred if its furniture and fittings were unrelated to the architectural design. So he designed furniture of all descriptions – carpets, fireplaces, tapestries, embroidery, plate and mirrors – to go in the houses he built.

Not only did Robert have the freshness of vision which speedily brought him to the head of his profession, but also he was a personable young man. He was quickly accepted into high society, where he made many valuable contacts. One of these was the diarist Fanny Burney,

who met Robert Adam soon after he arrived in London. She wrote that he was 'very sensible, very polite and very agreeable'. After supper on that occasion, the guests sang, but, she recorded, 'none shone more than Mr Adam; though, in truth, he had little or no voice... yet he sung with so much taste and feeling that few very fine voices could give such pleasure'.

Inspired by imperial Rome

Commissions poured in. And one of the first was Syon House, where Adam started work in 1762. There he designed the reception rooms as a unity, varying the form and height of the apartments to avoid monotony.

Syon House was the seat of Sir Hugh Smithson, who in 1750 had succeeded in laying claim to the ancient earldom of Northumberland. In keeping with his new status, the earl employed the most fashionable artists and craftsmen of the day. His portrait was painted by Thomas Gainsborough, his grounds laid out by Capability Brown and for his splendid apartments at Syon he chose Robert Adam, who was commissioned to refashion them 'in the antique style'. For his part, Adam 'endeavoured to render it a noble and elegant habitation, not unworthy of a proprietor who possessed not only wealth to execute a great design, but skill to judge of its merit'.

Adam's original plans were too ambitious, even for the purse of the proud earl, but his scheme for the principal rooms survived unchanged. In them he matched Classical simplicity of line with vibrant colours. Each interconnecting room varied in atmosphere and style, to give the visitor a succession of pleasing experiences.

The deliberate coolness of the neo-Classical Entrance Hall, dominated by a statue of the god Apollo, was designed to make a striking visual contrast with the following room, the Ante-Room, which is one of the most brilliantly glowing chambers that Adam ever designed.

The Ante-Room was enhanced still further by relics from imperial Rome itself. Adam had learnt that some ancient Roman columns made of green marble had been discovered on the bed of the River Tiber. He persuaded his patron to buy them, and ranged them around the walls of the ante-chamber. Each of the 12 columns was crowned by a gilded statue, and the atmosphere of glittering imperial luxury was enhanced by a highly polished floor.

The mood changed again with the restrained gracefulness of the State Dining Room. Adam gave this long, wide room a cool, detached atmosphere, where the earl and his male guests could engage in serious political debate over the after-dinner port. No wall-hangings or curtains which might retain the smell of

ARTISTIC GENIUS *The young Robert Adam took London by storm, and soon established himself as the most fashionable architect of the day.*

food were permitted. Copies of antique statues, painted in restrained shades of ivory, gazed at the diners from niches in the walls.

Beyond the dining room there followed the Red Drawing Room. Its walls were covered with Spitalsfield silk, in an explosion of rich colour. Adam himself designed the carpet, which was woven by Thomas More, a leading craftsman of the day. The blaze of painted medallions on the ceiling was executed by the fashionable artist Angelica Kauffman.

Palaces for the aristocracy

But it was the last of this great series of rooms which had the greatest impact. The Long Gallery – 136 ft in length and 14 ft wide – was designed, as Adam wrote, 'in a style to accord great variety and amusement'. The room also set him the greatest challenge, for its length and width meant that it was impossible to achieve the perfect balance of Classical proportions. So Adam filled it with columns, carved doorways and book-cases, installed clusters of furniture of his own design and crowned it with an exquisite moulded ceiling, designed to exaggerate the width.

At Syon, Adam showed his mastery of all forms of design. And, after his triumph there, British architecture was never the same again. Adam went on to greater and greater triumphs, such as Kenwood, near Hampstead, Osterley, near Brentford, and Keddlestone in Derbyshire. In the last year of his life alone, when he was 63, he designed 25 private houses and eight public buildings. And when he died he was buried in Westminster Abbey, with five great noblemen among his pall-bearers. They had reason to pay him tribute. For he had created a world in which they could display their dreams of classical grace and grandeur.

GRANDEUR OF ROME *Twelve columns of green marble dredged up from the muddy floor of the River Tiber in Rome, were brought to Syon House, London, by Robert Adam, for his classic Ante-Room.*

SYMPHONY IN RED *The Red Drawing Room, with its crimson Spitalsfield silk walls and carpet designed by Adam, is famous for its doorways which are decorated with ormolu on panels of ivory.*

INTRICATE DETAIL *The patterns in gold-leaf above the columns in the Ante-Room reveal Adam's love of elaborate ornament.*

TOTAL CONCEPT *Adam believed that décor and architecture should blend together. In the Long Gallery, the elaborate ceiling, the carpet, the 11 windows, the two fireplaces, the three doorways and all the furniture and materials were designed by Adam as matching parts of his overall concept.*

An unlikely hero fights for English liberty

'THAT DEVIL, WILKES'

John Wilkes is portrayed on this snuff-box, now in the British Museum. A gambler and rake, Wilkes seemed an unlikely man to stand up for a principle. But in the 1760's he fought George III's attempts to control the Press, thus winning a reputation as the heroic defender of English liberty.

In the 1760's, a clash took place which was to determine 'whether English liberty shall be a reality or a shadow'. These words were spoken by John Wilkes, Member of Parliament for Aylesbury, who took on the might and majesty of George III to establish the freedom of the Press. After five years of struggle, Wilkes was successful. His triumph established another bastion of English freedom.

Wilkes was an unlikely hero. Ugly, boss-eyed, yet a successful ladies' man and a notorious rake, he seemed more suited to carousing with his cronies of the Hell Fire Club than to standing for a principle.

'That devil, Wilkes'

The struggle began on April 23, 1763, when a warrant was issued for the arrest of the authors and printers of *The North Briton*, a satirical magazine edited by Wilkes. Urged on by Lord Temple, a leading member of the Opposition, Wilkes had used his magazine to launch a series of savage attacks on George III and the king's 'dearest friend', Lord Bute. In issue No. 45 Wilkes redoubled his insolence, portraying George III as the dupe of his ministers. The king decided to silence 'that devil, Wilkes' once and for all.

Wilkes was arrested on April 30, and taken for interrogation to the home of Lord Halifax, one of George's leading ministers. Undaunted, Wilkes harangued his captors at length, denying the legality of the government's 'general warrant'. If ministers, he argued, were allowed to arrest their opponents and search their houses on the vaguest of suspicions,

England had no claim to be a free country. Wilkes had a good case. The Prime Minister, George Grenville, had been in such a hurry to deal with Wilkes that he had not even consulted his law officers before ordering the arrest. And on May 6 Wilkes was released.

But the Prime Minister stepped up his attack. Parliament decreed that a member's privileges did not extend to seditious libel, and ordered the hangman to burn issue No. 45 of *The North Briton*.

Wilkes and liberty

On Christmas Eve, Wilkes fled to France. His failure to answer the charges against him ensured that he was formally proclaimed an outlaw and expelled from Parliament.

Wilkes remained in exile for five years. Then, in 1768, with Grenville out of power, he returned to claim his lost rights. News of his return spread swiftly. And enthusiasm increased still further when it became known that Wilkes was going to stand for Parliament. The cry went up 'Wilkes and Liberty!' It was a slogan that the government would ignore at its peril.

But the cry was resisted. Twice the electors of Middlesex returned Wilkes to Parliament and twice he was not allowed to take his seat. On April 27, Wilkes was arrested on the charge of outlawry and taken to the King's Bench prison. The building was immediately surrounded by his supporters, and the government ordered out the Guards.

Violence finally broke out on May 10, when the mob broke through the cordon of troops and began to stone them. Three guardsmen and an officer, Captain Murray, gave chase to one of their assailants, a man wearing a red waistcoat. They soon lost sight of their quarry, but they burst into a shed behind a nearby inn and found William Allen, the innkeeper's son, wearing a similar garment. They shot him dead.

With this news, pandemonium broke out. A magistrate read the Riot Act, ordering the mob to disperse. But they refused, and the Guards opened fire. Six people were killed outright; 10 died later.

That afternoon, there were as many as 15,000 of Wilkes's supporters in the streets. An observer exclaimed: 'This is the most glorious opportunity for a revolution that ever offered.' But George and his ministers backed down. Wilkes was freed and eventually allowed to take his seat in the Commons. The events of May 10, 1768, were a warning. Had they not been heeded, London, not Paris, might have led Europe into revolution.

WILKES THE VICTOR *Wilkes is carried in triumph through London after his victory in the 1768 Middlesex election.*

George III: 'I glory in the name of Briton'

PATRIOT KING *Though Hanoverian by descent, George III (1760–1820) was English-born, and determined to be as English as his subjects.*

At the age of 22, George III, the first English-born monarch to rule England since Queen Anne half a century before, came to the throne. At first it was thought that he would be a king in name only. He was easily flustered and nervous in public, speaking far too rapidly, with a lot of unnecessary 'what, what', if he could think of nothing to say. In these disconcerting mannerisms there was perhaps an ominous hint of the tragic illness that was to cloud his old age.

At first, many of his people believed that he was completely dominated by his autocratic mother, Augusta of Saxe Gotha, and her close friend, the Earl of Bute. But George's virtues soon won increasing respect.

He was tremendously hard working, and determined to master the business of government. Once he made up his mind, no argument could shake his convictions. He was calm in moments of crises when others lost their heads. When the Gordon Riots swept London in 1780, it was the king, rather than his ministers, who took action, exclaiming: 'I can answer for one who will do his duty.'

George III was never a glamorous figure. The one thing he knew about was farming; he loved talking to sheep farmers and estate workers at Windsor. He knew he was nicknamed 'Farmer George' – but he did not object. He was an ordinary man, but then so were most of his subjects. That was why they respected him so much. Few of Britain's kings have been so typically English – as George himself recognised when he proclaimed: 'I glory in the name of Briton.'

A man of vision launches Britain's canal age

When Francis, Duke of Bridgewater and James Brindley opened their first canal in 1765 all England was lost in admiration. At Barton Bridge the canal was carried high over the River Irwell on a three-arched stone aqueduct. Astonished visitors saw water carried over water. Barges sailed in mid-air, 40 ft higher than those in the river below. When the writer Arthur Young saw it, he declared that it surpassed 'the noblest work of the Romans when masters of the world'. To the Manchester correspondent of the *St James's Chronicle* it was the 'greatest artificial curiosity in the world'.

Underground, the canal was just as impressive. In its first mile it went deep into the workings it had been designed to serve. It passed beside underground quays, lit only by candles. There, half-naked miners loaded coal into barges, accompanied by the grating noises of engines and pumps, and the occasional sound of muffled explosions when gunpowder was used by the miners to clear rocks.

A new means of transport

Brindley and Bridgewater had triumphed. They had managed to find a solution to the one crucial problem that stood in the way of the Industrial Revolution. It had been essential to find a cheap and reliable way of transporting raw materials. There was no point in a would-be industrialist installing new machinery to increase production, if transport costs made his goods too dear for most people to buy. And transport was extremely backward. It was

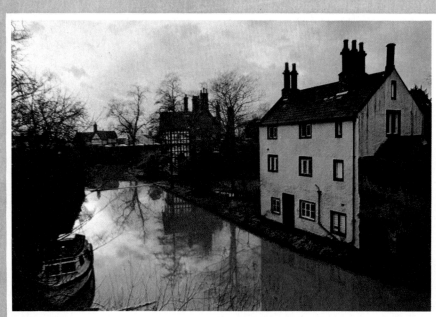

BIRTH OF THE CANAL AGE

Today the placid waters of the canal built by James Brindley at Worsley, Lancashire, no longer reflect the toil that went into the creation of this engineering feat. But canals like this were once the lifeline of England's industry in the 18th and early 19th centuries.

THE MASTER AND HIS WORK

James Brindley (right) masterminded the construction of the Duke of Bridgewater's first canal, providing brilliant solutions to the problems of canal engineering. His aqueduct over the River Irwell (above) was once considered a new wonder of the world. The ten locks at Runcorn (left) were described by Josiah Wedgwood as 'the work of Titans'.

still possible for a man to drown in the water-filled ruts of the Great North Road. River transport might have provided an alternative, but, particularly in the north, rivers were often too shallow or the current too fast to be of much use in transport.

Two men of bold ambitions

Canals were the answer. A packhorse stumbling along a rutted road could carry scarcely 200 lb. A horse pulling a barge on a canal could draw as much as 30 tons. The saving would be enormous.

The Duke of Bridgewater was only 22, and fresh from a visit to the *Canal du Midi* in France, when he decided to have a canal built to carry coal from his collieries at Worsley to Manchester and the River Mersey. To design the canal he chose another exceptional man, James Brindley, a millwright and surveyor.

Brindley had a hand in almost all of the early canals. He was a quarrelsome man, who always dressed in a gentleman's smart snuff-coloured coat and a white cravat. Above all, he was proud of his craft. His chief gift was a tremendous feeling for the lie of the land. By just looking at a landscape he could tell where a canal should go.

Work on the canal started in 1759. It was 10½ miles in length, and cost nearly £50,000 to build. In order to find the money, the duke lived on £500 a year. Even then it was not always easy to pay the workmen. But Bridge-water was willing to gamble on the future; and he knew that the canal was the only way to increase the sale of his coal.

The canal was finally opened in 1765. It was an immediate success. Not only was Bridge-water able to cut the cost of his coal by half, but the canal itself was soon earning him £75,000 a year. And the canal soon inspired more ambitious projects. By the late 1770's plans were well ahead for a canal system linking the Mersey with the rivers Trent, Severn and Thames. Noisy boatmen and their gaily decorated barges became a familiar sight throughout the country.

The barges might be carrying coal, grain, cotton, china clay, ironware, or a hundred other things. Canals linked the new centres of industry with the markets which were crying out for their wares. Trade began to go the way that man, not nature, intended. Compared to canals, rivers seemed unimportant. When a member of a Parliamentary Committee asked Brindley why God had created rivers, his rough reply to the question was: 'To feed navigable canals, of course!'

But this splendour was not to last. For out of the Industrial Revolution, which the canals did so much to create, was to come the invention which superseded them. Within 80 years they were to be almost completely abandoned. And, as men travelled along the new railways, they might see a solitary barge or two to remind them of the canals' former glory.

Wedgwood's pottery wins world-wide fame

One of the first men to grasp the possibilities of the new canal age was Josiah Wedgwood (right), a Staffordshire potter, who led the agitation for a canal to link the rivers Trent and Mersey. To achieve his aim, Wedgwood rode roughshod over all opposi-tion – but such single-mindedness was part and parcel of the character of this pioneer of the Industrial Revolution of the 18th century.

Josiah Wedgwood was born in Burslem in 1730 into a family of potters. But, by the time he was growing to manhood, the pottery produced by Staffordshire's kilns was losing its appeal. It was too clumsy, heavy and un-attractive to find favour with the aristocracy or the rising middle-classes; people who could afford it were eating off smooth bone china from Holland, Germany and China.

Wedgwood's fellow potters knew that their work was unsatisfactory, but it was Wedgwood alone who had the drive and determination to carry through decisive change. His aim was twofold – to mass-produce pottery at a price all could afford, but make it beautiful enough to be used by princes and emperors.

Wedgwood's proud boast was that 'all things yield to experiment'. At the age of 29 he was ready to set up in business on his own. His first great triumph came ten years later when he produced his 'Queen's Creamware', which was far more delicate than traditional English pottery. Then in 1775 he launched the earthenware which fulfilled his highest hopes – Jasper ware. This was impervious to water, did not need glazing and was easily polished. So high were his standards, that he made over 10,000 trial pieces before finally putting the ware on sale to the eager public.

A household word

The public's response repaid these efforts. 'Wedgwood' became a household word throughout the world. The wonder which impressed his contemporaries was that Wedgwood had managed to make mass-produced objects with 'hand-made' quality. The care and craftsmanship displayed in the superb 'Frog' service made for Catherine the Great of Russia was kept up in all his work. Napoleon took a Wedgwood service into exile with him on the island of St Helena.

Wedgwood's secret lay in his handling of men. Up to that time, potters had been inde-pendent, hard-drinking and undisciplined. Wedgwood's huge factories with carefully planned production lines changed all this. He passionately believed that he had a role to play in creating a better world and he paid his workers high wages, built them houses and

even founded schools for their children. And Wedgwood carried over this enlightened attitude into his politics – even at the risk of offending his customers. He advocated reform of Parliament, sympathised with the Americans in their War of Independence and was a prominent member of the Society for the Abolition of the Slave Trade. One of the finest cameos Wedgwood ever produced showed a kneeling, manacled slave, with the inscription 'Am I not a Man and a Brother?' Its impact on the public was tremendous.

But Wedgwood was no mere idealist. Above all, he was a practical man determined to succeed in his chosen career. He had a weak leg, the result of smallpox in childhood, and the slightest knock meant long periods spent in bed and away from his beloved kilns. So in an age without anaesthetics he took the extraordinary decision to have it amputated. Such single-minded determination was charac-teristic of this supremely confident man. His reward was success in his own lifetime, and fame which has lived after him.

RUSSIAN WEDGWOOD *A fruit dish from the service commissioned by Empress Catherine of Russia. The 2000 pieces Wedgwood made for the empress were decorated with specially chosen views of country houses and parks.*

FIT FOR A QUEEN *A hand-painted tureen of Wedgwood's 'Queen's Creamware'. The ware was named after George III's wife, Queen Char-lotte, in 1763, when she honoured Wedgwood by appointing him to be 'Potter to the Queen'.*

Secret orders take Cook
in search of the unknown

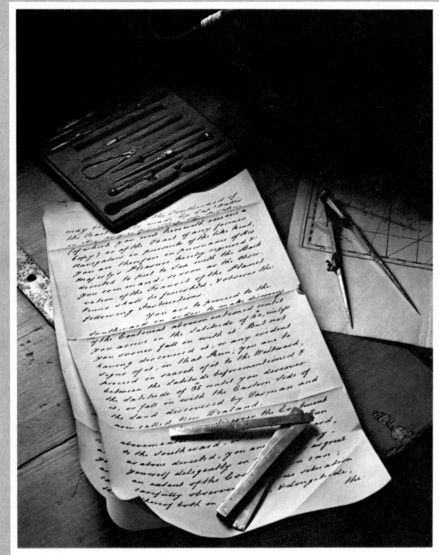

INSTRUCTIONS TO SEEK THE UNKNOWN
Having completed the first part of his expedition to the Pacific and observed and recorded in detail the orbit of the planet Venus, Cook opened these secret orders in his cabin on board the Endeavour *on June 3, 1769. They commanded him to 'make discovery' of the unknown southern continent, and are now in the Public Records Office, London.*

AUSTRALIA CLAIMED *Two spear-wielding Aborigines confront Cook's landing party in Botany Bay. Cook's discoveries in New Zealand and Australia were the first steps in winning Britain a Pacific empire. But 18 years were to pass before colonisation followed his exploration.*

Sailing out of Plymouth Sound on August 26, 1768, Lieutenant James Cook was embarked on a voyage into the unknown. For even he did not know his ultimate destination. Locked away in his cabin aboard his ship, the *Endeavour*, were secret orders from the Admiralty, which he was forbidden to open until he had reached the Pacific island of Tahiti.

Almost a year later, as the *Endeavour* floated peacefully at anchor off Tahiti, Cook opened his secret orders. These called on him to search for the 'great southern continent', whose existence had been confidently predicted by geographers for more than a century.

Rising from the ranks
The man chosen for this daunting task was a taciturn Yorkshireman, aged 40. He had risen through sheer ability from his humble background as an apprentice on a Whitby collier, plying the North Sea between the Yorkshire coast and London. Cook was a professional sailor, not a scientist. But he had the fore-

thought to take with him a scientific team, which was led by Joseph Banks, the outstanding young botanist of the day.

On August 9, 1769, Cook left Tahiti, heading southwards into uncharted waters. For two months the *Endeavour* was swallowed up in the vastness of the Pacific. As the weeks passed, its crew grew more and more eager in their search for land. Cook himself offered a gallon of rum to the man who made the first sighting. Suddenly, on the afternoon of October 7, a 12-year-old ship's boy, Nicholas Young, from his lofty perch high at the *Endeavour's* masthead, cried 'land ahead!' The cape he sighted was named after him – 'Young Nick's Head'. Cook had reached New Zealand.

Filled with exploring zeal
During the next five months Cook sailed round the islands, and proved with a brilliant series of charts that New Zealand was not part of the mysterious southern continent. Ashore, he met the Maoris, a suspicious and hostile people, who spurned his simple gifts and wanted only weapons. Cook had found a whole new world waiting exploration.

The *Endeavour's* weary crew now longed to return to Britain, but their leader's exploring zeal had not diminished. He decided to visit the totally uncharted island continent of Australia on his homeward voyage. The *Endeavour* dropped anchor in a sheltered bay

Triumph and tragedy – Cook dies at Hawaii

Only a year after Cook had returned to Britain, he was again on his way to the Pacific. Still in search of the southern continent, he sailed into the Antarctic, the first captain bold enough to venture deep into those ice-packed seas. Five years later he returned, having finally proved his belief that the continent did not exist.

This voyage had broken Cook's health, but the lure of exploration proved too strong for him to resist, and in 1776 he set sail again. This time he was in search of the north-west passage, a route from the Atlantic to the Pacific believed to lie north of Canada. The voyage was ill-fated; when his ships, the *Resolution* and *Discovery*, put into Hawaii for repairs, Cook lost his temper over the theft of a cutter by the natives and decided that 'violent measures' were needed. On February 14, 1779, he landed with a small party of armed marines, intending to seize an important chief, King Terreeoboo, and hold him hostage.

Disaster on the beach

The king protested that he knew nothing of the theft, but Cook asked him to return to the *Resolution* for more talks. Terreeoboo agreed, but a crowd of natives, fearing for their chief's life, gathered outside his hut and urged him not to go. The marines forced a path through the mob, but, as they were in sight of the beach, the king's favourite wife threw her arms around Terreeoboo and implored him to stay.

This was the trigger point; the menacing natives forced Cook and his men back towards the beach and suddenly fighting broke out. Cook was surrounded, struck from behind with a club and then stabbed to death. Belatedly, his ships opened fire and the natives withdrew, taking Cook's mutilated body with them to their village where it was ceremonially burnt. A handful of ashes were eventually recovered and committed to the deep at sunset on February 21 by Cook's grieving shipmates.

THE BOTANIST OF BOTANY BAY

On his first voyage to Australia, Cook had the services of a scientific team led by Joseph Banks (left), the ablest young botanist of the day. The red honeysuckle (right) was one of the plants found by Banks, which led Cook to name their Australian landfall Botany Bay. After the *Endeavour's* triumphant return, bearing thousands of new plants, it was Banks rather than the modest Cook who won instant fame. When Cook was given command of the *Resolution* for his second Pacific voyage,

Banks's demands for additional accommodation for his scientists and equipment made the ship so unseaworthy that one of the officers told him that he would 'go to sea in a grog-tub if required . . . but must say that I think her (the *Resolution*) by far the most unsafe ship I ever saw'. Cook rejected the plans and Banks withdrew from the voyage. The two were never to sail together again.

on April 28, 1770. By chance, Cook had arrived at one of the most fertile parts of Australia's coasts – and the scientists soon found that they were exploring a botanists' paradise. Cook named the place Botany Bay.

The first landing party was met by two hostile Aborigines, wearing white warpaint, who tried to fight off the intruders. Though one was shot and wounded, they hurled their spears at Cook and his men before retreating into the bush. Cook was impressed by their courage in the face of such odds. The natives' hunting weapons caused great puzzlement among the sailors, and they mistook the boomerang for a curved sword. Explanations were hard to come by, for the natives remained aloof. Cook wrote in his journal: 'All they seemed to want was for us to be gone.'

For two weeks the scientists roamed through woods and bushland, bringing back specimens of strange plants and animals which were puzzled over in the *Endeavour's* great cabin.

But perhaps the most startling discovery was made by Banks himself, when he shot and killed his first kangaroo, having first observed its amazing method of movement.

Before finally turning homeward, Cook landed on a tiny island, later christened Possession Island, and there in the glow of a tropical sunset he raised the British flag and, in the name of George III, formally claimed for Britain the 2000 miles of Australia's coastline which he had charted. On July 13, 1771, the *Endeavour* dropped anchor in the English Channel. Cook modestly disclaimed all credit, especially since he had failed to solve the riddle of the southern continent. But he was summoned to an audience with George III and the Admiralty wrote that 'their Lordships extremely well approve of the whole of your proceeding'. And as Charles Darwin recognised, he had 'added a hemisphere to the world', and he had also fulfilled his own ambition 'to go farther than anyone had done before'.

DEATH IN HAWAII *Cook meets his death in Hawaii in 1779. Such was his fame that his native assassins gave him a chieftain's burial.*

TWO GREAT ARTISTS CAPTURE ENGLAND'S GOLDEN AGE

PORTRAIT OF PROSPERITY *Thomas Gainsborough's earliest masterpiece was this portrait of 'Mr and Mrs Andrews'. The ripe corn, grazing sheep and glimpse of a manor house provide a background of assured prosperity.*

GAINSBOROUGH LADY *Mary, Countess of Howe, was painted by Gainsborough in the early days of his fame as the portrait painter of Bath. He drew on nature to dramatise her beauty, with a splash of light in the brooding sky.*

The aristocrats of the 18th century were the lords of all they surveyed, enjoying a style of graceful luxury which has seldom been equalled in the history of civilisation. They employed men of taste and genius, such as Capability Brown and Robert Adam, to create a suitable background for their lives. And they sought artists who could portray their world in all its enviable perfection.

Two painters of genius who brilliantly fulfilled this role were Thomas Gainsborough and George Stubbs. Gainsborough loved to paint the most beautiful women of the age, dwelling with pleasure on their expressions and their beautiful finery. Stubbs seemed equally infatuated with his subject – the graceful strength of the finest horses.

Two painters with a common purpose

Both men provided their works with a background that was subtly flattering to their proud land-owning patrons – a background of the well-tilled fields which were the source of England's great prosperity. Born within a few years of each other – Stubbs in 1724 and Gainsborough in 1727 – they belonged to the last generation of Englishmen who were to live their whole lives in a settled agricultural society, before the coming of the railways.

Gainsborough's love of nature came from his childhood days in Suffolk, where he spent his time roaming the countryside and sketching. At 19 he was made financially independent by his marriage to the beautiful Margaret Burr, said to be the illegitimate daughter of the Duke of Beaufort.

He moved to Ipswich where he produced his first masterpiece, 'Mr and Mrs Andrews' – a portrait of a minor Suffolk squire and his pretty young wife against a background of neat, prosperous fields, which summed up the whole mood of the era. At 32 the artist, his

ARTIST'S AUTUMN *At the peak of his success, Gainsborough grew tired of fashionable portraiture, and returned to his first love – the country scenes of his Suffolk childhood. In 'The Harvest Wagon' he painted a group of country people homeward-bound after a day's harvesting.*

wife and two young daughters, moved to Bath, the capital of fashion and the best place for an artist to make his name.

Gainsborough took a studio opposite the abbey and adopted a new style, closely founded on that of the most successful portrait painter ever to work in Britain, Sir Anthony van Dyck. Very soon he was able to raise his prices from five to 100 guineas for a full-length portrait. Among his patrons were the greatest art collectors of the day.

At the age of 47, Gainsborough decided to move to London into a mansion in Pall Mall, where he won royal patronage and great wealth. But portraits had begun to tire him. He had painted 700 of them 'to make the pot boil', as he explained, and now, in the last period of his life, he returned to his first love – rural England.

He wrote to a friend: 'I'm sick of portraits and wish very much to . . . walk off to some sweet village where I can paint Landskips and

ART IN SCIENCE

The first major work of George Stubbs's life was his illustrated study *The Anatomy of the Horse*, still the finest book on its subject. Stubbs probably conceived the idea during his tour of Italy, where he was impressed by the Italian tradition of scientist-artists which went back to Leonardo da Vinci.

It was an undertaking which only a man of Stubbs's remarkable singleness of mind would have undertaken. Dissection in the 18th century was an invitation to violent criticism, and Stubbs withdrew to the isolated village of Horkstow on the Humber in order to do the preliminary work of dissection and drawing in safety.

The long self-imposed task proved an invaluable apprenticeship for Stubbs's future career. After publishing his *Anatomy* in 1766 Stubbs emerged as Britain's finest painter of horses. His work has never been surpassed.

enjoy the fag End of Life in quietness and ease.' He painted a last series of mellow landscapes drawn from his memories of the East Anglian countryside where he had wandered as a boy.

Gainsborough died of cancer in 1788. Even on his death-bed he expressed his serene confidence: 'We are all going to heaven – and Van Dyck is of the company.'

George Stubbs would never have expected a place in such august company. He believed himself to be more of a scientist than an artist.

Yet in his devotion to horses he became the greatest equestrian artist of all time.

Stubbs's obsession with horses began in childhood in Liverpool, where his father was a leather merchant. Their yard was always filled with the carcasses of dead animals, and Stubbs was drawing anatomical details from them at the age of six. After a brief tour of Italy in 1754 he returned to the solitude of a Lincolnshire farm, to carry out the necessary dissections for his great work, *The Anatomy of the Horse*. At the age of 35 he went to London to look for a publisher for his book, and soon he was winning commissions for sporting pictures from many wealthy patrons.

Record of England's golden age

On working tours of the great estates of England, he painted the most renowned racehorses and hunters. But for his own pleasure he preferred to paint farming scenes. In these pictures, the patient horses, the crops and the trees, the men and women at their work and the luminous sky overhead are all imbued with a sense of tranquillity and order.

When Stubbs died at the age of 81, many of these pictures were still unsold in his studio. Only a later generation could perceive that the scientist-artist, with his obsessional interest in horseflesh, had transcended the narrow limits of his time. Just as Gainsborough's portraits had gone far beyond his patrons' requirements for flattering likenesses, so Stubbs had passed beyond the confines of the sporting picture or the pretty pastoral scene. Together, they had captured the spirit of the golden age before industry changed the face of Britain.

255

A free nation is born as Britain loses America

THE WEAPON THAT FAILED TO HOLD AMERICA

A 'Brown Bess' musket, now to be seen at the Tower of London. These muskets were the main weapons used by the British infantry against the American rebels. Though they had been a success in the battles of the Seven Years' War (1756-63), they proved to be of little use in the skirmishes and guerrilla fighting of the North American battlefield.

All hope of British victory in the War of American Independence came to an end on October 17, 1781. On that day, Lord Cornwallis surrendered his entire army of 3723 men to a mixed force of Americans and French at Yorktown, Virginia, after a grim 18 day siege.

Militarily, the surrender was no disgrace. Cornwallis's men were short of tools to build their defences, yet they had toiled throughout the heat of a Virginian August to strengthen their vulnerable position at the head of the Williamsburg Peninsula. In the absence of horses, they had fashioned harnesses for themselves to drag their guns into place. Surrender was not considered until nearly half the British force had been killed or wounded. And as the vanquished Redcoats marched out into captivity through their battered defences, British bands played the popular tune 'The World Turned Upside Down'.

This was a melancholy jest. Although peace was two long years away, this was the last important engagement in the battle for North America. But the dice had been loaded against the British from the start of the war in 1776. They had to reconquer a vast land, sending troops, arms and supplies 3000 miles across the Atlantic in ships which took four to six weeks to make the crossing. And the two commanders on the spot, Cornwallis and Sir Henry Clinton, the commander-in-chief, disastrously differed over the way the campaign to defeat the rebels was to be fought.

The British blunder

More important still, for once in her history, Britain did not rule the waves. Cornwallis's surrender would never have come about if his country had enjoyed what she had come to regard as her unchallengeable right – command of the sea. For the moment this had passed to France.

Cornwallis decided to march inland – northwards to Virginia, the stronghold of rebel defiance. Despite the odds against success, the British government cheered Cornwallis on. But the success of his campaign depended on good communications between his army and Clinton. For Clinton would have to send reinforcements quickly if Cornwallis got into trouble on his advance.

He soon did. By the time he had worked his way through the thickly forested hills of North Carolina, his army had been badly mauled by the Americans. In March 1781, with one-third of his men gone, he retreated towards the coast. In August he dug in at Yorktown and waited for relief.

Powerful forces were soon arrayed against Cornwallis's army: 9000 Americans, 8000 French and 40 French ships of the line. These were commanded by Admiral François de Grasse who, having trounced the British in the West Indies, sailed up to blockade Chesapeake Bay – the bay through which Cornwallis had confidently expected the Royal Navy to come to his rescue.

The siege began on September 30. The heavily outnumbered Cornwallis could not match his enemies' fire power. American artillery pounded the British and inflicted appalling casualties. In the heat of late summer, wounds quickly festered. For hundreds of Redcoats the struggle to hold America for the king ended in a painful death, far from home.

By October 14, only one of the British cannon was still able to fire. And it was on that day that Cornwallis made his fateful decision to surrender his army – a decision that was to cost Britain North America. The same day, Clinton sailed with a relieving force. When he heard the news, he turned back.

Taste of defeat

Yorktown's importance was both strategic and emotional. The Americans remained in control of Virginia – their revolution's heartland. And the British people, long accustomed to victory, learnt the bitter taste of defeat.

Despatches announcing the tragedy arrived in London on November 28. The Prime Minister, Lord North, broke down when he heard the news, sobbing: 'Oh God! It is all over.'

But North's royal master, George III, took a different view. At the start of the war he had declared that he would rather lose his crown than abandon the empire. He comforted himself with the thought that 'knavery seems to be so much the striking feature of America's Inhabitants that it may not in the end be an evil that they become Aliens to this kingdom'.

UNREST AT HOME

America was not the only battleground in the struggle against George III. In England, too, many politicians – including Lord Chatham (William Pitt) and the Whig leaders Charles James Fox and Edmund Burke – attacked the king for what they claimed was his tyrannical rule. Their discontent led them to support the American rebels and culminated in 1780, at the height of the revolution, in a famous parliamentary resolution passed in the House of Commons: 'That the influence of the Crown has increased, is increasing and ought to be diminished.'

Lord Chatham collapses in the House of Lords while urging the justice of the American cause. This was his last speech before his death.

THE FINAL DISASTER *To the sound of bands playing 'The World Turned Upside Down', the British army under Lord Cornwallis marches out of Yorktown to surrender to the Americans in 1781. This shattering defeat convinced the British people that victory in the war against the rebels was impossible to achieve.*

Democracy takes root in the New World

When war broke out between the North American colonies and Britain in 1775, it was the predictable climax to many years of bitter quarrels between the colonists and their homeland. In the past, the Americans had complained and rioted against attempts to raise taxation without their consent. They had protested against the arrogance of the officials sent to govern them. But they still regarded themselves as loyal subjects. They argued that it was the government of George III which was acting illegally, and that they had a right, even a duty, to resist attempts to destroy liberty.

Money was at the root of the problem. The Americans were virtually untaxed – they paid a paltry sixpence a year. On average, Englishmen paid 50 times as much. But, since the colonists returned no members to Parliament, they were affronted at being taxed at all. 'No taxation without representation' was their slogan.

Fiery leaders began to emerge – such as Patrick Henry in Virginia and Samuel Adams in Massachusetts. They cried out that the government's actions were illegal and stirred the colonists to riot. But George III refused to make concessions, and his government daily grew more repressive – especially after the Boston Tea Party on December 16, 1773.

Britain had authorised the almost-bankrupt East India Company to sell tea directly to the colonies. This would have ruined the American merchants who had been smuggling in cheap tea from Holland. When the first East India ship arrived in Boston, protesters dressed as Red Indians tipped its £10,000 cargo into the harbour. The British responded with martial law and soon open rebellion had begun.

An example to the world

On July 4, 1776, in a meeting at Philadelphia, representatives of all 13 colonies buried their differences to unite in accepting the Declaration of Independence. This historic document was dedicated to the principles that: 'All men are created equal; that they are endowed by their Creator with certain unalienable rights; that among these are life, liberty and the pursuit of happiness.'

These words were written by a Virginian lawyer, Thomas Jefferson, later to become the third President of the United States. But he wrote them in the spirit of an Englishman. In his justification of rebellion, Jefferson had argued that the case of George III in America was the same as that of James II in England. By breaking their obligations to their people, both had forfeited their right to govern.

Later, the United States would formally embody the principles of the Declaration in its constitution. The nation so founded was based on English concepts of justice, law and freedom – England's legacy to the New World.

SCIENTIFIC REVOLUTION IN A GARDEN BY THE THAMES

The forces that drove Britain forward into the 18th-century scientific revolution took many forms – from the self-interest of businessmen to the pleasures of gardening. Noblemen who created the great gardens of the 18th century vied with one another in the search for rare and beautiful plants, just as they competed for works of art to adorn the interiors of their houses. They could afford to send plant-hunters to seek specimens in Africa, South America and Australia. They were not content merely with ownership, but wished to understand and classify the secrets of botany.

Patronised by a queen

This scientific interest in plants and flowers resulted in the creation of the world's greatest botanical gardens; they were laid out at Kew, on the Surrey bank of the Thames, a few miles upstream from London. The gardens were a perfect expression of their age, combining beauty with practical usefulness and pure science, and in later generations they became the most influential gardens in history,

for Kew was the nursery for crops which transformed the economy of whole nations.

There had been impressive gardens at Kew House since the mid-17th century. In 1730 the estate was acquired by the Royal Family, and it was George III's mother, Princess Augusta, who started a 9 acre botanic garden and study centre there, with the botanist William Aiton as the first director in 1759.

Aiton had been director of Chelsea Physic Garden, where plants and herbs were grown mainly for their medicinal value. At Kew he was able to broaden his work. By 1789 he had catalogued 5500 plant species, classifying them and listing the country of origin and date they were introduced.

George III loved Kew. He enlarged the gardens and commissioned the landscape gardener Capability Brown to redesign them. In 1768, with the encouragement of George III, the botanist Joseph Banks sailed on Captain Cook's journey to the South Seas, in order to add specimens to the collections at

HEAD OF KEW *William Aiton, who was appointed director in 1759, as painted by John Zoffany.*

COLLECTOR *Francis Masson was one of the first gardeners sent abroad from Kew. He brought back 400 species, and painted this watercolour of a fleshy-leaved plant* (Mesembryanthemum digitatum) *after finding it in South Africa.*

TROPHIES FROM ABROAD *In 1772 Kew Gardens sent overseas Francis Masson, a Scotsman who was the first of its numerous plant collectors. He travelled principally in South Africa bringing back this species of heather* (Erica taxiflora), *popular in greenhouses and as a room plant.*

BOTANIC ART *Artists of delicate accuracy were needed to record rare botanical specimens. Francis Bauer, an accomplished artist who worked for 50 years at Kew Gardens and painted this Chinese orchid* (Limodorum tankervilliae), *was a master of fine detail.*

Kew. At one spot on the Australian coast Banks and his assistant gathered 1000 strange plants. The place was named Botany Bay.

Captain William Bligh supported the work of Kew. The celebrated mutiny occurred in 1789, while his ship the *Bounty* was on a botanical mission to collect breadfruit from the South Sea Islands. The mutineers threw the precious breadfruit plants overboard.

Bligh and 18 of his crew were set adrift in an open boat, but managed to navigate the 3618 miles to the Javanese island of Timor. One of the castaways was Banks's agent, who survived the three months of exposure but died soon after reaching the island.

After the deaths of George III and Banks in 1820, the gardens went into a decline. Then they passed from the crown to the nation, and Sir William Hooker became director. He started exchanging plants with other gardens, and also opened Kew to the public.

The gardens were improved, and the architect Decimus Burton designed the Palm House, a vast greenhouse which is more than 120 yds long, took four years to build and cost £30,000.

Sir William's son and director of Kew, Joseph Dalton Hooker, returned from Sikkim in the Himalayas. He brought back seeds of 43 species of rhododendron and other plants which, having acclimatised at Kew, brought about a revolution in the English garden.

The work of Kew has not been simply to collect and rear plants: healthy species from the gardens were transplanted abroad, often to countries where they had never grown before.

Tea from China was introduced to India through the gardens. Seeds of the *Cinchona* tree were taken there from Java, and when they had developed into seedlings were re-exported to India, where quinine prepared from the bark saved the lives of countless malaria sufferers.

A world-wide legacy
Cotton from Uganda and the Sudan passed through Kew on its way to Cyprus, while sultana grapevines from Cyprus spent a while in the Thames-side hothouses before being introduced into St Helena. Bananas have made a two-way journey via Kew: tropical African varieties to Trinidad and cultivated ones from the West Indies to West Africa and Australia.

Pineapples and coffee have made similar trips. Nowadays such tropical growths are kept in strict quarantine at Kew: this reduces the risks of carrying pests and diseases to their new homes.

The culminating achievement was Henry Wickham's mission, on Joseph Hooker's orders, to find the rubber plant in the Amazon jungle. Despite hardships, dangers and opposition from the Brazilians, he collected 70,000 of the precious seeds, and chartered a steamer to get them to Kew before they all died. From there, seedlings were sent to Malaya in the late 1870's, where they revolutionised the economy.

CREATING A NEW WORLD ON NIGHTS OF THE FULL MOON

Britain in the age of George III was fortunate in numbering among its citizens a group of practical men who grasped that science could be set to work. These men were among the creators of the modern world. Their inquiring minds, practical gifts and business acumen turned the pure speculation of the age of Newton into the force which was to transform Britain. They did not know the word, but they were changing science into technology.

Among the men who were to achieve this feat were the members of the Birmingham Lunar Society – so called because its monthly meetings were timed to coincide with the full moon, so that members could travel home safely by moonlight. It was an informal group, with a membership never higher than 14, and its leading light was the Birmingham engineer and factory owner Matthew Boulton.

Men of vision
Around 1760, Boulton struck up a fruitful friendship with Erasmus Darwin, an ambitious young doctor with wide-ranging interests. Boulton and Darwin were joined by John Whitehurst, a clockmaker who was also interested in mechanics, hydraulics and geology. The three of them established the Lunar Society as a forum for the discussion of scientific ideas and inventions.

Erasmus Darwin, a large, vigorous man with a stammer, was the society's most speculative mind. His projects included an intricate surveying machine, and a prototype steam and gas engine, which helped to stimulate the work of the Scotsman James Watt in the field of steam power. Darwin's work in optics, medicine, geology and meteorology was distinguished by careful observation and meticulous experiment. He even anticipated by half a century the discoveries of his grandson, Charles Darwin, in the field of evolution.

True to his own dictum that 'a fool is a man who never tried an experiment in his life', Darwin made frequent trips in a carriage he had designed to exploit the maximum power of a horse. In the course of these trials he broke his kneecap and acquired a lifelong limp.

In 1765 the society gained a valuable new member in the person of Dr William Small, introduced by the American scientist and statesman Benjamin Franklin, who had himself been in regular contact with the society since its foundation. Until his death in 1775, Small worked closely with Boulton on the development of Watt's steam engine.

Watt himself became a member of the Lunar Society, as did the great potter Josiah Wedgwood, who brought to it an interest in

INQUIRING MINDS *Joseph Priestley (left) and Erasmus Darwin (right) were members of the Lunar Society, whose influence was to help transform British science.*

canal construction and the chemistry of clays and glazes.

Outstanding among the later members of the society was Joseph Priestley, the chemist and dissenting churchman, who settled in Birmingham in 1780. Priestley's most important contributions to science were his experiments with electricity and the chemistry of gases. He discovered oxygen, which he called 'dephlogisticated air'.

Priestley, a gentle unworldly idealist and radical republican, supported the French Revolution. His political opinions so infuriated popular feeling that, in 1791, a mob broke into his house and laboratory, destroyed his apparatus and manuscripts, and set the building on fire. He fled to London and later emigrated to America.

A great task accomplished
In exile, Priestley wrote his memoirs. And he recalled that his ten years among the Lunar Society's members in Birmingham were the happiest and most fruitful of his life.

But the riot against Priestley, with its undertones of distrust for science, brought about the decline of the Lunar Society. The Birmingham mob's cry had been 'No philosophers – Church and King for ever!' Some of the society's members began to wonder whether their speculations were now unleashing a force they could not control. They faced a dilemma they could not solve – the relationship between scientific progress and the hard realities of politics. Besides, they were mostly elderly gentlemen who had prospered as a result of their diligence and sound application of enterprising ideas. Now, in a suddenly hostile world, they prudently withdrew into themselves, and their society with its curious name was soon forgotten.

But its activities laid the groundwork on which the achievements of the Industrial Revolution were based. Through the next 100 years, its influence continued to shape the character of science in Britain.

The quiet valley where a revolution was born

SYMBOL OF THE INDUSTRIAL REVOLUTION

The first bridge in the world to be built entirely of iron was opened at Ironbridge in Salop in 1780. Spanning the River Severn, the bridge took three months to build and is still in use today. It was designed by Abraham Darby, the manager of a nearby foundry, who was the first English engineer to realise the potential of iron as a building material.

What marble was to the ancient Greeks, iron was to Britain in the 18th and 19th centuries. The dramatic use of iron that changed the face of the land began with a bridge built across the River Severn at the Salop town of Ironbridge. It was the first bridge ever to be constructed entirely of iron, and it endures to the present day – a symbol of the Industrial Revolution.

When tenders were invited in 1776 for a bridge over the Severn, only one man, Abraham Darby, manager of the Coalbrookdale ironworks a mile upriver, was willing to take on the challenge. The stumbling block was that an exceptionally long central span – 120 ft – was required to reach across the gap.

Other engineers feared that stone could not do the job, but could offer no alternative solution. Darby had faith in the cast-iron his foundry was producing, even though the material had yet to be proved in so demanding a task. No one knows for certain who conceived the original design – possibly another iron-maker in the district, or an employee of the Coalbrookdale company. But Darby was

COALBROOKDALE BY NIGHT *A contemporary painting shows the iron foundries of the village of Coalbrookdale blazing in the night sky. There, the first Abraham Darby found the natural resources – iron ore and coal from which to make coke – that enabled him to begin the smelting of iron ore on a large scale in 1709. His family were to remain in the vanguard of technological change for over 50 years.*

responsible for actually executing the daring plan. It called for neither bolts nor rivets; the parts were slotted together and fixed with wedges. To test its practicability, Darby built a scale model. Then he stepped up production in his foundry. Even so, it took him most of his first winter's work to cast the 378½ tons of iron sections, some weighing over 5 tons each, that the design specified.

A 'most singular curiosity'

The bridge was erected in only three months in 1779. Using a giant scaffold, workmen lowered the ribs into position with ropes and chains until the ends met in the centre, 40 ft above the river.

Just over a year later, this 'most singular curiosity', as a local newspaper called it, was opened to traffic. Soon there was a profitable stream of horse-riders and pedestrians crossing and recrossing for a toll of a halfpenny each. The wealthy came in carriages, at a shilling a time, as much to marvel as to get from one side of the river to the other.

The bridge was a first in engineering history. But it was by no means the first technical breakthrough achieved by the Coalbrookdale Darbys, one of the founding families of the Industrial Revolution. The first Darby (the bridge-builder's grandfather) opened the way for the Industrial Revolution in 1709, when he successfully smelted iron for the first time with coke, making full use of the resources at his doorstep. There was iron ore in Coalbrookdale; there was coal from which to make the coke in the gorge of the Coalbrook stream, and the stream itself, with its fast-flowing waters, supplied the power that drove the bellows of Darby's furnaces.

Family of inventors

The use of coke was a highly significant innovation. Until then, England had depended upon charcoal for fuel; but now it was becoming scarce and expensive. Darby found the substitute, and with it transformed Coalbrookdale into the cradle of the modern iron age.

For more than half a century, the Darby family were in the van of technological advance. They made the first cast-iron cylinders for steam engines in 1722; the first pig iron for forge work in 1748 (under Abraham II); the first cast-iron rails for the horse-drawn predecessors of trains (under Abraham III), and then the first iron bridge. Thanks to the company's 'amazing scene of business', as the locals described it, Coalbrookdale became an industrial inferno, its rural slopes illuminated by night with the red glare of furnaces.

Towards the end of the 18th century, similar scenes were taking place all over Britain. After the marriage of cheap steam, discovered by James Watt, to cheap iron, provided by Abraham Darby, iron production trebled in less than 20 years. By 1850 Britain was producing half the world's iron.

Watt gives industry its 'lungs of steam'

According to legend, James Watt, when only a sickly schoolboy in Greenock, Scotland, watched the lid of a boiling tea-kettle as it rattled up and down. In a flash he recognised the potential power of steam.

What struck his imagination was not the built-up pressure that lifted the lid of his aunt's kettle. It was the way that the steam condensed into beads of water when it touched the metal spoon he held to the spout. That observation, so the story goes, was to be the basis of the vital discoveries he later made.

Watt did indeed become fascinated by steam. At the age of 19 he became an unpaid apprentice to a maker of scientific instruments in London. After a year he had mastered the basic skills of the trade, but so frugally had he been forced to live – on only eight shillings a week – that he went back to Scotland. There, the University of Glasgow took him on as a mathematical instrument-maker. In 1763 he came face to face with his first practical challenge in the realm of steam.

The model engine used by the university had broken down, and Watt was asked to repair it. It was a miniature of the primitive machines invented by Thomas Newcomen in 1705. Full-scale Newcomen engines were being used to pump water out of tin mines in Cornwall and coal mines in the Tyne basin. They were gigantic, unwieldy, profligate with fuel and monstrously inefficient.

As he worked on the model in his workshop, Watt was struck by the amount of steam that went to waste. The problem lay chiefly in the inefficient method of condensing the steam that powered the pistons.

Steam was let into a huge cylinder, and then cooled with a jet of cold water. This condensed the steam, creating a vacuum that forced the piston to plunge down the cylinder. But the water cooled the container as well; much of the next batch of steam was wasted reheating the cold metal of the cylinder.

Perfecting a dream

The solution came to Watt when he was out walking one Sunday afternoon in 1765. It was to suck the steam out and cool it in a separate condenser. It was to take him ten years, harassed by financial crises and mechanical failures, to perfect his improved design.

At one stage, Watt came close to giving up. He remarked 'there is nothing so foolish as inventing'. Finally, he was lucky enough to find a partner, Matthew Boulton, the owner of a factory outside Birmingham, who was prepared patiently to finance the new engine. From that partnership between inspired engineering and practical commerce the steam age was born. Both men were also interested in other fields of science. They belonged to the influential Lunar Society of Birmingham, a body formed to encourage new scientific ideas.

The first Boulton and Watt engine was publicly demonstrated at Birmingham in 1776. Soon, Boulton was able to boast that 'Britain had gone steam-mill mad'. By the time of Watt's death in 1819 the whole of British industry was powered by muscles of iron and lungs of steam.

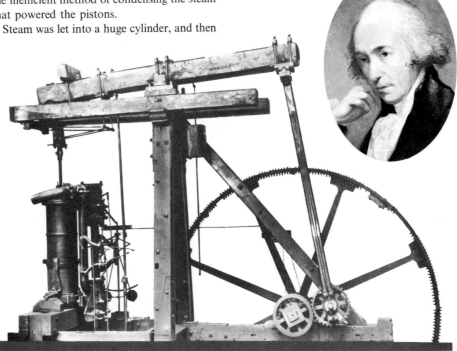

STEAM POWER *James Watt (above right) patented his rotative steam engine in 1781. Its unique features were its crank, flywheel and condensing cylinder, which stepped up efficiency and so enabled it to power the machinery of the Industrial Revolution. Its development marked the high point of the partnership between Watt and Matthew Boulton which began in 1774.*

THREE MEN OF TASTE FILL THEIR HOUSE WITH TREASURE

In the 18th century, a combination of affluence and family pride in the English aristocracy produced generations of collectors who delighted in amassing the richest and rarest furnishings and the finest works of art. Such men turned their mansions into treasure houses which were among the wonders of the world.

Among these treasure houses of Britain there are few to compare with Woburn Abbey in Bedfordshire. Woburn was the loving creation of three members of the Russell family, the 4th, 5th and 6th Dukes of Bedford, who lavished their wealth on making their home into a palace fit for an emperor. In their hands, Woburn became a temple to the 18th-century virtues of reason, sensibility and civilised good living; and year by year they added to its incomparable collections. Among many other visitors, the diarist Charles Greville was deeply impressed by the world their riches had created: 'The house, place and establishment and manner of living are the most magnificent I have ever seen.'

The riches that the Russells lavished on their creation came from the land they owned just west of the old city of London. As the capital expanded in the 18th century to become one of the biggest and wealthiest trading cities of the world, so the fortunes of the family increased.

In a money-spinning burst of development, their farmland in Covent Garden, Bloomsbury and Holborn was turned into fashionable terraces and squares.

Collections beyond price

It was John Russell, 4th Duke of Bedford, who began the transformation of Woburn. His important government posts, which often took him abroad, gave him the opportunity to start the great collections which were to become Woburn's glory. After a year on a mission to France, he returned with some superb French furniture and a magnificent 188-piece Sèvres dinner service given to him and his wife by Louis XV. Even in those days it cost more than £18,000.

But the Sèvres service was by no means the most important of John Russell's collections. He commissioned what in later years was to become Woburn's most famous and perhaps most valuable asset – the Canaletto collection. Giovanni Antonio Canal, known as Canaletto, was already famous when he came to London from Italy in 1746. It was there that the duke met him and persuaded the artist to paint 24 scenes of Venice.

Life at Woburn was now grander than it had ever been. John Russell, a plump good-humoured man described by the diarist Horace Walpole as 'the merry little duke', delighted to entertain and the house was always full. But his devotion to Woburn sometimes caused his colleagues in the government to grumble. Henry Pelham said that life for the duke seemed to be all 'jollity, boyishness and vanity'. A French cook presided in the kitchen and the menu was one of the best in England. Some British traditions, however, remained firmly entrenched. Beer was the staple drink and was always served first thing in the morning at the breakfast table.

Transforming a stately home

Francis Russell, the fifth duke, inherited Woburn in 1771. He had his father's artistic tastes and brought Henry Holland, the most celebrated architect of the day, to Woburn. Holland built the South Front, the library behind it, the sculpture gallery, the main staircase and the enchanting Chinese dairy.

But Holland's chief achievement was the creation of a fitting setting for the fabulous Canalettos. He made a perfect home for them in a glittering red, white and gold dining room. No room in England more perfectly expresses the ideal of the 18th-century aristocrat in his role as the patron of the arts.

Holland's work gave Woburn a new lightness from the outside and a new brightness within. And his patron was soon busily col-

VENETIAN GLORY *The private dining room is decorated with 21 views of Venice by Canaletto, ordered by John Russell, 4th Duke of Bedford.*

lecting new treasures to fill the showcases that Holland had created. Many extravagant gifts were given to him by his friend, the Prince of Wales, later George IV.

So impressive was the royal bounty that Edmund Burke, the politician and philosopher, wrote a tirade against the duke. The gifts lavished on Bedford by the prince, com-

MAKING THE GRAND TOUR

In the 18th century, no English aristocrat's education was considered complete unless he had made a Grand Tour of the Continent. These tours could last as long as three or four years. Those making them were expected to see the wonders of art and architecture, learn French and Italian, study fencing and horsemanship with the best masters, and acquire social grace and polish at the courts of the capitals of Europe. The whole Continent was seen as one vast finishing school.

Unfortunately, it did not always work out like that. The rich Englishman abroad was a target for swindlers and tricksters. Even the great British sculptor Joseph Nollekens was not above staining a new statue and passing it off as a Classical masterpiece. And many young travellers disliked what they found. Lord Fitzwilliam quickly decided that the French were 'a set of low, mean, impertinent people' whose houses were notable for 'a great want of furniture and a vast superabundance of dirt'.

But, like many of his fellows, Fitzwilliam returned home with a large collection of 'antiquities' with which to adorn his ancestral home. The impact of the Grand Tour upon such men played a vital part in transforming English taste, and in building up the great art collections which filled England's 18th-century treasure houses.

English travellers on the Grand Tour take breakfast at a French inn. Often the tour corrupted rather than educated. Many returned with 'the manners of a dancing master and the morals of a whore'.

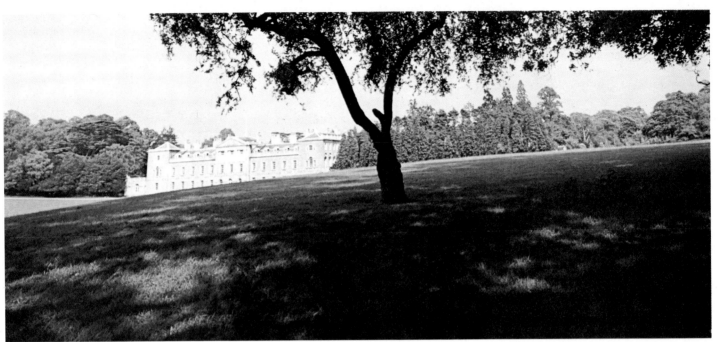

TREASURE HOUSE *Three members of the Russell family lavished time, wealth and ingenuity on making Woburn Abbey, Bedfordshire, into a treasure house whose riches would astonish the world. John Russell, the* *fourth duke, began the great Woburn collections in the mid-18th century and his work was continued by his sons, Francis and John. By the time John died in 1839, Woburn was a palace fit for a king.*

NOBLE PATRON *In keeping with his desire to give Woburn the best in art, John Russell, the fourth duke, filled the Blue Drawing Room (above) with works by Thomas Gainsborough. The two landscapes on the left-hand wall were his first purchase; the family portraits were specially commissioned.*

RIVAL ARTIST *Gainsborough's rival, Sir Joshua Reynolds, was also patronised by John Russell. Five of his works hang in the Breakfast Room.*

plained Burke, were 'so enormous as not only to outrage economy, but even to stagger credibility. The duke is the leviathan among the creatures of the crown'.

Francis lived and died a bachelor. His brother John inherited the title as sixth duke in 1803, and lost no time in expanding the collections still further. Within a year of succeeding his brother, he was in Paris buying Italian works of art from Napoleon. So vast were his purchases that 36 huge packing-cases were needed to ship them back to England. Ten years later he visited Pompeii where Queen Caroline of Naples presented him with a bronze satyr.

Such collecting called for further expansion, and in 1818 another royal architect, Sir Jeffrey Wyatville, was summoned by the duke to enlarge the sculpture gallery to house Woburn's new treasures.

As John Russell became too old himself to travel the roads of Europe looking for new treasures, he commissioned his eldest son, Francis, to collect for him. He advised Francis to inspire his own son 'with a taste for fine arts, that when I am dead and gone, the interesting pursuit may not be lost sight of at Woburn'.

Many later dukes fulfilled his hopes and shared the taste for the fine arts. But the incomparable treasure house was now complete. The role of later members of the family was to be custodians of the riches they had inherited, riches which are a lasting memorial to the 'interesting pursuit' as it was followed by three 18th-century aristocrats at Woburn.

GIFT FROM A KING *Three pieces from the Sèvres dinner service, given to John Russell and his wife by Louis XV of France. Now on display in the China Room, it cost £18,374.*

A VISIONARY GLIMPSES HIS 'GREEN AND PLEASANT LAND'

When William Blake was eight years old, he told his parents that he had seen the terrible face of God looking at him through a window, and 'a tree filled with angels'. These were the first of the visions which were to inspire and intoxicate him. He grew up to be a prolific artist and writer who believed that everything he produced was derived from a supernatural source.

Yet Blake was also a very practical man, with one foot firmly in the world of business. His father, a Soho hosier, was wise enough to encourage the boy's artistic bent by sending him to art school and, by the age of 14, Blake was an apprenticed engraver. In 1778 he completed his training and for the next 20 years he made a modest living executing commissions for booksellers and publishers.

In 1780 he gave his first exhibition of pictures at the Royal Academy. A year later he met Catherine Boucher, the uneducated daughter of a market gardener, and asked her to marry him. She could not share his visions, but devoted her life to the visionary.

Although many people thought that Blake was a little mad, Catherine's respect for the man and his work was shared by his fellow artists and writers. He struck his artist friend Samuel Palmer as 'a man without a mask'.

In 1789, when Blake was unable to find a publisher for his *Songs of Innocence*, Catherine was sent out with their last half-crown to buy printing materials. Blake then inscribed his poems on copper plates, embellishing the margins with his flowing designs; and Catherine learnt to print from these blocks. Husband and wife coloured the pages and Catherine stitched them together to form neat books. A sequel, *Songs of Experience*, followed five years later. In their appearance and their contents these two books were among the most original and profound works ever produced in Britain. They included the powerful short poems which have assured Blake of immortality, ranging from the fierce intensity of 'Tyger, Tyger, burning bright' to the tender innocence of 'Little lamb, who made thee?'

Blake spent most of his life in the crowded streets of 18th-century Soho. He was never far removed from poverty, and his feelings were aroused by his fellow prisoners of a cruel society, wronged heroes of the haunting lyric which he called simply, 'London':

In every cry of every man,
In every infant's cry of fear,
In every voice, in every ban,
The mind-forged manacles I hear.

How the chimney-sweeper's cry
Every blackening church appalls;
And the hapless soldier's sigh
Runs in blood down palace walls.

But most through midnight streets I hear
How the youthful harlot's curse
Blasts the newborn infant's tear,
And blights with plagues the marriage
*   hearse.*

In this mood of protest and compassion, Blake was keenly aware of all such victims, wearers of what he called 'mind-forged

SATAN'S CURSE *Job lies stricken as Lucifer smites him with a plague of sore boils. This comes from Blake's main artistic work, the 22 illustrations he produced for his* Book of Job *near the end of his life.*

FIERCE INTENSITY *In his attempts to express his visions in paint, Blake filled the space with colour and writhing forms. Paintings such as this – 'Elohim Creating Adam' – are alive with fire and energy.*

GLIMPSE OF HELL *The majesty of Blake's inspiration is seen in 'The Simoniac Pope', with its leaping flames and iridescent colours. The intensity of his poems and pictures has assured him immortality.*

STRANGE DREAMER *William Blake was the visionary of English art and poetry.*

manacles'. Such were the shaven-headed chimney-sweep boys, the soldiers doomed to die in futile wars and the unwanted babies born to London prostitutes. His sympathies extended to the other hapless sufferers from human cruelty, the animals:

A Robin Redbreast in a cage
Puts all Heaven in a rage.
A dog starv'd at his Master's gate
Predicts the ruin of the State,
A horse misus'd upon the road
Calls to Heaven for human blood.

When the Revolution broke out in France, the poet walked through the streets of London wearing the red cap of liberty. He was one of the first English writers to perceive the human costs of the Industrial Revolution, with its 'dark Satanic mills' spreading across a once 'green and pleasant land', and he pledged himself to a life-long crusade:

Bring me my Bow of burning gold!
Bring me my Arrows of desire!
Bring me my Spear! O clouds, unfold!
Bring me my Chariot of fire!

I will not cease from Mental Fight,
Nor shall my Sword sleep in my hand,
Till we have built Jerusalem
In England's green and pleasant land.

The same spirit of independence and revolt inspired his painting. He looked with utter derision on the work of his conventional contemporaries, and he had no interest in pictorial realism. He expressed his own aims in art in the form of an answer to an imaginary question from one of his critics: 'What,' it will be questioned, 'when the sun rises, do you not see a round disc of fire somewhat like a guinea?' To this Blake replied: 'O no, no I see an innumerable company of the heavenly host crying "Holy, Holy, Holy is the Lord God Almighty!"'

As both a major artist and a great poet, Blake stands alone in Britain's heritage. He represented no tendency, belonged to no school, but pursued his solitary path with heroic single-mindedness.

TWO PROPHETS OF NATURE TRANSFORM ENGLISH POETRY

The most productive friendship in the history of English literature took root in 1797. In that year William Wordsworth and his sister, Dorothy, moved to Alfoxden, on the Quantock Hills of Somerset, to be near Samuel Taylor Coleridge, whom they had met the year before. Together almost daily, they roamed the hills, discussing poetry – 'three persons and one soul', as Dorothy described them.

The friendship continued when the three moved to the Lake District, and over the next few years the creative force of these two young men was to change the course of English poetry. In his preface to their joint collection of poems, *Lyrical Ballads*, published a year later, Wordsworth explained their purpose: 'To choose incidents and situations from common life' and to describe them in 'language really used by men.'

In the first rapture of friendship, Coleridge wrote his greatest poems – 'The Ancient Mariner' and 'Kubla Khan'. But by 1802 Coleridge, dragged down by ill-health and a disastrous marriage, had fallen victim to despair:

A grief without a pang, void, dark
and drear,
A stifled, drowsy, unimpassioned grief.

In the same year Wordsworth also felt that his own inspiration was failing:

It is not now as it has been of yore;
Turn whereso'er I may,
By night or day,
The things which I have seen I now can
see no more.

Instinctively he turned back to the source of his power – his memories of childhood – and wrote his autobiographical masterpiece, the

CREATIVE FORCE *Samuel Taylor Coleridge achieved his greatest work during the few years of his friendship with the poet Wordsworth.*

'Prelude', which he dedicated to Coleridge.

In 1810 the great friendship ended in a bitter quarrel over Coleridge's dependence on drugs. Coleridge lived on to dazzle London with his conversation. But his poetic genius had died away.

In middle age Dorothy became insane, crying out like a naughty child to the tourists who came to catch a glimpse of her famous brother – by now Poet Laureate. Deprived of the companionship of the two people who had been his inspiration, the old poet spent his days pacing the mountain paths, producing moralistic verse. The glory had departed, and everything he saw reminded him of his loss:

But there's a tree, of many, one
A single field which I have looked upon,
Both of them speak of something that is
gone . . .
Whither is fled the visionary gleam?
Where is it now, the glory and the dream?

VALLEY OF CONTENTMENT *For half a century Grasmere (left) in the Lake District was the home of the poet William Wordsworth (right). He wrote of the valley's 'blended holiness of earth and sky . . . Made for itself and happy in itself, Perfect contentment, unity entire'.*

Triumph and tragedy as Nelson dies at Trafalgar

HEARTS OF OAK

Nelson chose the Victory *to be his flagship in 1803. Launched in 1765, she carried 800 officers and men and was armed with 104 guns. Today she is moored in Portsmouth Dockyard, a permanent memorial to Nelson's greatest victory – Trafalgar.*

THE BATTLE BEGINS *Nelson, flanked by his officers, stands on the quarter-deck of the* Victory, *issuing his orders as she goes into action for the first time. Within minutes, the first enemy broadsides struck the ship, inflicting heavy casualties. But, despite his subordinates' pleas, Nelson refused to take shelter.*

In the perilous year of 1805, England stood in daily fear of invasion. Napoleon's all-conquering *Grand Armée* was being made ready for the conquest of the country which for 12 years had stood between France and the domination of Europe.

Only one thing was lacking to fulfil Napoleon's plans – command of the sea. And this issue was decided off Cape Trafalgar, near the port of Cadiz. There, in a clash which was to decide the fate of two empires, the Royal Navy, commanded by Horatio, Lord Nelson, faced the combined French and Spanish fleets under the French Admiral Villeneuve.

Preparing for battle

Just before dawn on October 21, 1805, Nelson ordered his ships to prepare for battle. As the British fleet appeared on the horizon, Villeneuve realised that he must fight a decisive engagement. Nelson, too, had stressed that this was to be a battle of annihilation – of ships blown sky-high, not captured, of men drowned, not taken prisoner.

Until Nelson, naval strategy had been very simple. Fleets had sailed into action in two parallel lines, each ship taking on a single opponent. A fleet to the windward could always withdraw, so that overwhelming victories were rare.

At Trafalgar, Nelson broke completely with this tradition. He divided his fleet into two groups. One of them would attack sections of the enemy line and destroy them before other ships could come to their assistance. The other would attack the enemy at right angles, break through their line and cut off their retreat. The brilliance of the 'Nelson touch' marked a revolution in naval strategy.

But it was a risky business, for it demanded a very high standard of courage and seamanship. As Nelson's ships were advancing head-on, they would have to face the massed broadsides of the enemy for some time before they could bring their own guns to bear. When Nelson explained his plan to his captains they had never heard of anything like it. But Nelson was confident that his revolutionary new tactics would bring about the total destruction of the French fleet.

Soon after daybreak, Nelson came on to the deck of his flagship, HMS *Victory*. As usual, despite the protests of his officers, he showed his courage by wearing glittering full-dress

uniform, with the four stars of his orders pinned to his left breast. Action had not yet been joined and he returned to his cabin to add a codicil to his will. This commended Lady Hamilton and his daughter, Horatia, to the generosity of the nation.

'England expects'

Back on deck, Nelson told Captain Blackwood that he would 'amuse the fleet with a signal'. The words Nelson chose were 'England confides that every man will do his duty'. The signal officer, Lieutenant John Pascoe, explained that 'confides' would have to be spelt out, whereas one signal would be enough for 'expects'. 'That will do, Pascoe,' replied Nelson. 'Make it directly. As the cheers rang out, Nelson turned to Blackwood with the words: 'Now I can do no more. We must trust to the Great Disposer of all events, and the justice of our cause.'

The battle followed the course that Nelson had intended. The *Victory* led the northern or 'weather' column. The southern or 'lee' column was headed by the *Royal Sovereign*, under the second-in-command, Admiral Collingwood. As the British came within range of

THE NELSON TOUCH

The brilliant new ideas which Nelson introduced into naval strategy were not the product of careful study, but expressed his personal qualities of character. He was a single-minded and determined fighter, with little regard for his own or others' safety. He had no patience with the gentlemanly rules of war which declared that battles were more affairs of honour than ruthless fights to the finish. Nelson believed in risking all to reach a decisive conclusion. 'My disposition,' he wrote, 'cannot bear tame or slow measures.'

Nelson's preference for an open challenge and a fight to the finish had proved itself in his victory at the Battle of the Nile in 1798. But it was at Trafalgar, where he had a free hand for the first time, that his method reached perfection. His confidence inspired his officers when he told them of his battle plan. 'It was like an electric shock,' he wrote to his mistress, Lady Hamilton. 'Some shed tears, all approved. It was new, it was singular, it was simple.'

Before the battle Nelson explains his plan to his captains on board the Victory. *He divided his fleet into two squadrons – one to break the enemy line, the other to block retreat.*

A SCANDALOUS ROMANCE

Nelson's life was transformed by his love for the handsome Lady Emma Hamilton (left). Emma was born in Cheshire in 1765. She went to London as a nursemaid in 1788, but soon became the mistress of several men of fashion. Among them was Sir William Hamilton, British Ambassador to Naples, whom she married in 1791.

Nelson and Emma first met in Naples in 1792, but it was not until they both returned to England in 1800 that open scandal broke out. Cartoonists delighted in caricaturing the two lovers. When Emma bore Nelson a daughter, Horatia, in 1801, his wife left him.

Even on his deathbed at Trafalgar, Nelson's thoughts were of his mistress and his child. Almost his last words were: 'Remember, I leave Lady Hamilton and my daughter Horatia as a legacy to my country. And never forget Horatia.' But in 1813 Emma fled from England to avoid her creditors. She died at Calais a year later.

the enemy, Nelson exclaimed: 'I'll give them such a dressing as they've never had before.'

The column led by the *Victory* was now heading for the enemy centre, and the one led by the *Royal Sovereign* for the rear. Collingwood made for the towering and elaborately painted *Santa Anna*. As the *Royal Sovereign* turned her broadside against the Spanish flagship, Nelson called out: 'See how that noble fellow Collingwood carries his ship into action.'

The *Royal Sovereign* broke through the enemy line soon after noon. As she did so she

discharged one broadside into the *Fouqueux* and another into the *Indomptable*. Collingwood was followed by the *Belleisle*, which took on seven ships drifting northwards; the *Royal Sovereign* was being fired on by eight ships simultaneously.

Now it was Nelson's turn. Hitherto, his role had been one of deception, keeping the enemy uncertain where he would strike. The centre was his target and at 12.30 p.m. the *Victory* went into close action. One of its broadsides killed 100 men on the *Bucentaire* and, cutting

across another French ship, the *Redoubtable*, the *Victory* pierced the enemy line.

Nelson had trained his gunners to fire one broadside every 80 seconds. No ship in the world could match that rate of fire. All around, ships fought at point-blank range in a kind of sea-battle never attempted before. There was confusion, but it was clear who was winning.

'They have done for me at last'

As the battle raged, Nelson stood on his quarter-deck, one of the most exposed parts of the ship. Soon after 1.00 p.m. came the fatal shots from two snipers placed in the rigging of the *Redoubtable*, which was now in close conflict with the *Victory*.

Nelson was turning to go down a hatchway, when a musket ball struck the epaulette on his left shoulder and penetrated his chest. He fell flat on the deck, but was helped up. Nelson cried out to his friend, Captain Thomas Masterman Hardy: 'They have done for me at last, Hardy; my backbone is shot through.' The admiral was carried gently below.

To those who told Nelson that he might live, he replied: 'My sufferings are great but they will soon be over.' After making a brief examination, the *Victory's* surgeon, Beatty, had to agree. 'My Lord, unhappily for our country, nothing can be done for you.'

Nelson called for Hardy, who was able to assure the admiral that the Battle of Trafalgar was turning into a brilliant victory. Already, 14 enemy ships had struck their colours.

In a failing voice, Nelson implored Hardy: 'Take care of my dear Lady Hamilton,' and he added, scarcely audibly, 'Kiss me, Hardy!' The captain bent down and kissed Nelson's cheek. The dying admiral whispered: 'Now I am satisfied. Thank God I have done my duty.' As the captain was leaving, Nelson called out 'God bless you, Hardy.'

'I have done my duty'

Nelson lay dying for three hours. In his last conscious moments his words were again: 'Thank God I have done my duty.' A doctor massaged his chest, while an officer supported his shoulders. Then, as the *Victory's* log recorded: 'Partial firing continued until 4.30, when, a victory having been reported to the Right Honourable Viscount Nelson, KB and Commander in Chief, he died of his wound.'

After repairs in Gibraltar, the *Victory* sailed for England, bearing Nelson's body home for burial. His death marred the joyful celebrations of victory, but there was no mistaking the crucial significance of the battle in which he had perished.

Victory at Trafalgar ended French hopes of the conquest of England. Now that Napoleon's fleet was utterly vanquished, the danger of invasion had finally disappeared. No such threat would occur for another 135 years.

THE NEWS COMES HOME *A* Times *poster announces the victory – and the death of Nelson.*

THE DYING HERO *In the cramped space of the* Victory's *cockpit, Nelson lies mortally wounded. Two surgeons are in attendance, one taking his pulse, the other massaging his chest to relieve the pain. Leaning above Nelson is his closest friend, Captain Hardy.*

Nelson's navy – his 'Bequest to the Nation'

The news of Trafalgar and the death of Nelson reached England on November 5, 1805. In his despatch, Admiral Collingwood lamented 'the loss of a hero whose name will be immortal'. The spirit that Nelson had inspired in all ranks of the navy – from admiral to cabin boy – lived on. His legend inspired the continuing success of the navy throughout the 19th century.

Life in Nelson's navy was hard. Lack of space meant that even officers lived in cramped and uncomfortable quarters. They entered the service at the age of 13 and lived below the water line in the stinking after-cockpit, next to the supplies of rancid butter. The common seamen lived and slept among the weapons and gear of the gun decks. Their mess tables were fixed between the gun barrels and then hooked to beams when not in use.

At sea, officers and men ate the same food. There was 'ship's biscuit' – made of wheat flour usually adulterated with bone dust – which became infested with maggots on a long voyage. Meat had often been in salt for several years. It was shrunken and glistened with salt crystals. When it came to the cook, it was, according to one observer, 'believed to be salt horse, resembling very much a piece of mahogany, and often quite as sapless'.

A mutiny born of despair

In 1797 conditions became so bad that the squadrons stationed at Spithead and the Nore mutinied. At Spithead the men's demands were met, after a week's strike, by the one officer they trusted, Admiral Lord Howe. He rowed from ship to ship carrying letters of pardon from George III. The mutiny at the Nore was not so easily settled. It was apparently caused by the Admiralty's refusal to share out prize money equally. But when the mutineers began to quarrel among themselves, the Admiralty seized its chance and ruthlessly suppressed it. Richard Parker, the leader of the mutiny who had proclaimed 'the Floating Republic', was hanged.

After the mutinies, some increase in the pay of ordinary seamen and an improvement in the quality of supplies took place. But life was still astonishingly harsh. Offences such as drunkenness were often punished by death. The most usual punishment, though, was flogging with the cat-o'-nine tails; the cat was a short wooden stick covered with red baize, while the tails were pieces of knotted cord about 2 ft long. The flogging and the brutality of life in the Royal Navy horrified even the Prussians, whose army was the most savagely disciplined in Europe.

Punishment was at the discretion of the captain and might be anything from 36 to 72 strokes. Nelson and Collingwood were both noted for their humanity to their men, and seldom had more than one man flogged a month.

The men who survived on this diet and endured these punishments did not serve through choice. In the sea-ports of Britain the most dreaded sound was the marching steps of the press-gang. Law-abiding citizens could be seized in the streets and shanghaied to a waiting ship, to find themselves under the discipline of the Articles of War.

Bond of pride

Despite the brutality of life at sea, there was genuine friendship between officers and men. After a flogging, a man went back to his post and, by custom, his offence was never mentioned again. Jokes were usually taken in good part. A sailor found praying before going into action at Trafalgar explained: 'I was only praying that the enemy shot may be distributed in the same proportion as the purse money.' Seamen did not like weak officers because they knew this would only leave them in the power of harsh subordinates.

Captain and crew alike expected British and foreign merchant ships to lower their top-sails when passing a British man-of-war. Nelson's daring and his success in battle added to this feeling of pride. The impact of Nelson had been immense. He had given his country the supremacy of the seas. This was not to be challenged for the next 100 years. As Collingwood said of officers and men at Trafalgar: 'The spirit which animated all was the same.' A little of Nelson – his imagination, his fearless courage and his dedication to his duty – rubbed off on the whole of the Royal Navy. In that sense, he was immortal.

POPULAR HOMAGE

More than any other figure of his age, Nelson won the love and admiration of the British people. Through his cool courage, his dash and his flair he became the supreme popular hero of the day. Souvenirs of Nelson began to be made after the Battle of the Nile. They depicted either the admiral himself or his exploits, which had been so daring that they had cost him an arm and the sight of an eye. Such was the magic of Nelson's achievements that they continued to be produced throughout the 19th century.

Three snuff-boxes and a pottery group show Nelson's exploits, his ship and his death.

A march against time to save Britain's army

MEDAL OF HONOUR

To commemorate the brave stand of the British army against the French at Corunna, George III ordered the striking of a gold medal for the survivors. This example can be seen at the National Army Museum, London.

In 1808, Napoleon's empire stretched unchallenged over the continent of Europe. All the powers which had dared to challenge him on the field of battle had been overthrown. Ancient kingdoms had been reduced to powerless satellites and reluctant allies. Only Britain held out against the might of the 'Corsican tyrant' – but she had no foothold on the European continent from which her forces could attack him.

In that year, however, Napoleon invaded Spain and Portugal, where his forces met with desperate resistance. Britain was quick to send an army to the scene. Portugal was secured and British troops swiftly advanced into Spain.

In September 1808 Sir John Moore, the son of a Glasgow doctor, was appointed commander of the British forces in Spain and Portugal. Moore was 46, a handsome athletic man, with broad shoulders and penetrating eyes. He was adored by his men for, unlike many of his fellow generals, he treated them like intelligent human beings, not mere cannon fodder. He had given proof of his qualities of leadership in his creation of the Rifle Brigade, a corps of shock troops. A senior staff officer wrote: 'Everyone admires and loves him.'

Trapped deep in enemy country

But destiny was not on his side, for it was Moore's misfortune to find himself leading an army of 30,000 men against 300,000, commanded by the greatest military genius of the age. On November 1, Napoleon himself marched into Spain. In the face of this onslaught, the Spanish armies melted away. The British were trapped deep in hostile territory.

Napoleon was determined to annihilate Moore's army, even at the cost of delaying the conquest of Spain. Moore's only hope was to march 250 miles across the peninsula, threatening Napoleon's line of communication with France, to reach the sea where he and his men could be evacuated by the Royal Navy.

A French army of 18,000 seasoned troops under Marshal Soult was in the forefront of the pursuit. The British occasionally turned on Soult and inflicted heavy casualties. But they

A HERO'S FINEST HOUR *Only the inspired leadership of Sir John Moore (left) maintained order in the British army during its 250 mile retreat to Corunna in 1809. There the British fought a brilliant rearguard action (below) against the pursuing French, and embarked for home. But Moore himself was killed in his hour of triumph.*

FROM DEFEAT TO VICTORY

The British have always been good at turning a retreat into a triumph, and Sir John Moore's retreat to Corunna was only the beginning of an epic struggle by which the British army was to bring down Napoleon himself. The news of the retreat had spread dismay at home, but a new commander was soon chosen. He was a man whose spirit would not brook defeat – Arthur Wellesley, later Duke of Wellington.

His first task was to hold Britain's foothold in Portugal against Napoleon's army. For three years he played cat and mouse with the French, who outnumbered him by 250,000 to 45,000 men. But Wellington had two priceless advantages. The first were the Spanish guerrillas, who mercilessly harried the hated French. The other was the dauntless spirit of the British troops. 'Their soldiers,' Wellington said of the French generals, 'always got them into scrapes. Mine always got me out.' Triumph came in 1812 and 1813, after Napoleon had drained Spain of men for his ill-fated Russian campaign. In two great victories – Salamanca and Vittoria – Wellington liberated Spain. His success inspired the rest of enslaved Europe to throw off the French yoke.

Privates of the Rifle Brigade fight their way through the snow to Corunna in 1808. Their courage and resolution inspired the British army during the course of the long retreat.

could not afford to tarry for, by December 24, Napoleon and his vast force were only 20 miles behind.

Moore's men had been marching hard since October, but now their commander ordered them to double their speed – through mountain country at the worst possible time of year. By day, the roads were rivers of mud; at night, they became treacherous glaciers. Food was short, clothing in tatters, boots worn out.

The troops were still urged on. 'By Jesus, Master Hill,' demanded an exhausted private, 'where the devil is this you're taking us to?' The officer replied: 'To England, McLaughlin, if you can get there.'

Seeing their liberators in full retreat, the Spanish population became hostile. Some villagers even refused to give water to the British wounded. Under such provocation, discipline came close to breaking down. On several occasions soldiers burnt down villages in their quest for drink to relieve their misery. But, under Moore's resilient command, discipline was maintained and the British were able to hold off the Imperial Guard, the flower of the French army.

At last, the shoeless, scarecrow army reached the sea at Corunna on January 10, 1809. But they looked in vain for the transports which were to take them back to England. Moore could only dig himself in and hope that the navy would arrive before the French.

Eventually, the missing transports docked, and by January 16 the last stores and baggage had been embarked. At 2.00 p.m. Moore remarked: 'Now if there is no bungling, I hope we should get away in a few hours.'

At that moment, Soult's forces began to close in. With many of their guns already on board ship, the British were at a disadvantage

and the French swept forward. Their batteries poured shells into the British lines.

Moore had carefully kept two divisions in reserve. He now ordered them to join the fighting, and the French were driven back. Moore cried encouragement to the Black Watch: 'If you've fired your ammunition, you've still your bayonets!'

Sacrifice of a brave general

It was clear that the British would now be able to escape. But in his moment of triumph a French cannon ball struck Moore.

The shot carried away his left shoulder; part of his lungs was exposed to the air and his arm hung only from a tatter of flesh. His face appeared absolutely unmoved. He rejected all medical assistance, telling the surgeons: 'You can be of no service to me. Go to the wounded soldiers to whom you may be useful.' He insisted on keeping his sword, and ordered that his bearers should stop to let him see what was happening.

While the last of his troops embarked, Moore lay dying. He asked after his officers and commended Lord Paget. He whispered: 'I hope the people of England will be satisfied; I hope my country will do me justice.'

As dawn broke on the following morning, a small party of officers and men made its way along the landward ramparts of the Corunna citadel, bearing the body of their dead commander. Moore was wrapped in a military cloak and laid to rest with hurried ceremony.

By his selfless actions, Moore had saved his army; 24,000 men were safely evacuated. These veterans were to form the core of a new force which, under the Duke of Wellington, was to return to Spain, drive out the French and bring down the great Napoleon himself.

The twilight years of Britain's 'mad king'

For the whole of the Napoleonic Wars, England was ruled by George III, who has gone down in history as the 'mad king'. But George showed no sign of derangement until 1788; before that he enjoyed excellent health.

Total madness suddenly appeared on November 5. That night, at dinner in Windsor Castle, George seized the Prince of Wales by the collar and tried to smash his head against the wall. The other members of the Royal Family rushed to restrain him. Gradually the king's ravings degenerated into gibberish.

George's doctors, led by Francis Willis, believed that madness was evil, and that the only way to cure it was by punishment. Mustard plasters were placed on George's legs to cause blisters which would draw away his evil humours. When, in his agony, the king would try to tear them off he was put in a strait-jacket – on occasions for 24 hours.

In spite of Willis's treatment, George gradually regained his sanity. There were relapses in 1801 and 1804, but final madness did not descend until 1810. The king spent his last years shambling round a small set of rooms overlooking the North Terrace of Windsor Castle.

More and more, George's appearance came to resemble that of Shakespeare's King Lear. He became blind. He was almost completely bald and had grown a flowing white beard. The only thing to show that this pathetic old man was the King of England – and the last monarch of America – was the Star of the Garter which he kept pinned to his dressing-gown. So he lived, rambling on about events long forgotten and men long since dead, until he himself finally found peace at the end of January 1820.

MAD KING *A contemporary artist depicts the aged George III, bald, bearded and almost blind, as Shakespeare's tragic hero, King Lear.*

The struggle to win Reform

Triumph at Waterloo brings no peace to a nation divided into rich and poor, but the threat of revolution forces Britain along the road of reform

In 1810 the threat of French domination still hung over Europe. England, alone among the nations that had taken up arms against France, had managed to avoid defeat at the hands of Napoleon. But under the impetus of war, its two nations – rich and poor – had moved further apart. The poor suffered under the combined weight of low wages and high wartime prices, while the aristocracy flung itself into exuberant extravagance.

The spendthrifts of the aristocracy found their natural leader in George, Prince of Wales, who became Prince Regent when his father finally went mad in 1810. Gamblers and dicers lounged in the royal staterooms. Fashions came and went with the seasons. Low necklines and German waltzes gave the impression that the British upper classes had surrendered to frivolity and vice. At the Royal Pavilion in Brighton (pp. 278–9), the stately pleasure dome of Regency England, the Prince Regent escaped from the tedious business of government by indulging himself in gambling, drinking and 18-course banquets. And men of all classes followed his example (pp. 276–7).

While the Prince Regent dallied, the Duke of Wellington was winning the war for Britain. In the Peninsular War in Spain, his armies took the offensive against the French, forcing them back across the Pyrenees and into their own territory. For its part, the British government poured out subsidies to every nation in Europe willing to fight Napoleon. In 1812, Britain's expenditure rose to the unprecedented figure of £118 million; by the end of the war in 1814, when Napoleon abdicated, the National Debt had risen

A DIVIDED NATION

The rich of the West End rub shoulders with the poor from the slums of the East End during a parliamentary election held in Covent Garden in 1818. The popular mood was demonstrated in banners calling for 'Universal Suffrage' and 'Magna Charta'. But they went unheeded.

Covent Garden, little changed today (inset), was one of the few places where the great debate could be carried on, as elections in the City of Westminster were relatively free.

The two nations of Regency England were in constant conflict. The poor demanded greater freedom; the rich replied with repression.

But by 1832 the reformers' demands could only be resisted at the cost of revolution. In that year Parliament was finally reformed.

DEATH IN THE COMMONS *Spencer Perceval (left), Prime Minister of England, meets his death at the hands of the insane Francis Bellingham in the lobby of the House of Commons on May 12, 1812. Bellingham killed Perceval for personal reasons, but his crime was seen as part of the unrest that was sweeping England at the height of the Napoleonic Wars. The unrest stemmed from Napoleon's 'Continental System', which had closed Europe to British trade and thrown thousands out of work at home.*

REFORM AND REPRESSION *The coming of peace in 1815 did not diminish the suffering which led to demand for reform. A trade slump in 1819 gave rise to widespread agitation and, on August 16, some 50,000 people assembled at St Peter's Field, Manchester, to press for reform. The local magistrates panicked and sent in the yeomanry; in the 'Peterloo massacre' 11 were killed.*

POPULAR VOICE *The cartoonist George Cruikshank summed up the mood of popular discontent with England's system of government under the Regency. A Briton is shown in rags, with his mouth padlocked to stop him spreading sedition against king and constitution. The government's response to popular discontent was not reform but repression.*

from £252 million to £861 million. And when the 'Corsican tyrant' returned to France a year later, it was Wellington who again defeated him. By crushing Napoleon at the Battle of Waterloo in 1815 (pp. 280–3) he laid the foundations for a lasting peace. The duke arrived back in England as a conquering hero. By 1818 he had been made a cabinet minister and the leader of the Tory Party in the House of Lords. For the following 20 years, his prestige and influence were decisive factors in British politics. 'The duke is against it!' was often enough to damn any proposal.

The effect of peace was to turn men's minds either in hope or in fear away from the French peril, and towards those currents of change that had for so long been dammed up by the national effort against Napoleon. The country to which the duke returned seemed both to him and his colleagues in the government to be almost as dangerous a place as the Continent. Wellington had not fought revolutionary France to see its insidious principles established in his own country.

In the early 19th century, the House of Commons was an exclusive club rather than a body representing the people of Britain. Nearly all its members came from the land-owning aristocracy – most of them men who had little knowledge of or sympathy with the lives of men less fortunate than themselves. Peace brought great hardship and unemployment, as the soldiers returned and the demand for British manufactured goods, which had been stimulated by the war, fell off sharply.

The House of Commons, however, was only concerned to protect the wealth and privileges of the aristocracy. It repealed the income tax William Pitt had imposed in 1793 to help pay for the war; and it passed the Corn Laws, which forbade the import of foreign wheat at low prices. This kept up the high wartime price of food.

The result was deep unrest throughout the country. Mobs surrounded Parliament, holding up rope halters and crying 'No starvation! No landlords!' The home of the minister who had introduced the legislation was sacked. Riots by farm labourers in the south and strikes by coal miners in the north culminated in a great reform meeting in London in December 1816. Demands for the abolition of the Corn Laws and for the reform of Parliament swept the country, but the Tory government's frightened response was to suspend *Habeas Corpus*, so that agitators could be imprisoned without trial, and to outlaw 'seditious meetings'.

Two nations – bitterly divided

In 1819 trouble flared up again. This time the centre was not London but the north, the heart of the industrial challenge to the traditional power of the landed aristocracy. At Manchester, the home of the cotton industry and the most important of the growing towns which were still unrepresented in Parliament, a great meeting was held to petition the government for parliamentary reform. It attracted an enormous crowd of 50,000. The local magistrates ordered in the troops of the county yeomanry to disperse the crowd. In the resulting chaos 11 people were killed and 400 injured. The tragedy quickly became known as the 'Peterloo massacre', and a legend was born of popular resistance to repression and tyranny.

Peterloo did not stop the demand for reform and, in the following year, the monarchy itself became the subject of open attack. When George III at last died, his son, George IV, was determined that the wife he so hated, Caroline of Brunswick, should not be crowned queen, and demanded that the government bring in a Bill for her divorce (pp. 284–5). Caroline was a vulgar, brassy woman, but the mob thronged the streets of London in her support and, when the divorce was abandoned, howled with delight. Never had the prestige of the crown sunk so low in the eyes of the British people.

Contempt for George IV was reflected in the verses of Shelley, Keats and Byron, the greatest poets of the day (pp. 286–7). Shelley and Keats had both been inspired by the ideals of the French Revolution, while Byron, who was to die for the liberty of a foreign land, railed against 'the fourth of the fools and oppressors called George'.

But it was technological, not intellectual, ferment that was to speed reform. The Royal Institution spread the knowledge of modern science. Under its auspices, the most brilliant scientists of the day, among them Davy and Faraday (p. 287), lectured to vast audiences of both high and low. And their work in their laboratories – particularly in the field of electricity – was soon put to practical use in transforming Britain still further.

FIRST POLICE *In the 1820's the government realised that only reform would stave off revolution. One of the reforms introduced by Sir Robert Peel, the Home Secretary, was an efficient civilian police force. Its members were nicknamed 'Peelers' or 'Bobbies' after him. Previously, the only force that the government could call on to preserve law and order in times of unrest had been the army.*

Reform changes the face of Britain

Another revolution was the coming of railways. In 1829 Stephenson's *Rocket* (pp. 288–9) finally convinced sceptics that self-propelled locomotives were safe and efficient. So began the great railway boom that was to affect every aspect of life in Britain. The railways gave Englishmen the feeling that industrial success was a noble and glorious objective for any civilised nation. The liberal headmaster of Rugby School, Dr Thomas Arnold, looked down from a bridge on a passing train and exclaimed: 'I rejoice to see it and to think that feudality is gone for ever.' Any remaining 18th-century prejudice against trade was banished; 19th-century England saw the railways as portents of an ever-increasing prosperity. Their importance was reflected in the painting 'Rain, Steam and Speed' by William Turner, who gave artistic expression to the new age just as John Constable had to the old (pp. 292–3).

The pace of change was reflected in the politics of the 1820's. At the Foreign Office, George Canning turned his back on the despotic powers of Europe and recognised the new democratic republics of South America. At the Board of Trade, William Huskisson eased the lot of the poor and gave a spur to industrial advance by reducing the customs duties on imports, including food. In 1825 a major step was taken to secure the rights of workers. The Combination Acts, which prevented workers from forming Trades Unions to press for higher wages or better working conditions, were repealed. And at the end of the decade, even the Duke of Wellington, who had now become Prime Minister, was forced to yield. In 1829 Roman Catholics were allowed to become Members of Parliament.

But there was one demand the Tories would not concede – reform of Parliament. By 1830 this had become irresistible. Severe famine had provoked outbreaks of mob violence and arson, while the large industrial towns of the north and Midlands chafed under their exclusion from Parliament.

Two years of bitter agitation followed. At a General Election the Tories were thrown out of power and the Whigs took office after 50 years in Opposition. To save the constitution, Lord Grey's government introduced a sweeping Reform Bill (pp. 290–1), abolishing the corrupt 'rotten boroughs' and giving the middle classes the vote. But the House of Lords threw out the Bill, and for several weeks Britain stood on the brink of revolution.

Now a new figure had the decisive voice. For George IV had died in 1830 and his moderate brother, William IV, was on the throne. He promised to create new peers to ensure the Bill's passage. Opposition collapsed and the Reform Bill became law.

In spite of its name, the Reform Act achieved only a small measure of reform. But it was a symbol. It showed that the landed aristocracy could be forced to share its power. And its passage was a sign that new forces were arising to change the face of British society.

PLOT AND CONSPIRACY *Radical fervour reached its height in the Cato Street Conspiracy of 1820. A group of conspirators, led by Arthur Thistlewood, planned to blow up the entire British cabinet over their dinner. Their heads were to be exhibited to the mob at the Mansion House, where Thistlewood was to be proclaimed president of a provisional government. But the plot was betrayed and the conspirators were arrested at their Cato Street headquarters (above).*

REFORM AT LAST *The Duke of Wellington – once the hero of Waterloo but now a hated reactionary – is surrounded by an angry mob outside his London home, Apsley House, in 1832. In that year, the demand for parliamentary reform grew so great that a Whig government passed the Great Reform Bill. This was only achieved after a year-long resistance by the House of Lords had brought Britain to the brink of revolution.*

WHEN PLEASURE RULED

No era in Britain's history has ever been as devoted to pleasure as the Regency. Even though the country was involved in a war with France, this only gave an added zest to its citizens' pursuit of amusement. With the extravagant figure of the Prince Regent as their example, high and low-born alike flung themselves into every kind of enjoyment. The robust amusements of the age, such as bull-baiting, prize-fighting and cock-fighting, attracted an enthusiastic following from every class of society. One of the nation's greatest figures, the Duke of Wellington, observed that there was 'nothing the people of this country like so much as to see their great men take part in their amusements'. And the popular ideal of the gentleman was of a fighting sportsman, ready at the slightest excuse to defend his honour with his fists or his pistols. Even after duelling was made illegal in 1828, duels continued to be fought.

Excess was the keynote of the age. Lord Petersham, a prominent dandy, took extravagance to the point of eccentricity. He indulged his fondness for snuff by keeping 3000 lb. of it permanently in stock, using a different snuff-box every day of the year, and painting his carriage snuff brown. Gambling to extremes was a universal passion. The rich squandered fortunes at the card tables of clubs such as Crockford's – whose owner made £1 million from it – while the poor patronised fairground gaming booths. In their pleasures, if in nothing else, the British were united as never before.

NEW DANCE *Introduced from Austria, the waltz created a sensation in England. It was thought immodest, and it took years before the waltz was accepted in fashionable circles.*

IN THE COUNTRY *Shooting duck in winter was a favourite country sport – but confined to the upper classes. It was illegal for anyone but a squire or his eldest son to shoot game.*

RARE RELAXATION *An engraving by Rowlandson of a country fair. Seasonal fairs were the high points of the rural year, giving country folk a rare chance to enjoy themselves and buy small luxuries from travelling pedlars.*

NATIONAL SPORT *Boxing had the greatest claim to be considered the national sport of Regency England. Prize-fighters such as Tom Cribb, who fought 76 rounds to become British champion, had a special status in high society and could win huge rewards from their noble patrons. But the price of fame was high; there were few rules and boxers fought bare-fisted until they fell.*

STAGE-STRUCK *Edmund Kean, the great Shakespearian actor, falls to the ground in one of his most famous scenes – the death of Richard III. His other famous roles included King Lear and Othello. Well-known actors were idolised by working people as well as by aristocrats. Attempts to raise London gallery prices caused riots in the theatres during this period.*

COURAGE *Fencing was an upper-class sport, esteemed as a school for duelling. The Regency saw the heyday of duelling.*

SCANDAL AND ROMANCE *London's courtesans were patronised by the famous. A cartoon shows Harriette Wilson, once mistress of the Duke of York, receiving compliments from her admirers.*

DANDY *Though neither rich nor high-born, George 'Beau' Brummel was the arbiter of Regency taste. He dressed with exquisite care, preferring sober perfection to showy display.*

THE GAMBLERS *Card-playing was a favourite pastime. While rich rakes lost fortunes overnight in their clubs, families enjoyed whist (above).*

BLOOD SPORTS *Cruelty was no barrier to pleasure in Regency England. Standards were less squeamish than now, and men of all classes found amusement in any kind of blood sport – especially if it also provided an opportunity to indulge their passion for gambling. At the Westminster rat pit (above), bets were placed on the terrier most likely to kill the greatest number of rats in a given time.*

FANTASY PALACE BUILT FOR A PRINCE OF PLEASURE

A contemporary said of the Prince Regent that he was 'a bad son, a bad husband, a bad monarch and a bad friend'. But posterity has taken a kinder view because of the prince's one redeeming feature: bad in so much else, he had good taste and he was one of the greatest patrons of the arts ever to occupy the throne of England.

He created the royal collection of paintings; he was responsible for the foundation of the National Gallery in London; he encouraged the great plan for rebuilding the West End of London, including the creation of Trafalgar Square, Regent Street and the terraces of Regent's Park. Above all, he created at Brighton a seaside palace which ranks as one of the most inventive and enjoyable works of architecture in Britain.

In his role as art collector and builder of palaces, George's worst failings – his extraordinary vanity and egoism, his limitless extravagance and wild irresponsibility in money matters – were turned to virtues. His vanity prompted him to dream of palaces of unparalleled splendour. His extravagance permitted him to fulfil even his wildest dreams. The marine pavilion at Brighton evolved from 40 years of this royal folly.

George, Prince of Wales, was just 19 when he began a lifelong association with Brighton. In 1783 he was persuaded that sea water would help cure some uncomfortable glandular swel-

EGYPTIAN INFLUENCES

As the French armies swept through Egypt in 1798, their commander, General Bonaparte, became obsessed with the ancient world of the pharaohs. He sent antiquities back to Paris, where Egyptian design soon became the rage. Despite the barriers of war, the fashion spread to England, where the Prince Regent introduced it into Brighton Pavilion.

NILE-INSPIRED *A couch shaped like an Egyptian river boat.*

BACK IN TIME *A clock in an ancient setting.*

SPHINX *Armchair for state occasions.*

CHINESE EXTRAVAGANZA *The Prince Regent's taste for Chinese art was given full flight in the Banqueting Room. Its centrepiece, a 1 ton chandelier with a lotus flower motif, hung from a gilded dragon in the dome. A typical menu for a banquet there listed 116 dishes.*

ORIENTAL FANTASY *It fell to John Nash to try to unify the Prince Regent's fashionable fantasies with a plan for the pavilion, shown here in a cross-section. He was inspired in 1815 by a book of Indian scenes painted by Thomas Daniell, which he had borrowed from the prince's library. But the prince's finances were in a precarious state and the* Prime Minister, Lord Liverpool, the Foreign Secretary and the Chancellor of the Exchequer warned him that Parliament would never vote further expenditure on the house. At last work began with a gift of £50,000 from the prince's mother, Queen Caroline. By 1820, when work finished, the pavilion had cost the enormous sum of £155,000.

lings in his neck, and he travelled to the quiet fishing village of Brighton for the first time.

Two years later, the young prince secretly married Mrs Fitzherbert, a beautiful widow of 25 who, as a Roman Catholic, was ineligible as a wife for the heir to a Protestant throne. He brought her to Brighton where he leased a house overlooking the Steine, a wide stretch of grass where fishermen spread their nets to dry.

But no modest seaside house was good enough for 'Prinny', as his friends affectionately called him. In 1787 he commissioned the architect Henry Holland, who had re-built Carlton House in London for him, to design a 'marine pavilion' on the site. The first pavilion – a bow-fronted house of pure Classical design – was completed in the same year.

The prince's taste, however, was constantly changing. In 1802 he was given a roll of Chinese wallpaper, and he immediately made plans to add a Chinese gallery. This was the beginning of the oriental decorations which soon spread to other parts of the house.

Even as the designers and craftsmen were at work on these elaborate Chinese decorations, the fickle prince had fallen in love with a new fashion – the romantic and glittering style of India's Mughal emperors. His imagination had been fired by Thomas and William Daniell's *Views of Oriental Scenery*. He ordered the most elaborate stable block ever built in Britain, including an iron and glass cupola 80 ft wide and 65 ft high, all in Indian style.

This building took six years to complete, and cost £70,000 – well over £1000 for each of the royal horses. The prince liked to remark that even his horses were now housed in a palace. William Hazlitt, the contemporary writer, took a more critical view: 'The King's horses (if they were horses of taste) would petition against such irrational lodging.'

The Prince Regent now had two exotic styles – Chinese and Indian – warring with each other inside the shell of a conventional Classical house. He was in need of an architect with the inventive power to unite the styles into the 'stately pleasure dome' of his dreams. The one man in Britain with the type of skill that was needed was John Nash, a self-taught speculative builder, who was already at work on his superbly dramatic transformation of the West End of London.

A prince and his architect

Nash was appointed Surveyor-General of royal buildings, and in 1815 began work on the pavilion. It took five years to complete. The exterior was transformed into an exotic version of Indian architecture, with a large bulbous dome built over the central salon and flanked by smaller domes on either side.

But it was inside that the extravagant fantasy was at its most imaginative. Writhing dragons rioted across the walls of the Music and Banqueting rooms whose roofs were shaped like Saracen tents. In the Banqueting Room hung a magnificent chandelier, which cost over £5000.

Even in the Great Kitchen, the supporting pillars of the high roof were made to look like palm trees. Here, the most celebrated chef of the day, Carême, presided over the ovens, with 15 chefs under him.

A prince's legacy

The Prince Regent's guests found the enormous meals, the stuffy heat, the dazzling architecture and their host's endless mealtime monologues somewhat overpowering, but nevertheless impressive. The prince's subjects, suffering from unemployment and poverty, were less easily pleased. In Parliament, one member of the Whig opposition summed up the feelings of the people when he described the pavilion as 'that squanderous and lavish profusion which resembled more the pomp and magnificence of a Persian satrap than the sober dignity of a British prince seated in the bosom of his subjects'.

Throughout the rest of his reign the pavilion continued to arouse the wrath of George's subjects. It was not until 100 years later that his extravagant folly was to be fully appreciated and enjoyed by the British people.

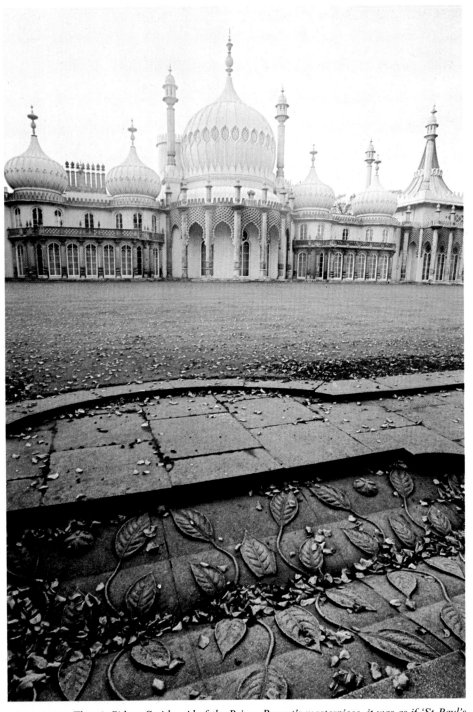

ROYAL WHIM *The wit Sidney Smith said of the Prince Regent's masterpiece, it was as if 'St Paul's had gone down to the sea and pupped'. But no sooner was the glittering oriental pavilion at Brighton completed in 1820, than the fickle prince lost interest and seldom visited it again.*

Victory at Waterloo–and Europe's fate is decided

WELLINGTON'S TRAVELLING CASE

The Duke of Wellington's travelling case, which accompanied him from his first campaigns in India to his last battle, Waterloo in 1815. It contains razors, nail scissors and medicine, and it now can be seen at Apsley House, London. But, unlike many of his junior officers, Wellington was a soldier, not a fashionable dandy.

NAPOLEON *In this contemporary picture, the French emperor is shown formed out of corpses and symbols of death – a reminder that his career as self-made master of Europe was built on pitiless conquest. Only the British, the 'nation of shopkeepers' he despised, held out; and at Waterloo in 1815 they brought him down.*

As the long afternoon of Sunday, June 18, 1815, wore on, the city of Brussels was in a state of panic. Since 3 p.m. refugees had been pouring in from south of the capital. Twelve miles away, on the field of Waterloo, the Duke of Wellington, with his Allied army, was barring the way of 70,000 French veterans under the command of Napoleon. The grumbling thunder of the guns grew louder, and rumours of Wellington's defeat swept through the city. 'I never saw such consternation,' wrote the diarist Fanny Burney. 'We could only gaze and tremble, listen and shudder.'

Only a few days previously, everyone in the Allied camp at Brussels had been supremely confident of victory. Leisurely preparations were being made for the invasion of France. Napoleon, whose untimely return from exile on the Mediterranean island of Elba had plunged Europe into renewed war, would finally be overthrown.

The Prussian army, under Marshal Blücher, numbered 113,000 men – almost as many as the largest striking force the French could possibly raise. Wellington's own army was 70,000 strong. And further east, 500,000 Austrians and Russians were massing.

But Napoleon struck first. He had made his reputation by daring – and now he risked everything on a lightning last throw, hoping to meet and defeat his enemies one by one. On June 15 his forces smashed through the feeble

frontier posts at the Belgian border. Wellington's main object was to keep in touch with the Prussians, so he ordered an immediate concentration of his forces. But the British were slow to obey their commander's orders, and by the end of the following day Napoleon had defeated the Prussians at Ligny.

Despite their defeat, the Prussians had managed to retire in good order. They kept in touch with the British, who now took up a defensive position at Waterloo and waited in a downpour for their allies to join them. Wellington was quietly confident as he went off to a glittering ball given by the Duchess of

THE IRON DUKE *Wellington's great victories against the French made him a popular hero.*

A GAMBLE THAT FAILED *Seeking the chance of a quick victory, Marshal Ney sent 5000 French horsemen against the British infantry squares at Waterloo. The French charged five times, but each time they were beaten back, suffering huge losses. The dead and wounded riders reminded Wellington of overturned turtles as they sprawled in the mud. Ney's gamble failed and the battle was lost when Blücher and his Prussians arrived to complete the French rout. A few days later Napoleon abdicated and went into exile. He had finally lost his throne.*

Richmond in Brussels. At 2 a.m. on June 18, Wellington retired to bed, slept for six hours and then rode out to see his troops. The French were there and about to attack – but the Prussians had not yet arrived. Wellington's plans had miscarried. He now had to face Napoleon's veterans alone; defeat seemed to many to be very near.

Two men of action

All would now depend on the quality of the two commanders and the bravery of the men they commanded. Wellington and Napoleon had both been born in the same year – 1769. Both men were outsiders. Wellington's family was poor, and its Irish peerage laughed at by English nobles. Napoleon's home, Corsica, only became a French possession in the year of his birth, and the emperor always spoke French with a strong Italian accent.

Both men had tremendous energy and were capable of going without sleep for days on end. Officially they denigrated each other's abilities, but there was a grudging respect between them. When he heard the details of one of the duke's campaigns, Napoleon remarked: 'Only Wellington and I are capable of carrying out such measures.'

In public, however, Napoleon scorned the duke. He told his chief-of-staff, Marshal Soult: 'You think he is a great general? I tell you that Wellington is a bad general, that the English are bad troops and that this will be a picnic.' The emperor also believed that there did not seem to be much greatness about a man who had made his reputation by always fighting on the defensive. Napoleon exclaimed contemptuously: 'There's a man for you! He is forced to flee from an army he dares not fight.' Now the two men were to meet on the battlefield for the first time – with Europe as the prize.

Man for man, Wellington's troops were probably inferior to the veterans of the *Grand Armée*. Out of every 100 men only 18 were actually British. The rest were Hanoverians, Brunswickers, Belgian and Dutch. The duke tersely described them as: 'The scum of the earth; they have all enlisted for drink.' But he valued their loyalty, and to this end he wore the national cockades of all the allies in his hat; he also forbade the playing of 'Rule Britannia' by his regimental bands.

Wellington's men wore more or less what they liked. One officer wrote: 'Provided we brought our men into the field well appointed, with the 60 lb. of ammunition each, Wellington never looked to see whether their trousers were black, blue or grey.' The smartest soldiers were probably the light dragoons, who wore blue coats with very tight breeches.

Most of the cavalry discarded their standard-issue swords, preferring to fight with captured French weapons. To even the score, Napoleon's men marched in boots made in Northampton. The British muskets were better than those of the French, but they were difficult to fire in wet weather.

On both sides, the men would do their duty – either from enthusiasm or from threat of punishment. Wellington stated: 'I have no idea of any great effect being produced on British soldiers but by the fear of immediate corporal punishment.' Napoleon, on the other hand, inspired devotion in his men. He always addressed his soldiers as *mes amis*, and did his best to provide for wounded veterans.

Now, both commanders were making their final preparations. By 11 a.m. Wellington was riding along the ridge at Mont St Jean. He was wearing a strange mixture of military and civilian dress – a low cocked hat, a plain blue coat, white buckskin breeches and highly polished top boots.

From his horse, Copenhagen, Wellington could see the French columns as they formed up ready for battle. He did his best to hide his concern, but he wrote later: 'It was already quite clear that we should have a terrible day.'

Soon afterwards, a fierce skirmish broke out between troops commanded by Jerome Bonaparte, Napoleon's youngest brother, and eight companies of guards around the Château Hougoumont, a manor house at the southern end of the British line. This was the weakest point in Wellington's defence, but Napoleon only meant this as a diversionary attack. He put his faith in one swift decisive blow on the British centre, which he believed would be enough to hurl the stiff-necked Redcoats into retreat. 'I shall hammer them with my artillery,' he declared to his staff, 'charge them with my cavalry to make them show themselves, and, when I am quite sure where the actual English are, I shall go straight at them with my Old Guard.'

'The French came on in the old style'

The first part of Napoleon's plan went into operation at 1 p.m., when 80 French guns began a ferocious bombardment of the centre. This lasted for 30 minutes and then 16,000 French grenadiers and *tirailleurs* (sharpshooters) moved forward, sending several Belgian units into panic-stricken flight.

But veterans of the war in Spain, such as the 79th Highlanders and the 95th Rifles, held their fire until the enemy were only 20 yds away. Then, from their extended line, they poured in a tremendous disciplined volley, and, as the startled French tried to deploy, the British charged with fixed bayonets. The French attackers broke and ran. Wellington later recalled: 'The French came on in the old style – and we drove them off in the old style.'

Then things started to go wrong for the British. The fleeing Frenchmen were pursued by the Household Cavalry and the Scots Greys. The Scots Greys had been given rum before the battle and their blood was up. They charged headlong into the centre of Napoleon's army, where they were cut to ribbons by a French counter-attack. With the loss of some of his

THE EMPEROR FLEES *With defeat inevitable, Napoleon's hand-picked Old Guard clears the way for his flight, which was so hasty that he left behind hat and sword. Two days later he abdicated.*

best cavalry, Wellington's position was critical.

A lull followed, during which Wellington decided to reposition some of his troops. It was at this moment that Napoleon's brilliant subordinate, Marshal Ney, made a disastrous error that was to cost his master the battle.

Determined to seize the chance of quick victory, Ney launched 5000 heavy cavalry, perhaps the finest in the world, against the British position. This move – sending cavalry against intact squares of infantry supported by artillery – was against all the textbook rules of

LAST STAND *As twilight fell, the survivors of the Old Guard were surrounded by the British. Even in defeat they refused to capitulate and managed to retreat to safety. Their commander, General Cambronne, is said to have shouted: 'The Old Guard dies, but does not surrender.'*

war. But by such unorthodoxy Napoleon's marshal had made his reputation.

Five times the French charged – and five times they were repulsed. The slaughter on both sides was prodigious. Inside each tightly packed British square was a small area for dying infantrymen and crude battlefield surgery. Between the squares lay the fallen French cavalrymen.

Ney did capture the farmhouse outpost of La Haye Sainte, giving the French a chance of overrunning Wellington's unreliable Hanoverian auxiliaries and breaking the British line. Had Napoleon given Ney infantry support, the French might still have won the day. But Napoleon refused to commit his reserves and Wellington had time to plug the gap.

As Wellington sent in British regiments to stiffen the Hanoverians, he replied to a mes-

Wellington described his men as 'the scum of the earth; they have all enlisted for drink'. And drunkenness, looting and rape were their chief preoccupations off the battlefield. But on duty, discipline was rigid. They obeyed orders without question and, at Waterloo, one-third of the British regulars were killed or wounded. A quick death was a blessing because wounds were usually fatal. A shattered limb meant amputation – without anaesthetics. Gangrene and tetanus killed thousands. Even for fit men conditions were appalling. They were ill-fed and badly paid (each private's prize for winning at Waterloo was £2 11s 4d). Disease was rife.

Nor could a soldier expect promotion. The purchase system, by which the wealthy could buy commissions, made it almost impossible to rise from the ranks.

The British Hussar took his name and his distinctive shoulder cape, worn by all such regiments, from Hungary.

In contrast to the red coats of the other regulars, the Rifle Brigade's green-and-black uniform was fine camouflage.

These infantrymen, the mainstay of the line, wore the red coats which distinguished the British army from all others.

sage from Sir Colin Halkett, commanding a brigade of the 3rd Division. Halkett asked if he could retreat a little. Wellington replied: 'Tell him what he asks is impossible. He and I and every Englishman on the field must die on the spot which we occupy.'

'À Bruxelles, mes enfants'

It was at this moment, when all seemed uncertain, that Wellington observed to his anxious staff: 'Hard pounding this, gentlemen, but we will see who can pound the longest.' Throughout, he had been glancing at his watch. Now, at long last, a staff-officer brought the message he had awaited: the Prussians were arriving. With their gun-carriages axle-deep in mud, Blücher and his men had taken a day to come 9 miles.

Napoleon, too, knew that his gamble was on the brink of failure. At 6.30 p.m. he ordered his last throw – an all-out attack by his finest troops, the hand-picked Imperial Guard. The emperor stood before his soldiers, shouting 'À Bruxelles, mes enfants, à Bruxelles'.

The Guard advanced in two massive columns to make a frontal assault on the British lines on the crest of the ridge. In front of each regiment rode a general – the hardened men who had marched in triumph into every European capital but one – London. In the face of this tremendous onslaught, the British held their formation, but the Guard pressed on.

Suddenly the initiative was taken from Wellington by the action of John Colbourne, commander of the 52nd Rifles, the most experienced regiment of the British Army. Without orders, Colbourne ordered his men to wheel out of line and take up position on the French left. It was dangerous to leave this gap, but the gamble succeeded. The astonished Guard halted, and poured a volley into the 52nd which brought down 140 of its men. But the 52nd's reply was decisive. Every British bullet seemed to find its mark. The Guard broke and fled.

Wellington had been appalled by Colbourne's recklessness. But, as he saw the Guard crumble, he muttered: 'Oh damn it! In for a penny, in for a pound!' He ordered a general advance.

'À damn near thing'

The drifting smoke and the low clouds brought on an early dusk. In the twilight, the French army dissolved. The day had been won by Wellington's men, and the arrival of Blücher made the enemy give up all hope. But the remnants of the Old Guard fought on to give their emperor the chance of escape.

The victorious commanders, Wellington and Blücher, met about 10 p.m. The 72-year-old German gasped *'Quelle affaire'* – as the duke observed, about the only French he knew.

Wellington rode on into the darkness. On the field lay 45,000 dead and wounded men, 15,000 of his own – the rest French. The bodies were still there as the sun rose. Many remained for days and all distinction between friend and foe was lost amid the cries of the dying.

Wellington had triumphed. His victory secured the peace of Europe for 33 years. But there had certainly been times when the French had the upper hand. Wellington observed that 'it was a damn near thing – the nearest run thing you ever saw in your life'.

The 'Iron Duke' who dominated a generation

After his triumph at Waterloo, Wellington had over 30 years of active life in front of him. His first decision was to abandon the army for politics. But his military reputation was a liability as well as an asset in his subsequent career. With Napoleon's example before them, many believed that the duke, too, might have dreams of supreme power.

There were alarming straws in the wind. Wellington, a diehard Tory, was on the side of repression at home and abroad. When anything went wrong, whether connected with politics or not, the duke was liable to exclaim: 'Hah! here's liberality again.'

Wellington believed that the British constitution was perfect and incapable of improvement. What others – particularly the less privileged – thought of as anomalies and abuses were to him its finest features. But for all his apparent rigidity, Wellington had his priorities clear. Experience as a soldier had taught him that exposed positions had sometimes to be given up to defend more crucial points. As Prime Minister, in 1828, he conceded Catholic emancipation – the right of Catholics to sit in Parliament – in the teeth of the opposition of his own party, to avoid revolution in Ireland.

Soon after the passage of the Great Reform Bill in 1832, Wellington returned to the army. He became commander-in-chief for life. 'Consult the Duke' was a precept for every statesman, diplomat and soldier. And when he died in 1852 the nation honoured its 83-year-old hero with a state funeral in St Paul's.

THE COACHMAN *Wellington became Prime Minister in 1828. 'The man wot drives the sovereign' was a jibe at the power he held.*

A scorned queen puts the monarchy on trial

WHERE A QUEEN SPENT HER EXILE
The Ranger's House in Greenwich Park, London, where Queen Caroline, wife of the Prince Regent, set up home after being forced to leave the court in 1798. She lived there for 16 years, learning to play the harp, paint, and even tending her own vegetable garden.

A QUEEN ON TRIAL *Caroline (seated, centre right) at the House of Lords in 1820. Her trial was held in the annexe of the House, which was specially built for the occasion. Although she was allowed to attend the hearings, she was refused the right to give evidence.*

In the mid-summer of 1821 England crowned its new king, George IV, in Westminster Abbey. No expense was spared to make the occasion unforgettable. In total, the coronation cost £250,000. Every resource of an age devoted to flamboyant display and luxury was brought into play by the king.

As the royal procession neared the sacred precincts of the abbey, George's efforts were rewarded. The spectators were reduced to stunned silence. Then the cheers rang out. At the head of the procession walked the King's Herb Woman and six handmaidens, scattering herbs along the way. They were followed by the officers of state, carrying the crown, orb, sceptre and the sword of state, and three bishops, bearing the paten, chalice and Bible. The peers and Privy Councillors, majestic in their state robes, came next. Finally, George himself appeared. He walked slowly beneath a cloth-of-gold canopy. Behind him, pages supported a 27 ft long train of crimson velvet decorated with gold stars.

One person, however, was missing from her place in the abbey – George's wife, Caroline of Brunswick. No invitation had been sent to the rightful Queen of England. Early on Corona-

tion Day she went to each of the abbey doors in turn and demanded admittance. But she was turned away by the ushers as the mob shouted 'Shame!' and 'Off! Off!'

Such was the end of a tragedy which had come close to shaking the throne of England to its foundations. George and Caroline had been estranged for years – almost since their first meeting in 1795.

On that occasion, George, then Prince of Wales, turned to his companion, Lord Malmesbury, and audibly whispered: 'I am not well, pray get me a glass of brandy.' He had been persuaded to marry her only as part of a bargain for Parliament to pay off his debts.

Scandal in Italy

Since 1814 Caroline had been living in Italy. While his father had lived, George was content with such a separation. But when he became king he determined to prevent Caroline from returning to England as queen. In February 1820 he laid papers before his cabinet relating to the adulterous conduct of his wife, and demanded a divorce. According to his charges, Caroline had been living in Milan 'in a most unbecoming and disgusting intimacy' with

Bartolemo Bergami, an Italian of low birth whom she had made her Chamberlain.

George's own reputation, however, did not bear close examination. His mistresses had been many – and his people knew it. And so the cabinet, while agreeing to omit Caroline's name from the royal prayers in the prayer book, refused to agree to the king's demand for a divorce. For four months, George fumed against his ministers.

It was Caroline herself who forced the issue. Beside herself with anger at George's attempts to deny her legal rights, she landed at Dover on June 5, 1820. She meant, she said, to secure those rights or blow her husband off his throne.

Caroline swiftly proceeded to London, where the mob gave her a tumultuous welcome. They believed her to be a wronged woman – and it was their duty as Englishmen to protect her.

The government made a last offer to Caroline – a life annuity, on condition that she stayed out of England. This she rejected, and on July 5 the cabinet reluctantly introduced a Bill of Pains and Penalties in the House of Lords, depriving Caroline of her crown and dissolving her marriage.

In the House of Lords the debates were long, the details fascinating. An Italian fisherman testified that Caroline and Bergami had kissed in his boat. There were tales of meetings in secret grottoes, noises behind locked doors and hints of an illegitimate child.

But the defence proved that Hanoverian

diplomats had bribed some of the Italian witnesses. Moreover, Caroline's English servants told a different story. Lady Charlotte Lindsay had observed no improprieties in the queen's conduct.

From triumph to humiliation

In November the bill was passed by nine votes. But this was too small a majority to take it to the House of Commons and the government abandoned it. They also played their trump card – they dissolved Parliament. By January, when it met again, support for the queen had died down, especially when it became known that she had accepted an

annuity of £50,000 from the government. Her appearance at the coronation was her last throw. In August she died, according to her supporters, of a broken heart, but according to her doctors, of an overdose of magnesia.

Caroline was the most unlikely symbol for a popular revolution. She was fat, unwashed and given to barrack-room language. In Italy she had gone about in a mother-of-pearl carriage supposed to look like a sea-shell, wearing large pink feathers in her hat, a low-cut pink bodice and a short white skirt, revealing her short fat legs. But for a few months her cause became the outlet for all the ills of an England ruled by a reactionary king.

George IV: A prince who lost his charm

George IV was one of the most controversial kings in British history. When he died in 1830, *The Times* wrote that 'there was never an individual less regretted by his fellow creatures than this deceased king'.

Yet, in his early years, George had been a handsome and witty prince, who had been idolised by society. He knew more about the arts than any prince in Europe. He was such an excellent mimic that his friend George 'Beau' Brummell declared that he could have been the finest comic actor in Europe.

Above all, George was a connoisseur of paintings and a generous patron of architecture. He did much to give his country objects and buildings of great beauty. The splendid pavilion at Brighton, with its domes, minarets and 'Chinese' furniture, was a permanent contribution to English life. And George persuaded the government to pay £300,000 for the Angerstein Collection of Dutch paintings, which was to become the nucleus of the National Gallery.

Corrupt and extravagant

But George was also the victim of a taste for self-indulgence. At the early age of 52 the once-slim Prince Charming had turned into a 'voluptuary' whose backside was one of the sights of society.

By the time George came to exercise political power, his character had been warped by the company of rakes. Moreover, George's extravagance did much to turn his people against him. At one time his debts amounted to as much as £600,000 – squandered, so his subjects believed, on drink, gambling and women. Leigh Hunt, a radical poet, described him as 'a man who has just closed half a century without one single claim on the gratitude of his country'.

George disliked ridicule more than anything else, and Hunt was imprisoned for two years for seditious libel. But such attacks swelled, and soon after he became king in 1820 George withdrew into isolation. He was now a sick man, troubled by insomnia and sapped of energy by the large doses of laudanum he took with cherry brandy for his gout.

Refuge in fantasy

George's last years were spent almost totally at Windsor. The rapidly ageing king was now filled with tortured longings for what he might have been, and what he might have done. He convinced himself that he had commanded a division at Waterloo and won the Goodwood Cup on his own horse. But at least he could meet his death with bravery. In the early hours of June 26, 1830, he awoke his page, Thomas Bachelor, with the cry: 'Good God, what is this?' Clutching Bachelor's hand, George continued: 'My boy, this is death.'

VICTIM OF THE SATIRISTS

Contemporary satirists had a field day with the luckless George IV. His size, his extravagance and his infidelity made him a constant butt for cartoonists such as George Cruikshank and James Gillray. The king hated their caricatures, which he referred to as 'licentious abominations'. And from 1819 to 1822 more than £2600 of taxpayers' money was paid out to cartoonists in a vain attempt to stop them ridiculing their king.

James Gillray's view of the king – 'A voluptuary under the horrors of digestion' – was one of many cartoons mocking George for his excesses.

A reflection published during the divorce crisis argues that the royal couple were as bad as each other – 'Kettle abusing the pot'.

A WORLD OF BEAUTY – THE VISION OF THREE POETS

Keats, Byron and Shelley, three of England's greatest Romantic poets, all died young. And all three lived and wrote as if they had some premonition of the tragic shortness of their lives. They were desperately aware of the need to cram a lifetime's experience into the years of youth.

Keats died in Rome, from tuberculosis, at the age of 25. Shelley drowned the next year, aged 30, while sailing off the Italian coast; and Byron was 36 when he died of fever, playing a leading role in the Greek struggle against the Turks.

'Mad, bad and dangerous to know,' Lady Caroline Lamb wrote in her diary, after her first meeting with George Gordon Noel, the 6th Lord Byron.

When the first two instalments of 'Childe Harold's Pilgrimage' appeared in 1812, Byron became the most notorious, most desirable guest in any fashionable drawing-room. His dark good looks coupled with the hints he let drop of strange doings in his past, made him irresistible to society women.

In 1815, partly to extricate himself from a tedious affair with Lady Caroline Lamb, and partly to solve his financial problems, he married Anna Isabella Milbanke, the spoilt and priggish daughter of a coal-owning squire. The marriage was a disaster. Byron awoke on his wedding night exclaiming: 'Good God, I am surely in hell.' Anna Isabella left him the next year after the birth of their daughter.

There was only one woman throughout his life whom Byron really loved: his half-sister Augusta Leigh. She laughed at him, coaxed him out of his black humours – and returned his love. In 1816, when the scandal of their affair broke in London, Byron was forced to leave the country. He lived the rest of his life trailing what he called his 'Pageant of a bleeding heart' through Europe.

Byron in exile became England's best-known poet, but towards the end of his life a note of world-weariness crept into his writing.

To his fellow poet Tom Moore, his former drinking companion, he bade farewell:

So we'll go no more a roving
So late into the night,
Though the heart be still as loving,
And the moon be still as bright.

For the sword outwears its sheath,
And the soul wears out the breast,
And the heart must pause to breathe,
And love itself have rest.

The end came suddenly. Byron was almost shipwrecked as he sailed to Greece to help in the struggle for independence against Turkey. He caught fever in the small swamp village of Missolonghi, and died four months later.

Two years before, Byron had been present at the scene of Shelley's death. When Percy Bysshe Shelley's body was washed ashore in the Bay of Lerici, in Italy, it was Byron who arranged the pagan funeral cremation.

ROMANTIC EXILES *Shelley, Keats and Byron.*

POET'S PYRE *After he was drowned, Shelley was cremated on the beach watched by his friends, including Lord Byron (in white scarf). One of them snatched the poet's heart from the pyre.*

The two poets had been close friends. Shelley had been forced to leave England in the same year as Byron, after the uproar caused when he declared himself an atheist and believer in free love. He eloped with Mary Godwin, author of *Frankenstein*, the world-famous horror story. His first wife, Harriet, drowned herself shortly afterwards.

From his earliest attempts at writing, Shelley had dreamt of reforming the world. But his real gift was for lyric poetry. In his years of exile, he wrote some of the most haunting songs in the English language, capturing with heart-rending poignancy what he saw as the fundamental human dilemma:

> *We look before and after,*
> *And pine for what is not:*
> *Our sincerest laughter*
> *With some pain is fraught;*
> *Our sweetest songs are those that*
> *tell of saddest thought.*

Shelley drowned with a copy of the poems Keats published in 1820 in his jacket pocket – the poems that were to bring Keats the recognition he had craved all his life. But fame came too late. He was already dying when the poems were published.

John Keats's father was a Finsbury innkeeper. Both his parents died while he was still young, and he was apprenticed to a surgeon. But he confessed: 'I find I cannot exist without Poetry – half the day will not do.'

Keats gave up medicine, and moved to Hampstead, where he fell in love with his 17-year-old neighbour, Fanny Brawne. Their relationship was at once a torment and a delight. Fanny loved parties and company; Keats was poor, jealous and possessive. Nevertheless, during 1818 and 1819, the years of his infatuation with Fanny, he wrote almost all his greatest poetry.

In 1818 Keats nursed his younger brother until his death from tuberculosis, and contracted the disease himself. Racked by coughing, desperately poor, and with his poetry as yet largely ignored, Keats knew there was no hope of his surviving the English winter of 1820. With grim foreboding he wrote:

> *When I have fears that I may cease to be*
> *Before my pen has glean'd my teeming*
> *brain,*
> *Before high-piled books in charactery*
> *Hold like rich garners the full ripen'd grain.*

But already he had written enough to assure him the place he craved 'among the English poets after my death'.

Keats's friends and publisher clubbed together to send him to spend the winter in Italy with the painter Joseph Severn. After a storm-racked and painful sea journey they reached Rome, and took lodgings in the Piazza di Spagna. There, far from home and all he loved, full of self-doubt, jealousy and bitterness, Keats passed his last few months.

MEN OF SCIENCE PURSUE THE MYSTERY OF ELECTRICITY

EXPERIMENTAL GENIUS *Michael Faraday, son of a blacksmith, pictured in his laboratory in the Royal Institution where he experimented with electromagnetism, giving the world the electric motor and the dynamo. His start in science was as laboratory assistant to Sir Humphry Davy.*

Few men made a greater impact on 19th-century science than Humphry Davy and Michael Faraday. As well as being prolific inventors, both were gifted lecturers and were able to kindle an enthusiasm for science in the minds of ordinary people.

Davy was the eldest of a large Cornish family and became fascinated by science when apprenticed to a Penzance surgeon. He became his own guinea pig. On one occasion he had to be revived by friends after inhaling nitrous oxide (laughing gas).

In 1801, at the age of 23, he was appointed assistant lecturer in chemistry at the newly founded Royal Institution in London, which provided working and lecturing facilities for scientists. He used voltaic cells (the first batteries) to discover and isolate the elements sodium, potassium, boron, calcium, magnesium, barium and strontium. Davy's studies of the explosive qualities of fire damp mixed with air led to his invention of the safety lamp. This was to save the lives of thousands of miners.

One of those who listened to his lectures at the Royal Institution was a bookseller's apprentice, Michael Faraday. In 1812 the 21-year-old Faraday applied to the great scientist for a post in the institution, and Davy made him his personal assistant. Around 1820 he turned to physics, concentrating on the newly discovered phenomenon of electromagnetism.

European scientists had discovered that an electric current would cause a pivoted magnetic needle to move. Faraday and Davy attempted to reverse the process. They failed. But Faraday continued with his tests.

On Christmas Day, 1821, the breakthrough came. Mrs Faraday, busy with the dinner, heard her name called. Rushing to the laboratory, she found her husband staring at a bar magnet standing in a bowl of mercury. A wire suspended above it was rotating around the magnet in response to an electric current. It was the prototype of all electric motors.

The principles of electricity

In a dazzling succession of linked discoveries, Faraday now proceeded to evolve the principles of the form of energy which in a few generations was to transform life on earth, providing heat, light and power for a multitude of purposes.

In the openness of his nature, the great scientist shared these findings with a wide audience. His Friday evening lectures inspired a whole generation.

Faraday achieved these later triumphs without the aid of his master and friend, Davy. The two men had quarrelled in the 1820's after Faraday published the results of his electromagnetic experiments without acknowledging Davy's efforts. But their joint achievements had laid the foundations for the partnership between science and industry; and it was this partnership which made Britain the leading industrial power of the 19th century.

Stephenson triumphs–and the railway age begins

HERALD OF THE RAILWAY AGE
George Stephenson's Rocket *launched a transport revolution when it made its first journey in 1829. Yet so quick was the pace of technical change it sparked off that it ran for less than ten years. In 1862 it was given to London's Science Museum. The steam breakthrough was said to have raised train speeds from 'those of a carthorse to more than those of the fastest racehorse'.*

LINE TO SUCCESS *The* Fury *on the Liverpool and Manchester Railway, the world's first successful commercial line. But its opening in 1830 was marred by tragedy. The politician William Huskisson was run down by a train and killed – the world's first railway casualty.*

A revolution that was to change the face of the world began in a field at Rainhill, just outside Liverpool, on an October day in 1829. Several thousand people had gathered to watch the trials the directors of the Liverpool and Manchester Railway were holding for a locomotive to be used on their new line. They had offered a prize of £500 for an engine that could meet the testing standards they had laid down – to pull 20 tons at a speed of not less than 10 mph.

The scene at Rainhill was like a race meeting. Bets were being laid and there was a special stand for the 'beauty and fashion' of the area. All the spectators were impatiently waiting for the contest to begin.

Resistance to the competition had lasted almost up to the last minute. Old-fashioned pessimists still advocated horsedrawn trains. Inventors were toying with madcap schemes for driving trains by hydrogen gas or carbonic acid. The engineering establishment argued that stationary steam engines hauling trains by ropes were both cheaper and safer. One engineer, Nicholas Wood, stated categorically that 'no locomotive can travel more than eight miles an hour'.

But the designer of the line, George Stephenson, argued that improvements in locomotive design had met these objections. He persuaded his reluctant directors to hold the competition. But Stephenson was not a disinterested party. He had already decided to try to win the prize for himself.

Building the 'Rocket'
At his Newcastle works, Stephenson built a revolutionary new steam engine and named it the *Rocket*. After tests on the Killingworth Colliery Railway, near Newcastle, the engine was dismantled and sent to Liverpool by sea.

Compared to the cumbersome machines in use on the Stockton and Darlington Railway, the *Rocket* was a streamlined masterpiece. Its most revolutionary feature, invisible to the casual spectator, was its boiler.

Earlier boilers had simply been large tanks of water. But the *Rocket's* consisted of 25 narrow copper tubes around which flames from the fire-box passed freely. The effect was a dramatic increase in the quantity of steam produced and thus in the power of the engine. At first, difficulties were experienced in preventing leaks in the boiler tubes. But in September, only a month before the all-important trials, George Stephenson's son and partner, Robert, announced that 'the engine is capable of doing as much, if not more, than set forth in the stipulations'.

The trials began on October 6, 1829. There were five entries, each of which had to make 20 trips up and down a flat stretch of line about 2 miles long. One entry, the *Cycloped*, was disqualified at the start, when it was discovered to consist of a horse in a frame. Of the others, the *Sans Pareil* was a copy of one of Stephenson's earlier designs and the *Perseverance* could manage only 5 mph. The only serious challenge came from the strange-looking *Novelty*, with its vertical boiler. It reached 28 mph, but it could not pull heavy trucks and frequently broke down.

GEORGE STEPHENSON *A fireman's son with little formal education, he created the railway age.*

The *Rocket* was tested at 8 a.m. on October 8. Tension increased in the crowd, for it took 57 minutes after the boiler fire was lit to raise a head of steam. But then the engine ran for 35 miles at an average speed of 15 mph.

The crowd was stunned by a performance beyond their wildest expectations. They were even more amazed when, running on its own, without carriages or trucks, the *Rocket* reached the undreamt of speed of 35 mph.

A new iron age

The Stephensons had triumphed; the argument of fixed engines versus locomotives had finally been settled. James Cropper, formerly a fervent advocate of the fixed-engine principle, threw up his hands and exclaimed: 'Now has George Stephenson at last delivered himself.'

At the end of the day, the crowds who had gathered that morning at Rainhill made their way home. They were smoke-grimed, excited and slightly incredulous. They had witnessed the first day in a new age of transportation. As one commentator wrote: 'The experiments have established principles which will give a greater impulse to civilisation than it has ever received from any single cause.'

For the next 16 years, until his retirement, Stephenson devoted himself to developing the railway age. There was hardly a scheme in which he was not consulted or an important line built without his help and advice. When he died in 1848, he had seen his country transformed by the locomotive that he had helped to create. Stephenson had won himself a high place in the great line of English inventors.

PIONEERS OF STEAM

The success of George Stephenson's *Rocket* on the Liverpool and Manchester Railway was the climax to over 20 years of hard work on the challenge of steam locomotion. Railways had been pioneered by the mining industry, which needed to transport coal and iron ore in bulk. In 1804, Richard Trevithick, a Cornish mining engineer, produced the first steam engine designed to run on rails. It hauled 10 tons of iron ore and 70 men along a colliery track in Wales at a speed of almost 5 mph. Trevithick and other pioneers improved this early invention, but it was George Stephenson who made the decisive breakthrough. In 1825 his experiments at Northumbrian mines were crowned by the opening of the 27 mile Stockton and Darlington Railway, where coal was carried partly by horse and partly by steam power. He went on to become the official engineer of the Liverpool and Manchester line. From these achievements sprang the railway age.

Richard Trevithick's engine Catch-me-who-can *running on its circular track at Euston in 1809. Crowds came to see it from all over London. He charged passengers 1s a ride.*

Iron rails transform the face of Britain

With the opening of the line linking Liverpool and Manchester on September 15, 1830, the railway age began in earnest. This was the first line to rely entirely on steam locomotives and to carry a high proportion of passenger traffic. Success was instantaneous. After this, there was no stopping the advance of the iron road.

Soon, armies of navvies were employed building railways. At the peak, in 1847, there were 250,000 of them at work all across the country. Their equipment was primitive. 'Spoil' (soil) was moved in small barrows; the great cuttings and embankments were literally created with pick and shovel. The navvies themselves were frequently undisciplined. They lived in squalid hutment townships and spread terror to the surrounding villages on pay nights.

But despite these handicaps, the results were astonishing. In the 15 years after the Liverpool and Manchester line was completed, there followed the London and Birmingham, the London and Southampton, the Grand Junction, the Great Western and many smaller lines. Railways brought travel to the lives of millions – particularly after third-class fares were fixed at 1d a mile in 1844. In stagecoach days, the return fare from Manchester to London was £3 10s. In 1851 the railways offered a special cheap ticket at 5s.

The impact of the railways changed the face of Britain. But their impact on ordinary people was even greater. Towns and villages, which had remained little changed since the days of the Middle Ages, were awakened into a new age by the coming of steam.

THE RAILWAY AGE

Railway companies mushroomed after the success of the Liverpool and Manchester Railway. But much railway development was haphazard. Even the Great Western (insignia below right), which was formed in 1835 to build a line from London to Bristol, went its own way by refusing to adopt Stephenson's standard gauge for its tracks. And many smaller companies ran uncoordinated lines.

It was not until 1921 that Parliament resolved the situation by authorising 120 companies to be merged into four. The London Midland and Scottish (insignia below left) was the largest of the merged companies.

BIRTH OF THE 'ROCKET' *This advertisement by the Liverpool and Manchester Railway was the chance George Stephenson had been waiting for to prove his theories. His* Rocket, *with its revolutionary boiler design, proved far superior to its four rivals during trials at Rainhill in 1829. The engine was the basis from which all future locomotive designs followed.*

Reform or revolution?
Britain makes its choice

SOUVENIR OF REFORM
The Great Reform Bill aroused passionate interest. When the House of Lords rejected the Bill, bells were tolled in a funeral dirge in Birmingham, and London newspapers produced black-bordered editions. Finally, the Bill passed into law on June 4, 1832, and popular relief found expression in attractive souvenirs, such as this Swansea-ware jug. Similar pieces are on view at the Glynn Vivian Art Gallery, Swansea.

In 1832 it seemed to many Englishmen that their country stood on the brink of revolution. Only two years before, the King of France had been overthrown. Could the same thing now happen in England?

Since the end of the Napoleonic wars against France 17 years earlier, England had been ruled by diehard Tories, who feared all change and were determined to keep things as they had been in the peaceful days of the 18th century. The power of these men – aristocrat, squire and parson – was based firmly on wealth from land. But the Industrial Revolution was rapidly sweeping this England away. And the pressures that resulted meant that political change could be resisted only at the government's peril.

The question of reforming Parliament had been debated for the previous 60 years. In the General Election of 1830 it became the key issue. Though the Tories managed to hold on to office for a few weeks, they were soon voted out. The Whigs came in, determined to carry through reform. Their Bill, which was to transform parliamentary government in Britain, was introduced into the House of Commons by the Paymaster-General, Lord John Russell, on the evening of March 1, 1831.

Russell declared that 56 'rotten' boroughs – seats such as Bossinney in Cornwall where the two members were elected by one voter – would be disfranchised. A further 30 would lose one of their two members. The seats gained would be given to the new towns.

As the names rolled from Russell's lips, most members looked stunned. Some grew purple with rage and a few just laughed at the absurdity of it all. To them, it seemed that Russell and the government had gone mad. But ardent reformers were delighted.

On the verge of revolution
At first, it seemed that the Bill would soon be passed. On March 23 its second reading was carried by one vote. But a ferocious struggle was to follow as the Tories fought to defeat the measure. In vain, the Whig politician Macaulay appealed to them to: 'Save property, divided against itself. Save the multitude, endangered by their ungovernable passions. Save the aristocracy, endangered by its own unpopular power. The danger is terrible. The time is short.' In April the government was defeated in committee. William IV dissolved Parliament and a General Election was called. The Whigs were returned with a majority of 130. They introduced a second Bill which passed the Commons in September 1831. But after five days of debate the Lords rejected it.

The details of the Bill were now the obsession of millions. At once, rioting broke out. The Tory leaders were soon in danger. Mobs attacked the Duke of Wellington's London home, Apsley House. In Bristol the Mansion House, the gaol, the customs house and the Bishop's Palace were destroyed by rioters and their contents looted. The bishop's champagne, claret and port were taken from his cellars and sold on College Green for 1d a bottle.

In this hour of peril, the government persevered and introduced yet another Bill in December. Again it passed through the House of Commons – but on May 7, 1832, in a last-ditch stand, the Lords wrecked it with a series of drastic amendments.

Now the decision between reform and revolution lay with one man – William IV. The Prime Minister, Lord Grey, asked the king to create enough peers to ensure the passage of the Bill. William IV refused, Grey resigned and the king begged the Duke of Wellington to form a government.

Armed resistance was planned if a Tory government looked like succeeding. And there were other ways of making things impossible for them. A leading agitator, Francis Place,

REFORMED PARLIAMENT *A painting of the first meeting of the reformed House of Commons in 1833. The Whig government benches are on the left. The Prime Minister, Lord Grey, stands third from the left. His adversary, Wellington, stands third from the right.*

launched the slogan – 'To stop the Duke, Go for Gold' – and people rushed to change their banknotes into sovereigns, threatening the national economy.

The triumph of reform
Wellington believed that his duty was, above all, to the king. He was prepared to pass a Reform Bill of his own to stave off revolution. But his supporters refused to follow him, and within a week Grey was back in office.

Grey called upon the king to give him a pledge that the Bill would be passed 'unimpaired in its principles and its essential provisions'. The king finally agreed to create Whig peers and the threat brought the House of Lords to heel. On June 4, the Great Reform Bill passed into law.

Few of those who had cried for 'the Bill, the whole Bill and nothing but the Bill' became voters when the measure was passed. In the new manufacturing towns, most of the seats were filled by the new industrialists – men who were, in fact, less sympathetic to the workers than the landed squires they replaced in Parliament. In 1831 there were about 300,000 voters. Russell's proposals increased the number to 500,000 – about 4 per cent of the population. Yet the flood-gates of change had been opened. Britain had taken a decisive step along the road to democracy.

William IV: A sailor sets a safe course

William IV, the third son of George III, was not expected to become king and so was not educated for monarchy. At the age of 13 he was sent to sea and there he acquired a nautical directness and a taste for strong language that he never lost. His chief characteristic was a blunt tactlessness which earned him the nickname 'Silly Billy'.

It was not until the Duke of York died in 1827 that William became heir to his eldest brother's throne. Yet he turned out to be a conscientious sovereign. Despite his age – he was 64 in 1830 – he was in robust fettle, and could scarcely contain his glee at becoming king. For months he had been practising his royal signature – 'William R'. There were 48,000 papers to deal with and he would work far into the night, with a basin of warm water to bathe his fingers. His delight was summed up in his stage whisper – 'Who is Silly Billy now?' – as the Privy Council gravely lined up to kneel before their new monarch.

William ruled England at the beginning of a hectic period in English history – and one which might have seen revolution. But, by consenting to a dissolution of Parliament in 1831 and agreeing to create Whig peers if necessary to pass the Reform Bill in 1832, William behaved, as his Prime Minister, Lord Grey, said, 'like an angel'. And his common sense helped to raise the public prestige of the monarchy from the depths of scandal to which his brother, George IV, had brought it.

FROM HUSTINGS TO POLLING BOX

The Great Reform Bill of 1832 was only a first step in Britain's long road to full democracy. Though Parliament itself had been reformed, the conditions under which its members were elected remained the same as in the 18th century. Votes were still cast in public on the hustings, and this inevitably encouraged open bribery and corruption. Candidates spent vast sums of money purchasing votes, particularly in small constituencies. Voters could sell their votes for a fixed price, or to the highest bidder. The novelist Charles Dickens captured such a scene in the 'Eatanswill' election in *The Pickwick Papers*.

At Ilchester in 1802 the price for each of the 60 voters was £30. Alternatively, the candidates 'treated' the electors, plying them with food, drink and entertainment in an attempt to win promises of support. The cost of such an election could be astronomical. In 1807 the three candidates fighting the Yorkshire seat spent almost £500,000 between them on their campaigns.

The other evil of public voting was that it opened the way for intimidation of the voters. A powerful landlord could easily browbeat his tenants into voting for the candidate of his choice. Any tenant who refused to do so risked eviction. This fate befell 100 voters in Cardiganshire after one election.

Some British politicians felt that there was nothing wrong with this state of affairs. The Whig politician, Lord Palmerston, remarked that 'to go sneaking to the ballot box is unworthy of the character of a straightforward and honest Englishman'. But most Parliamentary reformers knew that while voting was not secret, real democracy was impossible. They pressed for the introduction of the secret ballot. Two Bills to introduce it were defeated in 1870 and 1871, but the following year it became law. Britain had taken another step towards democracy.

One of the earliest by-elections to be held under the terms of the Ballot Act, which passed into law in 1872, was at Taunton in October 1873. These contemporary prints show a working man casting his vote by secret ballot, and policemen carrying off the sealed ballot boxes to the final count (right).

NEW BROOM *William IV was popularly welcomed as a sober contrast to the indulgent George IV. He is shown here as an exciseman, eager to clear the decks for a fresh start.*

A NEW ART DEDICATED TO THE WORSHIP OF NATURE

In the years that followed the French Revolution, another revolutionary force swept through Europe, profoundly affecting the works of man in poetry and art. This great new inspiration, known as Romanticism, drew its strength in Britain from the beauty of the countryside. In literature its prophets were the poets Wordsworth and Coleridge. In art, the Romantic movement found expression in the paintings of two of the world's finest landscape artists, John Constable and Joseph Turner.

Turner was born in 1775 and Constable a year later, and both devoted their lives to the task of capturing nature in paint. Yet the two men saw nature quite differently. Turner yearned for drama, emotion and passion in nature. He loved craggy mountains, thundering waterfalls, raging seas and storms. Constable, on the other hand, experienced nature simply and submissively. He loved tranquil summer scenes with a breeze fluttering the leaves and sending ripples across sparkling water. He wrote: 'The landscape painter must walk the fields with a humble mind.'

A struggle for recognition

Constable was a countryman, the son of a prosperous Suffolk miller, who sent him to London to the Royal Academy School. By the time he was aged 27 he realised that his talents lay exclusively in landscape painting. Although this form of art was then unfashionable, he spent most of his time in the countryside, his pockets filled with sketchbooks. He wrote: 'The sound of water escaping from mill dams, willows, old rotten planks, slimy posts and brickwork, I love such things... these scenes made me a painter and I am grateful.'

For years he could sell little of his work in Britain. His first recognition came from France. In 1824 his eldest son was dying and his wife was suffering from tuberculosis. Constable himself was 48 and ill from worry over expenses. To raise money, he decided to sacrifice his masterpiece, 'The Hay Wain', to a French dealer who had offered him £125 for it.

PRELIMINARY WORK *This was Constable's sketch for his 'Leaping Horse'.*

CLOUD EFFECTS *'Seascape Study with Rainclouds' was one of Constable's many studies of the drama of the skies.*

SUMMER IDYLL *Constable's masterpiece 'The Hay Wain', dated 1821, was sold to a French dealer for £125.*

VISION OF LIGHT *Turner painted this view of Petworth Park, Sussex, in his last years when he had become obsessed by the desire to depict the beauty of light in his work.*

VIOLENT SEAS *Turner was fascinated by the drama of nature. He found beauty in violence in his 'Shipwreck'.*

Later that year, the dealer exhibited the picture at the Paris Salon and it became famous overnight. The French king, Charles X, awarded Constable a gold medal and tried to buy the picture for the nation. But the dealer had already sold it to a private collector for £834.

But even this success did nothing for Constable's reputation in England. In France, the great painter Delacroix said that Constable was 'pursuing nature, while we are merely occupied in imitating pictures'. Constable, too, was conscious that he was breaking new ground. He wrote: 'When I sit down to make a sketch from nature, the first thing I try to do is to forget that I have ever seen a picture.'

It was precisely this break with convention that made it so difficult for Constable to win recognition. Year after year, his pictures were ridiculed at the Royal Academy's annual exhibition, and it took him ten years to win admission to its ranks.

But Constable was not a man to become embittered. He drew consolation from his love for his wife, his unswerving passion for the countryside and his simple fidelity to the things he thought important. He wrote: 'I never saw anything ugly in my life.'

Inspired by light and drama
Unlike Constable, Joseph Mallord William Turner, the son of a London barber, was quick to win both fame and fortune. As a child he had been starved of air, space, light and sun, and his life became a constant quest for all these things. For more than 60 years he lived almost all the daylight hours with either a pencil or a brush in his hand. He produced 25,000 oil paintings, watercolours, etchings and drawings in his lifetime. He never married.

At the age of 11, Turner left his father's cramped shop to go to the Soho Academy, where he received drawing lessons. It was not easy for a poor boy to gain the necessary training. One of his teachers gave him up as hopeless. 'Better make him a tinker or a cobbler,' his father was told. 'He will never make an artist.' But Turner possessed a single-minded ambition. It was this, and his father's sacrifices, that took him to the Royal Academy School and then to the studio of Sir Joshua

NEW IMAGES IN ART *In his 'Rain, Steam and Speed', Turner pictured the new age of transport that was transforming the English landscape. Ignoring his critics he developed a revolutionary impressionistic technique that was to inspire later generations of 19th-century artists.*

Reynolds. In 1802, at the age of 27, Turner was already exhibiting at the Royal Academy.

Contemporaries described Turner as blunt to the point of rudeness, careless in dress and, with his pronounced nose, far from good looking. But his intensity carried all before him. A friend wrote of him: 'His temperament was full of audacity, self-centred, self-reliant, eager for success . . . no man ever loved fame and money more than he did, and no man condescended less to opinion.'

Both artists were fascinated by the effects of the sky. For Constable, landscaping clouds was the ultimate expression of sentiment. For Turner, they had a symbolic meaning. Constable wrote of him: 'He seems to paint with tinted steam, so evanescent, so airy.' After his first visit to Italy his paintings achieved even greater lightness and brilliance.

Up to the age of 40, Turner enjoyed continuous success and recognition. But then he decided to paint only what suited him. He was

determined to push beyond the accepted frontiers in search of the mystery of light. In his dedicated pursuit he moved beyond the understanding of his contemporaries.

Paintings such as the masterpiece 'Rain, Steam and Speed' were dismissed as 'Mr Turner's little jokes'. A critic commented on another picture: 'It looks as if he has been throwing eggs at the canvas.' But by now Turner was painting for himself alone – and for the future. The radiant canvases found in his studio when he died aged 76 became the inspiration for later generations.

Rooted as they were in their absolute fidelity to the countryside, the two great landscape artists had moved into another world. In their struggle to reproduce such things as the glimmer of light through mist, the hint of rain in a spring sky, the dance of leaves stirred by a breeze or the reflections in a rippling stream, they anticipated the school of Impressionists who were to transform the art of the world.

The decades of triumphant change

Victoria's long reign sees Britain transformed – from a land of farmers and small shopkeepers to an industrial giant dominating the world and ruling over a vast empire

Queen Victoria's reign lasted 64 years, the longest in British history. When she came to the throne in 1837, she was an 18-year-old girl. By the time she died in 1901 she had made her impact felt on every part of British life. Between her coronation (pp. 298–9) and her death, she saw Britain change beyond recognition. She saw the country linked by railways; she saw electric trams and even the first motor-cars. She saw sail give way to steam at sea. She was, said her last Prime Minister, Lord Salisbury, 'the bridge over that great interval which separates old England from new England'.

Her reign saw the British Empire extended to the far corners of the globe. Industry sprawled its smoky cities over Britain and the population trebled. Modern politics were born. Religion came under attack. And the worship of progress became almost a new creed.

Queen Victoria reigned; she did not rule. But she made her preferences for one Prime Minister over another very clear. She deeply admired Lord Melbourne and Benjamin Disraeli, but could barely tolerate William Gladstone. She made no secret of her feelings in her voluminous private diaries. Power, however, had passed firmly from the crown into the hands of the politicians – and the people.

Victoria's influence on her people was direct. In her simplicity and honesty of manner and in her devotion to her husband, Prince Albert, and their nine children, she set the tone for the nation. Her concept of her 'duty'

THE GRANDMOTHER OF EUROPE

By the time of her Golden Jubilee in 1887, Queen Victoria had mellowed from the naïve young girl who had come to the throne in 1837 into the dominant figure among Europe's monarchs. Amongst the family group in this

painting with the 68-year-old Victoria (1) are her eldest son, the Prince of Wales later Edward VII (2), his wife, Princess Alexandra of Denmark (3) and the queen's eldest daughter, Victoria (4), who had married Crown Prince Frederick of Prussia in 1858 and was Empress of Germany for 99 days in 1888. Two grand-daughters who became queens are also shown. Princess Maud (5), youngest daughter of Edward VII, married King Haakon of Norway in 1896. Alix (6), daughter of Princess Alice, married Nicholas II, the last Tsar of Russia, in 1894. Also Sophie, one of Princess Victoria's daughters, married King Constantine of Greece in 1889. Queen Victoria's direct descendants also ruled Sweden, Spain and Romania.

REVOLUTION IN THE FIELDS *In the 64 years of Victoria's reign, a revolution transformed the traditional pattern of agriculture in Britain. The time-honoured methods of the harvesters (above) were swept away by the new machines that industry provided, such as the steam traction engine (below).*

IN THE CITIES *The bustling prosperity of Victorian life was reflected in the great cities of Britain. The demands of a growing population meant that old-fashioned traders (above) soon found themselves outclassed by modern shops (below). These provided cheap food from all over the world for the teeming millions of Victorian Britain. But agriculture at home declined in the face of this competition.*

never faltered. It was a concept that many Victorians extended to their own lives in an age when moral improvement and social reform were dominant topics. When she died, Archbishop Temple paid her a simple tribute: 'She was a good woman.'

Next to the queen, the chief figures of the Victorian age were the architects of change. These included engineers such as Isambard Kingdom Brunel (pp. 300–1), who built railways and the first great ocean liners. The average family travelled more and were better educated and better read than their ancestors. They were proud of the progress their society was making. The 'penny post' of 1840, the introduction of piped water and gas, the building of the London Underground were all objects of Victorian pride, and helped build confidence in the future. And the Great Exhibition of 1851 (pp. 302–3) was a fitting monument for this certainty. Held in Hyde Park beneath Joseph Paxton's glittering glass frame, it was a British workshop for the world to admire and a temple for the worship of progress.

But there were some who revolted against the material world. The Pre-Raphaelite movement (pp. 304–5), which began in 1848, produced works of art far removed from average Victorian taste. The paintings of Dante Gabriel Rossetti, John Everett Millais and William Holman Hunt evoked the romance of the long-past medieval age. Edward Burne-Jones and William Morris extended the influence into glass and furniture. But the freedom expressed in both the art and the lives of the Pre-Raphaelites scandalised many of Victoria's sober-minded subjects.

Spreading the benefits of civilisation

Such people preferred to admire the heroism of the rank-and-file soldiers of the Crimean War, fought against Russia from 1854 to 1856. Stories of their sufferings, and of the dedication of the war's great heroine, Florence Nightingale – 'the lady with the lamp' – touched and inspired ordinary people. And the Charge of the Light Brigade at the Battle of Balaclava (pp. 306–7) became one of the great stories of British heroism on foreign soil.

The Crimean War was the first to be fully reported in the daily Press by a group of war correspondents led by William Russell of *The Times*. Their reports gave a great boost to the new mass-circulation newspapers which were helping both to inform and to create public opinion.

Most novels, such as Charles Dickens's *Bleak House* and *David Copperfield*, first appeared in serialised form in newspapers or magazines. Dickens (p. 308) intended that his novels should not only entertain but also expose the evils of Victorian society. His vivid pictures of the life of the poor, huddled into airless factories and living in slums, were a direct appeal to the social conscience of the middle classes. At the other end of the literary scale, the romantic and passionate novels of the Brontë sisters (p. 309) were a reaction against the restrictions of middle-class society.

But whatever cruelties and injustices existed at home, Victorians believed that it was their mission to carry British civilisation to the far corners of the world. In India, it was believed that the slow introduction of British culture and standards would lead to the moral improvement of the people. So the outbreak of the Indian Mutiny (pp. 310–11) was a considerable shock to public opinion. But the crushing of the mutiny with the recapture of Cawnpore and the relief of Lucknow re-established confidence. The mutiny, too, ended the rule of the East India Company and substituted that of the crown. But it did more than that. It widened a gulf between rulers and ruled that could never be bridged.

At home, the functions of government grew more complex and there was an outcrop of both civic and national buildings to house them. Massive new town halls graced cities such as Manchester and Leeds. In London a disastrous fire at

Westminster gave the government a chance to create a new building to house Parliament (pp. 312–13). Charles Barry won the competition to build it, but it was not finally completed until after his death. Built in the Gothic style, it was the first palace for modern democracy.

'Wider still and wider'

But the House of Commons, echoing the sentiments of most of its members, still barred atheists, as the radical Charles Bradlaugh found when he tried to take his seat in the 1880's. Many regarded Charles Darwin's *Origin of the Species* (pp. 314–15), published in 1859 and the sensation of the age, as a blasphemy. By suggesting the revolutionary theory that man had developed from lower forms of life, Darwin was flying in the face of established religion and casting doubt on the biblical story of the Creation.

Religion, too, lay behind much of the ardent imperialism of the last decades of Victoria's reign. Christian conscience urged the campaign against slavery and encouraged the exploration of Africa – the 'Dark Continent'. For all his fame as an explorer, David Livingstone (pp. 316–17) considered himself first and foremost a missionary. H. M. Stanley, with whom Livingstone's name is forever linked, was a journalist turned explorer. But he, too, regarded it as his duty to spread the knowledge of civilisation to Africa.

Paradoxically, the age of imperialism coincided with a noticeable change in the Victorian mood. The boom years of prosperity which had produced the Great Exhibition had extended through the 1860's, but by the 1870's there was a feeling of economic uncertainty. Foreign competition seriously threatened Britain's exports for the first time.

But progress at home continued. The Reform Acts of 1867 and 1884 gave most men the right to vote. Trade unions were beginning to gather strength. Primary education became compulsory. All these factors combined to make politicians aware, almost for the first time, of the need to woo the electorate. William Gladstone's exhausting political speaking tour of 1879 was the first modern political campaign. His great rival, the Tory leader Benjamin Disraeli, denounced it as demagogy. But within a decade all politicians were following Gladstone's example.

The symbol of the age

Victorians turned to their queen as the true symbol of the age. Her two jubilees, the Golden Jubilee of 1887 and the Diamond Jubilee of 1897 (pp. 318–19), were displays of unashamed patriotism. They gave a chance to show the world, through the naval reviews at Spithead, that it was Britain's might at sea which had won her an empire.

But this confidence was shattered by the disastrous beginning of the Boer War in South Africa, when a handful of farmers inflicted three heavy defeats on Britain's highly trained regulars in the disastrous 'Black Week' of December 1899. Once again the queen spoke for the nation with the terse statement: 'We are not interested in the possibilities of defeat; they do not exist.' Soon the tide turned in Britain's favour. But the event of the war that brought the greatest enthusiasm was the relief of Mafeking (pp. 320–1).

Late Victorian confidence concealed the symptoms of an unhealthy society. With Germany in the ascendant in Europe, a policy of 'splendid isolation' was becoming unwise and outdated. And, at home, the worst results of over-hasty industrialisation were becoming clear. The Victorians bequeathed to the 20th century an unparalleled heritage of prosperity. But they also left a legacy of social problems which were to hamper their descendants in the changed circumstances of a new world.

NEW LEARNING *Under Victoria, many social reforms were introduced, especially in the field of education. A dame's school (above) was the only form of learning that most people received until the 1871 Education Act set up a state system of education and state schools (below).*

A REVOLUTION IN TRANSPORT *No innovation transformed Victorian Britain more than the rapid development of the railways. The stagecoach (above) was soon made obsolete by the train (below). And legislation to fix cheap fares meant that ordinary people were able to travel widely for the first time in history.*

The day Victoria remembered as the 'proudest of my life'

CROWN FOR A QUEEN

This new Crown of State was made for Victoria to wear towards the end of the Coronation Service – because the traditional St Edward's Crown was too heavy for the slender girl queen. The crown, which can be seen at the Tower of London, has 3000 precious stones, including the great ruby given to the Black Prince and worn by Henry V at the Battle of Agincourt.

One of the first things Victoria did after she became queen in 1837 was to deliver a colossal snub – to her mother.

It was an extraordinary thing for an 18-year-old to do, particularly as she had just attended her first Privy Council meeting, and delighted her ministers with her self-assurance and dignity.

'And now, Mamma, am I really and truly queen ?' she asked her mother.

'You see, my dear, that it is so.'

'Then, dear Mamma, I hope you will grant me the first request I make to you as queen. Let me be by myself for an hour.'

The snub had its justification.

Victoria's father had died when she was eight months old, and she was brought up by her mother, the Duchess of Kent, an ambitious and prudish woman who made Victoria wear a sprig of holly on her collar to make her sit erect at the table. The duchess disapproved of Victoria's uncle, the bluff William IV, and kept her daughter as much as possible away from his court, occupying frugal rooms in Kensington Palace. The princess was never allowed to be alone. She had to sleep in her mother's room, and her days were carefully arranged so she would always have the company of her governess, Baroness Lehzen, the daughter of a Hanoverian clergyman.

Nevertheless, Victoria loved and trusted this forbidding governess, as she admitted frequently in her diary. But she detested the Comptroller of her mother's household, Sir John Conroy, who had ambitions of carving for himself a career as the power behind the future throne. He had a dominating influence on the duchess – it was said the princess had once surprised him in her mother's arms. Certainly, Victoria disliked him, because, shortly after she became queen, she dismissed him with an annuity and made certain that his relationship with her mother was absolutely broken.

A new queen launches a new age

It was never completely certain that Victoria would inherit the throne. When George IV became king, she was only third in line to the throne, after the Duke of York, who died in 1827, and the Duke of Clarence, who became king as William IV in 1830. But the likelihood was always there.

Her mother and Sir John arranged a series of semi-royal progresses for the princess around the country, meeting county families and civic dignitaries. These tours aroused the fury of the king, particularly the salutes, and at a formal palace dinner he publicly expressed his fear that he might die before his niece came of age, and that a regency would fall into the hands of 'evil advisers'. Victoria was reduced to tears by this declaration, and the duchess made as dignified an exit as she could muster.

The king's fears were justified. When only 16 years old, Victoria caught typhoid fever in Ramsgate. Sir John, abetted by the duchess, tried to persuade her into signing a document which promised him the key position of her secretary when she became queen. Even though she was desperately ill, she found the strength and courage to refuse.

The hard lessons of her early years gave Victoria a mature self-confidence which, added to her youthful freshness and vivacity, made her a natural popular heroine, a perfect focus of the coronation festivities. It seemed to her subjects that she symbolised the dawning of a new era of peace and prosperity, a new spirit after a period of political discord and a succession of uninspiring monarchs.

The manner in which she was first hailed queen became a romantic legend even before she was crowned. William died in the small hours of June 20, 1837, and immediately the Archbishop of Canterbury drove to Kensington Palace.

Victoria donned her dressing-gown when she heard the archbishop had arrived – at 5 a.m. She stood in her night clothes while the elderly cleric knelt before her and broke the news of her uncle's death. 'Since it has pleased Providence,' she wrote in her diary that day, 'to place me in this station, I shall do my utmost to fulfil my duty towards my country.'

Immediately after she became queen, she gave orders that her bed should be removed from the duchess's room, and that her meals should be served with nobody else present. She recorded with pride that she had given audiences to the Archbishop of Canterbury, the Lord Chamberlain and the Prime Minister – 'of course, quite alone'.

At 4 a.m. on the day of her coronation on June 28, 1838, Victoria was woken by the guns of the Royal Horse Artillery thundering a royal salute. She ate only a little breakfast before she drove to Westminster Abbey, through rapturously cheering crowds. Her reception overwhelmed her.

The procession reached the abbey just after 11.30, but the ceremony was marred by hitches. The Archbishop of Canterbury got muddled, and gave the heavy orb to the new queen at the wrong moment. Then he put the coronation ring on the wrong finger, so that it proved painful and difficult to take off afterwards. And another incident came close to ruining the ceremony. The 82-year-old Lord Rolle overbalanced as he tottered up the stairs to the throne to kiss the royal hand. He fell backwards to the bottom of the steps, but Victoria rose from the throne and went to help the old man back again. It was a gesture that was taken as an indication of the new monarch's sympathy and generosity.

Pomp and pride

At the palace that evening, her Prime Minister, Lord Melbourne, had tears in his eyes when he told her she had carried off the whole occasion quite beautifully.

In public she had acquitted herself as a woman; now, in private, she could be a girl again. She rushed straight up to her private rooms, took off her ceremonial robes and gave her dog, Dash, his evening bath. With evident happiness in her heart, she noted in her diary – underlining her emotions – 'I cannot say how proud I feel to be the Queen of such a Nation. I shall remember this day as the proudest of my life.'

DAY OF SPLENDOUR *One month after her 19th birthday, Victoria was crowned at Westminster Abbey on June 28, 1838 in a service starting just after 11.30 a.m. She receives the Sacrament from the Archbishop of Canterbury (left) and is shown in her coronation robes (above). That evening she said that she had 'the gratifying feeling that her duty had been done' – but that her feet were tired after the long service.*

Victoria: The monarch who vowed 'to be good

FAMILY GROUP *Victoria and her husband, Albert, the Prince Consort, with (left to right) some of their children – Alfred, Edward, Prince of Wales, Alice, Helena and Victoria.*

The image of Queen Victoria which emerges from history is of a severe old lady dressed in black and with a white-ribboned bonnet – the symbol of an age of austere morality.

But this was far from being the whole story. When she died, she had been in mourning for 40 years for her adored husband, Prince Albert; and, with children and relatives occupying nearly every throne in Europe, her influence was immense. But these facts obscure the real woman.

In her youth she had been a pretty and fun-loving girl who loved to dance, and often lapsed into fits of giggles. Later, she became a devoted mother and doting wife. But she seemed unable throughout her life to manage without the support of a series of strong-willed masculine men. At various times she was popularly called 'Mrs Melbourne', after her elderly Prime Minister at the beginning of her reign, 'Queen Albertine', after her husband, and even Mrs Brown, after John Brown, her Highland servant. Another man whom she came to trust and rely on was the Conservative Prime Minister, Benjamin Disraeli.

But her passionate love for her husband eclipsed all others. She idolised him with an intensity almost cloying: 'I should like to fall at his feet ... for I feel how unworthy I must be of one so great and perfect as he.'

The 'widow of Windsor'

Albert's death, after 21 years of marriage, devastated Victoria. For the rest of her life she wore widow's weeds, and refused to have his room changed in the smallest detail, except for the fresh flowers she strewed on his bed. Even five years after his death, she excused herself from opening Parliament, because she did not wish to be a 'spectacle of a poor, broken-hearted widow, nervous and shrinking, dragged in deep mourning'.

The strange consolation of her widowhood was John Brown. He was brusque with everyone, and even called the queen 'wumman'. But nobody could communicate with her except through him, and she did not seem to mind when he drank too much whisky.

But she never forgot Albert – the one man who had shared her own naïve resolution 'to be good'. By her wish, she was buried beside him in the mausoleum at Frogmore, in the grounds of Windsor Castle.

FAVOURITE HOME *In the early years of her marriage, Victoria's favourite home was Osborne House on the Isle of Wight. She shared her desk with Albert, who sat on her left and helped her with state business. Bell pushes (near the right-hand table leg) summoned equerries or staff.*

A man of genius builds steamships of iron

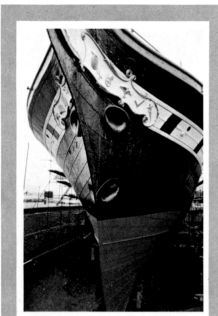

REVOLUTIONARY STEAMSHIP
Brunel's Great Britain, *constructed of iron and driven by propeller, revolutionised ocean travel. Abandoned in the Falkland Islands after being caught in a storm off Cape Horn in 1886, she was towed back to Bristol in 1969, exactly 126 years to the day after her launching there.*

Confidence was one of the hallmarks of the Victorian era. Confidence in progress and the ability of Britons to overcome any obstacle. Confidence in Britannia's mastery of the waves.

It took confidence on a massive scale, in the days of wooden-hulled ships, to build an ocean liner of metal and powered by steam. But Isambard Kingdom Brunel, designer of the *Great Britain*, and an outstanding engineer, had a faith in himself that was remarkable even by Victorian standards.

Revolution at sea

The *Great Britain* was the world's first all-metal liner. She had technical innovations which, though they had been experimented with before, were now combined for the first time. Iron hulls were now 20 years old, and screw propellers had been invented by Leonardo da Vinci in the 15th century, but nobody had brought them together before, and, above all, never on such a scale. The *Great Britain*, at 320 ft, was by far the biggest ship ever built, half as big again as the largest warship in the Royal Navy.

When she was launched, Brunel was just 37 years old and at the very height of his powers. He had already established his reputation by building the 110 mile London to Bristol railway for Great Western Railways.

When a critic questioned the wisdom of so long a rail link, he retorted: 'Why not have it longer and have a steamboat to go from Bristol to New York?' It was following up this idea which led Brunel into ship-building, and he started to design his first ship, the *Great Western*. Launched in 1836 with a length of 236 ft, she was already larger than any steam vessel afloat.

Quest for perfection

Brunel was determined to show that it was possible to make the transatlantic crossing by steam alone, which many thought impossible. The *Great Western*, however, made the crossing from Bristol to New York in a record 15 days, and with 200 tons of coal to spare. Before long, the ship was running the first regular steamship service across the Atlantic.

Immediately, Brunel set to work on the design of an even more ambitious ship, the *Great Britain*. In his constant search for perfection, he completely redesigned his original plans after deciding to have a propeller rather than paddles. Then he decided to build·in iron, rather than wood, even though the timber for the ship had already been bought. Once again, he redesigned the ship.

The following year, Queen Victoria visited the *Great Britain* when the ship was anchored in the Thames to be finally fitted out. She marvelled at the luxury of the 64 staterooms, the music rooms, the rich panelling and the 1200 yds of Brussels carpet.

Six months later the *Great Britain* made her maiden voyage to New York, but a year later disaster struck. She was outward bound when a navigational error ran her aground on rocks in Dundrum Bay, Ireland. All the passengers were safely landed, but the ship lay stranded with 10 ft of water in her holds; and there she stayed throughout the winter until she was refloated and repaired. The grounding was a financial disaster for her owners for the esti-

ROYAL LAUNCHING *An engraving of the launching of the* Great Britain, *Brunel's revolutionary iron-hulled, screw-driven liner, by Prince Albert on July 19, 1843. She plied a successful transatlantic steamship service for a year before she ran aground on the Irish coast. She was eventually towed off by the* Birkenhead.

STEAM AND SAIL *A contemporary lithograph of the* Great Western *crossing the Atlantic. The journey took her 15 days and five hours.*

mated cost of repairs was more than £21,000. But it vindicated Brunel's use of iron in ship-building, for any timber ship would have broken up in the winter storms.

Far from being dismayed, Brunel was soon busy with an even bigger ship-building scheme. His *Great Eastern*, 692 ft long, was the most ambitious construction project of her day, but was dogged with problems, few of Brunel's making. It took three and a half years to get her into the water, and broke Brunel's health.

An iron memorial

But the *Great Britain* sailed the seas for 41 years. After her grounding, she was sold, refitted and put on the Australia run as a passenger liner, where she worked for 23 years. She was a troop carrier in the Crimean War, carrying complements of 1650 troops and 30 horses. In 1882, an ageing ship, she was sold again, converted to carrying a cargo of coal, and put on the route to San Francisco. In 1886 she was caught in a storm while rounding the Horn and grounded, this time deliberately for safety, in the Falkland Islands. There she lay, rusting but indestructible, for 83 years, used only as a nesting place for sea birds.

But the *Great Britain* was to make one last voyage. In 1969, financed by public subscription, she came home on a specially designed raft, and sailed under Brunel's own Clifton suspension bridge and up to Bristol Docks – a permanent memorial of the revolution from sail to steam.

RAILWAY BUILDER

There was hardly any aspect of engineering in which Brunel's versatile genius did not make an impact. He was only 27 when in 1833 he was appointed engineer for the proposed London to Bristol Great Western Railway. He took to a horse to survey the route himself, rarely working less than 20 hours a day. He supervised every detail of the construction and design of the railway – bridges, tunnels, the architecture of the stations, even the quality of the coffee at a station hotel. He would throw off his coat and work alongside the navvies, who affectionately called him the 'Little Giant'.

The railway was built in stages and completed in 1841. Brunel left his mark everywhere – his bridge at Maidenhead, the 3000 yd long Box Tunnel near Bath, the 2 mile long Sonning cutting, and a new town for railway workers at Swindon. On the broad-gauge line he laid down, the London to Bristol express took four hours on its inaugural run. Brunel supervised the first journey from the footplate.

The Great Western's broad-gauge track took huge engines with 9 ft high driving wheels.

An engineer to whom nothing was impossible

On the flood tide of the Industrial Revolution a new breed of men began to emerge. Their confidence and dynamism were unbounded. They felt they were in possession of the materials and techniques for building a new world – and in many ways they succeeded.

In this vital age, which brought Britain to a peak of economic power, the outstanding man was Isambard Kingdom Brunel, son of a refugee from the French Revolution. His father, himself a brilliant mathematician and a successful engineer, sent the young Isambard to France to complete his education in mathematics, and afterwards took him into the family firm. It was typical of Brunel's ambition that, before he was 19, he was complaining in his diary of his father 'stifling' him. 'I will not suffer it,' he wrote. But by the age of 21, he was in charge of the Thames Tunnel, the world's first tunnel under a navigable river.

His energy was immense. No detail of any project in which he was involved escaped him. He worked 20 hours a day, chain-smoking cigars to keep himself going. Civil engineer, engine designer, bridge-builder – no branch of his profession seemed beyond his capacity. His bridges at Maidenhead, Saltash and Clifton stand today as monuments, not only to his engineering skill, but also to his artistic creativity; for nothing would satisfy him but perfection.

Looking to the future

Innovation was what he lived by, and luckily he had the knack of persuading committees and boards of directors of the practicability of his plans. Nothing was 'impossible' to him.

Brunel's unremitting search for new techniques, and his willingness to experiment, always made him a controversial figure. Although many of the projects he attempted were triumphantly successful, many others were judged disasters at the time.

His Thames Tunnel from Wapping to Rotherhithe was dubbed the 'Great Bore' by *The Times*, but it is still part of the London Underground rail system. His steamship *Great Britain* bankrupted the company which built it, but is now regarded as a milestone in the evolution of ship design. His *Great Eastern*, for over 40 years the largest ship ever built, was furiously attacked by the Press, who accused Brunel of 'megalomania' because of it. It was dogged by minor setbacks which seemed insoluble at the time, and was a financial disaster. Yet today it is regarded as the prototype of modern luxury liners.

The problems of the *Great Eastern* killed Brunel. The day before her trials, Brunel collapsed on her deck. And the news of a boiler explosion on board was the final blow. He died on September 15, 1859, aged 53.

FINAL PROJECT *An enormous shadow loomed over the last years of Brunel's life – that of the* Great Eastern. *Nearly 700 ft long, and popularly known as the 'Leviathan', it was more than 40 years before a bigger ship was built anywhere. She was intended for the Australia route, but changing circumstances, such as the opening of the Suez Canal, made her uneconomic even before she was launched – she ended up laying Atlantic telegraph cables. The difficulties of her construction (above) exhausted even the prodigious energies of Brunel (right), and led to his death shortly after she was completed in 1859.*

Prince Albert creates a showcase of British power

EXHIBITION SOUVENIRS
For six months in 1851, London was dominated by the Great Exhibition in Hyde Park. The 6 million visitors bought every kind of souvenir, such as this box (top) with a view of the Crystal Palace. A season ticket (bottom) cost 2 guineas for women, 3 guineas for men. Both are now in the Victoria and Albert Museum.

Throughout the gloriously hot summer of 1851, Englishmen from the provinces and visitors from abroad descended upon London to attend the Great Exhibition in Hyde Park. The world's first industrial giant, confident in its overpowering strength, had invited the nations to join it in the first international exhibition in history.

The exhibition was the brain-child of the queen's husband, Prince Albert. Albert was a true representative of his age, a passionate believer in the moral and material rewards to be reaped from the progress of science and industry. The world, he believed, stood at the threshold of a new age of international co-operation and prosperity. It was 'England's mission, duty, and interest', he said, 'to put herself at the head of the diffusion of civilisation and the attainment of liberty'.

The Great Exhibition, the most ambitious scheme of Albert's fertile imagination, was to proclaim both the dawning of that new world and Britain's leadership of it.

Albert first put the scheme forward in 1849. For two years he had to fight the opposition of rural squires and powerful organs like *The Times*, who feared the relentless march of industry. In the proposed felling of Hyde Park's trees to make room for the exhibition, they found a symbol of industry's indifference to the traditional world of agricultural England. Albert would not be beaten. He cajoled, argued and persuaded. He launched a public subscription. And by January 1851 he had won parliamentary approval for the exhibition.

Made of iron and glass
The first stage of Albert's great work was over. Ahead lay the more daunting task of getting everything ready for the opening in May, a mere 22 weeks away. The building itself, designed by Joseph Paxton, was 1500 ft long and covered 26 acres – three times the size of St Paul's Cathedral. To build it workmen laboured through the winter nights, aided by huge bonfires of scrapwood. Miraculously the building was finished, outfitted and filled with exhibits exactly on time, ready for the royal opening.

The completed exhibition hall was a splendid sight. Paxton's revolutionary building caught perfectly the note of confidence in Britain's industrial future. It was the first building made only of iron and glass. It was also the world's first prefabricated structure (which accounted for the speed with which it was put up). It silenced the critics who had stormed against the invasion of Hyde Park by bricks and mortar. Its glittering dome soared above the elm trees, and when the exhibition was over it was easily dismantled and moved to Sydenham, south of London.

A 'fairy-tale palace'
With the sun shining into it, Paxton's monumental building seemed to Queen Victoria like a 'fairy-tale palace'. The magazine *Punch* called it the Crystal Palace, and the name stuck. William Thackeray, the novelist, was moved to poetry:

> *As though 'twere by a wizard's rod*
> *A blazing arch of lucid glass*
> *Leaps like a fountain from the grass*
> *To meet the sun!*

Reporting the opening of the exhibition on May 1, *The Times* forgot its early hostility and spoke out in fulsome praise: 'There was yesterday witnessed a sight the like of which has never happened before, and which, in the nature of things, can never be repeated. They who were so fortunate as to see it hardly knew what most to admire, or in what form to clothe the sense of wonder, and even of mystery, which struggled within them.'

No one was more impressed than Queen Victoria herself. She left her own description of the opening day in her journal: 'The glimpse of the transept through the iron gates, the waving palms, flowers, statues, myriads of people filling the galleries and seats around, with the flourish of trumpets as we entered, gave us a sensation which I can never forget, and I felt much moved... The tremendous cheers, the joy expressed in every face, the immensity of the building – all this was moving indeed, and it was and is a day to live forever.'

On display were more than 100,000 objects from 14,000 exhibitors from all over the world. Though half the space was allocated to foreign products, the exhibition was no less a British showplace, and Britain provided the most impressive examples of engineering and invention. There were models of suspension bridges,

THE CRYSTAL PALACE *The Great Exhibition of 1851 is formally opened by Queen Victoria and Prince Albert. The queen wrote that she was 'filled with devotion' by the ceremony.*

EXHIBITION BUILDERS *Navvies, engaged on the construction of the Crystal Palace, breakfast beside the almost-completed glass building.*

a lighthouse and even a scale model of the entire Liverpool docks. Working machinery included a boiler house and steam pumps.

Among the mechanical marvels of the age were many weird inventions. There was a machine for folding envelopes; a sportsman's knife with 80 blades; a model of the floating Church for Seamen in Philadelphia; a stove designed in medieval Gothic style. In the clothing section could be seen Australian hats made of cabbage-tree leaves; cuffs spun and knitted from the wool of French poodles; and a shirt cut on mathematical principles.

Marvels of an age

The exhibition was a global supermarket, a gigantic jumble of hardware, textiles, precious metals, works of art and ornamental bric-à-brac.

Apart from its curiosities, the exhibition was an important event in the formation of Victorian life and manners. Its message was that Britain led the world in the manufacture of useful articles which were made to last, and which were available at reasonable prices.

After 1851 the label 'Made in Britain' was a guarantee respected throughout the world.

Just as important, the exhibition marked the entrance of the skilled working man into the ranks of the 'respectable' in Victorian society. It was from such men that the wonders of the festival had come. The 'swinish multitude' and the 'great unwashed' became phrases of memory only. The future lay with the 'respectable artisan'.

Great care had been taken to ensure that the exhibition would be open to all. Although admission on the first two days was restricted to those wealthy enough to pay £1, the cost was then lowered to 5s and after the first month there were 1s entrance tickets for four days each week.

All over Britain, special excursions to the exhibition were organised. Working men saved up a few pence every week, and many employers gave their workers extra holidays so that they could visit the exhibition. The Admiralty even offered to provide transport for the Portsmouth dockyard workers in case they could not afford the train fare. For the first time in Britain, people from all walks of life mingled together in a common celebration of their country's achievements.

Memorial to a prince

Financially, the exhibition was a greater success than anyone had dared to hope. In the six months that it was open, more than 6 million people attended it. It cost £335,742 to mount, but when the accounts were tallied – including the proceeds from the sale of 1,092,337 bottles of mineral waters, 934,691 Bath buns and 870,027 plain buns – the profit was discovered to be £186,437.

Paxton was rewarded with £5000. The rest went, as Albert desired, to help to pay for that ambitious project with which Queen Victoria permanently fixed the memory of Albert in the English mind. This was the great cluster of museums, including the Science Museum and the Natural History Museum, which now grace South Kensington. They stand just down the road from the site where the Crystal Palace had, for a season, held the attention of the world.

Victorian Britain – the 'workshop of the world'

The Great Exhibition was not simply a celebration of manufacturing invention. It was also a temple in praise of work. For the Victorians, work was more than an economic necessity; it was a moral virtue. The best-selling book of the mid-Victorian era was Samuel Smiles's *Self Help*, a long treatise on the rewards of industry, self-reliance and thrift, published in 1859.

Everywhere in Victorian England there was ceaseless activity. England had become the 'workshop of the world'. At the 1851 census it was discovered that, for the first time, more than half the population lived in towns. Manchester was the centre of the cotton industry. Knives, scissors, buckles, corkscrews and guns were made at Birmingham. Woollen stockings were made at Leicester and cotton ones at Nottingham.

'Dark satanic mills'

Much manufacture was still on a small scale – women and children in the textile industry often worked at home – so that men could still take personal pride in work which retained something of the craft about it.

But where factories sprang up – as at Northampton, centre of the 'sweated' shoe-making trade – hardship and cruelty followed. Children and women worked long hours for low wages. They went home in the evening to overcrowded tenements and unsanitary basements. And the air that they breathed was, for the first time, becoming polluted.

Two decades of prosperity were ushered in by the Great Exhibition. The number of men employed in ironworks rose from 80,000 to 200,000, exports nearly trebled, and savings deposits increased from £30 million to £53 million. The high expectations of 1851 were met. But they were only accomplished through the sufferings of thousands in Victorian England's 'dark satanic mills'.

HALL OF INVENTION *The machinery section of the exhibition housed much of the best of Britain's achievements in engineering.*

INGENIOUS DESIGNS

Though the Great Exhibition was a showplace for great inventions and massive machines, small-scale products were not neglected. The beginnings of mass production had not entirely destroyed the tradition of individual workmanship, and objects such as cutlery, chinaware and ornaments were examples of skilled craftwork. The style of the period was florid and elaborate, and characterised by dense decoration.

A cut-throat razor by Hawcroft & Sons of Sheffield, its blade engraved with a view of the Crystal Palace.

A heavily ornate fish-server in the Moorish style.

A papier-mâché plaque (above), and an inkstand (right) inset with a clock.

TURBULENT PASSIONS OF A BROTHERHOOD OF ARTISTS

The Pre-Raphaelites, the most striking, original group of English painters, first came together in 1848 – a significant date, for 1848 was a year of political revolutions throughout Europe. John Everett Millais, Dante Gabriel Rossetti, William Holman Hunt and their colleagues were idealistic young painters totally caught up in the revolutionary spirit of the age.

They were given the name Pre-Raphaelites because of their shared belief that art had pursued false objectives following the death of the 16th-century Italian master Raphael. They were determined to recapture the mystical interpretation of nature by earlier artists, and

they revolted against classical themes. Above all, they despised the artistic 'establishment' – in particular, the Royal Academy.

These precocious young men saw themselves not merely as the founders of a new movement, but as a closely knit band of devotees dedicated to the ideals of truth and beauty. For a while the studios in which they worked together, sharing models and inspiration, had the atmosphere of a monastic cloister.

They called their association the Brotherhood, savouring its suggestion of democracy and its overtones of the past. And their determination and solidarity were strengthened by the hostility of the Victorian art world to their

ideas. Few of their paintings were sympathetically received, and some Royal Academicians began a deliberate campaign to denigrate their work in the Press. Charles Dickens, in *The Atheneum*, launched a vitriolic attack on Millais's 'Christ in the House of His Parents' as 'revolting and loathsome'. He went on: 'In the foreground of that carpenter's shop is a hideous, wry-necked, blubbering red-haired boy in a night-gown who appears to have received a poke from the stick of another boy ... and to be holding it up for the contemplation of a woman so horrible in her ugliness that ... she would stand out from the rest of the company as a monster in the vilest cabaret in France or the lowest gin-shop in England.'

The Pre-Raphaelites, however, were not entirely without friends. John Ruskin, the respected author, critic and social reformer, was an ardent patron, and supported Millais and Rossetti with gifts and commissions, while also introducing them to prospective clients.

The Brotherhood broken

The collaboration was short-lived. The Brotherhood broke up, its members driven apart by their own differences. The wild and depressive Rossetti took a dislike to Ruskin and found co-operation with his former colleagues difficult. Holman Hunt left the group to travel in the Middle East. Millais fell in love with Mrs Ruskin, whom he later married; his financial success and his membership of the Royal Academy made him a member of the 'establishment', and earned him the contempt of the Brotherhood.

By 1854 the original Pre-Raphaelites had gone their separate ways, and the movement was dead. But its influence lived on. It was the inspiration for William Morris and his Arts and Crafts Movement, and it also inspired Aubrey Beardsley and the Art Nouveau of the early 20th century.

DROWNED BEAUTY *For full realism of effect Millais posed his model for 'Ophelia' in a bath.*

METICULOUS DETAIL *John Everett Millais (below), the son of an Anglo-French family from Jersey, paid little attention to his schooling, and was expelled for biting a master's hand. But his doting parents encouraged his gifts and helped him to establish a reputation as a painter of religious and historical subjects. He exhibited his first picture at the Royal Academy at the age of 17. Millais painted with meticulous attention to detail, recording every leaf and flower in the lush background of his painting of 'Ophelia' (above), and every woodshaving in 'Christ in the House of His Parents' (right). But Millais's allegiance to the Pre-Raphaelite Brotherhood was only an early phase in a brilliant career.*

RELIGIOUS OUTRAGE *Millais's 'Christ in the House of His Parents' was reviled by Charles Dickens.*

LEAVING THEIR HOMELAND *Ford Madox Brown's 'Last of England'.*

SEEKER FOR TRUTH *Ford Madox Brown (left), though never a member of the Brotherhood, was its most important single influence. Setting 'truth above originality . . . to be true no matter whence the truth comes', he was already an established artist when Rossetti became his pupil in 1848. That same year Brown eloped with a Herefordshire girl of 15. Both of them are shown in his 'Last of England' (above).*

PLEASURES OF LOVE *Holman Hunt's 'The Hireling Shepherd'.*

MORAL STRENGTH *None of the Pre-Raphaelites fought harder for his ideas than Holman Hunt (left). His parents were poor, and strongly opposed to his becoming a painter but he achieved his aim. He saw his task as 'to serve as high priest and expounder of the excellence of the works of the Creator', and many of his subjects were biblical in origin. 'The Hireling Shepherd' (above) describes the story of a young shepherd who neglected his sheep for love.*

ARTIST'S INSPIRATION *Elizabeth Siddal (left) and Jane Morris (right).*

IDEALISED LOVE *Rossetti's 'Dante's Dream' was painted in 1871.*

SPIRIT OF ROMANCE *Dante Gabriel Rossetti (left), central figure of the Pre-Raphaelites, worshipped women with a passionate, mystical devotion. But it was a platonic love, inspired by the pure emotion that his namesake, the Italian poet Dante, felt for his ideal, Beatrice.*

As a poor, unrecognised artist, Rossetti fell in love with Elizabeth Siddal, a milliner's daughter, whom the Pre-Raphaelites used as a model. They became engaged in 1850, but were not to marry for another ten strange and often tormented years. Rossetti adored her as a goddess of virginity and beauty, but at the same time took as his mistress another model, Sarah Cox, an exotic sensuous young woman, quite in contrast to the ethereal Elizabeth. Rossetti found another aspect of woman's 'ideal' beauty in Jane Burden, later the wife of the designer William Morris – and Rossetti's innocent attachment to her cost him Morris's friendship. He eventually married Elizabeth in 1860, but the marriage was short-lived. She gave birth to a dead child the following year, and never recovered from the experience. Suffering from consumption and depression, she committed suicide in 1862.

Rossetti's grief was so profound that he laid the manuscripts of his poems beside her in her coffin. But seven years later his friends persuaded him to have them exhumed, and they were published with enormous success in 1870. His last literary effort, Ballads and Sonnets, appeared in 1881. The rest of his life was riddled by ill-health, depression and drug addiction. Outbursts of anger and ingratitude lost him most of his friends, and towards the end he found comfort only in his work.

The Light Brigade charges into the 'valley of death'

The dashing, pointless sacrifice of the Light Brigade at the Battle of Balaclava in October 1854 came as the muddled climax to a foolish war – a war which had been muddled even in its origin.

Exactly a year before, Russia had gone to war with Turkey on the pretext of defending the Christian subjects of the Turkish empire. Britain saw this as evidence of Russian ambitions to threaten the Indian empire. Driven on by popular fervour, the British government, together with France, concluded an alliance with Turkey – the 'Sick Man of Europe'. An expedition was dispatched to the Black Sea in February 1854; war was declared in March. The Crimea was to remain the focus of the British war effort.

Britain had fought no major campaign since the Napoleonic wars 40 years earlier, and both government and people basked in the reflected glory of Waterloo. They believed that the same methods would bring them victory.

They were to be proved abysmally wrong. Britain's armies were untried; their organisation and administration were hopelessly defective. Worst of all, the standard of command was appalling. There was no general of outstanding ability, no one remotely approaching the stature of Wellington. The evils of the purchase system had eaten away at the standards of the entire officer corps. Promotions were bought and sold, and the effect was that high rank and command went not to the most able, but to the wealthiest. Such men were totally unequipped to face the taxing conditions of modern war. The fatal weaknesses of the structure were clearly demonstrated in the men who presided over the destruction of the Light Brigade.

Lord Raglan, the commander-in-chief, had not seen active service since Waterloo, and had never commanded an army in the field. Though a conscientious man, he completely lacked the power of decision. Lord Lucan, the commander of the cavalry division, was a

WAR COUNCIL *Lord Raglan, Omar Pasha and General Pélissier meet to discuss Allied strategy.*

INTO THE VALLEY OF DEATH *With Lord Cardigan galloping ahead, this Victorian lithograph shows the 17th Lancers leading the Charge of the Light Brigade. Confused orders led to this fatal attempt at a frontal assault on the massed Russian guns at Balaclava. The heroism of the charge was immortalised in Tennyson's famous poem 'Charge of the Light Brigade'.*

WAR AGAINST WINTER *An inadequate and disorganised supply system left most British troops ill-equipped to survive the rigours of a Russian winter. The lucky ones, like these sheepskin-coated soldiers, found their own supplies. But many more died, victims of official negligence.*

man of undeniable courage, but was quick-tempered, imperious and quarrelsome. And the man who led the Light Brigade itself, Lord Cardigan, was one of the most incompetent officers in the army.

Arrogant and self-satisfied, Cardigan had purchased the command of a regiment of the Light Brigade just two years after having been removed from a previous command in disgrace. His new regiment had been famous in peacetime London as the 'Cherry-Pickers' – in reference to the bright red trousers Cardigan had had designed for them. But, smart and disciplined though they were on the parade-ground, Cardigan and his resplendent troops had never been tested in the iron school of war.

Forewarned but not forearmed

Their test came on the afternoon of October 25, 1854, at Balaclava. It was to be one of the most gruelling in the history of British arms.

Balaclava was a small harbour on the south-western coast of the Crimea. It had been chosen by the French and British allies as their base for their assault on Sebastopol, the key to the Russian defensive system in the Crimea. The bombardment of Sebastopol had begun on October 17. Pounded by unceasing artillery fire, the Russians decided that their best hope of saving the fort lay in attacking Balaclava.

Early in the morning of October 25 the attack was launched. It took the British by surprise, for although Raglan had been forewarned, he had already been deceived by several false alarms and decided to ignore this fresh information. The battle was dominated by complete confusion from the very start.

Raglan chose to direct his army from a vantage point on the hills above the main field of battle, and it was from this remote command post that the fatal course of events was set in train. The Russians had captured a number of British guns and, anxious to recover them, Raglan dictated his famous order to his Quartermaster-General, General Airey: 'Lord Raglan wishes the cavalry to advance rapidly to the front – follow the enemy and try to prevent the enemy from carrying away the guns. Troop Horse Artillery may accompany. French cavalry is on your left. Immediate.' The order was signed by Airey.

Into the jaws of death

Raglan's brief order was disastrously ambiguous. It was carried down to Lucan's cavalry on the plain below by an enthusiastic young aide-de-camp, Captain Nolan. Nolan had watched with mounting frustration all day as his beloved light cavalry stood idle and inactive. Now, beside himself with irritation and anger, he swooped like an avenging angel from the heights, bearing the message that was to spell the doom of the Light Brigade.

Lucan, not having Raglan's bird's-eye view of the battlefield, could not understand which guns Raglan meant. Perplexed, he asked Nolan

for clarification. Impatient of the delay, Nolan flung out his arm in front of him. 'There, my Lord! There is your enemy! There are your guns!' he shouted.

But to Lucan, Nolan seemed to be pointing at the only guns he himself could see. These were not the captured guns, but a bristling Russian battery lying at the end of a valley protected on both sides by even more artillery. A frontal assault on these would be doomed to disaster. But standing orders laid down that the Commander-in-Chief's orders had to be obeyed without question. Despite his doubts, Lucan gave Cardigan the order to advance and the Light Brigade, immaculate and sparkling, trotted forward.

At first, nobody realised that a catastrophic error had been made. Then Nolan, suddenly seeing that the orders had been misinterpreted, galloped furiously across the front of the advancing cavalry, shouting and waving in an effort to halt the charge. But, before he could give warning, a Russian shell blew a hole in his chest.

The brigade continued its advance, moving towards the blazing guns at a steady pace. Its formation was perfect; not one man faltered, and as each trooper fell, so the ranks closed up.

On the heights above, the Allied General Staffs watched, appalled but powerless. The French general, Bosquet, was deeply impressed by the brigade's unwavering discipline under such shattering fire. But he commented: '*C'est magnifique, mais ce n'est pas la guerre* (It is magnificent, but it is not war).'

'A mad-brained trick'

Six hundred and seventy-three British cavalrymen dashed into an inferno of Russian fire. They reached the battery and began their hopeless hand-to-hand engagement with the 20,000 waiting Russian troops. But so shaken were the Russians by the disciplined courage of this charge that for a moment they lost their nerve. Had the Light Brigade received immediate support, they might have forced the enemy into retreat. But the brigade was alone. Faced with such desperate odds, it wheeled and retired, running the gauntlet of the Russian guns a second time. In 20 minutes, 247 men had been wounded or killed; over 500 horses also died; and the Light Brigade ceased to exist as a fighting unit.

Cardigan, turning to the remnants of his men, said tersely: 'Men, it is a mad-brained trick, but it is no fault of mine.' A voice replied: 'It was nothing, my lord, and we are ready to go again.' And late on the same evening, the shocked Raglan summoned Lucan to give his own bitter judgment: 'You have lost the Light Brigade.' But the loss of the Light Brigade was to develop into more than mere recriminations amongst generals. The disasters of the Crimea spelt the end of the old British army. In the future wealth would not be the sole key to advancement.

Heroine and hero of an inglorious war

The wild enthusiasm with which Britons greeted the outbreak of the Crimean War in 1854 had turned to disillusionment and anger by the time peace was made two years later. This remarkable turn-about was the work of two extraordinary people, Florence Nightingale (right) and William Russell, who made people aware for the first time of the sufferings which common soldiers had to endure in war.

Russell was the first great war correspondent. He sent back to *The Times* graphic descriptions of the lack of clothing, ammunition, proper quarters, food and medical supplies and treatment. The British were used to hearing that their soldiers were brave. Now they heard in addition that they were filthy, frozen, starved and badly led.

It was Russell's reports which fired the imagination of Florence Nightingale. With 38 volunteer nurses, she arrived at Scutari, the main British base, in November 1854.

The army hospital there was filthy – the wounded lay virtually unattended in beds infested with lice and fleas. More than half of the men who died in the war had contracted a fatal disease in the hospital.

With determination and patience, Florence Nightingale overcame the doctors' suspicions. Then she set to work, cleaning, repairing and providing new medical equipment.

Above all, she brought comfort and care to the virtually abandoned men, and was said never to leave the side of a dying man. The official medical staff were jealous to the last. But to the men she was a ministering angel – the 'lady with the lamp'. And to the British public she was the great heroine of the war.

WILLIAM RUSSELL *As* The Times *correspondent, he set a new style of realistic war reporting.*

LESSONS FROM LIFE INSPIRE A GREAT STORY-TELLER

On a December evening in 1833 Charles Dickens, an unknown political reporter of 21, was on his way to the House of Commons when he saw a new number of the *Monthly Magazine* in a Strand bookshop. Weeks before he had sent a story to its editor, but had heard nothing from him. He was supporting his entire family on his earnings and could ill afford the half-crown it cost, but he bought the magazine.

Turning the pages he saw his own name in print for the first time. His hands and knees shook, tears blinded his eyes; he was forced to step into Westminster Hall to recover his composure, and there he read the story before going on to his evening's work.

Nine years later, after the publication of his *Sketches by Boz*, and five other novels – among them *The Pickwick Papers*, *Oliver Twist* and *The Old Curiosity Shop* – Charles Dickens, now married and father of four children, was the most widely read author in the world.

A large part of Dickens' especial appeal for the sentimental Victorian reading public lay in his talent for presenting the grotesqueries of his world through the startled, bemused and innocent eyes of childhood. He never forgot the hardships of his own boyhood.

Stories drawn from life

Charles was only 12 when his father was gaoled for debt, and he was sent out to earn his living in a rat-infested factory. He lived alone in cheap London lodgings, and wandered the streets and wharves by night. The raggle-taggle low-life of London he knew so well during these years furnished much of the atmosphere and vast range of comic characters in his books; and his most touching descriptions of oppressed children, like David Copperfield, Nicholas Nickleby or Oliver Twist, are based on his own experiences.

Crusader and entertainer

Wilkie Collins, Dickens' close friend and fellow novelist, advised him that the best formula for the novel was to 'make 'em laugh, make 'em cry – but make 'em wait'. Dickens' books admirably bore out his advice. His range of comic characters is unequalled, and his readers were made to 'wait' by the serial form in which his books appeared, which called for a constant series of climaxes to sustain interest. So skilled was he in maintaining the excitement, that the ship taking the latest episode of *The Old Curiosity Shop* to America was met in New York by a crowd on the harbour which surged forward, shouting 'is Little Nell dead?'

But Dickens was more than just a great entertainer. Dedicated to social reform, he relentlessly attacked the abuses of Victorian

ASKING FOR MORE *Oliver Twist asks for more gruel in Cruikshank's illustration.*

CONVIVIALITY *Dickens' account of Mr Pickwick and his club brought him fame.*

FROM LIFE *The hapless Mr Micawber in* David Copperfield *is modelled on Dickens' father.*

NOVELIST
Dickens in middle life.

society. The wicked cruelty of schools and orphanages, the corruption and incompetence of the Poor Laws and the law courts were all mercilessly attacked in his books.

Throughout his life Dickens drove himself with an almost unbelievable energy, sometimes to the very limits of exhaustion – writing, editing, travelling, entertaining, dining out, acting and producing his own plays.

Year by year he drove himself on, digging deep into his childhood memories to create the countless fascinating characters that fill the pages of his books. And when he was more than 50 years of age he took up the even more arduous profession of public lecturer.

Dickens revelled in the chance to display his theatrical talent, and as fruit of this tireless energy he left £93,000 in his will. But he had worn himself out. He knew the end was at hand, and he wrote desperately, trying to finish his last great novel, *Edwin Drood*, before death came. For once he was defeated. On June 8, 1870, he collapsed after dinner with his daughter, and died the next day.

RESTING PLACE *In* Great Expectations, *Pip, the novel's hero, said that these graves – at Cooling, Kent – belonged to his family.*

HUMBLE BEGINNINGS *This forge and cottage in Chalk, Kent, were the model for Pip's home before he heard of his 'great expectations'.*

TRAGIC GENIUS FLOWERS IN A YORKSHIRE PARSONAGE

THREE SISTERS *Anne, Emily and Charlotte Brontë, painted by their brother, Branwell, who placed his self-portrait in the middle of the picture. He later painted it out. After an unrequited love affair, Branwell took to drink and drugs. He died of consumption at the age of 31 in 1848. Within seven years his three sisters had followed him to the grave.*

In July 1848 the publisher George Smith was working in his London offices in Cornhill when two small, shy, old-fashioned ladies were shown in. One handed him a letter written to Currer Bell, author of *Jane Eyre*, which he had published with resounding success the previous year. 'You see,' she explained 'we are three sisters.'

Her real name was Charlotte Brontë and her companion was her sister, Anne. A third sister, Emily, was at home in Yorkshire. All three had published books under pseudonyms, as Currer, Acton and Ellis Bell – for fear that prejudice against women would hinder their chances of success.

From success to tragedy

Charlotte, Emily and Anne, together with their brother, Branwell, were brought up in the bleak Yorkshire village of Haworth. Their father, a temperamental isolated Irishman, was rector; their mother died while they were very young. Few people visited the rectory, and the children, forced in on the world of their own imagination, inhabited a secret, self-centred literary realm, producing poems and romantic stories by the thousand. Charlotte and Branwell recorded the chronicles of Angria, a land entirely populated by handsome heroes and passionate women; Emily and Anne wrote of Gondal, an altogether sterner country of windswept moors and hills.

Charlotte and Emily, anxious to earn a living, attempted to teach as a career. Leaving Anne at home, they took up positions as student-teachers in a school in Brussels. Desperately homesick, they returned home, and turned to professional writing. In 1848 their first novels came out.

Anne's *Agnes Grey*, and her only other work, *The Tenant of Wildfell Hall*, were solid but uninspired books. Success eluded Emily's *Wuthering Heights* for many years, but Charlotte's *Jane Eyre* was an instant success.

Jane Eyre became one of the great heroines of English literature. Plain, passionate, intelligent, independent and, finally, triumphant, she was a projection of Charlotte's own nature, isolated at Haworth.

The inspiration for Emily's *Wuthering Heights*, on the other hand, was almost mystic. Emily rarely moved outside Haworth, her world was totally circumscribed by the Yorkshire moors and the vividness of her imagination. *Wuthering Heights*, one of the most remarkable novels in the English language, set the eternal drama of love and passion against the wild moors.

But just as success seemed within reach, the family was devastated by tragedy. In 1848 Branwell died of consumption, aged 31. Emily, a year younger, caught cold at his funeral, and died three months later, and Anne soon followed them to the grave.

Alone now, Charlotte stayed on at the rectory and wrote her last novel *Vilette*. In 1855, after years of spinsterhood, she married her father's curate. Her happiness was short-lived. Within a year she was struck down by fever, and died before she could give birth to the child she was carrying.

A handful of Britons–the heroes of the Indian Mutiny

SPARK OF REVOLT

A cartridge from the Royal Small Arms Factory, Enfield, of the same type as those which provoked the Indian Mutiny. Hindus and Muslims were outraged because some of the cartridges were greased with fat from cows and pigs – both of which had a religious significance.

DEFENDER *Sir Henry Havelock reinforced the besieged Lucknow garrison but could not fight his way out.*

RELIEVER *Sir Colin Campbell and his seasoned troops raised the siege of Lucknow in November 1857.*

On July 2 a shell hit his bedroom as he lay exhausted on his bed. Two days later he died, and was buried in a mass grave.

Now, without their leader, the British forces faced the ordeal of the long Indian summer. There were 1800 men, women and children, together with 1200 loyal native troops. The mutineers were not the only enemy, for the beleaguered garrison had to fight a second battle against heat and starvation. The garrison lived in daily hope of relief, but, as the weeks went by in silence, morale fell.

No source of food was neglected. On one occasion, 150 sparrows were shot and made into a curry. On another occasion, when a shell splinter shattered a cooking pot and plastered a group of officers with what was to be their meal, the ravenous men licked the food from their clothes and bodies. There was no room for pride.

Meanwhile, the guns of the besiegers took a daily toll. Those who were not killed out-

RELIEF ARRIVES *The Queen's Bays, part of Sir Colin Campbell's 5000-strong relief force, charge the rebel Indians outside Lucknow in November 1857. The cavalry charge was the final stage of Campbell's carefully organised relief expedition. His troops led the besieged British out of Lucknow to safety, but the city itself was abandoned to the Indians, and was not recaptured until March 1858.*

In 1857 British rule in India hung in the balance as thousands of rebels rose against the handful of Britons who held their country in thrall. The mutineers' aim was simple – to drive the British out. And to achieve this it was essential to capture the garrison cities which were the centres of imperial power.

Such a city was Lucknow, the capital of the northern province of Oudh. It was there that a siege took place which passed into Victorian history as an epic of courage against overwhelming odds.

The Indian Mutiny broke out in the middle of May 1857. Within a few days, Sir Henry

Lawrence, the Commissioner of Oudh, was facing the responsibility of protecting the lives of the terrified European community in Lucknow, now isolated in a sea of rebellion.

Cut off and alone

Hastily, Lawrence completed makeshift arrangements to withstand a siege. His own Residency building was chosen as the centre of refuge. Stores were hurriedly assembled. Earthworks were thrown up in a rough-and-ready system of fortifications. And outside them gathered the Indian rebels, whose numbers reached 20,000 at the height of the siege.

Lawrence was one of the first casualties.

right had to suffer the agonies of the primitive hospital. Without antiseptics or anaesthetics, operations were performed in a chaos of flies, dirt and filthy linen. Gangrene and death were the inevitable result. Outside the hospital, dysentery, diarrhoea, scurvy and lice made everyone's life a daily torment.

But on September 23 a loyal native reached Lucknow with the news that relief was at last on the way. And two days later, Sir Henry Havelock fought his way into the city. At a heavy cost, his troops joined the garrison and were met with frantic joy.

But this joy was short-lived. The force that Havelock had brought into the city was, even when joined with the surviving members of the garrison, too weak to fight its way out. The siege continued to take its toll.

However, Havelock's brave attempt had not been in vain. For Sir Colin Campbell, who had now arrived from Britain with reinforcements, determined to make the relief of Lucknow his first priority.

End of the ordeal

On November 9 Campbell began his advance from Calcutta. News of it soon reached Lucknow's garrison and a clerk, Henry Kavanagh, volunteered to disguise himself as a rebel and make his way through the enemy lines to guide Campbell and his forces. It was a hazardous venture, for Kavanagh was 6 ft tall, with red-gold hair and brilliant blue eyes. But he succeeded in his desperate mission and, even though he was a civilian, he was later given the supreme award for courage on the field of action – the Victoria Cross.

ROLL OF HONOUR *An unknown drummer boy painted this memorial to the men of the 32nd Light Infantry Regiment who died defending Lucknow. Rebel gunners took a heavy toll of the British during the long siege.*

By November 13 Campbell's army of 5000 men had reached the outskirts of the city. On the following day he began a carefully planned assault, capturing one by one the large buildings which lay as strongpoints along the route to the Residency. Meanwhile, Havelock led his troops out from the Residency to harass the enemy from the rear.

Finally, only a few hundred yards separated the two British armies. Heedless of the flying bullets, Havelock rushed forward to meet Sir Colin and congratulate him. The relief of Lucknow had finally been achieved.

Campbell had fulfilled his mission. The siege of the Residency had been raised. Those who survived it were evacuated to safety. For them, the four-month ordeal was at an end.

Ruling the 'brightest jewel' in the empire

The ferocity of the mutiny which swept India in 1857 came as a profound shock to the British. But only a blow of this magnitude could have forced home to them the inadequacies of their rule in India.

Starting in the 18th century, a commercial enterprise, the East India Company, had gradually taken over the administration of the ramshackle native states with which it came into conflict. By the 1850's, it controlled vast areas of India.

But no commercial concern could hope to rule so great an empire effectively. The British government had been forced to intervene, but all that it achieved was an uneasy system of dual control, which made efficient administration almost impossible.

And the physical problem of ruling an empire which lay so far from the centre of imperial power in Britain seemed almost insuperable. Britain's regular army was far too small to garrison India. So the East India Company was charged with raising locally recruited native troops. The largest was the Bengal Army. It was made up of Hindus from the provinces on the River Ganges, which had a long-established military tradition.

These soldiers were the famous Sepoys. But though they subdued their own country on behalf of their British masters, they were given little reward for their services. Though frequently men of high caste, they were treated with contempt by their British officers. Yet the British always took their loyalty for granted.

But in May 1857, the Sepoys of Meerut, near Delhi, rose against their officers. They had recently been issued with a new type of cartridge, which had to be bitten before being loaded into a rifle. And, ignoring official instructions, the manufacturers had greased some cartridges with the fat of cows and pigs – even though the cow was sacred to Hindus and the pig unclean to Muslims.

The Sepoy mutiny was welcomed by many Indian princes, who saw their chance to expel the British intruders. The revolt spread quickly over northern and central India. Delhi fell to the rebels, and Lucknow was besieged.

The tide turns

The British, surprised and outnumbered, fought back with desperate determination. Reinforcements were rushed out from Britain and, with the recapture of Delhi and the relief of Lucknow in the autumn, the tide turned against the rebels. After that came a long mopping-up operation, in which the British took savage reprisals.

But the mutiny at last inspired the British government to decisive action. In 1858 India was removed from the control of the East India Company and placed under the direct rule of the British government. And for the next 79 years, India remained Britain's proudest possession – the brightest jewel in her worldwide empire.

MILITARY LIFE *After the mutiny, the British Army played an increasingly important role in India. It was the rock on which the Indian Empire stood, and more than any other group it stamped the style of British India. Though native troops remained the backbone of the Indian army, many more British officers were appointed, including medical staff (above). Artillery was kept in British hands – even the Maxim gun detachment (left) is composed entirely of British soldiers. And every British regular regiment took its turn to serve in India.*

MASTER AND PUPIL BUILD A PALACE FOR DEMOCRACY

THE DESIGNERS *The talents of Augustus Pugin (left) and Charles Barry combined to create the new Palace of Westminster.*

FAMOUS SKYLINE *The Palace of Westminster, seen here from the Thames, was rebuilt after a fire in 1834. Completed in 1867, it has 1000 rooms, 100 staircases and 2 miles of corridors.*

Throughout centuries of monarchical rule, Britain's finest architects, artists and craftsmen devoted their talents to building and decorating magnificent palaces for royalty. In the 19th century the balance of power shifted irreversibly from the monarchy to the people. And, suitably, a new palace was built which was to become a unique monument – a palace for democracy.

It was a monument which came into being by accident. On the night of October 16, 1834, workmen burning a large pile of old wooden Exchequer tallies over-stoked the furnace in the old Westminster building which had been the home of Parliament. The flues became too hot and fire spread rapidly through the timber-framed building.

Firemen managed to save Westminster Hall, dating back to 1097, and St Stephen's Chapel. But the rest of the building was gutted.

Building from the ruins

Not everyone saw the fire as a disaster. *The Times* pointed to the deficiencies of the old building and urged that the new Houses of Parliament should be 'well considered of space, form, facility of hearing, facility of ventilation, facility of access and amplitude of accommodation for the public as well as for the members themselves'.

A national competition was held for the design of the new building with the stipulation that the prevailing style should be 'Gothic or Elizabethan', both of which were then fashionable. Charles, later Sir Charles, Barry won the competition. But his entry was based on a set of 'exquisite and minute drawings' which were largely the work of his brilliant 23-year-old assistant, Augustus Pugin.

Barry's own special interest was Classical architecture, evident in his earlier buildings such as the Travellers Club and the Reform Club in Pall Mall. In 1844, four years after construction of his new Westminster Palace began, he realised he would need considerable help with the ornate and complex Gothic detail. He turned again to Pugin, who was by now widely acclaimed as the master of the 19th-century Gothic style.

A partnership between equals

'I am in a regular fix,' Barry wrote to his former employee, begging him to help with the decoration of the House of Lords. Pugin at once accepted, and for the next seven years the two men – different in taste and character – worked together to produce one of the greatest British buildings of the 19th century.

While Barry was a staid, methodical architect, Pugin was an erratic genius. He dressed unconventionally in a wide-brimmed hat with a huge cloak to hide his shabby clothes. He often made his beautifully detailed sketches while sailing in the open sea, and he once said that the only two things worth living for were 'Christian architecture and boats'.

Pugin thought little of his fellow architects, calling them 'villains' and their work 'deplorable' and 'execrable'. Although he did not share Barry's love of Classical design, he later paid tribute to his skill, admitting that he could never have planned a building as large and logical as the Houses of Parliament. Barry, in turn, said that he himself did not have the inventiveness to produce the infinite variety and beauty of Pugin's details.

To Barry, the palace owes the surprising simplicity of its basic design: a single spine beginning with the House of Commons at the north and running southwards through the three major lobbies, the House of Lords, the Princes' Chamber and the Royal Gallery. Barry's great plan was completed by the two towers which balance one another at either end of the enormous building – the impressive Victoria Tower and the 320 ft high Westminster Clock Tower which houses Big Ben.

Wealth of detail

Inside, it is Pugin's brilliance that is supreme. He wrote: 'I strive to revive, not invent.' But when invention was called for, he produced a seemingly inexhaustible wealth of ideas, crowding thousands of tiny details into such rooms as the octagonal Central Lobby, the intricately patterned Queen's Robing Room and the moodily romantic corridors.

Into these spectacular chambers – lit by narrow shafts of light from hidden Gothic windows – Pugin put exquisite mosaic patterns, carved reliefs and tracery, intricate ceilings, carved panelling, gilt and bronze statuettes.

'Gravely gorgeous'

Nothing was too small for his inventiveness. Umbrella stands, coat-hooks, lamp-brackets and even inkstands were made in Gothic style to Pugin's design.

The culmination of the partnership between Barry and Pugin came in one magnificent chamber – the House of Lords. The great throne, with its huge canopy and metal candelabra, dominates the brown-and-gold chamber, vividly warmed by its scarlet morocco seats, its azure carpets and its rich gilding. Repeated intricate details, the panelled ceilings, the frescoes and hidden niches all contribute to the impression of breathtaking splendour. An early American visitor, the author Nathaniel Hawthorne, commented: 'Nothing could be more magnificent and gravely gorgeous.'

Yet the Palace of Westminster brought little but trouble to Barry, who was under constant attack from critics and various committees. He had many problems with the Royal Com-

ARCHITECT'S TRIUMPH *The House of Lords, with its brilliant colour and Gothic tracery, is dominated by Pugin's gilded throne, used by the monarch on State occasions.*

mission of Fine Arts which had been set up to help with the decoration of the palace. Eventually the commission took complete charge of the gigantic and melodramatic murals.

Barry also had a long-standing argument with Edmund Beckett Denison, the designer of the clock and Big Ben itself, the 14 ton bell which was named after Sir Benjamin Hall, the Commissioner of Works. Despite the varying problems – the initial failure of the clock to work, the cracking of Big Ben I and II – the bell, still cracked, has loudly chimed the time for over 100 years. And the 14 ft minute hand of the huge clock, 22·5 ft in diameter, has continued to travel over 100 miles a year ever since it was erected.

Both Barry and Pugin died before Westminster Palace was completed in 1867 – Pugin, only 40 years old and insane, died in 1852, and Barry in 1860. In the years that followed their deaths the building fulfilled its lofty purpose. Its magnificent debating chambers became the sounding board for great orators and the scene of dramatic events, a fitting stage for the triumph of the democratic ideal.

CLASH OF TWO GIANTS

The newly built Palace of Westminster was dominated during its first decades by two of the greatest Parliamentarians in Britain's history – William Ewart Gladstone and Benjamin Disraeli.

Disraeli, the unlikely leader of the Conservatives, was of Jewish origin, a dandy who wore his dyed hair in ringlets and looked on politics as an exciting game. When he became Prime Minister in 1868 he commented flippantly that he had reached the 'top of the greasy pole'.

Gladstone, the austere and high-minded leader of the Liberals, had no time for frivolities, and saw politics as a Christian mission. Disraeli said

he did not mind Gladstone always having an ace up his sleeve, but objected to his presumption that God had put it there.

Disraeli's flamboyance found an outlet in the empire-building adventures which Gladstone thought were reckless, expensive and immoral. Gladstone preferred reforms at home. His policy was 'peace, retrenchment and reform'.

The two great rivals disliked each other intensely. Facing one another across the floor of the House, they provided a long-running drama which perfectly matched the richly theatrical architecture that Barry and Pugin had created.

Souvenir plates of Gladstone (left) and Disraeli.

THE QUIET SCIENTIST WHO OUTRAGED VICTORIAN SOCIETY

THE VOYAGE OF THE 'BEAGLE' *Charles Darwin (above) was just 23 when he set sail as ship's naturalist in the* Beagle *(left). The voyage led to Darwin's theory on the evolution of species which shook religious beliefs.*

To the average Christian in the 19th century every word in the Bible was still literally true. The world had been created by God in six days and man had been created in his image. All the creatures of the world had survived the Flood only because Noah had taken two of each species on board the Ark. Charles Darwin's theory of evolution by natural selection shattered these beliefs. It struck at the very roots of society, undermining man's belief in his natural superiority, the inheritor of the universe.

Darwin developed this revolutionary theory during the five years he spent as naturalist on the survey ship HMS *Beagle*. On his return to London in 1837 he was already famous, simply because of the sheer volume of scientific material he had collected.

Voyage of discovery

Like so many men of genius, Darwin developed late. His interest in natural history was encouraged at Cambridge, where he became friends with the Cambridge botanist Professor John Henslow, to whom he confided his mania for collecting beetles: 'I will give a proof of my zeal: one day, on tearing off some old bark, I saw two rare beetles, and seized one in each hand; then I saw a third and new kind, which I could not bear to lose, so that I popped the one which I held in my right hand into my mouth.'

Professor Henslow recommended Darwin for the unpaid post of naturalist aboard the Admiralty's survey ship, HMS *Beagle*.

The *Beagle* sailed from Plymouth on December 27, 1831. By the time she returned five years later, Darwin was halfway to re-

shaping the landscape of 19th-century thought. At sea he was possessed by an almost superhuman energy, a magical vitality that he was never again to recover.

Whenever the ship touched land, he threw himself into energetic exploration and inquiry. He roamed the rain forests of South America; he climbed the Andes mountains; he undertook long and hazardous treks that would have exhausted the most seasoned explorers. And throughout it all he was collecting specimens of rare plants and animals.

Darwin recorded his observations, with painstaking detail, in *Zoology of the Voyage of HMS Beagle*. The birds, the animals and the flowers he saw only sharpened the conflict he now began to feel between his observations and his acceptance of the biblical account of the Creation of the natural world.

This conflict finally came to a head in the Galapagos Islands in the eastern Pacific. Darwin noticed that the islands had few varieties of land birds but that there were many different finches, all extremely similar except in the size of their beaks. He was struck by the thought that each species appeared to have been 'modified for different ends'. It was as if finches had developed on these isolated islands to fill roles normally filled by other birds.

Here at last was the clue to Darwin's dilemma. Either every one of these species had been separately created, or an ancestral pair of finches had arrived and their offspring, colonising new islands, had evolved into separate species.

With mounting excitement Darwin wrote at the time: 'Here we seem to be brought

somewhat near to that great fact, that mystery of mysteries, the first appearance of new beings on earth.'

He was 28 when he returned to London. Within weeks he was jotting down the beginnings of the theory that was to make him world famous and change the history of science: 'If we let conjecture run wild, then animals – our fellow brethren in pain, disease, death, suffering, and famine, our slaves in the most laborious works, our companions in our amusements – they may partake from our common origin in one ancestor, we may all be netted together.'

The final inspiration

In the following months this conjecture slowly became conviction. Darwin realised that species develop in different directions when isolated from one another – and that they are not immutable.

He was halfway to making his momentous discovery. But he still could not solve 'that mystery of mysteries' – the force which drives species to change, over many thousands of years, to suit varying environments.

The explanation came to him suddenly two years later. He was reading the *Essay on Population* by the Rev. Thomas Malthus. Malthus argued that human populations multiplied faster than the available food supply. If this were also true of animals, then they had to compete to survive. Darwin rightly concluded that in this deadly competition only those animals endowed with favourable characteristics – with slightly longer legs, thicker fur or stouter beaks – would survive. This was the basis for Darwin's theory of the

DARWIN'S FINCHES

Of all the thousands of species of animal life that Charles Darwin described during his five-year voyage on board the *Beagle,* the finches of the Galapagos were among the most important, for they eventually provided the most telling evidence for his epoch-making theory. Darwin noticed that there were about a dozen different species of finch and that they filled many different roles. One species feeds from the flowers of cacti and has a beak well suited for this purpose. Another species, with a tit-like beak, probes bark and leaves for insects; and others have parrot-like beaks, well adapted for cracking large seeds.

Darwin knew at once that the natural oddities of the Galapagos Islands had brought him near to 'that mystery of mysteries', the origin of species. But it was to be many years before he appreciated the full significance of the finches. Ten years after his voyage, he wrote hesitantly: 'One might almost fancy that, from an original paucity of birds on this archipelago, one species had been taken and modified for different ends.' And another 14 years were to pass before he set out to show that this 'fancy' was scientific fact. In Darwin's book, *The Origin of Species,* the finches finally emerged as perhaps his most convincing evidence that new species arise through the process he described as 'natural selection'.

This tree finch feeds like a European tit by probing bark and gleaning leaves for insects.

Ground finches have powerful beaks to crack large seeds.

Cactus-eaters have long pointed beaks to probe the flowers of cacti for their food.

Warbler finches glean insects with thin bills.

Another tree finch has a hooked beak for reaching insects.

THE PROTAGONISTS

When Darwin published his theory of evolution in *The Origin of Species* in 1859, Victorian society was incensed. The challenge to the biblical account of Creation threatened man's view of his God-given superiority, and the clergy took it up at a famous meeting of the British Association at Oxford in June 1860. Samuel Wilberforce, Bishop of Oxford, led the concerted attack and declared beforehand that he was out to 'smash Darwin'. He told a packed and hushed hall that the theory was 'casual', 'sensational' and contrary to the divine revelations of the Bible. He then turned on the biologist, T. H. Huxley, a champion of Darwin's theory, and demanded to know whether it was through his grandmother or grandfather that he claimed to be descended from the apes. Huxley was infuriated by the insolence of the question, and heatedly replied that he would prefer to be descended from an ape than from a cultivated man who prostituted his culture and eloquence to prejudice and falsehood. During the uproar that followed one woman fainted, and Wilberforce's supporters angrily demanded an apology. *The Descent of Man*, published in 1871, excited renewed public furore. But by Darwin's death in 1882, at the age of 73, his controversial theories were widely accepted. They form the basis for all modern biology today.

Thomas Huxley.

Bishop Samuel Wilberforce.

survival of the fittest, which he called the 'principle of natural selection'. This theory was to have far-reaching implications, not only in the scientific world, but on man's whole view of himself in the universe.

Darwin put up a tremendous fight against the conclusions he had been forced to draw. He wrote 'disbelief crept over me at a very slow rate but was at last complete'. He himself knew how reluctantly he had reached his conclusions, and he realised how outrageous they would appear to the public.

He made a rough outline of his theory, and locked it in a drawer with a letter to his wife, asking her to publish it in the event of his death. Then for 20 years he kept his heretical ideas from the public.

He had married his cousin Emma Wedgwood, and lived at Down in Kent. He adored his family, and when any of his ten children were ill, he would keep them beside him in his study while he worked. During these years his studies were hampered by daily headaches, and even these may have had their origin in the overwhelming guilt he felt at the ruthless implications of the theory he had developed.

Pilloried by the public

In the event his hand was forced by Alfred Wallace, another naturalist, who had independently arrived at a similar theory, and had written in June 1858 to tell Darwin of his findings. Papers from both men were read at the Linnean Society in London the following month; they caused little stir, but the following year Darwin published his theory as a book, *The Origin of Species.*

Public reaction was intense. Darwin was mercilessly criticised and abused. But he persevered with his work, and in 1871 he compounded the outrage he had already caused by publishing *The Descent of Man*, which advanced the belief that men and apes were descended from a common ancestry.

Darwin had expected the public execration. He knew that the acceptance of his theory would need time. He was prepared to sacrifice his private happiness to the cause of science.

When the outcry finally died down, the living world was seen to be a different place, and Charles Darwin was responsible for this change. The quiet, unassuming family man, working slowly but doggedly in his isolated country house, pursuing the solutions to the most basic questions about the natural world, became the father of modern biology. He wrote that his success was due to 'love of science, unbounded patience in long reflecting over any subject, industry in observing and collecting facts, and a fair share of invention as well as of common sense'.

He never stopped working: 'When I am obliged to give up observations,' he wrote, 'I shall die.' He collapsed at work on April 17, 1882. Two days later, he died of a heart attack at the age of 73.

Livingstone fulfils his destiny in darkest Africa

FIXING THE UNKNOWN
Livingstone kept accurate daily records on his journeys, no matter how terrible the conditions, with observations of his position, data on flora and geology. These went to the Royal Geographical Society, who still keep the sextant he used.

On April 18, 1874, Dr David Livingstone was buried in Westminster Abbey. Benjamin Disraeli, the Prime Minister, and the Prince of Wales attended. Dense crowds, many openly weeping, lined the funeral route. Florence Nightingale called him 'the greatest man of his generation'.

Livingstone was a national hero because he combined the virtues Victorians admired most – indomitable courage, stern morality and boundless faith. Yet by his own exacting standards, he had failed.

Tragically for him, it was only after his death that the ideas which drove him on were realised. Two months after his death the British brought to an end the slave trade in East Africa. And within 20 years, Nyasaland (now Malawi), Uganda and Kenya were incorporated into the empire.

Nothing exemplified the extraordinary tenacity of Livingstone more than his struggle to educate himself. From the age of ten, he had worked a 12½-hour day in the Blantyre cotton mills for six days a week – but somehow he found time to learn to read and write. Through sheer hard work he went on to graduate in medicine in Glasgow, and later to be ordained a priest.

Hardship and privation
He sailed for South Africa in 1841, aged 28, to a life of incredible hardship. But he was 40 when he made his first real expedition across Africa from west to east between 1853 and 1856. It was the first crossing of the continent by a white man, and followed for the most part the Zambesi River. On his way he discovered the Victoria Falls, one of the world's great scenic wonders, which he named after the queen.

His accomplishment made him an overnight hero in England, but it had fired him with a burning ambition which was to dominate the rest of his life. On his way he had encountered the horrors of the slave trade, and he determined that the only counter to it, and the inter-tribal wars in its wake, was the introduction of trade and settlement by British colonisers.

With government backing he returned to the Zambesi in 1858 to prove his conviction that the river was navigable. The Kebrabassa Rapids proved him disastrously wrong, and he turned his attention to the area around Lake Nyasa. Once again he failed, and he returned to England in 1864, now 51, with his reputation in ruins.

But nothing could keep him from his heroic quest to stamp out slavery. In 1866 he returned to Africa, hopelessly ill-equipped, short of money and without European companions. As well as the problem of slavery, he had also become obsessed with finding the source of the Nile, the great geographic question of the time. His previous guesses and conclusions had been wrong. He went south instead of north from Lake Tanganyika. His hardships were incredible, his money ran out, his bearers abandoned him. There were rumours of his death. To the outside world he was 'lost'.

The man sent to find him was the 28-year-old Henry Stanley, a journalist from the *New York Herald*. His editor's briefing was blunt: 'Find Livingstone if he's alive, or his boots

HISTORIC FRIENDS *Though Livingstone (above) and Stanley (left, in a studio pose) were only together five months after their historic meeting (right), Stanley was inspired to devote his life to African exploration. When Livingstone died, his loyal servants embalmed his body and carried it 1000 miles to the coast for burial in his homeland.*

if he's dead.' In accordance with these instructions, Stanley followed every clue and rumour he could find in the huge continent. His journey took him 236 days and 1000 miles to the village of Ujiji on the shore of Lake Tanganyika. On November 10, 1871, dressed in a freshly pressed flannel suit and with glistening boots, Stanley arrived at the village and pushed through the crowd of Africans who thronged around the sick, old man he had come to find. Raising his hat he uttered the words which have passed into history – 'Dr Livingstone, I presume?'

A national hero

Though the two men were only together five months, Livingstone made a deep impression on Stanley. The stories he published in England re-established Livingstone as a national hero, then he himself returned to Africa to follow in Livingstone's footsteps. He discovered the source of the Congo River, and finally discovered the source of the Nile.

Livingstone had died two years after their historic meeting. His servants had found him dead, kneeling as if in prayer next to his camp bed. Constant dysentery had killed him. One of the last things he wrote had been: 'Nothing earthly will make me give up my work in despair. I encourage myself to the Lord my God and go forward.'

Crusade to end the curse of slavery

The campaign against slavery was started by a small band of dedicated campaigners in Britain during the 18th century. But it took many years before the world accepted their views.

While William Wilberforce and the abolitionists were fighting against slavery, the trade had never before reached such a peak of intensity. Liverpool and Bristol founded their wealth on shipping cloth to West Africa on the so-called 'Middle Passage'. The cloth was bartered for slaves in the malaria-ridden swamps of the African coast. The slaves were in turn exchanged for tobacco, sugar and cotton in the West Indies and America.

Estimates from the logs of British ships alone are that the trade involved 85,000 slaves annually during the 18th century. Records for 1771 show that 58 slave ships sailed from London, 25 from Bristol and 107 from Liverpool. In these ships the slaves were packed literally like sardines, head to toe, with 18 in. width in which to lie and not enough headroom in which to sit up. Sometimes only half a slave cargo survived the crossing across the Atlantic to the plantations of the Americas.

Britain leads the way

The abolitionists, inspired by a vigorous evangelical Christianity, had their first success when a British judge, Lord Mansfield, ruled in 1772 that no one could be a slave in Britain itself. And from this time on, the British abolitionists built up an intense and relentless pressure on the government. In 1807 they succeeded at last in persuading Parliament to ban the carrying of slaves by British subjects in British ships.

But this was only a beginning. Britain's pioneering stand led her into a series of campaigns to ensure that first the slave trade, and eventually slavery itself, was outlawed throughout Africa, America and the European colonies of the Caribbean. By the 1820's, most European nations had followed Britain's example and forbidden their subjects to participate in the trade.

Fighting the slavers

Nevertheless, a vast illicit traffic in slaves flourished to supply the continuing demand for African manpower – for, though trading was illegal, slavery was still allowed.

Britain used her naval power to police the West African coast and arrest any ship engaged in the trade. The centre of this blockade was Sierra Leone, which was formerly called the Slave Coast. Its port, called Freetown, became a settlement for freed slaves, who prospered from re-victualling Royal Navy warships which often spent up to three years on patrol without the crew or its officers leaving the ship. Further north on the coast another settlement for freed American slaves

was established and called Liberia. But the slave smugglers, in order to maximise the profit of the risky voyage, now crammed slaves even more densely into their holds. If detection and arrest by a British patrol seemed likely, the entire human cargo was usually thrown overboard.

Nor were these cruelties confined to the slavers from Europe. The traders seldom left their ships to venture into the tractless and malaria-ridden interior of the continent. It was Africans themselves who initially caught the slaves, the strong preying on the weak, in constant, bloody slave wars.

In Britain the abolitionist campaign achieved its greatest success in 1833, when Parliament abolished slavery throughout the empire, and slaves already there were given their freedom. The British public cheerfully paid £20 million compensation to slave owners in the colonies. And in the course of the next 50 years the nations of Europe and the Americas followed Britain's example.

New horizons open

The ending of the slave trade was more than a mere philanthropic gesture. Until abolition, Europe's interest in Africa had been dominated by slavery. The Africans themselves were regarded more as animal resources than human beings. Abolition opened new horizons – Africa became a source of human and scientific interest, and attracted missionaries, explorers and settlers. The ending of the slave trade put a huge new continent on the map.

HUMAN GOODS
Manacles or logs to prevent escape were used by the Arab slave-trader Tippu Tip (above).

A queen and her people celebrate 60 glorious years

SIXTY GLORIOUS YEARS
An embroidered Diamond Jubilee memento (left) shows Queen Victoria at 18 when she ascended the throne. The brooch (right), with her photograph at 78, is now in the London Museum. Victoria's reign, the longest of any British monarch, spanned the final development of the empire 'on which the sun never sets'. By the 1890's, the British people's imagination was fired by the idea of empire, and the jubilee became a celebration of British pride in their far-flung possessions all over the world.

Londoners turned out in their thousands to pay affectionate homage to the woman who had won a lasting place in their hearts. In an age of rapid change, Queen Victoria had presided over the nation as a symbol of tradition and a guarantee of stability. In 1897 she was Britain's vital link with the past. Of all the great persons around her, she alone could look back on 60 years of supreme achievement. She could remember the day when she had first entered into her inheritance – a time when imperial fanfares were unimaginable, and industrial growth had not yet transformed the British countryside.

'I thank my beloved people'
Rising early on the morning of June 22, the queen began her day by pressing an electric button to send a telegraphic message to all the colonies: 'From my heart I thank my beloved people. May God bless them.'

In mid-morning, the sun streaming down, she set out in an open landau drawn by eight cream horses on the procession to St Paul's. Victoria had always been fortunate in the weather – so much so that the 'queen's weather' had become proverbial. Now the sun blazed on her for the supreme moment of her life and reign.

As the queen passed down Piccadilly, through Trafalgar Square to the Strand, waving flags, handkerchiefs and placards greeted her at every turn. At Lilywhites' sporting goods shop a banner was unfurled saying: 'Her Most Gracious Majesty's Grand and Glorious Innings – 60 Not Out.' But what touched the queen most of all was a group of veterans from the Charge of the Light Brigade, 43 years before, who had gathered on a

London has been the setting for many a royal pageant, but seldom has it seen a more emotional display than the rejoicing which marked the Diamond Jubilee of Queen Victoria's reign. For one day the life of the capital came to a halt, as its citizens indulged in an outpouring of pride in empire and affection for the longest-ruling monarch in Britain's history.

The jubilee was a double family gathering. From all over the world the queen's colonial premiers came to honour their sovereign. The vast empire over which she ruled now had more than 387 million subjects. From Europe came representatives of the great royal houses – including Victoria's daughter, the Dowager Empress of Germany, and the Crown Prince of Austria-Hungary. Most of them were relatives of the queen. By her children's marriages she had become the grandmother of Europe.

Pomp marked the occasion, but it was the people who gave the day its special meaning.

JUBILEE PROCESSION *The culmination of Queen Victoria's procession through London was a short service outside St Paul's Cathedral.*

balcony in Ludgate Hill to pay her homage. As she passed them she was seen to weep.

At noon the procession reached the steps of St Paul's. There, Victoria was greeted by Albert Edward, the 53-year-old Prince of Wales, mounted, and wearing a Field Marshal's uniform.

The queen was 78 years old and frail. Her eyesight was failing and rheumatism was causing her sleepless nights. Age and sorrow had sapped her of much of her former energy, so that she now received her guests in a wheelchair. Owing to her lameness, the service was held on the steps outside the cathedral and was kept short. The queen remained in her carriage as two bands struck up:

All people that on earth do dwell,
Sing to the Lord with cheerful voice.

When the service was over, the queen returned to Buckingham Palace by a route which took her south of the Thames and past the homes of some of the poorest of her subjects. There, her reception was just as tremendous as it had been in the West End.

'A never-to-be-forgotten day'

She arrived home very tired, but well pleased. That evening, while bonfires blazed on hills all over the country, Victoria recorded her satisfaction in her diary.

'A never-to-be-forgotten day. No one ever, I believe, has met with such an ovation as was given to me, passing through those six miles of streets... The crowds were quite indescribable and their enthusiasms truly marvellous and deeply touching... Every face seemed to be filled with real joy. I was much moved and gratified.'

Britannia rules – and the world marvels

Like all great empires, the British Empire was acquired and maintained by armed power. In 1897 that empire stood proudly at its highest peak, secure in the knowledge that it was guarded in the harbours and sea-routes of the world by the largest navy on earth.

The Royal Navy had 53 ironclads and armoured cruisers – 21 more than its nearest rival, the French fleet. The jubilee expressed the pomp and sentiment of empire, but it was the royal review of the navy four days later at Spithead that was the year's most memorable event for most foreign observers.

The queen herself was too tired to bear the strain of a long naval review. Her place was taken by the Prince of Wales, who inspected the fleet from a small convoy of elegant yachts and steamers. With him were all the colonial premiers, men who knew that the defence of their countries rested with the Royal Navy.

The Spithead review was the largest collection of warships ever gathered together at anchorage: five lines of 6 miles each, including 50 battleships. And this impressive array of strength was formed entirely from the home fleets. Not a single overseas base, it was carefully publicised, had been weakened to make the review possible.

Most of the ships were less than ten years old. All of them were ablaze with gleaming brass, and draped in yards of patriotic bunting. Brilliantly painted in white and yellow, they made, with their barbettes and torpedo-booms, their funnels and enormous guns, an impressive silhouette against the sky. 'We are a great people,' proclaimed the magazine *Vanity Fair*, 'and we realised it on Saturday as we never realised it before.'

In the intoxicating haze of that jubilee summer, it seemed to most Englishmen that their superiority at sea would last for ever. But the navy, though one of the nation's most ancient and proud institutions, was also one of the most insular and tradition-bound. Even at its height, the navy's supremacy was being undermined by the advance of technology.

For centuries, navies had consisted of wooden ships – 'Hearts of Oak' – which lasted for 60 years. The sheer number of ships in the Royal Navy gave Britain a lead which no foreign power could hope to overcome. By 1897, however, ironclads had replaced the old wooden hulks, and advances in gunnery and armour meant that entire navies could become obsolete in a decade. Ambitious powers like Germany were now able to compete with Britain on equal terms.

In 1897 – the very year that Britain's mighty fleet was gathered for review at Spithead – Kaiser Wilhelm II's government, inspired by Admiral von Tirpitz, drew up its own plans for an Imperial High Seas Fleet. This was to consist of 38 battleships, with a full strength of supporting craft. The German challenge had begun.

Responding to the challenge

Britain still had the advantage of highly trained and experienced sailors, but even that was more impressive on the surface than in reality. Officers had long been trained to regard seamanship as the supreme virtue. Some ships held gunnery practice only once a year, and in the annual gunnery competition of 1902, British warships missed the target with two rounds out of every three.

But if 1897 was the sunset of the old navy of Nelson, there were already signs that Britain was capable of responding to the challenge of German ship-building. In the first years of the century plans were laid which led to the proud moment when Britain launched the world's first 'Dreadnought' in 1906.

The British battle-fleet which sailed to war in 1914 was very different from the ships which had executed their stately war-dance at Spithead. But the resolution to control the seas survived into the new age of naval warfare.

BRITANNIA'S MIGHT *It was Britain's naval might which preserved her world-wide empire, and at the Spithead Review, four days after the Diamond Jubilee, the Royal Navy gave a convincing display of its power. The combined lengths of the warships in the review totalled an amazing 30 miles.*

Mafeking – the grim siege where a legend was born

MAFFICKERS *News of the victory at Mafeking was greeted by such wild rejoicing in London that a new verb was born – to maffick.*

MAFEKING MONEY

Food and entertainment were relatively plentiful for the troops in Mafeking, but cash soon ran short. The British commander, Robert Baden-Powell, solved the problem by printing special notes, one of which is in the National Army Museum, London.

In the eyes of a world jealous and suspicious of Britain's imperial ambitions, the Boer War was a brave challenge offered to a bullying Goliath by a gallant race of Davids. To the British public, steeped in a century of imperial glory, the confrontation with the Boers seemed more like an insult hurled at the world's greatest power by a handful of insolent farmers.

Yet, the longest episode of the war – a siege which held the British public spellbound – was a complete reversal of this classic contrast. For 217 long days, in the tiny town of Mafeking, 1000 British troops held over 8000 Boers at bay. And at the head of the British was the romantic and flamboyant Lieutenant-Colonel Robert Baden-Powell, while the Boers were led by one of their most seasoned commanders, General Piet Cronje.

Two fateful decisions

In normal times, Mafeking was an insignificant trading post, with a population of no more than 2000 settlers. What thrust this little town into the sudden prominence it was to enjoy from October 1899 to May 1900 was Baden-Powell's decision to make Mafeking his military headquarters and the base from which to organise the defence of the Cape's

northern frontiers. It was this action which made Mafeking a principal objective for the Boer forces. Yet the town would never have had the chance to achieve its fame had the Boers launched an immediate assault. Such was their superiority that they would have

easily overrun it. Cronje favoured such a bold action; but he was under orders not to risk any move liable to cause more than 50 casualties.

So, instead of direct attack, the Boers pounded the town every day with their 'Long Tom' siege guns; and at the end of the siege, not a building was left unscarred.

Life under siege

In other respects, life in the besieged town was startlingly unaffected. Food remained plentiful and Christmas at the Mafeking hotel was celebrated with a massive banquet which would not have disgraced a major city. There were regular concerts, receptions, dances and cycle races. For a time there was even polo on Sundays – until a Puritanical Boer commander threatened to shell the polo-ground unless sport on the Sabbath ceased.

Baden-Powell took the hint, and forebade polo, but he encouraged all other amusements as part of a campaign to maintain morale. His jaunty courage inspired his garrison's resistance, and his deliberately light-hearted official dispatches, which African messengers smug-

---

BIRTH OF THE SCOUTS

A group of Scouts at camp in 1909. The movement quickly spread.

A fourpenny booklet called *Scouting for boys* appeared in the shops on January 15, 1908. The writer was Robert Baden-Powell, by then a lieutenant-general and famous as the defender of Mafeking. Fathers bought the book for their sons; word quickly spread about the exciting world of adventure, sports and camp fires described by Baden-Powell; the Boy Scout movement began. He used his South African experiences to the full. Even his Scouts' hats were modelled on the one he had worn at Mafeking.

There were no barriers of class or religion. The first Scouts were often poor children, who wore rags and went about in bare feet. They met in alleyways and cellars, and camped on waste ground under a piece of tarpaulin slung over a plank against a wall. Inspired by Chief Scout 'B.-P.', boys from all over Britain flocked to join the new movement, and Baden-Powell retired from the army to give it all his time. Cubs, Rovers and the Girl Guides were established. When war broke out in 1914, 'Be Prepared' had become a national slogan. Scouts helped as War Office messengers, hospital orderlies and farmhands. More than 20,000 Sea Scouts did coastguard work and, during air-raids, Scouts' bugles signalled the 'All Clear'. Older members joined up – 11 of them won the Victoria Cross, but 10,000 were killed. In the Second World War, thousands of Scouts helped in the evacuation of children from the cities, as well as fire-watching and salvage-collecting. Baden-Powell died in 1941, aged 83.

PEOPLE'S IDOL *The Mafeking episode made Baden-Powell a national hero.*

gled through the Boer lines, became famous: 'October 21st. All well. Four hours' bombardment. Killed, one hen; wounded, one yellow dog; smashed, one hotel window.'

But the Boers were proving to be a far tougher enemy than had ever been expected, and it was not until Lord Roberts was sent out to replace Sir Redvers Buller as British Commander-in-Chief that the tide turned.

Relief at last

At the beginning of May 1900, Roberts ordered forces to be dispatched to Mafeking. Regiments of Rhodesians and Canadians under Colonel Herbert Plumer joined up with the official Mafeking Relief Force led by Colonel Bryan Mahon. Their combined force of some 2000 men drove the Boers off and, on May 17, Mafeking was finally relieved. Thanks largely to the resourcefulness of Baden-Powell, the long and wearying ordeal had cost only 35 lives.

Back in Britain, the news was greeted by unprecedented scenes of wild national rejoicing. Baden-Powell's example had restored the people's flagging faith in victory.

A handful of farmers challenge the empire

Fifty thousand British soldiers began arriving in South Africa at the beginning of November 1899, convinced they would put down the rebellious Boers within weeks. They were the best-equipped force ever to leave Britain, and they faced an enemy of undisciplined farmers commanded by bearded old men who looked like clergymen instead of fighters. The Boer Commandant-General, Piet Joubert, was 68 – 'a kindly, well-meaning old man bewildered at the heavy responsibility', wrote one of his men.

Britain expected victory by Christmas. The humiliation was numbing when her armies were defeated in the first major battles. The war dragged on for three years, in which time the force that went out that November had to be increased tenfold.

Mismanagement and incompetence

What the Boers lacked in war-craft and discipline, they made up for in determination. They were fighting for their homeland. President Kruger said of his people, 'If they must belong to England, then a price will be paid that will stagger humanity'.

In the ill-famed 'Black Week' of December 1899, three heavy defeats – on December 10 at Stormberg, on the following day at Magersfontein and on December 15 at Colenso – shocked British morale to the core. The men blamed the incompetence of their generals; the generals grudgingly admitted they had been unprepared for the courage of the Boers. It was soon clear that the British Commander-in-Chief, Sir Redvers Buller, would have to go.

A British doctor wrote from a hospital camp

in February 1900: 'Men are dying from actual starvation. It is all through mismanagement – in fact, there is no management at all. Buller has had ten weeks to move 18 miles and he has really done nothing except lose precious lives, messing up everything he has tried, encouraging the Boers and dispiriting our own soldiers.'

Lord Roberts was sent out to replace Buller. The full resources of the empire were mobilised to salvage Britain's self-respect. By October 1900 the Boer armies in the field had been defeated. It seemed the war had been won, but it was to drag on for another 18 months.

The Boers turned to guerrilla warfare and again Britain was unprepared. In May 1901 Lord Kitchener scraped together 80,000 untried mounted troops to combat the constant sabotage of railways and capture of army posts and convoys. These men were no match for the Boers, skilled at riding and accustomed to the terrain.

Desperate for victory, Britain introduced concentration camps to isolate the Boer women and children from their fighting men. This measure, and the burning of homes, put world opinion even more firmly on the side of the farmers. Not until May 1902 was peace finally achieved.

Learning the lesson

British pride had taken a heavy blow, yet there was some profit gained. The army's miserable performance caused reforms in training and tactics that were to prove invaluable when world war broke out in 1914. Most important of all, Britain began to abandon the policy of self-sufficiency that had left her alone and friendless. The Boer War started the alliance-making process which became so necessary for Britain to undertake in the next decade.

FAMILIES AT WAR *The Boer fighters were boys and men aged from 16 to 70. Families went to war as a team – son, father, grandfather and even great-grandfather. Women and children – and the family business – often went with their men, too (right). Boer soldiers rarely had uniforms. A rifle, a bandolier of ammunition and a satchel of food were their only equipment.*

The challenge
of modern times

*At great cost, the British people triumph in two wars,
then – abandoning their far-flung empire – they turn
to face the problems of a rapidly changing world*

In 1901, when Queen Victoria died, Britain was the foremost nation in the world. She owed her unmatched strength and power to her industrial and technological ascendancy, a stable political system at home, and a far-flung empire which covered a quarter of the earth's surface and to which a quarter of mankind belonged.

But two World Wars were to transform Britain's place in the world, and by the time Elizabeth II came to the throne in 1952 Britain was no longer a major world power. The empire, on which the Victorians had boasted that 'the sun never set', had entered its final stage of transformation into the Commonwealth of Nations. Other powers had successfully challenged Britain's industrial mastery. Confidence in the future was not shaken; but it had taken a different turn. Britain was choosing a new role for herself in a changing and changed world.

Progress came to be measured not simply by the accumulation of wealth but by the fairer distribution of it. In the 1970's romantics might cast wistful eyes back to the vanished golden days of Edwardian Britain when the world had seemed so predictable. But for the mass of people life had become more pleasant and more secure than it had been 75 years before.

Taking their example from their king, the people of Edwardian England enjoyed pleasure to the full (pp. 326–7). But the life that the rich enjoyed contrasted sharply with the severe poverty in which one-third of the nation lived. In 1906 the Liberal Party awoke Britain's conscience with promises

THE QUEST FOR POWER

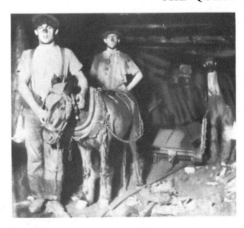

At the beginning of the 20th century, British industry, powered by the island's huge coal reserves, led the world. The price of this success was the appalling conditions in which many industrial workers, such as the miners (inset), spent their lives. The next 75 years transformed these conditions, improving the lot of most people in Britain. But, over the same period, Britain's industrial supremacy was successfully challenged by other nations. In addition, the cost of two World Wars was crippling. In the 1970's, however, vast oil fields were discovered in the North Sea, offering the prospect of new industrial vigour. Here (left) British Petroleum's platform, Sea Quest, drills for oil off Aberdeen.

323

THE TITANIC SINKS *British confidence in their technology was rudely shattered after the 'unsinkable' Titanic (below) set sail on her maiden voyage with 2224 passengers in April 1912. A few days later she rammed an iceberg and went down within hours. More than 1500 people died. A newsboy (right) breaks the news.*

of reform, and their landslide victory in the General Election of that year enabled them to lay the foundations of the welfare state.

The patriotic pomp and splendour of the Edwardian period found its expression in the music of Edward Elgar (p. 328), the first great composer produced by Britain for two centuries. The same patriotic spirit was aroused by the valiant but tragic attempt by Captain Robert Falcon Scott and his brave team to become the first men to reach the South Pole (pp. 330–1). In science, the period provided hints of great changes to come. The Cavendish Laboratory (p. 329) in Cambridge was becoming the centre for a new science that was to transform the world – atomic physics.

When Edward VII died in 1910 a sense of security seemed to die with him. At home, the suffragettes (pp. 332–3) turned to militancy to win women the vote. Abroad, the menace of war grew stronger as Germany strengthened her military might. Crisis followed crisis until in 1914 Europe was a powder-keg which needed only a spark to set it on fire.

Decades of crisis

The spark came with the assassination of the Archduke Franz Ferdinand, heir to the Austro-Hungarian throne. Within a few weeks, the whole of Europe was at war. More than 750,000 Britons and 200,000 soldiers from the empire were to die before the world found peace again.

In the early days, it was confidently predicted that the war would be 'over by Christmas'. But after the Battle of the Marne (pp. 334–5) in September 1914 the pattern for the next four years was set – stalemate. The battles that attempted to break this pattern, such as the British offensive on the Somme (pp. 336–7) in 1916, brought a terrible result. In that one battle, 420,000 British soldiers were killed or wounded – 19,000 of them died on the first day alone. As the horror of war struck home, the patriotic fervour expressed in Rupert Brooke's poetry gave way to the bitter disillusionment of Siegfried Sassoon and Wilfred Owen (pp. 338–9). At sea, too, the early years brought no great victory. The only full-scale naval battle of the war, at Jutland (pp. 340–1) in 1916, lasted a few hours and ended inconclusively. But in 1918 the tide turned. America's entry into the war the previous year was beginning to take effect. A string of Allied victories in the summer of 1918 (pp. 342–3) brought about the collapse of Germany, and in November she surrendered.

Peace raised expectations of a better life. But the returning soldiers did not find themselves in a land 'fit for heroes to live in', as the wartime Prime Minister, David Lloyd George, had promised. The firstfruits of peace were a severe economic recession and massive unemployment. Industrial strife dogged the 1920's, culminating in the General Strike of 1926 (pp. 344–5).

UNITED IN WAR *George V, his cousin Nicholas II of Russia, President Poincaré of France and Albert I of Belgium feature on this handkerchief, sold during the early months of the First World War. All expected the war to be over within months of its outbreak in August 1914. But it was to last four years, and 10 million men were to be killed. Of these, 750,000 were British troops and 200,000 from the empire.*

Britain faces her 'finest hour'

FRUITS OF EMPIRE *A vast exhibition was held at Wembley in 1924 to celebrate the glories of the British Empire. This poster shows the Palace of Industry. But many colonies were pressing for independence. India – the 'jewel in the imperial crown' – led the way.*

In the 1930's, the foreign situation became ominous. A few far-sighted prophets – most notably Winston Churchill – raised their voices to warn of the rebirth of German aggression under Adolf Hitler. The generation which had fought so hard for peace refused to listen. They were preoccupied with a more immediate crisis. In 1936 Edward VIII announced that he intended to marry Mrs Wallis Simpson, a twice-divorced American. His decision to abdicate rather than give her up (pp. 346–7) shocked the nation. But the devotion to duty of his younger brother, George VI, prevented any permanent damage to the monarchy.

In 1939, however, king and country faced their gravest test in 1000 years of history. Germany's attack on Britain's ally, Poland, in August 1939 left the British no option but to declare war. On September 3 the Second

World War broke out – just over 20 years after the triumphant conclusion of 'the war to end wars'.

It soon became clear that the country needed a new leader. The hour produced the man. Winston Churchill, eloquent, resolute and courageous, led Britain through what he stirringly described as her 'finest hour' – the Battle of Britain (pp. 348–51). Britain stood alone against Hitler and his ally, Italy, for almost a year. Then, in 1941, Russia and the United States entered the war. Japan came in to join Germany and Italy. Almost every nation in the world was now involved in bitter conflict.

Britain continued to play a decisive role – especially in North Africa. Victory at El Alamein in 1942 (pp. 352–3) and the defeat of Rommel's *Afrika Korps* was the turning point of the war. Germany herself was now suffering the horrors of heavy bombing which she had inflicted on Britain in 1940. With the success of the D-Day landings in France in June 1944 (pp. 354–5), her defeat became inevitable. In May 1945 she finally surrendered. Japan followed suit later in the year.

Peace had come at last. But two World Wars had taken their toll. In 1914 Britain had been a creditor to poorer countries all over the world. By 1945 she was herself heavily in debt, owing a staggering £4196 million. The responsibility of empire was now a burden beyond her means, and the granting of independence to India in 1947 was the first step in the abandonment of her Asian and African empires.

TROUBLED DECADE *As anger grew in the economic depression of the 1930's, some men looked to the example set by Hitler's Germany and Mussolini's Italy as a solution for Britain's problems. One of them was Sir Oswald Mosley, a former Labour minister, who founded first the New Party and then the British Union of Fascists in his bid for supreme power.*

New problems in a changing world

At home, too, the mood was for sweeping changes. Between 1945 and 1951 a Labour government introduced a series of revolutionary reforms, most notably the National Health Service, and the nationalisation of key industries, such as coal.

By the early 1950's, the austerity and hardship of the immediate post-war years was coming to an end. A lighter and more optimistic mood prevailed and found expression in the graceful modern architecture of the 1951 Festival of Britain. The conquest of Mount Everest, the world's highest mountain, by a Commonwealth team in June 1953 (pp. 356–7) gave a fillip to national pride. News of Hillary and Tensing's feat reached Londoners as they watched the coronation procession of Elizabeth II. During the first two decades of her reign successive Prime Ministers – both Labour and Conservative – grappled with the problems facing Britain in a rapidly changing world. Sir Anthony Eden's miscalculations about Britain's world role led to the landings at Suez in 1956. His successor, Harold Macmillan, showed a surer touch in his assessment of the new realities: abandoning the idea of empire in Africa, he prophesied a 'wind of change' sweeping through the African continent. But the loss of empire left a vacuum at home. As an American observer, the former Secretary of State Dean Acheson remarked: 'Great Britain has lost an empire, and has not yet found a role.'

As the last quarter of the century dawned, there were hopes that closer political and economic links with Europe could resolve this dilemma. The enmities which had cost Britain so dearly in two World Wars were now forgotten in shared aspirations. Meanwhile, Britain maintained ties of friendship with the countries of the old empire, now independent nations united in the Commonwealth.

At home, despite recurrent economic crises, most people enjoyed the 'consumer revolution' (pp. 358–9). The discovery, in the 1970's, of vast oil fields in the North Sea, brought the prospect of a fresh boost to Britain's economy. With this new wealth it was hoped that Britain would enjoy increasing prosperity, and once more assume a dynamic role in world politics.

FALSE PEACE *Neville Chamberlain announces 'peace in our time' after meeting with Hitler at Munich in 1938. But he was forced to go to war a year later.*

CROWNING GLORY *Elizabeth II and her family, after her coronation in 1953. Under her the British people became identified with the monarchy as never before. On Coronation eve, 30,000 people camped out in the Mall and almost half the nation watched the ceremony on television. For the first time, a monarch was crowned in full accordance with the ritual – 'in the sight of all the people'.*

AGE OF ENJOYMENT

With the death of Queen Victoria in 1901, Britain entered a new age. And for many it was an age of unbridled pleasure. The restraints that the old queen had symbolised were thrown off in an extravaganza of enjoyment.

No one epitomised the new mood better than the new king, Edward VII. With his obvious enjoyment of the good things in life – including enormous cigars, racehorses and pretty women – he set the pattern of social life for rich and poor alike. Both shouted their approval – 'Good old Teddy' – when the king's horse won the Derby in 1909. The politician Sir Edward Grey wrote that 'the humblest devotee of horse racing in a Derby day crowd knew that King Edward was there to enjoy the national festival in precisely the same spirit as themselves'. But some showed their disapproval of this new spirit. One of the king's secretaries, Frederick Ponsonby, regretted that 'eminent men were being knighted while comic songs were being played'.

Like his subjects, Edward adored the music halls. But new inventions were already providing forms of entertainment which would reach even larger audiences. Seated in their cluttered parlours, the Edwardians could enjoy the peerless soprano notes of Dame Nellie Melba or the inimitable singing of Marie Lloyd on their new wind-up gramophones. And in theatres and halls throughout the country they could marvel at the 'animated photographs' of the flickering bioscope, ancestor of the modern cinema. Out in the country, chickens scattered as glittering motor-cars swept along unmade lanes, and overhead the sound of flying machines disturbed the tranquil skies.

A contemporary described Edward and his aristocratic set as a 'race of gods and goddesses . . . upon a golden cloud'. But darker clouds were gathering over the Continent. When the storm broke in August 1914 the age of 'gods and goddesses' ended for ever, as the lights went out all over Europe.

VAUDEVILLE *Among the acrobats, jugglers and comics, male impersonators such as Vesta Tilley (above) were rapturously received.*

DRAMA AND INTRIGUE *Popular Edwardian melodrama, in the old-fashioned, full-blooded style, packed West End theatres in London.*

A BICYCLE MADE FOR THREE *By Edward VII's time the Victorian penny-farthing had given way to the pneumatic-tyred safety-bicycle. One oddity was a 'triplet' (above). But for single women, a tricycle was considered more convenient and more becoming. Bicycle parties cycled out to the country at weekends.*

STAR TURN *The famous music halls of the Edwardian age – the Alhambra and the Palace, the London Pavilion and the Tivoli – were all within five minutes' walk of Piccadilly Circus. All London went to watch Little Tich – 'The Droll Dancer' – the juggling of the great Cinquavelli, and the inimitable Marie Lloyd (above).*

VARIETY *The spirited dancing of the famous Gaiety girls dazzled the Edwardian audience.*

RAGTIME HIT *A new type of music made an instant impact on London audiences when the American revue 'Hullo Ragtime' arrived in 1912.*

GLORIOUS AMATEURS *The reigning county cricket champions in 1902–3 were the Yorkshire team captained by Lord Hawke (centre) and including F. S. Jackson (later Sir Stanley Jackson, Governor of Bengal). Hawke once said: 'Pray Heaven, a professional will never captain England.'*

LEADER OF FASHION *Edward VII takes his first drive in a motor-car, a 12 hp Daimler, driven by Lord Montagu of Beaulieu. Like many of his subjects, Edward was fascinated by the new pleasures of motoring. On one journey to Brighton, his chauffeur reached the speed of 60 mph.*

AIRBORNE *Londoners flocked to Hendon air display in 1913 to see the flying machines advertised on this London Underground poster.*

ANIMATION *The first films, appearing in the early 1900's, boasted that they could reproduce 'the latest events from all parts of the world'.*

HIGH SOCIETY *The life of the upper classes was dominated by a rigid calendar. Here spectators watch the regatta at Henley.*

A GREAT COMPOSER CAPTURES THE PAGEANTRY OF HIS ERA

The prosperous and patriotic mood of Edwardian England found perfect expression in the work of Edward Elgar, the first British composer to achieve wide recognition since Purcell.

No one could have been more suitable to portray the spirit of his native land. As English as the Malvern Hills of his birthplace, Elgar remained throughout his life something of the country gentleman, and was always more attached to the home comforts and middle-class respectability of his background than the bohemian life so often associated with great artists.

Edward William Elgar was born on June 2, 1857, in the village of Broadheath, near Worcester. His family was very musical and lived in a district where there was much music making. His father owned a music shop in Worcester, and from an early age Elgar learnt the piano and violin. At 16 he was a member of the orchestra at the local music centre, the Glee Club, and saving hard to get to London

and finance more serious study. By 1887 he had achieved his ambition and, 'living on two bags of nuts a day', as he claimed, he embarked on a series of violin lessons with the great Hungarian violinist, Adolf Pollitzer.

Elgar soon realised that he was never going to become a concert violinist. Pollitzer described him as a 'most earnest musician', and encouraged him to discuss his own music. Gradually Elgar realised that his real talent lay, not in mastering the violin, but in composition.

In the main, Elgar was self-taught. He had to earn his living, and for ten years he concentrated on learning his craft. He wrote a few pieces which met with considerable success in the provinces, and taught music at a girls' school in nearby Malvern. And it was when Elgar reached 30, that two incidents occurred which were to change his entire life and inspire the full flowering of his genius. The Czech composer Dvořák came to England, and this visit stirred the young Elgar's enthusiasm. And he met and married Caroline Alice

Roberts, his companion and inspiration for the next 30 years.

Alice persuaded her husband to move to London. Shortly after this move Elgar received his first general recognition with a short piano piece, 'Salut d'amour', which he sold to Schotts, the music publishers, for £5. Schotts arranged it for violin, piano and orchestra, and it became the best-selling piece of its time.

But real success still eluded Elgar. Money was scarce and Alice was forced to sell her pearls. After three years, depressed and suffering from a nervous illness, Elgar admitted defeat, and returned to the country and his old profession, teaching. To add to his income, he played with local orchestras.

Recognition at last

The recognition he craved finally came to him at the turn of the century. Slowly but solidly he built up his reputation, culminating with two great works, the 'Enigma Variations', a set of musical portraits of the composer's friends, performed in 1899, and the oratorio 'The Dream of Gerontius' (1900), which was acclaimed as a European masterpiece in 1902. Richard Strauss, the celebrated German composer, wrote of it: 'With that work England

DEVOTION *Elgar (left) and his wife, Alice, who encouraged him during his struggle for recognition. After her death in 1919, he composed very little.*

COMPOSER'S BIRTHPLACE *Elgar was born in this house at Broadheath, near Worcester, in 1857. It is now a museum dedicated to him.*

MASTERPIECE *The original manuscript of Elgar's second symphony. He wrote on the score 'Rarely, rarely comest thou, spirit of delight'.*

became for the first time one of the modern states.' A symphony soon followed, together with more oratorios. These included 'The Apostles' and 'The Kingdom' – both taking their theme from the New Testament and widely regarded as masterpieces.

Not all Elgar's work was so profound. In 1901 he wrote the 'Cockaigne Overture', a light-hearted work embodying the exuberant bustle of London. In the same year he composed the first 'Pomp and Circumstance' march in an unashamed outburst of patriotic fervour. With this one piece Elgar became Britain's best-loved composer. He later developed part of it as 'The Coronation Ode', celebrating Edward VII's accession to the throne. The king himself suggested that the patriotic poet A. C. Benson should write words for it, and it became almost a second national anthem – *Land Of Hope And Glory.*

'I am folk music'
Elgar genuinely admired Edward VII. The composer was, after all, a modest, self-made man from the provinces, and enthusiastic praise for his music from England's reigning monarch must have been overwhelmingly gratifying. After the king's death in 1910, Elgar's second symphony was dedicated to his memory, the noble slow movement expressing the composer's grief.

In the Edwardian period, Elgar became a well-known public figure. He was knighted, in 1902, and became Professor of Music at Birmingham University. He made lecture tours of America, and visited European capitals where he was rapturously received. The compliments of high society flattered him, but at the same time he was deeply moved by the appreciation of his music which came from ordinary people.

'I am folk music,' he would reply to critics who dismissed his music as too popular, even vulgar. Vulgarity, he declared, at least bore 'signs of initiative', often lacking in the work of his fellow composers.

He knew that he was capable of a solemn depth that was far removed from the hollow rhetoric of his contemporaries – and also of a fairy-like fantasy which no 'popular' composer could equal. One single work, the 'Enigma Variations', reveals the wide range of his style – the light-winged 'Dorabella' together with the stately processional 'Nimrod'.

Elgar outlasted the Edwardian age by 20 years, but wrote little after his wife's death in 1919. His last major work was the autumnal 'cello concerto. But on his 75th birthday in 1932 it was announced that Elgar was to break his long silence with his third symphony, commissioned by the British Broadcasting Corporation. However, only his sketches survive, as before the work could be completed, he contracted pneumonia. He died while listening to his own second symphony being played on the gramophone.

THE ATOMIC AGE IS BORN IN A CAMBRIDGE LABORATORY

SPLITTING THE ATOM *Ernest Rutherford (right) and the simple apparatus he used at the Cavendish Laboratory, Cambridge, in 1919, to split the nucleus of the nitrogen atom.*

In the first years of the 20th century a small group of dedicated men, working in a quiet laboratory in the university city of Cambridge, were providing the basis for a new science which was to change the shape of the world.

The science was nuclear physics, and the most brilliant of these scientists was Ernest Rutherford, later Baron Rutherford of Nelson. He was the first man 'to split the atom' and produce the world's first-ever artificial nuclear reaction.

Rutherford was born in New Zealand in 1871 – the same year the Cavendish Laboratory was founded. An outstanding scholar, whose early experiments were done in the cloakroom of Christchurch University, New Zealand, Rutherford joined the Cavendish at the age of 24 as its first post-graduate student, at a time when, under the leadership of the brilliant 28-year-old J. J. Thomson, the laboratory was entering its most creative and prolific period.

The discovery of X-rays by Wilhelm Rontgen had set in motion a whole new series of experiments in which Thomson enlisted the help of the young Rutherford. As a result of their research, Thomson discovered the electron, the minute particle which forms a part of all atoms. In this exhilarating atmosphere, Rutherford's genius flourished. His scientific curiosity was by now thoroughly aroused: if the electron was one part of the atom, what were its other components? More important, what was the overall structure of the atom?

It was in 1908 that Rutherford made the breakthrough that was to change the whole concept of physics. He found that if he fired radioactive particles at a thin foil of metal most particles passed straight through – but, more important, other particles were deflected. These deflected particles, Rutherford believed, had hit some sort of dense core

which occupied only a very small part of the volume of the atom.

Rutherford called the dense core the 'nucleus' of the atom around which he envisaged the systematic orbiting of electrons. Rutherford's model of the atom as a miniature solar system won him the Nobel Prize in 1908.

His greatest work, however, was still to come. Eleven years later, he used different radioactive particles – high-speed helium – to bombard a different substance – nitrogen. This time, instead of being deflected by the nitrogen nucleus, the particles shattered the nucleus to produce a totally different material, oxygen. The age-old dream of transmutation had been realised. Rutherford had 'split the atom' – and by doing so had unleashed the most powerful form of energy known to man.

'The nursery of genius'
Rutherford's discovery opened up a new field for research at the Cavendish. The great scientist himself published over 150 papers and his fellow scientists – 'the Cavendish Boys', as they were called – broke new ground in the understanding of nuclear physics, atomic energy and molecular biology. Sixteen Nobel Prize winners made their important discoveries at the Cavendish, which came to be called 'the nursery of genius'.

An amiable, robust man with a hearty laugh, Rutherford took over from J. J. Thomson at the Cavendish in 1919 and remained at its head until his death, at the age of 66, in 1937. He was fortunate not to live to see the horrific climax of the Second World War, for he had once expressed the hope that man would not learn to use atomic energy until the world had found lasting peace. As his fellow-scientist Lord Snow said: 'It was to this man we owe the entire atomic age.'

Heroism and self-sacrifice in the race to the Pole

we shall stick it out to the end but we are getting weaker of course and the end cannot be far.

It seems a pity but I do not think I can write more —

R Scott

Last Entry

For Gods Sake look after our people

SCOTT'S LAST WORDS

The final entry in Captain Scott's diary, to be seen at the British Museum, was written just before his death in the Antarctic. A last agonised scrawl, 'For God's sake look after our people', follows his signature.

The lure of the unknown, uncharted wilderness has long held a special appeal for the English spirit of adventure. In the early 20th century, Antarctica presented the greatest of all challenges left to explorers. Many men from many nations had explored Antarctica, but none had reached the Pole. One of these was the English naval officer, Robert Falcon Scott. On November 1, 1911, Scott and four companions set out from Hut Point, in the Ross Sea inlet, in a bid to become the first men to reach the South Pole, 1800 miles away. The expedition was financed by the government. National prestige was at stake.

Scott's attitude to exploration was a mixture of the romantic and the practical. Delicate and dreamy as a child – his father nicknamed him 'Old Mooney' – he had schooled himself for a life of strenuous excitement and privation by iron self-discipline. While preparing for his first polar expedition, he used to keep fit by running through the streets of London, and even, on occasion, took a Great Dane with him to pace his runs.

The journey to the Pole

Almost two years of planning preceded the departure of Scott and his 64-man expedition from London on June 15, 1910. At first, he had expected to have a clear run at the Pole. But when he arrived in Melbourne he learnt that the Norwegian explorer, Roald Amundsen, had decided to make it a race.

From the outset Scott ran into difficulties. On an earlier trip, in 1901, he had found it impossible to control his huskies because of his sentimental attitude towards dogs. Their harnesses became constantly entangled, they fought each other and they got lost chasing seals. This time Scott decided to use a mixture of three motor-sledges and 15 Manchurian ponies for haulage.

The decision to use ponies had meant that Scott was compelled to delay his expedition

until the onset of milder spring weather. Amundsen thus gained a head start on him. Despite pressing his men faster than planned – in the end, perhaps, at too great a cost – Scott could not overcome this disadvantage.

The motor-sledges proved to be a complete failure. One fell through thin ice; the others would not start because of the cold. Less than halfway to the Pole, the ponies – whose weight and sharp hooves caused them to sink into the snow up to their bellies – sickened and died. And so Scott was forced to fall back on manpower, which drained his men of energy.

Scott began the journey from Hut Point cheerfully enough. He recorded in his diary on October 31 that 'I can think of nothing left undone to deserve success'. But problems soon crowded in upon him. Progress was difficult and slow. Men and animals were both quickly exhausted by each day's tramping through the snow. And Scott was bitterly disappointed by the poor weather conditions: 'It is really time the luck turned in our favour,' he wrote on December 3. 'We have had all too little of it.'

Disappointment and disaster

On January 17, half a mile from the South Pole, one of Scott's party spotted a black speck on the horizon. It was a Norwegian flag. Scott and his men had been beaten. When they reached the point, they found a note asking Scott to inform the King of Norway of Amundsen's triumph. Tired, short of supplies and threatened by the approach of an early winter, the bitterly disappointed British party started the long trek back.

It was 800 miles to One Ton Depot, the first of the food stations. 'I wonder,' Scott wrote in his diary, 'if we can make it.'

At first favouring winds helped to speed them on their journey. But within a few days the onset of blizzards and blustering gales began to sap the strength of the five men. The wind lowered the temperature and increased the risk of frostbite. And Scott noted that their sleeping blankets and clothing were becoming steadily wetter.

There was also a shortage of food. The supplies had been carefully calculated to keep down the weight. Each man was given a daily ration of 4100 calories, which modern

SUPPLY LINES *Scott set up his base camp at Cape Evans on the Ross Sea (above). An intermediate camp was established on King Edward VII plateau (below). Ernest Shackleton, Scott's main British rival, had named this territory on his 1909 expedition, when he failed to reach the Pole by 97 miles. Scott succeeded, but he and his companions perished on their return journey.*

DESPAIR AT THE POLE *When Scott's party reached the South Pole on January 17, 1912, they found the Norwegian flag. Roald Amundsen had beaten them by a month. A last photograph of the five explorers who were to perish shows (left to right) Oates, Bowers, Scott, Wilson and Evans.*

research has shown to have been about 800 calories short. Lime juice, to ward off scurvy, was not provided.

Only a few days after leaving the Pole, a series of misadventures hit the party. Edward Wilson, an outstanding naturalist and artist and Scott's right-hand man, strained a tendon in his leg. Both Scott and Edgar Evans fell into crevasses hidden by a light cover of snow. Frostbite rendered Evans's hands useless.

The diary of Lieutenant H. R. Bowers was soon down to short, weary jottings: 'Very heavy surface – ice crystals – lower temperatures – Wilson's leg – Evans's fingers.'

'I may be some time'

Evans was the first to weaken. Scott was astonished by his breakdown. Evans had been a PT instructor in the navy and was physically robust. But though the largest of the team, he had to be nourished on the same meagre rations as the rest. A bad fall concussed him and he fell behind. He was found crawling aimlessly on hands and knees. That evening, as he lay insensible in the tent, it was reluctantly decided, for the safety of the others, to push on in the morning without him. Mercifully, he died before daybreak.

Four men now remained. But for Captain Lawrence Oates the ordeal was becoming unbearable. His feet were badly frostbitten and he found movement more and more exhausting; 29 miles from One Ton Depot he could go no further. The next morning, while a blizzard raged, he said quietly that he was going outside – 'and I may be some time'.

His three companions instantly realised what those words meant. Oates never came back. 'Though we tried to dissuade him,' Scott wrote, 'we knew it was the act of a brave man and an English gentleman. We all hope

to meet the end with a similar spirit, and assuredly the end is not far.' Scott, Wilson and Bowers managed to struggle on for another 18 miles. They got no further. Just 11 miles from the safety of One Ton Depot, they were pinned down in their tent by a blinding blizzard. They had only enough fuel for two cups of tea apiece and food for only two days. While they waited for the weather to clear, death claimed them. A few days earlier, Scott had written the last entry in his diary: 'It seems a pity, but I do not think I can write more . . . For God's sake look after our people.'

The expedition, which ended in failure and death, was ennobled by the heroism of Scott and his comrades in their defeat. 'For my own sake,' read one of Scott's last entries, 'I do not regret this journey, which has shown that Englishmen can endure hardship, help one another and meet with death with as great a fortitude as ever in the past.'

'We took risks'

Eight months later, one year after Scott nad set out with such high expectations from Hut Point, a search party came upon the explorers' last camp. Inside the tent lay the three bodies, their scientific instruments intact around them. A bottle of opium tablets was untouched, and a note written in a firm hand lay at Scott's side. 'We took risks, we knew we took them; things have come out against us, and therefore we have no cause for complaint.'

The searchers read the burial service. Then they built a cairn of ice and snow over the bodies, with a cross made from the pieces of two skis.

Another cross was set up at Hut Point, with Scott's favourite line from Tennyson's 'Ulysses' inscribed upon it: *'To strive, to seek, to find, and not to yield.'*

Edward VII: A king who loved pleasure

Edward VII was an old man when he came to the throne in January 1901 – over 60, and already a grandfather. Years of waiting for the crown had made him determined to enjoy the ceremonial of monarchy to the full. When appendicitis forced him to postpone his coronation in 1902, he pleaded in vain that he 'would rather die in the Abbey than put off the Coronation'.

Yet Edward's long years as Prince of Wales had scarcely equipped him for the life of a king. His mother, Queen Victoria, thought that he was weak and irresponsible. She also believed that his scandalous behaviour had hastened her beloved husband's death in 1861. As a result, she had rigidly excluded him from participation in affairs of state.

Edward spent his adult life under the shadow of his mother's disapproval. Lacking an official role, he spent most of his time in the pursuit of pleasure. He loved shooting, golf, croquet, cards, motoring, sailing and racing. And this delight in pleasure continued after he came to the throne. In 1909 he became the first reigning monarch to own a Derby winner.

One weakness endeared Edward to the public. He was quick to fall victim to the charm of a pretty face: his friendships ranged from aristocrats such as the Hon. Alice Keppel and Lady Warwick, to actresses such as Lillie Langtry and Sarah Bernhardt.

But though Edward's behaviour sometimes scandalised moralists, he inherited from his mother a strong conservative streak, and a powerful sense of royal dignity. He was not as diligent as his mother had been, but he knew how to deploy his considerable charm in the service of politics. On a state visit to Paris in 1903 his dignity won him the affection of what had been an anti-British crowd, and laid a firm foundation for the *Entente Cordiale* of 1904. Later, he saw better than many politicians the gathering clouds of war. Above all, he gave monarchy a personal touch. When he died in 1910, the nation mourned a man as well as a king. Showing that even monarchs can enjoy themselves, Edward had given royal approval to the pursuit of pleasure.

SPORTING KING *When Edward VII went out shooting, he liked the birds to be driven straight over his head by the beaters. This was so that he could not be seen to miss.*

Women stand 'shoulder to shoulder' to win the vote

TROPHIES OF STRUGGLE
The suffragettes were led in their struggle by Emmeline Pankhurst, whose portrait (above) is decorated with the suffrage colours. The medal (below) was awarded to hunger strikers. Both these mementoes are in the London Museum.

O n a hot summer Sunday in 1908, London's Hyde Park was the scene for one of the largest political demonstrations Britain has ever seen. Half a million people gathered on 'Women's Sunday' – June 21 – to hear speaker after speaker demand the right for women to cast their votes as equal citizens in British democracy.

In the fortnight leading up to 'Women's Sunday', squads of women on bicycles toured London, plastering the walls with posters and scattering the streets with leaflets. And on the day itself, thousands of women from every corner of England poured into the capital, marching in the brilliant sunshine to Hyde Park under their brightly embroidered banners. Many famous faces were among the thousands of sympathisers who thronged the park – among them the novelists Thomas Hardy and H. G. Wells, and the playwright

VOTES FOR WOMEN.
ELECTORS! Your representatives in the House of Commons by a majority of 110 voted for our Bill but M^c^ASQUITH put his Veto on it. Therefore we call on you to censure M^c^ASQUITH by voting against the Liberal Candidate.

On behalf of the Women's Social and Political Union. | EMMELINE PANKHURST. EMMELINE PETHICK LAWRENCE.

WAR TO THE KNIFE *The Liberal Prime Minister, Henry Herbert Asquith, was opposed to women's suffrage and so was vehemently attacked.*

George Bernard Shaw. The purpose that the demonstration was intended to prove was that the campaign for women's suffrage enjoyed overwhelming public support. And the suffragettes had worked painstakingly to ensure its success. The organisers carefully picked the 80 women speakers, and 20 separate platforms were erected in the park. Official colours were chosen for the suffragettes: purple for justice, white for purity and green for hope. Scarves, ribbons and dolls in the new colours were sold by the thousand.

The demonstration was a triumph for three of the staunchest fighters for women's suffrage: Mrs Emmeline Pankhurst and her daughters Christabel and Sylvia. Mrs Pankhurst was the widow of a radical Manchester lawyer, and already accustomed before her husband's death in 1898 to the drama of politics. Together, mother and daughters inspired the suffragette movement in England for over ten stormy years, winning the personal devotion of thousands of supporters.

Breaking the deadlock
It was the Pankhursts who, in 1903, founded the organisation which launched 'Women's Sunday' – the Women's Social and Political Union. The WSPU opened a new era in the struggle for women's rights.

By 1903, women had won some significant victories in their fight for equality. But they still did not have the most fundamental right of all – the right to vote. Many politicians, both Liberals and Conservatives, were beginning to recognise that women's suffrage was inevitable. But they were split on how to achieve it. Even men could not vote unless they possessed certain property qualifications. To apply the same qualifications to women would enfranchise only the wealthy – and this would obviously favour the Conservatives.

But universal female suffrage would, it was believed, favour the Liberals. Moreover, it would give the vote to many more women than men, and so lead to demands for the extension of the vote to all adults.

The Pankhursts founded the WSPU in a bid to break this deadlock. 'It is unendurable to think of another generation of women wasting their lives,' Christabel wrote. 'We must not lose any more time. We must act.'

Violence on the streets

The tireless work of the Pankhursts attracted ever-growing support. The suffragettes took their cause into the streets. They heckled politicians and were often arrested. When magistrates denounced them as lawbreakers, they retorted: 'We are here in our efforts to become lawmakers.'

The huge demonstration of 1908 was a turning point in the suffragette campaign. Despite this evidence of mass support, the Liberal Prime Minister, Herbert Asquith, refused to yield to the suffragettes' demands, and the Pankhursts decided that the time had come to change their tactics.

In London, women broke the windows of 10 Downing Street, tried to storm the House

LAWBREAKERS *Mrs Pankhurst is arrested outside Buckingham Palace in 1914 (left). Her example and that of her younger daughter, Christabel, photographed with her mother in prison (above), inspired the suffragettes.*

of Commons, and chained themselves to the railings of the Ladies' Gallery. In Birmingham, suffragettes stationed on a nearby roof stoned Asquith as he left a public meeting. In Newcastle, rowdy demonstrations greeted the Liberal Chancellor of the Exchequer, David Lloyd George. Pillar boxes were set on fire, mass window-smashing campaigns were organised, and politicians' homes were attacked.

Hundreds of suffragettes, including the Pankhursts, were arrested and thrown into prison. Their hunger strikes, and the forcible feeding used by the authorities, won them wide publicity and sympathy. Labour leaders such as Keir Hardie and George Lansbury spoke up for the suffragette movement in the House of Commons. But although several private members produced bills to give women the vote, their passage was blocked by government indifference. After each failure the suffragettes returned to their campaign with redoubled vigour.

Martyr for the cause

In March 1913 the government, fearing that the suffragettes would win martyrs for their cause if any hunger-strikers died in prison, passed the 'Cat and Mouse Act'. Under it, prisoners whose health was endangered were temporarily released, to be re-arrested when they had recovered.

Within months the suffragettes had found their first martyr. On Derby Day in June 1913, as George V's horse rounded Tattenham Corner on the Epsom racetrack, 32-year-old suffragette Emily Davison flung herself into its path and tried to snatch its reins. The jockey was thrown, and she herself was trampled by the horse as it fell. Four days later, she died of her injuries.

Emily Davison had not meant to die. The return half of her railway ticket was found in her pocket. But her funeral provoked the most moving demonstration in the entire history of the suffragette movement.

The vote at last

A long procession formed on June 14 to accompany her coffin through London. To solemn music from women's bands, suffragettes dressed in white, purple and black walked with the coffin to King's Cross station, where it was to be transported to Emily Davison's Northumberland home for burial.

It was the last great suffragette protest. Though militancy continued for another year, the outbreak of the First World War brought it abruptly and unexpectedly to an end. Led by Mrs Pankhurst, the majority of the suffragettes agreed to suspend their activities.

The reward for women came in 1918, when women over the age of 30 years were at last enfranchised. In a second Act, ten years later, the vote was given to all men and women over the age of 21. In the ballot-box, women had won their equality with men at last.

George V: As British as his loyal subjects

BLUNT KING *George V and his wife Mary. During his 26-year reign, George's bluff honesty won him the affection and respect of the subjects of the vast empire over which he ruled.*

In many ways, George V was the model of an ideal Englishman. Dignified, fair and conscientious, he held conventional views but was tolerant of those who differed from him. He used his influence for moderation, never sought popularity and was not afraid to speak his mind when it became necessary.

George came to the throne in 1910, at the age of 44, and was immediately plunged into a constitutional crisis between the Lords and the Commons. His statesmanlike neutrality in the dispute set the tone for his reign.

His feelings, if commonplace, were very human. Throughout the First World War, he was determined to set his people an example, taking the 'king's pledge' against alcohol to encourage their efforts. When the author H. G. Wells, in the anti-German fervour of 1917, condemned the court as 'alien and uninspiring', George replied with spirit: 'I may be uninspiring, but I'll be damned if I'm an alien!'

'They like me for myself'

After the war, George met new problems in the same spirit of understanding. He wrote to his mother, Queen Alexandra, of the first Labour government: 'They ought to be given a chance and treated fairly.' And at the end of the General Strike of 1926 he commented: 'Our old country can well be proud of itself . . . not a shot has been fired and no one killed; it shows what a wonderful people we are.'

Despite their failure to understand the new mood of the inter-war generation, the king and his wife, Queen Mary, forged closer links with their subjects. Such a link was George's Christmas Day radio message to the peoples of his far-flung empire.

George did not realise that his people could care for someone so old-fashioned and unbending as himself, and he was genuinely surprised by the warmth which greeted his Silver Jubilee in 1935. 'I am beginning to think they like me for myself,' he remarked. In fact they liked him because he had remained himself over so many hectic years – a fixed point in a rapidly changing world.

The 'contemptible little army' wins its first victory

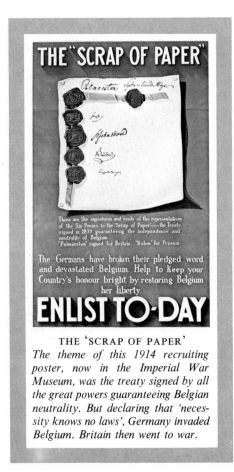

THE 'SCRAP OF PAPER'
The theme of this 1914 recruiting poster, now in the Imperial War Museum, was the treaty signed by all the great powers guaranteeing Belgian neutrality. But declaring that 'necessity knows no laws', Germany invaded Belgium. Britain then went to war.

The British army fought its first battle on the European continent since Waterloo, 99 years before, on Sunday, August 23, 1914. Three days earlier, the British Expeditionary Force had mustered on the Belgian border. There, under its commander Sir John French, it made ready to advance into Belgium. In accordance with the plans of the French high command, the British Expeditionary Force was to form the extreme left of the Allied line as it advanced.

But France's plans had already collapsed. The two French armies nearest the BEF were already in full retreat. The four infantry divisions and one cavalry division of the BEF – numbering nearly 90,000 men between them – were in mortal danger of being outflanked, enveloped and overwhelmed by the 320,000-strong German First Army.

Fortunately, the German commander, Colonel-General von Klück, was completely ignorant of the British whereabouts. His troops stumbled into battle against one of French's two corps, deployed between the mining towns of Mons and Condé on the Franco-Belgian border. It was the 19th day of the war and the British were about to meet

their first major test of the Great War.

All over the battlefield, church bells were ringing and families were preparing for church. In every way it was an unsuitable place for a battle – the ground covered with slag-heaps and dotted with mining villages, the soil broken by ditches and dykes. The calm was soon abruptly shattered.

As the German troops assaulted the British Second Corps along the Mons–Condé canal, the highly trained British regulars shot them down in heaps with furious and accurate rifle fire. British machine-guns fired until the water boiled in their cooling jackets. British 18-pounder field guns deluged the enemy in shrapnel. At the end of the day when – in a gesture smacking of the days of chivalry rather than those of modern war – the German bugles blew the ceasefire, two British divisions had fought off six German divisions.

That evening, the Germans counted their losses. One of their officers wrote: 'Our first battle is a heavy, unheard-of, defeat and against the English, the English we laughed at.' His battalion commander told him that same evening: 'You are the only company commander left in the battalion. The battalion is a wreck, my proud beautiful battalion!' No longer would the Germans accept the confident statement that the BEF was 'a contemptible little army'.

Attack and counter-attack
But the next day, with the entire centre and left of the Allied line buckling under German pressure, the BEF had no course but to retreat. Day after day the Allied armies fell back. Yet there was still plenty of fight in them. On August 26, the British First Corps fought a successful battle at Le Câteau. Three days later, the French counter-attacked at Guise.

Disrupted by this Allied resistance and also by quarrels among their own commanders, the German armies began to lose cohesion. But the BEF was still retreating further and further. At this moment, the volatile Sir John French told his superiors in London that he proposed to remove his army from the line and retreat behind the Seine. He was overruled by Lord Kitchener, the Secretary of State for War, and ordered to maintain contact with the French at all costs.

Birth of the Western Front
But Sir John's state of mind was a major worry to Marshal César Joffre, the French Commander-in-Chief. The BEF made up the extreme left of his line – the key to victory or defeat. Joffre therefore began to create a new

THE GENERALS *Sir John French (left), was forced to retreat by von Klück (above). But von Klück's mistakes led to Allied victory at the Marne.*

French army, the Sixth, to be positioned beyond the British.

Then, at this crucial moment, came the news that von Klück had altered the course of his advance. He had swung east towards the River Marne instead of marching west of Paris. Instead of the Germans enveloping the Allied flank, it was now von Klück's own flank which was exposed to a counter-attack by the French and British forces. Joffre ordered a general counter-offensive, and on September 6 the Battle of the Marne began.

Von Moltke, the German Commander-in-Chief, had already perceived his danger and ordered a retreat. The BEF slowly but decisively advanced into a gap opened up between the German First and Second Armies, and the Germans fell back to the River Aisne. Paris was saved, the Allied armies were saved and France itself was saved. German hopes of a quick victory were over.

But on the Aisne, it was the turn of the Allied offensive to fail. By November, the war of movement had finally ended in stalemate. Behind barriers of barbed wire, and with the pockmarked mud of no-man's land between the two sets of trenches, the Western Front was born.

THE ROAD TO WAR *Cavalry covered the long retreat of Sir John French's expeditionary force from the Belgian frontier to the Marne in September 1914. Profiting from their experiences in the Boer War in South Africa, the British had trained their cavalry to fight dismounted as infantry.*

THE END OF THE BEGINNING *German prisoners after the Battle of the Marne. The Allies were too exhausted to exploit the German defeat, so the hopes of a short war came to an end. The armies of both sides settled down into their trenches and the Western Front was born.*

The 'lights go out' as Britain goes to war

The Archduke Franz Ferdinand, heir to the Hapsburg throne, was assassinated by Serb nationalists in the Balkan town of Sarajevo on June 28, 1914. Less than six weeks later, Austria, Germany, Russia and France were at war, dragged into conflict by the iron chains of alliances and military timetables.

Alone among the great powers, Britain had no commitment to go to war. But, since the *Entente Cordiale* of 1904, Britain and France had been deepening their friendly relations. Even though no formal alliance had been signed, there were secret plans to send a British army to France in the event of war between France and Germany.

Yet, in the first days of August 1914, as Europe prepared to erupt in conflict, Britain was torn between a deep desire for peace and French appeals to her national honour. The Liberal government itself was deeply divided. The Foreign Secretary, Sir Edward Grey, was in an agony of indecision, and other ministers threatened to resign if war was declared.

Honouring a 'scrap of paper'

It was German ruthlessness which proved decisive in drawing Britain into war. Germany's long-prepared strategy was to outflank France's powerful frontier defences by marching through Belgium.

On August 4 the British government learnt that Germany had violated Belgian neutrality. And, under a treaty of 1839, Britain was a guarantor of Belgian neutrality – as was Germany herself.

Now, honouring this treaty – a 'scrap of paper', as the German Chancellor Bethmann-Hollweg derisively described it – Britain declared war on Germany at 11 p.m. on August 4, 1914. It was the end of an era.

COUSINS *George V (right) and Wilhelm II together in 1913. A year later, their countries were at war.*

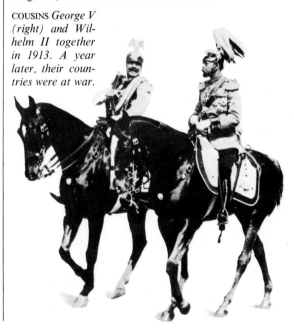

ON THE EVE OF THE GREAT WAR

Watching a lamp-lighter at work in Green Park, London, on the evening of August 3, 1914, Sir Edward Grey, the Foreign Secretary, remarked: 'The lights are going out all over Europe; we shall not see them lit again in our lifetime.' But Grey's forebodings were not shared by the vast majority of his fellow countrymen.

An eyewitness described the London scene on the following day as the excitement mounted. 'Parliament Square and Whitehall were thronged with people . . . A brilliant sun shone in a cloudless sky. Young men in straw hats were in the majority. Girls in calico dresses were numerous. All were already touched with war fever . . . Cries of "Down with Germany!" were raised . . . the singing of patriotic songs, such as "Rule Britannia" . . . and also the "Marseillaise" brought the crowds still closer together.'

But the densest crowds of all were outside Buckingham Palace. As Big Ben tolled 11 p.m. – signalling that the British ultimatum had expired – a sudden hush fell. And then the National Anthem swelled up. Singing and cheering, the British swept into war with Germany.

The KING'S MESSAGE TO HIS ARMY. BUCKINGHAM PALACE.

George V assured his departing troops that they were fighting for 'the safety and honour of my empire'.

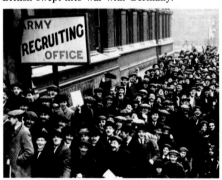

Volunteers outside a recruiting office, inspired by the call 'Your King and Country need you'.

A generation perishes in bloody battle on the Somme

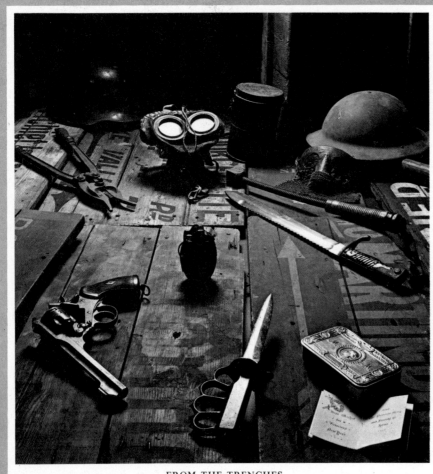

FROM THE TRENCHES

Among this collection of weapons issued for use on the Western Front, and now in the Imperial War Museum, are a Webley revolver, wire cutters and hand grenades. The tobacco box and Christmas card were presents from home to the men at the Front.

DAY OF DISASTER *British troops on the first day of the Somme offensive on July 1, 1916. Their commander, Sir Douglas Haig (right), was confident of victory. But the price paid was to be more than 400,000 British and empire casualties – 57,000 of them on the first day of battle.*

In 1916, two years after the outbreak of war, Britain launched her first great offensive on the Western Front. By then, the scale of British involvement in the war had grown to an extent undreamt of in 1914. The British armies in the west totalled over a million men – 57 divisions, compared with the four divisions of the original 90,000-strong British Expeditionary Force. Now, in July 1916, Britain's inexperienced mass army was ready to face its first great task.

Deluge of steel

Just before 7.30 a.m. on July 1, on a morning brilliant with summer sunshine, the thunder of the guns ceased. For a moment the waiting 13 British and five French divisions heard the sound of birds singing. Then, as they clambered out of their trenches on a 25 mile front

north of the River Somme, the guns recommenced their bombardment. Slowly the Allied troops advanced in the open towards the German defences.

General Sir Douglas Haig, the British Commander-in-Chief, and his colleagues were fully aware of the strength of the German line they hoped to break. The enemy lay on the commanding slopes and crest of chalk downland. Successive lines of dug-outs had been excavated deep into the chalk. Each village was a fortress, each valley a cul-de-sac. In front of the German positions were dense belts of barbed wire.

Yet the British commanders were convinced that their preliminary bombardment, a relentless deluge of steel lasting a week, had smashed the German defence positions and cut the wire to pieces. They believed the assaulting in-

fantry, now advancing against the German troops in their lines, would find a clear path and weak opposition.

They were tragically mistaken. At the end of the day, the British army had suffered a complete catastrophe. Out of some 150,000 attackers, more than 57,000 had become casualties, including over 19,000 killed. Nowhere except in the southern sector nearest the Somme had the British even dented the German line. But the extent of the disaster was not realised by the British high command.

Slaughter in no man's land

The British bombardment had cut only a few narrow gaps in the German wire. But no reports of this failure had filtered upwards to Haig or his subordinates before the battle. The German defenders survived in their deep dug-outs, and when the British infantry began to advance across no man's land, they swarmed out. They set up machine-guns in the ruins of their trenches or in shell-holes.

The Germans found a perfect target. While the French, old hands at the game, came on in small groups, making best use of the ground, the British infantry marched forward slowly and steadily in regular extended lines, as they

CASUALTIES OF WAR *Field dressing stations and hospitals could not keep pace with the wounded, who often had to wait hours for attention.*

THE TERROR OF TANKS

British inventive genius produced a weapon that was eventually to break the stalemate of trench warfare. It was the tank (below), the inspiration of Lieutenant-Colonel Ernest Swinton. The name 'tank' was deliberately chosen for security reasons.

Some doubted the tank's effectiveness. The War Minister, Lord Kitchener, said, 'the war will never be won by such machines'. Others, like Winston Churchill, encouraged their construction. Development began in utmost secrecy in early 1915. But, because of production delays, only 50 reached France by September 1916. And when the tanks made their debut in battle, breakdowns had reduced their number to 32. Their full potential was not seen until the Battle of Cambrai a year later.

had been instructed, rifle at the port. Each man was encumbered with over 60 lb. of kit and ammunition.

Bravely, doggedly, the attackers kept going through the smoke and crash of enemy gunfire, the merciless flail of the machine-guns. Then they reached the uncut wire – and stopped, helpless in the open. Even where there were gaps in the wire, the attackers were forced to bunch together in their attempts to struggle through – another gift to the German machine-gunners. Whole battalions were mown down like wheat before the sickle.

Nevertheless, Haig and his subordinates were prisoners of circumstance. The British artillery, expanded in frantic haste, lacked heavy guns. The shells produced in new factories or imported from America often failed to explode. And so the German defences had escaped decisive damage.

The citizen army

Haig's army was pitifully inexperienced – another inevitable result of hasty wartime expansion. Haig himself wrote in March 1916: 'I have not got an Army in France really, but a collection of divisions untrained for the field.'

Yet Haig had no alternative but to launch this raw citizen army against the most formidable army in Europe. For Marshal Joffre, the French Commander-in-Chief, had warned him that unless the British attacked to relieve the crushing German pressure on Verdun, the French army would cease to exist by August.

The tragedy of July 1, 1916, was only the beginning of a struggle which lasted for 140 days. Slowly, week by week, the armies of the British Empire forced the Germans back. But they never broke through.

On July 11, however, the Germans were forced to call off their attack on the French at Verdun. And the British continued to attack, struggling and dying in a wilderness of mud and destruction. But the Allied hopes of bringing Germany and Austria down in 1916 were not fulfilled. As winter drew nearer, the fighting died away everywhere. Haig brought the Somme battle to an end on November 18.

Legacy of loss

The value of the Somme offensive was mixed. The narrow tract of captured ground was certainly not worth the loss of some 400,000 attackers killed, wounded or missing. But, for the first time since 1914, another army had taken over from the French the main burden of the fighting. The Germans had suffered as never before. The Somme was the preliminary to Haig's victories in 1918.

Together with the Third Battle of Ypres (Passchendaele) in 1917, the Somme made a lasting and terrible impression on the British national memory. Nothing in their experience had accustomed them to such loss; and the loss fell this time not on the professional army but on civilians in uniform.

War leads to a social revolution at home

It took until the summer of 1915 – ten months after the outbreak of the First World War – for the British to begin to take the measure of the strength of Imperial Germany. The harsh facts were that Britain – for so long 'the workshop of the world' – had failed to develop the industries that were the key to modern warfare.

So the government embarked on a virtual revolution. New factories were built and, in the interests of the war effort, the trade unions were persuaded to allow the 'dilution' of skilled craftsmen by unskilled labour.

Women at war

The new machines, the manpower shortage and the insatiable demand for munitions ushered in another revolution in industry – the mass employment of women.

There were women in the shipyards, women sweeping chimneys, painting houses, working the land. Thousands of middle-class ladies went out to work for the first time in history, running offices, canteens and welfare services.

By the end of the war, women had even joined the armed forces. And with their new-found importance and independence came a growing equality with men. In 1918 this was recognised when women were given the vote.

In the shared effort, hardship and sacrifice of war, the British found a new sense of national community. And in David Lloyd George, who became Prime Minister in 1916, they found a magnetic leader with a single-minded determination to win victory.

The innovations of the war were to be permanent. By the time the armistice was signed in 1918, Britain had undergone the fastest social revolution in her history.

WOMEN AT WAR *Some 800,000 women were mobilised into Britain's armaments works in order to meet the demand for weapons.*

POETS AND PAINTERS RECORD THE NIGHTMARE OF WAR

After a century of peace the first major mechanised war in English history came as an appalling shock to the people of Britain. At the outset, the ideal of heroic patriotism still prevailed. Young men went to war in a spirit of adventurous romance; war still appealed to the imagination. As disillusionment set in, and the horrors and atrocities of modern warfare could no longer be concealed, this attitude changed – a change reflected in the poetry and painting the war inspired.

From illusion to reality

Typical of the early school of romantic patriotism bred by the war was Rupert Brooke, once described by his fellow poet W. B. Yeats as 'the handsomest young man in England'. The son of a Rugby housemaster, he was educated at Cambridge. The fashionable literary circles of the day fêted him for his talents and his extraordinary good looks. He was the last representative of the tranquil, sunlit world of Georgian Britain, a settled world of picnics and charades, tea-parties and bicycle rides.

The war was soon to destroy this peaceful complacency. But, at the beginning, war provided Brooke with an outlet for the sentimental and self-consciously romantic strain in his character. *1914 and Other Poems*, written on the theme of war, brought him instant recognition. One sonnet in particular, 'The Soldier', expressed the stirring ideal of sacrifice for country:

> *If I should die, think only this of me:*
> *That there's some corner of a foreign field*
> *That is forever England...*

Rupert Brooke did not live long enough to learn the cruel message of real warfare. He never saw action in the war he celebrated, dying of fever during the voyage to the Dardanelles in 1915 at the age of 28.

By this time the glory of war was already beginning to pall. Charles Sorley, a poet who was killed at the age of 20 on the Western Front, condemned the heroic attitude: 'The voice of our poets and men of letters is finely trained and sweet to hear... it pleases, it flatters, it charms, it soothes; it is a living lie.'

By 1916 the lie that charms and soothes was no longer able to disguise the great massacre of the stalemated armies in the mud of Flanders. Young poets such as Siegfried Sassoon and Wilfred Owen saw it as their duty to tell the civilian population the true facts about the carnage, and to correct the lies of the politicians and the Press.

Siegfried Sassoon, coming from a rich and respectable family, had spent a happily carefree youth reading and hunting. At the age of 28 he joined the Royal Welch Fusiliers, and distinguished himself for his bravery and enterprise. Known as 'Mad Jack', he won the MC, and was recommended for a DSO. But he was wounded in 1917, sent home to England, and there he became haunted by the suffering and horrors he had witnessed.

He described the common soldier's ordeals in the trenches:

> *Tripping, he grabbed the wall; saw some*
> *one lie,*
> *Humped at his feet, half-hidden by a rug...*
> *'God blast your neck!' (For days he'd had*
> *no sleep),*
> *'Get up and guide me through this stinking*
> *place.'*
> *Savage, he kicked a soft, unanswering heap,*
> *And flashed his beam across the livid face*
> *Terribly glaring up, whose eyes yet wore*
> *Agony dying hard ten days before...*

Sassoon was disgusted by the 'brass hats' and politicians who seemed to throw away lives so recklessly. He expressed this mood in his 1918 volume of poems *Counter Attack*. They are among the most savagely, anti-war poetry ever written. While Sassoon was convalescing in hospital near Edinburgh he met another young poet, Wilfred Owen.

Born in Shropshire in 1893, Owen did not go to a public school or a university. Until 1915 he worked as a private tutor in France, and on his return trained with the Artists' Rifles. In 1916 he was commissioned in the Manchester Regiment.

The meeting with Sassoon was a turning point in Owen's career. In a new burst of creative fervour he spoke out against the war in harsh, uncompromising terms.

In 'Anthem for Doomed Youth' he voiced his outrage at the mass slaughter:

> *What passing bells for those who die as*
> *cattle?*
> *Only the monstrous anger of the guns.*
> *Only the stuttering rifles' rapid rattle*
> *Can patter out their hasty orisons.*

His most famous poem, 'Strange Meeting', describes the poet's dream encounter with a dead soldier in Hell. It ends with the chilling words:

> *I am the enemy you killed, my friend.*
> *I knew you in this dark; for so you frowned*
> *Yesterday through me as you jabbed and*
> *killed.*
> *I parried; but my hands were loath and cold.*
> *Let us sleep now...*

Owen had been invalided home from the Front in 1916, suffering from a nervous disorder and it was during this convalescence that the historic meeting with Sassoon took place. Owen voluntarily returned to France in 1916. Life at the front, he felt, could not be worse than staying at home and watching 'the stink-

POET'S VOICE *Siegfried Sassoon was determined to voice his horror at the bloodshed he saw on the Western Front. Anxious not to make him a martyr, the army invalided him out, claiming that he was suffering from shell shock.*

THE PITY OF WAR *Wilfred Owen (right) belonged to a generation of poets who could no longer believe that it was glorious to die on the battlefield. He claimed: 'All a poet can do today is warn.'*

AN ENGLISH PATRIOT *Rupert Brooke had a brief but brilliant reputation before his premature death in 1915. The most English of writers, he delighted in the gentle pleasures of English country life. His poem 'The Soldier' was on everyone's lips at the outset of war.*

ing Leeds and Bradford war-profiteers now reading *John Bull* on Scarborough Sands'.

He was killed on November 4, 1918, during the crossing of the Sambre Canal, one week before the Armistice was signed. He was 25.

Among the papers found after Owen's death in 1918 was a draft preface to his planned volume of poems. It sums up his aims as a poet of pity, who saw his duty as to 'warn':

'This book is not about heroes. English poetry is not yet fit to speak of them.

Nor is it about deeds, or lands, nor anything about glory, honour, might, majesty, dominion, or power, except War.

Above all I am not concerned with Poetry. My subject is War, and the pity of War. The poetry is in the pity.'

In drawing attention to the pity of war, Sassoon and Owen, and the artists who also went to the Front, had lived up to their great ideal – to warn future generations. Determined to find new ways of communicating their indignation, these young poets and artists were the forerunners of the modern movements which were to transform literature and art in the next decades. Their influence survives in the arts of today.

NIGHTMARE LAND *Paul Nash served with the Artists' Rifles in France and was appalled by the landscape blasted by mortars and shells. 'I am no longer an artist interested and curious,' he wrote. 'I am a messenger who will bring back word from the men who are fighting to those who want the war to go on for ever . . . it will have a bitter truth and may it burn their lousy souls.' His picture of the 'Menin Road', painted in 1917, was intended to rob war of the 'last shred of glory'. For the rest of his life he suffered from the effects of poison gas.*

IMAGE OF VIOLENCE *Christopher Nevinson was unfit for active military service, but served in France in 1914 with the Friends' Ambulance Unit. His abstract pictures express his horror at the sufferings of the wounded and the ruthlessness of war. 'La Mitrailleuse' (The Machine Gun) is a terrifying view of mechanical efficiency.*

'MASS-MURDER' *Percy Wyndham Lewis was the founder-member of the most modern movement among artists – the Vorticists. Their aim was 'to build up a visual language as abstract as music'. In his painting of 'A Battery Shelled', Wyndham Lewis used the bleak war landscape of cogs and wheels and abandoned, inhuman machinery to build up an impression of mechanical violence. He himself went to the Front in 1914 as a Bombardier, and he wrote later: 'I have never been able to regard modern war as good or bad. Only supremely stupid. The greatest wickedness is the perpetuation of foolishness these carnivals of mass-murder involve.'*

Victory hangs in the balance off the coast of Jutland

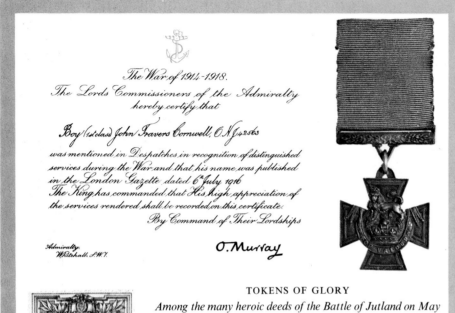

The War of 1914-1918.

The Lords Commissioners of the Admiralty hereby certify that

Boy (1st class) John Travers Cornwell, O.N. J42563

was mentioned in Despatches in recognition of distinguished services during the War and that his name was published in the London Gazette dated 6th July 1916

The King has commanded that His high appreciation of the services rendered shall be recorded on this certificate.

By Command of Their Lordships

Admiralty, Whitehall, S.W.1.

O. Murray

TOKENS OF GLORY

Among the many heroic deeds of the Battle of Jutland on May 31, 1916, the one that most deeply moved the British public was the story of the 'Boy VC', John Cornwell. Aged only 16, Cornwell was one of the gun-crew on board the light cruiser Chester *when she was attacked by four German ships. Within minutes, one-fifth of the* Chester's *crew were killed or wounded, including all of Cornwell's comrades. But he stuck to his post until he, too, was killed. He was awarded a posthumous VC. His medal (above right), the certificate of his mention in dispatches (above left) and a commemorative stamp (left) are all in the Imperial War Museum, London.*

A thickening North Sea mist enveloped the British Grand Fleet, steaming towards the Danish coast from its base at Scapa Flow. The 24 battleships advanced in six parallel columns, with cruiser squadrons scouting ahead. On the forebridge of the flagship, HMS *Iron Duke*, Admiral Sir John Jellicoe peered at the blurry line where sea and sky met. Listening to the thunder of gunfire from the south, the admiral's calm vanished for a moment. 'I wish,' he suddenly remarked to his staff, 'someone would tell me who is firing and what they're firing at.'

A battle with no room for error

It was about 6 p.m. on May 31, 1916. The Battle of Jutland, the only great sea battle of the First World War, was just beginning. During the afternoon, scant and contradictory reports had reached Jellicoe from the Commander-in-Chief of the Battle-Cruiser Fleet, Vice-Admiral Sir David Beatty. They indicated that Beatty's ships were in action with enemy battle-cruisers, and the whole German High Seas Fleet was steaming northwards. Now the two battle fleets were just concealed from Jellicoe's own ships by the misty horizon. At any moment he would have to decide how to deploy his great fleet for battle – and decide quickly.

Yet he lacked essential information – where exactly Beatty was, and how his ships had fared. Above all, Jellicoe did not know the precise location and course of the German fleet.

Shortly after 6 p.m., Jellicoe saw Beatty's flagship *Lion* emerge from the murk at full speed, smoke pouring from her fo'c'sle. A signal lamp blinked in *Lion*: 'Have sighted enemy Battle Fleet, bearing SSW.' Now, with the two main fleets still invisible to each other,

INTO BATTLE *Admiral Sir John Jellicoe (above left), the Commander-in-Chief of the Grand Fleet, refused to risk Britain's naval supremacy by over-hasty action against the German High Seas Fleet in the North Sea. But when the British broke the German radio code and thus secured advance knowledge of Admiral Scheer's plans, Jellicoe felt confident to go into action at Jutland. Vice-Admiral Sir David Beatty (above right) used his battle-cruisers to lure the German fleet into action against the British Grand Fleet of 24 battleships under Jellicoe. One of the worst-damaged German ships at Jutland was the battle-cruiser* Seydlitz *(right). She was hit by 21 heavy shells, and a torpedo which blew a 39 ft hole in her bows. Half-waterlogged, and with one in ten of her crew killed or wounded, the* Seydlitz *still managed to limp back to port at Wilhelmshaven.*

but converging at a combined speed of over 50 knots, Jellicoe had at last to decide his battle dispositions. An error of judgment on his part could, as Winston Churchill wrote, 'lose the war in an afternoon'.

At 6.15 p.m., Jellicoe ordered the deployment to begin, and his fleet formed into line of battle behind the port wing column. The moment Jellicoe had been waiting and hoping for since the war had begun in 1914 had arrived.

Except for occasional sorties, the German High Seas Fleet had so far remained in its heavily protected coastal waters. But in 1916 its new Commander-in-Chief, Vice-Admiral Reinhard Scheer, decided that, with the German army hard-pressed on every front, the German navy could no longer remain aloof. His plan was to bait a portion of the British fleet into a trap, and destroy it. His battle-cruisers, under Vice-Admiral Hipper, were to supply the bait, sailing northwards past the Danish province of Jutland.

Now, chasing Beatty's Battle-Cruiser Fleet northwards at top speed, Scheer believed that his plan had succeeded brilliantly. For he had no idea that Jellicoe's Grand Fleet was just out of sight ahead of him.

Suddenly, Scheer saw in the gloom ahead of him an interminable line of British battleships. At once he ordered his fleet to reverse course. Within minutes Jellicoe lost sight of his prey. Yet he hesitated to start an immediate pursuit, fearing that Scheer meant to entice him into a submarine ambush. Instead, he held to his course towards the south-east, so getting between Scheer and his base.

During this encounter, the British battle-cruiser, HMS *Invincible*, was hit in a magazine, blew up and sank. Soon after 7 p.m., Scheer started eastwards again – only to find Jellicoe across his course once more. The German fleet wallowed in confusion, pounded by ferocious British gunfire. In desperation, Scheer ordered his battle-cruisers on a 'death-ride' against the British line, in order to cover his fleet's escape.

Once more Hipper's ships steamed into action against the Grand Fleet. Then, having covered Scheer's retreat, they turned and steamed away. They had been in action all day and their crews were exhausted. Yet though appalling damage was inflicted on them, not a single German ship in the squadron was sunk.

Command of the seas assured

Between 8 and 9 p.m., the German fleet was sighted a third time, lying to the westward in the fading light. But neither Jellicoe nor Beatty steered to close with the enemy. The Grand Fleet held on a south-westerly course, still running between Scheer and his base at Wilhelmshaven.

That night, in a desperate dash for home, Scheer smashed through British cruisers and destroyers in the rear of the Grand Fleet. And so the greatest sea battle since Trafalgar sputtered out. By morning, the German High Seas Fleet, though badly mauled, had reached its base. The Germans claimed the victory, for they had sunk 111,980 tons of British ships against their own losses of 62,233 tons; and they had inflicted 6945 casualties while receiving only 2921.

But, strategically, success at Jutland lay with the British. The war saw no other naval battles. The German fleet only ventured to sea on three occasions during the rest of the war. An American journalist wrote: 'The German High Seas Fleet had assaulted its jailer; but it is still in jail.'

The unseen menace of Germany's U-boats

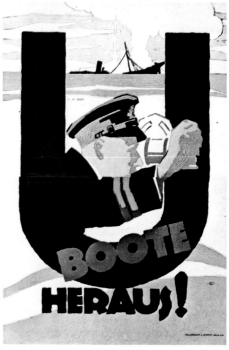

'THE U-BOATS ARE OUT !' *A German war poster glories in the work of the U-boats, which brought Britain to the verge of defeat in 1917.*

Throughout the First World War, the sea was Britain's jugular vein, for her national life depended on imports of food and raw materials. From the beginning of 1915, even though they were shackled by international law, which forbade sinking at sight without warning, the U-boats quadrupled the monthly British tonnage sunk. Then, in February 1917, Germany began to use her submarines in an even more deadly fashion, by freeing them of all restrictions under international law. The Germans knew that to sink ships on sight would probably bring America into the war. But they believed that this move would defeat Britain before America could mobilise her strength.

The effects were dramatic. In April, one out of every four ships that left Britain never returned. The First Sea Lord, Sir John Jellicoe, confessed that 'there is absolutely no solution that we can see'. With only six weeks' food left, Britain faced starvation.

But then, just as dramatically, the answer was found – the convoy system. Convoys could be protected by naval escorts and, by concentrating merchant ships in large groups, the number of targets for the U-boats to attack was drastically reduced.

By the autumn of 1917 all British vessels moved in convoys, and losses fell by nearly two-thirds. By the end of the war the U-boat had dwindled into a mere nuisance. But the margin between victory and defeat had been frighteningly narrow.

A summer of victories – and the First World War ends

THE FINAL BLOW
As the German armies crumbled in the summer of 1918, victory was at last in sight. This poster, now in the Imperial War Museum, called for one last national effort to beat the foe.

In the high summer of 1918, only months before the armistice, the British army won its most brilliant victory of the war. This time there was no long preliminary bombardment; none of the elaborate and obvious preparations which on previous occasions had warned the enemy long in advance that an offensive was imminent.

At 4.20 a.m. on August 8 the guns opened fire, creating a slowly advancing curtain of annihilation. Close behind came nearly 500 tanks, including the new 8 mph 'Whippets', grinding forward through the ground-mist. They were a shield of steel for the advancing British, French, Australian and Canadian infantry divisions.

The second Battle of the Somme was opening, and it was an astounding contrast to the first battle two years before. Yet it was planned and directed by the same Commander-in-Chief, Sir Douglas Haig, and the same army commander, Sir Henry Rawlinson.

Taken completely by surprise, the Germans collapsed. By nightfall, Canadian troops had advanced over 8 miles, and what General Ludendorff called 'the blackest day of the German army in the history of the war' had come to an end. German losses totalled 27,000 men killed, wounded and missing. But even

more alarming to Ludendorff than the collapse of the German front on the Somme was the disintegration of his soldiers' morale. Only three days later he warned the Kaiser that the war must be ended. This was the measure of Haig's success.

Yet barely six months earlier, on March 21, Ludendorff had launched the enormous spring offensive – the *Kaiserschlacht* (Emperor battle) – with which he intended to win the war for Germany. At first the Germans had achieved striking gains, breaking through the British Fifth Army front, and starting to drive a wedge between the British and French armies. But after the French Marshal Ferdinand Foch was appointed Allied Supreme Commander, dogged resistance brought the Germans to a halt just short of the key railway centre for the British front – Amiens.

From victory to victory

Later, but smaller, German offensives, first against the British in Flanders, then against the French along the Aisne and round Rheims, were also blocked after early successes. On July 18 the French opened the Allied counter-offensive with an attack led by tanks, at Villers-Cotterêts. Now, on August 8, it was the turn of the British.

The second Battle of the Somme was only the first of a series of crushing blows struck by Haig as part of the general Allied offensive of 1918. Nine more attacks were to follow before the armistice.

By the last week of September, Haig had

THE END IN SIGHT *German infantry surrender to Australian troops near the Hindenburg Line in September 1918. A few days later, the German commanders, Hindenburg and Ludendorff, told Kaiser Wilhelm II that Germany was defeated and warned him that the war must be ended.*

reached the Hindenburg Line, the most formidable of the German positions on the Western Front. It was a maze of strongpoints, trenches, pill-boxes and barbed wire. From England, the Chief of the Imperial General Staff, Sir Henry Wilson, warned Haig that the War Cabinet 'would become anxious if we receive heavy punishment in attacking the Hindenburg Line without success'.

The cabinet was still thinking in terms of the stalemate battles of 1916 and 1917. Its members were planning to achieve victory only in 1919. But Haig realised that the German army was tottering at last. The time had come to garner the fruits of the earlier terrible battles of attrition.

Between September 27 and 30 the armies of the British Empire smashed their way through the Hindenburg Line, and the French and Americans drove back the enemy on their sections of the front. On October 4 Germany

A NEW HORROR

By 1918 the new technology of war had reached its peak. Massed artillery bombardments, machine-guns, barbed wire, flame throwers – these and many other innovations had combined to make life in the trenches a living hell for soldiers of both sides.

Of all these new inventions it was poison gas that was most feared. The Germans first used gas at Ypres in 1915. It took the Allies by surprise, and French troops were seen clutching at their throats and choking as they ran. Though the Allies condemned this as an example of 'German barbarism', they were soon using gas in their turn. By 1918 millions of gas shells were being fired by both sides.

British gas victims line up for medical treatment at a dressing station. It took a year for an effective form of gas mask to be developed.

A menace from the air ends Britain's isolation

Britain suffered 52 air raids during the First World War, and 5806 tons of bombs were dropped, killing 557 people and injuring 1358. These casualties were slight by the standards of the Second World War, but even this limited toll had a profound effect on the morale of a people who had never experienced war at first hand.

At first, the German air threat to Britain was based on the Zeppelin, a hydrogen-filled airship. But the Zeppelin was only the first of a new race of war machines. In 1917 a new and more dangerous threat appeared in British skies – the Gotha bomber.

Terror in the skies
When an area was raided, industrial production would drop by 25 per cent because of absenteeism. And there was a public outcry at the lack of effective protection from air attack. Slowly an air-defence system was built up. By the end of the war, London and other important cities were protected by guns, searchlights, sound locators and fighters.

By 1918 the newly founded Royal Air Force numbered 22,000 planes. It was the largest air force in the world.

Yet the British were slow to learn the full lessons of air power. At the end of the war, the RAF was drastically run down. And 20 years later, on the eve of another war, British air power had once again to be built up almost from scratch.

The Daily Chronicle

✠ No. 17,702. LONDON, TUESDAY, NOVEMBER 12, 1918. ONE PENNY

END OF THE GREAT WORLD WAR.

Extra Late Edition.

SURRENDER
OF
GERMANY.

ARMISTICE SIGNED.

ALL FIGHTING SUBMARINES TO BE HANDED OVER.

The end of the world-wide war was announced yesterday in the House of Commons by the Prime Minister in the following historic declaration:—

The Armistice was signed at five o'clock this morning. Hostilities ceased on all fronts at 11 a.m. to-day. . . . Thus came to an end the cruellest and most terrible war that has ever scourged mankind. I hope we may say that thus, on this fateful morning, came to an end all wars.

CHIEF POINTS IN CONDITIONS OF ARMISTICE.

End of fighting by air, land and sea.	and all stocks, shares and money removed.
Evacuation of invaded lands—Belgium, France, Alsace-Lorraine, Luxemburg—and repatriation of all inhabitants of these lands. Within 14 days.	Restoration (to Allies in trust) of Russian or Rumanian gold yielded to, or taken by, Germany.
Evacuation of countries on left bank of Rhine within 31 days.	What Germany Surrenders, Germany to surrender, in good condition:—

EX-KAISER A FUGITIVE.

UNCONFIRMED REPORT OF THE SHOOTING OF CROWN PRINCE.

PROBABLE INTERNMENT OF WILLIAM II.

HINDENBURG REMAINS AT GERMAN MAIN HEADQUARTERS.

William II. has fled to Holland, and as he crossed the frontier wearing a military uniform and sword, it is believed he will be interned.

Hindenburg, contrary to report, has not fled with his fallen master, but accompanying the party were the Kaiserin and at least one of her sons.

The following message was received at a late hour last night:—

AMSTERDAM, Monday.

It is reported that the Crown Prince has been shot. Details are lacking.—Central News.

HOW THE KAISER CAME.

CHANGES INTO CIVILIAN ATTIRE REACHING HOLLAND.

HINDENBURG REMAINS.

TO RECEIVE SOLDIERS' COUNCIL AT HEADQUARTERS.

VICTORY AT LAST *The* Daily Chronicle *front page for November 12, 1918, proclaims the end of the war and the Kaiser's flight from Germany to exile in Holland. After four years of bloodshed, in which over 8 million soldiers on both sides perished, Germany had finally surrendered.*

---

asked President Woodrow Wilson of the United States to settle the terms of an armistice.

But throughout the month of October, while peace negotiations went on, the Allied armies kept up their remorseless offensives, first on one sector of the front and then another. They cleared the Belgian coast and drove the Germans steadily off French soil.

'The end of a frightful four years'
This pressure was not confined to the Western Front. Far off in Syria, the British pursued a routed Turkish army back to Damascus, and then beyond Aleppo. On October 30 Turkey signed an armistice. The day before, Bulgaria, defeated by an Allied army based on Salonika, had asked for terms. On November 3, Germany's sole remaining ally, Austria, signed an armistice.

In Germany itself, revolution broke out. Yet the German army fought on. Then, at last, on November 11, an armistice was signed by the new republican German government,

which had come into power two weeks earlier when the Kaiser abdicated.

It was the soldiers of the British Empire who played the greatest part in the final triumphant campaign on the Western Front. They took 188,700 prisoners, as against 196,070 by the French, Belgian and American forces. They captured 2840 guns, compared to the 3775 taken by their three allies.

In November 1918, the greatest war Britain had yet fought was over. On Armistice Day a British regular officer, Brigadier-General Jack, summed up the war in his diary: 'Incidents flash through the memory: the battle of the first four months: the awful winters in waterlogged trenches, cold and miserable: the terrible trench assaults and shell fire of the next three years: loss of friends, exhaustion and wounds: the stupendous victories of the last few months: our enemies all beaten to their knees.

Thank God! The end of a frightful four years . . .'

A NATION ON RATIONS
Air raids were only one of the dangers that the British had to face at home in the last two years of the war. By the middle of 1917, the success of the German U-boat campaign had brought Britain close to starvation. Thousands waited patiently in line outside the shops for food. A new word was borrowed from France to describe this phenomenon – the queue.

In February 1918, for the first time in Britain's history, rationing was introduced in response to popular demand. But, paradoxically, this revolutionary step was no longer necessary. The U-boat's moment of supremacy had been ended by the convoy system, and the consumption of food was not heavily restricted. It was in Germany – victim of the Royal Navy's blockade – that there was starvation.

A 1918 ration book. Rationing was not fully abolished until three years after the war.

Nine days that shook Britain to its foundation

TWO VOICES
*During the General Strike,
both the government and unions
produced newspapers, now in the
British Museum Newspaper Library.
The* British Gazette *was edited by Winston
Churchill, the Chancellor of the Exchequer.
The* British Worker *was published by the TUC.*

For nine days in May 1926, Britain's industrial life was brought to a standstill. On the orders of the Trades Union Congress, over 2 million workers in vital sectors of British industry – including miners, dockers, printworkers, shipbuilders and workers in transport, power and construction – downed tools from midnight on Monday, May 3. The stoppage was total.

A nation at a standstill

The threat of a General Strike had been looming over Britain for a year, provoked by the crisis in the mining industry. In April 1925 Britain had returned to the gold standard, restoring the old pre-war exchange rate between sterling and the dollar. But this step was inspired more by illusions about Britain's financial strength than by sound economic principles. It forced exporters to raise their prices abroad.

The coal industry was among the worst hit. In June 1925 its owners announced that the only way out of their crisis was to reduce wages and lengthen working hours.

The miners rallied under the slogan 'Not a penny off the pay, not a minute on the day', and prepared to resist the demands of the owners. A strike in the pits was averted at the last moment, when the government decided to grant a temporary subsidy to the mining industry, and to appoint a Royal Commission under Sir Herbert Samuel to investigate its problems. But the government had only bought time. In March 1926 both sides rejected the Samuel Commission's recommendations. On May 1 the miners were locked out by their employers.

Immediately, the TUC called for a nationwide stoppage in chosen sectors of British industry. Their object was to force the government to find a satisfactory solution to the mining dispute. And the government, the nation – even the TUC – was astounded by the response as Britain's workers rallied to support the miners. In most of the affected areas, the strike was almost 90 per cent solid. Britain had never seen anything like it.

Fear of revolution

In this situation, unprecedented countermeasures were adopted. The trade unions had taken on the government, and their challenge could not be allowed to succeed. The Prime Minister, Stanley Baldwin, was already prepared. His plans to meet the strike had been laid in the autumn of 1925, and now they swung smoothly into action.

The major tasks facing the government were the preservation of order, and the distribution of food and other essential supplies. Warships moved into position off major ports and rivers. The navy went into the docks to unload waiting ships. The army was given responsibility for food distribution. Civil commissioners were appointed to supervise operations in each of ten areas into which the country was divided. Hundreds of special constables were sworn in. Most heartening of all for Baldwin and his colleagues was the response to their appeal for volunteers. Thousands of them were soon at work.

But, though many feared that the strike was the first step on the road to a violent revolution, there was far less violence than had been expected. The peaceful nature of the strike had been foreseen by the socialist writer Beatrice Webb, who suggested that it would 'turn out to be a batch of compulsory Bank Holidays without any recreation and a lot of dreary walking to and fro'.

And for many, it was a nine-day Bank Holiday – including a good deal more entertainment than Beatrice Webb thought.

Volunteering to beat the strike

London was the centre of the tremendous volunteer operation to counter the strike's effects on the nation's political and commercial life. Thousands of people left their desks, their homes or their colleges to register for work.

Among them were hundreds of undergraduates who ran London's bus services with style and wit. To travel on their vehicles was more a jaunt than a journey, for their progress was unreliable. Many drivers were ignorant of the routes. Some made wide detours to deliver passengers to special destinations. Others were obstructed by angry pickets. The volunteers had their own answer to this last threat: 'The driver of this bus is a student of Guy's Hospital', was the notice chalked on one vehicle; 'The conductor of this bus is a student of Guy's. Anybody who interferes with either is liable to be a patient of Guy's.'

Victory for the government

Other volunteers had the chance to fulfil schoolboy ambitions to become engine-drivers. Westminster Underground station was manned by two lords, a knight, and an army major – all MPs. Volunteers kept some daily papers going. Lady Edwina Mountbatten became a telephonist for the *Daily Express*, and eminent readers of *The Times* – including two duchesses, a viscountess and the daughter of a marchioness – drove lorries to distribute the paper. And the government, too, produced its own newspaper – the *British Gazette*.

Only a handful of clashes disturbed the prevailing calm. Army escorts for food convoys were a common sight in London. But in general the strikers were orderly. In Plymouth there was even a football match between

Police and Strikers (the Strikers won 2–0).

On May 12 the TUC called off the strike. Never wholeheartedly in favour of such massive industrial action, the TUC had conducted negotiations with the government throughout the nine days. They reached a compromise settlement of the miners' issue: only when the mine-owners had adopted the Samuel Commission's reorganisation proposals would a wage reduction be permitted.

But the miners themselves rejected this plan. They stayed out for another six months, until starvation forced them back to the pits.

Lessons from failure

The miners felt betrayed by the failure of the General Strike. But for many trade unionists, the lessons of the strike were of lasting importance. They realised that they could not lead Britain's workers towards revolution. The threat of class war receded, and Britain's trade union and Labour leaders prepared for the time when the processes of democracy would give them a real chance to wield power.

VOLUNTEERS *Undergraduates unloading milk churns at King's Cross Station. Students from Oxford and Cambridge responded in their hundreds to the government's call for volunteers at the start of the strike. In London they ran buses and trains.*

SHOW OF FORCE *As the strike went on, the government resolved on an open show of strength. On Sunday, May 9, six days after the strike had begun, troops and armoured cars escorted a food convoy through the East End of London. Three days later, the strike was called off.*

MEN OF ACTION *Guarded by soldiers, sailors unload rations for their comrades sent into Neasden power station to supply electricity. Troops were also used in the docks, where pickets were deterred by the threat of machine-guns.*

In 25 years a new party rises to power

TO·MORROW – WHEN LABOUR RULES

NEW AGE *The men, women and children of Britain look forward to a better future 'when Labour rules' in this 1922 election poster.*

In January 1924 a new era dawned in British politics. Ramsay MacDonald became the country's first Labour Prime Minister. In the general election of December 1923 the Conservatives had lost over 90 seats, and their government was defeated when the new Parliament met. Since its foundation in 1900, the Labour Party had made dramatic progress. In less than 25 years, the number of Labour MPs had risen from two to 191. Now Labour, as the next largest party in Parliament, was called on to form a minority government.

Observing the conventions

Many traditionalists viewed the prospect of a Labour government with horror. But their fears that Britain was heading for revolution, proved groundless. For thoughts of revolution were far from Ramsay MacDonald's mind.

When George V invited him to form the new government, MacDonald assured the king that there would be no concessions to Labour's fiery left-wingers. He promised to prevent his followers from celebrating victory by singing the 'Red Flag' in the House of Commons. And MacDonald also insisted that his ministers must observe the customary etiquette by wearing court dress at Buckingham Palace.

Many Labour voters saw this as treachery to the ideals of the movement, and reacted with bitterness. But MacDonald's government needed the votes of the 158 Liberal MPs in order to survive. In this situation, Labour had no hope of adopting radical measures.

The first Labour government lasted only eight months. Five years later MacDonald formed a second government – again in a minority. And in 1931, in the throes of the economic depression, MacDonald agreed to form a National Government with the Conservatives and Liberals. Shocked by this 'betrayal', the Labour Party split in two. It was to be 14 years before a reunited Labour Party swept to power, with an overwhelming mandate, to fulfil the goals which its founders had cherished.

A king renounces his throne for 'the woman I love'

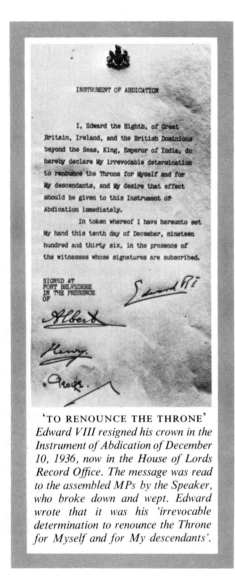

'TO RENOUNCE THE THRONE'
Edward VIII resigned his crown in the Instrument of Abdication of December 10, 1936, now in the House of Lords Record Office. The message was read to the assembled MPs by the Speaker, who broke down and wept. Edward wrote that it was his 'irrevocable determination to renounce the Throne for Myself and for My descendants'.

Edward Albert Christian George Andrew Patrick David Windsor reigned as Edward VIII for just 325 days. At 10 a.m. on Thursday, December 10, 1936, the still-uncrowned king-emperor abdicated. On the following evening, he broadcast to the people of Britain and the empire: 'A few hours ago I discharged my last duty as King and Emperor. I now quit altogether public affairs, and I lay down my burden.' Within hours of this statement, the ex-king had boarded the destroyer HMS *Fury* in Portsmouth Harbour, and slipped out of England to join the woman he loved, in a lifetime of exile.

In the quarter of a century since he became Prince of Wales in 1911, Edward had done much to endear himself to his subjects. Dashing and debonair, he had provided a refreshing contrast to the austere and restricted life of his parents, George V and Queen

Mary – to their disapproval. And in adult life, Edward reacted sharply against the atmosphere of hallowed tradition and strict convention that had enveloped his childhood upbringing. During the First World War, he asked to be allowed to fight at the Front, but had to be content with being attached to the General Staff in France. And in the 1920's he relaxed from official duties at parties, nightclubs and country weekends – a foretaste, it seemed, of the more informal style he would adopt as king.

There was another side to Edward's unorthodoxy. Notwithstanding his indulgence in fashionable pleasures, the prince also revealed a strong social conscience. In 1926 he shocked many of his subjects by contributing to the miners' relief fund after the General Strike. Ten years later, as king, he made his own views clear when he saw the misery of the depressed mining valleys of South Wales. His comment was: 'Terrible, terrible, something will be done about this.' It seemed evidence of more than formal sympathy with the plight of the unemployed.

Dislike of convention

Edward's party-going and his social concern were not contradictions, but the two sides of a single coin. The keynote of his character was a deeply felt dislike of the formal conventions that bound his life. Edward's ambition was to give the English monarchy a more modern appearance, to make it more accessible to millions of ordinary people.

It was this genuine commitment to the monarchy as an institution that led Edward to abdicate when he felt that he could not live up to its demands. He had often doubted his ability and, as he said in his abdication broadcast: 'I have found it impossible to carry the heavy burden of responsibility and to discharge my duties as a King as I would wish, without the help and support of the woman I love.'

Keeping the royal secret

That woman was an American, Mrs Wallis Ernest Simpson, whom Edward had met in 1931. The prince soon fell in love with her. Three years later, Henry 'Chips' Channon, a prominent member of high society, noted that Mrs Simpson 'already had the air of a personage who walks into a room as though she almost expected to be curtsied to'.

According to the rigid standards of the age, Mrs Simpson was an unsuitable candidate for the hand of the future King of England. She had divorced her first husband and was now in the process of dissolving her second marriage. Since the Church of England then refused to

SMILE THAT WON AMERICA *Edward conquered the United States during his tour of 1919, when this photograph was taken.*

bless the marriage of divorced people, Edward could neither go through a religious wedding ceremony with Mrs Simpson nor have her crowned as queen. As king, he was 'Supreme Governor of the Church of England', so his dilemma was more than a personal one.

The new king and Mrs Simpson were frequently in each other's company after his accession in January 1936, and in the summer went on a holiday cruise together. But for months after the royal romance was common knowledge throughout the world, the British Press voluntarily kept silent.

It was on December 1 that Bishop Blunt of Bradford made a public comment on the king's 'need for grace', and the long-awaited storm broke. The bishop's remarks were reported in the *Yorkshire Post*, and two days later an editorial in *The Times* spoke openly of a 'marriage incompatible with the Throne'.

Marriage or the throne

The crisis came at the end of a dismal year for Britain. Hitler had occupied the Rhineland in March; Mussolini's troops had conquered Ethiopia in May; and the Spanish Civil War had broken out in July. The world's political future looked grim. 'For the monarchy to lose the affection and respect of the people would be to imperil the continuance of the Empire, and thus to add immensely to the perils of this troubled world,' declared the *Church Times*. 'If the King marries Mrs Simpson, relations between the Church and the State must be fundamentally affected.'

Stanley Baldwin, the Prime Minister, rallied his cabinet firmly behind Church opinion. The king must choose between the crown and Mrs Simpson. Sympathisers with Edward wondered whether Baldwin's firmness had anything to do with the king's indignation at what he had seen in South Wales. His comments could have been taken as a criticism of the government's

THE SPORTING PRINCE *Edward is pictured after a successful partridge shoot on the estate of Sir Walford Selby, the British Ambassador to Austria. On such holiday visits abroad, Edward would combine business with pleasure, using his trips to show the British flag as well as to relax.*

VALLEYS OF GLOOM *Crowds surround Edward during his tour of industrial valleys in Monmouthshire in 1936. The poverty he found among the unemployed miners deeply shocked him, and he said that 'something will be done'. It was this social conscience which helped to establish his popularity.*

George VI: A shy man devoted to his duty

Albert, Duke of York, had not been trained for kingship. Aged 41 when he came to the throne, adopting the title of George VI, he was shy and nervous, and suffered from an acute stammer. On the first night of his reign he admitted his fear to his cousin, Lord Louis Mountbatten: 'I never wanted this to' happen. I'm only a naval officer, it's the only thing I know about.'

Yet, due to his courage, his doubts were not borne out and within a few years of his accession, the king was even more popular than his brother had been.

With medical assistance, George mastered his embarrassing stammer. He continued to support projects such as his Duke of York's camps – where, in shorts and shirtsleeves, he mingled with boys drawn from both public schools and slum areas.

But the supreme test of George's life came in 1939. In rising to this challenge, he leant heavily on the extraordinary gifts of his wife, Queen Elizabeth. The daughter of the Earl of

INTO THE LIMELIGHT *George VI said that he had 'never seen a state paper' before coming to the throne after his brother's abdication in 1936.*

Strathmore, she was the first British-born queen since the 17th century, and she was blessed with the rare gift of a popular touch.

In Britain's darkest hour, the king and queen lived and suffered in the midst of their people. They accepted rationing, they refused to leave England and, in September 1940, they even lived through the bombing of Buckingham Palace.

George personally introduced the George Cross and Medal, to recognise civilian heroism and, again on his own initiative, he bestowed the George Cross on the Mediterranean island-fortress of Malta. George's undemonstrative leadership was recognised by his wartime Prime Minister, Winston Churchill. He told the king: 'Your Majesties are more beloved by all classes and conditions than any of the princes of the past.'

policies. 'God save the King from Baldwin!' declared the demonstrators' placards.

But despite such proof of his public popularity, influential opinion was against the king. And in this ultimate test of duty, Edward did not fail. He knew he must marry the woman he loved, and his government had made it clear that he could not remain king if he did so. Less than a week after the crisis broke, on December 5, Edward agreed to abdicate.

'Now we all have a new King'

It took another five days for the legal and constitutional arrangements to be completed. Baldwin's government drew up the formal Instrument of Abdication and rushed it through both Houses of Parliament. On December 11, 1936, Edward spoke to the public as a private citizen, first declaring his allegiance to the new king, his brother Albert, Duke of York. He ended: 'Now we all have a new King.'I wish him, and you, his people, happiness and prosperity with all my heart. God bless you all. God save the King.'

IN EXILE *Edward married Mrs Simpson in June 1937 at Château de Cande, near Tours, France.*

347

Britain stands alone to face its 'finest hour'

Only two weeks after Germany launched her long-awaited offensive in the West on May 10, 1940, the British cabinet was discussing the possibility that France would soon be defeated. If this happened, could Britain survive alone?

This was the question that the newly appointed Prime Minister, Winston Churchill, put to the chiefs of staff at the end of May, just as the British army was beginning its evacuation from Dunkirk. They answered: 'The crux of the matter is air superiority.' For the British army, after its losses in France, did not have the strength to drive out an invader.

Battle in the sky

The Germans, too, were aware of the crucial importance of air power when, after the fall of France in June, they began to plan Operation Sealion – the invasion of England. Because of the strength of the Royal Navy, it would only be possible to launch an invasion if the *Luftwaffe* had first won air supremacy.

Reichsmarshal Hermann Göring, commander of the German air force, had no doubts that his invincible *Luftwaffe* would succeed. It had triumphed in the skies over Poland, Norway, France and the Low Countries: now it would crush the outnumbered Fighter Command of the Royal Air Force.

On July 10, Göring opened the first phase of his air offensive – attacks on Channel ports and shipping. But it was not until August 13 – *Adlerstag* – ('Eagle Day'), as the Germans optimistically dubbed it – that the Battle of Britain began in earnest. The pattern set on that day was to be followed throughout the

blue-skied summer of 1940. German planes took off in waves from their bases in northern France, took up formation high over the Channel and headed inland over the English coast. Their targets were the RAF airfields. For the first time, the British watched what was to become a familiar spectacle: vapour trails stretching across their skies; glinting specks twisting in combat, high in the sunshine.

The *Luftwaffe* had about 2500 aircraft available for its offensive; 800 of them were Messerschmitt 109 single-seat fighters. Fighter Command numbered no more than 700 serviceable Spitfires and Hurricanes. England's salvation depended on these aircraft and the 1400 men who were now to win immortality as 'the Few'.

But, though outnumbered in the air, the pilots had a major advantage over the Germans. Britain's southern and eastern shores bristled with a chain of radar stations, the first in the world. Radar provided accurate and early warning of the position and direction of approaching enemy squadrons.

And Fighter Command was the most advanced air-defence organisation in the world. Its centre lay in Command Headquarters at Stanmore, Middlesex, where the

'THEIR FINEST HOUR' *Fighter Command had a strength of just over 1400 pilots at the start of the battle, but in August alone 300 of them were lost. Waiting in their messes (above) until the alert sounded, pilots would 'scramble' for their planes – in this case Hurricanes (below). Fighter Command flew 600 sorties a day during July and August. Its great victory over the* Luftwaffe *on September 15 turned the tide of battle decisively in Britain's favour.*

information from radar stations and observation posts was plotted on maps and charts. These gave the head of Fighter Command, Air Chief Marshal Sir Hugh Dowding, a continuous picture of the fighting, enabling him to supervise and co-ordinate all operations.

Tactical control of the battle lay in the hands of group and sector commanders, who had their own subsidiary operations rooms. These 'ops rooms' gave the pilots in the air up-to-date information and instructions.

'Their finest hour'

From the very start of the battle, the Germans found that they were failing to achieve the decisive successes they had expected. Time and again their formations would find British fighter squadrons waiting for them. German aircraft losses were consistently higher than those of the British.

Then, on August 24, the Germans changed their tactics. Instead of dispersing their efforts over many targets, they began to concentrate on Fighter Command's own airfields and sector stations – and the sector stations, with their vital communications centres, were the key to British control of the battle.

Within a fortnight, the fighting had swung heavily against the defenders. As the airfields and sector stations were knocked out or badly damaged, Fighter Command's efficiency began to suffer. Losses in the air were mounting dangerously. Between August 24 and September 6, the British lost 295 fighters totally destroyed and another 171 badly damaged. But the aircraft factories only managed to produce 269 new machines.

The brave young pilots were as indispensable as their aircraft – and now the original band who had led the fight to defend their country only a few weeks earlier were sadly depleted in number. In August, 300 fighter pilots were lost, and the flying schools could provide only 260 young and inexperienced replacements. By the first week of September, Dowding knew that the tide of the battle was turning against him.

But then a German mistake gave Fighter Command a much-needed respite. On September 8, stung by a British raid on Berlin, Göring switched his offensive from the hard-hit airfields and sector stations to London. For Londoners, it was the start of the Blitz, but the Air Ministry was able to seize the opportunity to rebuild its strength. The pendulum of aircraft losses once again began to swing against the Germans, who now prepared for the climax of the battle. This came on September 15. The Germans launched a huge raid on London, intending it to be the final blow against both Fighter Command and British morale. It was to pave the way for invasion but instead, though much damage was done to London's docklands, the *Luftwaffe* lost 60 aircraft to the RAF's 26.

The events of the day made it plain to Hitler that the RAF was far from defeated, and therefore invasion was impossible. Two days later, he postponed the invasion.

The Battle of Britain, the first decisive battle in history to be fought solely in the air, had been won by the RAF. Hitler had met his first defeat. But when the *Luftwaffe* faced up to the fact that it had lost the Battle of Britain, it at once switched to another strategy – one that had never been known to fail – the terror bombing of cities. For the British people a new and brutal word was about to enter the language – the Blitz.

The first major raid on London came on September 8, 1940. From 5 p.m. onwards, hundreds of Nazi bombers struck at the docks of the East End. The first waves carried incendiaries and, guided by the light of the fires, successive waves of attacks continued into the night, and until 4.30 the following morning.

Striking at the capital

The destruction was immense, and London's civil defence was stretched to its limits. By the time the bombing ceased, there were nine huge fires, and countless smaller blazes. The fire officer trying to deal with the biggest blaze of all, in the Surrey Docks, sent a message to his superiors: 'Send all the bloody pumps you've got. The whole bloody world's on fire!' The casualties were equally tragic; 430 Londoners were killed, 1600 seriously injured and thousands made homeless.

This was the scene that the British and their leaders had dreaded for years. Thanks to the bravery and skill of the RAF, the *Luftwaffe* was soon prevented from bombing London

NERVE CENTRE *At Fighter Command headquarters at Stanmore, Middlesex, a constant watch was kept on the enemy. There, Sir Hugh Dowding commanded the battle which saved Britain.*

SPITFIRES IN THE SKY *Guided by the top-secret radar system, Spitfire squadrons such as these above, from Biggin Hill, Kent, helped to fight off the* Luftwaffe *during the Battle of Britain. The public collected scrap metal and gave their pots and pans to help build them.*

BACKROOM BOYS *While the 'few' were in the skies, ground teams worked unremittingly to provide new planes and ammunition.*

and the other cities of Britain by day. But for the next 76 nights, with the exception of November 2, when bad weather grounded Göring's planes, London was attacked as no city had ever been. Night after night, the anti-aircraft guns deployed in and around London kept up a non-stop barrage.

With these night attacks, the government had to come to terms with a new situation. Before the war, all civil defence plans were based on the belief that the enemy would strike one overwhelming blow by day. No one had foreseen continuous raids lasting from 14 to 16 hours. Nor had anyone expected that people would have to hibernate by night, nor that thousands of homeless would have to be cared for. By November, London had 250,000 of them – men, women and children.

Welfare services for the victims of the Blitz were swiftly organised. The Underground was opened as shelters, and the Aldwych branch was even completely closed and turned into a deep shelter. By the end of September, more than 177,000 people were taking refuge every night in the 'tube'. And some Londoners looked further afield for a shelter from the bombs. Several thousand took refuge in the

caves at Chislehurst in Kent. Special trains were run there each evening, and life soon became so organised that the inhabitants of the caves had their own concerts, church services – and even a barber's shop.

All the capital's citizens showed defiant courage. Thousands volunteered to serve as air-raid wardens or firewatchers. Despite the bombing, essential workers stuck to their posts. And, by widening their attacks over the whole capital, Göring's raiders created a unity of spirit never seen before.

'London can take it'

During the day 'Business as usual' was London's slogan. By night the need was for cool courage. When the BBC was bombed as the news was being read, listeners heard a muffled crash and a voice assuring the news reader that it was 'all right'. The news then continued without a break.

Throughout London, signs appeared in shattered shop-fronts. 'Blast!' was the briefest, 'More open than usual' the most common. Soon, bomb stories became so common that some Londoners wore badges bearing the slogan 'I've got a bomb story too!' London

was the country's only major sufferer for two months. Despite the black-out, the great U-bend of the Thames glinting in the dimmest moonlight made it impossible to hide the position of the city. The capital was the natural target of the *Luftwaffe* in its attempts to break British morale and force Britain to sue for peace.

Then, in November, the *Luftwaffe* again changed its tactics. London, it was clear, could not be bombed into submission. From November 18 to January 19, London experienced only six full-scale raids – though one of them, on December 29, was more destructive than any that had gone before. For the second time, 270 years after Sir Christopher Wren had rebuilt the city, all London seemed to be ablaze. Only the bad weather, which prevented the *Luftwaffe* returning to the attack, saved the city from complete destruction.

But, by this time, London was not alone. Göring's attack had spread over the entire country. And the luckless city of Coventry was its first victim.

On November 14, the *Luftwaffe* attacked Coventry for ten hours, using a new direction-finding method based on following radio

BANK STATION *The damage after the* Luftwaffe *hit the Bank Underground station in London in January 1941. Below – cheers for Winston Churchill as he meets Manchester bomb victims after the* Luftwaffe *struck the city.*

HITLER'S TARGET *The great U-bend of the River Thames made it easy for the* Luftwaffe's *bombers to pinpoint central London, even during the blackout. Much of the East End was soon reduced to rubble. Casualties were heavy, with thousands killed and many more made homeless. Many historic monuments were also destroyed – including the House of Commons in May 1941.*

MERCY MISSION *Rescuers freeing the landlord of a public house. Bombing united rich and poor. When Buckingham Palace was hit, the queen said: 'It makes me feel I can look the East End in the face.'*

waves – the *Knickebein*. It was a vital target as a centre of the British armaments industry. But no attempt was made to pinpoint its factories. Incendiary-carrying pathfinders first set fire to the medieval city centre which, with its 500-year-old cathedral, was soon totally destroyed. Then hundreds of tons of bombs were poured down in one concentrated attack. One-third of the city was destroyed, and over 4000 of its citizens were killed.

Climax of the offensive

Delighted with the success of their attack, the Germans coined a word to describe the fate of Coventry. It was the verb *Coventrieren* – 'to coventrise'.

Other cities soon came to understand the meaning of the word. On November 24, Bristol was 'coventrised'. Merseyside, Southampton, Portsmouth, Plymouth, Birmingham – even far-away Belfast – suffered the same blows. In Merseyside's 'May Week', Liverpool and its neighbours were bombed unmercifully for eight successive nights in May 1941. Morale shuddered – but it did not break. Even in Coventry itself, armaments production at the giant Morris Motors factory was back to

normal within six weeks of the devastating November raid.

Finally, on May 10, London itself was 'coventrised'. It was the worst air-raid the city experienced in the course of the war; 1436 were killed and 1792 were injured. Fires raged from Hammersmith in the west to Romford in the east. The House of Commons was burnt to the ground, the Tower of London and Westminster Abbey were hit. In the British Museum 250,000 books were burnt. More than 2200 separate fires were burning, and they raged for 11 days.

But the final blow never came. For, despairing of his attempts to break Britain's morale, Hitler had already ordered the abandonment of Operation Sealion – the invasion of Britain – and most of the *Luftwaffe* was now transferred to the east to prepare for action against Russia.

The Blitz was never to be resumed on the same scale. In its eight months, 43,000 had died, 86,000 had been seriously injured, and 151,000 more were slightly hurt. But Britons had shown that, in Churchill's words, they 'could take it'. And the experience had united them as never before.

Churchill's voice speaks for a united nation

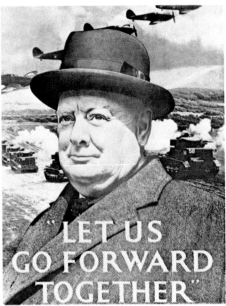

UNITED FRONT *This poster symbolised the new mood of defiance against the enemy after Winston Churchill became Prime Minister.*

Winston Churchill presented himself and his new war cabinet to the House of Commons on May 13, 1940, with these stirring words. 'You ask, what is our policy? I will say: It is to wage war, by sea, land and air, with all our might and with all the strength that God can give us; to wage war against a monstrous tyranny, never surpassed in the dark, lamentable catalogue of human crime. That is our policy. You ask, what is our aim? I can answer in one word: Victory – victory at all costs, victory in spite of all terror; victory, however long and hard the road may be; for without victory there is no survival.'

Churchill was 66 years old. Throughout the previous decade of mounting tension in Europe he had been a lone, scorned voice. Now he was Prime Minister when Britain was in the most desperate plight of her history. By the end of June, after the fall of France, it seemed impossible that she could survive against the combined power of Nazi Germany and Fascist Italy.

Yet Churchill knew that this was a time not for reason, but for faith: for a simple, stubborn refusal to give in. And the British people were at one with their Prime Minister.

Churchill gave superb expression to the nation's mood. His towering personality symbolised a Britain embattled and unafraid.

Churchill did not seek to disguise the tremendous challenge facing the British. He offered them, he said, 'nothing but blood, toil, tears and sweat'. By openly admitting the grim reality, and by inviting every citizen to join him in lifting Britain from the depths, Churchill rendered the greatest single service of his career to his fellow countrymen.

RAZED CITY *The Germans coined a word for their destruction of Coventry in November 1940 – the verb* Coventrieren, *'to coventrise'. The* Luftwaffe *used a complex system to guide their bombers on to the target. Transmissions from two radio stations were arranged so as to intersect, and the bombers were guided 'blind' to their destination. The British had hitherto been able to distort the beams, but the Germans had now improved their methods. The horror of Coventry was the result. Within hours the city was destroyed.*

ON GUARD *The threat of German troops landing was real, and air-raid wardens were taught to use a gun. The king practised shooting in the palace gardens.*

Victory in North Africa – and the tide of war turns

DECORATION OF WAR
The Africa Star was awarded to all the troops who fought in the desert campaign in North Africa, which lasted from June 10, 1940, to May 12, 1943. This medal can be seen in the Imperial War Museum, London.

In the summer of 1942, British fortunes in the Second World War had reached their lowest point since the grim days of the fall of France two years before. In the Far East, the Japanese had conquered the 'impregnable' fortress of Singapore. In North Africa, the only front on which the British army faced its German and Italian enemies, the Eighth Army had just suffered a resounding defeat.

Since May 26, Erwin Rommel, the brilliant commander of the German *Panzerarmee Afrika*, had driven the British back 400 miles across the burning North African desert and deep into Egypt. He had captured the key stronghold of Tobruk, taking over 30,000 prisoners and masses of equipment. Now the British prepared to make a last-ditch stand at El Alamein. Defeat would open the way to Cairo and the Suez Canal.

Although the advance had taken its toll by reducing Rommel's strength to less than

FOES IN THE DESERT *Montgomery (above) and Rommel (right) had very different ideas on generalship. Rommel was a gambler, full of dash and daring, while Montgomery was more cautious. He never took unnecessary risks. But both men possessed the ability to get the best out of their troops. Their methods – putting their men 'in the picture' – and their insistence on constant contact with the soldiers in the front line shocked some of their contemporaries.*

9000 German and Italian troops and 60 tanks, he believed that success lay within his grasp. On the morning of June 30, the last of the retreating British took up position at El Alamein. Towards noon a sandstorm swept up, as thick as a London fog but oven-hot. The British peered into the billowing murk, waiting for it to form into the shapes of the German tanks which were pursuing them into the heart of Egypt. Then, out in the west, something moved – tanks, trucks and guns. A salvo crashed out from a battery of British field artillery. These were the first shots in the two battles of El Alamein which were to decide the campaign in the Western Desert.

On July 1, Rommel attacked, swinging his forces south around the British position in a characteristically bold attempt to encircle his foe. But this time he found himself in trouble from the start. The German attack was hammered by British artillery from three sides.

Waiting to strike

For Rommel now faced a new opponent – General Sir Claude Auchinleck, the Commander-in-Chief Middle East, who had taken over direct command of the Eighth Army. Auchinleck told his troops: 'The enemy is stretching to his limit and thinks we are a beaten army. He hopes to take Egypt by bluff. Show him where he gets off.'

This was the beginning of a three-week duel between Rommel and Auchinleck. By mid-July Rommel was afraid that his own front would collapse under Auchinleck's blows.

In the last week of that month, Auchinleck tried to complete his success by destroying Rommel's army. Though his attacks failed to break through, he had saved Egypt.

But Churchill dismissed Auchinleck

when he refused to promise him an early renewal of the offensive. General Sir Harold Alexander was appointed C-in-C Middle East, and Lieutenant-General Sir Bernard Montgomery commander of the Eighth Army.

Montgomery, aged 55, was a master of the arts of leadership – a dedicated professional. He soon faced his first serious challenge. At the end of August, Rommel made a last attempt to break through to the Nile, but his gamble was defeated.

Despite Churchill's urgings, Montgomery refused to launch his own offensive until he was ready. He paused for nearly two months while the Eighth Army was reinforced with fresh troops and new equipment, including 300 American tanks. Montgomery's instructions to his men were to 'hit the enemy for six' and drive them out of North Africa.

Rommel knew that a British offensive was imminent and made his own preparations to meet it. He built a 4½ mile deep defensive zone between the Qattara Depression and the sea. There he had sown 'Devils' Gardens' of minefields, belts of barbed wire and pillboxes. Montgomery's solution to the problem that Rommel had set was to be equally methodical.

When the second Battle of El Alamein opened on October 23, Montgomery enjoyed complete superiority in the air and odds of two to one in men, tanks and guns over the combined German and Italian forces – despite the reinforcements they had received. At 9.40 p.m. the British artillery opened fire: 1000 guns began their barrage. The infantry advanced, their paths marked by shielded lamps and white tapes. But the attack failed to reach its objective, and co-operation between the armour and infantry broke down. Montgomery had to think again.

Defeat for the 'desert fox'

A 12 day struggle followed. It saw a piecemeal grinding forward by the Eighth Army, as Montgomery used his superior strength to wear the enemy down. On November 2, the British armour at last broke through into the open desert. Two days later, after a final tank battle at odds of 90 against 700, Rommel gave the order to retreat.

Thanks to Montgomery's resolution and his soldiers' dogged courage, Britain at last had a resounding victory to cheer after a grim year of defeat.

AT THE BATTLEFRONT *British troops capture a German tank and its crew at El Alamein. The Germans lost 15,000 men killed, wounded and captured during the battle, and over 200 of their 250 tanks were seized or destroyed.*

SURRENDER *German prisoners are rounded up at El Alamein. The Prime Minister, Winston Churchill, saw the victory as a turning point in the war. He said: 'This is not the end. It is not even the beginning of the end. But it is, perhaps, the end of the beginning.'*

Winning the battle of the Atlantic

SINK THE 'BISMARCK'! *It took the Royal Navy seven days to finally corner the battleship* Bismarck *(above). The end of the* Bismarck, *which Hitler had boasted was unsinkable, was master-minded by Admiral Sir John Tovey (right).*

El Alamein was the turning point for Britain on land. The war at sea was to be won, six months later, in the North Atlantic.

Until 1943, the Battle of the Atlantic had run very much in Germany's favour. A vital lifeline for Britain, the North Atlantic was also an essential supply route for the eventual invasion of Hitler's Europe.

'Our worst evil'

The British had one great success – the sinking of Germany's finest battleship, the *Bismarck* in May 1941, at the cost of Britain's most powerful battle-cruiser, HMS *Hood.* After this, the German surface fleet played little part in the Atlantic struggle. But the victory did not stop the U-boat menace. In 1942 the Allies lost 1664 ships, a total of nearly 8 million tons. And 1160 of them were sunk by U-boat attacks, which Winston Churchill described as 'our worst evil'.

In March 1943 500,000 tons of shipping were sunk in just 20 days. The Germans were on the point of finally cutting the North Atlantic lifeline. Yet within two months the U-boats had been defeated. An all-out effort mobilised escort carriers now released from the North African landings; 40 long-range bombers were made available by the USA; and improvements in radar meant that surface ships could now detect U-boats without themselves being detected.

In the first three weeks of May alone, no fewer than 31 U-boats were sunk. On May 24, 1943, Admiral Doenitz acknowledged defeat by withdrawing his submarines from the Atlantic. From now on the sea lanes were open to feed the final offensive in Europe.

The Allies invade France as the 'longest day' dawns

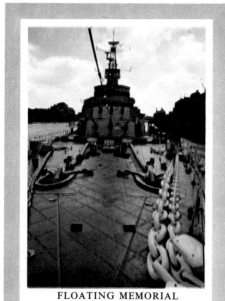

FLOATING MEMORIAL
The cruiser Belfast *took part in the bombardment which supported the Allied landings on the beaches of Normandy in June 1944. The ship is now a floating museum and is moored in the Thames near Tower Bridge.*

I n the spring and summer of 1944, the whole of southern England was one vast military camp. Quiet country lanes rang to the marching feet of Allied troops, while a never-ending stream of traffic – guns, tanks, lorries and jeeps – crammed the main roads. Both the men and their machines were heading in one direction – towards the sea.

The British knew full well that the long-awaited Second Front – the invasion of France – was imminent. Winston Churchill had broadcast that 'the hour of our greatest effort and action is approaching'. And across the Channel, the Germans, too, waited for the Allies to strike. Field-Marshal Rommel, commander of the Nazi defences on the French coast, commented to his aide: 'Believe me, Lang, the first 24 hours of the invasion will be decisive . . . for the Allies, as well as for Germany, it will be the longest day.'

'The sound of shells bursting'
On June 6, 1944, at 6.35 a.m., the longest day dawned as the first wave of landing craft grounded on the Normandy beaches. 'The wind was bringing them now the sound of shells bursting ashore,' wrote the novelist Alexander Baron, an official government observer of the D-Day landings. 'Each man could feel the thudding detonation somewhere

inside him. The talking stopped. Men took up their rifles and machine carbines; there was a clack of bolts being drawn and rammed home. The slow, wallowing motion of the landing craft eased; they were coming into shallower water. There was smoke across the beach ahead, and the black plumes of explosions, each with a cherry-red flicker at its heart. The landing craft nosed ashore through a mass of floating rubbish.' Operation Overlord was under way.

The Normandy invasion was a combined operation, the fruit of meticulous planning at every level. Since January 1943 plans for the Second Front had been going ahead. It was the British Combined Operations Headquarters which had originally studied the technical problems of seaborne landings and developed the necessary specialist equipment, such as landing-ships and craft with unloading ramps.

The supreme commander of the operation, General Dwight D. Eisenhower, was American. His deputy, Air Chief Marshal Sir Arthur Tedder, was a Briton. So, too, were the naval commander, Admiral Sir Bertram Ramsey, the air commander, Air Chief Marshal Sir Trafford Leigh-Mallory, and the commander of the ground forces, Field-Marshal Sir Bernard Montgomery. Montgomery was also responsible for drawing up the final assault plan for the Allied forces.

Battle of wits
The scale of the expedition and the numbers involved dwarfed all historical precedents. One and a half million American troops had been shipped across the Atlantic to join 2 million Allied soldiers, of a dozen different nationalities, already mustered in England. As Eisenhower joked: 'Only the great number of barrage balloons floating constantly in British skies kept the island from sinking under the seas.'

Over 5000 ships – transport vessels and warships – were assembled for the passage across the Channel. More than 10,000 aircraft took part. On the first two days of the invasion alone, 20,111 vehicles of all kinds and 176,475 men were to be landed.

The landing itself was only the first hurdle. Although the Germans had not completed their 'Atlantic Wall' of fortifications, they had made all French Channel ports impregnable. Hitler was convinced that, without a large port, the Allies would be unable to land enough troops to avoid being swept back into the sea.

It was British inventive genius that solved this crucial problem. As a substitute for a

INVASION FLEET *An armada of 2700 vessels loaded with men and equipment made the first landings. They went unnoticed by the Germans until dawn broke on June 6.*

THE D-DAY COMMANDERS *In the front from the left are Tedder, Eisenhower and Montgomery. At the back from the left: Bradley, Ramsey, Leigh-Mallory and Bedell Smith.*

seaport, two artificial harbours – called 'Mulberries' – were towed across the Channel after D-Day. Thanks to them 326,547 men, 54,186 vehicles and 104,428 tons of supplies were brought ashore during the first six days of Overlord. The Mulberries shattered the basis of German strategic calculations.

Taken by surprise
The Allied landing achieved complete tactical as well as strategic surprise. It was accomplished in poor weather during a period of full moon, and at low tide – a threefold feat that the Germans had thought impossible. And an elaborate deception plan had in any case convinced the German High Command that the invasion would come further north – in the Pas de Calais.

Months of bombing of German defences and communications reached their climax on

HEROES ON THE BEACHES *A commando unit sets out on one of the toughest assignments of the D-Day landings. They had been ordered to link up with the paratroops who had been dropped behind the German defences. They had been warned that they faced casualties of up to 84 per cent, but were told: 'No matter what happens we must get on to the beaches'.*

Welfare for all in the midst of war

CELEBRATION *The leading British field commander of the war, General Montgomery, is given due credit in this flag made for V-E Day.*

While Britain was still in the grip of war, the post-war future was already being shaped. Popular feeling ran strong. People were determined that this time they would create 'a land fit for heroes to live in'. The privations of war had united rich and poor in a common purpose. The end of the war, when it came, should signal a new dawn for a united Britain.

One wartime document best summed up the mood and aspirations of the average Briton. Published in 1942 under the unpromising title 'Social Insurance and Allied Services', and popularly known as the Beveridge Report, it was a blueprint for the kind of society which the British hoped to see emerge after the war.

The report had been prepared for the government by the economist Sir William Beveridge. It took as its starting point that every working person in the land should be able, with one weekly payment, to ensure his employment, sickness pay and pension.

Security for all

It was a revolutionary concept. Beveridge answered the demand for social justice sparked off by the sufferings of the 1930's, when millions had queued for the dole. His new society was based on equality not charity. Thus the Welfare State was born.

When the Labour government was swept to power in 1945, the Beveridge Report became the basis for its far-reaching social legislation. The new age, it seemed, had really arrived.

Out of the many measures that were passed into law, the most momentous was the founding of the National Health Service in July 1948. The Minister of Health, Aneurin Bevan, faced opposition from many doctors and surgeons when he introduced this ambitious venture. But the establishment of state medical treatment for all, regardless of income, was to remain a part of British life.

By the time the Conservatives returned to power in 1951, the Welfare State was accepted by all. The principles embodied in the Beveridge Report had come to stay.

D-Day itself, when heavy bombers alone dropped over 10,000 tons of bombs. The German defences along the coast were not totally destroyed by this onslaught, but they were badly damaged and disrupted.

There were only two serious hold-ups on D-Day itself; on an American beach – code-named 'Omaha' – where the assault force ran into a German infantry division on exercise, and near Caen in the British sector, where a counter-attack by a German Panzer division almost penetrated to the coast. But by nightfall on June 6 the Allies were firmly ashore. By the end of the following day, they were in occupation of a beachhead 60 miles long and up to 12 miles deep. Montgomery wrote that 'all anxiety had passed'. The months of preparation had been crowned with complete success: the Germans had lost the battle of the 'longest day'.

HITLER'S LAST THROW

As soon as the Allies landed in France, Britain came under bombardment by a new German weapon – the V1. This unmanned flying bomb was the first of Hitler's 'revenge' weapons developed at the Peenemünde testing grounds. Its range was 150 miles and its warhead was 1870 lb. Another was shortly to follow. In September the first V2 rocket (below) fell on Britain. Hitler had hoped to have these weapons in service earlier. But British Intelligence had discovered his plans. A massive bombing raid on Peenemünde in 1943 put back the German development programme by a year – and probably saved the D-Day invasion itself from disaster.

Team spirit takes the British to the summit of the world

THE VICTORS *Edmund Hillary (left) and Sherpa Tensing (right) prepare for the last assault. Tensing carries the Union Jack they were to plant on the summit. They had only enough oxygen for one attempt, and if the weather had broken they would have been forced to turn back. Their last meal was of sardines, crackers, honey and dates.*

DOUBLE CELEBRATION

News of Everest's conquest reached Britain on Coronation Day. Eager crowds bought newspapers outside the Abbey. A copy of the News Chronicle, *now in the British Museum Newspaper Library, captures the mood of the moment.*

TEAM SPIRIT *The 1953 Everest expedition, under the leadership of Colonel John Hunt, relied on flawless teamwork between Hunt and his carefully selected team and a band of 20 Sherpas recruited in Nepal. In this group photograph, Edmund Hillary, John Hunt and Sherpa Tensing are fifth, sixth and seventh from the left in the back row.*

BASE OF OPERATIONS *Base Camp for the assault was set up at 17,900 ft. From there, the equipment needed for the attempt on the summit was slowly carried up the mountain. It took a month to establish a camp on the South Col, but this slow progress was deliberately planned by Hunt to gradually acclimatise his men to greater and greater heights.*

Mount Everest has magnetised climbers ever since it was discovered to be the world's highest peak in 1852. But the supreme challenge of its 29,028 ft was not finally beaten until May 29, 1953 – after 12 unsuccessful attempts which had cost 12 lives. At 11.30 a.m., a New Zealander, Edmund Hillary, and a Nepalese Sherpa, Tensing Norkay, became the first men to stand on the summit of the world.

'I looked at Tensing,' Hillary wrote later, 'and in spite of the balaclava, goggles and oxygen mask all encrusted with long icicles that concealed his face there was no disguising his infectious grin of pure delight as he looked all round him. We shook hands and then Tensing threw his arms around my shoulders and we thumped each other on the back until we were almost breathless.'

This achievement was more than the work of just two men. Behind the 15 minutes that Hillary and Tensing spent on the summit of Everest lay months of planning and training, and years of hard-won experience.

Colonel John Hunt, a 42-year-old soldier and climber, was chosen to lead the expedition. His party numbered ten climbers – eight Englishmen and two New Zealanders – along with a doctor and a number of reserves. All were tough and experienced mountaineers. When the expedition reached Nepal in March 1953, its members were joined by a band of 20 Sherpas – the hardy hillmen of the Himalayas. Led by Tensing, five of the most experienced were picked out to join the assault team itself.

These men, climbers and Sherpas, were the backbone of the expedition as it set out on the assault from the Base Camp at 17,900 ft in April. Hunt and his men climbed higher and higher until, just over a month after the expedition had set out, the final camp was

established at 24,000 ft, 5028 ft below the summit. From there, Hunt had decided to launch two assaults on the summit itself. The first would use light-weight oxygen equipment; if it failed, a second attempt would be made, using a heavier but longer-lasting oxygen system.

The first assault, by Tom Bourdillon and Charles Evans, was made on May 26, but it was beaten back at 28,700 ft by lack of oxygen. Now Hillary and Tensing, assisted by a three-man support party, prepared for their own attempt.

On May 28, the five men established a camp on a ridge at 27,900 ft. At 2.30 that afternoon, the support group left Hillary and Tensing on their own to pitch their tent and rest before launching their attempt on the summit.

The final assault
As soon as it was light the next morning, the two men were ready to go. Their climb first took them through soft snow, then up a steeper slope of hard snow, broken by a formidable 40 ft rock face. After climbing this difficult obstacle, they found themselves on a hard snow ridge once more, fighting for every breath as they made their way up the steep slope. Then, suddenly, the summit itself stared them in the face. A few steps more and the climb was over.

On the summit, Tensing buried some biscuits and sweets, gifts to the mountain's gods. Beside them, Hillary laid his own religious offering – a small crucifix given to him by Hunt. Tensing posed for Hillary's camera, waving his ice-axe with a string of flags attached – the flag of the United Nations, the Union Jack and the flags of Nepal and India. Everest was conquered at last.

Elizabeth II: Symbol of Britain's future

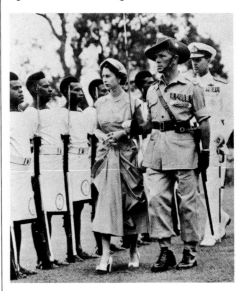

SYMBOL OF UNION *The first Commonwealth tour of the queen's reign was in 1954. It was the first of her many personal triumphs.*

The coronation of Elizabeth II, in June 1953, was the occasion for a display of public pageantry and loyalty unsurpassed in living memory. Winston Churchill spoke for all the new queen's subjects when, on Coronation Day, he hailed 'the gleaming figure whom providence has brought to us – and brought to us in times where the present is hard and the future veiled'.

Young, pretty and above all determined to do her duty, Elizabeth II symbolised, from the moment she came to the throne, values that her people hoped might inspire a new age. She was quick to seize on one invention that was transforming the life of Britain. At her personal insistence, television broadcast the coronation ceremony from within Westminster Abbey itself. And this direct link with millions of British people aptly heralded the new spirit of her reign.

Elizabeth's training for the throne began early. Edward VIII's abdication in 1936 made her the heir presumptive to the throne, and during the Blitz the 14-year-old Elizabeth broadcast to the children of an embattled Britain. As the war continued, she took on more and more public duties.

Duty has dominated the queen's life ever since. Her evident pleasure in the long-established routines of royal life, with its cycle of quiet domestic occasions in long-familiar places – Windsor, Sandringham and Balmoral – have made her a symbol of permanence in a changing world. At the same time, the innovations introduced into the monarchy, many of them by her forceful husband, Prince Philip, have brought the crown into closer touch with its subjects than ever before.

HUMAN CHAIN *A team of Sherpa porters make their way up the mountain with the vital supplies and equipment for the assault.*

ON TOP OF THE WORLD *Sherpa Tensing stands on the summit of Mount Everest at 11.30 a.m. on May 29, 1953. Hillary took the picture.*

THE WAY WE LIVE

The quarter century from 1950 to 1975 produced a revolutionary transformation in the British way of life. Despite recurrent economic crises, a new prosperity spread across the country – a prosperity in which every home seemed to share. 'You've never had it so good,' Prime Minister Harold Macmillan claimed in 1957.

Traditional barriers were swept away by this new and equally shared wealth. For millions, this well-being was expressed in the ownership of a car. Car-owners increased from just over 2 million in 1939 to 13 million in 1973. This was a social revolution.

The effect of television was even more momentous. It reached mass audiences in the 1950's. Independent television, financed by advertising, began in 1955, and the 1970's saw the spread of colour TV. By 1975, 92 per cent of homes had TV sets.

With its alluring advertisements and its stimulating new ideas, television encouraged the British to strive for an even higher standard of living. It also made people more informed and critical, and helped to widen their horizons by covering events all over the world.

The term teenager was invented to describe a generation with more money in their pockets than their parents had dreamt of. Rejecting accepted beliefs, they adopted an entirely new style of living. Their music, long hair, strange clothes and their permissiveness led to conflict with their elders. The 'generation gap' was born.

The vigour of creative change also found expression in more traditional art forms. Encouraged by ever-increasing popular interest and sustained by state patronage, British music, ballet, opera and theatre became the envy of the world.

PUBLIC EYE *Television changed the British way of life, largely replacing the cinema. Even Royalty collaborated with its probing cameras. Here, the Queen and Prince Philip are shown at a meal with their two elder children in the TV film 'The Royal Family at Home'.*

ARMCHAIR SPORT *Television also revolutionised sport, bringing major events into millions of homes all over the world. Here Bobby Moore beats a West German player to the ball in the match which won Britain the World Cup at Wembley in 1966.*

RECORD BREAKER *Britain's technological age produced a string of breathtaking achievements, such as the record set by Donald Campbell's jet hydroplane, Bluebird, in 1964. Here speeding on Coniston Water in 1966, he attempted to break his own water-speed record of 276.3 mph. He died a few weeks later when his boat hit a log on rough water and somersaulted.*

MINI REVOLUTION *Designed by Sir Alec Issigonis, and launched in 1959, the Austin and Morris mini cars represented a complete revolution in car design – and a breakthrough for Britain's export trade. More than 1½ million cars have been made since the mini was first launched at a basic price of £496 including tax. Early minis, such as this model pictured at Silverstone, proved themselves in races and rallies.*

BEATLEMANIA *The 1960's charted the pop world's greatest success, the discovery and rise of the Beatles. Found playing in the Cavern, a steamy, underground club in Liverpool, their Liverpudlian accents and irreverent humour, together with the catchy lyrics of their songs, captured the mood of the young. In April 1963 they had their first No. 1 hit 'From Me To You', and from* *then each of their songs was an instant success. They were mobbed, their concerts were the scenes of mass hysteria by young fans, and their records sold millions all over the world. Their most successful and most revolutionary record was 'Sergeant Pepper's Lonely Hearts Club Band' (detail from sleeve above), released in 1967. But fame brought problems for the four, and in 1971 the group split up.*

YOUTH CULT *In 1960 a young designer, Mary Quant, recognising a new generation of fashion-conscious teenage girls, began to make attractive cheap clothes. In 1964 she introduced the mini-skirt to a stunned world. Scores of small shops sprang up in Carnaby Street in London's West End and in the King's Road, Chelsea, to cater for the new market. The 'Swinging Sixties' were born. Twiggy (above), favourite model of the period, wears a mini-skirt.*

MAN OF MUSIC *Benjamin Britten, the composer.*

ARTS CENTRE *The Festival of Britain in 1951 gave a new drive to the arts. Over the following 24 years the exhibition site on the South Bank evolved to give Britain a new national arts centre. This view shows the Festival Hall on the right, opened in 1951, the Hayward Gallery on the left, opened in 1968, and the long-planned project for the new National Theatre, just visible above it. One of the founders of the National Theatre was the actor Sir Laurence Olivier (later Lord Olivier). He is seen (right) as Archie Rice in John Osborne's play* The Entertainer.

REVIVAL *There was an upsurge of interest in music and ballet during the 1950's and 1960's. Among composers, Benjamin Britten stood out, especially for his 'War Requiem', first performed at the consecration of Coventry Cathedral in May 1962. The Royal Ballet became the world's leading company. Much of its success was due to its prima ballerina, Dame Margot Fonteyn, shown here (above) in 'Paradise Lost' with Rudolf Nureyev.*

359

LAND OF HISTORY

An A–Z guide to the places where history was made

The currents of British history have swept like a tide across the land, affecting even the most remote villages and valleys. Every place has its story – meadows where kings and rebels clashed for the crown or mansions where nobles schemed for power. Individual places have also cast their spell over the history-makers – men and women who contributed to our cultural heritage or shaped the nation's destiny in the world of action. *Land of History* recounts the great events which have taken place at more than 300 sites in Scotland, England and Wales, and tells the stories of many famous men and women in their favourite places.

PROUD FORTRESS *Standing on a rocky site, the ruins of Dolwyddelan Castle in Gwynedd are a memorial to the medieval struggles between the English and the Welsh. It was the birthplace of the Welsh hero, Llewelyn the Great.*

Places which are open to the public are marked with an asterisk, but visitors should check opening times before going to see them.

Abbotsford, *Borders*

In 1811 Sir Walter Scott bought a farm on the banks of the River Tweed. The property consisted of 110 acres of rough land and a farmhouse, into which Scott, his family and his servants moved in 1812. He decided to call the place Abbotsford* because monks used to ford the river near the farm.

Two years after settling at Abbotsford, Scott began the *Waverley* novels, whose success made him a rich man. But he spent his income on buying more land, and by 1820 his estate had grown to 1400 acres.

Scott's ambitious plans for transforming the farmhouse into a man-

sion were not carried out until 1817. He first enlarged the house, but in 1822 he pulled it down and built the mansion of turrets and battlements that still stands today. It cost Scott £76,000 and untold energy to build Abbotsford. Every detail of its construction was carried out under his supervision.

In order to pay for Abbotsford, Scott became involved in publishing speculation. Disaster struck in 1826, when the publishing firm of Constable, and Ballantyne's the printers, which had become enormously successful through Scott's writings, overreached themselves and went bankrupt. Scott, who was closely connected with the affairs of both firms, found himself liable for debts of £117,000.

While desperately striving to hold on to Abbotsford, Scott set about repaying his debts through his writings. In six years he paid back £70,000, but the effort proved too much and by the beginning of 1832 he was too ill to work. After a visit to the Mediterranean, Scott returned to his beloved Abbotsford, where he died in September 1832.

DREAM CASTLE *Abbotsford was the mansion built by Sir Walter Scott (above right) to fulfil an ambition to live in baronial splendour.*

Aberdeen, *Grampian*

Until the mid-18th century Aberdeen was fought over by one army after another.

In 1296 Edward I garrisoned troops in Aberdeen Castle. Two years later the Scots patriot William Wallace tried to dislodge them, without success. The English set fire to the town to delay him, and Wallace retaliated by burning their fleet in the harbour.

Early in the 1300's, Robert Bruce

raised an army of Aberdonians for one of his campaigns. Returning home, his soldiers captured and destroyed Aberdeen Castle, killing all the English garrison, despite pleas for mercy from the local monks.

Aberdeen resisted the campaign by the Covenanting movement of 1638 against Anglicanism. The Covenanters occupied the city and held four burgesses hostage against payment of a heavy fine. Aberdeen surrendered, agreeing to adhere to

the Covenant. But during the following 12 years there was sporadic fighting in the streets of Aberdeen between the Covenanters and their opponents.

During the first Jacobite rising, in 1715, the Old Pretender, James Stuart, lodged in Castlegate*. Thirty years later the British commander-in-chief, Sir John Cope, camped at Aberdeen before going on to his defeat by Prince Charles Edward Stuart at the Battle of Prestonpans. (See p. 413.)

But disaster was in store for the prince. In February 1746 part of the rebel army reached the town after their long retreat from Derby, and left it again only two days before the arrival of British troops under the Duke of Cumberland. The duke stayed six weeks and gave a ball at Marischal College* before marching on to Culloden, where his troops routed the prince and his followers. (See map, p. 380.)

Abergavenny Castle, *Gwent*

The foulest deed in the history of Abergavenny was the massacre of the Welsh chiefs of Gwent by the Anglo-Norman Lord William de Braose. In 1176 he invited them to the castle* to celebrate Christmas, but at a signal from de Braose his men-at-arms slew them all. This was supposedly in revenge for the death of his uncle.

Fifty years later the Welsh avenged themselves on the de Braoses by killing William's grandson. In the reign of Henry VI, the castle was taken over by Richard Neville, Earl of Warwick, known as the Kingmaker, and its remains still belong to the Neville family.

Abingdon, *Oxon*

The final parting between Charles I and his queen, Henrietta Maria, took place at Abingdon on April 17, 1644. Early in the Civil War the queen went to live at the king's headquarters in Oxford. But when the position of the city became insecure in the spring of 1644, the king decided to move Henrietta Maria, then seven months pregnant, to Exeter.

The queen left Oxford, accompanied by the king, Prince Rupert and the Duke of York. At Abingdon the queen fell on her knees before her husband, pleading with him not to permit their separation. But Charles, raising and embracing

his wife, begged her not to distress him with further pleading. Overcome by grief, the queen fainted. When she recovered in the carriage taking her to Exeter, she was 30 miles away from Abingdon. Her daughter, Princess Henrietta, was born at Exeter in June, and in the following month the queen sailed from Falmouth for France.

Aldeburgh, *Suffolk*

This small seaside and fishing town among the marshes has been an important musical centre since Benjamin Britten founded a festival of music and the arts there in 1947. Britten's opera 'Peter Grimes' is set in Aldeburgh and is based on 'The Borough', a long poem by the local poet, George Crabbe (1754–1832).

The Victorian novelists George Meredith and Wilkie Collins lived there. Alde House was for long the home of Elizabeth Garrett Anderson (1836–1917), one of the first women doctors, who was elected mayor of Aldeburgh in 1908—the first woman mayor in England.

Alloway, *Strathclyde*

Robert Burns, Scotland's national poet, was born in 1759 at Alloway, in the kitchen of a two-roomed, clay-and-thatch cottage* built by his father. He went to school for a time at nearby Alloway Mill, and was later taught at a small private school set up by his father and some neighbours.

When Burns was eight, his father took an unprofitable farm at Mount Oliphant, 2 miles away. By his early

POET *Born at Alloway, Robert Burns lived his last years at Dumfries, where this silhouette was cut.*

teens Burns was his father's chief labourer. He took refuge from his hard life in poetry and love affairs. As he went about his work on the farm he composed verses for songs, and invented new ballad forms.

After his father's death, Burns moved to Mossgiel, where he fell in love with Jean Armour. Because Jean's father persistently refused to let her marry him, Burns decided to emigrate to Jamaica. In order to raise money for the journey, he published his *Poems, Chiefly in the Scottish Dialect* in 1786.

The acclaim with which these poems were received persuaded Burns to stay in Scotland. He went to Edinburgh, where he was lionised by fashionable society, and later he visited the Border country and the Highlands.

Burns married Jean Armour in 1788, obtained the post of excise officer at £50 a year, and settled at Ellisland Farm near Dumfries. When the farm failed in 1791, he moved to Dumfries. In his last unhappy years, the poet wrote prolifically. But his radical views offended friends and admirers, and his heavy drinking and womanising led to a breakdown in his health. He died prematurely, aged 37, on July 21, 1796.

Alnwick Castle, *Northld*
Alnwick Castle*, which survived centuries of siege and Scottish invasions, was the principal seat of the Percy family. (See pp. 98–99.)

War was a way of life for the Percys. Henry, 4th Lord Percy and Earl of Northumberland (1342–1408), joined Henry of Lancaster against Richard II. But, after Lancaster had become Henry IV, Northumberland felt he had not been sufficiently rewarded for his help and, with his son, Harry Hotspur, rebelled unsuccessfully. The Percys lost Alnwick as a result, but Henry V restored it to them. During the Wars of the Roses the Percys again managed to survive. But in the religious conflict of the Reformation the Roman Catholic Percys again fell foul of the throne. Sir Thomas Percy, brother of the sixth earl, was executed at Tyburn for his part in the Pilgrimage of Grace of 1536. And the seventh earl, Thomas, nephew of the sixth, was executed by Elizabeth I for conspiring with Mary, Queen of Scots, as was his son, Henry.

Disfavour persisted under James I. The ninth earl spent 15 years in the Tower on the suspicion of being involved in the Gunpowder Plot of 1605.

Alton, *Hants*
Scars on the main door and walls of the parish church of St Lawrence* tell of the final heroic scene in the Civil War Battle of Alton in 1643.

Royalist troops under Lord Crawford who were quartered in the town were surprised by Sir William Waller and his Roundheads. Crawford, who was unprepared, slipped away with the cavalry and fled to Winchester, leaving a Captain Bowles and the infantry to hold off the enemy.

Bowles was forced back into the town and with 80 men made a last stand in front of the church. As they were beaten back into the building the brave captain was killed and the survivors surrendered. Marks of cannonballs and even bullets themselves can be seen in the walls.

Anglesey, *Gwynedd*
When the Romans invaded Britain in AD 43, Anglesey was a stronghold of the Druid religion. Seeing the power of the Druid priests as a threat to their own dominance, the Romans launched an attack on the island in AD 61.

For a year, the Roman leader, Suetonius Paulinus, prepared for the invasion of Anglesey. Special ships were built to ferry his infantry across the Menai Strait. His cavalry swam the shallows on the night of the attack.

When the Romans reached the island, they were confronted by a line of fierce warriors standing on the shore. Behind the warriors ran frenzied black-clad women, bearing flaming torches. In the rear, where huge sacrificial fires blazed, stood the white-robed Druid priests, lifting their hands to heaven and uttering frightening curses.

Undaunted by this chilling sight, the Romans ruthlessly cut down the warriors, the women and the priests. Those who were not slain by the sword were thrown into the fires. When the slaughter ended, the Romans chopped down the thick groves of oak trees that were the sacred places of the Druids.

At the height of their onslaught

the Romans hastily withdrew to deal with Boudicca's uprising at Colchester. But they returned 17 years later, completed their conquest of the island and finally destroyed the Druids' stronghold.

Later, Anglesey became a stronghold of the Welsh princes of Gwynedd. It was not finally conquered by the English until 1282–4.

Antonine Wall, *Strathclyde-Central*
Three legions constructed Britain's second Roman wall* during the year AD 143. The wall, named after Emperor Antonius Pius, stretched for about 37 miles from Bridgeness on the Firth of Forth to Old Kilpatrick on the River Clyde. Built of turf on a stone foundation, the wall had a series of 12 forts, placed at intervals of 2 miles, on its southern side. The Romans hoped it would relieve the main frontier, Hadrian's Wall, from the attacks by Scottish tribes. (See pp. 38–39.)

The wall was breached in 155–8, and again in 184, when marauders overwhelmed the Roman garrisons and ravaged the Lowlands. Following this attack the Romans rebuilt the wall, but soon afterwards the legions were withdrawn from the fortifications and by 200 the Antonine Wall stood abandoned.

STONE OF SCONE *The custodian at Arbroath Abbey (right) uncovers the missing stone, left there by Scots Nationalists (below) in 1951.*

Arbroath, *Tayside*
Early on Christmas morning in 1950, three young Scotsmen and a girl raided Westminster Abbey. Their target was the ancient Stone of Scone, symbol of their nation's independence, which had been taken from Scotland 654 years before by Edward I.

With police looking for them throughout Britain, they lay low until the following April, when they conveyed the stone secretly to Arbroath and left it in the ruined abbey* there.

They did so remembering the Scottish Declaration of Independence, drawn up by the nobles and commons of the kingdom at Arbroath Abbey in 1320: 'For so long as a hundred of us are left alive, we will yield in no least way to English dominion. We fight not for glory nor for wealth nor honours; but only and alone we fight for freedom, which no good man surrenders but with his life.'

This ringing declaration was the culmination of a struggle between Scotland and England which had raged since 1290, when Margaret, the Maid of Norway and child-queen of Scots, died in the Orkneys at the age of seven. She was the last of the House of Canmore.

Edward I of England had betrothed his son to Margaret, and after her death considered himself master of Scotland. Since there were at least 13 claimants to the vacant throne, Edward faced a confused and disunited opposition. It was only after his death that Robert Bruce, who had rallied the Scots behind him, was able to expel the English at Bannockburn in 1314. (See pp. 88–89.)

Although the pope did not recognise the Arbroath Declaration until 1326, the document established Scottish sovereignty and acknowledged Bruce as king.

Arbury Hall, *Warks*

George Eliot, the 19th-century novelist, whose real name was Mary Ann Evans, was born in 1819 at South Farm on the Arbury estate, where her father was agent. She was christened in the 13th-century church at Chilvers Coton.

In 1820 the Evans family moved to nearby Griff House and lived there until 1841. From an early age Mary drove round the estate with her father. Her childhood memories of village life in the Warwickshire countryside are reflected in her early successful novels, such as *Adam Bede* (1859), *The Mill on the Floss* (1860) and *Silas Marner* (1861).

NOVELIST *Mary Ann Evans, born at South Farm, won fame as George Eliot, author of* Adam Bede.

Arbury Hall* is the 'Cheverel Manor' described in *Mr Gilfil's Love Story*; and Chilvers Coton, now a suburb of Nuneaton, is the 'Shepperton' of the same story, which appears in *Scenes of Clerical Life*.

Ardvreck Castle, *Highland*

In 1650, a year after Charles I was executed, James Graham, the Marquess of Montrose, led an invasion force into Scotland on behalf of the exiled Charles II. After the rout of the Royalist forces at Carbisdale, Montrose sought refuge at Ardvreck Castle*, the clan centre for the Macleods of Assynt.

The Roundheads' offer of £25,000 for Montrose's capture was too tempting for Macleod, who betrayed his guest to General Leslie at Tain. Montrose was taken to Edinburgh where, on May 21, 1650, he was hanged. (See Montrose, p. 408.)

Arundel Castle, *W Sussex*

For more than 700 years the Dukes of Norfolk and their ancestors have lived at Arundel Castle*. The 11th-century keep is the work of Robert Montgomery, who came over with the Conqueror; he also built a great gatehouse. The castle was destroyed by the Roundheads during a 17 day bombardment in the winter of 1643–4. It was rebuilt in the 18th century and extensively restored between 1890 and 1903.

The earldom of Arundel dates from 1139, when William de Albini acquired the castle and other estates by marrying Adeliza of Louvain, widow of Henry I.

During the 13th century the title and lands passed to John Fitzalan who, with Henry III, was captured at the Battle of Lewes in 1264 by Simon de Montfort.

Arundel Castle remained the home of the Fitzalans for 300 years until it passed by marriage to the Howard family, the Dukes of Norfolk, in 1580.

Spies and messengers connected with Catholic conspiracies against Elizabeth I passed through Arundel on their way to and from Flanders, but Elizabeth's spies were alert; the 4th Duke of Norfolk was arrested and executed. His son, Philip Howard, Earl of Arundel, was sent to the Tower in 1589, where he died six years later. Elizabeth confiscated Arundel town and castle, but the family earldom was restored by James I in 1604.

Ashby de la Zouch Castle, *Leics*

In the 12th century the Norman manor house of Ashby was held by a Breton nobleman, Alan la Zouch. By the time of the Wars of the Roses, Ashby had a Lancastrian owner, the Earl of Ormonde. When he was beheaded after the Battle of Towton in 1461, Ashby became the property of the crown. In 1464 the manor was granted to the first Lord Hastings, who was Lord Chamberlain to Edward IV.

Hastings rose swiftly to a prominent position in Edward's court, and in 1467 obtained permission to transform Ashby manor house into a castle*. But in 1483 he was found guilty of treason and executed by Richard III.

During the Civil War, one of Hastings' descendants, Colonel Henry Hastings, garrisoned Ashby for the king. The town was captured by Parliament in 1644, but the castle held out until forced by an outbreak of plague and lack of food to surrender on February 28, 1646. Three years later, following Parliament's order that the castle be 'slighted', the south wall and all the outer part of the building were destroyed by gunpowder.

Ashingdon, *Essex*

The Battle of Ashingdon in 1016 ended a campaign by Edmund Ironside, to keep Canute's Danes from capturing London.

Although far fewer in numbers, the Danes inflicted a heavy defeat on the Saxons. But Canute decided to come to terms with Edmund. They agreed that Edmund should rule Wessex and Canute be made ruler of London and the land north of the Thames. But Edmund died before the year was out and Canute became king of all England.

Ashridge, *Herts*

Ashridge House was one of the homes of the children of Henry VIII. In 1553 Princess Elizabeth, later queen, fled there from the court of her Catholic sister, Queen Mary.

In January 1554 Elizabeth was suspected of being involved in Sir Thomas Wyatt's rebellion in Kent. Mary sent three councillors to Ashridge to arrest her sister and bring her to London to be interrogated. When she came to court at the end of February, Mary refused to see her; Elizabeth stayed in apartments at Whitehall.

The evidence against Elizabeth was flimsy. Letters were found from Wyatt to her, but no written reply from her was found. She was imprisoned in the Tower and expected execution, but the government had no evidence to convict her of treason.

At his execution, Wyatt declared Elizabeth innocent of involvement in his conspiracy, and after two months in the Tower she was allowed to go to Woodstock, where she was closely watched by the government for another year.

At Ashridge only the barn remains of the Tudor building.

Aslockton, *Notts*

This tiny village was the birthplace of Thomas Cranmer, the first Protestant Archbishop of Canterbury, who bequeathed to Englishmen the 1549 Book of Common Prayer, most of which he compiled himself.

Henry VIII promoted Cranmer from divinity lecturer to archbishop in three years, because he had devised a means of annulling the king's marriage to Catharine of Aragon. Cranmer pronounced Henry legally married to Anne Boleyn, but only three years later he had to find grounds to undo that marriage.

Cranmer shifted his religious principles to suit Henry's changing views. But his career came to an end at the stake when he refused to abandon his beliefs under the Catholic Mary. (See pp. 136–7.)

Aston, *W Midlands*

Association football was transformed from an amateur pastime into a professional game during the late 19th century. One of the most successful clubs of the time was Aston Villa. Like many other clubs, it began as a church organisation. The first meeting was held in 1874 under a lamp post near Villa Cross Wesleyan Chapel, Aston.

During the 1880's most of the players became professionals. In the 1887 Cup Final at Kennington Oval, London, the club beat their neighbours, West Bromwich Albion, 2–0 to win the FA Challenge Cup.

By the end of the 19th century, Aston Villa had taken the FA Cup twice more and had been Football League champions five times; in 1897 it won both competitions, a feat not repeated for 64 years. The glory the club won did much to spread the professional game.

AMATEURS *England play Scotland in 1878. Many clubs, including Aston Villa, turned professional in 1885.*

Auchinleck, *Strathclyde*

The family of James Boswell (1740–95), diarist and biographer of Dr Johnson, became lairds of Auchinleck when Thomas Boswell obtained the estate from James IV. Thomas died with the Scottish king, fighting the English on the field of Flodden in 1513.

The present house was built by James's father, Lord Auchinleck, a judge who disapproved of his son's conduct and threatened to disinherit him. Upon his father's death in 1782, James became laird, and is buried in the church. After his death it was believed that his heirs had burnt his papers, but later his revealing and bawdy *London Journal* was found at Auchinleck.

Audley End, *Essex*
The lands of the Benedictine priory of Saffron Walden were granted at the Dissolution of the Monasteries to a firm supporter of Henry VIII. He was Thomas Audley who had, succeeded Sir Thomas More as Lord Chancellor.

As Lord Audley of Walden, he transformed the Prior's house into a comfortable home. On his death in 1544 the house passed to his daughter, Margaret, who was the second wife of Thomas Howard, 4th Duke of Norfolk. Howard was executed for treason by Elizabeth I and Walden passed to his elder son, Lord Thomas Howard.

Lord Thomas played a notable part in the defeat of the Armada. He was created Baron Howard de Walden in 1597, and became a favourite of James I.

In 1603 Howard, now Earl of Suffolk, had begun to build a new house at Audley End*. It took 13 years to build and is reputed to have cost £200,000—a gigantic sum for those days. Meanwhile, he was appointed Lord High Treasurer of England, and King James is said to have observed that Audley End was 'too big for a king, but might do for the Lord Treasurer!' But Howard's downfall came in 1618 when he was committed to the Tower of London and fined £30,000 for embezzlement.

Audley End became a royal palace after the restoration of Charles II in 1660. It reverted to the Suffolks in 1701 and later, on the advice of architect Sir John Vanbrugh, was greatly restored and much reduced in size. In 1745 the Suffolk line failed.

Lady Portsmouth bought the house and park and made further alterations. The property was bequeathed to her nephew, who

became a field-marshal, and in 1784 succeeded to the barony of Howard de Walden. Four years later he was created Baron Braybrooke. He employed Capability Brown to landscape the gardens and Robert Adam to build bridges and temples.

Title and property passed in 1797 to Braybrooke's kinsman, Richard Aldworth Neville. He and his son, the 3rd Lord Braybrooke, were responsible for the final embellishments to the house, now the property of the nation. Although little remains of Thomas Howard's Audley End, the successive restorations were carried out with such feeling for the original design that it still has the look of an early-17th-century mansion.

Avebury, *Wilts*
The village of Avebury lies inside a circle of earth-works and standing stones*—the largest stone circle in Europe. Its exact function is still a mystery. The structure dates from about 2000 BC—the close of the Stone Age and dawn of the Bronze Age. The site seems to have been some kind of ritual centre for the local herdsmen and farmers. But in the Middle Ages many of the stones were overthrown and buried because the inhabitants of Avebury feared their pagan associations. The vandalism claimed a victim: under a tumbled sarsen was found a crushed skeleton.

Aylesbury, *Bucks*
In the bitter divisions of the Civil War, the town of Aylesbury and the Pakington family, the lords of the manor, were on different sides. In these years of struggle the Pakingtons supported the king—and the town, Parliament.

On November 1, 1642, the Royalist general, Prince Rupert, entered the town by surprise. But the tables were turned when Roundhead reinforcements united with the garrison and forced Rupert to retreat.

The radical reformer John Wilkes, who was Aylesbury's MP from 1757 to 1764, kept up the tradition of struggle against arbitrary rule. Wilkes founded the journal, *The North Briton,* in which he attacked George III and the government of the day. He lived in the 18th-century Prebendal House, now a school. (See pp. 248–9.)

SHAW'S CORNER *The playwright George Bernard Shaw (left) settled in Ayot St Lawrence in 1906. He wrote some of his most famous plays in the study (above), preserved today as he left it.*

Ayot St Lawrence, *Herts*
When George Bernard Shaw and his wife were looking for a house near London in 1906, they came upon a tombstone in the graveyard of Ayot St Lawrence. 'Jane Eversley. Born 1825. Died 1895. Her time was short,' ran the inscription. Shaw instantly remarked: 'Then this is the place for me.'

Shaw bought the old rectory and retreated to its seclusion at weekends. He wrote there large portions of some of his most famous plays,

Ayr, *Strathclyde*
Ayr was the scene of one of the most appalling massacres in Scottish history. In 1297 the English captured the town and used the barns in Ayr as a barracks. Wallace set fire to them—with 500 soldiers inside—as a reprisal for the hanging of leading Scotsmen. He went on to sack the castle and, it is claimed, to slaughter 5000 more English soldiers.

In 1315, a year after the Scots victory at the Battle of Bannockburn, Robert Bruce called a Scots parliament at the old parish church of St John's to decide the Scottish succession. Eventually the crown passed to Robert II, Bruce's grandson, and from him descended the Stuarts. The church was incorporated into a fort built by Oliver Cromwell in 1652. Cromwell also gave money for the building of a new church*, which still stands.

John Loudon McAdam, the inventor of the 'macadamising' system of road-building, was born at Ayr in 1756. While he was still at school he built a model section of a local road, and began experimenting with different kinds of road-building materials in the 1780's. The first macadam road of crushed stone and tar was constructed at Maybole

including *Pygmalion, Heartbreak House, Back to Methuselah*, and *Saint Joan*. The villagers christened the house 'Shaw's Corner'*.

Even at the age of 94, in 1950, Shaw liked to prune and top the trees in his garden rather than leave it to his gardeners. It was in September of that year, while working on the trees, that he fell and broke his thigh. The injury was a major cause of his death three months later. His ashes were scattered in the garden he so loved.

in 1797. McAdam became surveyor of roads for Britain in 1827, and by the time of his death in 1836, his name was synonymous with his invention.

B

Bala, *Gwynedd*
In 1324 Edward II founded Bala as a royal borough. The town is situated at the northern end of Lake Bala, the largest natural lake in Wales. According to legend, the old town was swallowed up by the lake.

Bala was a stronghold of Welsh Methodism in the 18th century. In 1865 a group of Methodists left Bala to found a colony in Patagonia, a province of Argentina. Even today some of their South American descendants still speak the Welsh language as well as Spanish.

Balmoral Castle, *Grampian*

The manor house of Balmoral, set in the Scottish Highlands, was Queen Victoria's favourite retreat. As she wrote in her diary: 'Every year my heart becomes more fixed in this dear Paradise and so much more so now that all has become my dearest Albert's own creation, own work, own building, own laying out ... and his great taste and the impress of his dear hand have been stamped everywhere.'

Victoria and Albert fell in love with Balmoral in 1848 and they spent many happy holidays there, although the house was too small for the needs of a growing royal family. Between 1852 and 1855 the old dwelling was demolished and the present building erected under Prince Albert's direction.

After Albert's death in 1861 the queen looked on Balmoral as a permanent memorial to her husband. She rarely spent less than five months of each year there, and enjoyed being the laird of this private estate, visiting the cottages of the labourers and interesting herself in their lives.

None of Victoria's children and few of her visitors shared her affection for the Scottish home. But later generations of the royal family have rediscovered the walks, picnic sites and views so beloved by Victoria and Albert.

HIGHLAND VISITORS *Tsar Nicholas II (fourth left) and Empress Alexandra (third right) with Queen Victoria (centre) at Balmoral in 1896.*

Balquhidder, *Central*

The real Rob Roy—the model for Sir Walter Scott's novel—was a MacGregor, who spent much of his life in and around Balquhidder and is buried there.

Rob Roy started out as a cattle dealer with a good education and a mastery of swordsmanship. Taking advantage of the feuds and raids between the cattlemen of the area, Rob built up a flourishing protection racket.

Legend says that he once advanced the rent money owed by a tenant of the Duke of Montrose. Rob told the tenant to get a receipt from the agent when he came, then laid in wait for the man and stole the money back.

Once, hearing that soldiers were looking for him, he disguised himself as a beggar, lured the soldiers into a house in pairs, then bound and disarmed them.

When Rob lay dying at Inverlocharaig in 1734, he insisted on being dressed, sword and all, to receive a former enemy who came to call. Collapsing after his visitor had left, Rob bade his piper play 'Cha till mi tuille' (I shall never return) until he died.

Bamburgh Castle, *Northld*

Founded in the 6th century, Bamburgh Castle* was the seat of the Northumbrian kings. It was rebuilt by both Henry II and Henry III as a bastion against the Scots. David II of Scotland was imprisoned there after his defeat by Edward III at Neville's Cross in 1346.

In the churchyard of Bamburgh parish church is a monument to Grace Darling. On the stormy night of September 7, 1838, she rowed with her father—the Langstone Lighthouse keeper—to rescue the nine survivors of the *Forfarshire*, wrecked on the Farne Island rocks a mile away.

Banbury, *Oxon*

In AD 624 Banbury was given to St Birinus, a missionary to the West Saxons, who became Bishop of Dorchester on Thames, and for

FAMED CROSS *The medieval Banbury cross, celebrated in the nursery rhyme, was replaced in 1860.*

1000 years the town enjoyed peace under Church rule.

Tranquillity came to an end with the Civil War, when the town held out for Charles I. The 12th-century castle was twice besieged by Parliamentary forces. In 1644 it was relieved by the Royalists, but in 1646 it surrendered. The townsfolk then petitioned Parliament to destroy the castle which had caused them so much hardship, and in 1648 it was demolished.

Banbury's famous cross*, mentioned in the nursery rhyme 'Ride a cock-horse', was torn down by Puritans, who regarded it as popish. The 'fine lady' of the rhyme is thought to be Celia Fiennes, who became celebrated for her horseback journeys throughout England and published her *Journeys* in 1702. She was a member of the Fiennes family, who still live in nearby Broughton Castle.

Bannockburn, *Central* See p. 88

Bardsey Island, *Gwynedd*

The oldest monastery in Wales is said to have been founded on Bardsey in 516 by St Cadfan. The monks at Bangor-is-Coed are thought to have taken refuge on Bardsey after their monastery was destroyed in the 7th century.

Traditionally the burial ground of 20,000 monks, the island became famous as a place of pilgrimage in the Middle Ages.

In 1550 the monastery became a pirates' storehouse, and for the next century Bardsey was a centre of a flourishing smuggling industry.

Barnard Castle, *Durham*

Built in the early 12th century Barnard Castle, now in ruins*, was the stronghold of John Balliol, whom Edward I made King of Scotland in 1292, and also of his son, Edward, King of Scotland under Edward III's protection.

In the mid-15th century the castle passed to Richard, Duke of Gloucester, later Richard III, who had married Anne Neville, daughter of Warwick the Kingmaker.

It is said that Richard's brother, the Duke of Clarence, tried to stop the marriage, to prevent his brother from sharing in the vast Neville inheritance. He persuaded Anne to escape Richard's attentions by disguising herself as a kitchenmaid in his household. But Richard recognised Anne despite the disguise and abducted her from his brother.

Barnet, *Gtr London*

An obelisk* on Hadley Green, just north of Barnet, marks the spot where Edward IV defeated and killed Warwick the Kingmaker at the Battle of Barnet on Easter Day, April 14, 1471. Edward had originally been set up as a puppet king by the Earl of Warwick. When Edward showed signs of becoming his own master, Warwick plotted against him, and allied himself with the Lancastrians. He drove Edward into exile in the Low Countries, and restored the deposed Henry VI.

After six months, Edward came back to England with 2000 men. In a month he had captured Henry VI and gathered an army 10,000 strong. In a three hour battle in the morning mist near Barnet, the 15,000-strong Lancastrian army led by Warwick was routed by the Yorkists.

Bass Rock, *Lothian*

According to an old Scottish saying, an impossible task is 'like building a bridge to the Bass'. Bass Rock, a mile out in the Firth of Forth, its walls rising 350 ft from the sea, has been a refuge, prison and fortress.

St Baldred, the early Christian missionary, made his recluse's cell* there in the 7th century. A thousand years later the rock was a prison* for the extremist Scottish Protestants, known as the Covenanters.

After James II's flight from England in 1688, some of his followers were imprisoned on the rock. But they overpowered their gaolers and seized the rock. They held out against the government until 1694.

Bateman's, *E Sussex*

Although Rudyard Kipling was fervently patriotic, he had never put down roots in England until he bought Bateman's*, a 17th-century ironmaster's house, in 1902. He came across it down a 'rabbit-warren of a lane' on a motoring excursion. When he saw Bateman's, he exclaimed: 'That's her! Make an honest woman of her—quick!'

Kipling was born in India where he worked as a journalist. By the time he settled in England he had become a highly successful author. In the first years at Bateman's, he wrote some of his most famous works, including *Puck of Pook's Hill*, *Rewards and Fairies*, and *If*. He was awarded the Nobel Prize for Literature in 1907.

Kipling's later years at Bateman's were overshadowed by misfortune. His only son was killed early in the First World War. From about the same time Kipling was tormented by ceaseless pain, which was caused by an ulcer. He died in 1936.

PATRIOTIC POET *Born in India, Kipling roamed the world before settling at Bateman's near Burwash.*

Bath, *Avon*

Legend says that Bath was founded on the site of the only hot mineral springs in Britain by Bladud, father of King Lear, after his leprosy had been cured by the healing waters.

The Romans built a fine bathing establishment there about AD 54, with a temple dedicated to Sulis Minerva, the goddess of healing. The Saxons founded religious buildings there including an abbey where Edgar, first king of all England, was crowned in 973.

Bath was largely destroyed in the strife which followed the death of William the Conqueror, and in 1088 it was bought for £60 by John

ENGLISH DANDY *An arbiter of elegance, 'Beau' Nash made Bath into a fashionable centre.*

de Villula, a bishop and physician. He founded several hospitals, and the sick and poor went to bathe in the waters. Bath soon became a refuge for beggars from all over the kingdom.

Anne of Denmark, wife of James I, was the first royal visitor to the baths. She went there early in the 17th century, trying to find a cure for dropsy. Samuel Pepys arrived in 1668 and wrote in his diary: 'It cannot be clean to go so many bodies together in the same water.' The town prospered, though it was dirty and rowdy and the accommodation for the increasing numbers of visitors was inadequate.

In 1703 there arrived in Bath a man who was to transform it into a glittering centre of fashion. Richard 'Beau' Nash was a 29-year-old professional gambler, whose sense of taste and elegance re-created Bath in his own image. Nash became master of ceremonies and 'King of Bath'. (See pp. 228–9.)

Battle, *E Sussex*

Fulfilling a vow he made before his victory, William the Conqueror built a Benedictine abbey* on the site of the Battle of Hastings. Work began immediately after the Conquest and the building was conse-crated in 1094. The altar of the now-ruined abbey stood on the spot where King Harold died. A memorial set up in 1903 now marks the place of his death.

Beachy Head, *E Sussex*

The French inflicted a humiliating defeat on the Anglo-Dutch fleet off the chalk cliffs of Beachy Head on June 30, 1690. It was one of the engagements of the lengthy War of the League of Augsburg (1689–97), which was waged by Louis XIV against the Protestant powers.

A strong French fleet, consisting of 80 ships under Admiral Tourville, sailed up the Channel from Brest, and was sighted off the Isle of Wight on June 22. The Anglo-Dutch fleet, commanded by Arthur Herbert, Earl of Torrington, under strength and consisting of only 56 ships, withdrew.

On the evening of June 29, Torrington was ordered by William III to engage, no matter what the odds. The following morning he went into action against the French off Beachy Head.

Torrington's Dutch contingent, with whom he was on bad terms, rashly attacked and was mauled by the French. When Torrington retreated, Tourville and his fleet pursued him as far as Dover but then gave up the chase.

Torrington was arrested and tried by court-martial at Sheerness for not engaging the enemy. He was acquitted on all charges, but was never given another command.

Beaconsfield, *Bucks*

Best known for its association with Benjamin Disraeli, who became Earl of Beaconsfield in 1876, the town was also the home of poet Edmund Waller, and of the influential statesman and political philosopher Edmund Burke.

Burke lived at Gregories, now destroyed, from 1768 until his death in 1797. It was here that he entertained his many artistic and political friends, including Dr Johnson on his return from his Welsh tour in 1774. Burke is chiefly remembered for his belief that social and political change must be based on tradition and custom. In his *Reflections on the French Revolution*, he denounced the excesses of political upheaval. He is buried in the parish church.

Edmund Waller, who praised Cromwell, and later Charles II, in his poetry, lived at Hall Barn for most of his life (1606–87) and is buried in the churchyard. He was sent by Parliament to discuss peace terms with Charles in 1643, but was later banished for conspiring to reinstate the king.

Beaulieu Abbey, *Hants*

King John founded this abbey in 1204 to atone, it is said, for his violent anger against some Cistercian abbots who had refused his demands for money.

The abbey, consecrated in 1246 in the presence of John's son, Henry III, became a place of sanctuary for fugitives from justice. During the Wars of the Roses, Margaret of Anjou, wife of Henry VI, fled there with her son after being defeated by the Yorkists at the Battle of Barnet in 1471.

Another fugitive, the Yorkist pretender to the throne, Perkin Warbeck, fled to the abbey after vainly attacking Henry VII's forces at Exeter in 1497. In 1538, at the time of the Dissolution of the Monasteries, the abbey church was demolished and only the ruins* remain.

The abbey gatehouse became Palace House*, now the home of the Montagu family.

Beaumaris Castle, *Gwynedd*

Beaumaris Castle* was the eighth and last castle to be founded by Edward I in Wales. It was built between 1295 and 1298 by James of St George—the Savoyard engineer who built castles at Flint, Rhuddlan and Conway. (See pp. 86–87.)

In 1400 Henry IV gave the castle to Henry Percy, Earl of Northumberland—father of the famous Hotspur—in gratitude for his help in placing him on the throne.

During the Civil War, the castle, held for the king by the Constable, Colonel Richard Bulkeley, was attacked by the Parliamentarians under Colonel Mytton. He approached the castle from the landward side, and there were heavy casualties on both sides. To save further bloodshed, the fortress surrendered on June 25, 1646, and remained in Parliamentary hands until the Restoration in 1660. After 1705 the castle was abandoned and fell into ruin.

In the porch of the parish church at Beaumaris stands the carved stone sarcophagus of King John's illegitimate daughter, Joan. In 1206 Joan married the Welsh prince, Llewelyn the Great, after he had made peace with her father. She was buried at Llanfaes, near Beaumaris, in 1237.

Beddgelert, *Gwynedd*
The name of the village means 'Grave of Gellert'. According to legend, the Welsh Prince Llewelyn the Great returned to his castle to find his infant son missing and his faithful dog Gelert's jaws dripping with blood. Believing that the dog had slain his son, the prince in his distress stabbed the hound to death. But he then discovered his son, and lying near by a wolf, which the dog had killed.

This ancient legend was revived, to attract visitors in the 18th century, by David Pritchard, the landlord of the Royal Goat Inn, who erected a monument* to the dog in a meadow south of the village.

Bedford, *Beds*
John Bunyan was twice imprisoned at the county gaol in Bedford for illegal preaching. During his second brief imprisonment in 1676, he began writing his famous work, *Pilgrim's Progress*. (See p. 191.)

CHAMBER OF DEATH *The ill-starred Edward II was murdered in this room at Berkeley Castle in 1327. His cries were heard in the village.*

Berkeley Castle, *Glos*
The rose-pink and grey castle* has been held by the Berkeley family for over 800 years.

One of the Berkeleys, Thomas, 3rd Lord Berkeley, received the disgraced and captive Edward II into his custody in April 1327. After the discovery of two plots to rescue him, Edward's wife, Isabella, sent a cryptic message to his gaolers which they interpreted as an order to put Edward to death.

Slow starvation and ill-treatment

Berkhamsted, *Herts*
William the Conqueror's brother, Robert Mortain, built England's first Norman castle* at Berkhamsted. From 1155 until 1165 it was the home of Thomas Becket, Henry II's Chancellor. He was criticised for the great state he lived in and for spending too much money on rebuilding the castle.

Edward III's eldest son, the Black Prince, selected seven men from the town to fight the French at the Battle of Crécy, and ten years later, after the Battle of Poitiers, brought John II of France there as a prisoner.

Berwick-upon-Tweed, *Northld*
This ancient port has a turbulent history. Between 1147 and 1482 it changed hands 14 times. In the castle, of which little now remains, Edward I decided against the claim of Robert Bruce to the Scottish crown in 1291; and in 1306 the Countess of Buchan was imprisoned for four years in a cage for her part in Bruce's coronation.

Bewdley, *Herefs & Worcs*
Stanley Baldwin, Conservative Prime Minister during the General Strike (1926) and the abdication crisis (1936), was born at 15 Lower

having failed to break Edward's robust constitution, the king was murdered during the night of September 21. His piercing cries are said to have been heard by the villagers living outside the castle walls, but when witnesses were summoned on the following day to view the king's body they could find no outward signs of violence.

Edward Jenner (1749–1823), the pioneer of vaccination, was born and died in Berkeley, at what is now the vicarage.

Park, Bewdley. 'Honest Stanley'—the voters' pipe-smoking average Briton—left public life in a blaze of glory in 1937, taking the title Earl Baldwin of Bewdley. But he had not dealt effectively with Europe's dictatorships. And, at the outbreak of the Second World War, he was pilloried for failing to rearm Britain. He withdrew into isolation for the last years of his life and died in 1947.

BALDWIN *Cartoonist Low's view.*

Bideford, *Devon*
Sir Richard Grenville, born in 1542 at Bideford, is remembered as the hero of a sea battle unequalled for its gallantry.

He was admitted to the Inner Temple in 1559, fought on the Continent and in Ireland, and was knighted in 1577. In 1586 he commanded a fleet of ships taking Sir Walter Raleigh's colonists to Virginia, and two years later he joined Drake to fight the Spanish Armada.

In 1591 Grenville sailed to the Azores in the *Revenge*, as second-in-command to the fleet led by Lord Thomas Howard, to waylay the homeward-bound Spanish treasure fleet. While anchored at Flores, they learnt that 53 Spanish vessels were approaching to join the fleet.

Howard ordered his ships to stand out to sea, but the *Revenge* became separated from the rest. Sir Richard, instead of fleeing, turned to face 15 Spanish vessels. In the ensuing battle he sank two enemy ships and damaged two more, while 2000 men were killed. But the *Revenge* was completely wrecked. Sir Richard, mortally wounded, was carried on board the Spanish flagship, where he died a few days later.

SEADOG *Grenville of the* Revenge *fought to the death when he took on a Spanish fleet in 1591.*

Biggin Hill, *Gtr London*
During the Second World War, Biggin Hill airfield* was Britain's foremost fighter-plane station. Its squadrons destroyed well over 1000 enemy planes and its airmen earned more than 200 decorations.

On August 12, 1940, massive waves of German fighters and bombers began the attacks which Hitler intended should wipe out the RAF before Britain was invaded. Fierce air battles continued for ten weeks; on one day, August 15, the *Luftwaffe* threw in 1800 planes. For more than a week the airfield itself was continuously bombed, but the craters were filled in and the station remained operational.

On September 15, when the *Luftwaffe* launched its greatest daylight assault on Britain, the Biggin Hill fighters played a vital part in its defeat. That day, now known as Battle of Britain Day, was the turning point in the battle. Hitler then abandoned his plans to invade Britain.

Birmingham, *W Midlands*
In 1538 the geographer John Leland wrote of Birmingham, today the second city of England, as just 'a good market town, with many smiths that make knives and all manner of cutting tools'.

It was as knife-makers that the citizens of Birmingham first entered the pages of history. During the Civil War they supplied more than 15,000 swordblades to the Parliamentary army. They showed their loyalty to the Parliamentary cause by welcoming the army which came to besiege the king in Aston Hall* in 1642. Birmingham paid for its radical attitudes in the following year, when Prince Rupert's soldiers plundered the town. An enormous fine of £30,000 was levied on the citizens by the Royalists.

The Industrial Revolution made Birmingham a major industrial centre. Matthew Boulton set up his Soho Foundry here in 1796 in partnership with James Watt and William Murdock, the inventor of gas lighting. Using steam engines and water power, they produced a wide range of tools and metalwork, as well as casting parts to build new steam engines.

Nearly a century after Boulton and Watt, Birmingham saw a new kind of factory set up once more. In 1889 Richard and George Cadbury established one of the first 'garden suburbs', when they moved their cocoa business from the centre of Birmingham to the rural suburb of Bourneville*.

Birmingham, a city of small workshops and independent tradesmen, was a radical stronghold. In 1829 Thomas Attwood, a small-scale banker and industrialist, founded the Birmingham Political Union. Its object was to campaign for 'the real and effectual representation of the lower and middle classes in the House of Commons'. Theirs was the cause which triumphed when the Reform Bill was passed in 1832.

'Improvement'—clearing slums, taking gas and water companies into municipal ownership, and erecting fine public buildings—was the gospel of Victorian Birmingham, and Joseph Chamberlain was its missionary.

Chamberlain had arrived in Birmingham in 1854 at the age of 18, and quickly made his fortune as a manufacturer. He was mayor of Birmingham (1873–5), became a Birmingham MP in 1876, and a Cabinet Minister in 1880.

By his keen radicalism, and his efforts to bring about universal, compulsory, free, nondenominational education, Chamberlain won the loyal support of Birmingham citizens. This loyalty was extended to his two sons, Austen and Neville, who both began their political careers in Birmingham.

Austen Chamberlain (1863–1937), who entered Parliament in 1892, held many offices. He was Chancellor of the Exchequer, Foreign Secretary and the Leader of the House of Commons. But it was Austen's half-brother, Neville Chamberlain (1863–1940), who reached the highest political office of Prime Minister, although he once said: 'I don't take any interest in politics and I never shall.'

MISTAKEN LEADER *Neville Chamberlain trusted Hitler.*

Neville was a success as Minister of Health and Chancellor of the Exchequer. But his reputation has been eclipsed by his mistaken trust, when Prime Minister, in the worthless Munich Agreement, signed by Hitler in 1938. Chamberlain's belief that the agreement represented an end to Hitler's territorial aggression was tragically disproved by events. In September 1939 he led Britain into war, but in May 1940, after the British defeat in Norway, his party turned against him and he resigned as Prime Minister.

The cathedral of St Chad*, Birmingham, completed by the young Augustus Pugin in 1841, was the first Roman Catholic cathedral to be built in England since the Reformation. John Henry (later Cardinal) Newman came to Birmingham soon after his conversion from Anglicanism to Catholicism. Inspired by his hopes of bringing religion to the great industrial towns of England, Newman founded the Oratory of St Philip Neri* in 1848. Here he lived until his death in 1890.

Blackburn, *Lancs*

Refugees from Holland founded the cotton industry in the 16th century. In 1764 James Hargreaves of Stanhill, to the east of the town, invented the spinning-jenny. It spun several threads at once and enabled the spinners to keep pace with the increased demand for yarn created by the introduction of the flying shuttle. This device, invented by John Kay in 1738, greatly increased the speed at which weavers could work. These and other developments transformed cotton weaving from a cottage industry to a factory-based system.

Blantyre, *Strathclyde*

David Livingstone, the African missionary and explorer, was born at Blantyre in 1813 in a small weaver's cottage* in Shuttle Row. His father worked in one of the first cotton-spinning factories in Scotland, established at Blantyre in 1785, and at the age of ten Livingstone started work in the factory as a 'piercer'. He studied Latin, botany, zoology and geology at evening classes, at home, and even while working in the factory. The reward came at 23 when he was accepted for college courses in Glasgow. (See pp. 316–17.)

Blenheim Palace, *Oxon*

Blenheim Palace* is a permanent reminder of a great British general, a notable victory and a highly original architect. (See pp. 218–19.)

In 1704 John Churchill, 1st Duke of Marlborough, having defeated the French at the Battle of Blenheim, returned home to receive the acclaim of the English people. He was rewarded by a grateful nation, who gave vast sums to pay for the building of a palace at Woodstock. Work began almost immediately, under the architect Sir John Vanbrugh, but the great palace was not completed until 1722, the year the duke died. The most illustrious of the Spencer Churchills was Winston, grandson of the seventh duke. (The title passed to the Spencer Churchills through the first duke's daughters.)

Winston was born two months prematurely while his parents were visiting Blenheim in 1874, and although his home was in London, he spent holidays at Blenheim as a young boy. In 1908, while staying with his cousin and close friend, the ninth duke, Winston asked the beautiful Clementine Hozier to marry him. The couple were married three weeks later, and began their honeymoon at Blenheim. When Churchill died in 1965, he was buried within view of Blenheim Palace, in Bladon churchyard.

CHILD OF BLENHEIM *Winston Churchill (right), aged about 15, with his mother and younger brother, Jack. Winston was born at Blenheim in 1874.*

Bolton, *Gtr Manchester*

The importance of Bolton in the Industrial Revolution has overshadowed its earlier history. The area was settled in Roman and Anglo-Saxon times. During the Civil War the town was a Puritan stronghold, and in 1651 James, the 7th Earl of Derby, was executed there after being unjustly accused of ordering a massacre of townspeople during a Royalist attack in 1644.

Samuel Crompton (1753–1827) invented his spinning-mule in 1799, bringing wealth to his native town and ensuring the supremacy of Lancashire in cotton-spinning for the next century. The machine enabled Crompton to produce thread of exceptional quality.

Hall i' th' Wood*, Crompton's half-timbered house, was soon besieged by his rivals, trying to break their way in and steal his invention. Eventually Crompton, driven to distraction by the prying to which he was subjected, and with no money to purchase a patent, decided to reveal his secret for the paltry sum of £67 6s 6d. Other manufacturers made fortunes from his ideas. Crompton's later business ventures were failures, and only a small annuity kept him from poverty in his old age.

Boroughbridge, *N Yorks*

The ineffectual Edward II scored a rare triumph at this bridge over the River Ure in 1322. His troops, massed on the north bank, faced a rebel army led by his uncle, Thomas, Earl of Lancaster, and Humphrey de Bohun, Earl of Hereford. A spear thrust from under the bridge through a gap in the timbers killed Hereford as he tried to cross. Lancaster surrendered and was beheaded after a mockery of a trial. He was not even given a hearing by the triumphant king.

Because of his defiance of an unpopular king, Lancaster was revered as a martyr by the common people of England.

The town's manor house—now the Crown Hotel—was, in 1569, a meeting place of the rebel earls of the north who tried unsuccessfully to depose Elizabeth I and put her Catholic cousin, Mary, Queen of Scots, on the throne.

Borthwick Castle, Lothian
Shortly after their wedding in May 1567, Mary, Queen of Scots, and her third husband, the Earl of Bothwell, were besieged in Borthwick Castle* by the rebel Earl of Morton and his followers. Bothwell escaped, and Mary, refusing to be parted from her husband, slipped out of the castle disguised as a boy, to join Bothwell at Cakemuir.

Bosham, W Sussex
According to legend, it was at Bosham that Canute showed his flattering courtiers how foolish they were to say that by his command he could hold back the tide. The story was first recorded by the chronicler, Henry of Huntingdon, about 1130.

Harold Godwin, later King Harold II, sailed from Bosham in about 1064. Harold was shipwrecked off Normandy. He was captured by William, Duke of Normandy, and forced to swear to help William attain the crown of England on the death of Edward the Confessor. Harold's breach of the oath provided one pretext for the Norman Conquest.

Boston, Lincs
During the Middle Ages, Boston was a flourishing wool-exporting port. The guild chapels in the 15th-century church of St Botolph* —whose tower, 'the Boston Stump', is a landmark—recall the town's prosperous period.

The port's close association with America began in 1607, when the men who were to lead the Pilgrim Fathers to the New World were imprisoned in the Guildhall. In 1620 they finally sailed in the Mayflower. Ten years later, Boston citizens founded a New England settlement which they named after their home town—Boston, Massachusetts.

Bosworth, Leics See pp. 124–5.

Bourne, Lincs
After the Norman Conquest, Hereward the Wake, the Saxon noble who had his home at Bourne in the fenland, took on the leadership of the Anglo-Saxon struggle against William the Conqueror. In 1070 William gave the abbey of Peterborough to a French abbot called Turold, who arrived with a large band of French monks. Hereward, with the help of his native followers and some Danish seamen, descended on Peterborough. He burnt the monastic buildings, carrying off the treasure of the monks to his fenland base.

The rebels were joined by other Anglo-Saxon nobles and their retainers. With these reinforcements, Hereward held out in the fens for more than a year, surrounded by the armies of the Conqueror. In 1072 William's men finally overran the area. But Hereward escaped. He slipped through the Norman lines, and disappeared into legend.

Bournemouth, Dorset
'A Mediterranean lounging place on the English Channel,' is the description of Bournemouth given by Thomas Hardy in his novel, Tess of the D'Urbervilles, where he changed its name to 'Sandbourne'.

Robert Louis Stevenson, the novelist, and his wife came to Bournemouth in August 1884. They lived in a house, now demolished, in the Alum Chine Road, where Stevenson wrote Dr Jekyll and Mr Hyde in three days.

Annoyed by his wife's criticisms of his work, Stevenson threw the manuscript into the fire. Later, regretting this hasty action, he rewrote an improved version of this story. Another famous Stevenson novel, Kidnapped, was also written during this stay at Bournemouth.

Sir Charles Hubert Hastings Parry, the composer of 'Jerusalem', was born in Bournemouth in 1848. He was still at Eton when his first compositions were published.

In the churchyard of St Peter's lies Mary Shelley, the author of Frankenstein and wife of the poet.

Bradford, W Yorks
This industrial centre was once saved from destruction by a ghost. When the Royalists took Bradford in 1643, their commander, the Duke of Newcastle, ordered that it should be put to the sword. During the night, which he spent at Bolling Hall*, a spectre is said to have implored him to 'save poor Bradford', and the duke relented.

Two years later, in the summer of 1645, the plague struck Bradford.

COMPOSER Frederick Delius, sketched here by Augustus John, drew inspiration from his native Yorkshire.

Many died, and the wool trade which had brought the town to prominence almost collapsed.

The local water, which drains over peaty soil, is ideal for washing wool, and fulling mills are mentioned as early as 1311. In the 17th and 18th centuries the making of woollen cloth decreased, and worsted took its place. When steam-powered machinery was introduced in 1798, the industry grew rapidly.

The composer Frederick Delius was born in Bradford in 1862. He only wanted to study music, but was first ordered into the family business, and then sent to Florida as an orange-planter.

In 1886 his family finally gave in to Frederick's wishes, and sent him to the Leipzig Conservatorium. Although Delius lived in France from 1888, much of his music, such as 'Song of the High Hills', was inspired by memories of his native Yorkshire. After he became blind and paralysed in 1924, he dictated his music to his secretary-companion, Eric Fenby.

The author and playwright J. B. Priestley, who was also born in Bradford in 1894, writes of it in two of his greatest novels Bright Day and The Good Companions.

Bradgate Park, Leics
This 800 acre public park and nature reserve near Leicester contains the ruins of Bradgate House*, where Lady Jane Grey, uncrowned Queen of England for nine days in 1553 (see pp. 134–5), was born in 1537. She was the daughter of Henry VIII's niece, Frances, and Henry Grey, Duke of Suffolk. Jane was a studious girl, and the scholar Roger Ascham recalled finding her at Bradgate reading Plato while her family were out hunting in the park.

Braemar, Grampian
Braemar Castle*, built in 1628, was the home of the 6th Earl of Mar, who forfeited it after his part in the 1715 Jacobite rebellion. The castle was later garrisoned by the English, who rebuilt it in 1748.

The Braemar Royal Highland Gathering, usually attended by the queen, is held in September. The first games took place as early as the 11th century, when King Malcolm Canmore called the clans to meet at Braemar to select by competition 'his hardiest soldiers and his fleetest messengers'.

In the 1830's the British Highland Society, which wished to preserve and promote Highland customs, started an annual meeting at Braemar. Heralded by pipers, the participants at each event walked to the spot where the Highland Games were held. In 1848 Queen Victoria attended one of these meetings and bestowed upon the gathering the royal title it holds today.

SCOTTISH GAMES Highlanders take part in the sports of leaping (above) and tossing the caber (below).

Brecon Castle, Powys
Brecon Castle, built by Bernard de Newmarch in about 1092, was besieged by the Prince of Wales, Llewelyn ap Gruffydd, before he was defeated and killed by an

English force near Builth in 1282.

Two hundred years later, John Morton, Bishop of Ely, was imprisoned in the castle after quarrelling with Richard III. While still a prisoner, the bishop persuaded his gaoler, the Duke of Buckingham, to join in a plot to overthrow the king and put Henry Tudor, later Henry VII, on the throne. But their rebellion in 1483 was badly timed. Buckingham's uprising was crushed, and he was beheaded. Morton escaped to the Continent and joined Henry VII. He later became the king's chief minister.

In 1645, after the Royalist defeat at Naseby, the townspeople, fearing that Brecon would be besieged by the Parliamentarians, demolished the castle and the town walls. Some of the remains now form part of a hotel.

Bridgwater, *Somerset*
Robert Blake, one of England's greatest naval commanders, grew up among the coasters and colliers of Bridgwater docks. Born in 1598, he went to the local grammar school and then to Oxford University, before becoming MP for his native town in 1625.

During the Civil War, Blake defended Bristol and Lyme Regis against the Royalists, but his most notable exploit was his year-long defence of Taunton. He emerged from the war as an outstanding Parliamentarian commander.

Blake's real glory was yet to come. In 1649 he was given command of the navy and, two years later, destroyed most of Prince Rupert's fleet off Spain. His defeat of the Dutch navy in 1653 gave supremacy of the sea to the English.

Blake's last triumph was the destruction of the Spanish fleet at Tenerife in 1657. After cruising off Cadiz, Blake sailed homewards, a sick man, and died within sight of Plymouth. He was buried at Westminster Abbey, but at the Restoration his remains were transferred to the churchyard of St Margaret's.

Brighton, *E Sussex*
Until the middle of the 18th century, Brighton was just a small fishing village known as Brighthelmstone. Then Dr Richard Russell of Lewes wrote *A Dissertation Concerning the Uses of Sea Water in Diseases of the Glands.*

He recommended that people should not only bathe in 'the oceanic fluid' but also drink it, to prevent feverish infection and to strengthen the muscular fibres.

Soon, visits to the seaside at Brighton became fashionable. Sturdy attendants—'bathers' for men and 'dippers' for women—made sure that the patients were totally immersed. Mrs Thrale, the literary hostess, took a house in West Street, and among her guests in 1765 was her closest friend Dr Samuel Johnson, who at the age of 55 saw the sea for the first time in his life.

In 1783 the first visit by the Prince of Wales, later the Prince Regent and then George IV, set the seal on Brighton's popularity. In 1787 he commissioned Henry Holland to rebuild a small farmhouse as an elegant Classical villa, and this was later transformed into the Royal Pavilion* by John Nash. But, because of its vast cost, the pavilion was little appreciated by the Regent's subjects. On one occasion the mob daubed on the walls the slogan: 'More bread or the Regent's head!' (See pp. 278–9.)

Bristol, *Avon*
The sea has always given Bristol its livelihood. As early as the 12th century, the much travelled monk William of Malmesbury described its port as 'full of ships from every part of Europe'. And later the city took a leading part in the early voyages of discovery. John and Sebastian Cabot, financed chiefly by local merchants, sailed from Bristol in 1497 and surveyed Newfoundland. (See pp. 116–17.) The first English colonies in America, Virginia and Newfoundland, received their supplies and settlers in Bristol ships.

As the colonies expanded the demand for cheap labour grew, and Bristol merchants were among the first to supply it with Negro slaves. Some slaves were even kept at Bristol. A Mrs Dorothy Smith owned a Negro serving-woman called Dinah Black in 1665. In a Catholic chapel just outside the city, a simple entry in the parish register records all that is known about a Negro slave called Joseph Pope, who was 'born, we think, in about 1748'.

By the beginning of the 18th century, Bristol was second only to London as a trading port. After the 1760's, however, the canal system opened up the Midlands to Liverpool, which outstripped Bristol as a port for the Atlantic

trade. The Napoleonic Wars impeded Bristol's trade, and the end of the slave traffic brought about an economic decline.

Bristol's fortunes revived in the middle of the 19th century, with the opening of the Great Western Railway in 1840 and the building of new docks at Avonmouth in the 1860's.

One of the finest achievements of 19th-century Bristol was the completion of Brunel's Clifton suspension bridge*. Brunel was 'struck with the grandeur of the idea and the splendid effect which might be produced' by spanning Clifton Gorge, and in 1829 submitted his design, which was accepted. Work began seven years later, and was completed in 1864.

SAD MEMORIAL *An 18th-century tombstone in Bristol recalls the days of legal slavery in England.*

Brixham, *Devon*
The Dutch Prince William of Orange landed at Brixham on November 5, 1688, and so began the bloodless Glorious Revolution, which brought to an end the reign of James II. (See pp. 214–15.) William's ship ran aground in the harbour, and a fisherman waded out to give the future king a piggyback ashore. Next day William proclaimed: 'The liberties of England I will maintain.' These words were adopted by the people of Brixham as their motto.

A NEW MONARCH'S VICTORY MARCH

Thousands of William's cavalry and foot soldiers paraded through Exeter on November 9, 1688, after marching from Brixham. Their fine bearing and splendid uniforms impressed the townsfolk, but the Dutch prince was disturbed by the initial unwillingness of the local notables to come out on his side, although he was encouraged to hear of rebellions against James in other parts of England.

Meanwhile, in London, James was wrestling with indecision over whether to send his army to meet William, to call Parliament or to flee to France. The king sent envoys to negotiate with William who was advancing on London, collecting supporters and soldiers on the way.

James II joined his army at Salisbury on November 19, only to learn that Viscount Cornbury, eldest son of the Earl of Clarendon, had gone over to William—by now at Honiton—with 200 cavalry. Worse was to come. James called a council of war on November 24 to discuss whether to fight or retreat. Early next morning the commander of his troops at Salisbury, John Churchill, fled to William at Axminster with 400 cavalry.

As support for William grew, James headed sadly back to London with his troops. At Hungerford envoys from James met the Orange army, but William's terms proved unacceptable to the king.

On December 18 William entered London. That evening, bells rang out and bonfires blazed their welcome. William had taken 43 days to 'conquer' the English throne. James fled into exile in France.

Brodick Castle, *Strathclyde*
In February 1307, Robert Bruce captured Brodick Castle* from its English governor, Sir John Hastings. He waited there until the spring to renew his campaign.

Mistaking a chance fire for a signal that it was safe to return to the mainland, Robert and his followers sailed across the firth. On his arrival he found his wife, daughter and sister had been captured and many of his followers executed. However, this tragedy was only a temporary setback in his campaign for Scottish freedom.

Brookland, *Kent*
Like all the Romney Marsh villages, Brookland was for centuries a centre of smuggling. The village reached its greatest notoriety in 1821, with the so-called 'Battle of Brookland', between a gang of armed smugglers and the government's coast blockade. The customs men chased the smugglers across the marsh. Although their officer was shot dead, they killed four smugglers and wounded 16. The smugglers were tried at the Old Bailey in London and their leader was hanged.

Buckden, *Cambs*
In July 1533, Catharine of Aragon was brought to the palace* of the Bishop of Lincoln at Buckden, soon after her divorce from Henry VIII. Although Catharine was officially 'in retirement', and enjoyed the title Dowager Princess of Wales, she was virtually a prisoner.

By the end of 1533 the king was anxious to have Catharine confined elsewhere, because the local people were still loyal to her. Henry sent his brother-in-law, the Duke of Suffolk, to remove her to a royal manor far from London.

On his arrival at the palace on December 18, 1533, the duke found Catharine resolutely determined to stay there. When Suffolk lost his temper and shouted at Catharine, she shut herself in her room.

Hearing of the duke's plans, the men of Buckden lined the streets, silent but armed, as he passed through the village. Faced with such hostility, the duke dared not show force. He could only arrest a few of Catharine's attendants.

For six months Catharine refused to leave her room. But in May 1534 she gave in and was taken to Kimbolton, in Cambridgeshire. Catharine fell ill there towards the end of 1535. While rumours circulated that she was dying, her former Spanish lady-in-waiting, Maria de Salinas, nursed her.

The queen remained devoted to Henry until the end. In her final letter to the king, she wrote: 'Lastly, I make this vow that mine eyes desire you above all things.' According to one observer, this message brought tears to the king's eyes. But another witness records that on her death Henry dressed from top to toe in yellow, gave a ball at Greenwich and went among the guests crying: 'God be praised, the old harridan is dead.'

OUTCAST *After being divorced by Henry VIII, Catharine of Aragon spent ten months at Buckden.*

Bucklers Hard, *Hants*
Two miles south of Beaulieu lies the late 18th-century village of Bucklers Hard, which the 2nd Duke of Montagu intended to establish as a sugar port. His plans miscarried, but the inducements of low rent and free timber resulted in the village becoming a centre for shipbuilding from 1745 to 1822. Many Royal Navy ships were built at Bucklers Hard, including three which fought at Trafalgar in 1805: Nelson's favourite ship, the 64-gun *Agamemnon*, the 36-gun *Euryalus*, and the 74-gun *Swiftsure*.

Builth Wells, *Powys*
In 1282, Llewelyn ap Gruffydd, the first and last Welsh Prince of Wales, was killed in a skirmish near Builth Wells. He died because the garrison at Builth Castle* refused to give him protection from the pursuing English forces.

Late in the 1250's Llewelyn seized power from his brothers and proclaimed himself Prince of Wales. He began a successful campaign to drive the English out of the Welsh principality of Gwynedd, and establish his authority over Wales.

Llewelyn allied himself with the English barons, notably Simon de Montfort, who opposed Henry III. At the Treaty of Montgomery in 1267, Henry was forced to recognise Llewelyn's right to the title Prince of Wales, which he had assumed in 1258.

But Llewelyn underestimated Henry's successor, Edward I, whose ambition was to rule over an undivided kingdom. In 1277, after a series of Welsh attacks on the English borders, Edward led an army into North Wales.

Llewelyn, forced to make terms, was allowed to keep only the northern province of Gwynedd, although the king allowed him to retain his title. In 1282, however, following a further Welsh uprising led by Llewelyn and his brother, David, Edward again advanced into Wales.

Llewelyn, retreating southwards, was killed near Builth. With his death, all hope of maintaining Welsh independence was lost.

Buittle, *Dumf & Gall*
John de Balliol of Barnard Castle, one of the wealthiest and most powerful barons of England, married Devorguilla, descendant of David I of Scotland, in 1233.

For her he built a castle on the banks of the River Urr, called Buittle or Botel. Stones from it were used to build the 16th-century tower* that now stands on the site, 1½ miles west of Dalbeattie.

But Balliol over-reached himself by raiding Durham Cathedral. As a penance for this deed, Balliol agreed to found a hostelry for scholars at Oxford, but died in 1269 before the statutes were drawn up. Devorguilla went ahead with the plan and endowed Balliol College in her husband's memory.

New Abbey, east of Dalbeattie, was founded in 1273 by Devorguilla, who was later buried there beside her husband. With her was interred a silver and ivory casket, in which she had kept the embalmed heart of Balliol. Thus the abbey obtained its other name of Dulce Cor*, or Sweetheart. Only its ruins remain visible today.

Their son, John de Balliol, was born at Buittle. After his parents' death he was made puppet king of Scotland, nicknamed 'Toom Tabard', or Empty Coat.

Burbage, *Wilts*
Near Burbage is the site of Wolf Hall, which was the home of Jane Seymour, the best-loved of Henry VIII's wives. Her father, John Seymour, the warden of Savernake Forest, was a great favourite of Henry VIII. The king frequently visited Wolf Hall while in the West Country, and it was there that he first met Jane, who was to become his third wife.

Jane served as a lady-in-waiting to Anne Boleyn, Henry VIII's second wife. About 1534 the king fell in love with Jane. On May 30, 1536, only 11 days after Anne Boleyn's execution, he married her. Their wedding feast was held in a huge barn at Wolf Hall. The walls were hung with rich tapestries, and there was an abundance of game and drink.

Jane gave birth to Henry's only son, later Edward VI, but died 12 days later on October 24, 1537. The king was broken by the loss of his favourite wife, and at his death, by his own order, his body was placed beside hers in a tomb at St George's Chapel, Windsor.

Burnham Thorpe, *Norfolk*
England's great hero, Horatio Nelson, was a parson's son from this quiet coastal village behind the sand dunes. It is said that he was born on September 29, 1758, in the flint barn which still stands beside the inn; his mother, who had been out in a pony cart, had failed to reach the rectory in time.

Nelson was placed in the navy at the age of 12. His mother's brother, Captain Maurice Suckling, took him aboard his own ship, the *Raisonable*. He did not return to Burnham Thorpe until 1780, by which time, at the age of 20, he had commanded his first ship.

Early in the 1780's, while on service in the West Indies, Nelson married Frances (Fanny) Nisbet, a widow with one son. In 1787 they returned to Burnham Thorpe, where Nelson lived the life of a country gentleman. Now there was time for Nelson to study and reflect. He improved the rectory garden, spent many evenings at the inn and took up shooting.

At the outbreak of war with revolutionary France in 1794, Nelson obtained command of the *Agamemnon*. From then until 1800 he was on almost continuous active service, mostly in the Mediterranean. After his triumph at the Battle of the Nile in 1798, George III made him Lord Nelson of the Nile and Burnham Thorpe.

When he returned to England for a short time in 1800 he was already deep in his affair with Emma Hamilton, wife of the British Ambassador in Naples. There was a tense reunion with Fanny in London, but within a month they were separated. From now on his home was with Emma at Merton Place, Wimbledon. There were no more returns to Burnham Thorpe, although the great admiral loved his birthplace to the end of his life.

While cruising in the *Victory* off Ushant in May 1804, he wrote: 'Most probably I shall never see dear, dear Burnham again, but I have a satisfaction in thinking that my bones will probably lie with my father in the village that gave me birth.' But for the hero of his country there could be only one resting place—St Paul's.

NELSON'S WIFE *Fanny Nisbet lived at Burnham Thorpe before Nelson abandoned her for Emma Hamilton.*

Burntisland, *Fife*
A young French poet's passion for Mary, Queen of Scots, cost him his life. The queen was staying at Rossend Castle, Burntisland, when the poet, Pierre de Chastelard, was discovered hiding beneath her bed.

Mary was outraged by de Chastelard's conduct and ordered him from the court. But the next night he burst in on her when she was with one or two of her ladies and made such bold advances that Mary shrieked for help. Her halfbrother, the Earl of Moray rushed in and the lovesick poet was dragged off to the dungeons.

He was tried and sent to the block, his last words being 'Adieu, the most beautiful and the most cruel princess of the world'.

Burslem, *Staffs*
In middle age, the novelist Arnold Bennett said he hated the thought of his youth. But he wove his early experiences into the novels that made him famous and wealthy. *Anna of the Five Towns, Clayhanger* and *The Old Wives' Tale* derived their inspiration from the scenes of his boyhood in the Potteries— translated by him into the world of the Five Towns.

Bennett was born at Hanley, but spent most of his early years at 205 Waterloo Road*, Burslem—the Bursley of the Five Towns— living in a small, unsanitary house. A strict Methodist upbringing fostered industry and ambition. He did well at local schools and also studied music and painting. But any show of affection was unknown in the family. He was driven to work hard so as to rise in the world and escape the threat of poverty.

Bennett cut free from Burslem when he was 21. As a writer, he worked with incredible energy. In one year, for instance, he was able to write two long novels, two shorter books, one play, lectures, scores of articles for newspapers and numerous short stories.

He made frequent visits to Burslem. Once when being fêted there and asked to make a speech he rose and merely said: 'Ladies and gentlemen, I don't speak, I write.'

SUCCESS STORY *From a poor childhood in Burslem, Arnold Bennett rose to fame as a novelist.*

Bury St Edmunds, *Suffolk*
In 870 a Danish army which had been terrorising the East Angles captured their young king, Edmund, and offered to spare his life if he would renounce Christianity. He refused, and was scourged, tied to a tree and shot full of arrows. Finally his head was cut off and thrown into a wood.

Early accounts say that the king's followers, searching for the head so that it could be buried with the body, were led to it by a voice calling 'Here, here', and found it being guarded by a fierce wolf.

Edmund was buried at Hoxne, where he had died, and miracles were soon attributed to him. In 903 the body was moved to Beodricksworth Monastery, 21 miles to the south-west. King Sweyn Forkbeard of Denmark invaded in 1010, and legend says that when he demanded tribute money, Edmund appeared and threatened him with a lance, causing Sweyn's death from apoplexy.

The Dane's son, Canute, repaid the havoc wrought by his father by founding an abbey* in the name of the martyred and canonised Edmund. The shrine rapidly became a place of pilgrimage, and by 1065, Beodricksworth had become known as St Edmund's Bury.

On November 20, 1214—St Edmund's day—25 of the barons of England met in the abbey church, ostensibly to honour the martyr. Stephen Langton, Archbishop of Canterbury, placed before them a list of demands and they swore on the altar that they would force King John to accept them, which he did at Runnymede in 1215.

Bush Barrow, *Wilts* See pp. 20–21

Bushey Park, *Gtr London*
Bushey House in the park was the retirement home of Lord North (1732–92), George III's Prime Minister during the disastrous War of American Independence.

North was a heavy, ungainly man, with a puffy face, protuberant lips and bulging eyes. He was a close friend of George III, who chose him to form a government in 1770.

But North was a reluctant minister. On several occasions, George had to persuade him to stay on in office. He even paid off his debts of £20,000.

With the loss of America in 1782,

North finally resigned—to be labelled an ungrateful traitor by the king. And within three years, North's failing sight forced him to retire.

Cadbury Castle, *Som.* See pp. 46–47

Cadzow Castle, *Strathclyde*
The romantic position of Cadzow Castle, on a crag above the River Avon, inspired the 19th-century author Sir Walter Scott to write:

> *When princely Hamilton's*
> * abode*
> *Ennobled Cadzow's Gothic*
> * towers*
> *The song went round, the goblet*
> * flowed*
> *And revel sped the laughing*
> * hours.*

Mary, Queen of Scots, took refuge at Cadzow Castle*, stronghold of the powerful Hamilton family, after her escape from Lochleven Castle in 1568. From her base at Cadzow she attempted to save her throne against the revolt of the Earl of Moray's supporters. But at the Battle of Langside the Hamiltons ran away, and Mary fled to England. (See Carberry Hill, p. 375.)

Caerlaveroch Castle, *Dumf & Gall*
The English built Caerlaveroch Castle* late in the 13th century to command the Solway Firth.

It soon fell into the hands of the Scots, and by 1300 Edward I was forced to besiege it. For two days the English struggled to cross the bogs, moat ditches and finally the high walls. It was taken because the Scots left too few men to defend it.

Caerlaveroch was passed back and forth between the two countries over the next centuries. The Maxwell family owned it—on behalf of one side or the other—almost continuously.

In 1640 the Earl of Nithsdale, a Maxwell, held out for 13 weeks with 200 soldiers against the

Covenanters. But Caerlaveroch was eventually forced to yield, and its captors destroyed the fine furnishings of the castle.

Caerleon, *Gwent*

A permanent Roman camp, named Isca Silurum, after the local Welsh tribe, the Silures, was founded here in AD 75. It had timber buildings and earth and timber defences.

At the beginning of the 2nd century it was rebuilt in stone. The layout of the camp can still be traced in the roads and field boundaries of present-day Caerleon.

For 300 years, Isca Silurum was one of the busiest Roman settlements. It was the headquarters for one of the three legions which were quartered in Britain. From this base the legionaries manned a network of forts throughout Wales.

According to the chronicler Geoffrey of Monmouth, King Arthur was crowned at Caerleon.

PRINCE OF WALES *The future Edward VIII (centre), with his parents Queen Mary and George V, at his investiture at Caernarvon in 1911.*

Caernarvon Castle, *Gwynedd*

'Here is your prince, one who can speak neither Welsh nor English!' With these words, Edward I presented his new-born son, later Edward II, to the Welsh people at Caernarvon in 1284.

By creating a Prince of Wales, Edward was placating a conquered people, whose leader, Llewelyn ap Gruffydd, he had slain in battle. He hoped that the rule of a native-born prince would be less distasteful than that of an alien conqueror.

After his victories in Wales in

Caerphilly Castle, *Mid Glamorgan*

In 1268 Earl Gilbert de Clare built a castle at Caerphilly as a stronghold against his enemy, Llewelyn ap Gruffydd.

After construction of the castle began, Llewelyn invaded the district and destroyed it. Earl Gilbert decided to build a new fortress—the present castle*—encircled with three lines of defence. This 'concentric' design, a new development in Britain, had been used with success on the Continent.

Construction began in 1273, but once again Llewelyn attacked. This time, Earl Gilbert withstood the assault. The great Edwardian castles of Wales were modelled on Caerphilly. (See pp. 86–87.)

Calne, *Wilts*

The Witan, or king's council, met here in 978 and discussed whether priests should be allowed to marry. It is said that the debate was in full

1277, Edward I built eight new castles and strengthened many old ones throughout the country, to command his new dominions. The most important of these was the immense castle* at Caernarvon, which was not completed until 1330. (See pp. 86–87.)

In 1911, at a formal investiture ceremony at Caernarvon Castle, George V presented his son, later Edward VIII and the Duke of Windsor, as the Prince of Wales. The investiture of Prince Charles took place there in 1969.

flood when the floor gave way, injuring all those who supported a married clergy. The Archbishop of Canterbury, St Dunstan, who upheld the celibacy laws, was left sitting safely astride a beam.

Cambridge, *Cambs*

England's second university came into being almost by accident. In 1209 a riot broke out in Oxford when townsmen, resentful of the privileges of the university, stormed the student hostels. The university temporarily disbanded itself, and some of the students migrated to Cambridge, where they set up a new university. In 1228 the small community of scholars was reinforced by a new migration from Paris, where there had been similar riots. In 1318 the pope formally recognised Cambridge as a university.

Colleges were slow to appear, Peterhouse* was founded in 1284, and King's Hall (now part of Trinity College*) a few years later. Clare College* was endowed in 1326 by Lady Clare, a granddaughter of Edward I.

Relations between town and gown at Cambridge were always strained, and frequently led to bitter fighting. In 1381 the townsmen seized the opportunity presented by the Peasants' Revolt to settle old scores with the students. On the evening of June 15, when the great bell of St Mary's summoned the town to rebellion, the mob sacked Corpus Christi College*, and stole £80 worth of plate. Next morning they invaded the university library and cast the books into a bonfire in the Market Square.

Until the 16th century, few important scholars taught at Cambridge. The Dutch Renaissance scholar Erasmus was brought to the university in 1511 and took over the professorship of divinity. He introduced Greek and set up the first printing press at the university.

The ferment of ideas and rise of Protestantism led to the university becoming a stronghold of the Reformation. Leaders of the movement at Cambridge included Thomas Cranmer, the first Protestant archbishop, Nicholas Ridley and Hugh Latimer. All three were burnt—at Oxford—in the Catholic reaction under Mary Tudor.

Cambridge never lost its reputation for bold non-conformity. Isaac Newton, whose treatise on

gravitation challenged all the scientific views of his age, was a student at Trinity College, Cambridge, from 1661 to 1666.

Canterbury, *Kent*

Ever since AD 597 when St Augustine arrived with his band of missionaries, Canterbury Cathedral* has been the cradle of English Christianity. (See pp. 48–49.) The most momentous event in its history was the murder in 1170 of Thomas Becket. (See pp. 74–75.)

In 1174 the cathedral was destroyed by fire. On the afternoon of September 5 the cry went up that the church was on fire. As the monks and townsmen ran to fetch water and hatchets, the roof crashed down upon the choir stalls and set fire to the tapestries which hung on every wall. By nightfall, nothing was left of the great church but the arches of the nave.

The cathedral was rebuilt by the French architect William of Sens. As pilgrims' offerings flowed into the building fund, construction proceeded rapidly. By 1184 the monks were able to hold their first services in the completed church.

The choir of the cathedral is the burial place of the greatest English warrior of the Hundred Years' War. Edward, Prince of Wales, known to later generations as 'the Black Prince', was buried only a few feet away from St Thomas on his death in 1376

The Black Prince's tomb was to survive longer than that of the martyred archbishop. When Henry VIII waged his campaign against idolatry, Becket's shrine was removed by the royal commissioners. Its removal ended the pilgrimages which had paid for the building of the cathedral and made it the richest church in England.

WARRIOR *A 19th-century engraving of the bronze effigy on the tomb of the Black Prince at Canterbury.*

Carberry Hill, *Lothian*
Less than a month after marrying the Earl of Bothwell, Mary, Queen of Scots, was confronted at Carberry Hill, east of Edinburgh, by rebel lords objecting to the union. Mary was deserted by most of her troops and agreed to give herself up in return for Bothwell's safe conduct to Dunbar.

MARY'S DESPERATE FLIGHT FROM SCOTLAND

After the encounter with the rebel lords at Carberry Hill on June 15, 1567, Mary, Queen of Scots, was escorted to her own castle at Holyrood, then taken to Loch Leven and rowed over to the lonely island castle of Sir William Douglas.

Under pressure from the nobles she abdicated the throne and nominated her half-brother, the Earl of Moray, as regent. She was held at Loch Leven for ten months. George Douglas ('pretty Geordie'), Sir William's younger son, fell under the spell of the beautiful queen. On May 2, 1568, he helped her to escape to the mainland in disguise.

She crossed the Firth of Forth at Queensferry and slept at Lord Seton's home at Niddry Castle, near Kirkliston. The local folk welcomed her warmly, and in her haste to greet them she appeared with her auburn hair tumbling down her shoulders.

The Regent Moray was 'sore amazed' when he heard of the escape. He joined battle with her forces at Langside near Glasgow—now Queen's Park. The royalist commander, the Earl of Argyll, fainted at a critical moment, and Mary saw her army routed.

She fled 60 miles to Dumfries with Lord Herries, and rested at his castle at Corra before going on to Terregles. Of this arduous journey she later wrote: 'I have had to sleep upon the ground and drink sour milk, and eat oatmeal without bread, and have been three nights like the owls.'

She decided to seek refuge in England. Cutting her hair and in borrowed clothes and a hood, she made her way to Dundrennan Abbey, and with 20 supporters took a boat across the Solway Firth to Workington. Next day she moved on to Cockermouth and on May 18 reached Carlisle Castle—the first of her English 'prisons'. (See Fotheringhay, p. 387.)

Mary's flight. Loch Leven Castle, Firth of Forth, Edinburgh (Holyrood), Queensferry, Niddry Castle, Carberry Hill, Langside, Firth of Clyde, Terregles Castle, Dumfries, Corra Castle, Dundrennan Abbey, Carlisle, Solway Firth, Cockermouth, Workington. 0 50 miles

---

Carbisdale, *Highland*
The Marquis of Montrose's last campaign for the Royalist cause in the Civil War ended at Carbisdale on April 27, 1650.

Six years earlier, Montrose had raised the clans for Charles I and won a series of victories over the Covenanters, who supported Parliament. His support vanished when Parliament sent an army under General Leslie to Scotland. After being defeated at Philiphaugh, the marquis fled to the Continent.

In March 1650, Montrose landed in Orkney, gathered a force of 1200, and crossed to the mainland. His army, mostly untrained men, took up a strong position by the tarn of Carbisdale at the head of the Kyle of Sutherland.

Montrose's adversary, Colonel Strachan, who was moving up from Bonar Bridge, had a larger force than expected. The Orkney men were cut down by Strachan's cavalry or drowned trying to escape across the Kyle. Montrose had his horse shot from under him during the battle. The marquis escaped, but was later betrayed to the Covenanters and executed in Edinburgh.

Cardiff, *S Glamorgan*
The Norman castle* was once the prison of a rightful king of England. Upon the death of William the Conqueror, his eldest son, Robert, expected the crown, but it passed to William Rufus and then to Henry I. After years of quarrelling and fighting with his brothers, Robert was captured in battle in 1106, and Henry kept him prisoner until he died in 1134, aged about 80.

The castle was captured by the Welsh leader Owen Glendower during his revolt against Henry IV in the early 15th century.

Cardiff remained a walled township until the 17th century, but later expanded due to the coal and iron industries. It became the capital of Wales in 1955.

Carmarthen, *Dyfed*
Robert Ferrar, the Protestant Bishop of St David's, was burnt at the town cross at Carmarthen in 1555. A victim of the conflict between the Protestants and Catholics during the Reformation, he had been persecuted by both sides.

On taking up his appointment as bishop in 1548, Ferrar was suspected

MARTYR *Robert Ferrar, the Protestant Bishop of St David's, died for his faith at Carmarthen in 1555.*

of being a lukewarm Protestant by his Welsh diocese. After Ferrar exposed the financial misdeeds of the Cathedral Chapter, its members took revenge by bringing charges against him. He was tried and imprisoned for sanctioning superstitious practices.

At the accession of Queen Mary in 1553. Ferrar was still in prison. Ironically, the Catholics now persecuted him for the Protestantism which his parishoners had once found too weak.

Ferrar was condemned to death and went to the stake on March 30, 1555. A spectator in the crowd reported that the bishop spoke to him and said that 'if he saw him once to stir in the pains of his burning he should then give him no credit to his doctrine'. As the flames rose about him, Ferrar never moved. Only when a bystander struck him on the head did the bishop fall down.

Castle Rising, *Norfolk*
The castle* was built by the Normans on Roman fortifications which stand on immense prehistoric earthworks. In 1330 it became the chief residence of Queen Isabella, who lived there until her death in 1358. She was in disgrace because of her affair with Roger, Lord Mortimer, and their joint part in the downfall of her husband, Edward II, who was murdered at Berkeley Castle in 1327.

Henry Howard, 3rd Duke of Norfolk, obtained the castle in 1544, but two years later he and his son, the Earl of Surrey, angered Henry VIII by their opposition to the powerful Edward Seymour, Earl of Hertford. Father and son were imprisoned in the Tower and the earl was beheaded. The same sentence had been passed on the father, but the king died before the death warrant was signed, and his life was saved. The castle still belongs to the Norfolk family.

Chalfont St Giles, *Bucks*
The poet John Milton settled in a cottage* at Chalfont St Giles during 1665-6, while the Great Plague raged in London. (See p. 190.)

Here, Milton completed 'Paradise Lost' and began 'Paradise Regained'. His friend Thomas Ellwood, who read to Milton after he became blind in 1652, died here in 1713. Ellwood is said to have inspired 'Paradise Regained' after reading the manuscript of the first work. He said: 'Thou hast said much here of Paradise Lost, but what hast thou to say of Paradise Found?'

At Jordans, 2 miles south, are buried William Penn (1644–1718), Quaker founder of Pennsylvania, his two wives and five of his children. Penn's Quaker meeting house can still be seen.

Chalgrove Field, *Oxon*
Roundheads under Robert, Earl of Essex, clashed with Royalist cavalry led by Prince Rupert at Chalgrove Field on June 18, 1643.

Serving under Essex was Sir John Hampden, one of the leaders of the opposition to Charles I in both the Short and Long Parliaments. He fought the king over the Ship Money tax in 1636-7. (See pp. 172-3.)

Although Hampden had no military experience, he took a colonel's commission at the outbreak of the Civil War and raised an infantry regiment for the Parliamentary army. He distinguished himself at the battles of Edgehill and Reading.

Ordered to hold out at Chalgrove Field until help arrived, Hampden was badly wounded and retired to Thame, where he died six days later. His death was a blow to the Parliamentary cause, and was lamented even by the king.

Chard, *Somerset*

An early attempt at powered flight took place at Chard in 1848. In June of that year, John Stringfellow succeeded in flying his own model, a monoplane with a 10 ft wing span, inside a building at Chard. The model was powered by a light-weight steam engine which drove two twin-pusher propellers. The next year Stringfellow gave the model its first real test—an outdoor flight in London. The aeroplane was powerful enough to gain height during its flight. But after only 120 ft it crashed into a safety barrier. The remains of his 1848 model can be seen at Chard.

STEAM PLANE *The engineer John Stringfellow developed this model monoplane at Chard and flew it in London in 1849. Powered by a light-weight steam engine Stringfellow's flying machine was incapable of sustained flight, but his experiments helped advance the development of aircraft.*

Chartwell, *Kent*

For many years Chartwell* was the refuge and the inspiration of one of the greatest of English statesmen, Winston Churchill. When appendicitis prevented him from taking an active part in the general election of 1922, Churchill briefly lost his Parliamentary seat. He was, as he said, 'without an office, without a seat, without a party and without an appendix'. For a man with a varied political and military career behind him, inactivity was unthinkable. He bought Chartwell to provide himself with the setting he needed for his new life—a home where he could enjoy a variety of activities in a place which was a challenge in itself.

Chartwell was a heavily Victorianised Tudor house in a dilapidated condition with a jungle for a garden. It remained his working home for the remainder of his life. Here he wrote most of his books, painted most of his pictures and entertained most of the prominent people of the day. He greatly extended and altered the house, cleared the grounds, created lakes and built a swimming pool.

Churchill did a considerable amount of the work himself, his most notable achievement being the building of a 12 ft wall to enclose

STATESMAN AT HOME *Winston Churchill with his daughter, Mary, building a wall at Chartwell in 1928.*

300 acres of the grounds. Relatives, friends and visitors, no matter how eminent, might well find wellington boots and spades thrust into their hands before they were marched off as 'volunteers' to assist the latest of Churchill's undertakings. So closely did he identify with his home that he could say 'a day away from Chartwell is a day wasted'.

During his years in the political wilderness between 1933 and 1939, Churchill brooded on the growing power of Hitler's Germany and the impending catastrophe which he feared. He wrote letters and speeches advocating re-armament, and he prepared the policies which he put into operation when his country called on him.

Chawton, *Hants*

Between 1809 and 1817 Chawton Cottage*, then known as the Small House, was the home of the novelist Jane Austen. She moved there after several unhappy years at Bath and Southampton.

Inspired by her return to her native Hampshire, Jane soon began writing and thinking of publication. At Chawton she revised two of her manuscripts, *Elinor and Marianne* and *First Impressions*—to be published in 1811 and 1813 as *Sense and Sensibility* and *Pride and Prejudice*. There she also wrote her last three major novels, *Mansfield Park*, *Emma* and *Persuasion*.

Jane's work was widely acclaimed, but she still kept the secret of her authorship from all except her immediate family. She was dogged by ill-health and in 1817 died at Winchester, where she had gone for medical treatment. A year later, *Persuasion* and *Northanger Abbey*, begun in 1797, were published under Jane's name.

Chelmsford, *Essex*

On February 23, 1920, the first public radio broadcast in Britain was transmitted from Writtle, Chelmsford. It was the work of the Italian inventor and scientist Guglielmo Marconi, who came to England in 1896. In 1898 he established his wireless company at Hall Street, Chelmsford.

Despite the opinion of many scientists that the range of his signals could not exceed 200 miles, Marconi succeeded in making the

Cheltenham, *Glos*

The town began its rise to prominence when medicinal springs were discovered early in the 18th century, on the land of Henry Skillicorne, a retired Manx privateer. Skillicorne laid out a spa in 1738, and in 1788 George III spent five weeks there to drink the waters. This was to combat bilious attacks and fatigue brought on by the cares of office and the violent exercise he took in order to prevent corpulence.

While at Cheltenham the king, with Queen Charlotte and their daughters, stayed at Lord Fauconberg's house, Bays Hill Lodge. The journey was a great novelty to the king. Until then he had been so engrossed in his duties that he had rarely left London or Windsor. The king returned to Windsor in August, and in October, after going walking in the rain, became ill and began to show the first signs of madness.

Cheshunt, *Herts*

In 1603 James I of England and VI of Scotland was waiting with impatience for the death of Elizabeth I. Careful intrigue and the support of England's most powerful minister, Robert Cecil, had ensured that he would succeed to the vacant throne.

first trans-Atlantic broadcast in 1901. He was awarded the Nobel Prize for physics in 1907, and in 1920 his company began transmitting short programmes of music, talks and news from Chelmsford.

Among the personalities who broadcast from the station was Dame Nellie Melba, the greatest opera singer of the day. She was heard throughout Britain and much of Europe. Marconi's success was instrumental in bringing about the founding of the BBC.

INVENTOR AT WORK *The Italian Guglielmo Marconi demonstrates an early apparatus for wireless transmission, at his Chelmsford laboratory in 1902.*

At last the longed-for news was received and James set off for his new capital. At Theobalds (pronounced Tibbalds) Park, Cheshunt, one of his family estates, Cecil met his new master and entertained him with a diplomatic lavishness. The minister's support did not go unrewarded. He maintained his position as chief minister and was created Earl of Salisbury.

James took a fancy to the Tudor house and park at Theobalds, and in 1607 exchanged it with Cecil for Hatfield House. The celebrations for the house-warming included a masque written by the playwright Ben Jonson. The king frequently came to Theobalds to follow his favourite pastimes—hunting and falconry. On one occasion he entertained his Danish brother-in-law, Christian IV, at 'this most beautiful house' for what amounted to ten days of hard drinking. And it was there that James I died. Of the original palace, only the garden wall remains.

Chesterfield, *Derby*
For 1000 years Chesterfield has been an important market town, and with the coming of the railway it found new prosperity in industry. The Chesterfield line was part of the Derby to Leeds railway (afterwards known as the North Midland Line), and its building was supervised by George Stephenson, pioneer of the railway age.

During the building of the line, which began in 1837, a rich seam of coal was uncovered, and Stephenson formed a company to exploit this and the local ironstone. These were the local industries upon which the modern town was founded. While he was working in Chesterfield, Stephenson lived at Tapton House, remaining there when he retired. He died at Tapton in 1848, and is buried in Trinity Church.

Chichester, *W Sussex*
The cathedral town of Sussex has its own saint—St Richard of Chichester, born about 1197—who became Bishop of Chichester in 1245.

Bishop Richard, also known as Richard of Wyche, deprived corrupt clergy of their livings, excommunicated moneylenders, and suspended priests who mumbled or spoke too fast during services.

Renowned for the simplicity of his life, he died in 1253 and was canonised in 1262. Miraculous cures occurred at his tomb, which quickly became a place of pilgrimage. In 1276 a shrine to St Richard was consecrated in the cathedral* in the presence of Edward I. The shrine stood until the Reformation. But in 1538 Henry VIII's commissioners dismantled it and added its treasures to the royal coffers.

Claremont, *Surrey*
When Robert Clive, the great pioneer of British rule in India, returned home in 1767, he bought Claremont from the Duke of Newcastle. Clive was a wealthy man, and a large part of his fortune went into pulling down the old house and erecting a Palladian mansion*, designed for him by Lancelot 'Capability' Brown in 1772.

Unfortunately, Clive had many jealous enemies who accused him in Parliament of corruption and maladministration in Bengal. The result was a parliamentary inquiry into his conduct.

Although Clive's name was cleared of these accusations, he was a broken man. His health was poor and he suffered bouts of deep depression. On November 22, 1774, he took an overdose of opium and died at the age of 49.

Claremont's melancholy associations were not over. In 1816 the house was bought as a gift from the nation to the Prince Regent's daughter, Princess Charlotte, on the occasion of her marriage.

The public admired the princess and there was widespread rejoicing at her marriage to Prince Leopold of Saxe-Coburg. The couple settled at Claremont and Charlotte experienced the happiest period of her life. It proved all too short. Princess Charlotte died in child-birth on November 5, 1817, at Claremont.

Claydon House, *Bucks*
Florence Nightingale (1820–1910), the founder of modern nursing, was a frequent visitor to Claydon*, the home of Sir Harry Verney, who married Florence's sister, Parthenope, in 1858. The house had been the home of the Verneys since the early 17th century. The most famous of the family, Sir Edward Verney, was killed at the Battle of Edgehill.

Although forced by ill-health to lead the life of an invalid after her return from the Crimea in 1856, Florence was far from idle. A steady stream of visitors and letters seeking advice reached her from all over the world. She threw herself energetically into organising the proper training of nurses (her Nightingale Training School was opened at St Thomas's, London, in 1872). She also pressed for improvements in army medical care, sanitary reform in India, and improvement in hospital administration generally.

After his wife's death in 1890, Sir Harry Verney relied on Florence for companionship, and for the next few years she spent an increasing amount of time at Claydon.

With characteristic energy and thoroughness, Florence interested herself in the affairs of the estate and the surrounding villages. Discovering how urgently improvements were needed in rural health services, she initiated the training of Health Missioners in 1892, with the aid of the local Health Officer.

Sir Harry died in 1894, and Florence paid her last visit to Claydon in the winter of 1894–5.

Cliveden, *Bucks*
When the Astor family owned Cliveden house* before the Second World War, it was a meeting place of politicians and celebrities who became known as the 'Cliveden Set'. The vivacious Lady Astor, the first woman to take her seat in the Commons, presided over weekend gatherings which had a marked influence on foreign affairs during the 1930's.

The famous 'set' was accused of encouraging the appeasement of Hitler and Mussolini, although Lord and Lady Astor strongly denied the charge. German diplomats who met politicians such as Lord Halifax, Lord Lothian and Sir Thomas Inskip at Cliveden, came away believing that the British Establishment opposed Soviet Russia and wished to reach an understanding with Hitler's Germany. However, in 1940, Lady Astor was one of the Conservative MPs who helped bring Churchill to power.

Clouds Hill, *Dorset*
On May 13, 1935, Aircraftsman T. E. Shaw—known to the world as the First World War hero, Lawrence of Arabia—fell off his motor-cycle as he overtook two cyclists near his home, Clouds Hill, north of Bovington Camp. He died six days later.

A scholar and soldier, and author of *The Seven Pillars of Wisdom*, T. E. Lawrence had been the inspiring genius behind the Arab revolt against the Turks in the First World War. But after the war he rejected fame and rank for an obscure military career. To avoid publicity he changed his last name.

Early in the 1920's, Lawrence joined the Royal Tank Corps and was later transferred to the Royal Air Force. He was posted to Dorset and there bought a cottage* at Clouds Hill. He described it as 'very quiet, very lonely, very bare,' and the cottage remained his home until his death.

Speed was one of T. E. Lawrence's enthusiasms. The last six years of his life were spent testing, supervising and designing high-speed boats on the Solent and at Plymouth. It was while he was speeding on his motor-cycle that Lawrence suffered his fatal accident.

SHY HERO *Lawrence posed for this rare photograph, taken while he was serving in the RAF.*

Coalbrookdale, *Salop* See pp. 260–1.

Cockermouth, *Cumbria*
Fletcher Christian, first officer of the *Bounty* and leader of the mutineers against Captain Bligh, was born here in 1764.

The *Bounty* left England for Tahiti in 1787, and Bligh's harsh treatment of the crew led to his being set adrift in an open boat in the Pacific with a few loyal officers. They successfully reached Timor 4000 miles away.

Christian led the mutineers and some Polynesian women to Pitcairn Island. They destroyed the *Bounty* to cut off all links with the outside world. But there were quarrels with the natives and massacres. When an American ship called at the island 18 years later only one seaman had survived.

The poet William Wordsworth

was born at Cockermouth in 1770 and his sister Dorothy a year later. Eaglesfield, a village near by, was the birthplace of John Dalton (1766–1844), who laid the foundation of modern chemistry through his atomic theory.

Colchester, *Essex*

A thousand years before the Roman Conquest (AD 43) there was a Bronze Age settlement in the Colchester area. In the 1st century AD, the leader of the Catuvellauni tribe, Cunobelin—Shakespeare's Cymbeline—moved his capital to this ancient site. The ramparts of this British city, which was known as Camulodunum, can still be seen.

In AD 44 the city was captured by a Roman army under Emperor Claudius, who established the first Roman settlement in Britain for veteran soldiers. This walled Roman camp stood within the ramparts of the tribal capital. It had law courts, council chambers, public baths, a theatre and a temple to Emperor Claudius. The Roman town plan can still be traced in some of the streets—High Street, North Street and Head Street.

Camulodunum flourished until it was stormed, in 60, by Boudicca, queen of the Iceni tribe. The Iceni massacred the Romans and razed the city. When they were eventually defeated by the Romans, Colchester was rebuilt, but never recovered its importance. (See pp. 32–33.)

But, by the time of the Norman conquest, Colchester—known to the Saxons as Colnecester—was a thriving centre. In 1085, using Roman materials, the Normans constructed a huge castle keep*, which was twice the size of the White Tower, the keep of the Tower of London. The Normans left other legacies. St John's Abbey was built in 1086 and St Botolph's Priory*, the first Augustinian house in England, was established in 1100. The Normans also built up a thriving cloth industry.

In 1648 Colchester was besieged by Parliamentary forces, under Sir Thomas Fairfax, for 12 weeks. After the surrender of the town, the Royalist generals, Sir Charles Lucas and Sir George Lisle, were shot in the castle by a firing squad.

COLDSTREAMERS *The first regiment to wear a distinctive uniform, the Coldstream Guards as they appeared in 1650 (above) and in 1830 (right).*

Coldstream, *Borders*

In 1296 Edward I and his invading English army forded the Tweed at Coldstream, which had always been a crossing place for armies and raiding parties.

James IV of Scotland passed here on his way to his defeat at Flodden, a few miles south, in 1513. Covenanters used it to invade England in the Civil War, and General Monck took his Roundhead troops through the shallows on their way to subdue Scotland for Cromwell.

General Monck, who was later created Duke of Albemarle by Charles II, raised the Coldstream Guards for Parliament in 1650. At first known as Monck's Regiment, they acquired their present name after a stay at Coldstream in 1659–60. When quarrels between Parliament and army caused the breakdown of the Commonwealth after Cromwell's death, Monck marched his men to London. By this action, he restored order and helped pave the way for the Stuart restoration.

Coleridge Cottage, *Somerset*

On the last day of 1796 the poet Samuel Taylor Coleridge moved with his family to a cottage* at Nether Stowey, lent to him by his benefactor, Thomas Poole. During the two years of his stay Coleridge wrote two of his most famous poems, 'The Ancient Mariner' and 'Kubla Khan'.

Coleridge was born in 1772, the son of the vicar of Ottery St Mary, Devon. He was educated at Christ's Hospital and Cambridge, where he became a rationalist and a radical. After two years at Cambridge he ran away to London and enlisted in the army as Private Comberback.

His identity was discovered when he was unable to resist correcting two officers who were discussing a classical quotation. He left them 'as much astounded as if their dog had barked in Greek'.

Coleridge was always an eccentric, but after the age of 29 he became a pitiful figure because of his addiction to opium.

In the autumn of 1797, while away from home for a few days, he stayed at Culbone, probably at Ash Farm. One evening, according to Coleridge, he took 'two grams of opium to check a dysentery' and fell asleep over a book entitled *Purchas his Pilgrimage* at the line—'In Xamdu did Cublai Can build a stately Palace'. He dreamt one of the most famous poems in the English language, and after waking wrote 53 lines of 'Kubla Khan'.

Unfortunately Coleridge was interrupted in his task by an unknown person from Porlock who called on business. After the unwanted visitor left, Coleridge could not remember the ending of his poem and it remained unfinished.

Compton Castle, *Devon*

This 14th-century fortified manor house* was the family seat of Sir Humphrey Gilbert, navigator, pioneer of Newfoundland and half-brother of Sir Walter Raleigh.

In 1578 Queen Elizabeth granted her 'trusty and well-beloved servant Humphrey Gilbert' a charter which authorised him to 'discover, occupy, and possess remote heathen lands not actually possessed of any Christian prince or people, as should seem good to him or them'.

His first expedition ended in failure after eight months at sea, and it took Gilbert four years to raise enough money to fit out another expedition. He sailed from Plymouth in 1583, and two months later took possession of Newfoundland as England's first colony.

On the way home the ships met heavy weather in the Azores. As the 10 ton *Squirrel* was engulfed by waves, Gilbert shouted to the captain of the *Golden Hind,* 'We are as near to heaven by sea as by land'. That night the *Squirrel,* with Gilbert on board, was swallowed up by the sea. The *Golden Hind* reached England safely.

Coniston, *Cumbria*

Brantwood*, a simple roughcast cottage, together with 10 acres of fell country, was bought by John Ruskin, art critic, writer and social reformer, in 1871.

Ruskin had not even seen the property, but he loved the Lake District and wanted to move there from London after his mother's death. The cottage, which Ruskin described as 'a mere shed of rotten timber and loose stones', had a magnificent view of Coniston Water and the surrounding fells. He spent £4000 on enlarging and improving Brantwood, which was his home for the rest of his life.

In his early years at Brantwood, Ruskin wandered the lanes speaking to everyone he met, and calling in to chat with the village joiner, smith or boatbuilder. He loved children and would visit the local schools to see them.

Ruskin, who had been appointed the first Slade Professor of Fine Arts at Oxford in 1870, travelled frequently to lecture in London, but gradually his outbreaks of

RECLUSE *Victorian critic of art and society, John Ruskin spent his last secluded years at Coniston.*

insanity put an end to this work.

From 1884 he lived in increasing seclusion at Brantwood, and began to write his autobiography, *Praeterita*. He died early in 1890 and was buried in Coniston churchyard.

Conway, *Gwynedd*
Llewelyn ap Yorweth, called 'the Great', the most powerful medieval ruler in Wales died in Conway in 1240. A grandson of Owen Gwynedd, Llewelyn became ruler of the northern Welsh principality of Gwynedd in 1194.

In 1204, King John agreed to Llewelyn's marriage with his daughter Joan. Three years later Llewelyn conquered the neighbouring principality of Powys.

In 1215, Llewelyn sided with the English barons against King John and obtained recognition for Welsh rights in Magna Carta. In the same year he forced the surrender of many castles in South Wales. Three years later the English recognised his rule west of a line from Carmarthen to Montgomery.

A strong supporter of the monastic orders, Llewelyn took into his patronage a Cistercian abbey founded at Conway in 1185. In 1238 he himself entered the abbey, where he died two years later. The abbey was later destroyed by Henry VIII.

Richard II stayed at Conway Castle*—built by Edward I about 1283—on his return from Ireland in 1399. But he left the castle after being tricked by the Earl of Northumberland into agreeing to Henry (later Henry IV) Bolingbroke's terms. Later he was forced to abdicate after falling into an ambush of Henry's troops.

During the Civil War the castle was garrisoned for Charles I by John Williams, Archbishop of York and a native of Conway. But in 1646, after a three-month siege by the Parliamentarians, Williams arranged the castle's surrender to save it from destruction.

Corfe Castle, *Dorset*
The ruins of Corfe Castle* crown a steep hill where, 1000 years ago, a king was treacherously slain. The hill was first fortified by King Edgar, who died in 974, aged 33, leaving the crown to his eldest son, Edward. But the boy's stepmother, Elfthrith, wanted her own son, Ethelred, to have the kingdom.

One day in 978, the 18-year-old Edward called at Corfe to see little Ethelred. His stepmother met him at the gate and offered him a drink. The king, who remained mounted, accepted a glass of wine, but as he reached for it he was stabbed in the back, probably by a servant.

The king, who now lies at Shaftesbury Abbey, was canonised as Edward the Martyr, while his stepbrother became the unloved King Ethelred the Unready.

Treachery again overtook Corfe in the Civil War. The Norman castle was taken by the Roundheads in February 1645, after a prisoner had suborned some guards who seized the keep and let in the besiegers. The castle was then blown up.

Coventry, *W Midlands*
The city began when a convent was established there in the 7th century. Four hundred years later, the invading Danes destroyed it. When Leofric, Earl of Mercia, decided to rebuild, he founded a monastery, around which Coventry developed.

According to legend, Leofric imposed a heavy tax upon his tenants in 1040. His wife, Lady Godiva, pleaded with him to be more lenient. During their argument Leofric made an extravagant promise: the day that Godiva rode naked through the streets of Coventry, he would abolish the tax. When Godiva did so—covered only by her long flowing hair—the earl kept his promise to his wife.

This legend was first written down in the 13th century. It became so popular that an annual ride has been held in Coventry since 1768 to commemorate it. A statue* to Lady Godiva was put up in the 20th century by the city.

The story of the Peeping Tom was added to the Godiva legend during the reign of Charles II. According to this story, the townspeople went indoors to allow Godiva to pass unobserved. But Tom the tailor was unable to resist peeping at her as she rode by and was struck blind as a consequence of his deed.

Always famed for its crafts, Coventry ranked fourth among English cities of the Middle Ages, and wool was its most important trade. Later, it became an industrial centre, and during the Second World War, when the German air force started bombing major British cities, Coventry was one of the *Luftwaffe's* most important targets.

SURVIVING SPIRE *The 14th-century steeple of Coventry Cathedral survived the bombing of the city in 1940.*

The most devastating of all air attacks on the city came on the cold, moonlit night of November 14, 1940. The air-raid sirens were sounded at 7 o'clock. For the next 11 hours about 400 German bombers attempted to destroy the city in an all-out attack. By 3 o'clock the following morning, hundreds of uncontrollable fires were raging in Coventry.

As the bombs rained down, the fire engines were halted by the bomb craters in the streets. In many places firemen had no water to fight the flames because the exploding bombs had shattered the mains.

On the roof of the 14th-century cathedral three fire-watchers and the provost, desperately as they tried, could not stop the fires started by incendiary bombs. The bombs dropped through the roof, setting the structure on fire.

The following day, the extent of the destruction became known. Forty acres in the centre of the city had been flattened; of nearly 1000 buildings in the area only about 30 were still undamaged. There were over 500 civilians dead. Of the cathedral, only the 295 ft high spire and its chiming clock remained.

In 1954, work began on a new cathedral*, designed by Sir Basil Spence. Consecrated in 1964, the new cathedral, which stands by the shell of the old one, is a symbol of Coventry's survival.

Crichton Castle, *Lothian*
The castle* was the home of the reckless 4th Earl of Bothwell, third husband of Mary, Queen of Scots. During their brief marriage his first wife Jean Gordon, sister of the Earl of Huntly, remained there.

Bothwell could hardly turn Jean out, because her dowry had redeemed a mortgage he owed on the castle. A malicious adviser told the jealous queen that Bothwell had assured Jean that he still regarded her as his lawful wife—and Mary as his concubine.

The queen became increasingly influenced by the daring and resolute earl after her favourite, David Riccio, was murdered in her presence by Darnley, her husband, and other nobles. In 1566 her desire for revenge on him for this deed led to the conspiracy by Bothwell and other nobles to kill him at Kirk o' Fields in February 1567.

In April Bothwell carried the queen off with a show of force to Dunbar, where he forced her to agree to marry him. Bothwell had taken steps to have his marriage to Jean Gordon dissolved. A divorce was granted against him on May 3, and on May 15 he and Mary were married. She made him Duke of Orkney and Shetland.

Many of the Scottish nobility were horrified by the marriage and turned against Mary and her new husband. The queen was imprisoned, and Bothwell fled to Scandinavia, where he later died.

Culloden, *Highland*
An exhausted army of Highlanders was routed by the Duke of Cumberland's government forces on April 16, 1746—the last pitched battle on British soil. (See pp. 234–5.)

Bonnie Prince Charlie had drawn up his 5000 clansmen on Culloden, or Drummossie Muir. The 18-stone duke, later nicknamed 'Butcher' for his slaughter of the wounded and brutal suppression of the Highlanders, had celebrated his 25th birthday two days before, and was four months younger than the Stuart prince.

His efficient artillery pounded the badly placed supporters of the prince, who were outnumbered by nearly two to one. In a desperate charge which burst through the government front line, the clansmen on the right wing died in their hundreds under a hail of musket balls, and on the points of English bayonets.

On the prince's left wing, the Clan Donald regiments were left isolated, and had to meet an attack from two sides. Their leader,

Keppoch, died sword in hand. The whole Highland line was soon in full retreat, mercilessly harried by Cumberland's dragoons.

The prince eventually escaped into exile, having lost 1200 men against only 76 of the English. The defeat extinguished the last Stuart hope of regaining the crown, and hastened the breakup of the clan system.

ESCAPE INTO EXILE

After Prince Charles Edward Stuart was led in tears from Culloden by his faithful followers, he roamed the Highlands and islands with a price of £30,000 on his head.

In the small hours of April 17—the day after his defeat—his party reached Invergarry, rested, and rode along Loch Arkaig for a night at Glenpean. They left their horses and continued less noticeably on foot.

The prince was persuaded to make for the Hebrides and await rescue by a French ship. On April 25 he and four friends were rowed for 70 stormy miles to Rossinish in Benbecula.

The prince was welcomed almost everywhere, but had to turn back from Stornoway in Lewis because the local people feared punishment by the English troops. The prince made for remote Glen Corodale in South Uist, where he was able to relax for three weeks and even went shooting

and fishing. At midnight on June 21 he secretly met 23-year-old Flora MacDonald from Skye, who was visiting relatives. Though at first reluctant, she agreed to help him to get to Skye, as hopes of a ship from the islands had gone.

Flora secured a pass for herself and 'Betty Burke', her maid, who was the disguised prince.

From Benbecula the prince was rowed over the sea to Skye. At Kilbride they came across militia and Flora made conversation with their officer while 'Betty' slipped away. At Portree the prince bade farewell to Flora and gave her his portrait in a gold locket.

Six days later he crossed Skye and embarked at Elgol for Mallaig. For two months he was on the run until, early on September 20, he boarded a French ship in Loch nan Uamh and sailed away from Scotland for ever.

Cumnor Hall, *Oxon*

In 1560 Cumnor Hall was the scene of tragedy. Robert Dudley, later Earl of Leicester, was 28, a handsome, charming courtier, and Elizabeth I was in love with him. There was only one problem—Robert was already married.

Dudley's wife, Amy Robsart, stayed mainly in the country. On

September 8, 1560, Amy's servants returned to Cumnor from an outing to Abingdon Fair and found their mistress lying at the foot of the main staircase with a broken neck.

It seems now that Amy may have been suffering from advanced cancer of the breast, which caused a spontaneous fracture of the spine.

Dudley's many enemies spread

rumours that he had engineered the murder of his wife, and abroad it was even suggested that Elizabeth I had been involved as an accomplice.

D

Darlington, *Durham*

The railway age was born at Darlington on September 27, 1825, when George Stephenson drove his steam locomotive *Active* (later re-

Dartmouth, *Devon*

Dartmouth owed its early importance to its deep-water harbour sheltered by a circle of hills. An international fleet assembled there in 1147 to embark on the Second Crusade, against the Turks in the Holy Land. Richard I's squadron sailed from there for the Third Crusade in 1190, and in 1944 part of the Allied fleet sailed from Dartmouth for the Normandy landings.

Dartmouth's importance declined with the loss of England's French possessions in the 15th century. This ended the wine trade with France, which had flourished since Henry II's time.

But the port gained prominence again in Elizabethan times. The harbour was used by famous sailors and explorers, who explored the world for their queen and country. They included Sir Walter Raleigh,

named *Locomotion No. 1*) along the 38 mile track to the quayside at Stockton, on the River Tees. It was the first public passenger railway in the world.

The single track of the Stockton and Darlington Railway went beyond Darlington to Shildon in the Durham coalfield. There were passing bays every quarter of a mile. In its early years the 20 mph locomotive was used only for pulling goods, and passengers were drawn along by a horse. Where there were steep descents, the horse trotted behind the coaches or was carried on a special wagon. Stephenson and his son, Robert, went on to build many other lines.

INVENTOR *George Stephenson and his first steam locomotive,* Locomotion No. 1, *which can still be seen on Bank Top station platform at Darlington.*

his half-brother Sir Humphrey Gilbert, and John Davis, who explored the Labrador and Newfoundland coasts and discovered the Davis Strait.

Darvel, *Strathclyde*

In his later years Sir Alexander Fleming (1881–1955), discoverer of penicillin, gave credit to his birthplace on a sheep farm near Darvel for two of his qualities. His stamina, he said, came from the outdoor life of his boyhood, and the foundations of his learning were laid in his study of the catechism.

At 14, after 18 months at Kilmarnock Academy, he went to London, where he worked as a shipping clerk before enrolling at St Mary's Hospital medical school.

Fleming described his discovery of penicillin as 'a triumph of accident and shrewd observation'.

One day in 1928, while working in the laboratory at St Mary's, Fleming by chance exposed a culture plate of bacteria to the air. Later, he noticed that a mould had grown on the plate and destroyed the bacteria around it. After further experiments with this mould, Fleming produced penicillin—which destroys disease-producing bacteria—and thereby opened a new era in medicine.

The drug was perfected in 1940, in time to save thousands of lives during the Second World War. In 1945 Fleming and his fellow workers, Sir Howard Florey and Sir E. B. Chain, were awarded the Nobel Prize for medicine.

Denbigh Castle, *Clwyd*

Denbigh Castle*—a fortress dating from the reign of Edward I—became one of the last remaining strongholds of the Royalists during the Civil War.

After his defeat at Rowton Moor, outside Chester, Charles I stayed at Denbigh Castle for two nights before fleeing to Scotland. Colonel William Salesbury and the rest of the king's supporters were left to face Cromwell's forces.

The Parliamentarians besieged Denbigh Castle for 11 months. After surrendering in 1646, Salesbury mounted the Goblin Tower next to the castle and hurled the key of the fortress down into the moat. He shouted at the Roundheads in Welsh: 'The world is yours—make it your dung house.'

Derby, *Derbys*

In 1717 Derby won a place in British industrial history when the first true factory in the country—a silk mill—was built by Thomas Lombe. Thomas first sent his half-brother, John, to Italy, to learn the secrets of silk manufacturing, and then they built a five-storey building, whose working areas were lit by 500 windows. In the centre a water wheel, 18 ft in diameter, driven by the River Derwent, powered 26,000 machine wheels.

In the 1750's Derby began to produce high-quality porcelain and chinaware under the skilful direction of William Duesbury.

In 1906 the rapidly expanding car firm of Rolls-Royce moved from Manchester to a new site at Derby, and by the 1930's the town had become the centre of the aero-engineering industry. The Rolls-Royce Merlin engine, which powered the Spitfire and Hurricane fighters that won the Battle of Britain, was made there.

LADY WITH A LUTE
Derby has been famed for its porcelain since the middle of the 18th century. Among the early popular productions of the Derby porcelain-makers were modelled figures, such as this lady with a lute.

Devizes, *Wilts*

The castle at Devizes, built by the powerful Bishop Roger of Salisbury soon after the Norman Conquest, was seized by King Stephen during his struggle with Matilda. Refortified during the Civil War and held for the king, the castle was captured by Cromwell's forces in 1645 and later destroyed.

The Kennet and Avon Canal, which passes through the town, was the work of the Scottish engineer John Rennie (1761–1821). Outside the town, the canal is carried up Caen Hill by a spectacular series of 29 locks.

The father of the painter Sir Thomas Lawrence (1769–1830) kept the Black Bear Inn. Thomas, a precocious child, entertained guests at the age of five by reciting passages from the poetry of Milton and Pope, and drawing their portraits. His career as a fashionable portrait-painter culminated in his election as President of the Royal Academy in 1820.

Dorchester, *Dorset*

Thinly veiled as 'Wessex', the setting of Thomas Hardy's novels was Dorset and the surrounding countryside. Its capital 'Casterbridge', was Dorchester.

Hardy was born in a cottage* at nearby Higher Bockhampton, educated at local schools and apprenticed to a Dorchester architect.

In 1883 Hardy built himself a house, Max Gate, on the outskirts of the town. Here, where he lived for 44 years until his death in 1928, he wrote some of his greatest works, including *Tess of the D'Urbervilles* (1891) and *Jude the Obscure* (1896).

In 1685 the men of Dorchester took part in Monmouth's rebellion against James II. At Dorchester alone more than 300 were tried by the notorious Judge Jeffreys at the Bloody Assizes. Almost 300 were sentenced to death; 74 were hanged and 175 were transported.

In 1834 six labourers from the nearby village of Tolpuddle were tried in Dorchester for organising an agricultural trade union. Unions were no longer illegal; but the men were charged under the Unlawful Oaths Act of 1797 for a harmless initiatory ritual. The key witness, James Locke, described how he had been taken to the cottage of the organiser, George Loveless, and made to swear an oath which he did not understand.

A reduction in the men's wages, from 8s. to 7s. a week when they asked for a rise, had brought their families near starvation. But local farmers were alarmed and a hostile judge sentenced the men to be transported to Tasmania for seven years.

Persistent agitation caused the Home Secretary to remit the remainder of their sentences two years later. But it was only after reading an old newspaper in 1838 that the six 'Tolpuddle martyrs' realised that they were free to return to England.

Dover, *Kent*

One of William the Conqueror's first acts after the Battle of Hastings in 1066 was to capture Dover and refortify its castle*.

The present castle was built by Henry II, who spent £7000—about 70 per cent of his annual income—on it. It was completed by his son, King John. Dover Castle, though often attacked, was never stormed.

In May 1670 the castle was the setting for diplomatic intrigue. In utmost secrecy, four ministers of Charles II and the diplomatic agents of Louis XIV signed the Treaty of Dover. In return for a handsome subsidy, the impoverished Charles agreed to turn Roman Catholic and to support Louis' plans for European supremacy.

The intermediary between the two kings was Charles's favourite sister, Henrietta Anne, called 'Minette'. She was a Catholic, who was married to Louis' brother, the Duke of Orleans.

But Charles, well aware that he could not keep the Catholic part of the treaty, lost all interest in fulfilling his part of the bargain after Minette's sudden death from consumption a few weeks later. And when Louis realised he had been deceived, the payments stopped.

Matthew Webb, a 27-year-old Merchant Navy captain, was the first man to swim the English Channel without a life-jacket. On August 24, 1875, Webb, covered in a layer of insulating porpoise grease, stepped into the sea beside Admiralty Pier, Dover. Almost 22 hours later he reached Cap Gris Nez on the coast of France, having used only the breast-stroke to make his $39\frac{1}{2}$ mile crossing.

FIRST MAN *Captain Matthew Webb's heroic feat of swimming the Channel was depicted even on matchboxes.*

Down House, *Gtr London*

From 1842 until he died in 1882, Charles Darwin lived in this house* in the village of Downe. Between 1844 and 1858 he wrote *The Origin of Species,* which overturned the Victorians' belief that man had a special place in creation.

Darwin at first considered Down House ugly and its garden bleak, but he grew fond of it. 'Its chief merit is its extreme rurality. I think I never was in a more perfectly quiet country,' he wrote to his cousin.

Between the several short periods a day Darwin spent working he tended his pigeons and fowls, or lay on a sofa listening to novels read aloud by his wife. Owing to chronic ill health Darwin seldom left home, but maintained a steady stream of correspondence with the leading scientists of the day.

Drayton Bassett, *Staffs*
Sir Robert Peel, who was Prime Minister in 1834–5, 1839 and 1841–6, spent his boyhood at Drayton, near Tamworth, and always regarded it as his home. His father, a wealthy textile manufacturer, built a magnificent manor house, now demolished, on the estate.

When his father died in 1830, Peel and his wife settled at Drayton. But he was forced by his political duties to spend much of his time in London. As Home Secretary, he founded the first efficient London police force in 1829. The police were called 'bobbies' after Peel's nickname. In the 1840's, Peel was converted to Free Trade, but in pursuit of his policies, he split the Tory Party and fell from power. Only the 'Peelites', remained loyal to him.

Peel died in July 1850, after falling from his horse while riding in London, and was buried in the church at Drayton Bassett.

Dunbar, *Lothian*
On September 2, 1650, a despondent English army of 14,000 men under Oliver Cromwell, hemmed in between the open sea and 27,000 Scots above Dunbar, faced starvation or surrender. The Scottish general, David Leslie, rashly left his strong position and went down to meet the Roundheads. Cromwell launched a dawn attack on September 3. Within an hour his troops had inflicted 3000 casualties on the Scots and taken 10,000 prisoners, for the loss of 22 men.

The battle was the beginning of the end for the Scottish Covenanters, and for Charles II's hopes of being restored by them. Cromwell had tried to reason with this sect. 'I beseech you in the bowels of Christ,' he begged them, 'think it possible that you may be mistaken.'

Dunbar has had a turbulent history. Edward I, 'Hammer of the Scots', smashed a Scottish army at Spott, just south of Dunbar, in 1296. His son, Edward II, fled to Dunbar in 1314 to take ship for England, after defeat by Robert Bruce at Bannockburn. In 1338 'Black Agnes', the Countess of Dunbar, held the castle* against the English.

Mary, Queen of Scots, fled to Dunbar Castle in 1566 with her husband, Darnley, after the murder of her favourite, Riccio. After Darnley's murder in the following year, James Hepburn, the Earl of Bothwell, the main suspect in the crime, carried Mary off to Dunbar. They were married three weeks later in Edinburgh, but soon their cause met with disaster at Carberry Hill. (See p. 375.)

Bothwell fled to Dunbar, and then made his way to Norway. He was imprisoned at Dragsholm Castle in Denmark. For nine years his only activity was walking around the pillar to which he was chained. Before he died in prison in 1578, his strong nerve broke and he went insane.

DEFEATED CONSORT *Pursued by the Scottish nobility, the Earl of Bothwell fled from Dunbar to Scandinavia.*

Dundee, *Tayside*
The city was ravaged by English armies from the time of Edward I onwards. John of Gaunt destroyed it in 1385; it was plundered during Henry VIII's wars; a Royalist general, the Marquis of Montrose, sacked it in 1645; and in 1651 the Roundhead General Monck pillaged it, and killed 1000 people.

The dashing Scottish soldier, John Graham of Claverhouse, Viscount Dundee, lived at Dunhope Castle near the city from 1685 until 1688. After fighting for William of Orange, Claverhouse returned to Scotland to command the royal troops against the Covenanters. He was defeated by their army at Drumclog on June 1, 1679, but took part in the Duke of Monmouth's victory over them at Bothwell Brig 22 days later. Claverhouse's ruthless campaign against the Covenanters

DASHING SOLDIER *John Graham of Claverhouse raised the standard for James II against William and Mary.*

during the 'killing time' of 1679–88 earned him many honours. He became a hereditary constable of Dundee in 1683, and James II of England (VII of Scotland) made him Viscount Dundee in 1688.

A year later, when the Scots parliament declared that James had forfeited the Scots throne, Claverhouse raised a Highland army against William and Mary. At the Pass of Killiecrankie, he defeated the government forces under General Hugh Mackay. But, at the moment of victory, Claverhouse was mortally wounded and the rising of the Highlanders collapsed. (See Dunkeld, this page; also Killiecrankie, p. 393.)

Dunfermline, *Fife*
The town became the capital of Scotland during the reign of Malcolm III (1057–93), and succeeded Iona as the traditional burial place of the Scots kings.

Malcolm, called in Gaelic 'Canmore' (great head), slew Macbeth, who had slain his father Duncan in 1057. He and his Saxon queen, Margaret, a refugee from the Norman invaders of England, were married in 1070, in a chapel on the site of which she founded Dunfermline Abbey.

The saintly Margaret helped to civilise the primitive court and society of old Scotland: through her influence, English customs spread, and the declining Celtic Church was supplanted by the authority of Rome. Margaret fed orphans with her own spoon, and washed the feet of the poor. She revived the custom of giving thanks to God after meals, and the grace cup is still known in Scotland as St Margaret's Blessing.

The queen died after learning of the death of Malcolm and one of her sons while on a raid into England. Malcolm and Margaret were buried in the abbey, and in 1250 she was canonised by the pope.

Dunfermline Palace* (now in ruins) remained a favourite royal residence for centuries, and was the birthplace of Charles I in 1600. Here, in 1651, before his march to defeat at Worcester, Charles II was obliged to humble himself, in order to gain the allegiance of the Scots. They forced him to accept the Solemn League and Covenant of 1643—an agreement between England and Scotland to establish Presbyterianism in both countries. He also had to sign the humiliating Dunfermline Declaration. In this he had to concede that his father was to blame for the bloodshed of the Civil War, and that his mother, Henrietta Maria, as a Catholic, was guilty of idolatry. After his dealings with the Covenanters, Charles is said to have regretted that he had ever been born.

Dunkeld, *Tayside*
Five thousand victorious Highland clansmen, searching for their Covenanting enemies after Killiecrankie (1689), found that 1200 Cameronians, a newly formed Lowland regiment, had taken up position near the ruined Dunkeld Cathedral*. A terrible battle raged through the small burgh. Nearly every house was burnt. Lead was stripped from roofs to provide ammunition.

The Cameronians, despite the loss of their young colonel, the poet William Cleland, held on so grimly that the Highlanders gave up the struggle and retreated.

Dunnottar Castle, *Grampian*
The 7th Earl Marischal of Scotland watched from this fortress* in 1645 as troops of the Royalist Marquis of Montrose set his estates ablaze. The earl, who had shut himself up in the castle with 15 Presbyterian preachers, was comforted by one of them with the words: 'The reek will be a sweet-smelling savour in the nostrils of the Lord.'

In 1651 Dunnottar held out for eight months against Cromwell's troops before surrendering. But the prizes that the English hoped to find—the Scottish regalia and the private papers of the exiled Charles II—had been smuggled out of

Dunnottar Castle during the siege.

Anne Lindsay, a kinswoman of the governor's wife, left the castle with the papers stitched into a belt. The regalia were lowered over the wall to a serving woman, pretending to gather seaweed, who hid them in her basket. They remained concealed under the floor of the parish church at Kinneff, a few miles away, until the Restoration of 1660, and are now in Edinburgh Castle.

A terrible moment in the history of Dunnottar Castle came in 1685, during the rebellion of Monmouth and Argyll. A group of 122 men and 45 women—all zealous Covenanters—were herded into the dungeon, now known as the Whig's Vault.

Packed tight, the captives could not sit, lean or lie down, and many of them died. Some took the oaths of allegiance required of them to gain their freedom, but the others were sent into exile.

Dunstable, *Beds*
In 1533 Archbishop Cranmer held a court in the Lady Chapel of Dunstable Priory, for the divorce of Catharine of Aragon. The proceedings lasted two weeks.

On May 23 Cranmer pronounced the dissolution of the marriage between Henry VIII and Catharine, and confirmed the legality of the king's marriage to Anne Boleyn. Catharine stubbornly refused to take any part in the divorce proceedings. (See Buckden, p. 372.)

Dunstable was founded by the Romans who set up a small posting station at the point where Watling Street crossed the prehistoric Icknield Way. In 1132 Henry I founded an Augustinian priory, around which the town developed, and built a palace at nearby Kingsbury.

Dunwich, *Suffolk*
During a great storm of 1740, the town of Dunwich, the former capital of East Anglia, was almost completely destroyed by the sea.

In the early 7th century the Saxon king, Sigeberht, made Dunwich the centre of his kingdom. By 1086, the town had a bishop's palace, a mint and many richly appointed mansions belonging to local merchants.

Dunwich was one of the leading ports on the English east coast when the sea began slowly eroding the shore in the 11th century. The first storm, in 1287, caused havoc, and

the harbour was wrecked in 1347. Twenty years later 400 houses were overwhelmed by the waves, and by the end of the 14th century half of the town had disappeared.

These disasters reduced Dunwich from a prosperous town to a decaying village. Its fishing industry was ruined. In 1600 the town lost its economic importance when the market place vanished beneath the sea. The last church disappeared early this century. Only a few houses and a graveyard now remain.

Durham, *Durham*
In an age when bishops were powerful, none was greater than the prince-bishops of Durham. They defended by force of arms much of the border with Scotland. They conducted their own courts and minted their own money. The king's writ had no force in the Palatinate of Durham.

The bishops were well suited to their high office. William of St Carileph, who began to build the present cathedral in the 11th century, thought nothing of challenging William the Conqueror, and proudly boasted that he was exempt from the king's justice. Ranulf Flambard, the close confidant and minister of William Rufus and scourge of his fellow churchmen, was Bishop of Durham.

Two centuries later, Bishop Anthony Bek led his troops into battle against the Scots and twice defied the might of Edward I. 'The bishop,' proclaimed Bek's steward, 'is king in his own diocese.'

The present cathedral* was begun in the closing years of the 11th century. It was the first church in Europe to be built with pointed arches and ribbed vaulting. This was the first hint of the Gothic style which was to conquer the Christian world in the years to come. It was a seat fit for England's mightiest prelates. (See pp. 70–71.)

Dynevor Castle, *Dyfed*
Rhodri Mawr—Roderick the Great —who united Wales in the 9th century, built Dynevor Castle in 876 for his son, Cadell, whom he made ruler of Deheubarth (South Wales). From that time the castle became the residence of the Princes of Deheubarth. The old castle now lies in ruins and the present castle was built in 1856.

Late in the 12th century, the Welsh

hero Lord Rhys lived at Dynevor. Because he had become a menace to the English, Henry II determined to force him into obedience.

Rhys's men were afraid of the freckled-faced English king, because an ancient prophecy foretold that a freckled-faced man who crossed the ford of Pencarn would bring disaster to the Welsh.

Rhys was encouraged when Henry's army crossed the river at another point. But his relief was short-lived. A trumpet blast frightened the king's horse. Bolting along the river bank, the horse plunged into the water at Pencarn ford. After this incident, Lord Rhys paid homage to the king, who made him Justice of Deheubarth. South Wales prospered, and Lord Rhys encouraged a revival of the arts.

Towards the end of his reign, two of Rhys's sons rebelled, imprisoning their father and their brother, Howell, at Dynevor Castle. The brothers blinded Howell, but he knew the castle so well that he was able to find his father and release him. After escaping, Lord Rhys and his son recaptured the castle.

Eastchurch, *Kent*
The early pioneer air pilots, such as Moore-Brabazon, Rolls and Sopwith, made many flights from Eastchurch. They flew over the Swale, between the Isle of Sheppey and the Kentish mainland, and off Leysdown at the eastern end of Sheppey.

In 1909, at Shell Beach, near Leysdown, J. T. C. Moore-Brabazon, later Lord Brabazon, became the first pilot to fly a British-built aeroplane for a circular flight of 1 mile. He went on to fly 2 miles in $2\frac{1}{2}$ minutes at varying heights up to 30ft.

Winston Churchill learnt to fly at Eastchurch. In 1910 Short Brothers set up their workshops at the aerodrome. They built many flying-boats which they tested on the Swale. During the Second World War the

aerodrome was taken over by the Royal Air Force, and suffered heavy raids by German aircraft during the Battle of Britain.

Ecclefechan, *Dumf & Gall*
The historian Thomas Carlyle (1795–1881) was born here in a house* built by his father and uncle, who were master masons. The village is the 'Entepfuhl' of his satirical essay, *Sartor Resartus*.

Carlyle, who was a schoolmaster in his early years, wrote his first book, a life of the German poet Schiller, in 1825. His chief works were a work on the French Revolution and a life of Frederick the Great.

His wife, Jane Welsh, a doctor's daughter, suffered much from his gloom and ill-temper during the 40 years of their marriage. They were devoted to each other, but Carlyle often masked his affection for her by his gruff behaviour

She was a woman of wit and beauty, who enjoyed the social life of London. He preferred to shut himself away from the world for hours in a soundproof room at the top of their house in Chelsea, London.

Research was often a dreary burden; Carlyle complained of his thoughts 'all inarticulate, sour, fermenting, bottomless'. He was afflicted by dyspepsia, 'a rat gnawing at the pit of my stomach'. Bouts of sleeplessness and the crowing of 'demon fowls' from his neighbours' gardens drove him to distraction.

The sudden loss of his wife in 1866 was a bitter blow. She was found sitting dead in her carriage one day, just after her dog had been knocked down by another vehicle. Carlyle realised too late how much distress he had caused her, and made a yearly pilgrimage to her tomb.

LITERARY GIANT *Born in Ecclefechan, Thomas Carlyle was a major figure of 19th-century letters.*

Edinburgh, *Lothian*
Built on seven hills, Edinburgh has been Scotland's capital for 500 years. Its boundaries extend from the Firth of Forth to the Pentland Hills. Much of the city's grace and dignity derives from the 18th-century streets, squares and crescents of New Town, but its heart is the Royal Mile, linking Holyrood Palace with Castle Rock, the nucleus around which the city grew.

Edinburgh Castle
From its foundation on Castle Rock in the 12th century, Edinburgh Castle* has been the focus of many events in Scottish history.

In 1440 Chancellor Crichton lured his chief rivals, the young Earl of Douglas and his brother, to a banquet there and then treacherously had them beheaded. Half a century later the Duke of Albany, who had been imprisoned by his brother, James III, escaped over the battlements on a knotted rope.

In a small room looking south from the castle, on June 19, 1566, Mary, Queen of Scots, gave birth to a boy. She said: 'This is the son who, I hope, shall first unite the two kingdoms of Scotland and England.' Her wish came true, for the boy was to be crowned James VI of Scotland and James I of England.

Seven years after James was born, William Kirkcaldy of Grange fought desperately to save Edinburgh Castle for Queen Mary against rebel lords. After four months the castle fell, and Kirkcaldy was hanged. During the siege the Earl of Morton bombarded the castle. Later he rebuilt it and added the massive Half Moon Battery.

When Jacobite rebels seized Edinburgh in 1745, the British troops held the castle against them. If the Highlanders had gained access, they might have found the Scottish crown jewels, locked in a cellar. The treasures were discovered by Sir Walter Scott in 1818, and are on display.

Royal Mile
Until the 18th century the Royal Mile was the scene of turbulent upheavals in Edinburgh's life.

In 1520 the Hamiltons, followers of the Earl of Arran, and the Douglases, supporters of the Earl of Angus, met in the narrow street known as Blackfriars Wynd. Neither of the rival families would yield the crown of the road to the other. The resulting skirmish, known as the 'Cleanse the Causeway' riot, led to the Douglases gaining control of Scottish affairs.

Through these same wynds and closes Deacon William Brodie pursued the life of crime which brought him to the gallows in 1788. A respected town councillor and cabinetmaker by day, at night Brodie used impressions that he had taken of his customers' keys to burgle their houses. His career gave Robert Louis Stevenson the idea for *Dr Jekyll and Mr Hyde.*

In 1637 an Edinburgh woman, Jennie Geddes, struck a blow for religious liberty. At St Giles Kirk*, the Anglican order of service was being used when, seizing her stool, Jennie hurled it at the minister's head with the shout, 'Ye'll naesay your mass in my lug!'

A more vigorous protest by the citizens of the Old Town occurred outside St Giles in 1736—the Porteous Riot. A smuggler had earned popular sympathy by robbing the customs house, and when he was being hanged the mob began to throw stones. Captain Porteous, commander of the City Guard, opened fire and killed several townsfolk. He was tried and sentenced to death, but reprieved. The incensed crowd stormed the prison, dragged out Porteous and hanged him.

Princes Street and the New Town
Between 1767 and 1800 the New Town was built as a suburb of the city, with Princes Street as its main thoroughfare. James Craig, a young local architect, prepared the design, which was given its finishing touch by the Adam brothers.

People were reluctant to move beyond the protecting wall of the medieval city until £20 was offered to the first person to build a house in the New Town. Only then did fashionable society make the move.

As the New Town was being built, Edinburgh's importance as an 18th-century cultural centre grew. It produced a brilliant galaxy of men, including Adam Smith, the founder of political economy, the philosopher David Hume, and the engineer Thomas Telford.

Holyrood Palace
According to legend, the Abbey of Holyrood was founded by David I. Thrown from his horse in the marshy land where the abbey now

A KING IN PLAID *Dressed in a kilt, George IV delighted the people of Edinburgh during his 1822 visit.*

stands, the king was about to be gored by a stag when a miraculous vision of a cross appeared between its antlers, at which the animal bounded away. In gratitude the king founded the great church and monastery of the 'holy rood', or cross.

Mary, Queen of Scots, spent the greater part of her troubled reign at the royal palace*, which James IV began developing from the abbey guesthouse in 1501.

In 1745 royal ceremonial was briefly revived at Holyrood for the Jacobite court of Bonnie Prince Charlie. 'He came to the royal palace,' wrote an eyewitness, 'amidst a vast crowd of spectators who, from town and country, flocked to see this uncommon sight, expressing their joy and surprise by long and loud huzzas.'

From Holyrood, on September 20, 1745, Prince Charles marched out to meet the Hanoverian army at Prestonpans; and to the palace he returned victorious next day.

A similar reception greeted George IV on his arrival at Holyrood in 1822, the first official royal visit for two centuries. The king wore pink silk tights and an extremely short kilt. 'As he is to be with us so short a time,' said one Scots lady, 'the more we see of him the better!' It was Queen Victoria who established the present pattern of annual royal visits to Scotland.

Duddingston Village
The churchyard of Duddingston Village was a favourite hunting ground for body-snatchers in the early 19th century. They stole freshly buried corpses to sell to the anatomists, such as the surgeon Dr Robert Knox, at the University of Edinburgh. The array of iron grilles guarding the graves bears witness to this gruesome business.

Doctors did not inquire into the source of bodies which were used for dissection. In particular, an Irish labourer, William Burke, and his accomplice, William Hare, made a handsome profit from body-snatching and selling corpses.

At first Burke and Hare robbed fresh graves. But as the authorities took more precautions to prevent grave-robbing, these so-called 'Resurrection men' turned to murder. Helped by their wives, they lured 15 people to their deaths before discovery. In 1829 Hare, the more villainous of the two, turned king's evidence and Burke's career ended on the scaffold.

On one occasion a life was saved. When John Samuel and Martin Eccles broke into a coffin late one night, the corpse sat up and sneezed. The robbers fled, and the supposedly dead woman lived for several years.

VILLAINY *The gruesome trade of body-snatchers in 19th-century Edinburgh, shown in this contemporary engraving, was stopped in the 1830's.*

Colinton and Swanston

In the hills on the southern outskirts of Edinburgh is Colinton village, where the 19th-century poet and novelist Robert Louis Stevenson spent each summer of his boyhood at his grandfather's house. When he was older he lived at Swanston, 2 miles towards the hills. 'The road goes down through a valley and then finally begins to scale the main slope of the Pentlands,' he wrote. 'A banquet of old trees stands round a white farmhouse, and from a neighbouring dell you can see smoke rising and leaves ruffling in the breeze. This, with the hamlet lying behind, unseen, is Swanston.'

Throughout his later life, Stevenson looked back nostalgically to the peace of Swanston Cottage.

AN EXILE'S HOME *The novelist Robert Louis Stevenson (left), forced to leave Scotland because of ill-health, looked back nostalgically to his home at Swanston (above).*

Elstow, *Beds*

Born in 1628, John Bunyan, the author of *The Pilgrim's Progress,* grew up in Elstow, 2 miles south of Bedford. He was educated at a village school. After being drafted into the Parliamentary army in 1644, Bunyan returned to Elstow in June 1647 to become a tinker. Two years later he married a girl from the village.

During this time, Bunyan underwent a spiritual conflict, described in his autobiography, *Grace Abounding,* and changed from a lively and roisterous young man to a sober Puritan. (See p. 191.)

Ely, *Cambs.*

Saxon resistance to the Normans was centred on Ely, then an island amid the fens. The Saxon leader was Hereward the Wake, who cut his way through William the Conqueror's besieging troops, and vanished from history after 1072.

The cathedral*, on the site of a monastery founded in the 7th century by St Ethelreda, or Aethelthryth, daughter of a king of East Anglia, was begun in 1083, and work went on until the 16th century. An annual fair was held on the feast day of St Ethelreda, or St Awdrey as she became known, at which cheap trinkets were sold. From these trinkets is derived the word 'tawdry', an abbreviation of St Awdrey.

Epworth, *Humberside*

John Wesley, the leader of Methodism, was born on June 17, 1703, the 15th of 19 children. His father, Samuel Wesley, rector of Epworth, was a stern man, whose religious and political convictions brought him into conflict with parishioners. In 1709 a furious mob burnt down the Wesley home. It is said that John was rescued by his nurse only moments before the roof collapsed. Despite this incident, the Old Rectory* was rebuilt, and Samuel remained at Epworth until his death.

At Oxford in 1720, John joined a religious group formed there by his brother Charles. The members were derisively called 'Methodists', because of their strict religious observance.

Evesham, *Herefs & Worcs*

On August 4, 1265, Simon de Montfort and his supporters were defeated at Evesham by Henry III's son, Prince Edward, later Edward I. Two years before, the barons under Simon de Montfort had revolted against Henry III, and had captured the king and the prince at the Battle of Lewes. But after the revolt, the barons in the west refused to accept de Montfort's lead.

In April 1265 de Montfort marched towards the Welsh borders. At Hereford, Prince Edward escaped from imprisonment and joined his allies.

Prince Edward marched 40 miles overnight from Worcester to Kenilworth, where de Montfort's son was staying. He attacked at dawn, routing the unprepared force and taking the de Montfort banners. Carrying these banners at the head of his forces, Edward intercepted de Montfort at Evesham.

At first de Montfort believed that it was his son advancing towards him. When he realised that the prince had tricked him, he was trapped by the River Avon. His allies deserted him, and he died fighting as Edward's larger force surrounded and crushed his army.

Exeter, *Devon*

An ill-equipped force of 6000 stood before the gates of Exeter in September 1497. Their leader was Perkin Warbeck, a 23-year-old from Flanders, who claimed to be Richard of York, son of Edward IV, and the younger of the two princes in the Tower. The pretender to the English throne received support from the courts of Europe, who wished to embarrass Henry VII.

After landing at Whitesand Bay, near Land's End in Cornwall, the pretender raised an army and marched towards Exeter. But, on learning of the approach of the Earl of Devonshire, Perkin withdrew to Taunton, where he abandoned his followers to their fate.

Perkin finally surrendered to Henry VII who at first treated him with clemency, and he was lodged in the Tower. But, after a foolish attempt at seizing the Tower, he was hanged at Tyburn in 1499.

Perkin Warbeck's assault on Exeter was only one of many which the city has suffered. It was stormed by the Danes in AD 876, and two centuries later it yielded to William the Conqueror.

The Roundheads occupied Exeter at the outbreak of the Civil War, but it was later taken by the Royalists, led by Prince Maurice, in 1643. Charles I's daughter Henrietta was born there in 1644. Many of its historic buildings were destroyed by German bombing in 1942.

Falkirk, *Central*

Edward I marched north in 1298 with 2500 cavalry and 16,000 foot, mostly from Ireland and Wales, to crush William Wallace, the leader of Scots resistance to English rule.

At dawn on July 22 Edward engaged the Scots on the south side of Callendar Wood, near Falkirk. As the king was mounting his horse it was frightened by a trumpet blast and kicked him. With two broken ribs, Edward continued to direct his forces throughout the day.

The Scots infantry stood firm against the onslaught of Edward's cavalry. They eventually gave way before a hail of arrows from the Welsh archers and broke up. Wallace's cavalry fled and about 5000 Scots are said to have perished.

Despite this defeat, Wallace's rising had put steel into Scottish resistance and Edward was able to reoccupy only the southern part of the country.

The second battle of Falkirk took place in January 1746, when Bonnie Prince Charlie surprised and defeated government forces under General Henry Hawley at Bantaskyne, south-west of Falkirk, during the Scots' long retreat north.

Falkland Palace, *Fife*

The palace* was a favourite residence of the Stuart kings. Building began in the late 15th century, but the palace owes its present shape to the efforts of James V, who died there after Scotland's defeat at Solway Moss in 1542.

He had just become the father of a baby girl, the future Mary, Queen of Scots. Recalling that his dynasty had begun with Walter the Steward's marriage to Robert Bruce's daughter, Marjorie, the Scottish king said prophetically: 'It cam wi' a lass and it will gang wi' a lass.' The last Stuart monarch was not to be Mary but Queen Anne, who came to the throne 160 years later.

Falmouth, *Cornwall*

Until the 17th century Falmouth consisted of a hamlet, known as Pennycomequick, and a manor house, Arwennack. The owners of the manor, the Killigrew family,

developed Falmouth against opposition from the ancient Cornish ports of Truro, Penryn and Tregony.

Given its royal charter in 1661, Falmouth became a thriving port. In 1688 it became the headquarters of the mail boats or 'packets' to New York. After 1852, when it was replaced by Southampton as the mail port, Falmouth developed a docks industry and, later, it became a popular seaside resort.

AIR SHOW *George V and Queen Mary inspecting new aeroplanes at the Royal Army Aircraft Factory, Farnborough, in 1914.*

Farnborough, *Hants*

The systematic development of the British aircraft industry began at Farnborough in 1910 with the establishment of His Majesty's Balloon Factory. Two years earlier the town had been the scene of the first successful heavier-than-air flight in Britain. On October 16, 1908, the American-born pilot Sam Cody ascended 1390 ft in a demonstration

flight in an army aeroplane.

In 1910 Cody won the British Empire Michelin Cup for flying 185½ miles in 4 hours and 47 minutes at Farnborough. His achievement aroused the government's interest in aviation. Within a year the Balloon Factory had been expanded into the Royal Army Aircraft Factory, the beginnings of the present-day Royal Aircraft Establishment.

Farringford, *IOW*

Alfred, Lord Tennyson settled at a farmhouse near Farringford in 1853. He went there after being made Poet Laureate, with a pension of £200 a year granted him by Sir Robert Peel. With Tennyson came his wife, Emily, and their infant son.

Tennyson was a prudent, methodical man, who was prone to depressions. He was unusually tall and of almost Indian appearance with his black hair and beard, aquiline features and dark eyes and skin.

In his first secluded years at Farringford he wrote 'The Charge of the Light Brigade', and finished the first series of *Idylls of the King*, his romantic epic poems about King Arthur and his knights. This was an instant success, and 10,000 copies were sold within a month of publication. Tennyson's other works achieved a popularity unequalled by any other English poet. Among

BEST SELLER *In 1861, at the peak of his popularity, Tennyson, aged 52, posed for this photograph.*

his most ardent admirers was Queen Victoria.

Sightseers flocked to his home. He found them such a nuisance that in 1868 he set in hand the building of a summer residence, Aldworth,

in a then remote spot near Haslemere, Surrey. For the rest of his life he divided his time between Aldworth and Farringford.

Tennyson continued to write poetry prolifically until he was over 80. At the age of 74 he went with the Liberal Prime Minister, William Gladstone, on a voyage round Scotland to Scandinavia. On this voyage Gladstone at last persuaded him to accept a peerage, and he became Baron Tennyson of Aldworth and Farringford.

Faversham, *Kent*

In 1551 this estuary town was the scene of a notorious murder that provided the plot for the first domestic melodrama in the British theatre.

The murder victim, Thomas Arden, was a prosperous businessman, collector of the Customs at Faversham and a former mayor. His wife, Alice, fell in love with a tailor called Thomas Mosby. Alice and Mosby decided to murder Arden. They hired two assassins, Loosebagg and Black Will, and all four finally did away with Arden on the night of February 15, 1551, while he was playing draughts in his parlour.

Three of the murderers were caught almost immediately. Alice was burnt at Canterbury; Mosby was hanged at Smithfield; Black Will was burnt at Flushing; Loosebagg appears to have escaped. Arden's half-timbered house, the scene of the crime, still stands in the town.

The story found its way into Holinshed's *Chronicles*, published in 1577, which was the source of much of Shakespeare's historical material. In 1592 an unknown playwright wrote *The Lamentable and True Tragedie of M. Arden of Feversham in Kent*. At one time it was thought that the play was written, or at least retouched, by Shakespeare, but this theory is no longer taken seriously.

Fishbourne Palace, *W Sussex*
See pp. 34–35

Fishguard, *Dyfed*

The last invasion of Britain took place in 1797. On February 22, a small French force landed at a cove near Fishguard. They hoped to rouse the Welsh in an attempt to dethrone George III.

During the voyage to Wales, the leader of the force, General Tate,

an Irish-American, had kept his men on short rations. As a result the French satisfied their hunger and thirst by looting the inns and farms of their supposed allies.

The local people, instead of joining the French, fled in terror. However, a woman cobbler, Jemima Nicholas, seized her pitchfork and rounded up 12 French prisoners.

The Fishguard Fencibles, the local militia, were alerted, and the 700-strong South Pembrokeshire Yeomanry marched into the area. As the French were preparing for battle, they saw some figures in red cloaks and tall black hats approaching their assembled ranks.

Imagining that these were troop reinforcements, the terrified French surrendered. These reinforcements were in fact a group of Welsh women, dressed in the traditional costume of their country, who had come to watch the battle.

Flint Castle, *Clwyd*

Flint Castle* was the first of the great fortresses built by Edward I to control the Welsh countryside. Construction began in July 1277.

In 1399 Richard II, tricked by the treacherous Earl of Northumberland into leaving Wales for London, was ambushed on the way to the capital and escorted to Flint Castle. There, he was persuaded to abdicate in favour of his victorious rival, Henry Bolingbroke, Duke of Lancaster, later Henry IV.

A French noble who was with Richard II described the arrival of Henry's army at Flint Castle: 'The host approached the castle and entirely surrounded it, even to the sea, in very fair array. Then the Earl of Northumberland went to Duke Henry and they talked together rather a long while and concluded that he should not enter the castle till such a time as the King had dined, because he was fasting. The table being laid, the King sat down to dinner. The King was a very long time at table; not for anything he ate; but because he well knew, that as soon as he had dined, the Duke would come for him, to carry him off or put him to death.'

Flodden Field, *Northld*

The most crushing defeat in Scotland's history was inflicted by an English army at Flodden, near Branxton, on September 9, 1513.

Taking advantage of Henry VIII's absence in France with the main English army, James IV of Scotland (1488–1513) had crossed the border on August 22, 1513, with a force of about 30,000 men. James captured the castles of Norham and Ford from the English.

Henry's lieutenant in the north, Thomas Howard, Earl of Surrey, hurriedly mustered an army of about 25,000 men at Newcastle and formally challenged James to meet him in battle.

James waited in a strong position on Flodden ridge. Surrey reached Woller Hough, 6 miles from Flodden, on September 6. Failing to tempt the Scots to fight in the plain, he marched north and turned to attack them from the rear.

The battle began late in the afternoon. When the English artillery opened fire the undisciplined Scottish infantry charged forward.

James, believing that the English were in disarray, advanced swiftly downhill with two columns. But his pikemen lost their formation. The English cavalry routed the Scottish left wing, and the English archers, taking the Scottish extreme right wing by surprise, drove it back.

In the centre the Scottish king fought on foot with his nobles. The long and bloody battle continued until nightfall. But at last the shattered remnants of the Scottish army finally admitted defeat. James himself, many of his nobles and 10,000 of his subjects fell in the battle, as well as 4000 English.

Fonthill Abbey, *Wilts*
The wealthy and talented William Beckford (1759–1844) always hated the Classical mansion where he was born. Late in the 1790's he decided to replace it with one of the most exotic and extravagant edifices ever built in Britain.

A product of Beckford's romantic imagination, his new Gothic abbey had a 300 ft high octagonal tower, 120 ft high hall, and 8 miles of surrounding walls. Built at great speed by 600 men, sometimes working all night by the light of bonfires, Fonthill was structurally unsound. The tower collapsed twice during the building operations. In 1825, three years after Beckford had been forced by lack of money to sell Fonthill, the great tower crumbled. Hardly a stone of Beckford's abbey now remains.

Fotheringhay Castle, *Northants*
After the execution of Mary, Queen of Scots, in 1587, Fotheringhay crumbled into decay. The great hall in which the execution took place was built into Connington Manor, Huntingdonshire, now destroyed.

All that remains of Fotheringhay today is a mound, and some stonework surrounded by railings.

MARY'S CAPTIVE YEARS

After Mary, Queen of Scots, lost her crown and country at the Battle of Langside in May 1568, she was forced to flee to England. Mary was to spend 19 years in exile there, officially as Queen Elizabeth's guest, but in effect her prisoner. During these years she and her entourage were sent from place to place at Elizabeth's orders.

Mary was moved in 1568 from her first 'prison', at Carlisle, because it was near the Scottish border and possible rescue, and taken to the more isolated Bolton Castle.

In 1570 the Earl of Shrewsbury and his wife, 'Bess of Hardwick', were appointed gaolers to Mary. For 14 years the trio moved from one country house to another, and at first they got on well together. But the Scottish queen tricked the earl by sending secret messages to the Catholic Duke of Norfolk. And his wife added to his troubles by accusing him of having an affair with Mary.

Suffering from ill-health and depression, Mary also lived at Wingfield Manor. She stayed occasionally at Chatsworth while the manor was cleaned—as was the custom with large houses in that insanitary age. Buxton spa was not far from Chatsworth, and Mary took the waters there.

After a plot to free her by the northern earls, Mary was taken to Coventry and then to Sheffield, which had two residences fit for a queen—the castle and the manor.

At Chartley, in the autumn of 1586, there was an unsuccessful rescue attempt by Sir Anthony Babington. Then Mary made her last journey, to Fotheringhay. She was tried for plotting Elizabeth's overthrow and, on February 8, 1587, wearing a blood-red petticoat to signify martyrdom, the Queen of Scots was beheaded. (See pp. 144–5.)

Last of Mary's prisons (map, left) was Fotheringhay, where she was executed. A contemporary sketch (above) shows Mary being tried there.

Framlingham Castle, *Suffolk*
Mary Tudor, the rightful Queen of England, found refuge in this castle* during the nine days in which the Protestant claimant, Lady Jane Grey, was attempting to usurp her throne. (See pp. 134–5.)

At Framlingham Queen Mary was the guest of the Catholic Duke of Norfolk. She had been warned that the Protestants would attempt to keep her from the throne and so had stayed away from the death-bed of her half-brother, Edward VI.

At Framlingham, Mary's supporters rallied around her, and soon she was acknowledged as queen.

Gad's Hill Place, *Kent*
Charles Dickens bought Gad's Hill Place (now a school) in 1856, just before he and his wife agreed to separate. He lived there with nine of his ten children (the eldest having left with his wife) until the end of his life, and spent lavishly on improving the property.

He worked in a chalet in the garden editing the periodicals *Household Words* and, from 1859, *All the Year Round,* in which *The Tale of Two Cities* and *Great Expectations* first appeared. At Gad's Hill he also wrote *Our Mutual Friend* and the uncompleted mystery story, *Edwin Drood.* Dickens died suddenly at the dinner table in Gad's Hill Place on June 9, 1870. (See p. 308.)

Glamis Castle, *Tayside*
Sir Walter Scott declared Glamis Castle* to be the noblest specimen of a medieval castle he had ever seen.

The murder of Duncan I by Macbeth, Thane of Glamis, as told in Shakespeare's *Macbeth*, is reputed to have taken place here. In reality Duncan was slain by Macbeth in a battle at Bothouganan, near Elgin, in 1040.

The nucleus of the present castle, rebuilt in the late 17th century, is a 15th-century tower said to contain a secret chamber known only to the Earl of Strathmore and his heir. Reputedly, knowledge of a terrible family secret is similarly confined to the earl, who divulges it to his heir when he comes of age.

Glasgow, *Strathclyde*
The city of Glasgow—the Celtic name, *Gelschu,* means 'beloved green place'—grew up round a 6th-century church founded by St Mungo. Traditionally this was the site of the present cathedral*, which dates from the 12th century. Glasgow University, the second oldest university in Scotland after St Andrews, was founded in 1451.

In early times, this small university town was under the domination of the church. Situated on the River Clyde, it faced away from the profitable trade of the European ports and its river fisheries were its only source of wealth. But although Glasgow was a backwater, its citizens were caught up in the tumult of Scottish history. In 1568 the town joined forces with the Regent Moray to defeat Mary, Queen of Scots, at the Battle of Langside. The site of this conflict is now Queen's Park—named after her.

The city began to prosper after the Act of Union in 1707 opened up the English colonies in the Americas to Scottish traders; its merchants made fortunes out of the trade in sugar, rum and tobacco.

Shoals in the River Clyde prevented large vessels from reaching the city. In the mid-17th century the civic authorities bought 13 acres downstream near Greenock, and Port Glasgow came into being. A century later, engineers managed to clear a channel and large ships were able to reach Glasgow.

Although, in the 1770's, the War of American Independence wiped out the tobacco fortunes, the city had become a centre of trade and

ART NOUVEAU PIONEER

This high-backed chair is typical of the work of Charles Rennie Mackintosh, a Glasgow architect and pioneer of art nouveau. In 1895 he won a competition to produce designs for a new and enlarged art school in Glasgow.

commerce. And, with the coming of the Industrial Revolution, it began to surge forward again. The basis for Glasgow's industrial growth was the huge coal and iron deposits in the surrounding countryside.

By 1834 Scotland had 134 cotton factories, most of them within 25 miles of the centre of Glasgow. Between 1765 and 1861, Glasgow's population soared from 28,000 to almost half a million.

Glasgow and the Clyde achieved world leadership in shipbuilding. In 1811 a Port Glasgow firm built Henry Bell's 30 ton *Comet,* the first steam ship to run commercially in Europe.

Experiments with iron ships began. The *Fairy Queen* was built in a city foundry in 1831. But the peak of Clyde shipbuilding came with the famous liners, the *Queen Mary* (launched in 1936) and the *Queen Elizabeth* (1940).

Glasgow and its university have produced many great men. James Watt (1736–1819), Greenock-born designer of the first economical steam engine. Adam Smith (1723–90) held the chairs of logic and

philosophy at Glasgow, and wrote *Wealth of Nations,* one of the most influential of all books on political economy. David Livingstone (1813–73) studied medicine, applied science and divinity at the university, before he went to Africa as a missionary.

William Thomson, Lord Kelvin (1824–1907), professor of natural philosophy for 53 years, applied his theoretical knowledge of heat, light, sound and electricity to practical problems. Kelvin's research into submarine cables ensured the success of the Atlantic cable, and after it was laid in 1866 he was knighted and given the freedom of the city of Glasgow.

Sir Thomas Lipton (1850–1931), a native of Glasgow, built a butter-and-ham empire of grocery shops over Britain. He was an errand boy at the age of nine and, after working in America, opened his first grocer's shop in Glasgow in 1871. It was soon followed by other shops, and Lipton was a millionaire by the age of 30.

He succeeded in the tea trade because he prepared special blends for different towns after analysing their water supplies. He was a keen yachtsman and made repeated but unsuccessful attempts to win the America's Cup.

Glastonbury, *Somerset*
The ancient abbey* of Glastonbury was already old when St Dunstan restored it in the 10th century. The monks claimed to be able to trace its foundation back to King Arthur and St Patrick.

When, in 1184, the old wooden church was burnt down, the monks decided to rebuild it with the offerings of pilgrims. In 1191 they pretended that they had found the bodies of Arthur and Guinevere in their cemetery.

Later, the monks claimed to have the Holy Grail—a cup which Christ had used at the Last Supper. The pope granted an indulgence reducing the number of days spent by sinners in purgatory if they made a pilgrimage to Glastonbury.

The monks' myth-making may have been founded on fact. Glastonbury Tor is close to Cadbury Castle, and if the historical Arthur made his base at Cadbury, it is likely enough that Glastonbury was his burial place. In any event, the surviving ruins are a monument to the stories of King Arthur.

Glencoe, *Highland*
The massacre of 38 MacDonalds of Glencoe in 1692 is one of the most infamous acts in Scottish history. (See pp. 216–17.)

The man whom many Scots held responsible for this outrage was Sir John Dalrymple, later Earl of Stair (1648–1707). William III's chief adviser in Scotland. He said: 'It is a great work of charity to be exact in rooting out that damnable sect, the worst in all the Highlands.'

The legend persists that Stair, using William III's authority, wrote the 'extirpation' order on a nine of diamonds playing card which henceforth was known as 'the curse of Scotland'. This belief may have arisen because the pips on the card resemble the arms of Stair.

Glen Fruin, *Strathclyde*
West of Loch Lomond lies Glen Fruin ('Glen of Sorrow'), the scene of a bloody clan battle in 1603. Horsemen of the Colquhoun clan found themselves in boggy ground, and were helpless against the onslaught of the MacGregors. Two hundred Colquhouns fell to their enemies on the battlefield or in the merciless pursuit.

A hundred Colquhoun widows paraded before James VI (James I of England) at Stirling. Each rode a white horse and carried her husband's bloody shirt on a spear. James was so moved that he outlawed the MacGregors and forbade the use of their name.

Charles II reversed the decision in 1663 in gratitude for their help to the Royalist cause, but William III renewed the ban 30 years later. The MacGregors remained proscribed until 1755.

Gloucester, *Glos*
In the Civil War, Gloucester held out against a Royalist siege for four weeks in 1643. The city's governor, Colonel Edward Massey, was only 23.

This resistance, at a time when the king's cause seemed triumphant, heartened all supporters of Parliament. The trained bands, or militia, of London volunteered to help and marched westwards.

Meanwhile the Royalists had mined the city walls and, on September 5, Charles warned Massey to yield before they were blown up. But that night, with food running

out, the defenders saw a beacon fire signalling that relief was coming. Before morning heavy rain had flooded the Royalist mines and rendered them useless.

By September 8, when the trained bands sighted Gloucester Cathedral*, the besiegers had withdrawn. After the Restoration, as a final act of revenge, the walls which had defied Charles I were destroyed by order of his son, Charles II.

Gotham, *Notts*
During the Middle Ages, Gotham, near Nottingham, was known as 'a village of fools'. This reputation is said to date from the reign of King John in the 13th century.

According to tradition, the villagers purposely acted like fools in order to discourage the king from building a hunting lodge at Gotham. They were afraid that the presence of the court would involve them in great expense and disrupt the life of the village.

The king's servants, flabbergasted by the behaviour of the villagers, are said to have returned to the king and advised him to abandon his plan to live there.

After the success of their ruse, the inhabitants of Gotham are reputed to have said: 'We ween there are more fools pass through Gotham than remain in it.'

Grasmere, *Cumbria* See p. 281.

Gravesend, *Kent*
In the parish churchyard of Gravesend is a bronze statue* commemorating Pocahontas. In 1608, this 13-year-old Red Indian princess, daughter of the powerful chieftain,

INDIAN PRINCESS *Pocahontas, daughter of a chief, saved the life of an Englishman about to be killed.*

Powhattan, rescued Captain John Smith, who was the leader of the colonists in Virginia.

Smith was captured by the Indians, who condemned him to death. Pocahontas placed her head over his as a tomahawk was raised to strike the fatal blow. This act of bravery saved Smith's life and he was freed by Powhattan.

Pocahontas later became a Christian and married a settler named John Rolfe.

When Rolfe brought Pocahontas to England in 1616, together with their infant son, Thomas, she was fêted at the court of James I. In the following year while sailing down the Thames at the start of her return voyage to Virginia, Pocahontas caught a fever and died, aged 22, off Gravesend. The young Indian princess was buried in the chancel of St George's Church.

Greenock, *Strathclyde*
This town, at the 'Tail of the Bank' on the Firth of Clyde, was the deep-water port for Glasgow until the river was opened up for large

SEAFARER *Captain Kidd, shown in this print, was a notorious pirate whose birthplace was Greenock.*

ships in the late 18th and early 19th centuries.

Greenock's most notorious seafarer was Captain William Kidd, born there in about 1645. His father is thought to have been a Covenanting minister.

Kidd served in the West Indies against the French, and was voted £150 by the American colonial authorities for help during riots after the Glorious Revolution of 1688. By the time he was 50 he was prosperous, married and with a home in New York. Then he

went to London, where he received the King's Commission to hunt pirates and share the profits with peers of the realm, including the First Lord of the Admiralty and the Lord Chancellor.

Kidd went to Madagascar, but found few pirates, and began to plunder shipping in the Indian Ocean. He claimed afterwards that he was forced to do so for fear of revolt by the crew, and during a mutinous incident he killed a gunner with a wooden bucket.

Complaints of Kidd's activities began to reach England. The Great Mogul threatened to expel the East India Company from India if the piracy was not checked. Kidd was arrested on his return to America and sent back to England where he was tried and executed in 1701.

Gretna Green, *Dumf & Gall*
For a century runaway lovers made for Gretna Green just over the border where, under Scots law, they could be quickly married without the consent of their parents.

The smithy at Gretna Green still has the anvil over which they were married, but since 1940 the smith has no longer had the right to conduct the ceremony.

Grime's Graves, *Nflk* See pp. 16–17.

Guildford, *Surrey*
In Saxon times, Guildford was a fording place over the River Way. The town was first mentioned in the will of King Alfred of Wessex: 'To Ethelwald, my brother's son, I bequeath the manor at Godalming and at Gyldeford.'

The Norman castle, built in the 12th century, was visited on many occasions by King John, and became a favourite residence of his son, Henry III. Only the castle keep* remains today.

Flemish weavers, invited by Edward III to settle in Guildford during the 14th century, made the town a prosperous centre of the wool trade, which continued to flourish until the 18th century.

Gwennap Pit, *Cornwall*
In 1762 John Wesley, the founder of Methodism, preached at Gwennap Pit* to a crowd of 20,000. The natural amphitheatre is a circular depression, created possibly by the subsidence of a mine. Wesley continued to hold evangelical meetings

at Gwennap Pit until 1788, when he was 85. In 1803, the sides of the pit were terraced; it is still used for Methodist gatherings.

H

Haddington, *Lothian*
A servant girl putting a clotheshorse too near an open fire is said to have caused a blaze which destroyed the town in 1598.

Haddington had been burnt several times before by English invaders. They held it for more than a year in 1548–9 in the face of a Scottish siege, until relieved by the Earl of Rutland.

The county offices, dating from 1833, stand on the site of a palace where Alexander II, son of William the Lion, was born in 1198. The poet William Dunbar (1460–1520) and the religious reformer John Knox (1513–72) are believed to have been born in the town. Knox was educated at Haddington and spent several years as a notary there.

Another native of Haddington was Samuel Smiles (1812–1904), whose book *Self-help* (1857) encouraged many Victorians to better themselves by following the example of great men.

Haddon Hall, *Derby*
One of the finest medieval manor houses in existence, Haddon Hall was the scene in 1558 of the elopement of Sir John Manners and the heiress Dorothy Vernon during her sister's wedding celebrations.

Hadrian's Wall See pp. 38–39.

Hagley Hall *Herefs & Worcs*
After the failure of the Gunpowder Plot, Humphrey Lyttleton, whose family seat was Hagley Hall, hid two of the conspirators, his brother Stephen Lyttleton and Robert Winter, in the hall.

On January 9, 1606, one of the servants found the hiding place

and fetched the local constable, who arrested them. Humphrey was found guilty of harbouring the fugitives and sentenced to death.

Attempting to save his life, Humphrey betrayed the whereabouts of Jesuits thought to be implicated in the plot. But he was executed just the same.

In 1760 Hagley Hall was torn down by Lord Lyttleton and replaced by the present structure.

Halidon Hill, *Northld*
In 1333 Edward III decided to besiege Berwick to try to maintain his shaky control over Scotland. The English army was placed on Halidon Hill, which overlooked Berwick and the road to Duns. Around the hill lay a deep bog. Twice Berwick refused to yield, in the belief that aid was on the way. When help did arrive from Duns, the relief troops sank in the mire and were picked off by archers. The survivors fled before the English knights.

Hambledon, *Hants*
Cricket, originally a medieval game, was polished and organised by the men of Hambledon, whose matches were played in the mid-18th century on Broad Half Penny Down, a mile from the village. Afterwards, the players would gather at the Bat and Ball Inn which was owned by Richard Nyren, who founded the club in 1760 and became its captain and groundsman.

During a memorable match in June 1777, the Hambledon players beat the all-England side by an innings and 168 runs. And the club introduced a third stump to the wicket late in the 1770's. Hambledon lost its dominance when the Marylebone Cricket Club (MCC) was formed at Lord's in 1788. The Hambledon Club was finally disbanded in 1825.

EARLY CRICKETER *A player wields the curved bat popular at Hambledon in the 1700's.*

Harby, *Lincs*
Queen Eleanor, wife of Edward I, died in 1290 at Harby, where she and her husband were spending some weeks hunting. Her body was taken for burial at Westminster.

Each stopping place of the cortège was marked with a cross. Three survive—at Northampton, Geddington and Waltham Cross. The last stopping place was at Charing Cross, London, where a replica of the original stands.

Hardwick Hall, *Derby*

Elizabeth of Hardwick—'Bess of Hardwick'—was known for two great talents: marrying rich men and building great houses. Born in 1518, the daughter of a country squire, she spent the years of her childhood in a one-storey half-timbered house at Hardwick.

Bess was married at the age of 14 to a neighbour named Robert Barlow. He died when she was 15, leaving her a large estate.

Sixteen years later she married Sir William Cavendish, Treasurer of the Chamber. Bess persuaded her husband to buy an estate for them at Chatsworth, on which she built a magnificent mansion.

When Cavendish died, Bess was only 39. Her next husband, William St Loe, died in 1564 or 1565, leaving his entire estate to Bess. Still beautiful, witty and ambitious, and by now very rich, Bess now married her third husband, one of the most powerful men in England—George Talbot, 6th Earl of Shrewsbury.

In 1591 Shrewsbury died. Bess, now 63, promptly began building her final masterpiece—Hardwick Hall. This house is one of the most spectacular triumphs of Tudor architecture, remarkable for having more glass than stone in its walls. It is also an expression of its owner's pride and self-confidence. The old woman had her own initials carved in vast stone letters in the parapet—E. S. for Elizabeth Shrewsbury.

From her bedroom window, Elizabeth had a convenient view of her childhood home, from which she had travelled so far in status and wealth. She died at Hardwick Hall in her 90th year, a remarkable age for Tudor times.

Harlech Castle, *Gwynedd*

Edward I built Harlech Castle* between 1283 and 1290. Because the castle could be defended by fewer than 20 men, it became the stronghold for the desperate few in major wars in Wales.

In 1400, at the beginning of the revolt of the Welsh against the English, Harlech was held by five Englishmen and 16 Welshmen. After a four-year siege, the castle fell to the Welsh leader, Owen Glendower. He made it his capital and held one parliament within its walls before his eventual fall.

In 1460, during the Wars of the Roses, Henry VI's wife, Margaret of Anjou, fled to Harlech before going to Scotland to raise recruits against the Yorkists.

The constable of Harlech Castle, Dafydd ap Ieuan, was a staunch Lancastrian supporter. For eight years, he held out against the Yorkists. He boasted that once he had kept a castle so long in France that all the old women in Wales talked of it; and now he would keep Harlech until all the women of France talked about it.

But Dafydd was forced to surrender the castle in 1468 when, according to a contemporary account, the Earl of Pembroke, a Yorkist supporter, 'assaulted the castle in such a furious thundering manner that it yielded to his hands'. The song, 'Men of Harlech', commemorates this siege.

Hatfield House, *Herts*

Hatfield House has been the home of one of England's most illustrious families—the Cecils—for more than 350 years. The mansion was completed in 1612, only months after the death of its conceiver, Robert Cecil, Earl of Salisbury. Before then the old palace had belonged to the bishops of Ely and then to the crown. But in 1607, James I exchanged Hatfield House for Robert Cecil's nearby home at Theobalds.

In 1835 Hatfield House nearly came to an untimely end. The eccentric dowager marchioness lived then in the west wing. Though over 80 she still rode to hounds, entertained lavishly and used language outrageous for a lady. One November night in 1835 she caught her elaborate coiffure in a candle flame. Before aid could be summoned her apartments were ablaze. The marchioness died. The entire west wing was burnt down and only a change in wind direction saved the rest of the house.

The 3rd Marquess of Salisbury (1830–1903) was born at Hatfield. Described by Disraeli as 'the only man of real courage that it has been my lot to work with', Salisbury was Conservative Prime Minister three times from 1885 onwards.

Hawarden Castle, *Clwyd*

In 1839 William Ewart Gladstone, then a 30-year-old MP and 29 years away from his first term of office as Prime Minister, married Catherine Glynne, the heiress of Hawarden Castle.

For 60 years Gladstone and his wife lived at the castle. In 1847 the Glynne estates were badly hit by a financial panic. Gladstone had to work diligently to make the estates economically sound. As a result, he became the largest landowner in the county. His experience gave him training in economics. When he became Chancellor of the Exchequer in 1852, he said: 'It was always a matter of sailing close to the wind in running the estate, and from that I have learned much of benefit to my present administration.'

At Hawarden, Gladstone exercised by cutting down trees. When he became famous, tourists arrived to watch him, with his braces thrown off and his shirt collar unfastened, at work. After this exhibition, he would distribute wood-chippings as souvenirs.

Gladstone died at Hawarden in 1898 and was buried at Westminster Abbey. He had written, 'I desire to be buried where my wife may also be'. After her death in 1900, she was buried privately by his tomb.

TOURIST ATTRACTION *Gladstone (extreme right) loved to chop down trees on his estate at Hawarden. Tourists used to turn up to watch him at work.*

Hayes Place, *Gtr London*

William Pitt the Elder (1708–78), first Earl of Chatham, whose policies brought Britain victory in the Seven Years' War, bought Hayes Place as his country house in 1753. His second son and future Prime Minister, William, and the younger children were born at Hayes. Pitt rebuilt the house, giving it 24 bedrooms, and stabling for 16 horses.

In 1766 Pitt became Prime Minister. He sold Hayes Place to pay for enlarging a house that had been left to him at Burton Pynsent, in Somerset. Within a year Pitt suffered from a nervous breakdown. Believing that only at Hayes Place would he recover, he paid £17,400 to repurchase the house he had sold for £11,780. He died there in 1778.

Helpston, *Cambs*

John Clare, one of the greatest poets of the English countryside, was born in 1793 at Helpston, which he described as his 'old home of homes'. The son of a Northamptonshire labourer, Clare, although he had almost no schooling, began writing poetry at the early age of 12.

In 1820 Clare's first book, *Poems Descriptive of Rural Life*, was well received, but his other volumes failed to sell. Through patrons, Clare secured a small annuity, but it was not enough to keep his large family from sinking into poverty.

In 1841, after years of hardship, Clare went insane, and had to be confined to an asylum at Northampton, where he spent his last 23 years. In a lucid moment, he wrote to a friend: 'If life had a second edition, how I would correct the proofs.'

Holkham Hall, *Norfolk*

Thomas Coke (1752–1842) led the way in the 18th-century revolution in agricultural production. Coke developed the Norfolk system of crop rotation, modified versions of which are practised today. Four crops are grown in turn on the same soil. The first is turnips, introduced as a field crop in 1731 by 'Turnip Townshend'—Viscount Townshend of Rainham Hall, Norfolk.

Barley, oats or peas follow, and then the land is put under clover or grass. In the fourth year wheat is grown. This rotation saves the soil from exhaustion and checks the spread of pests and disease.

Coke also planted winter fodder, for feeding livestock in the cold months. He called farmers' meetings to explain the new methods which had greatly increased the value of his own estate.

Coke encouraged his tenants by granting them long leases. His contemporary, Robert Bakewell, founded modern stockbreeding by his clever crossing of animals.

Honiton, Devon
Late in the 16th century, Flemish refugees, whose skill was making fine Brussels lace, settled at Honiton, where they developed a new style. The town became the centre of lace-making in Britain during early Stuart times.

By the beginning of the 19th century, Honiton lace had gone out of fashion. But in Victorian times it enjoyed a revival in popularity. The lace for Queen Victoria's wedding dress was made near Honiton.

COTTAGE INDUSTRY
The typical Honiton style of richly worked flowers and fronds is shown on this lace sampler. Small amounts of this delicate, hand-made fabric are still produced at Honiton. The local industry—founded by Flemish refugees in the late 16th century —was badly hit by the introduction of machine-made lace a century ago.

Horsham, W. Sussex
Catharine Howard, one of the ten children of Lord Edmund Howard, was brought up by her grandmother, Duchess of Norfolk, at Horsham and later in London. Living in this free-and-easy household, Catharine, young and attractive, had several lovers—including Francis Dereham, a kinsman, and

her cousin Thomas Culpepper.

Catharine was introduced to the king in 1540 by Stephen Gardiner, Bishop of Winchester. Henry VIII, then 49 and already tiring of his new bride, Anne of Cleves, was captivated by the lively Catharine.

After his divorce from Anne on July 9, he married Catharine privately and publicly recognised her as his wife on August 8.

On November 2 Archbishop Cranmer informed Henry of Catharine's misconduct before their marriage. Henry began inquiries, which revealed meetings between Catharine and her former lovers. Dereham and Culpepper were executed in December 1541.

Catharine steadfastly denied any misconduct since marrying Henry. But on February 11, 1542, Parliament passed a bill of attainder against her, and two days later she was beheaded in the Tower.

Houghton Hall, Norfolk
Robert Walpole, Britain's first Prime Minister and the longest holder of that office (1721–42), was born at Houghton Hall, and inherited the estate when he was 24.

Houghton Hall was then shackled with debts. Although, by clever management, Walpole raised its annual income from £2000 to £8000, he remained always in debt because he lived in an extravagant and showy style.

It was on Houghton that Walpole spent the 1000 per cent profit he made on his stock in the South Sea Bubble. He spent 13 years having the hall rebuilt as a Palladian masterpiece. He lavishly refurnished the interior, built up a superb art collection, and had the village of Houghton moved because it was spoiling his view.

Walpole was a good-natured, vivacious, coarsely spoken man with a loud, ill-bred manner, a local accent all his life, and no interest in literature or oratory. But beneath all this he was a shrewd manager of men and money, an indefatigable worker, and a connoisseur of art. His passion was hunting; he kept a pack of harriers at Houghton, held hunts there each November, and was said to open letters from his huntsman before looking at any of his official mail.

When he retired from office, Walpole spent most of his time at Houghton, plagued by gout, and

often heavily drugged by opium administered to relieve his pain. He was buried in the church at Houghton Hall. (See pp. 230–1.)

LAVISH SPENDER *Robert Walpole, the first Prime Minister, lived extravagantly and was always deep in debt.*

Howe of Corrichie, Grampian
A great Highland family met its downfall in battle at this spot near Banchory in 1592. George Gordon, 4th Earl of Huntley, who had won the enmity of Mary, Queen of Scots, was making for Aberdeen when her troops defeated him and his followers.

Huntley had taken the advice of his wife. Witches had told her that by nightfall her husband would be lying in the city's tolbooth (town hall) without a wound on his body.

Their prophecy was fulfilled. The earl collapsed and died at his captors' feet. His unmarked corpse was thrown over a pair of fish baskets and taken to the tolbooth, where it lay that night.

Hughenden Manor, Bucks
Benjamin Disraeli bought this imposing mansion*, situated in 750 acres of parkland on a wooded spur of the Chilterns, in 1847.

Disraeli, who was Conservative Prime Minister in 1868 and in 1874–80, was devoted to Hughenden and retreated there to recuperate from the pressures of parliamentary life. 'When I come down to Hughenden I pass the first week sauntering about my park . . . and then I saunter in my library and survey my books,' he wrote in his memoirs. He informed a friend that he and his wife, Mary Anne, had 'restored the house to what it was before the Civil Wars, and we have made a garden of terraces in which cavaliers might roam and saunter with their lady loves.'

At his own request, Disraeli was buried next to his wife at Hughen-

den instead of receiving a state funeral. A few days after the burial, Queen Victoria herself visited Hughenden to lay a wreath on the tomb of her favourite minister.

Hull, See Kingston upon Hull, p. 394

Huntingdon, Cambs
A small, austere grammar school serves as the only reminder of Huntingdon's most famous citizen, Oliver Cromwell. It was here that he learnt Latin and Greek as a boy and passed his early manhood as a fenland farmer.

Nothing in Cromwell's early life marked him out for greatness. But in 1628 Cromwell began to champion the rights of local farmers and peasants. At the same time he underwent a deep spiritual crisis, from which he emerged as a committed Puritan and a bitter opponent of the High Church policies of Charles I.

Armed with these convictions, Cromwell attended the Parliament of 1628 as MP for Huntingdon. It was the threshold of his great career as a soldier and ruler.

THE PROTECTOR *Oliver Cromwell rose from fenland obscurity to become leader of his country.*

Huntingtower Castle, Tayside
The castle*, 2 miles north-west of Perth, was known as Ruthven (pronounced Riven) until 1600, and was the ancient seat of the earls of Gowrie. It was the scene of the 'Raid of Ruthven' in 1582, when a band of nobles, led by the earls of Gowrie and Mar, kidnapped the 16-year-old James VI of Scotland (the future James I of England) by luring him into the castle when he was hunting close by. The boy king wept when the Master of Glamis barred his escape.

The plotters had objected to James's favourite, the Earl of

Lennox. It took James a year to escape. Later he had his revenge. Gowrie was trapped into a confession of treason and executed.

Inveraray, *Strathclyde*
For centuries Inveraray has been the centre of the Campbell clan under their chiefs, the earls and dukes of Argyll. Archibald Campbell, the eighth earl (1598–1661), had 20,000 retainers and was said to be the most powerful subject of the crown in Scotland. A leading Covenanter, he made sure that the Scottish parliament and not Charles I exercised the real power in Scotland.

The king was reconciled with the Covenanters and made Argyll a marquis. Later, Argyll forged an alliance between Cromwell and the Scots against the king, but his plotting led to his execution after the Restoration of Charles II.

Another Archibald Campbell was created first duke in 1701 for his part in the Glorious Revolution of 1688. The second duke was an architect of the Union of Scotland and England in 1707, and helped to put down the 1715 Jacobite Rebellion. The early-15th-century castle* and the town were rebuilt in 1745–80 by the third duke.

Inverlochy Castle, *Highland*
After his early successes against the Covenanters in 1644, the Earl of Montrose, a supporter of Charles I, turned to attack the king's main opponent—the Earl of Argyll, a leader of the Covenanters.

In February 1645 he marched his men from Fort Augustus, through snowbound passes to Inverlochy, where Argyll and his Campbell clan were gathered.

Spearheaded by a force of cavalry, Montrose's wild clansmen, roaring their battlecries, swept down on the unsuspecting Campbells. Before the day ended, 1500 of the defenders lay dead under the walls of Inver-

lochy Castle*. Argyll fled down Loch Linnhe in his galley.

Montrose reported to the king: 'I am in the fairest hopes of reducing this kingdom to your Majesty's obedience.' (See Montrose p. 408.)

Inverness, *Highland*
In the 6th century, St Columba converted the Pictish King Brude to Christianity at his wooden fortress beside the River Ness. The fort is believed to have been where the present town lies. King Duncan's son, Malcolm III, who avenged his father's death at the hands of Macbeth, destroyed the castle.

A stone keep built by David I in the 12th century stood on a summit above the river for 600 years. James I of Scotland (1394–1437) invited 40 Highland chiefs to a parliament in the town in 1427, and then locked them up in the castle. Alexander, Lord of the Isles, celebrated his release a year later by pillaging and burning the town.

When Bonnie Prince Charlie occupied Inverness in 1746 he had the castle blown up, and the present one—used as a courthouse and offices—dates from the 1830's.

Iona, *Strathclyde*
This tiny island off the south-west tip of Mull was the cradle of Christianity in Scotland. St Columba (521–97), a scholar-monk of Irish royal blood, landed there in 563 and persuaded the Pictish king to give him Iona for a monastery.

Columba's conversion of the native Picts led to the gradual spread into their country by the saint's fellow countrymen from Ireland.

St Oran's cemetery* on Iona is the ancient burial place of Scotland's kings. Forty-eight of them lie there, with four kings of Ireland and eight of Norway. The last to be buried was Duncan, slain by Macbeth in 1040.

Thereafter, royal burials took place at Dunfermline.

Ipswich, *Suffolk*
Tudor intrigues may have prevented Ipswich from becoming a great centre of learning. Cardinal Wolsey, born there about 1475, planned to build a great college close to St Peter's Church. It was designed as a 'nursery' for Wolsey's Cardinal College at Oxford, which was later refounded as Christ Church. But the cardinal's enemies were gather-

ing against him and the project, like its creator, was doomed. Henry VIII suppressed the college, and all that remains is the red-brick Tudor gateway.

Charles Dickens stayed at the Great White Horse in Tavern Street, and it was here that one of his characters, Mr Pickwick, entered the wrong bedroom to discover an elderly lady in yellow curl papers.

Isle of Man
In the 9th century the Isle of Man was invaded by the Norwegians who established the island's parliament—the Tynwald. Fought over by the English and Scots in the 13th century, the island was finally taken by Edward III in 1333.

In 1405 Henry IV bestowed it on the Stanleys, who ruled the island for over 300 years.

When the seventh earl left to join forces with Charles II in January 1651, he entrusted the island to his wife. Later that year, the local landowners, led by William Christian, forced the countess to surrender the island to the Roundheads. Christian was tried and executed in 1663, after the restoration of Charles II.

In May 1765 the sovereignty of the island, by then a haunt of smugglers, was bought by the crown for £70,000. The crown's representative, the Lieutenant-Governor, presides over the Tynwald, which remains substantially independent of the British Parliament.

Jedburgh, *Borders*
In 1285 Alexander III of Scotland was married to Iolande, the Count of Dreux's daughter, at Jedburgh Abbey*. At the wedding banquet,

Jarrow, *Tyne & Wear*
Jarrow is identified with a modern tragedy—the depression of the 1930's and the 'hunger march' of the unemployed to London in 1936.

The inter-war slump closed down the town's shipbuilding and steel industries. Up to 80 per cent of the working people lost their jobs.

The view of Walter Runciman, later Lord Runciman, then President of the Board of Trade, was that 'Jarrow must work out its own salvation'. This phrase kindled a strong reaction which led to the march of 1936, the Jarrow Crusade.

The 200 thin, ill-nourished marchers, led by their militant Labour MP, the red-haired Ellen Wilkinson, took three weeks and

five days to cover the 295 miles.

The men slept in schools, drill halls or casualty wards. Local authorities and Labour and Conservative organisations provided baths and hot meals, while relays of medical students cared for blistered feet and minor ailments.

The shabbily dressed hunger marchers reached London in pouring rain. They presented, in the words of one observer, 'the picture of a walking depression'.

There was a huge meeting in Hyde Park and a visit to the House of Commons. Sympathy was widespread, and one or two new factories were set up, but it took the Second World War to give Jarrow's economy the boost it needed.

PROTEST MARCHERS *Widespread unemployment in Jarrow in the inter-war years led to the famous Jarrow 'hunger march' on London in 1936.*

which was held in the now vanished Jedburgh Castle, a ghost is said to have appeared to warn the king of his death. The following year Alexander fell from a cliff on his way to join his queen. His reign had been a period of peace and tranquility, and his death was followed by a struggle for the Scottish crown—a struggle in which Edward I of England intervened.

The abbey, one of David I's four great Border foundations of the 12th century, lay in the path of the English invaders and suffered much damage during the Middle Ages.

Kelmscott Manor, *Oxon*
'A heaven on earth,' was William Morris's first impression of the beautiful 16th-century Cotswold-stone manor which was his country home* from 1871 until his death in 1896. He was a man of extra-ordinary versatility and genius, who was not only a designer of furniture, wallpapers and textiles, but also an artist, writer and socialist thinker. And in the peace of Kelmscott Manor – 'this many-gabled old house built by the simple country-folk of the long-past times' – he found a refuge from the 19th-century industrialisation of Britain which he loathed.

He never reconciled himself to living in London and, when forced to do so for business reasons, consoled himself with the thought that he could step into a boat outside his home on Hammersmith Mall, Chiswick, and sail up-river 130 miles to Kelmscott.

Kendal, *Cumbria*
The 12th-century castle*, now in ruins, was the birthplace of Catharine Parr, daughter of Sir Thomas Parr of Kendal, the sixth and last wife of Henry VIII.

George Romney, the 18th-century portrait painter, came from his native Lancashire to Kendal in 1755.

PAINTER *George Romney, who did this self-portrait in 1784 at the height of his fame, learnt his art in Kendal.*

In 1762, having married and set up as a painter, he left for London, leaving part of his savings with his wife and children. He did not return, apart from brief visits, until 1799.

Romney quickly established a reputation as a fashionable portrait painter. His chief inspiration, Nelson's Emma Hamilton, appears in more than 30 of his pictures. At the age of 65, exhausted by his labours, Romney returned to his devoted wife in Kendal, and died there three years later.

Kenilworth Castle, *Warks*
The Norman castle*, now a ruin, was granted by Elizabeth I to her favourite, Robert Dudley, Earl of Leicester, in 1563.

During her Midlands progress in July 1575, the queen spent three glorious weeks at Kenilworth.

On arrival she was greeted by the porter, in the guise of Hercules, and then by a character from the Arthurian legend—The Lady of the Lake. The clock of Caesar's Tower was deliberately stopped to prolong the fantasy of a midsummer night's dream. Beneath a shower of fire-works—'a blaze of burning darts flying to and fro, gleams of stars coruscant'—devised by an Italian engineer, the queen entered the castle in procession over a bridge built in her honour and guarded by 'gods' and 'goddesses'.

Within the castle Elizabeth attended a series of sumptuous banquets, and was entertained by music, dancing and a performance of the Coventry players. Outdoors there was bear-baiting.

The climax of these lavish entertainments was a water pageant, the Delivery of the Lady of the Lake, with Triton riding on a mermaid

and Proteus upon a dolphin. But when Leicester died in 1588, the queen, still furious at his marriage to Lettice Knollys ten years earlier, insisted that Lettice sell the contents of the castle to meet Leicester's debts to Elizabeth of £34,000.

In 1648 Oliver Cromwell granted the castle to Colonel Hawkesworth and his regiment to meet their unpaid wages. They drained the lake, and pulled down most of the walls to sell the materials.

Kent's Cavern, *Devon* See pp. 14–15

Keston, *Gtr London*
William Pitt the Younger (1759–1806) bought Holwood House, a 16th to 17th-century residence at Keston, in 1785. The brilliant son of Lord Chatham, the great war leader, William himself became Prime Minister at the age of 24. For most of the 19 years of his first premiership, Pitt used Holwood, with its 200 acres of land, as his country house. He spent his weekends there to escape from politics, at first wholly occupied by his favourite recreation of landscape gardening.

The sheltered, lonely life of a delicate child had made Pitt shy and ill at ease among society. He would bring one or two friends with him to Holwood, where they breakfasted punctually at 9 o'clock, spent the day walking, riding or reading, and in the evenings, if there were no official papers to be worked on, enjoyed small dinner parties.

For a man whose reputation was made as a finance minister, Pitt's private finances were chaotic. Despite his comparatively simple bachelor life and his salary of about £900 a year over many years, Pitt had debts of £45,000 when his first ministry came to an end. Much to his sorrow, he had to sell Holwood in 1802 and put the proceeds towards paying off his debts.

Killiecrankie, Pass of, *Tayside*
John Graham of Claverhouse, Viscount Dundee, gathered a Highland army in 1689, and led the first attempt to put James II back on the British throne after the Glorious Revolution the year before.

He won a brilliant victory at the Pass of Killicrankie in July, but at the cost of his own life. Dundee had been urged to attack the army of William III, led by General Hugh

Mackay, in the pass itself. But his chivalry would not let him put his enemy at such a disadvantage, so the fight took place outside the northern entrance to the pass.

The Highlanders rushed wildly down on the government's inexperienced troops. In the resulting panic-stricken rout, 2000 of Mackay's men died and 500 were made prisoner, though the clansmen were outnumbered two to one.

But in the moment of victory, Dundee was shot beneath the breastplate as he led his troop of cavalry against Mackay's centre. According to Highland legend, he was invulnerable to bullets and was killed by a silver button torn off his own coat. He was taken to Blair Castle*, where he died, loyal to James II to the end. His last words were: 'It matters less for me, seeing that the day goes well for my master.' (See Dundee, p. 382.)

Mackay had left a sentry to guard the pass, and the soldier's first inkling of defeat was the sight of Highlanders rushing towards him. He saved himself with a tremendous 17 ft jump across the River Garry, at a spot which is still known as Soldier's Leap.

Despite this victory, Dundee's death put an end to James's hopes in Scotland—as William III realised. He refused to send troop reinforcements, saying: 'Armies are needless, the war is over with Dundee's life.'

King's Lynn, *Norfolk*
A small force of Royalists was sent to King's Lynn in August 1643. Under Sir Hamon L'Estrange they fortified the town and beat off the first enemy attacks. One ship crept up the Great Ouse with provisions, but when the enemy cut off the water supply, L'Estrange had to capitulate after a month's siege.

The Royalists, who by then were masters of the North, had missed an opportunity to relieve King's Lynn and overrun East Anglia, the area from which Parliament drew much of its strength.

The town thrived in medieval days on its trade with the Continent. Its importance declined in the 19th century with the development of steam navigation and railways.

Captain George Vancouver, born in New Conduit Street in 1758, discovered Vancouver Island in 1795 and charted the whole of the north coast of North America.

Fanny Burney, the famous 18th-century novelist and diarist, was born at King's Lynn in 1752.

Kingston Hill, *Gtr London*

John Galsworthy, author of *The Forsyte Saga,* was born at Parkfield, a house near Kingston Hill, in 1867. His father later built three houses on a 24-acre site at Combe Warren on Kingston Hill, where the family lived from 1867 until 1886. In the *Saga,* Galsworthy transformed Combe Warren into 'Robin Hill'. He peopled his great sequence of novels with imaginative renderings of his own family. His father, whom he adored, he immortalised as old Jolyon. His irritating mother he turned into silly Aunt Juley. His sister, Mabel, become the sympathetic June Forsyte.

Kingston upon Hull, *Humbside*

Edward I laid out a new town named Kingston (King's Town), on the site of a small trading settlement founded by the monks of Meaux Abbey.

During the Middle Ages, the prosperity of the town was based on trade with northern Germany and the export of wool. Shipbuilding was also important and by the 18th century Hull was famed for its warships.

In 1642 the governor, Sir John Hotham, closed Hull's gates to Charles I on the orders of Parliament. It was the first active defiance against the king at the beginning of the Civil War.

One of Hull's greatest citizens was the reformer William Wilberforce (1759–1833). His efforts in Parliament to abolish the slave trade were rewarded with success in 1807, when a bill prohibiting slave trading by British vessels and the import of slaves into British colonies was passed. He then fought for abolition of slavery abroad. A few weeks after his death in 1833, the government passed an act emancipating slaves throughout the British Empire.

Kirriemuir, *Tayside*

A cottage*, at 9 Brechin Road, Kirriemuir, was the birthplace of the novelist and playwright, Sir James M. Barrie. Barrie, whose passionate love of children sprang from his boyhood experiences, rechristened Kirriemuir 'Thrums', in many of his books.

Barrie's father, a poor weaver

with nine children, sacrificed to send him to school and then to university at Edinburgh. He then went to England where, after struggling as a journalist, he eventually won success with *The Little Minister* in 1897.

His other triumphs included *The Admirable Crichton* and *Dear Brutus.* But the play which won him undying fame was *Peter Pan,* first performed in New York in 1904.

Knaresborough Castle, *N Yorks*

Riding hard from Canterbury, the four murderers of Archbishop Thomas Becket took refuge at Knaresborough Castle* in 1170.

The castle was owned by one of the assassins, Hugh Mauclerk. He and his fellow-conspirators lay low at the castle for a year—riding out the storm of indignation over their action, which had shocked the whole Christian world. None of the neighbouring nobles would eat, drink or talk with them. Finally the pope gave them the penance of serving in the Crusades. The king's displeasure with the murderers soon passed.

By 1399 the castle was owned by Henry Bolingbroke, Duke of Lancaster, who ousted Richard II and supplanted him as king. Richard was briefly held prisoner at Knaresborough before being taken to Pontefract, where he was put to death. (See Pontefract, p. 412.)

The castle was reduced to ruins during the Civil War by the Parliamentary army, which captured it after a six-week siege.

Among Knaresborough's most notorious citizens was the prophetess Mother Shipton, born in 1488. She prophesied metal ships, aircraft and the end of the world in 1991.

Lacock Abbey, *Wilts*

Founded in 1229 by a pious widow, Ela Devereux, Countess of Salisbury, Lacock Abbey* was bought and converted into a mansion by Sir William Sharington after its

dissolution by Henry VIII in 1539.

In the 19th century it became 'the first house to have drawn its own picture'. William Henry Fox Talbot (1800–77), whose family had bought the abbey generations earlier, invented the 'calotype' process, forerunner of the modern photographic negative. In 1833 he made the first photographic prints, showing the exteriors and Gothic windows of Lacock Abbey. For this work he was honoured by the Royal Society, who awarded him two medals. These prints are preserved in the Science Museum in London.

INVENTOR *William Henry Fox Talbot, working at Lacock Abbey, made the first photographs in 1833.*

TAKING PICTURES *Talbot's assistants at his photographic studio in Reading, reproduced above from one of his early photographs.*

Lancaster, *Lancs*

Founded by the Norman, Roger of Poitou, Lancaster Castle* became, in the 14th century, the headquarters of the greatest and most powerful of all medieval baronies.

John of Gaunt, who became Duke of Lancaster in 1362, was the son and father of a king, but never became king himself. His frustrated ambition explains his varied and colourful career.

John, the fourth son of Edward III, took his name from the Flemish city of Ghent, where he was born in 1340. While his elder brother, the Black Prince, dissipated his inheritance at his court at Bordeaux, John developed and extended his estates in Lancashire, and made himself the richest and most influential man in England after the king.

In the 1370's John took advantage of his father's senility and the ineffectiveness of the Black Prince to claim a commanding role in English politics. He encouraged Parliament

to attack the clergy, especially the detested William of Wykeham, Bishop of Winchester. But he earned the hatred of the London mob by protecting the heretic John Wyclif at his trial in 1377.

The death of the Black Prince in 1376, and the king's death a year later, left John the most powerful man in England. For four years he ruled in the name of his young nephew, Richard II.

The irony of John's life was that his son, Henry, did win the crown. Within months of his father's death in 1399, he deposed his cousin and made himself king.

Taken by Parliament in 1643, during the Civil War, Lancaster Castle withstood two Royalist sieges successfully.

Bonnie Prince Charlie spent three days in Lancaster Castle in 1745 as he advanced south. It was the castle's last moment of glory. Between 1788 and 1823 the castle was largely rebuilt.

George Hepplewhite, the 18th-century furniture-maker, was apprenticed to a firm in Lancaster before moving to London, where he was to win fame.

ELEGANT FORM

After leaving Gillow and Son in Lancaster, George Hepplewhite set up a business in London. Hepplewhite was not a prominent craftsman and his reputation is based on the Cabinetmaker's and Upholsterer's Guide, *which was published by his wife two years after his death. Among the furniture designs in Hepplewhite's* Guide *is this chair with a motif of Prince of Wales feathers.*

Largs, *Strathclyde*
In 1263 at the Battle of Largs, the Scottish king, Alexander III, defeated the last attempt of the Norsemen to conquer Scotland. The Norwegian king, Haakon the Old, set out with a fleet of 60 ships, but it was dispersed and largely destroyed by a storm.

Alexander III defeated the remnants of the invading force at Largs. Alexander also regained the Hebrides and the Isle of Man, which had been Norse lands since the late 9th century.

Laugharne, *Dyfed*
In August 1936 the poet Dylan Thomas and his future wife, Caitlin, fell in love while staying at Laugharne Castle House*, the home of Richard Hughes, author of *A High Wind in Jamaica.* The couple stayed on there for two years because they had no money to leave. The poet's grave is in the churchyard at Laugharne.

Thomas claimed that the town of Llareggub in *Under Milk Wood,* was not modelled on Laugharne. But every three years a performance is given as a tribute to its most famous literary figure.

Laughton, *E Sussex*
The family seat at Laughton was the home of two Prime Ministers, the brothers Thomas and Henry Pelham. What the writer Horace Walpole said about Thomas would apply to both men: 'His life had been a proof that even in a free country, great abilities are not necessary to govern it.'

Henry Pelham (1695–1754) held office in Sir Robert Walpole's Whig government, and became Prime Minister in 1743. An able parliamentary tactician, he was too readily influenced by others to keep a firm policy of his own.

His brother, Thomas, Duke of Newcastle (1693–1768) succeeded him as Prime Minister when he died. Unable to find or keep a partner to take charge in the Commons, the vacillating Newcastle resigned in 1756, but returned to power in 1757 with Pitt. The partnership survived until George III appointed his favourite, Lord Bute.

Both brothers were buried at Laughton church.

Leeds, *W Yorks*
'The whole town standeth by clothing,' John Leland, the antiquary, wrote of Leeds in the reign of Henry VIII. The first wool merchants of Leeds were the monks of Kirkstall Abbey, whose ruins* still stand on the outskirts of the city. With the coming of the industrial age, the role of the monks was taken over by Leeds businessmen like Benjamin Gotte, the 18th-century entrepreneur whose original factory can still be seen in Wellington Street. In the 19th century Leeds became the largest town in Yorkshire and one of the great manufacturing cities of England.

The town hall* of Leeds is the most imposing of all monuments to the civic pride of the Victorians. The hall, opened in 1858, by Queen Victoria and Prince Albert, amid scenes of great rejoicing, had taken six years to build, and had cost the enormous sum of £122,000.

Leicester, *Leics*
The remains of Leicester's medieval castle* are a reminder that the city, now a thriving industrial centre, was once the possession of proud and rebellious baronial families.

The Grandmesnil family, which received the town from William the Conqueror, rebelled against his son in 1102; and the Beaumont family, who became earls of Leicester in 1107, proved equally fickle friends of the king. Robert Beaumont was one of the first to join the rebellion against King Stephen in 1138. Simon de Montfort, a descendant of Robert's and the ablest antagonist to face a medieval monarch, was Earl of Leicester from 1231 until his death at Evesham in 1265.

In the 15th century, Leicester became a centre of the wool trade and one of the richest towns in England. William Wyggeston was one of the town's leading wool merchants in the early 16th century. His legacy to the city included a chantry, which can still be seen, as well as a hospital and two schools.

Its warlike ways forgotten, Leicester allowed its castle to fall into decay. It was so ruinous that in 1485 Richard III had to sleep at the Blue Boar Inn, now demolished, on his way to fight Henry Tudor in Bosworth Field. After the battle, Richard's body, stripped by looters, was taken to the Grey Friars of Leicester for burial.

In 1530 Cardinal Wolsey, shorn of his power by Henry VIII and carried on a stretcher to be tried in London, reached Leicester and died there. 'I have come to leave my bones among you,' he told the Abbot of St Mary's*.

Eight years later St Mary's itself felt the wrath of Henry VIII and was dissolved. It was the last monument of an age when Leicester stood in the front rank of English towns.

Lemsford, *Herts*
Brocket Hall, near Lemsford, belonged to William Lamb, Viscount Melbourne (1779–1848), Queen Victoria's first Prime Minister. She became very attached to Melbourne and made him her sole adviser. Melbourne served the young queen well, teaching her the principles of constitutional government and the complexities of home and foreign affairs.

Melbourne's early life had little of the prim moral uprightness associated with Victoria. His father had been a dissolute politician, whose career had been advanced by the wit and beauty of his wife—the notorious Elizabeth Milbanke. She lavished attention on William, her favourite son, and according to contemporary gossip his father was Lord Egremont, one of Lady Melbourne's many lovers.

The greatest mistake of Melbourne's life was his marriage in 1805 to the wildly eccentric Lady Caroline Ponsonby. The most celebrated of her affairs was with the poet Byron. Melbourne obtained a separation from her in 1825. Mentally unstable, she died at Brocket Hall three years later.

Lewes, *E Sussex*
One of the major battles of the Middle Ages was fought in 1264, north-east of Lewes. The contestants were Simon de Montfort, leader of the rebellious barons, and Henry III. The aim of de Montfort was to curb the powers of the king, who had won back many of the rights granted to the barons by Magna Carta in 1215.

On May 14, de Montfort drew up his 50,000 men high above Lewes. The king, who commanded nearly twice that number, marched up from the town with his infantry.

De Montfort's left wing was swiftly routed by the king's cavalry. But the tide of battle turned against Henry when de Montfort's infantry and reserve cavalry launched a fierce attack on the king's infantry.

De Montfort captured both the king and his son, Edward. In the following months, he took the first steps towards founding the parliamentary system by summoning burgesses from the towns and knights from the shires.

Lincoln, *Lincs*
Just outside Lincoln, in February 1141, the greatest battle of King Stephen's turbulent reign was fought.

Ranulf, Earl of Chester, Stephen's most determined opponent, had seized Lincoln Castle* a few months earlier. In London, Stephen waited until he knew that Ranulf had disbanded most of his forces, then hurried north to Lincoln.

The citizens opened their gates to Stephen, who laid siege to the castle. But Ranulf, who had escaped, returned on February 2 with a formidable army.

When the rebels attacked, the king was left to face his enemies with only a few retainers. He fought with savage bravery, but at length was hit by a stone and taken alive.

The citizens paid dearly for their loyalty to Stephen. Many who fled across the river in flimsy boats were drowned. Those who remained were slain and their city was sacked. Stephen himself was imprisoned in Bristol Castle. (See pp. 72–73.)

Lindisfarne, *Northld* See pp. 52–53

Little Sodbury, *Avon*
William Tyndale (1492–1536) was the chaplain and tutor at the manor house at Little Sodbury. During his stay there he began his English translation of the New Testament, parts of which were eventually published in Germany. 'If God spares my life,' he said, 'I will see that a boy who drives the plough shall know more about the Bible than many priests.'

His work aroused intense controversy, both in England and on the Continent. Betrayed to the authorities in Antwerp by a Catholic zealot, Tyndale was tried for heresy, strangled and then burnt.

Liverpool, *Merseyside*
Ireland is the key to Liverpool's early history. King John's two expeditions to Ireland convinced him of the need for a safe harbour from which to embark an army. In 1207 he promised special privileges to all who settled in the small port of Liverpool, and from that time it began to grow.

The boom years of Liverpool began at the end of the 17th century, when it started to rival Bristol as the capital of the American trade. The first American cargo—it was probably tobacco—reached Liverpool in 1648. Cargoes of sugar and cotton followed. The West Indies slave trade was quickly dominated by Liverpool merchants, and contributed handsomely to the town's prosperity until the trade's abolition in 1807.

Victorian Liverpool became the centre of the Lancashire cotton industry, then Britain's largest export industry. The introduction of steamships and refrigerated cargo holds accelerated the town's expansion. Liverpool is still the second port of England.

Built on trade, Liverpool owes its wealth to its good communications. The first docks were completed in 1721, and building was still continuing at Birkenhead at the end of the 19th century. Liverpool's half-mile long landing stage, begun in 1847, is still the largest floating quay in the world.

Liverpool has always valued its links with the industrial Midlands. A network of canals connected it with Manchester and the great textile towns by the end of the 18th century. The first Mersey road tunnel, stretching more than 2 miles

under the river to Birkenhead, was opened in 1934. The second road tunnel, linking Liverpool with Wallasey, was completed in 1971.

Llangollen, *Clwyd*
In the spring of 1778 Lady Eleanor Butler and Sarah Ponsonby, aged 39 and 23 respectively, ran away from their homes in Ireland, determined to lead a life of intellectual retirement together.

Pursued and brought back by their outraged families, the two friends finally set off for Wales later in 1778, having steadfastly refused to be dissuaded from their purpose.

In 1780 they rented a cottage and 4 acres of land at Llangollen, which they named Plas Newydd*. Here they lived for the next 50 years.

The seclusion of their early life together—spent walking, gardening, painting and reading—gradually ceased as stories of their idyllic house and garden and the unconventional way of life attracted an increasing round of visitors. The Duke of Wellington, Sir Walter Scott, Thomas de Quincey and William Wordsworth were among the many celebrated people who came to pay their respects to the 'Ladies of Llangollen'.

Lady Eleanor died in 1829, and two years later Sarah Ponsonby was buried beside her lifelong friend in Llangollen churchyard.

Llantrisant Castle, *Mid Glamorgan*
'The Welsh will never fail you,' Edward II was told when he fled into Wales in 1326, pursued by an army led by his wife, Isabella, and her allies among the barons. The king took refuge at Neath Abbey, but left after a few days, fearing 'lest the Cistercians should suffer from harbouring him'.

Edward's destination was Llantrisant Castle*, which was the home of his companion, Hugh Despenser the Younger. Their guide was a Welsh clergyman, Rhys ap Howel, who betrayed the king's route.

The king and his party, with their baggage, had to struggle towards the castle through a gale. As they came to a bend in the road, they were captured by the Duke of Lancaster.

Edward and his treasure were taken by the duke. But, in the confusion of the skirmish, Hugh Despenser and three of the king's companions escaped to Llantrisant.

Two thousand pounds were offered for Despenser. He was hotly pursued and run to ground in a wood. On the following day, this proud court favourite was executed at Hereford, on the orders of the triumphant Isabella.

Llanystumdwy, *Gwynedd*
David Lloyd George, the Liberal Prime Minister (1916–22) who brought Britain through the First World War, was born in Manchester in 1863 and brought to Llanystumdwy at the age of two. His widowed mother and her three young sons were given a home by her brother, the village cobbler Richard Lloyd. The family was poor. In later years Lloyd George wrote: 'We never ate fresh meat and I remember that our greatest

WAR LEADER *An eloquent and persuasive orator, David Lloyd George, Prime Minister from 1916 to 1922, led Britain to victory in the First World War.*

After his capture, Edward spent the night at Llantrisant Castle and was then escorted to Monmouth, where he surrendered the Great Seal, the symbol of sovereignty. He was murdered ten months later. (See Berkeley Castle, p. 368.)

luxury was half an egg for each child on Sunday mornings.'

Lloyd George became a solicitor at 21 and Liberal MP for Caernarvon at 27, a seat he retained for 55 years. In 1916 he superseded Asquith as Prime Minister, leading Britain to victory and into the post-war period. His downfall came in 1922 when the Conservatives withdrew from his coalition; his attempts during the 1920's at a political comeback failed.

In 1939 Lloyd George bought a farm near Llanystumdwy (which now has a museum* in the grounds). He retired there in 1944 and died in the following year. He is buried in the local churchyard.

Lochindorb, *Highland*
The ruined, 12th-century fortress* on an island in the loch, was granted in 1371 by Robert II to his fourth son, Alexander, Earl of Buchan, the notorious 'Wolf of Badenoch'. In 1390, when the Church censured the earl for deserting his wife, he took his revenge by burning Elgin Cathedral. He was excommunicated and his half-brother, Robert III, afraid of the consequences of such sacrilege, forced the Wolf to repair it.

Lochranza, *Strathclyde*
Robert Bruce landed at Lochranza ('loch of safe anchorage') on the Isle of Arran in 1306, from Rathlin Island in Ireland, at the beginning

of his campaign for Scottish independence from England.

Although Bruce's army was only 300 strong, the Scottish leader was resolved to defeat the English. According to a legend, Bruce's determination had been inspired by watching a spider trying to weave its web again and again, while he was hiding in a cave on Rathlin. This story was first widely circulated by Sir Walter Scott.

After a year on the Isle of Arran, Bruce crossed to the mainland and began the campaign that was to culminate in the victory at Bannockburn. (See pp. 88–89.)

Longleat, *Wilts* See pp. 160–1.

London (*Inner Boroughs*)

For its first 1000 years London grew from a Roman settlement to a fortress and a port. Just before the Norman Conquest, Edward the Confessor built his palace to the west of the City of London and established the Abbey Church* of Westminster there. After William the Conqueror invaded England in 1066, he was crowned at the Confessor's church.

Outside the eastern walls of the city, the Conqueror erected a great castle, the Tower of London*, to overawe the capital's turbulent citizens. It soon won a grim reputation as the state prison.

A third medieval building of importance, Westminster Hall*, was erected by William Rufus. In 1264 the barons of Henry III gathered in the hall to hold the first Parliament. (See pp. 84–85.)

During the reign of Henry III, it was established that Westminster was the seat of the legislature and the courts, while the walled City of London was the centre of trading. But by the end of the Middle Ages the two cities were linked by the Strand, along which the great built their mansions. These conditions did not change until the Great Fire of 1666 destroyed the timber buildings of the City.

By the late 17th century a new city of brick and stone had arisen on the ground-plan of the old. The disaster gave Sir Christopher Wren the chance of rebuilding the churches of the city, more than 20 of which survive today. His greatest achievement, St Paul's Cathedral*, stood on the site of a 7th-century cathedral.

London's population rapidly grew, and in the 17th century the Earl of Bedford laid out the streets and the square in Covent Garden. Other developers, such as the Grosvenor family, began to build in Mayfair and St James's. In the mid-18th century George III bought Buckingham Palace, and the movement westwards to Belgravia and Kensington gained impetus.

In the 19th century the stucco terraces of John Nash and the termini of the new railways had transformed the city once again. By 1900 London stretched for more than 10 miles in every direction from Charing Cross, and had completely engulfed the surrounding villages and countryside.

NASH FAÇADE *Buckingham Palace was rebuilt in the 1820's by George IV's architect, John Nash, who placed the Marble Arch at the entrance.*

VICTORIAN FRONTAGE *A new wing, hiding Nash's forecourt, was added in 1847, and the Marble Arch was moved to the north-east corner of Hyde Park.*

Bank of England

The City of London has evolved from a crowded, plague-ridden medieval town into one of the world's great financial centres. Within the square mile of the City stand some of Britain's oldest and wealthiest institutions: Lloyd's of London*; the Stock Exchange*;

CITY STRONGHOLD *The builders of the Bank of England deliberately designed it to look like a fortress.*

and the banks, the most awesome being the Bank of England.

With its windowless outer walls, the Bank of England looks like an ancient temple modified to withstand a siege. The bank was founded in 1694, and acquired its present site in Threadneedle Street in 1724. An 18th-century cartoon depicted the Bank as a rich woman sitting on a money box; and so it won the nickname of 'The Old Lady of Threadneedle Street'. Today's building is a modern reconstruction.

Bloomsbury

Originally laid out by the Earl of Southampton during the 1660's, Bloomsbury was developed by successive dukes of Bedford until the mid-19th century. It has several fine squares—Bloomsbury, Bedford, Tavistock, Russell, Gordon, Woburn—around which were built the houses of the rich.

Montague House was bought to house a collection of documents, medals, precious stones and curiosities of natural history, belonging to Sir Hans Sloane (1660–1753). This collection was the nucleus of

Bloomsbury's most famous institution, the British Museum.

In the succeeding 70 years there were many additions to the original collection, and the museum outgrew Montague House. After George IV donated the great library of his father in the 1820's, the building of the present museum* began. It took 24 years to build, and was completed in 1847.

The great domed Reading Room was added in 1857. Since then it has been used by scholars from all over the world, and it was in the Reading Room that Karl Marx wrote *Das Kapital*.

During the first 40 years of this century, a closely knit set of writers, painters and intellectuals lived in Bloomsbury. The leading personalities of the 'Bloomsbury Group' included the biographer Lytton Strachey, the economist John Maynard Keynes and the novelist Virginia Woolf. Their remarkable influence on English letters survived until the Second World War, which dispersed their members and damaged many of the squares where they had lived.

Buckingham Palace

When George IV succeeded his father, he demanded that his favourite architect, John Nash, undertake the conversion of Buckingham Palace. Originally the home of the Duke of Buckingham, it had been bought by George III for Queen Charlotte in 1762.

Nash's rebuilding, in Bath stone at an estimated cost of £260,000, began in 1826. But his hastily drawn design was criticised—the dome was considered 'a common slop-pail turned upside down'.

Queen Victoria, who moved to Buckingham Palace after her accession in 1837, was appalled by the building's shabbiness. In accordance with her wishes, the deep forecourt was enclosed in 1847 by a frontage which provided more accommodation for her rapidly growing family.

But in the years of her widowhood Victoria rarely came to London. The Prince of Wales, later Edward VII, referred to the palace as the 'sepulchre', but after Victoria's death he moved the court from Marlborough House back to it. Buckingham Palace once again became the centre of the winter and summer seasons.

Chelsea

Famous for its writers, poets, painters and eccentrics, Chelsea was a rural hideaway beyond the limits of London until the 19th century. Its peace attracted Sir Thomas More, who built his house there in 1520 to get away from the bustle of Henry VIII's court. There, More was visited by such men as the Dutch theologian Erasmus, and the painter Hans Holbein.

Many others valued the seclusion of Chelsea—'away from the great roads, safe at the bend of the river', as one resident, the 19th-century author Thomas Carlyle, described it. They ranged from the dour Scottish novelist Tobias Smollett to the playwright Oscar Wilde.

Wilde moved to 16 (now 34) Tite Street in 1884. He had already established a brilliant reputation for his outrageousness, his audacious wit and his unconventional dress. His career ended with his arrest at the Cadogan Hotel, Sloane Street, and his trial and imprisonment.

A rival wit and eccentric, the American painter James McNeil Whistler settled in Chelsea in 1866. When his painting 'The Falling Rocket'—an impression of fireworks seen across the Thames from Chelsea—was exhibited in 1877, the art critic John Ruskin accused Whistler of 'flinging a pot of paint in the public's face'. This provoked a lawsuit in which Whistler was awarded a farthing in damages. The cost of the action bankrupted Whistler, who was forced to sell his new house in Tite Street.

Wilde and Whistler were not Chelsea's only eccentrics. The Pre-Raphaelite painter Dante Gabriel Rossetti kept a menagerie in his garden at Cheyne Walk. At various times the garden housed a laughing hyena, chameleons, snakes, wallabies and armadillos.

OPERA HOUSE ON FIRE *The second Covent Garden Theatre was destroyed by flames in 1856, but within two years the present opera house was built.*

CHELSEA ECCENTRICS *The cartoonist Max Beerbohm captured the artistic life of Chelsea in this caricature of a gathering in Dante Gabriel Rossetti's garden in Cheyne Walk. Among those included are Whistler and Swinburne, William Morris, John Ruskin and Rossetti himself.*

Covent Garden

The area is famous for both its opera house and for the fruit and vegetable market which stood there for more than 300 years. The name was originally Convent Garden, from a 13th-century monastery garden, which was seized from the church by Henry VIII.

The square was laid out as a residential quarter by Inigo Jones for the 4th Earl of Bedford (1593–1641), whose house (destroyed in 1700) and walled garden formed one side of the quadrangle. The earl asked the architect to put a church on the west side—something inexpensive, 'like a barn'. Jones told him he would get the handsomest barn in Europe, and the result was St Paul's Church*. The portico of the church is the setting for Eliza Doolittle's first encounter with Professor Higgins in Bernard Shaw's play, *Pygmalion*.

In 1661 the principal market for flowers, fruit and vegetables in London was established by royal charter at Covent Garden. The market began as a huddle of shacks and stalls under the Earl of Bedford's garden wall. But in the 19th century it was housed in the market buildings which remained in use until the market was removed to Nine Elms, south of the Thames, in 1974. It was in the market that Charles II is reputed to have found

---

STARS OF COVENT GARDEN AND DRURY LANE

When Covent Garden Theatre opened in 1732, there was only one other major playhouse in London—the Drury Lane, which had been established during the Restoration. For a century, the two theatres dominated the London stage.

The great actor-playwright David Garrick (1717–79) took over the management of Drury Lane in 1746, and for 30 years he ran the theatre, which was famed for the brilliance of its performances.

Sarah Siddons (1755–1831) failed in her first performance as Portia at Drury Lane in 1775, but when she returned seven years later in Thomas Southerne's *The Fatal Marriage*, all London acclaimed her. She and her brother, the tragedian John Philip Kemble (1757–1823), were the theatre's principal attractions, but they left to join Covent Garden after the Drury Lane management failed to pay their wages. Mrs Siddons made her farewell at Covent Garden in 1812, two years before the electrifying début of Edmund Kean (1789–1833) as Shylock. In later years Kean's supremacy was challenged by a new star, Charles Macready (1793–1873). In 1848 Covent Garden went over to opera, and Drury Lane struggled on until the 1880's, when it became the home of melodrama.

Mrs Sarah Siddons, shown here as Lady Macbeth, one of her greatest roles, was without equal in tragic and heroic parts. Off-stage this great beauty could be mercenary and formidable.

A versatile actor, David Garrick was acclaimed for his tragic roles, such as Richard III (left). As the actor-manager of the Drury Lane Theatre, he dominated the London stage for 30 years.

Edmund Kean triumphed in villainous parts, such as Iago, but his Hamlet (right) failed to impress. A brilliant but unpredictable actor, Kean's health was destroyed by his drinking.

Kean's chief rival, Charles Macready, shown here as Othello, was a fine, rather than a great, actor. Macready disliked his profession, but encouraged the best in the theatre of his time.

an orange-seller named Nell Gwynne, who later became a highly successful actress at the nearby Drury Lane Theatre.

The Royal Opera House*, the third theatre to stand on this spot, dates from 1858. When the second building was opened in 1809, there were serious disturbances because John Philip Kemble, the actor-manager, had put up the admission prices. Performances were marred by the audience shouting 'Old prices!' and Kemble brought in ruffians to keep order. But the nightly uproar grew worse, and the actor George Frederick Cooke had to mime his Richard III because his words could not be heard above the noise. After 68 nights Kemble was forced to yield to the rioters. He apologised and the old prices were restored. The affair was known as the 'O.P. Riots'.

Fleet Street

The short stretch from Temple Bar to Ludgate Hill is a synonym for journalism and the national press. Caxton's assistant, Wynkyn de Worde, set up here in the early 1500's, and printers, stationers and booksellers followed.

In their train came the writers. They lived, as did Dr Samuel Johnson, in the courts and the alleys abutting the street. The doctor's attic den in his Gough Square house* was the birthplace of his great dictionary.

The vitality of Fleet Street has

spawned a host of colourful characters. Greatest of them were the Press barons—men such as Lord Northcliffe and Beaverbrook —who used their publications and purses to champion causes or in attempts to make and unmake governments.

Lord Northcliffe, born Alfred Harmsworth in 1865, started a magazine at his London school when he was 15. He became a journalist, and in 1888 borrowed £1500 to launch a new weekly, *Answers to Correspondents*. After a shaky start, *Answers* achieved an enormous success with a competition which offered the winner £1 a week for life.

In 1896 he founded the *Daily Mail*, the first London paper to sell for ½d. In 1903 the *Daily Mirror* appeared. In 1908 Northcliffe secured control of *The Times*, but his delusions of grandeur grew and his behaviour became irrational. He died in 1922, aged 57.

Lord Beaverbrook, born Max Aitken in Canada in 1879, acquired a paper round at the age of 12 and employed sub-agents in order to make more money. When he grew up he went into finance and was a millionaire by the age of 26. In 1910 he went to London and entered politics as a Conservative. In 1918 he bought the *Daily Express* and founded the *Sunday Express,* using his newspapers as platforms for one of his favourite causes, Empire Free Trade.

Beaverbrook's influence on the political life of Britain was controversial, and his Press campaigns had little success. His finest hour was in the Second World War when, as Minister of Aircraft Production from May 1940, he supplied the aeroplanes which won the Battle of Britain. Lord Beaverbrook died in 1964.

Greenwich

In 1428 Henry V's brother, Humphrey, Duke of Gloucester, built a palace, Bella Court, on the site of Greenwich House, which had been used by English sovereigns since 1300.

On the duke's arrest for high treason in 1447, Queen Margaret of Anjou, wife of his nephew Henry VI, seized Bella Court. She lavished money on extensions and renamed it the Palace of Pleasance or Placentia. After the Wars of the Roses, Henry VII renovated Placentia and renamed it Greenwich Palace.

Elizabeth I's successor, James I, presented Greenwich Palace to his extravagant consort, Anne of Denmark, in 1613. Since the palace had remained unchanged for nearly a century, the architect Inigo Jones was commissioned to build a new residence—the Queen's House or the House of Delight—which was to become one of the finest examples of Renaissance architecture in England.

In 1618 Anne of Denmark died before her residence was completed and all work on it stopped. However, in 1635, after Charles I settled the house on his wife, Henrietta Maria, to mark their reconciliation, Jones returned to his task. The queen was never able to enjoy her House of Delight. Her husband's court left London in 1642—never to return.

After the Restoration, John Webb, son-in-law and pupil of Inigo Jones, enlarged the Queen's House. The house was later used as part of the Greenwich Hospital School, and in 1933 it became the National Maritime Museum*.

During the reign of Charles II, the derelict Greenwich Palace was demolished and Webb was ordered to build another royal residence— the King's House.

In 1688, when William and Mary took over this unfinished house,

they could not afford its completion and instead gave the riverside site to the navy for the construction of a royal hospital for wounded seamen. Sir Christopher Wren supervised the building of the hospital, which was one of his greatest architectural triumphs. After the hospital was closed in 1869, the building became the home of the Royal Naval College*.

It was in the Painted Hall of the Royal Hospital that Nelson's body lay in state for three days in 1805, after his death at the Battle of Trafalgar. According to a contemporary newspaper account, the hall was 'fitted up with peculiar taste and elegance', and many thousands struggled to see the body. 'When the doors finally closed, a multitude that almost extended from Greenwich to London was turned back.'

Hampstead

Since the 18th century, Hampstead has been the haunt of artists, writers and poets. Among the great names who have lived there are Coleridge, Keats, Romney, Constable, Charles Dickens and D. H. Lawrence.

Lawrence is now regarded as one of the most important novelists that Britain produced in this century. But at the time he lived in the Vale of Health in 1915, his pacificism and the fact that he had a German-born wife led to vitriolic attacks on his writings.

His novel *The Rainbow* was prosecuted at Bow Street, where it was described as 'a mass of obscenity of thought, idea and action throughout'. The whole edition of the book was ordered to be destroyed. Lawrence commented bitterly that this persecution marked 'the end of my writing for England'.

Hampstead was kinder to another great figure of the 20th century. In 1938 Sigmund Freud, the founder of psychoanalysis, came to live there after fleeing from the Nazi occupation of his native Austria. He wrote that he found 'the kindliest welcome in beautiful, free, generous England'. And he was delighted with his house in Maresfield Gardens.

Freud's house was inundated with visitors—H. G. Wells, Chaim Weizmann, Salvador Dali among them—and with flowers from well-

MASTER OF FLEET STREET *Taking advantage of a new mass market, Alfred Harmsworth (left) launched the* Daily Mail *(above) in 1896. It was the first newspaper in the world to sell a million copies a day.*

EXILE *Sigmund Freud arrives in London in 1938 after being driven from Austria by the Nazis.*

wishers and with hundreds of letters, some simply addressed to 'Dr Freud, London'.

Only three weeks after his arrival, Freud had to undergo a serious operation for cancer of the jaw, from which he had been suffering for 16 years. But, despite the constant pain, he continued to work on his book *The Outlines of Psychoanalysis* until a few weeks before his death.

On September 3, 1939, he heard the first air-raid siren of the Second World War from his Hampstead garden. Asked whether he thought it would be the last war, he answered that it would definitely be the last for him. He died three weeks later on September 23.

Highgate

In 1386 the Bishop of London agreed, because of the 'deepnesse and dirtie' passage of the highway from London to Barnet, to build a new road through his land on the hills north of London. He set up a gate where a toll could be collected; and from this landmark Highgate acquired its name.

For centuries Highgate, perched on the twin hill to Hampstead, was famed for health-giving qualities of its air. By the 18th century it had become a fashionable village.

In middle age the poet and critic

REVOLUTIONARIES IN LONDON

The tomb* of Karl Marx in Highgate Cemetery is a reminder that, for 34 years, the founder of modern Communism lived in obscurity and poverty in London.

From Grafton Street, Kentish Town, the family and a few Socialist friends made regular Sunday excursions to Hampstead Heath during the summer. The group would play games, and return home, singing songs and reciting poetry.

Marx's hours of reading in the British Museum culminated in the publication of the first volume of his major work, *Das Kapital*, a study of capitalism, in 1867. In 1883 Marx

died at his house in Finsbury and was buried in Highgate.

Lenin, the Russian Bolshevik leader, who was profoundly influenced by Marx's thought, first came to London in 1902 to supervise the publication of a left-wing newspaper, *Iskra* (the Spark). He and his wife, Krupskaya, rented two unfurnished rooms in a house (now demolished) in King's Cross.

During the next nine years Lenin returned to London to attend political meetings or to work in the British Museum. In his spare time he explored the city by bicycle or bus. He went to Speaker's Corner, in Hyde Park, to the theatre and the music hall. One landmark Lenin unfailingly went to on his visits was Marx's grave in Highgate Cemetery.

London was a refuge for the two exiled founders of Communism—Karl Marx (top) and Lenin (right). Marx lies buried in Highgate Cemetery (above).

Samuel Taylor Coleridge retired to Highgate to cure himself of opium addiction. He lived at the home of his doctor, James Gillman, until his death. According to Carlyle, Coleridge spent his last years 'looking down on London and its smoke-tumult like a sage escaped from the inanity of life's battle'.

Within 50 years of Coleridge's death, Highgate had become a

middle-class suburb of Victorian London. Men from the city, on which the poet had gazed with such contempt, were now able to reach the peace of Highgate.

Holland House

Only a wing of Holland House, a Jacobean mansion destroyed by bombs during the Second World War, remains in Holland Park. The

mansion took its name from James I's favourite, the 1st Earl of Holland, whose father-in-law began building it in 1605.

The third earl (who was also the Earl of Warwick) and his wife, Charlotte, were generous hosts to the literary men of the early 18th century. Among those who visited Holland House were the satirist Dean Swift, the poet Alexander Pope and the essayist and politician Joseph Addison. Fifteen years after her husband's death the countess married Addison in 1714. He died three years later.

In 1768 Holland House was bought by Henry Fox, who squandered his own large fortune before acquiring a second by eloping with an heiress. He made a third fortune as a notoriously corrupt minister.

From 1799 until 1840 Holland House was the centre of a brilliant literary and political circle entertained by Henry Richard Fox, the 3rd Lord Holland, and his formidable wife, Elizabeth. Among their guests were the European statesmen Metternich and Talleyrand, the novelists Sir Walter Scott and James Fenimore Cooper, and the celebrated wit Sidney Smith.

Hyde Park

Popularly christened the 'lungs of London' in Victorian times, the five royal parks—Hyde Park, St James's Park, Green Park, Regent's Park and Kensington Gardens—have long been places of recreation for the citizens of London.

Once an estate belonging to the monks of Westminster Abbey, Hyde Park is the oldest of the parks. It passed into royal hands when Henry VIII dissolved the monasteries, and it was transformed by him into a deer park, where his daughter Elizabeth I came to hunt. In 1637 Charles I opened the park to the public.

Charles II made Hyde Park a centre of fashion, but in the reign of William and Mary highway robberies there were common. A roadway leading to Kensington Palace* was hung with 300 lamps to make royal journeys safer. This lighted highway was known as *La Route du Roi*, from which the name 'Rotten Row' is probably derived. In the late 19th century the road was a resort for strollers and riders from Mayfair and Belgravia.

Another social spectacle was ice-skating on the Serpentine, an artificial lake created by George II's wife, Caroline. The queen was responsible for enclosing 300 acres of Hyde Park to make Kensington Gardens. It was her intention to include in the gardens the remainder of Hyde Park (and St James's Park). But when the queen asked the Prime Minister, Sir Robert Walpole, what the cost would be, he replied: 'Three crowns —England, Scotland, and Wales.'

Islington

This area was once a playground for Londoners during the 17th and 18th centuries. Pleasure gardens, teahouses, music and dance rooms, and the more robust attractions of archery, duck-shooting and prize-fights drew Londoners for a day's enjoyment. For the walk back to the city across robber-infested fields, people would gather at the Angel, a coaching inn now demolished, to be escorted in parties by a mounted and armed guard.

In 1683, when Thomas Sadler found an old well in his garden in Islington, he quickly promoted it as a miraculous spa, charging 3d for the waters and the entertainment provided. Out of this grew the first Sadler's Wells Theatre, which was built in 1783. Another popular establishment for entertainment, opened less than a century later, was Sam Collins's Music Hall beside Islington Green.

Kensington

Kensington's royal associations date back over many centuries to the time when it was a tiny village in the centre of a vast hunting preserve stretching west from Westminster. The first king to do more than hunt there was William III, who moved his court into Kensington Palace*.

William chose Kensington as his new abode because of its tranquillity and for reasons of health. The damp fogs rising from the Thames had aggravated his asthma. His taste was shared by his successors— Queen Anne, George I and George II, who all lived there.

Where the monarchy led, fashion followed. According to a foreign visitor of the 1780's, many wealthy Londoners 'who have no country seat of their own, in summer move into Kensington houses for the sake of the good air, the gardens, the fine prospect'. But the area was not safe from thieves. George II himself was accosted by a highwayman who climbed over the wall and 'with a manner of much deference, deprived the king of his purse, his watch and his buckles'.

By the 19th century Kensington was no longer a village, and it received the royal seal of approval when it was made a royal borough by Queen Victoria, who was born in Kensington Palace in 1819.

But it was Victoria's husband, Prince Albert, who gave Kensington its most lasting royal legacy. He inspired the Great Exhibition of 1851 in Hyde Park (see pp. 302–3). With its profits, he and his fellow commissioners embarked on a great programme of museum building which made South Kensington a national monument.

THE RISE AND FALL OF THE MUSIC HALL

Sam Collins's famous music hall as it was during the 1920's after its heyday.

Collins's Music Hall was one of the 500 halls which were built in late 19th-century London. Whatever their trade or class, Londoners who had a little money to spend and were eager for amusement flocked to these popular places of entertainment for nights of revelry.

The music halls began in alehouses and taverns, where the customers were entertained with songs and comic turns. In 1849 Charles Morton (1819–1904), the enterprising proprietor of the Canterbury Arms, Lambeth, created the first music hall by putting up a special building with a bar, tables and a platform for the performers. Morton's venture was so successful that competitors began building halls throughout London.

Morton, who became known as the 'father of the halls', opened the palatial Oxford Music Hall in the West End in 1861 and was later called upon to manage the London Pavilion (Piccadilly Circus) and the Palace (Cambridge Circus), which he transformed into 'temples of variety'. It was at the Palace that music hall received its highest honour, when George V ordered a command performance in 1912.

This was the heyday of the halls, many of which had become gilt-and-plush theatres and had created stars such as Harry Lauder, Dan Leno, Little Tich, Marie Lloyd, George Robey and Vesta Tilley. But by the 1920's the music halls began to decline in popularity, having lost their audiences to the films, one of whose most famous stars was the English-born music-hall comedian, Charlie Chaplin.

Singer Marie Lloyd (left) and comic Little Tich were idols of the halls.

Lambeth

For seven centuries Lambeth Palace has been the residence of the Archbishops of Canterbury. Stephen Langton, who was archbishop between 1207 and 1228, began making alterations to the original manor house. Over the next three centuries it was transformed into the rambling, turreted red-brick palace* of the present day.

A great part of the palace was built in the early 15th century by Archbishop Chichele, who added the Lollards Tower, reputed to have been a prison for the heretical followers of John Wyclif. Cardinal Morton, Henry VII's Chancellor, who was appointed archbishop in 1493, restored the palace, which had been neglected during the Wars of the Roses, and rebuilt the Gate-house. In Morton's time, Lambeth Palace became a centre of learning.

But in 1381 Wat Tyler's rebels plundered the building and beheaded its resident, Archbishop Sudbury, on Tower Hill. And during the Gordon Riots in 1780 Lambeth Palace was narrowly saved from destruction

Mansion House

Built by George Dance the Elder between 1739 and 1753, Mansion House* is the official residence of the Lord Mayor during his year of office. This dignified building stands on the site of the medieval Stocks Market, whose profits from the sale of fish and meat were used to pay for the upkeep of the old London Bridge.

Apart from private apartments

PRINCE'S LEGACY *Built to commemorate the life and work of Victoria's Prince Consort, the Royal Albert Hall was opened in 1871.*

the Mansion House has a number of chambers for balls, dinners and receptions. The most impressive of these is the grandiose Egyptian dining-hall, where mayoral banquets for up to 350 guests are held. These feasts are prepared in kitchens where, according to one Victorian observer, there were ovens 'large enough to roast an entire ox', and vessels for boiling meat and vegetables which were 'not pots but tanks'.

The tradition of lavish mayoral entertainment, which must be paid for partly by the citizen who holds this high office, dates from the Middle Ages. According to legend, on one splendid occasion, Richard Whittington, thrice Lord Mayor (1397–8, 1406–7, 1419–20), when entertaining Henry V and his queen, burnt not only costly cedar logs but also bonds worth £60,000 to keep his guests warm.

Marylebone

This area of London came into existence in the great building boom of the late 18th and early 19th centuries. It soon became the home of many of the rich and famous—and of a group of men who have added much to the lustre of British science. The area around Harley Street is well known for its medical specialists, and many celebrated doctors have worked there.

But one of the greatest figures of 19th-century medicine deliberately chose to live away from the London medical world which had poured scorn on his ideas. Joseph Lister (1827–1912) was 50 when he moved from Edinburgh to a house in Park Crescent in 1877, and began his long battle to win acceptance for his theory of antisepsis.

For years he fought against the prejudices of his London colleagues, who refused to accept his conviction that observing rules of hygiene during an operation would prevent wounds from becoming infected. But by his death in 1912, he had seen his theories accepted.

Among the other famous residents of the area were H. G. Wells and George Bernard Shaw, who lived there during his days as music critic of *The Star*. Writing under the pseudonym Corno di Bassetto, Shaw set London laughing by expounding his controversial views not only on music but also on such diverse subjects as women's rights, bicycles and socialism.

The most human story to emerge from Marylebone was the long romantic courtship—immortalised in the play and film, *The Barretts of Wimpole Street*—between the poetess Elizabeth Barrett and her suitor, Robert Browning. For 40 years Elizabeth had been dominated by an intractable father. Then, on the morning of September 12, 1846, she broke the knot that had held her captive by slipping out of the house to marry Browning in the parish church. In later years, Browning returned to kiss the altar stairs at which he and his wife 'had been made happy for life'.

DANCES AND DEBUTANTES *Queen Charlotte's Ball (above) was a high point of the inter-war Mayfair season. Below, a 'deb' advertises a charity ball.*

Mayfair

Speculators and aristocrats together created Mayfair, a name which evokes luxury, fashion and snobbery. The district now bounded by Piccadilly, Park Lane, Oxford Street and Regent Street was open country when Charles II gave his Lord Chancellor, the Earl of Clarendon, a large piece of land in 1664. Clarendon sold portions to his friends Lord Berkeley and Lord Burlington before spending £40,000 on a mansion and garden on his remaining piece. He moved into the house in 1667 but fled into exile the next year to escape trial for high treason. Bankers and speculators led by Sir Thomas Bond bought his estate and on it grew Bond Street, Dover Street, Albemarle Street and Stafford Street. The Great Fire of 1666 had destroyed half the city and noblemen were rushing to buy properties in the new West End.

When Lord Berkeley died, his widow leased his Palladian home to Princess (later Queen) Anne, who became Mayfair's first royal resident. Her presence made Mayfair even more fashionable.

The Earl of Scarborough laid out an estate in north-east Mayfair in 1717. Lord Burlington leased plots behind Burlington House, while the greatest developer of them all, Sir Richard Grosvenor, created the north-west section.

His mother, Mary Davies, had inherited lands between the Oxford Road and the River Thames. Mary married the wealthy Sir Thomas Grosvenor, and Richard, heir to Mary's land and Thomas's money, laid out Grosvenor Square, Grosvenor Street, Audley Street and the grid of streets around them.

Mary Davies's descendants became dukes of Westminster. The second duke's estate in Mayfair and Belgravia was charged duty of £12 million when he died in 1953.

Shepherd Market, a picturesque huddle of narrow streets, was laid out by Edward Shepherd in the mid-18th century, on the site of the May Fair which gave the district its name. James II had given permission in 1686 for a cattle fair every May. Around it gathered a host of rowdy characters. Finally the neighbours had the fair closed.

Gladstone, Disraeli, Nelson and Wellington lived in Mayfair. Clive of India died at 44 Berkeley Square in 1774 of drugs, either from addiction or to kill pain. Handel wrote the *Messiah* in Brook Street, and the infatuated Lady Caroline Lamb dressed up as a page boy to visit Byron in his chambers at Albany, off Piccadilly.

The rich kept their town houses into the 20th century, but after the First World War office blocks and hotels encroached. And if an era epitomises Mayfair it is the 1920's, when a fashionable Mayfair clique known as the 'Bright Young Things' lived in a whirl of dances, theatre-going, cocktail parties and uncon-

POET AND POETESS *Robert Browning (right) and Elizabeth Barrett, whose long courtship led to one of the greatest romantic correspondences in history.*

Yours very truly,
Robert Browning.

ventional behaviour. Writers such as Aldous Huxley, Evelyn Waugh and Noel Coward so enhanced this little world that it stands for everything that is gay and inconsequential. For the fortunate few, Mayfair in the 1920's was a golden age between the realities of two world wars.

Paddington

Before the 19th century, Paddington was notorious for its dark place in London's history. Within its bounds stood Tyburn, for centuries the capital's chief execution place.

Tyburn's first recorded victims perished in 1196. At first, the executions there were by hanging from the elm trees that grew in the vicinity. Later a gallows was erected. It was a large three-legged gantry, whose triple crossbeams enabled a dozen or more criminals to be hanged at the same time. Its services were much in demand; as late as the early 19th century over 200 petty

offences were punishable by death. (The site where the gallows stood is now marked by a stone on a traffic island near Marble Arch.)

Among the many thousands to die at Tyburn was Jonathan Wild, whose flamboyant career as a professional 'thief taker' had won him great notoriety in the 18th-century London. Operating in the days before there was a police force, Wild brought many criminals to justice. But his own career was more often illegal than legal.

With his intimate knowledge of all types of dishonesty, Wild was able to exploit crime from every angle. He got money from protection rackets, from blackmailing criminals, from the sale of stolen goods (which he might alternatively return to owners for a fat reward), and from rewards given for the criminals he turned over to the law.

Wild's disdain for legal processes was legendary. At his own trial in 1725, for trafficking in stolen goods, he circulated among the jury a list

MORAL EXAMPLE *The fate of Jonathan Wild, executed at Tyburn, is held up as a grim example to criminals.*

of those he had been instrumental in convicting. On the list were the names of 35 robbers, 22 housebreakers, and ten convicts who had returned from transportation—an offence punishable by death.

Many others followed Wild to the scaffold for offences ranging from murder to picking pockets. But Tyburn's day was drawing to a close. The last felon to be hanged there was John Austin in November 1783 for robbery and wounding.

With a new century came a revolution that was to transform the area. The building of Paddington Canal—part of the Grand Union System—in the early 1800's led to a wave of new building. The elegant houses that were erected there were deliberately intended to rival Belgravia—and the area became known as 'Tyburnia'. And the final transformation came about with the coming of the railway. In the 1830's the directors of the Great Western Railway and their engineer, Isambard Kingdom Brunel, decided to build a great terminus there for the line they were building to the west.

Regent Street

Nothing but the line of the street remains of architect John Nash's original plans for Regent Street. He designed it as part of the 'Royal Mile' to link the Prince Regent's proposed new country house in Marylebone (later Regent's) Park with the palace of Carlton House in Pall Mall. Carlton House was pulled down in 1827.

Because of the bankruptcy of the builders and the financial strains of the Napoleonic Wars, the park itself is only a shadow of Nash's grandiose scheme for a fashionable garden suburb. But Regent Street, begun about 1817, benefited from the building boom which began soon after the Battle of Waterloo, and was completed by 1823.

The County Fire Office marked the end of Lower Regent Street, which ran from Waterloo Place to Piccadilly Circus. From there Nash carried the street on a curve—the Quadrant—which led into the final stretch to Oxford Circus.

The original Quadrant consisted of a superb colonnade of 145 columns in front of regular rows of stucco-faced houses. But Regent Street did not long remain as Nash had planned it. The shopkeepers complained that their goods could not be seen in the dim light which filtered through the columns.

In 1848 the colonnade was removed (and part of it was added to one side of Drury Lane Theatre) and the frontages rebuilt. The lower part of the frontage was divided into shops. Above their windows was a long balcony which continued the horizontal curve as the colonnade had done.

Following the rebuilding of the Piccadilly Hotel in Portland stone in 1908, other buildings in Regent Street were gradually heightened and rebuilt in the same stone.

The completion of the rebuilding in 1927 was celebrated by cheering crowds, when George V and Queen Mary drove down a Regent Street decked with flags and flowers.

St James's

Although Britain's sovereigns no longer use St James's Palace as a permanent residence, it has remained the headquarters of court ceremonial, and foreign ambassadors are still accredited to 'the Court of St James's'.

Henry VIII built it on the site of a hospital for leprous women which was dedicated to St James the Less. The only remnants from Henry's time are the Chapel Royal*, and the clocktower gatehouse which faces St James's Street, for a disastrous fire destroyed much of the old palace in 1809.

It was the birthplace of Charles II, James II, Mary II, Anne and George IV. Mary Tudor used it

---

THE GROWTH OF UNDERGROUND LONDON

Digging the first underground.

The world's first passenger-carrying underground railway opened in London in 1863. It was the result of 30 years of struggle. Charles Pearson, an enterprising and far-sighted surveyor of the City of London, saw it as the only solution to the city's road-congestion problems.

The first underground line to be opened was a 3¾ mile stretch from Paddington to Farringdon Road, which was run by the North Metropolitan Railway Company. On the first day, Londoners flocked to the underground railway and in the first six months an average of 26,500 passengers used the line daily.

Pearson, who did not live to see

his scheme fulfilled, had also planned for an underground system linking all the main railway stations in London. In 1868, with the building of the Metropolitan and District line, this project became a reality. There quickly followed a vast network of underground railway tunnels.

Apart from its crucial role as part of London's transport system, the underground railway has served other important functions. During both world wars it was a refuge from bombing raids for thousands of Londoners, and a storehouse for some of London's great treasures, such as the Elgin Marbles from the British Museum.

as a private residence, and she died and was buried here. Charles I spent his last night in the guardroom before walking across St James's Park to the scaffold at Whitehall.

During the reign of William III the king granted apartments in the palace to Anne and her husband, Prince George of Denmark. Never happy at her brother-in-law's palace in Kensington, Queen Anne made St James's the royal household.

It was during the reign of George II that St James's became a centre for fashionable society. His queen consort, Charlotte, presided over brilliant balls and receptions.

St James's ceased to be the home of the monarch when George III bought Buckingham House in 1762. However, the west wing of St James's, which survived the fire of 1809, has been known as York House. It became the London home of the princes of Wales and was last used by Edward VIII before his accession. Clarence House and Marlborough House, which are built in the palace grounds, have been used as residences for other members of the royal family.

Soho

Now a maze of narrow streets and alleys, Soho was a small village until late in the 17th century. It derives its name from the cry 'So Ho' used by fox hunters who rode on their hunts through the surrounding green fields.

Soho was first settled in the 1680's by French Protestants who had fled from religious persecution in their own country. Since then other refugees have settled in this cosmopolitan quarter. Among the most famous was Karl Marx, the founder of Communism.

The adventurer Theodore de Neuhof, King of Corsica, is buried at the site of St Anne's Church. Theodore was crowned in Corsica in 1736 but had to flee the island a few months later. He settled in Soho, where he lived in poverty in Great Chapel Street.

Soho became fashionable when King Square, named after the developer Gregory King and now known as Soho Square, was laid out on the site of the Duke of Monmouth's house in 1681.

In the 1760's one of the great

mansions in the square was bought by Mrs Teresa Cornelys, a mistress of the Italian adventurer Casanova. She transformed the house into a sort of night club, where she staged balls and masquerades for the nobility. For 30 years this forerunner of modern Soho night life flourished until it was converted into a church in 1792.

Southwark

The name of the borough comes from the south works—the fortifications on the South Bank which protected London Bridge.

Southwark was famous for its taverns, brothels and prisons—the Clink (which became a slang term for all prisons) and the Marshalsea. Late in the 16th century, pleasure-seeking crowds flocked to its bear and bull-baiting rings, and to Shakespeare's Globe Theatre.

The Globe was an unroofed, six-sided wooden structure. The beams used in its construction came from the first London playhouse, the Theatre, which had been erected in Finsbury Fields in 1576. Performances at the Globe were given on summer afternoons, and audiences were summoned by the sound of a trumpet.

Stepney

The heart of London's East End, Stepney's first mention in history is in the Domesday Book, compiled by order of William I after his conquest of England in 1066.

By the 19th century the area was notorious for its slums. Charles Dickens captured their squalor in novels such as *Oliver Twist*. The horror of the poverty he found there inspired the young Dr Thomas Barnardo (1845–1905) to found refuges for destitute children—the Barnardo homes.

A visit to a boy's club in Stepney also changed the course of life for Clement Attlee (1883–1967), Labour Prime Minister for six years after the Second World War. His experiences in Stepney started his conversion to socialism. He gave up his career at the bar in 1910 to devote himself to social reform. In 1919 he became mayor of Stepney, and four years later he entered parliament.

The man who Winston Churchill described as 'a sheep in wolf's clothing' nevertheless became the leader of the Labour Party. And,

IN POWER *Once Mayor of Stepney, Clement Attlee led Labour to power in 1945.*

when he became Prime Minister after the war, his subordinates found him far from sheeplike. His government carried through a far-ranging nationalisation programme, introduced social services and health schemes and gave independence to India.

Strand

One of London's most famous streets, the Strand was once a riverside road linking the City of London to the Palace of Westminster, the residence built by Edward the Confessor in the 11th century. From that time until the 18th century this thoroughfare was lined with the houses of noblemen.

A great medieval mansion of the Strand was the 13th-century Savoy Palace. But in 1381 its owner, the powerful John of Gaunt, Edward III's son, witnessed its sacking by Wat Tyler's rebels. Henry VII transformed the Savoy into a hospital, which was demolished in the reign of Queen Anne. Only the Tudor chapel* was saved from destruction. And in the 16th century, the Duke of Somerset, who was Lord Protector of the kingdom during the reign of Edward VI, built his palace on the Strand.

In the 19th century the remaining great mansions of the Strand disappeared and were replaced by theatres and cafés. As if to mark this change in the character of the Strand, Richard d'Oyly Carte, who had made a fortune from presenting the Gilbert and Sullivan comic operas, opened his Savoy Theatre there in 1887.

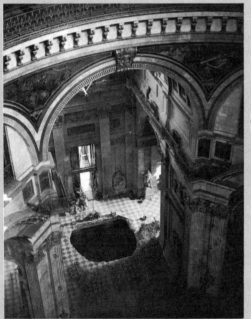

A story that must earn a man the V.C.

St. Paul's saved: 1-ton bomb

A MONSTER bomb weighing fully a ton which for three days has been buried near St. Paul's Cathedral in London, exploded yesterday—but not at St. Paul's.

The courage and tenacity of a bomb disposal section under Lieu-

CHURCH BOMBARDED *During the Blitz, St Paul's was constantly under fire. In one raid a bomb fell into the crypt (left). There were some near misses, as the* Daily Express *reported (above).*

St Paul's

One of London's most famous landmarks is the great dome of St Paul's Cathedral. Since the 7th century there has always been a cathedral on the site. During the Middle Ages it became one of the greatest churches of Europe, and pilgrims flocked to see its collection of relics, which included an arm of St Mellitus and St Ethelbert's head.

But by 1660 the cathedral had

degenerated into a market place. It was a haunt of courtesans and a short cut for porters with casks of beer and loads of fresh fish and vegetables. It was destroyed by the Great Fire of 1666.

The present cathedral* was rebuilt by Sir Christopher Wren. (See pp. 204–5.) It took Wren 36 years to complete his revolutionary building. He is buried in the crypt together with other national figures.

Lossiemouth, *Grampian*

James Ramsay MacDonald, the first Labour Prime Minister in 1924 and again in 1929–35, was born in a thatched cottage at 1 Gregory Place in the fishing village of Lossiemouth. Isabella Ramsay brought up her grandson, James, the illegitimate child of her youngest daughter Annie. Mac-Donald's grandmother was a woman of exceptional courage and determination, who had been left penniless when her husband deserted her and their four children.

While at a local school, Mac-Donald started reading the book collection of a watchmaker who had retired to Lossiemouth. This introduced him to the works of Scott and Dickens.

After leaving school he worked on a farm, but the 'dominie' persuaded him to come back as a pupil-teacher at £7 10s a year; he also allowed the boy the use of his library, which included works on socialism. In 1885, aged 18, MacDonald left for Bristol and then moved to London, where he began his political career as a socialist in the 1890's.

In later years, MacDonald and his family spent their holidays at Lossiemouth with his mother, who was always known as 'Miss Annie Ramsay'. In 1937 MacDonald died at sea, while on a cruise for his health; his ashes were taken back to Lossiemouth and laid to rest in the family grave.

Ludlow, *Salop*

The history of Ludlow, like the town itself, is overshadowed by the ruins of its imposing castle*. The castle was one of a great line of fortresses built to defend the border area between England and Wales, known as the Welsh Marches.

In the 1470's Edward IV established his court of the Marches at Ludlow, and his sons, the young Prince of Wales and his brother Richard, lived there for 11 years. From Ludlow they were taken by Richard III to the Tower of London, where they met their mysterious deaths.

In November 1501 Ludlow Castle became once more the home of a Prince of Wales. Prince Arthur, Henry VII's heir, set up his court in the castle with his Spanish bride, Catharine of Aragon. Although he

had been betrothed since the age of two, Arthur had never seen Catharine until she arrived from Spain for the wedding. Their time together at Ludlow was sadly brief. By the spring of 1502 he was dead, at the age of 16.

The changes in government in Wales made by Henry VIII in the 1530's meant the end of Ludlow's greatness. No longer did princes of Wales need to live there. When Milton's masque *Comus* had its first performance in the castle in 1624, part of the roof had already fallen in. By the beginning of the 18th century it was uninhabited, a grim reminder of forgotten Welsh wars.

Lumphanan, *Grampian*

Macbeth, King of Scotland, was killed at Lumphanan in 1057. He had been *mormaer*, or district chief, of Moray and Ross and rose to become commander of his master Duncan I's forces.

In 1040, after murdering Duncan, Macbeth seized the throne. His reign was a prosperous period, but several attempts to recover the throne were made by Duncan's family. Duncan's father, the Abbot of Dunkeld, tried in 1045, and Duncan's son, Malcolm Canmore, in alliance with the Northumbrians, made an unsuccessful attempt to overthrow Macbeth in 1054.

In 1057 Malcolm Canmore again invaded Scotland, and met Macbeth in battle at Lumphanan. Macbeth was killed. Malcolm became Malcolm II, and his reign lasted until his death in 1093.

Shakespeare took the story of Macbeth from the 1587 edition of Holinshed's *Chronicle of England and Scotland*, and wove it into one of the most powerful tragedies in the English language.

Lutterworth, *Leics*

The last, peaceful years of the philosopher and theologian John Wyclif were spent at Lutterworth.

Born in 1330, Wyclif became one of the most brilliant scholars of his time at Oxford. His attacks on the Church, first published during the 1370's, drew Wyclif into the turbulent politics of that decade. In 1382 Wyclif's opinions were condemned as heretical. Broken in health, Wyclif retired to Lutterworth, where he died in 1384.

Wyclif's followers, known as the

Lollards, carried on his attacks on the Church. They prepared an English translation of the Bible. But the movement was suppressed in the 15th century.

Lyme Regis, *Dorset*

The Duke of Monmouth, illegitimate son of Charles II, was a claimant to the throne of his uncle

James II. Banished from the English court in 1683, the duke responded to vague invitations from England and came back in the summer of 1685. With its radical and Protestant traditions, the West Country was an especially suitable choice for the landing. For in 1680 Monmouth had been warmly welcomed there during his tour of the country.

'KING MONMOUTH'S' ILL-FATED UPRISING

Encouraged by the crafty William of Orange, the Duke of Monmouth landed at Lyme Regis on June 11, 1685, at the start of his ill-fated attempt to overthrow James II. The Dutch leader saw in this escapade an opportunity to rid himself of his most dangerous rival for the crown.

Monmouth's three ships sailed in from Holland with 82 followers aboard, and the duke walked ashore at the beach later named after him, with only £100 to raise an army. He at once proclaimed his legal right to James II's throne. Parliament responded by issuing a writ for his arrest and offering £5000 for his capture, dead or alive.

But within 24 hours Monmouth had gathered a band of 1500 supporters and by the time he entered Taunton, his army had swollen to 7000. He was proclaimed king, his supporters styling him 'King Monmouth'. Twenty-six 'Fair Maids of Taunton' presented him with a Bible, a sword and flags.

Monmouth now assumed the royal style in his pronouncements, which included a warrant for the gathering in of scythes for use as weapons. Prayers were offered for him, and superstitious peasants asked him to touch their children in order to cure them of the skin disease known as

the 'King's Evil', or scrofula.

On June 21 Monmouth had an enthusiastic welcome at Bridgwater, but James's army was already advancing from London. After a skirmish with 200 Life Guards at Keynsham, the duke decided to forgo an attack on Bristol and made for Bath, which refused to surrender. At Frome his flagging spirits were further depressed by news that a simultaneous rebellion in the north by the Duke of Argyll had failed.

Monmouth returned to Bridgwater on the strength of false information that large numbers of peasants were joining his colours. From the tower of St Mary's Church, he watched his enemies assemble on Sedgmoor plain. (See pp. 210–11.)

A desperate night attack ended in disaster. Monmouth fled, was captured and executed at Tower Hill. His followers were delivered up to Judge Jeffreys, and in a series of trials they were cruelly punished.

M

Machynlleth, *Powys*

This small market town was briefly the capital of Wales under the rebel Owen Glendower.

Born in 1359, Glendower was a rich and aristocratic Welsh landowner. In 1400 a feud with a neighbour, Lord Grey of Ruthin,

led to Owen's attempt to raise the Welsh against Henry IV.

Within a year, his revolt had spread to the whole of North Wales, despite successful attacks by Henry's forces. In 1402 Glendower captured Lord Grey of Ruthin and Lord Edmund Mortimer, who allied themselves with their captors.

When the revolt spread to the whole of Wales, Glendower was joined in rebellion by the discontented Earl of Northumberland and his son Hotspur.

In 1404 Glendower was at the peak of his fortunes. After capturing the castles of Aberystwyth and Harlech and burning Cardiff, he was proclaimed King of Wales at a parliament summoned by him to meet at Machynlleth.

But the superiority of the English forces began to turn the scales against Glendower.

In 1405 the northern rebellion was crushed by Henry, and Wales was gradually recaptured. When Harlech fell in 1409 English rule was no longer disputed. Glendower himself, who is believed to have died in the mountains of central Wales in about 1416, never surrendered to the English.

Magus Muir, *Fife*

On May 3, 1679, a party of Covenanters stopped a coach carrying James Sharp, Archbishop of St Andrews, and his daughter, on Magus Muir, 3 miles from St Andrews. They ordered Sharp out, struck him as he knelt, hacked him and finally thrust a sword through his belly. The ghastly murder took three-quarters of an hour. A cairn marks the spot of the crime.

It was the Presbyterian extremists' revenge for an act of treachery, for Sharp had been sent to London to plead their cause. He returned as their oppressor, bribed with the title of archbishop.

John Balfour of Kinloch, a leader of the assassins, is said to have escaped to Holland. But David Hackston, laird of Rathiller, was hanged, drawn and quartered for his part in the deed.

Maiden Castle, *Dors* See pp. 30–31

Man, Isle of See Isle of Man, p. 392

Manchester, *GM*

Although the history of Manchester begins with the Romans, the city is a product of the Industrial Revolution. Industry began in the town as early as the 14th century when Flemish weavers introduced woollen and linen weaving. By Henry VIII's reign, the antiquary John Leland described Manchester as 'the fairest, best builded, and most populous town in all Lancashire'.

The old town was swept away during the boom of the 1770's and 1780's. Manchester's industrial development began in the 1730's when the first machines were introduced into the woollen and cotton industries. In 1761 the growth of industry was furthered by the completion of the Duke of Bridgewater's canal*. On this

waterway coal was brought from local mines to the heart of the town. By 1800 canals joined Manchester to the port of Liverpool and to other major manufacturing towns in Lancashire.

It was the cotton industry which transformed Manchester from a busy market town into a great industrial centre. Cotton had been imported by Manchester weavers in the 16th century. But after the tax on pure cotton was cut in 1774, the industry grew rapidly. Between 1740 and 1800 cotton imports increased in value from £1 million to £60 million.

The development of the cotton industry was advanced by the abundant coal supply, the damp climate and the improvements in machinery. The world's first cotton-spinning factory, powered by water, was built by Richard Arkwright in 1780. Nine years later, one of Boulton and Watt's steam engines was installed in a Manchester cotton-mill. By the beginning of the 19th century, cotton had superseded wool in the Lancashire mills.

In 1830 the opening of the Liverpool to Manchester railway set the seal on a century of progress. The population had climbed from 20,000 in 1759 to 142,000 in 1831. A by-product of this progress was squalor. 'The town is abominably filthy,' wrote a visitor in 1808. 'The steam engines are pestiferous, the dyehouses noisome and offensive, and the water of the river as black as ink or the Stygian lake.'

The appalling conditions in the factories and slums of Manchester resulted in the growth of the working-class movement. In 1817 the Blanketeers—each man carrying his own blanket to sleep in — set out from Manchester to lay their grievances before Parliament. They were arrested by government troops in Derbyshire, but later were discharged without trial.

Two years later, in 1819, a political reform meeting was violently suppressed by the yeomanry. The incident became known as the 'Peterloo Massacre'. Some 60,000 people had gathered in St Peter's fields, now the site of St Peter's Square, to hear the great radical politician, 'Orator' Hunt. The local magistrates, fearing that a riot was about to begin, ordered the troops to charge. Eleven people died and several hundred were wounded

before the field was cleared of demonstrators.

The memory of the massacre still rankled when Manchester men began to agitate against the high duties on corn in 1838. Eight years later, the Anti-Corn Law League, led by Richard Cobden and John Bright, triumphed when the hated Corn Laws were repealed by Parliament. It was a Manchester victory, and the Free Trade Hall was built to commemorate it.

The tradition of radicalism did not die with Cobden and Bright. Edwin Chadwick, the civil servant whose reports on working-class life stirred the conscience of Victorian England, was born in Manchester. The *Manchester Guardian,* which embodied the views of Manchester radicals, was founded in 1821.

Marlow, *Bucks*

The poet Percy Bysshe Shelley and his second wife, Mary, stayed in a house, now named Shelley House, in West Street in 1817.

It was while living here that Shelley wrote his impassioned vision of the French Revolution,

FRANKENSTEIN'S CREATOR *Mary Shelley, wife of the poet, wrote her famous novel at Marlow.*

'The Revolt of Islam', and also published some political tracts under the signature of 'The Hermit of Marlow'. Mary, who was expecting a baby, created her best-known work, *Frankenstein*. She had begun the story in rivalry with Byron, to see who could produce the most chilling Gothic horror novel. By the beginning of 1818, however, Shelley had become restless, and in March the family left England for Italy.

Marston Moor, *N Yorks*

On July 2, 1644, the largest battle of the Civil War between king and Parliament took place about 6 miles west of York on Marston Moor.

The Parliamentarians, led by Oliver Cromwell, the Earl of Manchester and Lord Fairfax, were forced to raise the siege of York by Prince Rupert, who had dashed from Lancashire to rescue the beleaguered Duke of Newcastle. But, unwisely, the prince decided to stay and fight the Parliamentarians at Marston Moor,

although he knew he had only 11,000 men to their 27,000.

Throughout that July day the Royalists faced the Roundheads, waiting for the battle to begin. Suddenly, at 7 o'clock the Parliamentary army hurled itself on the Royalists. The king's army scarcely had time to seize its muskets before it found itself driven back from its line. By nightfall it had been routed.

For the king, it was a disaster. He had lost control of the north, and 3000 of his most experienced soldiers lay dead.

DECISIVE BATTLE *A 19th-century painting of the Battle of Marston Moor, which shattered Royalist control of the north after a Roundhead victory.*

Medmenham, *Bucks*

Medmenham Abbey, a 15th-century mansion built on the site of a 12th-century Cistercian abbey, was the home of Sir Francis Dashwood (1708–81) from 1751 until his death.

Contemporaries supposed the abbey to be the secret meeting place of a group of Dashwood's fashionable friends, who indulged in blasphemous orgies and mock-religious rituals. Every conceivable type of vice was attributed to this group—later christened the Hell-Fire Club. Their motto was 'Do what you will'. But the club's members soon lost their enthusiasm when Dashwood let loose a baboon at one of the 'services'. They believed it to be the Devil and fled in terror.

These stories were exaggerated by the MP John Wilkes and the poet Charles Churchill in the Press from 1763 onwards. This was part of their campaign to discredit Lord Bute's government, in which Dashwood became Chancellor of the Exchequer in 1762.

The Medmenham legend was further embellished by stories of the club's activities in the golden dome* above West Wycombe church (restored by Dashwood in 1763), and in the nearby caves*, which had been excavated in 1751 to provide building materials for a road between West and High Wycombe.

Melbourne, *Derbs*

Thomas Cook the travel agent was born in a cottage in Quick Close in 1808. His widowed mother scraped a living from selling earthenware and evangelical books, and Thomas earned sixpence a week working in a market garden.

Both his first employer and a cabinet-maker to whom he was later apprenticed were heavy drinkers. While his employers caroused in the taverns Thomas, grandson of a Baptist minister, took to evangelism and the temperance movement.

When he was 17 he began to walk through the countryside selling Baptist books, covering 2106 miles on foot in one year. Then he had the idea of com-

bining temperance with the growing popularity of the railways, and in 1841 organised a temperance excursion from Leicester to Loughborough, with tea and a brass band thrown in. Cook had catered for 1000 trippers, but double that number showed up.

He had embarked on the career that was to make the world's most successful travel agents. Cook, who ran his first 'Great Circular' tour of Europe in 1856, changed the world's travelling habits by inventing the conducted tour.

Melrose Abbey, *Borders*

Scotland's struggle for independence and the stormy relations between the English and Scottish Churches feature in the story of ruined Melrose Abbey*, founded by David I early in the 12th century.

The king, who had estates in England and a rich English barony, brought Cistercian monks from Yorkshire, but refused to acknowledge that the Archbishop of York should be supreme over them. Alexander II (1198–1249) gave the monks Eskdale Forest as a source of income. Later, the king, the clergy and people of Scotland, were excommunicated because Alexander had sided with Louis of France against the pope. In 1217–18 all the Scots were released from the ban, except bishops and other clergy, who were summoned to York to receive absolution. But under Alexander's influence they refused.

In 1326 Robert Bruce granted the abbey £2000 worth of feudal dues, plus £100 income from farms in Berwickshire. Bruce's heart, brought back from the Holy Land, was probably buried beneath a window in the abbey.

The abbey was finally destroyed by English troops in 1543–4.

Middleham Castle, *N Yorks*

During the Wars of the Roses, Middleham Castle* was the stronghold of Warwick the Kingmaker—Richard Neville, Earl of Warwick. Edward IV became king in 1461 as a result of Warwick's support, but in 1470 Warwick restored to power the deposed Henry VI.

After Warwick was slain at the Battle of Barnet in 1471, Richard, Duke of Gloucester, later Richard III, was appointed viceroy of the north by his brother, Edward IV, in

1480. He made his headquarters at Middleham Castle.

Richard married Warwick's daughter, securing for himself a half share in the vast Neville inheritance, including Middleham itself. Their only son, Edward, was born at the castle and died there at the age of eight in 1484, the year after his father had become king.

Milford Haven, *Dyfed*

This natural harbour on the Welsh coast has for centuries been a back door into and out of Britain.

In 1171 Henry II gathered together a fleet of 200 ships at Milford Haven to carry his invasion force to Ireland. In 1399 Richard II landed there from Ireland before his surrender to the usurper Henry of Lancaster, later Henry IV.

Five years later, in August 1404, 12,000 French troops disembarked here to aid the Welsh rebel leader, Owen Glendower. They marched with the Welsh to Worcester, before retreating back into Wales. At the end of the year, they sailed back to France with their booty.

In 1485 the exiled Henry Tudor, later Henry VII, landed at Milford

with 2000 French mercenaries. This invasion ended with Henry's victory at the Battle of Bosworth.

In 1782 Sir William Hamilton inherited the harbour and village of Milford Haven, which was part of the estate of his Welsh wife.

Sir William authorised his nephew, Charles Greville, to develop the site. By 1790 Greville had built a dockyard, a customs house, a quay and warehouses, and was encouraging the development of trade with Ireland.

In the early 1780's Greville had introduced his mistress, Emma Lyon, to Sir William, who admired her beauty and vivacity. When Greville found himself in debt, he agreed to send Emma to Sir William. In exchange, Sir William agreed to pay Greville's debts.

In 1791 Sir William, the British envoy in Naples, married Emma. She became the darling of the Neapolitan court, where she met Lord Nelson in 1798.

In 1801 Nelson, the Hamiltons and Greville celebrated the fourth anniversary of the Battle of the Nile at a new hotel, later named after Lord Nelson.

FLYING HERO *The Hon. Charles Stewart Rolls, who grew up at Monmouth, made many pioneer aeroplane flights before his death in a crash in 1910.*

Monmouth, *Gwent*

The pioneer of motoring and flying, the Hon. C. S. Rolls, was born at Monmouth in 1877. Rolls carried out his first experiments in an old bathchair. Hauling the chair up the drive of his parents' mansion, the Hendre, he would jump on as it began to hurtle downhill. There were occasional accidents on his progress. 'One happy day,' Rolls remembered, 'I bagged a curate, a

butcher's boy and a dog cart.'

From 1904 Rolls was partner with Sir Frederick Henry Royce in the famous car firm, until he died in an aeroplane crash in 1910.

Monmouth's castle was built in 1071. Here, Henry of Monmouth, later Henry V, was born in 1387. Geoffrey of Monmouth—the chronicler of the *History of the Kings of the Britons*—was born in the town during the 12th century.

COOK'S WORLD TRAVEL SERVICE · EST 1841

Montrose, *Tayside*

On the western edge of the Montrose basin, in the parish of Maryton, are some stonework remains of a farming estate still known as Old Montrose of the Grahams.

This was the farm that bred Scotland's poet-soldier James Graham, the Great Montrose, who was born a marquis in 1612 and succeeded as earl when he was 14.

Montrose spent most of his life campaigning, first as a Covenanter against the Royalists of Charles I, then for the king against the rebels led by Argyll.

When, in 1638, Charles tried to force a revised prayer book on Scotland, Montrose was one of the first to sign the Covenant, the document binding the Scots in resistance to Charles's demands. To support the Covenant he marched into Aberdeen three times, and fought a battle at the Bridge of Dee.

But by the 1640's Montrose realised that Argyll and his western Highlanders were using the Covenanters' religious zeal as a cover for their own intrigues. The Covenanters split, and Montrose led the king's faction. He was a clever tactician and won six victories, including the burning of Inveraray, seat of the 'Glied Earl' of Argyll, so called for his squint.

Defeat came as quickly: in 1645 Montrose lost a battle at Philiphaugh. He was forced into exile by a deal between Charles I and the Scots. He went to Norway, then Belgium, where he fainted when he heard of the king's execution.

Montrose briefly tried to unite Scotland on behalf of Charles II when he landed at Orkney in December 1649. He was betrayed by the impoverished Macleod of Assynt, and taken to Edinburgh on a Shetland pony in May 1650. There he marched with courage and dignity to the gallows, while the 'Glied Earl' squinted through the shutters of a house near by.

Mortimer's Cross, *Herefs & Worcs*

On December 30, 1460, at the Battle of Wakefield, Richard, Duke of York, was defeated and slain by the Lancastrians. By order of Henry VI's queen, Margaret of Anjou, his severed head was displayed on the gate of York wearing a paper crown.

When his son, Edward Mortimer, later Edward IV, heard the news, he gathered together troops to avenge his father's death and win the crown. (See Wakefield, p. 424.)

Edward met the Lancastrian forces of Henry VI at Mortimer's Cross on February 2, 1461.

Edward took personal command of his troops and won the battle, in which 4000 men died. Among those taken prisoner was Owen Tudor, grandfather of Henry Tudor, later to become Henry VII. He was later beheaded at Hereford. After this decisive victory for the Yorkists, Edward was proclaimed king on March 5.

Naseby, *Northants* See pp. 182–3.

Neville's Cross, *Durham*

In October 1346 England was invaded by a Scots army under their king, David Bruce (1324–1371), who hoped to take advantage of Edward III's absence on his French campaigns. But the invasion was halted on October 17 at Neville's Cross, where the Scots met the combined English forces of the Nevilles, the Percies and the Archbishop of York.

The English archers and spearmen attacked the static formations of Scottish pikemen. The Scottish right and centre formations collapsed under a hail of arrows. The left held firm, but did not come to the aid of the others. 'We have played our part. Now let them play theirs,' said its commander, before withdrawing his pikemen.

David Bruce was wounded, captured and taken to the Tower of London. He remained a prisoner for 11 years, and was released in 1357 for a ransom of 100,000 marks which had to be paid in ten annual instalments.

Newark, *Notts*

As the Roundhead forces closed in on Royalist Oxford, Charles I fled from the city and surrendered here to the Scots on May 5, 1646.

A MONARCH IMPRISONED

The captive king, Charles I, in this broadsheet of 1648, makes an appeal from Carisbrooke Castle, one of his many prisons (see map below).

On May 13, 1646, a week after his surrender to the Scots Covenanters, at Newark, Charles I arrived at Newcastle upon Tyne.

After months of fruitless deliberation, the Scots marched home, leaving him in the hands of Cromwell's officials. On January 30, 1647, Charles was taken to Holmby House where, one morning in June, a party of soldiers appeared. Their leader, Cornet Joyce, said he had the army's authority to carry the king off. Asked for his warrant, Joyce pointed to the soldiers. Charles smiled and said that the 'warrant' seemed legible.

The king was first taken to Newmarket and then to Hampton Court, from which he escaped on November 11, despite a promise not to do so. He gave himself up to Sir Robert Hammond, governor of Carisbrooke Castle on the Isle of Wight, hoping for sympathy.

But Hammond was a supporter of Cromwell, and Charles was a prisoner again. To prevent the king from escaping, his favourite sport, hunting, was banned. Instead, he walked with his dogs, Rogue and Gypsy, and played bowls with his attendants. He intrigued busily, smuggling coded letters in and out of the castle in laundry baskets.

At Newport, Isle of Wight, in September 1648, there were more talks on a settlement, but the king played for time. His court was now pitifully small—a few rooms and a handful of attendants. But the common people still respected him, and mothers brought their children for him to touch for the skin disease known as the 'King's Evil', or scrofula.

Finally, the king was told that Parliament intended to put him on trial. On December 1, he was taken by coach to Yarmouth, then to Hurst Castle and on to Windsor.

While at Windsor he went to Winchester for a night. He was warmly welcomed by the mayor and aldermen, who were later reprimanded by Parliament. He rode past the ruins of Old Alresford near Winchester, a bitter moment, for the village had been burnt during his first serious defeat five years before.

After closely guarded nights at Farnham and Bagshot, Charles was ordered to stop all ceremony and not to dine in public. He was no longer recognised as king. In January 1649 he was taken to London and put on trial for his life.

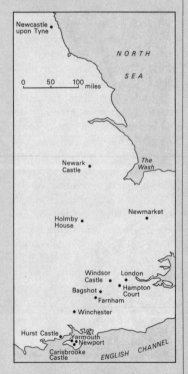

New Lanark, *Strathclyde*
David Dale (1739–1806), a non-conformist and humanitarian, set up a spinning mill by the Falls of Clyde in 1784. To attract labour he built the model village of New Lanark* near by for his workers.

Robert Owen (1771–1858), the Welsh social reformer, married Dale's daughter in 1799 and succeeded Dale as owner in 1814. Owen's efforts to improve conditions led to the passing of the Factory Act of 1819.

At New Lanark, Owen reduced the working day to 10½ hours and supplied employees with cost-price provisions. Each day Owen marked every worker's conduct by awarding him a 'silent monitors'—a label which by its colour indicated his degree of goodness or badness. Owen's belief in the importance of early education led to his opening the first infants' school at New Lanark in Britain.

Later, Owen exhausted his fortune by setting up experimental communities in Britain and the United States, but none of these succeeded.

Newmarket, *Suffolk*
Horse-racing has been the sport of kings since the reign of James I, who helped to start the meetings at Newmarket in 1605. He also began the practice of importing Arab stallions and cross-breeding them with English mares to produce the English thoroughbred.

Charles I was a frequent visitor to Newmarket, and instituted the autumn and spring meetings and the first cup race in 1634.

After a ban on horse-racing by the Puritans in the 1650's, racing was revived when Charles II came to the throne. The king made Newmarket the headquarters of the turf, which it has remained ever since. He himself was known as 'Old Rowley', after his favourite mount, and on several occasions rode his own horses in the Newmarket races.

In 1695 Tregonwell Frampton was appointed the 'Keeper of the Running Horses of His Sacred Majesty'. The first professional horse-trainer in the world, Frampton dominated Newmarket for 50 years, and received an annual royal stipend of £1000 from 1700.

Late in the 18th century, racing enthusiasts and horse-owners at Newmarket formed themselves into the Jockey Club to control the rules and conduct of the sport. It became so powerful that, in 1791, it forced the Prince Regent to dismiss one of his jockeys who was suspected of being bribed to lose a race.

Newport, *Gwent*
On November 3, 1839, a mob of local weavers, miners and ironworkers marched into Newport, protesting against low wages and rising food prices. They belonged to the Chartist movement, a working-class political organisation, campaigning for universal male suffrage.

A few of the Chartists were armed with muskets and pikes, and the rest carried pitchforks, picks and staves. Under the leadership of John Frost, the angry mob of demonstrators attacked the Westgate Hotel.

When they began to split open the wooden door of the hotel with their hatchets, the soldiers stationed inside opened fire, killing five members of the mob. Bullet scars can still be seen on the entrance pillars.

After this skirmish, which was known as the Newport Rising, John Frost and the other leaders were tried and condemned to death. The sentences were afterwards commuted to transportation.

Newstead Abbey, *Notts*
Lines written by Lord Byron salute the gloomy ruined mansion of Newstead Abbey*, which the poet inherited, with his title, in 1798 at the age of ten.

> 'Hail to thy pile, more honoured in thy fall
> Than modern mansions in their pillared state . . .'

Born in London, George Gordon, Lord Byron, was the son of Captain John Byron and Catherine Gight, a Scottish heiress. After Captain Byron had squandered his wife's fortune, he deserted her and his son.

Lame from birth, Byron spent his first ten years with his temperamental mother in shabby lodgings at Aberdeen. When his great uncle died at Newstead Abbey, mother and son moved to the estate which had been in the family since 1539. Their stay was brief. The abbey was too dilapidated to be habitable, and they settled in Nottingham.

After attending Harrow and Cambridge, Byron returned to Newstead Abbey, where he had a few rooms made fit for use. With his friends, he held parties, at which the guests, dressed as monks, drank from skull goblets.

Byron's attempts at improving the abbey included planting an oak in the treeless grounds and setting up a menagerie. A bear and a wolf were chained up at the entrance to the house. Bloodhounds galloped down the winding drive. When Byron's favourite Newfoundland dog died, the poet buried it in the family vault.

In 1808 Byron vowed to sell his unprofitable estate. But the next year, he wrote: 'Newstead and I stand and fall together.'

Byron's first poems began to appear in 1807. When the *Edinburgh Review* attacked his work, he sat down at his desk at Newstead Abbey and wrote a stinging rebuttal, *English Bards and Scottish Reviewers*.

In 1812 Byron published 'Childe Harold', a poem inspired by his continental travels, and 'awoke to find himself famous'. The idol of London society, Byron became a less-frequent visitor to Newstead Abbey.

In 1816 Byron said goodbye to England. Before leaving, he sold Newstead Abbey to a friend, Colonel Thomas Wildman, who preserved many of the poet's belongings. After Byron's death in Greece, his body was brought back and buried near Newstead Abbey in the church at Hucknall Torkard*.

Nonsuch, *Surrey*
In 1538 Henry VIII decided to create a palace near Cheam. For size and splendour, it was designed to surpass any royal residence in Christendom. An army of workmen were assembled, and slowly an incredible architectural extravagance grew up. Nonsuch was a forest of turrets, towers, pinnacles and cupolas. Its courtyard walls were garnished with plaster-work and life-size statues, and its upper storeys were hung with gilded tiles.

Mary Tudor hated Nonsuch because of its associations with her father. But Elizabeth I loved its wild extravagance and went there every summer to hunt.

During the reign of Charles II, Nonsuch came to a sad end. The king gave the palace to his mistress, Barbara Villiers, who had the house pulled down.

TUDOR EXTRAVAGANZA *Built by Henry VIII, Nonsuch was a favourite residence of Elizabeth I, who is shown arriving at the palace in this 1562 drawing.*

Northallerton, *N Yorks*
In Scotland's long and bitter struggle with England, few episodes were as savage as the great invasion of 1138, which ended on the heath a few miles north of Northallerton.

A large Scottish army, followed by a band of English bordermen, Norwegians from Orkney and the Isles, and Danish mercenaries rampaged through the northern counties, raping, murdering or enslaving the inhabitants.

The task of repelling the invaders fell upon Thurstan, the aged Archbishop of York. Thurstan sent his priests to preach a crusade in the north, and thousands gathered beneath his standard to defend their homes from the Scots.

This standard was the most remarkable that has ever rallied an English army. A tall ship's mast was mounted on a cart; at the top was hung a casket, containing a communion wafer. From its arms fluttered the banners of the four great saints of the north. These were St Peter of York, St John of Beverley, St Wilfrid of Ripon and St Cuthbert of Durham.

The battle of the Standard was fought on August 22. In a three hour struggle the invaders were put to flight. The Scottish king, David, was eventually forced to make peace.

Northampton, *Northants*
In the early morning of July 10, 1460, the Earl of Warwick established by force of arms his right to be called 'the Kingmaker'. For two years he had held out for the Yorkist cause at Calais, while the half-mad Lancastrian king, Henry VI, and his powerful queen, Margaret of Anjou, governed England. Then, in June 1460, he landed with an army at Sandwich. Within two weeks he occupied London and marched north to face the royal troops at Northampton.

The Lancastrian army, commanded by the Duke of Buckingham, waited for the enemy to attack. On the evening of July 9 Warwick, confident of victory, sent the Bishop of Salisbury to offer terms. Buckingham refused to allow him into the king's presence. This fateful decision was to cost Buckingham his life.

At 7 o'clock, on July 10, the Yorkists attacked in force. The Lancastrian gunners found that their powder had been soaked by rain. One wing of the Lancastrian army abandoned the field. 'Kill the knights and spare the common soldiers,' Warwick cried to his advancing soldiers. The battle was over in half an hour. Buckingham was found dead in front of the king's tent. Henry VI, seized by his enemies, spent his first night in captivity next to the battlefield.

Norwich, *Nflk*
Three times in 300 years the people of the prosperous East Anglian city of Norwich responded to the call to violence and rebellion.

The first rising came in 1272, when the increasing prosperity of the townspeople brought them into conflict with the jealous prelates of the Church. Rioting broke out, and Henry III went in person to punish the malcontents. St Ethelbert's Gate in the close of the Norman cathedral* was built in 1316 as a penance for the revolt.

After the introduction of Flemish weavers by Edward III in 1336, Norwich's prosperous wool trade grew even richer.

But the wealth of a few only emphasised the misery of the peasants, and when Wat Tyler's Peasants' Revolt began in Kent in 1381 it found a ready response in the city. Led by Geoffrey Litester, the rebels plundered and burnt the houses of the wealthy wool merchants, but were bloodily defeated at North Walsham by the 'fighting bishop', Henry Despenser.

A third uprising, in 1549, led by a local man, Robert Kett, was caused by discontent over the enclosure of common land. His force of 16,000 men captured the city, but seven weeks later, when they were driven out by Edward VI's troops, 3500 were slaughtered. Kett was hanged from the castle keep*.

Nottingham, *Notts*
The shell of Nottingham Castle* is all that remains of the great stone fortress built by Henry II in the 1160's. Partly demolished by the Roundheads in 1651, the castle was rebuilt as a palace by the Duke of Newcastle in 1674. This in turn was burnt by the mob during the Reform Bill riots of 1831, and pieced together again 30 years later.

This castle has witnessed a succession of stirring events in England's history. On October 18, 1330, the 17-year-old king, Edward III, arrived outside the castle with a baronial army, in pursuit of Roger Mortimer, Earl of March. Mortimer, who was the lover of the young king's mother, Isabella, had deposed Edward II in 1327 and governed England ever since in the name of Edward III. The intense hatred of the barons for Mortimer gave the young king his chance to free himself from the earl's control.

Tradition has it that the king and his men entered the castle through a secret passage in the rock, now known as 'Mortimer's Hole'. Mortimer was taken to London and

executed there for high treason.

In the 17th century Nottingham was once more in the forefront of national affairs. On August 22, 1642, Charles I raised his standard outside the castle gate, which signalled the opening of Civil War. This conflict ended, seven years later, with his own execution.

Nottingham had been a clothmaking town since the Middle Ages. In 1155 Henry II gave it a monopoly of manufacturing dyed cloth within a radius of 10 miles of the town; the tradition survived until this century.

Richard Arkwright set up his first spinning machine here in 1771. His new factories put skilled handspinners out of work and opened a violent chapter in Nottingham's history. In 1811 cloth workers smashed machinery in the mills and rioted outside the castle. The rioters were known as Luddites, after Ned Ludd, who had won notoriety by breaking machines some 30 years earlier. In 1812 the murder of a local textile manufacturer sparked off further disturbances which were suppressed only when seven regiments were sent to the town.

Oakham, *Leics*
A dwarf named Jeffery Hudson was born at Oakham in 1619. When he was nine, and only 18 in. high, he was concealed in a pie served to Queen Henrietta Maria, wife of Charles I, at a banquet.

Hudson became a favourite at the court of Charles I, and is said to have served in the Civil War as a captain of horse. In 1644 he fled with the queen to Paris, where he shot a man dead in a duel.

On a sea voyage he was captured by Turks and sold as a slave, but escaped to England before 1658. During his Turkish imprisonment he had grown to 3 ft 6 in. As a Roman Catholic, he was suspected

of complicity in the Popish Plot of 1678. Hudson was confined in the Gatehouse at Westminster, but was released and died in 1682.

Oban, *Strathclyde*
A massive circular structure, known as McCaig's folly*, dominates this harbour town. It was built in the 1890's by John Stuart McCaig, a banker, as a small replica of the Colosseum in Rome. He intended the project to encourage young artists and provide work for the unemployed. He also planned it as a memorial to his family. But it was never finished.

Old Cramond Bridge, *Lothian*
James V of Scotland (1512–42) was set upon by gypsies here. Jock Howieson, a local miller, rescued the king and brought water to bathe his wounds.

In gratitude, James bestowed the land of Braehead on the miller, on condition that Jock and his heirs always have a jug of water and a basin to present to their sovereign.

In 1952, the 25th Laird of Crawfordland and Braehead gave a silver ewer and a bowl of rose-water to Queen Elizabeth II when she visited the area.

Old Sarum, *Wilts*
Overlooking Salisbury is a windswept waterless mound called Old Sarum. It was the site of an overcrowded town, which was abandoned in 1219 for the valley below. Its buildings were pillaged for the new city of Salisbury.

Old Sarum continued to return two MPs to Westminster, though it had no electors. The owner of the land granted tenancies to two friends of his who met under an elm tree and elected the MPs he nominated.

Old Sarum was among the 'rotten boroughs' swept away by the Reform Bill of 1832. A stone stands where the elm once grew.

Olney, *Bucks*
The poet William Cowper (1731–1800) lived for 19 years with Mrs Unwin, the widow of a friend, in a red-brick house by the market place. The curate of Olney, John Newton, befriended Cowper and the two men collaborated in writing the *Olney Hymns* (1779)—the source of two famous hymns, 'God moves in a mysterious way' and 'How sweet the name of Jesus sounds'.

Osborne House, *IOW*

In 1844 Victoria asked her Prime Minister, Sir Robert Peel, to find an estate on the Isle of Wight where she, her husband Prince Albert and their four children could all enjoy sea air and privacy. She was delighted with his choice of Osborne. 'It is impossible to imagine a prettier spot,' she wrote. 'Valleys and woods which would be beautiful anywhere; but all this near the sea...is quite perfection.'

The existing house was enlarged, following a design prepared by Prince Albert himself and the architect Thomas Cubitt. A Swiss cottage was built in the grounds as a play-house. All the family enjoyed bathing from the private beach.

These happy days came to an end when Prince Albert died suddenly in the December of 1861. Victoria turned the house into a shrine sacred to the memory of her husband. Everything had to stay as Albert had left it, even to his hat hanging on the hat-stand. Osborne House was the scene of Victoria's last hours. She died there in January 1901.

FAMILY PARTY *Queen Victoria in a group at Osborne in 1898. To the left of her are the future George V with his second son, who became George VI.*

Otley, *W Yorks*

Thomas Chippendale, the cabinet-maker, was born at Otley in 1718, the son of a joiner.

As a young man, Chippendale left Otley for London to become an apprentice in furniture-making. He set up business first in Long Acre and then in St Martin's Lane. His inventive style soon won him a reputation as an outstanding maker of furniture. His designs enriched many of the great houses of the mid-18th century—among them Badminton in Gloucestershire.

Chippendale died of tuberculosis at the age of 61 in 1779 and is buried at St Martin-in-the-Fields, Westminster.

INFLUENTIAL DESIGN

Chippendale's fame rests on his skill as a designer rather than as a craftsman. In 1754 he published his Gentleman and Cabinet-maker's Director, *the first book to be devoted entirely to furniture design. It was immensely successful and influential. In the 1762 edition of the* Director, *Chippendale included designs for bookcases (see below), which had become fashionable.*

Otterburn, *Northld*

By the light of the harvest moon, Scots and English fought the Battle of Otterburn in August 1388. The antagonists were 'Hotspur'—Henry Percy, eldest son of the 3rd Earl of Northumberland—and James the 2nd Earl of Douglas, who had just raided England.

Hotspur attacked Douglas in his camp at Otterburn, and the battle raged through the night. Douglas was mortally wounded. As he lay dying he told his knights to keep his death a secret. They picked up his banner, shouted the warcry of 'Douglas!' and rallied the Scots. Soon the English were scattered, losing 800 dead and 1400 prisoners, including Hotspur. The Scots, who lost only 100 dead and wounded, returned home with the body of their leader, which they buried at Melrose Abbey. Hotspur was soon ransomed by the English.

The battle was celebrated in ballads by both sides—the Scots in 'The Battle of Otterburn', the English in 'The Hunting of the Cheviot' or 'Chevy Chase'.

Oxford, *Oxon*

In 1167 Henry II ordered all Englishmen studying abroad to return to England. Hundreds of these scholars settled in Oxford. (See pp. 78–79.)

During the Middle Ages there was a constant struggle between the townspeople and the scholars. This unrest came to a head in the riots of St Scholastica's Day in 1335. A brawl in the Swyndestock Tavern was followed by three days of fighting in which more than 20 scholars were killed, shops were burnt, and scores of townspeople were injured.

Late in the 15th century, Oxford began to profit from the new ideas of the Renaissance. Such men as the Greek scholar William Grocyn and the physician Thomas Linacre were encouraged by Erasmus, the Dutch humanist, who was a frequent visitor to Oxford.

During the Civil War, Oxford was the Royalist capital of England, when Charles I made his head-quarters there in 1642. He fled before the city surrendered in June 1646. Later in the 17th century, Oxford's intellectual life was dominated by a group of brilliant men. Among their number were John Wilkins, President of the Royal Society, and the scientists Robert Boyle and Robert Hooke.

Despite such men, Oxford University fell into decline until academic conditions were improved early in the 19th century.

Benjamin Jowett (1817–93), the greatest Oxford tutor of his time, was Master of Balliol from 1870 to 1893. He made his college the intellectual leader of Oxford.

In 1854 almost all fellowships and scholarships were thrown open to free competition. In 1871 religious tests for entry were abolished, and the university was opened to students of all denominations.

It was at Oxford that Britain's car industry began to develop in the 1920's. Thousands of Morris cars were made at the Cowley factory founded by William Morris, later Lord Nuffield, who had begun his career as a cycle repairer.

By 1930 his cars had made him a millionaire. Nuffield gave away £30 million in his lifetime to worthy causes—hospitals, charities and Oxford University.

Paisley, *Strathclyde*

The spinning mule invented by Samuel Crompton produced a very fine thread which brought prosperity to the weavers of Paisley at the beginning of the 19th century.

The weavers began to make shawls with a pattern featuring the Indian pine or cone motif—the Paisley pattern. But towards the end of the century the popularity of the Paisley shawls waned. Linen thread became the staple industry, and Paisley is the world's largest thread-producing centre.

Peel Castle, *IOM*

A castle* was built by William le Scrope, King of Man from 1392–9, on St Patrick's Isle at the mouth of Peel Harbour. The fortress was frequently used as a place of exile for state prisoners.

Pembroke Castle, *Dyfed*

Henry Tudor, the future Henry VII and founder of the Tudor dynasty, was born in 1457 in a tower next to the castle gatehouse. His claim to the throne was through his mother, Margaret Beaufort, great-grand-daughter of Edward III's son, John of Gaunt. Margaret was only 13 when Henry was born, and already a widow; her husband Edmund Tudor, Earl of Richmond, had died in captivity 12 weeks before.

Henry fled to Brittany in 1471 to escape from Edward IV; he stayed there for 14 years before returning to wrest the crown from Richard III at the Battle of Bosworth.

The castle* stands on a steep-sided promontory jutting into the

Pembroke River. It was first fortified in 1097. In 1648 Royalists held out there for six weeks before being forced to surrender.

Penshurst Place, *Kent*

One of the most admired and gifted men of the Elizabethan age, Sir Philip Sidney, who was poet, courtier and soldier, was born at Penshurst Place* on November 30, 1554. In 1585 he was appointed Governor of Flushing, in the Low Countries, where Queen Elizabeth had sent an army to support the Protestants against the Spanish occupying forces.

In September 1586, during a raid on the Spanish-held stronghold of Zutphen, Sidney's left thigh was shattered by a musket ball. After riding from the field of battle, he

IDEAL ELIZABETHAN *Sir Philip Sidney was famed as a soldier, courtier and writer of sonnets in the 16th century.*

was about to drink from a water flask when he saw a wounded soldier parched with thirst. Sidney handed him the flask, with the words that have won him immortality: 'Thy necessity is yet greater than mine.'

Sidney was taken to Arnhem to recover from his wound. But gangrene set in, and he died, aged 32, on October 17, 1586. The following February Sidney was buried in St Paul's Cathedral.

Perth, *Tayside*

A woman stopped James I of Scotland (1394–1437), poet-king of Scotland, as he was about to cross the Firth of Forth on his way to Perth, then the seat of Scottish government, where he intended to spend the Christmas of 1436. 'An ye pass

this water ye shall never return again alive,' she shouted.

The king went on to Perth, where he established his court at Blackfriars monastery. In February 1437 the woman appeared there and asked for an audience, but the king told her to come back to see him the following morning.

That night a group of nobles, angry at James's attempts to curb their power, burst in. Traitors had already removed the bar from the king's apartment door.

James hid beneath the floor. He was soon discovered and run through with a sword. Within a month the killers had been caught, tortured and executed. Later, Perth lost its status as capital when the king's widow and his heir, James II, moved the court to Edinburgh.

Philiphaugh, *Borders*

The fate of Scotland hung in the balance in the summer of 1645. The Highlanders under the Royalist Marquis of Montrose had mauled the Covenanters, who supported Parliament. But after their victories they began to drift away to their homes with their loot.

In September David Leslie, the commander of the Scottish Parliamentary army, crossed the Tweed at the head of 4000 troopers and surprised the remnants of the Highlanders at Philiphaugh near Selkirk. The battle ended in the massacre of the Royalist force, and Montrose himself became a fugitive. (See Montrose, p. 408.)

Pinkie, *Lothian*

In September 1547 the last battle between the English and Scottish crowns took place at Pinkie. The Duke of Somerset, Lord Protector of England, ruling for his ten-year-old nephew, Edward VI, had proposed the peaceful union of the two countries. After the Scots refused to consent, Somerset went to war. At Pinkie he defeated the Scots under the Earl of Arran, regent for the five-year-old Mary, Queen of Scots. But his dream of creating one kingdom was dashed. Mary went to France, and she married the Dauphin instead of Edward VI.

Plymouth, *Devon*

Plymouth Sound, 4 square miles of water with natural shelter on three sides, has been the source of Plymouth's importance. Seafaring has

been Plymouth's story, and the heroes of many adventures at sea —the Hawkins family (William, John and Richard), Sir Richard Grenville, Sir Francis Drake, Sir Humphrey Gilbert, John Davis, Sir Walter Raleigh, and many others—have set sail from its harbour. And it was in Plymouth Sound that, in 1588, the English fleet waited for the Armada.

When Francis Drake was mayor of Plymouth in 1582, he was responsible for bringing the town its first pure water supply. A 17-mile long watercourse had to be cut from the River Meve and carried in wooden chutes over Burrator Gorge. At its opening in 1591 Drake, in a scarlet cloak, rode ahead of the water as it advanced along the cutting towards the dignitaries walking out from the town along the dry bed. The annual corporation banquet includes the toast, 'To the pious memory of Sir Francis Drake, and may the descendants of him who brought us water never want wine'.

The *Mayflower*, a small vessel of about 180 tons, set sail from Plymouth on September 6, 1620, carrying 101 Pilgrim Fathers, mostly British, bound for the New World. (See pp. 168–9.)

Pontefract Castle, *W Yorks*

The town's Norman castle*, now in ruins, has dominated its history. The most famous of all its distinguished prisoners—Thomas, Earl of Lancaster and Archbishop Scrope among them—was Richard II. Deprived of his throne by Henry Bolingbroke (later Henry IV) in September 1399, Richard—disguised as a forester—was taken first to Leeds Castle in Kent and then to the castle at Pontefract.

How he died remains uncertain. In Shakespeare's play he is struck down by one of Henry's squires, Sir Piers Exton. But starvation appears to be the most likely cause, since no definite evidence of violence could be found when the king's tomb in Westminster Abbey was opened and the corpse examined in 1873.

Portland, Isle of, *Dorset*

On the night of June 5 and the grey morning of June 6, 1944, an army of 418,585 American troops and 144,093 vehicles were squeezed into a fleet of small, overloaded ships and landing craft in the

choppy Channel off Portland.

For months they had been preparing for the invasion of Europe; Portland had swarmed with soldiers. Beaches around the naval base were turned into 'hards'—reinforced surfaces for landing craft and vehicles. Despite bad weather and other delays, the Americans made their rendezvous at sea with British and Commonwealth forces and together landed on the beaches of Normandy.

Portsmouth, *Hants*

Portsmouth came into existence in the 12th century when Richard I, seeing the strategic advantage of the site, founded the town. It had already become an important naval station before Henry VII started the dockyard which his successor Henry VIII greatly enlarged.

The Duke of Buckingham, the favourite of James I and Charles I, restored Portsmouth to importance after a period of neglect. It was there in 1628 that the duke was attacked and stabbed to death by a disgruntled soldier.

Nelson always stayed at a hotel in the High Street. In 1805, early in the morning, before he sailed away on the *Victory** to the Battle of Trafalgar, the admiral left the hotel quietly by the back staircase to avoid the waiting throng outside.

Charles Dickens was born in 1812 at 393 Commercial Road, Landport, now a Dickens museum*. Sherlock Holmes's creator, Sir Arthur Conan Doyle, practised medicine in the Southsea district during the 1880's, and the impoverished 15-year-old H. G. Wells was a draper's assistant at Portsmouth for two years (1881–3). Isambard Kingdom Brunel, civil engineer, was born here in 1806.

Powick Bridge, *Herefs & Worcs*

A month after Charles I had raised the royal standard at Nottingham, the first clash in the Civil War took place at Powick Bridge on September 23, 1642.

Preston, *Lancs*

During the Civil War, Roundheads and Royalists fought for possession of Preston. It became a Royalist headquarters in 1642 before falling to the Roundheads in the following year. Scarcely a month after the Roundheads had entered Preston, the Earl of Derby recaptured it for the king. After the defeat of Marston Moor, in 1644, Prince Rupert seized the mayor and bailiffs and carried them off to Skipton Castle as hostages for the loyalty of the citizens to the Royalist cause.

The climax of Preston's dramatic part in the Civil War came in 1648 when 20,000 Scots, allies of Charles I, under the Duke of Hamilton, had advanced as far as the River Ribble.

On August 17, Cromwell attacked the Scots across Preston Moor, and routed their army in three hours. Pursued southwards by the relentless Roundheads, and cut off from their bases, the Scots finally surrendered at Warrington.

Richard Arkwright was born in Preston in 1732. While still in his teens, Arkwright opened a barber's shop in a Bolton cellar and charged less than the other barbers of the town. 'A clean shave for a half-penny,' was his slogan. Arkwright earned nothing from shaving, but made large profits by selling hair to wig-makers.

In 1767 Arkwright set up a textile factory at Preston with John Kay, a watchmaker. In the following year he moved to Nottingham where he patented his famous water-frame —the first machine in Europe capable of spinning a strong thread suitable for weaving.

The idea of the water-frame was not Arkwright's but Kay's. In 1785, after a decade of litigation, the courts quashed Arkwright's patent. But, by this time, Arkwright had already made his fortune. He was knighted in 1776.

Another Preston man, Joseph Livesay (1794–1884), founded the Temperance Movement and published England's first tee-total newspaper, the *Preston Temperance Advocate,* from 1834–8. The word 'tee-total' came from the efforts of a stammering friend of Livesay's to take the movement's pledge of 'te-te-total abstinence'.

Prestonpans, *Lothian*

The Jacobites under Bonnie Prince Charlie scored their biggest victory at Prestonpans on September 21, 1745. His 2500 Highlanders, with weapons ranging from guns to pitchforks and scythes, crept stealthily across a morass at 3 a.m. on September 21 and took Sir John Cope's 2200 redcoats completely by surprise. The Jacobites fired their muskets once, threw them down,

THE LAST RISING FOR THE STUARTS

The Rebel Prince, Charles Edward Stuart, was supported by the Highland Scots, who were loyal to the Stuarts. In a year he led them from victory at Prestonpans to defeat at Culloden (see map).

When Bonnie Prince Charlie landed on Eriskay on August 2, 1745, to regain the throne for the Stuarts, the local Highland chiefs were sceptical.

He had brought little money, few arms and seven companions. The chiefs advised him to go home. 'But I *am* come home,' he replied.

Charles and the seven sailed on to Loch nan Uamh and, on August 19, encouraged by the backing of the Cameron chief Lochiel, he raised the standard of the Stuarts at Glenfinnan. By the end of the day 1200 clansmen had rallied to him.

Aware that something was brewing, the British reinforced Fort William. But the prince was already heading for Edinburgh. On August 31 he was entertained to dinner at Blair Castle by the Marquess of Tullibardine, and on September 4 he rode into Perth clad in tartan trimmed with gold.

On the road to Edinburgh, the Highlanders won a skirmish without pain or bloodshed. They met two regiments of dragoons and fired their pistols, although well beyond range. The dragoons turned and fled without a fight, retreating into Edinburgh and out the other side in panic.

The Highlanders captured the city by rushing one of the gates as it opened to let a coach out. Once they entered Edinburgh, they encountered no opposition.

The victory at Prestonpans on

September 21 and the fall of Carlisle, gateway to England, on November 14, caused alarm in London. The British began mustering to oppose the Jacobites' southward march. But Kendal, Lancaster, Preston, Wigan and Manchester fell.

At Macclesfield the prince learnt that the Duke of Cumberland was bringing an army back from the Netherlands to put down the rebellion. When the Jacobites reached Derby, only 130 miles from London, there was a run on the banks and George II prepared to flee from England back to Hanover.

But Charles's advisers persuaded him to retreat. The French had not sent an army, and the English would not back him. Deeply disappointed, Charles led his men home, beating off cavalry attacks. Their reception at Glasgow was cool. Charles took Stirling on January 8, and on January 16 a Highland charge scattered British troops at Falkirk. But, at Culloden on April 16, his hopes vanished with his defeat by Cumberland. (See Culloden, p. 379.)

Charles escaped to Europe, where he wandered for years in disguise, a slave to the brandy bottle. He paid at least one secret visit to London and died in Rome in 1788. A monument, the gift of George III, marks the tomb in St Peter's of the last three Stuarts —James and his sons Henry and Bonnie Prince Charlie.

and charged with drawn broadswords. Cope's men fled in panic. Their rout is commemorated in the ballad 'Hey Johnny Cope'.

Princetown, *Devon*

In 1806, at the suggestion of Sir Thomas Tyrwhitt, a camp for thousands of prisoners captured during the Napoleonic Wars was built on this exposed site, 1430 ft above sea level. Tyrwhitt, who owned granite quarries near by, was convinced that a fortune could be made if Dartmoor were properly developed. The small town which grew up round the prison was named after the Prince of Wales (George IV).

Dartmoor, as the prison came to be called, was closed in 1816, but a new prison was built in 1850 for long-sentence prisoners.

The most notorious mutiny at Dartmoor took place in 1932. The rioting prisoners overpowered the staff, set fire to the administration block and took control of all the prison buildings. Having demonstrated their strength, the prisoners went back to their cells peacefully on the following day.

R

Raglan Castle, *Gwent*

The surrender of Raglan Castle* by the 1st Marquis of Worcester on August 19, 1646, after a ten-week siege, marked the end of the first phase of the Civil War.

The castle was the last of the great fortified houses to fall to the Roundheads. And, after its surrender, Charles I fled to seek the protection of the Scottish army.

The castle is largely 15th century; it suffered during the siege and afterwards was deliberately damaged to render it indefensible. The estates were forfeited to Parliament.

The Marquis of Worcester, who died in December of 1646, was one of England's richest men: he is

413

reputed to have given his vast fortune in support of the king's cause. Charles II later heaped honours on the family.

Ravenspur, *Humberside*

'Away with me in post to Ravenspurn,' exclaims the Earl of Northumberland, in Shakespeare's *Richard II*. During the Middle Ages, the now-vanished town of Ravenspur, at the mouth of the River Humber, was one of the wealthiest ports in England, and a major trading town. In 1332, John Balliol, the pretender to the Scottish throne, set sail from Ravenspur, with an invasion fleet, for Scotland. Edward VI landed there in 1471.

Late in the 15th century, Ravenspur was swallowed up by the North Sea, and its exact site is today unknown. Old maps of the Yorkshire coast show that the sites of other towns, such as Old Aldborough, Auburn and Withow, have also disappeared. Threatened by the onslaught of the sea, the townspeople were forced to move inland.

SUBMERGED SITES *Lying under the sea off the coast of Yorkshire are lost medieval towns, such as Ravenspur.*

Redruth, *Cornwall*

In this Cornish town is Murdock House, the first house in Britain to be lit by gas. In 1777 William Murdock, a Scottish engineer, was sent to supervise the installation of Watt's steam-engines at a mine near Redruth. He experimented in his backyard with the distillation of coal, and by 1792 had devised a retort to produce gas that he piped to light his cottage and office.

Richard Trevithick, 'father of the locomotive engine', was born and educated in nearby villages, and settled at Moreton House near Redruth in 1797. He led the way in the development of steam locomotion with his invention of the high-pressure steam-engine. Trevithick applied the invention first to a road vehicle which carried about ten people up Beacon Hill, Camborne, on Christmas Eve 1801—the first passengers ever carried by steam. Trevithick anticipated Stephenson's locomotive when, in 1804, he built a steam vehicle to run on the rails of a former horse tramway.

Rhuddlan, *Clwyd*

In August, 1277 Edward I, with 25 ships and an army of soldiers, artisans and builders, sailed up the coast from his military base at Flint Castle. At Rhuddlan they began building another castle* in stone. (See pp. 86–87.)

The towers and King's Hall were roofed by 1280, but building was stopped because of a Welsh uprising. The unfinished castle became Edward's headquarters during his victorious campaign against the Welsh. It was completed in 1282.

Edward had a deep-water channel dug from the sea to the castle. Three years later the River Clwyd was diverted to fill the channel, which was the first British canal.

Around the castle the king built a new town of Rhuddlan, which was enclosed by a timber palisade.

Inside this barrier, streets were laid out on a rectangular plan. Some of the streets remain today as High Street, Castle Street, Church Street and Parliament Street.

Richmond Castle, *N Yorks*

Richmond Castle* was begun about 1071 by Count Alan of Richmond, son of the Earl of Brittany, who had fought at the Battle of Hastings. Earl Conan enlarged the castle in 1146 and built the keep.

Two Scottish kings were imprisoned at the castle: William the Lion in 1174 after his capture at Alnwick, and David II after his defeat at Neville's Cross in 1346.

Henry Tudor, from birth the Earl of Richmond, retained his early title as Henry VII.

Richmond, *Gtr London*

This London borough takes its name from the sumptuous Palace of Richmond built by Henry VII late in the 15th century. The palace stood on the site of the royal manor of Sheen, where Edward III had died. It had been the favourite home of Richard II's wife, Anne of Bohemia. In his grief over her death in 1394, the king ordered that the palace should be demolished. A second manor house of Sheen, which was erected by Henry V, was burnt down at Christmas 1497.

Henry VII decided to rebuild Sheen as a magnificent palace. Within two years it was ready for occupation, and the king named it after his Yorkshire earldom. A contemporary observer said that it was 'most glorious and joyful to consider and behold'. In her later years, Elizabeth I thought of Richmond as a 'warm winter box to shelter her old age'. She died there in 1603.

After Cromwell's government sold the palace to pay the army's wages, it fell into decay. Three Tudor houses and a gatehouse are all that remain of Henry VII's palace today.

Rochester, *Kent*

In the Middle Ages, Rochester Cathedral* had its own place of pilgrimage, which rivalled the shrine of St Thomas Becket at Canterbury. Rochester's saint was St William of Perth. In 1201 this charitable Scottish baker was murdered outside the town, after he had spent the night in Rochester on the start of a pilgrimage to the Holy Land. The rich shrine built to house his remains no longer exists.

Romsey, *Hants*

Henry Temple, Viscount Palmerston (1784–1865), who dominated the political life of mid-19th-century Britain, was raised here on his father's estate, Broadlands.

As Whig Foreign Secretary (1830–41, 1846–51), Palmerston made Britain's power and prestige felt abroad. He established friendly relations with France, helped Belgium to gain independence, and supported Turkey against Russia. His aggressive policies made him popular with his countrymen, who affectionately called him 'Pam', and indispensable to the Whigs. But he offended Queen Victoria by going his own way without seeking or heeding her views.

When the Crimean War went badly for Britain, Queen Victoria was forced to ask Palmerston to form a government in 1855. He

BLUFF 'PAM' *Palmerston was held in high esteem by his countrymen, who admired his aggressive policies.*

brought the country successfully through the conflict and, with one short break, remained in office until he died.

Rottingdean, *E Sussex*

This little seaside village saw one of the grimmest episodes in the sea war between England and France, which flared up at different times during the 14th century.

In the summer of 1377, a force of several hundred Frenchmen landed at Rottingdean Gap. Looting and burning, they drove the surviving villagers up towards the church, where they took sanctuary. One horseman managed to escape, and rode over the downs to Lewes to summon help from the prior—in those days a military as well as spiritual leader.

The villagers in the church took refuge in the belfry and drew the ladder up after them. But the French set fire to the building and burnt them alive. The stone still shows the marks of scorching from the enormous heat. The prior arrived too late to save them. He engaged the French, but was captured and held in France until a ransom was paid.

Rothesay, *Strathclyde*

The Duke of Rothesay is the premier Scottish title, given usually to the British monarch's eldest son.

Robert III made Rothesay a royal burgh in 1401, and his ill-fated son, David, became the first duke. According to legend, David was starved to death by Robert's scheming brother, the Duke of Albany.

Roxburgh Castle, *Borders*

James II of Scotland, an artillery enthusiast, besieged the English-held Roxburgh Castle in 1460. He was standing watching the discharge of a cannon called 'The Lion' when it burst, and a wedge used to tighten the hoops round the barrel flew off and killed him. His widow, Queen Mary, inspired the Scots army to complete the capture of the castle.

Royal Tunbridge Wells, *Kent*

Ever since a jaded young courtier, Lord North, discovered the medicinal qualities of a spring near this Kentish town in 1606, the waters of Tunbridge Wells have been famous. They were popularised by the Stuarts, beginning in 1629, when Charles I's wife, Henrietta Maria, went there to recuperate after the birth of her first child. The royal family camped on the common for lack of houses near the spring.

Charles II's court spent the summer there on several occasions in the 1660's; Nell Gwynne is thought to have accompanied the king. Later the town was a favourite with Queen Victoria. But the prefix 'Royal' was not added to its name until 1909, when Edward VII gave it the ultimate seal of royal approval.

Rugby, *Warks*

The school founded here in 1567 became one of the most famous schools in the world.

A tablet on a wall overlooking the school close records how in 1823 William Webb Ellis 'first took the ball in his arms and ran with it, thus originating the distinctive feature of the Rugby game'. This famous violation of the rules of football as they then existed was at first condemned by the school. However, in the 1840's, it permitted players to run with the ball. The school's most famous headmaster

Rye, *E Sussex*

In 1898, when he was 55, Henry James, the American-born novelist, leased Lamb House*. After his busy social life in London, James at first found Rye lonely. He wrote 'the days depart and pass, laden somehow like processional camels, across the desert of one's solitude'. However, many other writers of the day, Joseph Conrad and H. G. Wells among them, soon called to relieve his solitude. The American novelist Edith Wharton often took him for long drives in the car he called 'The Chariot of Fire'.

During his later years James always dictated his novels to his secretary, who was allowed to

was Dr Thomas Arnold. He came to Rugby in 1828, at a time when bullying and flogging had damaged the reputation of public schools. The new headmaster did little to reform teaching at Rugby. But he tried to instil in his pupils a sense of duty and the Christian ideal of service. His example led to the founding of many other schools, which took Rugby as their model.

Arnold died at the early age of 47 in 1842. His headmastership is described in *Tom Brown's Schooldays*, which was written by a former pupil of Rugby, Thomas Hughes.

crochet during the long and frequent pauses. While at Rye James wrote some of his greatest novels. These Included *The Awkward Age*, *The Golden Bowl*, *The Wings of the Dove*, *The Ambassadors* and *The Sacred Fount*. He left Rye during his last illness, and died in London in 1916.

MAN OF LETTERS *American-born Henry James, who settled in England in 1869, lived at first in London, but later moved to secluded Lamb House in Rye.*

Rye House, *Herts*

In 1683 a plot to assassinate Charles II was concocted at Rye House, home of Richard Rumbold. The plan failed, the ringleaders were executed and the Duke of Monmouth, the king's illegitimate son, was exiled for his part in the plot. Rumbold was executed in 1685.

S

St Albans, *Herts*

As Verulamium, St Albans was one of the chief towns of Roman Britain. It lasted from AD 43 to about 400, and modern St Albans is still rich in remains of the period.

St Albans is named after Britain's first martyr, a Roman soldier who, in 303, sheltered a priest from his persecutors and was converted by him to Christianity. Alban put on the priest's clothes so that the fugi-

tive could escape and was himself arrested, beaten and beheaded.

His shrine was soon venerated, and in about 793 a Saxon monastery was founded in his memory. From the 11th to the 15th centuries the main parts of the present cathedral* were built—notably the longest medieval nave in England.

The first blood in the Wars of the Roses was shed at St Albans in 1455, when the forces of York and Lancaster clashed in the streets. Yorkists, under the Earl of Warwick, overwhelmed the Lancastrian positions from behind with small loss of life, and captured Henry VI.

In 1461, when the Yorkists and Lancastrians met again east of St Albans, Warwick's host was taken by surprise. His defensive man-traps were badly sited, and the new handguns either failed to work or exploded in his soldiers' hands. The treachery of the Kentishmen in Warwick's army and the failure of reinforcements to arrive completed the rout. Henry VI was rescued by the Lancastrians, led by his queen, Margaret of Anjou, Warwick escaped from the battle and, with the Earl of March, went to London. (See pp. 104–5.)

St Andrews, *Fife*

The oldest, most famous of all golf courses was already in existence at St Andrews in 1552. But golf, popular with Scotsmen since the 15th century, interfered with archery practice necessary for the country's defence, and James II (1430–60) forbade it entirely in 1457.

This royal prohibition lasted only a short period. Mary, Queen of Scots, played several rounds only a few days after the murder of her husband, Lord Darnley. Later Stuart monarchs—Charles I and James II—enjoyed the game.

Golf became a popular sport in England during the 19th century. The world's first tournament was held at Prestwick in 1860. But the present rules were first laid down at St Andrews in 1882.

St David's, *Dyfed*

St David's, the holy city of Wales, is traditionally held to have been founded by Dewi Ddyfrwr, or David the Water-Drinker, in about AD 500. It was a centre of Celtic Christianity, and the monks there lived a rigorous life. They had to vow that they would never eat meat;

RUGBY FEVER *By the 1860's, when the match in this picture was played, rugby football was popular at schools, universities and clubs throughout Britain.*

and, instead of oxen, the monks themselves pushed the plough.

After it came under the control of the Roman Church, St David's remained a place of great sanctity. In 1120 David was canonised and became the patron saint of Wales.

Destroyed by Danish pirates in 1087, the present cathedral*, the finest in Wales, was begun in 1187.

St Margaret's Hope, Orkney

Vowing to conquer Scotland, Haakon IV of Norway ordered his fleet to gather at the Orkney Islands in the summer of 1263. On the day Haakon's warships sailed into St Margaret's Hope, there was an eclipse of the sun, and many of the Norse sailors believed that this was a bad omen. They were to be proved right. The fleet sailed off with 120 ships. At the head was Haakon's own warship, which had a golden dragon's head carved on the prow.

Haakon's dream was dashed when storms in the Firth of Clyde wrecked much of his fleet. Defeated by the Scots at Largs, Haakon's few remaining ships sailed to Kirkwall, in the Orkneys, where he died.

St Michael's Mount, Cornwall

According to legend, St Michael's Mount was part of the fabled kingdom of Lyonesse, which stretched from Land's End to the Scilly Isles. From this land came King Arthur and one of the Knights of the Round Table, Tristram or Tristan.

The origins of the monastery* are vague. It was said that St Michael appeared on a rock on the island and instructed the local fishermen to set up a religious establishment. But it is more likely that the monastery was founded by Edward the Confessor in 1044 with the help of monks from Mont St Michel, which lies off the Normandy coast of France.

In the 12th century Henry de Pomerai, a supporter of King John, captured St Michael's Mount by a ruse. His men, disguised as pilgrims, landed on the island and expelled the monks, opponents of the king.

This trick was repeated in 1471, when the Earl of Oxford captured the island for Edward IV during the Wars of the Roses.

Salisbury, Wilts

England's first 'new town' came into existence on April 28, 1220, when Bishop Richard le Poore laid the foundation stone of the new cathedral on the site.

Only a year before, the bishop and his clergy had abandoned the city of Old Sarum for a new site on the plain. Old Sarum, perched on its steep hill, had been exposed to the weather and was short of water. Its site had been too small for an expanding city. Moreover, it was garrisoned by uncouth soldiers who were constantly quarrelling with the canons of the cathedral. 'Let us in God's name descend unto the level,' one of the canons suggested. And in 1217 the pope gave his permission for the move to Salisbury. (See Old Sarum, p. 410.)

In 1227 Henry III gave the new town of Salisbury trading privileges. The citizens prospered and money flowed into the cathedral building fund. Most of the cathedral* was completed by 1258, and the famous 404 ft spire was added in 1334.

In 1331 Old Sarum suffered the final blow to its self-esteem when the old cathedral the clergy had abandoned was demolished to provide stone for the new cathedral's close.

Salisbury, or 'New Sarum' as it was called for many years, continued to play its role in England's history. The Duke of Buckingham, a victim of the treachery of Richard III, was executed in the marketplace of Salisbury in 1483

In 1688 the city saw the ill-fated struggles of the discredited James II to cling to the throne. His army mustered in Salisbury to resist the triumphant advance of William of Orange. But the king lost his nerve and fled, while his army deserted to the other side. On December 4, 1688, William entered Salisbury and stayed at the bishop's palace, now the cathedral school. (See Brixham, p. 371.)

Salisbury Hall, Herts

Charles II remodelled this Tudor-built house* in the fashionable Restoration style for his mistress Nell Gwynne, the orange-seller who bore him a son who was created the Duke of St Albans.

The house is still surrounded by its medieval moat, and there are signs of Roman and Anglo-Saxon habitation. A Norman fortified building was still standing there in 1471, when Warwick the Kingmaker rode out to fight and die at the Battle of Barnet. It was during Warwick's ownership that the hall received its name, for he was also Earl of Salisbury.

Sandringham, Norfolk

The pleasure-loving Edward VII acquired the Sandringham estate when he was Prince of Wales, and he and his bride, Alexandra, settled there in 1863. Over the years the house grew as his whims demanded the addition of new rooms.

Sandringham became a gathering place for the fashionable set who surrounded the future king, and whose doings shocked Victorian public opinion. In the autumn of 1871 the prince lay there seriously ill with typhoid for several weeks,

and almost died from the disease.

Sandringham has been one of the homes of all subsequent generations of the royal family. A cottage on the estate became known as 'York Cottage' when the future George V (then Duke of York) and his bride, May of Teck, spent their honeymoon there. Both the king and queen loved the place and they brought their family to stay at the house every Christmas. It was from Sandringham that George V broadcast the first-ever Christmas message to the empire in 1932.

THE SPORTSMAN KING *Edward VII loved to go shooting on his estate at Sandringham, which became a gathering place for his fashionable friends.*

Sandwich, Kent

One of the original Cinque Ports—together with Dover, Hastings, Hythe and Romney—Sandwich is now stranded 2 miles inland, as a result of the silting-up of the River Stour. It was a target for French raiders throughout the Middle Ages. In 1457 a force pillaged the town and murdered the mayor. Since then, the Mayor of Sandwich has worn a black robe in mourning.

Sauchieburn, Central

The reign of James III of Scotland, who was crowned in 1460 at the age of nine, was ended in 1488 by mutinous nobles, who resented the favours he showed to their inferiors.

His troops met the barons' army at Sauchieburn in 1488. The rebels put a standard into the hands of the king's son, the young Prince James, and forced him to take part.

The king, a poor horseman, fled the field when his horse bolted and threw him. He sought refuge at a mill. He asked for a priest, and a rebel came along pretending to be one. But once inside the mill he stabbed the king to death.

The prince, later James IV (1473–1513), was so ashamed of his part in his father's murder that throughout life he wore an iron chain round his waist in penance.

Scarborough, N Yorks

John Paul Jones, naval commander of the American War of Independence, fought his most famous battle off Scarborough. He had been sent by the American rebels on a mission to France, and was given permission to cruise in European waters.

On September 23, 1779, when off Scarborough, Jones encountered the Baltic merchant fleet in a convoy protected by the British men-of-war *Serapis* and *Countess of Scarborough*. In a three-and-a-half-hour battle by moonlight Jones, on board the *Bon Homme Richard,* fought with the *Serapis*. Hundreds were killed or wounded. Jones's ship was sinking, so his men boarded and captured the *Serapis*.

Another of Jones's squadron, the *Pallas,* took the *Countess of Scarborough* and he made off with these prizes. Louis XVI gave Jones a gold-hilted sword and made him a chevalier of France.

During the Civil War, Scarborough Castle* was twice besieged by the Parliamentarians. It held out for 12 months the first time (1645–6) and three months the second time (1648). After the second surrender, Cromwell ordered it to be demolished. The north-west front was blown up with gunpowder, but other parts, including the dungeons, remained in use.

Early in the First World War, while Britain's Grand Fleet was at Scapa Flow, a German force from the Imperial High Seas Fleet put out in fog and heavy seas and shelled Scarborough and Hartlepools on December 16, 1914. They killed 120 civilians, wounded 400 and went on to lay mines off the coast.

As the Germans withdrew they met the British second battle squadron and battle-cruisers, which had been ordered to intercept them. The light vessels engaged in an indecisive fight. But the heavy ships missed each other in the fog, and the raiders escaped before the British could catch them.

REBEL HERO *An 18th century medal commemorating the American naval hero John Paul Jones.*

Scilly Isles

For centuries these islands were a shelter for pirates, and the islanders lived by pillaging wrecked ships.

In 1646, after the Royalist defeat in the west, the Prince of Wales, later Charles II, fled to the Scilly Isles. He and his party endured considerable privations. One of them recorded that 'we were destitute of clothes, and meat and fuel... was not to be had'. Charles escaped before the Roundheads arrived.

The Royalist Sir John Grenville and his 'pirates of Scilly' recaptured the islands, but in 1651 they passed back to the Parliamentarians.

In 1707 a British fleet under Admiral Sir Cloudesley Shovell was returning from the siege of Toulon when it was caught in a storm off the Scillies. Two thousand men were drowned. Shovell himself was among those who perished.

Scone, *Tayside*

Kenneth MacAlpin, King of Scots, united Scotland in the 9th century by treacherously slaughtering the Pictish king and nobles at a feast in their capital, Scone, which later became the coronation place of Scottish kings.

The Stone of Destiny—a block of red sandstone—was part of the crowning ritual. The Scots are said to have brought it from their original homeland, Ireland, during the 6th century AD, and for centuries it had rested at Dunstaffnage Castle.

The Scots used to carry the stone from the Abbey of Scone to a hill close by. Their new king was then seated upon it by the Earl of Fife, recognised as the leading noble of the realm.

Edward I of England seized the stone from the Scots in 1296 and carried it off to Westminster Abbey, where it is still kept today.

Sedgmoor, *Somerset* See pp. 210–11

Selborne, *Hants*

Gilbert White, the 18th century naturalist, lived at the Wakes* in Selborne. According to a contemporary: 'He was a little, thin, prim, upright man, who used to go poking about the lanes and hedges with his stick'.

At the age of 69, White published his only book, *The Natural History of Selborne,* written in the form of letters to two friends. Its observations about nature, in and around Selborne, made White and his village famous.

As a child, White and his brothers dragged a large stone from the village of Farringdon to the top of the Hanger, the hill which overlooks Selborne. It remains there still and can be approached by a path called the Zig Zag, cut by White in 1751.

NATURE LOVER *Gilbert White, one of Britain's first naturalists, in the robes of an Oxford Master of Arts.*

Seton Palace, *Lothian*

Lord Seton was a loyal friend of Mary, Queen of Scots. Many times she found refuge at his palace on the Firth of Forth, near Edinburgh, from the intrigues at her own court at Holyrood House. She paused there briefly to collect some followers on the night of Riccio's murder, when she and Darnley galloped away from Edinburgh.

A year later, following the murder of Darnley, the queen visited Seton Palace. James Bothwell, who had been accused of Lord Darnley's murder and then acquitted, followed her, paid suit and was refused. Soon afterwards, Mary left for Stirling, and on the way she was abducted by Bothwell.

Sevenoaks, *Kent*

A plaque on the wall at Solefields on the southern edge of Sevenoaks, marks the spot where, on June 7, 1450, Jack Cade, at the head of an army of Kentish rebels, defeated a force under Henry VI.

This uprising, which had begun in the previous month, was not a peasants' revolt but a rebellion of many of Kent's prominent citizens, including a great number of the gentry, mayors and constables. Angry at the corruption of the government and the petty tyranny of its officials, the rebels marched to Blackheath, outside London, where they set up a fortified camp.

The government was taken by surprise. It accepted Cade's demands, hoping to gain time in which to raise an army. After Cade's followers returned to Sevenoaks, the government assembled a force to pursue them. At the skirmish near Sevenoaks on June 7 the royal army was defeated, and Cade marched again on London with no opposition before him. There, Cade's supporters seized the king's favourite, Lord Saye, the royal treasurer, and Saye's son-in-law, William Crowmer, and beheaded them.

Cade lost the support of the citizens of London by his lawlessness, and the rebels were driven from the city. A price of 1000 marks was put on Cade's head. As his supporters began to return to their homes, Cade realised that he would have to flee. Pursued by the Sheriff of Kent, Cade was captured in a garden near Heathfield, Sussex, and was killed on the spot.

Thomas Bourchier, for 30 years Archbishop of Canterbury, conceived the idea of building a palace where he could spend the summer. In 1456 he bought the manor of Knole, Sevenoaks, for £266 1s 4d, and within a decade was able to move into one wing.

In 1532 Henry VIII seized the manor and began to convert it into a palace for himself. But little came of his grandiose plans and, in the reign of Elizabeth, Knole* was granted to the Sackville family who have owned the house ever since.

Shaftesbury, *Dorset*

This Dorset town has associations with three early English kings— Edward the Martyr, Canute and Alfred the Great.

Alfred the Great founded a convent for Benedictine nuns at Shaftesbury at the end of the 9th century AD. It became one of the most important and influential religious institutions for women in the Middle Ages. The ruins of the convent and the nuns' church can still be seen.

In 1861 the tomb of the Anglo-Saxon King Edward the Martyr was found in the abbey at Shaftesbury. The body had disappeared, but in 1931 a box containing bones, believed to be those of the king, was found near by. Edward, whose reign was brief (975–8), was murdered at the age of 16 by his stepmother at Corfe Castle.

In 1035 Canute died at Shaftesbury. Twenty years before, this Danish leader had landed in Dorset. Within a year he had conquered much of England and become its king.

Sheerness, *Kent*.

In May 1797, when the French navy was poised to invade England, the sailors of the Nore fleet, at anchor off Sheerness, mutinied. They were rebelling against the intolerable conditions afloat—brutal floggings for trivial offences, bad food, cramped quarters and poor pay.

Led by Richard Parker, who styled himself president of the 'Floating Republic', the mutineers threatened to attack London, but declared that they would fight the French fleet, if it appeared.

The mutineers depended for supplies on Sheerness. When the government stood firm, supplies were cut off, and the mutiny of the Nore collapsed on June 20.

Parker was hanged from the yardarm of his ship; a few of his associates were executed or flogged.

MUTINEER *Richard Parker, leader of the Nore Mutiny, seized control of 13 ships of the line during his uprising.*

Sheffield, *S Yorks*

Sheffield, the steel capital of England, is famed for its cutlery. By the 14th century it was noted for its knives, and by Elizabeth I's reign other cutting tools—sickles, scissors, scythes and shears—were also being manufactured.

In the early 18th century Thomas Boulsover's invention of 'Sheffield plate'—copper covered with a thin layer of silver—gave Sheffield a worldwide reputation. After 1850 the invention of electroplating

superseded Boulsover's invention. Sheffield's international reputation for steel-making dates from 1740, when Benjamin Huntsman discovered a method of making steel in clay crucibles. In 1856 the city's steel industry received an added impetus when Henry Bessemer, the pioneer of modern steel-making, set up a factory in Sheffield:

Sherborne Castle, *Dorset*

At first sight of Sherborne Castle, Sir Walter Raleigh wanted it for himself. (See pp. 166–7.)

Its owner, the Bishop of Salisbury, reluctantly agreed to give up the castle after Raleigh had presented Elizabeth I with a jewel worth £250 to bribe the bishop, and had agreed to pay an annual rent of £260.

At first Sir Walter tried to improve the 400-year-old building. But in 1594 he decided to build Sherborne New Castle* to the south of the old one, which is now in ruins.

James I gave Sherborne to his favourite, Robert Carr, after Raleigh was imprisoned for treason in 1603. After Carr's fall and execution, the king granted it to Sir John Digby, Earl of Bristol, in 1617. The Digby family has kept Sherborne ever since.

Sheriffmuir, *Tayside*

In 1715 Highland Scots loyal to the Stuart cause rebelled. They called themselves Jacobites, from *Jacobus,* the Latin name of their leader, Prince James Edward Stuart. The rising was led by the Earl of Mar on behalf of James. On November 13, Mar's army fought an indecisive battle with British forces at Sheriffmuir. This destroyed James's cause even before he arrived in Scotland. (See pp. 226–7.)

Sherwood Forest, *Notts*

The forest is the traditional setting for the exploits of Robin Hood, the legendary outlaw, who appears in popular ballads dating from the 14th century.

It has been suggested that Robin may have been one of those who fought for Simon de Montfort against Henry III's troops at the Battle of Evesham in 1265; or a Yorkshire fugitive from justice mentioned in the pipe roll of Henry III in 1230; or a Robin Hood born in Wakefield about 1285 and outlawed after the Battle of Boroughbridge in 1322.

Shoreham, *W Sussex*

On the run after his defeat at Worcester in 1651, the future Charles II made his way to Shoreham harbour disguised as a groom.

Captain Nicholas Tattersall took him over to France in his coal brig, the *Surprise*. After the Restoration the grateful Charles enrolled the brig in the fleet.

THE PERILOUS FLIGHT OF A YOUNG PRINCE

For six weeks after his army's defeat by Oliver Cromwell at Worcester on September 3, 1651, the future Charles II of England evaded his enemies.

With trusted companions, he rode north to the country seat of White Ladies. Next night he moved on to Boscobel House, where he was given peasant clothes by a family of woodcutters. Guided by one of them he tried to escape to Wales but found the Severn crossings too heavily guarded by Cromwell's troops.

Charles returned to Boscobel. During the day he reputedly hid in a hollow oak, and slept the night under the attic floor. Then he rode on to Moseley Old Hall, home of the royalist Thomas Whitgreave. The party's goal was Bristol, and a passage to the Continent.

On the way to Long Marston, Charles's horse lost a shoe and he had to visit a blacksmith who was anti-royalist. But he managed to avoid detection. After a night at Cirencester he stayed three days at Abbots Leigh, while trying in vain to arrange passage from Bristol.

Disguised as the servant of his companion, Lord Wilmot, Charles pushed on to Castle Cary, where he was told that the Roundheads were offering a reward of £1000 for his

capture. Charles decided to take refuge at Trent House, home of the loyal Colonel Francis Wyndham.

After a few days he left for Charmouth in the guise of a servant to an eloping couple—parts taken by Wilmot and the colonel's niece. They waited at Charmouth for a seaman to help them, but his wife had locked him up and hidden his trousers.

The fugitives pressed on to Bridport, where they found the streets swarming with soldiers. Charles said the best plan was to 'go impudently into the best inn in the town'. So they went into the Queen's Arms and asked for the finest accommodation.

Meanwhile, the troops had been alerted by a blacksmith at Charmouth. The fugitives hurriedly took the highway to Dorchester and fooled pursuing Roundheads by ducking up a lane. They lodged at the inn at Broadwindsor—where 40 soldiers were staying.

On October 6 Charles went into hiding at Heale House, near Salisbury, and spent a day examining Stonehenge. A week later he was escorted to Hambledon and on to Brighton. Disguised as a groom he reached Shoreham, and on October 15 embarked on a coal brig which took him to France.

Charles II wandered for 43 days before reaching Shoreham (see map), where he finally found a ship to take him to France. The king's concealment in an oak at Boscobel is commemorated in a symbolic 17th-century drawing (above right), which shows the royal crowns on the branches of the tree and the diehard Royalist fleet fighting in the background.

Shrewsbury, *Salop*
Standing on a rocky spur, above the River Severn, the town of Shrewsbury was the seat of the princes of Powys from the 5th to 8th centuries.

In the 11th century, Roger de Montgomery, the Conqueror's kinsman, built its castle* and founded the abbey.

Edward I made Shrewsbury his seat of government during the conquest of Wales (1277–83), and on October 2, 1283, Dafydd, the Welsh leader and the last of the native royal princes of Wales, was sentenced to death there by a hastily summoned Parliament.

The Battle of Shrewsbury in 1483 took place at Battlefield, just outside the town. (See pp. 98–99.)

Solway Moss, *Cumbria*
By the 1540's, England and Scotland were heading for war. Henry VIII felt threatened by the Franco-Scottish alliance and there were constant border raids.

The English marched into Scotland in 1542. Shortage of supplies caused them to fall back on Berwick, leaving Sir Thomas Wharton at Carlisle with 3000 men to face an army of 18,000 Scots.

On November 24 Wharton came out as the enemy were crossing the Esk, with the marshy tideland of Solway Moss behind them. The Scots floundered in the water of the ford or on the Moss, while Musgrave's lancers dashed in and out among them.

The tide was on the turn. Many Scots gave up hope of reaching higher ground and surrendered. Hundreds more drowned.

It was Scotland's greatest military disgrace. Two earls, five barons, 500 lairds and 20 guns were captured.

Southampton, *Hants*
From Roman times, Southampton has been one of Britain's greatest seaports. The original port, the Roman Clausentum, had a flourishing trade with the Continent.

After the Norman Conquest, it became a point of embarkation.

In 1189 Richard I sailed from the port for his Crusade. Edward III led his fleet from here in 1345 to embark on the Hundred Years' War.

Before leaving Southampton in 1415 to defeat the French at Agincourt, Henry V had to deal with a conspiracy to put Edward, Earl of March, on the throne.

The conspirators—Richard, Earl of Cambridge, Lord Scroop of Marham, and Sir Thomas Grey—were found guilty and beheaded at Southampton's Bargate*, the northern entrance to the old city.

In 1554 Philip II of Spain landed here. Before his journey to Winchester, where he was to marry Mary, the Spanish king heard a Thanksgiving Mass at the Church of the Holy Rood, now a ruin.

South Harting, *W Sussex*
In 1880 the novelist Anthony Trollope (1815–82) decided to move from London in the hope of relieving his severe asthma. He found a suitable house—The Grange*—at South Harting.

The Duke's Children, the last of Trollope's *Palliser* novels, was published in 1880, the year he settled in Sussex. The problems of old age were beginning to obsess him. There he wrote *An Old Man's Love, Mr Scarborough's Family, Kept in the Dark* and *The Landleaguers.*

At the age of 67 Trollope suffered a paralytic stroke and died, on December 6, 1882. He is buried at Kensal Green, London.

Southill Park, *Beds*
When, in 1757, the body of Admiral John Byng was laid to rest in the mausoleum at Southill Park*, his epitaph represented the feelings of many Englishmen: 'To the perpetual disgrace of public justice . . . when bravery and loyalty were insufficient securities for the life and honour of a naval officer.'

Byng was sent with an inadequate naval squadron to relieve the island of Minorca, then under French attack. The governor of Gibraltar refused him extra troops. He engaged the enemy fleet on May 20, but mishandled the battle, and eventually withdrew with several crippled ships. The government, furious at Byng's failure, ordered the admiral's court martial.

Byng was found guilty. The king, ignoring the court's recommendation of mercy, sanctioned the death penalty, which was carried out by a firing squad at Portsmouth on March 14, 1757.

Stafford, *Staffs*
In a jesting toast, the 18th-century wit and dramatist Richard Brinsley Sheridan said, 'May the trade of Stafford be trod underfoot by all the world'. He was referring to the town's long-established and thriving shoe-making industry.

Stafford may have been founded by St Bertelin, a Mercian prince, who built himself a hermitage there. This structure was later fortified against the Danes by Aethelflaed, Lady of the Mercians, King Alfred's daughter.

Izaak Walton, the 17th-century author of *The Compleat Angler, or the Contemplative Man's Recreation* (1653), was born in Stafford.

Stamford Bridge, *N Yorks*
On September 25, 1066, Harold of England defeated Harold Hardrada, King of Norway, and his own half-brother, Tostig, at Stamford Bridge, near York. The battle ended the Scandinavian threat to the power of the English monarchy.

Tostig, ousted from his lands by Harold, allied himself with Harold Hardrada in 1066. In September the Viking fleet reached the Tyne to join Tostig and his Scottish mercenaries.

Harold marched north to meet them, and on the morning of September 25 faced the enemy in battle at Stamford Bridge.

Both Tostig and Harold Hardrada fell in the battle and Harold's forces won a complete victory over the invaders.

But Harold did not enjoy his victory for long. Soon after the battle, news arrived that William of Normandy had invaded England. (See pp. 64–65.)

Staunton Harold Hall, *Leics*
For 900 years, from 1066 until the 1950's, Staunton Harold Hall belonged to the same family. One member, Laurence Shirley, 4th Earl Ferrers (1720–60), achieved notoriety. The earl's wife having obtained a separation, his steward, John Johnson, was appointed receiver of his rents. Infuriated, the earl shot him.

Ferrers' plea of 'occasional insanity of mind' was not borne out by the skill with which he conducted his case, and he was found guilty.

Stirling Castle, *Central*
Dominating the surrounding plain from its 250 ft high crag, Stirling Castle* changed hands more than any other fortress during the long Anglo-Scottish conflict.

Edward I of England took it in 1296 without a fight. In the following year William Wallace rallied the Scots and retook the castle, only to surrender it to Edward seven years later after a three-month siege. In 1314 the Scots turned the tables again by beating the English at Bannockburn. (See pp. 88–89.)

In 1452 the 8th Earl of Douglas refused to repudiate his alliance with the Earl of Crawford against James II of Scotland. Furious, James stabbed Douglas to death at Stirling.

Mary Stuart was crowned Queen of Scots in the castle chapel at the age of nine months in 1543. There, in 1566, she celebrated the baptism of her son, the future James VI of Scotland and James I of England.

Stockton-on-Tees, *Cleveland*
Thomas Sheraton, son of a Stockton cabinet-maker, was a designer not a maker of furniture. He published *The Cabinet-Maker and Upholsterer's Drawing-Book* early in the 1790's, soon after he had moved to Soho in London. In the book, Sheraton described the neo-Classic style and included plates of 113 of his designs, which hundreds of craftsmen copied.

Although his designs were widely appreciated, Sheraton was never accepted by fashionable society. He lived and died in near poverty.

SHERATON STYLE
This cylinder desk topped by a bookcase shows Sheraton's typical design features of usefulness, simple lines, a delicate and graceful appearance. The desk (left) has a tambour front—a roll of narrow wood strips on canvas backing.

Stonehaven, *Grampian*
Three Episcopal clergymen were imprisoned in the tolbooth*, or courthouse, in 1748 after failing to pray for the royal family while conducting services. They went on performing their duties out of the windows of the building.

Women wanting their babies baptised concealed them in fishing creels, or baskets, and took them to the back window of the tolbooth.

Stonehenge, *Wilts*

James I visited Stonehenge* while staying at nearby Wilton House in 1620. He was so impressed by what he saw that he instructed the architect, Inigo Jones, to make a plan of the stones and give him some account of their origin.

The publication of Jones's conclusions in 1655—that the stones were part of a Roman temple and came from the 'quarries about Albury'—led to increasing research into the monument's history.

The 16th-century antiquarian John Aubrey was the first to suggest that Stonehenge was a Druid temple. Cremated human bones were found in a ring of holes on the site, but the henge was certainly already a ruin before the first Druids reached Britain about 250 BC. (See pp. 18–19.)

Stow-on-the-Wold, *Glos*

One of the last battles of the Civil War was fought at Stow-on-the-Wold on March 2, 1646. A Royalist force of 3000 was on its way to Oxford when it was intercepted and defeated by a Parliamentarian army.

After the news of this defeat, the king renewed his efforts to make peace with Parliament. But after a month of fruitless negotiations, Charles left Oxford to surrender himself to the Scottish army at Newark. (See Newark, p. 408.)

Stowe, *Bucks* See pp. 240–1

Stranraer, *Dumf & Galloway*

The Arctic explorer John Ross, born near Stranraer in 1777, reached the Boothia Peninsula in 1829 and planted the British flag on the magnetic North Pole.

Stratford-upon-Avon, *Warks*

See pp. 154–5

Sudeley Castle, *Glos*

The present Sudeley Castle* was built on the site of a manor house belonging to Ethelred the Unready. Although the Normans confiscated most of the lands of Saxon nobles, Sudeley Castle was kept by its Saxon owner, Harold, because his wife was related to William the Conqueror. Harold's son, John de Sudeley, built the first castle during the reign of William the Conqueror.

In 1469 the victorious Yorkist king, Edward IV, took Sudeley from its Lancastrian owner and gave it to his brother, the Duke of Gloucester, later Richard III. During the reign of Henry VIII, Sudeley was still crown property; the king and Anne Boleyn visited the castle.

When Henry VIII died in 1547, the boy-king, Edward VI, gave Sudeley to his uncle, Sir Thomas Seymour. After Seymour had married Henry's widow, Catharine Parr, they went to live at Sudeley, accompanied by Lady Jane Grey and a large household of retainers.

In August 1548 Catharine, who died in childbirth, was buried in Sudeley chapel.

Sunderland, *Tyne & Wear*

Sir Joseph Swann, born in Sunderland in 1828, invented a process for carbon printing, bromide paper and photographic dry plates. In 1860 he anticipated the work of the American inventor Thomas Edison, by producing a rudimentary electric lamp.

Sutton Courtenay, *Oxon*

Here, Herbert Henry Asquith, Earl of Oxford and Asquith (1852–1928), converted three waterside cottages into his country home, The Wharf. The son of a West Riding cloth manufacturer, Asquith made his way at the bar without wealth or influence. As Liberal Prime Minister (1908–16) he restricted the power of the House of Lords, introduced old-age pensions and National Insurance, and steered the country through the early years of the First World War. His aloof but dominant style of government won him the title 'the last of the Romans'.

But he lost the premiership in 1916, when the clamour for an imaginative and energetic war leader forced him to resign, and Lloyd George took his place. In the 1918 General Election he lost his seat at East Fife, but he was later returned to Parliament in 1920 as the member for Paisley.

Out of office, Asquith turned for a living to books and newspaper articles. He lived mostly at The Wharf, where he died in 1928. He is buried in the churchyard.

Sutton Hoo, *Suffolk* See pp. 50–51

Syon House, *GL*

This mansion*, originally a convent, founded by Henry V to make amends for his father's overthrow of Richard II, has a tragic history.

It remained a convent, in the possession of the Order of St Bridget, until its dissolution by Henry VIII in 1534.

Henry's fifth wife, Catharine Howard, accused of adultery, was imprisoned in Syon House. She stayed there from November 1541 until the eve of her trial and execution at the Tower of London the following February.

In 1547 the new king, young Edward VI, granted Syon to the Lord Protector, the Duke of Somerset. After Somerset's death on the block in 1552, the house passed to the Duke of Northumberland, who himself was executed only a year later.

Northumberland's son, Guilford Dudley, married the claimant to the throne, 16-year-old Lady Jane Grey. In July 1553 Lady Jane was rowed down the Thames from Syon to the Tower, after being summoned to take the crown, in place of the rightful heir, Mary Tudor. But her reign only lasted nine days, and both she and her husband were beheaded in the Tower of London for treason in 1554. (See pp. 134–5.)

Under James I, Syon's owner, another Northumberland, was held in the Tower for 15 years. And in 1646 three of Charles I's children were imprisoned at Syon. Charles, himself a prisoner at Hampton Court, was occasionally allowed to visit them. The Duke of York, later James II, escaped in 1648, Prince Henry was later freed, but Princess Elizabeth died at Carisbrooke Castle in 1650.

Tain, *Highland*

Robert Bruce, crowned at Scone in 1306 when Scotland's fortunes were at a low ebb, spent the next few months with his wife and daughter avoiding capture by the armies of Edward I of England.

Eventually, the two women found sanctuary in a tiny chapel at Tain, built 100 years earlier to house the relics of St Duthac.

Their sanctuary was betrayed by the Earl of Ross. English soldiers dragged them out and took them into captivity. After seven years' imprisonment, they were released after Bruce's victory at Bannockburn in 1314.

The chapel was burnt down in 1470 and is now an ivy-covered ruin.

Tantallon Castle, *Lothian*

Standing on a high headland surrounded on three sides by the sea, with a high wall and a double moat protecting its landward side, Tantallon Castle* won a reputation for impregnability in the 16th century.

Tantallon's owners—the Earls of Angus—also won a reputation—for black treachery. For a century they played off the rulers of Scotland and England against each other. Sometimes they were forced into exile and twice—in 1491 and 1528—their castle successfully withstood a determined siege.

But though Tantallon resisted the heaviest guns in use in the 16th century, it could not withstand the new guns of the 17th century, used by the Roundheads in the Civil War. In 1651 General Monck laid siege to it, and Tantallon surrendered after 12 days of continuous bombardment. The once-proud stronghold was then plundered and demolished by Monck's victorious soldiers.

Taunton, *Somerset*

The Duke of Monmouth, illegitimate son of Charles II and cousin of James II, received a tumultuous welcome when he was proclaimed king in Taunton on June 20, 1685, during his short-lived rebellion.

A train of young girls presented him with a Bible, a sword and a gorgeously embroidered flag, before he marched out of the town to his defeat by James's troops at Sedgemoor on July 6. (See pp. 210–11.)

Three weeks later the duke's supporters were tried by Judge Jeffreys during the 'bloody assizes' in the great hall of Taunton Castle. Monmouth himself was taken to London, where he was tried and executed in the Tower.

The notoriously cruel Colonel James Kirke, left in command of the West Country, sat drinking wine at the White Hart Inn while 30 of the rebels who had been condemned were hanged from the inn sign.

Tay Railway Bridge, *Tayside-Fife*
On the stormy night of December 28, 1879, a train steamed slowly on to the Tay Bridge, which had been opened 18 months before.

Suddenly a violent, sleet-filled gust swept the firth. Within moments 13 spans of the bridge crumpled into the water, taking the train with them. About 80 died.

The story of the disaster began in 1870, when the North British Railway obtained Parliament's approval for the 2 mile viaduct from Angus to Fife. Its designer, Thomas Bouch, finding that the river bed was not firm all the way across, sank cast-iron piers in the middle of the Tay instead of building the more massive brick ones originally intended.

The bridge carried a single track 88 ft above the water. It was opened on June 1, 1878, and that summer Queen Victoria's train was diverted across the bridge on its journey to Balmoral, so that she could admire its wonders.

But the next winter the bridge began to show ominous signs of wear, when cracks in the iron piers started to appear. They were patched and bound with iron hoops. Trains were restricted to 25 mph for safety.

But Bouch had not tested his design for wind pressures, and nothing could save the bridge when the great gale blew. Public horror at the disaster led to a public inquiry. Bouch, who had been knighted and asked to draw up plans for a Forth bridge, never built another.

The new Tay rail viaduct, still in use, was built 60 ft upstream, using lattice girders that can withstand lateral pressures of up to 56 lb. per square inch. The piers of Thomas Bouch's bridge can still be seen.

RAILWAY DISASTER *A 19th-century engraving of the Tay Railway Bridge collapse, which carried a train and its passengers into the storm-tossed Tay.*

Tewkesbury, *Glos*
Beneath the walls of the Benedictine Abbey of Tewkesbury*, the hopes of the Lancastrians were shattered on May 4, 1471.

Henry VI, deposed ten years earlier, was a prisoner of the Yorkist Edward IV in the Tower. The king was half-mad and the leadership of the Lancastrians had passed to Queen Margaret and 18-year-old Prince Edward, exiles in France.

Prince Edward landed on the Humber in March 1471. York opened its gates to him and thousands flocked to join him. Edward IV faced his greatest crisis. His victory over Warwick the King-maker at Barnet still left him to face the prince and the queen in battle.

After weeks of energetic campaigning, the two sides faced each other across Bloody Meadow, just outside Tewkesbury, on May 4. The queen's host, 7000 strong, was led by the Duke of Somerset and Lord Wenlock, a former Yorkist.

Edward IV, however, had mustered a larger and better-equipped army, and when disputes broke out in the queen's camp, defeat was certain. Somerset, finding Wenlock taking no part in the battle, accused him of treachery, and killed him.

It was an act of folly which destroyed the Lancastrian army. Prince Edward was killed; Somerset and the queen were captured. Support for the Lancastrian cause evaporated, and Edward IV entered London in triumph a fortnight later. His rival, Henry VI, the figure-head of the invasion, was put to death in the Tower on the same night. (See pp. 104–5.)

Thetford, *Norfolk*
Thomas Paine, the radical whose books included *The Rights of Man* (1791), a defence of the French Revolution, and *Age of Reason* (1794), a rejection of Christianity, was born at Thetford in 1737.

First acclaimed in America, he became a member of the French revolutionary convention. He died in poverty in New York in 1809.

Tichborne House, *Hants*
This country house, just north of the village of Cherwell, was the home of the Tichborne family, which was involved in one of the most celebrated Victorian trials.

In April 1854 Sir Roger Doughty-Tichborne was lost at sea when the *Bella* sank in the South Atlantic. His mother refused to believe that he was dead, and advertised around the world for news of her son.

A detective agency in Sydney, Australia, found a man who in some ways fitted Sir Roger's description. He was known as Tom Castro, and worked as a butcher in the outback town of Wagga Wagga.

Sir Alfred Tichborne, who had succeeded his brother Roger, died in 1866. On December 25 of that year, Castro arrived in England to claim the title and the considerable Tichborne inheritance. He was an immensely fat man—5 ft 8 in tall and 27 st. in weight—an unlikely double for the well-proportioned Sir Roger.

But Lady Tichborne, who was living in Paris, was desperately anxious to find her son. After their meeting there, she declared him

INFAMOUS IMPERSONATOR *Tom Castro, otherwise Arthur Orton of Wapping, claimed to be the heir to the Tichborne fortune and title. A contemporary cartoon by 'Ape'.*

to be Roger. The rest of the family were equally convinced that Castro was an impostor.

In 1871 Castro brought a legal action claiming the family estates. He had been carefully schooled in details of Sir Roger's life, but as the 100-day trial in Westminster Hall went on, his story began to crumble. It turned out that he was Arthur Orton, the son of a butcher from London's East End.

The baronetcy then passed to the rightful heir, Alfred's son.

Orton was accused of perjury, and after a second, criminal, trial on that charge in 1873, he was sentenced to 14 years' hard labour. Released in 1884, he died a poor man, in London, 14 years later.

Tintagel Castle, *Cornwall*
According to legend, Tintagel Castle* was the birthplace of King Arthur. Some of the foundations date from 7th century AD, when he is believed to have lived, but most of the castle, which belonged to the earls of Cornwall, was built in the 13th century.

Tippermuir, *Tayside*
James Graham, Duke of Montrose —the Great Montrose—made a crucial decision in 1644.

He had signed the Covenant in 1638, opposing Anglican religious practice in Scotland, but his objections were only religious. When Charles I faced Civil War in England and a Covenanters' rebellion in Scotland, Montrose prepared to oppose his fellow Covenanters.

The Parliamentarians had recruited powerful support in Scotland, including the Earl of Argyll who held Perth on their behalf. Montrose raised a motley army, 3000 strong, with no artillery, little cavalry and few good weapons.

At Tippermuir, just west of Perth, on September 1, 1644, he met nearly 9000 well-equipped Covenanters, led by Lord Elcho. When fighting ceased, 2000 Covenanters were dead, another 2000 were captured and Montrose's men gained Perth, where they acquired a reputation for blood-thirsty plundering. (See Montrose, p. 408.)

Towton, *N Yorks*
On March 29, 1461, the flower of the Lancastrian chivalry was slaughtered in a field outside the small town of Towton.

421

At stake was the crown of Henry VI and the ambitions of his queen, Margaret of Anjou, whose 22,000-strong army was gathered on a ridge between Towton and Saxton.

But fate deprived the queen of victory. A swirling snowstorm blinded the Lancastrian army. The archers were unable to aim their arrows accurately as the Yorkists advanced towards them. The arrival of Yorkist reinforcements under the Duke of Norfolk decided the day.

The Lancastrians were routed and fled to Towton. As a result of this Yorkist victory, Henry VI was deposed, and the Duke of York, aged 19, was crowned Edward IV on June 26, 1461.

Turriff, *Grampian*

First blood in the events which led to the Civil War was shed here in 1639. In a skirmish known as the 'Trot o' Turra', a band of Covenanters, recruiting support against Charles I's religious policy, was chased out of Turriff by 1200 followers of the Gordon clan.

Wakefield, *W Yorks*

On December 30, 1460, at the Battle of Wakefield, Queen Margaret's Lancastrian army of 10,000 ambushed a force of 8000 under Richard, Duke of York, father of Edward IV. The duke and almost all the Yorkist leaders lost their lives in the battle. Spurred by this defeat, Edward avenged his father's death a month later at Mortimer's Cross. (See pp. 104–5.)

Throughout the Middle Ages, 'mystery plays', dramas dealing with the Christian story from the Creation to the Last Judgment, were performed by religious guilds in churches at Wakefield and other English towns. The author of the most famous cycle of these plays was an anonymous 'Wakefield Master', of the Middle Ages.

Before the rise of Leeds and Sheffield, Wakefield was the centre of the clothing trade in Yorkshire.

Walmer Castle, *Kent*

The castle*, just south of Deal, was built by Henry VIII in 1539 as one of a chain of forts for defence against invasion.

It has been the official residence of the Lords Warden of the Cinque Ports since the early 18th century. Many great statesmen have held the office, including William Pitt the Younger and Sir Winston Churchill.

Another famous Lord Warden, the Duke of Wellington, died at the castle in 1852.

The Iron Duke died suddenly and unexpectedly. On September 13 he went riding as usual. The following morning he was taken ill, and at 4 o'clock in the afternoon he was found dead in his armchair. Hundreds of people filed through the castle to see the duke's body before it was removed to London for the state funeral. His bedroom has been left virtually unaltered, and the room next door boasts a pair of original Wellington boots.

Warwick Castle, *Warks*

The infamous career of Piers Gaveston, the dissipated young favourite of Edward II, ended near Warwick Castle* in 1312.

Gaveston, banished from the court of Edward I for dissolute living, was instantly recalled by the new king, who made his handsome Gascon friend Earl of Cornwall. Twice more Gaveston was exiled and recalled. Finally, a group of earls, angered at the honours heaped on the favourite, held him in a dungeon at Warwick Castle.

Gaveston had nicknamed Guy Beauchamp, Earl of Warwick, the 'Black Dog of Arden', and the earl swore that he would feel the Black Dog's teeth. Gaveston was tried in the Great Hall by a council of barons and then taken to nearby Blacklow Hill, where he was beheaded.

Richard Neville, Earl of Warwick (1428–71), by his support for successive leaders in the Wars of the Roses, earned the title of 'the Kingmaker'. He began as a Yorkist, and for the first three years of Edward IV's reign was the real ruler of England. But he went over to the Lancastrians after Edward married Elizabeth Woodville and her family's influence increased. Warwick's efforts to restore the Lancastrians to the throne were finally shattered at the Battle of Barnet in 1471, when he was defeated and killed by Edward.

BEHEADED FAVOURITE *Piers Gaveston lies at the feet of the Earl of Warwick, one of his bitterest enemies.*

Warwick Castle, one of the few medieval fortresses that have been continuously inhabited, was converted into a mansion in the 17th century. The 14th-century curtain wall and tower defences are intact.

Wells, *Somerset* See pp. 82–83

Welton, *Humbside*

Early in 1739 Dick Turpin, the highwayman, was arrested at the Green Dragon Inn, Welton. At York, where he was taken, the authorities did not realise who their prisoner was. To local people, he was known as 'John Palmer', an outwardly respectable member of the community, who had been caught disposing of stolen horses.

Fearing that his true identity might be revealed, Turpin wrote to his brother in Essex; asking for someone to be sent to swear that he was Palmer. However, the postmaster in Essex, who had been Turpin's schoolmaster, recognised the handwriting and opened the letter. Hastening to York, he exposed Turpin. His reward for denouncing to the authorities the notorious highwayman was £200. Born in Hempstead, Essex, Dick

Weymouth, *Dorset*

In 1789 George III stayed at Gloucester House, now a hotel, in Weymouth—the first of several long holidays he took in the town.

Sea-bathing became a fashionable pastime in the 1760's and the king believed that the sea water would benefit his health.

On his first visit he was followed everywhere. At the seashore, as he stepped from his bathing-machine into the waves, an enthusiastic local band on another bathing-machine played 'God Save The King'.

Whitby, *N Yorks*

In 656 St Hilda established Whitby Abbey*, now in ruins, on a site given by the King of Northumbria, in thanksgiving for his victory over the Mercians. Seven years later the abbey was the scene of the Synod of Whitby, where the Celtic Church came to an agreement with the

Turpin was a butcher, but he was accused of finding meat for his shop by sheep-stealing. He then joined a gang of thieves and became expert in house-breaking, smuggling and cattle-stealing.

When the gang broke up, Turpin went into partnership with Tom King, and for a brief time they won fame as highwaymen. After his partner was wounded during a fight in London, Turpin fled to Yorkshire, where he started the trade in stolen horses that led to his arrest.

On the morning of April 7, 1739, the crowd which had gathered at the gallows of York gaol cheered Turpin, who was dressed in a new frock coat and followed by five hired mourners. The *Newgate Calendar* observed that the spectators 'seemed much affected by the fate of a man so distinguished by the comeliness of his appearance'.

HIGHWAYMAN *Dick Turpin, in this 18th-century woodcut, is shown fleeing London after his fight with the authorities.*

Roman Catholic Church.

Caedmon, the first known English Christian poet, was a herdsman on the abbey lands. One night, after dreaming that he heard a voice commanding him to sing about the beginning of Creation, he composed his hymn, the first recorded poem in the English language.

Whithorn, *Dumf & Galloway*
In AD 397 St Ninian, the first Christian missionary to Scotland, founded a monastery—the Candida Casa, or 'white house'—at Whithorn. The monastery church, the first in Scotland to be made of stone, was dedicated to St Martin of Tours, Ninian's patron.

In the 12th century, Fergus, Lord of Galloway, built a priory*, now in ruins, on the site of Candida Casa. A 5th-century oratory—probably part of the 'white house'—was excavated by archaeologists at the end of the priory church in 1949.

Wilton House, *Wilts* See pp. 192–3

Winchelsea, *E Sussex*
Present-day Winchelsea is an example of medieval town-planning. The original town lies buried forever under the sands to the east.

Throughout the 13th century immense storms swept the southeast coast of England, doing great damage to Old Winchelsea, which was built on a shingle spit at the mercy of the waves. The town and harbour were finally obliterated during the 'Great Storm' of 1287.

On the orders of Edward I, a new town was laid out, complete with churches and a grid pattern of streets, on a nearby hilly peninsula. But the storm had so altered the anchorages that this stretch of the Sussex coast never regained its former prosperity.

Winchester, *Hants*
Alfred the Great made Winchester his capital, and the city shared this role with London for nearly 200 years after the Norman Conquest. In 1070 William I built its first castle, and nine years later Bishop William Walkelin founded its great, 556 ft long Norman cathedral*.

Henry III had a special affection for his birthplace. He rebuilt the castle, and decorated it with murals. With the exception of the hall*, Henry's castle was destroyed by the Roundheads in the 17th century.

In 1382 William of Wykeham founded Winchester College, where many of Britain's famous statesmen have been educated.

Windsor Castle, *Berks*
For 900 years Windsor Castle* has been a royal home. William the Conqueror built the mound that became the nucleus of this fortress commanding the middle Thames and approaches to London.

Henry II replaced the wooden building on the mound with a stone keep—the original Round Tower—and set up the outer walls with watchtowers.

Edward III, the first sovereign to make Windsor a comfortable residence, was born in the castle. His architect, William of Wykeham, built apartments in the upper ward round a quadrangle. Edward also made striking changes in the lower ward, where a chapel dedicated to St George, patron saint of England, had stood for a century. In 1348 he founded the Order of the Garter, greatest of the orders of chivalry.

The choice of emblem is obscure. A chronicler reports that Edward picked up a garter dropped by the Countess of Salisbury at a festival and put it round his own knee, saying to his smiling courtiers: 'Honi soit qui mal y pense' (Shame to him who thinks evil of it). Another account has the king using his own garter as the signal for the attack on the French at Crécy in 1346.

Edward IV began building St George's Chapel in 1472, a Gothic masterpiece. Henry VIII provided a new castle gateway and tennis court, and was laid to rest in St George's beside the coffin of his third queen, Jane Seymour.

To young Edward VI, captive of the Protector Somerset, the castle seemed a prison. 'Here be no galleries nor no gardens to walk in,' the boy wrote. To Windsor came Queen Elizabeth, his sister, in times of crisis. Roundheads seized it early in the Civil War, and Charles I spent his last Christmas here as a prisoner of Cromwell's régime before his execution at Whitehall in 1649.

Charles II had the royal apartments rebuilt, with the Star Building embellished by Verrio and Grinling Gibbons. These improvements were overshadowed by George IV, whose architect was Jeffrey Wyatville. He rebuilt the apartments to the east and south of the quadrangle

in a revived Gothic that blends well with the old. He transformed Horn Court into the Waterloo Chamber where, on June 18 each year, the anniversary of the battle, a memorial banquet is held.

Queen Victoria became known as 'the widow of Windsor' for, in her grief at the Prince Consort's death in 1861, she confined herself to her private apartments for long periods.

In June 1917, at the height of the First World War, George V renounced his German names and titles, and adopted Windsor as his family name.

And it was from Windsor that his son, Edward VIII, made his farewell broadcast at his abdication in 1936. His successor, George VI, had told him that he intended to create him Duke of Windsor. 'It shall be the first act of my reign,' he said. He fulfilled his promise.

Woburn, *Beds* See pp. 192–3

Woodstock, *Oxon*
Henry II installed his mistress, the Fair Rosamund, in the royal manor of Woodstock.

The king's jealous wife, Eleanor of Aquitaine, is said to have pursued Rosamund into a maze in the grounds, offering her death by dagger or poison. In fact, Rosamund retired to a convent.

In 1554 Elizabeth I was held at Woodstock by her sister, Mary, for suspected involvement in Sir Thomas Wyatt's rebellion.

In 1704 Queen Anne gave the manor to John Churchill, 1st Duke of Marlborough, as the site for Blenheim Palace.

Worcester, *Herefs & Worcs*
Worcester owes its importance to its vital position dominating the crossing of the River Severn and to its ancient cathedral*.

The present cathedral was built by St Wulfstan, one of the few Saxon bishops to retain his see under William the Conqueror. Here, King John was buried, and here the body of Prince Arthur, first husband of Catharine of Aragon, was taken after his premature death.

In 1651 Cromwell fought his final battle in England at Worcester. Charles II and his army of 12,000 Scots were trapped in the city by 30,000 Parliamentarians. On the morning of September 3, Cromwell crossed the Severn and stormed vic-

toriously into Worcester. Only the courageous rearguard action of the Earl of Cleveland allowed Charles to escape. (See Shoreham p. 418.)

York, *N Yorks*
Eboracum, a Roman fortress built about AD 71 where York now stands, became one of the leading cities of the Roman Empire. It was here that Severus died in 211, and Constantine was proclaimed emperor in 306.

After the withdrawal of the Romans in 400, York became the capital of the kings of Northumbria. King Edwin was baptised in York in 627 by the Roman missionary Paulinus. A wooden church was hastily built for the purpose, but after the ceremony Edwin ordered a magnificent stone church to be erected to take its place.

After the Norman Conquest, York paid dearly for rebelling against the Conqueror, who ravaged the city and built a castle, Clifford's Tower, to keep its citizens in subjection. The castle was destroyed by fire in the anti-Jewish riots of 1190. Most of the city's Jewish colony, about 150 men, women and children, died inside the building.

During the Middle Ages, when the cathedral and many churches and religious houses were built, York became one of the main religious centres of England. (The church of St Peter* has always been both a cathedral and minster, or centre of religious training.)

York was also, until the 6th century, the centre of the wool trade. Its prosperous guilds were famous for their colourful processions and religious plays.

In 1813 a mass trial in York of the machine-breaking rioters, known as the Luddites, broke up the main Luddite movement. Seventeen rioters were hanged, and many others transported.

Wales
&
Southern England

Showing the historic places included in the Land of History *gazetteer*

Legend

Site or building ▲

Town or village ■

National boundary — + — + —

County boundary — — — — —

N

0 ——————— 20
Miles

MERSEY-SIDE
■ Liverpool

Anglesey
■ Beaumaris
■ Conway
■ Rhuddlan
Flint Castle ▲

CHESHIRE

■ Denbigh
Castle
Hawarden
Castle ▲

■ Caernarvon
Castle

GWYNEDD

CLWYD

■ Beddgelert
■ Llangollen

■ Llanystumdwy
■ Bala

▲ Harlech
Castle

Shrewsbury ■

*Bardsey
Island*

Coalbrookdale ■

SALOP

■ Machynlleth

*Cardigan
Bay*

Ludlow ■

POWYS

Mortimer's
Cross ▲

HEREFORD
&
WORCESTER

■ Builth
Wells

■ Fishguard

DYFED

Brecon ▲
Castle

*St David's
Head*
■ St David's

Abergavenny ■

■ Carmarthen

Dynevor ▲
Castle

Monmouth ■

■ Milford
Haven
■ Laugharne

Raglan ▲
Castle

WEST
GLAMORGAN

MID
GLAMORGAN

GWENT

▲ Pembroke
Castle

■ Caerleon

*Worms
Head*

Caerphilly
Castle ▲

■ Newport

Llantrisant
Castle ▲

Severn

■ Cardiff

Bristol ■

SOUTH
GLAMORGAN

AVON

Bristol Channel

Wells ■

Lundy

Glastonbury ■

Coleridge ▲
Cottage

▲ Sedgmoor

*Hartland
Point*

■ Bridgwater

■ Bideford

SOMERSET

Cadbury
Castle

■ Taunton

Sherborne
Castle

■ Chard

DEVON

Honiton ■

Lyme Regis ■

■ Exeter

*Lyme
Bay*

▲ Tintagel
Castle

■ Princetown

Compton ▲
Castle

▲ Kent's Cavern

CORNWALL

■ Plymouth

■ Dartmouth

■ Brixham

Start Point

Gwennap ▲
Pit

■ Redruth

■ Falmouth

*Land's
End*

*Scilly
Isles*

St Michael's
Mount

Lizard Point

424

GREATER
Manchester
MANCHESTER

SOUTH YORKSHIRE

■ Sheffield

Haddon ■ Chesterfield
Hall ■ Hardwick
Hall

Sherwood
Forest

Harby ■ ■ Lincoln

LINCOLN

NOTTINGHAM

Newark ■

■ Burslem

DERBY

Newstead ▲
Abbey

Nottingham ■
Aslockton ▲
Gotham ■

■ Boston

STAFFORD

■ Derby

The
Wash

Burnham ■ Holkham Hall
Thorpe

■ Stafford

Melbourne ■

Staunton ▲
Harold Hall

LEICESTER

■ Bourne

Castle ■ ▲ Houghton Hall
Rising
King's ■ Sandringham
Lynn

NORFOLK

■ Norwich

Drayton
Bassett

Ashby de la ▲ ▲ Bradgate
Zouch Castle Park

Leicester ■

■ Oakham

■ Helpston

WEST
MIDLANDS

Arbury
Aston ■ Hall ▲

Bosworth ▲
Field

Lutterworth

CAMBRIDGE

▲ Grime's Graves

Thetford

■ Birmingham

Coventry ■

Fotheringhay ▲
Castle

Hagley Hall ▲
Bewdley

Rugby ■

■ Naseby

NORTHAMPTON

■ Huntingdon

Newmarket ■

■ Ely

Dunwich

▲ Kenilworth
Castle

Northampton ■

■ Buckden

■ Cambridge

Bury St Edmunds ■

Framlingham ▲
Castle

■ Worcester

Warwick ▲
Castle

Stratford-upon-Avon

WARWICK

Olney ■

Bedford ■

SUFFOLK

Aldeburgh

Powick ▲
Bridge

Evesham ■

Elstow ■
Southill ▲
Park

Ipswich ■

Banbury ■

Tewkesbury ■

Sudeley ▲
Castle

Stowe ■

BEDFORD

Audley End ▲

Stow-on-
the-Wold ▲

Claydon ■
House

■ Woburn

Colchester ■

The Naze

Cheltenham ■

Blenheim ■ ▲ Woodstock
Palace

Dunstable ■

HERTFORD

Gloucester

GLOUCESTER

OXFORD

Aylesbury ■

BUCKINGHAM

Ayot St Lawrence ▲
Lemsford ▲ Rye ▲
House

Chelmsford ■

Berkeley
Castle

Cumnor ▲
Hall

Oxford ■

Ashridge ▲

St ■
Albans

Hatfield ▲
House

■ Cheshunt

ESSEX

Kelmscott ▲
Manor

Abingdon ■

Berkhamsted ■
Hughenden ▲

Salisbury ▲
Hall

Cheshunt ■

Chalgrove ▲
Field

Manor Chalfont
▲ ▲ St Giles

Ashingdon ■

Lyford ■

Sutton
Courtenay

Beaconsfield ■
Marlow ■

Barnet ▲

Thames

Little
Sodbury

Medmenham ■

Cliveden ▲

GREATER

Hayes ■
Place

Inner

London

North
Foreland

Lacock ▲
Abbey

Calne ■

Windsor ▲
Castle

Syon ▲
House

Richmond ■

LONDON

Sheerness ■
Eastchurch ■

Gravesend ■

Gad's Hill ▲
Place

Rochester ■

Avebury ■

Kingston ■
Hill

Nonsuch

Keston ▲

Sandwich ■

Bath

Devizes ■

Burbage ■

Claremont ▲

Biggin ▲
Hill

Bushy ▲
Park

Down ▲
House

Sevenoaks ■

Faversham ■

Canterbury ■

WILTSHIRE

Farnborough ■

BERKSHIRE

Chartwell ▲

KENT

Walmer ▲
Castle

Stonehenge ▲

■ Guildford

Penshurst ▲
Place

Royal ■
Tunbridge
Wells

Dover ■

Bush Barrow ▲
Old ▲
Sarum

SURREY

Wilton ■
House

Alton ■

Old ■
Alresford

Chawton ■

Horsham ■

EAST

Fonthill ▲
Abbey

Salisbury ■

Winchester ■

Tichborne ▲
House

Selborne ■

WEST

Brookland ■

Shaftesbury

HAMPSHIRE

Romsey ■

Hambledon ■

South ■
Harting

SUSSEX

SUSSEX

Bateman's ▲

Rye ■

Winchelsea ■

Southampton ■

Battle ▲
Abbey

Fishbourne ▲
Palace

Arundel ▲
Castle

Shoreham ■

Laughton ■
Lewes ■

Beaulieu ▲
Abbey

Chichester ■
Bosham ■

Brighton ■

DORSET

Buckler's ▲
Hard

Solent

Portsmouth ■

Rottingdean ■

Clouds ▲
Hill

Bournemouth ■

ISLE
Farringford ■ Osborne ■
House

Selsey
Bill

Beachy
Head

Dorchester

OF

Corfe ▲
Castle

Plymouth

WIGHT

Isle of
Portland

425

Scotland & Northern England

Cape Wrath

Butt of Lewis

WESTERN ISLES

North Minch

Little Minch

North Minch

▲ Ardvreck Castle

Carbisdale ▲

Tain ■

Moray Firth

Lossiemouth ■

Inverness ■   ▲ Culloden

HIGHLAND

Lochindorb

■ Turriff

GRAMPIAN

Lumphanan ▲   Aberdeen ■
                Howe of
                Corrichie ▲
▲ Balmoral
Castle
Braemar ■   Stonehaven ■
                 Dunnottar ▲
                 Castle

▲ Inverlochy
  Castle

Glencoe ●   Pass of
                 Killiecrankie ▲   Kirriemuir ■
                                   ■ Montrose
                 TAYSIDE
                         Glamis ▲
                         Castle
Dunkeld ■   Dundee ■
                 ■ Arbroath
Huntingtower ▲   Scone ▲
Castle   ■ ● Perth
Tippermuir ▲   Magnus ▲
                 Muir   ■ St Andrews
▲ Sheriffmuir   Falkland ▲
                        Palace   *FIFE*

Iona ●   Oban ■

Balquhidder ■

CENTRAL

Inveraray ■

Inchmahome Priory ▲

Stirling Castle ▲
Sauchieburn ▲ ▲ Dunfermline   Burntisland ■
Bannockburn ▲   *Firth of Forth*
*Glen   *Bass Rock*
Fruin*   Wall
         Antonine   Old   Seton ▲   ▲ Tantallon Castle
Greenock ■ ▲ Falkirk Cramond ▲ Palace   ■ Dunbar
                     Bridge   ▲ Haddington ■
Rothesay ■ Paisley ■ Edinburgh ● Prestonpans ■
Largs ■   Glasgow ■   *Carberry Hill* Pinkie
                                Crichton Castle ▲
Lochranza ■   Blantyre ■   Borthwick ▲
Brodick ▲   Cadzow ▲   Castle
Castle   Castle
STRATHCLYDE   New Lanark ■   Halidon Hill ▲
                               ■ Berwick-upon-Tweed
Darvel ■

Ayr ■   Auchinleck ■   Abbotsford ▲   Coldstream ■
Alloway ■   Melrose ▲   Bamburgh ▲
                    Philiphaugh ▲ Abbey   Castle
                               Roxburgh ▲ Flodden
                               Castle   Field
                               Jedburgh ■
                               BORDERS   Alnwick ▲
                                          Castle

DUMFRIES & GALLOWAY   ▲ Otterburn
                               NORTHUMBERLAND

Dumfries ■   Ecclefechan ■
Caerlaverock ▲ Gretna ▲   *Hadrian's Wall*   TYNE Jarrow ■
Castle   Green   &
                    ▲ Solway   WEAR   ■ Sunderland
Stranraer ■   ▲ Buittle Moss

Whithorn ■   Neville's ▲
                               Cross   ■ Durham
              Solway Firth

St Bees Head   Cockermouth ■   Stockton-on-Tees ■
                                              Darlington ■
                        CUMBRIA   DURHAM   CLEVELAND
                                    Barnard ■
                                    Castle ▲

                        Grasmere ■   Richmond ▲   ■ Whitby
                        Coniston ■   Castle ■ Northallerton
                        ■ Kendal   Middleham ▲
                                              Castle   ■ Scarborough

                                   NORTH YORKSHIRE   *Flamborough
                                                      Head*
Peel ▲   *Isle of   Boroughbridge ■
Castle   Man*   Knaresborough ▲ Stamford ▲
                             ■ Lancaster   Castle   Marston Bridge
                                                    Moor
                                          Otley ■   ● York
                             LANCASHIRE   HUMBERSIDE
                                          Leeds ■ ■ Towton
                             Preston ■   Bradford ■ Pontefract ■ Kingston upon Hull ■
                             Blackburn ■   Castle   ■ Welton
                                    WEST YORKSHIRE
                                          Wakefield ■   Ravenspur
                             Bolton ■
                             GREATER   SOUTH
                             MANCHESTER   YORKSHIRE   ■ Epworth
                    MERSEY-   Manchester ■   Sheffield ■
                    SIDE   *Humber*
             Liverpool ■   NOTTS
                        Mersey   LINCOLN
Anglesey ■ Beaumaris   Haddon ■
Conway ■   Rhuddlan ■ Flint ▲   CHESHIRE   Hall   Chesterfield ■
            Denbigh ▲   Castle   Hardwick ▲ *Sherwood Harby ■
            Castle   Hawarden ▲   Hall   Forest* ■ Lincoln
Caernarvon ▲   Castle
Castle   STAFFORD DERBY Newark ■

Orkney Islands inset:
ORKNEY ISLANDS
St Margaret's ■ Hope

Legend
Site or building ▲
Town or village ■
National boundary —+—+—
County boundary — — — —

N

0   20
Miles

426

INDEX

Page numbers in **bold type** refer to a main entry on a subject.
Figures in *italics* refer to illustrations, which are often accompanied by mention in the text
on the same page. The panels provide quick reference to some of the major themes
occurring throughout the book. (*Abbreviations—s.* son of; *w.* wife of)

ACKNOWLEDGMENTS

The publishers acknowledge their indebtedness to the following for permission to use their photographs. The details are arranged according to chapter and page number (**bold** figures) and the photographers are given in brackets.

Prehistory 12/13 Stonehenge: (Mike Taylor) **14** Artefacts from Kent's Cavern: Trustees of the British Museum (Natural History) **15** Barnfield Pit, Swanscombe: (Malcolm Aird); Swanscombe skull: Trustees of the British Museum (Natural History); bone fragment: Trustees of the British Museum **16** Grime's Graves: (Penny Tweedie); Grime's Graves Venus: Trustees of the British Museum **17** Clactonian flint: Colchester and Essex Museum (Mike Freeman); hand axe: Trustees of the British Museum (Natural History); flint blade, axe head and arrow head: Devizes Museum (Eileen Tweedy); pots: Devizes Museum (J. Beale) **18** Stonehenge: (Mike Taylor) **19** Silbury Hill: (Malcolm Aird); Avebury: (Penny Tweedie); Dolmen: Susan Griggs (Adam Woolfitt); Castlerigg Circle: Picturepoint **20** Bush Barrow: (Mike Taylor); belt hook and mace: Devizes Museum (Eileen Tweedy) **21** Bell beaker, axe head: Devizes Museum (Eileen Tweedy) **22** Waterloo helmets, Desborough mirror, Battersea shield: Trustees of the British Museum **23** Horse mask, torc: Trustees of the British Museum; limestone head: Gloucester City Museums **23** Mousa broch: Susan Griggs (Michael St Maur Sheil)

Romans 24/25 Hadrian's Wall: Brian Brake, from the John Hillelson Agency **26** Coins (Raymond Gardner) **28** Beach near Walmer: (Malcolm Aird) **29** Coin: (Raymond Gardner); statue of Caesar: Susan Griggs (Adam Woolfitt); the Dying Gaul: Scala **30** Maiden Castle: (Penny Tweedie); coin of Vespasian: (Raymond Gardner) **31** Head of Claudius: Colchester and Essex Museum (Mike Freeman); distance slab: National Museum of Antiquities of Scotland **32** Tombstone: Colchester and Essex Museum (Mike Freeman) **33** Pharos at Dover: Crown copyright by permission of the Controller HMSO; Roman road: (Penny Tweedie); diners and reciter: Colchester and Essex Museum (Mike Freeman) **34** Dolphin mosaic, boy's head: *Sunday Times* **35** Mosaics: Michael Holford; Pierce Bridge plough group: Trustees of the British Museum; hoe and plough share: Guildhall Museum, London (Mike Freeman) **36** Multangular Tower: (Mike Freeman); jet ornaments: Yorkshire Museum (Mike Freeman) **37** Tragic mask: National Museum of Wales; Colchester vase: Colchester and Essex Museum (Mike Freeman); Roman bath: (Michael Holford); strigil and oil-flask: Guildhall Museum, London (Mike Freeman) **38** Hadrian's Wall: Brian Brake, from the John Hillelson Agency; head of Hadrian: Trustees of the British Museum **39** Pictish slab: C. M. Dixon **40** Roman glass: Canterbury Royal Museum (Penny Tweedie); Lullingstone Chi-Rho, Lullingstone wall-painting: Trustees of the British Museum **41** Mildenhall dish and cover: Trustees of the British Museum; Jupiter: Colchester and Essex Museum (Mike Freeman); sphinx: Colchester and Essex Museum (Mike Freeman); dancing lar: Colchester and Essex Museum (Mike Freeman); head of Mithras: Guildhall Museum, London (Mike Freeman)

Saxons 42/43 Sompting church: (Mike Freeman) **44/45** Anglo-Saxon calendar: British Library MS.COT TIB'V (Colour Centre Slides Ltd) **46** Cadbury Castle: Camera Press (Ron Starr) **47** King Arthur: British Library MS.Roy. 20 AII f.4; Round Table: Bibliothèque Nationale MS.Fr.343 f.3; Noah's Ark: Bodleian Library roll 172D **48** St Martin's Church: (Malcolm Aird) **49** Bede: British Library ADD MS.39943 f.2; Ixworth cross: Ashmolean Museum (Colour Centre Slides Ltd); Franks casket: British Museum (Michael Holford) **50** Sutton Hoo: (Mike Taylor) **51** Sutton Hoo helmet and buckle: British Museum (Michael Holford); Offa's Dyke: (Keith Morris) **52** Lindisfarne: Tre Tryckare, Cagner and Co. (Brian Seed) **53** Relics of St Cuthbert: Durham Cathedral Library (Colour Centre Slides Ltd); Lindisfarne slab: Crown copyright by permission of the Controller HMSO **54** Coin of Alfred: (Raymond Gardner); the Alfred jewel: Ashmolean Museum, Oxford **55** Cnut: British Library MS.Stowe 944 f.6 **56** Shrine of the Confessor: Perfecta Press; Edward the Confessor: Bodleian Library roll 205B **58** Lindisfarne carpet page: British Library Lindisfarne Facsimile f.10v; the Church of St Lawrence: (Mike Freeman) **59** Mouth of Hell: British Library MS.NERO CIV f.39; reliquary cross: Victoria and Albert Museum; Kingston brooch: Merseyside County Museums; Winster Moor brooch: Sheffield City Museum (Colour Centre Slides Ltd); five senses brooch: British Museum (Michael Holford)

Medieval 60/61 Coronation of a king: Master and Fellows of Corpus Christi College, Cambridge; Chair: Woodmansterne **62** Feast, tournament, masons: Trustees of the British Museum **63** Monks cutting planks, dyers at work, reapers and harvestman: Trustees of the British Museum **64** Battlefield at Hastings: John Hillelson Agency (Erich Lessing) **64/65** Death of Harold, Bayeaux Tapestry: (Michael Holford) **65** Halley's Comet: Photo Science Museum, London; comet, Bayeaux Tapestry: (Michael Holford); William I: Dean and Chapter of Wells Cathedral (BPC) **66** White Tower: (Chris Ridley); St John's Chapel: A. F. Kersting **67** Tower of London, MS.illumination: Trustees of the British Museum; *Domesday Book*: Public Record Office; Hereward the Wake: Mansell Collection **68** New Forest: (Keith Morris); death of William Rufus: Mary Evans Picture Library **69** Hunting with bow and arrow: Bodleian Library roll 189A; hunting deer: Bodleian Library roll 189A; William Rufus: Trustees of the British Museum **70** Durham Cathedral, Nave, Durham Cathedral from bridge: (Patrick Thurston) **71** Durham Cathedral, Galilee Chapel: (Patrick Thurston); Durham Cathedral, wall-painting and sanctuary knocker: British Tourist Authority **72** Wreck of the *White Ship*: Trustees of the British Museum **73** Stephen: Bodleian Library roll 205b; illumination from Bury Bible: Master and Fellows of Corpus Christi College, Cambridge MS.2 (Colour Centre Slides Ltd) **74** Canterbury Cathedral: (Malcolm Aird) **75** Manuscript illumination of Becket's death: Trustees of the British Museum; Canterbury pilgrims, MS.illuminations: Trustees of the British Museum **76** Chertsey Abbey tile: Trustees of the British Museum **76/77** Massacre of Saracens: Bibliothèque Nationale Service Photographique **77** Effigy: (G. Cozal); Richard I: Trustees of the British Museum **78** Mob Quad, Merton College: (Alain Le Garsmeur); MS.illumination of William of Wykeham: Bodleian Library roll 214.8; Duke Humphrey's Library: Thomas-Photos, Oxford; Merton College Library: BPC (Chris Ridley) **79** Founder's cup: Queen's College, Oxford (Alain Le Garsmeur); giant salt: All Souls College, Oxford (Weidenfeld and Nicolson Ltd) **80** Runnymede: (Keith Morris); King John at Runnymede: Guildhall Library; King John's seal: Trustees of the British Museum; Magna Carta: Trustees of the British Museum **81** King John's tomb: Dean and Chapter of Worcester Cathedral (Derrick Witty) **82** Wells Cathedral, west front: Dean and Chapter of Wells Cathedral (Malcolm Aird); MS.illumination of Wells: Bodleian Library roll 214.8 **83** Wells Cathedral transept: Dean and Chapter of Wells Cathedral (Picturepoint Ltd); Wells Cathedral chapter house: Dean and Chapter of Wells Cathedral (Perfecta Publications Ltd); Wells Cathedral, prior's staircase: Dean and Chapter of Wells Cathedral (Michael Holford); Wells Cathedral, corbels: Dean and Chapter of Wells Cathedral (Malcolm Aird) **84** Westminster Hall: Perfecta Publications Ltd; seal of Simon de Montfort: Trustees of the British Museum **85** MS.illuminations of Parliament (detail): Copyright reserved; Henry III: Dean and Chapter of Westminster Abbey **86** Harlech Castle: (Penny Tweedie) **87** Stonemasons: Pierpont Morgan Library MS.638 f.3; coronation of Edward I: Bodleian Library roll 173G **88** Stirling Castle: (Patrick Thurston); Robert Bruce: Mansell Collection; Battle of Bannockburn: Master and Fellows of Corpus Christi College, Oxford MS.CCC 171 f.265r **89** Edward II: Trustees of the British Museum **90** The Black Prince's shield: Dean and Chapter of Canterbury Cathedral (Penny Tweedie); Battle of Crécy: Bibliothèque Nationale Service Photographique **91** Longbowmen: Trustees of the British Museum; Edward III: Mary Evans Picture Library **92** St Mary's, Ashwell: (Keith Morris); Burial of plague victims: Bibliothèque Royale de Belgique **93** Medical instruments: By permission of the President and Fellows of St John's College, Oxford **94** Groats of Richard II: British Museum (Christopher Barker); Death of Wat Tyler: Trustees of the British Museum **95** John of Gaunt: Mary Evans Picture Library; abdication of Richard II: Trustees of the British Museum **96** Page from *Piers Plowman*: Bodleian Library roll 175A **96/97** Six illuminations from the facsimile of the Ellesmere Chaucer: Trustees of the British Museum **98** Alnwick Castle: (M. Breese); Richard II surrenders: Trustees of the British Museum **99** Coronation of Henry IV: Trustees of the British Museum **100** Stone relief of Henry V: Dean and Chapter of Westminster Abbey (Alain Le Garsmeur); Henry's portrait: National Portrait Gallery (detail); Battle of Agincourt: By courtesy of the Archbishop of Canterbury and the Trustees of Lambeth Palace Library **101** Brasses: Victoria and Albert Museum **102** King's College Chapel – interior: (Michael Holford); King's College Chapel – exterior: Camera Press (Wim Swaan) **103** King's College Chapel – stained glass: (S. Newbury); Eton College – wall-painting: By courtesy of the Provost and Fellows of Eton (S. Newbury); Eton College – Canaletto: By courtesy of the National Gallery, London **104** Helmet: Victoria and Albert Museum (Chris Ridley); the Earl of Warwick: By courtesy of the Marquess of Abergavenny (BPC); Margaret of Anjou: Worshipful Company of Skinners (Percy Hennel); Plucking of the Red and White Roses: By permission of the Right Honourable The Speaker (John Freeman) **105** Battle of Tewkesbury: Bibliotek der Universiteit, Ghent; Henry VI (detail): National Portrait Gallery **106** *Dictes and Syenges*: The British Library (John Freeman); Anthony Woodville and Edward IV: By courtesy of the Archbishop of Canterbury and the Trustees of Lambeth Palace Library **107** Model of Caxton's Press: Crown copyright, Science Museum, London; Edward IV enthroned: Trustees of the British Museum **108** Bosworth: (Michael St Maur Sheil); Battle: Bibliotek der Universiteit, Ghent; Richard III (detail): National Portrait Gallery **109** Princes: by permission of the Trustees of the Wallace Collection

Tudors 110/11 The Ambassadors (Holbein): By courtesy of the National Gallery, London **112** Cellerer: Trustees of the British Museum; emigrants: British Museum (John Freeman); pedlar: British Museum (John Freeman) **113** Hunting at Nonesuch: reproduced by permission of the Syndics of the Fitzwilliam Museum, Cambridge; Campion: Mary Evans Picture Library; Virginia potato: Bodleian Library roll 196c; schoolroom: British Museum (John Freeman) **114** Earl of Dorset: Victoria and Albert Museum; children at table: By kind permission of the Marquess of Bath (John Freeman) **115** Elizabeth Vernon: By kind permission of His Grace the Duke of Buccleuch and Queensberry; Bradford table carpet and cushion cover: Victoria and Albert Museum; Court Musicians and Henry VIII: Trustees of the British Museum **116** Coins: British Museum (Christopher Barker); document: Crown copyright, Public Record Office E101/414/6 f.83V **116** Cabot: Bristol City Art Gallery; **117** Map: Museo Naval, Madrid (Archivo Mas); Henry VII: National Portrait Gallery **118/19** Compton Wynyates: By kind permission of the Marquess of Northampton **120** Clock salt: Goldsmiths Hall (Eileen Tweedy); Henry VIII: Walker Art Gallery, Liverpool; Francis I: Cliché Musées Nationaux, Paris **120** Field of the Cloth of Gold (detail): Copyright reserved **121** Catharine of Aragon (detail): National Portrait Gallery; Anne Boleyn (detail): By gracious permission of Her Majesty Queen Elizabeth II; Jane Seymour: Kunsthistorisches Museum, Vienna; Anne of Cleves: The President and Fellows of St John's College, Oxford (Thomas-Photos Oxford); Catharine Howard (detail): Copyright reserved; Catharine Parr (detail): National Portrait Gallery **122** Hampton Court: (Malcolm Aird); Hampton Court, engraving: Crown copyright by permission of the Controller HMSO **124** Missal: By permission of the Governing Body of Christ Church, Oxford (Alain Le Garsmeur); Wolsey: National Portrait Gallery **125** MS.illuminations: Bodleian Library roll 214.5 **126** Hever Castle and lock: By permission of the Hon. Gavin Astor (Malcolm Aird); Anne Boleyn (detail): National Portrait Gallery; Henry VIII and Anne (engraving): Mary Evans Picture Library **127** Thomas Boleyn (detail): By gracious permission of Her Majesty Queen Elizabeth II; Thomas, Duke of Norfolk (detail): Copyright reserved **128** Enamel: By kind permission of the Rector of Stonyhurst College (Alain Le Garsmeur); Utopia: British Museum (John Freeman); **128** More and his daughter: Tate Gallery, London (John Webb) **130** Glastonbury Abbey: (Malcolm Aird); Syon Nunnery: Bristol City Art Gallery; *Valor Ecclesiasticus*: Crown copyright, Public Record Office E344/22; Thomas Cromwell (detail): National Portrait Gallery **131** Mells Manor: By kind permission of the Earl of Oxford and Asquith (Gordon Moore); judge: Trustees of the British Museum **132** More and his family: Kunstmuseum, Basel; Fisher (detail): By gracious permission of Her Majesty Queen Elizabeth II; Holbein self-portrait: Weidenfeld and Nicolson Ltd **133** Henry VIII: Baron Thyssen Collection; Prince Edward: National Gallery of Art, Washington D.C. (Andrew Mellon Collection); Anne of Cleves: Cliché Musées Nationaux, Paris **134** Inscription: Crown copyright by permission of the Controller HMSO; Lady Jane Grey (detail): National Portrait Gallery **134** Beheading: Mary Evans Picture Library; document: Trustees of the British Museum **135** Prince Edward: Kunstmuseum, Basel (Hans Hinz, Basel); Prayer Book: Mansell Collection **136** St Mary's, Oxford: (Michael Freeman); Ridley (detail), Latimer (detail), Cranmer (detail), Mary I (detail): National Portrait Gallery; Woodcuts: British Museum (John Freeman) **138** *Liber Regalis*: By courtesy of the Dean and Chapter of Westminster; procession: College of Arms **139** Sir Edward Dymock: College of Arms; Elizabeth I: By kind permission of Lord Brooke, Warwick Castle (John Wright) **140** Hilliard: Victoria and Albert Museum; Leicester: National Portrait Gallery; Hatton: Victoria and Albert Museum; Mary, Queen of Scots: By kind permission of His Grace the Duke of Portland **141** Young Man and a Rose Bush: Victoria and Albert Museum; Elizabeth I: Victoria and Albert Museum; Henry Percy: Ashmolean Museum, Oxford **142** Silver casket: By permission of His Grace the Duke of Hamilton KT, and the National Museum of Antiquities of Scotland (Patrick Thurston); Death of Riccio: National Gallery of Scotland; Rizzio: Mary Evans Picture Library; Mary: Scottish National Portrait Gallery **143** Scene of Darnley's Murder: Crown copyright, Public Record Office SP 52/13* No. 1; Darnley (detail): Copyright reserved **144** Rosary and Prayer Book: By kind permission of His Grace the Duke of Norfolk (Penny Tweedie); Facsimile of warrant: Mary Evans Picture Library; Mary's portrait: National Portrait Gallery **145** Execution of Mary, Queen of Scots: Scottish National Portrait Gallery **146** Goblet: Plymouth City Art Gallery (Michael Freeman); coconut: British Museum (Time Inc. British Empire Series); Drake: National Portrait Gallery; Map: British Museum (John Freeman) **147** Frobisher: Bodleian Library, Oxford; Indians eating maize: British Museum (John Freeman) **148** Longleat – exterior: By kind permission of the Marquess of Bath (Penny Tweedie); Sir John Thynne: By kind permission of the Marquess of Bath (Photo Precision Ltd) **149** Painting of Longleat: By kind permission of the Marquess of Bath; Longleat – interior: By kind permission of the Marquess of Bath (Photo Precision Ltd) **150** Drake's Drum: Plymouth City Art Gallery; Philip II (detail): National Portrait Gallery; Elizabeth I (detail): from the Woburn Abbey Collection, by kind permission of His Grace the Duke of Bedford (Michael Freeman) **150/1** Armada painting: National Maritime Museum, London **151** Howard of Effingham (detail): National Portrait Gallery; Progress: St Faith's Church, King's Lynn (J. R. Freeman) **152** 1st Armada map: National Maritime Museum, London (Time Inc. British Empire Series); 2nd, 3rd and 4th Armada maps, Drake (detail): National Maritime Museum, London **152/3** Armada painting: Tiroler Landesmuseum **153** Armada Treasure: Transworld Feature Syndicate Inc. **154** Shakespeare: National Portrait Gallery; the Globe theatre: Trustees of the British Museum **156** Document: By kind permission of His Grace the Duke of Sutherland (British Museum); ring: Dean and Chapter, Westminster Abbey (Woodmansterne); Earl of Essex: from the Woburn Abbey Collection, by kind permission of His Grace the Duke of Bedford (Michael Freeman) **157** Burghley (detail): National Portrait Gallery; Cecil: By permission of the Marquess of Salisbury; Funeral of Elizabeth: Trustees of the British Museum

Early Stuarts 158/9 Execution of Charles I: By permission of Lord Primrose, Scottish National Portrait Gallery; Rubens ceiling: Crown copyright, by permission of the Controller HMSO **160** Arms: Radio Times Hulton Picture Library; St Paul's: Society of Antiquaries of London; James I and Prince Charles: Society of Antiquaries of London **161** Death of Buckingham: By kind permission of the Marquess of Northampton (Henry Cooper); Covenanters: Mary Evans Picture Library; Lord Mayor's procession: Guildhall Library; Hobbes (detail): National Portrait Gallery; Charles II's escape: By permission of the 6th Earl of Arran Will Trust (Christopher Barker) **162** Lantern: Ashmolean Museum, Oxford; gunpowder plotters: Mansell Collection; Fawkes apprehended: British Museum (John Freeman) **163** James I: Crown copyright, Public Record Office (E30/1705); Carr (detail), Buckingham (detail): National Portrait Gallery **164** Tradescant: Ashmolean Museum, Oxford; drawing of plum: Bodleian Library roll 208G **164** Hatfield – south front: By kind permission of the Marquess of Salisbury **165** Marble hall and grand staircase: By kind permission of the Marquess of Salisbury (John Freeman); deed: By kind permission of the Marquess of Salisbury (Basil King) **166** Raleigh's *History*: British Museum (John Freeman); execution: Mary Evans Picture Library; Raleigh: National Portrait Gallery **167** Raleigh in Trinidad: Mansell Collection **168** *Mayflower* model: Crown copyright, Science Museum, London; pilgrims: House of Lords (Phoebus Picture Library) **169** Page from the Bible: British Library (John Freeman) **170** Harvey demonstrating to Charles I: Ronan Picture Library; relics of Harvey: By permission of the Royal College of Physicians of London (Keith Morris); Harvey (detail): National Portrait Gallery **171** Bacon (detail): National Portrait Gallery **172** Account: Crown copyright, Public Record Office SP 116/284 No. 43; Hampden: Mary Evans Picture Library; *Sovereign of the Seas*: National Maritime Museum, London; Speaker of the House of Commons: By permission of the Right Honourable the Speaker (Derrick Witty) **173** Archbishop Laud: National Portrait Gallery **174** Block and axe: Crown copyright by permission of the Controller HMSO; execution: Radio Times Hulton Picture Library; Strafford (detail): National Portrait Gallery **175** Raising of the Standard: Phoebus Picture Library **176** Wilton – south front: By kind permission of the Earl of Pembroke (A. F. Kersting) **177** Double Cube Room: (A. F. Kersting); Inigo Jones (detail): National Portrait Gallery; Inigo Jones watercolour: Devonshire Collection, Chatsworth reproduced by permission of the Trustees of the Chatsworth Settlement **178** Triple portrait of Charles I (detail): Copyright reserved; children of Charles I (detail): Copyright reserved **179** Charles I on horseback: National Gallery, London; Henrietta Maria (detail): Copyright reserved **180** Battlefield: (Tony Evans); engraving of battle: National Army Museum;

Edgehill medal: Trustees of the British Museum (Christopher Barker) 181 Essex (detail): By kind permission of His Grace the Duke of Portland, on loan to the National Portrait Gallery; Drawing of Colours: Dr Williams Library (National Army Museum); Prince Rupert: Niedersachsisches Landesmuseum, Hanover 182 Priming flask: Cromwell Museum, Huntingdon; Battle of Naseby: Anne S. K. Browne Military Collection, Providence R.I. 183 Fairfax: The British Library (John Freeman); stained-glass figures: (C. M. Dixon); title page: Cromwell Museum, Huntingdon 184 Chair: Victoria and Albert Museum (Phoebus Picture Library); Charles I (detail): Copyright reserved; engraving of trial: Mary Evans Picture Library 185 Death warrant: House of Lords Record Office 186 Shirt: London Museum; engraving of execution: Mary Evans Picture Library 187 Funeral of Charles I: Phoebus Picture Library 188 Cromwell's hat: Cromwell Museum, Huntingdon; engraving: The British Library (John Freeman); Cromwell: National Portrait Gallery 189 And When Did You Last See Your Father?: Walker Art Gallery, Liverpool 190 All illustrations: Mary Evans Picture Library 191 Bunyan (detail), Milton (detail): National Portrait Gallery; Sin between Satan and Death by Henry Fuseli: Los Angeles County Museum of Art, gift of Mr and Mrs F. M. Nicholas, Mr and Mrs H. B. Swerdlow and Mr and Mrs W. K. Glikbarg

Later Stuarts 192/3 Painted ceiling, Greenwich: Crown copyright by permission of the Controller HMSO 194 Sea battle: Admiral Blake Museum, Bridgewater (Michael Freeman); Countess of Orleans (detail): National Portrait Gallery; John Locke (detail): National Portrait Gallery 195 News of William III's arrival: Tate Gallery, London; Britannia: Mansell Collection; William III (detail): National Portrait Gallery 196 The Compleate Gamster: Radio Times Hulton Picture Library; frost fair: London Museum (Eileen Tweedy) 197 Fox hunt: Radio Times Hulton Picture Library; Walton (detail), Killigrew (detail), Dryden (detail): National Portrait Gallery 197 Drury Lane Theatre, Davenant: Radio Times Hulton Picture Library; Coffee house: British Library (Penguin Books) 198 Boscobel House: By permission of the Department of the Environment (Keith Morris); wood panel: Victoria and Albert Museum (Eileen Tweedy); Duchess of Portsmouth (detail): National Portrait Gallery; Barbara Villiers: By kind permission of the Earl Spencer; Nell Gwynne (detail): National Portrait Gallery 199 Charles at Dover: House of Commons (Phoebus Picture Library); Charles II (detail): National Portrait Gallery 200 Eyam churchyard and register: (Keith Morris); burial of victims: Mary Evans Picture Library; plague doctor: By permission of the Wellcome Trustees 201 Charles II curing the 'King's Evil': British Library (John Freeman) 202 Fire-fighting equipment: London Museum (Eileen Tweedy); 202 Painting of the Fire of London: London Museum (Eileen Tweedy) 203 Pepys (detail): National Portrait Gallery 204 Wren (detail): National Portrait Gallery; Thames by Canaletto (detail): Copyright reserved 205 St Paul's – exterior: Expression Photo Library (Brian Shuel); St Paul's – Nave: Perfecta Publications Ltd; Gibbons carving: Feildon and Mawson (Alistair Smith) 206 Tiles: Victoria and Albert Museum (Eileen Tweedy); Edward Coleman: Mary Evans Picture Library; Titus Oates: British Library (John Freeman) 207 Shaftesbury: Victoria and Albert Museum; procession: Mansell Collection 208 Microscope, observatory: Photo Science Museum, London 209 title page: British Library (John Freeman) 210 Sedgemoor battlefield: Gordon Moore; Monmouth (detail): National Portrait Gallery; battle print: Mansell Collection 211 Trial: Graves Art Gallery, Sheffield; James II (detail): National Portrait Gallery 212 Jet engine: Ronan Picture Library 213 Newton (detail): National Portrait Gallery; Woolsthorpe Manor: National Trust; telescope: The Royal Society (Eileen Tweedy) 213 Newton's notebook: Bodleian Library MS.N.C. 361 roll 2 f.45v 214 Declaration of Rights: House of Lords Record Office 214 William at Torbay (detail): Copyright reserved 215 William and Mary: Photo. Hatchette 216 Glencoe: Picturepoint Ltd; Glencoe massacre: Museum and Art Gallery, Glasgow 217 Act of Union: Mary Evans Picture Library 218 Blenheim: Barnaby's Picture Library; Marlborough: By kind permission of His Grace the Duke of Marlborough; Blenheim tapestry: By kind permission of His Grace the Duke of Marlborough 219 Queen Anne (detail): National Portrait Gallery; Sarah Churchill: By kind permission of His Grace the Duke of Marlborough

Early Georgian 220/1 St James's Park and the Mall (detail): Copyright reserved 221 St James's Park today: (Mike Coles) 222 English family drinking tea (detail): Tate Gallery, London; Dr Hoadly (detail): Tate Gallery, London; sleeping congregation: Mary Evans Picture Library 223 Jethro Tull: Royal Agricultural Society of England (Eileen Tweedy); Tull's Wheat Drill: Mary Evans Picture Library; the orrery: Derby Museum and Art Gallery 224 Beggar's Opera: Tate Gallery, London; Vauxhall Gardens: Victoria and Albert Museum; hunting scene: British Library (John Freeman) 225 Acrobat, dancing bear, peasants dancing, minuet: British Library (John Freeman); mop sellers and hot pudding seller: (Michael Holford) 226 State swords: HM Tower of London, by courtesy of the Armouries; the Old Pretender (detail): National Portrait Gallery 227 Landing of the Old Pretender, George I (detail): National Portrait Gallery 228 View of Bath: British Library (John Freeman) 229 Views of Bath: (Christopher Ridley) 230 Houghton Hall: (A. F. Kersting) 231 Walpole:

British Library (John Freeman); George II (detail): National Portrait Gallery 232 Hogarth, self portrait (detail): Tate Gallery, London; Marriage à la Mode (detail): Courtesy of the National Gallery, London 233 Shrimp Girl (detail): Courtesy of the National Gallery, London; Chairing the Member: Trustees of Sir John Soane's Museum 234 Monument: Picturepoint; Bonnie Prince Charlie (detail): Scottish National Portrait Gallery; Culloden (detail): Copyright reserved 235 Secret portrait: West Highland Museum (R. Matassa) 236 Johnson's Dictionary: Courtesy of Courage Ltd, Brewers, London; Dr Johnson (detail), Boswell (detail), Handel (detail): National Portrait Gallery; Handel's organ: Courtesy of the Thomas Coram Foundation 238 Wolfe's dressing gown: Quebec House, Westerham (Eileen Tweedy) 239 The Taking of Quebec: National Army Museum, London; Death of Wolfe: Ickworth House (National Trust); Pitt: British Library (John Freeman) 240 Stowe House: (John Bethell); the gardens of Stowe: By kind permission of the Head Master of Stowe School (Keith Morris) 241 Capability Brown (detail): National Portrait Gallery

George III 242/3 Old Customs House quay: Victoria and Albert Museum (John Webb) 244 Factory children: Mary Evans Picture Library; toll gate: British Library (John Freeman); carriage and pair: National Gallery, London 245 Gordon riots: Radio Times Hulton Picture Library; Burke (detail): National Portrait Gallery; Pitt and George III: British Library (John Freeman) 246 Robert Adam (detail): National Portrait Gallery 247 Interiors of Syon House: (Jeremy Whitaker) 248 John Wilkes: Trustees of the British Museum 249 Wilkes' entry into London: Mansell Collection; George III (detail): Royal Academy of Art (Phoebus Picture Library) 250 Worsley Canal: Daily Telegraph (Clive Coote); Runcorn locks: Mary Evans Picture Library; James Brindley: Collection of the City Art Gallery, Salford (Patrick Thurston); Duke of Bridgewater's aqueduct: Mansell Collection 251 Wedgwood plaque, compotier, Queen's ware tureen: Courtesy of Josiah Wedgwood and Sons Ltd 252 Cook's secret orders: Crown copyright, Public Record Office ADM 2/1332 P.165 (Mike Freeman); Cook's landing: National Gallery of Victoria (Hamlyn Picture Library) 253 Joseph Banks (detail): National Portrait Gallery; Honeysuckle, death of Cook: (Michael Holford) 254 Mr and Mrs Andrews: National Gallery, London; Countess Howe: The GLC, Trustees of the Iveagh Bequest; The Harvest Wagon: The Barber Institute of Fine Arts, University of Birmingham 255 The Haymakers: Upton House, National Trust; 255 Anatomical drawings of horses: Royal Academy of Arts 256 Musket: HM Tower of London, by courtesy of the Master of the Armouries; surrender at Yorktown: Musée de Versailles (Service Photographique des Musées Nationaux) 258 William Aiton: Crown copyright, by permission of the Controller, Royal Botanical Gardens, Kew; erica, mesembryanthemum, limodorum: Trustees of the British Museum (Natural History) 259 Joseph Priestley (detail), Erasmus Darwin (detail): National Portrait Gallery 260 The Iron Bridge: Transworld Features Syndicate Ltd; Coalbrookdale: Photo. Science Museum, London 261 Boulton and Watt's beam engine: Crown copyright, Science Museum, London; James Watt (detail): National Portrait Gallery 262 Woburn Abbey Canaletto Room: By permission of His Grace the Duke of Bedford 263 Woburn Abbey: By permission of His Grace the Duke of Bedford (Mike Freeman); Blue Drawing Room: By permission of His Grace the Duke of Bedford; Reynolds Room: By permission of His Grace the Duke of Bedford (Aspect Picture Library); Sèvres china: By permission of His Grace the Duke of Bedford; Englishmen abroad: British Library (John Freeman) 264 Satan Visiting Job with Sore Boils, Elohim Creating Adam, The Simoniac Pope: Tate Gallery, London 265 William Blake (detail), Coleridge (detail): National Portrait Gallery; Grasmere: British Tourist Authority; Wordsworth: Radio Times Hulton Picture Library 266 HMS Victory: Aspect Picture Library; Nelson on the Victory: Nelson Museum, Monmouth (Eileen Tweedy) 267 Lady Hamilton: National Maritime Museum, London (John Bulmer); Council of war: National Maritime Museum, London 268 News vendor's bill: Radio Times Hulton Picture Library; death of Nelson: National Maritime Museum, London, Greenwich Hospital Collection 269 Patch boxes, pottery group: National Maritime Museum, London (Eileen Tweedy) 270 Corunna medal: National Army Museum; Sir John Moore (detail): National Portrait Gallery; Retreat to Corunna: British Library (John Webb) 271 Rifle brigade: National Army Museum; George III (detail): Copyright reserved

Regency 272/3 Covent Garden hustings (detail): Reproduced by gracious permission of Her Majesty Queen Elizabeth II 273 Covent Garden today: (Mike Coles) 274 Death of Perceval: Mary Evans Picture Library; Peterloo, freeborn Englishman: British Library (John Freeman) 275 Policeman: British Library (John Freeman); Cato Street Conspiracy: Mansell Collection; Duke of Wellington: Mary Evans Picture Library 276 Duck shooting, prize fight, country fair: British Library (John Freeman); the waltz: Mary Evans Picture Library 277 Fencers, Harriette Wilson, whist players, Westminster rat pit: British Library (John Freeman); Kean as Richard III: Victoria and Albert Museum; Beau Brummel: Mary Evans Picture Library 278 Furniture and clock from Brighton Pavilion: Royal Pavilion, Brighton; banquet, cross section of the Pavilion: British Library (John Freeman) 279 View of the Pavilion: (Keith Morris) 280 Wellington's

field set, Wellington (detail): Wellington Museum, Apsley House (Eileen Tweedy); Napoleon: Bibliothèque Nationale, Paris 281 Battle of Waterloo (detail): Wellington Museum, Apsley House (Eileen Tweedy) 282 Flight of Napoleon, Last Stand of the Imperial Guard: National Army Museum 283 Soldiers: National Army Museum; The Man Wot Drives . . .: British Library (John Freeman) 284 The Ranger's House: (John Couzins) 285 The Trial of Queen Caroline (detail): National Portrait Gallery; The Kettle and the Pot: British Library (John Freeman); Prince Regent: National Portrait Gallery 286 Shelley (detail), Keats (detail), Byron (detail): National Portrait Gallery; Fournier – Funeral of Shelley: Walker Art Gallery, Liverpool 287 Faraday in his Laboratory: Royal Institution, London (Eileen Tweedy) 288 The Rocket: Science Museum, London, Crown copyright; George Stephenson: Mary Evans Picture Library 289 Goods train: Science Museum, London (Eileen Tweedy); Trevithick's railroad and advertisement: Photo. Science Museum, London 290 Reform jug: Courtesy of J. & J. May Ltd (Eileen Tweedy) 291 Reformed House of Commons (detail): National Portrait Gallery; voters: Mary Evans Picture Library; William IV: British Library (Eileen Tweedy) 292 Constable – Study for the Leaping Horse: Victoria and Albert Museum; Constable – Seascape study: Royal Academy of Arts (Phaidon Ltd); Constable – The Haywain: Trustees of the National Gallery, London 293 Turner – Petworth House, Turner – The Shipwreck: Tate Gallery, London; Turner – Rain, Steam and Speed: Trustees of the National Gallery, London

Victoria 294/5 Victoria and family (detail): Copyright reserved 296 Wheat field: Mary Evans Picture Library; traction engine: Radio Times Hulton Picture Library; shop: Mary Evans Picture Library; Sainsbury's: Courtesy of J. Sainsbury Ltd 297 Dame school: Mary Evans Picture Library; council school: Mansell Collection; stage coach: Mary Evans Picture Library; steam engine: Science Museum, London, Crown copyright 298 Proclamation jug: Courtesy of J. & J. May Ltd (Eileen Tweedy); Coronation of Victoria: Copyright Reserved 299 Queen Victoria (detail): National Portrait Gallery; Victoria's desk at Osborne: Erich Lessing (Magnum) from the John Hillelson Agency 300 SS Great Britain: (Malcolm Aird); Launch of the SS Great Britain, SS Great Western: City Art Gallery, Bristol 301 SS Great Eastern: Radio Times Hulton Picture Library; I. K. Brunel: Brunel University Library; railway engine: Mansell Collection 302 Souvenirs of the Great Exhibition: By courtesy of the Victoria and Albert Museum (Eileen Tweedy); navvies: Radio Times Hulton Picture Library 303 Opening of the Great Exhibition (detail), Machinery Hall (detail): Reproduced by gracious permission of Her Majesty Queen Elizabeth II 304 Millais – Ophelia: Tate Gallery, London; Millais: Academy Editions; Holman Hunt – Christ in the House of His Parents: Tate Gallery, London 305 Ford Maddox Brown – The Last of England: Tate Gallery, London; Elizabeth Siddal: Ashmolean Museum, Oxford; Jane Morris: Academy Editions; Ford Maddox Brown (detail): National Portrait Gallery; Dante's Dream: Walker Art Gallery, Liverpool; Hireling Shepherd: City Art Gallery, Manchester; Rossetti, Holman Hunt: Academy Editions 306 Bugle: Museum of the 17th/21st Lancers, Belvoir (Eileen Tweedy); Council of War, Men of the 47th Foot: National Army Museum; Charge of the Light Brigade: (Eileen Tweedy) 307 W. H. Russell, Florence Nightingale: Radio Times Hulton Picture Library 308 Charles Dickens: Radio Times Hulton Picture Library 309 Cooling graveyard, Forge at Chalk: (John Bulmer); The Brontë Sisters (detail): National Portrait Gallery 310 Paper cartridge: Pattern Room, Royal Small Arms Factory, Enfield; Sir Henry Havelock, Sir Colin Campbell: Mansell Collection; Charge of the Queen's Bays: By permission of the Colonel, 1st The Queen's Dragoon Guards 311 Lucknow memorial, Medical Group No. 1, Maxim gun: National Army Museum 312 Houses of Parliament: (Brian Shuel); Pugin (detail), Barrie (detail): National Portrait Gallery 313 House of Lords: (Perfecta Press); Gladstone and Disraeli plates: (Eileen Tweedy) 314 The Beagle, Charles Darwin: Down House (Royal College of Surgeons) 315 Darwin's finches: Trustees of the British Museum (Natural History); T. H. Huxley, Bishop Wilberforce: Radio Times Hulton Picture Library 316 Livingstone's sextant: Royal Geographical Society; Stanley, Livingstone: Livingstone Memorial, Blantyre; the meeting: Mary Evans Picture Library 317 Tippu Tip, African Slave: United Society for the Propagation of the Gospel; slave chain: Royal Geographical Society 318 Victorian souvenirs: (Eileen Tweedy); Jubilee procession: Guildhall Art Gallery, London 319 Naval review at Spithead: National Maritime Museum, London 320 Mafeking siege money: National Army Museum; scout camp, Mafeking night: Radio Times Hulton Picture Library 321 Baden-Powell march: National Army Museum; Boer soldiers, Boer families: Radio Times Hulton Picture Library

Twentieth century 322/3 Oil rig: British Petroleum; miners: National Coal Board 324 Newsboy: Radio Times Hulton Picture Library; Titanic: Popperfoto Ltd; British Empire Exhibition poster: Lords Gallery; Allied leaders handkerchief: Leslie L. Hook (Eileen Tweedy) 325 Mosley: Keystone Press Agency; Neville Chamberlain, Royal Family: Popperfoto Ltd 326 Bicycle poster: Lords Gallery; Marie Lloyd poster: Victoria and Albert Museum; Vesta Tilley: Jasmine Spencer; 326 Edwardian melodrama advertisement: The Mander and Mitchenson

Theatre Collection; Gaiety Girl poster: Lords Gallery 327 'Hello Rag Time' programme cover: The Mander and Mitchenson Theatre Collection; Edward VII in a Daimler: Montague Motor Museum; Egyptian Hall poster: London Museum; Cricket team: Radio Times Hulton Picture Library; Flying at Hendon poster: London Transport; Henley Regatta: 328 Radio Times Hulton Picture Library Elgar: Mary Evans Picture Library; Lady Elgar, Elgar's house, still life: (John Bulmer) 329 Nucleus disintegrator: Cavendish Laboratory, Cambridge (Michael St Maur Shiel); Rutherford (detail): National Portrait Gallery 330 Page from Scott's journal: By kind permission of Sir Peter Scott and the Trustees of the British Museum (Popperfoto); Cape Evans, Camp on King Edward VII Plateau: Popperfoto Ltd 331 Group: Popperfoto Ltd; King Edward VII Keystone Press Agency 332 Suffragette poster: London Museum (Eileen Tweedy); Votes for Women poster: Mary Evans Picture Library; arrest of Mrs Pankhurst: Radio Times Hulton Picture Library 333 Pankhursts in Holloway: Radio Times Hulton Picture Library; Coronation souvenir poster: Jasmine Spencer 334 'Scrap of Paper' poster: Imperial War Museum (Eileen Tweedy); French, von Klück: Radio Times Hulton Picture Library 334 Mons retreat: Robert Hunt Library 335 German prisoners: Robert Hunt Library; King's message: Jasmine Spencer; recruiting office: Radio Times Hulton Picture Library; George V and the Kaiser: Popperfoto Ltd 336 Still life: Imperial War Museum (Michael Freeman); Haig: Radio Times Hulton Picture Library; troops: Imperial War Museum (Camera Press) 337 Field dressing station: Popperfoto Ltd; tank: RAC Tank Museum; ammunitions factory: Imperial War Museum (Camera Press); 338 Sassoon: Radio Times Hulton Picture Library; Owen: Journey from Obscurity, Wilfred Owen 1893-1918 by Harold Owen, published by Oxford University Press (National Portrait Gallery); Brooke: Radio Times Hulton Picture Library 339 Menin Road: Imperial War Museum; La Mitrailleuse: Tate Gallery, London (John Webb); A Battery Shelled: Imperial War Museum (Eileen Tweedy) 340 Cornwell relics: Imperial War Museum (Eileen Tweedy); Jellicoe: Radio Times Hulton Picture Library; Beatty: Robert Hunt Library; Seydlitz scuttled: Imperial War Museum (Camera Press) 341 U-boat poster: Imperial War Museum (Eileen Tweedy) 342 Poster: Imperial War Museum (Eileen Tweedy); gas victims: Imperial War Museum (Camera Press); Germans surrendering: Robert Hunt Library; front page of the Daily Chronicle: John Frost Historical Newspaper Service; ration book: Imperial War Museum (Eileen Tweedy) 344 Newspapers: John Frost Historical Newspaper Service; undergraduates unloading milk: Radio Times Hulton Picture Library 345 Food convoy, sailors at power station: Radio Times Hulton Picture Library; poster: Labour Party 346 Abdication document: Radio Times Hulton Picture Library; Prince of Wales in 1919: Popperfoto Ltd; 347 Prince of Wales hunting: Popperfoto Ltd; Edward VIII in Wales and George VI: Popperfoto Ltd; wedding: Radio Times Hulton Picture Library 348 Spitfire: RAF Museum, Hendon (Perfecta Publications Ltd); waiting pilots: Popperfoto Ltd; scramble: Imperial War Museum (Camera Press) 349 Operations room, Spitfires: Imperial War Museum (Camera Press); preparing bullets: Popperfoto Ltd 350 Bomber over London: Imperial War Museum (Camera Press); rescue workers: Keystone Press Agency; bomb damage, London: Popperfoto Ltd; Churchill in Manchester: Keystone Press Agency 351 bomb damage – Coventry, Air-raid Wardens: Keystone Press Agency; Churchill poster: Imperial War Museum (A. C. Cooper Ltd) 352 Medal: Spinks Ltd (Eileen Tweedy) Montgomery, Rommel: Popperfoto Ltd; action at El Alamein: Popperfoto Ltd; prisoners: Keystone Press Agency 353 Sinking of the Bismarck: Associated Press; Admiral Tovey: Keystone Press Agency 354 HMS Belfast: (Michael Freeman); Allied Commanders: Imperial War Museum (Camera Press); armada, commandos, V-2 rocket: Imperial War Museum (Camera Press); flag: Jasmine Spencer 356 Front page of the News Chronicle: John Frost Historical Newspaper Service; Members of the Expedition, Hillary and Tensing, Base Camp: Royal Geographical Society 357 Porters, Tensing on the summit: Royal Geographical Society; Her Majesty the Queen in Canberra: Popperfoto Ltd 358 The Royal Family: ITC; World Cup: Syndication International; Bluebird: Press Association; Mini: Syndication International 359 Twiggy: Syndication International; Beatles: EMI; Festival Hall: (Nicholas Sapieha); Lord Olivier: Camera Press (Bert Cann); Benjamin Britten: Popperfoto; Fonteyn and Nureyev: Camera Press (Reg Wilson)

Gazetteer 360 Castle: British Travel Authority; 362 Abbotsford: Mary Evans Picture Library; Sir Walter Scott (detail): National Portrait Gallery; Robert Burns: Trustees of the Burns Memorial, Alloway 363 Stone of Destiny (both pictures): Keystone Press Agency 364 George Eliot (detail): National Portrait Gallery; football match: Mary Evans Picture Library; 365 George Bernard Shaw (detail): National Portrait Gallery; Shaw's Corner: A. F. Kersting 366 Balmoral 1896: Radio Times Hulton Picture Library; Banbury Cross: Mary Evans Picture Library 367 Rudyard Kipling: Radio Times Hulton Picture Library; Beau Nash: Bath Municipal Libraries, Victoria Art Gallery; 368 Berkeley Castle: British Tourist Authority; Baldwin: Popperfoto Ltd; Sir Richard Grenville (detail): National Portrait Gallery 369 Neville Chamberlain: Popperfoto Ltd; Churchill: Mansell Collection 370 Delius: Mansell Collection; Highland Games: Mary

Evans Picture Library 371 Gravestone: City Museum, Bristol 372 Catharine of Aragon (detail): National Portrait Gallery 373 Lady Nelson: Radio Times Hulton Picture Library; Arnold Bennett (detail): National Portrait Gallery 374 Investiture of Edward VIII: Mary Evans Picture Library; Black Prince: Mansell Collection 375 Robert Ferrar: Radio Times Hulton Picture Library 376 Stringfellow aeroplanes: Crown copyright, Science Museum, London; Churchill: Radio Times Hulton Picture Library; Marconi: Marconi Ltd 377 Lawrence of Arabia: Radio Times Hulton Picture Library 378 Coldstream Guards: Radio Times Hulton Picture Library; Ruskin: Mary Evans Picture Library 379 Coventry: Fox Photos Ltd 380 George Stephenson (detail): National Portrait Gallery 381 Captain Webb: Mary Evans Picture Library; Captain Webb matches: Bryant & May Ltd; Bothwell, Viscount Dundee: Radio Times Hulton Picture Library; Thomas Carlyle: Mary Evans Picture Library 384 George IV: Radio Times Hulton Picture Library; Resurrectionists: Mansell Collection 385 R. L. Stevenson, Stevenson's home: Mansell Collection 386 Farnborough: Illustrated Newspapers Group; Tennyson: Mansell Collection 387 Trial of Mary, Queen of Scots: Trustees of the British Library 388 Pocahontas: Mary Evans Picture Library 389 Captain Kidd: Radio Times Hulton Picture Library; batsman: Mary Evans Picture Library 390 Hawarden: Mansell Collection 391 Sir Robert Walpole (detail): National Portrait Gallery; Cromwell: Radio Times Hulton Picture Library 392 Jarrow marchers: Radio Times Hulton Picture Library 393 George Romney (detail): National Portrait Gallery 394 Fox Talbot (both): Photo. Science Museum, London 396 Lloyd George: Radio Times Hulton Picture Library 397 Buckingham Palace (both): Radio Times Hulton Picture Library 398 Rossetti: from The Poet's Corner by Max Beerbohm, published by William Heinemann (Mansell Collection); Mrs Siddons: Royal Shakespeare Theatre, Stratford-upon-Avon; Garrick, Kean, Macready: The Mander and Mitchenson Theatre Collection 399 Northcliffe: Mary Evans Picture Library; Daily Mail: John Frost Historical Newspaper Service 400 Freud: Associated Press; Karl Marx: Mansell Collection; Marx's tomb: Camera Press (Peter Mitchell); Lenin: Mansell Collection 401 Collins Music Hall: The Mander and Mitchenson Theatre Collection; Marie Lloyd: Popperfoto Ltd; Little Tich, The Royal Albert Hall: Mary Evans Picture Library 402 Elizabeth Barrett Browning: Radio Times Hulton Picture Library; Robert Browning: Mary Evans Picture Library; Queen Charlotte's Ball, deb's parade: Radio Times Hulton Picture Library 403 King's Cross 1861, Jonathan Wild: Mary Evans Picture Library 404 Bomb damage in St Paul's: Fox Photos Ltd; press cuttings: Daily Express; Attlee: Keystone Press Agency 406 Mary Shelley (detail): National Portrait Gallery; Marston Moor: National Army Museum; Thomas Cook & Son trade mark: Mansell Collection 407 Rolls: Radio Times Hulton Picture Library 409 Nonsuch: Radio Times Hulton Picture Library 411 Royal Family at Osborne: Radio Times Hulton Picture Library 412 Sir Philip Sidney: Radio Times Hulton Picture Library 413 The Young Pretender: Radio Times Hulton Picture Library 414 Lord Palmerston: Mary Evans Picture Library 415 Henry James: Radio Times Hulton Picture Library; Football at Rugby: Illustrated Newspapers Group 416 Edward VII: Illustrated Newspapers Group 417 John Paul Jones: Mansell Collection; Gilbert White: Popperfoto Ltd 418 Richard Parker: Mansell Collection; Charles II: Mary Evans Picture Library; Tichborne claimant: Mary Evans Picture Library 421 Tay Bridge: Mansell Collection; Turpin: Radio Times Hulton Picture Library; Warwick: BPC

The publishers also acknowledge their indebtedness to the following books and journals which were consulted for reference:

Abbeys, Castles, and Ancient Halls of England and Wales by John Timbs and Alexander Gunn (Frederick Warne); Age by Age: Landmarks of British Archaeology by Ronald Jessup (Michael Joseph); The Age of Elegance by Arthur Bryant (Penguin); Alfred the Great by Eleanor Shipley Duckett (University of Chicago Press); Alfred The Great by H. R. Loyn (Oxford); Alfred The Great and His England by Eleanor Shipley Duckett (Collins); Anglo-Saxon Architecture by H. M. and J. Taylor (Cambridge); The Anglo-Saxon Chronicle edited by Dorothy Whitelock (Eyre and Spottiswoode); Anglo-Saxon England and the Norman Conquest by H. R. Loyn (Longman); Anglo-Saxon Saints and Scholars by Eleanor Shipley Duckett (The Macmillan Company); The Anglo-Saxons by David M. Wilson (Thames and Hudson); Anne Boleyn by Hester W. Chapman (Jonathan Cape); The Archaeology of Roman Britain by R. H. Collingwood & Sir Ian Archibald Richmond (Methuen); Art in Britain Under The Romans by J. M. C. Toynbee (Oxford); The Ascent of Man by J. Bronowski (BBC); Auchinleck by John Connell (Cassell); August 1914 by Barbara Tuchman (Constable); The Battles of Wales by O. M. Morgan (Salisbury

Hughes); Bede's Ecclesiastical History of the English People edited by Bertram Colgrave and R. A. B. Mynors (Oxford); Blue Guide to Wales edited by Stuart Rossiter (Ernest Benn); The Book of the City edited by Ian Norrie (High Hill Books); Britain, Rome's Most Northerly Province by G. M. Durant (G. Bell); Britain and her Army by Correlli Barnett (Allen Lane); Britain and Ireland in Early Christian Times AD 400–800 by Charles Thomas (Thames and Hudson); Britain in the Roman Empire by Joan Liversidge (Routledge); British Battle Series by Katherine Tomasson and Francis Buist (Pan Books); British Battlefields series by Philip Warner (Osprey); Britannia by Sheppard Frere (Routledge); The Bronze Age Round Barrow in Britain by Paul Ashbee (Phoenix House); Brunel and His World by John Pudney (Thames and Hudson); The Buildings of England series edited by Sir Nikolaus Pevsner (Penguin); Caesar by Irwin Isenberg (Cassell); Captain Cook, His Artists, His Voyages (Sydney Daily Telegraph); Captain Cook, the Seamen's Seaman by Alan Milliers (Penguin); Captain Cook and the South Pacific by Oliver Warner (Cassell); Castles of England by Garry Hogg (David and Charles); The Castles of England by Frederick Wilkinson (George Philip); The Castles of Scotland by Susan Ross (George Philip); The Castles of Wales by Alan Reid (George Philip); Celtic Britain by Nora K. Chadwick (Thames and Hudson); The Celts by Nora K. Chadwick (Penguin); Chambers Biographical Dictionary edited by J. O. Thorne (W. and R. Chambers); Charles Edward Stuart by David Daiches (Thames and Hudson); Charles II by Hesketh Pearson (Heinemann); Civilisation by Kenneth Clark (BBC/John Murray); The Collapse of British Power by Correlli Barnett (Eyre Methuen); The Coming of Christianity to Anglo-Saxon England by Henry Mayr-Harbing (Batsford); The Companion Guide to Kent and Sussex by Keith Spence (Collins); A Concise History of England by F. E. Halliday (Thames and Hudson); A Concise History of Scotland by Fitzroy Maclean (Thames and Hudson); Conquest of Gaul by Julius Caesar edited by S. A. Handford (Penguin); Costume: An Illustrated Survey from Ancient Times to the Twentieth Century by Margot Lister (Barrie and Jenkins); Costumes of Everyday Life by Margot Lister (Barrie and Jenkins); The County Books series edited by Brian Vesey Fitzgerald (Robert Hale); The Court at Windsor by Christopher Hibbert (Longman); Cricket: A History by Rowland Brown (Eyre and Spottiswoode); Cromwell, Our Chief of Men by Antonia Fraser (Weidenfeld and Nicolson); The Crystal Palace by Patrick Beaver (Hugh Evelyn); The Dark Ages edited by David Talbot Rice (Thames and Hudson); D-Day, Spearhead of Invasion by R. W. Thompson (Pan Ballantine); Defeat Into Victory by Sir William Slim (Cassell); The Deluge: British Society and the First World War by Arthur Marwick (Bodley Head); The Desert Generals by Correlli Barnett (William Kimber); The Dictionary of National Biography (Oxford); Discovering London by Norman Hillson (Herbert Jenkins); Douglas Haig: The Educated Soldier by John Terraine (Hutchinson); Drake by Ernle Bradford (Hodder and Stoughton); The Edwardians by J. B. Priestley (Heinemann); El Alamein by David Carver (Batsford); The Elizabethan Image by Roy Strong (Tate Gallery Publications); England in the Nineteenth Century by David Thomson (Penguin); England in the Reign of Charles II by David Ogg (Oxford); The English by J. B. Priestley (Heinemann); English Cathedrals by Peter Meyer (Thames and Hudson); English Costume from the 2nd Century BC to 1952 by D. Yarwood (Batsford); English, Furniture AD 43–1950 by E. T. Joy (Batsford); English Furniture of the 18th Century by David Nickerson (Weidenfeld and Nicolson); English Historical Documents c. 500–1042 edited by Dorothy Whitelock (Eyre and Spottiswoode); English History, A Survey by Sir George Clark; English Life series edited by Peter Quennell (Batsford/Putnam); English Social History by G. M. Trevelyan (Longman); The Escape of Charles II by Richard Ollard (Hodder and Stoughton); Excavations at Clickhimin, Shetland by J. R. C. Hamilton (Edinburgh: HMSO); Field Guide to Archaeology in Britain by Eric S. Wood (Collins); The First Battle of Britain 1917–18 by Raymond H. Fredette (Cassell); Fishbourne: A Roman Palace and Its Garden by Barry Cunliffe (Thames and Hudson); Forts and Castles by Terence Wise (Almark); George IV, Prince of Wales by Christopher Hibbert (Longman); George IV, Regent and King by Christopher Hibbert (Allen Lane); Glencoe by John Prebble (Penguin); Gloriana, The Years of Elizabeth I by Mary M. Luke (Gollancz); The Grand Tour by Christopher Hibbert (Spring Books); The Great Invasion by Leonard Cottrell (Evans Bros.); The Great War 1914–1918 by John Terraine (Hutchinson); The Greater Anglo-Saxon Churches by E. A. Fisher (Faber); Greater London by Christopher Trent (Phoenix House); A Guide to the Prehistoric and Roman Monuments in England and Wales by Jacquetta Hawkes (Sphere); Hanover to Windsor by Roger Fulford (Batsford); The Herberts of Wilton by Tresham Lever (John Murray); History of England by Sir Keith Feiling (Macmillan); History of England by Thomas Babington Macaulay (J. M. Dent); History of

England by G. M. Trevelyan (Longman); A History of Scotland by Rosalind Mitchinson (Methuen); History of the Second World War by B. H. Liddell-Hart (Cassell); A History of Wales by J. E. Lloyd (Longman); A History of Warfare by Field Marshal Viscount Montgomery of Alamein (Collins); The Home Fronts 1914–1918 by John Williams (Constable); How They Lived (Vol. I) Compiler: W. O. Hassall (Blackwell); How They Lived (Vol. II) Compilers: M. Harrison and O. M. Royston (Blackwell); How They Lived (Vol. III) Compiler: A. Briggs (Blackwell); The Ice Age by Björn Kurtén (Hart-Davis); The Ice Age in Britain by B. W. Sparks and R. G. West (Methuen); An Illustrated Cultural History of England by F. E. Halliday (Thames and Hudson); An Inventory of the Historical Monuments in the City of York (Vol. I, Eboracum, Roman York) (Royal Commission on Ancient and Historical Monuments of England); Iron Age Communities in Britain by Barry Cunliffe (Routledge); Isambard Kingdom Brunel by L. T. C. Rolt (Penguin); Jackdaw Publications (Founded and Distributed by Jonathan Cape Limited); James VI & I by D. H. Wilson (Cape); Julius Caesar by Michael Grant (Weidenfeld and Nicolson); King Arthur in Legend and History by Richard Barber (Boydell Press); King Edgar by Helen Panter (Morgan Books); King John by W. L. Warren (Penguin); Kings and Queens of England series, General Editor Antonia Fraser (Weidenfeld and Nicolson); The King's Arcadia: Inigo Jones and The Stuart Court by John Harris, Stephen Orgel and Roy Strong (Arts Council); The King's Peace by C. V. Wedgwood (Collins/Fontana); The King's War by C. V. Wedgwood (Collins/Fontana); Liaison 1914 by Sir Edward Spears (Eyre and Spottiswoode); The Life of Shakespeare by F. E. Halliday (Duckworth); Literature and Western Man by J. B. Priestley (Heinemann); Living History by Alan Sorrell (Batsford); London by David Piper (Thames and Hudson); London, A Pictorial History by John Hayes (Batsford); London, The Biography of a City by Christopher Hibbert (Longman); London Growing by Michael Harrison (Hutchinson); London on the Thames by Blake Erlich (Cassell); The Lowlands by Ian Finlay (Batsford); Maiden Castle, Dorset by R. E. M. Wheeler (The Society of Antiquaries); Making of a Nation 1689–1789 by A. J. Patrick (Penguin); The Making of Early England by D. P. Kirby (Batsford); Mayfair, a Town within London by Reginald Colby (Country Life); The Medieval Castle by Philip Warner (Arthur Barker); Men and Places by J. H. Plumb (Penguin); Mons: The Retreat to Victory by John Terraine (Batsford); Montgomery as Military Commander by Ronald Lewin (Cassell); The Mystery of Stonehenge by Franklyn M. Branley (David and Charles); The Narrow Margin by Derek Wood and Derek Dempster (Hutchinson); Nelson by Arthur Bryant (Collins/Fontana); Nelson and His World by Tom Pocock (Thames and Hudson); Nelson and the Age of Fighting Sail by the Editors of Horizon Magazine (Cassell); The Norman Achievement by David C. Douglas (Collins/Fontana); Northumberland and Durham by Iris Wedgwood (Faber); The North-West Frontier of Rome by David Divine (Macdonald); Old English Towns by F. R. Banks (Batsford); Orkney by Patrick Bailey (David and Charles); Oxford by Ralph Durand (Oxford); The Oxford Companion to the Theatre edited by Phyllis Hartnoll (Oxford); Oxford History of England (XV Volumes) edited by Sir George Clark (Oxford); Pagan Celtic Britain by Anne Ross (Routledge); The Pelican History of Art by Sir John Summerson (Penguin); The Pelican History of England series (Penguin); A Place in History by Paul Johnson (Weidenfeld and Nicolson); The Prince of Pleasure and His Regency by J. B. Priestley (Heinemann); The Private Papers of Douglas Haig edited by Robert Blake (Eyre and Spottiswoode); The Purnell History of the 20th Century A. J. P. Taylor, Editor-in-Chief (BPC); Queen Elizabeth I by J. E. Neale (Cape); The Quest for Arthur's Britain edited by Geoffrey Ashe (Pall Mall Press/Paladin); R.A.F. Biggin Hill by Graham Wallace (Putnam); The Rebellion of Boudicca by Donald R. Dudley and Graham Webster (Routledge); Richborough Excavations edited by Barry Cunliffe (Society of Antiquaries); The River Dart by Ruth Manning-Sanders (Westaway Books); Robert, Earl of Essex, an Elizabethan Icarus by Robert Lacey (Weidenfeld and Nicolson); Roman Archaeology and Art by Sir Ian Richmond (Faber); Roman Britain by Aileen Fox and Alan Sorrell (Lutterworth); Roman Britain by I. A. Richmond (Jonathan Cape); Roman Britain and Early England 55 BC–AD 871 by P. Hunter Blair (Nelson); The Roman Conquest of Britain (43–57) by D. R. Dudley and Graham Webster (Batsford); The Roman Imperial Army of the 1st and 2nd Centuries AD by Graham Webster (A. and C. Black); Roman Roads in Britain by Ivan D. Margary (John Baker); Rommel as Military Commander by Ronald Lewin (Batsford); The Rommel Papers edited by B. H. Liddell-Hart (Collins); Royal Dukes by Roger Fulford (Collins); Royal Homes by Neville Williams (Lutterworth); Saxon England by John Hamilton and Alan Sorrell (Lutterworth); Scotland by Gordon Donaldson (Oliver and Boyd); Scottish Revolution 1637–1644 by David Stevenson (David and Charles); The Second World War by Winston Churchill

(Cassell); Shakespeare, The Poet and His Background by Peter Quennell (Weidenfeld and Nicolson); Shakespeare's England by Levi Fox (Wayland); Shakespeare's England by the Editors of Horizon Magazine (Cassell); The Shape of History by Donald Turnbull (Macmillan); The Shell Book of Offa's Dyke Path by Frank Noble (Queen Anne Press); Shetland by J. R. Nicolson (David and Charles); A Short History of English Literature by Gilbert Phelps (Folio Society); A Short History of the Second World War by Basil Collier (Collins); Sir Walter Raleigh by Robert Lacey (Weidenfeld and Nicolson); The Somme by A. H. Farrar-Hockley (Batsford); The Spanish Armada by Jay Williams (Cassell); Sport in Society by P. C. McIntosh (C. A. Watts); Steel Bonnets by George MacDonald Fraser (Barrie and Jenkins); Steinberg's Dictionary of British History (Arnold); The Stuarts by J. P. Kenyon (Collins/Fontana); Sutton Hoo by Charles Green (Merlin Press); The Sutton Hoo Ship Burial by R. L. S. Bruce-Mitford (British Museum); The Swordbearers by Correlli Barnett (Eyre and Spottiswoode); Tacitus and Germania translated by H. Mattingley (Penguin); They Saw It Happen (1689–1897) edited by T. Charles Edwards and Brian Richardson (Blackwell); Tourist's England by Arthur Grand (Frank Graham); The Tower of London in the History of the Nation by A. L. Rowse (Weidenfeld and Nicolson); A Traveller's Guide to Battlefields of Europe Volume I edited by D. Chandler (Hugh Evelyn); A Traveller's Guide to Literary Europe Volume II edited by Margaret Crosland (Hugh Evelyn); The Trial of Charles I by C. V. Wedgwood (Collins/Fontana); Van Dyck: Charles I on Horseback by Roy Strong (Allen Lane); Victoria R.I. by Elizabeth Longford (Weidenfeld and Nicolson); Victorian Cities by Asa Briggs (Penguin); The Victorian Scene 1837–1901 by Nicholas Bentley (Weidenfeld and Nicolson); Wales by Gilbert Stone (George Harrap); The War for America by Piers Mackesy (Longman); Wedgwood Portrait Medallions by Robin Reilly (National Portrait Gallery); Wellington's Peninsular Victories by Michael Glover (Pan Books); Welsh Border Country by P. T. Jones (Batsford); The West Country by S. H. Burton (Robert Hale); Where They Lived in London by Maurice Rickards (David and Charles); Who's Who in History series, General Editor C. R. N. Routh (Blackwell); William and Mary by Henry and Barbara van der Zee (Macmillan); Windsor Castle in the History of the Nation by A. L. Rowse (Weidenfeld and Nicolson); The Works in Architecture of Robert and James Adam by John Swarbrick (Alec Tiranti); The World of Charles Dickens by Angus Wilson (Penguin); Wren by Margaret Whinney (Thames and Hudson)

The publishers wish to acknowledge their indebtedness to the following for permission to use quotations:

Richard Barber and The Boydell Press Ltd for an extract from King Arthur in Legend and History (1973) by Richard Barber; Eyre and Spottiswoode Ltd for an extract from The Anglo-Saxon Chronicle, a revised translation edited by Dorothy Whitelock with David C. Douglas and Susie I. Tucker; Eyre and Spottiswoode Ltd for extracts from English Historical Documents c. 500–1042 edited by Dorothy Whitelock; Faber & Faber Ltd and G. T. Sassoon for the extract from 'Counter Attack' in The Collected Poems of Siegfried Sassoon; The Estate of H. Mattingley (1948 and 1970) and Penguin Books Ltd for the extracts from Tacitus and Germania by Tacitus, translated by H. Mattingley; The Executors of the Estate of Harold Owen and Chatto & Windus for extracts from 'Anthem for Doomed Youth', 'Strange Meeting' and a quotation from the draft preface to Wilfred Owen's planned volume of poems, taken from The Collected Poems of Wilfred Owen edited by C. Day Lewis, 1963; The Pall Mall Press Ltd for an extract from The Quest for Arthur's Britain by Geoffrey Ashe; Penguin Books Ltd and Nevill Coghill for lines from The Canterbury Tales by Geoffrey Chaucer, translated by Nevill Coghill (Penguin Classics, Revised Edition 1960) © Nevill Coghill, 1951, 1958, 1960; Penguin Books Ltd for extracts from Conquest of Gaul by Julius Caesar, translated by S. A. Handford; Sidgwick & Jackson Ltd for lines from 'The Soldier' in The Complete Poems of Rupert Brooke; John Terraine for the quotation from General Jack's Diary by Brigadier General James Lochhead Jack, edited by John Terraine (Eyre and Spottiswoode, 1964)

Contributors The publishers gratefully acknowledge the assistance of the following contributors: Will Allan; Anne Angus; Dulcie Ashdown; Adrian Brink; Anthony Cheetham; John O. E. Clark; Gila Curtis; Diana de Deney; David Hunn; W. F. Inglis; Anne Kings; Patricia Ledward; David Levy; Maurice Rickards; Simon Rigge; Basil Skinner; Keith Spence; Judith Taylor; Margaret Willes

Artists Victor Ambrus; Gary Hinks

Photographers Malcolm Aird; Michael Coles; John Couzins; Mike Freeman; Alain Le Garsmeur; Keith Morris; Chris Ridley; Mike Taylor; Eileen Tweedy

Paper, Printing and Binding by: Bowater Paper Sales Ltd; Brown, Knight & Truscott Ltd, Tonbridge; Carlton Repro International, Winchester; Culver Graphics Ltd, Lane End; Jarrold & Sons Ltd, Norwich; Litra Machine Plates Ltd, Edenbridge; Redbridge Book Cloth Co. Ltd, Bolton; Reprocolor/Llovet SA, Barcelona; Thomson Litho Ltd, East Kilbride; Tullis Russell Ltd, Fife

Published by The Reader's Digest Association Limited, 25 Berkeley Square, London W1X 6AB